Nineteenth-Century
Literature Criticism

Guide to Gale Literary Criticism Series

When you need to review criticism of literary works, these are the Gale series to use:

If the author's death date is:	You should turn to:
After Dec. 31, 1959 (or author is still living)	***CONTEMPORARY LITERARY CRITICISM*** for example: Jorge Luis Borges, Anthony Burgess, William Faulkner, Mary Gordon, Ernest Hemingway, Iris Murdoch
1900 through 1959	***TWENTIETH-CENTURY LITERARY CRITICISM*** for example: Willa Cather, F. Scott Fitzgerald, Henry James, Mark Twain, Virginia Woolf
1800 through 1899	***NINETEENTH-CENTURY LITERATURE CRITICISM*** for example: Fedor Dostoevski, Nathaniel Hawthorne, George Sand, William Wordsworth
1400 through 1799	***LITERATURE CRITICISM FROM 1400 TO 1800 (excluding Shakespeare)*** for example: Anne Bradstreet, Daniel Defoe, Alexander Pope, François Rabelais, Jonathan Swift, Phillis Wheatley ***SHAKESPEAREAN CRITICISM*** Shakespeare's plays and poetry
Antiquity through 1399	***CLASSICAL AND MEDIEVAL LITERATURE CRITICISM*** for example: Dante, Homer, Plato, Sophocles, Vergil, the Beowulf Poet

---

Gale also publishes related criticism series:

CHILDREN'S LITERATURE REVIEW

This series covers authors of all eras who write for the preschool through high school audience.

SHORT STORY CRITICISM

This series covers the major short fiction writers of all nationalities and periods of literary history.

ISSN 0732-1864

Volume 18

Nineteenth-Century Literature Criticism

Excerpts from Criticism of the
Works of Novelists, Poets, Playwrights,
Short Story Writers, Philosophers, and Other
Creative Writers Who Died between 1800
and 1899, from the First Published Critical
Appraisals to Current Evaluations

Janet Mullane
Editor

Gail Ann Schulte
Robert Thomas Wilson
Associate Editors

 **Gale Research Inc.** · *DETROIT* · *LONDON*

STAFF

Janet Mullane, *Editor*

Gail Ann Schulte, Robert Thomas Wilson, *Associate Editors*

Rachel Carlson, *Senior Assistant Editor*

Grace Jeromski, Mary Nelson-Pulice, *Assistant Editors*

Cherie D. Abbey, Sheila Fitzgerald, Jelena Krstovic,
Phyllis Carmel Mendelson, Emily B. Tennyson, *Contributing Editors*
Denise Michlewicz Broderick, Robin DuBlanc,
Melissa Reiff Hug, Jay P. Pederson, Debra A. Wells, *Contributing Assistant Editors*

Jeanne A. Gough, *Permissions & Production Manager*
Lizbeth A. Purdy, *Production Supervisor*
Kathleen M. Cook, *Production Coordinator*
Cathy Beranek, Suzanne Powers, Kristine E. Tipton,
Lee Ann Welsh, *Editorial Assistants*
Linda Marcella Pugliese, *Manuscript Coordinator*
Maureen A. Puhl, *Senior Manuscript Assistant*
Donna Craft, Jennifer E. Gale, Rosetta Irene Simms, *Manuscript Assistants*

Victoria B. Cariappa, *Research Supervisor*
Maureen R. Richards, *Research Coordinator*
Mary D. Wise, *Senior Research Assistant*
Joyce E. Doyle, Kevin B. Hillstrom, Karen O. Kaus, Eric Priehs,
Filomena Sgambati, Laura B. Standley, *Research Assistants*

Janice M. Mach, *Text Permissions Supervisor*
Kathy Grell, *Text Permissions Coordinator*
Mabel E. Gurney, Josephine M. Keene, *Senior Permissions Assistants*
Eileen H. Baehr, H. Diane Cooper, Anita L. Ransom,
Kimberly F. Smilay, *Permissions Assistants*
Melissa A. Kamuyu, Martha A. Mulder, Lisa M. Wimmer, *Permissions Clerks*

Patricia A. Seefelt, *Picture Permissions Supervisor*
Margaret A. Chamberlain, *Permissions Coordinator, Pictures*
Pamela A. Hayes, Lillian Tyus, *Permissions Clerks*

Contents

Preface

The nineteenth century was a time of tremendous growth in human endeavor: in science, in social history, and particularly in literature. The era saw the development of the novel, witnessed radical changes from classicism to romanticism to realism, and fostered intellectual and artistic ideas that continue to inspire authors of our own century. The importance of the writers of the nineteenth century is twofold, for they provide insight into their own time as well as into the universal nature of human experience.

The literary criticism of an era can also give us insight into the moral and intellectual atmosphere of the past because the criteria by which a work of art is judged reflect current philosophical and social attitudes. Literary criticism takes many forms: the traditional essay, the book or play review, even the parodic poem. Criticism can also be of several types: normative, descriptive, interpretive, textual, appreciative, generic. Collectively, the range of critical response helps us to understand a work of art, an author, an era.

Scope of the Series

Nineteenth-Century Literature Criticism (NCLC) is designed to serve as an introduction for the student of nineteenth-century literature to the authors of that period and to the most significant commentators on these authors. Since the analysis of this literature spans almost two hundred years, a vast amount of critical material confronts the student. For that reason, *NCLC* presents significant passages from published criticism to aid students in the location and selection of commentaries on authors who died between 1800 and 1899. The need for *NCLC* was suggested by the usefulness of the Gale series *Twentieth-Century Literary Criticism (TCLC)* and *Contemporary Literary Criticism (CLC)*, which excerpt criticism of creative writing of the twentieth century. For further information about *TCLC, CLC,* and Gale's other criticism series, users should consult the Guide to Gale Literary Criticism Series preceding the title page in this volume.

Each volume of *NCLC* is carefully compiled to include authors who represent a variety of genres and nationalities and who are currently regarded as the most important writers of their era. In addition to major authors who have attained worldwide renown, *NCLC* also presents criticism on lesser-known figures whose significant contributions to literary history are important to the study of nineteenth-century literature. These authors are important artists in their own right, and often enjoy such an immense popularity in their own countries that English-speaking readers should become more familiar with their work.

Author entries in *NCLC* are intended to be definitive overviews. In order to devote more attention to each writer, approximately ten to fifteen authors are included in each 600-page volume, compared with about forty authors in a *CLC* volume of similar size. The length of each author entry is intended to reflect the amount of attention the author has received from critics writing in English and from foreign critics in translation. Articles and books that have not been translated into English are excluded. However, since many of the major foreign studies have been translated into English and are excerpted in *NCLC,* author entries reflect the viewpoints of many nationalities. Each author entry represents a historical overview of critical reaction to the author's work: early criticism is presented to indicate initial responses, later selections represent any rise or decline in the author's literary reputation, and current analyses provide students with a modern perspective. In each entry, we have attempted to identify and include excerpts from all seminal essays of criticism.

An author may appear more than once in the series because of the great quantity of critical material available or because of a resurgence of criticism generated by events such as an author's centennial or anniversary celebration, the republication or posthumous publication of an author's works, or the publication of a newly translated work. Usually, one or more author entries in each volume of *NCLC* are devoted to individual works or groups of works by major authors who have appeared previously in the series. Only those works that have been the subjects of extensive criticism and are widely studied in literature courses are selected for this in-depth treatment. Wilkie Collins's *The Moonstone* and Charles Dickens's *The Mystery of Edwin Drood* are the subjects of such entries in *NCLC,* Volume 18.

Organization of the Book

An author entry consists of the following elements: author heading, biographical and critical introduction, principal works, excerpts of criticism (each preceded by explanatory notes and followed by a bibliographical citation), and an additional bibliography for further reading.

- The *author heading* consists of the author's full name, followed by birth and death dates. The unbracketed portion of the name denotes the form under which the author most commonly wrote. If an author wrote consistently under a pseudonym, the pseudonym will be listed in the author heading and the real name given in parentheses on the first line of the biographical and critical introduction. Also located at the beginning of the introduction are any name variations under which an author wrote, including transliterated forms for authors whose languages use nonroman alphabets. Uncertainty as to a birth or death date is indicated by a question mark.

- A *portrait* of the author is included when available. Many entries also feature illustrations of materials pertinent to an author's career, including manuscript pages, letters, book illustrations, and representations of important people, places, and events in an author's life.

- The *biographical and critical introduction* contains background information that introduces the reader to an author and to the critical debate surrounding his or her work. When applicable, biographical and critical introductions are followed by references to additional entries on the author in other literary reference series published by Gale Research Inc., including *Dictionary of Literary Biography, Children's Literature Review,* and *Something about the Author.*

- The list of *principal works* is chronological by date of first book publication and identifies the genre of each work. In those instances where the first publication was in other than the English language, the title and date of the first English-language edition are given in brackets. Unless otherwise indicated, dramas are dated by the first performance, rather than first publication.

- *Criticism* is arranged chronologically in each author entry to provide a useful perspective on changes in critical evaluation over the years. All titles by the author featured in the critical entry are printed in boldface type to enable the user to ascertain without difficulty the works being discussed. Also for purposes of easier identification, the critic's name and the publication date of the essay are given at the beginning of each piece of criticism. Unsigned criticism is preceded by the title of the journal in which it appeared. When an anonymous essay is later attributed to a critic, the critic's name appears in brackets at the beginning of the excerpt and in the bibliographical citation. Publication information (such as publisher names and book prices) and parenthetical numerical references (such as footnotes or page and line references to specific editions of works) have been deleted at the editor's discretion to provide smoother reading of the text.

- Critical essays are prefaced with *explanatory notes* as an additional aid to students using *NCLC*. The explanatory notes provide several types of useful information, including the reputation of the critic, the importance of a work of criticism, a synopsis of the essay, the specific approach of the critic (biographical, psychoanalytic, structuralist, etc.), and the growth of critical controversy or changes in critical trends regarding an author's work. In some cases, these notes include cross-references to related criticism in the author's entry or in the additional bibliography. Dates in parentheses within the explanatory notes refer to the dates of other essays in the author entry.

- A complete *bibliographical citation* designed to facilitate the location of the original essay or book follows each piece of criticism.

- The *additional bibliography* appearing at the end of each author entry suggests further reading on the author. In some cases it includes essays for which the editors could not obtain reprint rights.

An appendix lists the sources from which material in the volume is reprinted. It does not, however, list every book or periodical consulted for the volume.

Cumulative Indexes

Each volume of *NCLC* includes a cumulative index listing all the authors who have appeared in *Contemporary Literary Criticism, Twentieth-Century Literary Criticism, Nineteenth-Century Literature Criticism, Literature*

Criticism from 1400 to 1800, Classical and Medieval Literature Criticism, and *Short Story Criticism,* along with cross-references to the Gale series *Children's Literature Review, Authors in the News, Contemporary Authors, Contemporary Authors Autobiography Series, Dictionary of Literary Biography, Concise Dictionary of American Literary Biography, Something about the Author, Something about the Author Autobiography Series,* and *Yesterday's Authors of Books for Children.* Readers will welcome this cumulated author index as a useful tool for locating an author within the various series. The index, which lists birth and death dates when available, will be particularly valuable for those authors who are identified with a certain period but whose death dates cause them to be placed in another, or for those authors whose careers span two periods. For example, Fedor Dostoevski is found in *NCLC,* yet Leo Tolstoy, another major nineteenth-century Russian novelist, is found in *TCLC.*

Each volume of *NCLC* also includes a cumulative nationality index to authors. Authors are listed alphabetically by nationality, followed by the volume numbers in which they appear.

New Index

An important feature now appearing in *NCLC* is a cumulative title index, an alphabetical listing of the literary works discussed in the series since its inception. Each title listing includes the corresponding volume and page numbers where criticism may be located. Foreign language titles that have been translated are followed by the titles of the translations, for example: *Die Leiden des jungen Werthers (The Sorrows of Young Werther).* Page numbers following these translated titles refer to all pages on which any form of the title, either foreign language or translated, appears. Titles of novels, dramas, nonfiction books, and poetry, short story, or essay collections are printed in italics, while all individual poems, short stories, and essays are printed in roman type within quotation marks. In cases where the same title is used by different authors, the author's surname is given in parentheses after the title, e.g., *Poems* (Wordsworth) and *Poems* (Coleridge).

Acknowledgments

No work of this scope can be accomplished without the cooperation of many people. The editors especially wish to thank the copyright holders of the excerpted criticism included in this volume, the permissions managers of many book and magazine publishing companies for assisting us in securing reprint rights, and Anthony Bogucki for assistance with copyright research. We are also grateful to the staffs of the Detroit Public Library, the Library of Congress, University of Michigan Library, and Wayne State University Library for making their resources available to us.

Suggestions Are Welcome

In response to various suggestions, several features have been added to *NCLC* since the series began, including: explanatory notes to excerpted criticism that provide important information regarding critics and their work; a cumulative author index listing authors in all Gale literary criticism series; entries devoted to criticism on a single work by a major author; more extensive illustrations; and a cumulative title index listing all the literary works discussed in the series.

The editors welcome additional comments and suggestions for expanding the coverage and enhancing the usefulness of the series.

Authors to Appear in Future Volumes

About, Edmond François 1828-1885
Aguilo I. Fuster, Maria 1825-1897
Aksakov, Konstantin 1817-1860
Aleardi, Aleardo 1812-1878
Alecsandri, Vasile 1821-1890
Alencar, José 1829-1877
Alfieri, Vittorio 1749-1803
Allingham, William 1824-1889
Almquist, Carl Jonas Love 1793-1866
Alorne, Leonor de Almeida 1750-1839
Alsop, Richard 1761-1815
Altimirano, Ignacio Manuel 1834-1893
Alvarenga, Manuel Inacio da Silva
    1749-1814
Alvares de Azevedo, Manuel Antonio
    1831-1852
Anzengruber, Ludwig 1839-1889
Arany, Janos 1817-1882
Arène, Paul 1843-1896
Aribau, Bonaventura Carlos 1798-1862
Arjona de Cubas, Manuel Maria de
    1771-1820
Arnault, Antoine Vincent 1766-1834
Arneth, Alfred von 1819-1897
Arnim, Bettina von 1785-1859
Arriaza y Superviela, Juan Bautista
    1770-1837
Asbjörnsen, Peter Christen 1812-1885
Ascasubi, Hilario 1807-1875
Atterbom, Per Daniel Amadeus
    1790-1855
Aubanel, Theodore 1829-1886
Auerbach, Berthold 1812-1882
Augier, Guillaume V.E. 1820-1889
Azeglio, Massimo D' 1798-1866
Azevedo, Guilherme de 1839-1882
Bakin (pseud. of Takizawa Okikani)
    1767-1848
Bakunin, Mikhail Aleksandrovich
    1814-1876
Baratynski, Jewgenij Abramovich
    1800-1844
Barnes, William 1801-1886
Batyushkov, Konstantin 1778-1855
Beattie, James 1735-1803
Becquer, Gustavo Adolfo 1836-1870
Bentham, Jeremy 1748-1832
Béranger, Jean-Pierre de 1780-1857
Berchet, Giovanni 1783-1851
Berzsenyi, Daniel 1776-1836
Black, William 1841-1898
Blair, Hugh 1718-1800
Blicher, Steen Steensen 1782-1848
Bocage, Manuel Maria Barbosa du
    1765-1805
Boratynsky, Yevgeny 1800-1844

Borel, Petrus 1809-1859
Boreman, Yokutiel 1825-1890
Borne, Ludwig 1786-1837
Botev, Hristo 1778-1842
Brinckman, John 1814-1870
Brown, Charles Brockden 1777-1810
Browning, Robert 1812-1889
Büchner, Georg 1813-1837
Campbell, James Edwin 1867-1895
Campbell, Thomas 1777-1844
Carlyle, Thomas 1795-1881
Castelo Branco, Camilo 1825-1890
Castro Alves, Antonio de 1847-1871
Chatterje, Bankin Chanda 1838-1894
Chivers, Thomas Holly 1807?-1858
Claudius, Matthias 1740-1815
Clough, Arthur Hugh 1819-1861
Cobbett, William 1762-1835
Colenso, John William 1814-1883
Coleridge, Hartley 1796-1849
Collett, Camilla 1813-1895
Comte, Auguste 1798-1857
Conrad, Robert T. 1810-1858
Conscience, Hendrik 1812-1883
Cooke, Philip Pendleton 1816-1850
Corbière, Edouard 1845-1875
Crabbe, George 1754-1832
Cruz E Sousa, João da 1861-1898
Desbordes-Valmore, Marceline
    1786-1859
Deschamps, Emile 1791-1871
Deus, João de 1830-1896
Dickinson, Emily 1830-1886
Dinis, Julio 1839-1871
Dinsmoor, Robert 1757-1836
Du Maurier, George 1834-1896
Eminescy, Mihai 1850-1889
Engels, Friedrich 1820-1895
Espronceda, José 1808-1842
Ettinger, Solomon 1799-1855
Euchel, Issac 1756-1804
Ferguson, Samuel 1810-1886
Fernández de Lizardi, José Joaquín
    1776-1827
Fernández de Moratín, Leandro
    1760-1828
Fet, Afanasy 1820-1892
Feuillet, Octave 1821-1890
Fontane, Theodor 1819-1898
Freiligrath, Hermann Ferdinand
    1810-1876
Freytag, Gustav 1816-1895
Ganivet, Angel 1865-1898
Garrett, Almeida 1799-1854
Garshin, Vsevolod Mikhaylovich
    1855-1888

Gezelle, Guido 1830-1899
Ghalib, Asadullah Khan 1797-1869
Goldschmidt, Meir Aaron 1819-1887
Goncalves Dias, Antonio 1823-1864
Griboyedov, Aleksander Sergeyevich
    1795-1829
Grigor'yev, Appolon Aleksandrovich
    1822-1864
Groth, Klaus 1819-1899
Grun, Anastasius (pseud. of Anton
    Alexander Graf von Auersperg)
    1806-1876
Guerrazzi, Francesco Domenico
    1804-1873
Gutierrez Najera, Manuel 1859-1895
Gutzkow, Karl Ferdinand 1811-1878
Ha-Kohen, Shalom 1772-1845
Halleck, Fitz-Greene 1790-1867
Harris, George Washington 1814-1869
Hayne, Paul Hamilton 1830-1886
Hazlitt, William 1778-1830
Hebbel, Christian Friedrich 1813-1863
Hebel, Johann Peter 1760-1826
Hegel, Georg Wilhelm Friedrich
    1770-1831
Heiberg, Johann Ludvig 1813-1863
Herculano, Alexandre 1810-1866
Hertz, Henrik 1798-1870
Herwegh, Georg 1817-1875
Hoffman, Charles Fenno 1806-1884
Hooper, Johnson Jones 1815-1863
Horton, George Moses 1798-1880
Howitt, William 1792-1879
Hughes, Thomas 1822-1896
Imlay, Gilbert 1754?-1828?
Irwin, Thomas Caulfield 1823-1892
Isaacs, Jorge 1837-1895
Jacobsen, Jens Peter 1847-1885
Jippensha, Ikku 1765-1831
Kant, Immanuel 1724-1804
Karr, Jean Baptiste Alphonse
    1808-1890
Keble, John 1792-1866
Khomyakov, Alexey S. 1804-1860
Kierkegaard, Søren 1813-1855
Kinglake, Alexander W. 1809-1891
Kingsley, Charles 1819-1875
Kivi, Alexis 1834-1872
Koltsov, Alexey Vasilyevich 1809-1842
Kotzebue, August von 1761-1819
Kraszewski, Josef Ignacy 1812-1887
Kreutzwald, Friedrich Reinhold
    1803-1882
Krochmal, Nahman 1785-1840
Krudener, Valeria Barbara Julia de
    Wietinghoff 1766-1824

Lampman, Archibald 1861-1899
Lebensohn, Micah Joseph 1828-1852
Leconte de Lisle, Charles-Marie-René 1818-1894
Leontyev, Konstantin 1831-1891
Leopardi, Giacoma 1798-1837
Leskov, Nikolai 1831-1895
Lever, Charles James 1806-1872
Levisohn, Solomon 1789-1822
Lewes, George Henry 1817-1878
Leyden, John 1775-1811
Lobensohn, Micah Gregory 1775-1810
Longstreet, Augustus Baldwin 1790-1870
López de Ayola y Herrera, Adelardo 1819-1871
Lover, Samuel 1797-1868
Luzzato, Samuel David 1800-1865
Macedo, Joaquim Manuel de 1820-1882
Macha, Karel Hynek 1810-1836
Mackenzie, Henry 1745-1831
Malmon, Solomon 1754-1800
Mangan, James Clarence 1803-1849
Manzoni, Alessandro 1785-1873
Marii, Jose 1853-1895
Markovic, Svetozar 1846-1875
Martínez de La Rosa, Francisco 1787-1862
Mathews, Cornelius 1817-1889
McCulloch, Thomas 1776-1843
Merriman, Brian 1747-1805
Meyer, Conrad Ferdinand 1825-1898
Montgomery, James 1771-1854
Morton, Sarah Wentworth 1759-1846
Müller, Friedrich 1749-1825
Murger, Henri 1822-1861
Neruda, Jan 1834-1891
Nestroy, Johann 1801-1862
Newman, John Henry 1801-1890
Niccolini, Giambattista 1782-1861
Nievo, Ippolito 1831-1861
Nodier, Charles 1780-1844
Obradovic, Dositej 1742-1811
Oehlenschlager, Adam 1779-1850

O'Neddy, Philothee (pseud. of Theophile Dondey) 1811-1875
O'Shaughnessy, Arthur William Edgar 1844-1881
Ostrovsky, Alexander 1823-1886
Paine, Thomas 1737-1809
Peacock, Thomas Love 1785-1866
Perk, Jacques 1859-1881
Pisemsky, Alexey F. 1820-1881
Pompeia, Raul D'Avila 1863-1895
Popovic, Jovan Sterija 1806-1856
Praed, Winthrop Mackworth 1802-1839
Prati, Giovanni 1814-1884
Preseren, France 1800-1849
Pringle, Thomas 1789-1834
Procter, Adelaide Ann 1825-1864
Procter, Bryan Waller 1787-1874
Pye, Henry James 1745-1813
Quental, Antero Tarquinio de 1842-1891
Quinet, Edgar 1803-1875
Quintana, Manuel José 1772-1857
Radishchev, Aleksander 1749-1802
Raftery, Anthony 1784-1835
Raimund, Ferdinand 1790-1836
Reid, Mayne 1818-1883
Renan, Ernest 1823-1892
Reuter, Fritz 1810-1874
Rogers, Samuel 1763-1855
Ruckert, Friedrich 1788-1866
Runeberg, Johan 1804-1877
Rydberg, Viktor 1828-1895
Saavedra y Ramírez de Boquedano, Angel de 1791-1865
Sacher-Mosoch, Leopold von 1836-1895
Satanov, Isaac 1732-1805
Schiller, Johann Friedrich von 1759-1805
Schlegel, Karl 1772-1829
Sedgwick, Catherine Maria 1789-1867
Senoa, August 1838-1881
Shulman, Kalman 1819-1899

Sigourney, Lydia Howard Huntley 1791-1856
Silva, Jose Asuncion 1865-1896
Slaveykov, Petko 1828-1895
Smith, Richard Penn 1799-1854
Smolenskin, Peretz 1842-1885
Stagnelius, Erik Johan 1793-1823
Staring, Antonie Christiaan Wynand 1767-1840
Stendhal (pseud. of Henri Beyle) 1783-1842
Stifter, Adalbert 1805-1868
Stone, John Augustus 1801-1834
Taunay, Alfredo d'Ecragnole 1843-1899
Taylor, Bayard 1825-1878
Tennyson, Alfred, Lord 1809-1892
Terry, Lucy (Lucy Terry Prince) 1730-1821
Thompson, Daniel Pierce 1795-1868
Thompson, Samuel 1766-1816
Tiedge, Christoph August 1752-1841
Timrod, Henry 1828-1867
Tommaseo, Nicolo 1802-1874
Tompa, Mihaly 1817-1888
Topelius, Zachris 1818-1898
Turgenev, Ivan 1818-1883
Tyutchev, Fedor I. 1803-1873
Uhland, Ludvig 1787-1862
Valaoritis, Aristotelis 1824-1879
Valles, Jules 1832-1885
Verde, Cesario 1855-1886
Villaverde, Cirilio 1812-1894
Vinje, Aasmund Olavsson 1818-1870
Vorosmarty, Mihaly 1800-1855
Weisse, Christian Felix 1726-1804
Welhaven, Johan S. 1807-1873
Werner, Zacharius 1768-1823
Wescott, Edward Noyes 1846-1898
Wessely, Nattali Herz 1725-1805
Whitman, Sarah Helen 1803-1878
Woolson, Constance Fenimore 1840-1894
Zhukovsky, Vasily 1783-1852

Thomas Arnold

1795-1842

English educator, historian, essayist, and sermonizer.

A prominent educational and religious figure in nineteenth-century England, Arnold is best known today as the great reforming headmaster of Rugby school and as a leading voice for liberal reform in the Anglican church. Under his guidance, the development of Christian standards of conscience and conduct became the focus of education at Rugby, and he also established government by sixth-form prefects as a sanctioned system of student self-regulation. These aspects of the Rugby program have, in various forms, become significant features of English public school life, thus distinguishing Arnold as one of England's most influential educators. Arnold is also known for the distinctive perspective that he brought to scriptural exegesis and to his writings on church reform. Minimizing the importance of traditional divisions between secular and religious matters, he helped demonstrate that reason was compatible with faith in biblical exegesis, while in his *Principles of Church Reform* and other essays, he promoted the liberal ideal of a unified, socially responsive national church in England.

Arnold was born in West Cowes, on the Isle of Wight, to Martha Delafield Arnold and her husband, William, a customs official. He attended Warminster Grammar School in Wiltshire and Winchester College as a youth, taking an avid interest in ancient and modern literature, and in 1811 began his undergraduate studies at Corpus Christi College, Oxford University. Arnold won first-class honors in 1814 and was subsequently elected a fellow of Oriel College at the university. He appears to have joined in the theological discussions of the Oriel Noetics, scholars known for examining traditional religious conventions and dogmas in the light of history and reason, and was ordained a deacon in the Anglican church in 1818. The following year Arnold moved to Laleham, near Staines on the Thames River, and established himself as a tutor. He married Mary Penrose in 1820, and the couple soon started a family that would eventually grow to nine children, including the renowned author Matthew Arnold. Arnold's most ambitious writing project during his eight-year stay at Laleham was a series of periodical articles on early Roman history that was posthumously published as *History of the Later Roman Commonwealth*.

In 1828, Arnold was elected headmaster of Rugby. He continued to study classical history, working on his *History of Rome* and editing Thucydides' *The History of the Peloponnesian War* in his spare time, but his primary interest lay in extending the influence of Christianity in English society. To this end, he made the inculcation of Christian moral standards the focus of education at Rugby and urged sweeping church reforms aimed at breaking down the barriers separating secular and religious life in England. In 1831, Arnold founded the *Englishman's Register,* a short-lived periodical in which he published articles on contemporary religious and social topics, and in 1833 he published *Principles of Church Reform,* his most comprehensive statement concerning religious affairs in England. This essay, which advanced such controversial concepts as a unified national church incorporating most of the dissenting sects in England, offended conservatives and liberals

alike and generally served to alienate Arnold from the religious mainstream. Arnold's 1836 essay "The Oxford Malignants and Dr Hampden," an attack on the leaders of the Oxford movement that was widely denounced as immoderate, further increased his isolation. Indeed, it was not until the late 1830s, when the Oxford movement began to weaken and his Rugby students graduated and went on to spread his fame at the universities, that Arnold's reputation improved. He was appointed Regius Professor of Modern History at Oxford in 1841, delivering a series of lectures there that was published as *Introductory Lectures on Modern History*. Arnold suffered a fatal attack of angina pectoris a short time later, dying at the age of forty-six.

Although Arnold rarely presented his ideas systematically, commentators generally regard his writings as a source of significant approaches to history, scriptural exegesis, and church and social reform. Arnold's major historical work is *History of Rome,* an unfinished chronicle brought up to the close of the Second Punic War. In the course of this work, he applied the lessons of the classical past to contemporary society, a practice based on a theory of parallel national development that he expressed in his "Essay on the Social Progress of States" and in *Introductory Lectures on Modern History*. Many recent critics observe that Arnold's theory owed much to the ideas of the Italian philosopher Giovanni Battista Vico and the German historian Barthold George Niebuhr. Arnold's approach to scriptural exegesis, although difficult to trace in his writings, is also considered significant. While he apparently made no major statement concerning exegetical theory, Arnold is often praised for bringing scholarly methods to bear on the study of Scripture without sacrificing his faith in the Bible as an instrument of divine truth. As some commentators have noted, for many Victorians this balanced approach to Scripture helped bridge the gap between faith and reason in an age of religious doubt.

Arnold's *Principles of Church Reform* and other statements concerning church renewal in England are the writings for which he is best known. Hoping to establish God's kingdom on earth, Arnold argued that the English church and state ought to be identical. Working from this premise, he proposed an agenda for reform aimed at unifying and revitalizing the English church. Impatient with such "external" hindrances to unity as disagreement on questions of church government and "over-definite" creeds, he envisioned a national church tolerant of a wide variety of Christian religious convictions and reorganized so as to reduce priestly religious prerogatives and financial abuses. Many commentators credit Arnold with attempting to put the unifying figure of Christ rather than historically divisive creeds at the center of church life and with trying to make the church more responsive to the needs of the new industrial society in England. At the same time, he has often drawn negative criticism for exhibiting what W. C. Lake, one of his former students, described as a "painful indifference to truth of doctrine," an attitude that some observers have faulted as unrealistic and inconsistent with Arnold's role as an ordained minister in the Church of England. One other aspect of his religious views has elicited intense scrutiny: his advocacy of mandatory religious tests for citizenship and his belief that Jews and other non-Christians should be denied full status as citizens. Although these propositions grew out of his concept of England as a Christian polity, they seem to many commentators symptomatic of a narrowness of mind on Arnold's part, which has troubled even his staunchest admirers.

Arnold's intellectual and literary reputation rests primarily on his historical and religious writings, but his general renown is firmly based on his achievements at Rugby. He was recommended for the Rugby headmastership by Edward Hawkins, the provost of Oriel College, as one who would "change the face of education all through the public schools of England." Remarkably, Arnold made good on this prediction by instituting a widely emulated system of student self-government at Rugby and by introducing a strong religious and ethical spirit into public school life. With regard to student government, Arnold gave the most advanced pupils—sixth-form boys—extensive powers in all aspects of school affairs, including the corporal punishment of those in lower forms. As boarding students largely left to their own devices, public school boys had previously been a self-regulating group given to hazing and insubordination; under Arnold's system, the schoolboy leaders' authority was legitimized by the headmaster and thereby subject to his influence. Arnold personally used this influence to realize his primary goal, which was to "introduce a religious principle into education." In addition to stressing the importance of duty and rectitude to his sixth-form prefects, he assumed the school chaplaincy, giving Sunday sermons before the assembled school that were usually focused on the practical moral issues arising in the schoolboys' lives. As an educator, Arnold has inspired both praise and blame. His emphasis on moral conduct has received special attention: detractors fre-

quently contend that he instilled in his students a premature and excessive moral self-consciousness that harmed their development, while supporters maintain that only exceptionally high-strung students were adversely affected by Arnold's zeal. These and other issues—including his reliance on sixth-form prefects and use of corporal punishment—often arise in discussions concerning Arnold's impact on English education and society as a whole.

Arnold has sustained a relatively high profile in England, largely due to his portrayal in several widely read works. According to Edward C. Mack, Arthur Penrhyn Stanley's inspiring 1844 biography caused Arnold to become known as the "outstanding schoolmaster of his generation" and the "dominating force in educational matters" in the years immediately following his death. Still, stringent criticisms—a few voiced by former students—were not unheard of, which some scholars believe led Matthew Arnold to write the famous poem "Rugby Chapel" extolling his father's spiritual leadership. Arnold's poem was written in the late 1850s, the same decade in which Thomas Hughes published his schoolboy classic, *Tom Brown's School Days*. This work, which was set at Rugby during Arnold's headmastership, conveys a glowing image of Arnold that continues to inform public opinion today. Lytton Strachey attempted to debunk this image in his *Eminent Victorians*, published in 1918, but Arnold has weathered this and other criticism well. His life, writings, and ideas are regularly examined today by commentators who generally agree that Arnold merits study and recognition for the important contributions that he made to England's religious, intellectual, and educational life in the nineteenth century.

(See also *Dictionary of Literary Biography*, Vol. 55: *Victorian Prose Writers Before 1867*.)

PRINCIPAL WORKS

The Christian Duty of Granting the Claims of the Roman Catholics (essay) 1829
Sermons. 3 vols. (sermons) 1829-34
Thucydides: The History of the Peloponnesian War. 3 vols. [editor] (history) 1830-35
Principles of Church Reform (essay) 1833
"The Oxford Malignants and Dr Hampden" (essay) 1836; published in periodical *The Edinburgh Review*
History of Rome. 3 vols. (unfinished history) 1838-43
Christian Life: Its Course, Its Hindrances, and Its Helps (sermons) 1841
Christian Life: Its Hopes, Its Fears, and Its Close (sermons) 1842
Introductory Lectures on Modern History (lectures) 1842
History of the Later Roman Commonwealth, from the End of the Second Punic War to the Death of Julius Caesar, and of the Reign of Augustus, with a Life of Trajan. 2 vols. (history) 1845
The Miscellaneous Works of Thomas Arnold (essays, letters, and lecture) 1845
Sermons Chiefly on the Interpretation of Scripture (sermons) 1845
Sermons by Thomas Arnold. 6 vols. (sermons) 1878

*This work includes "Essay on the Social Progress of States."

THE BRITISH CRITIC (essay date 1830)

[*In reviewing the first volume of Arnold's* Sermons, *the anonymous critic protests against Arnold's condemnation of "imperfect" Christian individuals and organizations and questions the logic of his attack on corruption in established churches.*]

[Dr. Arnold] professes, in his preface [to his *Sermons*], that his object has been to grapple at once with the understanding and conscience of his hearer; and that, in pursuit of this object, he has abjured all pretensions on the score of style, and this even at the hazard of being chargeable with homeliness and defect of skill. Points of criticism, or difficult questions of theology, he has deliberately avoided. The discourses, he tells us, "are directly practical;" and adds, that "it has been his endeavour, in all of them, to enforce what may be called peculiarly Christian practice—that is, such a perfection in thought, word and deed, as the Spirit of God should inspire to the enlightened understandings and willing hearts of those whom Christ redeemed, and who are now no longer under the law, but under grace."

In the execution of this purpose, it will appear that the preacher has set before his congregation a very lofty standard of Christian morals. He faithfully and urgently presses upon their attention how grievously the professors of the Gospel generally fall below the measure of a perfect man—below the stature, and the strength, and the fulness of a Christian: and in doing this he is, unquestionably, fulfilling one of the first duties of a preacher of Christian Righteousness. Nevertheless, while we render the amplest testimony to the fidelity with which he discharges this part of his office, we crave permission to express our doubts whether his anxiety to be *found faithful* in this matter, has always been under the guidance of a sound discretion. For ourselves, we must avow, that we have frequently risen from his statements with feelings widely different from those with which we rise from the perusal of the Bible. The devout and attentive study of the Scriptures can never fail to leave us under the influence of profound humility and self-abasement; but this lowliness of heart is always, more or less, accompanied and relieved by a sense of heavenly animation and energy. "The bones which are broken," nevertheless "rejoice." But the general result of Dr. Arnold's representations struck us as being, in this respect, occasionally, somewhat at variance with the teaching of the Holy Ghost. The mild and tender spirit of the Saviour seemed frequently to be wanting. The preacher is honestly intent on breaking the proud and worldly spirit, but sometimes appears to forget that he may be crushing the bruised reed. While he is labouring to consign us to the service which is perfect freedom, he little suspects, perhaps, that his style of preaching too often "gendereth unto bondage." The contrast between Christian perfection, and the present condition of the Christian world, is so formidably represented, and insisted upon with such incessant urgency, as often to send a deadly dejection into the very depths of the heart, and will nigh to blight our hopes of the improvement of the human race. (pp. 259-60)

[Dr. Arnold] has occasionally fallen into an application of the language of Scripture, which, as it appears to us, is at least productive of confusion; and which, moreover, tends to deepen the gloom that sometimes hangs over his doctrine. Is it, for instance, consistent with the doctrine of the Church of England, or with the mind of St. Paul, to describe as "children of wrath," all those members of the Christian Church, who are living in disregard or violation of their holy profession? "We *were* by nature," says the Apostle, addressing the whole Ephesian church collectively, "children of wrath, even as others;" implying manifestly that they were "children of wrath" no longer. "Being by nature born in sin" (says our Catechism) "and 'the children of wrath,' we are hereby" (that is, by the inward and spiritual grace of baptism) "made the children of grace." Can it, then, be properly said of any one who has received that grace, that he is a "child of wrath" in the sense contemplated by the Apostle, and, after him, by our own church?. . . [Certainly] the theology of the Church of England proclaims no man in her communion to be a "child of wrath," so long as there remains either hope or possibility of his being reclaimed to the blessedness of a "child of grace." We, therefore, cannot but regret that the language of one of her ministers should, in this respect, be so directly at variance with her scriptural charity and wisdom.

Another instance of disputable exposition may be found in Sermon XII. The general tendency of this discourse is admirable. Its text is Rom. vi. 14.—"Sin shall not have dominion over you, for ye are not under the law, but under grace;" and its purpose is to show that a genuine and sincere Christian obeys God, not so much from fear of violating his commandments, as from delight in fulfilling them. In illustrating this position, however, Dr. Arnold commences by a definition of law, which we cannot allow to pass wholly without question.— "By the word law the Apostle means any rule of life which puts a restraint on our natural inclination, and which we obey through fear, and with an effort." Now can this definition be just? Can it be proper to mix up the motive to obedience with the essence of the rule? Does a law cease to be such, because it is obeyed willingly, and without effort? The law says "thou shalt not kill;" and is not this equally a law to all, whether to Howard the philanthropist, or to Burke the wholesale and practised murderer?

It is true that the Apostle says,—"the Law was not made for a righteous man, but for the lawless and disobedient, for the ungodly and sinners, for the unholy and profane." But this seems to be little more than a popular and striking mode of saying, that if a perfectly righteous man could be found, the sanctions of a written law would be needless for him; he would, in the highest sense, be a law unto himself; and, if the human race had retained their moral perfection, the promulgation of a formal and positive commandment would have been comparatively useless. But man having now lost that perfection, it is necessary, not only that "Revelation should lay down a rule to be followed invariably in opposition to appearances; but that to the instructions of infinite wisdom, infinite power should add penal sanctions." But how can it follow from this, that the rule thus revealed must lose its imperative or prohibitory character, in every instance, in which it happens to meet with no opposition from the inclination of the individual who is under its dominion?

In another part of the same discourse the preacher enforces his views by the following passage from Gal. v. 4. "Christ is become of none effect to you, as many of you as would be acquitted by the law; ye are fallen from grace:"—a sentence which appears to us to be without the slightest application to the general purpose of the Sermon. It is clear from the preceding verses, that the Apostle is here speaking with reference to the pernicious notion, that the Gospel was merely suppletory to Judaism, and that the rite of circumcision was the only *effectual entrance* to the Christian dispensation; and he contends that this notion could not be maintained without an utter renunciation of Christianity. If, says he, you will insist on the necessity and the efficacy of circumcision, I tell you that, by so doing, you fall away from the œconomy of Grace, and place yourselves, to all intents and purposes, under the complete dominion of the Jewish system. All this is perfectly intelligible as addresses to the Galatians, under their peculiar circumstances; but what endless confusion must result from the application of such a passage to a Christian community at the present day! The Galatian Church was in danger of a principle which involved a virtual apostasy from the faith. But with what safety, or what charity, can it be said of the unworthier members of a modern congregation that they have "fallen from grace," that they are no better than apostates, and that they must henceforth stand or fall by the unmitigated letter of the law? (pp. 261-63)

According to the views and notions of the Apostle, a man is living "under the law," when he has nothing but the letter of the law to look to; when he has no promise of spiritual aid to give animation and steadiness to his obedience; when he has no assurance that his repentance for transgression of the law will be graciously accepted. Over such persons sin may very properly be said to exercise dominion; for they have no offer of heavenly support against the violence of their passions, no whispers of comfort to assuage the horrors of their bondage! And such would be the condition of all mankind, to the end of time, if they were never to be brought under the economy of grace. But when once a man is brought under this better dispensation, when he is federally invested with a right to claim its promises and blessings, what strange perplexity must result from speaking of him, as if he were still remaining under the power of any former dispensation? It may be very proper for a preacher to tell his hearers, that they may sin themselves into an eventual forfeiture of the privileges of the covenant of grace; but it is contrary to scripture, to charity, and to common sense, to pronounce of any man that he has actually been transferred from that covenant to the tyranny of the law, unless it can be shown that such forfeiture has been certainly incurred.

The whole complexion, indeed, of Dr. Arnold's divinity seems to us to betray the nurture and the training rather of the puritanical and sectarian school, than that of the great masters and doctors of the church of England. He appears to think that he cannot faithfully discharge his responsibility as a Christian minister, without representing those who are living in apparent disregard of their baptismal vows as persons who have not been taken into covenant with God, or else as persons who have positively abjured that covenant. He intimates that they "who are not walking according to the Christian love which the inward man approves, cannot reckon themselves as belonging to the flock of the good Shepherd." He urges that there is "a broad distinction between the Christian and the *unconverted* man—between the heir of heaven and the servant of the Devil." He therefore (unless we grossly misapprehend him) virtually contends for no less than this, that the reception of a child into the congregation of Christ's flock is a mere nullity *until* it shall appear, beyond all question, that his life is conformable to this beginning; that the titles of "a member of Christ, a child of God, and an inheritor of the kingdom of heaven," are, in a multitude of instances, prematurely, and almost presumptuously, bestowed by the Church; and that the very name of Christian ought, in strictness, to be withheld, wherever the life of the individual assimilates him to heathens, who have never entered the pale of the church, or to professed infidels, who have violently broken out of it. All this harmonizes admirably with the divinity of a certain school, but is, undeniably, at

variance with the sober, cautious, and charitable spirit of our Church. (pp. 264-65)

The vigour, with which Dr. Arnold has sometimes vaulted over the boundaries of moderation, is no where, perhaps, more remarkably exhibited, than in the xviith Sermon, in which, after observing that there are "many persons who, not disclaiming the name of Christians altogether, have yet no clear knowledge of what a Christian ought to be," he exclaims, "would that they would take one side or the other; that they would either be the servants of Christ in earnest, or renounce him openly, and say that they have nothing to do with Jesus of Nazareth, or his salvation! Happy, indeed, would it be for the Church of Christ, if all its false friends were to declare themselves its enemies." We protest that, to out apprehensions, there is something of temerity in this wish, which, if it came from the lips of an enthusiast, would almost make us shudder. For let us imagine the vow of the preacher to be heard. Let us suppose that all, who, at any given time, are nearly ignorant of the essentials of their religion, were openly and avowedly to desert the ranks of Christianity: what is the spectacle which, in that case, would be exhibited throughout the communities of Christendom? Why, neither more or less than this;—that on the one side we should have the company of the "true believers," and on the other side the whole assemblage of persons who might come under the description of the "false friends of Christ;" including every imaginable variety of character which falls short of a consistent profession of the Gospel,—from the irresolute, the thoughtless, and the unstable, down to the scandalous professor, and the disguised infidel. And what would be the consequence of thus building up a wall of partition between the best and sincerest believers, and the rest of the world? What,—but that we should have a vast portion of society permanently cut off from the ordinances and institutions of Christianity! The false or doubtful friends of Christ, having now finally separated themselves from his true followers, would cease to frequent the assemblies of the faithful. They would never hear the word of doctrine or of exhortation. They would have shut themselves out from the appointed means of grace. They would be publicly and solemnly pledged to unbelief. Their hearts would be sealed against the voice of the Church, which, otherwise, might win them back from their fatal alienation; and they would probably be fixed, to their life's end, among the desperate adversaries of their Redeemer! The existing condition of things is oppressive and discouraging enough; but it is a state of millennial bliss compared with that which would probably follow, if Heaven, in wrath, were to listen to the vows of our preacher. (pp. 266-67)

The degree to which the peculiar notions of Dr. Arnold have wrought themselves into the whole texture of his speculations, is signally exemplified in the Seventh Sermon, in which he has confounded the visible with the invisible Church; or rather (if we rightly comprehend him) has virtually denied that what men call the visible Church is anything better than a sort of perilous and hollow confederacy between Christ and Belial. "The Christian unity," he tells us, "was originally a unity of goodness, and affection of good men for one another, because they mutually loved God. But as soon as this was changed for another sort of unity, in which bad men could also be partakers, then the unity, of which St. Paul spoke so earnestly, was lost; and men ceased to be one with each other in the Father and the Son." He then proceeds to pourtray the evils which have rushed into the world in consequence of this departure from "Christian unity": and to assert that the abuse has actually averted and defeated, if we so may speak, the gracious designs of Providence, and thrown the world back into a condition very little, if at all better, than the worst darkness of heathenism. And then—''Is this,'' he asks, ''the kingdom of God upon earth, where every thought, and word, and deed, are brought into the obedience of Christ?''

We have, here, a notion of ''Christian unity'' which seems almost to revive the Novatian heresy, and the schism of the Donatists. The Novatians held the Church of Christ to be a society distinguished by universal innocence and virtue; and maintained that, consequently, no repentance could ever restore a heinous offender to her communion. Something of a similar spirit was manifested by the Donatist schismatics; for they relied on the language of the Apostolic Creed to prove, that any practice, at variance with *holiness*, destroys the pretensions of a community to the character of a Church. In like manner Dr. Arnold appears to have persuaded himself that there can be no true ''Christian unity'' in any society on earth, unless its members are all distinctly conscious of being engaged in *''one common strife*, not only against flesh and blood, but against all manner of spiritual evil.'' We believe it very safe to affirm, that no such ''unity'' of the *visible* Church was ever contemplated either by the Christian Fathers, or by the soundest divines of the Church of England.

But Dr. Arnold appeals to higher authority than that of Fathers or divines; for he produces the words of our Lord himself:— ''I pray for all who believe on me, that they all may be one; as thou, Father, art in me, and I in thee, that they also may be one in us.'' ''And the Apostles,'' he adds, ''in the spirit of their Lord, are earnest in recommending this same thing— that we should be of one heart, and one mind, forming, altogether, one undivided Christian body.''. . . When the Son of God came down from heaven to establish his kingdom on earth, it was to be expected that he should speak of it, for the most part, in language suited to its final and plenary success, rather than to the period of its agony and peril—to its triumphant, rather than to its militant, condition: and it would have been strange indeed if his Apostles had commended any less perfect exemplar to the imitation of their followers. Dr. Arnold, however, is not content to produce this entire unity of Christian holiness and affection as a model to which the hopes and desires of every Christian should be raised: he tells that, since this portraiture is nowhere realized on earth, the true Christian unity is wholly lost, and the Church is now fatally defective in that character, which the prayer of Christ assumes to be essential to her existence. But if this unity be now extinct, when—we desire to be informed—did it ever live and flourish? Certainly not (Dr. Arnold will probably reply) since the days of Constantine. But where, we demand, was it to be found before the days of Constantine? where in the times of the earliest Christian Fathers? where in the days of the holy Apostles themselves? If the mixture of unworthy members be a violation of Christian unity, where on earth is the body of Christians which has preserved its integrity from the day of our Lord's ascension to the present hour?

We had hitherto imagined that when our Lord was praying for the mysterious union of believers with the Father and with himself, he was contemplating that which is always devoutly to be desired, but which shall be fully realized only in that blessed company, whose names are written in heaven, but which, on earth, no man can sensibly discern. (pp. 268-70)

The imagination of Dr. Arnold . . . has been so intensely fixed upon the glorious integrity—the spotless and unwrinkled beauty—of the Church invisible, that he is unable to discern any form or comeliness in mortal societies which have no such unsullied purity to boast, and is almost unwilling to concede to them the honours of Christian communion. The Church of God, he tells us, is one and indivisible; but the societies which men call churches are scarcely better than sanctuaries of Romulus, and exhibit little else than a wretched multiformity of evil, disunion and corruption! . . . [This attitude threatens] all attachment to particular communions. It may tempt us to regard it as a matter of the profoundest indifference, whether Christian society wears an external appearance of concord, or whether it presents the semblance of a theatre, in which every imaginable experiment may be made in the formation of ecclesiastical constitutions. Episcopacy, Presbyterianism, Independency, all are to be perfectly or nearly indifferent in the estimation of man, because, eventually all of them may contribute members to the invisible Church of God! Nay, we know not where we are to stop, short of the persuasion, that any anxiety about such distinctions is a breach of Christian liberality and benevolence, if not a positive sacrifice of Christian sincerity and singleness of heart! All this may, perhaps, be exceedingly gratifying to ''the good and enlightened Dissenter,'' whom Dr. Arnold commends to the friendly and liberal notice of the Churchman; but what should we say to it if gravely propounded to us by a Presbyter and Doctor of the Church of England? (pp. 273-74)

[Dr. Arnold's] principles lead, almost directly, to the inference, that questions relating to ecclesiastical polity, have an interest and a value about as high as antiquarian discussions respecting the Roman College of Augurs, or the British Druids, or the Saxon Wittenagemote. If [as Dr. Arnold states] churchmanship be ''an earthly and unimportant'' matter, it, likewise, must signify little whether the Church be directed by bishops, or by elders, or by a lay committee. The unity and integrity of the Church of Christ would suffer no violent invasion by the utter destruction of episcopacy. If that institution were to be abolished to-morrow, there would be just one form of Church government the less—that is all! Doctrines like these will, of course, be received with glad acclaim throughout all the regions of non-conformity. But how will they be welcomed by the brethren of Dr. Arnold? What will be said to them by those whose studies have taught them, that, ''episcopal government being established by them, on whom the Holy Ghost was poured in such abundant measure for the ordering of Christ's Church, it had a Divine appointment beforehand, or Divine approbation afterwards, and is, in that respect, to be acknowledged as the ordinance of God.'' (p. 277)

[Dr. Arnold makes the following assertion in his Seventh Sermon:]

> The adoption of Christianity as the national religion in point of form and profession of opinions, whilst its spirit and principles were either unknown or hated, has introduced a confusion into our civil and ecclesiastical relations, under which we are at this moment labouring. It has led, for instance, to the maintenance of these two inconsistent propositions by the very same persons;—that the government may interfere in church matters, because in a Christian country the government is to be regarded as Christian, and the king must be a member of the church; and yet that Christianity does not meddle with political institutions, with forms of government, questions of public rights, legislation,

war and peace, &c. because Christ's kingdom is not of this world.

Precisely conformable to these views is another passage from the Sixteenth Sermon, in which, after describing the early success of the Gospel, and the lives and labours of the first Christians, he adds,—

> But soon Satan learnt to oppose their progress more artfully. Resistance appeared to fail before them; from being persecuted, they became triumphant; kings professed the name of Christ, and the idols of the heathen perished from before his face. His servants were ready to join in the hymn of the Apostle, 'The kingdoms of this world are become the kingdoms of the Lord and of his Christ.' But the snare of their enemy meanwhile fully succeeded: the kingdoms of the world became in name the kingdoms of Christ, only to make the kingdom of Christ in reality a kingdom of the world.

Now whether or not the notions here propounded or insinuated be just, is a distinct question. One thing, however, seems to us almost irresistibly clear, namely, that whoever adopts these notions must be prepared to avow, on the authority of a master of our Israel, . . . that a national profession of Christianity is not only inexpedient, but is little better than an abuse and an abomination. (p. 279)

We cannot . . . forbear to express our utter astonishment, that any one, bred in a school, which claims no humble character for logical precision of thought, should have failed to discern the fatal infirmity of this whole train of reasoning. One main objection here implied against a national profession of religion is, that all such professions have originated in illegitimate methods for propagating the Gospel; in methods tending to the production of an abominable miscellany, in which the celestial elements of a spiritual society are tossed into an unblest combination with the sordid, beggarly, and corrupt elements of the world,—the whole mixture being miscalled a Church. Now in order to see whether or not this objection is fatal, it will be necessary to consider for a moment what would have been the effect of a different mode of proceeding. Let us suppose for instance, that the secular power had, from the apostolic age to the present moment, suffered the Gospel to take its own course, and to depend solely on its own resources;—is it to be imagined that the result of this neutrality would have been a Christian Church of inviolate purity and integrity? Is it to be imagined that the world would at this day have witnessed a perfect exemplification of that Christian unity which is the object of Dr. Arnold's earnest and sincere desires? Can it be believed that a scrupulous abstinence from all secular alliance would have secured to the cause of Christianity such a powerful guidance and custody, as would have excluded all unsoundness from its communion? Is it to be supposed that there would, in that case, have been such a total separation between the kingdom of Christ, and the interests of this world, as would have enabled an Apostle (if he should revisit the earth) to say of the whole body of professing Christians, that they were strictly, and literally, and to a man, a royal priesthood, a chosen generation,—while the rest of the world were beyond the confines of God's marvellous light? Can all this be deliberately maintained? And if it cannot, why should the present state of things be arraigned as eminently destructive of Christian unity? Why should national professions of Christianity be objects of suspicion, for being deficient in a quality which, under no imaginable cir-

cumstances, could Christian society ever have exhibited? (pp. 282-83)

[Dr. Arnold] has recently been elevated to a post which will enable him to apply all the stores of his knowledge, and all the powers of his mind, to the solution of that hitherto unmanageable problem, the religious education of large bodies of youth. The failure of our most distinguished and popular schools to accomplish this purpose, has often been the subject of loud and bitter arraignment. Whether Dr. Arnold will be able to construct a system, the adoption of which shall efface this burning reproach, we shall not venture to anticipate. That he will omit no exertion which benevolence and piety can suggest, we are profoundly convinced. And should he succeed in this genuine labour of love—should he be enabled to convert that, which hitherto has frequently been considered as the "mere despair" of public tuition, into its "crown of rejoicing,"—we shall not hesitate to number him among the most distinguished benefactors to the human race. He must, however, forgive us, if,—with all our veneration for his virtues, and all our respect for his abilities and attainments,—we venture, very earnestly, to express one hope;—namely, that, in training his pupils for their Christian warfare, he will not think it an abandonment of his duty to abstain from language which may chance to impair their allegiance to our national communion. We regard it as a matter of the most urgent importance, that the British youth should be bred in sentiments of the deepest attachment for the constitution of England, both in Church and State; that they should be taught to understand the blessings of which our religious establishment has been made the honoured instrument, and that they should be trained rather in the school of her unrivalled masters of theology, than in that of her bitter though conscientious adversaries. All this may most assuredly be done, without the slightest sacrifice either of true religion, or of genuine liberality: without the sacrifice of religion,—for, (next to the Bible,) where is Christianity to be learned, if not from the mighty and venerable doctors of the English Church?—without any sacrifice of liberality,—for nonconformity itself has almost ceased its tragical complaints of high church bigotry, and is compelled to acknowledge the ample provision made by the present system for the independence—we had almost said, for the caprice—of private opinion and belief! We cannot therefore but reckon it among the most solemn obligations incident to the office of an instructor, to commend this sacred inheritance to the hearts of the youthful generation, and thus to secure its transmission, in unfading strength and honour, to our latest posterity. (pp. 293-94)

> *"Arnold's 'Sermons',"* in The British Critic, *n.s. Vol. VII, No. XIV, April, 1830, pp. 257-94.*

THOMAS ARNOLD   (letter date 1839)

[In the following extract from a letter to his friend and fellow Oxonian the Reverend Dr. Hawkins, Arnold defends the orthodoxy of his doctrinal opinions, maintaining that his reputation at Oxford for heterodoxy is "unfounded."]

When I found how entirely I agreed with your Sermon on Private Judgment, it struck me that I had taken rather too indifferently the sort of vague odium which has been attached to my opinions, or supposed opinions, for the last ten years in Oxford; that I had forfeited a means of influence which I might have had, and which would have been a valuable addition to what I have enjoyed among my own pupils at Rugby. I do not mean anything political, nor indeed as to the right or the wrong of my opinions on any matter, because I have held them decidedly and expressed them openly, and people who differ from me will of course think me wrong. But I think I have endured too quietly a suspicion affecting me more directly professionally; a suspicion of heterodoxy such as was raised against Hampden, and which would exclude me from preaching before the University; an office to which otherwise I think I should have a fair claim, from my standing, and from my continued connection with the University through the successive generations of my pupils. Now this suspicion is, I contend, perfectly unfounded in itself, and at the present moment it is ridiculous; because the Newmanites are far more at variance with the Articles, Liturgy, and Constitution of the Church of England than any clergymen have been within my memory; and yet even those who most differ from them do not endeavor, so far as I know, to hinder them from preaching in Oxford. I am perfectly aware that my opinion about the pretended Apostolical succession is different from that of most individual clergymen, but I defy any man to show that it is different from the opinion of the Church of England; and, if not, it is fairly an open question, on which any man may express his own opinion peaceably; and he is the schismatic who would insist upon determining in his own way what the Church has not determined. But in what is commonly called *doctrine*, as distinct from discipline, I do not think that anything can be found in any of my sermons, published or not published, which is more at variance with the doctrines of the Church than what is to be found in the sermons of any other man who has written as many; and not only so, but I think there is no *negative* difference; that is, I think there would be found no omission of any points which the Reformers would have thought essential, bating some particular questions which were important then, and are now gone by. I am perfectly willing to bear my portion of odium for all that I really have written, and the Newmanites may fairly speak against my opinions as I do against theirs. But a vague charge of holding, not *wrong,* but technically *unorthodox* opinions, affects a man's professional usefulness in a way that in any other profession would be thought intolerable; and, in fact, in other professions men would be ashamed or afraid to breathe it. I have gone on with it quietly for a long time, partly because no charge has ever been brought against me which I could answer, and partly because, whilst I was so fully engaged at Rugby, I was not practically reminded of it. But as I grow older, and the time is approaching more and more when I must, in the natural course of things, be thinking of leaving Rugby, and when I see a state of things in Oxford which greatly needs the help of every man interested about the University,—when I see that you are doing a great deal of good, and without any question of your orthodoxy, so far as I know, and yet know that in my constant preaching there is as little that anybody could call heterodox as in yours,—it makes me feel that I ought not silently to bear a sort of bad name, which to man or dog is little better than hanging; and that it would be desirable, if there really is a similar feeling against me to that which exists against Hampden, to get it if possible into some tangible shape. (pp. 134-36)

> *Thomas Arnold, in a letter to Rev. Hawkins on January 12, 1839, in* The Life and Correspondence of Thomas Arnold, D.D., *Vol. II by Arthur Penrhyn Stanley, 1844. Reprint by Charles Scribner's Sons, 1910, pp. 134-36.*

[WILLIAM GEORGE WARD]   (essay date 1841)

[*Ward was a prominent figure in the Oxford movement; a defender of Tractarian ideals, he was removed from his Oxford degree* following the publication of his 1844 treatise *The Ideal of a Christian Church and later converted to Roman Catholicism. In this excerpt from his review of Arnold's* Christian Life: Its Course, Its Hindrances, and Its Helps, *Ward remonstrates at length against what he perceives as Arnold's overemphasis on the "practical and external" aspects of Christian faith.*]

[Like its predecessors, **Christian Life: Its Course, Its Hindrances, and Its Helps**] is in many points most favorably distinguished from the ordinary run of sermons at the present day. It does not give us for exhortation vague and common place generalities, destitute of all direct practical and personal application; nor again barren admonitions, couched in a technical phraseology which no one would dream of using out of the pulpit, exhorting us to take care that our heart be rightly affected, without helping us on the practical question what means in our own power may help it to become so; neither for doctrine does it present loose and disjointed talk, contrived ingeniously to include contradictories, to give the appearance of holding major and minor premiss, and the appearance also of denying the conclusion, and exquisitely adapted to the purpose of concealing both from the author and his readers his want of any *consistent* scheme of doctrine whatever. No! Dr. Arnold knows his own mind, and says what he has to say in direct, forcible, and manly language; while there runs through his practical addresses a spirit of frank and affectionate earnestness, which shows clearly enough that his heart is in his work, and which would render it impossible, even were we inclined (which with us at least is far from being the case), and notwithstanding all that we find both to pain and perplex us, to feel otherwise than most kindly disposed to the writer, and much grieved at the wide interval of opinion which separates us from him.

Dr. Arnold's style is eminently *characteristic.* How many persons there are whose language is altogether a most untrue symbol of their mind! What a spell seems on them when they sit down to commit their thoughts to paper! how unlike their mode of writing to their mode of conversation!. . . But Dr. Arnold's language seems the exact correlative of his character: not calculated for the expression, whether of profound and accurate investigation, or of the cravings and perplexities of the more tender or more romantic class of minds; but not to be surpassed as a vehicle of historical and quasi historical narrative and discussion, or the expression of generous and manly sentiments in the way either of theory or exhortation. (pp. 298-99)

[Dr. Arnold] seems always, when in the pulpit, to bear in mind who are his hearers, what sort of advice they will want, and in what manner it may best be conveyed, so that they may understand it. When addressing his boys at Rugby, he is very short (hardly we should imagine exceeding a quarter of an hour in the delivery of a sermon), and usually confines himself to the plain and clear treatment of one subject in the simplest language, with a great deal of very apposite illustration from familiar objects, and with the introduction of the least possible extraneous matter. This homely and practical way of urging religious truths must be of especial value in a congregation of schoolboys, who are ever so singularly acute in the detection of unreality and inconsistency in those set over them. (p. 299)

The great idea which Dr. Arnold seems to us to have grasped and to put forth in every variety of shape in his sermons, is the duty of doing all to the glory of God; of considering our daily labours in the world, the duties of our station, the part we take in politics, to be as truly religious acts, and claiming to be done in a religious spirit, as prayer is. We *mean* of course by this no small praise; but when we come afterwards to add our explanations and qualifications, it will appear, we must confess, by no means so great as it does at first. But what makes the pointed enforcement of this great principle so especially valuable in a congregation of boys is, that while it is of course a truism to say that the notion of real religion without it is a delusion, in proportion as it is realized it may be made the foundation on which any amount of true doctrine may be reared. And while there must necessarily be so much danger at schools of duties being enforced on low and inadequate motives, and while the habit of looking to such, if encouraged so early, presents a fearful obstacle to subsequent real improvement, it is no slight blessing to have so much guarantee as these sermons may we hope be considered to give, that habits of good conduct and diligence shall be enforced, not from considerations of worldly prudence, but from first to last on the principle of pleasing God and doing His will. (p. 300)

But it must not be concealed that in this writer's *practical* religious system there are most grievous errors and deficiencies; sufficient indeed, as we must think, to deprive him altogether of weight as a *guide* in theological matters to the serious and humble enquirer; and the mention of some few of these is now our painful task.

He has himself said, and with great force and beauty of language, that in the Christian Revelation

> is contained the very food, and more than the food, of man's life: the remedy for all *troubles and sorrows,* from the simplest physical suffering of the rudest nature up to the mental conflicts which are the inevitable portion of the loftiest and most sensitive: the medicine for all *moral evil,* from the mere bodily appetites of the grossly ignorant to the most delicate forms of pride and selfishness in minds of the highest intelligence: the light to clear up every perplexity of practice, strengthening the judgment through the purified affections, the most exalted hope inseparably united with the greatest humility; because we believe in Christ Crucified, because we trust in Christ Risen.
> [*Principles of Church Reform*]

But we do not think that Dr. Arnold's *exhibition* of the Christian scheme in any way corresponds to this high language: indeed we must say that it bears a most suspicious resemblance to Dr. Arnold himself. Lemaistre, in speaking of that arrogant pretension to exclusive religious purity so common in Englishmen, and which is certainly grossly offensive in the eyes of foreigners, whatever we may think of it ourselves, says (we quote from memory, and we hope with no profaneness), that the English seem to imagine, "que Dieu s'est incarné *pour les Anglois:*" so we may say, also we hope with no profaneness and with rather a different application, that, if our author's representation of Christianity were true, we must consider that our religion was founded for the especial benefit of Dr. Arnold, unless indeed all mankind were counterparts of Dr. Arnold, which they most certainly are not. But if this seems rather more than he would himself claim, what remains but a strong presumption that the system whose wisdom he praises so highly, and which he seems able with undazzled eyes to behold in its length, breadth and depth, is rather, little as he thinks it, the unconscious developement of his own religious character, than the doctrine of the Bible: in a word, that he *makes* the system

first, and then he praises it? But on this subject we shall have hereafter to speak more at length.

It has been the especial line taken by heresy during the last three centuries, within or without the English Establishment, to deny or disregard what may be called *present* mysteries and wonders: and Dr. Arnold, who, with all his professions of independent study of Scripture, is on many points a complete slave to modern traditionary glosses, has fallen into the same snare. He has made, we rejoice to bear unequivocal testimony to it, the plainest avowals of orthodoxy on the great truths of the Trinity and Incarnation; but it is plain that belief in a Deity *once,* eighteen hundred years ago, incarnate, or *now* in mysterious Trinity governing the world as it were *at a distance* and by fixed laws, neither startles the reason nor irritates the imagination of minds of a certain class in the same degree as the news of unearthly and invisible agencies surrounding their common life, and close encircling them on all sides. It may be that disbelief in the latter class of doctrines is inconsistent with the hearty reception and appropriation of the former; but it need not perhaps lead, even *ultimately,* quite certainly in Dr. Arnold's case it has not *hitherto* led, to explicit *denial* of them. But such truths as the following (by way of example) are either practically neglected by the author, or plainly opposed.

1. That there is "a *particular* Providence under the Gospel," i.e., that by a chain of cause and effect, to us of course altogether incomprehensible, individual Christians who carefully live in God's faith and fear are so truly and fully regarded by Him as sons, so loved as though each severally were His only son, that, without deranging the universal machine, they are placed in those very external circumstances, exposed to those very trials, visited by those very favours, which He sees to be really the fittest for their spiritual discipline.

2. That even as to *general* laws, the Church is carried on by a vast system, unknown in its fulness to us, but including of course the whole subject of sacramental influences, and which moreover is of such a nature, that the simple and uncomplaining course of obedience and prayer in the humblest Christian, is as truly and, in the same sense, according to God's appointed way, a means and cause of the well-doing of the Church on earth (nay, affects the condition of the Church in Paradise or in Heaven) as the most active and best directed efforts of those called to a more prominent and obvious part in its support.

3. That Intercessory Prayer is in *reality and truth* efficacious.

4. That those of us who are in a state of grace here, are in a far closer communion with our fellow Christians on earth and with departed Saints, are far more truly in their presence and company, than we are in the presence and company of those who are discerned by our bodily senses. How far after death this communion becomes a *conscious* one, is of course a further question; but that it is *real,* even when unconscious, is no more *unmeaning* than to say that the indwelling in each Christian of the Holy Spirit is real, which is equally unconscious. "We walk by *faith,* not by sight;" and we are bound to aim at the *habitual* and *practical* belief in "the Communion of Saints" not less than in "the Holy Ghost."

5. That the holy Angels, "by God's appointment," as our Prayer-Book says, "succour and defend us on earth." That they are present when we are most alone, more especially when we pray and meditate, still more in church, most of all at the mysteries of the Sacrament of the Altar.

6. That an awful and mysterious gift beyond words is imparted to us in Holy Communion.

Now what is the practical effect of Dr. Arnold's omission of these and similar most consoling and transporting truths? His sermons will no doubt be of great use to that large class who are blessed with unfailing health and unflagging spirits, who take with pleasure to a life of active employment, who have warm and kindly, but not deep, affections, or who live naturally with a view to excellent and honourable, yet not romantic, objects. These will derive doubtless great benefit from his preaching: afterwards they may be led on by other guides to a fuller knowledge of the gracious scheme of redemption, and towards that specially *Christian* character of mind which Dr. Arnold's teaching is, we are persuaded, unable to create. But it is far otherwise with those whom sorrow or long sickness have disgusted with the world and with active life, or who, having warm and affectionate feelings, have been placed by God's Providence where there are no adequate human objects on which to rest them, or who by their very disposition are "keenly alive to the bitterly unsatisfying nature of earthly things," and are filled with a restless thirst for some unknown god, higher and more noble than the world around them, with unceasing aspirations after a scene of action more filled with the romantic and marvellous than at least the ordinary course of daily life can offer them. Such persons as these will find no rest in the exhibition of Christianity which the present volume would offer them. The thirst for something deep and true, to satisfy the cravings which arise from the causes we have referred to, in Dr. Arnold's own language, "will not be allayed by a draught so scanty and so vapid. . . ." Yet it has ever been the especial triumph of the Church, in her full developement, to reconcile all dispositions to the plain duties of practical obedience, and that, not by forbidding or checking such feelings as those just alluded to, but by guiding and directing them, and giving them their full scope in the performance of those very duties.

Where Catholic Christianity is purely taught, the more gentle and sensitive will be rescued from their tendency to a dreamy and unsatisfied indolence. There is not one of the many marvels which it teaches us, that does not in its place both raise the soul to heaven, and *also* stimulate and comfort it in its appointed sphere of earthly toil. Take for example that doctrine referred to above, which Dr. Arnold has pronounced not to be practical, and *therefore* not *revealed* in Scripture, viz. that angels are sent forth specially to minister for them who shall be heirs of salvation,—Is not the sympathy of Angels as much to be enjoyed in the most busy as in the most lonely scenes; nay, is it not *forfeited* by disobedience to the call of duty? And the thought of them, in proportion as it is dwelt upon and realized, will satisfy the needs of the most tender and most solitary heart; not as leading it to rest on them as the highest and adequate object for its affections, but as united with other parts of the Catholic doctrine and discipline to train it towards a habit, differing in kind not in degree from any attainable in the Protestant schools, both of love of God and sense of God's love, through His Son. And so, on the other hand, the more keen-minded and ardent, who under Protestant systems, if *well* principled, are cruelly oppressed through life with consciousness of deep feelings destitute of adequate objects whereon to rest, and if *not* rootedly well-principled, are tempted to a course of what may be called enthusiastic profligacy, have not been so overlooked by God in His pure Gospel. They need not go out of the routine of daily life in search of the marvellous and supernatural; it may be that they have plain duties to perform,

which *forbid* them to go out of it; let them only ponder and meditate on the mysteries which surround them *in* it. In the plain homely circle of common duties, their heart is not less the scene of combat between good and evil spirits than it would be in the wildest and most daring ventures; they are not less a spectacle to angels; they are not less by every small act of self-denial or self-indulgence acting for good or for evil on the fortunes of the Universal Church.

But such persons as these latter will not be contented without a more entire and ardent devotion of self to God, than that to which ordinary Christians feel themselves called. It will be not only the more mysterious truths, but the stricter and more severe *discipline* of the Gospel, which they will naturally need. And here too Dr. Arnold will meet and thwart them with his ready-made Procrustean system, "declaring that there is but one rule for all, a rule which the highest Christian can never go beyond,"—and showing but too clearly in his whole course of sermons what he considers that rule to be. This then brings us to another and much more serious complaint we are bound to urge against the author; his sadly inadequate notions of the strictness of discipline required by the Gospel scheme. . . . [Dr. Arnold] is unable even to *comprehend* the feeling which prompts many persons to aim at high and unusual strictness: it is not that he understands and condemns it, but that he cannot comprehend it. (pp. 303-08)

And now to begin our enumeration of some instances in which we find a very defective appreciation of the *strictness* and *spirituality*, as before of the *mysteriousness*, of the New Covenant: instances which will combine with our preceding observations in throwing light on Dr. Arnold's peculiar turn of mind.

1. Such teaching then as we have in the volume before us gives natural occasion to parties, whom the author would condemn as much as we should, to decry all inculcation of practical duties as "unspiritual." The impression generally conveyed is not so much that we are placed here as in a state of gradual preparation for our eternal Home, where prayer, praise and contemplation are to be our principal happiness, and that the course of daily practical life is admirably adapted, if we will but use it so, to serve as a *discipline* to that end, but rather as if this world, its duties and its history, were a final object of itself, the due carrying on of which was at least one principal end of our creation. A good life here below is represented as the *condition*, but is not put before us as the *preparation*, for happiness in the next. We do not accuse the author of really *holding* this view, but of creating the impression that he does, by the circumstance that he has not duly realized its opposite. (p. 309)

[There] is even a subtle worldliness in Dr. Arnold's *mode* of urging practical duties. We are not of course so hard-hearted, or paradoxical, or unthankful to God's mercy in leading us gently onwards, as to deny the great importance in the first instance of having our *heart* engaged in the worldly occupation which is our lot. Doubtless it was always intended that the beginnings of our obedience should be sweetened by the facility with which, in Dr. Arnold's words, "our tastes are disciplined to cling gracefully around that duty, to which else they must be helplessly fastened." And that to the end of our life we common men are in great need of such help, we are far from denying. But is it an extravagant suggestion, that we are not really pursuing a Christian course, unless we are making *progress* (however slowly) towards the habit of attachment to our duty, because it *is* our duty, because it is God's work on earth, because it is our preparation for His presence in Heaven? unless we at least find our comfort and happiness depend more than formerly on union with God, and *less* on our work, whatever it may be? is not, in fact, this progress the very business of most of us, the very end to which we should make all that befalls us, so far as may be, subservient? Yet we not only do not find this enforced with the urgency and prominence which are its due—we hardly think it is even alluded to in any of the four volumes. (pp. 310-11)

2. Accordingly, as might have been expected, Dr. Arnold makes little account of the hidden life of a Christian, of that habit of secret communion with God, which in His faithful servants is far more their real life than are their outward actions, and whose food is meditation and prayer. Thus we find neither rules to help us in the performance of habitual self-examination, nor even exhortations to that duty at all. Much less are his hearers advised to realize as best they may in the solitude of their hearts the depth and mysteriousness of the Gospel doctrines. His account of the Christian life is, short prayer morning and evening, occupation in our daily business, and necessary (worldly) relaxation; and this not only as a beginning on which higher attainments may be grafted; he seems a stranger (we are sorry to say it) to the very idea of spiritual progress. . . . [Dr. Arnold] does in general earnestly impress on [his peculiar congregation] the importance of so far keeping our Lord in remembrance throughout the day, as to preserve a consciousness that all should be done to His glory. But we are compelled to observe, that so much as *this* will never be accomplished without a far closer and more constant struggle with their old nature than he inculcates: and of a higher advance he seems to have no idea whatever. That as they make progress, they will feel some tendency to *love* the things most painful to the natural man, contempt, contumely, pain; or, again, that they will go on more and more to connect their work itself with holy thoughts, to employ short intervals of labour with holy aspirations, to find worldly relaxation less needed as religious exercises tend to supply its place; that such is the Christian's course heavenwards is the last thing that Dr. Arnold practically considers. (pp. 311-12)

3. We are naturally led by what has been said to mention the subject of Prayer, on which the plain language on the very surface of Scripture impresses us with a very different lesson from that which these sermons would suggest. . . .

4. From beginning to end of the four volumes *there is no exhortation to the regular habitual performance of intercessory Prayer.* (p. 313)

5. Dr. Arnold more than once professes belief in the doctrine so continually inculcated in Scripture of Judgment according to works; but he must excuse us for thinking that his usual language is by no means that of a person who realizes, that every hour of every day of every year of this mortal life has its account to give at the Great Day; that for the least act of obedience, in thought, word or work, we shall be for ever the happier, of *dis*obedience, for ever the less happy. As an instance which might be taken, it would be quite impossible for any one who *practically* understood this, to abstain from encouraging his hearers to continued acts of deprecation of God's wrath against their past sins; if for every one of them judgment is yet to come, how deeply does it concern them that that judgment may be merciful! Yet, for instance in his 26th sermon, when he speaks of those who "have not always been receiving the Holy Ghost *since they believed,* but are receiving him now," he gives no idea that there remains for them some

duty with reference to that time, be it long or short, during which they remained unfaithful to that grace, irreverent and disobedient to that Holy Ghost, who, as he tells them at the beginning of the very same sermon, was imparted to them at baptism. This will afford us an illustration also of what may be called (though it is much too strong a term) this writer's *heartlessness,* i. e. his want of any deep felt sympathy for the penitent's pangs and cravings. Were a depressed penitent to come before him, heart-broken with consciousness of past sin, and anxious, at whatever cost, for readmission to God's favour, he could give no other advice than "obey henceforward, and all will be as though you had never sinned!" Now we call this answer *heartless,* not *merciful;* for it will give no rest, let it not be imagined, to the really contrite and humble soul: his sense of God's justice, of the sinfulness of sin, of the voice of conscience, all will forbid it. We have no fear of his listening to Dr. Arnold, but we have great fear (and experience will be found to justify it) of his beginning to doubt the claims on his allegiance of that communion in which, should such opinions unhappily chance to be prevalent, he could obtain no other satisfaction for the purest feelings of his nature.

6. On the three preceding subjects we have referred to what appears on the very surface of Scripture, which is of course peculiarly an *argumentum ad hominem* in the case of the present author; we shall continue to do so on the following. We think then that the general tone of Scripture would give an idea that far more habitual self-denial and taming of the flesh is the Christian's duty than [*Christian Life: Its Course, Its Hindrances, and Its Helps*] would advocate. Scripture certainly does not represent Christians as gloomy (far otherwise indeed), rather as unceasingly rejoicing in the Lord; but this very joy seems ever in the sacred pages owing to that almost consciousness of divine realities which is obtained by and through mortification of the flesh; their rejoicing seems to be, that the world hangs so loosely upon them; and the world hangs so loosely, because "they are dead to it, and it to them." Any one must feel that such phrases as "taking up our cross daily," "whosoever leaveth not all that he hath cannot be my disciple," "that we must through much tribulation enter into the kingdom of God," "crucify the flesh with the affections and lusts," and a thousand others, do not somehow find a natural place in Dr. Arnold's system; that some forced and unnatural interpretation of them has to be given, which may serve to adjust in some way or other the language of the first century with the practice of the nineteenth. Again, with regard to the salutary effects of suffering and affliction, we find but little stress on such considerations; not so much (may we be pardoned for saying?) as judging from probabilities we should expect from a person of middle age, whose own lot in life had not been sunny far beyond the usual condition of men. On the subject of celibacy, as another instance, Dr. Arnold is in a difficulty; his own conscience does not lead him to consider it a higher state of life in itself than marriage, and he will not believe that any other person's conscience does either. In this he shows his usual imperfect knowledge of human nature, which his historical studies have done but little to improve; however, he is thus left to deal as he can with the text of Scripture, his own moral feelings preponderating on this point against, rather than for, the Catholic doctrine. St. Paul's advice he disposes of by considering it to rest mainly upon his (mistaken) impression "that the world would come to an end in the generation then existing." How he explains away our Lord's words (Matt. xix. 12), does not very clearly appear; nor will we here discuss the point whether a careful and *impartial* reading of the chapter of St. Paul will reconcile any one to this as the fair account

of it. But at least we may expect an answer to these two questions, 1st, are not Christians taught to live *always* as though the Day of Judgment were close at hand, nay in expectation of it? 2nd, unless the single life were *in itself* better, how would the proximity of the Last Day make it so? For there is no very obvious relation of cause and effect.

7. From what has been said it will have been expected that while Dr. Arnold will much admire "religious orders, especially of women, of different kinds and under different rules," so long as their function is the ministering of bodily and spiritual works of mercy to their fellow-creatures, he will not be tolerant of a life whose *chief* business shall not be active benevolence but contemplation. This will not be denied by any one, friend or foe; and therefore we need not be at the pains to prove from his writings that such is his feeling: the plea he would enter would be a *justification*. He might except the cases of persons who from age or sickness *cannot* be of direct service to their fellow-creatures; but others he would not except; nor is this any feeling peculiar to him, *we* rather are in the minority at the present day. Let us say then a very few words on this subject; for if we should succeed in occupying this position, we shall be in possession of the very key of the enemy's country. We all know how great is Dr. Arnold's veneration for Niebuhr; and we are willing for the present to admit the wonderful intellectual greatness of that writer, and that he well deserves nearly all that can be said in its favour. Now on what ground would Dr. Arnold justify this wonderful man in retiring from the line of direct and active benevolence, in order to devote himself to those close and intense studies, which have obtained for him that almost instinctive discernment of the historical truth latent amidst a mass of fable, so astonishing to all his intelligent readers? What would be said in answer to an indignant Utilitarian, who should rise up in arms against such an abandonment of the field of practical exertion, which may not much more be said in behalf of the old Catholic doctrine, which this busy age has learnt either lightly to scorn or seriously to condemn? "Of course if he had practical duties which he was plainly called to perform, he would *not* be justified in leaving them." *We* say the same of the religious life. "His wonderful talents seemed a direct call to that region of enquiry." It cannot, we suppose, be denied that some Christians also have endowments of mind which wonderfully qualify them for the life of prayer and contemplation. "He is really, though indirectly, of the utmost good to his brethren. History is most important for practical life; one man must study it in quiet, that many may profit by it in action. Again, he lives apart from the hurry and bustle of the world, and coming down among them from the calm field of historical enquiry, he tends to save them from that narrowing of the faculties which party action and practical life will certainly superinduce; and to infuse into this troubled scene a little of the gentle and humanizing atmosphere of patient and impartial investigation." And shall it be said that patient study, and removal from the bustle of active life, sharpens indeed the faculties and enlarges the intellectual vision in *history* or *literature;* but that in *religion*, to contemplate calmly is to obtain a distorted view, or to be removed from the sphere of practical action is to enter into that of monkish prejudice? Is a grammar and dictionary so *all sufficient* to interpret the sacred language of inspiration? Is it visionary to expect that he who leads the life most nearly of all earthly things resembling the divine, shall have truer sympathy with, and so fuller understanding of, words that are divine? Or is no good done indirectly to their brethren who are surrounded by the dust and heat of worldly cares, if there exist men who may come down among them from the regions of prayer and con-

templation, to preserve orthodoxy, to guide devotion, to infuse a purer and more heavenly atmosphere, to witness to the multitude the reality of unseen things? Lastly, is the intercession of holy men for their brethren no advantage to them? Let this be well considered: let it be observed whether those who are so loud in their protests on the *uselessness* of a life of seclusion, believe in any true sense the efficacy of intercessory prayer. But whatever comes of our reasonings, let us bring ourselves (it is no very usual thing with the present generation) to look facts fairly in the face. *Have there ever been times of zealous self-devotion in the cause of benevolence and humanity which have not been also times of retirement and contemplation?* Is it the active Protestant or the contemplative Catholic who has sent forth the sisters of charity and of mercy, the devoted priest, the zealous missionary? Let not the question then at least be *ruled* on the Protestant side, till something be done to make both reasoning and fact less exclusively on the Catholic; let us bear to think that twelve centuries and all the Church have *something* to say, when at issue with three centuries and a small part of it.

But we need not pursue farther our painful task. We may now sufficiently apprehend the ethical principles of that religious system which Dr. Arnold advocates. That his own character is to a very great extent moulded on those principles, may be assumed without discourtesy; rather indeed the discourtesy would consist in supposing him to aim at any other ideal than that which he proposes as the model to others. His support of history as a *foundation* for political science . . . is characteristic of the same turn of mind,—implying an exaggerated estimate of the practical and external; and his Erastian opinions . . . are all in the same direction. He *is rather attracted by the vision of good conduct in the many than of eminent holiness in the few;* and he will meet the usual fate of those who lack the faith to pursue God's end in God's way rather than their own; that his own principles would be found in practice far less efficacious for his *own* objects than is the polity which God has set up. . . . Yet the knowledge we derive from Dr. Arnold's sermons of the practical and (we must add) superficial turn of his mind, enables us to understand . . . that Dr. Arnold is himself an earnest and serious person labouring "in that state of life to which it has pleased God to call him," and because it is God's will he should there labour, with a zeal, energy and activity which may well serve both as an example and incentive to many who trust they have been led into far healthier views, and into a much purer and fuller knowledge of Gospel Truth. (pp. 314-18, 320)

[*William George Ward*], *in a review of "Christian Life, Its Course, Its Hindrances, and Its Helps," in* The British Critic, *Vol. XXX, No. LX, October, 1841, pp. 298-364.*

THOMAS ARNOLD (letter date 1842)

[*Writing to one of his assistant masters, Arnold here discusses his reaction to criticism of the disciplinary methods used at Rugby. Arnold's remarks are dated 1842, the year of his death, in the absence of information concerning the composition of his letter.*]

I do not choose to discuss the thickness of Præpostors' sticks, or the greater or less blackness of a boy's bruises, for the amusement of all the readers of the newspapers; nor do I care in the slightest degree about the attacks, if the masters themselves treat them with indifference. If they appear to mind them, or to fear their effect on the school, the apprehension in this, as in many other instances, will be likely to verify itself. For my own part, I confess that I will not condescend to justify the school against attacks, when I believe that it is going on not only not ill, but positively well. Were it really otherwise, I think I should be as sensitive as any one, and very soon give up the concern. But these attacks are merely what I bargained for, so far as they relate to my conduct in the school, because they are directed against points on which my 'ideas' were fixed before I came to Rugby, and are only more fixed now; e. g. that the authority of the Sixth Form is essential to the good of the school, and is to be upheld through all obstacles from within and from without, and that sending away boys is a necessary and regular part of a good system, not as a punishment to one, but as a protection to others. Undoubtedly it would be a better system if there was no evil; but evil being unavoidable we are not a jail to keep it in, but a place of education where we must cast it out, to prevent its taint from spreading. Meanwhile let us mind our own work, and try to perfect the execution of our own 'ideas,' and we shall have enough to do, and enough always to hinder us from being satisfied with ourselves; but when we are attacked we have some right to answer with Scipio, who, scorning to reply to a charge of corruption, said, 'Hoc die cum Hannibale benè et feliciter pugnavi:'—we have done enough good and undone enough evil, to allow us to hold our assailants cheap.

Thomas Arnold, in an extract of a letter in The Life and Correspondence of Thomas Arnold, D.D., *Vol. I, by Arthur Penrhyn Stanley, 1844. Reprint by Charles Scribner's Sons, 1910, p. 124.*

[HERMAN MERIVALE]   (essay date 1843)

[*Merivale highlights Arnold's intellectual penchant for controversy and for "rapid generalization," citing his views on the relationship between church and state as an example of these negative tendencies.*]

Dr Arnold was a 'crotchety' man: such appears to have been the general estimate of his character. It is an epithet of many meanings; but it seems to us to be commonly and significantly applied to those who endeavour to ascertain the truth on every separate subject of enquiry, instead of following the ordinary process of taking up whole bundles of opinions as they are commonly found connected together. Whoever does this, is very certain to agree in some points with one party, and in some with another; and equally certain to be called crotchety by both. But we must say in justice, that the epithet does to a certain extent describe his character, in some of its minute peculiarities. There was a rapidity of judgment about him—a haste in arriving at conclusions, which is apt to lead to the sudden formation of opinions—possibly to a little fickleness, on minor points, in adherence to them. His judgment seems to have been influenced at once by an abhorrence of dogmatism, commonly so called, and an impatience of scepticism. We do not mean in a religious sense only, but in historical and every other research. He could not, like Montaigne, *se reposer tranquillement sur l'oreiller du doute.* He had a mind averse from suspense, dissatisfied and uneasy under the pressure of doubt; and, therefore, disposed to generalize at once, where slower and more cold-blooded men would consider the process of induction hardly begun. To this was joined a strong moral perception, and a disposition particularly inclined towards ethical speculation—towards predicating moral right and wrong of every phenomenon which human history and human nature exhibit: a peculiarity which he seems to us to have caught in

great measure from association with his early friend Archbishop Whately, just as he caught his style of historical research from Niebuhr;—and a deep interest in the controversies of the day, with an eagerness to liberate his own mind by expressing his sentiments upon each of them. It is no disparagement of Dr Arnold to say, that this very eagerness sometimes appears to us to betray a secret uneasiness—a misgiving as to the results of his own conscientious enquiries. There are few, indeed, who, having deliberately rejected the idolatries of parties and systems, can rest undisturbedly on the ground they have chosen for themselves; for such thinkers have nothing of the ready support on which others so confidently lean. They would be more than men, if there were not moments when the very foundations seem to give way under them, and their own hearts to sink also—moments when they are tempted even to look with envy on those who march forward sternly or cheerfully, looking neither to the right nor the left, through regions in which they stumble and grope for light; yet their victory is not the less complete, although the enjoyment of its fruits, like all human enjoyment, is interrupted by obstinate questionings of its own reality.

It is a curious result of these tendencies, that Dr Arnold should have gone so far out of his way as to subjoin to his "Inaugural Lecture" [published in *Introductory Lectures on Modern History*] a special appendix on a subject certainly very remotely connected with the matters developed in it—namely, the refutation, by name, of the Archbishop of Dublin's views as to the separation of the duties of Church and State: and with him he has done us the honour to join ourselves, (alluding to an article in a late number of this Journal). He endeavours to unite 'one half of the Archbishop of Dublin's theory with one half of Mr Gladstone's: agreeing cordially with Mr Gladstone in the moral theory of the State, and agreeing as cordially with the Archbishop in the Christian theory of the Church; and deducing from the two the conclusion, that the perfect State and the perfect Church are identical.' It seems to us that there are at least four theories afloat on this much debated subject. One is, that the authorities which we commonly term 'the Church' ought to decide *circà sacra;* and that the authorities we call 'the State' have nothing to do but to enforce those decisions by civil penalties: this was the anciently received doctrine, so beautifully exemplified in the practice on the writ *de hæretico comburendo.* The next ascribes, if we may term it so, a sort of pre-existent harmony to Church and State; allotting to the State a power *circà sacra,* on a kind of assumption that it will proceed in harmony with the ecclesiastical authorities. The third is what, in the dictionary of theological hate, is called Erastian; namely, that the State has absolute authority *circà sacra,* to be enforced by civil penalties, irrespectively of the decisions of ecclesiastical authorities; and this is Dr Arnold's. The fourth is, that the civil governor has no such authority whatever, either in his legislative or executive character, although he may occasionally lend his aid, with benefit, for the attainment of purely religious objects; and this appears to be the Archbishop of Dublin's. We are far from wishing to revive the controversy on our own account; least of all, in commenting on the language of an antagonist, whose pure and lofty charity of soul deprived his tenets, if erroneous they be, of all the danger which commonly attends such error; and yet it is well to recollect that even Dr Arnold, with a spirit to which all religious despotism was abhorrent, was driven, by the force of his theory, to refuse to all avowed 'unbelievers in Christ,' a share in the legislature of a Christian country. Our object is much more to notice the peculiarities of the man, the eager, although tolerant, spirit with which he rushed into this as into other controversies; and the tendency of his mind to rapid generalization.

Now, one fruitful parent of theories is, the use of words (to employ a trite comparison) not as current coin, but as counters, to which the reasoner may affix his own imaginary value. The word 'Church,' is a very favourite counter with theorists; the word 'State,' is another, of which the meaning is quite as arbitrary. Before we can ascertain the truth of the 'moral theory' of the State, we must understand what the State is. Now, Dr Arnold's argument seems to rest entirely on the assumption, that Government, State, and Nation may be used as synonymous terms. Grant him this, and undoubtedly one great difficulty in the way of his theory is removed. 'When I speak of the Government,' he says, 'I am speaking of it as expressing the mind and will of the nation; and though a government may not impose its own law, human or divine, *upon an adverse people,* yet a nation, acting through its government, may certainly choose *for itself* such a law as it deems most for its good.'—'In a corrupt State, the government and people are wholly at variance; in a perfect State, they would be wholly one; in ordinary States, they are one more or less imperfectly.'—'For the right of a nation over its own territory must be at least as absolute as that of any individual over his own house and land; and it surely is not an absurdity to suppose that the voice of government can ever be the voice of the nation; although they unhappily too often differ, yet surely they may conceivably, *and very often do in practice,* completely agree.'— Here the right of a government to legislate *circà sacra* is rested, where all men of reasonable views must rest it, on its 'expressing the will of the nation.' Suppose the objector to take the ground, that the government, in point of fact, never does express the will of the nation except by accident; for that nine-tenths of mankind are governed by rulers who rest their authority on the principle, that they are not placed there to express, but to control, the will of the nation; while in those countries which are most democratically governed, the government can represent, at best, only the numerical majority of the nation;—a majority which may, or may not, comprehend the religious or intelligent portion of it; how is he to be answered on these premises? If the idea of a State could be realized with any reasonable probability, we can easily understand the value of a theory founded upon it—although actual States might be but imperfect agents to carry it out; but if the idea is one which history and common sense alike show us can never be realized at all, we do not understand how the theory can stand alone. In fact, Dr Arnold seems elsewhere to admit that his principle goes no further than this—that 'the favourite objections against the State's concerning itself with religion, apply no less to the theory of a Church. . . . The moral theory of a State is not open to the objection commonly brought against our actual constitution, namely, that Parliament is not a fit body to legislate on matters of religion; for the council of a *really Christian State* would consist of Christians at one good and sensible, quite as much as the council of a really Christian Church.'—Now, since we may very safely assume, that since Christendom began there has never been any thing approaching to a 'really Christian State'—since we may safely foretell that there never will be, until the kingdoms of this world are become the kingdoms of the Lord—this comparison seems to reduce the whole to a question of expediency; whether, upon the whole, it is best that the spiritual government of mankind should be left to those authorities whom we commonly term the Church, unarmed with coercive power, or to the temporal government which possesses it. Dr Arnold preferred the latter; and he had a perfect right to do so; but not to erect his own preference

into an axiom. He considered the Church 'a society far worse governed than most States.' It may be so; but other political philosophers may think that most States are, upon the whole, worse governed than the Church; and who is to decide between them?

And some may be disposed to think, that it was the weakness of the position which he had undertaken to maintain, which drove him to put forward such paradoxes as that excommunication is a *temporal* punishment, or, still more unworthy of himself, such vulgar arguments as that of the 'almost unanimous consent of all writers on government, whether heathen or Christian, down to the 18th century.' Dr Arnold, of all men, ought to have been best aware, that on the great questions which concern the government of mankind, so long as the consent of all writers is nearly unanimous, it is worthless. Consent is worthless, until people begin to think; and thought is only provoked by opposition. *Quot homines tot sententiæ,* as he elsewhere says, 'holds good only where there is any thinking at all: otherwise there may be an hundred millions of men, and only *una sententia,* if the minds of the 99,999,999 are wholly quiescent.' He might also have remembered, that if 'nearly unanimous consent' is conclusive for his views of a State, it is quite as conclusive against his views of a Church. We willingly quit so barren a subject; and could only wish that all who maintain similar views, whether on Dr Arnold's or any other premises, would represent to themselves and their readers their main position in its literal sense; namely, that it is the chief duty of the existing governor of every existing State, whether King or Majority, to take care of the spiritual welfare of every citizen. We by no means assert that they would change their opinions, but merely that they would see the subject in a very different light, if it were once freed from the endless fallacies of general words. When it was represented to the Emperor Ferdinand II., that the course which he was pursuing towards the Protestants of Bohemia, would render that kingdom a desert, his answer was, *'malumus regnum vastatum quàm damnatum.'* All we contend is, that on Dr Arnold's principles it is impossible to prove that the Emperor was wrong. (pp. 365-69)

[*Herman Merivale*], *"The Late Dr. Arnold," in* The Edinburgh Review, *Vol. LXXVI, No. CLIV, January, 1843, pp. 357-81.*

[W. R. GREG] (essay date 1843)

[*In assessing Arnold's accomplishments, Greg especially commends his ideas concerning Christian unity, yet notes "some singular inconsistencies" in Arnold's conduct and opinions in other religious matters.*]

Few names have been more widely known, and none have been more universally respected, in England, than that of Dr Arnold. As head master of Rugby school, his sphere of usefulness was extensive, and his reputation deservedly high; while his various theological writings insured him a corresponding estimation in the religious world; and, to say nothing of his valuable edition of Thucydides, his History of Rome, unhappily still a fragment, which was destined to supply a long felt desideratum in our literature, placed him at once in the very foremost rank among scholars and historians. Unfinished as it is, it will always retain its place as one of the finest historical fragments in our language; and in our humble opinion, enough even now remains to justify a conviction that, had he lived to complete it, it would have stood at the head of our classical literature in that department. It is a work, even in its present form, in which the experience of the Past is brought to bear, with singular force and discrimination, upon the exigencies of the Present; to solve many of the perplexing problems which are now evolving before our eyes; and to enlighten that dark cloud which, even to the most hopeful and trusting minds, involves much of the future destinies of our country and our kind. (p. 1)

In the year previous to his untimely death, Dr Arnold, to the great joy of all to whom historical pursuits were dear, was appointed to the professorship of modern history in the University of Oxford. It had not been customary for any lectures to be delivered from that chair; but Dr Arnold was not a man to make a sinecure of any office which he held. Moreover, his heart was in his subject, and he rejoiced in the opportunity thus afforded him of developing and promulgating his own well-considered conceptions of the moral and political philosophy to be deduced from history. Had he lived to complete his plan, his lectures would have been, we cannot doubt, one of the richest treasuries of wisdom and of learning extant; and he could scarcely have failed to instil some portion of his own lofty and upright principle into the minds of those whom he addressed: but, unhappily for us, it was otherwise decreed; and a brief sketch of what he had intended to do is all that he was permitted to accomplish. The volume of [*Introductory Lectures on Modern History*], which he delivered at the close of 1841, now lies before us; and though marked, perhaps, by a certain want both of terseness of language and concentration of thought (owing, no doubt, to the very short period allowed him for its preparation), it contains much valuable matter, and will furnish food for much careful reflection. (pp. 1-2)

[Had Dr Arnold lived to continue his duties in the Chair of Modern History at Oxford], he must incontestably have done much to liberalize the tone of opinion in that university, to redeem its character with the public, and to instil into the minds of those who attended his prelections, and who would hereafter be called upon to play their part as lawgivers and rulers, those lessons of enlightened patriotism, generous philanthropy, and uncompromising principle, which were never more needed than at present. By all the pupils who had been under his tuition at Rugby, and a large portion of whom afterwards graduated at Oxford, he was regarded with almost reverential admiration, and his influence over their feelings and opinions was almost unlimited; while the respect, both for his character and his intellectual endowments, which was entertained by all his colleagues in the university, must have greatly strengthened the Liberal party, of which he was one of the most distinguished ornaments; and must have contributed not a little to sweep back that tide of priestly intolerance which is striving to replace upon the nineteenth century the incubus which overshadowed the intellect and oppressed the energies of the middle ages. (pp. 20-1)

In his character and conduct throughout life, the most sincere and fervent piety was seen united with a clearness of vision, a depth of research, a logical sagacity, a comprehensive philosophy, a strength of purpose, a sympathy with the interests and a toleration for the feelings of the world, which are rarely its concomitants; and was at the same time utterly free from any taint either of spiritual pride, of intrusive sanctity, or of narrowness of heart. And this we believe to have been the secret of the almost universal estimation in which he was held by men of all classes and all diversities of opinion. Had he been a less sincere or a less pious Christian, the influence of his liberal and enlightened wisdom would have been unfelt by the religious world. Had his profound knowledge and philo-

sophical acumen been less indisputable, the influence of his piety would have been lost upon the world at large. By uniting the excellences of both characters, he was enabled to make religious sincerity lovely and respectable in the eyes of the indifferent and the worldly; he was able, also, to obtain from the less liberal of his priestly brethren, a patient consideration for doctrines of wise and charitable equity, which, coming from more ambiguous quarters, would have been scouted as impious, and condemned without a hearing.

Dr Arnold's clearness of intellect and genuine liberality of heart enabled him, and him alone of all his brethren of the church, to discover the true principle of mutual religious toleration, and the only basis on which harmony among Christians can ever be securely built; viz., the acknowledgment that *unity of practical aim,* not *unity of speculative faith,* should be the bond of brotherhood between them. (p. 22)

[Even] in a man of Dr Arnold's capacity and worth, [however, we find] what appear to us some singular inconsistencies of conduct and opinion; and, finding them in him, we shall believe that no man may flatter himself with the notion of being himself exempted from a similar imperfection. . . . Dr Arnold urged, in the strongest language, that unity of aim, and not unity of opinion, should form the bond and cement between the members of a Christian community: yet he retained his position as minister of a Church which binds all within its pale by the strictest shackles of a common creed. He maintained the right, and the obligation, of private judgment on religious points as sacred and inalienable, and the sin and danger of biassing the mind by the attachment of penalties or advantages to either decision: yet he more than once subscribed his allegiance to a Church which, whatever specious gloss it may put upon the matter, considers difference of opinion as criminal, and has long attached to it civil disabilities and spiritual menaces. He regarded as absurd and wicked every attempt to suppress heresy by force: yet every sabbath he prayed that the civil power might execute the duty of "maintaining truth." He repeatedly declared his conviction that mere error of belief was not culpable, because it was inevitable; that the sincerest inquirers would necessarily arrive at doctrines the most opposite on points the most important: yet he professed, and we doubt not conscientiously repeated, an unintelligible creed, which declares that whoever differs from that creed "without doubt shall perish everlastingly." Such are the melancholy anomalies which even the most upright minds cannot escape when hampered by a false position. (pp. 28-9)

Dr Arnold enjoyed [a] great source of happiness which, to a considerable extent, is within the reach of all. He felt that he was always doing good. His habitual occupations as an educator, though often no doubt irksome enough, were of a kind to produce certain, and generally profitable, results; their success, when successful, obvious and direct. The avocations of the generality of men have, for the most part, objects distinct from the good of their fellow creatures; and the benefit they produce to others is unseen, uncertain, and remote. In most other professions philanthropy forms not the staple labour, but at best the occasional recreation, or the ultimate and indirect aim. With the two to which Dr Arnold belonged, it was the actual business of every hour; and throughout his whole career he was able to repose on the conviction—the most soothing and supporting the human mind can entertain—that the world was the better for his labours, that he had not lived in vain.

Well may we repine at the early loss of so rare a pattern of human, and therefore of attainable, excellence. Had he reached the usual period allotted to man's earthly pilgrimage, and died as full of years as he did of honour, our only sentiment would have been

> A holy concord, and a bright regret,
> A glorious sympathy with suns that set.

But now this is mingled with the sadder feeling of disappointment which inevitably attends an unfulfilled purpose, an interrupted drama, an unfinished history; and with the perplexity consequent on a dispensation which we cannot understand. (pp. 31-2)

> [W. R. Greg], "Dr. Arnold," in The Westminster Review, *Vol. XXXIX, No. 1, February, 1843, pp. 1-33.*

A. LAMSON   (essay date 1844)

[*Lamson assesses Arnold's Rugby sermons, praising his practice of tailoring his remarks to meet the needs of his schoolboy audience.*]

The sermons contained in both [**Christian Life, Its Course, Its Hindrances, and Its Helps** and **Christian Life, Its Hopes, Its Fears, and Its Close**] were preached mostly in the Chapel of Rugby School, of which [Dr. Arnold] was head master. They are plain, serious, practical discourses, written without any attempt at eloquence. They exhibit no remarkable intellectual power, yet the thought is always fresh and vigorous, and they breathe an earnest and Christian spirit. Their peculiar excellence, as it appears to us, is their strict adaptation—this is true of most of them at least—to the condition and needs of the audience before which they were preached. They are not discourses on general subjects, which might be as well preached before one set of hearers as another. Many of them bear the form of direct addresses to the young, children at school; and consist not in vague declamation, but in a discussion of some definite subject, some principle of conduct or duty, connected with the wants, dangers, and temptations of youth. Others are upon the general duties of the Christian life, its "course, its hindrances, and its helps," "its hopes, its fears, and its close." Yet these topics are not treated in any formal way nor at all systematically, so as to form one regular whole. This the author does not pretend, though the title of the volumes would lead one to expect some such thing. Probably most persons who take up the volumes, allured by the title, will read them with a feeling of disappointment. Still we cannot but think, that the delivery of such sermons from Sabbath to Sabbath, marked, as they are, by a high moral and religious tone, and containing so much which was directly applicable, must have been attended with good, especially when we take into view the peculiar respect and affection, which, as we are told, Dr. Arnold had the happiness uniformly to inspire in his pupils. They certainly present a beautiful picture of the relation in which he stood to his pupils, not simply as their intellectual father, but a tender and faithful religious guide. Several of the sermons, however, have a direct reference to the principles and usages of his own Church, the Church of England, which will render them less acceptable elsewhere than at home and among the members of the Establishment. (pp. 38-9)

> A. Lamson, "Arnold's Sermons," in The Christian Examiner, *n.s. Vol. 1, No. 1, January, 1844, pp. 38-45.*

WILLIAM WORDSWORTH   (letter date 1844)

[*Wordsworth, who is considered by many scholars to be the greatest and most influential English Romantic poet, was Arnold's neighbor at the latter's country estate. Wordsworth comments on some of Arnold's intellectual and personal traits in the excerpt below.*]

Mrs. Wordsworth has read [Stanley's *Life* of Arnold] diligently. The first volume she read aloud to me, and I have more than skimmed the second. He was a truly good man; of too ardent a mind, however, to be always judicious on the great points of secular and ecclesiastical polity that occupied his mind, and upon which he often wrote and acted under strong prejudices and with hazardous confidence. But the book, notwithstanding these objections, must do good, and *great* good. His benevolence was so earnest, his life so industrious, his affections,—domestic and social—so intense, his faith so warm and firm, and his endeavour to regulate his life by it so constant, that his example cannot but be beneficial, even in quarters where his opinions may be most disliked. How he hated sin, and loved and thirsted after holiness! Oh, that on this path he were universally followed!

> William Wordsworth, in a letter to Henry Crabb Robinson on July 14, 1844, in Letters of the Wordsworth Family from 1787 to 1855, *Vol. III, edited by William Knight, 1907. Reprint by Haskell House Publishers Ltd., 1969, p. 305.*

ARTHUR PENRHYN STANLEY   (essay date 1844)

[*Stanley, who was one of Arnold's most outstanding pupils at Rugby, was appointed professor of ecclesiastical history at Oxford in 1856 and served as dean of Westminster from 1864 to 1881. In addition to numerous religious works, he wrote* The Life and Correspondence of Thomas Arnold, D.D., *a biography that is now valued as a seminal account of Arnold's character and career. Stanley attempts to explain the spirit of urgency and contention informing Arnold's writings in the following excerpt from the* Life.]

[Dr. Arnold's] works were not merely the inculcations of particular truths, but the expression of his whole mind; and excited in those who read them a sentiment almost of personal regard or of personal dislike, as the case might be, over and above the approbation or disapprobation of the opinions which they contained. Like himself, they partook at once of a practical and speculative character, which exposed them, like himself, to considerable misapprehension. On the one hand, even the most permanent of them seemed to express the feeling of the hour which dictated them. On the other hand, even the most transitory seemed to express no less the fixed ideas, by which his whole life was regulated: and it may be worth while, therefore, in regard to both these aspects . . . , to offer briefly a few remarks which may serve as a preface to all of them. (p. 175)

Secluded as he was, both by his occupations and his domestic habits, from contact with the world, even more than most men in his station, yet the interest with which . . . he entered into public affairs, was such as can rarely be felt by men not actually engaged in the government of the country. (p. 176)

It was of course only or chiefly through his writings that he could hope to act on the country at large: and they accordingly, almost all, became inseparably bound up with the course of public events. They were not, in fact, so much words as deeds; not so much the result of an intention to instruct, as of an incontrollable desire to give vent to the thoughts that were struggling within him. ''I have a testimony to deliver,'' was the motive which dictated almost all of them. ''I must write or die,'' was an expression which he used more than once in times of great public interest, and which was hardly too strong to describe what he felt. If he was editing Thucydides, it was with the thought that he was engaged, ''not on an idle inquiry about remote ages and forgotten institutions, but a living picture of things present, fitted not so much for the curiosity of the scholar, as for the instruction of the statesman and the citizen.'' If he felt himself called upon to write the history of Rome, one chief reason was, because it ''could be understood by none so well as by those who have grown up under the laws, who have been engaged in the parties, who are themselves citizens of our kingly commonwealth of England.'' If he was anxious to set on foot a Commentary of the Scriptures, it was mostly at times when he was struck by the reluctance or incapacity of the men of his own generation to apply to their own social state the warnings of the Apostles and Prophets. (pp. 176-77)

It is not, therefore, to be wondered at, if that impatience of present evil, which belonged alike to his principles and his disposition, appeared in his writings, and imparted to them— often, probably, unknown to himself—something, if not of a polemical aspect, at least of an attitude of opposition and attack, averse though he was himself to controversy, and carefully avoiding it with those whom he knew personally, even when frequently challenged to enter upon it. (p. 177)

Connected with this, was the peculiar vehemence of language which he often used, in speaking of the subjects and events of the day. This was indeed partly to be accounted for by his eagerness to speak out whatever was in his mind, especially when moved by his keen sense of what he thought evil—partly by the natural simplicity of his mode of speech, which led him to adopt phrases in their simplest sense, without stopping to explain them, or suspecting that they would be misunderstood. But with regard to public principles and parties, it was often more than this. With every wish to be impartial, yet his natural temperament, as he used himself to acknowledge, made it difficult for him to place himself completely in another's point of view; and thus he had a tendency to judge individuals, with whom he had no personal acquaintance, from his conception of the party to which they belonged, and to look at both through the medium of that strong power of association, which influenced materially his judgment, not only of events, but of men, and even of places. Living individuals, therefore, and existing principles, became lost to his view in the long line of images, past and future, in which they only formed one link. Every political or ecclesiastical movement suggested to him the recollection of its historical representative in past times,—and yet more, as by an instinct, half religious and half historical, the thought of what he conceived to be the prototypes of the various forms of error and wickedness denounced by the Prophets in the Old Testament, or by our Lord and his Apostles in the New. And looking not backwards only, but forwards, to their remotest consequences, and again guiding himself, as he thought, by the example of the language of St. Paul, who ''seemed to have had his eye fixed in vision rather upon the full-grown evil of later times, than upon the first imperfect show—the faint indications of it—in his own time,'' he saw in them the germs of mischief yet to come,—not only the mischief of their actual triumph, but the mischief of the reaction against them. (pp. 178-79)

[No] temporary interest or excitement was allowed to infringe on the loftiness or the unity of his ultimate ends, to which

every particular plan that he took up, and every particular line of thought which he followed, were completely subordinate. However open to objection may have been many of his practical suggestions, it must be remembered that they were never the result of accidental fancies, but of fixed and ruling ideas. However fertile he might be in supplying details when called for, it was never on them, but on principles, that he rested his claim to be heard; often and often he declared that if these could be received and acted upon, he cared nothing for the particular applications of them, which he might have proposed, and nothing for the failure of particular schemes, if he could hope that his example would excite others to execute them better. (pp. 182-83)

Vehement as he was in assailing evil, his whole mind was essentially not destructive but constructive; his love of reform was in exact proportion to his love of the institutions which he wished to reform; his hatred of shadows in exact proportion to his love of realities. ''He was an idoloclast,'' says Archdeacon Hare, ''at once zealous and fearless in demolishing the reigning idols, and at the same time animated with a reverent love for the ideas which those idols carnalize and stifle.'' Impatient as he was, even to restlessness, of evils which seemed to him capable of remedy, yet he was ready, as some have thought even to excess, to repose with the most undoubting confidence on what he held to be a general law.... ''We walk by faith and not by sight,'' was a truth on which in its widest sense he endeavored to dwell alike in his private and public relations,—alike in practice and in speculation. (p. 183)

It would often happen, from the necessity of the case, that his works were written in haste, and were therefore sometimes expressed nakedly and abruptly. But it would be wrong to infer from the unblotted, unrevised manuscript, which went to the press as it came from his pen, that it was not the result of much thought and reading; although he hardly ever corrected what he had once written, yet he often approached the same subject in various forms; the substance of every paragraph had, as he often said, been in his mind for years, and sometimes had been actually written at greater length or in another shape; his sense of deficient knowledge often deterred him from publishing on subjects of the greatest interest to him; he always made it a point to read far more than he expressed in writing, and to write much which he never gave to the world.

What he actually achieved in his works falls so far short of what he intended to achieve, that it seems almost like an injustice to judge of his aims and views by them. Yet, even in what he had already published in his lifetime, he was often the first to delineate in outline what others may hereafter fill up; the first to give expression in England to views which, on the continent, had been already attained; the first to propose, amidst obloquy or indifference, measures and principles which the rapid advance of public opinion has so generally adopted, as almost to obliterate the remembrance of who first gave utterance to them. And those who know the intentions which were interrupted by his premature death will form their notion of what he was as an historian, philosopher, and theologian, not so much from the actual writings which he lived to complete, as from the design of the three great works, to which he looked forward as the labors of his latest years, and which, as belonging not more to one period of his life than another, and as forming, even in his mere conception of them, the centres of all that he thought or wrote on whatever subject, would have furnished the key to all his views—a History of Rome, a Commentary on the New Testament, and, in some sense including both of these within itself, a Treatise on Church and State, or Christian Politics. (pp. 185-86)

> *Arthur Penrhyn Stanley, "General Life at Rugby," in his* The Life and Correspondence of Thomas Arnold, D.D., *Vol. I, 1844. Reprint by Charles Scribner's Sons, 1910, pp. 174-218.*

B. PRICE   (letter date 1844)

[*Price was a student of Arnold at Laleham and later worked with him as an assistant master at Rugby. In the excerpt below, Price extols Arnold's methods of scriptural exegesis, praising in particular his recognition of both human and divine elements in the Bible as well as his ability to identify the "eternal principles" in Holy Writ.*]

As an expounder of the word of God, Arnold always has seemed to me to be truly and emphatically great. . . . The amount . . . of interpretation which he has published to the world, though not inconsiderable, is still small in respect of what there remained to be done by him; but Arnold has furnished a method—has established principles and rules for interpreting Scripture, which, with God's blessing, will be the guide of many a future laborer, and promise to produce fruit of inestimable value. (pp. 194-95)

I am here concerned with the . . . strictly intellectual process; the scientific exposition of the Scriptures as a collection of ancient books, full of the mightiest intellectual truths; as the record of God's dealings with man: and the historical monument of the most wonderful facts in the history of the world. For the office of such an interpreter, Arnold possessed rare and eminent qualifications; learning, piety, judgment, historical tact, sagacity. The excellence of his method may be considered under two heads:—I. He had a very remarkable, I should rather say (if I might) wonderful discernment for the divine, as incorporated in the human element of Scripture; and the recognition of these two separate and most distinct elements,—the careful separation of the two, so that each shall be subject to its own laws, and determined on its own principles,—was the foundation, the grand characteristic principle of his Exegesis. Our Lord's words, that we must "render to Cæsar the things which are Cæsar's, and to God the things which are God's," seemed to him to be of universal application, and nowhere more so, than in the interpretation of Scripture. And his object was not, according to the usual practice, to establish by its means certain religious truths, but to study the contents themselves—to end, in short, instead of beginning with doctrine. Indeed, doctrine in the strict sense, doctrine as pure religious theory, such as it is exhibited in scientific articles and creeds, never was his object. Doctrine, in its practical and religious side, as bearing on religious feeling and character, not doctrine, in the sense of a direct disclosure of spiritual or material essences, as they are in themselves, was all that he endeavored to find, and all that he believed could be found, in the teaching of Scripture.

First of all he approached the human side of the Bible in the same real historical spirit, with the same methods, rules, and principles as he did Thucydides. He recognized in the writers of the Scriptures the use of a human instrument—language; and this he would ascertain and fix, as in any other authors, by the same philological rules. Further too, the Bible presents an assemblage of historical events, it announces an historical religion; and the historical element Arnold judged of historically by the established rules of history, substantiating the general veracity of Scripture even amidst occasional inaccuracies of detail, and proposing to himself, for his special end here, the reproduction, in the language and forms belonging to our own age, and therefore familiar to us, of the exact mode of thinking, feeling, and acting which prevailed in the days gone by.

But was this all? Is the Bible but a common book, recording, indeed, more remarkable occurrences, but in itself possessed of no higher authority than a faithful and trustworthy historian like Thucydides? Nothing could be further from Dr. Arnold's feeling. In the Bible, he found and acknowledged an oracle of God—a positive and supernatural revelation made to man, an immediate inspiration of the Spirit. No conviction was more deeply seated in his nature; and this conviction placed an impassable gulf between him and all rationalizing divines. Only it is very important to observe how this fact, in respect of scientific order, presented itself to his mind. He came upon it historically; he did not start with any preconceived theory of inspiration; but rather, in studying the writings of those who were commissioned by God to preach His Gospel to the world, he met with "the fact, that they claimed to be sent from God, to have a message from Him, to be filled with His Spirit. Any accurate, precise, and sharply-defined theory of inspiration, to the best of my knowledge, Arnold had not; and, if he had been asked to give one, I think he would have answered that the subject did not admit of one. I think he would have been content to realize the feelings of those who heard the Apostles; he would have been sure, on one side, that there was a voice of God in them; whilst on the other, he would have believed that probably no one in the apostolic age could have defined the exact limits of that inspiration. And this I am sure I may affirm with certainty, that never did a student feel his positive faith, his sure confidence that the Bible was the word of God, more indestructible, than in Arnold's hands. He was conscious that, whilst Arnold interpreted Scripture as a scholar, an antiquarian, and an historian, and that in the spirit and with the development of modern science, he had also placed the supernatural inspiration of the sacred writers on an imperishable historical basis, a basis that would be proof against any attack which the most refined modern learning could direct against it. Those only who are fully aware of the importance of harmonizing the progress of knowledge with Christianity, or rather, of asserting, admist every possible form of civilization, the objective truths of Christianity and its life-giving power, can duly appreciate the value of the confidence inspired by the firm faith of a man, at once liberal, unprejudiced, and, in the estimation of even the most worldly men, possessed of high historical ability.

II. But I have not yet mentioned the great merit of Arnold's Exegesis; it took a still higher range. It was not confined to a mere reproduction of a faithful image of the words and deeds recorded in the Bible, such as they were spoken, done, and understood at the times when they severally occurred. It was a great matter to perceive what Christianity was, such as it was felt and understood to be by the hearers of the Apostles. But the Christian prophet and interpreter had in his eyes a still more exalted office. God's dealings with any particular generation of men are but the application of the eternal truths of his Providence to their particular circumstances, and the form of that application has at different times greatly varied. Here it was that Arnold's most characteristic eminence lay. He seemed to me to possess . . . an insight not only into the actual form of the religion of any single age, but into the meaning and substance of God's moral government generally; a vision of the eternal principles by which it is guided; and such a profound

understanding of their application, as to be able to set forth
God's manifold wisdom, as manifested at divers times, and
under circumstances of the most opposite kind; nay, still more,
to reconcile with his unchangeable attributes those passages in
Holy Writ at which infidels had scoffed, and which pious men
had read in reverential silence. Thus, he vindicated God's command to Abraham to sacrifice his son, and to the Jews to
exterminate the nations of Canaan, by explaining the principles
on which these commands were given, and their reference to
the moral state of those to whom they were addressed; thereby
educing light out of darkness, unravelling the thread of God's
religious education of the human race, from its earliest infancy
down to the fulness of times, and holding up God's marvellous
counsels to the devout wonder and meditation of the thoughtful
believer. . . . Arnold has rather pointed out the path than followed it to any extent himself; the student will find in his
writings the principles of his method rather than its development. They are scattered, more or less, throughout all his
writings, but more especially in the Appendix to vol. ii. of the
Sermons, the Preface to the third, the Notes to the fourth, and
the *Two Sermons on Prophecy.* These last furnish to the student
a very instructive instance of his method; for whilst he will
recognize there the double sense of Prophecy, and much besides
that was held by the old commentators, he will also perceive
how different an import they assume, as treated by Arnold;
and how his wide and elevated view could find in Prophecy a
firm foundation for a Christian's hope and faith, without their
being coupled with that extravagance with which the study of
the Prophecies has been so often united. His sermons, also,
generally exhibit very striking illustrations of his faculty to
discern general truth under particular circumstances, and his
power to apply it in a very altered, nay often opposite form to
cases of a different nature; thus making God's word an everliving oracle, furnishing to every age those precise rules, principles, and laws of conduct which its actual circumstances may
require. (pp. 196-99)

> *B. Price, in a letter to Arthur Penrhyn Stanley, in*
> The Life and Correspondence of Thomas Arnold,
> D.D., Vol. I, *by Arthur Penrhyn Stanley, 1844. Re-*
> *print by Charles Scribner's Sons, 1910, pp. 194-200.*

[W. C. LAKE] (essay date 1844)

[*Lake was Arnold's disciple and Stanley's friend during his school
days at Rugby; ordained in 1842, he was appointed dean of Durham in 1869. In this excerpt from a review of Stanley's biography
(see excerpt dated 1844), Lake candidly depicts Arnold as a morally earnest but intellectually limited thinker.*]

Dr. Arnold is, in our view, an original rather than a profound
thinker—with a vigorous and clear, rather than a subtle or
comprehensive mind. 'He was deficient,' says Mr. Stanley,
'in the dramatic faculty on the one hand, and in the metaphysical faculty on the other:' *i. e.* he could not in proportion
to his other gifts enter into characters, or estimate many of the
most powerful motives that influence mankind—he had but
limited power of reproducing and analyzing various states of
feeling in himself, or of imagining them in others—he was
not, in fine, what is sometimes called *subjective* enough, and
knew too little of men to be much of a philosopher. This is
not to deny his greatness: nay, it is upon this view of him, and
this alone, that we consider his greatness tenable. We maintain
him to have been a most bold and vigorous thinker, rapid in
generalizing, fertile in illustration and association, and with a
moral earnestness which might have raised an intellect of lead;

and we believe that he has brought to light isolated truths of
the first importance: but we cannot think that he had the mind
which apprehends the great laws of truth and sees it as a whole—
and which, being a faithful representative of all human nature,
has a place in its system for all its phenomena. . . . [Thus] in
his religious teaching, while the oldest and simplest truths seem
new from the freshness with which they are enforced, he has
left utterly unworked (as if unconsciously) some of the deepest
mines of our nature: his political and social views (these last,
we think, his best) are always real and original, but often vague,
not seldom narrow; nor can we have a clearer proof of his want
of tendency to abstract speculation than the almost total absence
of discussion of any doctrine of this character amidst the varied
subjects which are treated with so much interest throughout
[Stanley's biography]. Aristotle, in fact, and Thucydides—the
love of law, rather than the love of beauty—the love of progress, rather than an apprehension of the goodness of the past—
the freedom, energy, and simplicity of Christianity, rather than
its more mysterious and devotional side, are the *ideas* of his
mind.

With this view all his virtues and all his defects agree: his
manly and simple character—his love of justice—his desire to
see Christianity recognized as the law of a Christian commonwealth—his keen sense of evils, and his impetuous warfare
against them; and, on the other hand, his inability to understand
the views of others, or to see the strong parts of any but his
own—an excessive self-confidence—and a vehemence of invective, intelligible indeed, but unjustifiable.

Standing as he did alone, looking up (in England at least) to
no set of men, the temptation was almost irresistible to be
sometimes unmeasured in his language. Vehement he always
was; but the Lentuli and Cethegi at Rome, or Prince Rupert's
bravoes in England, were what he calls them, 'the coarsest and
most profligate of the aristocracy;' *'men the most hateful and
contemptible—who have ever thwarted the cause of God and
of goodness;'* and we certainly cannot refute, though we almost
start to read, his attack upon 'the Movement party in France
and England,'—that Jacobinism which *'he detested in its root
and in its branches, with all its godless utilitarianism. Nothing,'* he adds, *'within my knowledge is more utterly wicked
than the party of. . . .—men who fairly and literally, as I fear,
blaspheme not the Son of Man, but the Spirit of God; they hate
Christ because He is of heaven, and they are of evil.'* But when
good men whom he *'knew to be thoroughly in earnest, fearing
God and loving Christ,'* scarcely ever appear in these pages
without some opprobrious epithet—when, after admitting that
he could see *'much of holy, just, and pure'* in their writings,
he can yet pour on them unmitigated expressions of stern and
contemptuous severity—and when with pain we remember that
even his Sermons are not free from certain missiles of the
Odium Theologicum (which in his own case he so sincerely
deprecated)—we cannot but think that his very earnestness and
love of truth sometimes led him into that error which he himself
denounced, of allowing our sense of intellectual error to over-
power our sense of moral goodness. This, we know, implied
no *habitual* bitterness; yet we cannot deny that—on the very
weak ground, as it seems to us, of attacking measures, not
men—he allowed himself too often to adopt a tone most inconsistent with Christian charity; and if some of those he assailed may be charged with similar intemperance, that can
afford neither excuse for him nor consolation to us.

Our general estimate of Dr. Arnold's character will exempt us
from the suspicion of alluding to these things without pain. It

would be, however, far greater if we thought the defect was chiefly a moral one. The fact is, he could not, as he tells us himself, the least enter into his opponents' views; and seeing nothing strong or good—no, not even *'any respectable weakness'*—in their system, and nothing feeble or difficult in his own, he spoke of views, and sometimes too of men, either with utter contempt, as in his earlier days of the 'Evangelicals,' or with bitter abhorrence, as later of what he called the Oxford school. (pp. 488-90)

Dr. Arnold's writings on History are those on which his literary reputation must principally rest. (p. 491)

He has not, we think, worked out a system—his views are rarely closed against attack: but his power of clear analysis and combination—his strong and true, though somewhat rude colouring—his passionate fondness for military details, and his remarkable geographical eye—are some of the greatest qualities in an historian. For vivid pictures his sketch of the sufferings during the siege of Genoa, and that real Epic Poem in which the struggle of one man against the whole might of the Roman people is so nobly depicted—the history of the second Punic war—can hardly be surpassed: while his power of analysis is well shown, when, comparing the seditions of Corcyra and of Marius, he paints the dangers which beset civilized society in the change from an aristocracy of wealth to a democracy—when, in the admirable Essay in his first volume of Thucydides, he traces the successive periods of a nation's life— when, in his view of the parties of the reign of Charles I., he follows from their birth to their death the history of the Puritans—their repression by the great qualities of Elizabeth—their advance under James I.—their full-blown vigour under Charles— distinguishing well the narrowness of their religious from the boldness of their political element—or, lastly, when in his [*Principles of Church Reform*] he sketches that 'awful time of trial for a nation, the first seventy years of the eighteenth century.'

Further, while he has sometimes discovered really extensive *principles*—we allude especially to the Essay in Thucydides— his exquisite feeling and tact about the ancient world led him to many isolated truths which, without actually coalescing into a system, threw a brilliant light upon all history. Such are several of the notes in his Roman history: his account, in the Preface to the third volume of Thucydides, of some distinctive features in the principles of antiquity; his clear exhibition of the changeableness of party principles—a popular party being often conservative, and conservatives joining with the mob; and the abundant illustrations of the good and evil of an aristocracy in every chapter of his Roman history.

The interest of his writings is increased by his hearty sympathies and antipathies, his store of analogies and illustrations, and his lively fancy. He loved and hated well: that dark frown which (as his boys knew) nothing but moral evil called forth, expressed itself in vehement and stern denunciation when he spoke of the merely selfish demagogue, aristocrat, or tyrant, as men 'in whom all virtue necessarily blighted; neither genius nor courage, nor occasional signs of human feeling, can atone for their deliberate wickedness;' and he luxuriated in illustrating a principle as much as in describing a country. His love of natural scenery and his study of history were indeed the main springs that freshened his style and his mind. Half his metaphors were the product of Westmoreland; and every page of the Roman history reflects that of Greece and of England. The principle which he maintained of looking to the present in writing of the past, is open perhaps to some objections, but

certainly not to that of dulness: and his comparison of Hannibal and Napoleon—his contrast between the war loans in England and the sacrifices made by the Romans in the Punic wars—his illustration of the long indifference of the plebeians to political rights, by the refusal of our own early parliaments to trouble themselves with questions of war and peace, give us, at least, the same pleasure that we derive from a lively traveller who can compare the men and manners of every country with his own.

A frequent fallacy, as we think with him is that old one of wise men who make words their counters, and give them their own meaning. The Liberal party to him is synonymous with 'advance in goodness'—the Conservative with 'resistance to all change;' when he speaks of a Democracy ('if there is any truth short of the highest, for which I would gladly die,' he once said, 'it is Democracy without Jacobinism') he never forgets the republics of Aristotle's *Politics;* when he turns to an Aristocracy, the old Claudii, Cethegi, and Lentuli rise up in all their horrors; and though his intense hatred of Jacobinism can never be concealed, and he occasionally speaks of an aristocracy of blood as the greatest element of national happiness, yet in his prevailing course of thought and exposition he seems to us at once to underrate the inherent (we do not say insuperable) dangers which all history as well as theory points to even in the purest republic, and the immense blessing (so long as it can exist) of that 'true guidance in return for living obedience,' which might and ought to be the aim of an aristocracy.

But here, as elsewhere, Dr. Arnold's vocation was to set forth one side of the truth most vividly, and (with a few modifications) in spite, or in consequence, of its giving us a liberal lesson, every one may read his Roman history with profit. (pp. 492-93)

[Dr. Arnold's] interest in social questions was still keener than in political ones: they lay (he thought) deeper, and their difficulties were greater. Thus, the most disastrous revolutions, he observes, have been caused by physical wants; it was their social changes which so grievously affected the character of the Roman people; it was the 'folly of letting evils go on unheeded' in the 18th century which is so startling to look back upon,—it is the growth of that vast body, which he styles our slave population, which is the worm at the root of our national power. (pp. 496-97)

[Speaking] of the 'devilish doctrine' which would make rich and poor natural enemies, he yet thought that the language of the Hebrew prophets was but too applicable to the neglect of our duties towards a population 'whom we treat with all the haughtiness and indifference with which we could treat slaves,'— and whose position in a free country he always said was one of the hardest questions of modern civilization. And then he asked earnestly—yet not in fact more earnestly than the wise and gentle Southey had done twenty years before—

> What is the good of a national Church if it be
> not to Christianize the nation, and to introduce
> the principles of Christianity into men's social
> and civil relations, and expose the wickedness
> of that spirit which maintains the game laws,
> and in agriculture and trade seems to think that
> there is no such sin as covetousness, and that
> if a man is not dishonest, he has nothing to do
> but to make all the profit of his capital that he
> can?

Artist's rendering of a classroom scene at Rugby in about 1816.

And this brings us to Dr. Arnold's great remedy for all our evils, moral, intellectual, and physical;—*'the vision which closed the vista of all his speculations,—his theory of the working of the Christian Church.'* (p. 497)

[Central to Dr. Arnold's theory was his belief that Church and State in England are identical],—that the Civil Power is far more able than the Clergy not only to govern but also to fix the doctrines of the Church,—that there is no difficulty in any important doctrines which a man of plain sense may not see through,—that errors about the doctrine of the Trinity are not *per se* seriously reprehensible,—that the Athanasian Creed, and like over-definite statements, are but that 'provoking and ill-judged language' of Trinitarians which has served 'as a stumbling-block to good Unitarians,' and are in truth only the natural products of 'the priestcraft heresy.' As to the last point,—he considered *Ordination* to be simply the appointment of important public officers by the Crown—'officers who are required to practise no virtue beyond the rest of their brethren;'—and practically, he wished to realise these views by a system of comprehension in which all bodies (except Jews, Quakers, some of the Unitarians, and the Roman Catholics) might worship together. So ample a fold might well, he thought, include 'good Arians,' because 'we are in no way injured by their praying with us to Christ as a glorified man, while we pray to Him as God,' and 'if an Arian will join in our worship of Christ, and will call Him God and Lord, there is neither wisdom

nor charity in wishing that he shall explain what he means by these terms;' and all whose bigoted views would prevent their entering this Church of England must be excluded also from the State. They must lose the right of citizens; they could but live among us, like the Jews, as aliens and sojourners:—if they did not like these terms they, like Louis XIV.'s Protestants, might emigrate. (pp. 498-99)

This Grotian scheme,—for in Grotius it may be read almost in Dr. Arnold's words,—certainly appears to us to be weak in its philosophy and history, and to lead to a painful indifference to truth of doctrine;—and as Mr. Hallam tells us that such a theory cannot appear tolerable to any zealous Churchman, so we may add that the obvious difficulties which Dr. Arnold does not solve will seem to most religious minds insurmountable. Indeed, the ease with which he cuts this knot is to us the clearest argument against the truth of his views. 'Objections,' he says to one of his doubting correspondents, 'do not bring us to the point; my view stands on four legs, and I think meets all the difficulties of the case.' (p. 499)

[It] may be well to look for an instant at the difficulties which are despatched thus summarily. They touch, as no thinking man will deny, on some of the hardest questions in theology and history—questions which perhaps no one has yet fully fathomed—and which are never entered into by Dr. Arnold, who continually assumes the point which he ought to prove!

The whole view, *e. g.*, that strict creeds and doctrinal statements are not important as a guard for true belief, is *assumed,* as if its author was not aware that there was much to be said on the other side—*assumed* against the almost universal consent of divines and good men, from Ignatius to Luther and Calvin—*assumed* too by one the manifest tendency of whose mind and studies hardly, we think, fitted him to estimate the importance of a precise doctrinal system. If there were much appearance of Dr. Arnold's having entered into the question whether such statements might not (say at the time of the Arian controversy) have been essential to protect the simple and unlearned against the insidious tone and feeling of 'good Arians,' we should (what, in opposition to the almost consentient voice of good men, we can hardly do now) have listened with deep respect to his authority; but we cannot forget that, while the sneer about the Christian world disputing for an *iota* came from Gibbon, the *iota* was the doctrine of the Holy Trinity, and the disputant was Athanasius. That great man's views, on this point at least, are the views of almost the whole Christian world. It is too much to be required to lay them aside at once; and Dr. Arnold, though on many points well fitted to be an *Athanasius contra mundum,* was not likely on this one to destroy, single-handed, the work of ages, and to substitute himself '*a system better and deeper than has satisfied the last seventeen centuries.*'

One or two other points are equally left *in ambiguo.* The belief that a mixed body, of whom the mass (unless we take a very mild view of human nature) will be neither religious nor instructed, nor under the same check of public opinion which must always influence the clergy—that, in fact, the Civil Executive will better guard the interests of religion than a Church government constituted *chiefly* of clergy—this *may* indeed be true; but it certainly needs proof, and this its advocate is so far from giving that many of his facts tell the other way. In one of our own recent Articles, if we may be allowed to refer to it, strong evidence has been adduced of the very extensive goodness and ability of the clergy even in the 'dark ages;' and as Dr. Arnold is himself constantly reminding us that in their conflicts with the civil power the clergy were almost always in the right, it is only his vehement and not, we think, very consistent 'anti-priestcraft' view, and his strong dislike of our own modern clerical history, which accounts for this *high-state* theory. Again, is it not almost chimerical to think that earnest men can be united in one church, on the basis of merging their peculiar opinions with men from the opposite poles of religious belief? Nor is the charge of persecution easily avoided, and persecution too of the most odious kind, when those who are earnest (or bigoted, as Dr. Arnold would say) are to be made men without a country because they cannot live on a system of negations.

Apart from the weakness of these details, the view was one that suited Arnold's nature well. His intensely national and political turn of mind, combined with those early studies in which the old Greek devotion to the State and the majesty of human law met him perpetually, strengthened the natural tendency of a practical intellect to look on active life as the scene in which alone religion is to be developed. Then came his conviction (how sadly true!) that the Church had *not* been doing its work; his horror of the overstrained distinction between worldly and religious duties; his prejudice against the existing clergy as a narrow-minded class; his want of subtlety and comprehensiveness; his very scanty knowledge of mankind; and hence a theory with little to support it in history, theology, or philosophy, yet well meriting attention for the great truths with which it is connected—faulty intellectually, but morally, in its

source at least, most noble. We look on it, in short, as an ideal mode of expressing the grand object of his life—to show that Christianity is at once real and universal—that it does not belong to one set of persons, but to all—not to one institution, but to all—not only to religious, but equally to what is called secular occupation—and ought to raise its voice not only in the pulpit, but in education, in literature, in Parliament—not only in questions between Churchmen and dissenters, but on every subject where there is a right and a wrong, of war or peace, of suffering or of injustice. (pp. 500-01)

[In estimating] Dr. Arnold's views we receive great help from his Sermons. There we may read much of his career and his opinions; and what Mr. Stanley has said of all his works is true especially of them—that they at once express the feeling of the hour which dictated them, and the fixed ideas by which the whole life of their writer was regulated. It is undeniable that late in life the speculative element came forward in them more clearly; but, even remembering that they are written for boys—to whom, of course, *frequent* discussions of doctrine would soon become tiresome—yet no one, we think, who reads the Sermons on Justification in the fifth volume, or who bears in mind how small are the traces in his three first volumes of any definite doctrinal views, will rise from them with the belief that Dr. Arnold was a great doctrinal theologian. But look to the practical side of any of his volumes—to the lesson which, in a vast variety of forms, he is ever inculcating—the paramount claims of Christianity not merely on our feelings or our respect, but on our actions—whether he describes the careless tone of worldly men or the thoughtlessness of boys, our coldness to friends or distance to the poor, or analyses the evils and shows the capabilities of a public school. . . . He was ever growing. Thus, though the earliest sermons are very full of interest as showing the first workings of his earnest mind, the last are far more beautiful; and each successive volume is more full of that which was so deep a feeling in him—his personal connexion with our Lord and Saviour. We will not venture to quote his words, but no one can fail to observe that it was not so much doctrine about Christ as the thought of Christ himself that was before him, and that he dwelt habitually on His words and acts with (if we may venture to call it so) the most affectionate reality; and let this be once more impressed upon us by Arnold's example, as a truth much needed in these controversial days, that however injurious we think the *tendency* of those opinions to which with pain we have drawn attention, yet their maintainer himself was in doctrine as in action '*rooted and grounded in love.*' His Sermons, but above all his Journals, exhibit a most earnestly religious man; but a man of no party, and whom for that very reason it will be good for men of every part to contemplate. (pp. 502-03)

[W. C. Lake], "Stanley's 'Life of Dr. Arnold'," in The Quarterly Review, Vol. LXXIV, No. CXLVIII, October, 1844, pp. 467-508.

[JAMES BOWLING MOZLEY]   (essay date 1844)

[Mozley was an influential English theologian and editor. In this excerpt from a review of Stanley's Life *(see excerpt dated 1844), he questions the Christological implications of Arnold's willingness to include Unitarians in his ideal of a multidenominational national church.]*

In spite of the haziness and perplexity of Arnold's whole state of mind and point of view on the subject of Unitarianism, so far is clear, that he had no objection to including sincere and earnest Unitarians in his [national] church. And he arrives at this conclusion by the following process—a most painful one for us to follow; because, say it we must, it puts Arnold's own individual belief on this doctrine in a most unsatisfactory light.

We take his letter to Mr. Smith of Norwich. Mr. Smith had written to complain of him for making the act of "addressing Christ as an object of worship" essential in his scheme of comprehension. Arnold, in reply, explains what that phrase of Christ being an object of worship means, in his view.

Does he say that it necessarily means addressing Christ as God? He does not. He says that common Unitarians make Christ virtually *dead,* and that they ought to think of him as *alive.* That is not the same with thinking him God. Again, he says the fault of the Unitarians is, that they approach God "in his own incomprehensible essence;" whereas they ought to approach him through Christ: and that, whereas a direct communion with God is reserved for a more spiritual state of being hereafter, they anticipate it here. Here the fault of the Unitarians is referred to the *mode* of worship only—not to the *object* of it; and they are blamed, not for refusing to regard Christ as God, but for refusing to regard him as the medium through which God is worshipped. And so far from there being an essential and eternal difference in the two relations to Christ,—which the Unitarian and orthodox side respectively suppose,—he distinctly intimates that the very relation to him which the orthodox side supposes, is only a function of our present earthly state of existence, and will not continue in our future spiritual one. A most painful expression of doctrine, by which he identifies the incomprehensible God with God the Father, ("God the Father, *that is,* God as he is in himself,") concentrates but too clearly the line of idea throughout; viz. that the Unitarians and the orthodox, having both the same Being before their minds as the object of worship, only approach him in different ways, the mediate and immediate; that there is, therefore, no fundamental difference in their respective doctrines, and that such worship as we pay to Christ, as being the medium of the worship we pay to God,—worship *in this sense* to Christ,—is not inconsistent in principle with the creed of Unitarians, and need not be objected to by them.

The question, in short, with Arnold was one of feeling, not of doctrine; and regarded the affection of the man to the Being, and not the essence of Being himself. It is not easy, indeed, to see how the two can be separated; for our feeling towards a being must be affected by the consideration of what that being is. But we state the view as he seems to hold it: "The feelings," he says, "with which we regard Christ are of much greater importance than the question of his humanity or proper divinity." And if Unitarians would think of him as *alive,* and would love and fear him, whether they thought him man or God, he regards them as true Christians. The word "fear" comes in strangely: "I never meant to deny the name of Christian to those who love and *fear* him." Religious fear is a feeling which applies ultimately to the Divine Being alone; and the notion of the "fear" of Christ going along with the simply human idea of him is a perplexing one. Indeed, in the general tone of Arnold's mind on this subject, we see no cold Unitarianism, but what might be taken for the vague foreshadowings of high uninstructed nature: and it is melancholy to see what would have delighted us so much as an aspiration toward revelation, thrown into such a different aspect by the fact of its being a relapse from it. What are we to think when Arnold could say what he did, and yet absolutely imagine that he thought the "central truth of Christianity was the doctrine of

our Lord's divinity." We can only suppose that he partly did not know what his own view was, and partly did not know what the doctrine was. "There was a vividness and tenderness," we are told, "in his conception of our Lord, which made all his feelings of human friendship and affection, all his range of historical interest—his instincts of reverence, his admiration of truth—fasten on Him as their natural object." "He seemed," says one, "to have the freshest view of our Lord's life and death that I ever knew a man to possess. His rich mind filled up the naked outline of the Gospel history:—it was to him the most interesting *fact* that had ever happened,—as real, as *exciting* (if I may use the expression) as any recent event in modern history of which the actual effects are visible." We must own we look fearfully on the richness and warmth of that feeling toward our Lord, which could tolerate the Unitarian view of them. (pp. 579-80)

[*James Bowling Mozley*], *"Dr. Arnold," in* The Christian Remembrancer, *n.s. Vol. VIII, No. XLVI, October-December, 1844, pp. 547-99.*

[WILLIAM EMPSON]   (essay date 1845)

[*In the following excerpt from his review of Stanley's* Life *(see excerpt dated 1844), Empson attempts to debunk Arnold's premise that all moral activity is spiritual in nature.*]

Arnold's Religion was at once attractive and commanding. We never recollect a religious life which so much affected us; which, while reading it, we wished so much to make our own; revolving which, we can so little justify ourselves that it should not be so. He was not afraid of the name of rationalist. He would trust no man who had turned fanatic. He forcibly reproved the tyranny of opposing faith to reason. Yet in any case, in which his Christian affections could possibly be moved, there was a great chance of his not allowing sufficient weight to other considerations; and, accordingly, of their preventing him from seeing the case in all its lights and bearings, and of properly judging it as a whole. (p. 221)

Arnold assumed it, as a first truth, that in all voluntary moral actions, there could be no distinction between civil acts and religious acts, between things secular and things spiritual. And yet to say, in the ordinary meaning of the words, that every voluntary moral action, to a Christian, must be spiritual as well as secular, is surely a hard saying. Such a maxim can only have proceeded from an excess of religious feeling; and in its logical consequences, it led him to conclusions against which we should strongly protest. It will be a verity or a fallacy according to the application of it. Let us see how Arnold applied it. On passing from the death-bed of one of the boys into the school-room, he was so troubled at the contrast between the two scenes, that, in addition to the general prayer before the whole school, he introduced a special one for the sixth form, with the observation, 'That if their work were made really a religious work, the transition to it from a death-bed would be slight.' Is this so? Can it be a true interpretation of human nature, or of God's word, that we ought to go about our ordinary business, and stand by the bed of a dying friend, with almost the same feelings? It is scarcely the doctrine of Epictetus and La Trappe; scarcely that of the Quakers—to whom Arnold paid the well-earned compliment, of being nobly distinguished from the multitude of fanatics, by seizing the true point of Christian advancement in the regulation of their daily lives. It is certainly not the lesson we should have drawn from Christ at the grave of Lazarus.

But even the general proposition—in what reasonable sense can it be true that all our works should be made religious works? Whether a proper sense of Christian obligation may be satisfied by its co-operating with the rest of our nature, according to circumstances, in the same manner as our sense of moral obligation does, or whether it must be infused into every specific act and motive, is not a question to be arbitrarily settled in favour of the last alternative, by direct assumption. Otherwise, we necessarily sin in all those thoughts and actions for which the common moral instincts of our nature are sufficient motives, unless we shall have spiritualized them simultaneously by a conscious reference of them to God. We think that Arnold himself has given the proper answer to any such requirement in another place. He has elsewhere remarked on the fearful way in which we live, as it were, out of God's atmosphere; not keeping that constant consciousness of His reality which, he conceived, we ought to have, and which should make Him more manifest to our souls, than the Schekinah was to the eyes of the Israelites. But is it possible that, if Arnold had heated the furnace hotter, he would have been better qualified for any of the duties for which man can be imagined to be here? Admitting, from his very peculiar nature, he might have made the experiment with impunity, we are not the less certain that, for ordinary persons, the attempt to carry it out would give us a hundred hypocrites, madmen, or fanatics, for every Christian of the kind that he himself could have cared to see.

On the fullest consideration we can give the subject, another of Arnold's applications of this first truth is almost as questionable. He declares, that the study of history and moral philosophy, if not based on Christianity, must be Antichristian, . . . and that their views of life must be so different, as to make it impossible to instruct Jews, Mohamedans, Hindoos, and Benthamites, together with Christians, in moral science. But the historian ought to write in the same spirit in which the student ought to study. To look, then, at histories. We agree that Gibbon's history is Antichristian. As far as it is so, it is false and offensive. By his imperfect representation of the importance of Christianity, as one of the peculiar elements in our civilization, he has left an enormous chasm to be filled up in the history of modern Europe. We can easily conceive, also, that a life of Christ might be written in a tone so purely historical—a neutrality so pregnant with indifference—as to deserve the character of Antichristian. But beyond this we cannot go. 'The historical tone,' to which Arnold objected in the case of a life of Christ, we should have understood, *ex vi termini*, to be the proper tone in *ordinary* history. And thus Arnold himself practically treated it. For, although one of his reasons for engaging on the Roman history was, in order to prevent the subject from being taken up by some one who might not write it like a Christian, yet, so little is the historical tone of his work affected by this specific object, that we have heard the difference between the spirit of his sermons and the spirit of his history gravely stated as a disgraceful and irreconcilable contradiction. We thought the charge a most absurd one; but it would cease to be absurd were the purely historical tone of a general history really Antichristian. In that case, we must be prepared to go the whole length of Foster's essay on the aversion of men of taste to evangelical religion. On any such supposition, Arnold would find it as hard to justify his passion for Greek and Latin, and his profession of a classical teacher, as his Roman History—or his appeal from the evil habits of his school, to its great and noble scenes. (pp. 222-24)

Arnold's favourite historians were Thucydides and Tacitus, Niebuhr and Carlyle. This could not possibly have been the case if he had considered them Antichristian. And yet to mention only the example of Niebuhr, if it were necessary for a good history that it should be based on Christianity, Arnold would, in this case, have seen at once in Niebuhr's history, without being obliged to wait for the further evidence of a personal interview with him, the groundlessness of the charge of scepticism which had been brought against him. For our part, we do not know the persons, to whose consummate wisdom we would dare commit the composition of Providential histories, and histories on Christian principles. We should dread letting loose a class of writers more likely than any others to bring both Providence and Christianity into contempt: And, the most we could hope in behalf of their readers, would be, that they might have the same cause for gratitude with one of the officers of the University of Cambridge, who, after attending the sermons at St Mary's for many years, thanked God he was a Christian still.

However, we would rather have Histories written upon Christian principles, than systems of Morals based on Christianity. . . . There is, we are firmly persuaded, a science of morals dependent upon the constitution of man, (*natura ad summum perducta,*) and therefore universal, notwithstanding the different standards of merit which, to a certain extent, have occasionally prevailed in a few cases. As such, it was cultivated, at all times and in all countries, upon its own proper grounds, and independent of religion. After the revelation of Christianity, it continued to be cultivated, as before, as a distinct science; which Christianity did not supersede or abrogate, only add to and complete. This is the almost unanimous doctrine of our truly great writers. Indeed, this was the view taken of it during that long period in which morality was only treated of in treatises of theology. Aquinas, 'the moral master of Christendom for three centuries, laid the grounds of duty solely in the nature of man, and in the well-being of society.' (Mackintosh.) In this sense, too, Dr Reynold Peacock, (the Erasmus of the fifteenth century,) writing against the 'Bible-men,' or Lollards, expressly affirmed, that 'Scripture does not contain all that is necessary for the grounding or supporting of moral virtues; and, therefore, it is not properly the foundation on which they stand.' (Lewis's *Life of Peacock*.) . . . Even writers with the opinions of Jeremy Taylor, (who held, no doubt, that morality proceeded directly from the will of God, independent of all moral distinctions,) admit that there are some rules which, being proportionable to our nature, will not be abrogated, while our nature remains the same. (pp. 224-25)

If we are to go further than this—if morals are to be based on Christianity, and not Christianity on morals, another difficulty immediately crosses our path. We shall want an interpreter of Scripture of a very different description from any one who has yet appeared. Of course, the authenticity of the canonical books must be first settled beyond all dispute. There ought to be no doubt about the book of Daniel; which Arnold believed 'to be most certainly a very late work of the Maccabees.' None about the Epistle to the Hebrews; which Arnold at one time suspected to have been written later than the Apostolical age; though he latterly 'inclined to the belief, that it might have been written, not merely under the guidance of St Paul, but by the Apostle himself.' Supposing the scriptural canon to be settled—how is it to be construed? In rude uncritical times, the authority of Scripture has been too often honestly relied on for too much guilt and folly, not to make us shrink from taking it nakedly as a guide; almost as much as from opening it at random for a *sortes Virgilianæ* text. (p. 226)

What a door has [Arnold] not thrown open on this question of questions, 'The True Use of Scripture,' in his **"Essay on Interpretation"**; the most important, in his own view of it, of all his writings. In the first place, it requires of us a competent philological and historical interpretation, that we may be able to separate the human element from the divine. In the next, it expects us to be endowed with a competent historical sagacity, that we may be able to apply the peculiar meaning of events and passages to our own times and to different stages of civilization. We may well ask who is sufficient for these things? or who can foresee the changes which must follow? Arnold was aware of the revolution in divinity, which opening the question of universal inspiration must of itself produce. He enquires of Mr Justice Coleridge,

> Have you seen your uncle's *Letters on Inspiration,* which I believe are to be published? They are well fitted to break ground in the approaches to that momentous question, which involves in it so great a shock to existing notions; the greatest, probably, that has ever been given, since the discovery of the falsehood of the Pope's infallibility. Yet it must come, and will end, in spite of the fears and clamours of the weak and bigoted, in the higher exalting and more sure establishing of Christian truth.

This may be very true at last: But meantime, while the problems of inspiration and interpretation are working out, surely the proper basis of morality ought not to be left at large. Is it a thing which can afford to wait for, or to vary with, the obscure, equivocal, and fluctuating answers that must precede the termination of debates, of which, if we once suppose them fairly launched, no man living can hope to see the end? (pp. 226-27)

> [*William Empson*], *in a review of "Life and Correspondence of Dr. Arnold," in* The Edinburgh Review, *Vol. LXXXI, No. CLXIII, January, 1845, pp. 190-234.*

[JAMES MARTINEAU]   (essay date 1845)

[*In the following discussion of Arnold's views on church and state, Martineau suggests that Arnold's advocacy of a religious test for citizenship contradicts his nondoctrinal conception of Christianity.*]

Arnold's all-prevailing moral nature made him seize with avidity, from every age, all the securities for human duty which genius had devised or inspiration imparted; and reject with indignation every counterfeit pretending to do the sterling work of a responsible will. He could not, for all his faith in revelation, forego one jot of the ancient reverence for law; or, for all his high doctrine of obedience, allow the priest to touch with one of his fingers the burthen of individual obligation. He would save government from degenerating into police, and Christianity into conjuring; and he had an unconquerable aversion to accept the constable as representative of the State, or the bishop of the Church. Both institutions were to him but incorporated expressions of the *conscience* of their members;— the one of its executive energy, the other of its meditative aspirations; neither therefore having an aim less or more comprehensive than the other; neither complete and healthy without the other; and requiring, in order to effectuate the ends of either, their coalescence into a living unity. (p. 294)

Arnold was [far] . . . from claiming coercive prerogatives for either ecclesiastical officers or worshipping assemblies: all ju-

dicial and executive authority he would leave where now it rests: only he would regard the functionaries who exercise it as deputed, not by the material interests, but by the moral sense of the community, and standing for the law of Christ by which all are bound. This ascription of a sacred character to authorised and constitutional rules is all that Arnold meant by his desire to make "the Church a sovereign society." He wanted, not more power to the Church, but a more Christian temper to the State. He could not endure that any part of life should escape the reach of obligation; that the process of social organization should be thought to give rise, at any step, to relations exempt from moral inspection; that any voluntary deeds between citizen and citizen, between subjects and rulers, between the commonwealth and foreign states, should be treated as less amenable to the divine rule of conscience, than the private conduct which is abandoned wholly to its sway. Hence he was impatient of the false distinction between "secular" and "spiritual" things; under cover of which he believed that countless questionable ways of thought and act passed without a just verdict or even an inquiring challenge, and whole provinces of life were ceded as irreclaimable for Christian cultivation. He felt how untruly this distinction presents the real difference between the pursuit of physical and that of moral good, as if they were each a separate business, to be achieved in society by different agents, in individuals by different acts. As in the case of private persons, there are not two sets of employments, one irresponsibly abandoned to the natural desires, the other the exclusive realm of duty; but moral good consists in the regulated pursuit of natural good according to a divine and holy law: so in communities, there are not two spheres of work and office, one with only physical ends, the other with only spiritual; but all parts of the body politic must serve one supreme intent, viz. that the whole natural life of society shall also be a moral life. Arnold, accordingly, with adventurous nobleness, insisted on carrying the Christian standard through every department of the state: sovereign and council, judges and ministers, legislators and magistrates, were to regard themselves as functionaries of a Christian church. Nay, he did not shrink from applying his principle to the province of government most difficult to reduce under the rule of truth, honesty, and justice,—we mean, the foreign relations of the commonwealth. He had no idea of leaving, in diplomacy, a privileged nest of retreat for chicanery and fraud; or, in war itself, a licensed escape from moral obligation. In all questions between nation and nation; in the conduct of all disputes, and the resistance of aggression, there actually *exists* a right and a wrong: and is it for Christian men to throw up these things in confusion and despair, and bid conscience turn the back till they have scrambled through a crisis they cannot manage by her rules? He was not to be scared, therefore, by any amount of Machiavellian practice from including ambassadors, army, and navy, in the staff of his national Church. . . . Arnold would have heartily adopted his favourite Aristotle's estimate of the religious character of wise and thoughtful sway, when he identified the rule of reason and law in states with the authority of God, and said that, to allow scope for the unregulated will of governors, was to give power to the brute. Of this sentiment, indeed, the following passage from the [*Fragment on the Church*], is little more than a Christian amplification:—

> It is obvious that the object of Christian society being thus extensive, and relating not to ritual observances, but to the improvement of the whole of our life, the natural and fit state of the Church is, that it should be a sovereign society or commonwealth; as long as it is subordinate and

municipal, it cannot fully carry its purposes into effect. This will be evident, if we consider that law and government are the sovereign influences on human society; that they in the last resort shape and control it at their pleasure; that institutions depend on them, and are by them formed and modified; that what they sanction will ever be generally considered innocent; that what they condemn is thereby made a crime, and if persisted in, becomes rebellion; and that those who hold in their hands the power of life and death, must be able greatly to obstruct the progress of whatever they disapprove of; and those who dispose of all the honours and rewards of society must, in the same way, be greatly able to advance whatever they think excellent. So long, then, as the sovereign society is not Christian, and the Church is not sovereign, we have two powers alike designed to act upon the whole of our being, but acting often in opposition to each other. Of these powers, the one has wisdom, the other external force and influence; and from the division of these things, which ought ever to go together, the wisdom of the Church cannot carry into effect the truths which it sees and loves; whilst the power of government, not being guided by wisdom, influences society for evil rather than for good. The natural and true state of things then is, that this power and this wisdom should be united: that human life should not be pulled to pieces between two claimants, each pretending to exercise control over it, not in some particular portion, but universally; that wisdom should be armed with power, power guided by wisdom; that the Christian Church should have no external force to thwart its beneficent purposes; that government should not be poisoned by its internal ignorance or wickedness, and thus advance the cause of God's enemy, rather than perform the part of God's vicegerent.

(pp. 295-98)

The views of Arnold, as to the perfect identity of aim in Church and State, set him directly at variance with the philosophy of his political party, and the theology of his ecclesiastical order. He could keep no terms with Warburton's principle, generally received by the Whigs, that—

> It was the care of the bodies, not the souls of men, that the magistrate undertook to give account of. Whatever, therefore, refers to the body is in his jurisdiction; whatever to the soul is not.

He maintained that, if this were so, the State could not be a "*sovereign* society;" inasmuch as there would be interests above its reach, and exempt from its command; and that as there is such a thing as spiritual good, which, in the form of personal perfection, constitutes the highest end of individuals, so can nothing less than this good, in the form of a moral civilization, present a true aim for the collective will of a community. He therefore regarded everything as within the province of the State, which might elevate the life of its people; and held it the duty of Government to provide for their education, to afford expression for their worship, to superintend

the construction of their dwellings, and the organization of their towns; and to control, with a view to moral results, the distribution of employments which might arise from the unrestrained operation of economical laws. While he separated himself thus from "the liberals," by asserting for the commonwealth higher aims than corporeal, he stood almost alone among ecclesiastics in denying to Christianity any function that was ritual. Religion and government met on the common ground of *moral* life,—the life of responsible *man*, not of a sentient creature on the one hand, or of a magical saint on the other. In short, from both extremities he dismissed all *physical* ends, simply as such; whether of the *zoological* kind, giving animal ease for this world,—or of the *theological* kind, providing an enchanted safety for the next. His theory would have been complete and self-consistent, if he could have adhered to his conception of the purely moral character of Christianity; and asked for no more, in his definition of a disciple, than a certain state of the conscience and affections. But this was impossible. Dealing with the Newmanites, he boldly vindicates a spiritual Gospel against a *ceremonial*. Dealing with Unitarians, he cannot allow a spiritual Gospel against a *doctrinal*. And were it even otherwise, the difficulty of managing this new ingredient of *belief*, cannot be overcome. Do what you will to give exclusive prominence to the *moral* element of Christianity, still, when all that is "sacramental" is cancelled, and the minimum of creed is spared,—it does not become identical with the law of conscience; it requires assent to some things not necessarily obvious to every man of good and honest heart; there is yet a residue of certain *historical* propositions to be embraced, to impose which as a condition of citizenship, is certainly to exceed your prerogative, as guardian of the moral life of the community. Arnold did not shrink from the practical consequences of his own scheme; he strenuously advocated the application of a theological test as a means of discriminating aliens from citizens; he resisted the removal of the Jewish disabilities; he wished to enforce a scriptural examination in the London University; he "would thank Parliament for having done away with distinctions between Christian and Christian;" but "would pray that distinctions be kept up between Christians and non-Christians." He struggled hard, but, in our opinion, ineffectually, to reconcile this adoption of a State creed with his principle that "union of action," not "union in belief," should constitute the social bond. In one mood, he maintained that every society "has a right to *establish its own ideas*;" but if so, it "chooses for its end truth, rather than good,"—the very thing which he emphatically condemns. At another time, he denies that the reception of Christianity implies any belief in "the truth of a proposition," and treats it as a purely practical allegiance, which any man may render at will, to a law of conduct; and in defence of this position, he adduces the example of the early Christians, among whom were some members "not even believing that there would be a resurrection of the dead." Then, if so, with what consistency could Dr. Arnold draw up a creed for the express purpose of defining the amount of belief sufficient to make a British citizen? He protests against Mr. Gladstone's doctrine, that the propagation and maintenance of "religious truth" are to be admitted among the proper ends of government; and considers himself as defending the very different proposition, that "man's highest perfection" should be the final aim of the State. But by including among the indispensable elements of human "perfection" a certain portion of "religious," and even historical "truth," he borrows the fundamental principle of the very theory he confutes, and lays himself open to every objection which can be brought against it, except as to the *extent* of its exclusiveness. There is not a consequence deducible from Mr. Gladstone's scheme, as to the treatment of dissidents, which does not equally follow from Dr. Arnold's,—with only the difference, that the sufferers are less numerous. The revival of a test-act; the enforcement of the law of religious libel; the punishment of active heresy as lawless disaffection,—are direct practical corollaries from a theory which inserts the New Testament among the statutes at large, and commits the estates of the realm to the maintenance of its authority in faith and practice. The truth is, Arnold's free and true nature led him to adopt in feeling the moral and affectionate conception of Christianity, as a simple aspiration towards the ideal of character presented in its records. But when, no longer reposing in the interior of this conception, he attempted to reach its boundary, and determine the *external* relations of the religion, he found that his definition must take in certain elements of theological *belief*; and what was meant to discriminate good from evil, turned out to be the old barrier between orthodox and heretic.

Such was the snare by which Arnold's divinity contrived to trip up his philosophy. (pp. 299-301)

> [*James Martineau*], *"Church and State," in* The Prospective Review, *Vol. I, No. II, 1845, pp. 283-321.*

DR. NEANDER (essay date 1846)

[*The German critic Neander hails Arnold as a liberalizing influence on English theology, demurring only with respect to his views concerning the identity of church and state.*]

We will not here enlarge on the [various] points of view in which Arnold's life and character may be contemplated, but will rather dwell on what is important as a sign of the times, in reference to the history, not only of the English Church, but of the Christian world, from the connection subsisting between all things that give promise of a brighter future. The view then, which we shall take of Dr. Arnold's character contemplates him as the representative of a new and more liberal theological system in the very country where what is old and established is hardest to eradicate, and where hitherto narrow and limited views have for the most part prevailed. Having been obliged in an earlier review to enter into controversy with a partisan of these narrow traditional views, and to uphold in opposition to him our freer German system of interpretation, we are the more rejoiced to be able to point out, even in England, a spirit akin to the Germans in his views, and who in this controversy would have perfectly agreed with us. And we consider this as an important sign of the times: it is the movement of a spirit which is abroad throughout Germany, and will probably bring about a revolution in many religious opinions. Where an intellectual movement is seen going on in different quarters, and in countries bearing the most opposite character, it has always been a sign that a new mental development is forming. Such truths, as they were spoken by this good and wise man, cannot remain without fruits; and he has left behind him a numerous band of disciples. (pp. 190-91)

It is not easy to see to what we are to ascribe the more liberal theological views which we see in this work. . . . [We are unable] to decide with certainty how far Arnold, who was led by Niebuhr's work on the Roman history to study the German language, was influenced by his acquaintance with the productions of the German divines. At all events, many of his opinions seem to have been formed from his own intellectual and theological developments in a manner peculiarly his own. In his mind are united many elements well calculated to have

a wholesome influence on theological development—a mind harmonized and cultivated by the study of the ancients, and habitually employed in criticism in other branches of learning,—and a truly Christian disposition, which must necessarily be opposed to all dry and narrow conceptions,—the true spirit of the gospel, which maketh free. It will be salutary for the German public likewise to hear from the lips of this man truths, which even with us find opponents in the adherents of antiquity.

Arnold justly designates those views which lay an undue stress on external forms, whether they consist in episcopal government and succession, a bigoted observance of Sunday, certain ideas respecting the sacraments, adherence to the letter of Scripture, or any others, as a renewal of the Judaizing element. . . . Thus he says, in a letter of the year 1834:

> To insist on the necessity of episcopacy is exactly like insisting on the necessity of circumcision: both are and were lawful, but to insist on either as *necessary* is unchristian, and binding the Church with a yoke of carnal ordinances; and the reason why circumcision, although expressly commanded once, was declared not binding upon Christians, is much stronger against the necessity of episcopacy, which never was commanded at all; the reason being, that all forms of government and ritual are in the Christian Church indifferent, and to be decided in the Church itself, *pro temporum et locorum ratione*—'the Church' not being the clergy, but the congregation of Christians.

Again, he speaks in a letter of the year 1836 of the errors of the Oxford Judaizers, as he calls the Puseyites, and designates as the subjects of their erroneous conceptions, the priesthood, the sacraments, the apostolical succession, tradition, and the church. And he sets forth as the positive opposite to this idolatry, as he calls it, the doctrine of the Person of Christ; not his church, not his sacraments, not his teaching, not even the truths about himself, nor the virtues which he enforces, but Himself, the only object which bars fanaticism and idolatry on the one hand, and gives life and power to all morality on the other. (pp. 191-92)

It is true that hostility against that form of Christianity justly described by Arnold as the Judaical element, may be carried too far. We must not refuse to acknowledge that a true and sound spirit of Christianity, even when assuming a peculiar form, has existed from the earliest periods, through the middle ages down to our own times; we must not forget that Christianity has been constantly liable to two opposite tendencies of exclusive devotion to what is inward, and to what is outward; that it is even a part of its divine character to be able to pervade these two extreme poles of opposite opinions, and all the intermediate steps which lie between them; and that without this it could not have been the leaven which was to leaven the whole world. If Arnold was sometimes moved, by his zeal for pure evangelical truth, to speak in various places very strongly against peculiar views, on the other hand, he was not wanting in that charity which can recognize Christianity even in this form; and no less did he possess that Christian insight into history which can perceive that each opposite tendency had in its beginning a relative use. (pp. 192-93)

It was indeed one of the most striking characteristics of this admirable man, that, rising completely above all narrow-minded dogmatism or bigoted sectarian prejudice, he always considered faith in Christ as the Saviour and the source of spiritual life, when it formed the basis of the mind, as the great foundation of Christianity, and the common bond of union between those who differed from each other in subordinate matters. Hence he could recognize the spirit of Christianity in various systems and opinions; hence he could even form a more correct judgment of Unitarianism, and could distinguish the Unitarianism which refers chiefly to dogmatical questions from that which affects the Christian life itself. He believed that this common faith would become the foundation of a more entire and perfect unity, taking its rise from within the Church; while the efforts after dogmatical uniformity and external agreement would only occasion further divisions, and lead to a new form of Judaism. Here, too, we see in Arnold a man who belongs to the forerunners of a purified and enlightened Church. (pp. 193-94)

We learn from [Arnold's] biographer that he applied the words of Christ, ''Render unto Cæsar the things that are Cæsar's, and unto God the things that are God's,'' in a new and significant sense to the separation of what is divine and what is human in the holy Scriptures.

The practical application of this principle, united as it was with his love of truth, and his mind highly cultivated by philological and historical studies, led him likewise to a freer and more fearless criticism of the books of the holy Scriptures, and especially the Bible history. (p. 195)

He complains that Bible criticism, at least as far as regards the Old Testament, is in England almost non-existent. He thought he discovered in Daniel traces of a later period. ''The self same criticism,'' he says, ''which has established the authenticity of St. John's Gospel against all questionings, does, I think, equally prove the non-authenticity of great part of Daniel.'' In treating of the prophecies of the Old Testament, he drew a distinction between the historical sense and the deeper meaning which lies beneath, and which has always reference to Christ. Thus he looked on the prophecy of Immanuel, Isaiah vii., declaring that it had not reference in its primary or historical sense to Christ. He observed that prophetic vision could see the fullness of the future in the imperfect germ of the present. He considered the various great epochs in the history of the world as various comings of Christ, forerunners of his last coming. And to this he refers the great events in church history. (p. 196)

Arnold could completely separate the two branches of religious and secular learning. He could also discern on which side religious doubts could be solved by intellectual inquiry, and on which side they could only be overcome by an effort of will, by a resignation of mind, and the power of feeling. Much that is excellent on this subject, much that shows an abundant Christian experience and a deep knowledge of human nature, may be found in his letters. Most admirably does he speak on the so-called negative impartiality and freedom from prejudice in the examination of religious subjects. On this subject he says, in reference to an article on the life of Christ:—

> To read an account of Christ written as by an indifferent person, is to read an unchristian account of Him; because no one who acknowledges Him can be indifferent to Him, but stands in such relation to Him, that the highest reverence must ever be predominant in his mind when thinking or writing of Him. And again, what is the impartiality that is required? Is it

that a man shall neither be a Christian, nor yet not a Christian? The fact is, that religious veneration is inconsistent with what is called impartiality; which means, that as you see some good and some evil on both sides, you identify yourself with neither, and are able to judge of both. And this holds good with all human parties and characters, but not with what is divine, and consequently perfect; for then we should identify ourselves with it, and are perfectly incapable of passing judgment upon it. If I think that Christ was no more than Socrates (I do not mean in degree, but in kind), I can of course speak of Him impartially, that is, I assume at once that there are faults and imperfections in His character, and on these I pass my judgment; but if I believe in Him, I am not His judge, but His servant and creature, and He claims the devotion of my whole nature, because He is identical with goodness, wisdom, and holiness. Nor can I for the sake of strangers assume another feeling and another language, because this is compromising the highest duty,—it is like denying Him, instead of confessing Him.

His judgment on Strauss's *Life of Christ* . . . is remarkable. He says—

> This book seems to me to show the ill effects of that division of labour which prevails so much amongst the literary men of Germany. Strauss writes about history and myths, without appearing to have studied the question, but having heard that some pretended histories are mythical, he borrows this notion as an engine to help him out of Christianity. But the idea of men writing mythic histories between the times of Livy and Tacitus, and St. Paul mistaking such for realities!

What Arnold says here agrees with his opinion of the necessity of uniting theology with general cultivation of mind. On this subject much that is excellent and deserving of particular attention, even in Germany, may be found in the third volume of his **Sermons**. But perhaps he may not have sufficiently appreciated the advantages for deep research into the more abstruse parts of theology which are gained by our division of labour, and which again reflects back on the more ordinary branches of study. Strauss's views are certainly not referable to his want of universal cultivation, as is the case with some others of his school: still there is much truth in Arnold's observation, that one who had been formerly conversant with independent research and historical criticism in other provinces, would not easily have been led to the strange theories which have been formed by the advocates of the mystical interpretation of Scripture History. (pp. 196-97)

There is but one point, and a point which appeared very important to Arnold, with regard to which we entirely differ from him. We mean his view of the desirableness of the identity of Church and State. But even here we recognize in him . . . that deep feeling for the highest merits of Christianity, that anti-hierarchical spirit, that full and complete recognition of the common priesthood of all Christians, which need to be more and more brought forward,—together with an earnest longing to see Christianity made more and more the leaven for the whole world, penetrating all the relations of life. But we think this can only spring from the inward, subjective working of Christianity in the Church through each individual receiving it from his own free conviction. Such an influence can only spread widely from this inward operation of Christian principles; in all cases it must be limited by the law of each man's own convictions.... Arnold continually opposes, as Jacobinism, with the disgust which the noble-hearted man ever shewed to what was low and mean, the view which considered the State as only intended for the bodily well-being, the material interests of man. In this we cordially agree with him. But we should not be led by the converse of this error to desire that the highest good should be realized in the form of the State which would answer to the condition of the old world, afterwards subdued by Christianity. We think that the State should ensure a free scope for all that is good for mankind, and therefore for the Church, from whence alone Christianity is enabled to exercise that influence with genuine and direct operative power, which in all other cases must be of only an *indirect* nature. (pp. 197-98)

> *Dr. Neander, "The Influence of Thomas Arnold on the Present State of the Church," translated by Rd. Dublin, in* Bentley's Miscellany, *Vol. XX, 1846, pp. 190-98.*

FRASER'S MAGAZINE FOR TOWN AND COUNTRY (essay date 1846)

[*In the following excerpt from a review of Arnold's* Introductory Lectures on Modern History, *the anonymous critic draws a devastating portrait of Arnold's intellectual shortcomings, characterizing him as a "parochial sage" whose ideas and judgments are distorted by intolerance, precipitateness, narrowness, harshness, and dogmatism.*]

Dr. Arnold, with all his gifts, was pre-eminently a parochial sage. While gazing on the universe and contemplating its past and present progress, he seems to have been spell-bound by the local influences which surrounded him. His school was a miniature world, whence he drew his pictures of human passions and affections, and he the king, who presided with despotic authority over the unruly microcosm; and when he went abroad into life, or attempted to delineate the great world without, we at once recognise the hastiness and the intolerance of one who was a stranger to contradiction, and whose confidence in himself was the result of a consciousness of his superiority to those around him rather than of a fair comparison of himself with his equals. This peculiarity is remarkably conspicuous in some of his professional writings. We have no evidence, for example, that he had studied ecclesiastical history with more than ordinary attention, and none whatever that he excelled in his knowledge of ecclesiastical polity, and yet his dogmatism upon both these subjects is literally overwhelming. His scheme of a comprehensive union of Christians may be considered complimentary to his liberality, but at the expense of his judgment; while his theory of priesthood and his hatred of clerical organisation clearly demonstrate his incapacity to deal with questions of so comprehensive a character. The legitimacy of the episcopate was another stumbling-block which impeded his path and disturbed his serenity throughout life, but which he at last overleaped at a bound, as an insufferable hinderance to the evolutions of a free spirit. Indeed, the scorn with which he treats the received hypothesis of prelatical descent is absolutely withering, and in a Churchman far from becoming. No greater horror could have been manifested had he been combating some hideous sophism which involved the peace of

the world and the well-being of the human race, instead of an opinion which, in the present age at least, is practically innocent, and which, for aught he knew to the contrary, might be historically correct. But on such points he was not an authority, and both the bent of his mind and his impatience of control, to say nothing of his contempt for scholastic antiquity, disqualified him in a remarkable manner for estimating the value of the testimony on which such conclusions rest. (pp. 597-98)

Dr. Arnold's temperament was ardent, and ... his zeal in all things, great or small, was irrepressible. To use a homely phrase, he could take nothing easily; and the result of this extreme anxiety to realise his own convictions was an intense manifestation of *individualism*. He was neither of Paul, nor Apollos, nor Cephas, in religion; nor of Socrates or Plato in morals; nor of Bacon or Descartes in modern literature; nor of Pitt or Fox, Russell or Peel, in politics; but of Thomas Arnold, and of Thomas Arnold alone. It was his business to think for himself, and he did so; but he seemed to forget that others had an equal right to the liberty of private judgment, and would probably use it; and that to differ from him was neither a religious, a political, nor a moral heresy. Nothing, indeed, strikes us as more remarkable in his history than the fact that his own very circumscribed sphere of observation, and his separation from the practical business of life, never suggested a single doubt as to his competency to grapple with matters of acknowledged difficulty in the moral and physical government of the world. Hesitation was not one of his defects; on the contrary, his practice was to rush *in medius res*, and to dispense his censure with no measured hand to the right and to the left. All the previous rules and maxims of social existence he stretched upon a Procrustean bed of his own formation, and chopped them down to its dimensions. The process was summary and generally neat, but it was arbitrary and often capricious, and it caused the force of circumstances, for good or for evil, in a great measure to escape him. In no writer of modern times of the same distinction do we remember of so little allowance being made for their operation; perhaps because their recognition would have been inconvenient to a very daring theorist, but more probably because their influence was inadequately apprehended. They obstructed his progress, and he turned aside from them with scorn. In like manner he delighted in abstractions, and was sometimes happy in their application; but it may be doubted whether he possessed the subtlety or the comprehensiveness of mind necessary for a successful metaphysician; and it is quite certain that if he did, he carefully concealed them. The common apology for these extravagancies is, his limited experience of mankind; nor shall we deny that the almost monastic seclusion of Rugby may have tended to corroborate instead of to soften those strong impressions which he adopted so readily and retained so tenaciously: but the fault would appear to us to have lain deeper, since it cannot be disputed that many men with as little knowledge of life have taken juster views of the organisation and objects of human society.... In our judgment, ... neither Winchester nor Oxford are answerable for the peculiarities discernible in Dr. Arnold, but Nature herself. She formed the man and made him what he was,—not the cloister or the school, the Academe or the Porch; a man whom a difficulty could not dismay nor a paradox startle; a man of high moral resolution and of strong passions, who was impatient of control and resented contradiction; a man who thought, felt, and acted energetically at all times and in all circumstances; a man of large benevolence, but who had resolved that the world should be virtuous only after a fashion of his own; a truthful but a severe man, from whom the weaknesses of humanity received little mercy; a respectable man, undoubtedly, and a good man, but one whose creed and precepts were unnecessarily harsh; and, beyond all controversy, a man the expansion of whose mind was cramped by the early adoption of a system of political ethics, which in after-life narrowed the field of his usefulness, and has cast over the most ambitious of his performances the shadow of a speedy decay. But it is time to turn to [*Introductory Lectures on Modern History*].

The lectures of which it consists . . . make up a small volume of remarkable interest in every respect; the question, therefore, naturally occurs, In what does that interest reside? Partly, no doubt, in the subject, which is attractive in itself, but in no small degree in the novelty of the enterprise, and in the very able manner in which it has been executed. We make the latter admission with the greater cheerfulness that many positions are laid down by Dr. Arnold as incontrovertible, in the sound-ness of which we cannot acquiesce; but, as our intention is not so much to review the book professionally as to offer some general remarks on its tone and tendency, we shall confine ourselves as much as possible to the consideration of these two points. (pp. 598-600)

Dr. Arnold's sketches are fresh, vivid, and striking, whether they be correct or not. The limning is perfect even where the details are scanty, and we easily discern the hand of a master in the vigorously executed draughts which are placed before us; but the accompanying logic is often faulty, sometimes vi-cious, and it has always appeared to us as if his chief difficulty on these occasions was to get beyond the charmed circle by which he was surrounded. We may admit, with the *Quarterly Reviewer* [see excerpt by Lake dated 1844], that the rapid outlines of the reigns of Elizabeth and James I., the account of the state of parties under Charles I., and the glance at the Puritans, contained in this volume, are, as he terms them, "admirable," without granting, as would seem to be required, that they are models of the highest style of historical compo-sition, for such we can by no means consider them; but we must utterly deny that "his sketch of the sufferings during the siege of Genoa," so much commended by this and other writ-ers, ought to be received as a sound specimen of political induction. We, on the contrary, look upon its reasoning with extreme suspicion, and would be disposed to refer to it rather as an illustration of the force and prominency of the author's personal predilections, than as a proof of his argumentative talent. The passage runs thus:—

> In the autumn of 1799, the Austrians had driven the French out of Lombardy and Piedmont; their last victory of Fossano or Genola had won the fortress of Coni or Cuneo, close under the Alps, and at the very extremity of the plain of the Po; the French clung to Italy only by their hold of the Riviera of Genoa, the narrow strip of coast between the Apennines and the sea, which extends from the frontiers of France almost to the mouth of the Arno. Hither the remains of the French force were collected, commanded by General Massena, and the point of chief importance to his defence was the city of Genoa. Napoleon had just returned from Egypt, and was become first consul; but he could not be expected to take the field till the following spring, and till then Massena was hopeless of relief from without, every thing was to depend on his

own pertinacity. The strength of his army made it impossible to force it in such a position as Genoa; but its very numbers, added to the pop-ulation of a great city, held out to the enemy a hope of reducing it by famine; and as Genoa derives most of its supplies by sea, Lord Keith, the British naval commander-in-chief in the Mediterranean, lent the assistance of his naval force to the Austrians, and by the vigilance of his cruisers, the whole coasting trade right and left along the Riviera was effectually cut off. It is not at once that the inhabitants of a great city, accustomed to the daily sight of well-stored shops and an abundant market, begin to realise the idea of scarcity; or that the wealthy classes of society, who have never known any other state than one of abundance and luxury, begin seriously to conceive of famine. But the shops were emptied, and the storehouses began to be drawn upon; and no fresh supply or hope of supply appeared. Winter passed away, and spring returned, so early and so beautiful on that gar-den-like coast, sheltered as it is from the north winds by its belt of mountains, and open to the full range of the southern sun. Spring returned, and clothed the hill-sides with its fresh verdure. But that verdure was no longer the mere delight of the careless eye of luxury, refreshing the citizens with its liveliness and softness when they rode or walked up thither from the city to enjoy the surpassing beauty of the prospect. The green hill-sides were now visited for a very different object: ladies of the highest rank might be seen cutting up every plant which it was possible to turn to food, and bearing home the common weeds of our road-sides as a most precious treasure. The French general pitied the distress of the people, but the lives and strength of his garrison seemed to him more important than the lives of the Genoese; and such pro-visions as remained were reserved in the first place for the French army. Scarcity became utter want, and want became famine. In the most gorgeous palaces of that gorgeous city, no less than in the humblest tenements of its humblest poor, death was busy; not the mo-mentary death of battle or massacre, nor the speedy death of pestilence, but the lingering and most miserable death of famine. Infants died before their parents' eyes; husbands and wives lay down to expire together. A man whom I saw at Genoa in 1825, told me that his father and two of his brothers had been starved to death in this fatal siege. So it went on, till, in the month of June, when Napoleon had already descended from the Alps into the plains of Lombardy, the misery became unendurable, and Massena surrendered. But before he did so, 20,000 innocent persons, old and young, women and children, had died by the most horrible of deaths which humanity can endure.

Dr. Arnold then considers shortly, and very generally, with whom "the guilt of most atrocious murder" lay, whether on both sides equally, or on one side only, and concludes his review of the "tragedy," by triumphantly exclaiming, "if any man can defend the lawfulness, in the abstract, of the starvation of the inhabitants of Genoa, I will engage also, to establish the lawfulness of the massacre of September.''

We are not surprised that this passage should have excited admiration. As a picture it is complete, and those who read here or elsewhere of the sufferings of the miserable inhabitants of Genoa during the blockade, which lasted forty-one days, will unite with us, as they would have united with Dr. Arnold, in considering war in all its aspects as one of the most dreadful scourges which ever desolated the earth: the analogy, however, with which it closes, appears to us to be both false and dangerous; and for these reasons we shall request the attention of the reader for a few minutes, while we endeavour to estimate its value.

The defence of the ''lawfulness in the abstract,'' of starving the inhabitants of the city of Genoa, or any other city, is scarcely within the limits of any discussion growing out of the history of that melancholy transaction, and was a demand which Dr. Arnold had no right to make, either as a casuist or as a critic on maritime law: while it must be painfully obvious to all that Lord Keith's share in that memorable incident is unfavourably contrasted with that of the revolutionary general who held Genoa for the French Republic. His office, nevertheless, was as purely ministerial as the office of Massena. They both did what their respective governments ordered them to do, and in their circumstances they could do nothing else; but the point to be observed is this, that the object of the allies was to force Massena out of Genoa, not to starve the Genoese;

Break time at Rugby, circa 1816.

and that, consequently, if the Genoese were starved because Massena would not abandon their city, the weight of that grave offence should lie upon him and those whom he served, and not upon the British admiral or the British government, who had no alternative between the institution of a blockade with all its attendant horrors, and the abandonment of that line of political action upon which they had entered for arresting the progress of the French arms in Italy. Morally speaking, the ''lawfulness'' of slaughtering men in battle may be doubted; and no one ever yet read the history of an assault without feeling his blood run cold at the recital of the atrocities which accompanied it; but the civilian who defines the rules of war, or the politician who justifies its necessity, is not to be held as destitute of humanity because he cannot abate its cruelties; for the assumption that it will and must be attended with cruelties is one of the conditions of his argument, which by the nature of the case he is compelled to adopt, and which, let us hope, he adopts with reluctance. . . . Look at it . . . in what light you will, suffering and sorrow must attend war. It is not, and never has been the herald of happiness, but the servant of desolation: but dreadful thing as it is, and inevitable as it would seem to be so long as man is constituted as he is, it still has its laws—in civilised countries, at least—and we must protest as energetically as we can against the extraordinary doctrine here announced by Dr. Arnold, that its incidental calamities may be balanced by the frightful atrocities committed in Paris in 1792, and known as the ''September massacres.'' If this be more than an antithetical ornament, we must pronounce it to be one of the most singular illustrations upon record of a confusion of moral ideas; for while legitimate war forbids murder, massacre is murder—more than that, it is murder in cold blood, without an aim or an object but the brutal lust of destruction and the fiendish love of slaughter; and such was the character of the ''September massacres'' which Dr. Arnold thought himself justified in setting off against the sufferings of the Genoese. These massacres lasted for three days, during which short time the wretches who officiated at these orgies sacrificed from 6000 to 12,000 victims (for the number is uncertain), of all ages and ranks, and of both sexes, including the Princess de Lamballe; and it must be remembered that these enormities were not perpetrated by enemies on their foes, which would have been bad enough, but by devils in human shape on their own hapless countrymen and kindred; that no plea of necessity, good, bad, or indifferent, could be alleged in defence of these atrocities, except the foul passions of their execrable authors, and that after the lapse of half a century they stand out in bold relief as one of the most dismal tragedies which stain the page of modern history. That they should be likened to any of the ordinary casualties of war by a man of Dr. Arnold's reputation, is truly wonderful; but if our estimate of his character be correct, perhaps this anomaly may be explained. The story which he heard a Genoa in 1825 made a strong impression upon his imagination, and like most of his impressions it was as durable as it was strong. Nothing could be more natural than that while in the city itself he should inquire about the siege, and to a mind constituted and pre-occupied as his was, the transition from gratified curiosity to anger was easy. From that hour we may reasonably suppose that the siege of Genoa would occupy a considerable place in his recollections. It was an incident well suited to his tastes, and he has made an episode out of it, which would have been perfect but for its excessive narrowness; and which, as it at present stands, is cruelly unjust to the actors in that melancholy enterprise, as well as illogical in its philosophical conclusions, if regard be had to the recognised principles of warfare in ancient and modern times. The truth, we apprehend to be, that Dr. Arnold had an inexact conception of nationality, if, indeed, that phrase conveyed to his mind any definite idea whatever. Upon no other hypothesis can we account for the stress which he lays upon what would appear to be individual in contradistinction to imperial interests, or for his anxiety to measure the latter by a standard which falls infinitely short of their true proportions. These lectures, beautiful and instructive as they often are, when critically examined, abound in proofs of this peculiarity. There were not, perhaps, twenty men in Britain who felt as acutely on all subjects as he himself did, or who could invest the passing occurrences of the day, or the events of remote times, with the charm which he threw around both: but he wrote as if he thought otherwise, and he reasoned as if he believed that every man might become ''a law unto himself,'' for it was far from his purpose to inculcate any such demoralising creed. His system of isolation has here its just issue. It confines his vision as a philosophical critic, as in other instances it confines his sympathies as a man: and the result is, a contracted appreciation of the force of those great influences which act on the common family of nations, which are in all probability a part of the scheme of creation, and which have been in conspicuous operation since the dawn of history downwards. The consideration of these, Dr. Arnold, as we venture to think, neglected; and if his book be taken as a whole, and be carefully examined, it will be found to be, if we mistake not, an ingenious defence of individual independency, and a softly worded apology for the ''rights of man.'' What is it, we should be glad to know, which he spares that bears the name or impress of power? The word, except in some sense proper to himself, was as offensive as the thing which it represented; and whether the question be of ecclesiastical subordination, of magisterial authority, of natural law, or even of moral obedience, there is at least a tacit reservation of the privileges of the individual which it is impossible to overlook. Compare him in this respect with Burke, and his most ardent admirers could desire no higher analogy. In the one you find the majesty and integrity of society strenuously enforced, and our ''glorious constitution'' set forth as an object of almost idolatrous veneration; in the other you will discover nothing of the kind, but you may learn that society is, upon the whole, rather an oppression than a benefit; that in various ways it has abridged your liberties, forced your will, and restricted your sphere of enjoyment; and that this or any other constitution—unless, perhaps, some unreal form of democracy—is as remarkable for its defects as its excellencies. Dr. Arnold was of the statutory school, and had unlimited confidence in the beneficial effects of legislation, and little in the undisturbed play of the social affections; and whatever of vice or folly may disfigure the world, would seem to be less a consequence of the propensity of man to err than of the neglect of his rulers to keep him right. The effects of this plaintive habit are very remarkable. All his pictures want relief. There is no sunshine, no *chiaro oscuro,* no light and shade, to diversify the landscape and to soften its angularities; but all is darkness and gloom, until the mind, saddened by the perpetual contemplation of an unavailing contest between feebleness and strength, and humility and tyranny, turns in dismay from a spectacle which is all the more terrible for the severe fidelity with which its several lineaments are displayed. We live in an age in which there is an unnatural appetite for the bare anatomies of life. The skin, the muscles, the bones, are each in their turn exposed to public view. Every social wound is probed till it bleeds and festers, and he is the most profound philosopher who is the most dexterous operator; but this disposition to luxuriate over human suffering and sordidness has the worst

possible effect upon the national mind and taste. The humanity which it inculcates is melo-dramatic and false, and may be indulged to any extent at the smallest expense to the individual; but there is nothing practical and nothing useful about it. Dr. Arnold's nature was too noble and too pure to allow of his personally participating in this degrading pastime; but there can be no doubt that there is a querulous and an unhealthy tone about his miscellaneous writings, which may tend to foster the growth of a disease which a wise man would repress, and that they may afford food to those who, without one particle of his ability or his benevolence, would have no objections to feed a passion which they consider respectable merely because it is prevalent. His otherwise admirable sketches will not teach contentment, nor will they inspire the uncritical reader with respect for the past or the present, for the author himself felt none: but surely there are some bright spots even in human history; surely there have been times when man was happy and deserved to be so; surely there is a tolerably equal admixture of good and evil in the world; and surely it is the duty of the moralist and the historian not to neglect these, were it only for example's sake. Dr. Arnold would seem to have thought differently. His theory of imaginary perfection precluded the possibility of a compromise, and what was not positively good he was obliged to condemn as positively bad. He had viewed society so long in one light that the power of contrast failed him, hence his characters are either heroes or devils. For mere humanity, such as God has made it, there was no place in his system; and between the paradisaical state of being on which his fancy loved to dwell, and the ''desolation of woe,'' there was no middle spot on which man could rest, and fulfil some of the purposes of his being. In his anxiety to be just, he became stern and exclusive; and in his dread of being lenient to vice, he forgot the existence, the authority, and the elasticity of virtue. (pp. 600-04)

''*Arnold's Lectures on Modern History,*'' *in* Fraser's Magazine for Town and Country, *Vol. XXXIII, No. CXCVII, May, 1846, pp. 596-605.*

ARTHUR HUGH CLOUGH   (essay date 1850)

[*Clough, a well-known English poet, is considered one of Arnold's foremost disciples. While he thrived under Arnold at Rugby, Clough suffered a religious crisis at Oxford. Hence, many critics cite his experience as evidence that Arnold overstimulated the moral sensibilities of his students and left them ill prepared for challenges to their faith and values. Clough himself took up some of these issues in 1850, when he wrote an epilogue to his poem* Dipsychus, *which was posthumously published in 1865. In the following extract from the epilogue, the fictive poet discusses with his uncle Arnold's role in fostering the ''over-excitation of the religious sense'' then noticeable in English schoolboys.*]

'You see, dear sir, the thing which [the poem] is attempted to represent is the conflict between the tender conscience and the world. Now, the over-tender conscience will, of course, exaggerate the wickedness of the world; and the Spirit in my poem may be merely the hypothesis or subjective imagination, formed—'

'Oh, for goodness' sake, my dear boy,' interrupted my uncle, 'don't go into the theory of it. If you're wrong in it, it makes bad worse; if you're right, you may be a critic, but you can't be a poet. And then you know very well I don't understand all those new words. But as for that, I quite agree that consciences are often much too tender in your generation—schoolboys' consciences, too! As my old friend the Canon says of the Westminster students, ''They're all so pious.'' It's all Arnold's doing; he spoilt the public schools.'

'My dear uncle,' said I, 'how can so venerable a sexagenarian utter so juvenile a paradox? How often have I not heard you lament the idleness and listlessness, the boorishness and vulgar tyranny, the brutish manners alike, and minds—'

'Ah!' said my uncle, 'I may have fallen in occasionally with the talk of the day; but at seventy one begins to see clearer into the bottom of one's mind. In middle life one says so many things in the way of business. Not that I mean to say that the old schools were perfect, any more than we old boys that were there. But whatever else they were or did, they certainly were in harmony with the world, and they certainly did not disqualify the country's youth for after-life and the country's service.'

'But, my dear sir, this bringing the schools of the country into harmony with public opinion is exactly—'

'Don't interrupt me with public opinion, my dear nephew; you'll quote me a leading article next. ''Young men must be young men,'' as the worthy head of your college said to me touching a case of rustication. ''My dear sir,'' answered I, ''I only wish to heaven they would be; but as for my own nephews, they seem to me a sort of hobbadi-hoy cherub, too big to be innocent, and too simple for anything else. They're full of the notion of the world being so wicked, and of their taking a higher line, as they call it. I only fear they'll never take any at all.'' What is the true purpose of education? Simply to make plain to the young understanding the laws of the life they will have to enter. For example—that lying won't do, thieving still less; that idleness will get punished; that if they are cowards, the whole world will be against them; that if they will have their own way, they must fight for it. Etc. etc. As for the conscience, mamma, I take it—such as mammas are now-a-days, at any rate—has probably set that a-going fast enough already. What a blessing to see her good little child come back a brave young devil-may-care!'

'Exactly, my dear sir. As if at twelve or fourteen a roundabout boy, with his three meals a day inside him, is likely to be over-troubled with scruples.'

'Put him through a course of confirmation and sacraments, backed up with sermons and private admonitions, and what is much the same as auricular confession, and really, my dear nephew, I can't answer for it but he mayn't turn out as great a goose as you—pardon me—*were* about the age of eighteen or nineteen.'

'But to have passed *through* that, my dear sir! surely that can be no harm.'

'I don't know. Your constitutions don't seem to recover it, quite. We did without these foolish measles well enough in my time.'

'Westminster had its Cowper, my dear sir; other schools theirs also, mute and inglorious, but surely not few.'

'Ah, ah! the beginning of troubles—'

'You see, my dear sir, you must not refer it to Arnold, at all at all. Anything that Arnold did in this direction—'

'Why, my dear boy, how often have I not heard from you, how he used to attack offences, not as offences—the right view—against discipline, but as sin, heinous guilt, I don't know what beside! Why didn't he flog them and hold his tongue? Flog them he did, but why preach?'

'If he did err in this way, sir, which I hardly think, I ascribe it to the spirit of the time. The real cause of the evil you complain of, which to a certain extent I admit, was, I take it, the religious movement of the last century, beginning with Wesleyanism, and culminating at last in Puseyism. This over-excitation of the religious sense, resulting in this irrational, almost animal irritability of conscience, was, in many ways, as foreign to Arnold as it is proper to—'

'Well, well, my dear nephew, if you like to make a theory of it, pray write it out for yourself nicely in full; but your poor old uncle does not like theories, and is moreover sadly sleepy.'

'Good night, dear uncle, good night. Only let me say you six more verses.'

'Ah, whose are those?—ah—what? well . . .'

'Good night, dear uncle, good night.' (pp. 292-94)

> *Arthur Hugh Clough, in an epilogue to "Dipsychus," in his* The Poems of Arthur Hugh Clough, *edited by F. L. Mulhauser, second edition, Oxford at the Clarendon Press, Oxford, 1974, pp. 292-94.*

[THOMAS HUGHES] (essay date 1857)

[*Hughes is best known as the author of* Tom Brown's School Days, *a classic story of English public school life that is set at Rugby during Arnold's headmastership. In the following excerpt from that work, which helped greatly to form the public image of Arnold, the protagonist reflects on the impact of Arnold's sermons on his schoolboy audience.*]

What was it [about his sermons] that moved and held us reckless childish boys, who feared the Doctor with all our hearts, and very little besides in heaven or earth; who thought more of our sets in the school than of the Church of Christ, and put the traditions of Rugby and the public opinion of boys in our daily life above the laws of God? We couldn't enter into half that we heard; we hadn't the knowledge of our own hearts or the knowledge of one another, and little enough of the faith, hope, and love needed to that end. But we listened, as all boys in their better moods will listen (aye and man too for the matter of that), to a man who we felt to be with all his heart and soul and strength striving against whatever was mean and unmanly and unrighteous in our little world. It was not the cold clear voice of one giving advice and warning from serene heights, to those who were struggling and sinning below, but the warm living voice of one who was fighting for us and by our sides, and calling on us to keep him and ourselves and one another. And so, wearily and little by little, but surely and steadily on the whole, was brought home to the young boy, for the first time, the meaning of his life: that it was no fool's or sluggard's paradise into which he had wandered by chance, but a battle-field ordained from of old, where there are no spectators, but the youngest must take his side, and the stakes are life and death. And he who roused this consciousness in them, showed them at the same time, by every word he spoke in the pulpit, and by his whole daily life, how that battle was to be fought; and stood there before them their fellow-soldier and the captain of their band. The true sort of captain too for a boys' army, one who had no misgivings and gave no uncertain word of command, and, let who would yield or make truce, would fight the fight out (so every boy felt) to the last gasp, and the last drop of blood. Other sides of his character might take hold of and influence boys here and there, but it was his thoroughness and undaunted courage which more than anything else won his way to the hearts of the great mass of those on whom he left his mark, and made them believe first in him, and then in his Master. (pp. 340-41)

[Thomas Hughes], in an extract from a review of "Tom Brown's School Days," in The Quarterly Review, Vol. 102, No. 204, October, 1857, pp. 340-41.

MATTHEW ARNOLD (poem date 1857)

[*Arnold's eldest son, Matthew, is considered one of the most influential authors of the later Victorian period. Well known today for his poetry, he exercised his greatest influence in his own time through his prose writings, especially his social and literary criticism. While Matthew disagreed with some of his father's religious views, he wrote the following elegy, "Rugby Chapel," extolling the elder Arnold as a noble and courageous spiritual guide. Matthew Arnold dated this poem 1857, but he also stated that he wrote it in response to comments that James Fitzjames Stephen made concerning his father in 1858 (see Additional Bibliography).*]

Coldly, sadly descends
The autumn-evening. The field
Strewn with its dank yellow drifts
Of wither'd leaves, and the elms,
Fade into dimness apace,
Silent;—hardly a shout
From a few boys late at their play!
The lights come out in the street,
In the school-room windows;—but cold,
Solemn, unlighted, austere,
Through the gathering darkness, arise
The chapel-walls, in whose bound
Thou, my father! art laid.

There thou dost lie, in the gloom
Of the autumn evening. But ah!
That word, *gloom,* to my mind
Brings thee back, in the light
Of thy radiant vigour, again;
In the gloom of November we pass'd
Days not dark at thy side;
Seasons impair'd not the ray
Of thy buoyant cheerfulness clear.
Such thou wast! and I stand
In the autumn evening, and think
Of bygone autumns with thee.

Fifteen years have gone round
Since thou arosest to tread,
In the summer-morning, the road
Of death, at a call unforeseen,
Sudden. For fifteen years,
We who till then in thy shade
Rested as under the boughs
Of a mighty oak, have endured
Sunshine and rain as we might,
Bare, unshaded, alone,
Lacking the shelter of thee.

O strong soul, by what shore
Tarriest thou now? For that force,
Surely, has not been left vain!
Somewhere, surely, afar,
In the sounding labour-house vast
Of being, is practised that strength,
Zealous, beneficent, firm!

Yes, in some far-shining sphere,
Conscious or not of the past,
Still thou performest the word
Of the Spirit in whom thou dost live—
Prompt, unwearied, as here!
Still thou upraisest with zeal
The humble good from the ground,
Sternly repressest the bad!
Still, like a trumpet, dost rouse
Those who with half-open eyes
Tread the border-land dim
'Twixt vice and virtue; reviv'st,
Succourest!—this was thy work,
This was thy life upon earth.

What is the course of the life
Of mortal men on the earth?—
Most men eddy about
Here and there—eat and drink,
Chatter and love and hate,
Gather and squander, are raised
Aloft, are hurl'd in the dust,
Striving blindly, achieving
Nothing; and then they die—
Perish;—and no one asks
Who or what they have been,
More than he asks what waves,
In the moonlit solitudes mild
Of the midmost Ocean, have swell'd,
Foam'd for a moment, and gone.

And there are some, whom a thirst
Ardent, unquenchable, fires,
Not with the crowd to be spent,
Not without aim to go round
In an eddy of purposeless dust,
Effort unmeaning and vain.
Ah yes! some of us strive
Not without action to die
Fruitless, but something to snatch
From dull oblivion, nor all
Glut the devouring grave!
We, we have chosen our path—
Path to a clear-purposed goal,
Path of advance!—but it leads
A long, steep journey, through sunk
Gorges, o'er mountains in snow.
Cheerful, with friends, we set forth—
Then, on the height, comes the storm.
Thunder crashes from rock
To rock, the cataracts reply,
Lightnings dazzle our eyes.
Roaring torrents have breach'd
The track, the stream-bed descends
In the place where the wayfarer once
Planted his footstep—the spray
Boils o'er its borders! aloft
The unseen snow-beds dislodge
Their hanging ruin; alas,
Havoc is made in our train!
Friends, who set forth at our side,
Falter, are lost in the storm.
We, we only are left!
With frowning foreheads, with lips
Sternly compress'd, we strain on,
On—and at nightfall at last
Come to the end of our way,
To the lonely inn 'mid the rocks;

Where the gaunt and taciturn host
Stands on the threshold, the wind
Shaking his thin white hairs—
Holds his lantern to scan
Our storm-beat figures, and asks:
Whom in our party we bring?
Whom we have left in the snow?

Sadly we answer: We bring
Only ourselves! we lost
Sight of the rest in the storm.
Hardly ourselves we fought through,
Stripp'd, without friends, as we are.
Friends, companions, and train,
The avalanche swept from our side.

But thou would'st not *alone*
Be saved, my father! *alone*
Conquer and come to thy goal,
Leaving the rest in the wild.
We were weary, and we
Fearful, and we in our march
Fain to drop down and to die.
Still thou turnedst, and still
Beckonedst the trembler, and still
Gavest the weary thy hand.

If, in the paths of the world,
Stones might have wounded thy feet,
Toil or dejection have tried
Thy spirit, of that we saw
Nothing—to us thou wast still
Cheerful, and helpful, and firm!
Therefore to thee it was given
Many to save with thyself;
And, at the end of thy day,
O faithful shepherd! to come,
Bringing thy sheep in thy hand.

And through thee I believe
In the noble and great who are gone;
Pure souls honour'd and blest
By former ages, who else—
Such, so soulless, so poor,
Is the race of men whom I see—
Seem'd but a dream of the heart,
Seem'd but a cry of desire.
Yes! I believe that there lived
Others like thee in the past,
Not like the men of the crowd
Who all round me to-day
Bluster or cringe, and make life
Hideous, and arid, and vile;
But souls temper'd with fire,
Fervent, heroic, and good,
Helpers and friends of mankind.

Servants of God!—or sons
Shall I not call you? because
Not as servants ye knew
Your Father's innermost mind,
His, who unwillingly sees
One of his little ones lost—
Yours is the praise, if mankind
Hath not as yet in its march
Fainted, and fallen, and died!

See! In the rocks of the world
Marches the host of mankind,
A feeble, wavering line.
Where are they tending?—A God
Marshall'd them, gave them their goal.
Ah, but the way is so long!
Years they have been in the wild!
Sore thirst plagues them, the rocks,
Rising all round, overawe;
Factions divide them, their host
Threatens to break, to dissolve.
—Ah, keep, keep them combined!
Else, of the myriads who fill
That army, not one shall arrive;
Sole they shall stray; in the rocks
Stagger for ever in vain,
Die one by one in the waste.

Then, in such hour of need
Of your fainting, dispirited race,
Ye, like angels, appear,
Radiant with ardour divine!
Beacons of hope, ye appear!
Languor is not in your heart,
Weakness is not in your word,
Weariness not on your brow.
Ye alight in our van! at your voice,
Panic, despair, flee away.
Ye move through the ranks, recall
The stragglers, refresh the outworn,
Praise, re-inspire the brave!
Order, courage, return.
Eyes rekindling, and prayers,
Follow your steps as ye go.
Ye fill up the gaps in our files,
Strengthen the wavering line,
Stablish, continue our march,
On, to the bound of the waste,
On, to the City of God.

(pp. 269-76)

Matthew Arnold, "Rugby Chapel," in his The Works
of Matthew Arnold: Poems, Vol. I, *1903-04. Reprint
by AMS Press, 1970, pp. 269-76.*

THE SPECTATOR   (essay date 1892)

[*The anonymous critic contends that by stressing the importance
of satisfying one's own conscience in religious matters, Arnold
inadvertently undermined the Christian faith of his followers.*]

The meeting last Monday in the school dining-hall adjoining
the cloisters of Westminster Abbey to raise a monument in the
Abbey to Dr. Arnold, fifty years after his death, was, as the
speakers evidently felt, not so much a reminiscence of his
life,—though it was that too,—as a testimony to the astonishing
growth of Dr. Arnold's influence since the date of his death.
Those who felt most keenly what England had lost in losing
him, felt still more keenly what England had gained by the fall
of that seed into the ground, and the much fruit that its death
had brought forth. Yet even that great gain has not been without
its compensating elements of loss. The impressive, almost
majestic earnestness which effected a transformation in the
whole tone of English ideals of character and the whole type
of English school life, has in some directions, and those the
directions in which its influence has been most keenly felt,

proved to be negative as well as positive. The great poet who celebrated Dr. Arnold in the noble verses on ''Rugby Chapel'' [see poem by Matthew Arnold dated 1857], was not only Arnold's pupil but his son; and yet he represented and disseminated a religious attitude of mind very different from his father's,—indeed, resembling his father's only in the somewhat imperious character of his intellectual make. Again, the poet and pupil who was perhaps even more powerfully affected by Arnold's moral genius than his son himself, Arthur Hugh Clough, represented and disseminated an attitude of mind towards the Christian religion very different from his master's. Further, Arnold's pupil and biographer, Arthur Stanley, who, by his *Life,* laid the foundation of Arnold's vast popularity, did perhaps as much to dissipate confidence in the historical Christianity which Arnold accepted, as he did to create for him an enduring fame. And the novelist who now best represents not only the *ethos* of Arnold's earnestness, but the eagerness of his wish to stamp the younger generation with that type of character,—we mean, of course, his granddaughter, Mrs. Humphry Ward,—is devoting her genius to what Dr. Arnold himself would have thought a negative crusade as regards faith and doctrine, no less than to a positive crusade as regards life and work. . . . [It] is rather curious that the two who are his descendants as well as his disciples, have had a decidedly greater influence in breaking down confidence in his historical Christianity, than the two who were his disciples only. Matthew Arnold's writings on Christian dogma are decidedly more subversive of his father's Christianity than Clough's more moderate and more dubious criticism. Mrs. Humphry Ward's onslaught on historical Christianity has been far more vehement than Arthur Stanley's pleas for universal comprehension. It looks as if Dr. Arnold's intensity of moral purpose contained implicit germs of a solvent for the Christian creed which he himself firmly held, no less than a commanding ethical impulse to share with others whatever the believer could believe, as well as the disbelief in whatever he was compelled to reject. Matthew Arnold certainly thought so. For though in ''Rugby Chapel'' he delineated only the great moral force of his father's courage and compassion, in the exquisite stanzas ''From the Grande Chartreuse'' he certainly includes him as one of the teachers who had saved him from the Catholic reaction in which many of his contemporaries had been involved, and plunged him into doubt:—

> For rigorous teachers seized my youth,
>   And purged its faith and trimmed its fire,
> Showed me the high white star of Truth,
>   There bade me gaze, and there aspire.
> E'en now their whispers pierce the gloom,
> *What dost thou in this living tomb?*
>
> Forgive me, masters of the mind,
>   At whose behest I long ago
> So much unlearnt, so much resigned—
>   I come not here to be your foe,
> I seek these anchorites not in ruth,
> To curse and to deny your truth.
>
> Not as their friend or child I speak!
>   But as, on some far Northern strand,
> Thinking of his own Gods, a Greek
>   In pity and mournful awe might stand
> Before some fallen Runic stone—
> For both were faiths, and both are gone.
>
> Wandering between two worlds, one dead,
>   The other powerless to be born,
> With nowhere yet to rest my head

> Like these, on earth I wait forlorn.
> Their faith, my tears the world deride—
> I come to shed them at their side.

And now Dr. Arnold's granddaughter, too, has just told us with that impressive earnestness which dignifies the vagueness of her aspirations, how necessary she thinks it that children should be taught to regard the belief of the early Church in Christ's resurrection as a mere subjective measure of the love his disciples bore to him, and has acquainted us how well she can even imagine, though she does not teach, a Christianity ''without the hope of God.'' No doubt she can imagine any number of religious hospices constructed of mere cards which will never shelter any one. But is it the severe critic of historical evidence who should tell us what she can imagine, rather than what she must believe?

What was it in Dr. Arnold's ''earnestness'' that seemed to have the effect of denuding those whom he most powerfully influenced, of so much belief which he himself continued to hold, no less than of spurring them on to an enthusiastic career of missionary zeal for the rescue of others from the contagion of indifference, and of careless, pleasure-loving ease? We suspect it was partly his eager historical craving to grope about the roots of all great institutions and analyse their origin, but much more that moral intolerance of any kind of authority not itself sternly and exclusively moral, which showed itself in his vehement attacks on the Anglican movement. It seems to us that what we may call the Arnold school of religion challenges all authority which does not proceed wholly from the conscience; and we venture to say that, great as the sphere of the conscience is, it is not competent, unassisted and without the help of high intellectual guidance, to lay the foundations of any revelation. The stern ''earnestness'' of the Arnold school is a grand earnestness, but an earnestness almost unaccompanied by humility. Even in Dr. Arnold's own writings, inspiring and noble as they are, we feel something of that want. It was the want which F. D. Maurice, who shared fully the earnestness, without sharing the seductively imperious attitude of mind with which in Arnold it was associated, supplied, but which is more or less wanting in all the most characteristic disciples of the Arnold school, especially in the great poet [Matthew Arnold], and the powerful novelist [Mrs. Humphry Ward] who told us the story of Robert Elsmere's collapse of creed and painful efforts at reconstructing faith on the airy basis of his own arbitrary selections from the traditions concerning Christ's teaching and life. It is surely quite unreasonable to take Christ as the very moral type of human nature, and then to assume that there was no higher and deeper intellectual knowledge of God in the spiritual atmosphere which was generated by his presence and teaching in the world, than is consistent with those modern theories which make the most theological of all the Gospels, and the most theological passages even of the first three Gospels, as well as the whole theology of the Epistles, a mere dream-world that has reared itself upon no historical basis at all. It will be said, of course, and with perfect truth, that this was not Dr. Arnold's own view, though it has been the view of two of the most illustrious of his descendants, and of his two most eminent pupils. No doubt. And it is more than possible that if Dr. Arnold had foreseen this solvent influence of his stern moral teaching, he would have recoiled from it, and discerned the deficiencies in that too imperiously ethical spirit which was destined apparently to undermine the foundations of the teaching best fitted to sustain its eager life. Nevertheless, we do think that ''that severe, that earnest air'' which characterised Dr. Arnold, and which made his attacks on the Anglicans of his day so fierce, had in it an implicit tendency to generate this dictatorial Liberalism that now appears to be decomposing Christianity, while it professes to be shielding and reconstructing it. We can never understand that so-called "Liberal" disposition to depreciate the whole intellectual environment of Christianity amongst those who hold up Christ as the ideal standard of human perfection. Surely the moral ideal of the race could not have been bound up with so feeble an intellectual insight into its own character, prospects, and history. And glad as we are to point out that Dr. Arnold himself gave no sanction to the paradox which has obtained so much credence amongst his school, we cannot help thinking that the imperious and scornful intellectual attitude which characterises that school, was caught at the feet of the great but rather aggressive ecclesiastical Liberal who inspired, and himself initiated, the mighty reformation which he has brought about in the educational life of this great country. Clough used to speak of "the ruinous force of the will" which enables men to believe what they want to believe. Dr. Arnold probably rather over-stimulated the will of his more sensitive disciples, and in the reaction, they lost almost as much as they had gained, though for the ordinary pachydermatous British schoolboy Dr. Arnold's influence was the best tonic that could have been applied. But what Dr. Arnold failed to teach was intellectual humility. In some of the stronger minds which felt his noble and chivalric enthusiasm, he inspired too great a trust in their own judgments. That is why, as it seems to us, so many of his disciples throw off with the greatest equanimity all the accessories, as they think them, of our Lord's teaching, and discover that that teaching was sheathed deep in error from the very day of the Crucifixion. Revelation, indeed, in the hands of these confident persons, needs all sorts of human reflecting and refracting and sifting agencies before it can be trusted as divine teaching, so that the external institution which Christ left in the world is valuable chiefly as testimony to what his teaching was *not*, rather than as to what it was. Could any group who had learned a lesson of true humility have transmitted so strange a lesson as this? Dr. Arnold's power to reform the whole tenor of our school life, was partly due, no doubt, to this grand self-confidence and imperious volition. But we doubt whether his intellectual influence over the convictions of posterity was at all as invigorating as his moral influence over education. He was a great practical reformer, but he was too self-confident to give the right key-note to a school of religious thinkers and critics. (pp. 840-41)

> *"Dr. Arnold after Fifty Years," in* The Spectator, *Vol. 68, No. 3338, June 18, 1892, pp. 840-41.*

THE TIMES, LONDON   (essay date 1896)

[*In this extract from an anonymous review first published in the London* Times *on 17 July 1896, the critic credits Arnold with improving English society through the values that he instilled in his students.*]

No one made a deeper change in education, a change which profited those who had never been at a public school. As much as any one who could be named, Arnold helped to form the standard of manly worth by which Englishmen judge and submit to be judged. A man of action himself, he sent out from Rugby men fit to do the work of the world. The virtues which his favourite Aristotle extolled—courage, justice, and temperance—were his, and the influence of his character and teaching was calculated to make brave, high-minded soldiers, zealous enlightened clergymen, lawyers with a just sense of the nature

of their vocation, and useful and public-spirited members of the State. The width and range of his teaching are apt to be forgotten by those who dwell on his personal influence. If he offered no large interpretation of life, if in his writings there are rarely 'thoughts beyond the reaches of the soul,' if as an historian he seems more at home in dealing with the geographical aspects of his subject, or in clear delineation of the movements of events, than in discovering the hidden springs of action, if he never or rarely let fall a pregnant unforgettable word, he had conceptions, new in his time, first and foremost his lofty conception of education, his conception of the Church as a great agency of social amelioration, his idea of each citizen's duty to the State, his view of history as a whole, with no real division between ancient and modern, the interest, new in his time, which he felt in the elevation of the masses. One must have been at Rugby or Oxford in the thirties to appreciate the effect of Arnold's sermons on generous, susceptible youth. Even in the volume of national life as it flows to-day, there may be detected the effect of the pure, bracing stream which long ago joined it.

> *An extract in* Thomas and Matthew Arnold and Their Influence on English Education *by Sir Joshua Fitch, Charles Scribner's Sons, 1897, p. 156.*

OTTO PFLEIDERER   (essay date 1909)

[*Pfleiderer, who was a professor of theology at the University of Berlin, acclaims Arnold as a liberating force in English theology.*]

It is Thomas Arnold, if any one, who must be regarded as the pioneer of free theology in England. It is true he wrote no considerable theological work—his vocation led him into the field of scholarship and history: and his views with regard to the interpretation of the Bible were neither quite new, nor do they meet completely the present requirements of historical criticism. But Arnold was the first to show to his countrymen the possibility and to make the demand, that the Bible should be read with honest human eyes without the spectacles of orthodox dogmatic presuppositions, and that it can at the same time be revered with Christian piety and made truly productive in moral life. He was the first who dared to leave on one side the traditional phraseology of the High-Churchmen and the Evangelicals, and to look upon Christianity, not as a sacred treasure of the Churches and sects, but as a Divine beneficent power for every believer; not as a dead heritage from the past, but as a living spiritual power for the moral advancement of individuals and nations in the present. If the universality of his interests and occupations was a hindrance to strictly scientific theological inquiry, it was really very favourable to his true mission: he showed how classical and general historical studies may be pursued in the light of the moral ideas of Christianity, and how, on the other hand, a free and clear way of looking at things may be obtained by means of wide historical knowledge, and then applied to the interpretation of the Bible and the solution of current ecclesiastical questions. Thus he began to pull down the wall of separation which had cut off the religious life of his fellow-countrymen, with their sects and churches and rigid theological formulas and usages, from the general life and pursuits of the nation. (p. 367)

> *Otto Pfleiderer, "A Survey of the Progress of Theology in Great Britain since 1825: Parties and Movements in the Theology," in his* The Development of Theology in Germany since Kant and Its Progress in Great Britain since 1825, *translated by J. Frederick*

Smith, third edition, Swan Sonnenschein & Co., Ltd., 1909, pp. 355-401.

G. P. GOOCH   (essay date 1913)

[Gooch describes Arnold's History of Rome *as the work of a promising historian.]*

The critical study of Roman history in England was inaugurated by the translation of Niebuhr; but next to Hare and Thirlwall his fame owes most to Thomas Arnold. No English scholar hailed the revised volumes [of Niebuhr's *Römische Geschichte*] with greater delight, and no one entertained a deeper veneration for the author, whom he visited at Bonn. 'It is a work,' he wrote, 'of such extraordinary ability and learning that it opened wide before my eyes the extent of my own ignorance.' He planned a history of Rome, not to rival the production of so great a man but because it was not likely to become popular in England. When Niebuhr died, he was more desirous than ever to restate and continue his work to the coronation of Charles the Great. His ambition was to imitate his method of inquiry, 'to practise his master art of doubting rightly and believing rightly.' He approached his task with becoming modesty. 'As to any man being a fit continuator of Niebuhr,' he wrote to Hare, 'that is absurd; but I have at least the qualification of an unbounded veneration for what he has done, and I should like to try to embody the thoughts and notions I have learnt from him.' The first volume of the ***History of Rome*** appeared in 1838, and covered the period before the invasion of the Gauls. The legends are related in archaic style to suggest that they are only romances. In the story of the Kings he finds a little, but only a little, that is historical. In this part of his work it is the pen of Arnold and the voice of Niebuhr. Even the hypothesis of the ballads is accepted. The second volume reaches the end of the First Punic War. The third, bringing the narrative within sight of the end of the Second Punic War, was almost completed when the author died in 1841. Thus Arnold's book, like that of his master, remained a fragment.

His early death decreed that his ***History*** should be remembered mainly as an adaptation of Niebuhr. Had he lived longer he would have shown how capable he was of walking alone. He was far better fitted to portray the life of a State than to reconstruct the faint outlines of an early civilisation. His strength grows as he advances, and his third volume is as superior to the second as the second to the first. 'The most remarkable of his talents,' wrote his friend Hare, 'was his singular geographical eye, which enabled him to find as much pleasure in looking at a map as lovers of painting in a Raphael.' This gift, added to his interest in military affairs, enabled him to interpret Hannibal. His admirable style, easy and flowing yet full of colour, found in the Second Punic War a theme worthy of itself. It is a grievous loss to literature that the hand which traced the portrait of the great Carthaginian was not spared to recount the fortunes of the Gracchi and the closing years of the Republic. The later part of his early sketch of Roman history was reprinted as a continuation; but it is a very poor substitute for the unwritten volumes, and is chiefly of interest for the outspoken condemnation of Cæsar. 'In moral character the whole range of history can hardly furnish a picture of greater deformity. Never did any man occasion so large an amount of human misery with so little provocation.' The portrait of Augustus is scarcely less severe, and the work forms a passionate indictment of Cæsarism. (pp. 319-20)

G. P. Gooch, "Thirlwall, Grote and Arnold," in his History and Historians in the Nineteenth Century, *second edition, 1913. Reprint by Longmans, Green and Co., 1920, pp. 308-22.*

LYTTON STRACHEY   (essay date 1918)

[Strachey was an early twentieth-century English biographer, critic, essayist, and short story writer. He is best known for his works Eminent Victorians, Queen Victoria, *and* Elizabeth and Essex: A Tragic History, *in which he disclosed previously overlooked complexities of personality in some of the most prominent and revered figures of English history. Arnold was one of those figures. In the following extract from* Eminent Victorians, *Strachey focuses on Arnold's position regarding moral and educational reform at Rugby, suggesting that many aspects of his program were ill advised. Strachey's remarks are addressed by G. F. Bradby (1932) and Edward C. Mack (1938).]*

[The] task before [Dr. Arnold at Rugby] was sufficiently perplexing. The public schools of those days were still virgin forests, untouched by the hand of reform. Keate was still reigning at Eton; and we possess, in the records of his pupils, a picture of the public school education of the early nineteenth century, in its most characteristic state. It was a system of anarchy tempered by despotism. Hundreds of boys, herded together in miscellaneous boarding-houses, or in that grim "Long Chamber" at whose name in after years aged statesmen and warriors would turn pale, lived, badgered and over-awed by the furious incursions of an irascible little old man carrying a bundle of birch-twigs, a life in which licensed barbarism was mingled with the daily and hourly study of the niceties of Ovidian verse. It was a life of freedom and terror, of prosody and rebellion, of interminable floggings and appalling practical jokes. Keate ruled, unaided—for the undermasters were few and of no account—by sheer force of character. But there were times when even that indomitable will was overwhelmed by the flood of lawlessness. Every Sunday afternoon he attempted to read sermons to the whole school assembled; and every Sunday afternoon the whole school assembled shouted him down. The scenes in Chapel were far from edifying: while some antique Fellow doddered in the pulpit, rats would be let loose to scurry among the legs of the exploding boys. But next morning the hand of discipline would re-assert itself; and the savage ritual of the whipping-block would remind a batch of whimpering children that, though sins against man and God might be forgiven them, a false quantity could only be expiated in tears and blood.

From two sides, this system of education was beginning to be assailed by the awakening public opinion of the upper middle classes. On the one hand, there was a desire for a more liberal curriculum; on the other, there was a demand for a higher moral tone. The growing utilitarianism of the age viewed with impatience a course of instruction which excluded every branch of knowledge except classical philology; while its growing respectability was shocked by such a spectacle of disorder and brutality as was afforded by the Eton of Keate. (pp. 211-12)

[Dr. Arnold] was convinced of the necessity for reform. But it was only natural that to one of his temperament and education it should have been the moral rather than the intellectual side of the question which impressed itself upon his mind. Doubtless it was important to teach boys something more than the bleak rigidities of the ancient tongues; but how much more important to instil into them the elements of character and the principles of conduct! His great object, throughout his career at Rugby, was, as he repeatedly said, to "make the school a place of really Christian education." To introduce "a religious principle into education," was his "most earnest wish," he wrote to a friend when he first became headmaster; "but to do this would be to succeed beyond all my hopes; it would be a happiness so great, that, I think, the world would yield me nothing comparable to it." And he was constantly impressing these sentiments upon his pupils. "What I have often said before," he told them, "I repeat now: what we must look for here is, first, religious and moral principle; secondly, gentlemanly conduct; thirdly, intellectual ability."

There can be no doubt that Dr. Arnold's point of view was shared by the great mass of English parents. They cared very little for classical scholarship; no doubt they would be pleased to find that their sons were being instructed in history or in French, but their real hopes, their real wishes, were of a very different kind. "Shall I tell him to mind his work, and say he's sent to school to make himself a good scholar?" meditated old Squire Brown when he was sending off Tom for the first time to Rugby.

> Well, but he isn't sent to school for that—at any rate, not for that mainly. I don't care a straw for Greek particles, or the digamma; no more does his mother. What is he sent to school for? . . . If he'll only turn out a brave, helpful, truth-telling Englishman, and a Christian, that's all I want.

That was all; and it was that that Dr. Arnold set himself to accomplish. But how was he to achieve his end? Was he to improve the character of his pupils by gradually spreading round them an atmosphere of cultivation and intelligence? By bringing them into close and friendly contact with civilised men, and even, perhaps, with civilised women? By introducing into the life of his school all that he could of the humane, enlightened, and progressive elements in the life of the community? On the whole, he thought not. Such considerations left him cold, and he preferred to be guided by the general laws of Providence. It only remained to discover what those general laws were. He consulted the Old Testament, and could doubt no longer. He would apply to his scholars, as he himself explained to them in one of his sermons, "the principle which seemed to him to have been adopted in the training of the childhood of the human race itself." He would treat the boys at Rugby as Jehovah had treated the Chosen People: he would found a theocracy; and there should be Judges in Israel.

For this purpose, the system, prevalent in most of the public schools of the day, by which the elder boys were deputed to keep order in the class-rooms, lay ready to Dr. Arnold's hand. He found the "Præpostor" a mere disciplinary convenience, and he converted him into an organ of government. Every boy in the Sixth Form became *ipso facto* a Præpostor, with powers extending over every department of school life; and the Sixth Form as a body was erected into an authority responsible to the headmaster, and to the headmaster alone, for the internal management of the school.

This was the means by which Dr. Arnold hoped to turn Rugby into "a place of really Christian education." The boys were to work out their own salvation, like the human race. He himself, involved in awful grandeur, ruled remotely, through his chosen instruments, from an inaccessible heaven. Remotely and yet with an omnipresent force. As the Israelite of old knew that his almighty Lawgiver might at any moment thunder to

him from the whirlwind, or appear before his very eyes, the visible embodiment of power or wrath, so the Rugby schoolboy walked in a holy dread of some sudden manifestation of the sweeping gown, the majestic tone, the piercing glance, of Dr. Arnold. Among the lower forms of the school his appearances were rare and transitory, and upon these young children "the chief impression," we are told, "was of extreme fear." The older boys saw more of him, but they did not see much. Outside the Sixth Form, no part of the school came into close intercourse with him; and it would often happen that a boy would leave Rugby without having had any personal communication with him at all. Yet the effect which he produced upon the great mass of his pupils was remarkable. The prestige of his presence and the elevation of his sentiments were things which it was impossible to forget. In class, every line of his countenance, every shade of his manner imprinted themselves indelibly on the minds of the boys who sat under him. (pp. 212-15)

To be rebuked, however mildly, by Dr. Arnold was a notable experience. One boy could never forget how he drew a distinction between "mere amusement" and "such as encroached on the next day's duties," nor the tone of voice with which the Doctor added "and then it immediately becomes what St. Paul calls *revelling*." Another remembered to his dying day his reproof of some boys who had behaved badly during prayers. "Nowhere," said Dr. Arnold, "nowhere is Satan's work more evidently manifest than in turning holy things to ridicule." On such occasions, as another of his pupils described it, it was impossible to avoid "a consciousness almost amounting to solemnity" that, "when his eye was upon you, he looked into your inmost heart." (pp. 215-16)

It was obvious that the primitive methods of discipline which had reached their apogee under the dominion of Keate were altogether incompatible with Dr. Arnold's view of the functions of a headmaster and the proper governance of a public school. Clearly, it was not for such as he to demean himself by bellowing and cuffing, by losing his temper once an hour, and by wreaking his vengeance with indiscriminate flagellations. Order must be kept in other ways. The worst boys were publicly expelled; many were silently removed; and, when Dr. Arnold considered that a flogging was necessary, he administered it with gravity. For he had no theoretical objection to corporal punishment. On the contrary, he supported it, as was his wont, by an appeal to general principles. "There is," he said, "an essential inferiority in a boy as compared with a man"; and hence "where there is no equality, the exercise of superiority implied in personal chastisement" inevitably followed. He was particularly disgusted by the view that "personal correction," as he phrased it, was an insult or a degradation to the boy upon whom it was inflicted; and to accustom young boys to think so appeared to him to be "positively mischievous."

> At an age [he wrote] when it is almost impossible to find a true, manly sense of the degradation of guilt or faults, where is the wisdom of encouraging a fantastic sense of the degradation of personal correction? What can be more false, or more adverse to the simplicity, sobriety, and humbleness of mind which are the best ornaments of youth, and offer the best promise of a noble manhood?

One had not to look far, he added, for "the fruits of such a system." In Paris, during the Revolution of 1830, an officer observed a boy of twelve insulting the soldiers and though the action was then raging, merely struck him with the flat part of his sword, as the fit chastisement for boyish impertinence. But the boy had been taught to consider his person sacred, and that a blow was a deadly insult; he therefore followed the officer, and having watched his opportunity, took deliberate aim at him with a pistol and murdered him.

Such were the alarming results of insufficient whipping.

Dr. Arnold did not apply this doctrine to the Præpostors; but the boys in the lower parts of the school felt its benefits with a double force. The Sixth Form was not only excused from chastisement; it was given the right to chastise. The younger children, scourged both by Dr. Arnold and by the elder children, were given every opportunity of acquiring the simplicity, sobriety, and humbleness of mind, which are the best ornaments of youth.

In the actual sphere of teaching, Dr. Arnold's reforms were tentative and few. He introduced modern history, modern languages, and mathematics into the school curriculum; but the results were not encouraging. He devoted to the teaching of history one hour a week; yet, though he took care to inculcate in these lessons a wholesome hatred of moral evil, and to point out from time to time the indications of the providential government of the world, his pupils never seemed to make much progress in the subject. Could it have been that the time allotted to it was insufficient? Dr. Arnold had some suspicions that this might be the case. With modern languages there was the same difficulty. Here his hopes were certainly not excessive. "I assume it," he wrote, "as the foundation of all my view of the case, that boys at a public school never will learn to speak or pronounce French well, under any circumstances." It would be enough if they could "learn it grammatically as a dead language." But even this they very seldom managed to do.

> I know too well [he was obliged to confess] that most of the boys would pass a very poor examination even in French grammar. But so it is with their mathematics; and so it will be with any branch of knowledge that is taught but seldom, and is felt to be quite subordinate to the boys' main study.

The boys' main study remained the dead languages of Greece and Rome. That the classics should form the basis of all teaching was an axiom with Dr. Arnold. "The study of language," he said, "seems to me as if it was given for the very purpose of forming the human mind in youth; and the Greek and Latin languages seem the very instruments by which this is to be effected." Certainly, there was something providential about it—from the point of view of the teacher as well as of the taught. If Greek and Latin had not been "given" in that convenient manner, Dr. Arnold, who had spent his life in acquiring those languages, might have discovered that he had acquired them in vain. As it was, he could set the noses of his pupils to the grindstone of syntax and prosody with a clear conscience. Latin verses and Greek prepositions divided between them the labours of the week. As time went on, he became, he declared, "increasingly convinced that it is not knowledge, but the means of gaining knowledge which I have to teach." The reading of the school was devoted almost entirely to selected passages from the prose writers of antiquity. (pp. 216-19)

Physical science was not taught at Rugby. Since, in Dr. Arnold's opinion, it was "too great a subject to be studied [in-

cidentally]," obviously only two alternatives were possible:— it must either take the chief place in the school curriculum, or it must be left out altogether. Before such a choice, Dr. Arnold did not hesitate for a moment.

> Rather than have physical science the principal thing in my son's mind [he exclaimed in a letter to a friend], I would gladly have him think that the sun went round the earth, and that the stars were so many spangles set in the bright blue firmament. Surely the one thing needful for a Christian and an Englishman to study is Christian and moral and political philosophy.

A Christian and an Englishman! After all, it was not in the class-room, nor in the boarding-house, that the essential elements of instruction could be imparted which should qualify the youthful neophyte to deserve those names. The final, the fundamental lesson could only be taught in the school chapel; in the school chapel the centre of Dr. Arnold's system of education was inevitably fixed. There, too, the Doctor himself appeared in the plentitude of his dignity and his enthusiasm. There, with the morning sun shining on the freshly scrubbed faces of his three hundred pupils, or, in the dusk of evening, through a glimmer of candles, his stately form, rapt in devotion or vibrant with exhortation, would dominate the scene. Every phase of the Church service seemed to receive its supreme expression in his voice, his attitude, his look. (pp. 219-20)

At the end of the evening service the culminating moment of the week had come: the Doctor delivered his sermon. It was not until then, as all who had known him agreed, it was not until one had heard and seen him in the pulpit, that one could fully realise what it was to be face to face with Dr. Arnold. The whole character of the man—so we are assured—stood at last revealed. His congregation sat in fixed attention (with the exception of the younger boys, whose thoughts occasionally wandered), while he propounded the general principles both of his own conduct and that of the Almighty, or indicated the bearing of the incidents of Jewish history in the sixth century B.C. upon the conduct of English schoolboys in 1830. Then, more than ever, his deep consciousness of the invisible world became evident; then, more than ever, he seemed to be battling with the wicked one. For his sermons ran on the eternal themes of the darkness of evil, the craft of the tempter, the punishment of obliquity, and he justified the persistence with which he dwelt upon these painful subjects by an appeal to a general principle: "the spirit of Elijah," he said, "must ever precede the spirit of Christ." The impression produced upon the boys was remarkable. It was noticed that even the most careless would sometimes, during the course of the week, refer almost involuntarily to the sermon of the past Sunday, as a condemnation of what they were doing. Others were heard to wonder how it was that the Doctor's preaching, to which they had attended at the time so assiduously, seemed, after all, to have such a small effect upon what they did. An old gentleman, recalling those vanished hours, tried to recapture in words his state of mind as he sat in the darkened chapel, while Dr. Arnold's sermons, with their high-toned exhortations, their grave and sombre messages of incalculable import, clothed, like Dr. Arnold's body in its gown and bands, in the traditional stiffness of a formal phraseology, reverberated through his adolescent ears. "I used," he said, "to listen to those sermons from first to last with a kind of awe." (pp. 221-22)

There were moments when [Dr. Arnold] almost lost faith in his whole system of education, when he began to doubt whether some far more radical reforms than any he had attempted might not be necessary, before the multitude of children under his charge—shouting and gamboling, and yet plunged all the while deep in moral evil—could ever be transformed into a set of Christian gentlemen. But then he remembered his general principles, the conduct of Jehovah with the Chosen People, and the childhood of the human race. No, it was for him to make himself, as one of his pupils afterwards described him, in the words of Bacon, "kin to God in spirit"; he would rule the school majestically from on high. He would deliver a series of sermons analysing "the six vices" by which "great schools were corrupted, and changed from the likeness of God's temple to that of a den of thieves." He would exhort, he would denounce, he would sweep through the corridors, he would turn the pages of Facciolati's lexicon more imposingly than ever; and the rest he would leave to the Præpostors in the Sixth Form. (pp. 233-34)

At their best, it may be supposed that the Præpostors administered a kind of barbaric justice; but they were not always at their best, and the pages of *Tom Brown's Schooldays* show us what was no doubt the normal condition of affairs under Dr. Arnold, when the boys in the Sixth Form were weak or brutal, and the blackguard Flashman, in the intervals of swigging brandy-punch with his boon companions, amused himself by roasting fags before the fire.

But there was an exceptional kind of boy, upon whom the high-pitched exhortations of Dr. Arnold produced a very different effect. A minority of susceptible and serious youths fell completely under his sway, responded like wax to the pressure of his influence, and moulded their whole lives with passionate reverence upon the teaching of their adored master. Conspicuous among these was Arthur Clough. Having been sent to Rugby at the age of ten, he quickly entered into every phase of school life, though, we are told, "a weakness in his ankles prevented him from taking a prominent part in the games of the place." At the age of sixteen, he was in the Sixth Form, and not merely a Præpostor, but head of the School House. Never did Dr. Arnold have an apter pupil. This earnest adolescent, with the weak ankles and the solemn face, lived entirely with the highest ends in view. He thought of nothing but moral good, moral evil, moral influence, and moral responsibility. Some of his early letters have been preserved, and they reveal both the intensity with which he felt the importance of his own position, and the strange stress of spirit under which he laboured. "I have been in one continued state of excitement for at least the last three years," he wrote when he was not yet seventeen, "and now comes the time of exhaustion." But he did not allow himself to rest, and a few months later he was writing to a schoolfellow as follows:—

> I verily believe my whole being is soaked through with the wishing and hoping and striving to do the school good, or rather to keep it up and hinder it from falling in this, I do think, very critical time, so that my cares and affections and conversations, thoughts, words, and deeds look to that involuntarily. I am afraid you will be inclined to think this "cant," and I am conscious that even one's truest feelings, if very frequently put out in the light, do make a bad and disagreeable appearance; but this, however, is true, and even if I am carrying it too far, I do not think it has made me really forgetful of my personal friends, such as, in par-

ticular, Gell and Burbidge and Walrond, and yourself, my dear Simpkinson.

Perhaps it was not surprising that a young man brought up in such an atmosphere should have fallen a prey, at Oxford, to the frenzies of religious controversy; that he should have been driven almost out of his wits by the ratiocinations of W. G. Ward; that he should have lost his faith; that he should have spent the rest of his existence lamenting that loss, both in prose and verse; and that he should have eventually succumbed, conscientiously doing up brown paper parcels for Florence Nightingale.

In the earlier years of his headmastership Dr. Arnold had to face a good deal of opposition. His advanced religious views were disliked, and there were many parents to whom his system of school government did not commend itself. But in time this hostility melted away. Succeeding generations of favourite pupils began to spread his fame through the Universities. At Oxford especially men were profoundly impressed by the pious aims of the boys from Rugby. It was a new thing to see undergraduates going to Chapel more often than they were obliged, and visiting the good poor. Their reverent admiration for Dr. Arnold was no less remarkable. Whenever two of his old pupils met they joined in his praises; and the sight of his picture had been known to call forth, from one who had not even reached the Sixth, exclamations of rapture lasting for ten minutes and filling with astonishment the young men from other schools who happened to be present. He became a celebrity; he became at last a great man. (pp. 234-36)

There can be little doubt that what [Dr. Arnold achieved at Rugby] justified the prediction of the Provost of Oriel that he would "change the face of education all through the public schools of England." It is true that, so far as the actual machinery of education was concerned, Dr. Arnold not only failed to effect a change, but deliberately adhered to the old system. The monastic and literary conceptions of education, which had their roots in the Middle Ages, and had been accepted and strengthened at the revival of Learning, he adopted almost without hesitation. Under him, the public school remained, in essentials, a conventual establishment, devoted to the teaching of Greek and Latin grammar. Had he set on foot reforms in these directions, it seems probable that he might have succeeded in carrying the parents of England with him. The moment was ripe; there was a general desire for educational changes; and Dr. Arnold's great reputation could hardly have been resisted. As it was, he threw the whole weight of his influence into the opposite scale, and the ancient system became more firmly established than ever.

The changes which he did effect were of a very different nature. By introducing morals and religion into his scheme of education, he altered the whole atmosphere of Public School life. Henceforward the old rough-and-tumble, which was typified by the régime of Keate at Eton, became impossible. After Dr. Arnold, no publics school could venture to ignore the virtues of respectability. Again, by his introduction of the prefectorial system, Dr. Arnold produced far-reaching effects—effects which he himself, perhaps, would have found perplexing. In his day, when the school hours were over, the boys were free to enjoy themselves as they liked; to bathe, to fish, to ramble for long afternoons in the country, collecting eggs or gathering flowers. "The taste of the boys at this period," writes an old Rugbæan who had been under Arnold, "leaned strongly towards flowers"; the words have an odd look to-day. The modern reader of *Tom Brown's Schooldays* searches in vain for any reference to compulsory games, house colours, or cricket averages. In those days, when boys played games they played them for pleasure; but in those days the prefectorial system—the system which hands over the life of a school to an oligarchy of a dozen youths of seventeen—was still in its infancy, and had not yet borne its fruit. Teachers and prophets have strange after-histories; and that of Dr. Arnold has been no exception. The earnest enthusiast who strove to make his pupils Christian gentlemen and who governed his school according to the principles of the Old Testament has proved to be the founder of the worship of athletics and the worship of good form. Upon those two poles our public schools have turned for so long that we have almost come to believe that such is their essential nature, and that an English public schoolboy who wears the wrong clothes and takes no interest in football is a contradiction in terms. Yet it was not so before Dr. Arnold; will it always be so after him? We shall see. (pp. 240-41)

> *Lytton Strachey, ''Dr. Arnold,'' in his* Eminent Victorians: Cardinal Manning, Florence Nightingale, Dr. Arnold, General Gordon, *G. P. Putnam's Sons, 1918, pp. 205-42.*

BERTRAND RUSSELL (essay date 1926)

[*A respected and prolific writer, Russell was an English philosopher known for his support of humanistic causes. Here, he calls attention to the negative social effects of Arnold's educational system. Russell's remarks are addressed by Mack (see excerpt dated 1938).*]

Dr. Arnold was the great reformer of our public schools, which are viewed as one of the glories of England, and are still conducted largely according to his principles. In discussing Dr. Arnold, therefore, we are dealing, not with something belonging to the remote past. but with something which to this day is efficacious in moulding upper-class Englishmen. Dr. Arnold diminished flogging, retaining it only for the younger boys, and confining it, so his biographer tells us, to ''moral offences, such as lying, drinking, and habitual idleness''. But when a liberal journal suggested that flogging was a degrading punishment, which ought to be abolished altogether, he was amazingly indignant. He replied in print:

> I know well of what feeling this is the expression; it originates in that proud notion of personal independence which is neither reasonable nor Christian, but essentially barbarian. It visited Europe with all the curses of the age of chivalry, and is threatening us now with those of Jacobinism. . . . At an age when it is almost impossible to find a true manly sense of the degradation of guilt or faults, where is the wisdom of encouraging a fantastic sense of the degradation of personal correction? What can be more false, or more adverse to the simplicity, sobriety and humbleness of mind, which are the best ornament of youth, and the best promise of a noble manhood?

The pupils of his disciples, not unnaturally, believe in flogging natives of India when they are deficient in ''humbleness of mind''.

There is another passage, already quoted in part by Mr. Strachey in *Eminent Victorians,* but so apt that I cannot forbear to quote it again. Dr. Arnold was away on a holiday, enjoying the beauties of the Lake of Como. The form his enjoyment took is recorded in a letter to his wife, as follows:

> It is almost awful to look at the overwhelming beauty around me, and then think of moral evil; it seems as if heaven and hell, instead of being separated by a great gulf from one another, were absolutely on each other's confines, and indeed not far from every one of us. Might the sense of moral evil be as strong in me as my delight in external beauty, for in a deep sense of moral evil, more perhaps than in anything else, abides a saving knowledge of God! It is not so much to admire moral good; that we may do, and yet not be ourselves conformed to it; but if we really do abhor that which is evil, not the persons in whom evil resides, but the evil which dwelleth in them, and much more manifestly and certainly to our own knowledge, in our own hearts—this is to have the feeling of God and of Christ, and to have our Spirit in sympathy with the Spirit of God. Alas! how easy to see this and say it—how hard to do it and to feel it! Who is sufficient for these things? No one, but he who feels and really laments his own insufficiency. God bless you, my dearest wife, and our beloved children, now and evermore, through Christ Jesus.

It is pathetic to see this naturally kindly gentleman lashing himself into a mood of sadism, in which he can flog little boys without compunction, and all under the impression that he is conforming to the religion of Love. It is pathetic when we consider the deluded individual; but it is tragic when we think of the generations of cruelty that he put into the world by creating an atmosphere of abhorrence of ''moral evil'', which, it will be remembered, includes habitual idleness in children. I shudder when I think of the wars, the tortures, the oppressions, of which upright men have been guilty, under the impression that they were righteously castigating ''moral evil''. Mercifully, educators no longer regard little children as limbs of Satan. There is still too much of this view in dealings with adults, particularly in the punishment of crime; but in the nursery and the school it has almost disappeared. (pp. 38-40)

Dr. Arnold's system, which has remained in force in English public schools to the present day, had another defect, namely that it was aristocratic. The aim was to train men for positions of authority and power, whether at home or in distant parts of the empire. An aristocracy, if it is to survive, needs certain virtues; these were to be imparted at school. The product was to be energetic, stoical, physically fit, possessed of certain unalterable beliefs, with high standards of rectitude, and convinced that it had an important mission in the world. To a surprising extent, these results were achieved. Intellect was sacrificed to them, because intellect might produce doubt. Sympathy was sacrificed, because it might interfere with governing ''inferior'' races or classes. Kindliness was sacrificed for the sake of toughness; imagination, for the sake of firmness. In an unchanging world, the result might have been a permanent aristocracy, possessing the merits and defects of the Spartans. But aristocracy is out of date, and subject populations will no longer obey even the most wise and virtuous rulers. The rulers are driven into brutality, and brutality further encourages revolt. The complexity of the modern world increasingly requires intelligence, and Dr. Arnold sacrificed intelligence to ''virtue''. The battle of Waterloo may have been won on the playing-fields of Eton, but the British Empire is being lost there. The modern world needs a different type, with more imaginative sympathy, more intellectual suppleness, less belief in bulldog courage and more belief in technical knowledge. The administrator of the future must be the servant of free citizens, not the benevolent ruler of admiring subjects. The aristocratic tradition embedded in British higher education is its bane. Perhaps this tradition can be eliminated gradually; perhaps the older educational institutions will be found incapable of adapting themselves. As to that, I do not venture an opinion. (pp. 53-5)

> *Bertrand Russell, "Postulates of Modern Educational Theory" and "The Aims of Education," in his* Education and the Good Life, *Boni & Liveright, 1926, pp. 15-46, 47-83.*

G. F. BRADBY (essay date 1932)

[Bradby here challenges many of Strachey's negative insinuations concerning Arnold's approach to education (see excerpt dated 1918).]

In *Eminent Victorians* Mr. Lytton Strachey took full advantage of his opportunities for poking grave, ironical fun, and if his gibes are sometimes a little cheap, at their best they are extremely diverting. By treating Dr. Arnold as if he had died yesterday and not in 1842, by detaching him from his surroundings and setting him in the midst of our own social conditions and conventions, Mr. Strachey was able to present him as an incongruous and amusing figure. The admirers of Dr. Arnold have no real quarrel with Mr. Strachey. It is good for all of us to be laughed at; it helps us not to get ourselves out of perspective. It would have been good for Dr. Arnold. Whatever is great in a man survives ridicule, and he does not cease to be great because his greatness is interwoven with foibles. (pp. 51-2)

But, if we really wish to discover why certain people were regarded as eminent in their own age, we must not detach them from their surroundings. However original a man may be, his attitude of mind is inevitably affected by the beliefs and conventions of his day, and not least by the limitations in the accumulated store of knowledge and experience which is available for him. The problems with which he has to deal, though they may be fundamentally the same as our own, do not present themselves in precisely the same form and are not capable of the same solutions. If he is a man of action, eager to build a New Jerusalem, he will be compelled to make compromises with the slower spirits of his age, and however free he may be from the worst prejudices of his day, he is sure to carry with him something of the atmosphere which surrounded his childhood. Dr. Arnold was serious in an age which was accustomed to talk seriously, and which was not afraid of expressing its religious convictions. It expressed them on occasions which we should regard as inappropriate. It was fond of quoting from the Bible; it was more tolerant of cant than of levity. It would not have understood our reluctance to commit ourselves to binding religious dogmas or our habit of understating our deeper emotions and convictions. Dr. Arnold was a deeply religious man, at times perhaps almost morbidly so. Religion coloured the whole of his life, and though his attempts to rationalize his intuitive convictions were not always very happy, he was a dynamic spiritual force of immense power. But there was always a struggle going on in the centre of his soul, a clash of conflicting emotions. His attitude to sin was

that of the great Hebrew prophets; he feared it, he hated it, with a peculiar intensity of feeling. But his favourite reading was St. John. In his dealings with boys the voices of the prophets sometimes drowned the voice of the Apostle. Love, if it is to be fruitful, must needs be stern, but in his hatred of their offences the head master was inclined to forget the immaturity of the offenders and the strength of their temptations.

In the seriousness of his outlook and the language in which he expressed it, Dr. Arnold reflected, on the whole, the attitude of the thinking part of his own generation. He would no doubt have thought us flippant; our grandchildren will perhaps think the same. For the tone and temper of any age are peculiar to itself and pass with it. In order to understand what our grandfathers really meant, we have often to translate their words into a more modern style. Thus when Dr. Arnold wrote:

> Rather than have Physical Science the principal thing in my son's mind, I would gladly have him think that the sun went round the earth and that the stars were mere spangles set in a bright blue firmament. Surely the one thing needful for a Christian and an Englishman to study is Christian, and moral and political philosophy?

What he really meant was that, if he had to choose between Natural Science and the Humanities as the sole basis of education, he would unhesitatingly choose the Humanities. There are still many people who will subscribe to that sentiment. (pp. 52-4)

[Dr. Arnold] certainly succeeded in impressing his pupils with his own belief that life was a serious business—as perhaps it is. But he did not impose his own views on them unduly. His zeal was not that of the fanatic, but of one who is a passionate seeker after truth, and the boys who grew up under his influence grew up with independent minds and judgements. It could never be said of men so different as Dean Stanley, Tom Hughes, Clough, Matthew Arnold, and Conington, that they had been forced into a single mould. And so it came about that, by the second half of the 1830's, a number of quite intelligent people, who did not always see eye to eye with Dr. Arnold on questions of religion or politics, and who would not otherwise have sent their sons to a public school at all, were sending them to Rugby, to grow up under the eye of its head master.

What was the secret of Dr. Arnold's success as a head master, at least in his own day? Acting on what principles did he manage to make of Rugby a place to which people, not otherwise favourably disposed to the public schools, were anxious to send their sons?

It must be admitted frankly that those principles were, in the main, not of the kind that is likely to commend itself to the more advanced school of modern educational thought. But one step forward Dr. Arnold did take on what was admittedly the path of progress. He recognized the necessity of broadening the then very narrow basis of education, and he admitted modern history, mathematics, and French into the school curriculum—in small doses, it is true, and not very effectively. Science he rejected, not because he was uninterested in science, but because he thought that, if it was to be studied profitably, it would take up more time than he was prepared to spare from the classics. It is easy to scoff at the meagreness of Dr. Arnold's achievement on these lines, but critics are apt to forget that new subjects cannot be taught at school without new teachers, and that a head master cannot create new teachers with a stroke of the pen. Even at the present day the curricula of the public schools are to some extent controlled by the Universities, and in the 1830's Oxford and Cambridge were almost sovereign and could 'dispose and bid what shall be right'. With the teaching at his disposal and under the circumstances of the time, it is questionable whether Dr. Arnold could have gone farther than he did. In any case, he lit a candle in England, even though it were a small one, which was destined not to be put out. (pp. 54-6)

The educational system which he built up at Rugby was based upon two ideas. In the first place he held that the ultimate value of knowledge to the learner depends on the kind of character on to which it is grafted, and that the mere acquisition of knowledge is not the purpose of life. In other words, he put character first. In the second place he had grasped the unpalatable truth that a boarding-school is not a place for everybody, and that (the words are his own) the first, second, and third duty of a head master is to get rid of unpromising material. This aphorism must sound so harshly in many ears, that a few words of explanation are necessary.

Life at a boarding-school is of necessity in some of its aspects an unnatural life. Boys are removed from the influences of home and more particularly from those of mother and sisters. As they are inevitably segregated into small communities, the traditions of their house and school, the public opinion and moral standards of their companions, exert a heavy and continuous pressure on them, especially in their earlier years. The dangers inherent in the system were even more pronounced in the 1830's than they are to-day, because boys often came to school at a very early age, and, as there were only two terms in the year, and, with fewer facilities for travelling, parents seldom visited their sons at school, the separation from home was longer and more complete. At its best a boarding-house is as happy and wholesome a place for boys as could well be devised; at its worst it is a nightmare, especially for the younger boys. Whether it is a wholesome or an unwholesome place depends on whether its public opinion is formed by the right kind of boy or by the wrong kind of boy. Dr. Arnold did not make the mistake (a not uncommon one) of supposing that boys are so much raw material which, poured into the school machine, will come out of it automatically stamped with the required pattern. For different boys respond very differently to ideals. There are some whom the healthiest school cannot assimilate, any more than the soundest timber can assimilate dry rot. Their continued presence is a danger both to themselves and to others. This, of course, does not mean that such boys are wholly bad. It only means that at a public school they develop their worst qualities, while they help to make the system unworkable and, too often, a sham. Holding these convictions, Dr. Arnold could not but come to the conclusion that one of his principal duties was to eliminate the wrong boys. (pp. 56-7)

The right boys Dr. Arnold defined as 'Christian gentlemen', a claim which had almost the sting of a paradox at a time when it was hardly expected of schoolboys that they would behave like Christians or like gentlemen, but which now sounds rather pretentious. What, in practice, Dr. Arnold meant by his 'Christian gentlemen' was boys who were capable of responding to Christian ethical ideals, and therefore capable of learning to regard themselves as members of a community in which the personal inclinations of the individual must often be subordinated to the interests of the community as a whole. By whatever name we choose to call it, that spirit, and that only, wherever it prevails, makes of the public schools a national asset. (p. 58)

In making his Sixth Form automatically a ruling body in the School, Dr. Arnold set a precedent which has not generally been followed by other head masters. The Prefect system which selects those 'by choice or place the worthiest' is not Arnold's system. He definitely meant to make of his Sixth Form a governing class, and believed that they would rise to the occasion. It is not the purpose of this essay to discuss which of the two systems is the better. Both have worked well, and both have failed. Everything depends on the judgement of the head master, his power of inspiring others, and his example. If he does not enforce discipline himself, he can hardly expect his boys to do so.

Dr. Arnold was certainly a stern disciplinarian, but his severity has been not a little exaggerated, and much too much is made of his use of the rod. A birching was in the 1830's, and for some time afterwards, the traditional punishment for school offences, many of which would now be treated far more leniently. But it was not felt to be cruel either by the boys or by their parents. Probably Dr. Arnold, like many other head masters, regarded these whippings as one of the more repugnant of the duties imposed on him by his office, and as the boys recognized in him a man of genuine convictions and not a bully, they did not cease to respect him because he could on occasions be severe. A certain fear of his head master is the beginning (though not the end) of wisdom in a schoolboy, if by fear is meant a certainty that the head master is not afraid of boys, that he cannot be humbugged, and that he will not overlook wrongdoing. Boys are seldom averse from discipline, when it is enforced impartially. They like to know exactly how they stand, what will be tolerated, and what not. It saves them from temptations, and makes life far easier and happier for the

A contemporary painting of Arnold as a young man.

smaller boys. What they do dislike is a capricious code of justice which varies with the mood of those who administer it, and which gives preferential treatment to favoured or important individuals. Dr. Arnold was a thoroughly known quantity, and his impartiality was above suspicion. To the new boys he was Black Tom, a figure inspiring awe rather than terror. As they grew and came under his personal influence, the feeling of awe changed to one of profound respect, and often of affection. Perhaps the rising generation will be inclined to wonder whether a man of such a stern exterior and of such unbending principles could have inspired so gentle a feeling as affection in his pupils; but for anybody who in his youth heard old Rugbeians talking of their great head master there is no room for doubt. Dr. Arnold undoubtedly had his limitations, some of them peculiar to his epoch, some inherent in his own character, whose strength lay in the concentration of his purpose rather than in the breadth of his sympathies. But he was capable of winning a devotion which is never given to those who are merely high-principled, and zealous, and stern. (pp. 59-61)

> G. F. Bradby, "Dr. Arnold," in his The Brontës and Other Essays, *Oxford University Press, London, 1932, pp. 51-64.*

EDWARD C. MACK (essay date 1938)

[Mack examines the issue of whether Arnold is responsible for fostering antiliberal conditions in English schools and English society, as claimed by Strachey (1918) and Russell (1926).]

Since Arnold's day there have been many writers who have denied . . . that Arnold was a liberal. Of these the most important has been a group of modern progressives led by Lytton Strachey and Bertrand Russell. For this group, besides accusing Arnold of being a black reactionary, has held him responsible for most of the anti-liberal conditions which they feel exist in our day both within the Public School and in the outside world.

Strachey has insisted that Arnold's emphasis on morality and religion and his deification of the prefect have meant slavery for the young and the creation of a type of older boy who follows orders blindly and is at the same time ruthless in enforcing on others a rigorous and repressive code. He has blamed Arnold for modern anti-intellectualism, athleticism, and the worship of good form. Russell has emphasized chiefly the effect of Arnold's system on the outside world. Arnold, he contended, was responsible for the creation of the modern empire builder, a man who, because he was 'energetic, stoical, physically fit, possessed of certain unalterable beliefs', imbued with 'high standards of rectitude, and convinced that [he] . . . had an important mission in the world', was adapted to exert authority at home and in the empire. His mission was to reform the benighted heathen. 'Not unnaturally,' adds Russell, 'the pupils of his [Arnold's] disciples . . . believe in flogging natives of India when they are deficient in "humbleness of mind".' 'It is tragic when we think of the generations of cruelty that he put into the world by creating an atmosphere of abhorrence of "moral evil".' According to Russell, 'Dr. Arnold sacrificed intelligence to "virtue".' The battle of Waterloo may have been won on the playing-fields of Eton, but the British Empire is being lost there. The modern world needs a different type, with more imaginative sympathy, more intellectual suppleness, less belief in bulldog courage and more belief in technical knowledge.'

Even if we are convinced of the liberal nature of some of Arnold's intentions and of the liberal effect of his teachings at Rugby, Strachey's and Russell's accusations cannot be lightly dismissed, for they raise questions that go beyond such considerations. Was the ultimate outcome of Arnold's teachings in accordance with his liberal aims? If it was not, how much of the responsibility for the failure of his designs must Arnold bear?

Of the answer to the first question there can be little doubt. Arnold's system has not, on the whole, borne liberal fruit in the years since his death. Public Schools have seldom been places of kindness or freedom, places where intellectual originality, individual happiness, and democratic co-operation have been cultivated. Arnold's educational instruments have been retained, but they have been used to further ends very different from any that Arnold desired.

Particularly has this been true of the central feature of his system, prefectorial government. Certain achievements of Arnold with respect to boy self-government have been of momentous and lasting importance. In the first place, Arnold established prefectorial government as the most unassailable part of the idea of a Public School. In the second place, he fixed as its permanent working principle the ideas of loyalty, *esprit de corps,* and self-sacrifice. If the system has functioned successfully, it is because prefects have always worked as a loyal and united body. In the third place, Arnold made enduring the idea that it was the duty of prefects to instil loyalty and self-sacrifice in others. Finally, and most important, he made of the prefect system an instrument of government not only recognized but deliberately used by the masters. Indeed, that it was so recognized is what gave it its increased power. Arnold actually did, with qualifications, break down the barrier between boy and master. Prefects were from Arnold's day on to be as universally recognized instruments of master government as flogging and religious instruction. This meant, on the one hand, that prefects were nominally, at any rate, loyal to and defenders of master ideals. Never again, except in certain respects, have boys and masters run separate governments with separate laws. On the other hand, this has meant that the masters have become part of a Public School. Loyalty and romantic attachment have, ever since Arnold, had as their object an institution belonging to boy and master alike.

But Arnold's prefect system has not always been used to further Arnold's ends; it has seldom protected the weak, encouraged real moral idealism, or instilled liberal principles. In the first place, prefects, enormously strengthened in their positions and considering themselves morally superior to others, have felt entitled vigorously to stamp out individuality and to enforce conformity. When they have left school, it may be added, they have been only too ready to assume their share of the 'white man's burden' in distant lands. In the second place, they have demanded standardization in the name of relatively vulgar ideals. Were such standardization enforced for the sake of promoting Arnold's purposes, one might possibly forgive the suppression of individuality. This has, however, usually not been the case. Prefects have become, once again, the administrators of boy ideals. They have asked boys to conform merely because conformity was considered a virtue, and have held up boy ideals like strength and competitive power as standards for imitation. Thus Arnold's prefect system has indirectly resulted in the worship of mere 'good form', and the deification and imitation of the athlete. As far as the outside world was concerned, it has meant the creation of a large group willing to die to preserve the upper classes in power at home and abroad.

In connexion with this question of Arnold's prefect system and the fruits which it bore, an interesting parallel between educational and politico-economic developments presents itself. That it is more than a parallel I do not venture to say. In a previous chapter I suggested that the condition of boy society before Arnold was analogous to the *laissez-faire* system that prevailed in the outside world. On top were decayed, powerless institutions that, because they embodied legitimate power, thwarted economic advance without checking its evils. Underneath was a seething, chaotic, and yet living society. In Arnold's day Whigs and Tories united to rehabilitate old institutions and make them the instruments for checking the greed and tyranny of the new manufacturing classes through Factory Acts and the like. Of this movement, called by M. Cazamian paternalistic interventionism, Arnold was himself a part. It left *laissez-faire* as the dominant characteristic of society but attempted to control it in the interests of the weak. Though it made some notable advances, it did not really check the advance of a ruthless and powerful monopolistic capitalism. It seems to me that Arnold's work at Rugby may well be called paternalistic interventionism. He left the old system of self-government of the boys intact, but tried to control it from above in the interests of humanity and morality. The ultimate outcome was, despite an improvement in moral tone, chiefly a strengthening of the power of the older boys and a greater crushing of the individuality of the small boy.

For what happened to Arnold's system after his death he cannot be held entirely without responsibility. In the first place, he did create the elements out of which subsequent difficulties developed. He over-emphasized worship of absolute ideals in comparison with independent thought, and obedience, loyalty, and self-sacrifice in comparison with freedom and originality. He was primarily concerned with producing boys who cared for *esprit de corps* rather than individuality. Moreover, he glorified the self-reliant prefect and made him a virtually independent educational instrument. He is responsible for future events in the sense that had he not emphasized these purposes and methods there might have been no deadening conformity, no cruelty, no imperialist leaders. Or, to put it more exactly, had Arnold had other ideas he might have stemmed the tide in those directions.

In the second place, he seems to have been curiously blind to the potentialities for evil that existed in his ideas. He seems not to have realized just how dangerous the delegating of power to boys was, how few were capable of using this power for their own benefit or for that of their fellows. On the one hand, he was oblivious to the harm that he was doing to those who, like Clough and Stanley, absorbed his purposes. On the other hand, he was equally unconscious of how few could be expected to comprehend those purposes in the way that Clough did, or administer them without the constant supervision of an Arnold. He failed, in short, to realize that he was strengthening a system which could yield libertarian and democratic fruit only in exceptional hands.

The same thing may be said with regard to Arnold's political views. Arnold believed that it was the duty of the morally superior English state to be helpful to weaker or less civilized peoples. The sincerity of the purely ethical motives which inspired such a belief is beyond question. Yet one cannot help feeling Arnold was unforgivably blind: one is even justified in feeling that, because of his blindness, he was not an inappropriate leader for the future Public School boy who was to conquer the world in the name of humanity and British capital.

The worst that one can say of Arnold, however, is that he was blind to the implications of his ideas. He was not only not directly responsible for most of what occurred after his death, but would have disliked it as heartily as do Strachey and Russell. Athleticism, the worship of good form, rigid uniformity, and imperialism would have shocked him profoundly. If Arnold preached conformity it was only in essentials, it was never blind, and it was in part obedience to liberal standards. Obedience to 'what is done' was the very opposite of what he wanted. Loyalty to my school, my country, right or wrong, was never even implicit in Arnold's ideals; he preached loyalty and self-sacrifice only for a worthy end. And that end was a moral, not a class end. Whether Arnold could have approved the sacrifice of millions of lives on the altar of capitalist profits would have depended on whether or not he would have been fooled into thinking he was saving the world for democracy. Loyalty to a nation, because it is your nation, or a class because it is your class, was foreign to Arnold's teaching. Even more important, the morality for which he was crusading was at least partly a democratic and humane one. His attitude towards natives, the poor, and small boys in the school may have been one of moral superiority, but it was never one of cruelty. Humanitarianism has been proved to be too weak to stop cruelty in the economic world, but to say this is not to accuse Arnold of fomenting cruelty. He fought for protection and sympathy for the small boy in school as well as for the poor outside. The very essence of Arnold's conception was the control of his prefects in the interests of the happiness of the weak. Finally, Arnold taught individuality and free thought within limits to all who were capable of profiting by his teaching. Arnold did not want unthinking servants of even the finest moral principles.

The ultimate responsibility for the failure of Arnold's system to develop in a liberal direction must rest elsewhere than on Arnold's shoulders. In the first place, a good deal of illiberalism, of conformity, and of prefect tyranny existed before 1830, and was merely not permanently destroyed by Arnold. When less powerful masters than he attempted to use his system, evils which had always been inherent in the Public School system gained the upper hand once more. . . . [The] moral success of Rugby was in good part the result of Arnold's forceful personality. When weaker rulers attempted to use his system, they failed to achieve his ends. They were forced, in order to preserve the friendship with boys which Arnold had won, to accede to boy demands, to allow prefects to administer schools in the name of boy ideals. In the second place, much that occurred was the result of new ideals in society which Arnold could neither have foreseen nor forestalled. Arnold's death in 1842 took place at the dawn of a new era. In the forties and fifties new forces working through other men than Arnold used Arnold's methods for their own ends. (pp. 275-81)

Edward C. Mack, "Three Reformers: Arnold," in his Public Schools and British Opinion, 1780-1860: The Relationship between Contemporary Ideas and the Evolution of an English Institution, *1938. Reprint by Columbia University Press, 1939, pp. 236-81.*

CYRIL KENNARD GLOYN (essay date 1942)

[*Gloyn elucidates and briefly critiques Arnold's ideas concerning social reform in England, focusing on his theory of the Christian state.*]

I: A National Church for Moral Reform

As Arnold looked about him, particularly in the years 1831 and 1832, he saw . . . a widening rift between the upper and lower classes. "One half of society was moving forward," he wrote, "the other half sinking backward, the distance between them in feelings and habits . . . continually becoming greater." He recognized that the two classes were separated in almost every relation of life; shared nothing in common, not even language. This separation of tastes and interests resulted, he believed, in a lack of understanding and sympathy between the two classes. The want of amicable and fraternal contact between the rich and the poor was *the* evil of the time and concerned him most. (p. 87)

Arnold's articles in the [*Englishman's Register*] and the letters he contributed in 1832 to the *Sheffield Courant* indicate clearly his conviction that educational and moral reform was the need of the time. The task as outlined in these articles and letters was fourfold: to instruct the poor as to the causes of their distress, to enlighten the rich as to the needs of the poor, to remove both the hatred felt by the poor toward the rich and the callous indifference of the rich to the poor.

The poor should be educated to see how difficult would be a solution of existing social problems so that they would not succumb to the appeals of those who would "destroy rather than reform" existing institutions. Arnold was certain that ignorance among the poor was the major cause of the "fires, outrages, riots and disturbances" taking place. "So long as the people are allowed to live in ignorance and insensible to the arguments of reason," he said in reference to a riot at one of the Welsh iron works, "so long will the political horizon present signs indicative of the bursting of storms from whose fury neither life nor property can hope to be safe." His analysis of the causes of social distress paralleled Coleridge's. Basic to other causes of the social maladjustments of the times, Arnold, held, was an excess of the commercial spirit which he attributed to the continental wars and the monopoly in foreign trade enjoyed by Great Britain. He considered related causes: the public debt; increase in population; the Poor Laws; the "excess of aristocracy"; the plight of the small farmer driven out of the market by the large farmer, and the small tradesmen unable to compete against the united powers of capital and machinery; the consequent increase in the number of those dependent solely on their labor and the resulting low wages. Some may think, he warned, that they know a short and effectual remedy for these ills—to despoil the rich, to overthrow the peerage and the Church, to divide great properties. Let them beware, was his advice to the working class, of men who advocated such remedies. There was no short-cut to social reform.

Meanwhile, in the same articles, he instructed the upper classes regarding their responsibilities. He called on them to "come forward manfully, . . . to state fairly the amount of their past neglect, and their hearty wish to make up for it. They may then meet the mere agitators boldly face to face and indignantly deny their outrageous and shameless falsehood." He advised the upper classes to demonstrate personal interest in their workmen, warning them that their tendency to think of workers as factory hands or laborers rather than as persons was a powerful factor in creating class antagonism. If the upper class would temper their mercenary spirit and show a greater interest in the welfare of the poor, social chaos, Arnold declared, might still be averted. (pp. 88-9)

In a final letter to the *Courant*, Arnold summarized his convictions.

Take the facts, and place them by the side of each other. On the part of the working classes, there is a mass of imperfect and ill-digested knowledge, on the part of the rich there is a . . . half-informed and half-awakened attention to the poor; newly risen, after a long continuance of great neglect. Surely here are the elements of a most happy state of things, if this imperfect knowledge on the one hand, and partial attention on the other, are by all means brought to assist in improving each other—if the past, instead of being for ever appealed to to inflame angry passions, be forgotten as if by common consent, like an evil dream, from which we are most thankful to have been awakened. But if the poor, instead of looking to be helped on by the rich, think to get on faster by plundering and pulling them down—or if the rich, instead of increasing their efforts a hundred fold, and in a wiser spirit, now stand aloof in fear or in disgust, the consequences will be that both rich and poor will suffer, or rather that all good men will suffer, whether rich or poor; while they who profit by the general ruin will be the dregs of either party, perhaps of both.

This was Arnold's message, delivered not only in 1831 and 1832 but in subsequent years. The choice before the nation was between intellectual and moral reform and revolution. Out of this conviction was born a conception of the national Church which was peculiarly his own.

Arnold believed that a national Church was essential to the well-being of the nation as offering the best means for providing the moral and intellectual enlightenment which he considered the alternative to revolution. This belief he expressed in his ***Principles of Church Reform***, a pamphlet presenting the most comprehensive view yet offered of what should be the basis and function of the national Church. (pp. 90-1)

Arnold saw no great obstacle to the realization of his plan for [a national Church] . . . which would unite men of different opinions, attached to various forms of church government, and of worship. All Christians, he held, are in agreement on certain points: God, Christ, and the Bible. All Christians have, with few exceptions, the same notions of right and wrong. Let them unite, then, on this common ground. With respect to church government, Arnold's plan involved an episcopacy (he believed the Establishment was entitled to this concession from the Dissenters) but an episcopacy not of divine right but as a practical matter only, and divested of all those aspects to which the Dissenters particularly objected. There would be lay councils to assist the bishops, who would be incapable of acting without them, diocesan general assemblies, election of ministers and a check on their appointment by the inhabitants of the parishes, with church officers in every parish, lay as well as episcopal. With regard to worship, all parish churches would be thrown open to various forms of ritual, different services being performed at different times of the day and week within the same church. "Not only," Arnold contended, "do the various tastes and degree of knowledge amongst men require varieties in the form of religious services, but the very same men are not always in the mood for the same things; there are times when we should feel most in unison with the deep solemnity of the Liturgy; there are times also, when we should enjoy a freer and more social service; and for the sake of the greater familiarity, should pardon some insipidity and some extravagance." Such, to Arnold's mind, was the ecclesiastical reform needed "to make the Church truly and effectually the 'Church of England'." (pp. 93-4)

Arnold developed further his concept of the Church in his **"Ends of the Church"**, written during the same period as his Church Reform pamphlet. In this he stressed the moral ends of the Church, defining it as a "great society, for the putting down of moral evil." The Church should "not . . . be thought of as a society or government in the common meaning of the words; but in that other sense in which we speak of civil society . . . to . . . which all men who are not savages belong." Men will, of course, belong to many different churches and these churches will have different laws. But the only thing required by Christian teaching is that Christians form themselves into communities for mutual help in moral duty; the particular form of ecclesiastical organization is of secondary importance. If this idea of the Church seems strange to anyone let him consider, said Arnold, "whether, if he consults the Scriptures, he will not find this notion of Christianity everywhere prominent; whether the most peculiar ordinances of the Christian religion are not grounded upon it and imply it." Arnold recognized that neither in their use of the term "religion" nor in speaking of "the Church" did men generally have any idea of the social character of Christianity; too often religion implied only certain individual relations of man towards God, and the Church was taken as synonymous with "the Clergy" who were purveyors of "religious instruction" to the people, not as "the Society of Christians" cooperating in the "putting down of moral evil." If the latter view were held there would be no separation of the laity from Church responsibilities, nor such separation of things religious and secular as existed. Arnold intimated that the social ineffectiveness of Christianity might be due to this misunderstanding of the true character of the Church.

The existing Church, Arnold held, was failing in this moral undertaking. It was failing for two reasons: "first, because it (had) substituted for its true object another, less extensive and much more liable to be perverted." . . . The different Christian sects, he complained, had been formed for religious instruction and religious instruction had meant instruction in doctrine, the predominant character of which had been conceived as "truth" not, as it should be, "efficacy as a means of moral good." (pp. 94-5)

The second reason given by Arnold for the failure of the existing Church to fulfill its moral purpose was its acceptance of a priesthood. The Church had, he said, "abandoned its social character and become an order rather than a society." Virtually all Arnold's writing on the Church reflect in one way or another his intense feeling with respect to the drawing of distinctions, other than those of administrative convenience, between clergy and laity. The conception of such a priesthood as the Tractarians upheld in their doctrine of Apostolical Succession was anathema to him. It struck at the heart of his idea of the Church as a "society for the putting down of moral evil," an idea with which two things, he thought, were utterly inconsistent: first, the substitution of a system in which a few were active and the great mass passive for a system in which the varied talents of all the communicants would be enlisted; and secondly, the removal of any segments of human life from religious control by a pretended distinction between things spiritual and secular. According to Arnold, a priesthood inevitably produces both of these results. They are evidenced, on the one hand, in those

members of the Church, who fancy that they, not being ministers of Christ, may be permitted to live less strictly and who hold that religious matters are not their business, and, on the other hand, in those clergymen who, exalting an apostolical succession and talking about secular interference with sacred things, thereby artifically separate religious and secular activities and indirectly undermine the authority of civil law. (pp. 95-6)

The conception of the Church as a "society for the putting down of moral evil" indicates Coleridge's influence upon Arnold's thinking. . . . Coleridge thought moral activity would prove valid the insights given men through reason and preached that social unity could be attained only by following the principles of reason. Similarly, Arnold stressed the unifying power of moral endeavor and criticized the sectarians for accenting unity of opinion rather than principles. "Make the (Church) a living and active society, like that of the first Christians," he wrote, "and differences of opinion will either cease or will signify nothing." Like Coleridge, he believed that men could be united only by moral and religious principles. He was, therefore, critical of all attempts to solve the problem of social disunity through intellectual enlightenment alone. This conviction that intellectual and moral enlightenment must go together caused him to agree with both Coleridge and the Tractarians that the Church was the answer to society's need. But . . . he abhorred the Tractarian sacerdotalism and, similar though he was to Coleridge in his view of the ends of the Church, he differed with Coleridge as to what constituted the Church.

II: The Church State: Its Basis and Its Duties

Arnold's concept of the State was as distinctive as his concept of the national Church. . . . For Arnold, the aim of the State, as of the Church, was moral in that the State sought the highest happiness of the people, which should include their moral and intellectual as well as their physical welfare. Furthermore, he did not, like many Broad Churchmen, regard Church and State as two agencies mutually interrelated, each working toward the same ends. For him the State was the Church in its perfect form; the proper development of the Church of Christ was its growth into a Christian State. "I can understand no perfect Church, or perfect State," he wrote James Marshall, "without their blending into one in this ultimate form." (pp. 96-7)

Arnold's lofty notions of the State's functions were an outgrowth of his unwillingness to permit any part of life to escape the reach of moral obligation. Separation of the spiritual and secular realms was, as he expressed it, groundless, "for in one sense all things are secular, for they are done in time and on earth; in another, all things are spiritual, for they affect us morally either for the better or the worse." The division rested, he said, "on principles of heathenism," tending to make Christianity, like the old world religions, "not a sovereign discipline for every part and act of life; but a system for communicating certain abstract truths and for the performance of certain visible rites." It had been promised that the kingdoms of this world were to become the kingdoms of Christ and, to the extent that English society was already Christian, in name if not in spirit, to divorce religion and politics, as both Utilitarians and ritualists were recommending, was to go backward, although the means were in their hands for moving forward to the completion of that promise.

This moral theory of the State would never have been disputed, Arnold thought, had it not been for the two mistaken notions which we have already briefly considered: the confusion of "moral ends" and "religious truth", and the belief in a priesthood apostolically ordained. When "man's highest perfection" is confused with "religious truth", the moral theory of the State is misinterpreted, for this confusion implies that the object of the State is to uphold some particular church and to discountenance those who are not members of it. The consequence of such an interpretation is that, to the extent that religious dissent exists in a nation, an Established Church becomes a dead weight on the shoulders of any government which supports it, for the enemies of the Establishment are driven to become enemies of the State. Little wonder, therefore, that man had been reluctant to acknowledge the sovereignty of the State over man's moral, as they had acknowledged its sovereignty over his civil, life.

The other error which had worked against the acceptance of a moral theory of the State was the confusion of Christian clergy with a priesthood. The supposition "that the Church has certain governors unalterably defined by God Himself, and that these governors possess certain inherent and essential powers which can only be communicable through their medium," inevitably tended to exacerbate Church and State relations since it caused churchmen accepting the supposition to make a sharp distinction between spiritual and secular activities. But Arnold could find in Christian teaching no grounds for the supposition. The concept of a Christian priesthood, he said, was not to be found in the New Testament or in the writings of the early Church Fathers, the specific basis of Tractarian pleading. Nor could it be supported theoretically by Protestants. Furthermore, what was meant, he asked, when it was said that the clergy "derive their authority from their apostolical descent"? When men said that the power of ordaining ministers was thus transmitted, there was a confusion, he thought, in the use of the word power. Bishops could give "neither piety, nor wisdom, nor learning, nor eloquence"—in short, they conferred only a legal qualification for the ministry. So, too, in Arnold's opinion, the particular schemes of organization by which churches should be maintained and governed had been left to the discretion of successive ages. Church organization was changeable "not in its object, which is for ever one and the same, but in its means for affecting that object; changeable in its details, because the same treatment cannot suit various diseases, various climates, various constitutional peculiarities, various external influences." In matters of church government, therefore, no particular form had been instituted; Christians were free to choose that form which they believed most effective.

Believing that a sovereign body must pursue moral ends or be an evil agency and that Christianity neither contained any idea of a priesthood nor demanded a particular order of church government, he thought the way was open for a merging of Church and State. Not only was the way open; it was essential that it be followed. The natural and fit state of the Church because its objects were all-embracing—relating to the improvement of the whole of man's life—was that it should be sovereign. Law and government are, however, Arnold recognized, the sovereign influences in human society, and so long as these take cognizance only of physical ends, its rulers can never be the rulers of the Church. Thus, he argued, "we have two powers alike designed to act upon the whole of our being but acting often in opposition to one another. Of these powers, the one has wisdom, the other external force and influence; and from the division of these things, which ought ever to go together, the wisdom of the Church cannot carry into effect the truths which it sees and loves; whilst the power of government, not being guided by wisdom, influences society for evil rather than for good." The conclusion is obvious: "that

this power and this wisdom should be united . . . that wisdom should be armed with power, power guided by wisdom."

The moral theory of the State, then, "agrees and matches" the true theory of the Church. In a Christian State, State and Church are fused: "the State's sovereign power . . . chooses for itself the true religion as it would choose also the truest system of political science in the lowest sense of the term . . . in other words, it declares itself Christian . . . By so doing, it becomes part of Christ's Holy Catholic Church." This is not an alliance which would imply distinctness; rather, the State is transformed into the Church. "A Christian society," Arnold wrote to the *Hertford Reformer*, "with a general control over human life, with a direct interest in the moral welfare of its members and a sovereign power of affecting this welfare by laws, rewards and punishments, is already a church." The Church, as ordinarily conceived, is also transformed. "The spirit of the Church is transfused into a more perfect body, and its former external organization dies away. The form is that of the State, the spirit is that of the Church; . . . but in that sense in which 'Church' denotes the . . . social organization of Christians in any one particular place, it is no longer a Christian Church, but what is far higher and better, a Christian Kingdom." There is no problem of a divided authority; the governors of the State become the governors of the Church. "When this sovereign power then directs and controls its inferior ministers, the clergy, and legislates for the great objects of the society . . . it is not that the State is governing the Church but that the Church, through the medium of its supreme government, is ruling itself." (pp. 98-101)

Arnold did not ignore the objections raised against his theory of the Christian State: that religion is not within the province of the civil magistrate; that secular coercion, "the temporal sword", may not be employed in the cause of the Gospel; that such a Christian State interferes with the political rights of men by making them dependent on their religious opinions, non-Christians being excluded from membership therein. The first objection had been answered, he stated, in the works of practically all the writers on government down to the eighteenth century, and in later times by Burke and Coleridge. The words "secular" and "temporal" in the second objection were used confusedly, he maintained, by the adversaries of the moral theory of a state, since everything done on earth was secular and temporal and in this sense no society, whether it be called Church or State, could have for its direct objects any but secular and temporal ends. With respect to "secular" coercion it was manifest that no coercion could be applied to a man without affecting his present well-being; excommunication was "secular" coercion as much as imprisonment. It was the third objection—that such a State interfered with political rights—which Arnold took greatest care in answering. In doing so, he defined Christian citizenship, and his Christian beliefs triumphed over his moralism.

The concept of citizenship, Arnold said, raised two questions: what is the true bond of political society and what are the political rights of individuals? We have already encountered his belief that men could be united only on the basis of moral principles. For Christian citizenship, *i.e.*, citizenship in the Christian State, Arnold maintained these must be Christian principles. Thus, to compare him again with Coleridge, where Coleridge considered the idea of the nation the bond which united the members of society, Arnold substituted their Christian interests; where Coleridge would have as legislators only men acting in the light of moral principles, Arnold would have only Christians. "Christianity forms so broad a line morally between those who embrace it and other men, that a man who is not a Christian is most justly excluded from citizenship in a Christian state, not merely on grounds furnished by Revelation, but according to the highest and noblest views of the nature of political society." He pointed out that even the ancient non-Christian world had recognized that the bond of political society must be something other than the possession of property or the payment of taxes. With the ancients citizenship had been racially derived. . . . Arnold could not accept race as the best bond of political society since he thought the mingling of races was essential to cultural progress. In his opinion, the problem of how this progress might be attained without confusion in a commonwealth had been answered by Christianity, which made religion and moral agreement independent of race or national customs, furnishing men "with a sure criterion to distinguish between what is essential . . . and what is indifferent." In the Christian State the profession of Christianity replaced race as the bond of citizenship. It was on this basis that Arnold objected so strenuously to the Jewish Relief Bill. He would give Jews "the honorary citizenship . . . so often given by Romans—*i.e.*, the private rights of citizens . . . but not the public rights." To admit Jews into the legislature would utterly confound the constitution of the Christian State, "for then Parliament cannot be the legislature of the Church, not being an assembly of Christians."

Respecting the second question—the political rights of individuals—Arnold spoke bluntly: "We hear a great deal too much in the present day of political rights of *individuals* . . . Individuals in a political sense are necessarily members; as distinct from the body they are nothing. Against society they have no political rights whatever." On this basis he argued that the State could make political rights dependent on religious agreement. "The State aiming at the highest perfection of its members can require them to conform their conduct to a certain law; and it may exclude from its benefits those who dispute this law's authority." To ask if the government can impose its religion upon the people was similar to asking if the government could impose its own law upon the people. "As states require declarations of allegiance to the sovereign, so they may require declarations of submission to the authority of a particular law." Because England had declared itself a Christian State Arnold held that only one conclusion could be drawn: "If a man believes himself bound to refuse obedience to the law of Christianity, or will not pledge himself to regard it as paramount in authority to any human legislation, he cannot properly be a member of a society which conceives itself bound to regulate all its proceedings by this law." Arnold recognized the threat to liberty of conscience entailed by a state religion. He sought to mitigate this threat by emphasizing that it was desirable to require obedience rather than belief. The obedience required, at least at the beginning, should be only the most general confession of faith. On this basis all Christians in England were entitled to political rights. Dissenters need not be excluded from the legislature, the differences between Christians being "not on such great points of principle or practice as to hinder them from taking the same estimate of the great business of human life." As members of the Christian State, and hence trustees for the nation's benefit of the immense advantages of a national establishment, Dissenters might legislate for a communion to which they themselves did not belong. But the State's prerogative to make political rights depend upon an initial confession of Christianity was not to be questioned; "individuals can plead no rights in opposition to society."

Such was Arnold's Christian State: its purpose, aiding men to attain their highest happiness; its duties, the provision for the whole life of citizens—social, intellectual, political, moral, religious; its method, education, legislation, and religion (in the sense of the insight given men through Christianity); its membership, Christians; its characteristic, sovereignty. Arnold acknowledged that England had not yet become the ideal Christian State. But for the same reason that Coleridge had sought to interpret Church and State "according to the Idea of each" in order that men might be guided thereby, Arnold presented his theory of the Christian State. "Though it never will be wholly realized," he admitted to Whately, "yet if men can be brought to look at it as the true theory, the practical approximations to it may, in the course of time, be indefinitely great."

One practical approximation, Arnold believed, would be the gradual extension of political representation to include the lower classes. Not that Arnold, in advocating an extension of political representation, envisaged a state in which rank would be abolished. Equality was, he thought, "the dream of a madman, or the passion of a fiend;" monarchy and an aristocracy of birth were too precious to lose. His belief in the virtues of caste did not, however, imply that he would regret a further extension of democracy. His ideal was "Democracy without Jacobinism"—a greater equality of physical and cultural advantages and political representation without the overthrow of ancient institutions. This ideal he did not believe immediately realizable in England. History taught that when the political struggle became a contest between parties who had nothing in common—no knowledge of each other's feelings, no sympathy in each other's pursuits—it was inevitably accompanied by atrocious crimes and despotism. This was one reason Arnold so earnestly desired to see the national Church and the aristocracy reformed and preserved. Their destruction, he thought, would make peaceful and rational social transition hopeless; could they be reformed, however, they might aid in the peaceful transition from one state of society to another. (pp. 102-05)

Another practical approximation to the ideal Christian State, Arnold held, would be to recognize the authority of the government to deal with the whole realm of national life. It would not do, he said, to continue to think of government as a necessary evil "of which the smallest possible dose . . . is the most desirable." In contrast to both Coleridge and the Tractarians, who had carefully delimited the functions of government, Arnold nowhere gives a hint of anything the government of his Christian State cannot do. To achieve its end of promoting man's greatest happiness, the Christian State through its government, must necessarily concern itself with all national life—education, the morals of all classes, the condition of the poor, economic questions—in short, "every outward thing having a tendency to affect man's moral character, either for the better or for the worse."

Thus, in Arnold's opinion, the State should provide that moral and intellectual enlightenment which he thought was the major need of the time. It was as much the State's task "to provide for the Christian education of the young, for the Christian instruction of the ignorant and for the constant public dissemination of Christian principles amongst all classes of its people" as it was "to provide for the external security of society, or for the regular administration of justice." (pp. 105-06)

So, too, it was the State's responsibility to deal with economic conditions and problems. Arnold, like the Tractarians, was particularly concerned with the economic condition of the poor. One activity on which he believed the State should concentrate was colonization at home and abroad. Colonization he thought essential, since, arguing from Malthusian premises, Arnold maintained that overpopulation was the basic cause of the suffering of the poor, not the unequal distribution of property nor the enclosure of land, as some reformers believed. (p. 107)

Because there was so little reclaimable waste land left in England—though what there was, he would have the State take over for settlements for the poor—Arnold looked primarily to emigration to improve the welfare of the country. The State should encourage this, informing the poor about countries to which they could go—ignorance, in his opinion, being one of the greatest obstacles to emigration—and supplying aid when they arrived. Only by encouraging emigration could England avoid one of two intolerable evils: the existence on the one hand of a free but impecunious population which would be inconsistent with the idea of a Christian State, or, on the other, a total overthrow of society by the division of property, which would, he believed, "of necessity make the well-being of mankind impossible."

One may justly conclude that Arnold was more adept at describing the existing social evils than diagnosing their causes or prescribing their cure. He admitted that he could do little more "than pull the bell, as it were, and try to give the alarm as to the magnitude of the danger." A critical economic analysis of the ills of industrial England was not to be expected of a man who was primarily a churchman and educator. It was to his credit that, in contrast to many of his associates, he realized that the lower classes had just claims for complaint and that preaching blind obedience or prating about England's "glorious constitution" neither clothed them, fed them, nor promoted their spiritual or cultural welfare. Equally commendable was his insistence on education for the poor, in order that they might secure some of the cultural advantages enjoyed by the upper classes. His theory of a nation in which people shared a community of interest, presented during a period when the extremes of society were drifting further and further apart, was greatly needed. To foresee a time when all men within the nation would stand in relation to one another as citizen to citizen, exercising their elective rights, took courage in a day when the majority of his own class bridled at the mere mention of democracy. But it cannot be maintained that Arnold's theory of the Christian State—even had it been accepted, which was hardly possible—would have resolved the basic conflicts of the period. The sovereignty with which he would endow the governing body was excessive, especially when we remember the composition of that body in the 1830's. Despite the fact that theoretically it was above all classes, the existing government too often revealed that it had other interests than the welfare of every member of the community. Arnold's totalitarianism would have left no channels for individual influences or, except in the limited degree that they were represented in the legislative body itself, for any interplay of social forces. He gave only negative answers as to what could be done if the sovereign power should fail to meet the needs of all. He advised the poorer classes whose needs were not being met, to shun violence, not to form trade unions, to respect property, and to beware of dangerous writers in the penny magazines. In his theory of the Christian State, he exhibited the same weakness as Coleridge. Both men failed to recognize that a solution of the problems of the time required a change in the economic arrangement of society and that a solution could not be expected from moral and intellectual enlightenment alone or from a philsophy of *noblesse oblige*. (pp. 107-09)

Cyril Kennard Gloyn, "Thomas Arnold," in his The Church in the Social Order: A Study of Anglican Social Theory from Coleridge to Maurice, *Pacific University, 1942, pp. 85-109.*

M. J. JACKSON AND J. ROGAN   (essay date 1961)

[*Jackson and Rogan examine Arnold's commitment to social and ecclesiastical reform, hailing him as a "powerful critic of the spirit and events of his own times."*]

The discovery of leading thinkers of the nineteenth century continues, but it is only now reaching Thomas Arnold. He is known, of course, as a famous headmaster who exercised considerable influence over his pupils and set a pattern for the public schools. In so far as he is supposed to have possessed any ideas they are popularly thought to be centered upon the classics and organized sports. Those who take the trouble to read his letters and works will soon perceive that they are in contact with a powerful critic of the spirit and events of his own times, whose basic ideas, even yet, are not without significance for the student of Church and society. Regrettable though it is that he never produced an extended creative work, it is possible to build a coherent picture of his thoughts from his occasional pieces. Though his observations about society were from the side-lines, pulling the bell to give the alarm, as he said, Arnold was headmaster of a leading school, he maintained his contact with Oxford, whose chair of modern history he held at the close of his life, and his correspondence shows him not to have been without influence in public affairs. Melbourne considered him for a bishopric but passed him over, fearing an uproar if he were appointed. Arnold in the 1830s was a controversial figure.

As a public critic of the emergent industrial society Arnold made his first appearance through his own short-lived paper the *Englishman's Register*. He continued his criticism in the *Sheffield Courant*. In later years he returned to the same themes in the *Hertford Reformer*. He was amazed to find the missionary and anti-slavery societies labouring at the corners of the earth when in their own midst lurked "the worst evils of slavery and heathenism". He was particularly sensitive to the affront to human dignity in the factory system and in the new industrial towns. In his view the evil for the manufacturing populations lay in the fact that "it implies the congregation of a vast multitude within a comparatively narrow space and with an object purely commercial. In other words they are regarded as *hands*—not as heads, hearts or souls." (p. 200)

Like many other Englishmen he attributed the distresses of the 1820s and 30s to the Napoleonic Wars, which, he thought, deranged the state of society. He saw that there was a growing indigenous working class society of which he did not entirely approve. They were "without the organisation of regular society" so that "the organisation which they have among themselves is rather mischievous than beneficial—they are formed into clubs and unions—associations which breathe a narrow and selfish spirit at best, but which, under favourable circumstances become mere gangs of conspirators". It was the common fear of a Jacobin revolution on the French model. Industrialism might create a slave society. If it did, an explosion would be engineered by the slaves' leaders. He believed that in Chartism he saw such a rebellion burning under the surface of the kingdom. The Chartists' indifference to old institutions and their carelessness about history were indications both of their menace and their slavish mentality. Arnold stood firmly for the education of the working class and the raising of its standard of living. . . .

While he attributed in part the troubles of the times "to the excess of aristocracy in our whole system", nonetheless he hoped that the aristocracy, whose power was already being checked by the new merchant classes, would join working class organizations to provide an alternative leadership and to help prepare the workers for responsible use of the benefits of parliamentary reform. Unlike some he did not regard parliamentary reform as the one change needful. While he supported it along with other items of reform from emigration to a new deal in local government, he held that the *malaise* of society went deeper. It called into question the meaning of politics—the purpose of society, its goals, and thus its relation with the Church. (p. 201)

[Arnold] opposed "that wretched doctrine of Warburton's that the State had only to look after body and goods". The State had a nobler end—the improvement of mankind. Given this distant goal, politics was the art of achieving approximations to this end, an improvement here and an abuse corrected there. In his political philosophy Arnold built a strong theological and philosophical basis for reform.

In his political philosophy there was an emphasis on the corporate nature of the State. Of course the individual still had its place, but there was too much talk of individual political rights. Such talk encouraged men to look upon themselves as independent of their fellows. The State had greater claims than the individual had. "Individuals, in a political sense, are necessarily members; as distinct from the body, they are nothing." . . . The aims and purposes of the State confined men in certain ways. As in ancient commonwealths religion and morals were the tests of citizenship, he thought, therefore, that the individual should profess the State's religion and thus disapproved of giving Jews full citizenship. The contemporary movement towards a secular, neutralist State, which held the ring was foreign to the Christian moralist, whose studies had also taken him deep into Greek political history and thought.

Christianity was in a special sense the bond of society, for Church and State shared the same moral ends. If the State is really Christian how can it have a different end from that of the Church? The doctrine of the King's Supremacy was "the very cornerstone of all my political belief", Arnold wrote. Popery, High Churchism, Independency, and all advocacy of separation came under his fire. (p. 202)

This identity of Church and State removes any false distinction between sacred and secular. "I cannot understand what is the good of a national Church if it be not to Christianize the Nation, and introduce the principles of Christianity into man's social and civil relations, and expose the wickedness of that spirit which maintains the game laws, and in agriculture and trade seems to think that there is no such sin as covetousness, and that if a man is not dishonest; he has nothing to do but to make all the profit of his capital that he can." . . .

A noble theory; but the Church was failing. An international fellowship had partly broken down into national units, which in turn splintered into dissenting groups. Dissenters prevented a national appeal. No progress could be made till these divisions were remedied. (p. 203)

[Arnold's] idea of a comprehensive national Church brought him into conflict with much orthodox opinion including the new Oxford Movement. Union with the Free Churches is still talked of and continues to be the subject of reports. Arnold's *Principles of Church Reform* was the first recall to unity since the failure of noble designs at the Glorious Revolution, but unlike the previous appeals his was edged with the constant awareness that Christianity was called to minister in a society changing with ever increasing rapidity. As a new world came to birth the division of the Church left Christians more averse to each other than to ungodliness and wickedness. The scorn which greeted his proposal of comprehension revealed the truth of his criticism.

A comprehensive national Church, embracing all denominations, required certain reforms in the existing Established Church, so that the new Church could be an effective instrument of mission in industrial society. Arnold advocated the commutation of tithes, an entire remodelling of the episcopal order, the redivision of dioceses, the creation of new parishes in industrial towns, and proper discipline over the clergy. Tithes he thought irritated more than they achieved financially. The remodelled episcopacy needed to remove the scandals of "High and Dry" prelacy. The redivided dioceses would give the Church efficient government, with a better distribution of income, which would principally benefit new industrial parishes. A better form of discipline would lift the standard of clerical conduct by reducing the scope of sporting parsons.

To many the main offence of the *Principles of Church Reform* lay in its advocacy of union without insistence upon doctrinal agreement: Arnold having concluded that theology as such had not been the major cause of schism but rather social factors. Underneath disputes about liturgy and dogma he saw a large measure of practical and doctrinal agreement. The moral precepts of the Gospel, the doctrine of the Trinity, the uniqueness of the saving works of Christ were common to all. It is true Roman Catholics and Unitarians presented difficulties; but these he thought could be overcome. The national Church of England should allow variety of opinion. It was foolish to think that all men at all times and in all places could or would think alike. The acceptance of a common faith in God and our Saviour should be the sole requirement. (pp. 203-04)

Arnold was an early and powerful critic of the Oxford Movement. His opposition was simple. He thought that the new movement sharpened the distinction between secular and sacred, transformed the Church into a sect and then narrowed it to the priesthood. From this position he went on to attack rites, ceremonies, and doctrines, especially that of Apostolic Succession. His article in the *Edinburgh Review* was a severe counter attack upon the Tractarians for their own assault upon Dr Hampden, though no worse than they had delivered to their opponents. When editing Arnold's works and compiling his biography Stanley did not see fit to reprint this polemic, so far had the tide followed towards concern about the internal life of the Church; and indeed the more personal side of *odium theologicum* is best forgiven and forgotten. It was fair to raise the question, however, whether the contemporary situation in new industrial England, did not make the churchman's concern for Apostolic Succession, the dominical authority of episcopacy and the Catholicity of the Church either superstitious or irrelevant. Behind this question were others about the purpose of the Church and its relation to society, which was Keble's starting point in the Assize Sermon on national apostasy. Arnold was quick to grasp that the new movement was no continuation of the old ineffective "High and Dry" Church but one with assumptions and attitudes which ran counter to his own. In its first years the Oxford Movement showed few signs of that later social concern, which sent devoted priests to work in industrial slums, and Arnold's early death denied him the chance of seeing it.

In recent years there has been much talk about the pattern of the Church's ministry. Part-time priests and a permanent order of deacons have been mooted. Arnold had views on this subject within the context of the Church's mission to society. His call for permanent deacons was based upon the need to minister more effectively in new industrial areas. A diaconate would supply ministry without the burden of great expense while supplying the Church's lack of non-commissioned officers. Such men would bridge the gap between clergy and laity by following their secular callings and by giving their spare time to ministerial work. Such an order would, moreover, enable men to enter the ministry who would not otherwise be able to do so. Men "of inferior rank and fortune, who cannot afford the expense of a university education . . . but who may have gifts which enable them to serve the Church effectually and who may naturally and lawfully wish not to let these gifts lie idle".

Work of this kind, he thought, could bring a closer unity between the churches, as those who became dissenting preachers might well become deacons in the national Church. Many became preachers of that sort he believed, not because they objected to Church doctrine but because they had no means of following what they felt their calling to be, in their own Church. Such part-time ministry would be a step towards a truly national Church. It was a bold proposal for 1840. To-day advocates of part-time ministry blur the rôle of laymen. No such accusation could be brought against Arnold, whose greatest achievement, perhaps, was the forming of conscientious lay Christians, who gave distinguished service to Church and State. (pp. 204-06)

To review some of Thomas Arnold's thinking is to liberate him from Lytton Strachey [see excerpt dated 1918] and the prison of his headmastership, with its echoes of fresh air, organized games, public school Christianity, upright pious English colonists and missionaries "doing good" to natives beyond Calais. He is revealed as an acute social and ecclesiastical critic. Moreover, he gives us a new and more healthy view of the history of the nineteenth-century Church, where the dust of internal controversies has obscured the whole question of the Church's obligation to society. As for his appeals for reform, Stephen Neill has written: "Many of the ideals of Arnold came to be quietly adopted in the Church, though not yet in their fullness or in every detail; Arnold and Stanley would have felt themselves quite at home as members of the joint gathering of Anglicans and Free Churchmen which in 1950 produced the report *Church Relations in England*", but his contribution lay at a deeper level, for if all that Arnold advocated had been put into immediate effect the deeper problems of mission and culture in an industrial society would still remain. His significance lies in his perspective, in his vision as a social critic, and as a missionary theologian. He thought sociologically. He understood the social context within which the Church was placed by the Industrial Revolution and perceived that an effective strategy of mission must be based upon such an understanding, or else it must fail. Arnold understood that there were social pressures upon men which affected their religious attitudes and behaviour; the crude conflict of the factory system; the miserable "East ends" of industrial cities; the impossibility of transplanting religious practice from country to town and the Church's apparent inability to make provision for the multitudes drifting into them. A new expression of Christianity was

called for with new structures, which would be relevant to the new society.

Arnold built his thinking as a missionary theologian upon the tradition of Anglican theology stemming from Hooker that held Church and State as religious and political aspects of the same society. In nineteenth-century England, as to-day, this was far from the case but remained an aspiration and also a criterion for judging the Church's relations with society. The attacks showered upon him from Evangelicals and Tractarians were often in reply to the implied charge that they isolated religion from its social context. The one preached a personal religion and the other a City of God withdrawn from the world in the life of its own purity. A private religion and morality was a scandal to Arnold given the many social evils of the day; it was in fact to condone the conventional morality and ideology of the age, perhaps not of the whole nation but at any rate a section of it. To withdraw into a private religious preserve was to be sectarian and abdicate from Christian responsibility for the good ordering of society. The Hookerian ideal, which Arnold tried to reinterpret in the new industrial society of the nineteenth century, set the Church certain social goals. This implied on the part of the Church a continuing involvement with and critique of the institutions of society. What Arnold did himself in his own theological and social writings and comments, he desired the Church as a whole to do. When large sections of the Church including some of its best minds were apparently failing to commit themselves to this task, they came under his fire. (pp. 206-07)

M. J. Jackson and J. Rogan, "Thomas Arnold," in The Church Quarterly Review, *Vol. CLXII, April-June, 1961, pp. 200-09.*

T. W. BAMFORD   (essay date 1970)

[*Bamford comments on the style and tone of Arnold's compositions and speculates on the impetus behind his compulsive writing habits.*]

Once written, [Arnold] very rarely went over [his] work again and was not really concerned with niceties of style. This apparent fact is obvious to anyone who has studied and compared his letters and printed works, but is somewhat surprising in view of his emphasis upon the use of the correct style in Latin or Greek translation, and his insistence upon finding the exact words to suit the passages under discussion. Apparently he felt no urge to polish the words and arguments in an attempt to seek the final form of the message, and, as they were committed to paper at first thought, so they remained in the final version. One natural consequence is the constancy of his style. Only minor differences show themselves between his letters, his sermons and his other published works. The rapid conversational style which suited him, meant that arguments were frequently interspersed with interesting if irrelevant digressions. With few exceptions, chiefly in the religious field, the printed pages do not present Arnold's ideas in any concentrated form; and we have to gather material for related themes from a variety of sources. This failure to link and connect is undoubtedly related to the lack of revision. Yet it is puzzling; most writers find it quite compulsive. It is difficult to believe that Arnold's standards of appreciation were low or that he was easy to please—more likely he was impatient and his mind had already passed on to more urgent things. Certainly his life was busy, and there was little enough time to tidy up the ends of work already done. He rarely gave titles to his works, and even the evocative heading of the anti-Newman article in the *Edinburgh*

Review [the **"Oxford Malignants"**] was chosen by someone else. (p. 38)

Arnold was not a cautious writer. If he felt strongly, as he often did, then the words matched his mood. When he felt outraged the denunciation is fierce; when he was despondent the spirit is one of despair. His friends often cautioned him on this point, knowing that he could rush and commit himself to paper in the first flush of outrage, expressing views which were ill-considered and conveying a totally false impression. It is not difficult to find such extremes in the **"Oxford Malignants"**, his writings on social reform, and particularly in some of the Sermons, where the feeling is sometimes matched by that passionate delivery from the pulpit which struck some of the more sensitive boys. (p. 39)

Arnold had an immense output—letters, diaries, sermons, histories, articles, religious and classical books. He was always writing, even on holidays. He was interested, if critical, about everything but music, and had the urge to set it all down while it was fresh in the mind. At the same time it is difficult not to believe that he found in writing a compulsive release, with a certain therapeutic value. He passed out through his pen his hopes, fears, feelings, ideas. He seemed to need a positive outlet for expressing these views over and above the printed word. The fact that he had already written about and published his thoughts on a particular point did not satisfy him—he seemed compelled to go on reproducing the same arguments time and time again to different correspondents, even to the use of the same phrases. (pp. 39-40)

> *T. W. Bamford, in an introduction to* Thomas Arnold on Education: A Selection from His Writings *by Thomas Arnold, edited by T. W. Bamford, Cambridge at the University Press, 1970, pp. 1-40.*

A. DWIGHT CULLER (essay date 1982)

[*Culler elucidates Arnold's cyclic theory of history, discussing its origin, influence, and modernity.*]

[In] the 1820s there was imported into England from continental sources, where it had long been used, the phrase "the spirit of the age," and with it the idea that every age had its own distinctive character which differed from that of the proceding age and of the age to follow. The reason for the emergence of this idea at this time was undoubtedly the sense the English had of unprecedentedly rapid social change. The repeal of the Test and Corporation Acts, the bill for Catholic emancipation, the Revolution of 1830 in France, and the passage of the First Reform Bill in England gave all thoughtful men the sense that they were living in the stream of history, coming from some point in the past, through the cataract of the modern age, toward some undetermined point in the future. Hence the efforts made to characterize the present age; in Fichte's *Characteristics of the Present Age*, in Hazlitt's *Spirit of the Age*, in R. H. Horne's *New Spirit of the Age*, and especially in Carlyle's "Characteristics" and "Signs of the Times" and Mill's "Spirit of the Age," all written within two years of one another in 1829-31. Mill's conclusion . . . was that the Victorian Age was "an age of transition," but if so, from what to what? For "the spirit of the times," said Landor, "is only to be made useful by catching it as it rises."

One way of doing this was to look into the mirror of history, and Thomas Arnold, a young liberal historian who in 1828 had just been made Headmaster of Rugby School, was ideally equipped for doing this. He had deep convictions about the relevance of the classics to the lives of his students and was so imbued with the narratives of Herodotus and Thucydides that his students were under the impression he had actually been present at the Siege of Syracuse and the Battle of Marathon. "The images of the past," wrote his pupil Stanley, "were habitually in his mind, and haunted him even in sleep. . . ." It is no wonder, then, that, inspired by the alarming state of the country, he could not avoid making application. "I think daily," he wrote at the time of the Peterloo Massacre, "of Thucydides, and the Corcyrean sedition, and of the story of the French Revolution, and of the Cassandra-like fate of history, whose lessons are read in vain even to the very next generation." Meditating on this, he thought that "a noble work might be written on the Philosophy of Parties and Revolutions, showing what are the essential points of division in all civil contests, and what are but accidents. For the want of this," he declared, "history as a collection of facts is of no use at all to many persons; they mistake essential resemblances, and dwell upon accidental differences, especially when those accidental differences are in themselves matters of great importance."

Unfortunately, Arnold never wrote this work, but he did write a sketch of it in the **"Essay on the Social Progress of States,"** initially published as an appendix to his edition of Thucydides. His basic philosophic scheme was adapted from Vico's *Scienza Nuova*, which Arnold probably read in Michelet's translation of 1827. Vico, as is well known, divided human history into cycles of three periods each, an Age of Gods, an Age of Heroes, and an Age of Men, each with its own characteristic language, mode of literature, and jurisprudence. Arnold evidently regarded much of Vico's system as fantastic, but he imitated its broad outlines, for he too divided history into cycles of three periods each. In his case the periods are based on an analogy with the individual human life and are called Childhood, Manhood, and Old Age (or sometimes Childhood, Youth, and Maturity). As in Vico, these are not phases of world history but of individual nation-states or civilizations. There is some confusion as to just how this would work out, but it appears that Greek and Roman civilization each has its three periods and that modern civilization is then regarded as a single cycle with the Middle Ages as the Childhood of the Christian world, the Renaissance as its young Manhood, and the period from 1688 to 1830 as a transition into the period of Maturity. These periods are conceived in social and political terms. The first is dominated by the Aristocracy, whose attribute is noble birth; the second by the Middle Classes, whose attribute is wealth; and the third by the Common People, whose attribute is numbers. Thus, Arnold finds himself at that crisis-point in history where power is being transferred from the Middle Classes to the Common People, and his concern is that the wealthy shall not cling so stubbornly to their privileges as to provoke violent revolution. The transition between aristocracy and wealth is not normally dangerous, but in the contest between wealth and numbers, says Arnold, "I know not that it has in any instance terminated favorably." In his anxiety about England's situation, therefore, he looks back to parallel moments in the history of Greece and Rome. The parallel moment in Greek history is the time of Thucydides, particularly the Corcyrean revolution; and the parallel moment in Roman history is the time from the Gracchi to the Antonines, particularly the conflict over the Agrarian Laws.

In the Agrarian Laws Arnold saw the solution to England's social problems. For this he was indebted to Barthold Niebuhr, whose great *Römische Geschichte* revolutionized Arnold's ideas about history and opened up for him an entirely new intellectual world. The thing that Arnold was most grateful for and which he regarded as Niebuhr's greatest contribution was his explanation of the true nature and significance of the Agrarian Laws. The matter is too complicated to go into in detail here, but suffice it to say that Arnold saw in the Roman situation an analogy to the monopolization of land in England through the enclosure system, primogeniture, and the entailing of estates. And in the Agrarian Laws he saw the remedy. They were, he said, ''among the fairest means ever devised for obviating the necessity of poor laws, and providing for the wants of a redundant people.'' If England could learn from the Corcyrean revolution in Greece and the Agrarian Laws in Rome, then it might avoid the savagery of the French Revolution in England.

It is a paradox that Arnold was appointed Professor of Modern History at Oxford, for his reputation as a historian was entirely founded on his edition of Thucydides and his ***History of Rome***. Moreover, history at Oxford was divided at that time into only two segments, Ancient and Modern, and therefore Arnold's province included the Middle Ages, about which he knew nothing, and the Renaissance, about which he knew little more. He was not seriously disturbed by this, however, for he had already proposed in his Thucydides ''a more sensible division of history than that which is commonly adopted of ancient and modern. We shall see,'' he says, ''that there is in fact an ancient and a modern period in the history of every people. . . . Thus the largest portion of that history which we commonly call ancient is practically modern, as it describes society in a stage analogous to that in which it now is; while, on the other hand, much of what is called modern history is practically ancient, as it relates to a state of things which has passed away.'' ''The period to which the work of Thucydides refers,'' he adds in the Preface to his edition, ''belongs properly to modern and not to ancient history: and it is this circumstance, over and above the great ability of the historian himself, which makes it so peculiarly deserving of our study. . . . Where Thucydides, in his reflections on the bloody dissensions at Corcyra, notices the decay and extinction of the simplicity of old times, he marks the great transition from ancient history to modern, the transition from an age of feeling to one of reflection, from a period of ignorance and credulity to one of inquiry and scepticism.'' Such a transition also took place in the sixteenth century, says Arnold, but it was less radical and thoroughgoing than that in Greece and much less so than the comparable transition in Rome. Thus, though we would do well to read any distinguished historian of ''the third period of full civilization, that of modern Europe,'' there is really no equivalent in pure modernity to Tacitus and Thucydides.

I do not know whether anyone has traced the idea of modernity to its roots—whether it has been determined, that is, at what point the word ''modern'' ceased to be used in a predominantly unfavorable sense and came to be used favorably. In the Quarrel between the Ancients and the Moderns there were those, of course, who favored the Moderns, but they did not do so specifically because of their modernity. The idea of ''modernity'' as designating not simply a chronological period but an intrinsic character that may be present in any age (so that, for example, it is possible to speak intelligibly of a ''post-modern'' age) is undoubtedly associated with the idea of the ''spirit of the age'' and particularly with the early nineteenth-century view of itself as an age of inquiry and skepticism following after an age of faith. Thus, the conception probably arose on the continent among those responsible for the new historical

outlook of the eighteenth and early nineteenth century. Certainly its chief purveyor in England was Thomas Arnold, and the persons who handed it down from him to our own day were, first, his son Matthew and then Walter Pater.

In his youth Matthew Arnold reacted against his father, but by the time he turned from poetry to prose he regarded himself as the continuator of his father's work. An example of this is in his essay on Marcus Aurelius, where, after complimenting George Long, the translator of the *Meditations,* for treating Aurelius as a ''truly modern striver and thinker,'' he adds, ''Why may not a son of Dr. Arnold say, what might naturally here be said by any other critic, that in this lively and fruitful way of considering the men and affairs of ancient Greece and Rome, Mr. Long resembles Dr. Arnold?'' An even more signal tribute is offered by the series of lectures, ''The Modern Element in Literature,'' which Arnold delivered on first being appointed Professor of Poetry at Oxford. As these lectures came just fifteen years after his father's death, an event which cut tragically short his father's career as Professor of Modern History at Oxford, Arnold could hardly have delivered them without thinking of that former occasion. . . . [The ideas in his **''Inaugural Lecture on the Study of Modern History''**] are almost entirely his father's. By analyzing a passage from Thucydides on the one hand, and from Raleigh's *History of the World* on the other, he demonstrates that it is the former which has the modern, critical attitude, whereas the latter is antique and fantastic. In general, he asserts that fifth-century Greece and the culminating period of Roman history are both significant, modern periods in the world's history, but that the former has an adequate literature interpreting that period whereas the latter does not. (pp. 18-23)

Matthew Arnold has more deeply influenced our current conception of the classics than his father because his very agreeable writings have carried his ideas down to our own day. But in his own time his father was equally influential. Edward Hawkins, indeed, predicted in recommending Arnold for the Headmastership of Rugby School that, if elected, he would ''change the face of education all through the public schools in England.'' Lytton Strachey, of course, has said that he did no such thing, that he continued the same classical curriculum that had obtained since the Renaissance [see excerpt dated 1918]. There are, however, different ways of teaching the classics. Prior to Arnold the emphasis had been on construing, verse-writing, and other elegant accomplishments. Arnold taught the Greek and Latin classics for their substance as guides in the conduct of one's own life and in the training of civil servants. He was not original in this. He arrived at Oxford just as Oxford had finished a similar reformation in its own method of instruction, and as two Fellows of his own college, Edward Copleston and John Davison, had completed a classic defense of the Oxford education against an attack by the *Edinburgh Review* which urged the inutility of all classical studies. Their line of defense, later used by Newman in the *Idea of a University*, was that a liberal education, though not directly useful in that its end is simply the cultivation of the intellect for its own sake, is ultimately useful in that it places the individual in the way of handling, flexibly and intelligently, any situation which may arise. This process is called ''transfer of training,'' and it used to be said by educational psychologists that it does not occur. Doubtless in narrow experimental circumstances it does not, but the whole purpose of the abstract element in mathematics, logic, rhetoric, language, and the other liberal disciplines is that training gained in one situation may be transferred to another, and the Oxford defenders were simply saying that it may be transferred from classic texts to modern situations. Arnold's revolution is simply the application of this Oxford theory to secondary education. He made the theory more specific and plausible by saying, on the basis of a cyclic theory of history, that there is an element of modernity in certain periods of ancient history which makes transfer less difficult. Whereas the eighteenth-century view that history is "philosophy teaching by example" tended to emphasize individual episodes, which might or might not be applicable to current situations, Arnold emphasized the broad analogy between two cultures that were in the same stage of their development. In this way the second culture might see in which direction things were moving and determine which was the party of the future. For Arnold divided all parties into Conservatives and Advancers, those who opposed and those who facilitated the movement of history. What their actual doctrines might be at any particular moment depended on the point they occupied in the cycle of history. The Advancers might be aristocrats or democrats, Catholics or Protestants, but the important thing was to remove prejudices, take off bonds, facilitate progress. All government had its origin in injustice, and hence the progress to perfection was through change. Arnold had no doubt that the final advance was to be found in liberal Christianity, and in this faith that the Christian church could solve the problems that had baffled the classical world he seems peculiarly limited and provincial. His son is more than a generation ahead of him in that respect. Still, in his general approach to the problem he is "a truly modern striver and thinker," and his son, on reading J. T. Coleridge's *Memoir of Keble* many years after his father's death, wrote to his mother: "There is much to interest me, and there must be more to interest you; but my one feeling when I close the book is of papa's immense superiority to all the set, mainly because, owing to his historic sense, he was so wonderfully, for his nation, time, and profession, European, and thus so got himself out of the narrow medium in which, after all, his English friends lived. I said this to Stanley last night, and he quite agreed." (pp. 23-5)

> *A. Dwight Culler, "Thomas Arnold and the Mirror of History," in* Browning Institute Studies, *Vol. 10, 1982, pp. 15-25.*

A. O. J. COCKSHUT (essay date 1982)

[*Cockshut briefly discusses Arnold's religious views, assessing their influence on many of his students and other contemporaries.*]

[Arnold's aim in his *Principles of Church Reform*] was a comprehensive English Church. He was too realistic to believe that his future Church of England could be absolutely comprehensive. He was troubled particularly by the cases of Catholics and Quakers, not only because they seemed more obstinately attached to their traditions than the sects but because he detected in them a more fundamental opposition to his favourite national principle. He does tentatively suggest that one day Catholics may come to feel that they belong more to the Church of England than to the 'Church of central Italy'. But this is not much more than a vague pious wish, which, as perhaps he really knew, fails to come to grips with the real issue. It is nevertheless revealing, because it could not have been written at all by a man who did not see religion very much in practical administrative terms, closely akin to the political.

But his main concern, of course, is with Protestants, especially the older traditional Protestant sects whose creed is more or less orthodox. He lays down as the principle of reunion with them a simple creed, which contains all that he considers absolutely indispensable. There is One God, and Jesus Christ was His Incarnate Son. He redeemed mankind on the Cross and rose from the Dead. Scripture is authoritative, but no particular interpretation of it is so. The two commandments to love God and neighbour sum up all the law.

It is a striking, and, in some ways, surprising programme. Brief and simple as it is, there is nothing tentative or mealy-mouthed about it. It is radically Christian, and with characteristic boldness and honesty, he meets head-on the difficult case of the Unitarians. Clearly they cannot adhere to this programme, and therefore, in principle, they must be excluded. But, partly anticipating the looser religious system of his son, who saw liturgy as far more important than doctrine, he hopes that, if they attend Anglican churches, then the venerable phrases of the Prayer Book may gradually soften and perhaps eventually remove their objections.

Plain, simple, orthodox, and practical though it is, there is one anomaly in the programme, and Arnold was far too intelligent, and far too much of a historian not to see it. It is, indeed, obvious to anyone who gives a few moments' thought to the matter. The authority of scripture cannot rest on nothing. The Acts of the Apostles speak of a time when the New Testament did not exist, but the Church did. Jesus Christ founded a Church; He did not write a book. The selection of the canon, and the whole idea of authoritative Christian writings (to say nothing of the incorporation of the Jewish Scriptures and the interpretation of them as prophecy) was the work of the Church. But Arnold was a practical man. The notion of the Bible as authoritative still had an immense grip on the people of England, and neither Arnold nor anyone else in 1830 could guess how very soon this would fade. The idea of Church authority, on which alone the idea of Biblical inspiration and authority could rationally be based, had much less appeal, and was actively disliked by many. Moreover, it raised questions which Arnold was determined to avoid. You could not consider the question of the authority of the Church without entering into all the difficulties involved in a consideration of England's place in the Christian world. Arnold's was an English programme.

This leads us to the question, on which it was very easy to go astray, 'Was Arnold insular?' In a certain limited sense no doubt he was, for his programme did not seriously consider other countries, or any Christian community except those which he hoped could be merged in the Anglican. But in another sense, he was breaking away from the traditional insularity of English culture and the Anglican church. . . . Intellectually, he owed a lot to German and something to French influences. As a historian he was a disciple of Niebuhr. His exclusive concentration on the English religious scene is really due to something else. He saw England as his diocese, one might almost say his parish. Gifted with superhuman energy, great practical ability, and an extraordinary personal magnetism, he really thought he could alter the religious face of England. Just as a busy civil servant never needs to think during working hours of territories outside the Crown's jurisdiction, but may yet be, when travelling abroad, a cultivated cosmopolitan gentleman, so with Arnold. As a practical man he had no time for speculative problems. This, in part, explains the silliest episode in his career, over which we may pass lightly, his very unfair attack on Newman and the Oxford Movement in the *Edinburgh Review* of 1836. In many ways he misunderstood his opponents, attributing to them, for instance, a pedantic ritualism that was alien to them. But he also saw that Newman was

Rugby school: A view from the close.

asking questions, that he was attempting the herculean task of framing a complete historical theory of the Church into which the Church of England could be fitted; and if the Church of England finally could not be fitted into it, then so much the worse for the Church of England. *Magis amica veritas.* This was, from Arnold's point of view terribly subversive, and, as it appeared in the short term—impatience was one of Arnold's leading characteristics—terribly destructive of future prospects.

So far we have been considering Arnold as a religious thinker; but to confine consideration to that would be to do him a serious injustice. His greatness lies in a disciplined and consecrated force. Characteristically, and possibly with a slightly wry tone, he wrote in a letter of 29 November 1829: 'there is always something to interest me even in the very sight of the weeds and litter, for then I know how much improved the place will be when they are removed.'

The weeds and litter perhaps included by extension the Oxford Movement, toryism, 'feudalism' (as he liked to call the habit of subservience to landed property), and the worldly vices, idleness, and sullenness, of ordinary English schoolboys. (pp. 383-86)

Arnold's educational theory and practice have been fully studied, and in any case education is not my theme. What we have to ask is, what was it in Arnold's religion that made it a powerful influence, despite the humdrum and simplistic character of his theology. We can get a hint, perhaps, from his sermons.

As biblical exegesis, they are in no way remarkable. Their striking quality is one which is very rare in the Protestant tradition, rarer still in the Erastian, to both of which he belonged. He breaks away from the simple idea of obedience to a moral law, following upon a single event of conversion to the acceptance of the merits of Christ. He sees every moment of every life as battleground of spiritual powers. His moral precepts have a real spiritual content, which was almost intoxicating to a generation that had been brought up on dull notions of duty, with duty to King and Country and respect for parents and social superiors, often, in practice, pretending to be the major part of duty to God. Though he is free with phrases like 'Satan's invention of Popery' and 'poison of prayers to Our Lady', he is unwittingly close to the tradition of Jesuit spirituality. Every worldly decision is important because of its spiritual content, because its issue will be a movement towards God's love or away from it. In Arnold's re-creation, life ceases to be a static round of duties to be fitted more or less comfortably into worldly ambitions. Every moment is a turning-point; every trivial act may be crucial. It was characteristic of him, despite his strong anti-Catholic sentiments, to preach on the feast of All Souls. It answered to his deep interest in the state and destiny of every soul. Though he asserts, of course, the impossibility of probing God's judgements, he yet seems to be straining his vision towards the actual condition of individual members of the army of the dead, personally known to himself or to his audience. And he revives the idea of the supreme spiritual importance of the moment of death itself. One can easily imagine that, as with Newman himself, many of his listeners may have wondered with uneasy admiration whether he really knew all their secrets, and was speaking directly and separately to each one of them. And we know that all this had an effect, sometimes a lasting effect both on the intellectual elite, of whom he expected so much in the way of maturity and leadership, and on the ordinary, unimpressionable, apple-eating, birds-nesting English youth.

But it affected them, naturally, in different ways. . . . [John D'Ewes Firth] captured the point very well, when he wrote: 'the whole spirit of an improving and moralizing age spoke through him to his best pupils. . . . Drawing his message from a thousand springs, he first canalized it within himself, and then released a fertilizing flood.'

The *canalization* is the point. Arnold's teaching was overwhelmingly, almost suffocatingly, personal. And this may have been more healthy for the ordinary apple-eating youth, whose nerves were too coarse-grained to be overstrained than for the elite. There is a sense in which the brilliant Clough never quite adjusted, as a mature adult, to the after-effects of the intellectual and spiritual precocity of Rugby days. And Stanley's letter to A. C. Tait, when he was chosen to succeed Arnold as Headmaster of Rugby, may have led the latter to bitter thoughts about the sense of proportion retained by those who were most under the sway of Arnold's memory. [In a footnote, Cockshut quotes from Stanley's letter to Tait: 'I conjure you by your friendship for me, your sense of the sacredness of your office . . . to lay aside every thought for the present except that of repairing your deficiencies. Read Arnold's sermons.'] (pp. 386-88)

> A. O. J. Cockshut, "Arnold, Hook, Ward: A Wiccamical Sidelight on Nineteenth-Century Religion," in *Winchester College: Sixth-Centenary Essays,* edited by Roger Custance, Oxford University Press, Oxford, 1982, pp. 375-402.

ADDITIONAL BIBLIOGRAPHY

Bamford, T. W. *Thomas Arnold.* London: Cresset Press, 1960, 232 p.
    A modern biography. Bamford includes chapters on such topics as the sources of Arnold's ideas, his response to the Oxford movement, and the growth of the Arnold legend.

Bolgar, R. R. "Classical Elements in the Social, Political and Educational Thought of Thomas and Matthew Arnold." In *Classical Influences on Western Thought, A.D. 1650-1870: Proceedings of an International Conference Held at King's College, Cambridge, March 1977,* edited by R. R. Bolgar, pp. 327-38. Cambridge: Cambridge University Press, 1979.
    Links selected aspects of the Arnolds' social, political, and educational views to their study of classical literature.

Campbell, Rev. R. J. *Thomas Arnold.* Great English Churchmen Series. London: Macmillan and Co., 1927, 242 p.
    A biography focused on "Arnold the churchman and patriot."

Cockshut, A. O. J. "Stanley's Arnold." In his *Truth to Life: The Art of Biography in the Nineteenth Century,* pp. 87-104. London: Collins, 1974.
    Critiques prominent aspects of Arnold's character, thought, and reputation in the course of appraising Stanley's *Life* (see excerpt dated 1844).

Fitch, Sir Joshua. *Thomas and Matthew Arnold and Their Influence on English Education.* The Great Educators, edited by Nicholas Murray Butler. New York: Charles Scribner's Sons, 1899, 277 p.

A comprehensive examination of the Arnolds' careers, ideas, and influence as educators.

Forbes, Duncan. *The Liberal Anglican Idea of History.* Cambridge: Cambridge University Press, 1952, 208 p.
    Studies the new historical outlook developed by Arnold and other liberal Anglican thinkers of his period.

[Ford, Richard]. Review of *Tom Brown's School Days,* by Thomas Hughes, and *The Book of Rugby School, Its History, and Its Daily Life. The Quarterly Review* 102, No. 204 (October 1857): 330-54.
    Includes a favorable account of Arnold's educational principles and methods.

Henderson-Howat, G. M. D. "Thomas Arnold and the Teaching of History." *The Quarterly Review* 302, No. 640 (April 1964): 213-21.
    Discusses Arnold's influential role in establishing modern history as a subject of study in English schools and universities.

Jann, Rosemary. "Changing Styles in Victorian Military History." *Clio* 11, No. 2 (Winter 1982): 155-64.
    Cites Arnold and Thomas Carlyle as practitioners of the "literary" style of military historiography favored in the early and middle years of the Victorian era.

Moyer, Charles R. "The Idea of History in Thomas and Matthew Arnold." *Modern Philology* 67, No. 2 (November 1969): 160-67.
    Explores the influence of Arnold's historical views on his son Matthew's poetry.

Newsome, David. "The Ideal: Godliness and Good Learning." In his *Godliness and Good Learning: Four Studies on a Victorian Ideal,* pp. 28-91. London: John Murray, 1961.
    Treats Arnold as a leading exponent of the mid-Victorian ideal of "godliness and good learning."

Nicholls, David. "The Totalitarianism of Thomas Arnold." *The Review of Politics* 29, No. 4 (October 1967): 518-25.
    Underscores the totalitarian aspects of Arnold's views on education and on the relationship between church and state.

Saintsbury, George. "Life till Marriage, and Work till the Publication of the *Poems* of 1853." In his *Matthew Arnold,* pp. 1-46. Modern English Writers. Edinburgh: William Blackwood and Sons, 1899.
    Includes a concise assessment of Thomas Arnold's strengths and weaknesses as a historian, scholar, prose stylist, and religious thinker.

Sanders, Charles Richard. "Dr. Thomas Arnold of Rugby (1795-1842)." In his *Coleridge and the Broad Church Movement: Studies in S. T. Coleridge, Dr. Arnold of Rugby, J. C. Hare, Thomas Carlyle, and F. D. Maurice,* pp. 91-122. Durham, N.C.: Duke University Press, 1942.
    Regards Arnold's teachings as a source of the Broad Church movement in England, comparing many of his views with those of Samuel Taylor Coleridge.

Smith, Julia A. "Thomas Arnold and the Genesis of *Past and Present." The Arnoldian* 3, No. 2 (Winter 1976): 14-16.
    Detects the influence of Arnold's *Introductory Lectures on Modern History* in Carlyle's *Past and Present.*

[Stephen, James Fitzjames]. Review of *Tom Brown's School Days,* by Thomas Hughes. *The Edinburgh Review* CVII, No. CCXVII (January 1858): 172-93.
    Maintains that Arnold's emphasis on moral earnestness had an unwholesome effect on his students.

Storr, Vernon F. "The Rise of Biblical Criticism in England." In his *The Development of English Theology in the Nineteenth Century, 1800-1860,* pp. 177-98. London: Longmans, Green and Co., 1913.
    Discusses the growth of biblical criticism in England, commenting on the pioneering role played by Arnold, Coleridge, and other nineteenth-century thinkers.

"Arnold of Rugby: A Revaluation." *The Times Educational Supplement,* No. 636 (9 July 1927): 317.

Maintains that Arnold's fame is founded not upon what he did but "on the creative personality that was his, and which transformed all that he did."

Trilling, Lionel. "His Father and His England." In his *Matthew Arnold*, pp. 36-76. The Works of Lionel Trilling, Uniform Edition. New York: Harcourt Brace Jovanovich, 1977.
Gives a generally favorable account of Thomas Arnold's headmastership at Rugby.

Waller, John O. "Matthew and Thomas Arnold: Soteriology." *Anglican Theological Review* XLIV, No. 1 (January 1962): 57-70.
Compares the Arnolds' views on spiritual salvation.

Whitridge, Arnold. *Dr Arnold of Rugby*. London: Constable & Co., 1928, 246 p.
A biographical study by Arnold's great-grandson that includes an extensive discussion of Arnold's educational philosophy and practices.

Willey, Basil. "Thomas Arnold." In his *Nineteenth Century Studies: Coleridge to Matthew Arnold*, pp. 51-72. New York: Columbia University Press, 1949.
Examines Arnold's contribution to the development of religious and moral thought in the nineteenth century.

Williamson, Eugene L., Jr. *The Liberalism of Thomas Arnold: A Study of His Religious and Political Writings*. University: University of Alabama Press, 1964, 261 p.
Provides a detailed analysis and historical evaluation of Arnold's religious and political ideas.

Woodward, Frances J. "Thomas Arnold." In her *The Doctor's Disciples, A Study of Four Pupils of Arnold of Rugby: Stanley, Gell, Clough, William Arnold*, pp. 1-19. London: Oxford University Press, 1954.
Discerns a conflicting allegiance in Arnold between the ideals of goodness and truth.

(William) Wilkie Collins

1824-1889

English novelist, short story writer, and dramatist.

The following entry presents criticism of Collins's novel *The Moonstone* (1868). For additional information on Collins's career and *The Moonstone,* see *NCLC,* Vol. 1.

The Moonstone is considered a pioneer work in the genre of detective fiction as well as a significant contribution to Victorian literature. Described by T. S. Eliot as "the first, the longest, and the best of the English detective novels," *The Moonstone* introduced literary devices that, through wide imitation, have become conventional features of the genre, including a clever but eccentric detective, a number of equally plausible suspects, and the disclosure of the solution to the crime before a gathering of those suspects. In addition, several critics have noted that in its delineation of character and narrative complexity, *The Moonstone* achieves a level of intellectual sophistication superior to that of most other Victorian popular novels.

The Moonstone was Collins's eighth novel, written when the phenomenal success of his earlier mystery *The Woman in White* had already brought him immense popularity. He began work on the novel early in 1867 but was forced to set it aside later that year in order to assist Charles Dickens, his longtime friend and collaborator, with the Christmas issue of Dickens's magazine, *All the Year Round.* Collins resumed writing in January of the following year, at which time the initial chapters of *The Moonstone* began appearing as a serial in *All the Year Round.* However, progress was slowed by Collins's distress over his mother's rapidly failing health and, after her death in March of 1868, by the worsening of his chronic gout. Indeed, Collins later reported that, despite large doses of laudanum, he was prevented by excruciating pain even from holding a pen during much of this period, forcing him to dictate large sections of the novel from his bed. Nevertheless, Collins was determined that Dickens's readers should not be disappointed by the discontinuation of the serial, and he persisted until the entire novel was completed late in 1868. Following its serialization, *The Moonstone* was published in book form, its immediate and enormous popularity necessitating three printings in as many years.

The events of *The Moonstone* unfold in a fairly straightforward fashion: a valuable diamond, said to be cursed, is bequeathed to a young English heiress, is subsequently stolen and sought by the eccentric detective, Sergeant Cuff, and is eventually recovered after a number of revelations concerning the various suspects. In the manner of many Victorian detective novels, elements of the plot were drawn from current news stories, most notably the character of Cuff, who was patterned after the Scotland Yard investigator in charge of the grisly "Road Murder" case of 1860. Yet critics note that Collins's handling of such materials was more complex than that of other writers of popular fiction. Composed of a series of monologues by several of the characters, *The Moonstone* reveals the subjective awareness of the various narrators and thus allows Collins to subtly critique their respective preconceptions. In the section told by the fundamentalist spinster Druscilla Clack, for ex-

ample, her distorted perception of events enables Collins to suggest the moral ambiguity inherent in her pious religiosity. Similarly, by creating a wide disparity between the true facts of the case and the conclusions of Gabriel Betteredge, who relies upon strict empiricism in formulating his interpretation, Collins exposed what R. P. Laidlaw has called the "naive realism" of Betteredge's point of view. Moreover, since no one character is aware of all the facts surrounding the case and many express interpretations that are completely incorrect, the novel creates a multifaceted portrait of reality that, in the opinion of William Marshall, "anticipated the greater fragmentation of the sensibility of modern man, as perhaps no other major Victorian novel was to do."

Enormously popular among English readers, *The Moonstone* elicited widely divergent responses from contemporary critics. Many early critics faulted its sensationalism and also insisted that the plot was tawdry, the construction clumsy, and the characters mere puppets. But on the other hand, some reviews of *The Moonstone* praised its suspense and intricately woven narrative structure. For several decades following its publication, appraisals of the novel—whether positive or negative— tended to focus on its importance as detective fiction and so stressed its value (or lack of value) as pure entertainment. In the mid-twentieth century, however, critics began to examine such issues as the social commentary inherent in the ambiguous morality of certain characters and the marked difference between Collins's portrayal of various social classes and that typical of Victorian popular fiction. Subsequent critics frequently discussed the surprising modernity of Collins's understanding of human psychology, with several noting that in his use of dreams and symbols to reveal the unconscious motivations and repressed sexuality of his characters, Collins anticipated the theories of Sigmund Freud. Based on the discovery of such elements underlying the detective-story structure of *The Moonstone*, modern scholars have reevaluated its merits. Currently, while critics often discuss the novel as an outstanding and well-wrought example of classic detective fiction and concentrate upon its influence in the development of that genre, many find greater significance in the way Collins departed from the traditions of popular fiction to create an insightful and subtly critical portrait of Victorian society.

(See also *Dictionary of Literary Biography*, Vol. 18: *Victorian Novelists after 1885*.)

CHARLES DICKENS   (letter date 1867)

[*A nineteenth-century English novelist, short story writer, and dramatist, Dickens is one of the greatest and most popular novelists in world literature. His works display his comic gifts, his deep social concerns, and his extraordinary talent for characterization. Collins showed Dickens several installments of* The Moonstone *prior to its publication in 1868 in his journal* All the Year Round. *In the following excerpt from a letter to W. H. Wills, Dickens offers high praise for the first three numbers of the novel.*]

I have read the first three numbers of Wilkie's story [*The Moonstone*] this morning [June 13, 1867], and have gone minutely through the plot of the rest to the last line. It gives a series of 'narratives,' but it is a very curious story, wild, and yet domestic, with excellent character in it, and great mystery. It is prepared with extraordinary care, and has every chance of being a hit. It is in many respects much better than anything he has done.

> *Charles Dickens, in a letter to W. H. Wills on June 13, 1867, in his* Letters of Charles Dickens to Wilkie Collins: 1851-1870, *edited by Georgina Hogarth and Laurence Hutton, James R. Osgood, McIlvaine & Co., 1892, p. 163.*

WILKIE COLLINS   (essay date 1868)

[*In the following preface to the first edition of* The Moonstone, *Collins states that the object of the work is "to trace the influence of character on circumstances."*]

In some of my former novels, the object proposed has been to trace the influence of circumstances upon character. In the present story I have reversed the process. The attempt made here is to trace the influence of character on circumstances. The conduct pursued, under a sudden emergency, by a young girl, supplies the foundation on which I have built this book.

The same object has been kept in view in the handling of the other characters, which appear in these pages. Their course of thought and action under the circumstances which surround them is shown to be (what it would most probably have been in real life) sometimes right and sometimes wrong. Right or wrong, their conduct, in either event, equally directs the course of those portions of the story in which they are concerned.

In the case of the physiological experiment which occupies a prominent place in the closing scenes of *The Moonstone*, the same principle has guided me once more. Having first ascertained, not only from books, but from living authorities as well, what the result of that experiment would really have been, I have declined to avail myself of the novelist's privilege of supposing something which might have happened, and have so shaped the story as to make it grow out of what actually would have happened—which, I beg to inform my readers, is also what actually does happen, in these pages.

With reference to the story of the Diamond, as here set forth, I have to acknowledge that it is founded, in some important particulars, on the stories of two of the royal diamonds of Europe. The magnificent stone which adorns the top of the Russian Imperial Sceptre was once the eye of an Indian idol. The famous Koh-i-Noor is also supposed to have been one of the sacred gems of India; and, more than this, to have been the subject of a prediction which prophesied certain misfortune to the persons who should divert it from its ancient uses. (pp. ix-x)

> *Wilkie Collins, in a preface to his* The Moonstone, *1868. Reprint by The Press of the Readers Club, 1943, pp. ix-x.*

THE NATION, NEW YORK   (essay date 1868)

[*In this excerpt from an anonymous review of* The Moonstone, *the critic denigrates Collins's art, particularly censuring his lifeless characters.*]

Mr. Wilkie Collins's new book [*The Moonstone*] is very suggestive of a game called "button," which children used to play, and probably play now. A number of little folks being seated in a circle, each with hands placed palm to palm in front of him, one of the party, who holds a button, comes in turn to each of the others, and ostensibly drops it into his closed hands. Of course, but one of the party can receive it, but in each case the same motions are gone through with; and having made his rounds, the principal performer enquires, "Who's got the button?" Each one, including him who has it, but who intentionally misleads the rest, guesses at the puzzle, and he who guesses right carries the button at the next trial. The Moonstone riddle is so like in its essential features to this child's-play, that it might very well have been suggested by it. Mr. Collins's art consists, in this particular case, in converting the button into a yellow diamond, worth thirty thousand pounds; in calling the players Hindoos, detective policemen, reformed thieves, noble ladies, and so on, and in thus more effectually distracting his reader's attention from the puzzle itself, which turns out at last, like most of Mr. Collins's mysteries, to have no vital connection with his characters, considered as human beings, but to be merely an extraneous matter thrown violently into the current of his story. It would perhaps be more correct to say that there is no story at all, and that the characters are mere puppets, grouped with more or less art around the thing the conjurer wishes to conceal until the time comes for displaying it. These books of his are, in their way, curiosities of literature. The word "novel," as applied to them, is an absurd misnomer, however that word is understood. There is nothing new in Mr. Collins's stories, if the reader has ever read a book of puzzles, and they serve none of the recognized purposes of the novel. They reflect neither nature nor human life; the actors whom they introduce are nothing but more or less ingenious pieces of mechanism, and they are all alike—like each other and like nothing else. They teach no moral lessons; they are unsuggestive of thought, and they appeal to no sentiment profounder than the idlest curiosity. They are simply conundrums. It is for this reason that Mr. Collins, wise in his generation, deprecates any attempts on the part of his critics to tell the plot of his stories. One commits, however, no breach of trust in speaking of the theatrical properties which supply, in our author's case, the place of dramatic ability. He cannot create a character, unless the solitary instance of Count Fosco be an exception; he can only dress a lay-figure with more or less of skill. Take his Moonstone, for instance—which, as far as the real business of the plot is concerned, might as well have been a black bean or a horn button—call it a yellow diamond, stolen, centuries ago, from the forehead of an Indian idol, and make its recovery a part of the religion of three mysterious, lithe, swarthy East Indians in flowing white robes, and there is a chance of awakening, in the most hardened of novel-readers, a curiosity which would assuredly have slept over the possible whereabouts of a button.

But it is hardly worth while to go on. One might say of the book, that it is like a pantomime—the characters appear to speak, but really say nothing, and are merely conventional figures, and not characters at all. Mr. Collins ventriloquizes behind each of his puppets, in order to give a sufficient number of misleading sounds. But his art is bad, and he has not art enough—his voice always betrays him, and the reader is never deceived into thinking that it is anybody but Mr. Collins that is talking. We do not know of any books of which it is truer than of Mr. Collins's to make the damaging remark, that nobody reads them twice, and that when the end of the first perusal is reached, everybody thinks his time has been wasted.

A review of "The Moonstone," in The Nation, *New York, Vol. VII, No. 168, September 17, 1868, p. 235.*

THE TIMES, LONDON   (essay date 1868)

[*In the following excerpt from a review of* The Moonstone, *the critic examines the story in relation to Collins's preface (see essay dated 1868). In addition, the critic analyzes the techniques Collins uses to keep the reader in constant suspense.*]

It would be unjust to the memory of Edgar Poe, or perhaps—to look further back still—to Mrs. Radcliffe, to style Mr. Wilkie Collins the founder of the sensational school in novels, but he long ago placed himself at its head. He proved, indeed, at so early a period his skill in the construction of a plot that he has since been his own most formidable rival. His **Basil** displayed a more intense concentration than, perhaps, any of his later tales of tragic interest, of however painful a kind, but about one or two characters only; in **The Woman in White** he evinced that he could preserve the unity and concentration of interest while multiplying his actors and circumstances; and in the present story [**The Moonstone**] he has shown himself a master in the art of amalgamating the most unmalleable and inconsistent of facts—fatalism and Hindoo mysticism and devotion, English squirearchy, detectives, and housemaids—and seems to have taken by choice difficulties for his resources. . . .

Mr. Wilkie Collins explains that the distinction between the present and former tales of his is that the attempt made in this is to "trace the influence of character on circumstances," and to show that the conduct of the several actors directs the course of those portions of the story in which they are concerned. . . .

The character of each of the real actors in the story is the centre of attraction within the orbit of its own circumstances, the actions of each in conformity with such person's character becoming in their turn circumstances on which the characters of the others have to operate. The robbery of the sacred diamond is in conformity with Herncastle's sullen obstinacy and defiance of opinion, combined with his brooding imaginativeness. His sister's somewhat unbending haughtiness predisposed her to find the stigma affecting her daughter's name unbearable. Her daughter's morbid habit of reticence involved her in a maze of doubt and reproach, and postponed a general clearing up of the mystery, to the reader's signal profit, who has thereby gained Miss Clack, but to Rachel's misery, for a whole year. Rosanna's experiences as a thief render her ready to suspect that Franklin Blake is a thief too; her love makes her desire to find him one, that there may not stand between her and him "the dreadful reproach which honest people are in themselves to a woman like her;" and it makes her, in the resolution to save him from the discovery of his imagined crime, take a course which wonderfully complicates the difficulties of the plot. Finally, Franklin's own manysidedness of character, which leads him through various phases of controversy till he politely informs his antagonist, a surgeon, that medical men are all impostors, puts him up as a mark for a little medical experiment of very serious consequences to himself.

So much for Mr. Wilkie Collins's theory. His readers, probably far too soon for their retention of the scientific placidity necessary for the due weighing of the principles laid down in his preface, if they ever read it, will be caught in the vortex of his plot. The essence and secret of sensational novel-writing is to keep flashing a metaphorical bullseye up the particular dark archways where the thief is not lurking; to make the circumstances agree with one given explanation, which is not the true one; and to disguise as long as possible the fact that they agree also with a perfectly different conclusion. It is to present a real clue and a pseudo clue, and tempt the reader on to follow the pseudo clue till past the middle of the third volume. The whole school has this habit of laying eggs and hiding them. But Mr. Wilkie Collins has a complex variety of this propensity for secretiveness. He is not satisfied with one false clue, but is perpetually dropping clues, and, like a bird, by his demonstrative employment of various arts to lead his readers elsewhere, away from the spot where he originally induced them to fancy the nest was, only makes them more eagerly bent on keeping the old path. Every character in the book has his or her theory as to the mystery, and each of the theories is partly true. But then it is also partly, and that manifestly, false. So when, as often, a hint of the truth is let fall by one of them, the reader has by this time grown so suspicious that he refuses to accept it. "No one has stolen the Diamond," says Sergeant Cuff, and Sergeant Cuff is a very king among detectives. But, as Sergeant Cuff says also "Your young lady has got a travelling companion, Mr. Betteredge, and the name of it is the Moonstone," in which he is certainly wrong, the reader disbelieves the true part of his theory. The idea at the foundation of the story is the discovery by a young girl, given to act for herself and not fond of sympathy, that her lover is a thief and has robbed herself;—and the question is what her consequent conduct will be. The author's main object throughout seems to be to conceal this. For this purpose the second volume, direct and positive as are the merits of Miss Clack, is interpolated. Almost everything of materiality to the plot is given in the first and third. If all from Rosanna's suicide, and Rachel's departure from home, at the end of the first, to the discovery made by Franklin on the seashore at the end of the second, were omitted, the plot would remain whole and entire. The creation of a rival heroine to Rachel in the person of Rosanna Spearman has the same object. Rosanna and her whole story do not, in fact, advance the action of the novel one inch. It is not any reflection of her suspicion of Franklin's dishonesty, which lowers him in Rachel's eyes. It does not expose him to the suspicions of Cuff. An old intimacy which she is stated to have had with Luker leads to nothing. Her love does not make Rachel jealous. She might have gone on living without the course of this story being slackened or quickened. Franklin himself discovers what it was she had hidden; and the revelations in her posthumous letter are made to him. He uses them to force on an explanation from Rachel of her strange aversion from him. But that must have come on scarcely later of itself. She is made, perhaps, the most interesting personage in the book; and a larger space is devoted to her character and doings than to those of any one else;—and all solely for the sake of throwing the reader out, and seducing him from a too exclusive concentration of attention on the simple facts of Rachel's change of demeanour to her lover.

Mr. Wilkie Collins never once quits his hold of his readers' interest. When one part of the mystery is solved, the interest in what remains becomes still more eager. The true test of writings like this, and one which *The Moonstone* will stand, is whether at each stage and break of the story a negative answer must be returned to the question whether the final denouement be yet seen. When the diamond is first found to be stolen the reader suspects the Indians. By the time that it is clear that it is not they, it becomes apparent that Rachel knows something, but is hiding it to shelter some one, not herself. It seems equally clear that there is knowledge, and probably, but not so certainly, not directly guilty knowledge, in Rosanna. The reader suspects, with the sergeant, that there is collusion between them, though not, as the sergeant fancies, to shield Rachel. When the absence of this is proved at Rosanna's death, there still lurks a doubt as to Rosanna's freedom from innocent connexion with the theft. A suspicion now also arises, and goes on gaining strength continually, that another person has, at all events, the benefit of the theft, and that either Rachel or Rosanna has known this. When Rachel's indignation at the rumour against that person exonerates her from such knowledge, there is still nothing to clear Rosanna of collusion. When the discovery on the sea shore and her letter show this is not so, but it becomes more and more certain who has the diamond, the double difficulty how it has been taken and how the possessor became such, appears no nearer its solution. When the author shows his whole hand, and while he is revealing the procedure by which it was taken by the one and came into the hands of the other, the interest even yet does not flag, and the reader traces each step to the goal which he sees before him in eager suspense and uncertainty, up to the last page, whether the real catastrophe be not still behind. Mr. Wilkie Collins has built his plot like an iron ship with the several compartments combining perfectly, but isolated and all watertight. It is not till every one has been burst open that the plot sinks, and the reader's interest with it;—although it must be confessed that when it does sink it sinks, after the manner of sensational plots, utterly, and can never be weighed up again. Or to explain our meaning by another comparison, the plot of *The Moonstone* has the quality which was fixed as a condition of the competition for the new law courts. One made free of the building will find all the rooms communicating with each other as soon as he gets inside; but the public, coming out of curiosity, can make their way from one court into another only by going outside and entering it by its own special door.

The book has its shortcomings. There are some petty ambiguities and flaws in the plot. . . . There is, again, a certain pervading high-pressure tone about the characters which is exhausting. The medical men are so very medical; the lawyers are so very legal, and peruse abstracts of title with "breathless excitement;" the politicians are so very political, and are seen "amusing" themselves "at home with the Parliamentary plaything which they call a Private Bill." "Eminent" professional personages outside the action of the book are so extremely pompous and silly, and philanthropists such hypocrites and cheats at bottom. Those who are retained for the narrative are so extremely sagacious, and, if by their special profession trained to be bitter, display for that reason natural tempers so much the more benevolent and kindly. Every character is sure to have his pet theory as to life, and to be exceedingly epigrammatic. There is a superabundance of law; and lastly, and above all, every narrator makes too much a point of giving to his simplest statements the air of depositions taken before a police magistrate.

But some of these faults are very closely allied to the merits of the book. We could not spare one item of Miss Clack's "patience" and "abstinence from judging" others, though all pious ladies are not malignant; Betteredge's frequent stumblings into epigram are none too many; and the legal tediousness and preciseness of the ordinary course of the narrative arises from the same intellectual quality whence come the minute touches (each doing its own work without projecting the smallest shadow in front), which work up the reader's interest at any important crisis to boiling point. To object again, as some ungrateful readers probably may, that there is no desire to turn back to the first volume when the last is read and con over each separate detail fondly, is to complain that the tale belongs to a class in which in proportion to the intensity of interest in the catastrophe is the suddenness of the descent into acquiescence when that is reached; it is to murmur at Mr. Wilkie Collins because his primary aims are not those of Miss Austen or even Mr. Anthony Trollope. There is one positive and intrinsic defect in Mr. Wilkie Collins as a novelist. It is a want of what Mr. Matthew Arnold has called "sweetness" and "charm." But those who admire the spectacle of ingenuity in the construction of a plot, and of the power of bringing home to the imagination the dreariness and terror of dreary and terrible scenes should seek, and will find, it in *The Moonstone*.

A review of "The Moonstone," in The Times, *London, October 3, 1868, p. 4.*

LIPPINCOTT'S MAGAZINE OF LITERATURE, SCIENCE AND EDUCATION (essay date 1868)

[*This anonymous critic praises* The Moonstone *as "a perfect work of art."*]

[*The Moonstone* is the best novel] that Mr. Collins has of late years given to the world, and we are inclined to consider it, with the one exception of *The Woman in White*, the best he has ever written. The story is singularly original; and when we remember the force and extent of Hindoo superstition, we can scarcely venture to pronounce it improbable. And how admirably is the story told! Clear, lucid and forcible in style, never straying into the alluring but pernicious paths of description or dissertation, the narrative moves onward in its unbroken and entrancing course. Let the impatient reader, hurrying to reach the dénouement, skip half a dozen pages. Instantly the thread of the story is broken, the tale becomes incomprehensible, the incidents lose their coherence. *The Moonstone* is a perfect work of art, and to remove any portion of the cunningly constructed fabric destroys the completeness and beauty of the whole. (p. 679)

It would be well if some of the New England writers, who look upon a novel as a mere vehicle for the introduction of morbid and unwholesome metaphysical and psychological studies, or long dissertations on Art—well enough in their way perhaps, but strangely out of place in a story—would study the elements of their art from Wilkie Collins. Then would the words ''American novel'' cease to be synonymous with weariness of spirit and much yawning on the part of the reader; and arguments for amalgamation would be placed before the public in their naked deformity, instead of under the thin disguise of novels possessing little plot and less probability. (p. 680)

> *A review of ''The Moonstone,'' in* Lippincott's Magazine of Literature, Science and Education, *Vol. II, December, 1868, pp. 679-80.*

WILKIE COLLINS   (essay date 1871)

[*In the following preface to the 1871 edition of* The Moonstone, *Collins recounts the personal difficulties he faced while composing the novel.*]

The circumstances under which *The Moonstone* was originally written, have invested the book—in the author's mind—with an interest peculiarly its own.

While this work was still in course of periodical publication in England, and in the United States, and when not more than one third of it was completed, the bitterest affliction of my life and the severest illness from which I have ever suffered, fell on me together. At the time when my mother lay dying in her little cottage in the country, I was struck prostrate, in London: crippled in every limb by the torture of rheumatic gout. Under the weight of this double calamity, I had my duty to the public still to bear in mind. My good readers in England and in America, whom I had never yet disappointed, were expecting their regular weekly instalments of the new story. I held to the story—for my own sake, as well as for theirs. In the intervals of grief, in the occasional remissions of pain, I dictated from my bed that portion of *The Moonstone* which has since proved most successful in amusing the public—the ''Narrative of Miss Clack.'' Of the physical sacrifice which the effort cost me I shall say nothing. I only look back now at the blessed relief which my occupation (forced as it was) brought to my mind. The Art which had been always the pride and the pleasure of my life, became now more than ever ''its own exceeding great reward.'' I doubt if I should have lived to write another book, if the responsibility of the weekly publication of this story had not forced me to rally my sinking energies of body and mind—to dry my useless tears, and to conquer my merciless pains.

The novel completed, I awaited its reception by the public with an eagerness of anxiety, which I have never felt before or since for the fate of any other writings of mine. If *The Moonstone* had failed, my mortification would have been bitter indeed. As it was, the welcome accorded to the story in England, in America, and on the Continent of Europe was instantly and universally favourable. Never have I had better reason than this work has given me to feel gratefully to novel-readers of all nations. Everywhere my characters made friends, and my story roused interest. Everywhere the public favour looked over my faults—and repaid me a hundred-fold for the hard toil which these pages cost me in the dark time of sickness and grief.

I have only to add that the present edition has had the benefit of my careful revision. All that I can do towards making the book worthy of the readers' continued approval has now been done. (pp. xv-xvi)

> *Wilkie Collins, in a preface to his* The Moonstone, *1871. Reprint by Dent, 1944, pp. xv-xvi.*

[MEREDITH WHITE TOWNSEND]   (essay date 1889)

[*Townsend claims that* The Moonstone *is the best work in detective fiction.*]

The position of Mr. Wilkie Collins in literature was a very unusual one. He was an extremely popular writer—deservedly popular, as we think—who was not very highly esteemed. Of all the Englishmen who read novels, few have failed to read some of his best stories; fewer, having begun them, ever laid them down unfinished; and fewest of all ended their reading without some criticism of more or less depreciatory friendliness. That is an odd position, and we do not know that it has been quite satisfactorily explained. That which Mr. Collins pretended to do, he did, when he was doing his best work, admirably; and it is by his best work, and not by his early failures, or the inferior stuff he wrote after he took, as his friend Mr. Yates explains, to opium-eating on the grand scale, opium-eating like Coleridge's or De Quincey's, that he ought to be judged. In four of his books, *The Woman in White, No Name, The Moonstone,* and *Man and Wife,* he showed himself exactly as he was,—that is, as a literary chess-player of the first force, with the power of carrying his plan right through the game and making every move tell. His method was to introduce a certain number of characters, set before them a well-defined object, such as the discovery of a secret, the revindication of a fortune, the tracking of a crime, or the establishment of a doubted marriage, and then bring on other characters to resist and counterplot their efforts. Each side makes moves, almost invariably well-considered and promising moves; the counter-moves are equally good; the interest goes on accumulating till the looker-on—the reader is always placed in that attitude—is rapt out of himself by strained attention; and then there is a sudden and totally unexpected mate. It is chess which is being played; and in the best of all the stories, the one which will live for years, *The Moonstone,* the pretence that it is anything else is openly discarded. There are two games going on at once,—that of the Indians who are seeking their diamond, against the heirs of Major Herncastle; and afterwards that of Frank Blake against his traducers. Both are fought out with a slow skill which enchains the observer, and both end in admirably contrived and most surprising mates. (p. 395)

We doubt if there are stories in English in which the plots are more perfect than in the four we have named, in which the situations are more dramatic, or in which the mystery is more perfectly preserved to the very end. The surprise is usually complete, so complete that it excites a kind of involuntary laughter, and usually, in *The Moonstone* in particular, it is led up to with a high degree of artistic skill. Every detail of the story leads up to the *dénouement,* yet not one in a thousand readers guesses it till it has arrived. When the present writer . . . , a most experienced novel-reader, and a bit of a detective besides, first read the book, he hugged himself warmly over the certainty that the thief was Rachel Verinder's mother, the only unsuspected character, she having stolen the diamond to avert from her daughter the assassination which she saw her brother's legacy had been intended to involve; and even when Rachel bore witness that she *saw* her lover steal the diamond, and the reader was full on the track of the true criminal, Godfrey Ablewhite, he had no conception of the means by which the real offender would ultimately be tracked, and Frank Blake cleared. The story is a very triumph of cleverness, is, in fact, the best detective-story ever written, and there is nothing surprising about its immense success, a success which we believe still continues. The reader has his hunting instinct excited to the full, while he is at the same time amused by the brightness of the narrative, and by an exhibition of humour which, though occasionally farcical, is always genuine and provocative of mirth. Mr. Wilkie Collins's humour was sometimes quite detestable—witness the scenes in the inn in **Man and Wife,** and the scenes with Mrs. Wragge in *No Name*—but in *The Moonstone,* Betteredge is admirably comic, and so, for the little we see of him, is the melancholy, rose-growing Inspector of Police. The reader wants to find that diamond as much as any one of the characters; and to produce that feeling is, we maintain, of its kind a literary triumph. It is not of the highest kind, or perhaps of a high kind at all; but still, it is literary skill quite great in degree. (pp. 395-96)

[*Meredith White Townsend*], *"Wilkie Collins," in* The Spectator, *Vol. 63, No. 3196, September 28, 1889, pp. 395-96.*

T. S. ELIOT   (essay date 1928)

[*Perhaps the most influential poet and critic to write in the English language during the first half of the twentieth century, Eliot is closely identified with many of the qualities denoted by the term Modernism: experimentation, formal complexity, artistic and intellectual eclecticism, and a classicist's view of the artist working at an emotional distance from his or her creation. The following excerpt is taken from Eliot's introduction to* The Moonstone, *which contains his often-quoted statement that the work is "the first, the longest, and the best of the modern English detective novels." For additional commentary by Eliot on* The Moonstone, *see excerpt dated 1927 in NCLC, Vol. 1.*]

The Moonstone contains no characters as memorable as [*The Woman in White*'s] Count Fosco and Marion, but it exhibits all of Collins's qualities in more perfect proportion than any other of his novels. The feeling of fatality is always present, but it is never overworked. It is given by the Prologue, which is accordingly essential to the story. The diamond has always been acquired by lawless means, is brought to England by a disreputable man in a disreputable way and brings misfortune to whoever possesses himself of it. Yet this fatality of the diamond puts no strain on our credulity; we are not expected to accept any occult powers or incredible coincidences. The position of the diamond in *The Moonstone* should be compared with the law case of Jarndyce *versus* Jarndyce in *Bleak House.* Like the Jarndyce suit it blights the lives of whoever come near it.

The tone thus established is intensified by the atmosphere which in this book Collins manages to create about his characters. The dinner party at the country house on the evening before the diamond disappears, with all its apparent irrelevances, arouses a feeling of ominous expectation. The terrible scene on the Shivering Sands is almost worthy of Dickens; it reminds one of the shipwreck of Steerforth in *David Copperfield.* And indeed in such scenes as this Collins must have learned much from Dickens. He learned a great deal also, all that a man of talent could learn from a man of genius, about the making of

character. Most of the characters in *The Moonstone* belong to the comedy of humours: Franklin Blake with his polyglot education, Godfrey Ablewhite and his friends with their philanthropic activities, Betteredge with his beehive chair and his divination by Robinson Crusoe, and Sergeant Cuff with his interminable disputes about the dog-rose.

In *The Moonstone* the characterization assists and is assisted by the method of narration. Collins was always addicted to the method of composing his story out of separate accounts in the first person by various witnesses each relating his part. In some of his books this method becomes tedious and even highly improbable. . . . In his efforts to obtain verisimilitude Collins sometimes over-reached himself; but in *The Moonstone* this method is kept well within bounds. (pp. xi-xii)

The Moonstone is the first, the longest, and the best of the modern English detective novels. We may even say that everything that is good and effective in the modern detective story can be found in *The Moonstone.* Modern detective writers have added the use of fingerprints and such other trifles, but they have not materially improved upon either the personality or the methods of Sergeant Cuff. Sergeant Cuff is the perfect detective. Our modern detectives are most often either efficient but featureless machines, forgotten the moment we lay the book down, or else they have too many features, like Sherlock Holmes. Sherlock Holmes is so heavily weighted with abilities, accomplishments, and peculiarities that he becomes an almost static figure; he is described to us rather than revealed in his actions. Sergeant Cuff is a real and attractive personality, and he is brilliant without being infallible. (p. xii)

T. S. Eliot, in an introduction to The Moonstone, *by Wilkie Collins, Oxford University Press, London, 1928, pp. v-xii.*

DOROTHY L. SAYERS   (essay date 1944)

[*An English writer, Sayers is known as the creator of Lord Peter Wimsey, the sophisticated detective-hero of such acclaimed mystery novels as* Murder Must Advertise, The Nine Taylors, *and* Gaudy Night. *In these works, Sayers attempted to fuse the detective story with the novel of manners. In so doing, she not only lent literary respectability to the genre of detective fiction, but also helped pioneer new directions for writers in that field. In the following excerpt, Sayers praises Collins for establishing the rules of detective fiction with* The Moonstone. *In addition, she notes several aspects of Collins's art that have been underrated by critics, including his ability to create believable characters and to realistically depict Victorian society. For additional commentary by Sayers on* The Moonstone, *see excerpt dated 1928 in NCLC, Vol. 1.*]

"Classical works," says Ezra Jennings in *The Moonstone,* "all (of course) immeasurably superior to anything produced in later times; and all (from my present point of view) possessing the one great merit of enchaining nobody's interest and exciting nobody's brain."

From what we know of Wilkie Collins, the sentiment has every appearance of being his own. It is one of time's ironic revenges that *The Moonstone* should have come to be accepted as a classic of detective fiction.

Our habit with accepted classics is to accept them obediently, and take them as read. If we except those isolated and timeless classics which speak to every age with a voice as new as on the day of their creation, the classic work of art suffers in our eyes by the very virtue that made it a classic. It is a work that achieves perfection in its own kind, and by so doing sums up and contains, not merely everything that preceded, but also everything that follows it. It is not only a "standard" work, the best of its class: it actually makes the class and sets the standard, so that what was the new and brilliant invention of its to-day becomes the commonplace of its to-morrow. One man, as in Tennyson's poem, plants a seed and grows a new flower; and the seed is taken by others and cast far and wide. When the thing has been done once, everybody can do it; and when we have grown familiar with its successors and imitators the original classic no longer appears to us to have anything original about it. Consequently, it is apt to "enchain nobody's interest and excite nobody's brain," because, the formula having become standardized, we forget what an enterprise it was to plant the standard in that particular region.

Thus to-day we accept as a "classical standard" of detective fiction the thing we call the "fair-play rule." We take it for granted that "no vital clue should be concealed," that reader and detective should start from scratch and run neck and neck to the finish. Yet the formulation of the rule belongs to the present century, and the rule itself is seldom kept by, for example, the *Sherlock Holmes* stories, which for so long held the centre of the detective stage. Even to-day, few readers and few reviewers attempt to distinguish accurately between the "detective story," which acknowledges the rule, and the "thriller," which does not.

Now, if you will examine carefully the first ten chapters of *The Moonstone,* you will find that practically every clue necessary to the unravelling of the mystery is as scrupulously set out in them as they would be in a story written yesterday by Freeman Wills Crofts. Judged by the standard of seventy years later, and across a great gap which acknowledged no fair-play standards at all, *The Moonstone* is impeccable. What has happened, in fact, is that *The Moonstone* set the standard, and that it has taken us all this time to recognize it. Having at last got so far, we observe the fair play of Wilkie Collins without reverence or surprise:

> Most can raise the flowers now,
> For all have got the seed.

Collins, however, had for models only the short stories of Edgar Allan Poe, and a couple of novels by Gaboriau, who is not by any means consistently fair in his methods. Nor, I think, was this quality in *The Moonstone* recognized in its own day for the admirable thing it was; the tendency of critics was rather to protest at being expected to remember details and dates, and to concentrate on the mere "thriller" surprises of the story. Collins, in fact, was called a master of "sensation fiction"; whereas his peculiar mastery was in the presentation of those clues for which the modern reader displays so keen an appetite.

Similarly, the actual scientific machinery used to fasten the theft of the moonstone, in the "classical" manner, on the most unlikely person is of a kind very familiar to us to-day; but it was Collins who first thought of it. And in this connection we may notice how many decades he is ahead of his followers in the scrupulous exactness of his medical, legal, and police details. When he wrote this book he was already using opium to relieve the agonies of rheumatic gout from which he suffered all his life; and his "clinical picture" of it is drawn from experience and drawn with care. The "law" of *The Moonstone* has been examined by experts and found correct; indeed, Collins was exact on these points in all his books, and painstakingly sought professional advice on all doubtful points. . . . His po-

lice work, too, is studied from real life. Dickens, whose colleague and close friend he was for many years, took a great interest in the "New Police" at Scotland Yard, and the detective work of Sergeant Cuff in *The Moonstone* is based upon that of the famous Sergeant Whicher in the case known as the "Road Murder" (1860). Whicher was known to Dickens, and doubtless to Collins also; in various articles in *Household Words* his exploits are recorded under the name of "Sergeant Witchem." The modern reader will observe, perhaps with some surprise, that Sergeant Cuff is hired by Lady Verinder to investigate the loss of the diamond, and dismissed by her when the inquiry appears to be taking an awkward direction. This is strictly in accordance with contemporary practice. (pp. v-vii)

Like many later detective novelists, Collins uses both amateur and professional investigators. It is noticeable that he uses them, not to compete with, but to complement each other; there is no "showing up" of incompetent police methods by the brilliant amateurs. The only real antagonism occurs between the stupid local constabulary and the trained Scotland Yard man; and this episode again is founded on the facts of the Road Murder, where the preposterous Inspector Foley played the part allotted by Collins to Superintendent Seegrave. Collins has subdued rather than exaggerated the picture.

Of period interest also is Collins's picture of mid-Victorian society. His handling of life in a household of gentlefolk, both above and below stairs, is convincingly truthful and sympathetic. He displays none of the snobbery of Thackeray, and none of the curious uneasiness with which Dickens is apt to handle the relations between a normal master and servant. The dignified and confidential position of an old and valued family steward is a thing perfectly seen and reported in the narratives of Gabriel Betteredge and Franklin Blake. We also get a glimpse of the (to us) unaccountable fashion which swept the middle decades of the reign for genteel piety and charitable activities. For these Collins has indeed very little use; he is savage in his ridicule both of Godfrey Ablewhite, the "ladies' committeeman," and of Miss Drusilla Clack, with her basketful of tracts and her censorious disposition. Miss Clack, by the way, has a considerable "rarity value." It is very seldom indeed that Collins presents us with a disagreeable spinster; in all his books there is no trace of any spitefulness about "ingrowing virginity" or old maids as such. In the vulgar Victorian manner he frequently made fun of exuberant fertility, but he never, in the vulgar and cruel Victorian manner, made fun of barrenness, or age, or ugliness in women.

In his whole treatment of women he stands leagues apart from his period—infinitely more "modern" than Meredith and (strange as it may seem) in certain ways more penetrating. He was not interested in feminine movements—in fact, he disliked what he knew of them; yet he is the most genuinely feminist of all the nineteenth-century novelists, because he is the only one capable of seeing women without sexual bias and of respecting them as human individuals in their own right, and not as "the ladies, God bless them!"

The women of Collins are strong, resolute, and intellectual; they move actively towards a purpose, which is not always, nor indeed usually, conditioned by their attitude to a husband or a lover. They are not unfeminine; yet they are capable, like men, of desiring knowledge or action for its own sake, rather than for its personal implications. Marion Halcombe in *The Woman in White,* Magdalen Vanstone in *No Name,* Madame Pratolungo in *Poor Miss Finch,* cannot be classed as "female characters''; they are simply characters, for whom other things than passion guide the plot.

Not that Collins could not deal with the passion of love if he wanted to. *The Moonstone,* less rich than some of his books in powerful ''character'' women, contains two of his finest and subtlest studies of women in love. In Rachel Verinder he has done beautifully a supremely difficult thing: he has drawn a young girl, virtuous, lively, a gentlewoman, and capable of passionate affection for a man, without subduing her individuality and without making her either a simpleton or a hoyden. Nor has the unhappy desire of the moth for the star ever been more delicately handled than in the hopeless passion of Rosanna Spearman for Franklin Blake. It is beautiful, pathetic, and not in the least sentimentalized. (How insufferable a thing it might have been in hands less sure we can readily imagine; suppose, for example, that Dickens had thought fit to afflict Jenny Wren with a powerful physical passion for Eugene Wrayburn, or that Thackeray had added to his patronage of Fanny Bolton, by making her not only a young person in a humble station of life, but a hunchback with a past in the penitentiary.) When Rosanna first sees Franklin Blake:

> Her complexion turned of a beautiful red, which I had never seen in it before; she brightened all over with a kind of speechless and breathless surprise. ''Who is it?'' I asked. Rosanna gave me back my own question. ''Oh! who is it?'' she said softly, more to herself than to me.

Not only the fact, but also the sensual quality of this love at first sight is conveyed in three or four lines. And Collins does not make the mistake of leaving the girl on the height of that moment. He is ruthless in depicting the humiliating shifts to which her infatuation drives her, and the spiteful bitterness which it engenders. And the spiritual problem which confronts all attempts to reinstate social sinners has seldom been seen more shrewdly or stated more concisely than in Rosanna's words:

> My life was not a very hard life to bear, while I was a thief. It was only when they had taught me at the reformatory to feel my own degradation, and to try for better things that the days grew long and weary. . . . I felt the dreadful reproach that honest people—even the kindest of honest people—were to me in themselves. A heartbreaking sense of loneliness kept with me, go where I might, and do what I might, and see what persons I might.

Collins, in fact, though he enjoyed a staggering success in his own day as a ''sensation-novelist,'' and has been accorded classical status in the C.I.D. of literature, has always been very much underrated as regards his competence to create living character, and to handle social themes. There are several reasons for this. He was in his lifetime, and has been ever since, put in the shade by a cluster of exceptionally brilliant contemporaries. Then, he is always a writer of mysteries—books ''with a secret,'' to use his own phrase—and we are accustomed to read such books merely with an eye to their detective plot, and not to look to them for a serious commentary on life. This point of view would have surprised and distressed him, as it would also have distressed Dickens, Le Fanu, or Gaboriau. They saw themselves primarily, not as puzzle-makers only, but as novelists, working in the main tradition of the novel. They specialized in telling interesting and exciting stories, but

with no idea of any deep gulf fixed between their kind of novel and the ''novel of manners.'' To this concept, which is much more truly English than the short-story puzzle-formula first used by Poe and expanded by Conan Doyle and his imitators to full novel length, the detective story has only gradually and tardily returned.

The Moonstone is, of all Collins's important books, the most strictly ''plot-founded,'' and the least openly preoccupied with social commentary. For that reason it is technically more rounded and satisfactory, though less powerful and less ambitious, than *No Name, Armadale,* or *Man and Wife,* which are ''theme-founded'' and embody a serious and searching social criticism. These are, in a sense, greater books, but they move less easily within the compass of the writer's technique. They are more affected by time and social change, and they suffer more from the limitations of Collins's mental equipment. Religion and philosophy in their profounder aspects were a closed book to him; nor was he, in any real sense of the words, a man of education. Like Dickens (who suffered from much the same limitations), his outlook is that of the Victorian town-bred middle class—narrow, prosaic, and unspiritual; and although there were certain subjects on which he felt strongly and passionately, he had neither the intellectual weight and training of a George Eliot nor the inner mystical experience of an Emily Brontë that could enable him to relate his fictions to a universal philosophy.

It must also be admitted that Collins's style is on the whole sober and pedestrian. It has not the vivid picturesqueness, the poetry, the soaring imaginative humour of Dickens at his best, or the emotional intensity of Charlotte Brontë, or the civilized wit of Thackeray, or the easy charm of Mrs. Gaskell. It is uneven; and when he strives after a boisterous humour or a high-falutin sentiment alien to his temperament, the results can be disastrous. Yet, when we have said that he cannot equal the giants of his age, the fact remains that it is with the giants that we compare him, and not with the lesser sensation-writers. . . . [His] serious portraits, especially of women and young children, are solidly conceived in the round—they make the women and children of Dickens look like sawdust dolls, and can take rank above Amelia Sedley, and not far below Becky Sharp; his landscapes, like that of the Shivering Sand in *The Moonstone,* or the lake sunset in *Armadale,* frequently have a sombre and restrained power; and when he is not trying to be funny in the dreadful rib-tickling manner of his worst contemporaries, he can produce a tart epigrammatic humour which is excellent and very much his own. . . . (pp. vii-x)

Finally, it is worth noticing that Collins, better than almost any of his contemporaries, evaded the falsification of character and situation which was almost forced on novelists by the early Victorian taboos on sex. Just because he can really suggest sensual passion, his seductions and marriages never come with that suggestion of cold indecency which attends, for example, Edith Dombey's affair with Carker or the repellent wedding of Merry Pecksniff to Jonas Chuzzlewit. He can mention, without fuss or emphasis, that Franklin Blake had been entangled with undesirable women; a feat quite beyond Thackeray, whose treatment of the Fanny Bolton affair in *Pendennis* is made oddly disagreeable as well as unconvincing by its hero's unnatural and priggish chastity. . . . [Collins] is, in fact, sane and sincere at the very point where the novelists of his day were tempted to hysteria and falsification; and this is an achievement of which any Victorian writer might well be proud. Needless to say, he was attacked for his immorality at the time; while to-day we have gone so far in the opposite direction that his boldness looks to us like timidity. The fact remains that he is one of the very few male writers who can write realistically about women without prejudice and about sex without exaggeration.

And he shares, of course, one great quality with the other novelists of his time—the power to invent a spacious world populated with interesting and entertaining people. True, it is a world only relatively spacious—a middle-class and professional world with a sprinkling of artists; it contains no great nobility, no fashionable society, no statesman, no universities, and practically no church; it knows little of the "teeming, squalid, vivid life of the democracy." But within its own compass it is a rich and full world. To turn from a modern detective story and to open *The Moonstone* is to escape from a narrow artificial stage to the crowded reality of the market-place. Collins's people do not exist simply and solely in order to make their moves on the chequer-board of intrigue; they have a full and lasting existence ouside the story through which they pass; they are solid characters living in a real world. Collins, in short, is a writer of genuine creative imagination; and it is this which, quite apart from his "classic" contribution to detective development, gives to his work a perennial interest and a permanent literary value. (pp. x-xi)

> *Dorothy L. Sayers, in an introduction to* The Moonstone *by Wilkie Collins, Dent, 1944, pp. v-xi.*

G. F. McCLEARY   (essay date 1946)

[*Declaring* The Moonstone *a masterpiece unrivalled by twentieth-century detective stories, McCleary points out differences between Sergeant Cuff and several later fictional detectives.*]

"Though we are mighty fine fellows nowadays," wrote Stevenson seventy years ago, "we cannot write like Hazlitt." Similarly, it may be said that though since the beginning of the century we have produced an enormous output of detective stories, many of high quality, there is not one that can rival that old Victorian masterpiece, *The Moonstone*. (p. 137)

Readers of *The Moonstone* will surely agree with Dickens that its characterization is excellent [see excerpt dated 1867]. One of the most admirably drawn figures is Franklin Blake, the young Englishman educated in France, Germany, and Italy, in whom the influence of each country sometimes became disconcertingly apparent, as at the dinner party on the evening before the jewel disappeared. At cheese and salad time, he fell into argument with the county member of Parliament, who, becoming heated about the spread of democracy in England, burst out with the question: "If we lose our ancient safeguards, Mr. Blake, I beg to ask you, what have we left?" To which Franklin replied from the Italian point of view: "We have got three things left, Sir—Love, Music, and Salad."

Sergeant Cuff, the detective in *The Moonstone*, is probably the most life-like and convincing sleuth in the whole of mystery fiction. In several noteworthy respects he differs from more recently created popular detectives. Unlike Sherlock Holmes and Lord Peter Wimsey, he was not a votary of detectivism; he detected not because he liked it but because he earned his living by it. When he could afford to retire he did retire, and devoted himself to rose-growing. That was his sole non-professional interest. How different from the great Sherlock, whose interests and proficiencies ranged over a vast field; who was an expert chemist, a wide reader—did he not quote from Flaubert, Goethe, Hafiz, and Petrarch?—an assiduous student of

Black Letter texts, a violinist, and a writer of authority on the polyphonic motets of Lassus. Lord Peter Wimsey is also a man of many varied interests. . . . With his piano he habitually communes with the mighty spirit of Bach, and he has a European reputation as a connoisseur of wine and brandy.

Sergeant Cuff had no such varied attainments. Nor had he the scientific equipment of Dr. Thorndyke, who was a master of microscopic technique. Cuff achieved eminence in his profession by reason of his keen observation, the extraordinary rapidity of his mental processes, his power of drawing inferences from facts, and his many-sided experience of the seamy sides of life. He did not solve the mystery of the moonstone's disappearance, but that is no reflection on his professional competence. On the data available no one could have solved the mystery. No one did solve the mystery. It was revealed by a series of events that followed one another naturally in a certain order. A clue to each event is given; Wilkie Collins plays fair with his readers. The difficulty is in combining the clues and attaching due importance to each. Cuff's failure to solve the mystery is almost unparalleled in detective fiction. Though the novelists' imaginary police officers who first appear upon the scene are often described as unable to solve the problem, the star detective, the hero of the story, is almost invariably successful.

There is another important difference between Sergeant Cuff and the detectives of modern fiction; he appears in one book only. If he had been created by a post-Victorian writer he would probably have been brought into one book after another. In *The Moonstone* he makes his last as well as his first appearance, and the chapters in which he appears form little more than one-fourth of the book. (pp. 138-39)

[Collins] was a man of mark in Victorian England. Nobody, of course, would place him with the towering figures of Dickens, Thackeray, George Eliot, and Charlotte Brontë; he could hardly be ranked with Meredith, Hardy, Trollope, or Stevenson. But apart from these immortals he holds his own among Victorian novelists. *The Woman in White* and *The Moonstone* are still living things, read by ordinary men and women for enjoyment, not merely "classics" for students of what is called by irreverent young people "Eng. Lit." He had his limitations. He was not much endowed with humour; it must be confessed that Gabriel Betteredge with his *Robinson Crusoe* becomes rather wearisome. Nor had he any charm of style. He lacked the golden pen of Stevenson. . . . But as a teller of tales he takes a commanding position. In the rare power of gripping the reader's interest from the first and holding it to the end he has few equals. *The Moonstone* was read for the first time by the writer of these lines in 1883, when he was studying music in Brussels. Out of curiosity, he took it up one fine summer morning as an after-breakfast preliminary to a hard day's work—"and nothing else saw all day long." Not even Beethoven could release the grip of the enchanter, which closes like a vice in the opening sentences:

> I address these lines—written in India—to my relatives in England.
>
> My object is to explain the motive which has induced me to refuse the right hand of friendship to my cousin, John Herncastle.

The present writer has read that beginning, and everything that follows, many times; always with the same thrill, and never without a deep sense of thankfulness to the brain that conceived and the hand that wrote *The Moonstone*. (p. 141)

Franklin and Rachel painting the door of her sitting room. From The Moonstone, *by Wilkie Collins. The Heritage Press, 1959. Copyright © 1959 by The George Macy Companies.*

G. F. McCleary, "A Victorian Classic," *in* The Fortnightly Review, *n.s. Vol. CLX, No. 956, August, 1946, pp. 137-41.*

A. A. MILNE (essay date 1951)

[*Although today known almost exclusively for his Christopher Robin books for children, Milne was also a poet, essayist, and dramatist, as well as the author of the classic* Red House Mystery. *In the following excerpt, Milne challenges the assessments of* The Moonstone *offered by Eliot (see excerpt dated 1928) and Sayers (see excerpt above dated 1944 and excerpt dated 1928 in* NCLC, *Vol. 1).*]

Mr. Howard Haycraft, in his great historical work *Murder for Pleasure* [see Additional Bibliography], attributed to Mr. T. S. Eliot the opinion that *The Moonstone* was "the first, the longest and the best of detective novels." A pronouncement so uncompromising seemed hardly in character. The authorised (or, possibly, revised) version, given . . . in an introductory note [to a 1951 edition of *The Moonstone*], calls it the first, longest and best of "modern English" detective novels. Reckoning modernity as starting on publication day in 1868 (and it must start somewhere), one would be reasonably safe in saying that *The Moonstone* was the first of them; whether it is in fact the longest is a matter of no great interest. But to call it the best, or, as Miss Dorothy Sayers, Emeritus Professor of the art, puts it, "probably the very finest detective story ever written," is

to make a claim for it which is more disputable. I can never quite believe in these solitary heights of pre-eminence. There is no best-dressed woman in Europe, not even the annual American elected by American votes; there is no worst-dressed politician in the House of Commons, as pilloried annually by *The Tailor and Cutter*, not even—well, look at the others. It may be tough at the top, but it is reasonably roomy.

The modern English detective novel—and by modern I mean something a little later than 1868—falls inevitably into one of two classes. Chesterton once said, and I think truly, that the right and natural medium for a tale of crime and detection was the short story. His feeling seems to have been that, if a detective wanted 80,000 words in which to solve a problem he wasn't a very good detective, and that in any case he couldn't be detecting all the time. A detective novel, then, tends to become either a Short Story Expanded or a Short Story Delayed. *The Moonstone* is an outstanding example of the first sort. As a detective story it could be told completely in 10,000 words. As a romance, with a mysterious jewel and a mysterious theft in it, and if nobody is in any hurry, it can be told in as many words as you like. Wilkie Collins limited himself for some reason to 200,000. I won't say that he couldn't have spared one of them, but the total is extremely readable, being as difficult to put down as it is heavy to pick up. Miss Sayers speaks of the marvellous variety and soundness of the characterisation; and though, in the fashion of the day, the characters border on caricatures, there is certainly the variety which such a long acquaintance needs. There are those, including Mr. Eliot, who think particularly highly of Sergeant Cuff "of the Detective Police." I am not of his admirers. He failed to detect anything, though the identity of the ostensible thief was written as clearly in every action of the heroine as in the behaviour of the supposed accomplice. He merely added a second mystery to the first: the mystery of himself. Who and what was Cuff? Of nation-wide fame as a detective, yet still only a sergeant; only a sergeant, yet on terms of professional equality with the local Superintendent; sent down to the scene of the crime by the Chief Commissioner, yet accepting a cheque from the lady of the house for his services; he is the real, unsolved problem of the book. . . .

Miss Sayers has said that by comparison with the wide scope of *The Moonstone* and its dovetailed completeness, . . . modern mystery fiction looks thin and mechanical. True. But by comparison with the wide scope of *War and Peace* or *The Origin of Species*, a modern crossword looks thin and mechanical, and no clue dovetails into the next. Yet the crossword addict makes no complaint of this. With equal reason the detective-story addict is happy to have the bare bones of the mystery laid before him, so that he can try to articulate them. If he fails to do so before the last chapter, then he can listen, mouth open, to the detectives' clearer articulation, kicking himself gently the while; the crossword solver kicks himself next morning for missing an obvious clue. A character in one of Anthony Hope's books was of opinion that though port tasted better without the conflicting aroma of tobacco, and though a cigar tasted better without the conflicting savour of port, yet port and a cigar together made a better effect on the palate than either separately. If you are of opinion that romance and detection together make a more pleasing effect on the mind than either separately, even though each a little spoils the other, then *The Moonstone* will give you all you want. But for myself I prefer my detection fuller-bodied and neater. And perhaps I should add that in saying this I am not referring to the Whisky Straight school of America; in which the interest is transferred to the number of drinks, blondes and beatings-up the ''private eye'' can absorb in a day's induction.

A. A. Milne, in a review of ''The Moonstone,'' in
The Spectator, *Vol. 186, No. 6406, April 6, 1951,*
p. 452.

KENNETH ROBINSON (essay date 1951)

[*Robinson discusses the sources of* The Moonstone *and analyzes Collins's narrative technique and method of characterization.*]

The Moonstone is from many points of view Wilkie Collins' most remarkable performance. In this, above all his books, he achieved precisely what he set out to do, and more—for it is unlikely that he intended to produce the archetype of a new branch of English fiction. To the modern reader *The Moonstone* has the special interest of being the first, and indeed the classic, example of the English detective-novel. In support of such a claim no more expert witness need be called than Dorothy L. Sayers, who wrote in her introduction to the Everyman edition: 'Judged by the standard of seventy years later, and across a great gap which acknowledged no fair-play standards at all, *The Moonstone* is impeccable. What has happened, in fact, is that *The Moonstone* set the standard, and that it has taken us all this time to recognise it' [see excerpt dated 1944].

If, in this book, Collins' art reached its zenith, the reason is not difficult to determine. He chose, consciously or otherwise, a subject fully within his limitations, a subject unentangled with social themes and problems better suited to the talents of a Reade or the genius of a Dickens. The canvas, though crowded, is smaller than that of *Armadale* or *The Woman in White* and, compared with the complexities of the earlier books, the plot of *The Moonstone* is in essence simple. The ingenuity which he brings to bear on its unfolding could hardly be surpassed, and the construction stands as a model. Within this smaller compass the flame of his imagination burned the more brightly, penetrating deep into human emotions and shedding upon the story in places a strange, almost magical glow.

The Diamond itself, as large as a plover's egg, seems almost a living thing:

> The light that streamed from it was like the light of the harvest moon. When you looked down into the stone, you looked into a yellow deep that drew your eyes into it so that they saw nothing else. It seemed unfathomable; this jewel, that you could hold between your finger and thumb, seemed as unfathomable as the heavens themselves. We set it in the sun, and then shut the light out of the room, and it shone awfully out of the depths of its own brightness, with a moony gleam, in the dark.

Wilkie acknowledges in the Preface [see excerpt dated 1868] that he was in part inspired by stories of two famous gems, the Koh-i-Noor and the stone that adorned the Russian Imperial sceptre. There may have been other sources, however. Lady Russell records that he used to be a frequent guest of Sir George Russell at Swallowfields and that the idea of *The Moonstone* arose from stories he heard there of the family heirloom, the famous Pitt diamond. Walter de la Mare, on the other hand, in a footnote to his essay on Collins' Early Novels, claims that the story was suggested by a moonstone which used to belong to Charles Reade, having been brought from India by his brother, and which is still in the possession of the Reade family.

The other main source of *The Moonstone* is less romantic. The newspapers of 1861 had given great prominence to the sensational Road Murder, in which a young woman named Constance Kent murdered her small brother in particularly brutal circumstances. She did not confess until four years after the murder, and at her trial two important pieces of evidence were a blood-stained shift and a washing-book. Although the crime itself plays no part in *The Moonstone,* there is much ado about a washing-book and a paint-stained nightdress. More important is the undoubted fact that Wilkie's detective, Sergeant Cuff, is founded upon the Scotland Yard detective in charge of the Road case, Inspector Whicher. Certain of Whicher's earlier cases were described in a series of articles in *Household Words,* where he is thinly disguised as 'Sergeant Witchem,' and he was in all probability known personally to Wilkie. Similarly Superintendent Seegrave, the stupid local policeman, had his real-life counterpart in Inspector Foley, who played an even more inept part in the Road case when supposed to be helping Whicher.

Since Sergeant Cuff has fathered such a multitudinous progeny in the literature of detection, he is worth examining at close quarters.

> A grizzled, elderly man, so miserably lean that he looked as if he had not got an ounce of flesh on his bones in any part of him. He was dressed all in decent black, with a white cravat round his neck. His face was as sharp as a hatchet, and the skin of it was as yellow and dry and withered as an autumn leaf. His eyes, of a steely light grey, had a very disconcerting trick when they encountered your eyes, of looking as if they expected something more from you than you were aware of yourself. His walk was soft; his voice was melancholy; his long lanky fingers were hooked like claws. He might have been a parson, or an undertaker—or anything else you like, except what he really was.

Thus he struck Betteredge, the house-steward, on his arrival to investigate the disappearance of the Moonstone. But Cuff's disagreeable appearance hides some very human qualities, such as his dry, salty humour and his passion for rose-growing. His most endearing quality, however, to those of us who may be satiated with detectives of super-human intellect, is his fallibility. Brilliant as are Cuff's deductions, he makes mistakes; he is a human creature after all.

For our part, we follow the detective happily along his false trails, drawing with faultless logic our wrong conclusions while all the essential clues to the mystery are, if not staring us in the face, at least within our knowledge. The secret is well kept until the moment when the author decides to enlighten us; and even then, with the main mystery solved, he contrives by sheer ingenuity to sustain, and perhaps heighten, our interest in the ultimate fate of the Moonstone.

The narrative method follows the pattern of *The Woman in White.* The book comprises a similar series of 'narratives' by different hands, but here they reflect more the personalities of their respective 'authors' and less that of Wilkie himself. Admittedly, in the case of Betteredge's story and of Rosanna's letter to Blake, there is a convention to be accepted in that these two characters are permitted a fluency of expression they would hardly have attained in reality, but the feelings they express are essentially their own.

Gabriel Betteredge, whose narrative is the first and the longest, combines the functions of Greek chorus and amateur detective. As the house-steward, he is both in the midst of, and outside the drama, which he records with a solid, earthy humour. 'A drop of tea,' he tells us, 'is to a woman's tongue what a drop of oil is to a wasting lamp.' If one can forgive his untiring reverence for *Robinson Crusoe*, the book which is his oracle and friend, and some of his more arch 'asides' to the reader, he proves an entertaining companion. Not only is Wilkie's choice of a family retainer as his narrator a device of some subtlety, but it shows once again his genuine interest in the lives of those who live 'below stairs,' a world which he, unlike nearly all his contemporaries, could describe faithfully, and without either condescension or embarrassment. We can recognise Collins' signature, too, in the portrait of Rosanna Spearman, the deformed housemaid with a prison record. He brings to it real understanding and compassion. Nothing in all his work is more moving than the growth of her hopeless love for Franklin Blake, which leads ultimately to her suicide; it is handled with rare sensitiveness and with a complete absence of sentimentality.

Miss Clack, authoress of the 'narrative' that follows, is pure caricature, and caricature with a touch of malice. Always repelled by ostentatious piety, Wilkie had doubtless suffered in many a drawing-room at the hands of evangelistic females. For one such lady he found himself in the position of trustee, a duty which he discharged with less than his usual courtesy, as the following peevish letter to Charles Ward indicates.

> Is the Jones-fund (may ''the Lord'' soon take her!) paid into *my* account regularly? . . . If it only rests with *me* to decide the matter, pay this pious bitch the two quarters together—so that we may be the longer rid of her . . . Tell me whether (by the help of the Lord) Mrs. Jones's dividends are now regularly paid into my account only. I don't want to pay Mrs. Jones (and the Lord) out of my own pocket.

The ridiculous Miss Clack, indiscriminately scattering her religious tracts, indefatigable in the exercise of 'Christian duty,' was his revenge. His armoury lacked the equipment for effective satire, and the satire is here applied with a heavy hand. As broad comic relief, however, Drusilla Clack serves her turn.

Of the heroine, Rachel Verinder, Betteredge tells us: 'She judged for herself, as few women of twice her age judge in general; never asked your advice; never told you beforehand what she was going to do; never came with secrets and confidences to anybody, from her mother downwards. In little things and great, with people she loved, and people she hated (and she did both with equal heartiness), Miss Rachel always went on a way of her own, sufficient for herself in the joys and sorrows of her life.' Rachel is no ordinary heroine, to whom events just happen, as for example Laura Fairlie; she is a young woman of intelligence and spirit, fully in command of the situation. Similarly Franklin Blake is far removed from the wooden hero of so many novels of the period. His experience of the world, and of women, is frankly acknowledged. Among a host of minor characters, most of whom are sketched with a deft and imaginative touch, mention must be made of Ezra Jennings. Into this striking portrait of a man haunted by past misfortune, torn by pain and kept alive by opium, Wilkie put much of his own suffering. There is a terrible authenticity about Jennings' confession:

> To that all-potent and all-merciful drug I am indebted for a respite of many years from my sentence of death. But even the virtues of opium have their limit. The progress of the disease has gradually forced me from the use of opium to the abuse of it. I am feeling the penalty at last. My nervous system is shattered; my nights are nights of horror. The end is not far off now.

Who can doubt that Wilkie had endured many a night such as that described in Ezra Jennings' Journal?

> June 16th—Rose late, after a dreadful night; the vengeance of yesterday's opium, pursuing me through a series of frightful dreams. At one time I was whirling through empty space with the phantoms of the dead, friends and enemies together. At another, the one beloved face which I shall never see again, rose at my bedside, hideously phosphorescent in the black darkness, and glared and grinned at me. A slight return of the old pains, and at the usual time in the early morning, was welcome as a change. It dispelled the visions—and it was bearable because it did that.

The *mise-en-scène* is done with all Wilkie's flair for creating atmosphere. The closing pages in particular linger in one's memory long after the book is put aside. The diamond has been restored at last to the sacred Indian city of Somnauth where its story began; a vast throng of pilgrims have gathered from afar to witness the ceremony, and the scene culminates in our final glimpse of the Moonstone:

> There, raised high on a throne—seated on his typical antelope, with his four arms stretching towards the four corners of the earth—there soared above us, dark and awful in the mystic light of heaven, the god of the Moon. And there, in the forehead of the deity, gleamed the yellow Diamond, whose splendour had last shone on me in England, from the bosom of a woman's dress.

There is imaginative power too in his conception of the Shivering Sand, and the uncanny spell it cast upon poor Rosanna whose life it claimed.

> The last of the evening light was fading away; and over all the desolate place there hung a still and awful calm. The heave of the main ocean on the great sand-bank out in the bay was a heave that made no sound. The inner sea lay lost and dim, without a breath of wind to stir it. Patches of nasty ooze floated, yellow-white, on the dead surface of the water. Scum and slime shone faintly in certain places, where the last of the light still caught them on the two great spits of rock jutting out, north and south, into the sea. It was now the time of the turn of the tide: and even as I stood there waiting, the broad brown face of the quicksand began to dimple and quiver—the only moving thing in all the horrid place.

When we recall the circumstances in which the greater part of this novel was written, we can only marvel at the courage and endurance with which he conquered afflictions that would reduce almost any man to utter helplessness. *The Moonstone* has held, and deserved, its special place in fiction as, to quote T. S. Eliot, 'the first, the longest, and the best of the modern English detective novels' [see excerpt dated 1928]. (pp. 218-24)

Kenneth Robinson, in his Wilkie Collins: A Biography, *1951. Reprint by Greenwood Press, Publishers, 1972, 348 p.*

CHARLES RYCROFT (lecture date 1956)

[*Rycroft provides a Freudian interpretation of* The Moonstone. *His remarks were originally delivered as a lecture in 1956.*]

I should like to discuss the theme of *The Moonstone* . . . starting from a sociological or historical observation. *The Moonstone* was written in the late eighteen-sixties and purports to describe events occurring in an upper middle-class setting some twenty years earlier. Now this was a time and an environment in which what later came to be called the 'double standard' of morality operated in theory if not entirely in practice. Young women of good family were assumed to be without sexual feelings and were expected to be not only innocent but also ignorant when they married. The future husband however could, perhaps even should, have had sexual relationships with women outside his own class. For the man, therefore, women were divided into two categories: those of his own class, who were idealized, one of whom he must eventually love and marry but must never think of sexually until after marriage; and those outside his own class, who were depreciated and with whom he could have sexual relationships but must never love and marry. Franklin is openly depicted as a young man with experience of the world and of women, while Rachel is an innocent girl. She is, however, proud, high-spirited, and independent, a woman who might, one surmises, have difficulty in making the type of submissive surrender which the Victorian male, in theory at least, demanded of his wife. I mention this in view of the well-known unconscious connection between loss of virginity and renunciation of the fantasy of having a penis.

If one views *The Moonstone* from the masculine point of view, the theft can be interpreted as a symbolic or symptomatic act or dream of a man in sexual conflict. Accustomed to casual sexual relationships with women outside his own class, [Franklin] finds himself in love with his cousin whom he wishes to marry. Her status as an idealized nonsexual woman makes her, however, unavailable as an object of either sexual activity or fantasy. As a result he gives up cigar smoking and suffers from insomnia and nervous irritation, i.e., he develops an actual neurosis. Under the influence of opium he then performs an act which is a symbolic fulfilment of his unadmitted wishes. The author exonerates him from guilt . . . by providing him with a respectable, altruistic motive and by having the Moonstone restolen from him. Ablewhite, the scapegoat, is however a personification of Franklin's own unconscious impulses. Franklin and Ablewhite are both maternal first cousins of Rachel and on the night of the crime they sleep in adjoining rooms. Ablewhite is also depicted as living according to the double standard, but unlike Franklin he does so hypocritically. He lives two lives, one with his mistress whom he maintains in luxury in the suburbs, the other as the devoted attendant on fashionable women in town and the secretary of numerous women's charitable organizations. Unlike Franklin he is prepared to degrade the idealized woman by marrying her for money.

Rachel's unconscious connivance in the crime can be interpreted in a complementary fashion. She falls in love with Franklin but her upbringing makes her blind to the physical aspects of being in love and to the problems and hazards that attach to the attainment of physical maturity. As a result she denies there is any risk that the Moonstone may be stolen—'Are there thieves in the house?'—but when she sees her lover stealing it she is powerless to stop him and yet overcome with fury and mortification at his having done so, even though she remains intensely in love with him. This ambivalent reaction is reminiscent of the outburst of hostility that the woman may feel toward the man to whom she loses her virginity and which Freud discusses at length.

Like Franklin, Rachel also has a double who personifies her repressed sexuality. Her maid, Rosanna, who is a reformed thief and the daughter of a prostitute, falls in love with Franklin at first sight and shows all the signs of physical infatuation with him. She is the first, excepting Rachel, to realize that the Moonstone has been stolen and it is she who discovers that the missing stained garment is Franklin's nightshirt. Her love for Franklin leads her to suppress this vital clue and so she shares with Rachel the responsibility for making the theft of the Moonstone a mystery. The different motives that the author attributes to Rachel and Rosanna for their silence and suppression of evidence provide an interesting contrast. Rachel is actuated by injured pride; she is disgusted with herself for loving a man who has proven himself capable of such an ignoble act. Her maid has simpler and more straightforward motives; she loves and wishes to protect him. She also wishes to hold on to something which might enable her to make Franklin, who has always been oblivious of her as a person, notice her and be indebted to her. So far from being shocked by discovering that Franklin is the thief, she is quite prepared to use her former contacts with the criminal world to help him dispose of the Moonstone. She also considers quite realistically the possibility that there may have been sexual reasons for Franklin's presence in Rachel's room on the night of the crime.

These considerations lead to the conclusion not only that the theme of *The Moonstone* is an unconscious representation of a sexual act, but also that its four leading characters, Franklin, Ablewhite, Rachel, and Rosanna, represent different aspects of the sexual conflicts that arise in a society which sanctions the tendency of the man to deal with his oedipal conflicts by dissociated conceptions of woman, one idealized and asexual, the other degraded and sexual. That the conflict underlying this tendency to dissociation does in fact stem from the oedipus complex and the taboo of incest is represented by the fact that Franklin, Ablewhite, and Rachel, the three upper-class characters, are all first cousins. Franklin and Rachel are indeed described as having as small children been brought up together as brother and sister. (pp. 236-39)

Charles Rycroft, "Detective Story: Psychoanalytic Observations," in The Psychoanalytic Quarterly, *Vol. XXVI, No. 2, April, 1957, pp. 229-45.*

A. E. MURCH (essay date 1958)

[*Murch discusses the importance of* The Moonstone *in the evolution of English detective fiction, focusing on the character of the police detective.*]

The Moonstone contains some of Collins's most powerful descriptive writing and his finest characterisation, but is even more remarkable for its extremely intricate plot, which gives ample scope for the working out of several lines of enquiry, curiosity and suspense mounting as the circle of suspects narrows. As in *The Woman in White,* the tale is unfolded in a series of reports, with various characters relating what they have each seen, heard or discovered, and though these amateurs all contribute something to the progress of the enquiry, in *The Moonstone* Collins also introduces a police detective, Sergeant Cuff. (p. 109)

The moment Sergeant Cuff arrives at Rachel Verinder's home, he assumes control with perfect composure, interviewing each guest and servant in turn, examining the house with minute care. It is worth noting his appearance, as described by the steward, Gabriel Betteredge:—

> —a grizzled, elderly man, so miserably lean that he looked as if he had not got an ounce of flesh on his bones in any part of him. He was dressed all in decent black, with a white cravat around his neck. His face was as sharp as a hatchet, and the skin of it was as yellow and dry and withered as an autumn leaf. His eyes, of a steely light grey, had a very disconcerting trick when they encountered your eyes as if they expected something more from you than you were aware of yourself. His walk was soft, his voice melancholy, his long lanky fingers were hooked like claws. He might have been a parson, or an undertaker, or anything else you like, except what he really was.

This might well serve as a composite picture of many later nineteenth century detectives of fiction. In it we catch glimpses that instantly link Sergeant Cuff with his near-contemporaries, Detective-Inspector Bucket and Gaboriau's Père Tabaret, as well as with such later figures as Ebenezer Gryce; Baroness Orczy's "Old Man in the Corner," whose long thin fingers played incessantly with a piece of string; even with Sherlock Holmes himself, hatchet-faced and lean, while Betteredge's concluding sentence has served to describe innumerable detective heroes. To complete the picture of Sergeant Cuff, Collins adds one or two individual touches—a dry humour, a passion for growing roses, and the human failing of being sometimes wrong in his conclusions. He is methodical, rather than brilliant, and though he makes a good start by proving that the diamond was taken between midnight and three o'clock in the morning by someone whose clothing must bear traces of paint, thereafter he makes only slow progress, disappearing from the scene for long periods and leaving various amateur investigators to unravel much of the mystery until he re-appears towards the end to weave the threads into a decisive pattern.

In *The Moonstone,* even more than in *The Woman in White,* the complicated plot was devised as a game of skill between writer and reader. Collins's technique of making different characters relate various episodes is most valuable in this connection because it enables the author to keep secret anything he does not wish the reader to know, and also allows him to convey impressions, false in themselves, but necessary for the development of the plot. Dickens had already used this technique in *Barnaby Rudge,* with the same purpose. It was Dickens's plan to make his readers believe that the steward, Rudge, had been killed when his master was attacked, but he does not say so himself, which would have misled the reader unfairly. Instead, he makes Solomon Daisy relate how "the body of poor Mr. Rudge was found," expressing the general belief. Dickens does, nevertheless, fall into the error of referring to Mrs. Rudge

as 'the widow,' though, as he reveals later, her husband is still alive. In Collins's hands the technique is employed more meticulously and more extensively, becoming a special feature, a convention of 'fair play' which he observes to perfection. Anything stated by one of his characters may possibly be inaccurate, but whatever Collins states himself, as author, can be accepted by the reader as true.

For the rest, *The Moonstone* is a kaleidoscope of changing suspicions, red herrings and doubtful alibis. For the first time in English fiction there is an ingenious juggling with details of time and place, careful reconstruction to determine how long certain actions would take, and though the secret is skilfully guarded till the end, Collins is scrupulous in giving the reader enough clues to enable him to deduce the solution for himself, if he is sufficiently perspicacious.

One detail which stands out in both these novels, and in all Collins's work, is his attitude towards domestic servants, so far in advance of his time as to seem almost revolutionary to his Victorian readers. To him, far more than to any other contemporary writer, even Charles Dickens, a servant was not a being to be patronised, regarded as humorous or of negligible importance, but a real person with a heart and mind, eyes and ears, as likely as his master to be truthful or observant. The detective story, perhaps more readily than any other type of fiction, takes the same democratic standpoint, giving impartial consideration to statements made by duke or farm-labourer, mistress or char-woman, and Wilkie Collins is the first English writer to express that view with perfect naturalness. (pp. 110-12)

At the time when *The Moonstone* was delighting English readers, detective fiction in France reached a new level of popularity in the novels of Emile Gaboriau, and it is possible to note the striking contrast between this first English detective novel and the typical contemporary *roman policier,* in atmosphere, in the nature of the central problem, and in the technique of plot construction. In the works of Gaboriau and his imitators, the story generally opens with the discovery of a brutal murder, every wound, every blood stain, all the wild disorder at the scene of the crime being described in gruesome detail. The victim is unknown to the reader until his (or, more often, her) disreputable past is gradually uncovered by the police, and the murderer is usually a melodramatic 'wicked baronet.' The other characters, with the exception of the detective, are little more than stock figures. The interest of the plot lies solely in the well-devised puzzle and its solution, the background being almost invariably a long drawn out tale of intrigue, passion and violence in aristocratic circles.

The Moonstone, notwithstanding its steadily mounting drama and suspense, has a quieter tempo, an atmosphere of gracious living, and deals with theft, not murder. We know the characters as individuals living their normal lives before the robbery takes place, and when Sergeant Cuff examines the scene of the crime he finds no greater disturbance than a small smudge upon a newly painted door. But the puzzle is quite as baffling as any solved by [Gaboriau's] Monsieur Lecoq, the plot even more intricate, the human drama far more credible, the contest of wits between writer and reader conducted with a precise regard for 'fair play' that is virtually unknown in the *roman policier* of the same period.

The credit for creating the English detective novel, and giving it characteristic features which still persist, belongs almost wholly to Charles Dickens and Wilkie Collins. (pp. 112-13)

[Dickens's] Detective-Inspector Bucket and Sergeant Cuff, taken jointly, form the prototype for the characteristic English police detective in later fiction. They are sound, dependable, self-respecting men of the middle-class, taking a pride in their work and very conscious that they function not merely as individuals but as members of a great organisation. They perform their duties with all the energy and efficiency of which they are capable, but they are not infallible. Sometimes they are at a loss, sometimes they are helped by amateurs, sometimes they must rely on their own dogged persistence, but eventually they bring their cases to a successful conclusion, enjoying the lime-light while they explain just how this has come about. They are happy in their home life, devoting their leisure to hobbies as other men do, so that the reader feels he knows them personally.

Amateur detectives differ widely in their personal character-istics, and have been particularly susceptible to influences from France and from America. But when an English detective novel has an English police-officer for a hero it is remarkable how often, even in the middle years of the twentieth century, that hero retains qualities linking him with Detective-Inspector Bucket and Sergeant Cuff. In this, as in the management of plot and the method of presentation, the example set by Charles Dickens and Wilkie Collins still exerts an active influence on the English detective novel. (pp. 113-14)

> *A. E. Murch, "Detective Themes in the Works of Charles Dickens and Wilkie Collins," in her* The Development of the Detective Novel, *1958. Reprint by Greenwood Press, Publishers, 1968, pp. 92-114.*

LEWIS A. LAWSON   (essay date 1963)

> [*In this Freudian interpretation of* The Moonstone, *Lawson ana-lyzes the sexual symbolism in the work and Collins's use of dream psychology. Lawson concludes that the novel is "based upon the Oedipal wish phantasy of its author's unconscious."*]

When the conditions of its composition are recalled, it is not surprising that *The Moonstone* abounds with references to dreams. For years forced by the pain of the gout to seek relief in laudanum, Wilkie Collins was consuming it in such quantities when he dictated the novel that he later admitted not recog-nizing the last part as his own work. As he well knew, and as he has Ezra Jennings write in the novel, the penalty of excessive opium is "the frightful dreams." But Ezra Jennings is not the only character in the novel who dreams. Franklin Blake writes at one point, "When I did get to sleep, my waking fancies pursued me in dreams." Both women who love Blake admit dreaming of him. Rachel Verinder, the well-born heiress, is the more restrained in her admission; she merely thinks of him by day and dreams of him by night. Rosanna Spearman, the poor servant, writing from the safety of the grave, is freer in describing her attraction to Blake; he was, she writes to him, like "a prince in a fairy story . . . like a lover in a dream." Her dreams are not always of Blake, however, for she early dreams of the quicksand in which she ends her life. And at the time when her thoughts are turning from the frustrations of love to the solace of death, Gabriel Betteredge, the steward of the household, repeatedly describes her actions as those of a person in a dream. It is Ezra Jennings, the doctor's assistant who is addicted to narcotics himself, though, who utters the most important words about dreams in the novel: "an ordinary dream subordinates to itself . . . judgment and . . . will." What Jennings says provides a basis for much of twentieth century

dream psychology. As Erich Fromm puts it, "Most of our dreams have one characteristic in common: they do not follow the laws of logic that govern our waking thought."

Collins does not elaborate upon the dream-content of his char-acters in *The Moonstone*. Both Rachel Verinder and Rosanna Spearman simply say that they dream of Franklin Blake, and there is no hint that their dreams are illogical, symbolical, or sensual. Franklin Blake comes closer to a modern understand-ing of dream-content when he says that his dreams were filled with fancies, but he never describes any of these fancies. And so Collins, although realizing the significance of dreams in portraying the total personality of his characters, left it to other writers to incorporate dream-content into the novel.

In another respect, Collins was profound in his use of the dream. Ezra Jennings knows that his dreams are the result of his narcotics addiction. The other dreams in the novel, though, the dreams of the ordinary characters, belong to those char-acters who constitute a love relationship. Collins must have recognized the strong connection between dreams and the sex-ual impulse. And either his knowledge of dream psychology went no farther beyond that point or he knew that Victorian propriety would not accept novels in which sexual relations were discussed not with moral disapprobation but with sci-entific objectivity. As it is, Collins' treatment of sex in the novel is considered daring by Victorian standards. The mere mention that Franklin Blake has had amorous entanglements or that Godfrey Ablewhite has carnal desires is said to be an uncommon honesty for a Victorian novelist, especially in the case of Franklin Blake, who is after all the hero of the novel. It would be a little more acceptable for Collins to acknowledge that Godfrey Ablewhite kept a mistress in the suburbs, for moral turpitude would be expected of the villain. But it is in his insinuations that women, even Victorian maidens, have a sexual impulse that Collins really shows his daring. In a country whose moral riches were firmly based upon the double stan-dard, Collins was a danger to the state in implying that maidens dreamed of men. Of course, he does nothing to suggest that Rachel Verinder, a member of the Establishment, has any knowledge of such bestial impulses: she simply dreams, in apparent romantic innocence, of Franklin Blake just as she thinks of him, and her purity is emphasized in the novel when she is referred to as a "lily." With the maidservant, Rosanna Spearman, Collins can be more truthful; she frankly dreams of a lover. After all, his audience could believe what he wrote of the belowstairs people. Still, the characterization of Rosanna Spearman is an achievement, when it is remembered that Dick-ens could write all of *Oliver Twist* without once mentioning that Nancy, like Rosanna a member of the criminal class, was the mistress of Bill Sykes.

It was perhaps because one member of the love relationship was a servant that Collins' imagination allowed him to treat sex more honestly than many of his contemporaries. Certainly the description of Rosanna Spearman's thoughts and actions are more sex-oriented, and hence more human to the post-Freudian mind, than Rachel Verinder's—at least on the literal level of the novel. Dorothy Sayers has called attention to the sensual quality of Rosanna's first glimpse of Franklin Blake [see excerpt dated 1944] and the scene *is* sensual, but not, as the Victorian mind would have it, repulsive. As Gabriel Bet-teredge describes the scene,

> Her complexion turned of a beautiful red, which
> I had never seen in it before; she brightened all
> over with a kind of speechless and breathless

surprise. 'Who is it?' I asked. Rosanna gave me back my own question. 'Oh! who is it?' she said softly, more to herself than to me.

The scene is, in fact, imbued with a pathetic charm that lifts it to the level of the fairy tale of the hunchback servant girl who falls in love with the prince. Collins apparently knew, too, of the connection between dream and fairy tale that Freud and his followers would elaborate fifty years later. An even more revealing description of the sex-orientation of Rosanna's mind is beheld when Blake receives the letter from Rosanna that she had entrusted to Limping Lucy before committing suicide. In the letter she tells of her thoughts on the morning that the diamond was discovered missing. Although Superintendent Seegrave had already arrived and the investigation of the theft had begun, Rosanna admits to Blake that the thought of his being the thief had not entered her mind, even when she discovered the paint-smeared nightgown in his room:

> I was so startled by the discovery that I ran out, with the nightgown in my hand, and made for the back stairs, and locked myself into my own room, to look at it in a place where nobody could intrude and interrupt me.
>
> As soon as I got my breath again, I called to mind my talk with Penelope, and I said to myself, 'Here's proof that he was in Miss Rachel's sitting-room between twelve last night, and three this morning!'
>
> I shall not tell you in plain words what was the first suspicion that crossed my mind, when I had made that discovery.

Nor does Collins rely solely upon literal description to depict Rosanna Spearman's obsession with sex. Immediately after Gabriel Betteredge describes Rosanna's first reaction to Franklin Blake, he describes Blake's appearance: "There, coming out on us from among the hills, was a bright-eyed young gentleman, dressed in a beautiful fawn-coloured suit, with gloves and hat to match, with a rose in his button-hole. . . ." As Collins later characterizes Franklin Blake, this is not the only rose that he has plucked, and Rosanna's name forecasts her pathetic captivation by her handsome superior. The rose is, indeed, as important an image to the modern reader of the novel as the moonstone itself. It is not always invested with symbolic importance; Collins makes Sergeant Cuff, a rose fancier, and Cuff and the gardener frequently argue about their respective favorites, but the rose is used here only to suggest an incongruous love of beauty in a police officer—a trait which later detective novelists, following Collins, have made into a convention of that genre. It is when the rose is utilized to describe the love relationship that it assumes symbolic importance. When Blake brings the moonstone as a present for Rachel Verinder's eighteenth birthday, Gabriel Betteredge wonders whether Rachel will marry Franklin Blake or Godfrey Ablewhite. To the eyes of society, Ablewhite would be the better choice, but Penelope Betteredge, Rachel's maid, soon informs her father that Blake is the favored one. And the information is quickly confirmed when Rachel takes Godfrey into the rose garden and refuses his offer of marriage. Then she begins to present Blake with roses for his button-hole. The action does not go unnoticed by the unfortunate Rosanna, however, and she begins to substitute roses which she has picked for those of Rachel Verinder. As she confesses in the letter that Blake receives after her suicide: "She used to give you roses to wear in your button-hole. Ah, Mr. Franklin, you wore *my* roses oftener than either you or she thought! The only comfort I had at that time, was putting my rose secretly in your glass of water, in place of hers—and then throwing her rose away."

Now certainly the rose has been a symbol of ambiguous meaning for thousand of years. But, as Barbara Seward writes in *The Symbolic Rose,* "In Freudian belief the explanation is sexual. Blossoms and flowers in general are said to represent the female sexual organs, while the particular shape of the rose associates it most directly with the shape of the vulva." Though the sexual meaning for the rose may fit perfectly for *The Moonstone,* the objection may be raised immediately that such interpretation is invalid because, first, Collins wrote the novel a half century before Freud and second, even granted the application of the meaning of the rose in *The Moonstone,* Collins' use of it was merely adventitious. The first objection may be answered by reference to two sources. As Roy Basler writes in *Sex, Symbolism, and Psychology in Literature,* it is a fallacy to suggest "that no literature of the past should be interpreted in light of what we now know." Maud Bodkin is even more specific:

> I hold that we cannot, when we experience a Greek or Elizabethan play, cancel the psychological awareness that our own age has conferred on us, nor should we seek to do so. It is with the complete resources of our minds that we must appreciate, if appreciation is to be genuine. If, for instance, we have found certain elements in experience made newly explicit through the teaching of Freud, that new awareness will enter into our apprehension of *Othello,* or of *Hamlet,* though it was not present in Shakespeare's own thought, nor in the audience for whom he wrote.

The second objection may be answered by a consideration of the mental condition of Collins during the period of the composition of *The Moonstone* and of the prevalence of a myriad of other sexual dream symbols that appear in the novel.

When it is remembered that Collins was consuming enough laudanum daily in these years to kill an ordinary man, it can easily be seen that Collins' state of mind would have been quite literally that of dreaming. One of Collins' biographers, Nuel Pharr Davis, has stressed the "weird, dreamlike consistency of mood and setting, if not of plot" of *Armadale* [see Additional Bibliography], and certainly the same judgment can be applied to *The Moonstone,* written just after *Armadale.* Freud has discussed the close connection that exists between the day-dream (which to him is similar to the night-dream) and the poetic imagination of the ordinary writer. How much closer to the dream-state would be a mind partially free of conscious restraint?

Underlying the detective plot of *The Moonstone* is a sexual schema involving four people. When Franklin Blake brings Rachel Verinder the moonstone, he is, symbolically, recognizing her maturity, for the diamond is after all in commemoration of her eighteenth birthday. The diamond is, in at least two ways, symbolic of femininity; first, the moon has immemorially been considered feminine, and as such it is a direct contrast to Franklin Blake, the "sunbeam," and, second, jewels, because of their great value, are symbolically significant as feminine genitals. Rachel Verinder recognizes her new status as an adult, for she refuses to let her mother take charge of the diamond on the night that it is presented to her. Even

Gabriel Betteredge, who has doubted Rachel's attraction for Blake, is impressed by a scene which occurs between the two just before they part for the night:

> What words passed between them I can't say. But standing near the old oak frame which holds our large looking glass, I saw her reflected in it, slyly slipping the locket (containing the diamond) which Mr. Franklin had given to her out of the bosom of her dress, and showing it to him for a moment, with a smile which certainly meant something out of the common, before she tripped off to bed.

In defiance of her mother, Rachel places the diamond in a cabinet of her own sitting room.

The next morning, at the discovery of the theft of the diamond, Rachel Verinder's attitude toward Franklin Blake is unaccountably hostile. She even refuses to leave her bedroom to discuss the theft, and when Superintendent Seegrave comes, she refuses to see him. For all of his bumbling, Seegrave does notice that the newly-painted door to Rachel's sitting room has been smeared, though he does not realize that the door provides him with an important clue to the mystery of the diamond. Rosanna Spearman realizes its significance, though, when she discovers from Penelope Betteredge that the painting would have been dry by three o'clock in the morning, and when she finds the paint smear on Blake's nightgown, her thoughts are instinctively sexually oriented. As she writes to Blake, "I shall not tell you in plain words what was the first suspicion that crossed my mind, when I had made that discovery." Symbolically, a paint-smeared door would be a defloration, so perhaps Rosanna should be forgiven for her suspicions.

When Rosanna does discover the significance of the nightgown as a clue, she determines to keep it, to see "what use . . . love or . . . revenge . . . could turn it to in the future. . . ." For the present, she decides, she will keep the nightgown hidden. Since her room is likely to be searched, she wears it under her own clothes, and she admits in her letter to Blake, "You had worn it—and I have another little moment of pleasure in wearing it after you." To Rosanna's fanciful imagination, her discovery that Blake is a thief suggests that she now has the opportunity to come between Rachel and Blake. Again she symbolically offers herself to him; using the pretext of giving him a ring that he had misplaced in his room she goes to the room where he is writing. She is rebuffed. The next day, she attempts to talk to him again, but, repelled by her ugliness, Blake concentrates upon the billiard cue which he has in his hand and upon the balls which he knocks about. As he later tells Betteredge,

> It was an awkward position; and I dare say I got out of it awkwardly enough. I said to her, 'I don't quite understand you. Is there anything you want me to do?' Mind, Betteredge, I didn't speak unkindly! The poor girl can't help being ugly—I felt that, at the time. The cue was still in my hand, and I went on knocking the balls about, to take off the awkwardness of the thing. As it turned out, I only made matters worse still. I'm afraid I mortified her without meaning it! She suddenly turned away. 'He looks at the billiard balls,' I heard her say. 'Anything rather than look at *me!*'

And again both feminine, the ring, and masculine, the cue, symbols have been utilized in conjunction.

After being rebuffed for the second time, Rosanna decides to hide the nightgown in a box in the Shivering Sand, and having done this, to approach Franklin Blake one last time. When she does approach him, she only overhears him say, "I take no interest whatever in Rosanna Spearman." And it is after that encounter with Blake that she throws herself into the sea.

But Rosanna was correct in her fantasy; she had been able to come between Rachel and Blake. At the same time that she is killing herself, Rachel Verinder, suspected of the theft of her own jewel and ostensibly unable to stand the presence of the police in her home, leaves for her aunt's home. Before the carriage pulls away, Franklin Blake attempts to speak to her, but she refuses even to look at him. At that action, Gabriel Betteredge thinks, "For the moment, Miss Rachel had completely unmanned him." As in every aspect of this novel, however, appearance is always the farthest thing from reality. By depriving Franklin Blake of the knowledge of his (unconscious, as it later turns out) participation in the theft, Rosanna is the person responsible for the unmanning of Franklin Blake.

The events that occur after the separation of Rachel and Franklin are significant to the detective level of the novel, but not to the symbolic. Franklin tours the world, traditionally symbolic of death, while Rachel removes to London. Only after Franklin is called back to England because of a death in his family does the symbolic element return to the novel, specifically in the letter from Rosanna Spearman and in the notes of Ezra Jennings taken from the fevered rantings of Dr. Candy. From the letter of Rosanna, Franklin discovers that he is the person who entered the room, and he cannot deny the act, for he has the nightgown to prove it. It is only after Franklin Blake recovers his nightgown that he regains his manhood. Thinking that the next step in the puzzle should be a conference with Rachel Verinder, he returns to London to talk with Mr. Bruff, the family lawyer. When Bruff has heard the story, he agrees to betray Rachel, who has refused to see Blake, into a conference with him. Blake is given a key to a door in Bruff's house which will admit him to the room where Rachel is unknowingly waiting. Here there is a combining of the literal and the symbolic; holding the key in his hand, Blake pauses for a moment in the garden, and then, as he described the event, "After the lapse of a minute, I roused my manhood, and opened the door." The conference with Rachel reveals that she saw him take the diamond, and her unaccountable animosity toward him on the morning of the discovery of the theft is now explained. (pp. 61-9)

[From] Ezra Jennings, Franklin Blake discovers how his taking of the diamond could have occurred without his knowledge: being given a narcotic before retiring the night of the theft, he had gone to sleep, worried about the safety of the diamond. In a sleep-walking state, he had arisen and gotten the diamond, an action which is psychologically valid. (p. 70)

But though the actual taking of the diamond is now known, the disposition of the diamond is not known. Blake and Bruff suspect that the diamond has been placed in a London bank for a year: since the time for the redemption of the diamond is almost up, they determine to watch the bank. Through action too detailed to recount here, the plot is played out. The mysterious Indians, who have sought the moonstone throughout the novel, make their reappearance, murdering Godfrey Ablewhite, the real thief, and taking the diamond back to India, from whence it began its journey many years before. Franklin Blake marries Rachel Verinder, and thus both the detective and the romantic lines of the novel are neatly knotted.

Rachel admiring the Moonstone. From The Moonstone, *by Wilkie Collins. The Heritage Press, 1959. Copyright © 1959 by The George Macy Companies.*

But what of the dream-symbolic line that has been suggested? Objects or actions that have Freudian significance can be found everywhere. Does that mean that every billiard cue mentioned in literature, for instance, is a phallic symbol? Such a question is obviously fatuous. An object or an action, to be a symbol, must appear in a consistent pattern of other symbols. . . . The pattern of symbols in *The Moonstone* has shown that there is a residual sexual layer in the novel lying beneath the consciously censored literal layer. Unlike most twentieth century literature, there is no conscious clinical absorption with sexual activities in the novel. Yet, because of the symbolism, it is clear that the unconscious creative imagination of the author was aware of the potential sex relationships between his characters. Since the characters themselves have symbolic importance to the phantasy-making part of the mind of the author, the id, what did it matter to Collins that Franklin Blake rejected Rosanna Spearman, that Rachel Verinder rejected Godfrey Ablewhite, that both Rosanna Spearman and Godfrey Ablewhite are dead at the end of the novel, that the Indians succeed in recapturing the diamond, and that Rachel Verinder and Franklin Blake, after their agreement-separation-reconciliation, finally marry and live happily ever after?

The attempt at an answer to the preceding questions must be delayed until a brief summary of the Freudian theory of aes-

thetics is given. What follows in this paragraph is a paraphrase of the theory as outline in Patrick Mullahy's valuable *Oedipus Myth and Complex.* The artist turns to phantasy to fulfill the wishes which he cannot fulfill in reality. Other people do this also, but the artist knows how to make his own phantasy enjoyable to people in general. Consciously, he adds continuity, logical motive, background, characterization, and other elements which will make his phantasy more ''literary.'' Unconsciously, because of the ''censor,'' that part of the mind charged with the protection of the ego, the artist uses ''various representations and disguises: transposition of motive, inversion to the opposite, weakening of the connection (as in an allusion), splitting of one figure into several, duplication, condensation, and especially fixed symbolism.'' As a result of both conscious and unconscious shifting and changing of phantasy materials in the mind of the author, art has countless possibilities for variety. But, for all the diversity, only a few repressed wish phantasy types are the force behind all art. The sexual force is responsible for much of the wish phantasy that accounts for art. The usual expression of the sexual wish fulfillment phantasy is through some form of the Oedipus situation, the sexual desire of the child for his parent of the opposite sex.

Now, to return to *The Moonstone,* what do the characters symbolize to their creator? The obvious character with which to begin an assignment of symbolistic meaning is Franklin Blake, the hero. ''The hero of all day-dreams and all novels'' is, as Freud so grandly puts it, ''His Majesty the Ego.'' To support himself, Freud asks,

> Shall we dare really to compare an imaginative
> writer with 'one who dreams in broad daylight,'
> and his creations with day-dreams? Here, surely,
> a first distinction is forced upon us: we must
> distinguish between poets who, like the bygone
> creators of epics and tragedies, take over their
> material ready-made, and those who seem to
> create their material spontaneously. Let us keep
> to the latter, and let us also not choose for our
> comparison those writers who are most highly
> esteemed by critics. We will choose the less
> pretentious writers of romances, novels and sto-
> ries, who are read all the same by the widest
> circles of men and women. There is one very
> marked characteristic in the productions of these
> writers which must strike us all: they all have
> a hero who is the centre of interest, for whom
> the author tries to win our sympathy by every
> possible means, and whom he places under the
> protection of a special providence.

The category of literature to which Freud proposes to confine his attentions is the category that *The Moonstone* would quite aptly fall into. On the very lowermost level of the unconscious, then, Blake symbolizes Collins' consciously forbidden incestuous wish.

Since Rachel is Blake's sexual choice, she becomes the mother-image. Nor is her portrayal incongruous, for the mother-image often has no superficial resemblance to the mother of actuality. More frequently, some figure not apparently resembling the mother of actuality at all emerges who symbolizes the mother-image. There are several elements in the composition of the novel that support this designation. The peculiar family relationship of Franklin Blake, Rachel Verinder, and Godfrey Ablewhite is important: all three of them are cousins, for their respective mothers were sisters. ''Members of the dreamer's family constitute a fairly high percentage of dream characters,'' and in eighty-five dreams of a hundred, there are two major characters in addition to the dreamer, one of his sex and one of the opposite sex. And in art, as in dreams, though their symbolic significance is to be interpreted and understood, the characters are often disguised. In other words, while Collins was really discussing his relations with his own psychic images, his ''censor'' forced him to substitute a relationship which, while not incestuous, was familial. Second, the possession of the moonstone by Rachel Verinder after its presentation to her by Blake is symbolically significant. Collins' first title for the novel was *The Serpent's Eye,* and his notes suggest that he intended at first to emphasize the Indian aspect of his materials. The finished work is, though, more of a domestic novel, with the emphasis on familial relationship. The title which he finally selected retains some of the Indian connotation while pleasing the desire of his unconscious. The moonstone is the important symbol of the novel, for it symbolizes the culmination of Collins' wish-fulfillment. Third, Rachel possesses another characteristic that suggests her function as a mother-image; of the three sisters, her mother is the one to have married nobility, and mother-images are often represented in dreams as being of the nobility. Finally, Rachel's fictional address in London is Portland Place. Collins' actual address at this time was Portman Place. With very little disguise, Collins' unconscious is stating the wish that Rachel, the mother-image, resided with him.

In the dream-triangle, Godfrey Ablewhite is the father-image, for he is, first of all, the defeated rival of Blake. The defeat is anticipated when he does not receive the roses in the rose garden; Rachel refuses to accept his offer of marriage there. Second, Godfrey's name suggests his function; the dreamer's father often appears in the dream as God. Third, Ablewhite attempts to steal the moonstone, the mother-symbol.

Rosanna Spearman, though not a member of the important triangle on the dream-symbolic level of the novel (as she is on the literal level), is nevertheless an important symbolic figure. She is, in effect, one of the disrupters of the relationship between the incestuous wish and its consummation. She represents the id, the willful, instinctual desires of sex, aimed not at the ideal mother image, but at any female sexual object. Quite naturally she is ugly and inferior in the unconscious creative imagination to the idealized mother-image, for she represents a threat to that idealization. Though she complains at her inferiority by saying, ''If she had been really as pretty as you thought her, I might have borne it better. No; I believe I should have been more spiteful against her still. Suppose you put Miss Rachel into a servant's dress, and took her ornaments off—?'', she really never had a chance at Franklin Blake's love, even though he seems to protest too strongly that he had never recognized her love of him. Speaking as the id, Rosanna attempts to tear the ego away from an idealized conception of the mother-image. When she takes Blake's nightgown, which is a phallic symbol, Collins specifically notes, as has been mentioned, that Blake's manhood had been taken. And only when Rosanna Spearman, the castrator that her family name suggests, has died and the nightgown has been returned does Collins note that Blake's manhood has returned.

In Freud's scheme of the mental state of humanity the ego and the id are joined to the super-ego, which represents the ''demands of morality and society.'' The function of the super-ego is to guard against trangressions against the outside world by the ego. In *The Moonstone* the symbolization of the super-

ego is split; both Sergeant Cuff and the Indians represent super-ego symbols. As Brahmins the Indians represent the religious aspect of the super-ego. On the literal level of the novel, they are priests who have traced the diamond to Rachel Verinder, whose grand-uncle had looted it from an Indian temple, and throughout the novel, they wander about the periphery of the plot, awaiting their chance to regain their possession. On the symbolic level of the novel they represent an idea which goes back to the pre-history of man, the taboo against incest. If *The Moonstone* is taken as an extended, artistically modified daydream, the Indians represent a vague injunction against incest which occurs from time to time. Sergeant Cuff, the police officer, the ''moral authority or conscience,'' represents the social aspect of the super-ego. He is attempting, on the literal level , to restore the diamond to Rachel Verinder, for theft is an act which society has designated as anti-social, as a crime. On the symbolic level he, like the Indians, represents a force determined to prevent the fulfillment of the wish. As he says, symbolic in a way that Collins would never understand, ''For the last twenty years, . . . I have been largely employed in cases of family scandal, acting in the capacity of confidential man.'' Certainly, the super-ego acts to prevent family scandal.

The Moonstone is, then, with artistically-induced modifications and amplifications, based upon the Oedipal wish phantasy of its author's unconscious. Though little is known of Collins' personal life, some of the details which are known support the theory which has been presented here. Ordinarily by the end of puberty, according to Freud, the Oedipal situation passes, and the child's sexuality is channeled by various factors into a socially approved heterosexual orientation. . . . But consider Collins' first known romantic attraction, for instance, in 1836, when his father was still alive. ''When he was only twelve years old he conceived a passionate affection for a married woman three times his age. So intense was his jealousy of the woman's husband that he could not bear to be in the same room, and ran away whenever he saw him approaching.'' It would appear that at the age of twelve, Collins was beginning to have difficulty making the change of love-objects that leads to a normal personality.

From the little which is known, a strong father-rivalry can be deduced. Though born ''William Wilkie Collins,'' the ''William'' after his father, within a year after his father's death, he had begun to change his usual form of address from ''Willie,'' the diminutive of his father's name, to ''W. Wilkie,'' and by 1854, used plain ''Wilkie Collins'' on all of his correspondence.

And though he never married, Collins lived with one mistress and sometimes two, for the remainder of his life. There is no reason to doubt that Collins was abnormal in the performance of his physically sexual role. He had three children by Martha Rudd, his second mistress, the last of whom was born in 1875, when Collins was fifty-one years old. But there is reason to believe that Collins could never unconsciously allow himself to establish a rival for his mother-image. ''(The Oedipus complex) also explains why some people never get married. A son feels that he must look after his mother and a daughter after her father. Of course they usually find good excuses to justify not getting married but below the surface one discerns the real reason, a strong attachment for the mother or father.'' Collins accepted quite openly the child of his first mistress by her husband and the three children of his own by Martha Rudd, and he left all four provided for in his will. But he never legitimized his relationship with either mistress, and though apparently fond of them, was capable of the utmost callousness. (pp. 70-7)

Kenneth Robinson has written in the summary of his biography of Collins, "there remains a sense of incompleteness about this picture of one who was in many respects an extraordinary man." He was, for example, extraordinary in his knowledge and use of nineteenth-century dream psychology in *The Moonstone*—but twentieth-century dream psychology may be the key to the door to his inner life that he had deliberately locked. He left few notes, little correspondence, and no diaries. Recollections of him by others tell little of the inner man. In such a case, perhaps speculation is justifiable, not for the gossip content of the author's personal life, but for the clues which may shed light on the man as an artist. In the author's preface dated May, 1871, Collins discussed his mental and physical condition at the time of the composition of *The Moonstone* by writing, "The Art which had been always the pride and pleasure of my life, became now more than ever 'its own exceeding great reward'" [see excerpt above]. He was referring to pain that the gout was causing him, but it can be suggested that art at this time provided him with the fulfillment of his lowermost unconscious desire. It is generally agreed that *The Moonstone* is the apex of his career. Perhaps, having succeeded in satisfying in his own mind his wish to capture the mother-image, Collins' frustration was dissipated, and without frustration great art is impossible. It is ironically appropriate that *The Moonstone* was inscribed *In Memoriam Matris*. (pp. 77-8)

> Lewis A. Lawson, "Wilkie Collins and 'The Moonstone'," in American Imago, Vol. 20, No. 1, Spring, 1963, pp. 61-79.

WILLIAM H. MARSHALL   (essay date 1970)

[*Marshall contends that, of equal importance to its place as a pioneering detective novel, is* The Moonstone*'s status as "one of the first major works in the fiction of the unconscious."*]

Of the two novels for which Wilkie Collins has been best known, *The Moonstone* has perhaps received more attention than *The Woman in White* because it is regarded as the first English detective novel. In fact, Dorothy L. Sayers described it as "probably the very finest detective story ever written" [see excerpt dated 1928 in *NCLC*, Vol. 1]. At times, however, the various aspects of the quality of the book are obscured by considerations of its historical position in the development of a particular *sous-genre*. Admittedly a triumph in the exploitation of man's rational faculty for fictional purposes, as indeed all significant detective stories must be, it also utilizes, as a means of explaining the mystery that reason seeks to solve, the potential offered by the nether side of the human mind: it becomes one of the first major works in the fiction of the unconscious.

Between the two extreme aspects of man's response stands man himself—and that he is neither wholly rational nor fully reacting below the level of consciousness is presented here with extraordinary skill. Rarely in the nineteenth century have the ambiguities of individual character, set against a partly incomprehensible world, been more clearly revealed than in the protracted dramatic monologues of such characters in *The Moonstone* as Gabriel Betteredge and Druscilla Clack. Most obscured has been the seriousness of *The Moonstone*, which implies the question that from the collapse of the Enlightenment, the committed literary artist has increasingly asked: What is the nature of identity or of the Self, and for what must it be held responsible? (p. 77)

The philosophic implications lying at the base of the question of identity posed by the narrative, ultimately devastating to the belief of a large number of readers, exist too far below the surface of the narrative itself to be grasped. For Collins' public, therefore, *The Moonstone* was without ambiguities; a work posing no unpleasant questions, it might be trusted to entertain. Tightly constructed as it is, *The Moonstone* sustained the readers at an almost consistently high level of response to the game of reason and motive which they saw the characters playing. In its presentation of the game itself, it was a serious work which set the standard for the detective novels that were to follow.

The emergence of the detective story as a literary form is a characteristic development of the nineteenth century. In the English tradition there had been the Newgate Calendar—the profitable recording and publication by "the Ordinary Chaplain" of the stories told by those poor souls, like Moll Flanders' comrades, who were about to go "out of the world by the steps and the string"; and from this developed a fiction of rogues and villains, of which Fielding's *Jonathan Wild the Great* (1743) was an early instance. There had also been the Gothic novel and the tales of terror, emphasizing the mystery and sometimes the supernatural elements not part of the literature of criminal life. Adapting the tale of terror to the novel of ideas in *Caleb Williams* (1794), William Godwin brought to the English tradition a novel depending for its resolution upon the characters' rational activity.

To this point the English tradition failed to repudiate popular hostility to the police and the representatives of authority, preserved even by the middle classes from the long centuries of oppression by aristocratic government. For the detective novel to develop significantly, the image of the police had first to become unsullied in the popular mind. The English popularity of the *Mémoires* of François-Jules Vidocq (1775-1857), published in Paris in 1829, did much to establish the figure of the detective as an agent of good; and the emerging middle-class readers increasingly depended for their survival as a group upon the enforcement of law. Nevertheless, the official policeman remained sufficiently tainted that a compromise was often reached in detective fiction that was expressed by the use of a private detective or, as in *The Moonstone*, a police officer from outside the immediate region. The development of a new kind of fiction thus established also depended upon the growth of a large reading public that made possible the expansion of the novel itself, but in this instance the readers had to have developed their rational capacities sufficiently to be able to follow the logical sequence on which the solution rested.

Finally, the detective story offered a means by which those as yet unprepared or unwilling to face the ethical implications of some of the leading ideas of the nineteenth century could retain the traditional differentiation between good and evil without concerning themselves with the question of the validity of the ontological structure on which such a differentiation implicitly rests. No work illustrates this fact so much as *The Moonstone*, which, when it is read exclusively at the level of action, remains a detective story and does not really press the implications of the meaning of identity or of the nature of moral responsibility. Stated another way, the detective story implies the grounds of its own existence: that, by the exercise of reason to discover and destroy some form of evil, man might attain good—an implication which is thereafter subject to no very close scrutiny. The question of the reason for the existence of evil in the first place remains unvoiced, as does the proposal that somehow, after triumphing over evil, the individual may achieve a state higher than that which he had experienced before he encountered evil. And, for those few readers ordinarily moved by intellectual doubt, the firm and rationalized distinction between good and evil might continue as part of the work of fiction and offer to its readers a form of satisfaction not found in the same way in life or in other intellectual activities.

The method which Collins brought near perfection in *The Woman in White*, by which the narrative is developed through the protagonist's editing of individual documents, was clearly suited to the needs of the kind of fiction given direction by *The Moonstone*. Encountering a group of dramatic monologues significantly arranged, the reader is able to learn more about the total situation than any one of the active characters knows. (pp. 78-80)

The principal quality of the resulting narrative structure is the organic unity that is derived to a great degree from the exploitation of either the dramatic irony or the incomplete knowledge apparent in nearly every individual narration. Rachel Verinder writes to Ezra Jennings not long before the crucial experiment is conducted upon Franklin Blake: "I want to have something to do with it, even in the unimportant character of a mere looker-on." . . . She here describes the situation to some degree of each of the participants in the episode: in terms of deducible meaning, none is really more than "a mere looker-on." Even the villain, Godfrey Ablewhite, begins his involvement by watching what is in front of him, and makes the significant commitment only somewhat later. Sergeant Cuff, in his letter of explanation to Franklin Blake—reconstructing the moment when the unknowingly drugged Blake took the Moonstone so that he might protect Rachel from the three Indians pledged to its recovery—remarks of the ultimate thief of the gem: "In that position he [Godfrey Ablewhite] not only detected you in taking the Diamond out of the drawer—he also detected Miss Verinder silently watching you from her bedroom, through her open door. He saw that *she* saw you take the Diamond too." The very *seeing*, a form of *knowing*, gives each character a degree of power in relation to other characters, each of whom may in return have a species of knowledge about him. The structure of the total narrative resembles an arrangement of mirrors reflecting mirrors, no one of which directly reflects full reality.

In some instances, dramatic irony arises from the fact that the narrator's total viewpoint is insufficiently complex to comprehend the significance of what he experiences or reveals. Thus, Gabriel Betteredge, judging Sergeant Cuff entirely by appearances that do not conform to Betteredge's image of what Cuff should be, distrusts him:

> A fly from the railway drove up as I reached the lodge; and out got a grizzled, elderly man, so miserably lean that he looked as if he had not got an ounce of flesh on his bones in any part of him. He was dressed all in decent black, with a white cravat round his neck. His face was as sharp as a hatchet, and the skin of it was as yellow and dry and withered as an autumn leaf. His eyes, of a steely light gray, had a very disconcerting trick, when they encountered your eyes, of looking as if they expected something more from you than you were aware of yourself. His walk was soft; his voice was melancholy; his long lanky fingers were hooked like claws. He might have been a parson, or

an undertaker, or any thing else you like, except what he really was. A more complete opposite to Superintendent Seegrave than Sergeant Cuff, and a less comforting officer to look at for a family in distress, I defy you to discover, search where you may.

And the evangelical old maid, Druscilla Clack, secure in the deep sense of her own rectitude, learns nothing from any experience. Elsewhere, the narrator, though acquiring information in the course of the events recalled, has as yet insufficient knowledge to interpret it correctly. The narrative of Mr. Matthew Bruff, the solicitor, serves as a device to bring together certain strands of information that are to be fully exploited by others.

The traditional literary juxtaposition of reality and appearance is a significant aspect of the method informing *The Moonstone*; yet the appearance of Sergeant Cuff, whose very strength as a character comes from his lack of flamboyance, has misled some of the modern critics as well as Gabriel Betteredge. Each character, operating within the structure of the novel, must continually discriminate between what is real and what merely appears to be; not every confusion of the two is so humorous as Betteredge's judgment of Cuff. Rosanna Spearman, possessing the half-knowledge that is more deceptive than total ignorance, tragically misunderstands Franklin Blake's *apparent* snub of her. Ezra Jennings, Mr. Candy's inventive assistant, is the most striking instance of the confusion of appearance and reality in the human person. Franklin Blake, recurringly upset at seeing Jennings ("the man with the piebald hair twice in one day!"), develops a compulsion to find some means to identify this man who will actually identify Blake—that is, return to Blake his moral identity by revealing the capacities of his unconscious self to be amoral.

To the ordinary reader of 1868, the juxtaposition between appearance and reality would have no further importance than in the deception marking the activities of certain characters, with the resulting momentary confusion of the reader in his attempts to distinguish between the "good" and the "bad" characters. Beyond this point such a reader would not go; he was unconcerned. But in this novel, in the dramatic and ironic manipulation of character, in the exploration of the reality of the self lying beneath the personality, Collins reflected some of the serious intellectual concerns of his age.

Gabriel Betteredge, the aging house-steward to Lady Verinder, the man whose narratives follow the Prologue and precede the Epilogue, is one of the most striking of the characters through whom the relation of several sensibilities is explored. Apparently a patient and long-suffering husband of a shrewish wife—in whose departure from life he finds reason to infer the reality of "an all-wise Providence"—and a devoted father, Betteredge has passed through life entirely unable, except in matters related to survival, to distinguish between appearance and reality; and his world view is the accumulation of the intellectual fragments cast forth by several passing centuries. He is fully aware of his role as narrator, but, with an even intensified irony, he cannot recognize how truthfully he writes when he remarks, "I am asked to tell the story of the Diamond, and, instead of that, I have been telling the story of my own self. Curious, and quite beyond me to account for."

Betteredge's classic misvaluation of Sergeant Cuff is reflected in his handling of other characters, notably Godfrey Ablewhite, whom he introduces, and Rosanna Spearman, whom he rightfully regards as innocent but for the wrong reasons. He can approach what he believes is an understanding of the sophisticated Franklin Blake only by reducing him to a composite of national roles and by attributing a given action to the momentary supremacy of "the German side" or "the French side." With his important place in the hierarchy below stairs, Gabriel Betteredge is a man whose learning has been esteemed by those whom he directs; he is accustomed to making pronouncements and completely believes in the authority of what he says. If he has not read widely, he has read repeatedly in the works that support and strengthen his own point of view; his narrative is, somewhat pompously, calculated to reflect the wisdom born of this reading.

Yet, his narrative reflects, more than all else, the fact that Betteredge remains totally simplistic in his view of life. An empiricist in his consideration of all that he regards as practical affairs, Betteredge considers himself "a good Protestant" who is ever mindful of his moral duty. His world view rests upon a firm belief in Christian revelation tempered by a flexible commitment to the proposition that by the exercise of reason man can triumph over all adversity. Not surprisingly, Betteredge has taken as his guide in life Defoe's *Robinson Crusoe* (1719), itself a monumental fusion of Protestant providentialism and empirical rationalism.

Though he has worn out a number of copies, Betteredge does not regard the *whole* book as a significant comment upon human experience so much as he uses it as Crusoe himself used the Bible, opening it at random to a passage which he then takes as a comment upon his situation of the moment because, as he asserts, he has been led to this passage by providential means. Avowedly anticlerical and insistently "not superstitious," Gabriel Betteredge has established *Robinson Crusoe* as an indisputable authority that only he can interpret, a substitute for Scriptures bestowed by the Enlightenment upon those modern beings who, failing to discriminate between their reason and their faith, lost all real sense of the value of either.

Betteredge becomes an amiable parody of the woman whose fundamentalism he so despises, Druscilla Clack. As she judges others by their reactions to her use of Scriptures, Gabriel judges men by their response to *Robinson Crusoe*: Ezra Jennings is to be pitied because he has not read the book since childhood, and Franklin Blake is to be esteemed after he appears to have accepted the providential usefulness of Defoe's novel. And in the conclusion of his first, and major, portion of narrative, Gabriel Betteredge demonstrates by the manner of his insistence upon the moral balance (which, in the narratives that follow, is to be seen as working through human agency) how truly incompetent he is to judge the very events that he has been recording: "May you find in these leaves of my writing what Robinson Crusoe found in his Experience on the desert island—namely, 'something to comfort yourselves from, and to set, in the description of Good and Evil, on the Credit Side of the Account.'—Farewell." Never aware of his inability to give significant order to his experiences and ideas, Gabriel sustains his image of his own being, of the self on which all interpretation of experience must rest.

Franklin Blake, on the other hand, experiences the fragmentation of sensibility and, through the restorative activities of Ezra Jennings, is even made fully aware of the nature of his experience. Jennings' view, that the mind has faculties operating at various levels of capacity and awareness, would hardly pose for Blake a disturbing possibility. In the case of the stricken Mr. Candy, now Jennings' patient, Jennings remarks upon "the superior faculty of thinking going on, more or less connectedly . . . while the inferior faculty of expression was in a state of almost complete incapacity and confusion"; with this understanding, Jennings can reconstruct the old man's meaning from fragments of speech, thereby establishing the central fact that Mr. Candy administered laudanum to the sleepless and unsuspecting Blake on the night that the Moonstone disappeared.

From this position Jennings can propose that Blake was "unconscious of what you were about when you entered the room [of Rachel Verinder]"—an idea with which Blake cannot disagree, in part because, since the moment he discovered the stain of paint upon his own nightgown, he has existed in moral alienation, unable either to endure or to explain the guilt that seems to be his. From the time that he suspects that Ezra Jennings may be able to lead him out of his dilemma, Franklin Blake feels "physically incapable of remaining still in any one place, and morally incapable of speaking to any one human being" until Jennings can reveal his plans. In effect, Blake has no choice but to submit to Jennings' proposed experiment, by which, through the calculated fragmentation of his personality, he might retrieve his moral identity.

The Moonstone may well be Collins' most skillfully constructed work, as it has been called, and it fully deserves its place as the first English detective novel. Of at least equal importance, however, in its use of the unconscious as the means by which reason is enabled to explain the disappearance of the Indian gem, *The Moonstone* anticipated the greater fragmentation of the sensibility of modern man, as perhaps no other major Victorian novel was to do. Paradoxically, the moment Franklin Blake rose guiltless from the fragments of his former self, the philosophic assumption on which the rational frame of the detective story rests showed evidence of collapse. (pp. 80-5)

> *William H. Marshall, in his* Wilkie Collins, *Twayne Publishers, Inc., 1970, 159 p.*

JOHN R. REED (essay date 1975)

> [*Reed briefly describes how Collins used the device of "disguise," or concealed identity, in* The Moonstone. *For additional commentary by Reed on* The Moonstone, *see excerpt dated 1973 in NCLC, Vol. 1.*]

[In *The Moonstone* Collins exploited the device of disguise] more elaborately and more successfully than elsewhere in his writings. William H. Marshall says of this novel that in "the dramatic and ironic manipulation of character, in the exploration of the reality of the self lying beneath the personality, Collins reflected some of the serious intellectual concerns of his age" [see excerpt dated 1970]. Collins was always concerned with the ordinarily unexamined layers of character, but here the many levels of character are more explicitly revealed. The stodgy Gabriel Betteredge is disturbed by Franklin Blake's multiple personality with its German, French, Italian, and English sides. Yet it is because of his ability to recognize the multiplicity of personality in himself that Blake can function as well as he does. It is one of the great ironies of the novel that Blake, with such a varied character, should be ignorant of a critically important region of his personality, the unconscious.

Blake is one of the few characters in the novel to acknowledge his own multiple nature. Cuff can recognize at least a dual personality in the reformed thief, Rosanna Spearman, and Godfrey Ablewhite knows his own duplicity; but awareness of man's potential for mutability or flexibility of character is limited. Instead, characters are forced by a society that requires appearances to be kept up to suppress that part of their character that would most benefit from exposure. It is this easily recognizable form of disguise that signals the shortcomings of English society. Rosanna Spearman, though she has reformed, is obliged to disguise her past, for society would not otherwise accept her. Yet when she dies she reveals that the "imposture" of respectability is her true identity. Her previous identity is now perceivable as the false one. In death she is proven no thief, but a woman willing to sacrifice herself for the man she loves. Rosanna's case is neatly contrasted with that of Godfrey Ablewhite; this spokesman of respectability in reality leads a double life. He is a sensualist, a swindler, and a thief. He too reveals his true identity in death. When the police officer snatches away the false beard from Godfrey's corpse, he discloses the man as a thief whose respectable role was a disguise. At the same time, on a larger scale, in removing Godfrey's disguise, the officer strips the mask from an entire culture that values its Ablewhites and its appearances above the realities of human nature. *The Moonstone* provided England with a means of looking past the many masks it wore, but few were willing to look at the undisguised truth. (pp. 320-21)

> John R. Reed, "Disguise," in his Victorian Conventions, *Ohio University Press, 1975, pp. 289-361.*

R. P. LAIDLAW (essay date 1976)

[*Laidlaw explores the dichotomy between objective and subjective reality in* The Moonstone, *arguing that Collins's handling of the theme "should lead to a revaluation of the novel from its present late-Gothic-cum-early-detective labelling to place it with the serious and significant works of Victorian fiction."*]

Most of the works of Collins's major period of writing share a basic structuring motif in studying the relationship between a totally secular and objective order and the subjective, or perhaps even supernatural, forces which continue to operate upon mankind. Indeed, it is frequently the flaws in man's own self-created secular world which allow these darker forces to tempt the individual to his destruction, since those who suffer or profit by the loopholes in the system become isolated either by shame and outrage or guilt and public revulsion. . . .

Many of the novels have explicit reference to supernatural possibilities, generally involving some idea of an ordering fate, but the central conflict is not so much between the real and the unreal as between objective and subjective versions of reality. (p. 211)

In brief, we have in these novels two extremes which are definable, in the terms which Franklin Blake uses in *The Moonstone,* as objective and subjective reality. It would be futile to suggest that, one or two novels apart, this basic pattern is not developed with a fairly depressing degree of crude complexity of construction, shallowness of psychological motivation and overplaying of the melodramatic, but even allowing for this the working towards a synthesis of objective and subjective realities is clear. . . . [It] is the writer's intention to suggest that in *The Moonstone,* at least, Collins develops his concerns with a sophistication and success which should lead to a revaluation of the novel from its present late-Gothic-cum-early-detective labelling to place it with the serious and significant works of Victorian fiction.

The Moonstone adds a further profession to the list of those who place their faith in objectivity and appearance: that of the

detective, Sergeant Cuff. Seeing Cuff as one of a group of believers in primary reality may do something to counter the overemphasis placed upon the role of the detective in this novel: an important thing to do, since probably nothing has stultified modern critical response to the novel as much as T. S. Eliot's much quoted comment that this was "the first and greatest of English detective novels" [see excerpt dated 1927 in *NCLC,* Vol. 1]. *The Moonstone* in fact, is written quite explicitly in an ironic relationship with an existing tradition of the detective novel: "It's only in books that the officers of the detective force are superior to the weakness of making a mistake," says Sergeant Cuff himself, and while this kind of irony is clearly what Eliot had in mind when he went on to define the specifically *English* tradition of the detective story, the emphasis on the importance of the detective without this qualifying context has led to distortion. Cuff, like Collins's lawyers here and elsewhere has, at least in his professional life, total belief in objective reality, or the power of appearance, and, like lawyer Bruff, is powerless to do anything in the direction of recovering the stolen diamond, however knowledgeable he may be after the event. Indeed the link between the names of Bruff and Cuff follows a favourite Dickensian satiric device, echoing the Coodles and Doodles of politics in *Bleak House,* or the Messrs. Aggs, Baggs and Caggs, and Alley, Balley and Calley of the legal world of *Our Mutual Friend,* and certainly argues against the uniqueness of Cuff.

Cuff recognizes a dualism operating in life, but sees no synthesis, restricting his business life to one half, and saving the other for his retirement:

> 'If you will look about you (which most people won't do),' says Sergeant Cuff, 'you will see that the nature of a man's tastes is, most times, as opposite as possible to the nature of a man's business. Show me any two things more opposite one from the other than a rose and a thief; and I'll correct my tastes accordingly—if it isn't too late at my time of life.'

In fact, there are possible ironies in Cuff's choice of a comfortable retirement in Surrey and rose hunting trips to Ireland in a novel in which others who wish to get away from it all choose the wastes of Hindustan or the deserts of the Near East (or in Ezra Jennings's case, opium and death), just as there are fairly well defined limits to a second Eden whose chief triumphs are the use of grass, rather than gravel, for its walks, and the growing of the white moss rose without first budding it on the dog rose. Cuff's biggest mistake is in part due to his separation of the rose from the thief: he has grave suspicions of Rosanna Spearman when she hides in the shrubbery, as he does of Rachel with her continuing silence, and in each case assumes that their motives are those of material gain rather than love of Franklin Blake.

The Preface to the First Edition of *The Moonstone* places the dichotomy between kinds of reality on a non-supernatural level:

> In some of my former novels, the object proposed has been to trace the influence of circumstances upon character. In the present story I have reversed the process. The attempt made, here, is to trace the influence of character on circumstances [see excerpt dated 1868].

Apart from the supposed curse on the stone and the Indian dabbling in clairvoyance, this is probably the least Gothic of Collins's novels. Circumstance, as the novel defines it, is the level of primary reality, of observed phenomena, and the world with which Bruff and Cuff can cope: thus Cuff observes Rachel's behaviour after the loss of the stone and forms what are logical conclusions by the standards of primary reality, deducing that she invented the story of the theft in order to cover the need to raise money on the stone. Bruff, betrayed for once into subjectivity by his faith in Rachel, forms what is, in fact, the correct opinion, that the stone was taken by Godfrey Ablewhite, only to have this blown away by the total objectivity of Rachel's knowledge that Godfrey did not take the stone.

The union of the Objective with the Subjective towards which Franklin strives in his philosophical moments, is basically a union of character and circumstance: in the first half of the novel he fails totally. Thus his "Subjective/Objective" explanation of why the wicked uncle should give his niece a valuable diamond—"to prove to his sister that he had died forgiving her"—carries no greater force than Gabriel Betteredge's totally Subjective, character-based, explanation, that the Colonel had "purposely left a legacy of trouble and danger to his sister" as a last act of vengeance. Blake's synthesis breaks down completely after the loss of the diamond, when appearance both for Franklin and, one assumes, for Rachel, can only be explained in terms of the total loss of character by the other: from Rachel's viewpoint, Franklin's loss of character is the loss of his good name (Rosanna Spearman and Ezra Jennings have both lost their "characters" in this way), while for Franklin, Rachel seems to have lost her own identity, and he discovers in the end a parody of his earlier synthesis:

> Good Heavens! the Objective-Subjective explanation follows, of course! Rachel, properly speaking, is *not* Rachel, but Somebody Else. Do I mind being cruelly treated by Somebody Else? You are unreasonable enough, Betteredge; but you can hardly accuse me of that.

It is only when Blake is presented with evidence that his own identity is linked with circumstances of which he has no knowledge that a new synthesis can develop with Rachel. Circumstances have obliterated character after the loss of the stone, but with the recovery of the nightgown from the Shivering Sands, a new confrontation of the two takes place:

> The nightgown itself would reveal the truth; for, in all probability, the nightgown was marked with its owner's name.
>
> It took it up from the sand, and looked for the mark.
>
> I found the mark and read—
>
> MY OWN NAME.
>
> . . . on the unanswerable evidence of the paint stain, I had discovered myself as a thief.

The novel traces a process of fragmentation and partial subsequent reintegration. After the loss of the diamond there is a swift movement away from the house in Yorkshire: Rachel, in particular, becomes increasingly isolated, as the death of her mother is followed by the rift with the Ablewhites and Miss Clack, while Franklin Blake, rejected by his father, leaves the country and is rediscovered on the edge of a desert. Although Rachel and Franklin marry and the family union is restored, permanent isolation is the fate which Collins chooses, as so often, for those who hold themselves beyond redemption, and Miss Clack ends in exile in Boulogne, while Godfrey Able-

white dies, alone and disguised, at the hands of his murderers. The novel has, as one of its final touches, Murthwaite's picture of total isolation and fragmentation which surely outweighs the story of new domestic bliss that Betteredge has offered from Yorkshire:

> The god had commanded that their [the Indians'] purification should be the purification by pilgrimage. On that night, the three men were to part. In three separate directions, they were to set forth as pilgrims to the shrines of India. Never more were they to look on each other's faces. Never more were they to rest on their wanderings, from the day which witnessed their separation, to the day which witnessed their death. . . . They rose—they looked on one another—they embraced. Then they descended separately among the people. The people made way for them in dead silence. In three different directions, I saw the crowd part, at one and the same moment. Slowly the grand white mass of the people closed together again. The track of the doomed men through the ranks of their fellow mortals was obliterated. We saw them no more.

The Indians have stepped outside a non-secular order, and have lost caste by pursuing the stone: Godfrey Ablewhite rejects the secular order by breaching both the law and the family trust in stealing the diamond, and this mirror-image version of the two extremes is an important one for the process of the novel, at times finding a comic form in parody. The Indians are "romantic"; Murthwaite describes their faith in clairvoyance as "simply a development of the romantic side of the Indian character." Clairvoyance, as they practise it, he claims, is totally subjective, since the medium reflects "what was already in the mind of the person mesmerising him": again the novel offers a clear totally objective version, since the clairvoyance of the Indians' hypnotized boy is mirrored by the clear-sightedness of the all-seeing boy detective, Gooseberry, whose only failure comes from a lack of subjectivity which makes him unable to comprehend the conflicting characters of the Indians' spy.

For all the avowed rejection of the efficacy of clairvoyance, the Indians are remarkably efficient. I suspect that this is because their existence and their link in the novel with the Moonstone are not only tied to the level of primary reality as they affect the other protagonists, but also have a close link with the most meaningful level of subjectivity, that of absolute inner consciousness. There has been at least one highly persuasive, if perhaps over-Freudian analysis of the novel [see excerpt by Lawson dated 1963], drawing particular attention to the pervasiveness of dreams; but beyond this, the Indians (and the stone itself) are strongly linked with scarcely expressed fears and desires, close to the identity of the protagonists, and probably find their origin in the book which Ezra Jennings recommends to Franklin Blake, De Quincey's *Confessions of an English Opium Eater*, a work which was doubtless close to the heart of a great English opium drinker like Collins. . . . In *The Moonstone*, Collins stresses the Indians' denial of the validity of individual life: Murthwaite's description of their attitude to murder—"they care just as much about killing a man as you care about emptying the ashes out of your pipe"—links with the whole nature of the conspiracy in which one Indian is replaceable by another for successive generations. Further, the central narrative of the book is sandwiched between descriptions of large sweeps of time as they appear from India, beginning with the chronicle which traces the history of the diamond through the centuries up to the Colonel's acquisition of it at Seringapatam, and ending with Murthwaite's view into the future:

> So the years pass, and repeat each other; so the same events revolve in the cycles of time. What will be the next adventure of the Moonstone? Who can tell!

The historical emphasis, particularly in Murthwaite's description, is upon the non-uniqueness of the individual, upon sameness and repetition—"the same events revolve in the cycles of time"—overshadowing the somewhat fussy concern with dates and individual happenings which recur so frequently in the novel. (pp. 212-16)

The Moonstone with its traditional moonlike qualities of uniting permanence with change, and objectivity with subjectivity, should be the resolution of Blake's dichotomies: in fact, the diamond mandala which is a symbol of total unity. It is described by Betteredge as an absolute microcosm: "It seemed unfathomable; this jewel, that you could hold between your finger and thumb, seemed unfathomable as the heavens themselves," but it does have a literal flaw, which serves to split its objective value away from its subjective meaning. To the Indians, it has subjective meaning only while it remains intact, while to Godfrey Ablewhite it would become more objectively valuable if it were cut into a number of perfect stones. On an even more objective level, Mr Candy offers to destroy the stone altogether, by evaporating it in the interests of science.

The vision of enclosed totality which the Moonstone offers to Gabriel Betteredge finds its opposite in the opium nightmare of Ezra Jennings:

> Rose late, after a dreadful night; the vengeance of yesterday's opium, pursuing me through a series of frightful dreams. At one time, I was whirling through empty space with the phantoms of the dead, friends and enemies together. At another, the one beloved face which I shall never see again, rose at my bedside, hideously phosphorescent in the black darkness and glared and grinned at me.

The "hideously phosphorescent face" is undoubtedly a parodic development of the diamond's "taking to shining of itself . . . in the dead of night," but the whole description is of unenclosed chaos, a jumble of contraries, "friends and enemies together." It is precisely because Jennings is forced to look on contraries, is himself, with his piebald appearance, a living expression of contrariety, that he is able to explain, if not reconcile, contradictions, while others, who fail to do so, cling to singleness of vision, whether it be faith in circumstances (Cuff) or faith in character (Betteredge).

Jennings is able to demonstrate that contraries are not merely an extension of the character/circumstance dichotomy; demonstrating with the aid of medical work, that a man may have two separate characters with appropriate sets of actions. The case which is cited is of an Irish porter, who had one character when drunk, and an entirely separate one when sober: this same Philip drunk/Philip sober contrast, parodied in the behaviour of the Indians' spy, is later to confuse Gooseberry at The Wheel of Fortune. For Jennings, the human mind takes

An enraged Betteredge objecting to Sergeant Cuff's suspicions concerning Rachel.

on the microcosmic quality which Betteredge attributes to the Moonstone; he quotes another medical authority:

> There seems much ground for the belief, that *every* sensory impression which has once been recognised by the perceptive consciousness, is registered (so to speak) in the brain, and may be reproduced at some subsequent time, although there may be no consciousness of its existence in the mind during the whole intermediate period.

Apart from its mystic significance, the Moonstone has, of course, the functional role of linking the mundane world of Yorkshire, with the romantic world of India:

> here was our quiet English house suddenly invaded by a devilish Indian diamond—bringing with it a conspiracy of living rogues, set loose on us by the vengeance of a dead man. There was our situation, as revealed to me in Mr Franklin's last words! Who ever heard the like of it—in the nineteenth century, mind; in an age of progress, and in a country which rejoices in the blessings of the British constitution

says Betteredge, and later Rachel and Godfrey's bouncing sisters get a thrill from the same strange connections; at the birthday dinner, Mr. Murthwaite comments:

> 'If you ever go to India, Miss Verinder, don't take your uncle's birthday gift with you. A Hindoo diamond is sometimes part of a Hindoo religion. I know a certain city, and a certain temple in that city, where, dressed as you are now, your life would not be worth five minutes' purchase.' Miss Rachel, safe in England, was quite delighted to hear of her danger in India. The Bouncers were more delighted still; they dropped their knives and forks with a crash, and burst out together vehemently. 'O! how interesting!'
>
> (pp. 217-18)

One of the things which *The Moonstone* is quite explicit about is the process of its own writing. Most of the first chapter, and a fair proportion of the next two of Betteredge's narrative are taken up with his response to the invitation to contribute and his difficulties in doing so. There are few periods in the novel, in fact, when the Moonstone narrative is allowed undisputed dominance, even though Chapter 6 of Miss Clack's Narrative (her correspondence with Blake upon her desire to include comments upon Lady Verinder's death in the form of "copious Extracts from precious publications" is the only other authorial intrusion of comparable length. Betteredge describes the process of the novel's writing as one of witnessing, rather than reporting:

> In this matter of the Moonstone the plan is, not to present reports, but to produce witnesses. I picture to myself a member of the family reading these pages fifty years hence. Lord! what a compliment he will feel it, to be asked to take nothing on hearsay, and to be treated in all respects like a Judge on a bench.

Betteredge's ideas on the form and function of the novel are, however, as open to question as anything else he says, and the comparison of the reader with "a Judge on a bench," in a novel in which the inability of the law to cope with the subjective and the imaginative is amply demonstrated, cannot be accepted unironically. The phrase "a member of the family" is the clue to Betteredge's position, picking up as it does the intention of the opening document on the storming of Seringapatam. From a purely legal point of view, there is no opportunity for final judgement, since the guilt of Godfrey Ablewhite is demonstrated absolutely: the only function of the papers collected by Franklin Blake could possibly be that of family reconciliation. Betteredge's version of objectivity has, in fact, a totally subjective ring about it.

A more obvious function of the divided narrative might seem to be that of extending the suspense of the plot by giving incomplete information; quite obviously, for instance, there is little in Betteredge's opening to implicate Godfrey Ablewhite in the theft of the diamond, while, indeed, there are things which might lead a reader to have doubts about Franklin Blake. While Betteredge's theories on the form of the novel are not inconsistent with this function, it is difficult to reconcile it with the continuing authorial intrusiveness, since absorption in the plot would seem to work more efficiently towards the maintenance of suspense; again, the shift in narrative viewpoint ultimately limits the field of suspicion: one can hardly suspect

Franklin Blake after sharing (rather than witnessing) his amazement at the discovery of the nightshirt, the most damaging piece of evidence against him.

The most crucial effect of the form of the novel is to establish the centrality of the subjective in human consciousness. For all the claims to strict objectivity, it is clear that the narrators stay within not only a limited range of experience, but also a limited range of assumptions. While Betteredge sets out "to keep strictly within the limits of my own experience, and . . . not to inform you of what other persons told me," his narrative is structured by absolute subjective assumptions, notably his faith in the incorruptible goodness of Rachel and Lady Verinder. Apart from clashes of narrative viewpoint, the plot itself offers continuing confrontations between totally enclosed sets of assumptions. The conflicting judgements of Cuff and the family in the First Narrative, the clash between Franklin Blake and Rachel in the fourth, and that between Jennings and Bruff and Betteredge in the fifth all parallel what is probably the most effective confrontation of all, that over the assumptions which lie behind the responses to Lady Verinder's death. Miss Clack's totally subjective view that Lady Verinder is damned because she did not die a Christian death collides head on with Rachel's subjective/objective view that a good life on earth assumes a good death and a sure passage to heaven:

> Oh, think of my poor mother's harmless, useful, beautiful life! . . . And that wretch stands there, and tries to make me doubt that my mother, who was an angel on earth is an angel in heaven now!

What is established above all is, to use a phrase from Scott Fitzgerald, the unreality of reality: a process in which the mundane Gabriel Betteredge becomes subjective, while the spiritual Miss Clack becomes mundane.

The assumptions of Gabriel Betteredge are crystallized in his faith in *Robinson Crusoe*. As Marshall points out [see excerpt dated 1970], *Robinson Crusoe* replaces the Bible for Betteredge as a source of truth and prophecy. The choice of a novel by Defoe may be seen simply as an expression of the naïve realism which Betteredge would claim as the key to his viewpoint: certainly, as the converse of this, as Betteredge's faith takes a beating, *Robinson Crusoe* seems to him less objective, and the two major references in the early part of the second half of *The Moonstone* are to "I stood like one Thunderstruck, or as if I had seen an Apparition" and to the "Secret Dictate." (pp. 220-22)

The challenge brought by the Moonstone to the isolation of the house and family in Yorkshire brings with it a doubting of the power of *Robinson Crusoe:*

> This was the first trouble I remember for many a long year which wasn't to be blown off by a whiff of tobacco; and which was even beyond the reach of *Robinson Crusoe*.

When the crisis comes, and Cuff actually accuses Rachel, Betteredge has chiefly a full desire to restore Defoe's fictional isolation:

> *Robinson Crusoe*—God knows how—has got into my muddled old head. If Sergeant Cuff had found himself, at that moment, transported to a desert island, without a man Friday to keep him company, or a ship to take him off—he

would have found himself exactly where I wished him to be!

(p. 222)

Apart from his own dabblings in literature, Betteredge's theories about the place of art in polite society are interesting, for he sees it primarily as an alternative to a more dangerous dabbling in the unknown. Science is a confrontation with mortality: not on the fully realized level of Franklin Blake's experience in Jennings's surgery, perhaps, but certainly involving a "cruel nastiness" which is out of place in a well-ordered household:

> I have seen them (ladies, I am sorry to say, as well as gentlemen) go out, day after day, for example, with empty pill-boxes, and catch newts and beetles, and spiders, and frogs, and come home and stick pins through the miserable wretches, or cut them up, without a pang of remorse, into little pieces. You see my young master, or my young mistress, poring over one of their spiders' insides with a magnifying-glass; or you meet one of their frogs walking downstairs without his head. . . .

Art has its own, lesser, nastiness: the "vehicle" with which Franklin and Rachel decorate a bedroom door "stank," and made Penelope sick. The door is decorated with "griffins, birds, flowers, cupids and such like," but the whole decoration appears primarily as a fairly grotesque parody of the whole appearance/character dichotomy, through a linking of imagery; Franklin's first act is to scrape off "all the nice varnish with pumice-stone," which parallels the repeated reference to Franklin's own "foreign varnish," which masks his real self, an image which is later used by Miss Clack about the imperturbable features of Bruff ("the smooth varnish on *his* wicked old face never cracked"). Blake, in fact, scrapes off the varnish, only to replace it with a decoration which partakes of the same falsely assumed separateness of the decorative world from actuality which leads Cuff to separate roses from thieves, since, according to Betteredge, the style is that of the "famous Italian painter . . . who stocked the world with Virgin Maries, and had a sweetheart at the baker's." This art work, in fact, very rapidly belongs to the world of objectivity, since it is smudged, and so gains the flaw which seems to offer the vital clue to the Moonstone's disappearance; the mirror image of this, on the other hand, is the Indian art work which traps Godfrey Ablewhite and Septimus Luker, which is totally impenetrable, incomprehensible and fascinating surface reality.

If Franklin Blake's door decoration is a false version of a movement below surface reality, the clearest genuine version of the duplicity of surface appearance is offered by the Shivering Sands: as with the varnish on the door, the terms of the description of the Sands have a grotesque development, linking their "false brown face" with the inscrutable dark faces of the Indians (and Godfrey Ablewhite's disguise). The Sands come to represent for Franklin a frontier between the mundane living world, and a kind of anti-world of living death, just as Rosanna Spearman, whose body lies below their surface, is quite clearly an antithesis to Rachel: indeed, since he expects to find the proof of Rosanna's guilt beneath the Sands, thereby clearing Rachel of all suspicion, his confrontation with the anti-world is an attempt to vindicate Cuff's sort of separation of the worlds of thieves and roses. The attempt to separate fails, of course, since he finds himself (or at least his own nightshirt) beneath the surface; the Sands become, in fact, a more terrible version

of the Moonstone, for like the stone, they have "unfathomable depths," and like the stone, they have "awful associations" with a non-material terror which Blake is forced to recognize:

> I saw the preliminary heaving of the Sand, and then the awful shiver that crept over its surface—as if some spirit of terror lived and moved and shuddered in the fathomless depths beneath.

(pp. 223-24)

The "false brown face" of the quicksand quite literally hides an identity: that of the one who took the Moonstone. However, while undoubtedly Blake has a moment of equally literal self-revelation, it is hardly a moment of self-knowledge, and the resolution of the English part of the novel takes on the aspect of a comic, at times, indeed, ritualistic, "expiation" of the inner terrors which have been revealed. Ezra Jennings, for instance, the man who refuses to be anyone other than himself (and will not live under a false name, even though he has lost his character), has, for all this, a horrifying exterior to show to the world: there is a ritual testing of the response to Jennings's surface appearance as the witnesses arrive at the house in Yorkshire. All but Rachel fail, in some degree, to see beyond the one hopeful version of a "false" brown face.

Quite apart from the actual repetition of Rachel's birthday dinner, which finally vindicates Blake, full expiation comes in the discovery of the true identity of the thief, which is hidden beneath the brown face of Godfrey's disguise. . . . The discovery of a nightshirt on the seashore is expiated by the discovery of a sailor in a bedroom, and the reading of the letter and discovery of the name point up the parallel closely; the wheel has gone full circle, and Godfrey dies in a hotel called "The Wheel of Fortune."

The Wheel is, of course, not only a working out of contraries as fortune decides, but also an enclosed cycle, returning the whole process to the place where it began. For most of the characters who survive, the novel ends where it began, at the house in Yorkshire with the establishment of a new generation of Verinder-Blakes and a restoration of Betteredge's faith in the prophetic efficiency of *Robinson Crusoe*. Only Murthwaite breaks away by an act of will, and closes the novel with a more chilling version of the Wheel, a version in which sameness dominates individual distinction:

> So the years pass, and repeat each other; so the same events revolve in the cycles of time. What will be the next adventures of the Moonstone? Who can tell!

(pp. 225-26)

> *R. P. Laidlaw, "'Awful Images and Associations': A Study of Wilkie Collins's 'The Moonstone'," in* Southern Review, Australia, *Vol. IX, No. 3, 1976, pp. 211-27.*

JOHN G. CAWELTI (essay date 1976)

[*Cawelti discusses* The Moonstone *in relation to the classical detective story of the twentieth century.*]

[With regard to] the boundaries of the classical detective formula, I would like to call attention to a fairly complex novel which, though it develops a great variety of other elements, remains essentially within the limits of the detective story. The work I have in mind is Wilkie Collins's **The Moonstone,** which was historically a precursor of the great body of detective fiction, and yet, like Poe's stories, is properly judged as one of the major creations of the classical genre. *The Moonstone* has many elaborate complications and a scale of time and space much larger than the majority of the works that have succeeded it. It has a variety of narrators and a number of inquiring protagonists who play the role of detective at various phases of the inquiry. In addition, the hidden secret that is finally uncovered at the end does concern the guilt or innocence of the most important of the inquiring protagonists. These characteristics indicate the degree to which *The Moonstone* is at some point on the line of development between the nineteenth-century novel of sensation and the twentieth-century classical detective story. Despite all its complications, however, the central narrative line of Collins's novel is the inquiry into the missing moonstone and correlatively into the guilt or innocence of Franklin Blake. As in the classical detective genre, the novel moves from detection to mystification with one reversal piled upon another until the solution is finally reached. Though that final revelation does concern the fate of the inquiring protagonist, the fact that he is a basically sympathetic, romantic character whose innocence is finally established makes a very important structural difference. I would argue that the romantic conventions of true love triumphant and the way in which we are associated through narrative method with the fate of Franklin Blake reassure us that somehow the circumstantial evidence against him will be disproved. With this reassurance we are able to concentrate on the pleasures of detection and mystification without having to spend emotional energy preparing ourselves for a possible catastrophe to a character about whose situation we have increasingly come to care. In addition, *The Moonstone* presents a professional detective—one of the first in literature—as a central figure. Though Sergeant Cuff is not exactly a protagonist in the fashion of the fully developed classical formula, and though he initially arrives at an incorrect solution to the crime, his presence suggests the extent to which Collins foresaw the fascination of the detective-mystification structure. In sum, I would say that the difference between *The Moonstone* and the classical detective is not so much a matter of kind as of degree. A little more emphasis on Sergeant Cuff and a more external treatment of a complex romantic relation between Franklin Blake and Rachel Verinder, and *The Moonstone* would be indistinguishable in structure from a work by Agatha Christie or Dorothy Sayers. Because of its affinity to the emphasis on detection and mystification in the classical detective genre, it is not surprising that it is considered by some to be one of the most perfectly plotted works in English literature. . . . (pp. 134-35)

> *John G. Cawelti, "The Art of the Classical Detective Story," in his* Adventure, Mystery, and Romance: Formula Stories as Art and Popular Culture, *The University of Chicago Press, 1976, pp. 106-38.*

D. A. MILLER (essay date 1980)

[*Miller argues that Collins modified the traditional pattern of the detective story by dismissing Sergeant Cuff early in the novel and allowing the community as a whole to solve the mystery. Miller also draws an analogy between the language of the novel and the idea that the power of surveillance resides in the community: "just as common detection transcends the single efforts of various detective figures, a common narration subsumes the individual reports of various narrators." Miller's essay has been printed in revised form in his* The Novel and the Police, *published in 1988.*]

The classical detective story disposes of an interestingly paradoxical economy, at once parsimonious and squandering. On one hand, the form is based on the hypothesis that *everything might count*: every character might be the culprit, and every action or speech might be belying its apparent banality or literalism by making surreptitious reference to an incriminating Truth. From the layout of the country house (frequently given in all the exactitude of a diagram) to the cigar ash found on the floor at the scene of the crime, no detail can be dismissed *a priori*. Yet if the criterion of total relevance is continually invoked by the text, it turns out to have a highly restricted applicability in the end. At the moment of truth, the text winnows grain from chaff, separating the relevant signifiers from the much larger number of irrelevant ones, which are now revealed to be as banal and trivial as we originally suspected they might *not* be. . . . It is hardly an accident that most readers of detective fiction can afterwards remember "whodunit?" but have totally forgotten the false clues and suspects that temporarily obscured his identity. For the detective's final summation offers not a maximal integration of parts into whole, but a minimal one: what is totalized is just—and no more than—what is needed to solve the crime. Everything and everybody else is returned to a blandly mute positivity.

This observation, of course, is meant to shift the emphasis from where it normally falls in discussions of the detective story: away from the mystery that it solves towards a recognition of the hypothetical significances that it finally dissolves. Though the detective story postulates a world in which everything might have a meaningful bearing on the solution of the crime, it concludes with an extensive repudiation of meanings that simply "drop out." It is often argued that the detective story seeks to totalize its signifiers in a complete and all-encompassing order. On the contrary, it is concerned to restrict and localize the province of meaning: to guarantee large areas of irrelevance. One easily sees, moreover, what else is guaranteed in such a form. For as the fantasy of total relevance yields to the reality of a more selective meaningfulness, the universality of suspicion gives way to a highly specific guilt. Engaged in producing a social innocence, the detective story might well take for its motto "The truth shall set you free."

One might take a step further: the detective story is invariably the story of a power-play. The quasi-universal suspicion is only another way of putting a quasi-total investigation. When the sheer fact of meaningfulness incriminates and has a policing force, the limits of the detective's knowledge become the limits of his power as well: his astonishing explications double for a control exercised in the interests of law and order. Detective fiction is thus always implicitly punning on the detective's brilliant "super-vision" and the police *supervision* that it embodies. (pp. 153-54)

Typically, the detective's super-vision is dramatized by being exercised on what would seem to resist it most: the ordinary, "trivial" facts of everyday life. During the police investigation in *The Moonstone,* for example, a smear is noticed on Rachel Verinder's newly varnished door. Superintendent Seegrave, an impressive-looking but incompetent local, dismisses the detail as a "trifle." Expert Sergeant Cuff, however, knows better: "'In all my experience along the dirtiest ways of this dirty little world, I have never met with such a thing as a trifle yet.'" He goes on to discover that the varnish dries after twelve hours; that it was applied at 3 p.m.; that it was still intact at midnight. Therefore, he concludes, the theft of the Moonstone was committed between midnight and 3 a.m. by someone whose dress—possibly a nightgown—is stained with varnish. The whole sequence makes a neat parable of the detective's work: to turn trifles into "telling" details, telling—what else?—a story of dirty linen.

Yet, as we know, the investigation from which nothing seems safe is also subject to clear and strict limits, and so ultimately reassures the community that it initially frightens. In the first place, it restricts its scope to a socially approved enterprise: the identification and apprehension of a criminal who is by definition the "other"; and it lasts no longer than the criminal goes uncaught. In the second place, it is characterized as a dramatic instance of intervention and, as such, it is marked with a high degree of visibility. In this sense, the detective's extraordinary power of vision can be seen in turn by the community he appears to investigate. And just as the community invariably perceives the detective's personality as "eccentric," it views the sheer disruptiveness of his investigation (think of the hysterical housemaids in *The Moonstone*) as an anomaly, a dramatic exception to a routine social order in which police and surveillance play no part. Thus seen, the investigation is fixed in place: outside a social normativeness, which it finally leaves untouched, free to be itself once more.

The final localization of culpability might thus be thought of as a single tactic in the wider and more important strategy of *localizing the investigation*: limiting its scope (the apprehension of a single criminal), limiting its agency (a single eccentric detective), and foregrounding its interventionary character (exceptional, out-of-the-ordinary). I said a moment ago that the detective story worked to produce a social innocence—an innocence that we can now formulate as substantially more than a mere freedom from guilt. For if the community is not finally the object of detection, neither is it the *subject* of detection: innocent of crime, it is—*a fortiori*—innocent of criminology too. Its most radical innocence, then, derives from its sheer ignorance of power, its incapacity to assume a machinery of surveillance, control, and punishment. The crime and the failure to solve it both testify to the community's naive state of vulnerability. Taken charge of by an eccentric outsider, the investigation preserves such naivete at the same time as it neutralizes the vulnerability attending it. If one were to speak of an ideology produced by the form of the detective story, here would be one of its major sites: in the perception of everyday life as fundamentally "outside" the network of policing power.

It is not difficult to recognize that *The Moonstone* begins by invoking and observing the norms of detective fiction. Rachel Verinder's Indian diamond is mysteriously stolen, and her mother, Lady Julia, has "no alternative but to send for the police." The police investigation quickly proves to require "a cleverer head than Superintendent Seegrave's," and the brilliant Sergeant Cuff—of whom " 'when it comes to unravelling a mystery, there isn't the equal in England' "—is called in to take charge. Cuff's powers of penetration are anticipated in the description of his gaze: "His eyes, of a steely light grey, had a very disconcerting trick, when they encountered your eyes, of looking as if they expected something more from you than you were aware of yourself." And such promise is soon made good in the impressive piece of reasoning about the varnish-smear. In short order, the text organizes itself as a movement from mystery to solution supervised by an extraordinary police detective. It comes somewhat as a puzzle, then, when the text abandons the scenario it has so conscientiously set up. Cuff's investigation is broken off, suspended, and even its provisional conclusions are revealed to be erroneous. The detective disappears from what remains a novel of detection, and although he reappears to clear up some incidental matters at the end, the mystery is solved *without his doing*. With Cuff's failure and departure, *The Moonstone* stages a conspicuous modification of what had seemed to be its program.

We can begin to elaborate what is at stake in this modification by looking at what motivates it in the novel. For Cuff's failure and departure are precisely what the novelistic community *has wished for*. In the First Period of the novel, his sheer presence is a disgrace, and he bears the burden of a general dislike.... Part of what [the] characters are responding to is the obvious affront of police intervention. Cuff is considered largely responsible for the fact that, as Betteredge's daughter puts it, "nothing is like what it used to be." The natural order of the Verinder estate is brutally democratized, in the sense that all members of its hierarchy stand equal before Cuff's inquiry and suspicion. In his search for the stained garment, he intends " 'to examine the wardrobes of *everybody*—from her ladyship downwards,' " and he is capable of advancing an hypothesis that links in guilt a maidservant who is a former convict and a young lady who is the mistress's daughter. His, indeed, is "an abominable justice that favoured nobody."

Cuff's investigation threatens the community in even more radical ways as well. Systematically, his "roundabout" and "underground" practices undertake to violate the common decencies and genteel forebearances on which daily social life is based. He trails Rosanna Spearman "privately" on her walk; he eavesdrops on Betteredge and Blake on a couple of occasions; and he sets a spy on the rumble of Rachel's carriage. Ordinary actions and encounters are no longer protected by the socially given obviousness that precludes scrutiny, or by the socially accepted conventions that prohibit it. The First Period of the novel is dominated by the community's shocked sense of violation. It has been invaded by an outsider, who not only watches what is not supposed to be watched, but also construes what he sees according to other rules than those by which this community is used to regulating itself.

It is just this "heteronomous" reconstruction of its world that the community resists. Practically, resistance takes the form of a reluctance and even refusal to collaborate with Cuff.... Cuff's interventions always strike the community as being unfair, and it is easy to see why. The very "manners" whose traditional, taken-for-granted authority has maintained the self-identity of the community are now exploited to produce an alienated knowledge that rives it apart. Not the least of Cuff's sins in this perspective is that he is a liar, one who abuses the conventional stability of language and contexts of communication in order to mislead and deceive. (pp. 154-57)

If Cuff's methods are troubling, their findings are untenable. Superintendent Seegrave has already implied a willingness to suspect Betteredge's own daughter, and Cuff proves even more perverse in suspecting Rachel Verinder herself. " 'I don't suspect,' " claims Cuff, moreover, " 'I know.' " Unable rationally to extricate Rachel from Cuff's impressively taut weave of evidence, the community relies most simply on a strategy of disavowal. (p. 157)

Now, before all else, Cuff's intervention is a sign that the community has failed to know itself. And if the results of his inquiry were verified, that failure of self-knowledge would become definitive. As it happens, however, Cuff is positively wrong. The diamond has been stolen not by Rachel or Rosanna (whose suspicious behavior is only intended to screen Franklin Blake, the man they love and think has stolen it), but by Godfrey Ablewhite, who needs ready cash to pay off his debts. By producing a solution that contradicts Cuff's conclusions but is consonant with the community's intuitions, the text blatantly endorses the latter. At a moment in Cuff's investigation, he scolds Betteredge for doing some detection on his own: " 'For the future, perhaps you will be so obliging as to do your detective business along with me.' " In fact, in a striking reversal of the pattern of detective fiction, it is rather the blinded Cuff who ought to have done his "detective business" along with the community. And the main effect of Cuff's departure is to turn over the work of detection to prominent members of this community, like Matthew Bruff, its lawyer, and Franklin Blake, its *jeune premier.*

In a way, such a shift is bound to remind us of the typical displacements of detective fiction, where the function of detection passes either from a local to a national agent (from Seegrave to Cuff in the First Period of *The Moonstone*), from a police to a private detective (from Scotland Yard to Sherlock Holmes in "The Naval Treaty"), or from a professional to an amateur (from Inspector G_____ to Dupin in the Poe stories). Taken as a whole, *The Moonstone* obviously exemplifies the third type of displacement. Yet too many "amateurs" are involved here for the term to be wholly adequate. It is not just Betteredge who contracts "the detective fever." Nor is it merely the obvious detective figures (Blake, Bruff, Ezra Jennings) who together with their helpers (Murthwaite, Gooseberry) prosecute the case to a successful conclusion. Necessary information is provided by Rachel (who confesses that she saw Blake take the diamond), Mr. Candy (whose partially recovered memory helps bring his drugging of Blake to light), Limping Lucy (who delivers Rosanna's letter), and even Rosanna herself (whose letter puts Blake in possession of the missing nightgown). That none of these characters *intends* to assist the work of detection is irrelevant to the fact of their practical collaboration, without which the mystery would never be solved. In effect, the work of detection is carried forward by the novel's entire cast of characters, shifted not just from professional to amateur, but from an outsider to a whole community. Thus, the move to discredit and finally dismiss the *role of the detective* is at the same time a move to diffuse and disperse the *function of detection.*

It might of course be thought that the community simply represents an alternative agency of detection, just as unified and localizable as that embodied in Sergeant Cuff. At its most radical, however, the dissemination of the detective-function precludes the very possibility of identifying the agency in charge of it. For not only does the work of detection fail to correspond to any one character's design, it never even corresponds to an implicitly "collective" intentionality. What integrates and consolidates the efforts of characters is a master-plan that no one governs or even anticipates. The community serves such a master-plan but is not its master. Significantly, the work of detection is prosecuted in large degree as a result of chance and coincidence. It would have been impossible to calculate on Mr. Candy's recovery from amnesia, or on an Ezra Jennings turning up in the right place at the right time. Such happy chances, moreover, are produced only in the course of time, which is also invested with the detective-function. . . . What needs to come out somehow does, and the work of detection advances, an intentionality without a subject, a design that no one is allowed to assume responsibility for forming.

Confronted with this phenomenon, critics like Ian Ousby [see excerpt dated 1976 in *NCLC*, Vol. 1] have been tempted to invoke the familiar notion of Providence, which would enable us to ascribe the work of detection to an agency in control of it. Yet one should beware of using the notion of Providence to neutralize the ways in which the "providential" is characterized in the novel. Contrary to Collins's practice, say, in *Armadale,* the "providential" here is divested of any explicit religious dimension. We are meant to respond with a very worldly smile when Betteredge speaks, like a good Protestant, of the Devil, and only in hypocrites like Miss Clack or Ablewhite do we find the traditional pious belief in divine will. Moreover, if such a will is at work in the novel, it functions only through the established logic of a thoroughly ordinary world. The providential effect of detection in *The Moonstone* does not depend on its proximate causes. These are individual psychologies, social institutions and scenarios, even ontological laws that operate in overwhelmingly conventional ways. Rather, it depends on the fact that detection, working exclusively through its agents' intentions, uncannily but benignly transcends them. Discreet and, in the last analysis, agentless, the detective-function is able to organize the text without raising the moral problems posed by Cuff's interventionary police enquiry.

It is this "discreet" detection, blandly and automatically attaching to the way things are, that our reading needs to foreground. We might begin by noticing that Cuff's morally unacceptable investigation has its pre-condition in a prior investigation. In his clever deduction regarding the door-smear, all Cuff really does is assemble and co-ordinate the information gathered and given to him by members of the community. . . . Natural curiosity and common gossip double for an informal system of surveillance that is in force on the estate well before the Moonstone is stolen.

In a more diffuse way, the system is implied in the very "knowledge" characters have of one another. Everyone's behavior in this world is being continuously encoded according to shared norms of psychological and moral verisimilitude. Invariably, the points at which behavior seems insufficiently "motivated" by these norms are points of *suspicion.* (pp. 158-61)

In effect, then, a policing power is inscribed in the ordinary practices and institutions of the world from the start. The full extent of this inscription can already be measured in the Prologue, where a cousin writing to relatives in England accuses Colonel John Herncastle of stealing the Moonstone from its Indian shrine. "I declare, on my word of honour, that what I am now about to write is, strictly and literally, the truth." Beginning like a legal deposition, the cousin's manuscript proceeds to marshal the "moral evidence" for his accusation, and concludes by submitting the case to the family's judgment. And the family network that detects and judges crime is also empowered to enforce its own sentence. . . . The quasi-legal status of the Prologue extends to the entire novel, as a "record in writing" containing "the attestations of witnesses who can speak to the facts.". . . In the most active sense of the term, the community is concerned to "justify" itself—*to make its own justice.* If this community can afford to dispense with the legal systems of surveillance, trial, and punishment, this is because its own organization anticipates and contains them.

With one crucial difference: its policing apparatus is inscribed not just "in" but "as" the ordinary practices of the world. Everyday roles, motivations, scenarios *naturalize* this apparatus effortlessly. Herncastle's cousin swears not in the name of God, as he would in a court of law, but on his honor, as he would in ordinary intercourse among ladies and gentlemen.

The institution of justice to which he appeals is also, on its most visible face, the institution of the Family. Herncastle is not so much "punished" as he is "snubbed"—the natural response of gentility to someone with a bad character. Penelope's spying is perceived as "the natural curiosity of women," a young girl's innocent interest in the love-relationships of her mistress and her fellow-servants. She doesn't, moreover, go tattle to the head servant; she quite properly confides in her father. As for the washing-book, its function is presumably to make sure the nothing is lost. Even many of the deposition-like narratives that record the story are no more than everyday forms of writing (letters, journals, diaries), or are at least derived from them.

In a similar pattern, detective figures such as Blake, Bruff and Jennings have no intrinsic interest in detection at all. Blake needs to clear up the mystery in order to gain Rachel's hand. A close family friend, Bruff is naturally concerned to protect the fatherless and soon altogether orphaned Rachel from adventurers, as well as to promote an obvious love-match between her and Blake. And Jennings gets involved because he feels sorry for Blake, whom he sees as a double of himself. (pp. 162-63)

In general, the effects of a police apparatus are secured as side-effects of their motivation *in another register*. They surface as incidental consequences of actions and institutions that have other, more obvious and "natural" explanations for their being. Thus, without having to serve police functions in an *ex officio* way, gossip and domestic familiarity produce the effect of surveillance; letters and diaries, the effect of "dossiers"; closed clubs and homes, the effect of punishment. The intention to detect is visible only at a "microscopic" level, casually implied in self-evident moral imperatives (to love, to take care of, to feel sorry for), or at a "macroscopic" level, inscribed in the fullness of time and in the moral-ontological law that compels guilt to confess itself. In either case, a direct assumption of policing power by the community is avoided. In a way, then, ***The Moonstone*** displaces the structures of detective fiction only to restage its ideology of everyday life in more ambitious ways. The detective story, I claimed, put policing power at the margins of everyday life, from which it made an occasional, anomalous incursion. More radically, ***The Moonstone*** dismisses the police altogether, and the mysterious crime is worked to a solution by a power that no one has charge of. The equivocal role of the "providential"—immanent in the social world yet distinct from its intentionalities—is thus part of a strategy whose ideological implications should be plain. The exercise of policing power inheres in the logic of the world, but only as a discreet "accident" of normative social practices and models of conduct. The community does not mobilize in a concerted scheme of police action, and yet things turn out as though it did. ***The Moonstone*** satisfies a double exigency: how to keep the everyday world entirely outside a network of police power and at the same time preserve the effects of such power within it. Indeed, the novel *increases* this power in the very act of arranging for it to "disappear," absorbed into (as) the sheer positivity of being in the world. It cannot be decried as an intervention because it is already everywhere. It cannot be resisted for long since it exerts the permanent pressure of "reality" itself. Finally, it cannot even be seen, for it is a power that never passes as such: therein lies its power.

Students of detective fiction commonly grow wistful when discussing its ancestors in the nineteenth-century novel. Such novels, it is usually lamented, approach the "classical" detective story, but stop disappointingly short of realizing its program fully and point by point. Yet if these novels are not detective stories, it is, as we say, because they do not wish to be. In the case of ***The Moonstone***, this is a quite literal truth. The text, we have seen, invokes the norms of detective fiction precisely to rework and pass beyond them. It moves from a story of police action to a story of human relationships in less "specialized" social contexts. Simultaneously, the move is a shift in genre: away from the detective novel to what can only be called the "novel" *tout court*. In superseding detective fiction, the text might thus be taken to elaborate a certain "genealogy of the Novel." The Novel, as it were, would be the form that results when the detective story is exploded and diffused. The genealogy, of course, is not a genesis. It would be absurd to claim that the novel emerged historically from the literature of crime and detection. Although examples of detective fiction were certainly available in the nineteenth century (Collins, for instance, knew the work of both Poe and Gaboriau), the genre did not really come into its own until the turn of the century and after, with Doyle, Christie, Leroux, et al. Generic labels here are simply a convenient way to foreground a double pattern of revision that the Novel typically enacts: the circumscription of professional offices of detection and punishment, and the reinscription of their functions in everyday life.

Traces of this pattern may be found throughout nineteenth-century fiction, where a police apparatus, legally charged with the detection of crime and the punishment of criminals, frequently stands on the periphery of the representation. Quarantined at the margins of the world, its status too seems "marginal," its pertinence limited. At the same time as a legal police apparatus is thus restricted, however, its powers are extended by attaching to other, extrajudicial and fully ordinary agencies. Dickens's *Great Expectations* and *Bleak House* rewrite the concerns of a police apparatus into the logic of an individual psychology or a whole society. Similarly, the professional detective work in Balzac's *Père Goriot* merely presents in miniature the general social expertise that Rastignac needs to master.... In George Eliot's *Middlemarch,* the public unmasking of Bulstrode's murderous attentions to Raffles represents a clear-cut police action on the part of the community; like the outlaw in a western, the banker is virtually ridden out of town.... Typically, then, the nineteenth-century novel "domesticates" a police apparatus—at a legal level, held in check on the periphery of the representation; at an extrajudicial level, diffused throughout it.

If such a pattern is not explained by literary history, it may make sense in a history of another kind. I have in mind Michel Foucault's "history" of the new modalities of surveillance and punishment that begin to permeate Western societies around the end of the eighteenth century [*Surveiller et punir*]. In place of the corporeal and spectacular forms of *punishment* that had previously been dominant, the nineteenth century substitutes an intangible and secluded *discipline*. (pp. 163-66)

Unlike the prison, which, despite its reformist pretensions, inescapably refers to a legal scenario of crime and punishment, everyday forms of discipline regulate areas of social life that have no felt connection with the law or the police. They operate on the surfaces of ordinary social practice from which the very idea of the police seems far removed. Paradoxically, their policing power is manifest only by remaining latent: carried in agencies that enjoy the alibi of nobler—or simply blander—intentionalities. In a sleight-of-hand that only increases its efficiency, disciplinary power shows up *where it can hardly be*.

Now the shift from a professional detective to lay detection in the story of *The Moonstone* is clearly a version of the move from punishment to discipline in Foucault's history of policing power. Indeed, we have claimed that the functions of a "disciplinary apparatus" are taken over by the world of the novel in an even more diffuse form than Foucault recognizes, carried in far more informal institutions than school or factory. Yet I shouldn't want to limit the relevance of Foucault's history by seeing discipline as simply the characteristic *content* of the nineteenth-century novel. For if the shift is a general one, then the texts we call nineteenth-century novels would not merely register it (as a feature of a referent in the real world), but relay it as well (within the literary institution of the Novel). According to Foucault, the disciplinary apparatus does not merely "reflect" certain arrangements of power, but *enacts* them in the formal details of its set-up. Similarly, although I have argued that *The Moonstone* tells a story of modern power analogous to Foucault's it would ultimately be more pertinent to show how this story is also the story of the novel's own telling. If Foucault is right , the text would do more than dramatize a certain ideology of power. It would produce this ideology as an effect—and in the mode—of its being read as a novel. Accordingly, our attention needs to turn from the "discipline" that is represented in the novel the "discipline" that inheres in the machinery of representation itself.

Unlike the majority of Victorian novels, *The Moonstone* is not related by an "omniscient narrator," whose unimpeachable authority imposes itself on the reader. Instead, the story is told in a succession of narratives written by some of the characters and organized through their limited points of view. The "modernity" of such a procedure is seductively apparent, as are the implications that a post-Jamesian criticism might wish to draw from it. Thus, *The Moonstone* is currently thought to offer "a narrative structure that is thoroughly subjective and unreliable" [see entry by Hutter in the Additional Bibliography] and "to provide a continually shifting viewpoint on the action, offering not merely different but sometimes contradictory views of the same event or character" (Ian Ousby). The text, it is implied in such claims, opens up the notion of truth to radically relativistic challenge—in a manner, say, of *Rashomon.* In Kurosawa's film (1950), one remembers, a crime is recounted four times, each time by a different protagonist. Not only are the accounts incompatible, but there is no compelling standard of plausibility by which the contradictions might be adjudicated. The "truth" is dissolved into four conflicting interpretations. Contrary to the example of *Rashomon,* however, the "unreliable" and "contradictory" narrative structure of *The Moonstone* works only as a ruse. To be sure, the text *claims* for itself all that Hutter and Ousby are ready to grant it. A reader is supposed to listen to the various witnesses, and to make up his mind about the validity of their reports as he will, "like a Judge on the bench." To all formal appearances, his reading is deprived of any grounding in an authoritative version. Yet the possibility of an authentic "dialogism" in the text disappears once we recognize that, in every crucial case, all readers (including Hutter and Ousby) pass *the same judgment.* The different points of view, degrees of information, tendencies of suspicion are never allowed to tamper with more basic interpretative securities about character and language. Characters may be *known* because they are always equipped with stable, centered identities; and they may be known *in language* because it is incapable of ever escaping from its own veridicity.

For all its apparent "subjectivity," for example, Betteredge's narrative can be counted on to give us a valid cognition of its "subject": the faithful retainer himself, whose very naivete is a guarantor of the truthfulness of his self-presentation. Moreover, to the degree that Betteredge's language unproblematically "names" him, we know exactly what weight to give to its cognitive claims about other matters in the novel. To suspect this language, as a reader of *The Murder of Roger Ackroyd* might well try to do, is to play a more strenuous interpretative game against the text than it is ever willing to reward: Betteredge's normative-seeming perceptions are normative in fact, fully borne out in the rest of the novel. . . . Whatever Betteredge doesn't know, he knows he doesn't know, and so do we. In this sense, the actual cognitive problems posed by his language are infrequent and strictly minor. Thus, when he introduces Godfrey Ablewhite . . . , it is unclear whether he means his language to be "straight" or sarcastic. The undecidability of what Betteredge means, however, never carries over into what his language actually says. The reader inevitably recognizes that, with or without Betteredge's knowledge, his text refuses to endorse Godfrey in any full way. That Betteredge's language is ambiguously motivated is irrelevant to a more fundamental readerly certainly about Godfrey's unique and suspicious hollowness.

The Moonstone, I am arguing, is more fundamentally about the securities of perception and language than about the problems they pose. To use Mikhail Bakhtin's term, the novel is thoroughly *monological*—always speaking a mastervoice that corrects, overrides, subordinates, or sublates all other voices it allows to speak. The basic monologism shows up best, in fact, precisely where it seems threatened most: in the narrative of Miss Clack. In obvious ways, Clack's perception differs radically from that of the rest of the community: she suspects Rachel, dislikes Franklin Blake, and adores Godfrey Ablewhite. Yet at least when it comes to representing the self-deceived spinster herself, Clack's language is incontestably truthful. At the start of her narrative, Blake appends a footnote telling us that

> 'the person chiefly concerned' in Miss Clack's narrative, is happy enough at the present moment, not only to brave the smartest exercise of Miss Clack's pen, but even to recognize its unquestionable value as an instrument for the exhibition of Miss Clack's character.

In addition to exculpating Rachel (who is, of course, "the person chiefly concerned"), the note invites us to read Clack's narrative against its grain—to locate its truth in the blinds of its narrator's *inconscience.* Even without the invitation, Clack's perceptions are so blatantly self-betraying that a reader inevitably revises them to mean something very different from what Clack imagines. (pp. 166-69)

There is a further point to be made. Not only is *The Moonstone* a monological text, but also its monologism quite literally *goes without saying.* Formally and linguistically, the master-discourse that organizes the text is unwritten: carried only through the subjective narratives that are unwittingly but regularly obliged to postulate it. Collins's technique is a way to inscribe the *effects* of monologism in the text without ascribing them to the *agency* of an actual monologist. As a result, monologism doesn't strictly seem *in* the text (like the shifters and first-personal pronouns that identify the narrator in George Eliot or Trollope); nor does it seem fully *outside* the text (like an interpretative choice that one may, or may not, impose on it). Rather, it is staged like an "invisible hand," programming the text without needing to be programmed into it. As such, of course, the monologism of the narration is exactly analogous to the work of detection in the representation. Just as a common detection transcends the single efforts of various detective-figures, a common narration subsumes the individual reports of various narrators. The world resolves its difficulties, and language finds its truth, according to the same principle of quasi-automatic self-regulation.

At both levels, *The Moonstone* promotes a single perception of power. In a consistent pattern, power in the novel is never gathered into an identifiable (and hence attackable) center. Neither is it radically "disseminated" so that the totality it claims to organize breaks down into discontinuities and incoherencies. Its paradoxical efficiency lies in the fact that an apparent lack of center at the level of *agency* secures a total mastery at the level of *effect*. What finally justifies us in calling the novel's perception of power "ideological" is that *The Moonstone* never really perceives power as such at all. The novel is itself blinded by the mystificatory strategy of power in the very act of tracing it. In practical terms, this means the novel must always "say" power as though it were saying *something else*. As I've tried to suggest, the "something else" is no less than the irresistible positivity of words and things "as they are." Just as detection surfaces only in the ordinary activities of amateurs, and monological narration only in subjective narratives, so too the discourse on power only comes to light in (as) a discourse on "the way things are." "Revealing" the character of modern power only insofar as it "masks" it as an ontology, *The Moonstone* is thus perfectly obedient to the imperatives of such power. Accordingly, the novel's discourse on power must finally be taken as a discourse *of* power—a discourse *spoken through* by a power that is simply extending its blinding strategy of displacement.

An argument might even be made that monologism forwards (is forwarded by) this "discourse of power" in novels that make use of an omniscient narrator as well. For the omniscient narrator (say, as he appears in George Eliot or Trollope) is typically presented as one who merely *tells* a story that is assumed to have happened already. The staging of the text as the narration of an autonomous story thus advances both the reality-effect of the story and the reality-effect of its self-regulation. Power, on this showing, is not felt to lie in the hands of the teller (who in general appears to regret the adventures he recounts). Instead, power is seen to coincide with the "reality" that is merely being re-presented: a reality whose authority may be lamented, but is never finally arguable. The "case" of *The Moonstone* raises the possibility of a wider investigation to be pursued under the hypothesis that traditional novels—whatever stories they may choose to tell—always repeat and reimpose the same story of power. (pp. 169-70)

> *D. A. Miller, "From 'Roman Policier' to 'Roman-Police': Wilkie Collins's 'The Moonstone'," in* Novel: A Forum on Fiction, *Vol. 13, No. 2, Winter, 1980, pp. 153-70.*

PATRICIA MILLER FRICK   (essay date 1984)

[*Frick cites* Memoirs of a Picture, *a novel by Collins's grandfather, as a source for* The Moonstone. *According to Frick, both authors depict the corruption of English society through the value it attaches to an aesthetic object.*]

Wilkie Collins's *The Moonstone* has often been hailed as the first and finest English detective novel. One natural consequence of this high regard for *The Moonstone*'s contribution to detective literature has been a preoccupation with its plot and structure, or the "spectacle of ingenuity" [see excerpt from the *Times* dated 1868] that the novel provides. Contemporary reviewers paid enthusiastic tribute to its "carefully elaborate workmanship," "entrancing narrative," and "the admirable manner in which every circumstance is fitted together" [see excerpt by Jewsbury dated 1868 in *NCLC*, Vol. 1]. Even Anthony Trollope, who considered plot "the most insignificant part of a tale," grudgingly praised *The Moonstone*'s "most minute and wonderful construction." In the twentieth century, it has continued to earn strong praise from, among others, T. S. Eliot [see excerpt above dated 1928 and excerpt dated 1927 in *NCLC*, Vol. 1], Dorothy Sayers [see excerpt above dated 1944 and excerpt dated 1928 in *NCLC*, Vol. 1], and J.I.M. Stewart, who has ranked it along with Sophocles' *Oedipus Tyrannus*, Ben Jonson's *The Alchemist*, and Fielding's *Tom Jones* as one of the "most perfectly plotted works in universal literature."

This enthusiasm for the plot of *The Moonstone* has undoubtedly helped to secure Collins's place in literary history, but it fails to focus on the novel's main interest—the Yellow Diamond itself. For those critics who primarily regard the novel as a detective masterpiece, the Moonstone is harmless enough. Materially valuable and compellingly beautiful, it is nevertheless only a missing piece of evidence in an intricate mystery. Yet this same diamond, "as large as a plover's egg" and as "unfathomable as the heavens themselves," engenders confusion, fear, admiration, doubt, obsession, and avarice in all of the novel's characters and radically transforms their lives by its disappearance. If a discussion of the detective aspects of the novel will not account for the power and centrality of the Moonstone, what will?

A previously unrecognized source for *The Moonstone* will help us to go beyond the detective elements of the novel and to see

Adriano Cecioni's Vanity Fair *cartoon of Collins, "The Master of Sensation."*

the Diamond's importance more fully. This source is the *Memoirs of a Picture,* a combination biography and picaresque novel, written by Collins's grandfather, William Collins, Sr., an art dealer and man of letters. Collins acknowledges his awareness of and interest in his grandfather's novel in his first work, a biography of his father, **Memoirs of William Collins, Esq., R.A.**:

> Before, however, I proceed to occupy myself with the incidents of Mr. Collins's boyhood, I would offer a few remarks on the principal work which his father produced,—the *Memoirs of a Picture*. Ihave been told that this book enjoyed in its day, no inconsiderable share of popularity. It is so novel in arrangement, it belongs so completely both in style and matter, to a school of fiction now abandoned by modern writers, it is so thoroughly devoted to painters and painting, and so amusingly characteristic of the manners and customs of the patrons and picture-dealers of the day, (and I might add, of the hardihood of the author himself, in venturing to expose the secret politics of the pursuit to which he was attached,) that a short analysis of its characters and story, whether it be considered as a family curiosity, a literary antiquity, or an illustration of the art and position of the artists of a bygone age, can hardly be condemned as an intrusion on the purposes, or an obstacle to the progress of the present biography.

So keen is Collins's interest in his grandfather's novel that he digresses at length to outline its complicated plot. The *Memoirs* tells the story of a painting, ''an unique and inestimable jewel, painted by the immortal Guido,'' which has been stolen from its rightful position in the Royal Gallery of France, ''where it had shone unrivalled amidst a blaze of beauty for so many years.'' The Picture undergoes a series of exploits and mishaps which form the basis for the remainder of the narrative. (pp. 313-14)

Once the relationship has been noticed, it is easy to see important parallels between the plots of the *Memoirs of a Picture*, and **The Moonstone**. In each work, the central figure is an inanimate object of great value which becomes the focal point for the novel's carefully constructed events. Just as the *Memoirs* opens with an account of the disappearance of Guido's painting from the Royal Gallery in France, **The Moonstone** begins with an account of the Diamond's disappearance from the Sultan of Seringapatam's Palace in India. Both thefts take place in ''sacred'' places, and both are perpetrated by unscrupulous men, the Chevalier and John Herncastle.

Other parallels are also significant. Like Guido's painting, the Moonstone undergoes a series of adventures after its theft, as it passed from one owner to another, and as it is pursued by its original Indian retainers. From Herncastle, who steals it from the Palace and brings it to England, the gem passes to Franklin Blake, to the tainted philanthropist Godfrey Ablewhite, to the moneylender Septimus Luker, and finally back to its original owners, the three Hindu priests who have followed it across the ocean. Moreover, the fate of the Moonstone, like that of Guido's painting, remains shrouded in mystery, as the celebrated traveller and mystic, Mr. Murthwaite, concludes in his narrative: ''You have lost sight of [the Moonstone] in

England, and (if I know anything of this people) you have lost sight of it forever.''

It is furthermore notable that many times throughout the *Memoirs* Collins, Sr. refers to Guido's painting either as ''that unique and inestimable jewel'' or ''that unparalleled gem.'' It is possible that these and alternative epithets for Guido's painting suggested to Wilkie Collins the idea of using a precious gem, a diamond, as the central object in **The Moonstone.**

These obvious similarities in plot and structure secure the possibility of establishing the *Memoirs* as a previously unacknowledged source for **The Moonstone.** Yet there is even stronger evidence of **The Moonstone**'s indebtedness to the *Memoirs* when one considers the symbolic function of the central objects in each work—the painting and the diamond—and how these objects help us to assess the integrity of the individuals and societies that covet them.

Collins, Sr. wrote the *Memoirs of a Picture* as a satire against that ''chosen band of Philistines . . . The professors of picture-craft.'' As an art-dealer in eighteenth-century England, he had witnessed first-hand, among painters and other art-dealers of his day, what he called in the *Memoirs* a ''general perversion of taste.'' To expose the artistic abuses which he hated, Collins, Sr., chose as the central focus for the *Memoirs* the logical object of such abuses—a painting. Guido's masterpiece acts as a catalyst, directly creating by its presence the conditions under which most of the novel's characters reveal the base reality of their own corruption and avarice. (pp. 315-16)

Like his grandfather, Wilkie Collins was also profoundly aware of the social, political, and moral ills of his own society and directly addressed many of them in **The Moonstone.** Just as Guido's painting provided a moral center for the *Memoirs*, the Yellow Diamond enables Collins to expose and to assess the many false assumptions and dubious values underlying Victorian life. In characters such as Gabriel Betteredge, the Verinder's house steward, and Miss Clack, the religious reformer, the Moonstone underscores the comic limitations of Sabbatarianism and Evangelicalism. For Betteredge, the Diamond introduces the perils of coming into contact with foreigners or strangers: ''Here was our quiet English home suddenly invaded by a devilish Indian Diamond—bringing with it a company of living rogues, set loose upon us by the vengeance of a dead man!'' For Miss Clack, the gem and its accompanying curse are even further evidence of her conviction that ''the Evil one lies in wait for us in all the most apparently innocent actions of our daily lives.''

While the Moonstone makes it possible for Collins to make fun of these ''common and petty hypocrisies of everyday British life,'' it establishes even more serious flaws, with often tragic consequences, in other characters. Sergeant Cuff's extraordinary powers of ratiocination fail him when he attempts to locate the missing jewel, and he wrongfully accuses Rosanna Spearman, the Verinder's melancholy and hopeless servant, of perpetrating the theft; his error in judgment tragically results in Rosanna's suicide beneath the Shivering Sand. Franklin Blake, the fiancé of Rachel Verinder and the unfortunate object of Rosanna's unrequited love, also succumbs to doubt and confusion when he becomes the prime suspect in the crime. Lacking the self-confidence and self-knowledge to vindicate himself, he severs his engagement to Rachel and disassociates himself from her family. John Herncastle totally defies all social and moral codes in his violent theft of the Moonstone during the British seige of Seringapatam, and in transferring the Diamond and its curse to his family, he further demonstrates his cruel and obsessive need for revenge. Finally, the Moonstone enables Collins to deride the officious philanthropy of Godfrey Ablewhite. Before the disappearance of the gem, Ablewhite is held in the highest regard by his devoted followers, but its theft raises many questions about his seemingly flawless character. He is seen in the company of Septimus Luker, a money-lender and an unlikely companion for a Christian hero, and he is also discovered to have examined Lady Verinder's will shortly before proposing to her daughter, Rachel. His theft of the diamond is not an attempt to further feed the starving masses but to save himself by paying his considerable gambling debts. Without the Moonstone, however, these devious aspects of his personality would remain submerged beneath his polished exterior.

Provincialism, self-doubt, confusion, fallibility, suspicion, hypocrisy, greed, and revenge: the portrait of English society that emerges from these brief analyses of the Moonstone's influence upon individual characters is hardly respectable or flattering, and it stresses the disorder and disharmony underlying the English characters' relationships with one another. The Moonstone acts as a destructive force in the lives of the English narrators, separating them, pitting them against one another in suspicion and mistrust. This shattering impact which the Diamond has is best summarized in Franklin Blake's remark to Gabriel Betteredge:

> When I came here from London with that horrible diamond . . . I don't think that there was a happier household in England than this. Look at the household now! Scattered, disunited— the very air of the place poisoned with mystery and suspicion! Do you remember that morning at the Shivering Sand, when we talked about my uncle Herncastle and his birthday gift? The Moonstone has served the Colonel's vengeance, Betteredge, by means which the Colonel himself never dreamt of!

However, the Moonstone has a completely different effect upon the Indian characters who pursue it in the novel. The Indians regard it as a sacred object which binds them together in their desire to retrieve it. For them, the gem is a symbol of unity, and it emphasizes their positive qualities of loyalty, persistence, and faith, which contrast with the doubt and disorder of the English narrators. The Indians are sensitive to the spiritual significance which the Moonstone has, and by sacrificing their caste to regain the Diamond, they show themselves to be morally superior to the English characters who seek the gem for vain and self-serving reasons.

In this contrast between the sincerity of the Indian figures in **The Moonstone** and their frequently hypocritical English counterparts, we are reminded of the contrast between those sincere artists and picture-dealers of eighteenth-century England, like William Collins, Sr., and their corrupt rivals, for whom the value of art was determined by profit, not aesthetic or moral integrity. It is reasonable to conclude on the basis of this evidence that in Collins, Sr.'s attack on the hypocrisy of the eighteenth-century art world, grandson Wilkie found the raw materials for his own criticism of nineteenth-century genteel life in England. In **The Moonstone,** as in the *Memoirs of a Picture,* an understanding of the true meaning of the central aesthetic object ultimately lies not in the active process of discovering its whereabouts but in the contemplation of its symbolic value as a permanent record of the virtues and lim-

itations of human nature, and as an impressive portrait of Victorian life. (pp. 317-19)

> *Patricia Miller Frick, "Wilkie Collins's 'Little Jewel':*
> *The Meaning of 'The Moonstone',"* in *Philological*
> *Quarterly, Vol. 63, No. 3, Summer, 1984, pp. 313-21.*

ADDITIONAL BIBLIOGRAPHY

Anderson, Patrick. "Detective Story." *Spectator* 217, No. 7226 (23 December 1966): 820.
    Recommends *The Moonstone* as "magnificent entertainment."

Ashley, Robert. "Master Craftsman (1860-1870): *The Moonstone* and *Man and Wife.*" In his *Wilkie Collins*, pp. 88-100. The English Novelists, edited by Herbert van Thal. London: Arthur Barker, 1952.
    Analyzes various aspects of *The Moonstone*, including its "hide and seek" theme, contrasting characters, and detective-story elements.

Baker, Ernest A. "The Kingsleys, Wilkie Collins, Reade, and Others." In his *The History of the English Novel: From the Brontës to Meredith, Romanticism in the English Novel*, pp. 161-220. London: H. F. & G. Witherby, 1937.
    Includes a brief discussion of characterization and structure in *The Moonstone.*

Beetz, Kirk H. *Wilkie Collins: An Annotated Bibliography, 1889-1976.* The Scarecrow Author Bibliographies, no. 35. Metuchen, N.J.: Scarecrow Press, 1978, 167 p.
    An annotated guide to criticism of Collins's works from 1889 through 1976.

Brantlinger, Patrick. "What Is 'Sensational' about the 'Sensation Novel'?" *Nineteenth-Century Fiction* 37, No. 1 (June 1982): 1-28.
    Attempts to define the sensational novel by analyzing it from historical, structural, and psychological perspectives. *The Moonstone* is one of several works that figure prominently in Brantlinger's commentary.

Davis, Nuel Pharr. "Out in the Dark." In his *The Life of Wilkie Collins*, pp. 239-60. Urbana: University of Illinois Press, 1956.
    Contains a discussion of the sources, composition, and contemporary reception of *The Moonstone.*

Gregory, E. R. "Murder in Fact." *The New Republic* 179, No. 4 (22 July 1978): 33-4.
    Analyzes the reasons for the continuing appeal of *The Moonstone.*

Haycraft, Howard. "The In-Between Years." In his *Murder for Pleasure: The Life and Times of the Detective Story*, pp. 28-44. New York: D. Appleton-Century Co., 1941.
    Argues that rather than creating a new literary form with *The Moonstone*, Collins wrote "a full-bodied novel in the fashion of his time, using detection as a central theme to catalyze the elaborate ingredients." Haycraft also briefly discusses several other aspects of *The Moonstone*, including its sources, humor, and characters.

Hennelly, Mark M., Jr. "Detecting Collins' Diamond: From Serpentstone to Moonstone." *Nineteenth-Century Fiction* 39, No. 1 (June 1984): 25-47.
    Examines the significance of the Moonstone diamond as the central object in the novel. According to Hennelly, the Moonstone not only "informs the novel's narrative and plot structures, its presentation of character, and its thematic concerns," but it also "coordinates some concerns of both detective and Victorian fiction."

Hutter, Albert D. "Dreams, Transformations, and Literature: The Implications of Detective Fiction." *Victorian Studies* XIX, No. 2 (December 1975): 181-209.

Develops a theory of literary criticism based on dream psychology, using *The Moonstone* to illustrate how this theory can be applied to detective fiction.

Lambert, Gavin. "Enemy Country." In his *The Dangerous Edge*, pp. 1-30. New York: Viking Press, Grossman Publishers, 1976.
Connects details of Collins's life—his personal relationships, ill-health, and antagonism toward conventional society—with the creation of *The Moonstone*. Lambert also describes the way Collins used the characters and plot of *The Moonstone* to explore the subsurface of Victorian society.

Lonoff, Sue. "Multiple Narratives & Relative Truths: A Study of *The Ring and the Book*, *The Woman in White*, and *The Moonstone*." In *Browning Institute Studies: An Annual of Victorian Literary and Cultural History*, Vol. 10, edited by Gerhard Joseph and William S. Peterson, pp. 143-61. New York: The Browning Institute and The Graduate School and University Center, City University of New York, 1982.
Compares Collins's use of multiple narratives in *The Woman in White* and *The Moonstone* with Robert Browning's narrative method in *The Ring and the Book*. Lonoff states that all three works point "the way toward a literature in which truth is perceived as conjectural and relative and point-of-view becomes a major issue."

———. "*The Moonstone* and Its Audience." In her *Wilkie Collins and His Victorian Readers: A Study in the Rhetoric of Authorship*, pp. 170-227. AMS Studies in the Nineteenth Century, no. 2. New York: AMS Press, 1982.
A wide-ranging study of *The Moonstone*, covering such topics as Collins's sources and literary models, the serial publication of the work, and its influence upon readers. Lonoff also assesses numerous other critics' interpretations of the novel.

Milley, Henry James Wye. "*The Eustace Diamonds* and *The Moonstone*." *Studies in Philology* XXXVI, No. 4 (October 1939): 651-63.
Maintains that Anthony Trollope satirizes *The Moonstone* in his novel *The Eustace Diamonds*.

Murfin, Ross C. "The Art of Representation: Collins' *The Moonstone* and Dickens' Example." *ELH* 49, No. 3 (Fall 1983): 653-72.
Analyzes the influence of Dickens's *Bleak House* on *The Moonstone*, focusing on the authors' interest in the power of writing.

Nadel, Ira Bruce. "Science and *The Moonstone*." In *Dickens Studies Annual: Essays on Victorian Fiction*, Vol. 11, edited by Michael Timko, Fred Kaplan, and Edward Guiliano, pp. 239-59. New York: AMS Press, 1983.
Contends that, with *The Moonstone*, Collins made science an "essential element" of the genre of detective fiction.

Nelson, Bill. "Evil as Illusion in the Detective Story." *Clues* 1, No. 1 (Spring 1980): 9-14.

Explores the concept of evil presented in two detective stories— *The Moonstone* and Graham Greene's *Brighton Rock*.

Page, Norman, ed. "*The Moonstone* (1868)." In *Wilkie Collins: The Critical Heritage*, pp. 168-81. The Critical Heritage Series, edited by B. C. Southam. London: Routledge & Kegan Paul, 1974.
Reprints selections from nineteenth-century commentary on *The Moonstone*.

Palmer, Jerry. "In Historical Perspective: Edgar Allan Poe and Wilkie Collins." In his *Thrillers: Genesis and Structure of a Popular Genre*, pp. 107-14. New York: St. Martin's Press, 1979.
Assesses *The Moonstone*'s impact upon the development of detective fiction.

Porter, Dennis. "Backward Construction and the Art of Suspense." In his *The Pursuit of Crime: Art and Ideology in Detective Fiction*, pp. 24-52. New Haven: Yale University Press, 1981.
Examines the relationship between structure and suspense in *The Moonstone*.

Starrett, Vincent. Introduction to *The Moonstone*, by Wilkie Collins, pp. vii-xvi. New York: Heritage Press, 1959.
Describes the contemporary reception of *The Moonstone* and emphasizes its historical significance.

Stewart, R. F. "Doubts and Suspicions." In his *. . . And Always a Detective: Chapters on the History of Detective Fiction*, pp. 27-40. Newton Abbot, England: David & Charles, 1980.
Disputes the notion that the genre of detective fiction began with Edgar Allan Poe's short stories and Collins's *The Moonstone*.

Symons, Julian. "Dickens, Collins, Gaboriau: The Pattern Forms." In his *Bloody Murder: From the Detective Story to the Crime Novel, a History*, pp. 42-56. New York: Viking, 1985.
Assesses *The Moonstone*'s importance in the development of detective fiction and praises the novel's ingenious plot. Symons maintains that, along with Émile Gaboriau, Collins established the character of the detective as "the protector of the innocent."

Wagenknecht, Edward. "The Disciples of Dickens." In his *Cavalcade of the English Novel*, pp. 234-67. New York: Henry Holt and Co., 1954.
Contains a broad survey of Collins's novels, including *The Moonstone*.

Wallace, Irving. "Hardly Coincidental." In his *The Fabulous Originals: Lives of Extraordinary People Who Inspired Memorable Characters in Fiction*, pp. 259-317. New York: Alfred A. Knopf, 1955.
Includes a description of Inspector Jonathan Whicher of Scotland Yard, the prototype of *The Moonstone*'s Sergeant Cuff.

Charles Dickens

1812-1870

(Also wrote under pseudonym of Boz) English novelist, short story writer, dramatist, poet, and essayist.

The following entry presents criticism of Dickens's novel *The Mystery of Edwin Drood* (1870). For additional information on Dickens's career and *The Mystery of Edwin Drood*, see *NCLC*, Vols. 3 and 8.

Dickens's novel *The Mystery of Edwin Drood* is one of the great puzzles of English literature. Left unfinished when Dickens died, *Edwin Drood* has baffled scholars, biographers, and amateur sleuths in their attempts to solve the riddle of how the novelist intended to conclude its plot. Although the vast majority of commentary on *Edwin Drood* seeks to explain how Dickens planned to work out the various unanswered questions posed by the novel, *Edwin Drood* has also been admired by both critics and readers for its intrinsic literary merits as well as for what it reveals about the direction of Dickens's art in the final year of his life. Thus, while *Edwin Drood* is one of Dickens's lesser-known works, it remains not only a fascinating literary enigma, but also a work honored for its own sake and for the interest naturally attached to it as the last novel of one of English literature's greatest authors.

At the time he wrote *Edwin Drood*, Dickens was established as perhaps the world's best-known author writing in English. His previous novel, *Our Mutual Friend*, had been published in 1865, and he spent much of his time and energy during the period from 1867 to 1869 on a series of highly successful but physically and mentally exhausting public reading tours in England and the United States. Biographical evidence suggests that he first began working on the idea for *Edwin Drood* in July of 1869; his notes for the novel show that in August he was searching for a title. By the end of September he had settled on what to call the book and commenced writing in early October. Scheduled to appear in twelve monthly parts, the first of which was published on 31 March 1870, *Edwin Drood* was cut short when Dickens died on 9 June, just after he had completed the sixth installment.

Set in the English cathedral town of Cloisterham (modeled upon Rochester, England), the complex plot of *Edwin Drood* centers around Edwin Drood and Rosa Bud, two orphans betrothed to one another by their parents. As the novel opens, Edwin comes to Cloisterham on one of his regular visits to see Rosa and stays with his uncle and guardian, John Jasper, the cathedral choirmaster. Unbeknownst to Edwin, Jasper leads a secret life as an opium addict and has conceived a violent passion for Rosa. When Edwin inexplicably disappears on Christmas Eve, suspicion of foul play initially falls on Neville Landless, a newcomer to Cloisterham who admires Rosa and who has previously quarreled with Edwin over the latter's patronizing treatment of her. No conclusive evidence against Landless surfaces, however, despite the choirmaster's attempts to incriminate him. With Edwin gone, Jasper openly and menacingly proclaims his desires to Rosa, causing her to flee to her guardian, a London lawyer named Hiram Grewgious. Shortly thereafter a mysterious stranger named Dick Datchery appears in Cloisterham. It is apparent that Datchery is really someone

else in disguise and that he has come to Cloisterham for the purpose of watching Jasper. Dickens's novel ends at this point, with little concrete evidence to suggest whether Edwin is alive or dead, who his assailant may have been, or who Datchery is.

Edwin Drood met with a generally favorable reception when originally published. Reviews of the first monthly number praised the work's descriptive passages and dialogue as they welcomed a new narrative from Dickens's pen after what was for him a relatively long interval between novels. When the final completed monthly part appeared on 31 August 1870, commentators were again primarily positive in their assessments, although divided over whether *Edwin Drood* showed an advance or a decline in Dickens's artistic powers. Among the most frequently discussed aspects of the novel were its characters and its place in Dickens's works as a whole.

Dickens died leaving no clear indication of how he intended to conclude his mystery, but important (if ultimately inconclusive) evidence about his plans came to light in the years following his death and continued to appear over time, creating a body of secondary materials now closely associated with the novel. The nature of this evidence and the chance it offered for the solution of the mystery helped to determine the course of critical commentary on *Edwin Drood* for the remainder of the nineteenth century and virtually the first half of the twentieth. The publication of the final volume of John Forster's *The Life of Charles Dickens* in 1874 provided the first and perhaps most consequential evidence concerning Dickens's designs for *Edwin Drood,* but the appearance in 1887 of Richard A. Proctor's monograph entitled *Watched by the Dead* marked the beginning of the trend that would dominate *Edwin Drood* studies for the next fifty years. The vast majority of commentary to appear on the novel during this period concerned itself with the key aspects of the plot that Dickens had left unanswered: was Edwin Drood indeed murdered (and if so, who was the assailant?), and who was Datchery? Critical and popular debate over these questions and other related aspects of the mystery produced numerous articles and books attempting to explain how Dickens would have proceeded with the novel—so many that as early as 1914, Montagu Saunders, in a preface to his own *The Mystery in the Drood Family,* was prompted to remark, ''It needs a considerable amount of assurance to add yet another book to the comparatively long list of those which have been written upon the subject of Dickens's unfinished story.'' Attempts to resolve the riddle of the novel continued, however, and in their search for clues, critics drew on a wide range of materials, including the original illustrations to the monthly parts by Charles Collins and Luke Fildes, the recollections of Forster, Fildes, and Dickens's family, and the text of the work itself. Various prominent scholars endeavored to prove either that Drood was alive or that he was dead; that he had been strangled; that Jasper was either guilty or completely innocent of the crime; that Datchery was Grewgious, Grewgious's clerk Bazzard, Landless or his sister, Helena, or even Drood himself—all with no conclusive results. A number of writers also undertook to supply the missing chapters of the novel by writing conclusions of their own; few of their efforts, however, are regarded as of more than passing interest.

With the publication in the 1930s of influential essays by Howard Duffield and Edmund Wilson, the flood of ''Droodiana'' attempting to solve the mystery began to abate somewhat and was in part replaced by more traditional literary analyses of various aspects of the novel. Interest gradually shifted from the details of Drood's murder and the identity of Datchery to the psychology of Jasper and the question of his guilt. Duffield's discovery that Jasper's activities in *Edwin Drood* bear a striking resemblance to the rituals of the sect of Indian professional murderers known as Thugs and Wilson's suggestion that Jasper's divided personality reflects conflicts and contradictions in Dickens's own personality both had a significant effect on subsequent studies. Thus, while many post-World War II evaluations of *Edwin Drood* have continued to speculate about the ending, including book-length investigations of the problem by Richard M. Baker and Felix Aylmer, scholars have also delved with greater frequency into such subjects as Dickens's handling of setting and description, his concern with social problems, and the autobiographical implications of Jasper's violent and repressed character. In addition, the novel's place within Dickens's writings as a whole and the evidence it shows of new developments in his literary art remain the topics of much critical debate, despite general agreement that it is not one of his greatest works. The proliferation of recent scholarly studies, as well as the publication in 1980 of two major fictional attempts to conclude the story, suggest not only that *The Mystery of Edwin Drood* will probably never be solved, but also that Dickens's unfinished final novel is likely to attract both critical and popular interest for some time to come.

(See also *Something about the Author,* Vol. 15, and *Dictionary of Literary Biography,* Vol. 21: *Victorian Novelists Before 1885* and Vol. 55: *Victorian Prose Writers Before 1867.*)

THE TIMES, London   (essay date 1870)

[*The following excerpt is drawn from an anonymous review of the first monthly number of* Edwin Drood. *The critic praises various aspects of the novel, including Dickens's descriptions, characterization, and dialogue.*]

The novel reading world have been on the tip-toe of expectation since the announcement of a new work by their favourite author. We have perused the first instalment, and venture to express the public pleasure, and to thank Mr. Dickens for having added a zest to the season. It is a zest, too, which will not pass away with the season, for the welcome number in its light-green uniform will await the tourist *poste-restante,* will be an addition to the delights of autumn holydays, and even when the winter comes again no more than a half-light may have been let in upon what is as yet a very dark scene of fiction. . . .

As far as a novel can be judged by the first five chapters, we judge well of this; it seems to be in its author's best manner; his pen is new-pointed, and dipped in fresher fancies than of late; his descriptions are as simple and as natural as ever; his dialogue is full of the old happy and unexpected turns. We need hardly say that the mystery of Edwin Drood is a mystery still; it would be strange, indeed, if a novelist were to answer the riddle of his title in the first few pages, although we can even now declare that the book will have many other attractions than the curious entanglement of its plot. . . .

[The story] as far as it has gone is excellently told. Persons and interiors are sketched with the easy pencil of an adept, and, though space is occupied by passages of description, we are surprised at the considerable progress made with the story in 32 pages. We are also a little surprised at finding ourselves in a cathedral town, and in company with a Dean. Mr. Trollope has so long worked with this machinery that it seems at first sight a bold and unlawful thing for Mr. Dickens to avail himself of it. But this uneasiness altogether vanishes before we have read two pages. There are Deans and Deans, and in Mr. Dickens's Cloisterham we are already introduced to life and character very different from that of Barchester, though as real, delighting us as much but delighting us for other reasons. The manner, the whole style and art of the two authors are entirely opposed, and yet one is not condemned in the least degree by the other. They may tread the same ground, might event tell the same story without clashing. Besides, it by no means follows that Cloisterham is to be the only theatre of this Mystery. As it stands at present, Edwin Drood is shortly to marry Miss Rosa Bud, now at school at the Nuns'-house Seminary for Young Ladies, and to proceed to Egypt, there to pursue his profession of civil engineer. But he may never see the Pyramids, and, if we have any experience in marriages as they are made in novels, he will be single for longer than he thinks, and will go very near to lose Rosa altogether.

Mr. Dickens has given us some admirable photographs of still life, and has cut out in prose which is close as ivory some dozen of distinct characters. So far from losing his old touch, it is, we think, more delicate than ever, and yet as firm. The scene at the Nuns'-house during Edwin's visit to his betrothed is as charming as almost anything ever written by its author. The saucy girl, who will not kiss her lover ''because I have got an acidulated drop in my mouth;'' Miss Twinkleton, the schoolmistress; and Mrs. Tisher, her companion, who is described as ''a deferential widow, with a weak back, a chronic sigh, and a suppressed voice,'' all these combine to make a most amusing episode. . . . Mr. Sapsea, the Cloisterham auctioneer, promises to be a great source of entertainment. He is the butt of the story, and we look forward to his absurdities with an appetite stimulated by the morsels already given to us. Stony Durdles, the sepulchral mason, is a thoroughly original conception, though if we *must* make one stricture, the chapter devoted to him seems to us a trifle drawn out, and a little defaced by some of Mr. Dickens's time-honoured excrescences of style and taste. But taken with all its faults, which are few, we are very much mistaken if ninety-nine hundredths of its readers do not see in this first number of the ***Mystery of Edwin Drood*** the promise of a novel well worthy of its author. One piece of even higher praise we must venture—it is that Edwin Drood himself shows signs of freeing Mr. Dickens from the reproach which has sometimes been made against him, that though he can sketch admirably many eccentricities of characters, he cannot draw a hero who is simply a gentleman. We look forward with great pleasure to the next and subsequent numbers; we believe that Mr. Dickens will show himself artist enough to interest us in each, and yet to preserve the unity and continuity of his story. Veteran of letters as he is, he cannot say that

> A sprightlier age
> Comes tittering on and shoves him from the stage.

As he delighted the fathers, so he delights the children, and this his latest effort promises to be received with interest and pleasure as wide-spread as that which greeted those glorious *Papers* which built at once the whole edifice of his fame. Its perusal will leave his readers still hoping and still asking, like the irrepressible Oliver, for "more."

> *A review of "The Mystery of Edwin Drood," in* The Times, *London, April 2, 1870, p. 4.*

[CHARLES H. ROSS?] (essay date 1870)

[*The following excerpt is drawn from a parody of* Edwin Drood *first published in* Judy; or, The London Serio-Comic Journal *sometime between April and June 1870. The author of the piece is thought to have been Charles H. Ross, editor of* Judy *and the son of an early friend of Dickens.*]

PROLOGUE

The other day a great author called upon Judy, to read the proof-sheets of a forthcoming work, and to ask her opinion on its merits. "By all means," said Judy; "pray begin." And he commenced as follows:—

CHAPTER I.—FOUR IN A BED

"The clock tower with its eye out! But how can the clock tower be upside down! The well-known clock at Bestminster standing on its head with its feet in hot water? But then you know what the bear said. Why did he want the soap? Therein lies the mystery. Won't fifty billion dancing dervishes do as well; if not, let's go in for white elephants. Confound the clock! why won't it stand the right end up? Why don't it strike? I'll strike it if it don't. Aha! it isn't a clock after all, but an old woman in a frilled nightcap, and I'm lying one of four in bed, and feel very particularly jolly uncomfortable."

"But ain't that rather disconnected?" asked Judy.

"Isn't it powerful, though?" said the great author.

"Very," said Judy.

And the great author proceeded:—

The man who has these fantastic imaginings arises from the bed, and knocks his head against the wall to settle his senses.

"Have another pipe," says an indistinct female, in a querulous rattling whisper. "Deary, dear! the Lascar gentleman whose toes is in the air is a reg'lar customer, and so's John Chinaman, here, twisted up like a pair of lazytongs struck by lightning. We're opium-eaters, we is. I got drunk on gin for sixteen years, and now I've took to opium. It's generally allowed I've a good constitution."

"Get out," says the man of the fantastic imaginings. "I play the organ in Bestminster Cathedral, and they're waiting for me to begin evening service. It's a way they have."

CHAPTER II.—A DEAN AND A CHAPTER TOO.

"Whosoever has observed that extremely useful, though homely, vegetable, the potato, may have noticed, in a sackful, how like each bulb is to its brother. In like fashion there is a sort of semblance twixt the Dorrits, Dombeys, Micawbers, and Pecksniffs of other days, and the Sapseas, Tokes, and Crisparkles of to-day. But what does it matter?"

"Mr. Rasper is late to-night," says the Dean.

"Oncommon," says the person addressed. (You must read it over once or twice, and you may, perhaps, find out whom it is.)

"Say uncommonly," says the Dean blandly; "and is he ill?"

"*Un*—common," says the other.

"—ly," adds the Dean, with increased blandness; as who should say, If you don't mind your terminations, where will you end?

• • • • •

Crack, crack.

"I have these sorts of fits," says Mr. Rasper, "but don't mind me, Rude Teddy. If you were boxed up in an organ-loft all day long (with a comprehensive glance including the clock tower and a large portion of the Thames Embankment) you'd almost like them, even, for a change. Have a nut?"

Crack.

"It's a bad 'un, but never mind," says Rude Teddy; "I'm going to be married, you know, to the girl I was betrothed to by my parents. You may remember a similar state of things in several old farces, also in a novel called ***Our Mutual Friend***."

"I do," replies Mr. Rasper, with a comprehensive glance, including all Smith's Library and the greater part of the railway bookstalls. "Wait till I have another fit. Take another nut while I do so."

Crack, crack.

"Thank you."

Then Mr. Rasper dissolves his attitude with a little hot water, and takes it without sugar.

"Thank you kindly," says Judy, "It seems so far, extremely amusing, and very easy to follow."

CHAPTER III.—"STICKY."

Suppose, for the fun of the thing, we go on calling Westminster Bestminster. It's an awful lark, looked at one way. In Barley-sugarment Street (there's a fantastic imagining for you), is situate Miss Tinkleton's "Young Ladies' School." It is an old house repainted, and naturally puts the most unimaginative persons in mind of a withered coquette who has been Rachelized.

Miss Tinkleton's pet pupil's name is Pitt: they called her Poppit, as a matter of course. She is the young lady Rude Teddy is engaged to.

She doesn't love him very particularly, but she has a fine taste for bulls-eyes. When he comes to call on her they buy them together.

Then they make love, and she looks very pretty with her mouth full.

"Don't," cried Poppit, "I'm all sticky."

CHAPTER IV.—PAPSY.

There was a jackass of the name of Papsy. He carried on the trade of auctioneer, and in his leisure hours wrote comic tombstone inscriptions.

"My own name," said the auctioneer, with his legs stretched out, and solemnly enjoying himself, "is not Pecksniff, as at first you might imagine, but Papsy. I chose it because it was funny. I married a woman of the name of Ethelinda, for the same reason. I also knock off little things of this sort (poetry to comic tombstone), which occur to me quite naturally on reading over a book of epitaphs. But here comes Murdles."

Murdles is a sexton. He has a way of getting drunk. He also carries his dinner in a bundle. When he taps the cathedral floor, he can tell directly whether there is a vault underneath. If there is, he breaks it open, and stirs up the ashes of the illustrious departed with his pickaxe.

The cathedral authorities are much pleased at his so doing.

When he is drunk enough to go home to sleep, and yet can't go of his own accord, he hires a street Arab to fling stones at him at a halfpenny per evening.

The street Arab does so, and very frequently knocks his brains out; but Murdles don't mind that.

He rather likes it.

CHAPTER V.—GOOD NIGHT.

Mr. Rasper goes home to bed. Rude Dedwin is already slumbering. Mr. Rasper contemplates him, as he sleeps, with one of those comprehensive glances before alluded to. Then with great care he steals, thief-like, to his room, and summons up, beneath the potent demon's influence the weird spectres of the previous night.

Again the eyeless tower.

Again the dancing dervishes.

Again the bear who wanted soap.

Chaos!——Oblivion!!——Crack!!!

"Sweetly pretty!" and Judy, when the great author had finished; "but what's the Mystery?"

"It must go no further, if I tell you," the great author said.

"I swear!" said Judy.

"The MYSTERY is, then," whispered the great author—"*the Mystery is—How-it sells!*" (pp. 16-19)

[Charles H. Ross?], "The Mysterious Mystery of Rude Dedwin," in The Dickensian, Vol. 62, No. 348, January, 1966, pp. 14-20.

THE SATURDAY REVIEW, LONDON (essay date 1870)

[*In the following excerpt from an early review of* Edwin Drood, *the anonymous critic suggests that the novel shows evidence of creative exhaustion on Dickens's part, noting the absence of the spontaneity and inventiveness characteristic of his earlier fiction.*]

There is an obvious difficulty in criticizing a work which appears under such circumstances as ***Edwin Drood.*** We can hardly look at it as a detached performance, and form a simple judgment of its intrinsic merits. We remember at every page that we are reading the last words of a man who, whatever place he may occupy in the opinion of posterity, certainly possessed some faculties in almost unequalled perfection. Like other last words they may be trivial or eloquent, but this accidental interest eclipses, for the first time at least, any more permanent interest which they might possess if read simply for themselves. We read about Edwin Drood and John Jasper and Durdles and Mr. Crisparkle, but we cannot help thinking of Sam Weller and Mrs. Gamp and Dick Swiveller and Oliver Twist, and all the numerous family of predecessors who acknowledge the same parent. We have indeed a feeling, which it would be impossible to disguise, that the younger branches are by no means distinguised by the freshness and vigour which charmed us in the old days. Mr. Dickens had undoubtedly a wonderful fertility of invention within certain limits, but no human brain could supply so many successive crops without showing some distinct symptoms of exhaustion. Indeed the most unequivocal merits of Mr. Dickens's writings are precisely those which are least able to bear the influence of time. . . . Mr. Dickens, like many other distinguished writers, was to a considerable extent the slave of his own success, and was hampered by the inevitable rivalry of his former self. He played his old tricks with something of his old humour; but the spontaneous impulse decayed, and the unconscious quaintness degenerated into a mannerism which was not seldom unequivocally tedious. Nor can it be said that the decline in freshness was compensated by any remarkable display of the more substantial qualities which ripen, rather than decay, in maturer life. There was a certain thinness about his characters at the best of times. There was little depth of sentiment or power of reflection. With an extraordinary capacity for catching the external aspects of things, and seeing with incredible rapidity all that a man could see in a glance, he seldom penetrated to any of the deeper springs of emotion, or gave much proof of purely intellectual power. For this reason his pathos was generally rather repulsive to his more thoughtful readers, and his characters, though admirable sketches, never rose to the level of portraits by the great masters. To the last he showed many flashes of the old inimitable spirit of fun; but yet, as that power grew inevitably weaker, one could not but feel more strongly his comparative incapacity for appealing to other sources of interest.

The ***Mystery of Edwin Drood*** might serve as an illustration of some of these remarks. To take one trifling but significant peculiarity, we have Mr. Dickens's old taste for extraordinary collections of proper names. The chief characters are named Drood, Jasper, Crisparkle, Bud, Twinkleton, Sapsea, Durdles, Landless, Grewgious, Honeythunder, Datchery, Bazzard, Tartar, and Billickin, besides a street urchin known as Deputy or Winks. Where, one asks, in the name of all that is wonderful, did Mr. Dickens ever rake together so amazing a museum?

We have discovered at different times that many of his queerest appellatives were genuine surnames under which some of our fellow-creatures are suffering at the present moment; and, for anything we know, every one of the above may have a precedent in real life. Still it almost passes the degree of belief which one is apt to concede even to a novel, to imagine that three such persons as Grewgious, Honeythunder, and Crisparkle could ever come together in this world. The system is, however, characteristic enough. Balzac in one of his novels is very eloquent upon the influence of names, and explains with apparently cogent reasoning that a person named Z. Marcas must necessarily be an unrecognised man of genius. If Mr. Dickens's creations were the victims of a similar influence, we should fancy ourselves from the above enumeration to be entering a museum of human oddities. And unluckily there is too much truth in the supposition. Each of the unlucky beings marked in this singular manner has some personal peculiarity almost as distinctive as his name; and, as a general rule, one can more or less faintly trace the association of ideas which led to the system of naming. Honeythunder, for example, is a fresh example of that race of mankind which seems above all others to have excited Mr. Dickens's most irrepressible disgust—the sham philanthropist whose virtue is of the most combative, ostentatious, and uncharitable type. We do not doubt that such people exist, as, for all that we know to the contrary, there may be a real family of Honeythunders; but the character is about as unusual as the name; and the almost infantile notion of satire which is implied in calling a man Honeythunder in order to make him ridiculous is exemplified only too consistently in the language and actions attributed to the bearer of the name. Mr. Honeythunder is a mere wooden figure, as lifeless as that which Mr. Quilp was in the habit of belabouring, pretty much in the same spirit as that in which Mr. Dickens belabours sham philanthropists, though from less amiable motives. The worst of it is that Honeythunder, whilst fully as grotesque as any of Mr. Dickens's earlier creations, is far less amusing, simply because a man when he is over fifty cannot design grotesques with the spirit which he possessed when he was under thirty. The oddity, as we have said, remains, but oddity requires to be carried off by a certain reckless audacity which is only to be expected from a youthful writer. Honeythunder, it is to be added, is only a subsidiary character, as he is one of the least satisfactory in the book; but the same taint of mannerism and forced humour is more or less evident in most of the other actors.

To make a more serious criticism, the pathetic and passionate parts of the book are, as usual with the author, the least satisfactory. There is some love-making which reminds us of Dora in *David Copperfield*, and there is a murderer (so at least we infer, though the mystery is not fully revealed) of the melodramatic type. This person endeavours to recommend himself to a young lady, whom, after the fashion of his kind, he regards with a certain wolfish admiration, by insinuating that if she marries him he will not procure the execution of another young man for a crime which he has himself committed. The general situation of the brutal villain threatening the amiable heroine into compliance with his wishes by revealing part of his diabolical character is familiar enough. We quote a fragment of his address as a specimen of the more high-flown passages:—

> "Rosa," says the villain, "even when my dear boy was affianced to you, I loved you madly; even when I thought his happiness in having you for his wife was certain, I loved you madly; even when I strove to make him more ardently

devoted to you, I loved you madly; even when he gave me the picture of your lovely face, so carelessly traduced by him, which I feigned to hang always in my sight for his sake, but worshipped in torment for years, I loved you madly; in the distasteful work of the day, in the wakeful misery of the night, girded by sordid realities, or wandering through Paradises and Hells of visions into which I rushed, carrying your vision in my arms, I loved you madly."

In this precious oration we recognise the worst style of Mr. Dickens, "ticking off" each point (as Mr. Grewgious expresses it on a similar occasion) by the burden of "I loved you madly." But do we recognise anything like the language of a passionate and blackhearted villain trying to bully a timid girl? It is the sort of oration which a silly boy, nourished on bad novels, might prepare for such an occasion; but it is stiff and artificial and jerky to a degree which excludes any belief in real passion. It is rounded off prettily enough for a peroration in a debating society; or it might be a fair piece of acting for a romantic young tradesman who fancied himself doing his love-making in the high poetic style; but it has an air of affectation and mock-heroics which is palpably inappropriate to the place. It is really curious that so keen an observer should diverge into such poor and stilted bombast whenever he tries the note of intense emotion.

In spite, however, of this and more which might be fairly said, there is much in *Edwin Drood* to remind us more pleasantly of the author's best days. There are a good many passages of genuine and easy humour; and, if the manner is apt to be rather cramped and deficient in the old flow and vivacity, there is yet abundant fertility in inventing really telling characters. There is nothing indeed to set beside our old familiar friends, such as Sam Weller and Mrs. Gamp, but there is something which nobody but Mr. Dickens himself could have written. The story, too, so far as we can judge from a fragment, is more skilfully put together than was usually the case, and may be read with interest in spite of the absence of a conclusion. We may guess pretty safely how the schemes of the bad characters would have been defeated, and all the good people portioned off with comfortable incomes and abundance of olive-branches. And we may welcome many touches of scenery and the picturesque description of the old cathedral town, whose identity may be recognised under its alias of Cloisterham.

> *A review of "The Mystery of Edwin Drood," in* The Saturday Review, *London, Vol. 30, No. 777, September 17, 1870, p. 369.*

THE SPECTATOR (essay date 1870)

[In this excerpt from an anonymous review of Edwin Drood, *the critic dismisses the idea that the novel represents a decline in Dickens's artistic powers.]*

We have seen it asserted by the critics that Mr. Dickens had lost, long before he wrote *Edwin Drood,* the power of giving to his grotesque conceptions that youthful *élan* which is essential to their perfection after their kind, and consequently to their fascination. But may not a great part of the explanation be that the critics, before they read *Edwin Drood,* had lost that youthful *élan* which was essential to enjoying it,—and that they continue to enjoy even Mr. Dickens's younger works more by the force of memory and tradition, than by virtue of any vivid and present appreciation of their humour? At least, so far as we can judge by close observation of those who now read *Edwin Drood* at the same age at which most of us first learnt to enjoy the *Old Curiosity Shop* and *Martin Chuzzlewit*, there does not seem to be any deficiency in the capacity of the rising generation to enter heartily into its still fresh humour. We sincerely believe that the picture of Durdles, the Cathedral stonemason, and of the young imp who stones him home at night, would have been welcomed twenty-five years ago with as much delight as was at that time the picture of Poll Sweedle-pipes, barber and bird-fancier, and his distinguished customer, Bailey Junior. We do not, of course, mean that *Edwin Drood* is nearly as brimful of humour as *Martin Chuzzlewit*. Few men ever reach a second time the standard of their most character-istic works, and the American tour of Mr. Dickens evidently gave a stimulus to his sense of humour which brought it all at once into its fullest flower. But *Edwin Drood* does seem to us nearer the standard of his first few works than anything he had written for many years back. It shows his peculiar power of grasping the local colour and detail of all characteristic *physical* life, in the exceedingly powerful sketch of the den of the East-End opium-smoker; it shows a different side of the same faculty in the abundant and marvellous detail as to the precincts and interior of the Cathedral; while all his old humour comes out in the picture of Miss Twinkleton's girls'-school, of Billickin the lodging-house keeper, and in the figures to which we have before referred, of the Cathedral stone mason and his attendant imp. No doubt there are all Mr. Dickens's faults in this story quite unchanged. He never learned to draw a human being as distinct from an oddity, and all his characters which are not oddities are false. Again he never learned the distinguishing signs of genuine sentiment; and just as nothing can be vulgarer than the sentimental passages of *Nicholas Nickleby* and *Martin Chuzzlewit*, so nothing can, at any rate, be much falser or in worse taste than the sentimental scenes in *Edwin Drood*. Mr. Dickens could not get over the notion that a love scene was a rich and luscious sort of juice, to be sucked up in the sort of way in which a bowl of punch and a Christmas dinner are so often enjoyed in his tales; and not only so, but all beauty, all that he thinks loveable, is apt to be treated by him as if it were a pot of raspberry jam, something luscious to the palate, instead of something fascinating to the imagination and those finer powers by which harmony of expression is perceived. All these faults, which have appeared in every tale of Mr. Dickens from the very first, have not, of course, in any way disappeared from this. But they are certainly not more obtrusive than usual, while the very unusual phenomenon of a story constructed with great care and ingenuity, relieves the ill-drawn and over-col-oured characters of much of their ordinary tedium. As more incidental evidence how little his greatest and most character-istic power of close humorous observation had decayed, take this perfect sketch of the two waiters from Furnival's Inn who attend the little dinner which Mr. Grewgious gives in his chambers.

> Bazzard returned accompanied by two wait-ers—an immovable waiter and a flying waiter; and the three brought in with them as much fog as gave a new roar to the fire. The flying waiter, who had brought everything on his shoulders, laid the cloth with amazing rapidity and dex-terity; while the immovable waiter, who had brought nothing, found fault with him. The flying waiter then highly polished all the glasses he had brought, and the immovable waiter looked through them. The flying waiter then flew across Holborn for the soup, and flew back again, and then took another flight for the made-dish, and flew back again, and then took another flight for the joint and poultry, and flew back again, and between whiles took supplementary flights for a great variety of articles, as it was discov-ered from time to time that the immovable waiter had forgotten them all. But let the flying waiter cleave the air as he might, he was always re-proached on his return by the immovable waiter for bringing fog with him and being out of breath. At the conclusion of the repast, by which time the flying waiter was severely blown, the immovable waiter gathered up the table-cloth under his arm with a grand air, and having sternly, not to say with indignation, looked on at the flying waiter while he set clean glasses round, directed a valedictory glance towards Mr. Grewgious, conveying, 'let it clearly be understood between us that the reward is mine, and that Nil is the claim of this slave,' and pushed the flying waiter before him out of the room. . . . And here let it be noticed paren-thetically, that the leg of this young man [the flying waiter], in its application to the door, evinced the finest sense of touch, always pre-ceding himself and tray (with something of an angling air about it), and always lingering after he and the tray had disappeared, like Macbeth's leg when accompanying him off the stage with reluctance to the assassination of Duncan.

Did Dickens in his best book ever write a passage of more closely observing humour than that, or finish it off with a finer stroke than that touch about the flying waiter's leg preceding himself and tray into the room "with something of an angling air about it?" Any critic who holds that Dickens had lost the youthful *élan* of his humour in writing that passage, must clearly have himself lost all the youthful *élan* essential to the full appreciation of humour. Or take another very different touch, in which "the Billickin" rises almost to the imaginative level of Wordsworth himself, while recalling the fatal influence which the poor diet at her boarding-school has exercised on her life:—"I was put in life," she says to Miss Twinkleton, "to a very genteel boarding-school, the mistress being no less a lady than yourself, of about your own age, or it may be, some years younger, *and a poorness of blood flowed from the table which has run through my life.*" It is possible to miss the analogy to Wordsworth's fine passage in the Prelude?—

> Was it for this
> That one, the fairest of all rivers, loved
> To blend his murmurs with my nurse's song,
> And from his alder shades and rocky falls
> And from his fords and shallows, *sent a voice*
> *That flowed along my dreams?*

We think it will be admitted that the Billickin's metaphor, though not exactly the grander of the two, is, at least, the bolder imaginative flight.

However characteristic the faults of the fragment which em-bodies Mr. Dickens's last literary effort, we feel no doubt that it will be read, admired, and remembered for the display of his equally characteristic powers, long after such performances as *Little Dorrit* and *Bleak House* are utterly neglected and for-gotten. (pp. 1176-77)

A review of ''The Mystery of Edwin Drood,'' in The Spectator, *Vol. 43, No. 2205, October 1, 1870, pp. 1176-77.*

JOHN FORSTER   (essay date 1874)

[*Forster was a Victorian biographer, historian, and critic who became Dickens's lifelong friend and literary advisor. Forster's* The Life of Charles Dickens, *from which the following excerpt is drawn, is considered one of the greatest biographies of a literary figure in the English language. In his comments on* Edwin Drood, *Forster provides what has proved to be a controversial account of Dickens's conception of the novel and ultimate plans for completing it. Despite widespread debate over the accuracy of Forster's assertions, his recollections are regarded as the most important evidence as to how Dickens intended to conclude* Edwin Drood. *Forster's comments were first published in 1874.*]

[Dickens's] first fancy for the tale [*Edwin Drood*] was expressed in a letter in the middle of July. ''What should you think of the idea of a story beginning in this way?—Two people, boy and girl, or very young, going apart from one another, pledged to be married after many years—at the end of the book. The interest to arise out of the tracing of their separate ways, and the impossibility of telling what will be done with that impending fate.'' This was laid aside; but it left a marked trace on the story as afterwards designed, in the position of Edwin Drood and his betrothed.

I first heard of the later design in a letter dated ''Friday the 6th of August 1869,'' in which after speaking, with the usual unstinted praise he bestowed always on what moved him in others, of a little tale he had received for his journal, he spoke of the change that had occurred to him for the new tale by himself. ''I laid aside the fancy I told you of, and have a very curious and new idea for my new story. Not a communicable idea (or the interest of the book would be gone), but a very strong one, though difficult to work.'' The story, I learnt immediately afterward, was to be that of the murder of a nephew by his uncle; the originality of which was to consist in the review of the murderer's career by himself at the close, when its temptations were to be dwelt upon as if, not he the culprit, but some other man, were the tempted. The last chapters were to be written in the condemned cell, to which his wickedness, all elaborately elicited from him as if told of another, had brought him. Discovery by the murderer of the utter needlessness of the murder for its object, was to follow hard upon commission of the deed; but all discovery of the murderer was to be baffled till towards the close, when, by means of a gold ring which had resisted the corrosive effects of the lime into which he had thrown the body, not only the person murdered was to be identified but the locality of the crime and the man who committed it. So much was told to me before any of the book was written; and it will be recollected that the ring, taken by Drood to be given to his betrothed only if their engagement went on, was brought away with him from their last interview. Rosa was to marry Tartar, and Crisparkle the sister of Landless, who was himself, I think, to have perished in assisting Tartar finally to unmask and seize the murderer.

Nothing had been written, however, of the main parts of the design excepting what is found in the published numbers; there was no hint or preparation for the sequel in any notes of chapters in advance; and there remained not even what he had himself so sadly written of the book by Thackeray also interrupted by death. The evidence of matured designs never to be accomplished, intentions planned never to be executed, roads of thought marked out never to be traversed, goals shining in the distance never to be reached, was wanting here. It was all a blank. Enough had been completed nevertheless to give promise of a much greater book than its immediate predecessor. ''I hope his book is finished,'' wrote Longfellow when the news of his death was flashed to America. ''It is certainly one of his most beautiful works, if not the most beautiful of all. It would be too sad to think the pen had fallen from his hand, and left it incomplete.'' Some of its characters are touched with subtlety, and in its description his imaginative power was at its best. Not a line was wanting to the reality, in the most minute local detail, of places the most widely contrasted; and we saw with equal vividness the lazy cathedral town and the lurid opium-eater's den. Something like the old lightness and buoyancy of animal spirits gave a new freshness to the humour; the scenes of the child-heroine and her luckless betrothed had both novelty and nicety of character in them; and Mr. Grewgious in chambers with his clerk and the two waiters, the conceited fool Sapsea, and the blustering philanthropist Honeythunder, were first-rate comedy. (pp. 807-09)

• • • • •

This reference to the last effort of Dickens's genius had been written as it thus stands, when a discovery of some interest was made by the writer. Within the leaves of one of Dickens's other manuscripts were found some detached slips of his writing, on paper only half the size of that used for the tale, so cramped, interlined, and blotted as to be nearly illegible, which on close inspection proved to be a scene in which Sapsea the auctioneer is introduced as the principal figure, among a group of characters new to the story. The explanation of it perhaps is, that, having become a little nervous about the course of the tale, from a fear that he might have plunged too soon into the incidents leading on to the catastrophe, such as the Datchery assumption in the fifth number (a misgiving he had certainly expressed to his sister-in-law), it had occurred to him to open some fresh veins of character incidental to the interest, though not directly part of it, and so to handle them in connection with Sapsea as a little to suspend the final development even while assisting to strengthen it. Before beginning any number of a serial, he used . . . to plan briefly what he intended to put into it chapter by chapter; and his first number-plan of *Drood* had the following: ''Mr. Sapsea. Old Tory jackass. Connect Jasper with him. (He will want a solemn donkey by and by)'': which was effected by bringing together both Durdles and Jasper, for connection with Sapsea, in the matter of the epitaph for Mrs. Sapsea's tomb. The scene now discovered might in this view have been designed to strengthen and carry forward that element in the tale; and otherwise it very sufficiently expresses itself. It would supply an answer, if such were needed, to those who have asserted that the hopeless decadence of Dickens as a writer had set in before his death. Among the lines last written by him, these are the very last we can ever hope to receive; and they seem to me a delightful specimen of the power possessed by him in his prime, and the rarest which any novelist can have, of revealing a character by a touch. Here are a couple of people, Kimber and Peartree, not known to us before, whom we read off thoroughly in a dozen words; and as to Sapsea himself, auctioneer and mayor of Cloisterham, we are face to face with what before we only dimly realized, and we see the solemn jackass, in his business pulpit, playing off the airs of Mr. Dean in his Cathedral pulpit, with Cloisterham laughing at the imposter. (pp. 810-11)

John Forster, in his The Life of Charles Dickens, *edited by J. W. T. Ley, Cecil Palmer, 1928, 893 p.*

LUKE FILDES (letter date 1905)

[*Fildes took over as illustrator of the original monthly parts of* Edwin Drood *when Charles Collins became ill. In the following excerpt from a letter to the editor of the* Times Literary Supplement, *Fildes gives an account of a conversation with Dickens regarding the illustrations. His assertion that Dickens had revealed to him that Jasper strangled Drood with a scarf has figured prominently in most attempts to solve the mystery, even when critics have questioned Fildes's truthfulness and accuracy.*]

Sir,—In an article entitled "The Mysteries of *Edwin Drood*" in your issue of to-day, the writer, speculating on the various theories advanced as solutions of the mystery, ventures to say:—

> Nor do we attach much importance to any of the hints Dickens dropped, whether to John Forster, to any member of his family, or to either of his illustrators. He was very anxious that his secret should not be guessed, and the hints which he dropped may very well have been intentionally misleading.

I know Charles Dickens was very anxious that his secret should not be guessed, but it surprises me to read that he could be thought capable of the deceit so lightly attributed to him.

The "hints he dropped" to me, his sole illustrator, for Charles Collins, his son-in-law, only designed the green cover for the monthly parts, and Collins told me he did not in the least know the significance of the various groups in the design; that they were drawn from instructions personally given by Charles Dickens and not from any text—these "hints" to me were the outcome of a request of mine that he would explain some matters, the meaning of which I could not comprehend and which were for me, his illustrator, embarrassingly hidden.

I instanced in the printers' rough proof of the monthly part sent to me to illustrate where he particularly described John Jasper as wearing a neckerchief of such dimensions as to go twice around his neck; I called his attention to the circumstance that I had previously dressed Jasper as wearing a little black tie once round the neck, and I asked him if he had any special reasons for the alteration of Jasper's attire, and, if so, I submitted I ought to know. He, Dickens, appeared for a moment to be disconcerted by my remark, and said something meaning he was afraid he was "getting on too fast" and revealing more than he meant at that early stage, and after a short silence, cogitating, he suddenly said, "Can you keep a secret?" I assured him he could rely on me. He then said, "I must have the double necktie! It is necessary, for Jasper strangles Edwin Drood with it."

I was impressed by his earnestness, as indeed, I was at all my interviews with him—also by the confidence which he said he reposed in me, trusting that I would not in any way refer to it, as he feared even a chance remark might find its way into the "papers" and thus anticipate his "mystery"; and it is a little startling, after more than 35 years of profound belief in the nobility of character and sincerity of Charles Dickens, to be told now that he probably was more or less of a humbug on such occasions.

> *Luke Fildes, in a letter to the editor of* The Times Literary Supplement, *No. 199, November 3, 1905, p. 373.*

KATE PERUGINI (essay date 1906)

[*Dickens's second daughter, Perugini was also married to Charles Collins, the artist originally engaged by Dickens to illustrate the monthly parts of* Edwin Drood. *In the following excerpt, Perugini corroborates the account of Dickens's plans for* Edwin Drood *given by John Forster in his* The Life of Charles Dickens (see excerpt dated 1874). *Perugini also provides her own impression of the course the novel was to have taken and summarizes what both her husband and the other members of Dickens's family knew about his intentions. Perugini's account is considered one of the most important pieces of evidence about Dickens's plans.*]

The Mystery of Edwin Drood is a story, or, to speak more correctly, the half of a story, that has excited so much general interest and so many speculations as to its ultimate disclosures, that it has given rise to various imaginary theories on the part of several clever writers; and to much discussion among those who are not writers, but merely fervent admirers and thoughtful readers of my father's writings. All these attach different meanings to the extraordinary number of clues my father has offered them to follow, and they are even more keen at the present day than they were when the book made its first appearance, to find their way through the tangled maze and arrive at the very heart of the mystery. Among the numerous books, pamphlets and articles that have been written upon *Edwin Drood* there are some that are extremely interesting and well worth attention, for they contain many clever and possible suggestions, and although they do not entirely convince us, yet they add still more to the almost painful anxiety we all feel in wandering through the lonely precincts of Cloisterham Cathedral, or along the banks of the river that runs through Cloisterham town and lead to the Weir of which we are told in the story.

In following these writers to the end of their subtle imaginings as to how the mystery might be solved, we may sometimes be inclined to pause for an instant and ask ourselves whether my father did not perhaps intend his story to have an ending less complicated, although quite as interesting, as any that are suggested. We find ourselves turning to John Forster's *Life of Charles Dickens,* to help us in our perplexity; and this is what we read in his chapter headed "Last Book." Mr. Forster begins by telling us that *Edwin Drood* was to be published in twelve illustrated monthly parts, and that it closed prematurely with the sixth number, which was itself underwritten by two pages; therefore my father had exactly six numbers and two pages to write, when he left his little Châlet in the shrubbery of Gad's Hill Place on June 8th, 1870, to which he never returned. Mr. Foster goes on to say: "His first fancy for the tale was expressed in July (meaning the July of 1869), in a letter which runs thus:

> What should you think of the idea of a story beginning in this way?—Two people, boy and girl, or very young, going apart from one another, pledged to be married after many years—at the end of the book. The interest to arise out of the tracing of their separate ways, and the impossibility of telling what will be done with that impending fate."

This idea my father relinquished, although he left distinct traces of it in his tale; and in a letter to Mr. Forster, dated August 6th, 1869, tells him:

> I laid aside the fancy I told you of, and have a very curious and new idea for my new story. Not a communicable idea (or the interest of the

book would be gone), but a very strong one, though difficult to work.

Mr. Forster then says that he immediately afterwards learnt that the story was to be "the murder of a nephew by his uncle"; the originality of which was to consist in the review of the murderer's career by himself at the close, when its temptations were to be dwelt upon as if not he, the culprit, but some other man, were the tempted.

> The last chapters were to be written in the condemned cell, to which his wickedness, all elaborately elicited from him as if told of another, had brought him. Discovery by the murderer of the utter needlessness of the murder for its object, was to follow hard upon commission of the deed; but all discovery of the murderer was to be baffled till towards the close, when by means of a gold ring which had resisted the corrosive effects of the lime into which he had thrown the body, not only the person murdered was to be identified, but the locality of the crime, and the man who committed it.

Mr. Forster adds a little information as to the marriages at the close of the book, and makes use of the expression "I think," in speaking of Neville Landless, as though he were not quite certain of what he remembered concerning him. This "I think" has been seized upon by some of Mr. Forster's critics, who appear to argue that because he did not clearly recollect one detail of the story he may therefore have been mistaken in the whole. But we see for ourselves that Mr. Forster is perfectly well informed as to the nature of the plot, and the fate of the two principal characters concerned, the murdered and the murderer; and the only thing upon which he is not positive is the ending of Neville Landless, to which he confesses in the words "I think," thus making his testimony to the more important facts the more impressive. If we have any doubts as to whether Mr. Forster correctly stated what he was told, we have only to turn to the story of *Edwin Drood* and we find, as far as it goes, that his statement is entirely corroborated by what we read in the book.

If those who are interested in the subject will carefully read what I have quoted, they will not be able to detect any word or hint from my father that it was upon the Mystery alone that he relied for the interest and originality of his idea. The originality was to be shown, as he tells us, in what we may call the psychological description the murderer gives us of his temptations, temperament, and character, as if told by another; and my father speaks openly of the ring to Mr. Forster. Moreover, he refers to it often in his story, and we all recognise it, whatever our other convictions may be, as the instrument by which Jasper's wickedness and guilt are to be established in the end. I do not mean to imply that the mystery itself had no strong hold on my father's imagination; but, greatly as he was interested in the intricacies of that tangled skein, the information he voluntarily gave to Mr. Forster, from whom he had withheld nothing for thirty-three years, certainly points to the fact that he was quite as deeply fascinated and absorbed in the study of the criminal Jasper, as in the dark and sinister crime that has given the book its title. And he also speaks to Mr. Forster of the murder of a nephew by an uncle. He does not say that he is uncertain whether he shall save the nephew, but has evidently made up his mind that the crime is to be committed. And so he told his plot to Mr. Forster, as he had been accustomed to tell his plots for years past; and those who knew him must feel

it impossible to believe that in this, the last year of his life, he should suddenly become underhand, and we might say treacherous, to his old friend, by inventing for his private edification a plot that he had no intention of carrying into execution. This is incredible, and the nature of the friendship that existed between Mr. Forster and himself makes the idea unworthy of consideration.

Mr. Forster was devotedly attached to my father, but as years passed by, this engrossing friendship made him a little jealous of his confidence, and more than a little exacting in his demands upon it. My father was perfectly aware of this weakness in his friend, and although the knowledge of it made him smile at times, and even joke about it when we were at home and alone, he was always singularly tender-hearted where Mr. Forster was concerned, and was particularly careful never to wound the very sensitive nature of one who, from the first moment of their acquaintance, had devoted his time and energy to making my father's path in life as smooth as so intricate a path could be made. In all business transactions Mr. Forster acted for him, and generally brought him through those troubles triumphantly, whereas, if left to himself, his impetuosity and impatience might have spoilt all chances of success; while in all his private troubles my father instinctively turned to his friend, and even when not invariably following his advice, had yet so much confidence in his judgment as to be rendered not only uneasy but unhappy if Mr. Forster did not approve of the decision at which he ultimately arrived. From the beginning of their friendship to the end of my father's life the relations between the two friends remained unchanged; and the notion that has been spread abroad that my father wilfully misled Mr. Forster in what he told him of the plot of *Edwin Drood* should be abandoned, as it does not correspond with the knowledge of those who understood the dignity of my father's character, and were also aware of the perfectly frank terms upon which he lived with Mr. Forster.

If my father again changed his plan for the story of *Edwin Drood,* the first thing he would naturally do would be to write to Mr. Forster and inform him of the alteration. We might imagine for an instant that he would perhaps desire to keep the change as a surprise for his friend, but what I have just stated with regard to Mr. Forster's character renders this supposition out of the question, as my father knew for a certainty that his jealousy would debar him from appreciating such a surprise, and that he would in all probability strongly resent what he might with justice be allowed to consider as a piece of unnecessary caution on my father's part. That he did not write to Mr. Forster to tell him of any divergence from his second plan for the book we all know, and we know also that my eldest brother, Charles, positively declared that he had heard from his father's lips that Edwin Drood was dead. Here, therefore, are two very important witnesses to a fact that is still doubted by those who never met my father, and were never impressed by the grave sincerity with which he would have given this assurance.

It is very often those who most doubt Mr. Forster's accuracy on this point who are in the habit of turning to his book when they are in search of facts to establish some theory of their own; and they do not hesitate to do this, because they know that whatever views they may hold upon the work itself, or the manner in which it is written, absolute truth is to be found in its pages. Why should they refuse, therefore, to believe a statement made upon one page of his three volumes, when they willingly and gratefully accept the rest if it is to their interest to do so? This is a difficult question to answer, but it is not without importance when we are discussing the subject of *Edwin Drood*. . . . [In] the third volume of Mr. Forster's *Life* is to be found the simple explanation of my father's plot for his story, as given to him by my father himself. It is true that Mr. Forster speaks from remembrance, but how often does he not speak from remembrance, and yet how seldom are we inclined to doubt his word! Only here, because what he tells us does not exactly fit in with our preconceived views as to how the tale shall be finished, are we disposed to quarrel with him, for the simple reason that we flatter ourselves we have discovered a better ending to the book than the one originally intended for it by the author. And so we put his statement aside and ignore it, while we grope in the dark for a thing we shall never find; and we obstinately refuse to allow even the little glimmer of light my father has himself thrown upon the obscurity to help us in our search. It was not, I imagine, for the intricate working out of his plot alone, that my father cared to write this story; but it was through his wonderful observation of character, and his strange insight into the tragic secrets of the human heart, that he desired his greatest triumph to be achieved.

I do not write upon these things because I have any fresh or startling theories to offer upon the subject of *Edwin Drood*. I cannot say that I am without my own opinions, but I am fully conscious that after what has been already so ably said, they would have but little interest for the general public; so I shrink from venturing upon any suggestions respecting the solution of my father's last book. My chief object in writing is to remind the readers of this paper that there are certain facts connected with this story that cannot lightly be put aside, and these facts are to be found in John Forster's *Life of Charles Dickens*, and in the declaration made by my brother Charles. Having known both Mr. Forster and my brother intimately, I cannot for a moment believe that either of them would speak or write that which he did not know to be strictly true; and it is on these grounds alone that I think I have a right to be heard when I insist upon the assertion that Edwin Drood was undoubtedly murdered by his uncle Jasper. As to the unravelling of the mystery, and the way in which the murder was perpetrated, we are all at liberty to have our own views, seeing that no explanations were as yet arrived at in the story; but we should remember that only vague speculations can be indulged in when we try to imagine them for ourselves.

It has been pointed out, and very justly, that although Jasper removed the watch, chain, and scarf-pin from Edwin's body, there would possibly remain on it money of some kind, keys, and the metal buttons on his clothes, which the action of the quicklime could not destroy, and by which his identity would be made known. This has been looked upon as an oversight, a mere piece of forgetfulness on my father's part. But remembering, as I do very well, what he often said, that the most clever criminals were constantly detected through some small defect in their calculations, I cannot but think it most probable that this was not an oversight, but was intended to lead up to the pet theory that he so frequently mentioned whenever a murder case was brought to trial. After reading *Edwin Drood* many times, as most of us have read it, we must, I think, come to the conclusion that not a word of this tale was written without full consideration; that in this story at least my father left nothing to chance; and that therefore the money, and the buttons, were destined to take their proper place in the book, and might turn out to be a weak spot in Jasper's well-arranged and complicated plot, *the* weak spot my father insisted upon, as being inseparable from the commission of a great crime, how-

ever skillfully planned. The keys spoken of need not be taken seriously into account, for Edwin was a careless young fellow, and it is not unreasonable to suppose that he did not always carry them upon his person; he was staying with his uncle, and he may have left them in the portmanteau, which was most likely at the time of the murder lying unfastened in his room, with the key belonging to it in the lock. It would be unfair to suggest that my father wrote unadvisedly of this or that, for he had still the half of his story to finish, and plenty of time, as he thought, in which to gather up the broken threads and weave them into a symmetrical and harmonious whole, which he was so eminently capable of completing.

That my father's brain was more than usually clear and bright during the writing of *Edwin Drood,* no one who lived with him could possibly doubt; and the extraordinary interest he took in the development of this story was apparent in all that he said or did, and was often the subject of conversation between those who anxiously watched him as he wrote, and feared that he was trying his strength too far. For although my father's death was sudden and unexpected, the knowledge that his bodily health was failing had been for some time too forcibly brought to the notice of those who loved him, for them to be blind to the fact that the book he was now engaged in, and the concentration of his devotion and energy upon it, were a tax too great for his fast ebbing strength. Any attempt to stay him, however, in work that he had undertaken was as idle as stretching one's hands to a river and bidding it cease to flow; and beyond a few remonstrances now and again urged, no such attempt was made, knowing as we did that it would be entirely useless. And so the work sped on, carrying with it my father's few remaining days of life, and the end came all too soon, as it was bound to come, to one who never ceased to labour for those who were dear to him, in the hope of gaining for them that which he was destined never to enjoy. And in my father's grave lies buried the secret of his story.

The scene of the Eight Club, which Mr. Forster discovered after his death, in which there figure two new characters, Mr. Peartree and Mr. Kimber, bears no relation as we read it to the unfolding of the plot; and although the young man Poker, who is also introduced in this fragment for the first time, seems to be of more significance, we see too little of him to be certain that we may not already have made his acquaintance. In Mr. Sapsea my father evidently took much pleasure, and we are here reminded of the note made for him in the first number-plan of *Edwin Drood*: ''Mr. Sapsea, Old Tory Jackass. Connect Jasper with him. (He will want a solemn donkey by-and-by).'' My father also wanted the solemn donkey, and not only brought him in for the purposes of his story, but because, as in the case of ''the Billickin,'' he took delight in dwelling upon the absurdities of the character.

As to the cover of *Edwin Drood,* that has been the subject of so much discussion, there is very little to tell. It was designed and drawn by Mr. Charles A. Collins, my first husband. The same reasons that prevented me from teasing my father with questions respecting his story made me refrain from asking any of Mr. Collins; but from what he said I certainly gathered that he was not in possession of my father's secret, although he had made his designs from my father's directions. There are a few things in this cover that I fancy have been a little misunderstood. In the book only Jasper and Neville Landless are described as dark young men. Edwin Drood is fair, and so is Crisparkle. Tartar is burnt by the sun; but when Rosa asks ''the Unlimited head chambermaid'' at the hotel in Furnival's Inn if the gentleman who has just called is dark, she replies:

"No, Miss, more of a brown gentleman."

"You are sure not with black hair?" asked Rosa, taking courage.

"Quite sure of that, Miss. Brown hair and blue eyes."

Now in a drawing it would be difficult to make a distinction between the fair hair of Edwin and the slightly darker hair of Tartar; and in the picture, where we see a girl—Rosa we imagine her to be—seated in a garden, the young man at her feet is, I feel pretty sure, intended for Tartar. Edwin it cannot be, nor Neville, as has been supposed, for he was decidedly dark. Besides this, Neville would not have told his affection to Rosa, for Helena was far too quick-witted not to understand from Rosa's first mention of Tartar that she is already in love with him, and she would have warned and saved the brother to whom she was so ardently attached from making any such confession. The figure is not intended for Jasper, because we know that Jasper did not move from the sundial in the scene where he declares his mad passion for Rosa, and Jasper had black hair and whiskers. And, again, the drawing cannot be meant to represent Helena and Crisparkle, for the young man is not in clerical dress. The figures going up the stairs are still more difficult to make out; but there can be little doubt that the active higher one is the same young man we see at Rosa's feet, and must therefore be Tartar. Of the remaining two, one may be Crisparkle, although there is still no clerical attire, and the other either Grewgious or Neville, though the drawing certainly bears but little resemblance to either of those characters.

The lower and middle picture is, of course, the great scene of the book; but whether the young man standing calm, and inexorable as Fate, is intended to be the ghost of Edwin as seen by Jasper in his half-dazed and drugged condition, or whether it is Helena dressed as Datchery, as one writer has ingeniously suggested (although there are reasons in the story against the supposition that Helena is Datchery, and many to support the theory that the "old buffer" is Bazzard),—these are puzzles that will never be cleared up, except to the minds of those who have positively determined that they hold the clue to the mystery, and can only see its interpretation from one point of view. The girl's figure with streaming hair, in the picture where the word "Lost" is written, has been supposed to represent Rosa after her parting from Edwin; but it may more likely, I think, indicate some scene in the book which has yet to be described in the story. This is another enigma; but my father, it may be presumed, intended to puzzle his readers by the cover, and he had every legitimate right to do so, for had his meaning been made perfectly clear "the interest of the book would be gone." Some surprise has been expressed because Mr. Forster did not ask Mr. Collins for the meaning of his designs; but if he already knew the plot, why should he seek information from Mr. Collins?—particularly as my father may have told him that he had not disclosed the secret of his story to his illustrators, for I believe I am right in affirming that Mr. Luke Fildes [see excerpt dated 1905] was no better informed as to the plan of the book than was Mr. Collins. (pp. 643-52)

There is one other fact connected with my father and *Edwin Drood* that I think my readers would like to know, and I must be forgiven if I again speak from my own experience in order to relate it. Upon reading the book once more, as I have already told, after an interval of a great number of years, the story took such entire possession of me that for a long time I could think of nothing else; and one day, my aunt, Miss Hogarth,

being with me, I asked her if she knew anything more definite than I did as to how the ending was to be brought about. For I should explain that when my father was unusually reticent we seldom, if ever, attempted to break his silence by remarks or hints that might lead him to suppose that we were anxious to learn what he had no doubt good reasons for desiring to keep from us. And we made it a point of honour among ourselves never, in talking to him on the subject of *Edwin Drood*, to show the impatience we naturally felt to arrive at the end of so engrossing a tale.

My aunt said that she knew absolutely nothing, but she told me that shortly before my father's death, and after he had been speaking of some difficulty he was in with his work, without explaining what it was, she found it impossible to refrain from asking him, "I hope you haven't really killed poor Edwin Drood?" To which he gravely replied, "I call my book the Mystery, not the History, of Edwin Drood." And that was all he would answer. My aunt could not make out from his reply, or from his manner of giving it, whether he wished to convey that the Mystery was to remain a mystery for ever, of if he desired gently to remind her that he would not disclose his secret until the proper time arrived for telling it. But I think his words are so suggestive, and may carry with them so much meaning, that I offer them now, with my aunt's permission, to those who take a delight in trying to unravel the impenetrable secrets of a story that has within its sadly shortened pages a most curious fascination, and is "gifted with invincible force to hold and drag." (p. 654)

Kate Perugini, "'Edwin Drood' and the Last Days of Charles Dickens," in The Pall Mall Magazine, *Vol. XXXVII, No. 158, June, 1906, pp. 643-54.*

HOWARD DUFFIELD   (essay date 1930)

[Duffield was the first critic to put forth the widely discussed theory that Jasper strangled or attempted to strangle Drood in a manner similar to that employed by the Indian sect of professional murderers known as Thugs. In the following excerpt from the article in which Duffield advanced his theory, he identifies numerous passages in Edwin Drood *in which Jasper's actions seem to closely resemble the ritual performed by practitioners of Thuggee prior to murdering their victims.]*

Among the unsolved puzzles of literature few are more intricate and fascinating than *The Mystery of Edwin Drood.* (p. 581)

From the outset John Jasper takes the limelight, as a study in criminal psychology, the exponent of an idea which Dickens asserted was "very curious", "very strong", "not communicable" and "difficult to work" [see excerpt by John Forster dated 1874]. It becomes quickly apparent that the clue to the rôle for which Jasper is cast must be sought for in Oriental antecedents. The story is enveloped in Oriental atmosphere. All the impulses which give it movement and direction come out of the East. Sultans, Turkish robbers, cymbals, scimitars, dancing-girls and parading elephants, like the fantastic figures of an Eastern rug, are woven into the web of the narrative by its introductory sentences. The moment the covers are opened a waft of opium is released, and every crisis reeks with opium fumes. The short prefatory chapter, which the author originally designated as the "Prologue", and at the close of which, as he himself says, he "touches the keynote", is wholly concerned with an East Indian opium den near the London docks, that great gateway through which the life of the Orient streams into England.

The occupants of the den are a Chinaman and a Lascar. Its proprietress is a hag who is an opium addict, and who "has opium-smoked herself into a strange likeness of the Chinaman". As he enters, Edwin Drood announces, "I shall go engineering into the East". In her first conversation with her betrothed, Edwin's fiancée drags in allusions to "Arabs, . . . and Fellahs, and people", to "Isises, and Ibises, and Cheopses, and Pharaohses", descants concerning the Pyramids and the Oriental trick of divining the future by gazing at a drop of ink in the palm of the hand. Mr. Sapsea, an auctioneer, pompously refers to "Pekin, Nankin and Canton", and proclaims that he comes in touch "with Japan, with Egypt, with bamboo and sandalwood from the East Indies". Neville and Helena Landless hail from Ceylon and the author, after due consideration, endows them with a "mixture of Oriental blood". Sapsea harps on their "un-English" appearance. Edwin opens conversation with Neville by proclaiming that "he was going to wake Egypt a little", and incessantly alludes to that "part of the world in which Neville was brought up". A sneering reference to Oriental manners, intensified by a contemptuous comment on Neville's "dark color", provokes an angry collision between the young men, which is a vital element of the plot. One of the most prominent characters has pinned upon him the grotesque title of "Tartar", a name as redolent of the East as a whiff of hashish.

Concerning the background of John Jasper, who occupies the center of the stage, Dickens intentionally left the reader in ignorance. A solitary remark as to personal appearance suggests an Oriental origin: "He is a dark man with thick, lustrous, well-arranged black hair and whiskers, and he looks older than he is, as dark men often do". Incidentally, he is shown to be familiar with the languages of the East for, when he listens to the mutterings of the opium-drenched Chinaman and the Lascar, he recognizes them as "unintelligible gibberish".

The revealing clue as to Jasper's personality is furnished by Dickens himself. With sedulous care he kept out of the story everything which might disclose its central secret, but in a confidential conversation with Luke Fildes, the illustrator of the novel, he made a statement which unveils Jasper with startling clearness. In a letter to the London *Times* of November 3rd, 1905, Fildes wrote that he had requested Dickens to explain a matter which he did not comprehend, and without an understanding of which he was unable properly to prepare his drawings [see excerpt above]. "I instanced," he writes, "the printer's rough proof, where he (Dickens) particularly described John Jasper as wearing a neckcloth of such dimensions as to go twice around his neck. I called his attention to the fact that I had previously sketched Jasper as wearing a little black tie around the neck, and I asked him if he had any special reason for the alteration of Jasper's attire; and if so,—I submitted to him,—I ought to know. He (Dickens) appeared for the moment to be disconcerted by my remark, and said something, meaning he was afraid he was 'getting on too fast' and revealing more than he meant to at that early stage. After a short silence, cogitating, he suddenly said, 'Can you keep a secret?' I assured him he could rely upon me. He then said, 'I must have the double tie. It is necessary, for Jasper strangles Edwin Drood with it'."

That this ample "neckcloth" was central to Dickens's thought is cried aloud by Fildes's letter. The insisted substitution of that long black scarf, for the "little black tie"; his anxiety, lest he might let into the open the very idea which he was so strenuously concealing; his brooding silence; his deliberate

weighing of the situation; his exaction of a pledge of absolute secrecy; his stressing the pivotal relation to the narrative, of Jasper's neck-gear—"I *must* have the double tie. It is *necessary*"—his explanation that Jasper is to *strangle* Drood with it, form a combination of circumstances which proclaim with cumulative emphasis that Fildes's inquiry went, like a probe, close to the heart of the "Mystery".

To anyone familiar with the habits and history of the East, the discovery that in a novel saturated with Orientalisms the chief character was to figure as "A Strangler" is electrifying. During two-thirds of the nineteenth century, the period spanned by the life of Charles Dickens, the outstanding feature of English rule in India was the effort to suppress the Phansigars, popularly known as "Thugs", whose victims were invariably strangled. Read in the light of this illuminating fact, the pages of the Drood fragment are found to be bristling with intimations that when Dickens told Fildes that a long black neckcloth *must* be in the picture, because it was *necessary* for a *strangling*, he made known what he had so earnestly striven to hide, that in the lore of this Oriental cult of death was to be found the major clue to the mystery which he was weaving.

The history of the Stranglers is a weird and gruesome chapter in the annals of crime. The bare conception of such a guild of murderers is so abhorrent and appalling that until the most convincing evidence had been secured the English Government refused to admit its existence, and it was not until the beginning of the nineteenth century that its presence as a cancerous factor in the social life of India became definitely acknowledged. In 1829 the Supreme Government of India established a Special Police Department, known as "Thuggee and Dacoity", to ferret out and suppress this savage brotherhood. Annual reports were made to the British Parliament until 1904, when it was believed that Thuggee had been finally wiped off the map.

The basal fact of the Drood story is a mysterious disappearance, and it was the frequency of "mysterious disappearances" (to quote the Police Reports) which first arrested the attention of the Government. Murder by a Thug was invariably a "mysterious disappearance". Travellers who set out upon a journey never reached their journey's end. Neighbors vanished. Soldiers on furlough failed to return to the rank. Nothing was ever known concerning a Strangler's victim, except that he was gone. The whole story of a Strangler's crime is contained in Dickens's repeated words, "No trace of Edwin Drood revisited the light of the sun".

The roster of these "mysterious disappearances" became so significantly large as to demand explanation, and the curtain lifted upon as repugnant and terrifying a spectacle as has ever been played in the drama of humanity. The Government of India found itself at close grips with a secret cult of "religious assassins". This craft of murder was sanctified, and its practice hallowed as a sort of ancestral rite. A member of that order would be running true to form if, as Jasper did, he wore a surplice over a murderous heart. A Strangler regarded himself as a votary of Kali, the Goddess of Destruction. Victims were never "murdered", but always "destroyed", as a sacrificial offering to her. The fact that, in the Drood fragment, Dickens has repeatedly used the term "destruction" in a very peculiar and sinister sense, flashes into light the thought that he is picturing Jasper as an adept in this unholy sect. When Jasper registers a vow of vengeance, consecrating his life to the pursuit of the supposed murderer of Drood, Dickens makes him say, "I *devote* myself to his *destruction*". This is a very strange and a very significant fancy expression. The natural statement would have been, "I will do all in my power to lead to his discovery, or secure his arrest, or bring him to justice, or insure his punishment". When he couches his determination in the term "I devote myself to his destruction", he is employing keywords in the vocabulary of the Stranglers. That Dickens was thoroughly aware of the baleful purpose of this phraseology and used it with set purpose is strikingly indicated by his selection as a heading for that chapter in which he records this incident of Jasper's dedication of himself as missionary of "destruction"—the one word "Devoted". To a Thug, that word could have but a single meaning. The presence of this idea in Dickens's mind is made still more apparent by his description of Jasper as endowed with an uncanny potency of "destruction". Dickens writes that Jasper gazed at young Landless, "as though his eye were at the trigger of a loaded rifle"—"with a sense of destructive power so expressed in his face" that his companion, who was a thick-skinned and stony-hearted bumpkin, shivered.

Not only did Dickens brand the Precentor of Cloisterham Cathedral with his hallmark of the Oriental Stranglers, but he has depicted him as a practitioner of every principle which is laid down in their science of death. The initial requirement of their system was the identification of themselves with the most respectable classes of the community, precisely after the fashion in which Jasper is introduced as having made for himself a place of high regard among the Cloisterham folk. Thugs became traders, farmers, men of business, even members of the learned professions. Commercially, they were trusted. Socially, they were courted. It was of prime importance that they should pose as good citizens and friendly neighbors. English officers testify to having lived on excellent terms with men whose affability and seeming integrity were only a mask for the instincts and practice of Thuggee. The language of the official records as to the favorable impression invariably created by a Strangler is distinctly re-echoed in the detailed stressing of Jasper's social standing:—"so much respected", "enjoying the reputation of having done wonders as a music teacher", "choosing his society and holding such an independent position".

It was a fundamental principle of Thuggee that the prelude to a murder should be the deception of the victim by pretended kindness. So important and imperative was this step, that its practice was assigned to a group specially trained for this purpose, and known as "Inveiglers". It was their treacherous task to insinuate themselves into the intimacy of their unsuspecting prey to the end that they might strike the death-blow behind the shield of a recognized attachment. Dickens has "writ large" such a relationship between Jasper and Edwin Drood. Underscored in the first pages, it is played up persistently and consistently throughout the story. Jasper was over-affectionate to Drood. He deluged him with affection. Cloisterham's name for Edwin was "John Jasper's beloved nephew". The Dean remarks, "I hope Mr. Jasper's heart may not be too much set upon his nephew". The Minor Canon, when told that a visit from Edwin was expected, says, "He will do you more good than a doctor, Jasper". Time and again Edwin protested against being so perpetually "moddley-coddleyed". The affection with which Jasper overloaded Edwin was ostentatious, almost unctuous. Acts of kindness were superabundant. Terms of endearment were employed with studious and exaggerated frequency. Such behavior would seem to mark him, and would certainly qualify him, as a Sothae, or Inveigler, in any circle of Thugs.

The "destruction" of a victim by a Strangler was wrought in accordance with a rigid ritual of procedure. Murder was never committed until a burial place had been prepared. Certain members of the band were chosen as a sort of committee on graves. An out-of-the-way spot was carefully selected in which the body could be instantly and secretly hidden. So expert were the Thugs in the concealment of the dead that the places in which the bodies of their victims were buried could seldom be discovered, except by the confession of the slayer. Jasper is represented as an expert in sepulture. Sounding the keys of the vaults, as if they were tuning forks; cultivating Durdles, the tombkeeper of the Cathedral, as a companion; continually rambling through the domain of the dead; arranging a night-time picnic in the crypt, during which every nook and cranny in which a corpse might be concealed was explored; taking note of a near-by heap of lime in which a body might be disintegrated, Jasper notably performed this cardinal duty of a Thug.

The observance of omens was regarded by a Strangler as absolutely essential, before attempting the "destruction" of his victim. Upon the eve of an assassination, watchers scanned the sky and air and landscape with piercing vigilance, searching for some token from the Goddess of Destruction. An elaborate code of such signs is catalogued in the governmental records of India. In a recent novel which vividly describes a murder by strangulation, a brace of Anglicized Thugs prefaced their assault by an "unaccountable expedition" across the Scottish countryside. For days their victim had been within reach, but

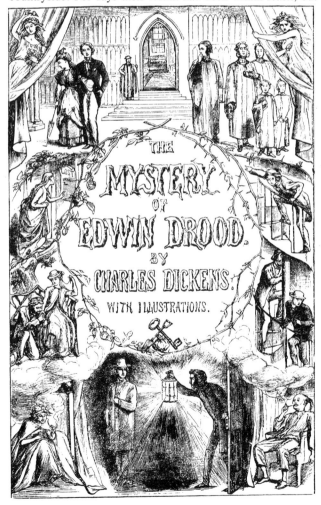

The cover design for the original monthly parts of Edwin Drood.

before the attack could be made, the omens must be noted. Jasper, accompanied by the grave-digger Durdles, made just such an unaccountable expedition to the top of the Cathedral Tower which has all the marks of an omen-hunt. It was undertaken at the proper time. The Christmas Eve party, which circumstances had denoted as the moment when Jasper must strike his blow, was at hand. The hour had come when it was necessary to consult the oracle of "destruction", and as he and Durdles made a midnight ascent of the Tower they received one of the most auspicious tokens known to Thuggee. Near the summit, they heard "the chirp of some startled jackdaw or rook". At the next step, as they emerged upon the top, they were greeted with a view of "the river, winding down from the mists of the horizon". The call of a rook in sight of a river, known as "Julkajura", was the most favorable omen which could possibly befall. In the lore of the Phansigar, the Goddess had spoken and had given to whatever plan ws in Jasper's heart her frightful benediction. The pair of Stranglers in the story referred to above, during their expedition through the fields heard the cawing of a rook as they caught sight of a river. "Sign and river!" cried the one to the other, in a kind of ecstasy. "The sign of signs!" That same occult token came to Jasper in the Tower. What he proposed to do was blessed by Kali.

In the earliest pages of the novel Dickens had called attention to the rooks which were fluttering about the Cathedral Tower, and embroidered the incident with some clever and whimsical notions. What was really in the back of his head when he wrote that paragraph slipped into view as he proceeded to say that onlookers might almost fancy that the behavior of the rooks was a matter of "some occult importance". Evidently he was so obsessed with the thought that the cawing of a rook in the Tower at the crisis of his story *would* be surcharged with occult importance, that the idea tinctured his ink and dripped from the point of his pen. The paragraph is most ingeniously devised to hoodwink the reader, but in its very excess of cunning it seems to whisper "If, by and by, the call of a rook is heard in the Tower, 'stop, look and listen', for that will be a cry of '*occult* importance'". Those rooks in the second chapter were really red herrings.

The Strangler was directed by Thuggee ritual to use but a single instrument of death,—a fold of cloth known as the "roomal". This strip of fabric had the sanctity of a relic. It was regarded as a fragment of the gown of Kali. Ordinarily it was white or yellow. Such colored stuffs in Jasper's possession would require explanation, Dickens therefore pictures him, when he went up the postern stair to his rendezvous with fate, as pulling off "a great *black* scarf and hanging it in a loop upon his arm". The hint as to color was given in the Kali mythology, which relates that the gown of the Goddess was black; and that grimly suggested "loop" is also distinctly inventoried in the Thugs' handbook of murder. This strangling cloth was invariably worn as part of one's dress, either as a turban or a girdle. Adapting it to English custom, Jasper wore it as a neckcloth, in the fashion of that old-time stock which Fildes was told he must put into the picture, because it was necessary for a strangling. That necessity was created by the rules of Thuggee. If Edwin was to be done to death by an Oriental Strangler, he "must" be murdered in just that way.

The death rubric of the Stranglers directed that the "destruction" of the victim must be wrought by at least two assailants. Captain Sleeman, Superintendent of the Thug Police, writes, "Two Phansigars are considered indispensable to effect the

murder of one man". For Jasper to undertake to strangle Edwin single-handed was contrary to the accepted practice, and the futility of his endeavor is definitely foreshadowed. In the first conversation between Edwin and his betrothed, Dickens represents Rosa as interpolating a far-fetched dissertation on Belzoni, the Oriental traveller, into their badinage. "There was Belzoni, or somebody," she said, "dragged out by the legs, *half choked* with bats and dust. All the girls say, they wish he had been *quite choked*. . . . But how can his legs and his chokes concern you?" Nothing in the story, as told to us, makes this prattle about "chokes" anything more than the whimsy of a schoolgirl. But when thirty-five years later Fildes announces that Dickens had confidentially advised him that a pivotal feature of the plot was an attempt by Jasper to strangle Drood, those apparently offhand sentences wear another look, and begin to shine with a strange light. Those "chokes" did concern Edwin, much more than Belzoni, and were not due to the "bats and dust" which, with such careful carelessness, are thrust upon the reader's attention. Those "half chokes", and that "not quite choked", carry one far deeper into Mr. Dickens's confidence than Luke Fildes ever penetrated.

"Half choked" victims were sufficiently frequent to have embalmed themselves in the Thug vocabulary. To quote from their dictionary of evil, "bisul purna" meant "to be awkwardly handled in strangling; to have the roomal round the face or head instead of the neck". "Bisul" is defined as "a person intended to be killed, on whom the roomal falls untowardly, either on his head or face". "Jywaloo" describes a person left for dead, but afterwards found to have life in him. This singular reference to Belzoni shows that Dickens had clearly in mind the intention of representing Jasper as only "half choking" Edwin in his unassisted assault upon him, an idea for which there is abundant authority both in history and in the court records; and it may be fairly claimed that he had laid the ground for such a frustrated attack by selecting the only kind of an attempt at murder which permitted it. A thrust with a dagger, a shot from a pistol, a pinch of poison in a wine glass—these would have meant certain death.

Had Dickens lived to relate what happened on the night of Edwin's mysterious disappearance, the tale would in all likelihood be a replica of much that is inscribed on the police blotters of the "Thuggee and Docoity" Department. To quote a single entry: "The Stranglers contrived to keep company with their victim, and watch for an opportunity to destroy him. This they sometimes create by persuading him to quit his lodging place, a little after midnight, pretending it is near daybreak; or by detaching him from his companions, lead him under various pretences to some solitary spot. In the destruction of their victims they first use some deleterious substance, which they contrive to administer in food or drink. As soon as the poison begins to take effect by inducing a stupor or languor, they strangle him to prevent his crying out. . . . The deed is completed on the brink of a well, into which they plunge the body". To those familiar with the Drood story, such a memorandum reads like a scenario for the Cloisterham affair. But it is actually a paragraph from "General Orders by Major General St. Leger, Commanding the Forces, Headquarters, Cawnpore, 28 April, 1810". It is printed in full in Captain Sleeman's book, *The Thugs*, which was widely circulated in England, and could not have escaped the attention of any writer interested in the subject of strangling.

A Phansigar motif would be peculiarly alluring to Dickens. The mystery which cloaked the very existence of this murder guild, the weird psychology of its members, the uncanny dexterity with which they wrought at their fiendish craft, would strongly appeal to one so temperamentally attracted by the melodramatic elements of human expression and who was such a keen and constant observer of their expression in criminality. During Dickens's entire lifetime, Thuggee was a topic which was more or less constantly in the air. The reports of Captain Sleeman, Superintendent of the force organized for the suppression of the Phansigars, were embodied in a volume which stirred and startled all England about 1835. The *Edinburgh Review* devoted a leading article to the subject in 1837. A little later Meadows Taylor, a high police official in personal touch with all the facts, presented them in the guise of a novel, entitled *The Confessions of a Thug*. This book had an immense vogue. De Quincey mentions it in his essays. Its composition was suggested by Bulwer-Lytton, Dickens's literary comrade, who declared that ignorance of the subject alone prevented him from devoting his own pen to its treatment.

In 1847 Eugène Sue entertained Dickens in Paris at the moment when his recently written *The Wandering Jew* was at its meridian. One of the high lights of that book is a detailed account of Thuggee. Foremost among its characters was a Strangler who practised in Europe the fell craft he had acquired in India. The French author was familiar with Captain Sleeman's reports, for the name of his Phanisgar villain is copied from its pages. Dickens could not have been in touch with Sue at just that time without coming to some extent under the spell of the Oriental clan of assassins, any more than a writer of novels at the present day could be the guest of John Galsworthy and remain indifferent to the fortunes of the Forsytes. In 1857, writing of an epidemic of garroting which had broken out in London, Dickens himself refers to the curios in the British Museum which illustrated the art of strangulation as practised by the Thugs. An American novel, called *Cord and Creese*, centered upon a mysterious murder by an Englishman who had become affiliated with the Thugs, and which, in similarity of incident, noticeably parallels the Drood story, was published and widely read upon both sides of the Atlantic in 1869, the year in which Dickens began to spin the "mystery" of his final plot. In that same year, the novel-reading world was gripped by *The Moonstone*, that masterpiece of Wilkie Collins, Dickens's literary friend, which is a tale of three Hindu devotees, members of an Oriental cult, who went skulking around England on a secret mission which culminated in murder. The literary atmosphere in which *The Mystery of Edwin Drood* was cradled was dense with a kind of germ for which Dickens's imagination was genial soil, and which would inevitably fructify into a story essentially akin to *The Moonstone*—which novel, it is worth noting, contributed, almost verbatim, at least one crucial paragraph to the Drood narrative. A conspiracy of circumstances seemed to thrust upon Charles Dickens, as a ready-to-hand theme for his final bit of pen-work, the malign activities in England of one whose antecedents in the Far East linked him with the most subtle and abhorrent fraternity of crime known to history. (pp. 582-88)

Howard Duffield, "John Jasper—Strangler," in The Bookman, *New York, Vol. LXX, No. 6, February, 1930, pp. 581-88.*

EDMUND WILSON (essay date 1939)

[*Wilson is generally considered one of the foremost American men of letters in the twentieth century. A prolific reviewer, creative writer, and social and literary critic endowed with formidable intellectual powers, he exercised his greatest literary influence as the author of* Axel's Castle, *a seminal study of literary symbolism, and as the author of widely read reviews and essays in which he introduced the best works of modern literature to the reading public. Wilson's 1939 essay "The Two Scrooges," from which the following excerpt is drawn, is regarded as a landmark in Dickens criticism. In his remarks on Edwin Drood, Wilson pursues the notion that Jasper was not merely a Thug and a mesmerist, but also a divided personality, one whose character reflects the conflicts and contradictions in Dickens's own psyche.*]

Dickens never lived to finish [*The Mystery of Edwin Drood*], and it is supposed to have been left an enigma. We must first try to solve this enigma; and to do so we must proceed with a consciousness of the real meaning of Dickens' work. For though it is true that **Edwin Drood** has been enormously written about, it has been always from the point of view of trying to find out what Dickens intended to do with the plot. None of the more serious critics of Dickens has ever been able to take the novel very seriously. They persist in dismissing it as a detective story with good touches and promising characters, but of no interest in the development of Dickens' genius. Bernard Shaw, who is interested in the social side of Dickens, declares that it is 'only a gesture by a man three quarters dead' [see Additional Bibliography]; and it is true, as Forster remarked, that **The Mystery of Edwin Drood** seems quite free from the social criticism which had grown more biting as Dickens grew older [see excerpt dated 1874]; but what Forster and Shaw do not see is that the psychological interest which had been a feature of Dickens' later period is carried farther in **Edwin Drood**. Like all the books that Dickens wrote under the strain of his later years, it has behind it bitter judgments and desperate emotions. Here as elsewhere the solution of the mystery was to have said something that Dickens wanted to say.

It did not, it is true, become possible to gauge the full significance of the novel until certain key discoveries had been made in regard to the plot itself; but the creation of such a character as John Jasper at this point in Dickens' development should have had its significance for any student of Dickens and should have led to a more careful consideration, in the light of certain hints supplied by Forster, of the psychological possibilities of the character. It has remained for two American scholars to hit upon the cardinal secrets that explain the personality of Jasper. As both these discoveries have been made since the publication in 1912 of W. Robertson Nicoll's otherwise comprehensive book, *The Problem of Edwin Drood* [see Additional Bibliography], they have not received attention there; they are not included by Thomas Wright in the bibliography of **Edwin Drood** in his *Life of Charles Dickens*, published in 1936; and so far as I know, up to the present time, nobody who has written about Dickens has been in a position to combine these ideas. Yet what happens when one puts them together is startling: the old novel acquires a sudden new value. As one can revive invisible ink by holding it over a lamp or bring out three dimensions in a photograph by looking at it through certain lenses, so it is possible to recall to life the character of John Jasper as he must have been conceived by Dickens.

The most important revelation about **Edwin Drood** has been made by Mr. Howard Duffield, who published an article called "John Jasper—Strangler" in *The American Bookman* of February, 1930 [see excerpt above]. Mr. Duffield has here shown conclusively that Jasper is supposed to be a member of the Indian sect of Thugs, who made a profession of ingratiating themselves with travelers and then strangling them with a handkerchief and robbing them. This brotherhood, which had been operating for centuries pretty much all over India and which had given the British government a great deal of trouble before it succeeded in putting them down during the thirties, had already attracted a good deal of attention. Two of the British officers who had been engaged in the suppression of the Thugs had written books about them—one of them in the form of a story, Meadows Taylor's *Confessions of a Thug,* supposed to be narrated by the Thug himself. Eugène Sue had introduced into *The Wandering Jew* a Thug strangler practicing in Europe; and an American novelist, James de Mille, was publishing a novel called *Cord and Creese,* which dealt with an Englishman affiliated with the Thugs, the same year, 1869, that Dickens began *Edwin Drood.* Dickens' friend, Edward Bulwer Lytton, had already considered using this theme. Dickens himself had mentioned the Thugs in 1857 in connection with a garrotting epidemic in London. The publication in 1868 of Wilkie Collins' detective story, *The Moonstone,* in which a band of Hindu devotees commit a secret murder in England, seems to have inspired Dickens with the idea of outdoing his friend the next year with a story of a similar kind.

Now we know from the statement of Sir Luke Fildes, Dickens' illustrator in *Edwin Drood,* that Dickens intended to have Jasper strangle Drood with the long scarf which he (Jasper) wears around his neck [see excerpt above]; and we know from many circumstances and certain hints that the story is to have its roots in the East. Neville and Helena Landless are supposed to come from Ceylon; and Mr. Jasper, who smokes opium and sees elephants in his trances, is described as having 'thick, lustrous, well-arranged black hair and whiskers' and a voice that sometimes sounds 'womanish'—in short, as something very much like a Hindu. Furthermore, as Mr. Duffield has established, John Jasper—and this explains a good deal that has never been understood—has been trying to fulfill the ritualistic requirements for a sanctified and successful Thug murder. The Thugs were worshipers of Kali, the Hindu goddess of destruction, and their methods had been prescribed by the goddess. (pp. 84-7)

Since Jasper is eventually to be caught, he is evidently to have slipped up in the ritual. Mr. Duffield suggests that his mistake has been to commit the murder without an assistant; but he has overlooked the Thug superstition (recorded by Edward Thornton in *Illustrations of the History and Practices of the Thugs,* published in 1837) that nothing but evil could come of murdering a man with any gold in his possession. Now Drood, unknown to Jasper, is carrying the gold ring which Grewgious has given him for Rosa; and we have it on Dickens' own testimony to Forster that the body is to be identified by this ring, which has survived the effects of the quicklime. True, Edwin had also been wearing the stickpin and the gold watch; but as Jasper knew about these and took care to leave them in the weir, he may have removed them before the murder when Edwin was drugged.

Supplementing this interesting discovery we find a paper by Mr. Aubrey Boyd . . . in which he shows that Jasper is also a hypnotist [see Additional Bibliography]. Dickens had always been interested in hypnotism. Forster speaks of his first seriously studying it in 1841. He even found that he himself, with that extraordinarily magnetic personality which made it possible for him so to fascinate his audiences and which exerted, as Mrs. Perugini testifies, so irresistible a power over his family, was able to hypnotize people. (pp. 88-9)

It was obviously on the cards that Dickens would do something with [mesmerism] in his novels; and it should have given the

Drood experts a lead when they encountered a reference to it in the third chapter of *Edwin Drood.* Robertson Nicoll, disregarding this key passage, mentions the matter in another connection: he sees that Jasper has 'willed' Crisparkle to go to the weir, where he will find the watch and stickpin of Edwin; but he does not inquire farther. It remained for Mr. Boyd, who has some special knowledge of Mesmer and his writings, to recognize that Dickens has introduced the whole repertory of the supposed feats of mesmerism—called also 'animal magnetism' at the time—just as he has reproduced the practices of the Thugs. Mr. Jasper is clearly exercising 'animal magnetism,' in this case the kind known as 'malicious,' on Rosa Bud in the scene where he accompanies her at the piano; he is exercising it on Edwin and Neville when he causes them to quarrel in his rooms. It was supposed in Dickens' time that this influence could be projected through the agency of mere sound: hence the insistent keynote in the piano scene and the swelling note of the organ that frightens Rosa in the garden. And it was also supposed to penetrate matter: hence Rosa's remark to Helena that she feels as if Jasper could reach her through a wall. It could be made to impregnate objects in such a way as to remain effective after the master of the magnetic fluid was no longer himself on the scene: Jasper has put a spell on the water where Edwin's watch and stickpin are to be found. And it is possible, though Mr. Boyd does not suggest it, that the transmission of Jasper's influence from a distance may also explain the behavior, of which the implausible character has been noted, of the men who pursue and waylay Landless.

The revealing hint here, however, is the passage in the third chapter, of which Boyd has understood the significance and which has led him to a brilliant conjecture: 'As, in some cases of drunkenness,' writes Dickens, 'and in others of animal magnetism, there are two states of consciousness that never clash, but each of which pursues its separate course as though it were continuous instead of broken (thus, if I hide my watch when I am drunk, I must be drunk again before I can remember where), so Miss Twinkleton has two distinct and separate phases of being.' Dickens had told Forster that the originality of his idea for *Drood,* 'a very strong one, though difficult to work' (Dickens' words in a letter), was to consist (Forster's words in recounting a conversation with Dickens) 'in the review of the murderer's career by himself at the close, when its temptations were to be dwelt upon as if, not he the culprit, but some other man, were the tempted. The last chapters were to be written in the condemned cell, to which his wickedness, all elaborately elicited from him as if told of another, had brought him.'

John Jasper has then 'two states of consciousness'; he is, in short, what we have come to call a dual personality. On the principle that 'if I hide my watch when I am drunk, I must be drunk again before I can remember where,' it will be necessary, in order to extort his confession, to find access to that state of consciousness, evidently not the one with which he meets the cathedral world, in which he has committed the murder. The possibility of opium, suggested by Robertson Nicoll, is excluded. Wilkie Collins had just made use of precisely this device in *The Moonstone:* the man who has taken the Moonstone under the influence of laudanum, which has been given him without his being aware of it, is made to repeat his action under the influence of a second dose. The drunkenness in which Jasper will betray himself will not, then, be produced by a drug. Dickens must go Collins one better. Mr. Boyd has evidently solved the puzzle in guessing that Helena Landless is eventually to hypnotize Jasper. In the scene at the piano, where he is working on Rosa with the effect of making her hysterical, Helena maintains an attitude of defiance and announces that she is not afraid of him. It had already been established by Cuming Walters—it was the first of the important discoveries about *Drood*—that Datchery, the mysterious character who comes to Cloisterham to spy on Jasper, is Helena in disguise [see Additional Bibliography]. We have been told that Helena used to masquerade and pass herself off as a boy; and Dickens' alterations in his text, both the amplifications of the written copy and the later excisions from the proofs, indicate very clearly that he was aiming—in dealing with such details as Helena's wig and her attempts to conceal her feminine hands— to insinuate evidences of her real identity without allowing the reader to find it out too soon. Helena is to get the goods on Jasper, and in the end, having no doubt acquired in India the same secret which he has been exploiting (there may be also, as so often in Dickens, some question of a family relationship), she will put him in a trance and make him speak.

What Mr. Boyd, however, was not in a position to do was combine this idea with the Thug theme. The Thugs were all in a sense divided personalities. Colonel James L. Sleeman, in his book on the subject, emphasizes what he calls this 'Jekyll-and-Hyde' aspect of their activities. The Thugs were devoted husbands and loving fathers; they made a point—again like Mr. Jasper—of holding positions of honor in the community. And in their own eyes they were virtuous persons: they were serving the cult of the goddess. In their case, the Jekyll-and-Hyde aspect of their careers existed only for profane outsiders. They would proudly confess, when they were caught, to the number of lives they had taken. But in the case of Mr. Jasper, there is a respectable and cultivated Christian gentleman living in the same soul and body with a worshiper of the goddess Kali. The murder has been rehearsed in his opium dreams: he has evidently gone to the opium den for that purpose. He has kept himself under the influence of opium all the time he has been plotting the murder. But those who are to put him in prison will not be able to make him take opium. Helena, with her will stronger than his, will have to come to the rescue and hypnotize him.

And now what has all this to do with the Dickens we . . . know? Why should he have occupied the last years of his life in concocting this sinister detective story?

Let us [turn] to his situation at this period. He is still living between Gadshill and the house of Ellen Lawless Ternan [who had appeared in *Great Expectations* as Estella and] who appears now in *Edwin Drood* with the even closer identification of the name of Helena Landless. The motif of the disagreeable scene [in *Our Mutual Friend*] between Bradley Headstone and Lizzie Hexam is repeated in the even more unpleasant, though theatrical and unconvincing, interview between Jasper and Rosa Bud—Jasper presenting, like Headstone, a gruesome travesty of the respectable Victorian. The Ellen Ternan heroine is here frankly made an actress: Helena Landless is an impersonator so accomplished that she can successfully play a male character in real life; and she is even more formidable than Estella because she is to stand up to and unmask Jasper. Her strength is to be contrasted not only with the fatal duplicity of Jasper, but with the weakness of Drood and Neville. All of these three men are to perish, and Helena is to marry Mr. Tartar, the four-square young ex-Navy man, bursting with good spirits, agility and a perhaps rather overdone good health.

Dickens had just finished his public appearances and had said his farewell to the platform. The great feature of his last series

of readings had been the murder of Nancy by Sikes, a performance which he had previously tried on his friends and from which Forster and others had tried to dissuade him. He was warned by a woman's doctor of his acquaintance that 'if only one woman cries out when you murder the girl, there will be a contagion of hysteria all over the place.' But Dickens obviously derived from thus horrifying his hearers some sort of satisfaction. The scene was perhaps a symbolical representation of his behavior in banishing his wife. Certainly the murder of Nancy had taken on something of the nature of an obsessive hallucination. Dickens' imagination had always been subject to a tendency of this kind. It had been pointed out by Taine that the fantasies and monomanias of his lunatics only exaggerate characteristics which are apparent in Dickens' whole work—the concentration on and reiteration of some isolated aspect or detail of a person or a place, as Mr. Dick in *David Copperfield* was haunted by King Charles' head. In one of the sketches of *The Uncommercial Traveller,* written during these later years, Dickens tells of being obsessed by the image of a drowned and bloated corpse that he had seen in the Paris morgue, which for days kept popping up among the people and things he encountered and sometimes compelled him to leave public places, though it eventually drove him back to the morgue. In the case of the woman in Italy whose delusions he attempted to dispel, one gets the impression that these bloody visions were almost as real to him as they were to her. And now, at the time of these readings, he jokes about his 'murderous instincts' and says that he goes about the street feeling as if he were 'wanted' by the police.

He threw himself at any rate into the murder scene with a passion that became quite hysterical, as if reading it had become at this point in his life a real means of self-expression. At Clinton, he wrote Forster, 'we had a contagion of fainting; and yet the place was not hot. I should think we had from a dozen to twenty ladies taken out stiff and rigid, at various times!' At Leeds, whether to intensify the effect or to avert the possible objections of the audience, he hired a man to rise from the stalls and protest in the middle of the murder scene against daring to read such a thing before ladies—with the result that the people hissed him and put him out. It was the opinion of Dickens' doctor that the excitement and strain of acting this episode were the immediate cause of Dickens' death. It took a long time for him to calm himself after he had performed it, and the doctor, who noted his pulse at the end of each selection, saw that it invariably ran higher after Nancy and Sikes than after any of the other scenes. . . . The doctors eventually compelled him to interrupt his tour and take a rest.

His son, Sir Henry Dickens, who speaks in his memoir of his father of the latter's 'heavy moods of deep depression, of intense nervous irritability, when he was silent and oppressed,' tells of an incident that occurred at a Christmas party the winter before Dickens died: 'He had been ailing very much and greatly troubled with his leg, which had been giving him much pain; so he was lying on a sofa one evening after dinner, while the rest of the family were playing games.' Dickens participated in one of these games, in which you had to remember long strings of words, contributed by the players in rotation. When it came around to Dickens, he gave a name which meant nothing to anybody: 'Warren's Blacking, 30, Strand.' He did this, says his son, who knew nothing at that time of this episode in his father's childhood, 'with an odd twinkle and strange inflection in his voice which at once forcibly arrested my attention and left a vivid impression on my mind for some time afterwards. Why, I could not, for the life of me, understand. . . .

At that time, when the stroke that killed him was gradually overpowering him, his mind reverted to the struggles and degradation of his childhood, which had caused him such intense agony of mind, and which he had never been able entirely to cast from him.'

Two weeks before his death, he went to a dinner arranged by Lord and Lady Houghton in order that the Prince of Wales and the King of Belgium might meet him. Lady Houghton was a granddaughter of that Lord Crewe in whose house Dickens' grandfather had been butler. She well remembered going as a child to the housekeeper's room to hear his grandmother tell wonderful stories. Dickens' neuritic foot was giving him such trouble at this time that up till almost an hour before dinner he could not be sure of going. He did finally decide to go; but when he got to the Houghton house, he found that he could not mount the stairs, and the Prince and the Belgian king had to come down to meet him.

But now the Dickens who has been cut off from society has discarded the theme of the rebel and is carrying the theme of the criminal, which has haunted him all his life, to its logical development in his fiction. He is to explore the deep entanglement and conflict of the bad and the good in one man. The subject of *Edwin Drood* is the subject of Poe's *William Wilson,* the subject of *Dr. Jekyll and Mr. Hyde,* the subject of *Dorian Gray.* It is also the subject of that greater work than any of these, Dostoevsky's *Crime and Punishment.* Dostoevsky, who owed so much to Dickens and who was probably influenced by the murder in *Chuzzlewit,* had produced in 1866 a masterpiece on the theme at which Dickens is only just arriving in 1869. Raskólnikov—*raskólnik* means dissenter—combines in his single person the two antisocial types of the deliberate criminal and the rebel, which since Hugh in *Barnaby Rudge* have always been kept distinct by Dickens. Dostoevsky, with the courage of his insight, has studied the states of mind which are the results of a secession from society: the contemptuous, will to spurn and to crush confused with the impulse toward human brotherhood, the desire to be loved twisted tragically with the desire to destroy and to kill. But the English Dickens with his middle-class audience would not be able to tell such a story even if he dared to imagine it. In order to stage the 'war in the members,' he must contrive a whole machinery of mystification: of drugs, of telepathic powers, of remote oriental cults.

How far he has come and to how strange a goal we recognize when we note that he has returned to that Rochester he had so loved in his boyhood—the Rochester where he had made Mr. Pickwick put up at the Bull Inn and picnic on good wine and cold fowl out of the hampers of the Wardles' barouche. Gadshill was next door to Rochester, and the Cloisterham of the novel is Rochester; but what Dickens finds in Rochester today is the nightmare of John Jasper. There is plenty of brightness in *Edwin Drood* and something of the good things of life: Mrs. Crisparkle's spices, jams and jellies, Mr. Tartar's shipshape rooms; but this brightness has a quality new and queer. The vivid colors of *Edwin Drood* make an impression more disturbing than the dustiness, the weariness, the dreariness, which set the tone for *Our Mutual Friend.* In this new novel, which is to be his last, Dickens has found a new intensity. The descriptions of Cloisterham are among the best written in all his fiction: they have a nervous (in the old sense) concentration and economy rather different from anything one remembers in the work of his previous phases. We are far from the lavish improvisation of the poetical early Dickens: here every de-

scriptive phrase is loaded with implication. It is as if his art, which in *Our Mutual Friend* had seemed to him so sorely fatigued, had rested and found a revival. Dickens has dropped away here all the burden of analyzing society—British imperialism in the East is evidently to play some part in the story, but it is impossible to tell whether or not this is to have any moral implications. . . . Dickens, so far as we can see, is exclusively concerned with a psychological problem. The dualism of high and low, rich and poor, has here completely given place to the dualism of good and evil. The remarkable opening pages in which the Victorian choirmaster, with his side whiskers and tall hat, mixes in his opium-vision the picture of the English cathedral with memories of the East and comes to in the squalid den to stagger out, short of breath, to his services, is perhaps the most complex piece of writing from the psychological point of view to be found in the whole of Dickens. But the characters that are healthy, bright and good—Rosa Bud, with her silly name, for example—seem almost as two-dimensional as colored paper dolls. We have got back to the fairy tale again. But this fairy tale contains no Pickwick: its realest figure is Mr. Jasper; and its most powerful artistic effect is procured by an instillation into the greenery, the cathedral, the winter sun, the sober and tranquil old town, of the suggestion of moral uncertainty, of evil. Even the English rooks, which in *The Old Curiosity Shop* had figured simply as a familiar feature of the pleasant old English countryside in which Nell and her grandfather wandered, are here the omens of an invisible terror that comes from outside that English world. The Christmas season itself, of which Dickens has been the laureate, which he has celebrated so often with warm charity, candid hopes and hearty cheer, is now the appointed moment for the murder by an uncle of his nephew.

Mr. Jasper is, like Dickens, an artist: he is a musician, he has a beautiful voice. He smokes opium, and so, like Dickens, leads a life of the imagination apart from the life of men. Like Dickens, he is a skilful magician, whose power over his fellows may be dangerous. Like Dickens, he is an alien from another world; yet, like Dickens, he has made himself respected in the conventional English community. Is he a villain? From the point of view of the cathedral congregation of Cloisterham, who have admired his ability as an artist, he will have been playing a diabolic rôle. All that sentiment, all those edifying high spirits, which Dickens has been dispensing so long, which he is still making the effort to dispense—has all this now grown as false as those hymns to the glory of the Christian God which are performed by the worshiper of Kali? And yet in another land there is another point of view from which Jasper is a good and faithful servant. It is at the command of his imaginative *alter ego* and acting in the name of his goddess that Jasper has committed his crime.

None the less, he is a damned soul here and now. All this bright and pious foreground of England is to open or fade away, and to show a man condemned to death. But it will not be the innocent Pickwick, the innocent Micawber, the innocent Dorrit, whom we are now to meet in jail: nor yet the wicked Fagin, the wicked Dennis, the wicked elder Rudge. It will be a man who is both innocent and wicked. The protest against the age has turned into a protest against self. In this last moment, the old hierarchy of England does enjoy a sort of triumph over the weary and debilitated Dickens, because it has made him accept its ruling that he is a creature irretrievably tainted; and the mercantile middle-class England has had its triumph, too. For the Victorian hypocrite has developed—from Pecksniff, through Murdstone, through Headstone to his final transformation in

Jasper—into an insoluble moral problem which is identified with Dickens' own. As Headstone makes his own knuckles bleed in striking them against the church and drowns himself in order to drown Riderhood, so Jasper is eventually to destroy himself. When he announces in the language of the Thugs that he 'devotes' himself to the 'destruction' of the murderer, he is preparing his own execution. (He is evidently quite sincere in making this entry in his diary, because he has now sobered up from the opium and resumed his ecclesiastical personality. It is exclusively of this personality that the diary is a record.) So Dickens, in putting his nerves to the torture by enacting the murder of Nancy, has been invoking his own death.

In this last condemned cell of Dickens, one of the halves of the divided John Jasper was to have confronted the other half. But this confrontation—'difficult to work,' as Dickens told Forster—was never, as it turned out, to take place. Dickens in his moral confusion was never to dramatize himself completely, was never in this last phase of his art to succeed in coming quite clear. He was to leave *Edwin Drood* half-finished, with Jasper's confession just around the corner—just about to come to life in those final instalments which he was never to live to write. (pp. 90-104)

Edmund Wilson, "*Dickens: The Two Scrooges,*" in his *The Wound and the Bow: Seven Studies in Literature, Houghton Mifflin Company, 1941, pp. 1-104.*

EDGAR JOHNSON (essay date 1952)

[*Johnson is a major Dickens scholar whose* Charles Dickens: His Tragedy and Triumph *is considered the definitive biography of the novelist. In the following excerpt from that work, Johnson discusses the major social concerns addressed in* Edwin Drood, *as well as the novel's principal themes and prevailing atmosphere.*]

The Mystery of Edwin Drood is Dickens's swan song. In its very heart there is a core of death. All its atmosphere is sunset and autumnal. Though the Cloisterham of the story, with its old Cathedral and moldering crypt, its ruined Monks' Vineyard and crumbling houses, is again the Rochester Dickens loved, it is no longer the spring-drenched Rochester of his *Pickwick* days, but a city where darkness already dims the bright colors and the first frost sprinkles the grass of the Cathedral close. Christmas in Cloisterham is no season of glowing cheer; it is a time when murder lurks to strangle its predestined victim and lock his remains within a hollow tomb. The dying mutter of a voice among the choir, sounding through the murky arches and sepulchral vaults until the sea of music rises high and beats its life out, is echoed by the dying chords of this dirge whose notes are broken out unfinished.

Never before has Dickens's control of scene and tone been more masterly. The black rooks flying around the tower, the black-robed Dean and clergy, the waning day and the waning year, the low sun "fiery and yet cold behind the monastery wall," the fallen red leaves of the Virginia creeper on the pavement, the wintry shudder that goes through the little pools on the cracked flagstones, the giant elms shedding their gust of tears, all are heavy and ominous with mortality. When Mr. Jasper goes for an exploratory midnight ramble through the galleries and tower of the Cathedral, he comes in the yard upon the saws of two journeymen, looking like the tools of "two skeleton journeymen out of the Dance of Death" who might be "grinning in the shadow." As Helena Landless leaves her brother at the little postern stair of Jasper's gatehouse, both notice the sky hung with copperous clouds and feel a strange

dead weight in the air. Throughout the entire book there is an elegiac precision of observation that not only harmonizes with its dark and secretive story but is as if Dickens were wandering in a last farewell through these familiar haunts and impressing on his mind all the loveliness that he must leave ere long.

This poetic and mournful tone, no doubt, is what led Longfellow to feel that *Edwin Drood* was "certainly one of the most beautiful of his works, if not the most beautiful of all." And it impelled Chesterton to compare this somber half-told mystery to the performance of a dying magician making a final splendid and staggering appearance before mankind [see Additional Bibliography]. Shaw, more impatiently, dismissed the book as only "a gesture by a man already three quarters dead" [see Additional Bibliography]. Only a few readers have called attention to its curious psychological overtones, and almost none have observed its brooding social implications. Though more commentators have expended their ingenuity upon it than upon any of Dickens's other books, for the most part they have been fascinated, to the exclusion of almost every other interest, by the puzzle of its plot. (pp. 1115-16)

Two things emerge darkly from the shadows of the story: that there is a strange fusion and tension between Cloisterham and the Orient, and that Jasper's mad jealousy of the nephew whom he also loves is only one facet of a much more deeply involved division in his soul. In his dreams at Opium Sal's, horrible deeds and dreadful journeys mingle Eastern visions with the Cathedral town; bending over the tumbled bed where he has been lying beside a Chinese and a Lascar, he listens to their mutterings suspiciously before dismissing them with the word, "Unintelligible!" The Landless twins, from Ceylon, are dark, gypsyish, and rich in coloring, and it is insinuated that they may have oriental blood. There is a hint of secrets having their roots somewhere in the Drood family business and the family background in Egypt. Descriptions of the dust of monastic graves in Cloisterham dissolve into allusions to the explorers of Egyptian tombs, "half-choked with bats and dust," and these in turn into Jasper's explorations of the crypt with its debris and moldering dead. In this mingling of East and West, all the imperialist tentacles of England are tangled in a network with this sleepy and decaying old cathedral town.

Jasper, tormented soul, drug addict, dark enigma, is the central figure in this web. It is significant that he is the single major character of whose thoughts we are told nothing. Only when he starts awake from a nightmare and when the opium woman draws ambiguous revelations from him while he is lying in a drugged daze does he give any unintended glimpse of the fiery furnace of his heart. When he knows what he is saying, almost all his words seem moves in his hidden plans. Not until Edwin has vanished does Jasper ever voice his feelings to Rosa, and even then he is careful to ensure that nobody else can hear. There is the possibility, though, that Jasper is a divided personality, and that in his normal state he does not remember what he does under the influence of opium, or know in what ways his everyday doings are influenced by the hidden self that then emerges. He may thus be entirely sincere in writing that he devotes himself to the destruction of a murderer whom he does not realize to be himself. (p. 1120)

There are probably "two states of consciousness" in Jasper; certainly he is at war within himself and a man of dreadful passions. In the garden scene, where he at last speaks his love for Rosa, his voice and vehemence are those of Bradley Headstone: "Rosa, even when my dear boy was affianced to you, I loved you madly; even when I thought his happiness in having you for his wife was certain, I loved you madly; . . . even when he gave me the picture of your lovely face so carelessly traduced by him, which I feigned to hang always in my sight for his sake, but worshipped in torment for years, I loved you madly; in the distasteful work of the day, in the wakeful misery of the night, girded by sordid realities, or wandering through Paradises and Hells of visions into which I rushed, carrying your image in my arms, I loved you madly.''

To Rosa this speech is a gross hypocrisy which makes her forget her fear in indignation. "How beautiful you are!" he responds. "You are more beautiful in anger than in repose. I don't ask for your love; give me yourself and your hatred; give me yourself and that pretty rage; give me yourself and that enchanting scorn; it will be enough for me." "There is my past and my present wasted life. There is the desolation of my heart and my soul. There is my peace; there is my despair. Stamp them into the dust; so that you take me, were it even mortally hating me!"

Jasper repeats with frightful intensity the agony of frustrated love Dickens had put into each book he had written since the time of *A Tale of Two Cities* and *Great Expectations*. Rosa Bud and Helena Landless echo in divided and inverted forms the two heroines of *Our Mutual Friend*. Rosa shares with Bella her teasing, coaxing, half-petulant charm, and both have Ellen Ternan's fair-haired prettiness. But Jasper feels for her the same painful infatuation Bradley Headstone did for Lizzie Hexam. And as Lizzie unintentionally drew the schoolmaster to his ruin, Helena Landless is prefigured as the Choirmaster's nemesis—Helena Landless, the very syllables of whose name evoke those of Ellen Lawless. Originally Dickens had intended to call her Olympia Heyridge or Heyfort, but he could not banish from his mind reverberations of Ellen's name. Is Helena more than a name?—is that defiant something in her between a crouch and a bound, is that foreshadowed struggle of wills between her and Jasper, a transmuted version of a struggle Dickens had known?

And what of Jasper, with his strange mesmeric power and his fierce longing for the delicate Rosa Bud, who shrinks from him in terror? Like George Silverman, who believed himself to be a wronged and misunderstood man, Jasper poses the problem of what are the truths in the abysses of a man's heart. He becomes a dark rendering of elements his creator had felt within himself. Seen in one light, Jasper is deeply suspect. In another, perhaps, he is a man misjudged, not guilty after all, or, at the very least, a man for whom there are explanations or extenuations not taken into account. And more profoundly still, there is a possibility that Jasper may be the projection of a dilemma Dickens had partly symbolized in *Hard Times*: the position of the artist and his relation to Victorian society.

In Jasper's dreams, visions of oriental splendor mingle with the rook-haunted towers of gray cathedrals. His outwardly staid life is darkened by a life of inward rebellion, in which he sinks down into the filth of the Ratcliffe Highway and ascends to the skies in the musical aspiration of his art. He has disguised himself as a sober choirmaster, just as Dickens appears on the surface a responsible middle-class citizen, but he burns with the fiercest and most violent passions. In the everyday world he, the artist, is a secret misfit, but is it he or that world which is in the wrong? Since the time of Plato the judgment of the world has again and again branded him as evil, but there is another realm, and another vision, in which he is a good and faithful servant. Is the artist a traitor in society's midst, a subverter of its moral standards, or is he a heroic rebel fighting its corruptions, its moldering values, its charnel decay?

Certainly this vision of a dead world lies heavy and brooding over *Edwin Drood*. Forster thought this last book "quite free from the social criticism which grew more biting as Dickens had grown older," but apparently he did not perceive the criticism implicit in its picture of a crumbling Cloisterham sinking into the dry rot of the dead past. That past, however, is linked to the present in ways no less sinister than those Dickens had seen extending from the Dedlocks and the Tite Barnacles to the Dombeys and Bounderbys and Gradgrinds and Merdles. Deep below the surface, the old forces of privilege and exploitation, which dominated the business and industrial world, had swollen out in a far-flung entanglement of occidental aggression swallowing up the remotest regions of the globe. It is not only the London docks and slums, the smoke-blackened cities of the north, that are strangled in its coils, but India, Egypt, China, the victims of the opium trade, subject peoples, everywhere, falling prey to a greedy imperialism.

Young Drood mouths the catchwords of that imperialism in their most infuriating form. He is "Going to wake up Egypt a little," he says patronizingly. Like any acquisitive materialist, he is condescending about the life of reflective thought. "Reading?" he asks with a trace of contempt. "No. Doing, working, engineering." He talks with insolent and insular contempt of other races. "Pooh, pooh," he sneers to the dark-skinned Neville Landless. "You may know a black comon fellow . . . but you are no judge of white men." His words briefly epitomize the whole vainglorious gospel of backward races and the white man's mission.

Instead, therefore, of abandoning the analysis of society, Dickens has deepened it, for he has sensed the extension of the struggle to take in the entire world. Despite its somnolent air of peace, behind Cloisterham lurk all those inhumanities he has spent his life in fighting, grown more monstrous than ever as they threaten now a dark resentful conflict of East and West. Felt more as subtle undercurrents than as sharply defined issues, they breed poisonously in the squalor of stale streets and miserable courts festering off the East India Docks. As personal antagonisms they well up in Drood's race-proud superiority, in Neville Landless's rancor against him, in Helena's hostility to Jasper, and in Opium Sal's malignant fist shaken behind the Cathedral pillar. And just as in the London of *Our Mutual Friend*, all industrial England, though unseen, is sensed in the shadows beyond the slums of Whitechapel and Millbank—the coal mines, the looms of Manchester, the lead mills, the iron foundries, and the potteries—so, in *Edwin Drood*, the shrunken symbols of authority—Mr. Sapsea the Mayor of Cloisterham, the Dean of the Cathedral, the overbearing philanthropist Honeythunder—reveal the insolvency of the institutions for which they stand.

The Mayor of Cloisterham, who is also its leading estate agent, represents both the outlook of its businessmen and the pompous conceit of officialdom. He exemplifies in the moribund world of this provincial backwater the same values that are at work in Lombard Street, Westminster, and Whitehall. The town's chief magistrate, he is easily blinded by any adroit manipulator, and serves Dickens as the instrument for a last fling at the law. "It is not enough that Justice should be morally certain," the egregious old fool observes sententiously; "she must be immorally certain—legally, that is." "His Honour reminds me," Datchery says respectfully, "of the nature of the law. Immoral. How true!"

The smooth, time-serving timidity of the Dean of the Cathedral is morally lower than Sapsea's imbecility. Disturbed by the mere unproved suspicion against Neville Landless, ''The days of taking sanctuary are past,'' he tells Mr. Crisparkle. ''This young man must not take sanctuary among us.'' He has rejected the merciful teachings of his church for a cautious conformity. The clergy, he says, must not ''be partisans. Not partisans. We clergy must keep our hearts warm and our heads cool, and we hold a judicious middle course'' and ''do nothing emphatically.''

Honeythunder, however, with his bellowing and intolerant reformatory zeal, is nothing if not emphatic. Love and good works in him are only catchword pretexts for a truculent violence. ''Though it was not literally true, as was facetiously charged against him by public unbelievers,'' Dickens remarks, ''that he called aloud to his fellow-creatures, 'Curse your souls and bodies, come here and be blessed!' still his philanthropy was of that gunpowdery sort that the difference between it and animosity was hard to determine.'' All dissent from his dogmas he tries to bluster down by abuse and distorted misrepresentation. As Sapsea embodies a valedictory jibe at administrative authority, Honeythunder is Dickens's final thrust at Sir Andrew Agnew and the rabid would-be legislators of public virtue. With the Dean, they form a striking secular trinity: the regnant jackass enthroned between the spiritual trimmer and the bigot of reform.

There is no hope for society in the forces represented by these three. But, as always, Dickens's trust is not in the official or self-appointed powers of church and state; it is in the health of human nature itself. And even here in Cloisterham, despite its atmosphere of mortality and the deadly passions seething below its sleepy surface, that vitality is latent. It dwells in the honesty and courage of Mr. Crisparkle, in the awkward rectitude of Mr. Grewgious, in the mysterious operations of Datchery; in Rosa's impulsive warmth of feeling, Neville Landless's quick responsiveness, and Helena's fiery devotion. All these breathe the promise of final victory. Like the gardens of Cloisterham, growing from the graves of abbots and abbesses, this world of graves will again bring forth life. Brought to a burning focus of concealed struggle through the forms of this murder allegory, Dickens portrayed for the last time the fundamental antagonisms and the fundamental problems of his world. And here for the last time he reaffirmed his fundamental creed: his belief in the generous loyalties and affections of the human spirit. (pp. 1122-26)

> *Edgar Johnson, in his* Charles Dickens: His Tragedy and Triumph, *Vol. 2,* Simon and Schuster, 1952, *1159 p.*

PHILIP COLLINS (essay date 1962)

[In this excerpt from his full-length study of crime in Dickens's fiction, Collins focuses primarily on Edmund Wilson's close identification of Dickens with Jasper in his essay ''The Two Scrooges'' (see excerpt dated 1939), challenging Wilson's notion that Jasper's character can be seen as a reflection of Dickens's own divided life and personality.]

'If the accumulation of comment means anything, it means that we need no longer expect a solution in which all our perplexities will magically vanish.' Professor [A. J. A.] Waldock's sentence refers, not to *Edwin Drood*, but to another of the great brain-teasers of English literature—though it is, of course, much more than that—*Hamlet;* and much of what he says in his

'Study of Critical Method' about this play applies also to our novel. 'Unfortunately, it is not of the slightest consequence how very reasonably all such considerations are urged,' he remarks of some suggestions, '*if the play does not urge them.* How much *Hamlet* criticism need not have been written if this self-evident principle had been kept in mind!' He refers to A. C. Bradley's famous lectures, with their tendency to 'treat *Hamlet* as if it had actually occurred in real life, as if it were, authentically, *le cas Hamlet*'. Bradley's account, he says, is 'an exposition built up with deft skill and masterly thoroughness. His *Hamlet* stands four-square: every joint is neat, every buttress seems solid. . . . Bradley's *Hamlet* is better than Shakespeare's: it is better in the sense that it has a firmer consistency, that it hangs together with a more irresistible logic'. And he concludes: 'A play is not a mine of secret motives. We persist in digging for them; what happens usually is that our spade goes through the other side of the drama.''

We are, certainly, more entitled to dig for 'secret motives' in *Edwin Drood* than in *Hamlet*, since no assessment of the novel, or of its relation to the rest of Dickens's work, is possible without our making some surmise about the unwritten second half in which Jasper's personality would have been more fully exposed. But it remains a novel (or rather, half one), as *Hamlet* is a play and not a baffling fragment from Danish history: and Dickens wrote it, not Dostoevsky or Strindberg or Wilkie Collins or any of the other ghosts who seem to have taken over in the minds of some of its commentators. Recent Droodiana, like most of the best and most of the worst Dickens-criticism of the past two decades, has been strongly influenced by Mr Edmund Wilson, whose pages on *Edwin Drood* unfortunately are, in my opinion, among his most precipitate and questionable. He makes optimistic use of that convenient phrase 'in short'. Jasper is described by Dickens as dark, etc, 'in short, as something very much like a Hindu'—he 'has, then, ''two states of consciousness;'' he is, in short, what we have come to call a dual personality'. Rounding some very tight bends by this handy device, Mr Wilson is able to present, with considerable confidence, an *Edwin Drood* as much 'better' than what Dickens was likely to produce as Bradley's *Hamlet* was superior to Shakespeare's: not a very difficult task, since Mr Wilson is a more intelligent critic than Bradley, and Dickens is habitually a worse craftsman and artist than Shakespeare.

Edwin Drood, he maintains, is carrying to its logical conclusion the criminal theme which had haunted Dickens all his life. 'He is to explore the deep entanglement and conflict of the bad and the good in one man. The subject of *Edwin Drood* is the subject of Poe's *William Wilson*, the subject of *Dr Jekyll and Mr Hyde*, the subject of *Dorian Gray*. It is also the subject of that greater work than any of these, Dostoevsky's *Crime and Punishment*.' Mr Wilson's *Edwin Drood* is, indeed, the work of an English, and therefore a less bold and extreme, Dostoevsky: but there is a salutary comment on these fashionable parallels between Dickens and Dostoevsky or Lawrence or Joyce or Kafka— Professor G. H. Ford's reminder that, after all, 'Dickens is more like Dickens than he is like any other writer.' . . . [Throughout] his fiction and journalism, Dickens regards murderers as unequivocally and entirely wicked men. Where, one wonders, does Mr Wilson detect 'the good' in John Jasper? As he admits, Jasper is 'a damned soul here and now', though he is 'a man who is both innocent and wicked'. His only apparent virtue—if it is one—is his fondness for the nephew he murders. Whenever he looks towards Edwin, we are told of their first meeting in the book, his face bears 'a look of intentness and intensity—a look of hungry, exacting, watchful, and yet devoted affection'. The Dean expresses the hope that Jasper's heart may not be 'too much set upon his nephew', and Edwin himself describes his uncle's manner towards him as 'almost womanish'. How genuine this affection was, and thus how much it cost Jasper to kill Edwin to gain possession of Rosa, whom he certainly loved more, we cannot tell. Necessarily, Dickens's expressions about his villain are ambiguous. It is difficult, however, to discover any other virtue even ambiguously imputed to Jasper. His association with the cathedral is, by his own confession, gross hypocrisy; his appearance of loving Edwin may well be the same.

Certainly his alleged love for his nephew does not prevent his killing him, doing the deed 'hundreds of thousands of times' in anticipation, and finding, when the decisive moment came, that 'It *was* pleasant to do'. These evil thoughts, it may be objected, belong to his 'opium' self; they are expressed, certainly, during an opium session at the Princess Puffer's. Mr Wilson, adhering to the 'Thug' theory of Jasper, makes a sharp division between these two selves. Jasper, he says, is eventually to destroy himself: 'When he announces in the language of the Thugs that he "devotes" himself to the "destruction" of the murderer, he is preparing his own execution. (He is evidently quite sincere in making this entry in his diary, because he has now sobered up from the opium and resumed his ecclesiastical personality. It is exclusively of this personality that the diary is a record.)' But . . . when Dickens spoke of Jasper's 'ecclesiastical personality' ('exercising an Art which brought him into mechanical harmony with others'), he noted the paradox that 'the spirit of the man was in moral accordance or interchange with nothing around him'. Given the conventions of the novel, he could hardly be more explicit about the wickedness of the normal 'ecclesiastical' Jasper.

The diary was, of course, to be relevant. It contained Jasper's careful record of Neville's 'demoniacal passion' against Edwin (largely induced by the drugs Jasper had put into their drinks) and his fear that Neville would murder Edwin in a fit of jealous rage. On the day of the murder he told Mr Crisparkle, to whom he had earlier shown these entries, that he would burn the diary in a few days' time, because it contained these 'exaggerative' thoughts; but Edwin's disappearance, and the subsequent suspicions against Neville, make it indispensable evidence (this, of course, was why it had been written at all), so Jasper preserved it, and showed Mr Crisparkle his further entry in it, to the effect that he would discover and destroy the murderer.

Certainly it is Jasper, as the murderer, who is to suffer destruction, and doubtless this diary-entry (given additional emphasis by coming at the end of a chapter and of an instalment) was to have come true, in some sense—but not, I think, in the way Mr Wilson suggests. Jasper is no Dostoevskian character, nor a King Oedipus virtuously but blindly proving his own guilt. Dickens projected a less interesting irony, I would guess: merely that, by some miscalculation or over-reaching himself—such as, he firmly believed, all murderers made at some point in their most cunning plans—Jasper would betray his own guilt through trying to convict Neville. Charles Collins . . . noted that, in his cover-design for the novel, the pursuit of the murderer is led by Jasper, 'who points unconsciously to his own figure in the drawing at the head of the title.' It is most unlikely that he portrayed Jasper with this gesture, except under Dickens's explicit instructions; and thus it seems likely (as Lady Pansy Pakenham has suggested) that the 'very curious and new idea' which Dickens cryptically told Forster the novel would contain, was to have been 'the pursuit and destruction

of Jasper *by himself*'. His accidental self-incrimination would, I guess, have been followed by an obdurate refusal to confess: and thus, probably, would have ensued the ending which Dickens sketched to Forster—the murderer would review his own career 'as if, not he the culprit, but some other man, were the tempted', and his wickedness, 'all elaborately elicited from him as if told of another,' would bring him to the condemned cell [see excerpt dated 1874]. His composure would be pierced, either through opium, or, more probably, through hypnosis, for in the earlier opium scenes he had not referred to himself in the third person. Helena Landless, I agree, was most likely to be the hypnotist.

Such are my hypotheses about *Edwin Drood*: not very original, I fear. They are much less exciting and ambitious than Mr Wilson's. . . . But I think I can see why Mr Wilson was, too easily, betrayed into accepting theories which gave such a conclusive note to his final pages—and I nag at him in this way, not because I lack respect for him (on the contrary: I pore over him with continual delight and benefit), but because his very persuasive account of Dickens has become, in too many respects, the unquestionable orthodoxy of recent years.

First, the *Edwin Drood* he posits is decidedly interesting, as the Dickens he describes throughout his essay was a figure much more likely to command attention and respect in 1941 than the *bonhomme* reformist Dickens of most earlier commentators. But his accounts, both of this novel and of the whole *œuvre*, omit too much, and make claims which cannot be sustained. Dickens is, as he insists, a very great writer, whose merits had been undervalued; but his greatness does not, I think, like just where Mr Wilson sees it. . . . More of his greatness resides in his comedy than Mr Wilson ever recognises; his vision of capitalist society was less complete, coherent, and hostile than he claims; and the concern with crime and violence belongs more to the 'Sensation Novel', and less to the higher reaches of art, than he seeks to show. The comparisons with Dostoevsky, like Macready's cry of 'two Macbeths!', only remind us that this aspect of Dickens is, at best, second-rate. That he had some insight into the psychology of guilt is shown more clearly by . . . *Martin Chuzzlewit, Little Dorrit* and *Our Mutual Friend,* than by surmises about *Edwin Drood*—at least to me, who am dubious about the notable development which Mr Wilson and others have asserted this novel would have shown. It would, indeed, be pleasant to accept Mr Wilson's claim that at last, after the disjunction of the 'two Scrooges' type, Dickens was now to have explored 'the deep entanglement and conflict of the bad and the good in one man'—but, I have argued, there is no evidence that Jasper was ever 'good' (as distinct from outwardly respectable).

I wish that Dickens had been capable of writing the novel that Mr Wilson thinks up for him. Instead, I think, he was plotting a better novel of the kind he already knew how to write—a Sensation Novel, but with a firmer plot-line, and less hackneyed sensations (hypnosis, opium, some unpredictable connection with the East). There were to be mysteries, including the enigma of Jasper's personality, but Mr V. S. Pritchett is nearer the truth, I believe, than Mr Wilson, through seeing *Edwin Drood* in the context of English fiction rather than European and American [see excerpt dated 1964]. With this novel and *The Moonstone,* he says, 'we begin the long career of murder for murder's sake, murder which illustrates nothing and is there only to stimulate our skill in detection and to distract us with mystery.' Indeed, long before comparisons with Dostoevsky had become *de rigueur,* George Gissing had noted in his excellent study of Dickens both the superficial similarities and the basic differences between the two novelists. Compared with the 'indescribably powerful and finely tragic' conception of *Crime and Punishment,* he wrote, 'the murders in Dickens are too vulgar of motive greatly to impress us, and lack the touch of high imaginativeness.' *Edwin Drood* shows Jasper 'picturesquely, and little more. We discover no hint of real tragedy. The man seems to us a very vulgar assassin, and we care not at all what becomes of him.'

Mr Wilson's second reason for misreading *Edwin Drood* (as I think) is equally instructive, and is suggested by these sentences, which follow his assertion that the man we are now to meet in gaol is not an innocent Pickwick, Micawber or Dorrit, and not a wicked Fagin, Rudge or Dennis, but 'a man who is both innocent and wicked'.

> The protest against the age has turned into a protest against self. In this last moment, the old hierarchy of England does enjoy a sort of triumph over the weary and debilitated Dickens, because it made him accept its ruling that he was a man irretrievably tainted; and the mercantile middle-class England has had its triumph, too. For the Victorian hypocrite has developed—from Pecksniff, through Murdstone, through Headstone, to his final transformation in Jasper—into an insoluble moral problem which is identified with Dickens's own.... Jasper is eventually to destroy himself.... So Dickens, in putting his nerves to the torture by enacting the murder of Nancy, has been invoking his own death.

This passage, too, has a satisfying conclusiveness, which seems to me unwarranted by the facts.

It is part of Mr Wilson's case that 'Of all the great Victorian writers, he was probably the most antagonistic to the Victorian Age itself', that emotionally he was almost as unstable as Dostoevsky, and that he was indeed 'the victim of a manic-depressive cycle, and a very uncomfortable person'. Certainly, in 1941, the popular notion of the Inimitable Boz needed correcting by a thorough immersion in the destructive elements of his character and behaviour. And certainly the Dickens who wrote *Edwin Drood* was still exciting himself by the *Sikes and Nancy* Reading, and was contravening the *mores* of his ages by sleeping with Ellen Ternan. But how deeply was he 'antagonistic to the Victorian Age itself'? and how far was Jasper a projection of his author? Of course, Dickens was exasperated by many features of his society—both what we would regard as its faults and what now seem its more benignant aspects (those penal reforms, for instance, which he deplored). But his *Child's History of England,* and all his other comments on the past, show how much better and more hopeful he thought his own age than any preceding age: and, despite his many criticisms of its institutions and social organisation, he seems to have had no expectation or desire that the future would be radically different. 'He frequently touched on political subjects,' wrote Sala of his conversation, '—always from that which was then a strong Radical point of view, but which at present [1894] I imagine would be thought more Conservative than Democratic.'

It was easy, during the first flush of excitement about the newly-discovered Ellen Ternan affair, to exaggerate his moral alienation from his age, and then to blow up the more ag-

gressive and anti-social aspects of his behaviour until a thoroughly split personality, a manic-depressive victim, emerged. One of the few pre-Ternan studies of Dickens that Mr Wilson respected, Ralph Straus's *Charles Dickens: a Portrait in Pencil* (1928), had increased the darker shades of the picture, but Dickens's surviving son Henry protested, at the time, that Straus's book, though good in many ways, presented his character and disposition 'in far too gloomy a light'. No doubt, he wrote, 'at certain periods of his life my father was intensely depressed and most unhappy. But these phases were intermittent and ... on the whole he got a keen enjoyment out of life. Speaking of my own experience of him, although like most geniuses he was liable to moods, his general disposition was singularly bright and joyous....'' Henry, of course, was a devoted son, and like the rest of the family, and like the official biographer Forster, he loyally suppressed some of the facts. (It was left to Katey Dickens to spill the beans about Ellen—but posthumously, through Gladys Storey's book *Dickens and Daughter.*) But, granted these pious omissions, Henry's picture is juster than Straus's and Mr Wilson's, and it is confirmed by the consensus of hundreds of reminiscences of Dickens by his contemporaries.

A theory about his personality which condemns these many witnesses as white liars or imperceptive fools should have been submitted to more careful scrutiny than it got. It was welcomed, however, without too much examination, because it provided a very acceptable change from 'the jolly Dickens': also because a Freudian and left-wing age expected its literary heroes to be suitably neurotic and alienated, and because even in the 1940s there remained a special relish in every fresh discovery that the Victorians were not so inhumanly respectable as they purported to be. The wrath of the more orthodox Dickensians at these imputations against their hero's character and conduct gave the iconoclasts a happy sensation of being champions of Enlightenment. Neither spirit was conductive to a quiet stock-taking. Both embattled parties were pushed into taking up positions more extreme than was wise.

Imperfections of character and temperament, as of intellect and art, Dickens certainly had. He behaved badly over the Separation business, and very strangely over the 'Murder' Reading—to mention only two obvious examples. His contemporaries had not been unaware of these defects. 'A *unique* of talents suddenly extinct, and has "eclipsed . . . the harmless gaiety of nations",' wrote Carlyle when he died. 'The good, the gentle, ever friendly noble Dickens—every inch of him an Honest Man!' A few years later, after reading Forster's *Life,* he noted that, beneath his 'sparkling, clear, and sunny utterance, . . . his bright and joyful sympathy with everything around him', there lay, 'deeper than all, if one has the eye to see deep enough, dark, fateful silent elements, tragical to look upon. . . .' As the sharp-tongued Mrs Lynn Linton observed, Dickens could be very inflexible—'his nearest and dearest friends were unable to deflect the passionate pride which suffered neither counsel nor rebuke. . . . [Although he] wrote so tenderly, so sentimentally, so gushingly, he had a strain of hardness in his nature which was like a rod of iron in his soul. . . . Nervous and arbitrary, he was of the kind to whom whims are laws, and self-control in contrary circumstances was simply an impossibility.' But, she added, he 'had very warm sympathies, too, and his true friends never found him wanting'.

Sometimes Dickens recognised his own faults, generally putting them down to artistic temperament—'the restlessness which is the penalty of an imaginative life and constitution.' Thus, he lectured his wife about her jealousy of a lady he had been helping: 'You know my life . . . and character, and what has had its part in making them successful; and the more you see of me, the better perhaps you may understand that the intense pursuit of any idea that takes complete possession of me, is one of the qualities that makes me different—sometimes for good, sometimes I dare say for evil,—from other men.' Late in 1857, when the Ellen Ternan infatuation had begun, he described his state of mind just after he had finished writing a story: 'It leaves me—as my Art always finds and always leaves me—the most restless of created Beings. I am the modern embodiment of the old Enchanters, whose Familiars tore them to pieces. I weary of rest, and have no satisfaction but in fatigue.' A few months later, he was writing to Forster, about his marital difficulties:

> You are not so tolerant as perhaps you might be of the wayward and unsettled feeling which is part (I suppose) of the tenure on which one holds an imaginative life, and which I have, as you ought to know well, often only kept down by riding over it like a dragoon—but let that go by. I make no maudlin complaint. . . . I am always deeply sensible of the wonderful exercise I have of life and its highest sensations, and have said to myself for years, and have honestly and truly felt, This is the draw-back to such a career, and is not to be complained of. . . . Nor are you to suppose that I disguise from myself what might be urged on the other side. I claim no immunity from blame. There is plenty of fault on my side, I dare say, in the way of a thousand uncertainties, caprices, and difficulties of disposition. . . .

His self-accusations were rarely more specific, or more severe, than this. He was not a very self-critical, nor a self-aware, man.

In what ways, then, was he akin to John Jasper? What could Mr Wilson be meaning when he spoke of Jasper's as being 'an insoluble moral problem which was identified with Dickens's own'? The resemblances do not strike me as impressive. Unhappy though Dickens was about some aspects of his society, he was very far from being 'in moral accordance or interchange with nothing around him', a man living 'apart from human life'. He revelled in being the world's most popular novelist, and much more often spoke for his society than he questioned its assumptions. Jasper, as has often been pointed out, is a sort of artist: not a creative one, but a musical executant. He is a mesmerist, and certainly this is a feature common to him and his creator. He is an opium-addict: the nearest I can find Dickens getting to this, is a reference in a letter written a month before his death to his taking laudanum for insomnia. He is passionately and wickedly in love with his nephew's girl, and will stop at nothing to obtain her, though he knows that she loathes him: and Dickens had made Ellen Ternan his mistress. . . . Dickens's heroines became more interesting and convincing after he knew Ellen (though they are still only passable, by quite ordinary fictional standards), and . . . it is only at this period that his murderers have a sexual motive. Many commentators have pointed out that the names of three of his latest heroines—Estella, Bella Wilfer, and Helena Landless—seem to echo the name of Ellen Lawless Ternan, and they have tried to deduce Ellen's character, and the course of Dickens's feelings for her, from these novels. It is tempting to do so, since

there is practically no other evidence about the emotions of either party in this intriguing episode. Dickens apparently confided his secret to only a very few intimate friends, and they or his executors seem to have destroyed most of the letters which contained any reference to the affair and to his feelings about Ellen. His letters to her have never been recovered, and his friends and family of course maintained a discreet silence about the matter. Ellen is reported as saying, many years later, that 'she loathed the very thought of this intimacy', but it is not clear whether this represents her feelings during the liaison, or her subsequent regrets and remorse as the respectable wife of a clergyman and headmaster.

If this paucity of evidence tempts one to reconstruct Ellen and Dickens's love for her from the novels, it should also suggest that any surmises thus arrived at must be very tentative. There are too few facts, to act as controls to the imaginative hypotheses. But recent biographers have tended to repeat, at a more sophisticated level, the error of the old-style Dickensian 'duffers' they deplored or patronised: for, as in the old-style hunt after the 'originals' of Dickens's scenes and characters, so also in the pursuit of Ellen, enthusiasm has far outrun a respect for facts and probable inference. Dickens may have felt the anguish and frustration that his later heroines induce in their lovers (though Estella, Bella and Helena have little in common with one another, except the more-or-less close resemblance between their names and Ellen's). But there is no evidence either way, in the letters or reminiscences. Moreover, it is not Helena Landless that Jasper loves, of course, but Rosa Bud, whose name no more resembles Ellen Ternan's than her character resembles the other heroines'. There are other weak points in the Jasper-Dickens, Helena-Ellen, theory. Jasper, like Headstone, has a successful rival, but no-one has yet produced an Edwin Drood or a Eugene Wrayburn in the Dickens-Ellen story. To this, of course, it is replied that Ellen was less forthcoming than Dickens wished (or so it is surmised—from the novels, not the facts), so he may well therefore have imagined that he had a rival, or realised how it must feel to have one. By such shifting devices one can prove almost anything.

I find it difficult, indeed, to see any 'insoluble moral problem' in Jasper or in his creator. Jasper, I have insisted, is a wicked man who murders for lust; there is no evidence in the book about his moral processes, except his opium confession that he greatly enjoyed the act of murder. As for Dickens, his life was, in general, morally unremarkable: he had his faults, and his virtues: the latter, in my judgment, predominated. (pp. 304-13)

> *Philip Collins, in his* Dickens and Crime, *1962. Reprint by Indiana University Press, 1968, 371 p.*

A. O. J. COCKSHUT (essay date 1962)

[*Cockshut suggests that* Edwin Drood *represents a reconciliation between the tendencies of Dickens's early and late fiction, specifically examining his handling of the novel's setting, characters, and plot.*]

In Rusholme, Manchester, near where I live, there is a dingy barber's shop; and outside it is a rotting plywood figure, approximately human in size and form, which bears the caption, 'Shave, sir'. One of the main reasons why we admire Dickens, I think, is that he has so far been the only English writer (with the possible exception of Lawrence) who has given artistic meaning to sights like these. And we know that this is no superficial gift of impressionism, but an outward sign of his wonderful use of the material of industrial civilization, which other novelists have found intractable, or have ignored. The railways and the commerce of *Dombey and Son,* the mounds in *Our Mutual Friend,* the disused mines in the country outside Coketown, the treatment of income from investment in *Great Expectations*—these things now seem to be his greatest and most characteristic achievement. No doubt fashion, and the reaction from the Chestertonian coaching Dickens, play some part in this; but on the whole this preference seems to me justified.

The fact that all this is absent from *Edwin Drood* is one reason why we are apt to feel uneasy with it. Cloisterham is very fine, the cathedral and elms are fine, but they are in a well-worn tradition of fictional settings. They are not quite a sufficient substitute, we may feel, for the Marshalsea, or for the rotting Thames of *Our Mutual Friend.*

A second reason for uneasiness is fortuitous, but can, nevertheless, be important. As the book is a mystery story, and unfinished, it attracts the type of critical attention which is given by those who do not care for literature at all. The people who are most eager to invent a new theory about Drood's murder are the same as those who wish to prove that the *real* old curiosity shop was in the Brompton Road, or to disentangle the topical references in *romans à clef.* Those of us who do not share this kind of interest are put off.

A third handicap to the full enjoyment of *Drood* is linked with the first. It seems to be in some ways a regression to the author's more superficial early style. Durdles seems at first sight (I hope to show that he is not) a stock early Dickens eccentric like

Dick Swiveller. The moral evil associated with Jasper and Honeythunder seems purely external and melodramatic, like that of Ralph Nickleby or Quilp. We have no sense of uneasily watching the portrayal of our own vices and shortcomings, as we do when we read about Pip. Still less do we feel that the author is comprehending and defining his own moral weaknesses as he does when he portrays Harold Skimpole. If the late Dickens is the best, as I believe it is, his last book may at first sight look very like the second childhood of his talent. The very names of the characters point to this, with their reversion to early Dickensian fantasy, and in some cases, their obvious allegorical suggestions—Honeythunder, Crisparkle, Rosa Budd. Both the name and the nature of the crusty, jocular old uncle, Grewgious, remind us very much of the high jinks and Christmassy pseudo-benevolence of some of the worst early passages. He is not as bad as the Cheeryble brothers, but he is much inferior as a guardian angel to Joe Gargery.

Of course, all this may seem, even if its general truth is accepted, to be disparaging the early Dickens too much. If so, we can point to Sapsea's monument:

ETHELINDA
Reverential Wife of
Mr. THOMAS SAPSEA,
AUCTIONEER, VALUER, ESTATE AGENT, &c.
OF THIS CITY,
Whose Knowledge of the World,
Though somewhat extensive,
Never brought him acquainted with
A SPIRIT
More capable of

An illustration by Luke Fildes of Drood, Jasper, and Landless together at Jasper's lodgings.

LOOKING UP TO HIM.
STRANGER, PAUSE
And ask thyself the question,
CANST THOU DO LIKEWISE?
If Not,
WITH A BLUSH RETIRE

This is early Dickens at his exuberant best. This is the humour of Mrs. Gamp and Pecksniff, the humour that escapes satire, and creates unanswerable new absurdities that no living person could ever really contemplate. When a mature artist reverts to the style of his early popular successes, we are apt to diagnose fatigue and loss of interest; particularly, perhaps, when we know that his health was failing and that he died with the book unfinished.

A first glance at the plot may yield a similar result. I take it to be established by scholarship, ignorant though I am myself on the subject, that every indication points to the presence of Indian thuggery in the story. The following indications among others have been noticed: Jasper's black scarf, the call of a rook in sight of a river, the fact that the murdered man is a traveller and is treated by the probable murderer with great kindness just before the deed. So, even if any doubt remains about the murderer's identity, it is clear that Dickens set out to produce a flavour of Eastern mystery, that he used opium addiction mainly for this purpose, that Jasper is an addict and that he goes through many of the rituals which were supposed to be performed by the Indian thug. Now this choice of plot is obviously important. It is true, and we have often been reminded, that Dickens's friend Wilkie Collins had recently published *The Moonstone,* which has a superficial similarity as a story of Eastern mystery. But the word 'influence' is apt to be misleading when applied to Dickens. It would seem that he was incapable of being influenced except in the way he wanted to go. His imaginative system could not assimilate matter alien to it; it was one of the benefits he derived from his anti-intellectualism. George Eliot paid the penalty for being an intellectual open to wide cultural influences in *Romola.*

And so the Eastern plot is very surprising. Dickens had always been so very English in the settings of his novels. The Paris of *A Tale of Two Cities* is a solitary exception which proves the rule. For after Carlyle the French Revolution had come to be regarded as a great event in English history. Apart from this, I can only recall the very 'English, grand tour' Italian travels of the Dorrit family. It looks as if the man is fatigued, is wearily seeking for factitious novelty, is deserting the field of his triumphs because the effort of true artistic creation is too great. For Dickens may have read and heard a lot about Indian thuggery. But he could not really have known about it in the way he knew the subjects with which he had achieved his most brilliant successes, the Thames, railways, money, dirt, prisons. He knew these with penetrating eyes, with memories of childhood agony and joy. Why travel so far from these obsessive and fruitful interests?

Weariness is the obvious diagnosis, and it would seem there was something to be said for Bernard Shaw's summary, 'only a gesture by a man three quarters dead' [see Additional Bibliography]. Though I believe this plausible judgment to be quite mistaken about the book as a whole, I fancy that I do detect some weariness in the last four or five chapters, though it is difficult to be quite sure that one is not unconsciously influenced by the knowledge that Dickens collapsed and died shortly after writing the words 'fall to with an appetite'. But whether or not we diagnose a weary searching after novelty in the choice

of opium-dens and thuggery, it is certain that such an explanation is totally incomplete. Consider the opening passage:

> An ancient English Cathedral Tower? How can the ancient English Cathedral tower be here! The well-known massive grey square tower of its old Cathedral? How can that be here! There is no spike of rusty iron in the air, between the eye and it, from any point of the real prospect. What is the spike that intervenes, and who has set it up? Maybe it is set up by the Sultan's orders for the impaling of a horde of Turkish robbers, one by one. It is so, for cymbals clash, and the Sultan goes by to his palace in long procession. Ten thousand scimitars flash in the sunlight, and thrice ten thousand dancing-girls strew flowers. Then follow white elephants caparisoned in countless gorgeous colours, and infinite in number and attendants. Still the Cathedral Tower rises in the background, where it cannot be, and still no writhing figure is on the grim spike. Stay! Is the spike so low a thing as the rusty spike on the top of a post of an old bedstead that has tumbled all awry?

This brilliant simultaneous evocation of the split mind, and of one culture superimposed upon another, perfectly introduced the whole text that we have. Taking the hint from it, we can see that *Drood* was never just a story with a titillating spice of Eastern mystery for jaded English palates, like *The Moonstone.* It was going to set the known and the unknown side by side, to reveal the value or the decadence (or both) of English society by means of the intrusion of an alien and destructive ethos. No doubt Dickens was wise, or lucky, in his choice of India, rather than (say) Italy, and not merely on the tactical ground that it would be more unfamiliar and exciting to his readers. The elementary John Bull in Dickens, as in later Arabophiles and Bengal Lancers, was far more at home with something truly alien than with the repudiated and misunderstood roots of our common European culture. Dickens could have written an excellent Asiatic travel book, but he only revealed his limitations in *Pictures from Italy.*

A startling contrast of cultures, and the split minds that go with it—that is the theme, and once that is understood, we are in a better position to evaluate the reversion to early Dickens humour, early Dickens macabre and murder, and early Dickens Christmas conviviality. Take the cathedral, for instance. Here no doubt nostalgic boyhood memories mingle with his new purpose. On the whole a cathedral does not seem a promising subject for Dickens. His Anglicanism was sincere enough, despite heretical tendencies towards Unitarianism. But he lacked several qualities needed to make the most of a cathedral as a symbol and of the Close as a social fact. He lacked a sense of history. The mediaeval past, of which cathedrals are the abiding monument, was to him an object of ignorant distaste and contempt. We remember that revealing row of dummy books he was so proud of—'The Wisdom of our Ancestors' series, all with titles like 'The Rack' and 'Disease'. One would expect the life of the Close to forfeit all his sympathy. Whether it is thought of as a life of old-world gentlemanly ease, or as a life of prayer, liturgical devotion, and scholarship, Dickens the 'practical', low-church philanthropist, despised, ignored, misunderstood both. Ancient churches had, for many years past, made few appearances in his work. He had given in *Our Mutual Friend* a word of praise to Mr. Milvey, the hard-working and impoverished guardian of a slum parish. But that is a different matter. That was an aspect of the new, swarming proletarian society of the nineteenth century. That was (as Dickens, like his own Mr. Meagles, would have said) 'practical'. On the other hand, when, many years before in *The Old Curiosity Shop* he had used the ancient peace and charm of the English village church, the presentation had been devoid of religious content. It had only been a sentimental setting for the enjoyment of the factitious agonies of Little Nell. The precedents were certainly not encouraging. And in the light of them Dickens's achievement in the treatment of the cathedral here becomes impressive. Not only is it solid, truly observed, not only is its setting of dripping elm trees and fallen leaves memorable, but it has an unexpectedly powerful symbolic force as well.

It seems as if the superimposition upon the cathedral of the mysteries of Eastern civilization and of the opium dream helped Dickens to see its positive aspects for the first time; and hence eventually its negative aspect also. For the cathedral is dreary and decaying; it is the home of the dead; it almost becomes in the end a monument to a dying civilization; dying, unregretted. We are very far from the smart sneering of dummy books, though the new message may be no more comforting in the last resort for supporters of conservative Anglicanism.

The book is full of little hints of decay and of split mind: 'Mr. Crisparkle, minor canon and good man, lately "Coach" upon the chief Pagan high roads, but since promoted by a patron (grateful for a well-taught son) to his present Christian beat.' An ordinary enough point; nothing is more likely than that a canon would have been a tutor in Latin and Greek. But in the context of the split mind and bestial pagan tendencies of the musical director of the cathedral's worship such little points are significant.

The past of Cloisterham is seen as a patchwork of ill-connected traditions, hence the description of its stones:

> Fragments of old wall, saint's chapel, chapter-house, convent, and monastery, have got incongruously or obstructively built into many of its houses and gardens, much as kindred jumbled notions have become incorporated into many of its citizens' minds. All things in it are of the past.

The choir has white robes but they are sullied. Jasper is in the middle of them. The old ways are in decline. 'Not only the day is waning but the year.' It seems at first like the disintegration which precedes death.

And so we come to the importance of Durdles. It is here that we can see most clearly how the old and new Dickens are united in an exciting new pattern. The distinction I make between the early and the late Dickens is in no way original and can be briefly summarized. In books like *Pickwick* and *Nicholas Nickleby* we have a spirited macabre and humorous development of the traditions of English melodrama. Grotesque fantasy of plot and character is made tolerable by that marvellous gift which never deserted Dickens throughout his career, his obsessive power of communicating the reality of physical objects. But in *Little Dorrit, Great Expectations,* and *Our Mutual Friend,* we have controlled symbolic comment on society, largely conveyed through the development of simple ideas which haunted him throughout his life—dirt, money, prisons, and the like. On the whole, except in *David Copperfield,* which is a rather unsatisfactory special case, there is little mingling of the two methods, and certainly no earlier satisfactory synthesis.

When we first meet Durdles we could easily mistake him for an inhabitant of the crude world of *Nicholas Nickleby*:

> He often speaks of himself in the third person; perhaps, being a little misty as to his own identity, when he narrates; perhaps impartially adopting the Cloisterham nomenclature in reference to a character of acknowledged distinction. Thus he will say, touching his strange sights: 'Durdles came upon the old chap', in reference to a buried magnate of ancient time and high degree, 'by striking right into the coffin with his pick'. The old chap gave Durdles a look with his open eyes, as much as to say, 'Is your name Durdles? Why, my man, I've been waiting for you a devil of a time!' And then he turned to powder.

But the meaning is deepened when we come to passages like this, in which Mr. Grewgious is shown the crypt:

> Old Time heaved a mouldy sigh from tomb and arch and vault; and gloomy shadows began to deepen in corners; and damps began to rise from green patches of stone; and jewels, cast upon the pavement of the nave from stained glass by the declining sun, began to perish. Within the grill-gate of the chancel, up the steps surmounted loomingly by the fast-darkening organ, white robes could be dimly seen, and one feeble voice, rising and falling in a cracked monotonous mutter, could at intervals be faintly heard.

Durdles, as a character, is bizarre early Dickens. As a symbol of the decay of the cathedral, of the collapse of the civilization of the country town, he is comparable in his symbolic status to the river in *Our Mutual Friend.* Such a synthesis is perhaps not completely unprecedented. A case could be made for Rogue Riderhood and Gaffer Hexam in *Our Mutual Friend* as achieving it partially. But Durdles is at any rate the most developed case. And it was a difficult achievement to synthesize two periods of a great career.

Durdles may be said to represent, too, both the two poles round which the novel historically turns—the intellectual, symbolical, 'artistic' type of Flaubert, James, etc., and the realistic, social-critical type of Balzac and Tolstoy. The few great masters who have achieved a synthesis have done so only occasionally in their careers. *Moby Dick* achieves it, but not *Pierre* or *The Confidence Man.* Durdles's death-obsession is much more than a psychological quirk. We can now examine briefly the way in which the other characters fit into this synthesis or opposition of early and late Dickens's styles. Deputy, Durdles's young imp, is another fine example of synthesis. As a character he might come straight from the pages of *Pickwick.* He is vivid, superficial, redolent, in spite of the Cloisterham setting, of the London streets on which Dickens had brooded for so long. Durdles explains how Deputy earns a halfpenny a day by driving him home with stones when he is drunk. Jasper comments: 'I wonder he has no competitors', and Durdles replies: 'He has plenty, Mr. Jasper, but he stones 'em all away.' A subtler, briefer, and more blistering comment even than is to be found in *Hard Times* upon the Manchester school, the commercial greatness of England, and the 'immutable laws of supply and demand'.

In Honeythunder, the synthesis of old and new is not successfully achieved. He has all the vigorous memorability of an early Dickens hypocrite. But the moral criticism of the uncharitable type of philanthropic temperament is crude. His ill-temper and rudeness become simply incredible, and his hypocrisy is vague, general, and improbable. It is a comedown from the brilliant portraits of Bounderby and Harthouse in *Hard Times,* each with his special, calculated, and entirely credible type of hypocrisy lurking behind certain agreed social stereotypes. (pp. 227-34)

Of Drood himself little need be said; he is a workmanlike hero, colourless perhaps by the author's intention. The Landless family and the amusing Miss Twinkleton contain little that is original. But the character of Crisparkle reveals a new respect for the priestly office, and, though not a profound character study, he is conceived with a balanced sympathy which the early Dickens had lacked.

But, of course, Jasper is the prime example of the successful synthesis of old and new. Here, clearly, there was much more to come; and we must speak tentatively. It would seem that he is a genuine split personality, not a melodramatic hypocrite. And so, he draws together in his person the threads of a story of clashing civilizations. He has his crude, early-Dickensian moments, as when he shows his jealousy of Rosa. But the mesmeric effect of his personality rings true. We cannot tell how the author would have resolved the apparent contradiction of motives. (Jasper shows signs of being at the same time a psychopath, and a conscientious devotee of thuggery.) But a reconciliation of these two strains is not impossible. It seems that Dickens had partly achieved at his death, and might have fully achieved, had he lived, the feat he had so often failed to achieve, the feat Dostoevsky, after learning from him, triumphantly achieved, the total analysis of the murderer's soul.

There are lapses, then, in this synthesis of old and new, and there are special problems, which are due to the work's unfinished state. But when we consider the extraordinary difficulty of telescoping the achievements of a great career, we may be amazed at the degree of success achieved. One thing is certain; whatever the effect on him as a man, Dickens as artist had not been spoiled by success. He refused to do over again what the public expected. As ill-health strengthened its hold, he was still seeking that true originality which includes and develops the achievements of the past.

Let us now examine briefly some of the hints which the text gives about the working-out of the plot. Perhaps the most obvious is given when Grewgious, Rosa's guardian, presents Drood with the ring which belonged to Rosa's mother. The understanding is that Drood will either place it solemnly on Rosa's finger as a sign of irrevocable promise of marriage, or return it to Grewgious, if the engagement is brought to an end. Grewgious says, 'I charge you once more, by the living and by the dead, to bring that ring back to me.' 'By the dead' means literally Rosa's dead parent. But it is scarcely a large assumption that it would have had an ironic meaning, in that the ring would have returned from Drood's dead body into Grewgious's possession, and (probably) given a clue to the identity of the murderer. There is partial confirmation of this in Forster's account of his conversation with Dickens on the subject [see excerpt dated 1874]. In spite of various more subtle theories, it still seems overwhelmingly probable that Jasper really was the murderer; but it is just conceivable that he was not, *although he thought he was.* That is, moving into a world of illusion through opium, he began to conform to the thug

rituals, until he imagined that he had really committed another man's crime. In either case, it is relevant that it was contrary to the thug doctrine to murder a man with gold in his possession. Perhaps we have here something more than a melodramatic device for detecting a criminal. We may be in that late Dickens world where material objects glow with a strange sacramental power—where things which, in the early Dickens would have been mere convenient coincidences, now testify to a vaguely-conceived but powerfully felt conviction of divine power and destiny. Such, for instance, is the destroying and healing power of the prison in *Little Dorrit* and of the river in *Our Mutual Friend.* A start is made towards achieving this in the following passage, which immediately succeeds Drood's decision to tell Rosa nothing about the ring he received from Grewgious, now that their engagement is at an end:

> Let them be. Let them lie unspoken of, in his
> breast. However distinctly or indistinctly he en-
> tertained these thoughts, he arrived at the con-
> clusion, Let them be. Among the mighty store
> of wonderful chains that are for ever forging,
> day and night, in the vast ironworks of time
> and circumstance, there was one chain forged
> in the moment of that small conclusion, riveted
> to the foundations of heaven and earth, and
> gifted with invincible force to hold and drag.

The quick-lime and the hidden chamber in the cathedral provide an obvious clue about the disposal of the body; and if the clue is not misleading, we can take it that another reinforcing version of death-in-life in the cathedral was in preparation. Finally we have a broad hint in the title of Ch. 14, 'When shall these three meet again?' The three are Jasper, Drood, and Neville Landless, who dine together on Christmas Eve. One can only assume that some sort of terrible dramatic tableau had been planned. The most likely form of it would have been this: Jasper (the murderer) is revisiting the dead body of Drood (? in the crypt), perhaps for the purpose of recovering the neglected ring from the body, when Neville Landless, wrongly suspected of the murder, catches him in the act. No doubt there are other possible variants which the reader may like to amuse himself by supplying.

Speaking tentatively, we may say that in the plot, also, we have a synthesis of early and late Dickens, though the early features predominate here more than they do in characters or in the symbolism of the cathedral. The plot is intensely melodramatic, just as much so as that of *Oliver Twist.* The old unbalanced excitement about murder, strong at all stages of Dickens's career, but softened in his best later books, is back again in its full force. The masked villain is there, and preparations are going on for a thrilling discovery scene. Yet there is something, less obtrusive and less easy to characterize, which is 'late'. Signs are already present, and destined perhaps to be stronger in the complete work, of a deeper meaning behind the melodrama and coincidence. In the early Dickens, if an opium addict had been a respected servant of a cathedral, it could only have been for the sake of disguise and the device of 'the most unlikely person'. Now it is more. It is a comment on the traditional cathedral world. There is a deadly irony in

> Mr. Jasper is in beautiful voice this day. In the
> pathetic supplication to have his heart inclined
> to keep this law, he quite astonishes his fellows
> by his melodious power. He has never sung
> difficult music with such skill and harmony, as
> in this day's anthem. His nervous temperament

is occasionally prone to take difficult music a little too quickly; to-day, his time is perfect.

There is even a point in the effects of the storm, which tore off the hands of the cathedral clock. The cathedral is being contaminated; official Christianity is losing touch with the time. The European way of life is losing its cultural purity. Jasper is, in his way, prophetic of 'Les Demoiselles d'Avignon'.

One crucial question remains, and I can only ask it, not answer it. What, in the last resort, is Dickens's attitude to all the things he collectively symbolized by the cathedral? What I have just said, and indeed any detailed analysis of all the images of death and decay associated with the cathedral, might suggest the author really believed that the old way of life was dead, and official Christianity with it. Yet I am not satisfied that this is the final impression the reader receives. It is not merely that Eastern and pagan influences are presented in their most repellent form, so that old English things, even if stupid and out-of-date, seem by comparison attractive. It is not only that, at the political and social level, as George Orwell and others have shown, Dickens is nearly always much more conservative than he thinks he is. It is more a question of a new development in his religious sensibility—as if the cathedral, rotting within, and wracked with storms without, had at last become for Dickens a convincing image of the Christian civilization he had so long ignored or sneered at, or misunderstood. The storm comes at a great festival of the Church, Christmas, as if to emphasize the danger; but it emphasizes also the value of what is threatened. And in the last few pages that Dickens ever wrote, there is a passage which hints at the revival of the cathedral life:

> A brilliant morning shines on the old city. Its antiquities and ruins are surprisingly beautiful, with a lusty ivy gleaming in the sun, and the rich trees waving in the balmy air. Changes of glorious light from moving boughs, songs of birds, scents from gardens, woods, and fields— or, rather, from the one great garden of the whole cultivated island in its yielding time— penetrate into the Cathedral, subdue its earthy odour, and preach the Resurrection and the Life.

Or is this too far-fetched? Would the images of death and decay have dominated in the end? In writing of this strange book, mysterious in intention, and still more mysterious in its unfinished state, I make no apology for ending with a question mark. (pp. 234-38)

> *A. O. J. Cockshut, " 'Edwin Drood': Early and Late Dickens Reconciled," in* Dickens and the Twentieth Century, *edited by John Gross and Gabriel Pearson, Routledge and Kegan Paul, 1962, pp. 227-38.*

V. S. PRITCHETT (essay date 1964)

[*Considered one of the modern masters of the short story, Pritchett is also one of the world's most respected literary critics. In the following excerpt, Pritchett discusses the ways in which* Edwin Drood *differs from Dickens's previous works.*]

When lately I was reading *The Mystery of Edwin Drood* I felt extremely the want of some sort of guidance on the Victorian fascination with violent crime. What explains the exorbitant preoccupation with murder, above all? In earlier periods, when life was cheaper, rape, seduction, incest were the crimes favored by literature. If we look to literature rather than to life, it is certain the Victorian writers took over murder from the popular taste of the eighteenth century, and succeeded—against the outcry of the older critics—in making it respectable. But in the nineteenth century one detects, also, the rise of a feeling (so curiously expressed by a popular writer on the melodrama a few years ago; I have forgotten his name) that "murder is cleaner than sex." There is a clue there, I think. There is a clue, too, in the fact that organized police forces and systems of detection were not established until the Napoleonic wars— we are bound to become fascinated by the thing we punish— and another more sinister clue lies in the relative freedom from war after 1815. A peaceful age was horrified and fascinated, for example, by the ritual murders of the Indian thugs. Where else can we look? To the megalomania that was a natural field for the Romantic movement? To the guilt that is deposited in the mind after a ruthless exertion of the will, such as the Victorians made at the time of the Industrial Revolution? To the social chaos before the fifties, when tens of thousands were uprooted, and if they did not rise with the rising tide were left to sink into the slums or to stand out alone in violent rebellion? The more one reads of the unrest and catastrophes of the nineteenth century, in social or in private life, the more one is appalled by the pressure which is revolution applied to human beings. And when we read again the rant of the melodramas, when we listen to the theatre organ of Bulwer-Lytton in *Eugene Aram,* and read the theatrical pages of Dickens, we feel, after the first shock of distaste, that these people are responding to a pressure which is not exerted upon us in the same degree. The violence of the scene suggests a hidden violence in the mind, and we begin to understand how assuaging it must have been, in novels like *Oliver Twist* or *The Mystery of Edwin Drood,* to see the murderer's conscience displayed in terms of nightmare and hysteria.

Assuaging to the Victorians, but not to us. We are not driven by the same dynamo. *Edwin Drood* stands at the parting of the ways between the early Victorian and the modern attitude to murder in literature, and also, I suspect, at the beginnings of a change in Dickens himself. The earlier murders of Dickens belong to the more turbulent decades of the nineteenth century. By the late fifties a calm had been reached; the lid had been levered back on to the pot of society and its seething had become a prosperous simmer. When Wilkie Collins wrote *The Moonstone* and Dickens, not to be outdone, followed it with *Edwin Drood,* we begin the long career of murder for murder's sake, murder which illustrates nothing and is there only to stimulate our skill in detection and to distract us with mystery. The sense of guilt is so transformed that we do not seek to expiate it vicariously on the stage; we turn upon the murderer and hunt him down. Presently, in our time, the hunt degenerates into the conundrums of the detective novel which, by a supreme irony, distracts us from our part in the mass murders of two wars. One or two critics have suggested that the struggle with the unfamiliar technique of the hunt was too much for Dickens and that it killed him and his novel. We cannot know whether this is so; but both those who dismiss the book as the last leaden effort of a worn-out man, and those who observe that it is the most careful and private of Dickens's novels, are agreed that it is pitched in a key he has never struck before.

What is that key? Before I add my answer to the dozens that have been made, it seems important to define one's own attitude to Dickens. I am totally out of sympathy with the hostile criticism of Dickens which has been made during the last twenty years, which has ignored his huge vitality and imaginative range and has done no more than to say he lacked taste and that he sacrificed a profound view of human nature to the sentimentalities and falsities of self-dramatization. To me it is a perversion of criticism to suggest that you can have the virtues of a writer without his vices, and the discovery of Dickens's failure does not make his achievement less. I swallow Dickens whole and put up with the indigestion. I confess I am not greatly interested in the literary criticism which tells me where he is good and where he is bad. I am glad to be instructed, but for us, at the present time, I think there is far more value in trying to appreciate the nature of his creative vitality and the experience that fed it—a vitality notably lacking in our own fiction. Now when we turn to *Edwin Drood* we do find some of the old Dickens. There is Mr. Sapsea, for example, with his own account of his courtship, that beautiful shot plumb in the middle of romantic love and Victorian marriage:

> Miss Brobity's Being, young man, was deeply imbued with homage to Mind. She revered Mind, when launched or, as I say, precipitated, on an extensive knowledge of the world. When I made my prosposal, she did me the honor of being so over-shadowed with a species of Awe, as to be able to articulate only the two words 'Oh Thou!' meaning myself. Her limpid blue eyes were fixed upon me, her semi-transparent hands were clapsed together, pallor overspread her aquiline features, and, though encouraged to proceed, she never did proceed a word further. . . . She never did and never could find a phrase satisfactory to her perhaps—too—favorable estimate of my intellect. To the very last (feeble action of the liver) she addressed me in the same unfinished terms.

That is the old Dickens, but a shadow is upon Mr. Sapsea. The tomb of Mrs. Sapsea is, we are told, to be used by Jasper, the murderer, for his own purpose. Durdles, the drunken verger, tapping the walls of the Cathedral for evidence of the "old uns," is to be roped in. The muscular Christian, Mr. Crisparkle, sparring before his mirror in the morning, is marked down by the plot; and that terrifying small boy, the Imp or Deputy, who is employed by Durdles to stone him homewards when he is drunk, will evidently be frog-marched into the witness box. Dickens is submitting to discipline, and how fantastically severe it was may be seen in Edmund Wilson's *The Wound and the Bow* [see excerpt dated 1939]. The background loses some of its fantasy, but the best things in *Edwin Drood* are the descriptions of the cathedral, the town and countryside of Rochester which are recorded with the attentive love one feels for things that are gracious and real. Chesterton thought that something of the mad, original Dickens was lost in this realism; other critics explain it as the influence of mid-Victorian settling down. Mr. Edmund Wilson seems to suggest that in *Edwin Drood* one finds the mellowness and the bitterness of the man who sets out with some confidence equipped to master his devil and to dominate his wound. I do not find a loss in this picture of Cloisterham:

> Cloisterham is so bright and sunny in these summer days, that the cathedral and the monastery-ruin show as if their strong walls were transparent. A soft glow seems to shine from within them, rather than upon them from without, such is their mellowness as they look forth on the hot cornfields and the smoking roads that distantly wind among them. The Cloisterham gardens blush with ripening fruit. Time

was when travel-stained pilgrims rode in clattering parties through the city's welcome shades; time is when wayfarers, leading a gypsy life between haymaking time and harvest, and looking as if they were just made of the dust of the earth, so very dusty are they, lounge about on cool doorsteps, trying to mend their unmendable shoes, or giving them to the city kennels as a hopeless job, and seeking others in the bundles that they carry, along with their yet unused sickles swathed in bands of straw. At all the more public pumps there is much cooling of the bare feet, together with much bubbling and gurgling of drinking with hand to spout on the part of these Bedouins; the Cloisterham police meanwhile looking askant from their beats with suspicion, and manifest impatience that the intruders should depart from within the civic bounds, and once more fry themselves on the simmering high roads.

The shocks in *Edwin Drood* come not from the sudden leveling of his fantasy and the appearance of realism. They occur when Dickens acts his realism—see the showdown between Jasper and Rosa—and we realize that it is really alien to Dickens's gift that his people should be made to talk to each other. When he attempts this he merely succeeds in making them talk *at* each other, like actors. His natural genius is for human soliloquy not human intercourse.

In criticism of the English novel and in appeals to what is called "the English tradition," there has been a misunderstanding, I think, about this intrinsic quality of Dickens. One hears the word Dickensian on all sides. One hears of Dickens's influence on the English novel on the one hand, and of the failure of the English novel to produce a comparable genius. While the word Dickensian lasts, the English novel will be suffocated. For the convivial and gregarious extravagance and the picaresque disorder which are supposedly Dickensian are not Dickens's especial contribution to the English novel. They are his inheritance from Sterne, Smollett and, on the sentimental side, from Richardson, an inheritance which may be traced back to the comedy of Jonson. What Dickens really contributed may be seen by a glance at the only novelists who have seriously developed his contribution—in Dostoevsky above all and, to a lesser degree, in Gogol. (There is more of Dickens, to my mind, in James Joyce's *Ulysses* than in books like *Kipps* or *Tono Bungay*.) For the distinguishing quality of Dickens's people is that they are solitaries. They are people caught living in a world of their own. They soliloquize in it. They do not talk to one another; they talk to themselves. The pressure of society has created fits of twitching in mind and speech, and fantasies in the soul. It has been said that Dickens creates merely external caricatures, but Mr. Sapsea's musings on his "somewhat extensive knowledge" and Mr. Crisparkle's sparrings in front of his mirror are fragments of inner life. In how many of that famous congress of "characters"—Micawber, Barkis, Moddles, Jingle, Mrs. Gamp or Miss Twitteron: take them at random—and in how many of the straight personages, like Jasper and Neville Landless in *Edwin Drood*, are we chiefly made aware of the individual's obliviousness of any existence but his own? The whole of Dickens's emotional radicalism, his hatred of the Utilitarians and philanthropists and all his attacks on institutions, are based on his strongest and fiercest sense: isolation. In every kind of way Dickens was isolated. Isolation was the foundation not only of his fantasy and his hysteria, but also—I am sure Mr. Edmund Wilson is correct here—of the twin strains of rebel and criminal in his nature. The solitariness of people is paralleled by the solitariness of things. Fog operates as a separate presence, houses quietly rot or boisterously prosper on their own. The veneer of the Veneerings becomes almost tangible, whipped up by the repetitions. Cloisterham believes itself more important than the world at large, the Law sports like some stale and dilapidated circus across human lives. Philanthropy attacks people like a humor or an observable germ. The people and the things of Dickens are all out of touch and out of hearing of each other, each conducting its own inner monologue, grandiloquent or dismaying. By this dissociation Dickens brings to us something of the fright of childhood, and the kind of realism employed in *Edwin Drood* reads like an attempt to reconstruct and coordinate his world, like a preparation for a final confession of guilt. (pp. 81-7)

> *V. S. Pritchett, "Edwin Drood," in his* The Living Novel & Later Appreciations, *revised edition, Random House, 1964, pp. 81-7.*

PAUL GOTTSCHALK (essay date 1970)

[*Gottschalk explores the importance of time as a motif in* Edwin Drood.]

About a third of the way through *The Mystery of Edwin Drood*, Mr. Grewgious pauses by the door of Cloisterham Cathedral and peeps in. "Dear me," he says, "it's like looking down the throat of Old Time." It is a rather imaginative notion for such a singularly angular man. It is also only one of many instances in the novel in which the architecture and people of Cloisterham are set against the background of things past and passing and to come. The revolutions of time, indeed, are a major *leitmotif* in *Edwin Drood;* the purpose of the present essay is to examine the nature and significance of this motif.

The novel itself is carefully set in time, a time that Dickens sees as extending from out of the almost immemorial past into the workaday present. Our first view of Cloisterham, the major scene of the book, establishes this continuum as the town's chief feature:

> An ancient city, Cloisterham, and no meet dwelling-place for anyone with hankerings after the noisy world. A monotonous, silent city, deriving an earthy flavour throughout from its Cathedral crypt, and so abounding in vestiges of monastic graves, that the Cloisterham children grow small salad in the dust of abbots and abbesses, and make dirt-pies of nuns and friars; while every ploughman in its outlying fields renders to once puissant Lord Treasurers, Archbishops, Bishops, and such-like the attention which the Ogre in the story-book desired to render to his unbidden visitor, and grinds their bones to make his bread.

The passage does more than establish Cloisterham as an immemorially old town: it shows the impingement of the past on the present, as the dead literally provide sustenance for the living in accordance with the natural cycle of decay and growth, and as the dead peacefully intrude themselves upon their successors—a theme to which the discovery of Edwin's body will provide a singular and horrifying variation. The architectural

transfusion of past into present, so common in English towns, extends even into the souls of the townspeople:

> In a word, a city of another and a bygone time is Cloisterham, with its hoarse Cathedral bell, its hoarse rooks hovering about the Cathedral tower, its hoarser and less distinct rooks in the stalls far beneath. Fragments of old wall, saint's chapel, chapter-house, convent and monastery, have got incongruously or obstructively built into many of its houses and gardens, much as kindred jumbled notions have become incorporated into many of its citizens' minds. All things in it are of the past.

Stones, notions, and even the very sounds carried through the air link the town serenely with its past. And, in addition to the Cathedral and the ancient gatehouse, which is the residence of Jasper, one of the chief settings of the Cloisterham chapters is Rosa's school, the Nuns' House, "a venerable brick edifice, whose present appellation is doubtless derived from the legend of its conventual uses"—note that these uses are legendary: again, the past is not cold history but part of the "notions" of the townsmen. Cloisterham is the natural habitat of Durdles, the bibulous sexton who lives among the dead—the "old 'uns,"—treating them with the familiarity of everyday professional acquaintances.

The England of *Edwin Drood*, then, is an England of shifting history with an underlying permanence. The people of Cloisterham go about their daily business in the comfortable shadow of the past; Mr. Grewgious, Rosa's guardian, goes about his with exemplary regularity in London under the sign of P.J.T. 1747. Even that great symbol of change, the railroad, has not yet reached Cloisterham (and when it does, Dickens observes, the trains will not stop there):

> Some remote fragment of Main Line to somewhere else, there was, which was going to ruin the Money Market if it failed, and Church and State if it succeeded, and (of course), the Constitution, whether or no. . . .

Plus ça change, plus c'est la même chose.

In this world of continuity, Jasper is at once in time and out of it. In a town where the citizens fear ghosts, have that "innate shrinking of dust with the breath of life in it from dust out of which the breath of life has passed," his very dwelling, the old gatehouse between the high street and the ancient cathedral close, places him on the borderline between the present and the past, the living and the dead. At night in Cloisterham, the close is deserted, cut off from life:

> One might fancy that the tide of life was stemmed by Mr. Jasper's own gatehouse. The murmur of the tide is heard beyond; but no wave passes the archway, over which his lamp burns red behind his curtain, as if the building were a Lighthouse.

His own personal life shows this double time. On the one hand, as choirmaster he lives in the tempo of Cloisterham and literally keeps the ecclesiastical hours of the Church. On the other, off in the city, he lives in the timeless world of opium. (The midnight scene in the crypt with Durdles, as Jasper scouts the territory for his murder and obtains the key for Mrs. Sapsea's monument under the pretense of seeking the picturesque, is a horrible combination of the diabolic and the ecclesiastical in the figurative seas beyond the tide of life.) While most men's memories are continuous, Jasper's breaks into two different parts, that of the choirmaster and that of the opium addict, neither of which holds communication with the other. He is, of course, the classic example of the divided self that Dickens mentions in the oft-quoted passage on animal magnetism, and at the end, it has been argued convincingly, it will take hypnosis to make him realize what he has done. This discontinuity sets him apart from his fellow townsmen, who live unseparated from their own past. And we never know when he conceives the murder: it seems present in his mind from the very first ambiguous encounter with his nephew; it is the creation of his other, timeless self, a scheme imposed upon life from an existence outside of time. "Well; I have told you that I did it here hundreds of thousands of times," he says to the old opium seller. "What do I say? I did it millions and billions of times. I did it so often, and through such vast expanses of time, that when it was really done, it seemed not worth the doing, it was done so soon."

In this context, it is especially interesting that Edwin Drood himself is characterized as a young man with a future—not that he has particularly great expectations, but that Dickens stresses over and over what lies ahead for him. Most obviously, he is betrothed to Rosa—a betrothal established by their respective parents, now dead, and one more example of the past's impingement on the present and the future. (It is a benevolent scheme, designed for the young people's happiness: if, as Grewgious hastens to make clear, they do not want to marry after all, they are not obliged to, and Edwin's one major act is to cut himself off from what is arbitrary in the past, to free himself for the future.) It is this tie with the past and future that links Edwin to Cloisterham and to the plot itself. In addition, over and over again in his conversation and his actions, his thoughts turn habitually to what is supposed to come, to the future that, for him, will never be. When we first see him, he is about to turn twenty-one and inherit the future laid out for him in the past. His conversation with Jasper and with Rosa turns naturally upon his impending marriage, upon his domestic and professional establishment in the Egypt that he will never see. In addition, he continually makes small plans for the immediate future. Ironically, he plans to break the news gently to Jasper that his engagement is off. He plans to return to Grewgious the ring that instead will be buried with his corpse. He has the Cloisterham jeweler wind and set his watch, though he will not live the time it will take for it to run down again. And Dickens goes even further by hinting several times of Edwin's growing interest in the newly-arrived Helena Landless, thus establishing a whole series of conventional romantic expectations on the part of the reader himself, expectations that are abruptly cut short just as Edwin's expectations are cut short: the hints are red herrings drawn across the path of the experienced novel-reader to involve him in a conventional future that is not, in fact, to occur.

We are accustomed to learning a great deal about an important character's past the first time we see him in a novel—especially if the character is to be the victim in a murder mystery—but Edwin has no past to speak of, only a future, near and distant, which he has partly laid out himself and partly received, tentatively, at the hopeful and loving hands of the past. He has no achievements, only promise. Jasper, on the other hand, has a great deal of past. What lies behind Edwin is irrelevant; behind his uncle, however, lies something dark and evil and—the refrain of chapter i—"unintelligible," a prior existence that the unfinished part of the novel would have brought to

light. But Jasper has no future. "The cramped monotony of my existence grinds me away by the grain," he tells his nephew, in the same conversation in which his nephew elaborates his future plans. "I must subdue myself to my vocation. . . . It's too late to find another now." The murder of Edwin Drood is horrible not simply because the villain is cruel and cunning and the victim charming and innocent, but because it is the murder of a young man with a future by a man who has none. In killing Edwin, Jasper murders time.

Other details of the murder bring out this theme still more clearly. The murder occurs on Christmas Eve—itself a symbolic crisis in time, a commemoration of a moving from old to new, just as Edwin is about to enter into a new life. The murder is shortly after midnight, and, symbolically, it stops time itself. A fierce storm rages that night that only subsides early Christmas morning:

> It is then seen that the hands of the Cathedral clock are torn off; that lead from the roof has been stripped away, rolled up, and blown into the Close; and that some stones have been displaced upon the summit of the great tower. Christmas morning though it be, it is necessary to send up workmen to ascertain the extent of the damage done. These, led by Durdles, go aloft; while Mr. Tope and a crowd of early idlers gather down in Minor Canon Corner, shading their eyes and watching for their appearance up there.

> This cluster is suddenly broken and put aside by the hands of Mr. Jasper; all the gazing eyes are brought down to the earth by his loudly inquiring of Mr. Crisparkle, at an open window:

> "Where is my nephew?"

The hands of Jasper have, figuratively, stopped the hands of the Cathedral clock—and the hands of Edwin's watch, so recently set and wound and now, its owner dead, once more allowed to run down. Jasper has immured Edwin's body in Mrs. Sapsea's monument and covered the body with some of Durdles' quick-lime: he hopes to *annihilate* Edwin, to put him outside of time, into the irrecoverable world of the "old 'uns," to violate the natural cycle of death, decay, and life that Dickens establishes at the outset of the novel. It is thus, perhaps, that Jasper reacts with scorn and apparent reluctance to Durdles' assertion that he once had heard a mysterious cry:

> "What do you mean?" is the very abrupt, and, one might say, fierce retort.

> "I mean that I made inquiries everywhere about, and that no living ears but mine heard either that cry or that howl. So I say they was both ghosts; though why they came to me, I've never made out."

> "I thought you were another kind of man," says Jasper, scornfully.

> "So I thought myself," answers Durdles with his usual composure; "and yet I was picked out for it."

> Jasper had risen suddenly, when he asked him what he meant, and he now says, "Come; we shall freeze here; lead the way."

If, as Dickens hints, Jasper's reaction here is rather in excess of the facts as they appear, the reason is that he plans to commit a murder, to put Edwin Drood out of time; in his own mind, he must insist on the discontinuity of time, of the dead and the living. And to get the key to Mrs. Sapsea's monument, Jasper must ply Durdles with liquor until he loses all sense of time, until he falls asleep, dreaming that he counts Jasper's footsteps and "that the footsteps die away into distance of time and of space"; when Durdles at last awakens, he must ask:

"What's the time?"

"Hark! The bells are going in the Tower!"

They strike four quarters, and then the great bell strikes.

"Two!" cries Durdles, scrambling up; "why didn't you try to wake me, Mister Jarsper?"

"I did. I might as well have tried to wake the dead."

Cloisterham—and the moral universe of the novel—lives comfortably with its past, and its future is just as comfortably secure in the hands of its young citizens, who, at the end of the novel, will be paired off to continue the natural cycle of life, death, and new life that Dickens has established at the outset. But meanwhile, one of these young people has been murdered, the cycle interrupted, and the unfinished half of the novel must have dealt with its reestablishment. Meanwhile, the *leitmotif* of time has served one of its purposes: we can see that the storm that accompanies the murder is not simply melodramatic embellishment, any more than the storm that accompanies the murder of Duncan in *Macbeth* or even the trembling of nature that accompanies the original sin in *Paradise Lost*. The murder of Edwin Drood is not simply repulsive in itself: it is a violation of the natural order.

Finally, the natural cycle will be reestablished; time will be fulfilled. The ring that Edwin receives from Grewgious and that is buried with his corpse is at once the means and the symbol of this fulfillment. Through the ring, of course, the body will be identified and justice ultimately accomplished. Dickens develops the theme in his own comment on Edwin's decision not to mention the ring to Rosa, a decision that means that it will remain hidden in his inner pocket, where Jasper will not find it:

Let them [the jewels of the ring] be. Let them lie unspoken of, in his breast. However distinctly or indistinctly he entertained these thoughts, he arrived at the conclusion, Let them be. Among the mighty store of wonderful chains that are for ever forging, day and night, in the vast iron-works of time and circumstance, there was one chain forged in the moment of that small conclusion, riveted to the foundations of heaven and earth, and gifted with invincible force to hold and drag.

Time is not simply a matter of coincidence—it is a moral force. The image of the chain, of course, is a recollection of *Great Expectations*:

That was a memorable day to me, for it made great changes in me. But it is the same with any life. Imagine one selected day struck out of it, and think how different its course would have been. Pause you who read this, and think

for a moment of the long chain of iron or gold, of thorns or flowers, that would never have bound you, but for the formation of the first link on one memorable day.

Here even more, there is the feeling that the course of time is more than merely consequential, that the past will come full circle in the future, that it is "gifted with invincible force to hold and drag." *Drag*: Rosa has used the same word only a few pages earlier, explaining her relief that the prearranged engagement is at last broken off:

"And you know," said Rosa innocently, "you couldn't like me then; and you can always like me now, for I shall not be a drag upon you, or a worry to you."

Rosa uses the word in abnegating her hold on Edwin, in freeing him from an unnatural situation that the past has laid on him—for among the good people of the novel, what is unnatural in the past can ultimately be laid aside, The chief unnatural act, however, and one that cannot be laid aside, is the murder, and now the ring will be a "drag" on Jasper as his past catches up with him. Edwin has been charged "by the living and by the dead" to return the ring should his engagement to Rosa be broken off. Ironically, gruesomely, he will keep this charge, and the ring will return again to Mr. Grewgious' keeping, where it will take its place among the bitter-sweet memories of things dead until, like the many other ghosts in *The Mystery of Edwin Drood*, it once more rejoins the living, returning "into circulation again, to repeat [its] former round."

In *Great Expectations* the metaphysical chains that bind day to day are man made, just as are the physical chains that bind Magwitch or that stretch across the door of Satis House. And in other Dickens' novels in which the evil lies predominantly in some social institution, the central symbol will commonly be a symbol of that institution, such as the disease-ridden fog that represents Chancery in *Bleak House* or the prison in *Little Dorrit*. His last novel, however, takes place out of the mainstream of Victorian society, in a universe that is morally ordered, and where evil is the act of individual men. The central symbol, then, is of this order itself, this force which underlies those acts of men and by which those acts are to be judged. Against the background of time the tale of Jasper and Edwin Drood unfolds. Against the background of time we see Jasper's unnaturalness and the particular unnaturalness of the murder he commits. And time itself will bring about the solution to the mystery of Edwin Drood.

The keynote to the completed half of the novel is sounded at the end of the first chapter when, "awakening muttered thunder," a passage from Proverbs is intoned in the Cathedral. Dickens cites (incorrectly) only the first four words, but the rest of the verse and the one following are what he evidently had in mind:

When a wicked man dieth, his expectation shall perish: and the hope of unjust men perisheth. The righteous is delivered out of trouble, and the wicked cometh in his stead.

The keynote to the unwritten half of the novel, I think, comes in another Cathedral scene and another, less somber biblical allusion; it is on almost the last page that Dickens wrote:

A brilliant morning shines on the old city. Its antiquities and ruins are surpassingly beautiful, with a lusty ivy gleaming in the sun, and the rich trees waving in the balmy air. Changes of glorious light from moving boughs, songs of birds, scents from gardens, woods, and fields—or, rather, from the one great garden of the whole cultivated island in its yielding time—penetrate into the Cathedral, subdue its earthy odour, and preach the Resurrection and the Life. The cold stone tombs of centuries ago grow warm; and flecks of brightness dart into the sternest marble corners of the building, fluttering there like wings.

"I am the resurrection, and the life: he that believeth in me, though he were dead, yet shall he live" (John, 11:25). The Gospel is describing the greatest miracle: the raising of Lazarus. In Dickens' hands, however, the specifically miraculous disappears, replaced by the recurrent, cyclical pattern of time, as spring comes to Cloisterham Cathedral, where past and present daily meet, at a moment when the novel begins hastening toward the deliverance of the righteous out of trouble and the coming of the wicked in his stead.

Earlier, a man of the church had confronted and consoled a righteous man in trouble:

> "And you must expect no miracle to help you, Neville," said Mr. Crisparkle, compassionately.
>
> "No, sir, I know that. The ordinary fulness of time and circumstances is all I have to trust to."

It is the sort of thing an earnest young minor canon might well say to his earnest young charge; in the context of *Edwin Drood*, however, it makes far deeper sense than a casual eavesdropper would suspect. (pp. 265-72)

Paul Gottschalk, "Time in 'Edwin Drood'," in Dickens Studies Annual, *Vol. 1, 1970, pp. 265-72.*

A. E. DYSON   (essay date 1970)

[*Dyson discusses the nature of Jasper's personality, probing the question of his guilt and sanity.*]

[Jasper is central to *Edwin Drood*]. Just as we enter the novel through his scattered consciousness, so he permeates much of its mood and tone. In his distinctive manner Dickens projects Jasper into the world around him: into his room, where the congruence between the man and his surroundings goes beyond the fairly normal perception that a man may colour a room, or even that a room may symbolise a man, to some more dynamic sense of the man incarnating himself in his surroundings and possibly enjoying the revelation and the concealment of himself in such a way:

> Mr Jasper is a dark man of some six-and-twenty, with thick, lustrous, well-arranged black hair and whiskers. He looks older than he is, as dark men often do. His voice is deep and good, his face and figure are good, his manner is a little sombre. His room is a little sombre, and may have had its influence in forming his manner. It is mostly in shadow. Even when the sun shines brilliantly it seldom touches the grand piano in the recess, or the folio music-books on the stand, or the bookshelves on the wall, or the unfinished picture of a blooming school-girl hanging over the chimney piece . . .

This blends in turn with the more sinister description of Jasper in his room, watching his nephew:

> Once for all, a look of intentness and intensity—a look of hungry, exacting, watchful, and yet devoted affection—is always, now and ever afterwards, on the Jasper face whenever the Jasper face is addressed in this direction. And whenever it is so addressed it is never, on this occasion or on any other, dividedly addressed; it is always concentrated.

In a novel of the hunters and hunted 'the Jasper face' suggests a degree of dislocation between reality and appearance that is highly sinister ('There's no art / To read the mind's construction in the face'). It is as though the look, 'hungry, exacting, watchful' were a cloak to cover whatever obsession underlies 'affection'; or as though only a constant effort, such as that required to overcome the 'unclean spirit of imitation' under opium, could keep the Jasper face from relapsing into other shapes—the 'strange and sudden smile' and the 'sense of destructive power' which Durdles sees, or the even fuller revelation to Rosa at the sun-dial: 'But his face looks so wicked and menacing, as he stands leaning against the sun-dial—setting, as it were, his black mark upon the very face of day—that her flight is arrested by horror as she looks at him.' In the affinity between Jasper and his room it may not be fanciful to discern a further suggestion: that just as the room appears dimly respectable, except in such moments as it becomes a place of rage and violence (Edwin's quarrel with Neville, and the night of Edwin's disappearance), so Jasper appears dimly respectable for much of the time, to his own nephew (who 'can't' be warned) as to the world.

As with Jasper's room, so with Cloisterham; it is as though the darker undercurrents of morbidity to be discerned there, in crypt and cloister, emanate somehow from this man. This may be why Jasper's impatience with Cloisterham and hatred of its deadness strikes us not as justification for his escape—we know the terms of that escape, after all—but rather as the source of infection, projecting what is seen. Just as the strange world of *The Ancient Mariner* takes on aridity and horror for the guilty mariner, so Cloisterham's evil seems strangely like Jasper's consciousness in decay. Jasper's Cloisterham is at best a place of sultry brooding, shot through with sharp flashes of fear and terror, where Rosa's fear of the man, exaggerated though it may be by aversion, is an index of his malign power for ill. Our release from *this* Cloisterham, as readers, comes not from Jasper's own escape into opium, which merely turns the cathedral into a nightmare stage for ritual murder, but from a different consciousness altogether: that of Canon Crisparkle and his mother—for whom a closet can turn to paradise, and the very cathedral proclaim, on sunlit mornings, the Resurrection and the Life.

The chief enigma for the reader is not then whether Jasper is malign and tormented—that is stamped on everything—but whether he is evil, or mad, or conceivably both. (pp. 279-81)

Is Jasper mad? The question, perhaps no more finally solvable than the plot riddles, has fascinating interest in the Dickens world. To my mind he is mad only as he drives himself mad, and he drives himself mad through evil designs. In *Great Expectations* there is a most revealing insight of Pip's about Mrs Joe's rampages: 'I must remark of my sister, what is equally true of all the violent women I have ever seen, that passion was no excuse for her, because it is undeniable that instead of lapsing into passion, she consciously and deliberately took extraordinary pains to force herself into it, and became blindly furious by regular stages.' Mrs Joe is an ordinary callous woman, certainly not a 'horrible wonder apart' like Jasper, yet the process of degradation may be the same. A nearer instance is Bradley Headstone, who, although slower and stupider than Jasper, is like him in passion, and is described during the genesis of murder in these terms:

> The state of the man was murderous, and he knew it. More; he irritated it, with a kind of perverse pleasure akin to that which a sick man sometimes has in irritating a wound upon his body. Tied up all day with his disciplined show upon him, subdued to the performance of his routine of educational tricks, encircled by a gabbling crowd, he broke loose at night like an ill-tamed wild animal. Under his daily restraint, it was his compensation, not his trouble, to give a glance towards his state at night and to the freedom of its being indulged. If great criminals told the truth—which, being great criminals, they do not—they would very rarely tell of their struggles against the crime. Their struggles are towards it. They buffet with opposing waves, to gain the bloody shore, not to recede from it. This man perfectly comprehended that he hated his rival with his strongest and worst forces, and that if he tracked him to Lizzie Hexam, his so doing would never serve himself with her, or serve her. All his pains were taken to the end that he might incense himself with the sight of the detested figure in her company and favour, in her place of concealment. And he knew as well what act of his would follow, if he did, as he knew that his mother had borne him.

We have only to think back over the great tormented minds in Dickens to notice that he regarded madness as almost self-induced, the final and worst stage of an evil will. At a certain stage the process may be irreversible, with the madman no longer accountable to himself or anyone for what he does, but this still remains a natural punishment for sin. There are certain energies which alienate from humanity, and enfold in torment: revenge for instance, as we see it in Carker, Edith Dombey, Alice Marwood, Rosa Dartle, Mrs Clennam, Miss Wade, Miss Havisham: and murder (where the men start to preponderate)— Bill Sikes, Rudge, Jonas Chuzzlewit, Tulkinghorn (who can be numbered here), Rigaud, Orlick, Headstone. All of these might be, or come to be 'mad' clinically, but Dickens finds wickedness at the core. These people do not belong with the deranged people who are victims of defects of birth (Barnaby), intolerable sufferings borne with gentleness (Miss Flite), or clinical disorders (Mr F's Aunt), and who deserve pity. They present themselves rather as the reverse of those characters who, responding to suffering with patience, courage, selflessness and other difficult virtues, become the salt of the earth.

Merely to reflect upon the men and women on both sides of this equation is to remember that Dickens never repeated characters or situations, and that his depiction of the endless byways of virtue and vice is as far-ranging as any in literature. Yet it remains true that all his really wicked characters violate certain clear rules of virtue and reason, and bring their worst derangements upon themselves. Dickens's greatest fear, both

touching individuals and society, was anarchy. No doubt he was led to this partly by self-knowledge; the capacities for destruction as well as creation in his own great energy are always clear. It is with this in mind that we can properly acknowledge his more remarkable villains as partial self-portraits; just as we might feel that Macbeth lurked in Shakespeare himself. 'Partial' is, however, the qualification, with all the difference implied in it between heaven and hell. If a writer can not only create a Macbeth but place him as Shakespeare does, the gulf cannot properly be described in lesser terms.

I make these observations because Jasper has actually been identified with Dickens by some critics (I shall return to this), and because others have seen him as pitiable because clinically mad. The confusion arises from the nature of the split in Jasper's character. Is he indeed one person, or two or more persons inhabiting one frame? When Mr Tope has been describing Jasper's 'daze' in the second chapter, the Dean replies 'And Mr Jasper has gone home quite himself, has he?' The 'daze' we know to be an after-effect of opium, and the mystery of what 'quite himself' might imply, with a man like Jasper, already obtrudes itself as cause for concern. James Wright has followed the critics who see the case as one of schizophrenia, with Jasper as a kind of Jekyll and Hyde. He quotes an innocent-seeming remark about Miss Twinkleton, and ponders whether Miss Twinkleton is the 'only one':

> As, in some cases of drunkenness, and in others of animal magnetism, there are two states of consciousness which never clash, but each of which pursues its separate course as though it were continuous instead of broken (thus, if I hide my watch when I am drunk, I must be drunk again before I can remember where), so Miss Twinkleton has two different and distinct phases of being . . .

In my own view this passage undoubtedly conceals some hidden clue, possibly in the parenthesis (it would turn out to be relevant perhaps to whatever arts Jasper has practised on Crisparkle which lead him to the weir), but I cannot see it as having any analogy to Jasper's frame of mind. The 'split' in him is not between two personalities, but between two deliberate *personae*—the respectable public self of Cloisterham and the exotic private self of the Limehouse den. At all times in his 'normal' life Jasper commands both *personae*. The suppressed excitement of his manner with Edwin comes of their ironic tension, and his only forgetfulness is during the spell of the drugs. Indeed, he so hates his public *persona* even while adopting it, that he tells Edwin it is the merest façade.

It is the same with the main action of the novel, Jasper's plan to make away with Edwin and Neville and to possess Rosa, to which all his waking words and deeds are attuned. The 'warning' he gives to Edwin, in the safe knowledge that Edwin will not understand it, is true enough as far as it goes. Jasper is already 'madly' in love with Rosa, and determined to control her, while murder is enacted as yet only in opium dreams. Jasper's attitude to Edwin obviously reflects a dark obsession with him, but an obsession which he consciously intensifies in his Limehouse life. When Neville comes on the scene, Jasper organises their quarrel, and takes care that the whole town shall be told. His morbid 'fears' are clearly intended for Crisparkle, and his diary exists chiefly—perhaps solely—to this end.

Jasper's plans for murder of Edwin include the public role which he builds up for himself as doting uncle, and his mysterious visit to the cathedral with Durdles, with its patent design (there are no doubt other designs also) on Durdles's keys. On the final day of Edwin's life we see Jasper wearing his long black scarf in readiness, and fully tuned, almost certainly with drugs, to his deed. Edwin also discovers on this day—too late for him to understand the import or to profit from it—that his uncle has a clear mental image of every scrap of his personal jewellery, and, moreover, that there is a dire threat to someone in Cloisterham called Ned ('not an inspiriting close to a dull day').

In all these plans Jasper the choir-master is engaged most fully, and there is no evidence of any 'self' in ignorance of what he does. His careful planning is, rather, an expression of moral deterioration, encouraged and accelerated in himself. The most obvious example of this is his recourse to opium, and to the Limehouse setting where we meet him first. In taking to drugs he renounces reason and normal consciousness in favour of 'scattered consciousness' outside reason's writ. This in turn follows his calculated rejection of the twin pillars on which his civilisation remains stable, the respectability of Cloisterham, and the demands and promises of the Christian faith. His hypocrisy in remaining outwardly conformist has none of the Pecksniffian panache; rather, its tone is sardonic and sultry, as evidenced in his revelation to Edwin:

> 'You were going to say (but that I interrupted you in spite of myself) what a quiet life mine is. No whirl and uproar around me, no distracting commerce or calculation, no risk, no change of place, myself devoted to the art I pursue, my business my pleasure.'
>
> 'I really was going to say something of the kind, Jack . . .'
>
> 'Yes, I saw what you were tending to. I hate it.'
>
> 'Hate it, Jack?' (Much bewildered.)
>
> 'I hate it. The cramped monotony of my existence grinds me away by the grain. How does our service sound to you?'
>
> 'Beautiful! Quite celestial!'
>
> 'It often sounds to me quite devilish. I am so weary of it. The echoes of my own voice among the arches seem to mock me with my daily drudging round. No wretched monk who droned his life away in that gloomy place before me can have been more tired of it than I am. He could take for relief (and did take) to carving demons out of the stalls and seats and desks. What shall I do? Must I take to carving them out of my heart?'

At the present time, Jasper's tone of social protest might seem almost standard; and Dickens would not have been wholly out of sympathy himself. He had no brief for the cloister and would not have relished it, though on the other hand he would scarcely have seen himself, as Jasper does, as a secluded drudge. But Jasper's tone is at once too urbane and too elusive to be sympathetic; surely he *relishes* Edwin's failure to glimpse the carvings in his heart? When he reveals himself more fully to Rosa at the sun-dial, we see behind the mask of his tone:

> 'There is my past and my present wasted life. There is the desolation of my heart and my soul.

> There is my peace; there is my despair. Stamp them into the dust, so that you take me, were it even mortally hating me!'

> The frightful vehemence of the man, now reaching its full height, so additionally terrifies her as to break the spell that has held her to the spot.

Even if this torment is somehow familiar—especially if it is somehow familiar—we might as well pity as cobra about to strike. Jasper is so mad here, that we can merely hope his own destruction will be upon him before other victims fall to his despair. The rejection of restraint and reason has so far been accomplished in him, that he is incapable also by now of love and trust. It is apparent that the 'love' he now declares is nightmarish, and that surrender to egotism has made a horror of the word.

The fact that he *is* passing into real madness becomes first fully apparent in his night with Durdles. From the start, Durdles asserts a kind of complicity which ought to warn him; but, watching Neville and Crisparkle in the moonlight, Jasper gives way to a fit of uncontrolled laughter which leaves Durdles pale. As the novel progressed, Jasper's madness would have deepened, and the scene in the condemned cell would have revealed the total derangement of his mind. If Dickens had lived longer, he might have surpassed his previous summits in this depiction. As it is, the image of Jasper at the sun-dial remains impressed on our minds.

There is surely then a curious irony in Edmund Wilson's famous suggestion that in important aspects Jasper is a final portrait of Dickens himself [see excerpt dated 1939]. . . . There is no major and seminal piece of literary criticism known to me—and Wilson's essay did more than any other piece of critical writing to introduce the modern world to Dickens's greatness—where a more damnable piece of nonsense can be found. I use the word advisedly, since the notion that Jasper's damnation should be justifiable from any valid point of view, and most of all from the author's, partakes of damnation itself. If Jasper worships Kali, and is regarded by the cult as a good and faithful servant, then are not Kali's worshippers a sect of murderous rogues? And is it not damnable to imagine that a murdering scoundrel like Jasper can in any serious manner be compared with one of the greatest creative minds of his own or any other age?

Wilson's error seems to me here so depressing, and yet so distinctively modern, that it is hard to know in what spirit it should be opposed. Who but a modern would imagine that the escape world of opium could have anything to do, except in the sickest parody, with the creative artist's power? Jasper's drugs are a rejection of consciousness for uncontrolled fantasy, not that union of consciousness and reason which fuse in all creative art. Drugs might be compatible with intelligent rubbish like the novels of William Burroughs, but never with the creation of a novel like *Edwin Drood*. As creator, Dickens confers beauty and significance of the kind which come only from the world of rational morality which Jasper spurns beneath his feet and kicks away. Wilson's suggestion is a melancholy reminder that Jasper is not only a wicked man but a surprisingly modern one; an *exemplum* who has surprising relevance to our scattered consciousness today.

He is, to be more precise, a precursor of our own last-ditch romanticism, a condition more prevalent and dangerous at the centenary of Dickens's death than it was when the novel was

An illustration by Luke Fildes of Jasper threatening Rosa in the garden of the Nun's House.

new. The early Romantics had directed the mind of man inwards to his personal psyche and the quest for its fulfilment. The prognosis seemed excellent. Only cast off the old chains of law and custom and man might be free and noble, loving and joyful; might be a great hero; might be a god. Literature since has offered tragic overtones to this splendid optimism, yet its lure is as potent now as it ever was. The Victorian novelists discovered that a tragic destiny might attend such freedom; in the twentieth century the prospects have further declined. Through desolate tracts of waste land to absurdist nightmares, the modern romantic pilgrimage wends its way. (pp. 285-92)

The importance of *Edwin Drood* to an insane climate—its peculiar relevance, I am suggesting—lies then in Jasper's prophetic gropings towards ourselves. From inside his consciousness, he is naturally a victim, to be pitied all the more as he becomes a 'horrible wonder apart'. From anywhere outside his consciousness he is an extreme evil, to be locked up if at all possible, and perhaps even killed.

What could more justify Crisparkle, with his Christian cheerfulness, and when called upon for it his Christian sternness, than the nightmare loosed on and into Cloisterham in this tale? Crisparkle holds out to Neville, also tigerishly tempted, the salutary hope of discipline and pure love. Love *itself* will not do: Jasper 'loves' Rosa, after all. For love to be purified, something else is needed. Decency, sanity, wisdom: these above all are the healing things.

If we consider *Edwin Drood* as a genre novel, it might seem a regression, a return beyond the moral realism of Jane Austen's dealings with cathedral cities to the wild world of gothic ro-

mance. A closer look dispels this notion. Eighteenth-century gothic pressed madness, drugs, unbridled passion and so forth into the service of sensationalism. With no pressure from realism, they arrived at 'mere entertainment', in a disabling sense. *Edwin Drood* looks not backward to this but forward, to our modern probing of madness, and our modern situation itself. It is as though Jane Austen's world becomes, in the light of *Edwin Drood*, the illusion, a mere dream of stable and decorous society in the human world. Dickens takes us to the battlefield where good and evil engage each other, and Cloisterham reflects the purities and nightmares of these rival worlds.

The wheel has indeed come full circle, when one can feel Jane Austen's as the world where a modern reader is likely to seek his escapism, and *Edwin Drood* as an image of life as it normally is. Dickens depicts in Jasper a path of despair and damnation which stands in its relevance to the individual much as the Terror in *A Tale of Two Cities* does to society at large. His final novel is his most striking picture of the human situation in its starkest relationship to good and evil. It is also his most striking justification of reason and sanity as the grounds for all human activity, the true pearls beyond price. (pp. 292-93)

> *A. E. Dyson, in his* The Inimitable Dickens: A Reading of the Novels, *Macmillan and Co. Ltd., 1970, 303 p.*

ANGUS WILSON (essay date 1974)

[*Wilson is one of the most important English novelists of the post-World War II era. He is also an esteemed critic of English literature who has written extensively on Dickens, including the following excerpt from his introduction to* Edwin Drood. *After faulting many critics' preoccupation with the novel's unresolved ending rather than with its intrinsic literary merits, Wilson compares the plot and other aspects of* Edwin Drood *with those of Dickens's earlier works and provides an extended analysis of its thematic concerns.*]

The first monthly number of *The Mystery of Edwin Drood* was published in April 1870. The novel was designed to be complete in twelve parts—a short novel by Victorian standards, a very short novel by Dickens's standards. It was, in fact, to prove even shorter, for on 8 June Charles Dickens suffered an apoplectic stroke. He died the next day. Six numbers only of *The Mystery of Edwin Drood* were completed.

This fact is central to the mass of discussion that the novel has aroused in later generations. A half-finished book by a man of genius is not something which it is easy for critics to assess. It is doubtful whether we truly can judge the literary value of *The Mystery of Edwin Drood*, we can only point to individual merits or imperfections, and try to put them into perspective beside those of the complete novels which had gone before.

Until quite recently most critics have evaded even this comparatively satisfying approach to what is inevitably a tantalizing, unsatisfying thing—an unfinished product of an artist of genius. They have attempted to compensate by laying exceptional stress on the circumstances under which the book was written.

Some few, knowing that Dickens's health was in serious decline in the last years of his life, have dismissed the book altogether. His friend, Wilkie Collins, later declared it to be 'Dickens' last laboured effort, the melancholy work of a worn-out brain' [see Additional Bibliography]. Bernard Shaw spoke of it as 'a gesture by a man who was already three quarters dead' [see Additional Bibliography]. This is not the view of most modern critics. More relevant, perhaps, it was not the view of critics in *The Times* [see excerpt dated 1870], *The Athenaeum,* or *The Graphic* at the date of the publication of the first number. Then *The Mystery of Edwin Drood* was not seen as the book of a dying man, but as a remarkable sign of the persistence of Dickens's vitality, evidence that he could entertain a whole new generation as he had entertained their fathers. There *were* hostile notices of the new novel. Most of Dickens's novels had received some. But the general reception of *The Mystery of Edwin Drood* when it first appeared was far more friendly, far more sure of his continued artistic vitality than it had been on the publication of *Our Mutual Friend* in 1865, four and a half years before, or, indeed, than it had been of *Little Dorrit* between 1855 and 1857, or, certainly, of *Martin Chuzzlewit* in 1843-4. The dismissive view of Collins and Shaw may be itself dismissed as an easy and insufficient hindsight.

The more usual approach to *Edwin Drood* is, I think, almost as insufficient, but not so easy to dismiss. For decades, from around the turn of the century until the outbreak of the last war, the concern of Dickens's admirers was entirely with the mystery aspect of the story—who killed Edwin Drood? Sometimes, was Edwin Drood really dead at all? And, in addition, who was the mysterious Datchery, the stranger who visits Cloisterham after Drood's disappearance? Certainly these questions come into our minds when we read the book, and, as they are not answered, they are bound to nag us. The title of the book, too, seems to lay emphasis on this purely 'whodunnit' aspect of the novel. But Dickens's titles do not as a rule run deep into the heart of the significance of his novels; and about this one . . . he was very undecided. There had been mysteries

in all his novels since *Oliver Twist*. If he had died before finishing *Barnaby Rudge,* certainly before he had reached Book Two of that novel, we might be asking, who killed Barnaby's father, or was his father really dead at all? These seem minor questions now beside that novel's extraordinary insight into the nature of violent revolution. And so with the murder of Mr Tulkinghorn in *Bleak House,* or the mystery of Rigaud's hold over Mrs Clenham in *Little Dorrit;* it would be an absurdity to see those two great social novels in such narrow terms. These mysteries are the essence of Dickens's plots. These plots are indeed essential to the novels, but they are only the mechanism by which the great imaginative magic lantern works; the total significance of what Dickens shows us in his novels is a hundred times greater than his plots. In fact he was a very clumsy contriver of plots, and often, as in *Little Dorrit,* the 'mysteries' are only unravelled in the last chapters in a mass of complicated and suddenly revealed events that have taken place before the action of the novel began. There is a hint of something of the sort in the complicated family relationships in *The Mystery of Edwin Drood.*

Nevertheless, it has to be admitted that the book, as we have it, *is* organized around Edwin's disappearance; and the book was to be a short one—perhaps, as a result, what might have been his next most skilfully organized novel after *Great Expectations,* another comparatively short novel. The mystery, the plot, that is, in so condensed a book, inevitably becomes more identical with the whole of the work of art than in the more sprawling novels, where digression, sub-plot and sheer comic performance may take off from the central story without at all reducing the profundity of the book's total insight. To this extent, the conventional detective-story concern of most commentators on *Edwin Drood* in the first half of our century has some justification, but only if by asking about Edwin's murder or Jasper's guilt we are exploring the deeper nature of the novel. There is really no evidence that Charles Dickens in his last novel had departed completely from the kind of novels that he had previously produced, nothing to suggest that he was intent upon creating a novel whose major interest lay solely in suspense and mystery, like his friend Wilkie Collins's *The Moonstone,* which had appeared as a serial in *All the Year Round* in 1868, less still upon writing the sort of complex technical mystery story which so many of the ingenious unravellers of Drood's puzzle have invented. Such technical perfections do not indeed belong to the Victorian period, they are the products of our century's mastery of the detective-story form. It is not surprising that at the height of the Dickensian passion for solving Drood's mystery, Sir Arthur Conan Doyle, and even Sherlock Holmes himself, to say nothing of the spirits with whom Sir Arthur was in touch in 'the world beyond the grave', should all have shown interest in how and if Edwin Drood met his end. From 1905, in its first issue, until at least 1930, contributors to the *Dickensian,* the journal of the Dickens Fellowship, were preoccupied with Jasper's guilt or innocence, and the real identity of Datchery. . . . Perhaps Sir Felix Aylmer's book, *The Drood Case* of 1964 [see Additional Bibliography], defending Jasper's innocence in a complicated, closely argued, but to me inherently improbable solution based upon the old Islamic family feud code, may be seen as the last magnificent rocket in [the] long firework display of detective ingenuity that has dazzled and distracted the readers of Dickens's novel. Most of this today seems hardly more than an enjoyable but irrelevant parlour game. All too few of these mystery solvers are concerned with the fact that the mystery was invented by Dickens and not by themselves; none are content to discuss the unfinished book as a part of his whole canon.

Here once again it is interesting to turn to contemporary reviews of the unfinished novel. What struck contemporaries as new was its un-Dickensian cathedral setting and clerical cast. Comparisons were made with Trollope rather than with Wilkie Collins's world of oriental mysteries and hypnotic powers. I do not myself think that the changed social setting of *Edwin Drood* is the absolute core of the book's significance, but it is certainly quite as unexpected in his work as the elements of the exotic. The latter are surely to be seen only as a new aspect of the gothic and the supernatural that had persisted—especially in his short magazine tales—from the days of the interpolated stories in *The Pickwick Papers* back in 1836.

Such evidence of Dickens's intentions in *Edwin Drood* as we have from his relations and friends is all agreed upon the simple solution to the mystery that Jasper murdered his nephew Edwin Drood. Such a solution is naturally not satisfying to those who look to the book for the kind of cleverly designed false clues and motives that mark twentieth-century detective fiction. In most cases these critics have found it possible to dismiss contemporary evidence in favour of certain very tantalizing puzzles in the half-finished text, and, above all, in the implications of the designs for the cover of the monthly parts. These puzzles are both genuine and fascinating. Yet I cannot feel that they should outweigh the account of the book given by those who knew Dickens, particularly as this account, though unsatisfactory to readers who are looking for a brilliant 'whodunnit', accords most satisfactorily with that concentration upon the fight between the forces of Good and Evil as exemplified in contemporary society, with particular emphasis upon the analysis and personification of Evil, which had been Dickens's preoccupation in all his novels. (pp. 11-14)

Dickens's previous novel, *Our Mutual Friend,* had ended serial publication in November 1865. There is, therefore, a four and a half year gap between the two novels, the longest in Dickens's writing life. This fact itself has been used by those who dismiss *Edwin Drood* as the work of a dying man to bolster their opinion. Yet the gap between *Our Mutual Friend* and its predecessor *Great Expectations* is about three and a half years, almost as long. It would be easy to suggest that, despite all the social and metaphysical profundity, above all the extraordinary 'modernity' of *Our Mutual Friend,* its spun-out length and its periodic slackness of texture after the remarkable tautness of *Great Expectations* was the work of an ailing man, only, of course, Charles Dickens did not die before he completed it. Beside *Our Mutual Friend, The Mystery of Edwin Drood* is a model of compression and, above all, a continuously and rapidly active book. I suspect that this compression and its consequent vitality were the product of Dickens's recognition of the need to conserve his energies in view of his physical weakening—but this only rebukes those who write off *Edwin Drood,* supporting rather Doctor Johnson's view that 'when a man knows he is to be hanged in a fortnight, it concentrates his mind wonderfully.' (pp. 14-15)

What of the half-book we have? Its opening is one of the most dramatic of Dickens's many arresting first pages. . . . [With] first a vision of the whole cathedral town, then moving down to the cathedral tower, we have a familiar Dickensian literary device, highly cinematic, as in *Bleak House* where the camera moves down through the fog to London, and at last on down to the Chancery and into its court in session. The merging of

the oriental dream with the cathedral town brings two unfamiliar worlds together and both are unique in a novel by Dickens.

We know that he had been fascinated since childhood with *The Arabian Nights,* but we also know that the Orient, always a matter of disgust for him, as embodied in the ancient, static, opium-laden civilization of 'John Chinaman', had become doubly hateful since the treachery of the Indian Mutiny in 1857. We can therefore expect the horror-attraction of Jasper's oriental vision. And, on the whole, the horror of the actual Asia of England's experience in the Mutiny is likely by this time consciously to outweigh his childhood fascination with *The Arabian Nights.*

I believe that in this embodiment of evil in Jasper's opium dreams, we penetrate very deeply into developments within Dickens's imaginative consciousness. There is little doubt, surely, that the oriental dream *is* evil—it is both erotic and violent, and, more important, it is the outcome of that necessary preliminary dream journey of Jasper's, mysteriously described in the last chapter, which surely relates closely to murder. Now, in identifying this oriental world—and the dream is Turkish rather than Indian or Chinese—Dickens is identifying the world of *The Arabian Nights* with the erotic and the violent, those parts of it which we may suppose he was unconscious when as a child he so loved it that it remained (with Shakespeare) his main source of quotation well on into his maturity. It is worth noting that the other literary reference of *Edwin Drood* is *Macbeth*—the darkest, most murderous of all Shakespeare's plays, though it is quoted very characteristically in a facetious context more than once in Dickens's novel. Now, if we take Jasper to be the symbol of evil, we must then conclude that his evil dreams are identified with one of the earliest sources of Dickens's literary imagination.

That, in this source, Dickens has picked out the erotic and the violent, perhaps, backs up Edmund Wilson's suspicion that Jasper embodies the submerged part of Dickens himself [see excerpt dated 1939]. It is certainly likely that a fear of his own violent side (we need not stress the erotic) may lie under Dickens's obsession with murder as the supreme evil. Mr. Dyson, who gives us a fine account of Jasper as the embodiment of evil, is deeply shocked at Wilson's attempt to see any part of so great a creative genius as Dickens in his evil fictive creation [see excerpt dated 1970]. I believe that Wilson's thesis does have some validity and need not shock us so greatly, if, first, we consider that a great number of responsible Englishmen of the last century spent much of their energies in suppressing the erotic-violent side of their natures, and, more particularly, if we accept Forster's account of Dickens's intentions with Jasper, namely that he was a divided man whose evil side was cut off from his everyday self [see excerpt dated 1874]. This does not mean that Dickens would have condemned him the less, for he was by this time an implacable foe to any excuse for crime.

In any case, for me, the important thing about this identification of the Arabian Night dream with evil does not lie in Dickens's fear, conscious or otherwise, of his own animal nature, but in its suggestion—a suggestion amplified in the whole treatment of opium escape and dreams—that Dickens had, perhaps partly consciously, become very mistrustful of fiction, of the art he practised, of the fancy and the imagination as weapons on behalf of the Good in life. If this is so, it corroborates or extends my detection of the same distrust of storytelling and art in *Great Expectations* when Pip's invented fantasies about Miss Havisham's house (so akin to Dickens's own fanciful powers) are reprehended by Jo as 'Lies'. Whether this reflects regrets by Dickens about his own life as an artist, a fiction-maker, is the concern of the speculative biographer; what we are concerned with here is its relation to the view of life embodied in his fiction, his fictional identification of the forces of good and evil as they worked in the world around him. I think it suggests a continuing, perhaps even a final disillusionment with child-likeness, with wonder and fancy as adequate positive forces. His idea of Sleary's circus folk as the antidote to the deadening factual world of Gradgrind—the armies of Good and Evil as he saw them back in 1854 in *Hard Times,* the logical culmination of all his early work—is now quite changed. Fancy and wonder have been taken over by the black, the gothic and the evil forces of Jasper. Good has shrunk to the small world of private responsible individuals ready to pit their courage against the forces of dark fancy—Rosebud's courage, Tartar's naval manliness and powers of practical invention, Helena's tough pride, and, most unlikely of all Dickensian 'good' people, a lawyer, Mr Grewgious, and a clergyman, the muscular, classically trained Canon Crisparkle—for in his earlier books all lawyers had been villains or, at least, ambiguous characters associated with crime like Jaggers, and until his previous novel, *Our Mutual Friend,* so had all clergymen.

This small army of the good, strong in its resolution, even, like Rosebud in flight from Jasper, ready to give way in order to oppose, is primarily middle-class and primarily private. It does not preclude Dickens's continued concern with the poor and the outcast, whom he had championed all his life, although in this novel their form is ambiguous—Puffer, Tope, above all, Deputy. But it does directly continue that small world of private doing of good, of professional-class heroes and heroines, that we see in the close of *Bleak House* or *Little Dorrit.*

Does this private good mean the world of Cloisterham close, so small compared with Dickens's previous vast social canvases? Not entirely, I think, for Cloisterham is not wholly good—the progressive, radical Dickens is not so changed that an old mouldering cathedral can be a positive value for him; and the Orient, too, as represented by England's Imperial Mission has also its good side. Let me take the last point first. Professor Edgar Johnson has seen in *The Mystery of Edwin Drood* a radical anti-imperial attitude by Dickens [see excerpt dated 1952]. He speaks of 'India, China, the victims of the opium trade, subject peoples everywhere, falling prey to a greedy Imperialism.' 'Young Drood', he says, 'mouths the catchwords of that imperialism in their most infuriating form. He is "going to wake Egypt up a little", he says patronisingly.' Dickens's suggestion in all this is surely quite the opposite. He believed firmly in the superiority of the white races over the brown and the black. His dislike for missionary activities, and what he thought to be some sentimentalization of the negroes of Africa among the members of the anti-slavery lobby, had originally been due to his feeling that concern for the black race abroad had made good men and women neglectful of the evils and poverty at home in England. That is the meaning of Mrs Jellyby in *Bleak House.* But gradually, and markedly after the Indian Mutiny in 1857, he had gone further and had come to believe that the white man must dominate and order the world of the blacks and the browns. This surely is the meaning of his support for Governor Eyre's harsh measures in Jamaica in 1865. His views expressed in letters about the basic racial inferiority of the blacks after his 1867-8 visit to the United States were definite. *The Mystery of Edwin Drood* continues to state these views, hence the absurd rumours against Neville in Cloisterham—'Before coming to England he had caused to be whipped to death sundry "Natives"—nomadic persons, encamping now in Asia, now in Africa, now in the West Indies, and now at the North Pole—vaguely supposed in Cloisterham to be always black, always of great virtue, always calling themselves Me, and everybody else Massa or Missie (according to sex)', and so on—the typical heavy irony about those who misguidedly respected black people. Edwin's fault is not, I am sure, to have an Imperial mission, but rather, in his youthful callowness, to make light of it. Perhaps Dickens had in mind the failure his son Walter had made in India, to which Dickens had sent him with such high hopes. In any case, if there is a public dimension to the little band of those who do good, it lies beyond seas, fighting the treacherous, colourful Oriental source of Jasper's dreams.

Certainly it does not lie at home. There are only three public figures in the book and all are stupid, bullying and cowardly. First we have Mr Honeythunder. We should note that he is a *general* philanthropist, for, although in *Bleak House,* Dickens had confined his satire to Exeter House missionaries and Tractarian busybodies, in the last decade of his life he extended his attacks to include all penal reformers, anti-Imperialists, supporters of women's rights and a host of other wrong-meaning enthusiasts. Second comes the Mayor, Mr Sapsea, the representative of reaction, the oldest of Dickens's enemies—the Tories. The 'Sapsea Fragment' . . . is very important in this respect, for it underlies Mayor Sapsea's Tory prejudices, his devotion to the old order, his snobbery. Without that, we might fear that the old radical Dickens had gone altogether, but this is not so. For the same reason the authority of the Cathedral is represented so odiously in the Dean.

The Mystery of Edwin Drood, as well as telling us much about Dickens's developing attitude to the young and to the Empire, also speaks of that very evasive thing, his religious beliefs. Dickens's faith was always strong but he preferred not to examine sacred subjects too closely. He was always a simple New Testament Christian. In earlier times a Unitarian, he had been increasingly reconciled to the Church of England he was baptized in, by the emergence of a broad church school without the Calvinism of Exeter Hall or the Romanism of the Tractarians; especially was he attracted by the muscular Christianity of Tom Hughes and Charles Kingsley. Canon Crisparkle is surely a tribute to this. But, of the Church as an institution, he still preserved, as he did towards all institutions, an instinctive radical suspicion; it is this that the Dean represents. Even more he remained, what he had been when he wrote *A Child's History of England* to prevent his eldest boy growing up into a High Church Tory, an unshakeable hater of the past, especially of the Middle Ages. We are reminded again and again in the novel of the unnaturalness of the cloistered life for men and women. The Cathedral is not a force for good, except in the last chapter, when it is seen through the believer Canon Crisparkle's good eyes. Because Jaspter hates it as a prison does not mean that we should revere it. Indeed Cloisterham itself is a place from which the good characters must escape. And here we have a final paradox, typical of the unresolved tensions which underlie the greatness of Charles Dickens's art. We know that in his last years Dickens sought refuge at Gad's Hill from a London he had come to loathe, but we also know that, as in the winter preceding his death, he was drawn to the bustle of London. So it is in the novel: the good characters, save for the Crisparkles, are more and more collected in London, have fled from the petty meanness of Cloisterham; yet London is the scene of the evil opium dreams of Jasper, though Cloisterham is the scene of his black deed. In London, too, is to be found the only purely comic character, the Billickin; but it is to be noted that her verbal comedy is the most stale thing in the novel, a repetition of Mrs Gamp and David Copperfield's London landlady, creations of the 1840s.

We are left, at last, with Jasper at the centre. Much has been written about the nature of his evil. Certainly mesmerism would seem to be part of his evil powers—mesmerism which Dickens had used beneficently to heal Mrs De La Rue, the consul's wife in Genoa, in 1844. Jasper's dissatisfaction, however, his willingness neither to endure the cathedral monotony manfully nor to make another life for himself, but to seek refuge in drugged dreams, are what set him apart among the damned in Dickens's world, where the good forces are always energetic and outward-looking, but never more so than at the end of his life. Some critics of the novel at the time of its publication dismissed Jasper as a melodramatic gesture. I could not do that, but neither could I take the character as we have it in this half-book for the tremendous achievement of depicting evil that it is sometimes said to be nowadays. This is one more reason for me to accept Forster's version of the book's entirety, for surely the last scenes as he suggests them, with Jasper's confession in the condemned cell, would have been tremendous and entirely Jasper's own. The character might well have been more terrible than any of Dickens's previous men of violence.

In fact, all unwillingly, one is always brought back to the simple distress that the book was not finished. We could have known more had Queen Victoria only been more inquisitive. In March 1870, two months and a half before his death, he had been received by the Queen in an hour and a half private interview. He wrote afterwards to his friend, Sir Arthur Helps, the Clerk of the Privy Council, 'If Her Majesty should ever be sufficiently interested in my tale to desire to know a little more of it in advance of her subjects, you know how proud I shall be to anticipate publication.' Alas, she was not. (pp. 22-8)

> *Angus Wilson, in an introduction to* The Mystery of Edwin Drood *by Charles Dickens, edited by Arthur J. Cox, Penguin Books, 1974, pp. 11-28.*

ROY ROUSSEL   (essay date 1978)

[Roussel provides an extended commentary on the theme of completion in Edwin Drood, *examining its implications in terms of both the unfulfilled lives of various characters in the novel and the relationship between the narrator and the narrative.]*

> For Minor Canon Corner was a quiet place in the shadow of the Cathedral, which the cawing of the rooks, the echoing footsteps of rare passers, the sound of the Cathedral-bell, or the roll of the Cathedral organ, seemed to render more quiet than absolute silence. Swaggering fighting men had had their centuries of ramping and raving about Minor Canon Corner, and beaten serfs had had their centuries of drudging and dying there . . . and behold they were all gone out of Minor Canon Corner, and so much the better. Perhaps one of the highest uses of their ever having been there was that there might be left behind that blessed air of tranquility which pervaded Minor Canon Corner, and that serenely romantic state of mind—productive for the most part of pity and forebearance—which is engendered by a sorrowful story that is all told, or a pathetic play that is played out.

> Red brick walls harmoniously toned down in color by the time . . . and stone-walled gardens where annual fruit yet ripened upon monkish trees, were the principal surroundings of pretty old Mrs. Crisparkle and the Reverend Septimus as they sat at breakfast.

The Mystery of Edwin Drood is an incomplete novel which raises the issue of completion on several levels. Most obviously, it is a narrative which precisely because it is a mystery story makes the reader aware it is unfinished in a particularly maddening way. Understandably, many of the critics who have given it their attention have been concerned with finishing the work by identifying Edwin's murderer. In their efforts to realize the completed work, however, these critics are only mirroring the action of the novel itself. *The Mystery of Edwin Drood* has as its central question the possibility of its characters completing or fulfilling their lives. In the opening chapters of the novel both John Jasper and Rosa Bud feel themselves trapped in unfinished states. Both their stories are concerned with their attempts to realize their dreams and, in this sense, finish their stories.

The narrator's reference to the completed story in his description of Minor Canon Corner suggests, moreover, that his relation to his narrative is dominated by a similar desire for completion. His association of the "serenely romantic" state of mind which pervades the Corner with the "tranquility . . . engendered by a sorrowful story that is all told" reminds us that the narrator frequently insists that his story, too, is a "history" set "in those days" before the coming of the railroad. Like Minor Canon Corner, his narrative would seem to derive its meaning from the fact that it frames an action which is finished and which can be presented as a "play that is played out." His art, then, is an art which privileges in a special way his use of the past tense. It is this tense which defines events as completed and enforces an historical perspective. And, evidently, it is only when the story is seen in its completed form, when it recedes into this historical past, that the mood of serene romanticism which defines its meaning can appear. His narrative is a process whose value is realized only in its completion.

Yet if this description of Minor Canon Corner exists in the text as an image of the text's own completion—an image which draws the narrator as surely as Jasper's dreams of "great landscapes" draw him back to Princess Puffer's—it is clear that it exists as the image of an unrealized and problematic ideal. This is not simply the result of Dickens' sudden death. The narrator's efforts to present the history of Edwin's disappearance as a completed story are compromised from the very first chapter. We only have to realize the narrator's commitment to the past tense to remember that this tense neither begins nor entirely dominates the book. Of the twenty-three chapters in *The Mystery of Edwin Drood* fourteen are written in the past tense. But seven are in the present and two juxtapose past and present in striking ways. The chapters written in the present, moreover, deliberately seem to emphasize the ways in which they violate any ideal historical perspective. In them the narrator is swallowed in the immediacy of events, constantly emphasizing the problematic outcome of a character's actions, and narrative becomes the record of an ongoing and apparently open-ended process.

The juxtaposition of these two tenses implies that the opposition between the narrative as a completed story and the narrative as an open-ended process was fundamental to Dickens' conception of *The Mystery of Edwin Drood*. The narrator's comment that events have their "highest uses" only when they are completed suggests, moreover, why completion should be such a central issue, not only for Dickens but for the novel as a genre. The concept that the value of a story lies in its completion is in this context more than a statement of the necessity of a well-constructed plot. It implies that the text should be grounded in—should be the revelation of—some principle of completion. (pp. 383-85)

The Mystery of Edwin Drood seems to have been intended by Dickens as a search for alternative grounds for the text's completion, of possible sources for the tranquility of Minor Canon Corner. For this reason it is one of Dickens' most complex and most important novels despite the fact that its mystery remains unsolved. In particular, *The Mystery of Edwin Drood* investigates two possibilities for the completed story—one which is implied in the stories of Jasper and Rosa and one which involves a radical transformation of the relation between the narrator and his narrative.

> A brilliant morning shines on the old city. Its antiquities and ruins are surpassingly beautiful, with a lusty ivy gleaming in the sun, and the rich trees waving in the balmy air. Changes of glorious light from moving boughs, songs of birds, scents from gardens, woods, and fields— or, rather, from the one great garden of the whole cultivated island in its yielding time— penetrate into the Cathedral, subdue its earthy odour, and preach the Resurrection and the Life. The cold stone tombs of centuries ago grow warm, and flecks of brightness dart into the sternest marble corners of the building, fluttering there like wings.

The first of these alternative possibilities is suggested by the way in which this description inverts the usual relation between Cathedral and garden. In the description of the Cathedral cited [previously] the glow which transfigured its walls seemed to shine "from within them." Here, however, the narrator describes the glow not as the manifestation of something present in the Cathedral but as the intrusion within these walls of the natural principle of fertility present in the "great garden" of the island. It is the "vegetable life" which is "the most abundant and agreeable" evidence "of progressing life in Cloisterham," which penetrates its shadows and preaches "the Resurrection and the Life." And this intrusion implies a different relationship between the life of man and the life of nature, between the cycle of man's life and the "revolving year" which fills the "cultivated island" with "ripening fruit." (pp. 387-88)

In *The Mystery of Edwin Drood* men experience the movement toward ripening which dominates the natural descriptions in the novel as desire. The stories of the major characters in the novel imply a vision of human life as the movement of desire toward satisfaction in a way which is apparently the expression of the movement of the natural world toward maturity. If it is true, moreover, that desire has its origin in the natural world, then perhaps it has its completion there as well. Perhaps there is a parallel between the "revolving year" and the "circle of [men's] lives," so that men are not only born buds but come to maturity and ripeness as part of the same natural process. The sense of tranquility and completeness which the narrator celebrates will be found in man's immediate involvement in nature.

Such an interpretation would alter radically the meaning of the narrator's description of Minor Canon Corner. Its center would

no longer be the Cathedral but rather the gardens "where annual fruit yet ripened upon monkish trees." The narrator would remain an historian but he now would address himself to a desacramentalized history. If it is true that human and vegetable life are co-extensive, then the fulfillment of human existence will lie in the way the cycle of human life is intertwined with the cycle of the natural world. A history which recorded this cycle would never transcend the temporality of the natural. But it could still be a history written in the past tense because it would find in this temporality a process which carries man to fulfillment.

The stories of Rosa and Jasper are concerned with this happy union of man and nature. Like all mystery novels, *The Mystery of Edwin Drood* intends a demystification, and part of this intention is realized in the narrator's discovery of the principle of "Progressing life" in the apparently timeless world of Cloisterham. This principle appears now not only in the life of its gardens but also in the "unexplored romantic nooks" of its inhabitants. Mrs. Twinkleton's relationship to "foolish Mr. Porters," Jasper's desire for Rosa, Edwin's attraction to Helena, and, in a wider sense, all the secret relationships which tie the East—associated throughout the novel with dreams and desire—to Cloisterham and the West, can now be seen as the manifestations of a natural process which should carry man to fulfillment. Only the Cathedral and the society of oppressive respectability centered around it seems to inhibit this process. They appear now as dead structures which give the past an unnatural and confining power over the present. The only thing necessary, it seems, is one act which would break the hold these structures have on the life of Cloisterham. Once their tyranny has been cast off, men will be free to complete themselves in the "fullness of time."

Jasper's murder of Edwin is such an act. This "journey" which he had performed "hundreds of thousands of times" in his opium dreams is intended to break this hold and to allow his dreams to be realized in the world.

Yet although this act does free desire to express itself and to realize itself in the future, it does not bring Jasper satisfaction. The removal of Edwin, although it does open the way to Rosa, does not bring her any closer to him. Quite the contrary, it only drives her further away. The scene between Jasper and Rosa in the garden of the Nuns' house is at once the moment in which his passion achieves its fullest expression and the moment its fulfillment becomes totally impossible. It is this encounter which drives Rosa away, which more than anything crystalizes the suspicions of Rosa, Grewgious and Crisparkle, brings them in league with one another against him, and results, if we can believe Forster's account of Dickens' plan, in his eventual imprisonment. The act intended to liberate and complete his life results, evidently, in his being confined to an even more monotonous and cramped "niche" than he occupied as choirmaster. Jasper himself recognizes the failure of his intentions' "new medicine" when he returns to Princess Puffer's to enjoy again in his dreams the journey which "when it was really done . . . seemed not worth the doing, it was done so soon." His dissatisfaction points directly to his failure by this journey to win Rosa and to realize in the real garden of Mrs. Twinkleton's, and in the true temporality of the world which is symbolized by its sundial, his visions of "great landscapes."

One way to understand Jasper's failure is to see reflected in it Dickens' persistent distrust of any aggressive action. Jasper's deliberate and willful choice of Rosa makes explicit, more than any other aspect of this novel, the growing sense of individual freedom which surfaces in Dickens' later novels. Yet the fact that Dickens makes Jasper's choice require the removal of Edwin reveals that Dickens still retains an inherent suspicion of positive action and, in Jasper's growing isolation, we can see the well-documented tendency of such action in Dickens to imprison the self.

There is, however, another implication of Jasper's failure, one which becomes apparent when we juxtapose certain elements of Jasper's story with certain elements of Rosa's. Like Jasper, Rosa feels herself to be a prisoner in the past. In chapter II her dissatisfaction with her engagement to Edwin is contrasted to the pleasure she feels eating Turkish candy in the "Lumps-of-Delight shop" in a way that is obviously meant to suggest in a different key the tension between Jasper's Eastern dreams and his role in Cloisterham. In a similar manner, her decision to abandon their engagement is, like Jasper's decision to murder Edwin, a rejection of the past. But there are obvious and important differences. Rosa's and Edwin's decision is mutually agreed to. More importantly, it is not a positive act aimed at the achievement of a chosen object but rather an act of resignation; and it lacks, therefore, the qualities of self-assertion which are associated by Dickens with isolation and imprisonment. It is not, the narrator tells us, "willful, or capricious" but "something more self-denying, honorable, affectionate, and true." Jasper's act results, obviously, in the destruction of his relationship to Edwin. Rosa's decision on the other hand results in the transformation of her relationship to Edwin from fiancé to brother. (pp. 388-91)

Rosa's self-denial in breaking her engagement to Edwin would seem to allow the future to manifest itself and desire to free itself in . . . a natural way. Her decision makes Jasper's unnecessary. If he had only waited the way to Rosa would have been opened to him in the normal progress of events, and this suggests that his intense sense of confinement in Cloisterham is a false one. The future opens naturally to Rosa without any conscious aggressive action on her part. Consequently, this future should bring her a satisfaction unmarred by the isolation and guilt which seemed to Dickens the inevitable result of such action.

The story of Rosa after Edwin's disappearance is an investigation of this possibility. Her journey to London, a journey which parallels Jasper's, retains these qualities of self-effacement. Just as she did not leave Edwin for another but only resigned her engagement to him, so her move to London is not a movement toward a chosen end but, as the title of this chapter tells us, a "flight" from Jasper. And this difference seems to have important implications for her involvement in relationship to the "progressing life" of the novel. Jasper's attempt to choose his future results in his being caught in the "wonderful chains that are forever forging, day and night, in the vast iron-works of time and circumstance." His willfulness determines not only his relation to Rosa and the other characters in the novel, it also determines his relation to time and circumstance. Rosa's flight, on the other hand, implies a more open attitude which is free to accept the ripeness which the natural movement of life will bring. "When one is in a difficulty or at a loss," Mr. Grewgious tells her, "one never knows in what direction a way may chance to open." It is this "business principle" of Grewgious' "not to close up any direction, but to keep an eye in every direction" which introduces Tartar into Rosa's life.

Rosa's relationship to Tartar seems, in fact, to promise the completion of her budding nature. Their chance encounter, which is certainly intended to be one of the "developing changes" which will move the "depths" of a self which "had never been moved," is described throughout these last chapters in ways which appear to set it in opposition to the scene between Jasper and Rosa in the garden of the Nuns' house. Rosa, on Tartar's arm, ascends "unexpectedly" to "his garden in the air, and seemed to get into a marvellous country that came into sudden bloom like the country on the summit of the magic bean-stalk." Here, in this world which is "like a dream" and yet is an actual garden, Rosa and Tartar enjoy an "enchanted repast." And this experience is repeated later in their excursion on the Thames to "dine in some everlastingly green garden."

These interludes in these gardens which seem at once real and enchanted do seem to indicate that Mr. Grewgious' principle of openness to the future is vindicated and that through an acceptance of what the future brings the union of dream and reality can take place as a matter of course. Yet there are elements in the novel which imply that the seemingly obvious contrast between Rosa's experience of the union between dream and actual garden and Jasper's experience of the distance between the gardens of Cloisterham and the "great landscapes" of his dreams is misleading. *The Mystery of Edwin Drood* is, of course, an unfinished work, and it is impossible to say what the final form of Rosa's and Tartar's relation would have been. But we must see that at the same time the narrator seems to imply that their enchanted gardens are realized in the natural world, he is carefully setting these occasions in opposition to the flow of time. Rosa's enchanted repast in Tartar's apartments ends because "Mr. Tartar could not make time stand still; and time, with his hard-hearted fleetness, strode on so fast that Rosa was obliged to come down from the bean-stalk country to earth." In a similar manner their afternoon on the Thames ends when "all too soon, the great black city cast its shadow on the waters, and its dark bridges spanned them as death spans life, and the everlastingly green garden seemed to be left for everlasting, unregainable and far away."

Such passages emphasize that no human garden is everlastingly green and that both Rosa and Tartar will inevitably travel "the silent road into which all earthly pilgrimages merge." The most obvious example of Grewgious' "business principle" of chance is, in fact, the drowning of Rosa's mother "at a party of pleasure" not unlike Rosa's and Tartar's afternoon on the Thames. These references to death remind us that if the characters in *The Mystery of Edwin Drood* can attain any sense of completion it is, at best, a temporary one. (pp. 391-93)

Although the romantic side of the characters in *The Mystery of Edwin Drood* has its origin in the "fermenting world" of nature, it finds its expression in visions—Jasper's dreams of "great landscapes," Rosa's enchanted gardens—which are incompatible with the gardens of the real world and the principle of "progressing life" which they express. Because the natural progress of life does not satisfy their dreams, the characters in this novel find themselves imprisoned by desire in particularly intense and frustrating ways. They define themselves by their desire but find themselves separated from its satisfaction by the very force of time and circumstance which, seen as the principle of ongoing life, is its source. Not only are the last chapters of the novel, as we have it, dominated by the imprisonment of its characters in this sort of endless dissatisfaction. The logic of the novel implies that this will not be transcended in the second half, and that all the characters will suffer the fate of Grewgious at the hands of a Nature who says "I really cannot be worried to finish off this man; let him go as he is."

The histories of Rosa and Jasper, then, have complementary meanings. Together they imply that man will never find fulfillment in the temporal world, either through his own actions or through the natural processes of life. Such a conclusion makes it clear that any vision of a completed story will never be realized in the imitation of history. In this context, Rosa's unfinished portrait describes the limit of a mimetic approach. "Humorously—one might almost say, revengefully—like the original," its incompleteness can only reflect and emphasize the incompleteness of its subject. An historical narrative, based on a principle of imitation, will never become the "globular" "picture of a true lover's state of mind" which occurs when the "true lover has no existence separable from that of the beloved object." Since a story which mirrors history will never record the historical union of a self with the object of its desire, this story, too, must remain unfinished.

If Rosa's story marks the inevitable failure of historical narrative, it does point to the ways in which the narrator's method represents a search for an alternative ground for the completed story. The direction of this search is implicit in the final situations of Rosa and Jasper. Both have turned from the frustrations of the world to experience their dreams in another way—Jasper in a return to Princess Puffer's and Rosa in the fantasies provoked by Mrs. Twinkleton's reading. If dreams cannot be realized, and the self completed, in history, then perhaps they can be incarnated and completed in some more appropriate form—in the world of language. Language is, after all, the product of consciousness and not of nature. Perhaps it would offer the proper medium for these visions which define the self's fulfillment. Such a language would not, of course, be tied to the real world. While it might find its subject in history, it would transform history into story—into a linguistic structure which is separate, and free, from the temporality of the natural world. To attempt this would be to follow Princess Puffer's advice when she tells Jasper "never take opium your own way . . . take it in an artful form."

The narrator himself suggests this interpretation of his story when he ends his description of the flying waiter and the immovable waiter who serve Edwin and Grewgious by remarking that "it was like a highly finished miniature painting representing my Lords of the Circumlocution Department, Commandership-in-Chief of any sort, Government." The finished quality of this painting which refers only to the fictional Circumlocution Department is meant obviously to contrast with Grewgious' picture of a true lover's state of mind whose realization in the world must be forever incomplete. But this passage alerts us as well to the way in which its finished quality has been achieved through a process of transformation. The metaphors of the immovable waiter and the flying waiter appear initially as ways of describing the actual dinner. But in the course of the long passage, they lose their referential quality and become instead the thing being described. The passage, in other words, becomes a finished picture only by absorbing the "real" subject of the passage into a self-referential world of language.

The technique of the extended metaphor in which the linguistic surface of the description becomes gradually opaque and the reader's gaze becomes concentrated on this surface is only one of the techniques which the narrator uses to emphasize the verbal texture of the story and to detach this texture from any

reference to the natural world. The translation of characters into objects—Mrs. Crisparkle into a "china shepherdess"—or the anthropomorphization of objects—the wine bottles which push at their corks like "prisoners helping rioters to force the gates" and the extreme lyricism of passages such as Dickens' description of the "one great garden of the . . . island," which in its verbal extravagance makes the reader constantly aware that it is more language than description, all invite us to see the novel as a purely "artful form."

From this point of view we can see one other possible way to understand the narrator's celebration of the completed story in his description of Minor Canon Corner. Perhaps this is not a description of some real quality of the Corner or of the history which has occurred there, but instead a product of the displacement of this history into story. This would be one way to explain why the "highest uses" of these events are realized in their absence. The distance between event and narrative is no longer simply a temporal perspective but a much more radically conceived hiatus between history and fiction. The air of tranquility which characterizes the Corner occurs only when the narrator separates it from the world of progressing life and makes it the location of a separate and independent world of story. By the same token, the narrator's use of the past tense can be seen not as the past tense of history but of narrative, where the two are understood to exist in opposition to one another. If the tranquility of completion can appear only when the "ramping and raving" of history has departed—then the past tense becomes one of the primary agencies by which the narrator distances the open-ended temporality of life and creates a world of story which can be "all told." (pp. 394-97)

The narrator's intention is . . . clear. He assumes both Jasper's failure to choose actively a self in the world and Rosa's failure to find completion through the workings of chance. Consequently he turns his intention not toward the world but away from it toward the creation of a "finished painting." The center of the Corner's serene romanticism would be no longer either the cathedral or the garden, but Mrs. Crisparkle's "wonderful closet, worthy of Cloisterham, and Minor Canon Corner" which she turns to whenever her son "wanted support." In the narrator's description of this closet the Cathedral bell and organ whose sounds "had made sublimated honey of everything in store" appear not the echo of a transcendental harmony but as the expression of a more human art represented by the portrait of Handel who "beamed down at the spectator, with a knowing air of being up to the contents of the closet, and a musical air of intending to combine all its harmonies in one delicious fugue." And it is presumably this human art which is responsible for the fact that everyone who dips into these contents returns "mellow-faced, and seeming to have undergone a saccharine transfiguration." (p. 398)

An important critic of the novel [Georg Lukács] has remarked that "certain fairy-tales still retain fragments" of an epic totality in which immanent and transcendental were inextricably interwoven. The association of Mrs. Crisparkle's closet with the harmony of the cathedral bell certainly expresses Dickens' nostalgia for such totality. But more than this, the a-historical world of the fairy-story seems to become for Dickens, as it did for some German Romantics, the appropriate mode to express the ability of consciousness to separate itself from the natural and create a realm which is the expression of this freedom. In this context the meetings of Tartar and Rosa in his "marvellous" garden and in "everlastingly green garden" where they dine on their excursion become the locus of this attempt to separate story from history. These passages can now be seen to accept the irreconcilability of human dreams and ongoing life which is figured in Rosa's and Tartar's return to London, and to concentrate instead on the narrator's ability to embody a sense of completion by transforming these events into fairy-story.

The relationship between the story of Rosa and Tartar and the narrator's assertion of his power to transform is suggested by the similarity between the locker from which Tartar, "by merely touching the spring knob . . . and the handle of a drawer," produces "wonderful macaroons, glittering liqueurs, magically-preserved tropical spices, and jellies of celestial tropical fruits" which make up their "enchanted repast," and Mrs. Crisparkle's closet. This similarity provides the proper context for the "transfiguration" which takes place when the narrator describes Tartar as a "water-giant" taking Rosa, the "fairy queen," or "First Fairy of the Sea," to his "garden in the air . . . a marvellous country that came into sudden bloom like the country on the summit of the magic beanstalk."

The allusions to fairy-stories which are concentrated in this description suggest that if *The Mystery of Edwin Drood* was going to record "a tale that was all told" it would do so only on the level of fairy-story. Such a completion would ground the tranquility which the narrator attributes to the Corner securely in the power of the narrator and would represent the novel as an aesthetic object over the idea of the novel as a realistic history. Yet the idea that *The Mystery of Edwin Drood* was intended to dramatize the narrator's transformation of history into story returns us to the tension in this book between past and present tenses, for the awareness that the past tense is an important agency in this transformation only underscores the conflict. Unfinished novels allow only probable conclusions, of course, and there is no way of establishing with any certainty the final success or failure of the narrator's effort. Yet the strong awareness of the present tense in a story which, from the narrator's point of view, should appear from its beginning as something completed would seem to compromise the success of his efforts, and consequently, to undermine the ability of consciousness to define itself in language.

One key to understanding this failure lies in what might be called the centripetal movement of the important passage in which the narrator's description of Grewgious' and Edwin's dinner transforms it into a picture "like a highly finished miniature painting representing my Lords of the Circumlocution Department." As we have seen, this passage located the narrator's vision of completion in his power to translate history into story, and centers the narration in the intentionality of the narrator's consciousness. But at the same time this description seems to be affirming the possibility of such a transformation effecting a completed story, it breaks the idea of the story as a closed, completed system by referring it to another text by way of the description of the Circumlocution Office in *Little Dorrit*.

It might be argued that what is at issue here is simply the distinction between an individual work and the totality of an author's writing, and that Dickens is merely inviting us to see him embodied and defined by his presence in the entire corpus of his work. But this possibility is not borne out by the way in which the narrator's power of transformation is associated with the fairy-tale motif in the book. The narrator does not choose a single fairy-tale as the basis of his narrative in a way which would allow us to see his use of this motif as the expression of an authorial intentionality. The case is quite the opposite. The references to fairy-tales appear in this work either in general allusions to enchanted gardens or in specific references to individual tales such as Jack and the beanstalk. But in neither instance are they integrated into a single narrative structure. The effect of these references, consequently, is to dissolve the narrator's story through a series of intertextual references which make it appear no longer centered in the narrator's act of transformation but force us to see it as one repetition of a set of narrative motifs. These are motifs, moreover, which are not themselves the expression of an intentionality. They do not, in other words, embody the presence of an individual consciousness. Like myths, fairy-tales have no specific individual source but exist as elements in an essentially infinite series of variations which cannot be referred either to an authorial consciousness or to some independent, "real" world of which they are an imitation.

From this point of view, the narrator's story can never be finished in the sense that it might become a closed structure which affirms the individual existence of his consciousness. Instead, the act of writing opens out into a field of language which denies the centrality of the narrator who apparently brings it into being. The translation of history into story, which begins as the positive assertion of this individuality, ends in the impersonal play of narrative motifs. This is precisely the implication of his reference to the Circumlocution Department, where the intentionality of human actions is swallowed up and dissipated in the endless circularity of language.

These histories of Rosa and Jasper show that man is limited, finally, by an unbridgeable gap between himself and the natural world. Now, since it is apparently the nature of language that stories can never be self-contained, the narrator is faced with an equivalent rupture in his relation to his narration. He finds himself defined by a two-fold separation, distanced at once from the world of nature and the world of language.

This awareness leaves both the narrator and the reader in a double bind. Dickens' works, from the beginning of his career, have balanced themselves between realism and a kind of artful burlesque. On the one hand, he shares with most English novelists a distrust of purely aesthetic solutions. On the other hand, his writings are characterized by a kind of verbal excess which is always violating the limits of realism and seeming to assert the validity of linguistic structures. In this sense the narrator of *Oliver Twist,* who describes himself as a biographer, has always lived uneasily with the narrator who describes himself as a melodramatist.

The Mystery of Edwin Drood is not unusual, then, in the fact that it addresses these opposing tendencies. All of Dickens' work . . . can be read as a dialectic between the ideas of history and story. What is important in this novel is the relentlessly precise way in which Dickens demystifies both history and story as possible grounds for completion. The narrator, it seems, can only record the inevitable tension between the idea of completion and the conditions which inevitably frustrate its realization. *The Mystery of Edwin Drood* seems, in this way, Dickens' final comment on his own search for tranquility. It is undoubtedly accidental that he did not live to finish the novel. But the ironic awareness of the narrator suggests that its unfinished state mirrors, in an uncanny way, its theme and that even if Dickens had lived to end it, we would have found ourselves, like Rosa in London, awaiting a completion that never comes. (pp. 399-402)

Roy Roussel, "The Completed Story in the Mystery of Edwin Drood," in Criticism, Vol. XX, No. 4, Fall, 1978, pp. 383-402.

MARILYN THOMAS (essay date 1985)

[*Thomas investigates the relationship between the atmosphere of death and decay surrounding Cloisterham cathedral and the decline of the social and religious life that the cathedral represents. According to Thomas, "city and church are so intricately bound together and paralyzed by each other that forces affecting the city necessarily impact on its citizens."*]

While *The Mystery of Edwin Drood* explores the mystery of a young man's sudden disappearance and probable murder, it also explores the larger mystery of a society and the effect a dying social institution has on it. Significantly, everyone in Cloisterham dwells in the shadow of this institutional demise, some more affected by it than others, starting with Jasper on the high end of the scale and moving down to Crisparkle on the low end.

Cloisterham began, we are told, as a monastic enclosure whose purpose was to preserve "sacred" values from barbaric profanation. As the story opens, however, we see a city bypassed by history, a shell whose material signs of age reflect the psychological ennui of its citizens.

In name as well as fact, city and church are so intricately bound together and paralyzed by each other that forces affecting the city necessarily impact on its citizens.

To understand better the psychological motivation of its citizens, therefore, it is enlightening to focus on the city-church conglomerate Dickens has created in Cloisterham.

Like the archetypal city of history and legend, Cloisterham was founded on a graveyard. In ancient days, cemeteries were considered sacred as meeting places between the living and the dead. Death was celebrated as a source of life. The church, too, grew out of an act of faith (or perhaps terror) in the face of immortality as a possible outcome of physical death. In the case of both city and church, early man was setting up a social institution to help him deal with these mysteries of life and death when he founded the institutions we now know as city and church. Both institutions attempted to transcend the imminent threat of death by making themselves as institutions superior to the biological cycles that confirm man's mortality.

It is against this ideal of transcending mortality that Dickens measures his own century's city and church. In the novel the narrator recognizes how pretentious it is for the city to even try to deny its temporal nature when it is the biological and therefore mortal "leaven of busy mother Nature" that keeps "the fermenting world alive." It is, for example, within the city precincts that those close to the soil naturally celebrate time and death as the necessary preconditions for rejuvenation. In the "vestiges of monastic graves . . .

> the Cloisterham children grow small salad in the dust of abbots and abbesses, and make dirt-pies of nuns and friars; while every ploughman in its outlying fields renders to once puissant Lord Treasurers, Archbishops, Bishops, and such-like, the attention which the Ogre in the story-book desired to render to his unbidden visitor, and grinds their bones to make his bread.

From earliest times, as fairy tales affirm, mankind recognized death as a source of life. At the heart of Cloisterham, however, there stands a Cathedral which reminds passersby of "Time and Death" without recalling as well nature's promise of "the Resurrection and the Life." With the passing of centuries the promise of life, symbolized by lofty stone structures, has died in crumbling stone that leaves only reminders of death and decay. The problem with Cloisterham, city and church, is that it is an institution built for permanence in a world where life is defined by constant change.

The church's failure to instill life within its members and represent life to them as well is manifested by its crypt, where the "dead breath of the old 'uns" penetrates nave as well as tower with a damp "earthy flavour." Instead of the breath of life, it fills its members' nostrils with evidence of corruption. In addition to physical decay, a sense of moral deterioration lurks in the shadows and finds a voice in the account Durdles relates to Jasper. According to the story, it was on Christmas Eve, ironically the feast of life, that Durdles heard a scream of death "followed by the ghost of a howl of a dog . . . a long dismal howl, such as a dog gives when a person's dead." Later his suspicions of foul play seem verified when he discovers an extra body in Mrs. Sapsea's tomb.

Significantly, a church loses its consecration when murder has been committed within its walls and must be reconsecrated before worship services may lawfully be celebrated there. Having lost its sacred character through defilement, Cloisterham Cathedral receives the attention of "excursion parties" rather than worshipers. And Mr. Tope is as much "Showman" for them as he is verger for priest and worshiper. Suggesting evil, the Cathedral echoes the words intoned by its choir: "WHEN THE WICKED MAN—". Furthermore, on the morning when Edwin is found ominously missing, the Cathedral is likewise found defiled, the hands of its clock "torn off," pieces of roofing "blown into the Close," and stones from the tower "displaced." Just as the cry of murder was heard on the previous Christmas Eve, it is again Christmas when signs of death and destruction replace expectancies of life. The Cathedral no longer serves the purpose for which it was founded (if, indeed, it ever did).

Murder, defilement, and a prevailing sense of ruin indicative of the Cathedral's need for a dawn of restoration and resurrection pervade the Cathedral's crypt, which seems to await the pick of Durdles' axe as though he were an angel of mercy come to release its bones from bondage. Durdles, who boasts knowing more about the dead than any man living and is therefore qualified to speak for them, imagines the response of one dead "un" to his knocking on a tombstone: "I've been waiting for you a devil of a time." It is indeed a "devil" of a time in Cloisterham for its citizens and members when death and ruin have obliterated all signs of life. As there is not much to separate "dust with the breath of life in it from dust out of which the breath of life has passed" in Cloisterham, it becomes evident that the power of death and the consequences of denying time and change have also penetrated city dwellings, architecturally associated with the Cathedral as they are and reflecting, in general, the tenor of the city's sanctuary.

John Jasper, Cloisterham's choirmaster and precentor, is a guilt-ridden citizen whose outward respectability belies an interior nature at least as violent as Deputy's. Jasper's house, like the rest of the city's dwellings, is built out of church stone and adjoins the Cathedral by way of Tope's place. Living midway between Cathedral and gatehouse, Tope is verger for both, his life dependent upon the Cathedral. Jasper, too, "appertains" to the Cathedral much as he resents that association. His gatehouse, though at a first remove, still lies within the shadow of the city's Cathedral. In spite of physical proximity, however, "the massive grey square town" that dominates the scene from any perspective on the horizon is confused in Jasper's mind with an obtruding vision of a "spike of rusty iron . . . for the impaling of a horde of Turkish robbers, one by one." In Jasper's opium-twisted mind, the Cathedral has non-Christian associations and invokes a past memory of which he needs purging. Whatever the memory, it is clear that Jasper's heart is not in his work as Christian choirmaster. Outwardly a respectable member of Cloisterham's religious establishment as its precentor, inwardly Jasper inhabits a world of opium-induced trances, sinister visions, and evil ambitions. Like the dual aspect of the Cathedral itself, beneath whose "grave and beautiful" exterior lie the skeletons of its dead, Jasper has a buried self opposed to the "face and figure" he shows the world, a face that looks "good," but which is dead; for the living Jasper lies in the self concealed from the city. Just as the Cathedral has its literal bones buried beneath the nave and hidden from public view, Jasper has a figurative skeleton concealed in the closet of his mind. In a candid conversation with Ned, Jasper insinuates as much: "There is said to be a hidden skeleton in every house, but you thought there was none in mine, dear Ned."

Living in the shadow of the Cathedral, Jasper lives a secret life in the dimension of his subconscious, which allows him release of those aggressive and erotic drives not acceptable in the daylight world of social convention. At the same time, he has mesmeric powers by which to control others. Instead of feeling the social communion and divine sanction traditionally associated with physical proximity to the church and social affiliation with it, Jasper confesses the deadening effect church affiliation has on his life. His days pass, he remarks, in "cramped monotony" and the sacred music he conducts rather than instilling peace to his soul makes him "quite devilish." Moreover, he admits to having demons in his heart which resemble those carved by monks of a bygone era into stall, seat and desk. Just as the Cathedral is enveloped in shadow, Jasper's living quarters also lie "mostly in shadow." His principal furnishings—which include a grand piano, music books and bookshelves, and a portrait of Rosa—are seldom touched by the sun. And the wind that ripples the "pendant masses of ivy and creeper covering the building's front" is the same wind that hums "through tomb and tower, broken niche and defaced statue in the pile close at hand." As his house indicates, Jasper lives psychologically in the shadow world of the subconscious as an escape from what he calls "the monotonous round of daylight consciousness and the meaningless routine of church service."

The duality of Jasper's personality, publicly respectable but privately demonic, is reflected in the gatehouse he inhabits. Guarding the entrance between city close and precinct, Jasper's gatehouse commands a vision of both periphery and center. Built over the city's central archway, his house has two windows opposite each other. Consequently, when Jasper stands between them, he commands a dual perspective. Like the gateway to his house that opens onto the private and public domains simultaneously, Jasper inhabits the domain of his subconscious even as he leads a life of public respectability. While he receives public acknowledgement for excellence in teaching and conducting the music whose resonating chords fill the Cathedral, Jasper lives a private life not subject to law and conven-

tion. Like Durdles, who joins the world of a dead past by identifying with the Cathedral, Jasper escapes to a world within where he can live an exterior life of conformity, but an interior one of forbidden pleasure. Consequently, though Edwin publicly courts Rosa, it is Jasper who possesses her through him. Jasper's ownership of Edwin's portrait of her, and his influence over her as piano instructor, signify the power he exercises over them both, even though Edwin remains oblivious of it. It is Rosa who shudders at the sound of a chord of Jasper's music and faints at one of his glances. Then, too, the look of watchful benevolence with which Jasper gazes at the sleeping Edwin is coupled with its hungry aspect. In his relationship with Edwin, Jasper is both benevolent (since he confides in Edwin as a brother rather than an uncle) and jealous (since they are rivals for the same woman). Because Jasper's situation outwardly resembles that of Neville, Jasper confesses to him the nature of the jealousy that possesses him:

> You and I have no prospect of stirring work
> and interest, or of change and excitement, or
> of domestic ease and love. You and I have no
> prospect . . . but the tedious unchanging round
> of this dull place.

At this point Jasper does not perceive Neville as another rival for Rosa's hand. And as long as Edwin is alive, Jasper must possess Rosa through his nephew. It is only after Edwin's disappearance that Jasper approaches Rosa directly himself. The mesmeric power of his gaze is illustrated particularly in the convent garden scene. When Rosa looks at him, she feels she is "being compelled by him." There is a look "so wicked and menacing as he stands leaning against the sun-dial—setting, as it were, his black mark upon the very face of day—that her flight is arrested by horror as she looks at him." What makes Jasper so horrible in Rosa's eyes is her recognition of the demon that possesses him; a demon that cannot be exorcised until Jasper is freed from the dualism of his personality, a dualism fostered by outdated institutionalism and conventions that force him to suppress his own psychological needs and drives.

In his opium trances Jasper's demonic drives, publicly concealed, are given full expression. Much as Deputy finds psychic release for his frustrated will to power in stone-throwing, Jasper gets temporary relief in opium-puffing. Falling into a momentary relapse in the presence of Edwin, Jasper makes a rare confession that elicits sympathy, but not understanding. For to Edwin, Jasper confesses both a likeness and a difference between himself and monks of old. Both he and they were possessed by demons, but for them the church provided an outlet, whereas for him it provides none.

Finding the daylight world of consciousness too confining and monotonous, Jasper lives in the shadow world of the subconscious, a world in which time is abolished; for in his subconscious the same deed can be committed mentally many times and always as though it were the first time; neither does duration limit the amount of experience that can be lived.

Even though he is misled by following his own interior drives, Jasper is not confined to the narrow existence defined by society for a churchman. Such an escape is encouraged by an ecclesiastical institution which is both overly restrictive and unbending with regard to change.

The narrator muses about the church as an institution that attempts to deny change. Fear of participation in the fermenting cycle of mother Nature, for example, is evident in Miss Twink-

Dickens's handwritten manuscript of the last completed page of Edwin Drood.

leton's secret dalliance with a certain Mr. Porter, a dalliance supposedly concealed by the darkness of night, since Miss Twinkleton prizes her image as impeccable directress of the former convent. Rosa's fear of Jasper is largely of a sexual nature as well. Even though Rosa preserves her bodily integrity, she feels the diabolic power of Jasper's glance, a glance that compromises her innocence by its penetrating potency. Although he remains an unsuccessful suitor, Jasper is not blind, but rather frightfully perceptive in exercising power over her. At the same time, her broken engagement to Edwin, surrounded by more immediate causes as it is, represents ultimately Rosa's fear of experiencing her own sexuality, of undergoing the maturing process that will separate her from the Nuns' House, that hothouse for roses in their budding stage. Denial of sexuality in this church-affiliated House is a denial of life itself. Rosa, raised within these walls, is also a victim of its fears and denials. She will consent to kiss Edwin only after they have agreed to love each other as brother and sister rather than as husband and wife. And when Edwin arrives to see her, Miss Twinkleton "turns to the sacrifice" to announce his arrival. Aware that from the convent's point of view her virginity is in imminent danger of being lost, a deplorable state to be moaned if not avoided, Rosa covers her head with her apron in bashful reticence when entering Edwin's presence. When Rosa does seriously contemplate the prospect of a marriage to Edwin, her mind immediately suggests images of death, since

their home, as she envisions it, will be Egypt with its "tiresome old burying grounds."

While the evidence of fermenting mother Nature can also be found in Crisparkle's house, and although Minor Canon Corner lies in the shadow of the Cathedral's general influence, the Cathedral rooks that fly overhead and the sound of its bell and organ that penetrate his walls have a mellowing effect on Crisparkle. He is the model Dickens sets up as a healthy response to an institution in a state of demise. Unlike the spark of fire that lurks within the recesses of the Cathedral, the kind of flame characteristic of Jasper's nature, Crisparkle's personality has about it the quality of the lamplighter's dot of flame. Even though sepulchral gloom dominates the Cathedral, the city's lamplighter still makes his silent, nightly round. Cloisterham "would have stood aghast at the idea of abolishing" this ancient tradition, even though its citizens regard "the sacred shadow" cast by his ladder when caught in the fire's glow as an "inconvenience."

While his house forms part of the close and his dwelling is "not a stone's throw" from Jasper's, Crisparkle has managed to integrate his personality within the daylight world of consciousness. As an outlet for his repressed, inner needs. Crisparkle engages in a program of physical fitness, which includes boxing, swimming, and jogging. Into the gloom of the ancient city's general state of decline, Crisparkle brings the sunshine of charity and creative endeavor.

His house, like his person, is a picture of stability rendered harmonious by time's mingled consonance and dissonance. While Crisparkle is a minor character as far as the novel got written, Dickens may have intended him as a norm against which to appraise the other personalities of Cloisterham. On the outside Minor Canon Corner mirrors the Christian athlete who dwells within. Its brick walls covered with "strong-rooted ivy" enclose small rooms rendered mighty by "big oaken beams." Within its "strong-walled gardens," the same trees that yielded fruit for monks of a bygone era continue to bear fruit for Mr. Crisparkle and his mother. The strength of his house outside is matched by its integrity within. While Jasper teases Edwin with the insinuation of "a hidden skeleton" being locked up in the closet of every house, Crisparkle's closet is as accessible to inspection as his home is open to guests a "glorious cupboard" from which "every dipper" among its shelves emerges "seeming to have undergone a saccharine transfiguration." Living within time's narrowing confines, Crisparkle is a connoisseur of the cupboard's hidden potential, preserving the sweetness it yields and doing what he can to distill good even from the bitter that comes with the sweet.

When the institutional church no longer provides an adequate guiding light to its members, it is to the individual that Dickens turns. While Crisparkle serves as a model of Christian deportment and uprightness, the city as a whole remains in need of purgation. It is in the disappearance of Edwin Drood that the city's guilt is revealed and, in the exposure of that guilt, readied for its expurgation. Because of Edwin's mysterious departure from Cloisterham and the violent nature of Neville's previous animosity toward him suspicions of foul play and cries of "Bloodshed! Abel! Cain" resound through Cloisterham's streets. Subsequently, like the Biblical Cain, Neville is banished from society to go "withersoever he would, or could, with a blight upon his name and fame." The curse placed on Neville is, in truth, a displacement of the curse of Cain that lies over the whole city of Cloisterham. Rather than admit its own complicity in a crime whose social nature demands expiation by society as a whole, Cloisterham's citizens find a scapegoat. Neville, an outsider with a history of violent behavior, becomes the likely choice. Yet in spite of the city's success in driving him out, guilt remains. For society's mental stoning of Neville is a bogus one, whereas Deputy's is justified defiance of a society blameworthy in denying him all social and religious communion. And until the murder mystery is solved, the whole city bears the mark of Cain.

Although Cloisterham Cathedral emphasizes death in its architectural ruins, empty nave, and crypt full of bones, there is the hope of a resurrection, a rebirth that must come through individuals, however, rather than through a social or religious movement. For just as detection and removal of the murdered in the city is equivalent to opening city closets and having their skeletons revealed, grave-opening (a necessary clue to the solution of Edwin's disappearance) will symbolically reestablish the church as a potentially life-affirming institution through its openness to change and renewal. Even though Dickens satirizes a character like Sapsea, who denies temporality and death in his boasting and in the external show of his dwelling, Dickens does not deny the possibility of transcending mortality. In *Edwin Drood*, Durdles' "Tombatism" is an ailment to be cured rather than a natural condition to be accepted in this city with its roots in antiquity. As Datchery begins his job of lifting Cloisterham out of its curse of darkness and guilt, "a brilliant morning shines on the old city. Its antiquities and ruins are surpassingly beautiful, with a lusty ivy" gracing its walls in contrast to Jasper's shivering climbers lost in shadow. Civilization and nature unite in expressing the renewal of life.

Without the passage of time, the seed that is sown in death cannot come to flower and fruition. Something besides ruin and decay does remain as a result of time's passing, a faith to which Crisparkle's closet bears witness. Including every delicacy from jams and spices to pickles and wines, his closet of preserves combines "all its harmonies in one delicious fugue." And that which makes him nauseous is kept separately and accepted for its medicinal uses. In a rapid transition from the mundane to the profound, the narrator compares Crisparkle's willing submission to this "herbaceous penitentiary" with that of "the highly popular lamb who has so long and unresistingly been led to the slaughter." Like the Lamb of sacrifice (in Christian symbolism, the Lamb of God), in whose blood believers are ritualistically purified, Crisparkle would go from that closet to Cloisterham Weir and ascend again as hopeful of being cleansed "as Lady Macbeth was hopeless . . . of all the seas that roll."

Reminiscent of Tartar's rooftop garden and the "everlastingly green garden" to which he rows Grewgious and Rosa, Cloisterham itself seems to breathe the air "from the one great garden of the whole cultivated island in its yielding time" about the time that Datchery arrives. Like the city, the Cathedral's earthy odor is subdued as it then preaches "the Resurrection and the Life." Even "the cold stone tombs of centuries grow warm, and the flecks of brightness dart into the sternest corners of the building, fluttering there like wings." Participating in the dynamics of a labyrinth, the bewildering city of London gives Rosa the impression of always "waiting for something that never came." Cloisterham on its periphery, however, is the secluded center where life's essential mystery, that of life rising out of death, is explored and reaffirmed. Although Dickens never go so far, it is safe to deduce from the available evidence that the demons were to be expelled and Cloisterham was to be delivered from the same demonic possession and experience a rebirth. (pp. 12-18)

> *Marilyn Thomas, "'Edwin Drood': A Bone Yard Awaiting Resurrection," in* Dickens Quarterly, *Vol. II, No. 1, March, 1985, pp. 12-18.*

ADDITIONAL BIBLIOGRAPHY

Aylmer, Felix. *The Drood Case.* London: Rupert Hart-Davis, 1964, 218 p.

A controversial but influential and much-discussed solution to the questions posed by the novel. Aylmer's conclusions—foremost among them the notion that Jasper is innocent—are widely regarded as ingenious, if often farfetched.

Baker, Richard M. *The Drood Murder Case: Five Studies in Dickens's "Edwin Drood."* Berkeley and Los Angeles: University of California Press, 1951, 195 p.

With Aylmer's study (see entry above), considered one of the most important modern attempts to solve the riddles posed by Dickens's incomplete text. Baker offers a series of reasoned conjectures about such problems as the identity of Datchery and whether or not Drood was indeed murdered.

Beer, John. "*Edwin Drood* and the Mystery of Apartness." In *Dickens Studies Annual: Essays on Victorian Fiction,* Vol. 13, edited by Michael Timko, Fred Kaplan, and Edward Guiliano, pp. 143-91. New York: AMS Press, 1984.

Argues that *Edwin Drood* displays "contradictions that were deeply interwoven into [Dickens's] own personality, particularly as an artist, and which, at the time of his death, remained still unresolved."

Bleiler, Everett F. "The Names in *Drood:* Parts One and Two." *Dickens Quarterly* I, Nos. 3, 4 (September 1984; December 1984): 88-93, 137-42.
Explores the significance of names in the novel.

Boyd, Aubrey. "A New Angle on the *Drood* Mystery." *Washington University Studies: Humanistic Series* 9 (October 1921): 35-85.
A landmark in *Edwin Drood* studies. Boyd was the first critic to explore the possible role of mesmerism in the novel.

Burgan, William M. "The Refinement of Contrast: Manuscript Revision in *Edwin Drood*." In *Dickens Studies Annual,* Vol. 6, edited by Robert B. Partlow, Jr., pp. 167-82. Carbondale: Southern Illinois University Press, 1977.
A study of prose style in *Edwin Drood* that focuses on Dickens's manuscript revisions.

Carden, Percy T. *The Murder of Edwin Drood Recounted by John Jasper: Being an Attempted Solution of the Mystery Based on Dickens' Manuscript and Memoranda.* New York: G. P. Putnam's Sons, 1920, 125 p.
One of the first studies of *Edwin Drood* to make use of not only Dickens's notes but also the manuscript in attempting to explain how Dickens might have completed the novel.

Cardwell, Margaret, ed. *The Mystery of Edwin Drood,* by Charles Dickens. The Clarendon Dickens, edited by John Butt and Kathleen Tillotson. Oxford: Clarendon Press, 1972, 269 p.
A definitive text of the novel, accompanied by a detailed discussion of its genesis, possible sources, composition, textual history, and publication. The editor also provides a series of appendices that include Dickens's working notes for *Edwin Drood* and a discussion of the original illustrations.

Chesterton, G. K. "Later Life and Works." In his *Charles Dickens, the Last of the Great Men,* pp. 150-72. New York: Press of the Readers Club, 1942.
A discussion of Dickens's late novels that includes brief comments on *Edwin Drood.* Chesterton is considered one of the most important Dickens critics of the early twentieth century.

Churchill, R. C., ed. *A Bibliography of Dickensian Criticism, 1836-1975.* Garland Reference Library of the Humanities, vol. 12. New York: Garland Publishing, 1975, 314 p.
A guide to writings on Dickens published between 1836 and 1975.

Cohen, Jane Rabb. "Dickens's Artists and Artistry in *The Mystery of Edwin Drood.*" *Dickens Studies* III, No. 2 (October 1967): 126-45.
Argues that Jasper and other characters in *Edwin Drood* reflect the dilemmas faced by Dickens as an artist.

Cohn, Alan M., and Collins, K. K. *The Cumulated Dickens Checklist, 1970-1979.* Troy, N.Y.: Whitson Publishing Co., 1982, 391 p.
A listing of writings on Dickens and his works published during the 1970s.

Cordery, Gareth. "The Cathedral as Setting and Symbol in *The Mystery of Edwin Drood.*" *Dickens Studies Newsletter* X, No. 4 (December 1979): 97-103.
Explores the symbolic implications of the cathedral in *Edwin Drood* and its function as a backdrop for the story.

Cox, Arthur J. "The Morals of *Edwin Drood.*" *The Dickensian* LVIII, No. 336 (January 1962): 32-42.
A study focusing on "the psychology of murder, which so many writers have agreed is the actual subject of *Drood.*"

———. "The *Drood* Remains." *Dickens Studies* II, No. 1 (January 1966): 33-44.
Discusses various questions associated with the portion of the *Edwin Drood* manuscript that had not yet been published at the time of Dickens's death.

"*Edwin Drood* (1870)." In *Dickens: The Critical Heritage,* edited by Philip Collins, pp. 542-64. The Critical Heritage Series, edited by B. C. Southam. New York: Barnes & Noble, 1971.
Reprints excerpts from selected early reviews of *Edwin Drood.*

Flynn, Judith Prescott. "'Fugitive and Cloistered Virtue': Innocence and Evil in *Edwin Drood.*" *English Studies in Canada* IX, No. 3 (September 1983): 312-25.
Contends that *Edwin Drood* differs from both Dickens's early comic writings and his later "dark" novels because it is "ultimately an optimistic work in its emphasis, not on the rescue of innocence, but on the possibility of the redemption of the wicked, the resurrection of the dead."

Forsyte, Charles. *The Decoding of "Edwin Drood."* New York: Charles Scribner's Sons, 1980, 222 p.
A recent attempt to complete the novel. Forsyte divides his book into two parts: an extended discussion of the evidence supporting his conclusions and a fictional realization of his ideas about how the novel might have been completed.

Gantz, Jeffrey Michael. "Notes on the Identity of Dick Datchery." *Dickens Studies Newsletter* VIII, No. 3 (September 1977): 72-78.
A summary of the evidence in favor of various identities for Dick Datchery.

Garfield, Leon. Chapters 23-41. In *The Mystery of Edwin Drood,* by Charles Dickens, concluded by Leon Garfield, pp. 205-327. New York: Pantheon Books, 1980.
A proposed ending to Dickens's text, written in close imitation of the novelist's prose style.

Garner, Jim. "*The Mystery of Edwin Drood.*" *Harvard Magazine* 89, No. 3 (January-February 1983): 44-8.
Explores the possible connection between the plot of *Edwin Drood* and a murder that occurred at the Harvard Medical School in 1849.

Gold, Joseph. *The Stature of Dickens: A Centenary Bibliography.* Toronto: University of Toronto Press, 1971, 236 p.
A guide to biographical and critical studies of Dickens.

Hark, Ina Rae. "Marriage in the Symbolic Framework of *The Mystery of Edwin Drood.*" *Studies in the Novel* 9, No. 2 (Summer 1977): 154-68.
Examines the theme of matrimony in *Edwin Drood.*

[Jackson, Henry]. *About "Edwin Drood."* 1911. Reprint. Folcroft, Pa.: Folcroft Library Editions, 1973, 90 p.
A response to Andrew Lang's and J. Cuming Walters's theories about *Edwin Drood* (see entries below). Jackson asserts that Drood was actually murdered and that Helena Landless was Datchery.

Jacobson, Wendy S. "John Jasper and Thuggee." *The Modern Language Review* 72, No. 3 (July 1977): 526-37.
Disputes the widely discussed theory that Jasper was a Thug.

———. *The Companion to "The Mystery of Edwin Drood."* The Dickens Companions, edited by Susan Shatto and Michael Cotsell. London: Allen & Unwin, 1986, 209 p.
An annotated guide to the text of the Clarendon edition of *Edwin Drood* (see Cardwell entry above) that includes extensive notes on people, places, things, events, and quotations within the novel.

Kostelnick, Charles. "Dickens's Quarrel with the Gothic: Ruskin, Durdles, and *Edwin Drood.*" *Dickens Studies Newsletter* VIII, No. 4 (December 1977): 104-08.
Examines Dickens's attitudes toward neo-Gothicism as expressed in *Edwin Drood.*

Lang, Andrew. *The Puzzle of Dickens's Last Plot.* London: Chapman & Hall, 1905, 100 p.
An early effort by a prominent critic to resolve the perplexities of the unfinished novel. Lang maintains that Jasper tried to kill Drood but failed, and that Datchery was Drood in disguise.

Mitchell, Charles. "*The Mystery of Edwin Drood:* The Interior and Exterior of Self." *ELH* 33, No. 2 (June 1966): 228-46.

A study of the inner and outer selves of various characters in *Edwin Drood*. Mitchell argues that the novel is a complex exploration of human personality in both its surface and hidden manifestations.

Nicoll, W. Robertson. *The Problem of "Edwin Drood": A Study in the Methods of Dickens*. London: Hodder and Stoughton, 1912, 212 p.
An influential early twentieth-century study. Nicoll was one of the first scholars to reprint Dickens's plans and notes for *Edwin Drood* and to publish the testimonies of various people close to the novelist regarding how the work was to have progressed. *The Problem* also contains a bibliography of "Droodiana" by B. W. Matz.

"Wilkie Collins about Charles Dickens." *Pall Mall Gazette* (20 January 1890): 3.
Includes comments on Dickens's works that Collins made in the margins of a copy of John Forster's *The Life of Charles Dickens*. This article is the source of Collins's often-quoted description of *Edwin Drood* as Dickens's "last laboured effort, the melancholy work of a worn-out brain."

Proctor, Richard Anthony. *Watched by the Dead: A Loving Study of Dickens' Half-Told Tale*. London: W. H. Allen & Co., 1887, 166 p.
The first full-length attempt to solve the "mysteries of *Edwin Drood*." Proctor's work was notable for his contention that Drood had not been murdered and had disguised himself as Datchery.

Saunders, Montagu. *The Mystery in the Drood Family*. Cambridge: Cambridge University Press, 1914, 159 p.
Attempts to answer the principal questions posed by the unfinished novel.

Shaw, Bernard. "Foreword to *Great Expectations*." In his *Shaw on Dickens*, edited by Dan H. Laurence and Martin Quinn, pp. 45-59. New York: Frederick Ungar Publishing Co., 1985.
Contains Shaw's frequently quoted parenthetical remark that "*Edwin Drood* is only a gesture by a man three-quarters dead."

Wales, Kathleen. "Dickens and Interior Monologue: The Opening of *Edwin Drood* Reconsidered." *Language and Style* 17, No. 3 (Summer 1984): 234-50.
Closely examines the first paragraph of *Edwin Drood*, probing its "status as interior monologue, its relations to the themes of the novel, and its supposed originality as an opening device."

Walters, J. Cuming. "The History" and "The Sequels and Solutions." In *The Complete "Mystery of Edwin Drood,"* by Charles Dickens and J. Cuming Walters, pp. xi-xxxiv, pp. 207-67. 1912. Reprint. Folcroft, Pa.: Folcroft Library Editions, 1974.
Dickens's text of the novel accompanied by what in 1912 was considered a thorough compendium of commentary, evidence, proposed conclusions, sequels, and illustrations relating to the unfinished novel.

Werner, Craig. "Fugal Structure in *The Mystery of Edwin Drood*." *Dickens Studies Newsletter* IX, No. 3 (September 1978): 77-80.
Argues that the thematic design of *Edwin Drood* is similar in many ways to that of a musical fugue.

(José) Esteban (Antonino) Echeverría

1805-1851

Argentine poet, essayist, and short story writer.

Echeverría was an influential proponent of Romantic literary and political ideals in Argentina. At a time when the newly independent country struggled to find direction, Echeverría encouraged Argentinians through his writings and activities to embrace the principles of national intellectual and political self-expression espoused by the European Romantics. Echeverría distinguished himself as a writer by composing and promoting verse that took native American life as its point of departure, thereby rejecting Spanish cultural influence and pointing the way toward independence in Argentine letters. As a political activist, he played a leading role in the fight to effect democratic reforms in government, helping to organize a group of young intellectuals dedicated to such reforms—the Asociación de Mayo—and formulating its credo, *Dogma socialista*. While Echeverría is best known as a poet and political activist, he has also won acclaim as the author of a highly regarded short story, ''El matadero'' (*The Slaughter House*).

Born in Buenos Aires, Echeverría was raised by his widowed mother. After attending school and working for a time, he became dissatisfied with his business career, leaving Argentina in 1825 to continue his education in Paris. From 1826 to 1830 Echeverría studied such diverse subjects as history, geography, mathematics, political economy, and law. Apart from this formal training, he assimilated the liberal Romantic philosophy of Victor Hugo and other leading writers, and he also took especial interest in the works of William Shakespeare, Johann Christoph Friedrich von Schiller, Johann Wolfgang von Goethe, and Lord Byron.

Echeverría returned in 1830 to Argentina, where he gradually established himself in the ensuing decade as an influential literary and political figure. He published two volumes of poetry in the early 1830s, *Elvira* and *Los consuelos,* but made his most profound literary impact with the appearance of his poem *La cautiva (The Captive Woman)* in 1837. This work, an evocation of life on the Argentine pampa accompanied by a prefatory statement encouraging the use of indigenous sources of inspiration in Argentine literature, greatly appealed to Echeverría's compatriots and helped establish his leadership among the intelligentsia. In about 1838, Echeverría helped form the Asociación de Mayo, a group committed to establishing democracy in Argentina. Echeverría wrote the organization's statement of principles, which was published in a newspaper and later issued in book form as *Dogma socialista,* and he was subsequently forced by the Argentine dictator Juan Manuel de Rosas to flee Argentina. He moved to Uruguay in 1840, continuing to write in exile but never equaling his previous literary achievements. Echeverría died in Montevideo in 1851, one year before Rosas fell from power.

Echeverría's poetry is largely discussed in terms of the vital contribution that it made to the development of Argentine literature. His early poem *Elvira* is generally acknowledged as the first Romantic work produced in Argentina. Along with his other verse, it helped inspire a whole generation of Romantic writers and encouraged the growth of a native literature

in the country. Echeverría consciously abetted Argentine cultural independence, most notably in *The Captive Woman,* his best-known poem. In his preface to the work, Echeverría wrote that ''the desert is our richest patrimony and we ought to try and draw from its breast not only wealth for our well-being, but also poetry for our moral pleasure and the encouragement of our literature.'' Most critics agree that he admirably exemplified this principle in *The Captive Woman,* a narrative poem detailing the escape of two captives from an Indian raiding party, their dramatic struggle to stay alive on the Argentine pampa, and their eventual death. While commentators seldom praise the poem for its intrinsic artistic merit, most critics would concur with Enrique Anderson-Imbert in describing it as the first Argentine work ''that displayed with skill the aim of a poetry that looked to the local scene, tradition, local color, the people, and history'' for inspiration, a distinction that has earned *The Captive Woman* an important place in the country's literary history.

Echeverría is generally considered a better prose writer than poet. While critics note that he used his talents to advantage in such politically oriented works as *Dogma socialista,* in which he promoted democracy, freedom of assembly, universal suffrage, and other concepts, they regard *The Slaughter House* as his finest prose piece. In this work, alternately labeled by commentators as a short story or part of an unfinished novel, Echeverría depicts Rosas's supporters, known as Federalists, as denizens of the Buenos Aires slaughter house; described as cruel and bestial, they climax a day of carnage by capturing and tormenting a passerby whom they assume to be a member of the anti-Rosas Unitarian party, and who dies as a result of their persecution. Commentators consistently commend the work as a passionate, powerful, and realistic exposé of the barbarism of Rosas's supporters and of the degraded state of Argentine society under his rule.

Echeverría was highly regarded by his Argentine contemporaries, and the numerous modern studies on Echeverría written in Spanish attest to his continuing interest as a literary figure. Criticism in English, however, is scarce and almost solely restricted to the twentieth century. English-language commentators stress Echeverría's historical importance, observing that his Romantic approach to literature and cultural independence was not only admired but assimilated by a generation of Argentine intellectuals, including Juan Bautista Alberdi, Juan María Gutiérrez, Domingo Faustino Sarmiento, and Bartolomé Mitre. Echeverría is thus recognized, in the words of Marguerite Suarez-Murias, as the "leader of the romantic movement in Argentina" and as an important proponent of intellectual emancipation. Since he and his followers helped spread these ideals to other South American countries during their years as political exiles, Echeverría is regarded as a key figure in the development of Romanticism in Spanish American literature as well. Echeverría additionally is credited with helping shape the political and social ideals of Argentina for, as many critics note, his followers in the Asociación de Mayo were instrumental in framing Argentina's constitution and in leading its government following Rosas's fall. Collectively, these signal contributions form the basis of Echeverría's current reputation as an important figure in the development of Argentine and Spanish American literary and political culture.

*PRINCIPAL WORKS

Elvira; o, La novia del Plata (poetry) 1832
Los consuelos (poetry) 1834
La cautiva (poetry) 1837; published in *Rimas*
  [*The Captive Woman*, 1905]
Rimas (poetry) 1837
**Dogma socialista de la Asociación de Mayo, precedido de
  una ojeada retrospectiva sobre el movimiento
  intelectual en el Plata desde el año 37* (essay) 1846
Obras completas de D. Esteban Echeverría. 5 vols.
  (poetry, prose, and short story) 1870-74
"El matadero" (short story) 1871; published in *Obras
  completas de D. Esteban Echeverría*
  [*El matadero (The Slaughter House)*, 1959]
Páginas autobiográficas (autobiography) 1962

*The principal source of information for this list is *Diccionario de la
literatura latinoamericana: Argentina, primera parte*, published in
1960 by the Union Panamericana.

**An earlier edition of this work was published in the newspaper *El
iniciador* in 1839 under the title "Código o declaración de los
principios que constituyen la creencia social de la República
Argentina."

ALFRED COESTER   (essay date 1916)

[*In the following excerpt from his pioneering study,* The Literary History of Spanish America, *Coester identifies and briefly discusses the importance of two key aspects of Echeverría's aesthetic theory: his advocacy of a native American literature and his belief in the "civilizing" function of poetry.*]

Before the worst days of Rosas' control there occurred an event of the first magnitude in the history of Spanish-American letters, the introduction of romanticism through the publication of Esteban Echeverría's poem *Elvira* in 1832. This date is noteworthy because it is the same year in which appeared the Duque de Rivas' *Moro espósito*, the first important production of Spanish romanticism. Argentina thus received directly the French type of romanticism whereas other countries absorbed the romantic spirit at second hand through the medium of Spanish works. (p. 106)

Esteban Echeverría . . . at the age of twenty, went to Europe in search of educational advantages not to be found then in his native land. The study of literature appears to have been his chief occupation, the works of Shakespeare, Goethe and especially Byron. . . . Warmly received [upon his return to Argentina], he published a few gratulatory verses and then withdrew from public intercourse to work on a poem which was published in 1832, entitled *Elvira ó la novia del Plata*. The public was too violently agitated by politics to give much attention to this production, but his next volume of verse, *Los Consuelos*, made their author immediately popular.

Los Consuelos are short poems in the Byronic manner. The romantic pose maintained throughout the collection was new to readers in Argentina and delighted them. The author explains the title by the words: "They solaced my grief and have been my only consolation in days of bitterness." The practice which he adopted from Byron of heading each poem by a quotation gives an excellent clue to their contents and character. For the entire collection he chose two lines from Auzías March which, after quoting in the original Catalan, he gave in the Spanish of Luis de León:

> Let no one see my writings who is not sad, or
> who at some time has not been sad.

> (pp. 107-08)

The most original poem of the collection is, "Él y Ella," a love dialogue which especially delighted the young ladies of Buenos Aires. The form of this poem departs from all classic standards as the strophes vary in length from twenty-four lines to a single line of passionate utterance. The volume also contained several patriotic appeals which expressed the feelings of the public at the moment and helped to arouse enthusiasm.

The success of this volume encouraged Echeverría to bring out in 1837, *Las Rimas*. Besides short pieces it contained a long poem, *La Cautiva*, which put into practice a doctrine previously expressed by the author, in a note to *Los Consuelos*. Poetry, he declared, does not enjoy in America the influence which it possesses in Europe.

> If it wishes to gain influence, it must have an
> original character of its own, reflecting the colors
> of the physical nature which surrounds us and
> be the most elevated expression of our predom-
> inant ideas and of the sentiments and passions
> which spring from the shock of our social in-
> terests. Only thus, free from the bonds of all
> foreign influence, will our poetry come to be

as sublime as the Andes; strange, beautiful and varied as the fertile earth, which produces it.

As a preface to *La Cautiva*, he wrote:

> The main purpose of the author has been to paint a few outlines of the poetical character of the desert; and in order not to reduce his work to a mere description, he has placed in the vast solitude of the pampa two ideal beings, or two souls united by the double bond of love and misfortune. The desert is our richest patrimony and we ought to try and draw from its breast not only wealth for our well-being, but also poetry for our moral pleasure and the encouragement of our literature.

Thus Echeverría first expressed a doctrine which Spanish Americans have generally felt to be true and according to which, consciously or otherwise, they have produced in literature, whatever is really valuable. (pp. 108-10)

The literary significance of *La Cautiva* lies in its revolutionary departure in form from the classic Spanish ideal and the author's success in carrying out his purpose. The Argentine critic, J. M. Gutíerrez, writes that "*La Cautiva* is a masterpiece, whose perspectives give the most complete idea of the sunburnt immensity of the pampa." (p. 111)

[Another long poem, *Avellaneda,* was] intended to celebrate the heroism of a man by that name who died in the struggle against Rosas. The scene is laid in the province of Tucumán. In depicting its natural beauties Echeverría again demonstrated his principles concerning the Americanization of literature. The political element of the poem is of course less attractive.

These two peculiarities dominate all Argentine literature, and as Echeverría put them forth as a sort of theory of aesthetics, it may be said that his influence has prevailed during most of the century. The Americanization of literature which he advocated in a note to the *Cautiva* had a long and varied development in Argentina and found in other countries at the advent of naturalism a responsive echo. And his conception of poetry as a moral or civilizing agent became the literary creed of later romanticists. (p. 113)

> *Alfred Coester, "Argentina," in his* The Literary History of Spanish America, *Macmillan Publishing Company, 1916, pp. 104-68.*

PEDRO HENRÍQUEZ-UREÑA (essay date 1945)

> [*Distinguished as a poet and scholar, Henríquez-Ureña wrote numerous works on Hispanic culture, including* Literary Currents in Hispanic America, *a revision of the Charles Eliot Norton lectures that he gave at Harvard in 1940-41. In the following excerpt from that book, Henríquez-Ureña discusses Echeverría's literary career in light of his desire to promote an authentic Argentine literature.*]

In 1825 a young man from Buenos Aires, Esteban Echeverría . . . , went to Paris, where he spent five years in the midst of the romantic insurrection. He discovered romanticism as a spiritual revolution that opened to every national or regional group the road to self-expression, to the full revelation of its soul, in contrast with the cold ultra-rational universality of academic classicism. The *Stimmen der Völker* were to be set free, the *Zeitgeist* commanded; "the spirit of the century leads nations to become emancipated, to enjoy independence,

not only political but also philosophical and literary independence," says Echeverría, who knew his Herder and his Mme. de Staël. Romanticism was a battle of the nations, waged on many fronts, from Norway to Russia and from Scotland to Catalonia. Echeverría wished to extend the field of battle to our hemisphere and conceived this purpose as a patriotic duty. When he sailed for Europe he did not think himself a poet, although he must have written a poem or two, like every self-respecting young man of our "good families" at the time. Now he made the decision to study the Spanish literature of the past in order to acquire skill in language and verse. He acquired it, though he never became a true poet—his lines yield only opaque sounds, magic of imagery is lacking in his style. His only merit lies in simplicity and clearness of design. It is a misfortune that he should have chosen verse as his vehicle, but the prejudice in favor of poetry was still too great in Hispanic America. His prose is far better—excellent, in fact—both in his lucid philosophical essays and in the bold realistic descriptions of *The Slaughter-House,* a vigorous piece which he seems to have valued little, since he never printed it. Yet his success as a poet was extraordinary—the success, it is true, of a discoverer rather than that of an artist.

The first poem he published after his return to Buenos Aires was [*Elvira*]. The date—1832—is significant; *Elvira* procedes by a year the first acknowledged work of the romantic school in Spain, *The Moorish Bastard,* by the Duke of Rivas. . . . Our literary emancipation proved true in regard to Spain; we adopted the new movement without waiting for her signal.

But *Elvira* drew little attention. It had failed of its purpose—Echeverría had only exchanged one European allegiance for another. His poem is a story in the manner of Bürger's ballads, with phantoms and all; it is South American only in its subtitle, "The Argentine Bride." Two years later he brought out a volume of romantic lyrics, [*Los consuelos*], with another ballad-like story, "**Laida,**" and they were more warmly received than *Elvira.* His crowning success came in 1837 with his volume of [*Rimas*], which included a third story in verse, *The Captive Woman.* Here, at last, he fulfilled his promise: *The Captive* conveyed to the reader a faithful semblance of nature and life in Argentina—the "open and immeasurable" pampa, all grass and no trees, with its persistent winds and its elongated clouds, its rains, its droughts, and its fires, its pugnacious howling Indians who had already mastered the horse and the European weapons, and its *criollos* struggling to lead a civilized life, surrounded by the vast emptiness of the land and perturbed by the ever present fear of attack from the savages. Echeverría is the ancestor of the great line of Argentine painters of nature—one of them a master of English prose, W. H. Hudson, the naturalist. The style of *The Captive* was direct, clear, simple; so simple, indeed, that it attained originality, though it did not attain distinction. (pp. 117-18)

[Echeverría] wrote four long poems after *The Captive,* all on Argentine subjects. Usually they are deemed inferior to his earlier work; they are not really very inferior, but they came after it, and the novelty had now worn off. Only a canto in *Avellaneda* found many admirers, because it described a new type of landscape, tropical Tucuman, entirely different from the pampas. (p. 119)

> *Pedro Henríquez-Ureña, "Romanticism and Anarchy: 1830-1860," in his* Literary Currents in Hispanic America, *Cambridge, Mass.: Harvard University Press, 1945, pp. 112-36.*

EDWARD LAROCQUE TINKER   (essay date 1947)

[*Tinker, an American writer who was interested in linguistics, literature, and other fields, briefly discusses Echeverría's contribution to gaucho literature.*]

Bartolomé Hidalgo lifted the oral folk songs of the *payador* to a recognized position as printed poetry. Hilario Ascasubi developed it as a political weapon and increased its importance and popularity; and these two writers together laid the foundation for the eventual canonization of the gaucho.

Both had slavishly imitated gaucho speech and *payador* verse form; but with Esteban Echeverría . . . a new school was born that regarded pampa talk as an illiterate jargon, and wrote their gaucho poems in correct Castilian, with only an occasional patois term to give color.

With him, the gaucho epopœia passed from the pampa to the plaza, from the pen of the countryman to that of the cosmopolitan. . . . (pp. 322-23)

[Echeverría tried his hand at romantic poetry] in *Elvira, ó la Novia de la Plata,* which appeared in 1832, and was followed by *Los Consuelos* two years later. They were distinctly Byronic in flavor and met with little or no success. Annoyed and disappointed, he published a bitter attack on the critics, and retired to Mercedes, a tiny town on the Rio Negro, to immerse himself in the simple gaucho life of the countryside. *La Cautiva,* the first national epic worthy of the name, was born of this sojourn, and appeared in 1837 in a collection of his verse called *Rimas.* (p. 323)

La Cautiva is notable because it introduced for the first time in Argentine literature the Indian and the white woman captive, and also because it is the initial gaucho poem to be written in pure Castilian. The previous authors, like Hidalgo and Ascasubi, had accented their Creolism and reproduced with complete fidelity every intonation of the pampa patois; but Echeverría, with his European education, believed that to follow this course was to promote a rhymed jargon to the rank of poetry. True poetry, he insisted, was never a servile copy, but must be a poetic interpretation of nature.

Far more than a mere *costumbrista* rhymster, he was a writer of vivid prose as well, and his novelette, **"Matadero,"** written to expose the brutality of Rosas' henchmen, is as passionately realistic as anything Steinbeck has ever done. He also published many political and literary essays that have preserved a clear picture of the thought of his day; and he taught his countrymen the same lesson [regarding literary originality and independence that] Emerson taught us in his "American Scholar." (p. 324)

> Edward Larocque Tinker, *"The Cult of the Gaucho and the Creation of a Literature,"* in Proceedings of the American Antiquarian Society, *Vol. 57, 1947, pp. 308-48.*

SEYMOUR MENTON   (essay date 1964)

[*Menton briefly discusses the qualities that contribute to the "high degree of artistry" evident in* The Slaughter House. *His remarks were first published in Spanish in 1964.*]

The Slaughterhouse, considering that it is one of the first Spanish American short stories, reveals a high degree of artistry. Although it was written at the peak of the Romantic era, by the "official importer" of Romanticism from France, about

the typical Romantic theme of the struggle against tyranny, and in a predominantly exalted Romantic tone, **The Slaughterhouse** transcends Romanticism and reveals characteristics of a surprising number of previous as well as subsequent literary movements. While its pungent wit and its anti-clericalism link it to the Encyclopedists of the eighteenth century, its minute descriptions, its obscene details, its multisensory tableaux, and its anonymous dialogues with a bold use of dialect herald respectively Realism, Naturalism, Modernism, and Criollismo.

Although the representation of a bloody dictatorship by a slaughterhouse does not require great imagination, the story surpasses the many other anti-Rosas works by its superb execution enhanced by the unimpassioned introduction. In the first paragraph, Echeverría adopts a Voltaire-like attitude to introduce the theme of meat in Lent and in order to indicate the complicity of the Church in the sufferings of the Argentine people. Immediately thereafter, he establishes the connection among the Church, the slaughterhouse, and the government. The description of the heavy rains, which at first appears to be a digression, actually echoes the reference to Noah in the first sentence and serves as a transition to the description of the hunger that was devastating the city.

Once the reader is projected into the slaughterhouse, the narrative becomes more vivid because of the concentration on the action in one specific place. The sketch of the slaughterhouse places the reader within the "Roman circus." He witnesses the slaughter of the animals, taking note of every detail. The Federalists are represented by the rabble which acts as a single character. Two hundred or four hundred human beasts are cornering forty-nine steers. Although the narrator distinguishes individuals—"two black women," "two boys," "one child"— he insists on the anonymity of his characters in order not to break the image of the mob's unity. Except for one allusion to Ño Juan, the only character with a name—probably a nickname at that—is Matasiete, the throatcutting executioner of bulls and Unitarians. The name of Rosas's dead wife, Doña Encarnación, although historical, reinforces the emphasis on the carnal, the carnage, and the carnivorous Argentineans. The spectacle is repulsive to every one of the five senses: the blood and the fat of the quartered steers, the hounds' growls, the sea gulls' squawks, the decapitated boy, and the cries of the animalistic mob.

The dynamic nature of the scene is captured stylistically by the use of many verbal adjectives and a series of long but intense compound sentences. In the original Spanish, the author's insistence on the imperfect tense (used for customary or repetitive actions) creates the effect of a prolonged nightmare until he focuses on the pursuit of the bull when he switches to the preterit. This episode, in which Matasiete distinguishes himself, represents the transition from the "Roman circus" with its epic proportions to the torture of the anonymous Unitarian, in which Matasiete is also one of the principal actors.

The episode of the Unitarian dragged through the street, stripped and tied to the four legs of the table, seems at first sight to be anti-climactic to the slaughterhouse scene. Nevertheless, it is justified structurally by its parallelism with the death of the bull and by the fact that everything takes place on the day before Good Friday. The violent death of the Unitarian obviously evokes the image of the passion of Christ and makes the anomalous alliance between the Church and the Federalist government even more poignant.

Given the absence of a prose fiction tradition in Argentina and Spanish America in general at the time this story was written, the author's talent is truly amazing both in his conception of the story's structural unity and in his relatively rich vocabulary. For the taste of the sophisticated contemporary reader, the symbolism may be too obvious and the occasional moralizing interventions of the narrator superfluous, but those defects are more than outbalanced by the vivid, brilliant, and moving nature of the story.

Beyond its intrinsic literary values, *The Slaughterhouse* reflects the strong antipathy held by the upper class Unitarian intellectuals for the riffraff, the rabble, the mob . . . the common man who supported the Rosas dictatorship. Over a hundred years later, a very similar situation occurred during the government of Juan Perón. Many of the more famous Argentine authors from Echeverría to Borges, unlike their Mexican colleagues, do not identify at all with the masses. They consider themselves an intellectual elite and treat the rabble (*la chusma* rather than *el pueblo*) with contempt. (pp. 21-2)

> *Seymour Menton, in a commentary on "The Slaughterhouse," in* The Spanish American Short Story: A Critical Anthology, *edited by Seymour Menton, University of California Press, 1980, pp. 21-2.*

ANGEL FLORES   (essay date 1967)

[*Flores is the author of an English translation of* The Slaughter House. *Although he disparages Echeverría's poetry in the following excerpt, Flores commends* The Slaughter House, *praising in particular its juxtaposition of real and surreal elements.*]

Seen in the light of objective appraisal, Echeverría's poetry contains all the weaknesses of Romantic poetry and few of its virtues. Such a "classic" as *La cautiva* is far-fetched to the point of banality and its rhetoric is hollow to the core.

Perhaps it is by his prose work and by his political activity that Echeverría's stature may best be judged. In 1838 he rallied together and organized a group of young intellectuals into a secret society, the revolutionary Asociación de Mayo. Echeverría drafted its manifesto which was in essence an expression of republican fervor and had little to do with its forbidding title *Dogma Socialista*. Echeverría's vivid depiction of the struggle of the Unitarians vs. Federalists, however, a deeply felt plea for liberalism and tolerance took the form of a short story: "**El Matadero.**" Buenos Aires' slaughter house [*el matadero*] is presented here in a grotesque realism reminiscent of the Flemish school, although the specific grows in dimension and the reader comes to realize that Echeverría's slaughter house was not just the Buenos Aires of the 1830's but the entire Argentine nation under the despotism of Dictator Rosas and his henchmen. Echeverría utilizes in its naive style a terse, colorful idiom unmistakably Argentine. But what is equally remarkable is his juxtaposition of realism and surrealism, which makes any comparison to the paintings of Breughel so rewarding. By way of illustration: into the filth and mire of the slaughter house, so truthfully depicted in the realistic tradition of the Spanish picaresque, there suddenly falls the severed head of a child (surrealist surprise) while its trunk propped on a forked pole of the corral squirts blood from innumerable jets. Even the denouement—the undaunted Unitarian hero, congested with anger, bursting like a ripe fruit—is highly surrealistic. In Echeverría, as in Kafka, unreality blossoms from the most mediocre, everyday reality. "**El Matadero**" is significant, therefore, both as a social document and as a literary achievement. (pp. 54-5)

> *Angel Flores, "Esteban Echeverría," in* The Literature of Spanish America, 1825-1885: A Critical Anthology, Vol. 2, *edited by Angel Flores, Las Américas Publishing Company, 1967, pp. 53-88.*

JEAN FRANCO   (essay date 1969)

[*Franco is an English scholar specializing in Latin American literature. In the excerpt below, she observes that by attacking "primitive native barbarism" in Argentina, Echeverría departed from the European Romantic convention of idealizing the common people and primitive ways of life. For related commentary by Franco, see excerpt dated 1973.*]

Echeverría did more than introduce Romantic ideas into Argentina. He expressed the dilemma of his time, the dilemma of a man whose artistic theories teach him to love the countryside and the 'folk' and whose living experience teaches him that the countryside and its inhabitants constitute a threat to all the values. The dilemma had its origin in the difference between the European context of Romanticism and the Latin-American context. The Industrial Revolution in Europe encouraged the European writer to idealise the countryside and the integrated, meaningful life of the peasant. In the Argentine, on the other hand, it was not industry but the vast, threatening pampa with its tribes of savage Indians and half-wild gauchos that constituted the chief danger to the good life. Thus, in Echeverría's work, Romantic conventions borrowed from European literature come into conflict with Argentinian reality. Aware of the Romantic idealisation of the common people and the noble savage, he saw in his country a bloodthirsty dictatorship which had come to power on the shoulders of the gauchos; and a nomadic Indian community that appeared to have little nobility. In both his main literary works—*La cautiva* [*The Captive*] and "**El matadero**" [*The Slaughter-House*]—Echeverría defends European values and attacks primitive native barbarism.

La cautiva is a narrative poem which, though Romantic in conception, nevertheless has roots in Argentine reality; for the white woman captured by Indians was one of the pathetic figures of contemporary folk-lore. In one of his best stories, "Marta Riquelme," the English writer William Henry Hudson, whose youth was spent in Argentina, related a haunting 'cautiva' story, and it is easy to see why the theme should also have appealed to Echeverría. His poem relates the tragic story of María, a captive amongst the Indians who finds that her husband Brian has been badly wounded and captured by them in a raid. She frees her husband and they flee across the pampa but he dies before reaching civilisation. The chief interest of the poem today lies in the contrast between Echeverría's treatment of his hero and heroine and his treatment of the Indians. Brian and María are spoken of only in ideal terms. Brian is a 'noble espíritu valiente' (noble valiant spirit) and María a 'sublime mujer' (sublime woman). The Indians are utterly ferocious and evil and are described in correspondingly bestial terms, as in the following passage in which the Indians stagger about after drinking in celebration of their victory:

> Y al regocijo sin rienda
> Se da la tribu; aquel ebrio
> Se levanta, bambolea,
> A plomo cae, y gruñendo
> Como animal se revuelca,
> Este chilla, algunos lloran,
> Y otros a beber empiezan
> De la chusma toda al cabo

La embriaguez se enseñorea,
Y hace andar en remolino
Sus delirantes cabezas.

[In a footnote, the critic adds this translation:

> And the tribe gives itself up to unbridled rejoicings; that drunkard gets up, staggers, falls flat and, groaning, wallows like an animal; one sobs, some cry and others begin to drink. Finally the whole crowd is under the influence of the intoxication which makes their delirious heads spin.]

The passage is an apt comment on Echeverría's hatred of the Indian, a hatred he shared with his enemy, Rosas.

This 'repugnancia' is nowhere more vividly expressed than in Echeverría's prose work, the short story, **"El matadero,"** written in about 1840 and published posthumously. Though the prose is high-sounding and rhetorical, there is a vigour and intensity of emotion that is unrivalled in the literature of the period.

Like *La cautiva*, **"El matadero"** describes the conflict between the forces of primitive darkness (the tribe or the mass) and the civilised individual. But **"El matadero"** is also a political allegory which attacks the dictatorship of Rosas and the barbarism of his supporters. The story relates an incident that took place in the slaughter-house of Buenos Aires during the Lenten fast. . . . An attentive reader will be aware of more than the literal description of the slaughter-house. The butchers wear the traditional *chiripá* and poncho of the gaucho; many of the women are mulatto. Hence the butchers are precisely those sections of the nation on whom Rosas relied for support. Even the seagulls are symbolic, for they are returned emigrants eager for scraps and attracted by the smell of blood. In **"El matadero,"** the gauchos and the dregs of society are in command, with one or two treacherous émigrés ready to snatch some advantage from the carnage. Echeverría draws a picture of a degraded society in which children play with 'bolas de carne' (balls of meat), in which men are only too ready to draw knives against one another and in which Negro and mulatto women are too insensitive to realise the disgusting nature of their work:

> Hacia otra parte, entretanto, dos africanas llevaban arrastrando las entrañas de un animal; allá una mulata se alejaban con un ovillo de tripas y resbalando de repente sobre un charco de sangre, caía a plomo, cubriendo con su cuerpo la codiciada presa. Acullá se veían acurrucadas en hilera cuatrocientas negras destejiendo sobre las faldas el ovillo y arrancando, uno a uno, los sebitos que el avaro cuchillo del carnicero había dejado en la tripa como rezagados, al paso que otras vaciaban panzas y vejigas y las henchían de aire de sus pulmones para depositar en ellas, luego de secas, la achura.

[In a footnote, the critic adds this translation:

> In another area, meanwhile, two African women dragged away the entrails of an animal; over there a mulatto went off with a ball of guts and slipping suddenly in a pool of blood, fell flat, covering the precious booty with her body. Over here, four hundred negresses were crouched in a row unravelling the ball on their laps and taking out the fat which the miserly butcher's

knife had spared within the bowels, while others emptied stomachs and bladders and filled them with air from their lungs in order to deposit the strips of meat there as soon as they were dry.]

There is no doubt that we are intended to draw the conclusion that in the slaughter-house of Argentina only the worst elements thrive. But worse is to come. At the height of the slaughter, a bull 'emperrado y arisco como un unitario' (as stubborn and churlish as a 'Unitarian') escapes and causes the death of a boy. The butchers recapture the animal, ritually slaughter it and then, whipped to a pitch of excitement, turn on a passer-by, a young man who wears European dress and who is not carrying the Rosas colours. He courageously stands up to the butchers but they torment him and when he suddenly has a haemorrhage, they leave him for dead. **"El matadero"** is thus the story of the forces of civilisation defeated by those of barbarism.

How different from Echeverría's own blueprint for a literature 'que armonice con la virgen, grandiosa naturaleza americana' (which may harmonise with the virginal and grandiose American nature)! The exaltation of this 'virgen naturaleza' could not be reconciled with sympathy for those who wished to control nature and civilise the backlands. Whereas the Lakeland shepherd was a type of common man who could be idealised by poets conscious of the fragmentation of the human personality in an industrial society, the American gaucho, the Indian and Negro could not be thus idealised by men who were still struggling for the recognition of law and order. (pp. 49-52)

> *Jean Franco, "Literature and Nationalism," in her*
> An Introduction to Spanish-American Literature,
> *Cambridge at the University Press, 1969, pp. 46-73.*

ENRIQUE ANDERSON-IMBERT (essay date 1969)

[*Anderson-Imbert, an Argentine literary scholar and fiction writer, here portrays Echeverría as the leader of a generation of Argentine Romantics who helped lay the foundation of their country's literary and political life.*]

[Unlike] other Hispanic-American countries, [Argentina] had a clearly romantic generation. 1830 is the boundary year. Until this year the educated men of Buenos Aires lived in the rationalistic and humanitarian "Age of Reason." The May revolution, the Independence and the first political and cultural organization of the republic from Moreno to Rivadavia were carried on under the sign of the enlightenment. From 1830 on, Buenos Aires came under the influences of French romanticism, and the generation of Echeverría, Alberdi, Gutiérrez, López, Sarmiento and Mitre was formed, all agreeing to justify the total break with Spain, to express the new emotions aroused by the American scene, and to put a liberal political system to the test.

Of the young men who had not become involved in the civil wars between federalists and centralists (known as *Unitarios*), but whom the tyrant Rosas had forced into exile, Esteban Echeverría . . . was the standard-bearer. In 1825 Echeverría left for France. . . . Through what he revealed later in his writings, and from the information left by his friends, we infer that Echeverría attentively observed, during the four years in Paris, the synthesis of romanticism and liberalism that was being produced precisely at that time. But of the rich canvas that France presented, Echeverría profited only from a few aspects.

Illustration by Eleodoro E. Marenco from La Cautiva. El Matadero, *by Esteban Echeverría. Ediciones Peuser.*

Between 1826 and 1830 important books appeared by Vigny, Hugo, Lamartine, Musset, Sainte-Beuve, Dumas. But more than these Frenchmen, it was the English and German who had influenced them, who oriented Echeverría's taste. He studied the philosophy of history and society which, evolving from the German historical school from Herder to Savigny, lent new accents to the French thought of Leroux, Guizot, Lerminier, Cousin, and others. Echeverría left Paris, if not educated by romanticism, at least with his mind sharpened by his romantic readings. By then he had projected two romantic formulas upon the Argentinian reality: political liberalism, which came to justify the break of the American colonies with Spain and advocated the continuance of the revolutionary line of May, 1810; and sympathy in the arts with the way of life of the people, through which he discovered the possibilities of an autochthonous literature based on the historical and geographical peculiarities of the pampas. Although the first formula was the more significant in the history of political ideas of Argentina, in a literary history we are obliged to refer only to the second. He had no calling or genius for poetry. He fulfilled, nevertheless, the function of a forerunner in the external history of our literature. . . . *Elvira, o la novia del Plata* was the first seedling transplanted directly from France, independent of Spanish Romanticism; . . . *Los consuelos* was the first volume of verses published in Argentina; [*La cautiva*], one of the compositions in . . . *Las rimas,* was the first work that displayed with skill the aim of a poetry that looked to the local scene, tradition, local color, the people, and history. In the immense pampa the Indian was seen as the appraiser of civilization.

The young set, dissatisfied with academic "good taste," became enthusiastic about Echeverría. They believed that with . . . *La cautiva* national literature had been established. Its simplicity sounded like sincerity to them; its emotional abundance,

poetic richness. This consecration no doubt flattered Echeverría. His life had been difficult—it would be so to the very end. He was poor, sickly, tormented. These were his misanthrophic years; and the literary reputation he earned from 1832 to 1837 must have alleviated his sadness. But, as his friend Gutiérrez noted, he felt more like the "hero of a novel," and reputation was not enough—it had to be glory, glory, and nothing else! "I renounce reputation," he wrote to Gutiérrez in 1836, "glory, yes, I would want if it were given me . . ." Today Echeverría is one of the glories of Argentine history, not because of his verses, but because he put his reputation as a versifier—that reputation that The renounced—to the service of the political regeneration of his country. Because of his literary reputation, young men followed the battle standard that he had once raised. From then on his prose works would surpass his poetry. He was, indeed, a better prosist than a poet; for this reason, . . . **"El matadero"** takes a place of honor in literary history. It is a sketch of customs of extraordinary realist vigor, differing from what had been written earlier because of the intensity of pathos and climax. As a sketch of customs it has a political and reformist purpose: to expose the despicable rabble that supported Rosas. But suddenly certain figures take on life and the sketch becomes a story. Then, in spite of the muckiness of the description, the romantic outlines become clear: the contrast between the horrifying note about the child whose throat is cut and the humorous note about the Englishman knocked down in the mud; a feeling for the "picturesque" and the "grotesque"; an aura of misfortune, fatality, death; the literary beautifying of the ugliness of the riffraff by comparing it with extreme ugliness; the curious spectacle of hundreds of "African" Negroes; the presentation of the young "Centralist," the gallant hero who loudly hurls challenges at society, in counterpoint as in a melodrama with musical background of guitars and popular song, and who, before he can be assaulted, dies of indignation, bursting into "rivers of blood." In other, more serene prose writings, Echeverría left lucid road signs that led out of the mire in which "federals" and "centralists" were having their disputes. Echeverría had a serious plan. Aware of the respect in which he was held, he decided to rally all youths around a clear doctrine. Thus the Young Argentina or the May Association was constituted in 1838; it branched out quickly throughout the remotest corners of the country. Thanks to Echeverría and his May Association, Argentine romanticism became the distinctive feature of the Hispanic American literary movement that swept a whole generation into its orbit. Romantic voices made themselves heard here and there through all Hispanic-America; it was only in Argentina however, in the decade of 1830, that there arose a generation of young romantics, educated by the same books, tied together by the same vital attitude toward historical reality. Witnesses to the calamities of their fatherland, they were friends who, in their assiduous personal associations, concurred in fundamental points of view, worked and talked together in clubs and newspapers, and while sounding the death knell of past norms, expressed the repertory of their own yearnings in a new style. Echeverría gave them their initial discipline. The work they accomplished is amazing. Argentina has never again had such a group of men thinking great thoughts. (pp. 220-23)

Enrique Anderson-Imbert, "1824-1860: Authors Born between 1800 and 1835," in his Spanish American Literature: A History, *edited by Elaine Malley, translated by John V. Falconieri and Elaine Malley, second edition, Wayne State University Press, 1969, pp. 208-57.*

JEAN FRANCO (essay date 1973)

[*Franco discusses Echeverría's treatment of civilization and barbarism in* The Captive Woman *and* The Slaughter House, *focusing on the contrast between the dynamism of the barbaric population and the impotence of the civilized characters. For additional commentary by Franco, see excerpt dated 1969.*]

[*La cautiva*] is Romantic in conception—the poetic narration of a flight from the Indian tents and an unsuccessful bid to reach civilization. But note how Argentine circumstance reverses the usual Romantic *escapes* from civilisation. We are not in industrialised Europe where lovers must find refuge in the countryside. The flight here is *from* barbarism. And although the loneliness of the pampa is evoked in terms of the 'sublime' of contemporary European Romanticism, there are also elements of fear and horror in the natural environment which totally mar its beauty. A description of a pampa fire, for instance, emphasises the loathsome force of wind and elements.

> Lodo, paja, restos viles
> De animales y reptiles
> Quema el fuego vencedor,
> Que el viento iracundo atiza:

The animal and reptile world are all part of the hostile force which is nature.

The poem centres upon a Romantic heroine, María, who represents the most delicate of civilisation's products, brought face to face with the most brutal of natural forces. Captured by the Indians, she kills the chief rather than succumb and then, on discovering that her husband is captive, also helps him to escape. There is certainly no hint of noble savage in Echeverría's picture of the drunken Indians:

> Mas allá alguno degüella
> Con afilado cuchillo
> La yegua al lazo sujeta,
> Ya la boca de la herida
> Por donde ronca y resuella,
> Ya borbollones arroja
> La caliente sangre fuera,
> En pie, trémula y convulsa.
> Dos o tres indios se pagan.
> Como sedientos vampiros,
> Sorban, chupan, saborean
> La sangre . . .

This is a primitive energy which is in total contrast to the impotence of the white hero Brian who is first glimpsed tied between four lances. Throughout the poem, Brian plays a purely passive role and is more helpless even than María. He almost refuses to run away with her for fear that her honour has been stained. Nor does he make a better showing once they leave the Indian camp, for nature has a repulsive rather than a beautiful aspect. They find themselves in a 'páramo yerto' with 'feos, inmundos despojos de la muerte'. The lovers, though in flight, often appear curiously immobile:

> En el vasto pajonal
> Permanecen inactivos.
> Su astro, al parecer, declina
> Como la luz vespertina
> Entre sombra funeral.

Despite the eruptions of violence—there is a pampa fire and an encounter with a tiger—it is this impression of inactivity and helplessness which is overwhelming. Fittingly Brian dies calling deliriously for his lance, a weapon he has never been able to use in the course of the poem. María, the more active of the two, has no will left once her man has gone and she too dies heartbroken on learning that her son had also perished.

The poem is not a literary masterpiece and is more of interest for what it tells us about Echeverría than for any intrinsic beauty. Certainly the contrast between the savage energy of Indian and nature and the passiveness and impotence of the white couple appears to reflect not the sturdy values of a pioneer civilisation but the tired resignation of a dying race. The vital forces of the poem are those which Echeverría fears, not those which he wishes to prevail. *La cautiva* forms a complete contrast in style to Echeverría's story **"El matadero,"** although the theme of the two works—the confrontation of an idealistic but impotent white race with a powerful, cruel, indigenous element—is similar. In the poetry, there has to be idealisation, for as Echeverría explained in the introduction to his *Rimas*:

> El verdadero poeta idealiza. Idealizar es sustituir a la tosca e imperfecta realidad de la naturaleza, el vivo trasunto de la acabada y sublime realidad que nuestro espíritu alcanza.

The prose work, on the other hand, is realistic, modelled on the *costumbrista* literature which purported to give a faithful depiction of types. Like his Spanish model, Larra, Echeverría transcends the picturesque and makes his *costumbrismo* the pretext for a savage attack. (pp. 39-41)

The story is set during the floods of the Lenten season when animals could not be brought into the slaughterhouse, thus causing famine on top of fasting. Echeverría, liberal and anticlerical, takes the opportunity to expose the Church's collusion with the Rosas régime and is savagely ironic about the 'intestine war between the conscience and the stomach' which their ordinances bring about. However, he continues:

> no es extraño, supuesto que el diablo, con la carne suele meterse en el cuerpo, y que la Iglesia tiene el poder de conjurarlo; el caso es reducir al hombre a una máquina cuyo móvil principal no sea su voluntad sino la de la Iglesia y el gobierno.

But though Echeverría attacks directly as in the above passage, he also uses symbolism to heighten the effect. The slaughterhouse is Argentina under Rosas, the workers—negroes and mulattos—are barbarian forces dedicated to the slaughter of everything that comes their way. They are so brutal that they play with balls of flesh and fight together like the dogs around them:

> De repente caía un bofe sangriento sobre la cabeza de alguno, que de allí pasaba a la de otro, hasta que algún deforme mastín lo hacía buena presa, y una cuadrilla de otros, por si estrujo o no estrujo, armaba una tremenda de gruñidos y mordiscones.

Notice that it is the 'deforme mastín' who wins the prize. Echeverría does not spare his feelings about the blacks and mulattos. The violence of dogs, of children, and of men is similar to the violence of the country as a whole.

Violence, cruelty, and hypocrisy are the prevailing forces, but they are not the only ones. Echeverría now introduces defiance in the form of a proud bull 'emperrado y arisco como un unitario' which escapes, is recaptured, and, in a primitive rite, is slaughtered and the testicles, the symbol of its potency, are given to the chief butcher, Matasiete. As they finish the slaughter, a young man passes on horseback and is seen to be riding with a European saddle. He is dragged off his mount and his hair is cut as a punishment. As he shouts his protest against these men whom he compares to animals, the butchers torment him more and more until he dies of haemorrhage brought on by his anger.

"El matadero" reflects a similar impotence against the forces of violence as *La cautiva.* The young Unitarian is held powerless by the butchers and forced to submit to humiliating torments. The reader cannot help being struck by the parallel of this young man, choked by his own rage, and Echeverría and his generation. Perhaps he himself suffered the feeling that verbal assaults on Rosas were finally useless. Certainly, in **"El matadero"** he attempted to use literature as a weapon. Yet there is the curious feature that in both his major works, the forces of barbarism and civilisation are unequal, the former being vigorous and dynamic, the latter weak, effeminate, reduced to verbal gestures. (pp. 41-2)

> Jean Franco, *"Civilisation and Barbarism,"* in her
> Spanish American Literature Since Independence,
> *Ernest Benn Limited, 1973, pp. 37-54.*

EDGAR C. KNOWLTON, JR.   (essay date 1986)

[*Knowlton here evaluates* The Captive Woman, *assessing the poem in light of Echeverría's preface to the work and the commentary of several latter-day critics.*]

[Juan María Gutiérrez, editor of **Obras completas de D. Esteban Echeverría,**] separated Echeverría's "Advertencia" or "Notice" to **The Captive Woman** from the poem, since it is in prose and also has individual value as a work of literary criticism which clarifies a poet's ideals about his own poetry. Evaluation of the poem, the one which is the chief basis of Echeverría's reputation as poet nowadays, cannot be fairly made without reference to this statement. . . . Because of its length, use will be made of paraphrase of certain portions, and of our own translation, enclosed in quotation marks. . . . (p. 34)

> The principal design of the author of **The Captive Woman** has been to depict some characteristics of the poetic face of the desert; and in order not to reduce his work to a mere description, he has placed, on the vast solitudes of the pampas, two ideal beings, or two souls united by the double bond of love and of misfortune. The event which he puts into poetry, if not certain, at least enters the realm of the possible; and since it is not for a poet to relate in minute detail all the circumstances like a chronicler or novelist, he has selected for building his portrait only those circumstances that might afford more local color to the brush of poetry: or, rather, he has scattered about the two figures that compose it some of the most characteristic ornaments of the surrounding nature. The Desert belongs to us, it is our richest patrimony, and we must try to derive from it not only wealth for our growth and well-being but also poetry for our moral delight and the encouragement of our national literature.

Echeverría goes on to explain that there are two dominant sides to the poem: externally, the energy of passion becomes manifest through actions, whereas internally, the struggle of this activity gradually consumes and, finally, annihilates like a lightning bolt its feeble existence. Intense passions are either satisfied when they are dissipated, or frustrated, in which case they also evaporate. The condition of being in the grip of strong passions is feverish and abnormal, not capable of being sustained, and the prelude to a crisis.

Purposely he uses colloquial expressions and names things by their name, because he thinks that poetry consists principally of ideas, and because not always, like them, do circumlocutions succeed in placing the object concretely before the reader's eyes. If this shocks those accustomed to high-sounding words and pompous ornamentation in poetry for the senses only, they will be at fault, for they are seeking not what is contained in the intent of the author, but rather what most pleases them.

Highly ornamental poetry, he continues, has its staunch advocates; this has given rise to the impression that poetry exaggerates and lies; poetry neither lies nor exaggerates. Only preachers like Brother Gerund (the hero of Padre Isla's novel of the eighteenth century in which excesses of church preachers are satirized) and soulless poets confuse tinsel and reverberation of words with eloquence and poetry. The poet only occasionally copies reality as it appears to view; since it is the basic principle of art to represent the beautiful, he must eliminate some of the blemishes. He takes what is natural or real just as the potter takes clay, the sculptor marble, the painter his colors, and then transforms them in accordance with his skill, into the likeness of the archetypes conceived by his mind. Nature and man give the poet primitive colors to be mixed and combined, sketches which he puts into relief, retouches, and gives character to impulses and ideas converted into models of intelligence and freedom, impressed with the most brilliant and elevated form capable of being conceived by the human mind. The true poet idealizes, replacing an imperfect reality with the likeness of a higher one. "Physical and moral beauty, thus conceived, both in the ideas and affects of man and in his acts, both in God and in His magnificent creations—here lies the inexhaustible source of poetry, the principle and goal of Art, and the lofty sphere in which its marvelous creations move." (pp. 34-5)

"Form, that is, the choice of meter, the exposition and structure of the **Captive Woman**, are exclusively the author's; not recognizing any form normal in the mould of which artistic conceptions necessarily must be put, he has had to select the one that best suited the realization of his thought." . . .

"With regard to the octosyllabic meter in which this volume is written, he will say only that one day he fell in love with it in spite of the discredit to which writers of couplets had reduced it. It seemed to him one of the most beautiful and flexible of our language, and he tried to make it recover the luster which it enjoyed in the most flourishing periods of Castilian poetry, applying it to the expression of elevated ideas with deep feelings. He will have attained his purpose if the reader, upon reading through his **Rimas** . . . does not notice that he is reading octosyllables.

Meter, or better, rhythm, is the music by means of which poetry captivates the sentiments and works with most efficacy on the soul." (p. 35)

Echeverría says: "There is, then, no complete poetry without rhythm. An instrument of art must in the poet's hands harmonize with his inspiration and adjust its measures to the various movement of the feelings. Hence rises the necessity of changing at times the meter in order to slow down or accelerate the voice, and give, as it were, to the song the intonations in accordance with the effect that is intended.'' (p. 36)

Echeverría's comment on the use of the octosyllable in this poem may have misled critics; it should be read in relation to the need later expressed by him in the same notice for change in meter. In part two there are two stanzas with six-syllable lines; in part four, there are seven stanzas with lines of twelve and six syllables; in part seven, there are five stanzas with six-syllable lines. No part is without octosyllables, and this type of line is dominant. Assonance in *é-a* is found only in part two. There is one section in part two where use is made of lines of four syllables, the fight between Brian and the Indians—the four-syllable lines are devoted to Brian, his appearance in battle, his raising his sword to send rolling the heads of the Indians Quitur and Callupán, his facing the remaining Indians like an enraged bull, and then his fall, like a colt on the plain, felled by the *bolas,* that Indian instrument of the pampa used to bring cattle or horses to the ground. It is worth focussing attention on parts of the poem with six (or twelve) syllable lines. The first one is the fight between Brian and the strongest of the pampa Indians, Chañil, told in sixteen lines. This ends with Chañil's death, and Echeverría closes with the ambiguous exhortation: ''Lloremos la muerte / Del indio más fuerte / Que la pampa crió.'' (''Let us bemoan the death of the strongest Indian that the pampa has reared.'') There may be some grim humor here, but the passage may also be interpreted as a tribute to strength in a redoubtable enemy.

The next variation in syllabic lines takes place in part four at the sudden attack by the Christians on the Indians, beginning with the alarm:

> Entonces, el grito, ''Cristiano, Cristiano''
> Resuena en el llano.
> ''Cristiano'' repite confuso clamor,
> La turba que duerme despierta turbada,
> Clamando azorada,
> ''Cristiano nos cerca, cristiano traidor.''

(''Then, the cry, 'Christian, Christian' resounds on the plain, 'Christian' repeats a confused clamor. The horde which sleeps wakes up disturbed, exclaiming in panic, 'Christian surrounds us, treacherous Christian.''') The translation suggests that the Indians' Spanish here may be limited to key words, without the adornment of articles or qualifiers other than *traidor,* ''treacherous.'' Here we have six-syllable lines separated by couplets of twelve-syllable lines.

Six-syllable lines are used also in part seven in the description of the pampas fire, to express the rapid, unexpected spread of the flames: ''Raudal vomitando, / Venía de llama, / Que hirviendo, silbando, / Se encrosca Y derrama / Con velocidad.'' (''Vomiting a torrent, it came as a flame, that seething, hissing, coils up and spreads rapidly.'')

It is clear that Echeverría reserved the changes in meter for moments of crisis, the arm-to-arm combat of Brian against individual Indians, the surprise attack by the Christians on the pagan Indians, the sudden appearance of the pampas fire which confronts María and Brian; María's reaction is brought into the stanza of which the first part has just been quoted: ''Sentada María / Con su Brian la vía: / 'Dios mio! decía, / De nos ten piedad'.'' (''María, seated, could see it with her Brian: 'My God!' she said, 'Have pity on us!''') This is, after all, the purpose of metrical variation, that the poet shifts the meter to

accord with the changing action or mood of the narrative. The fact that other exciting moments in the poem, such as the raid and the feast, do not occasion the use of lines other than the octosyllable, shows that these variations are not applied mechanically by Echeverría, and that lines may be varied in length so as to accord with different emotions and needs. (pp. 36-7)

In his credo, Echeverría pointed out the need for the poet to reflect the setting (the pampas), local manners and customs (the *malón* or Indian raid, the use of the horse, the use of the *bolas* would be concrete examples), and the inclusion of the ideas or thought of the time. One of the most important ideas of Echeverría and the young liberal thinkers in his circle was, of course, the concept of May, or of the independence of the nation. This is brought into the poem in the passage where Brian reviews his past days of glory, fighting under General San Martín, under the blue banner, just before his death. Another of the most important of Hispanic concepts, living in the Romantics as well as in the Golden Age, is the idea of honor, the idea of unsullied feminine virtue, something a woman must live up to completely, no matter what the purity of the father, husband, brothers, or sons might be. This is brought out early in the poem when María reaches the side of the captured Brian. When he recognizes her, at first kissing and embracing her, he suddenly realizes the logical explanation of her presence with him there, that her honor has been stained by the lust of a savage Indian. It is impossible for him to love her any more. This section of the poem has displeased some readers, but is in complete accord with the tradition of honor and with Romantic dramatic literature. A parallel, familiar to opera lovers who know Verdi's *Il trovatore (The Troubadour),* is found in the source of that opera, the Spanish play *El trovador (The Troubadour)* of García Gutiérrez. (p. 39)

Faith in God on the part of the Christians of the poem is another aspect of the life view of the civilized Argentinian of Echeverría's day. The female captives silently raise their humble prayers to God. God sends to Brian and María a star to guide their flight by; María compares this star with the red cloud seen by Israel, likewise sent by God. When María gives Brian water to drink to restore his energy, she expresses the idea that they should courageously wait for the end implored by them from God. . . . [The poet also addresses God thus:] ''. . .— ¿Adónde / Tu poder ¡oh Dios! se esconde? / Está por ventura exhausto? / Más dolor en holocausto / Pide a una flaca mujer?'' (''Where doth Thy power, oh God, hide? Is it perchance exhausted? Does it ask of a frail woman for more grief in sacrifice?'') The answer comes almost at once in the cry of the bird of the pampas, the *yajá* (or *chajá*), a term from the language of the Guaraní Indians of Paraguay and northern Argentina, applied to a type of wading bird of that area; this cry gives hope. The bird's name is derived from its cry, which has the meaning ''let's go'' in Guaraní. At its first appearance in the poem, Echeverría supplies an interesting note in which he refers to its significance as an alarm; it is nocturnal and repeats its call when it hears the noise of people approaching. People familiar with this characteristic of the bird prepare themselves for a possible attack from an enemy. A sort of syncretism of genuine Christianity and traditional folk superstition, not infrequent in parts of the Americas, may be glimpsed in this passage.

A solitary cross, too, marks María's grave, shaded by the characteristic tree of the pampas, the *ombú*. The birds nesting in the tree join in protecting the grave. There is some appeal to the supernatural, the mysterious appearance of two *luces* or "lights" at the spot where María is buried, the reaction of Indians who pass near, shouting "allí está la cruz" ("there lies the cross"). Thereupon they turn their heads back as if fearful of seeing the angry, terrifying spectre of Brian. References to the bird called *yajá* and the ombú tree are merely two of the poem's localisms; there are such words as *toldería,* "group of wigwams of the Indians," *ranchos,* here equated with "straw cabins of the countryside," *huinca,* word used by the Indian to refer to the Christian or person of a different race, somewhat like the English "paleface," *Valichu,* the evil spirit of the pampas.

Some of the negative criticism, particularly in recent years, valuable for showing flaws of the poem for the twentieth-century reader, can be used to show that Echeverría achieved his purpose well. It is his concept that may be viewed as flawed, rather than his ability to accomplish his goal. And flaws of this sort are quite possibly flaws for the moment, and may have been virtues in the past, and even, given the tendency for vogues in taste to change, again in the future. Americans who find interesting the narrative poems of Henry Wadsworth Longfellow should have little difficulty in regarding **The Captive Woman** as a meritorious work, even if they have not nationalistic or historical bias, as natives of Argentina might.

One critic has written: "The poem is not a literary masterpiece and is more of interest for what it tells us about Echeverría than for any intrinsic beauty. Certainly the contrast between the savage energy of Indian and nature and the passiveness and impotence of the white couple appears to reflect not the sturdy values of a pioneer civilization but the tired resignation of a dying race" [see excerpt by Franco dated 1973]. Masterpiece is a rather ambiguous term; it will be agreed that **The Captive Woman** does not have the scope of the Homeric poems or of Domingo Faustino Sarmiento's *Facundo,* but to deny it intrinsic beauty seems harsh. Nature and hostile Indians are powerful forces; if a reader recalls that Brian has been wounded—presumably his wounds are the cause of his death, rather than his passive impotence; and remembers his prowess in using his sword to make dread Indian warriors' heads roll, and that Echeverría has depicted in him a Romantic hero comparable in regard to the concept of honor with the hero of *El trovador,* he may not concur in this judgment. María, too, has been forced by circumstances to commit murder, to take a badly wounded and beloved husband away from his captivity and to set out over a hostile pampa; beset by pampas fire, afraid of discovery by the Indians, attacked by the merciless heat of the summer sun, she is able to carry her wounded husband on her back, and cross a swollen stream bearing her husband on the surface of the water. The reader may recall that in the raid the Indians killed her parents as well as her son, as well as severely wounding her husband. How many readers of either sex, in the twentieth century, would not be silent if the sound of the *tigre,* "New World tiger or mountain lion," in search of prey, were in the vicinity? Even the dread *caudillo* Facundo found the *tigre* of Argentina a worthy foe, as related by Sarmiento in his masterly account of this rival of Rosas in barbaric qualities.

If this critic senses savage energy in the Indian and passiveness and impotence in the whites, a reader may in challenge point to part four, where the Christians attack the Indians, not sparing woman, or man, or child of the tribe responsible for the abduction of Brian and María. The female captives are moved to tears of joy at being saved by their husbands, and sons, but the rescuers are sad not to find Brian, his valor and his loyalty

there. Rather than showing savage energy in the Indian and resignation of a dying race in the white man, Echeverría shows that on both sides there is savagery. The special significance of the vengeance on the Indians and the rescue of all the captives except María and Brian is the irony of a fate that would permit the superhuman energy of María to rescue her husband, when, had she only waited, the rescue of both of them might have been effected and Brian might have recovered from the effects of his wounds. Fate, some might say, but Echeverría, a Romantic who had great admiration for women, attributed María's fate to love:

> El destino de tu vida
> Fue amar, amor tu delirio,
> Amor causó tu martirio,
> Te dio sobrehumano ser;
> Y amor, en edad florida,
> Sofocó la pasión tierna,
> Que omnipotencia de eterna
> Trajo consigo al nacer

("The destiny of your life was to love, love your delirium, love caused your martyrdom, giving you superhuman existence; and love, in the flower of your age, suffocated the tender passion, which with your birth brought with it the omnipotence of being eternal.")

Another critic feels that María is as manly as Brian. It is true that Echeverría begins the epilogue of the poem with these words: "¡Oh María! Tu Heroísmo, / Tu varonil fortaleza, / Tu juventud y belleza / Merecieran fin mejor." ("Oh María! Your heroism, your manly strength, your youth and beauty had merited a better end.") But it is only her strength, under the stress of special circumstances, that earns the adjective *varonil,* "manly." The criticism has some point, but Brian was seriously wounded and Maria was motivated by the power of love to perform her superhuman, "manly" deeds. The masculine qualities of María are not emphasized in such passages as the following: "... ya no siente, / Ni llora, porque la fuente / Del sentimiento fecunda, / Que el feminil pecho inunda, / Consumió el voraz dolor." ("... no longer does she feel, nor weep, because the abundant source of feelings which floods the feminine breast was consumed by voracious grief.") and "... silenciosa ella, / Como tímida doncella, / Besa su entreabierta boca..." ("... silently she, like a timid maiden, kisses his half-open mouth"). Echeverría answers his question as to what María would be without love by saying, "Frágil caña / Que el más leve impulso quiebra, / Ser delicado, fina hebra, / Sensible y flaca mujer." ("A fragile reed that the slightest impulse breaks, a delicate being, a fine thread, a sensitive, a frail woman.") But Love converts her into a divine being, a powerful and tender angel, whom Hell would not cause to waver, nor to tremble. None of this is appropriate, really, to Brian, as described by Echeverría—more than once the reader is told by the poet that it is the power of love that has given María this very special strength. In the discussion of Brian's energy, examples have been given of the poet's depiction of his manliness; actually critics seem to have been worried about María's womanliness less than about Brian's manliness. They have not recognized sufficiently the seriousness of his wounds, nor noted the clues given by the poet of his courage, strength, and heroic qualities.

One charge levelled against Echeverría's poem is that it is not an authentic expression of the pampa, inasmuch as the gaucho does not appear at all. It is a temptation to answer the charge by appealing to Jorge Luis Borges's "conviction that one's expression of national or group identity need not, and should not, be deliberately set forth." Borges cited with approval Gibbon's observation that in the *Koran* there are no camels, and stated in this connection: ". . . si hubiera alguna duda sobre la autenticidad del *Alcorán,* bastaría esta ausencia de camellos para probar que es árabe. (". . . if there were some doubt about the authenticity of the *Koran,* this absence of camels would suffice to prove that it is Arabic.")

The gaucho, however, does appear in the poem by allusion: "Pero tú la tempestad, / Día y noche vigilante, / Anuncias al gaucho errante"; ("But you announce to the wandering gaucho the storm, watching day and night.") Echeverría here is apostrophizing the *yajá* bird. It is true that no character is portrayed in the role of gaucho in the poem, but some gaucho characteristics appear. The barbaric, untutored quality of the gaucho is visible in the impious voice of the soldier who raucously announces to María that her son had been beheaded by the Indians. Brian, too, in delirium shares the fondness of the gaucho for his horse and his weapon, when he calls for his horse and his lance.

Not necessary, but not inappropriate to the appreciation of the poem's value is the possibility that it be read for its parallels with the political and social situation of Argentina. María may symbolize Argentina, and the savages who murder her child may represent the barbarism of the pampa as exemplified by the cruelties of the despot Rosas. Brian, too, as a brave fighter in the War of Independence, can symbolize the spirit of May (Argentina's independence).

Criticism directed against the portrayal of credible, individualized characters is inappropriate since Echeverría desired to depict idealized beings. It can only serve to explain lack of enthusiasm for reading the poem nowadays, since many modern readers expect psychologically convincing characterization. Psychology as a handmaid to literary criticism does not always lead to like views. There are opposed opinions about María's apparent inconsistency with regard to knowledge of the poet's part, or superior knowledge of the psychology of grief. The latter interpretation may be defended, certainly, but hardly can be proved correct beyond doubt. The fact that such discussion is possible means that readers can take seriously the motives and actions of this "ideal(ized) being," and that Echeverría's narrative is not beyond the realm of what could have happened.

Professor Juan Collantes de Terán of the University of Seville has published the fullest literary discussion in recent years of *The Captive Woman,* focussing attention on the first eleven stanzas of the first part of the poem. To close the assessment of this poem, it is convenient to review his findings. Collantes de Terán finds perfection in the structuring of the poem through the predominance of a great expository unity. He gives examples of the creation of tone or mood through attention to the time of day, the coloring and emotional setting of the landscape. His analysis finds that Echeverría's technique is in accord with the Romantic taste of his day, new at the time. *The Captive Woman* displays the exaltation of the feelings characteristic of Romanticism, the sensations associated with the coming of night, for example, with its accompanying sorrow, the effect of the moods of Nature on the feelings of the poet; solitude intensifies sorrow. (pp. 40-4)

Echeverría is seen to be a careful user of appropriate color-terms, particularly those related to black, darkness, yellow,

brown, blue, green, with a view to intensifying emotion. Echeverría exemplifies the philosophical opposition of reason against feelings or emotions. Collantes de Terán also finds in *The Captive Woman* an innovation—its closeness to the sketch of manners, or the form of writing of the *costumbristas,* those who write on customs. As a specific example, he refers to the presence of the word *toldería* applied to the Indian dwellings, "wigwams" for the North American, made of wood and hide; attention to this sort of detail, Collantes de Terán feels, is significant in appearing during the first half of the nineteenth century, the historical moment in which the writers on manners and customs dedicated their attention to careful observation of the milieu. Another example is the reference to the *yajá* bird. Lastly, Collantes de Terán finds worthy of esteem Echeverría's versification, his use of eight-syllable lines in *The Captive Woman,* siding with critics like Emilio Carilla and against those like Enrique Anderson Imbert and Rafael Alberto Arrieta. When experts in literary criticism and history, native speakers of Spanish, disagree, the most that an outsider can do is state that Echeverría's versification is successful enough to win praise from some, if not all, qualified critics.

All in all, the continued popularity of *The Captive Woman,* frequently reprinted, as a true, albeit minor, masterpiece seems fully justified; for the student of Romanticism in Argentina and in Spanish America or for the reader of Echeverría, it is full of interest. (pp. 44-5)

> *Edgar C. Knowlton, Jr., in his* Esteban Echeverría, *Dorrance & Company, Incorporated, 1986, 125 p.*

ADDITIONAL BIBLIOGRAPHY

Anderson Imbert, Enrique. "Argentina's Pioneer Liberal." *The Américas* 4, No. 4 (April 1952): 21-3, 46.
   A biographical sketch focused on Echeverría's pioneering role in Argentine politics and literature.

Crawford, William Rex. "Independence and Nationhood: Esteban Echeverría (1805-1851)." In his *A Century of Latin-American Thought,* rev. ed., pp. 12-18. Cambridge: Harvard University Press, 1961.
   Outlines the principle political and social ideals that Echeverría expressed in *Dogma socialista* and other works.

Foster, David William. "Paschal Symbology in Echeverria's 'El matadero'." *Studies in Short Fiction* VII, No. 2 (Spring 1970): 257-63.
   An examination of Christ-related motifs in *The Slaughter House.*

———. "Echeverría, Esteban (1805-1851)." In his *Argentine Literature: A Research Guide,* 2d ed., pp. 350-60. Garland Reference Library of the Humanities, vol. 338. New York: Garland Publishing, 1982.
   An extensive list of critical monographs, dissertations, and essays on Echeverría, most of them written in Spanish.

Knowlton, Edgar C., Jr. "The Epigraphs in Esteban Echeverría's *La cautiva.*" *Hispania* XLIV, No. 2 (May 1961): 212-17.
   Discusses the sources, meanings, and functions of the epigraphs in *The Captive Woman.*

McMahon, Dorothy. "The Indian in Romantic Literature of the Argentine." *Modern Philology* LVI, No. 1 (August 1958): 17-23.
   Includes a brief discussion of Echeverría's attitude toward Indians, primarily as revealed in *The Captive Woman.*

''The Poetry of Spanish America.'' *North American Review* LXVIII, No. 142 (January 1849): 129-60.
> Contains a notice of Echeverría's *Rimas*.

Schwartz, Kessel. ''Costumbrismo and Romanticism.'' In his *A New History of Spanish American Fiction*. Vol. 1, *From Colonial Times to the Mexican Revolution and Beyond,* pp. 23-71. Coral Gables, Fla.: University of Miami Press, 1972.
> Briefly analyzes *The Slaughter House* and discusses its importance in the development of Spanish American fiction.

Suarez-Murias, Marguerite. ''The Influence of Victor Hugo on Esteban Echeverría's Ideology.'' *Latin American Literary Review* VI, No. 11 (Fall-Winter 1977): 13-21.
> Explores Hugo's influence on Echeverría's works and political philosophy.

Fanny Kemble

1809-1893

(Born Frances Anne Kemble; later Frances Anne Butler) English journal writer, autobiographer, dramatist, poet, critic, and novelist.

A celebrated actress and Shakespearean dramatic reader in England and America, Kemble is remembered in the literary world primarily for her *Journal of a Residence in America* and *Journal of a Residence on a Georgian Plantation in 1838-1839.* These two works—the former a source of controversy in the nineteenth century due to its outspoken, often provocative descriptions of American life and society, and the latter noted for its searing denunciation of slavery—are today valued both as compelling accounts of antebellum America and as insightful reflections of the character and personality of their author.

Kemble was born in London to an illustrious and extremely popular theatrical family. Educated chiefly in France, Kemble showed an early interest in literature: she completed her first work, *Francis the First,* at the age of seventeen, though the drama was neither published nor performed until several years later. Despite the example of her parents and of her uncle John Philip Kemble and aunt Sara Siddons, two of the most renowned actors of nineteenth-century England, Kemble apparently had little interest in an acting career. But in 1829 she agreed to play the female lead in a production of *Romeo and Juliet* to help her father out of financial difficulties. To her surprise, she was an immediate success, and during the next few years she appeared frequently in leading roles, delighting both critics and the public. Charles Kemble's financial situation failed to improve, however, and in 1832 the two embarked on an American theatrical tour in hopes of raising money. Kemble's reception in America was as enthusiastic as in England. Nonetheless, she abandoned her profession in 1834, when she agreed to marry Pierce Butler, a wealthy Philadelphian. Yet the new marriage quickly showed signs of strain because Kemble's husband strongly disapproved of her plans to publish a journal about her experiences in America. Although Butler attempted to block its publication, *Journal of a Residence in America* appeared in 1835, causing an uproar due to the author's forthright—and not always favorable—comments on various American people and on American society in general. A greater conflict between Kemble and her husband arose over the issue of slavery. Holding abolitionist sentiments, Kemble was astounded to learn that Butler not only condoned slavery, but owned and derived his wealth from Georgia plantations run by slave labor. In 1838 Kemble accompanied Butler on a visit to the plantations, an experience she described in a journal that remained unpublished for twenty-five years. Horrified at the plight of the slaves, Kemble repeatedly appealed to her husband on their behalf, while Butler, though he granted some of her requests, increasingly resented her interference.

Biographers note that the Butlers' discord over the slavery issue, like their conflict over the publication of *Journal of a Residence in America,* was symptomatic of a more fundamental disagreement between the two: Butler expected his wife always to accede to his wishes, while Kemble refused to do so. Relations between them continued to deteriorate, and in 1845 Kemble left her husband and their two daughters to move back

to England. She thereafter embarked on a year's tour of Italy, described in another journal, *A Year of Consolation.* Upon her return to England, Kemble briefly resumed her acting career, but soon abandoned it in favor of giving public readings of Shakespeare's plays. In 1848 Butler sued for divorce, charging desertion; after a widely publicized and acrimonious trial, the divorce was granted and Kemble lost custody of her children. For the next twenty years, she divided her time between America and England, continuing her dramatic readings of Shakespeare and composing her memoirs. Kemble died in London at the age of eighty-three.

Of her varied writings, Kemble's two journals of her experiences in America are of most interest to scholars. Both *Journal of a Residence in America* and *Journal of a Residence on a Georgian Plantation* reveal their author's personality: direct, candid, self-confident, at times iconoclastic. The earlier of the two, *Journal of a Residence in America,* is a vivid account of Kemble's impressions of America during her travels on the theatrical tour. Reportorial, anecdotal, and ruminative, *Journal of a Residence in America* ranges over a variety of subjects, including Kemble's daily activities, her thoughts concerning herself and her profession, her descriptions of people and landscapes, and her observations on social, cultural, and political institutions and issues. These lighthearted and, in the opinion of some, impudent impressions of American life caused a furor in the nineteenth century among American readers, many of whom were insulted by Kemble's assessments. One aspect of *Journal of a Residence in America* faulted by early commentators was Kemble's frank opinions of her acquaintances, whose names, though replaced by asterisks, were readily surmised by her contemporaries. Nineteenth-century reviewers also objected to the work's alleged vulgarity: many censured Kemble's coarse and indecorous style, which they deemed unbecoming in a female writer. Despite the hostility provoked by *Journal of a Residence in America*, many critics were inclined to forgive the author. Attacks on her outspokenness and vulgarity were frequently tempered with praise for the work's "spirit" and spontaneity, and the furor eventually abated.

Unlike *Journal of a Residence in America, Journal of a Residence on a Georgian Plantation* has a tone of impassioned earnestness. Written in the form of letters to a friend, Elizabeth Sedgwick, this journal details the hardships of the slaves on the Butler plantations—their unremitting labor, their lives spent in ignorance and squalor, the cruel punishments inflicted upon them—as well as Kemble's ineffectual efforts to help them. Scholars agree that *Journal of a Residence on a Georgian Plantation* contains, in addition to this emotional narrative, reasoned, cogent arguments against slavery, and the work was praised as a shattering exposé of the institution. Indeed, one commentator hailed it as "the most thrilling and remarkable picture of the interior social life of the slaveholding section in this country that has ever been published." But because it was largely ignored by proponents of slavery, *Journal of a Residence on a Georgian Plantation* failed to excite the sustained critical dialogue and controversy called forth by the earlier journal.

Kemble's other works are considered minor and have received comparatively little attention in the twentieth century, though they were often reviewed in the nineteenth. *Record of a Girlhood, Records of Later Life,* and *Further Records* form a continuing series of autobiography. While these works, along with *A Year of Consolation*, were praised for many of the same qualities admired in the earlier journals—namely, candor and vivid descriptive power—most critics believed that the autobiographies lacked the spirited wit of *Journal of a Residence in America* and the passionate conviction of *Journal of a Residence on a Georgian Plantation*. Nineteenth-century reviewers of Kemble's dramas and poetry focused more on the unrealized potential of the author than on her actual achievement. *Francis the First*, a sweeping historical drama, and *The Star of Seville*, a tragic love story, were admired for their Elizabethan-inspired blank verse and striking dramatic moments, but were considered too diffuse and lacking in dramatic focus to succeed. In addition, some critics found the plays indecorous and vulgar. Kemble's poetry also failed to achieve success. Primarily passionate and melancholy in tone, the poems were deemed promising but curiously unfinished, fragmentary, and unpolished.

At the time of their publication, Kemble's works were widely reviewed, arousing her contemporaries' enthusiasm, approbation, and censure. Interest in Kemble began to subside at the turn of the century, but since then, renewed attention has been given to *Journal of a Residence in America* and *Journal of a Residence on a Georgian Plantation*. While *Journal of a Residence in America* has received little formal critical analysis, its continuing appeal is demonstrated by numerous recent biographers who have relied upon its testimony and relished its spirited portrayal of Kemble's personality. As a historical

document, the work is valued for its lively descriptions and impressions of nineteenth-century America. *Journal of a Residence on a Georgian Plantation*, the recipient of the most sustained critical attention accorded any of Kemble's works in the twentieth century, is esteemed for both its literary and historical worth. Although some recent writers have condemned the journal as, in the words of Clement Eaton, "bitterly prejudiced" against the South, and a few have faulted its view of slave life as exaggerated and inaccurate, most critics have admired *Journal of a Residence on a Georgian Plantation* for the compelling urgency of its prose and for its stance on racial equality. In addition, many underscore its importance as a record of life in the antebellum South. Finally, there remains the enduring interest imparted to both *Journal of a Residence in America* and *Journal of a Residence on a Georgian Plantation* by the force of their author's personality, for, as her friend Henry James claimed, "She wrote exactly as she talked, observing, asserting, complaining, confiding, contradicting, crying out and bounding off, always effectually communicating."

(See also *Dictionary of Literary Biography*, Vol. 32: *Victorian Poets Before 1850.*)

PRINCIPAL WORKS

Francis the First   (drama)   1832
Journal of F. A. Butler   (journal)   1835; also published as
      Journal of a Residence in America, 1835
The Star of Seville   (drama)   1837
Poems   (poetry)   1844; also published as *Poems* [enlarged
      edition], 1859, and in revised form, 1883
A Year of Consolation   (journal)   1847
*Journal of a Residence on a Georgian Plantation in
      1838-1839*   (journal)   1863
*Record of a Girlhood   (autobiography)   1878
**Notes upon Some of Shakespeare's Plays   (criticism)
      1882
Records of Later Life   (autobiography)   1882
Far Away and Long Ago   (novel)   1889
Further Records: 1848-1883   (autobiography)   1890

*This work was partially published in the periodical *Atlantic Monthly* from 1875 to 1877 under the title "Old Woman's Gossip."

**This work includes the critical essay "On the Stage," which was first published in the periodical *Cornhill Magazine* in 1863.

[H. H. MILMAN]   (essay date 1832)

[*Milman is chiefly remembered for his historical works and for his verse dramas, particularly* Fazio, *in which Kemble played a leading role. In this excerpt from his review of* Francis the First, *Milman considers the play a first dramatic effort of bright promise.*]

From the announcement of **Francis the First,** it appeared, that the distinguished young actress [Miss Kemble], who has suddenly burst forth, to support the fortunes of her house, with powers of a very high order, and with indications of a depth and originality of conception rarely witnessed in a performer so unstudied and new to the stage, had . . . the high ambition of renewing the older days of our drama, and of reuniting the poet and the actor in their former close alliance. The most remarkable characteristic, however, of the tragedy before us, is its total and disdainful want of conformity to the present state of the stage. Far from accommodating itself with servile docility to the taste of the day, and displaying the nice tact, which might be acquired by familiarity with the incidents and situations—with the tone and manner of composition which produce the strongest effect on a modern audience—the tragedy of *Francis the First* is conceived in the spirit and conducted on the plan of a far different period. We mean not that an effective tragedy may not be cut out of this poem, as out of those of our older dramatists: but, according to its original conception, instead of condensing the whole interest, and concentrating it on two or three of the leading characters,—and keeping down the subordinate parts, which must necessarily be entrusted to the dangerous hands of inferior performers, as nearly as possible to mutes;—the piece before us is crowded with characters of the greatest variety, all of considerable importance in the conduct of the piece, engaged in the most striking situations, and contributing essentially to the main design. Instead of that simple unity of interest, from which modern tragic writers have rarely ventured to depart, it takes the wider range of that historic unity, which is the characteristic of our elder drama; moulds together, and connects by some common agent employed in both, incidents which have no necessary connexion; and—what in the present tragedy strikes us as on many accounts especially noticeable—unites by a fine though less perceptible moral link, remote but highly tragic events with the immediate, if we may so speak, the domestic interest of the play. There is something, in our opinion, singularly bold and striking in the manner in which not only the dark intrigues of the Queen Mother and the ingratitude of the court towards the Constable de Bourbon are revenged in the battle of Pavia, but at the same time the Nemesis of the injured Françoise de Foix pursues the King to the fatal field. The double current of interest is made to flow again in one stream, if, as hereafter will appear, more languidly than might be likely to keep up the excitement of a spectator, or even of a reader, yet with so much Shakspearianism in the conception as to afford a remarkable indication of the noble school in which the young authoress has studied, and the high models, which, with courage, in the present day, fairly to be called originality, she has dared to set before her. In fact, *Francis the First* is cast entirely in the mould of one of Shakespeare's historical tragedies. Miss Kemble has aspired to manage all the infinite variety of character, the complication of plot, the succession of interest, which make our great dramatic poems of that class not merely full of scenic effect, but living pictures of the whole period to which their personages belong.

The secret, however, of the total dissimilarity of Miss Kemble's tragedy to the modern race of successful dramas is extremely simple. It was written, we have been informed by persons who long ago perused the work in manuscript, several years before she appeared upon the stage, and at a time when she little anticipated the probability that she herself might be called upon to impersonate the conceptions of her own imagination. We believe that we are quite safe when we state that the drama, in its present form, was written when the authoress was not more than seventeen. We do not make this statement either to deprecate the severer criticism of others, or to account for any unusual tenderness in our own, but merely as explaining the singular anomaly of a tragedy, written by a successful actress, requiring as much alteration, we fear that we may add mutilation, in order to adapt it to the stage, as one of the most lawless and irregular compositions of the days of Elizabeth or James I.

Without doubt, every work of imagination must eventually stand or fall by its own intrinsic merit. Though the adventitious circumstances under which a poem has been composed may excite a strong interest at the moment of its appearance, yet this artificial life, where there is no inherent principle of vitality, will quickly wither and expire. While, therefore, we are unwilling that the authoress should plead either youth or sex in bar of the sternest justice of criticism, it is unquestionably a remarkable phenomenon, that a youthful poetess, however nurtured in Shakspeare, should begin her dramatic career by placing her main strength in the vigorous delineation of historic character. In this respect there is certainly no dramatic author of the present day who might not be proud to own the *Francis the First* of Miss Kemble; while, in the skill and intricacy with which the more dramatic part of the plot is managed, and the double interest, as it were, linked together by means of the Monk Gonzales, she may fairly compete with the most ingenious playwrights of modern times; nor are the masculine strength, and sustained vigour of the language, breaking out occasionally into gleams of very sweet poetry, unworthy of the bold conception and powerful execution of the general design. Throughout there is that spirit and animation, without which neither forcible delineation of character nor cleverness of plot will excite or keep possession of the reader's mind. The tragedy is alive from the beginning to the end; although it must be acknowledged, that the main impulse is exhausted at the close of the fourth act, and the fifth, therefore, must depend on its administering, as it were, the poetic justice of the whole, and on the lofty, historical, and almost romantic associations, which give an interest and importance to the 'Battle of Pavia,'—the close, as it were, of the splendid and chivalrous warfare of the feudal period; the last in which a great monarch fought with his knightly lance, hand to hand, in the thickest of the fray. (pp. 244-46)

[It] is certainly worth remarking, that from the disguised Monk Gonzales to Clement Marot the poet and Triboulet the jester, [the play's various personages] have all some character. We have, perhaps, too much of the passion of revenge; Gonzales himself may be drawn rather too nearly in the spirit of the Radcliffe school of modern romance, with a touch of not the better part of Byronism,—but still the delineation is one of great force and distinctness; and though among the female characters there is some slight similitude between Margaret and Françoise de Foix, they, too, are yet clearly discriminated; while both are drawn with much feminine gentleness and with words 'attuned to love,' the very different situations in which they are cast keep up a sufficient contrast and dissimilitude. (p. 246)

We must acknowledge, that, while reading the tragedy . . . , we have frequently paused to ask whether this could be the conception or the writing of a young girl, hardly ripening into womanhood. . . . Should she continue to write for the stage, [Miss Kemble] will derive some advantage from her intimate and experimental acquaintance with scenic effect, with the power of situation on the minds of the audience, with the style of language best suited to find its way to the heart. In this respect she will perhaps become less uniformly sustained, more simple and condensed, than she appears in her first effort. She will discover how far she may follow, in the conception and conduct of her plot, the bold irregularity, the free historic outline of the 'chartered libertines of our drama,' and beyond what limits she may endanger her command over the attention of her audience. She will judge of scenic effect, though with the fine tact which can only be acquired by familiarity with the stage, by no means on those narrow and technical rules which have made the judgment of the actors as to the success of a play proverbially fallible. If we remember right, it is in *Gil Blas* that an author expresses his innocent surprise, that when the actors foretell the failure of a piece, it is sure of success,—if its success, it is as certain to fail. She will preserve the independence of a poetic mind, and with that intuitive perception of the essentially dramatic, which cannot be acquired but by practice on the stage—she will retain that higher sense of tragic excellence which belongs exclusively to the poet—she will never condescend to sink the tragic poetess in the actress. Above all, she must set herself above her audience; she must not consider what *has* pleased, but what, according to her own genuine feeling of the noble, the pathetic, ought to have pleased. She must aspire to give the tone, not condescend to take it from the noisy and capricious arbiters of theatric taste. (pp. 259-60)

How high Miss Kemble's young aspirings have been—what conceptions she has formed to herself of the dignity of tragic poetry—may be discovered from this most remarkable work; at this height she must maintain herself, or soar a still bolder flight. The turmoil, the hurry, the business, the toil, even the celebrity of a theatric life must yield her up at times to that repose, that undistracted retirement within her own mind, which, however brief, is essential to the perfection of the noblest work of the imagination—genuine tragedy. Amidst her highest successes on the stage, she must remember that the world regards her as one to whom a still higher part is fallen. She must not be content with the fame of the most extraordinary work which has ever been produced by a female at her age, (for as such we scruple not to describe her *Francis the First,*)—with having sprung at once to the foremost rank, not only of living actors but of modern dramatists;—she must consider that she has given us a pledge and earnest for a long and brightening course of distinction, in the devotion of all but unrivalled talents in two distinct, though congenial, capacities, to the revival of the waning glories of the English theatre. (p. 261)

> [*H. H. Milman*], "'Francis the First', by Miss Kemble," in The Quarterly Review, Vol. XLVII, No. XCIII, March, 1832, pp. 243-61.

THE MONTHLY REVIEW, LONDON (essay date 1832)

[*This critic views* Francis the First *as not without merit, but faults Kemble's indecorous characterization and lack of dramatic focus.*]

There has been a good deal of scenic preparation as well off the stage as upon it, for the presentation of [*Francis the First*] to the public. It has long since been announced in the newspapers and the playbills that such a production was in existence, and was to be brought forward with the assistance of all the resources of Covent Garden theatre. A favourable review of it was written and published in a journal of considerable circulation and authority, before the drama itself saw the light; and its performance was so timed as to follow, we think within a day or two, the publication of the criticism, which was so well calculated to secure it a gracious reception. The night of trial came, and the succeeding morning was ushered in with the newspaper trumpets proclaiming on all sides the decided success of the new play, and the bills—those celebrated dispensers of theatric fame—have ever since continued to tell us of the rapturous applause with which *Francis the First* has been hailed by the most crowded and fashionable audiences of the season.

Do we object to all these proceedings, or to any of them? Not we. Miss Fanny Kemble is a lucky author, in being able from her connexions and her position in society, to command all the

assistance which her father's theatre and the journals could possibly have afforded her. It was something new, moreover, for a lady, and so young a lady, to appear before the world at once in the double capacity of an author and an actress, the delineator on the stage of one of the characters which she had imagined and painted in the closet. The attempt was in every respect a bold one, and deserved all the indulgence which it has universally experienced. (pp. 524-25)

Nor is it to be denied that the drama—the fair author does not call it a tragedy—now before us, is as a mere literary work, a production of some merit. There are some passages which, we confess, we did not expect from a pen necessarily so unpractised in the arts of poetical composition. But taking the piece as a whole, and forgetting—as impartial critics looking only to the character of our national drama we ought to forget—all the extraneous circumstances attending it, we are bound in our honest judgment to say that it is marked by many glaring faults, and wants most of the requisites which we believe to be essential to excellence in this department of our literature.

We discard from our consideration all those canons of criticism which are founded upon arbitrary principles with respect to the unities of time and place, and other such exploded doctrines of the French school. It is sufficient in our estimation, if the piece succeed in fixing the attention during the time of its performance so steadfastly on the stage, as to kindle the imagination, and induce it to identify the characters of the drama with the persons whom they are intended to pourtray. This species of mental illusion it is the great object of dramatic compositions of every class to excite; it may be in the power of the actor to mar that object by his incapacity, or to heighten it beyond our conception by his talents; but we can put the piece to the test in our study as well as in the theatre, and either way it will, generally speaking, lead us to a right decision as to the merits of the composition. Judging *Francis the First* by this simple rule, we should say that, neither in the closet nor on the stage, is it capable of attaining the object which the drama has in view.

The plot turns in the first place upon the sufferings and final success of the Duke of Bourbon, a vindictive traitor, who does not, like Coriolanus, redeem his treason by the grandeur of his character. There is a meanness in his motives, a littleness in his ambition, a falsehood in his conduct, which enlist all our best feelings against him, and would induce us to wrest from him, if we could, the triumph with which his proceedings are crowned. This could not be avoided, for it is matter of history, and it could not have been otherwise represented. But then it was not a matter of necessity for the author to choose that particular passage in history for her subject; and it must be admitted, that she was unfortunate in a choice, which, instead of engaging our feelings in favour of her hero, points them, on the contrary, against him.

Again:—few persons, we believe, have read the history of Francis the First without rising from it with the impression, that, however gross the faults which he committed during his reign, whether as a politician, a soldier, or a man, there was still a gallant bearing in his conduct, a chivalry in his soul, which after all make us think of him as one of the most generous and amiable sovereigns who have wielded the sceptre of France. Miss Fanny Kemble, however, appears to have read his history in a very different sense. She has here represented him as no better than Louis the Fifteenth in intellectual capacity, and quite equal to that monarch in all his infamies of debauchery. The attention of the king seems, throughout the first four acts of the play, to be almost exclusively devoted to the gratification of his passions, and the seduction of the innocent, at the same time that he appears to be kept in leading-strings by his mother. This inferiority of character to that which we read of him in history, may very well suit the purposes of the plot, but it does not at all correspond with our previous notions; it is in every way beneath them. And in the fifth act, where alone Francis appears himself for a scene or two, he scarcely has time to recover himself in our esteem, when he is abandoned by fortune and taken prisoner. This finale is in strict conformity with history, but it is a very undignified conclusion for the dramatic career of a monarch, to whom we should be so much inclined to wish success. Thus Bourbon rejoices in victory, whom we should desire to see humbled by defeat; and Francis is degraded by the surrender of his sword, whom we should be happy to see triumphant.

But the monstrous error of this drama is the king's mother, Louisa of Savoy—a woman whose conduct, in every instance where she appears on the stage, is repulsive in the extreme, and a violation of all the decencies of her sex. The author has here less excuse from history, as the passion which she imputes to Louisa for the Constable Bourbon, is altogether gratuitous. Bourbon had betrayed his allegiance, by joining Charles the Fifth before Francis turned his arms against the Milanese. It is notorious that the Constable's treason was the result of the persecutions which he had suffered from the king, and the confiscation of his property. Yet Miss F. Kemble makes Bourbon a governor of the Milanese for France before it was conquered, and she makes the queen mother, who actually detested him, recall him from his post, under an impulse of irresistible love, at the very period when he was in open arms against her son.

But even if history warranted the story which the fair author has invented, she would, in our judgment, have not the less violated all the rules of good taste, in drawing the character which she has here given to the queen. When that personage first makes her appearance, she, a woman of nearly sixty years of age, is made to speak of the passion of love with all the fervour of youth! (pp. 525-26)

She *loves* the Duke de Bourbon, and for the gratification of her passion she recalled him to France! If we can outrage nature so far, as to suppose that the queen was in fact actuated so powerfully by such a passion at that period of her life, womanly decorum would at all events forbid her to disclose it in such unqualified terms to a mere stranger, and that too without the slightest necessity upon her part. Nor is it, to us at least, a recommendation in Louisa's character, that she can swear 'by heaven,' like any trooper. (p. 528)

Such language as this in the mouth of a young man, ardently attached to a beautiful mistress, might be endurable, but in that of the mother of Francis, at the age of threescore, it is unnatural; and even if it were consistent with fact, is grossly unbecoming. Not content, however, with talking of her love to Gonzales, she next confesses it to Bourbon himself. (p. 529)

It is impossible not to be sensible, that the queen is left at the conclusion of this scene in a state the most degraded and most painful that a woman has ever experienced. Who can sympathize in the passion which is said to burn in her blood? or, if there be those who could sympathize with her feelings, could they further tolerate the bold unfeminine precipitancy with which she reveals her folly? (p. 530)

We rejoice in the final humiliation of such a monster of a woman, and we are glad that the curtain falls upon her crimes. But we have still a fifth act before us, which is in effect altogether a new and distinct drama. Francis, who through the four first acts appeared little more than a profligate courtier still in the leading strings of his mother, now at length puts on the king, and the scene changes from France to Italy; from domestic intrigue to foreign war. Hitherto the queen had been the heroine of the play; her passion and her crimes demanded our attention, and excited our horror; but now Bourbon becomes the hero,—we are to witness the consummation of his revenge, and the triumph of his perfidy.

We need scarcely remark, that this mode of conducting a drama, necessarily tends to divide the interest between too many prominent objects, and, by consequence, to weaken, if not to destroy it altogether. We care nothing about the unities of time or place, for the imagination can without difficulty shift with the scenery from one country to another, and can just as easily suppose the lapse of months or years in a moment. But no composition, whether intended for the closet or the stage, can be ranked in the order of excellence, which fails to produce a unity, or rather, perhaps we should say, a symmetry of impression. It may possibly be considered by some philosophers as a defect in the constitution of our powers of vision, that no object can be clearly figured upon the retina, unless the rays of light that emanate from it be previously brought to a single point of convergence in the pupil of the eye. The same defect, if such it be, appertains to the mind, which can receive no decided or permanent impression from any number of objects presented to its attention, unless they are capable of being collected into a focus. It is impossible for the mind to perform such an operation as this, with the passion of the queen for Bourbon, her hatred of Françoise, and the ultimate revenge of the traitor. These three leading points of interest do not converge: they spring from sources widely distant from each other, and might form so many different themes for the exercise of the author's dramatic powers.

The composition has its title from the king: yet, strange to say, although Francis is much seen and heard through the first four acts, he always appears in a secondary character. In the fifth act, he becomes the sovereign more completely; yet even here, though he commands armies, and fights battles, his star turns pale, while that of Bourbon is in the ascendant.

The fifth act opens with a scene which is altogether inconsistent with Bourbon's fiery character. He comes before us whining like a gentle swain for the absence of his lady love, Margaret, the sister of Francis! But this is not all. Lautrec, the brother of Françoise, who we now learn for the first time had been seduced by the king, goes over to the enemy, and asks permission to join the standard of Bourbon. But he, good rebel, all at once becomes scrupulous. He has grown old, he says, and cautious. His character was slandered in France. He, forsooth, was called a traitor, whereas he was only the instrument of his own revenge! He who was in arms against his sovereign, and at the moment on the march to encounter him, was afraid of offending Providence! Excellent, faithful Bourbon, he could not think of making his army (chiefly composed of brigands, by the way), a retreat for rebels! Moreover, Lautrec had sworn that he would be revenged on the king. It was therefore out of the question. Bourbon could not accept the assistance of such a person! All this is perfectly ridiculous.

We then come to the second scene, which displays more poetic beauty of composition than any other part of the drama. It will remind the reader at once of that fine scene in *Richard the Third,* the morning before the battle, of which, indeed, it is little better than an imitation; but an imitation, it must be confessed, of no mean order. (pp. 537-38)

The battle, however, is not yet begun, and as a battle on the stage cannot be of very long duration, and it was still necessary to eke out the act, Triboulet, the court jester, makes his appearance with the last batch of recruits from Paris, and entertains the king with his swaggering gallantry and pointless humour. This same Triboulet is evidently a great favourite with the author. His character is with her, what in the north would be called a "fond idea." It is the creation of an unsound vein of the fancy—a sort of nympholeptic indulgence, arising probably out of some girlish recollections of a story book, in which some jester of the olden time figured as the hero. A council of war is then held, the debates in which are nearly as drowsy as those on the reform bill, and at length the battle roars in right earnest. The fortune of the field turns against Francis—*Triboulet dies!* As if this jump from the sublime to the ludicrous were not sufficient, Triboulet, in the very hour of defeat, is borne to his tomb with all the honours of a dirge; at which Francis not only appears as chief mourner, but actually makes the responses in the *De Profundis*—and in Latin too! This introduction upon the stage, at the burial of a jester, of one of the most pathetic psalms in the whole of the Sacred Writings is, to say the least of it, an innovation, which we should not desire to see converted into a precedent. The whole scene is a mockery and an error, even dramatically speaking, for it cannot be supposed that at such a moment, Francis, who was already a prisoner, had either time or thought for such a ceremony as this, over the body of a reputed fool.

Now, with all these faults, which we have pointed out with the frankness and freedom that are absolutely necessary in a critical journal, whose sole and straightforward object it is to attend to the interests of the national literature, we are still willing to acknowledge that Miss F. Kemble has displayed in this composition intellectual powers that may, if rightly directed, enable her to produce a much better drama than *Francis the First.* She has evidently a fine perception of character, and a good idea of stage effect. We suspect the originality and extent of her poetical faculty; but the best poets are not always the best dramatic writers. We think her style sufficiently dignified and energetic when the occasion requires it, and her blank verse subsides without difficulty into the tone of excited conversation. We hope that she will select a theme for her next effort from English or Scottish history. (pp. 539-40)

> *A review of "Francis the First: An Historical Drama,"*
> *in* The Monthly Review, *London, n.s. Vol. 127, No.*
> *4, April, 1832, pp. 524-40.*

FRANCES ANNE BUTLER [FANNY KEMBLE]   (essay date 1835)

[In her preface to Journal of a Residence in America, *Kemble explains the intent of her book.]*

A preface appears to me necessary to this book [*Journal of a Residence in America*], in order that the expectation with which the English reader might open it should not be disappointed.

Some curiosity has of late been excited in England with regard to America: its political existence is a momentous experiment, upon which many eyes are fixed, in anxious watching of the result; and such accounts as have been published of the customs and manners of its societies, and the natural wonders and beau-

ties of its scenery, have been received and read with considerable interest in Europe. This being the case, I should be loth to present these volumes to the English public without disclaiming both the intention and the capability of adding the slightest detail of any interest to those which other travellers have already furnished upon these subjects.

This book is, what it professes to be, my personal journal, and not a history or a description of men and manners in the United States.

Engaged in an arduous profession, and travelling from city to city in its exercise, my leisure and my opportunities would have been alike inadequate to such a task. The portion of America which I have visited has been a very small one, and, I imagine, by no means that from which the most interesting details are to be drawn. I have been neither to the south nor to the west; consequently have had no opportunity of seeing two large portions of the population of this country,—the enterprising explorers of the late wildernesses on the shores of the Mississippi,—and the black race of the slave states,—both classes of men presenting peculiarities of infinite interest to the traveller: the one, a source of energy and growing strength, the other, of disease and decay, in this vast political body.

My sphere of observation has been confined to the Atlantic cities, whose astonishing mercantile prosperity, and motley mongrel societies, though curious under many aspects, are interesting but under few.

What I registered were my immediate impressions of what I saw and heard; of course, liable to all the errors attendant upon first perceptions, and want of time and occasion for maturer investigation. The notes I have added while preparing the text for the press; and such opinions and details as they contain are the result of a longer residence in this country, and a somewhat better acquaintance with the people of it.

Written, as my journal was, day by day, and often after the fatigues of a laborious evening's duty at the theatre, it has infinite sins of carelessness to answer for; and but that it would have taken less time and trouble to re-write the whole book, or rather write a better, I would have endeavoured to correct them. . . . (pp. v-vi)

However, my purpose is not to write an apology for my book, or its defects, but simply to warn the English reader, before he is betrayed into its perusal, that it is a purely egotistical record, and by no means a history of America. (p. vi)

> *Frances Anne Butler* [*Fanny Kemble*], *in a preface*
> *to her* Journal of a Residence in America, *A. and W.*
> *Galignani and Co., 1835, pp. v-vi.*

[EDGAR ALLAN POE?]   (essay date 1835)

[Considered one of America's most outstanding men of letters, Poe was a distinguished poet, novelist, essayist, journalist, short story writer, editor, and critic. Poe stressed an analytical, rather than emotive, approach to literature, emphasizing the technical details of a work, instead of its ideological statement. Although Poe and his literary criticism were subject to controversy in his own lifetime, he is now valued for his literary theories. The review of Journal of a Residence in America *excerpted below has been frequently but not conclusively attributed to Poe. The critic discusses the work's portrait of its author, as well as its style, language, and descriptions of Americans, rating the* Journal *an uneven production.]*

Perhaps no book has, for many years, been looked for, long previous to its publication, with such intense curiosity, as this record of Miss Fanny Kemble's observations and opinions of men and women, manners and customs, in the United States. . . . It is impossible to consider [*Journal of a Residence in America*] in any other than a personal point of view. Its very form forbids our separating the author from the work—the opinions and sentiments, from the individual who utters them. The idea of both exist in an indivisible amalgamation. Nor we fear, will it be possible for nine-tenths of her readers to weigh a single expression of Fanny Kemble the authoress, unmingled with the idea of Fanny Kemble the actress, the star—the "observed of all observers." Hence this [*Journal of a Residence in America*] will have an effect probably far beyond the anticipations of its writer. It will not only be looked upon as the test of Mrs. Butler's ability as an author; but it will, whether justly or not, convey to the thousands who have already perused, and the tens of thousands who will hereafter peruse it, a picture of her character and dispositions. The picture may, and doubtless will be an exaggerated one—few *pictures* are otherwise; but still it will be received as true, because the outlines have been traced by the original herself. We are sorry to say that the "counterfeit resemblance" of the fair authoress, presented by her book, displays many harsh and ill-favored lineaments, and the traces of passions which we could wish did not disfigure its many noble and magnanimous features. Mrs. Butler cannot claim for herself the immunity which she awards with great justice to poetical writers, of a distinction between their *real* and their *written* sentiments. If this book contains as we suppose, the faithful transcripts of her daily observations and opinions, revised long after they were penned, and thus exhibiting her true, unexaggerated impressions, by them must she be judged—and in passing judgment upon her work, a candid critic will find much, very much, to admire and approve, and much also to censure and condemn.

We have read Mrs. Butler's work with untiring interest—indeed the vivacity of its style, the frequent occurrence of beautiful descriptions, of just and forcible observations, and many sound views of the condition of society in this country—the numerous characteristic anecdotes, and some most discriminating criticisms of actors and acting, must stamp her work as one of no ordinary merit. And these attractions in a great measure neutralize, although they cannot redeem, her innumerable faults of language, her sturdy prejudices, her hasty opinions, and her ungenerous sarcasms—These abound in the [*Journal of a Residence in America*], and yet it is more than probable that her censorious spirit has to a great extent been suppressed, as almost every page is studded with asterisks, indicating, we may presume, that her sins of hasty censure have been greatly diminished to the public eye, by the saving grace of omission.

The defects of the work are not confined to the exhibition of prejudices and the expression of unjust opinions: the style and language is often coarse, we might say vulgar; and her more impassioned exclamations are often characterized by a vehemence which is very like *profanity,* an offence that would not be tolerated in a writer of the other sex. We cite a few, from among the many passages which we have noted, as specimens of undignified, unfeminine and unscholarlike phraseology: The word "*dawdled*" seems a great favorite with Mrs. Butler—as, for instance: "Rose at eight, *dawdled* about," &c. "Rose at half past eight, *dawdled* about as usual." "Came up and *dawdled* upon deck." "Came home, *daudled* about my room."—And in numberless other instances this word is used,

apparently, to signify loitering or dallying, spelled indiscriminately da*w*dled, or da*u*dled. Indeed so much does our fair authoress seem to have been addicted to the habit which the word implies—be it what it may—that in the second volume she speaks of having "dressed for once without *dawdling*," as an uncommon occurrence. She is also fond of the word "gulp," and uses it in strange combinations, as—"My dear father, who was a little elated, made me sing to him, which I greatly *gulped* at." "I *gulped*, sat down, and was measured," (for a pair of shoes,)—"on the edge of a precipice, several hundred feet down into the valley: it made me *gulp* to look at it," &c. (pp. 524-26)

She thus describes the motions of persons on ship-board, in rough weather: "Rushing hither and thither in all directions but the one they purpose going, and making as many angles, fetches, and ridiculous deviations from the point they aim at, as if the *devil had tied a string to their legs,* and jerked it every now and then in spite."

At page 99: "Supped, lay down on the floor in absolute *meltiness away,* and then came to bed." "When I went on, I was all but tumbling down at the sight of my Jaffier, who looked like the apothecary in *Romeo and Juliet,* with the addition of some *devilish* red slashes along his thighs and arms." "Away *walloped* the four horses,"&c. "How they did *wallop* and shamble about," &c. "Now I'll go to bed; my cough's enough to kill a *horse*." "Heaven bless the world, for a *conglomerated amalgamation* of fools." "He talked an amazing quantity of *thickish* philosophy, and moral and sentimental *potter*." In truth, "*potter*" and "*pottering*," seem to be favorites equally with *daudling,* and she as frequently makes use of them. (p. 526)

Such blemishes as these, apparently uniting the slang of the boarding school and the green room, deform the work of Mrs. Butler, and are much to be lamented, because they may have the effect of blinding the hasty, prejudiced or fastidious reader, to the many beauties which are to be found in its pages. Indeed the work has already encountered the severest criticisms from the newspaper press, imbittered by the many censorious remarks of Mrs. B. upon the manners and institutions of the country; her severe, and in many instances just strictures upon the state of society in the cities in which she sojourned; and the supercilious sneers which she has uttered against the editorial fraternity, "the press gang," as she uncourteously denominates that numerous and powerful body. The censures of her book, are doubtless, in the main, well deserved; but in their excess, the merits which the [*Journal of a Residence in America*] unquestionably possesses in great abundance and of a high order, have in many cases been passed by unheeded by her indignant critics. And here we cannot refrain from the utterance of a remark which has frequently occurred to us, and which is brought forcibly to mind by the reception which Mrs. Butler's criticisms upon America have met with: we think that too much sensitiveness is felt by our countrymen, at the unfavorable opinions expressed by foreigners, in regard to our social, political, and moral condition—and that the press, as the organ of public sentiment, is prone to work itself into a superfluous frenzy of indignation, at what are generally considered "foreign libels" upon us. . . . Entertaining these views, we have read Mrs. Butler's work, with a disposition to judge of it impartially; and while we have perceived many instances of captious complaints in regard to matters of trifling importance in themselves; and frequently a disposition to build up general censures upon partial, individual causes of disgust, displeasure or disappointment—we feel bound to say, that, taking the work as a whole, we do not think a deliberate disposition to misrepresent, or a desire to depreciate us, can be discovered in it. The strictures upon our modes of living, our social relations, &c. are often unworthy the writer. She complains for instance, that "the things (at the hotel in New York,) were put on the table in a slovenly, outlandish fashion; fish, soup, and meat, at once, and puddings, and tarts, and cheese, at another once; no finger glasses, and a patched table cloth— in short, a want of that style and neatness which is found in every hotel in England. The waiters too, remind us of the half-savage highland lads, that used to torment us under that denomination in Glasgow—only that they were wild Irish instead of Scotch."

Frequently too, she complains of the audiences before whom she performed, with occasional reproofs of their ungracious conduct in not sufficiently applauding her father or herself. . . . (pp. 526-27)

At the Philadelphia audiences, she grumbles as follows:

> The audiences here, are without exception, the most disagreeable I ever played to. Not a single hand did they give the balcony scene, or my father's scene with the friar; they are literally immoveable. They applauded vehemently at the end of my draught scene, and a great deal at the end of the play; but they are nevertheless intolerably dull, and it is all but impossible to act to them.

Of the ladies of this country, she seems to have formed a low estimate in many respects, and to look upon them generally with no little contempt. (p. 527)

As few matters, worldly or spiritual, escaped the observation of our authoress, it is not wonderful that her pen was occasionally dipped in the political cauldron. But as her ideas are in most instances tinged with her own national prejudices, we shall not dwell upon them longer than to say that she sees already a decided aristocratic tendency among us, and to quote the following summary of her opinion as to the permanence of our institutions and government:—"I believe in my heart that a republic is the noblest, highest, and purest form of government; but I believe that according to the present disposition of human creatures, 'tis a mere beau ideal, totally incapable of realization. What the world may be fit for six hundred years hence, I cannot exactly perceive—but in the mean time, 'tis my conviction that America will be a monarchy before I am a skeleton." If argument with a lady on such a subject could be reconciled to the precepts of gallantry, it would certainly be unprofitable where the causes of her belief are so vaguely stated. And we think she has furnished the best argument against herself in her frequent comparisons of the condition of the mass of the people of this country to that of the laboring class in England, in which she constantly decides in favor of America. It will scarcely be argued that a people enjoying such blessings as she ascribes to the condition of the mass of American citizens, could easily be induced to change their government, and yield up a certain good for a doubtful improvement—far less that they would willingly submit to a form of government which they look upon as particularly odious. (p. 528)

We have thus endeavored to give our readers an idea of this very remarkable book—a task of no little difficulty from its variable features, its mixture of sense and silliness, of prejudice and liberality—almost every page bearing a distinct and peculiar character. There are many things which have elicited censure, on which we have not laid any stress, and among these are the frequent exhibitions of attachment to her native country, and preference of its people, its customs, its laws, &c. to those of America. We cannot find fault with her for so noble and so natural a sentiment, even though it should lead her to depreciate and underrate us. Besides, she acknowledges the blindness of her partiality to England, and speaks of it with great candor, as a national characteristic:

> How we English folks do cling to our own habits, our own views, our own things, our own people; how in spite of all our wanderings and scatterings over the whole face of the earth, like so many Jews, we never lose our distinct and national individuality; nor fail to lay hold of one another's skirts, to laugh at and depreciate all that differs from that country, which we delight in forsaking for any and all others.

(p. 530)

The chief fault of the work will be found in the dictatorial manner of the writer. A female, and a young one too, cannot speak with the self-confidence which marks this book, without jarring somewhat upon American notions of the retiring delicacy of the female character. But the early induction of Mrs. B. upon the stage, has evidently given her a precocious self-dependence and a habit of forming her own opinions. There is perhaps no situation in which human vanity is so powerfully excited, as that of the favorite actor. The directness of the applause which greets his successful efforts is most intoxicating, and mingles so much admiration of the performer with delight at the performance, that he or she, whose vanity should resist its fascinations, must be a stoic indeed. The effects of this personal homage, added to the advantages of her birth, and her really masculine intellect, are apparent in Mrs. B's [*Journal of a Residence in America*]. But she also displays some fine feminine traits, which the flatteries of delighted audiences, the admiration of ambitious fashionables, and the consciousness of being the chief Lion of the day, could not destroy. Her sympathy for a sick lady, lodging in the same house in Philadelphia, is frequently and delicately expressed; and various other incidents shew that kindness and generosity are among her prominent qualities. Many pages are devoted to the subject of religion, and as appears from them, she was attentive to the performance of her devotions: Yet we cannot but think her religion as displayed in this book, more a sentiment than a principle; rather the imbodying of a poetical fancy, than that pervading feeling of the heart which enters into and characterizes the actions of those who feel its influence.—In conclusion, we will repeat what we have said before, that there is much to admire and much to condemn in this work—enough of the former to render it one of the most attractive (as it is one of the most original) that has recently issued from the press; and in censuring its faults it will be but justice to bear in mind a sentiment of Mrs. B.; "After all, if people generally did but know the difficulty of doing well, they would be less damnatory upon those who do ill." (pp. 530-31)

> *[Edgar Allan Poe?], in a review of "Journal of a Residence in America," in* The Southern Literary Messenger, *Vol. I, No. 1, May, 1835, pp. 524-31.*

[E.G.E. BULWER-LYTTON?]   (essay date 1835)

[One of the most versatile writers of the nineteenth century, Bulwer-Lytton was also one of the most popular; his success once rivaled

that of his friend Charles Dickens. An author whose works occupy a middle ground between popular and serious fiction, he wrote embellished accounts of the lives of criminals, historical novels, occult fiction, dramas, and fictional family chronicles, exhibiting in his writings almost all the trends of nineteenth-century literature. In the following excerpt from an anonymous review generally attributed to Bulwer-Lytton, the critic denies that Americans have cause to be offended by Journal of a Residence in America, *alleging that Kemble's treatment of American themes is honest and good-natured.*]

Mrs Butler's [*Journal of a Residence in America*] has all the freshness, confidence, and indiscretion of an intercepted correspondence. Among its many indiscretions, her declarations against 'the Press-gang'—that body before whom statesmen tremble—is pre-eminently indiscreet. But the sort of temptation, under which foolish and fearless schoolboys provoke a nest of hornets, appears to have been irresistible.... While some of our writers are shocked at her vulgarity, the Americans, it is said, are likely to be as much offended with the freedom of her remarks upon their manners. Is there any, and what degree of reason in these objections?

We take the book as it is, having neither means nor inclination to read the stars scattered over its pages. For any thing we can tell one way or the other, they may be very improper mischief-making stars, or 'the maidenliest stars in the firmament.' Confining ourselves, then, to the printed text, we should like to know, whom and what the public can have imagined the present journal was to place before them?—a pure and shrinking snow-drop, just brought out of the nunnery of an English nursery?—the milliners' flower—one of the curtseying conventional nonentities of fashion?—or some more stately personification of matronly reserve, sculptured out from our native granite? If so, the public may well be surprised. But, in fact, the absurdity of such a representation, in the present instance, would probably have been surpassed only by its stupidity. Mrs Butler has dealt more kindly by us. Instead of getting up for the booksellers a book which a hundred other travellers could have manufactured as skilfully as herself, she has given us one of those vivid realities which it is beyond the faculty of authorship to create. Her picture is a picture from the life—the original drawings taken on the spot. Our surprise, however, is perhaps as great as that of our neighbours, only of a more agreeable kind; first, at the extraordinary rapidity and truth with which the impression of the moment has been committed to paper—so little lost, so little added; next, at the frankness and good faith with which she has retained these, her first impressions, in spite of the thousand and one terrors, temptations, and prudential considerations of preparing for the press. The genuine juice of the grape, unmedicated and unmixed, is not a rarer phenomenon in the cellars of a wine merchant, than a production so perfectly natural, in the literary market. It is more like thinking aloud than any thing of personal history we ever expected to see in print. Now, thinking aloud, which would be rather a hazardous practise with most people, is not likely to be less hazardous than usual in the person of a young and lively actress—the writer, while in her teens, of so *bold* a play as that of *Francis the First*. We do not offer the result of the experiment as the precedent of a pattern-girl, whose manners, feelings, and expressions may be safely received by governesses as authority for their pupils. That is another question. There are too many impulses and contingencies belonging to most kinds of talent to make talents desirable, but as an exception in life. This must be particularly true in the case of women. All the arrangements of society proceed so completely on the contrary supposition! What allowances, then, ought

justice and charity to interpose, where, in addition to the common risks of wayward genius, its youthful destiny has been identified with the literature of the drama, the habits of the green-room, and the excitement of the stage? In case a juvenile actress should contract from her profession only a certain quantity of bad taste, and a little more of mobility and self-confidence than would be found in a young thing, who, although naturally as excitable, had been but just taken out of its country nest, she will have come out of the terrible ordeal marvellously little spoiled by it.

The way in which the supposed specimens of bad taste have been selected, in the newspapers and other publications, for exposure—sentences or half sentences detached from their quick and flowing context—makes them appear infinitely worse than they really are. For, the head and front of her offending amount to little more than occasional instances of a vehement and random style, which (though it has nothing improper in it in itself, yet) as it is not the language of good company, it is somewhat startling to hear a gentlewoman indulging in. For instance, she has no timid misgivings about the personality of Satan. An old magician could not speak of him with greater familiarity. The difficulty which the ladies of New York experience in pronouncing broadly and distinctly the first syllable of Hell-gate (the name of one of the wonders of the neighbourhood) passes her comprehension.... It is a bad sign to be over fastidious. Without knowing more of the matter, we should not conclude that Mrs Montague was less of a lady for having once in a way told Charles Fox, that she did not care 'three skips of a louse' for him. We say the same of the equivalent *étourderies* of Mrs Butler. A lady of the old school—successor and more than successor to Mrs Montague's authority—once repeated to us a list of expressions, from the use of which ladies had been excluded during her lifetime; and added her apprehension that, if things went on so, the time must come, when English men and English women would be speaking different languages.... For our own part, ... we feel obliged to Mrs Butler for refusing to be put into the mould.

The anger of our good cousins over the water would be still more ridiculous than the sensitiveness of our purists. We shall always be forward to denounce (Americans themselves not more so) spiteful one-sided exaggerations—splenetic attempts to depreciate their institutions or their people—more especially the childishness of making institutions answerable for matters of fact, which properly belong to other causes. The caricatures of Mrs Trollope and of Captain Basil Hall were much more disagreeable to us than the assumption and arrogance of Mr Cooper. But this is not enough of favour! No small portion of the American population regard advocates of our complexion as little better than enemies in disguise. They reject every thing as an insult which stops short of unqualified panegyric. What may be the value of Mrs Butler's opinions on America, is itself a matter of opinion. Sensible persons will have regard to the subject of which she may be speaking at the time. She says she knows nothing about politics. We believe her. Nevertheless, she lampoons the English Whigs; lauds the American institutions for things they have no merit in; and opines about the tendency of America to monarchy—about the necessary modifications of the Roman Catholic religion under a republic—and about the peculiar congeniality of Unitarianism with the character of New England, as peremptorily as if her knowledge of politics entitled her to have an opinion of her own. Her decisions concerning actors, scenery (out of doors' scenery we mean), literature, and society, are much more likely to be correct. But let her judgments be what they may—right or wrong—they occupy a small space. She appears principally as a witness; mentioning the particular facts which fell within her personal experience, and communicating the impression which the whole of what she saw and heard made upon her mind. Are there any marks of want of understanding for this purpose? Did she carry out with her the evil eye—observing the world before her in a mocking spirit? Or is the honesty of her revised descriptions open to suspicion? On these points, it is easy to show that the Americans must be exacting and quarrelsome indeed, who shall conceive that they have any just reason for complaint. Her book, it should be remembered, is no history of America. She expressly declares in the preface, that it does not pretend to be so. It is simply the journal of her twelve-months' professional sojourn in some of the principal commercial towns, with the addition of a few later notes. (pp. 379-83)

The first thing that a national caricaturist seeks to misrepresent is the condition of the body of the people. Not only is Mrs Butler sensible that a greater degree of comfort is enjoyed by the population at large in the non-slaving states than by the same class in the Old World; but she attributes their well-being to their democracy, with as much ignorance of the real nature of the case as their novelist, Cooper, could desire. (p. 384)

The next thing in which national unfairness generally betrays itself, is in the colour given to estimates of the general character of a people. But Mrs Butler is apparently quite as ready to do full justice to all that she has admired or liked in them, as to speak her mind on what was disagreeable to her. (p. 385)

She has passed to the credit of their account the several items of political greatness, honesty, courtesy, and humanity; and has added her own personal obligation for boundless kindness. After this, is she to be all but stoned for setting down in her tablets, day by day, as they occurred, the opposite matters, whether serious or trifling, which have most annoyed or most amused her? And what, in truth, does the burden of her imputed testimony against America actually amount to? For the most part her troubles and horrors are those of a quick and susceptible and somewhat romantic girl, who is pining after home, and is comparing every thing with the standards which she had left behind her; the riding school at New York with Fossard's; an evening among the rank and fashion of Chestnut Street with her last evening at Devonshire House. It may be truly a blessed country for the vast majority of mankind notwithstanding the following deductions:

There is no such thing as a good lady's horse to be got through-out the Union for love or money; horses are called well broken when they are only no longer wild; a decent rider, man or woman, is scarcely ever to be seen; their actors are in general an ignorant and inattentive set, and the audience cannot find it out; an election at the Quaker city of Philadelphia is as noisy as in London, and a clever Jacksonite can contrive to vote for 'old Hickory' nine times over; the division of labour and capital is not yet visible in their shop windows; while the dependence of the rich upon the poor (instead of the European alternative, the dependence of the poor upon the rich), is visible enough in the conduct of careless innkeepers, conversible shopmen, and washerwomen, who sit down while their mistresses are standing; for three years together a pretty woman may not get a single article of dress which shall not be ill made; what is almost as bad—poetical mountains are degraded by the ap-pellations of Crow's Nest and Butter Hill; no nightingales are to be heard in New England, nor rivulets singing through the fields; the people are given up to the realities of life, and mainly to that dull reality, the making money; they are in too great a

hurry to allow themselves time to perfect any thing, and will scarcely pause to keep a Christmas or a birth-day; the want of a class with independent means, and, therefore, able to com-mand literary leisure, and follow up the higher intellectual pursuits, is a national misfortune; the population, in conse-quence, is marvellously indisposed to humour, which is fancy laughing, and to poetry, which is fancy sad; the principal effort of national drollery or romance, consists in going to Lem-priere's Dictionary for the names of their wooden villages and negro slaves; drunkenness, while it is much less common among the poor than in England, is a frequent recreation of the rich; spitting on floor and carpet is so general that a clean white gown may be covered with yellow spots from the gentlemen's tobacco in a single afternoon; a nasal inflection is a national characteristic, while sundry peculiarities of pronunciation and accent more or less distinguish the principal divisions of the country; they play such queer tricks in modernizing the English of our liturgy, that their language must run a great chance of being driven from the solid anchorage which our ancestors had laid down in our old translation of the Bible; privacy any where is out of the question; an officer in the American army considers his commission to be a sufficient right of introduction to any body—young ladies included; visitors, once acquainted, walk in without leaving the visitees an option in the matter; the fair sex have a great dislike to being called 'women;' their feminine refined appearance is in singular contrast with their style of dress (French gone mad), and with their practice of talking across each other, five or six at a time, at the top of the shrillest voices in the world; the thorough-bred look and manners of our noble English ladies are seldom seen; married women be-come at once household drudges or nursery-maids; you will not find a lady at home in the morning six or seven times in three years—she is in the storeroom, while her husband is at the counting-house; for the most part society is led by chits—of whom the girls are brought up *en evidence* and in a bustle, and the boys are made men of business at sixteen; these dem-ocrats are as title-sick as a banker's wife in England; the dis-tinguishing points on which American *exclusives* pride them-selves, find, however, ample scope for variety in different parts of the country; the aristocracy of New York rests its pretensions upon its wealth, that of Boston upon its intellect, that of Phil-adelphia and of the south upon birth; a curious novel might be made in illustration of the struggle between the levelling spirit of American institutions and the separating and dividing spirit of American society; the effect of universal suffrage is to check mental cultivation, and give them an inferior government,—just, honest, and rational perhaps, but not enlarged or liberal; finally, and to conclude—the working of the whole brings out in the higher classes a system of life and manners any thing but agreeable to gentlefolks fresh from Europe.

A great deal of this may not be very pleasant hearing; but it is all told, meaning to tell the truth, and not meaning to be impertinent. Where this is the case, it is more absurd in nations, even than in individuals, to take offence. Mrs Butler says what she thinks of other nations as unreservedly as of the Americans. She goes out of her way to mention the vanity and blasphemies of the French. She speaks as ill of the filth of London hackney-coaches as of the paces of American saddle-horses, and was as sensible to the dirtiness of her hotel at Dublin, and to the savageness of the Highland serving-man at Glasgow, as to her similar miseries in the Northern States. . . . What then? Neither nation, nor French nor English, she is well aware, will think of directing the columns of a single newspaper against her, by reason of these hard sayings. . . . Europeans have learned that 'these things must not be thought of after this fashion; they would make us mad else.' The Americans, on the other hand, appear in this respect to be little better than so many spoiled children, unaccustomed to contradiction. They cannot play at cards unless they are allowed to call the trump. (pp. 388-91)

Though Mrs Butler has said nothing about the Americans, which, whether we look at the matter or the manner, she had not a perfect right to say; on the other hand, she has given the Americans, without any breach of gallantry, certain rights as against herself. An ornamental tube is not a barometer, unless it is properly constructed, the quicksilver what it ought to be, and the scale correctly noted. Now, this is not the nature of Mrs Butler's book. It is, at the best, a mirror; and not so much a mirror reflecting an image of America as of herself. General Jackson appears to have suspected her of belonging to the family of scribbling ladies, when he told her that the South Carolina disturbances had no larger source than 'the nib of a lady's pen.' It is curious to see the influence of the sex as powerful over American politics, as in the court of Queen Anne or Louis the Fifteenth. But the representation which Mrs Butler has given of herself, is a conclusive proof that the possibility of making a national or political use of her pages never entered into her head. Otherwise she would have been upon her guard; and written less in the headlong capricious style of 'a moonish youth, changeable, longing, and liking, for every passion something, and for no passion truly any thing, as boys and women are for the most part cattle of this colour.' Now, this is too much her way of going on, upon her own showing; her book being a window to her mind, in which all is seen that for the time is uppermost in it. (p. 394)

> [*E.G.E. Bulwer-Lytton?*], ''Mrs. Butler's 'American Journal','' in The Edinburgh Review, *Vol. LXI, No. CXXIV, July, 1835, pp. 379-406.*

[J. W. CROKER] (essay date 1835)

[*Nicknamed the ''slashing critic'' for his vitriolic literary reviews, Croker made extensive contributions to the periodical the* Quarterly Review, *the most prominent conservative Tory organ of the early nineteenth century. Here, he attacks the indecorum and affectation of* Journal of a Residence in America, *but acknowledges that the work is amusing and basically sensible.*]

[The *Journal of F. A. Butler*] is a work of very considerable talent, but, both in its conception and execution, of exceeding bad taste. There is something overbold, not to say indelicate, in the very idea of a young woman's *publishing* her private Journal; but when we found . . . [*Journal of F. A. Butler*] treating—besides her own personal concerns—of the manners and characters of her family, her friends, and even of the strangers into whose society she had been admitted, in a style of *free and easy* criticism, we confess that we were even less surprised by the abilities than at the self-confidence of this young lady. Nor is this fundamental error much alleviated by the style of execution, which is often colloquial almost to vulgarity, and occasionally bold even to coarseness. Such are the first, and not very agreeable, impressions that the work creates; and we doubt whether all the amusement it may give, and the admiration that particular passages will excite, can compensate, to the generality of readers, for those—considering the writer's age and sex—*unnatural* defects.

But there is, we are glad to say, a view of Miss Kemble's (or, as we must now call her, Mrs. Butler's) personal position, which will not only explain away much of the anomaly, but will serve as an excuse, if not an apology, for many of those

particulars which at first sight create the most surprise, and seem to deserve the least approbation. She is in years a young woman, but she has had considerable practice in the ways of the world. In many passages she expresses herself concerning her *profession* in very strong terms, sometimes of contempt and sometimes of disgust; but she never appears to have considered it in that particular point of view which bears most directly on her own case. The life of an *actress*—the habits of individual thought, study, and exertion—the familiarity with bargains, business, and bustle—the various and ever-varying situations and society into which she is thrown—the crossings and jostlings of the dramatic *race*—the acquired confidence which enables her to outface multitudinous audiences—and the activity and firmness of personal character which are necessary to maintain her rights from the encroachments of rivals and the tyranny of managers—must all tend to blunt the feelings of youthful timidity, to weaken the sense of feminine dependence, and to *force,* as in a hot-bed, to premature exuberance, all the more vigorous qualities both of mind and body. An actress lives fast: her existence is a perpetual wrestling-match, and one *season* gives her more experience—and with experience, more of the nerve and hard features of the world—than a whole life of domestic duties could do. In short, a *young actress* may be in mind and character an *old woman*; and when it happens, as in 'Master Fanny's' case, that the mind is originally of a vigorous and hardy cast, it is clear that she ought not to be measured by the standard of those more delicate young persons whose mental complexions have not been *bronzed* by the alternate sun and breezes of the stage, the green-room, and the box-office.

Again—the variety of characters with which she is obliged to identify herself (some of them not the most moral—Calista or Milwood, for instance—and some of them not the most feminine—as Lady Macbeth or Constance) must familiarize her with ideas and manners which never could approach a young woman in private life; and the infinite variety of such exhibitions gives her a kind of off-hand indifference to appearing before the public in *any* new character which may offer—even *that of a journalist.* Again—the general applause, and the individual attention, which actresses are in the habit of receiving, gives them inevitably a degree of self-confidence, a reliance on their own talents and judgment, and an idea of their own capacity and *importance,* which no other female mind is likely to attain. And, finally, all their thoughts and actions are calculated on familiarity with the *public*—they dress for the public, they read for the public, they write for the public, they live for the public—and accordingly think nothing of making the public their confidants in matters which an ordinary female conceals in the bosom of her family.

These are the considerations by which we account for Mrs. Butler's having thought of publishing her [*Journal of F. A. Butler*] at all—for the strange frankness in which she brings herself and all her friends on the literary stage—and for the decided tone and hardy expressions in which she exhibits her opinions: and if they do not constitute a sufficient excuse, we are satisfied that they afford at least the only rational explanation of the (otherwise unaccountable) step which Mrs. Butler has taken, in admitting the public into her dressing-room, and inviting them to the dinner and tea tables, and even into the *sick-chambers* of her friends and admirers.

But while Mrs. Butler's *profession* (should we say her *late* profession?) may be thus advanced in palliation of what we know has surprised the generality of readers, it has also, as might have been expected, influenced her literary style. If she is at times colloquial to vulgarity, she is at others pompous even to bombast, and in both cases she is *acting*. Her [*Journal of F. A. Butler*], we are satisfied, was from an early period, if not from the first line, destined for publication; and the whole thing is arranged for *stage effect*. She is pompous, to prove that she can be dignified; and then she interposes trivialities, in order to appear natural. She wishes to show that she can play Lady Macbeth and Nell in the same volume; but it seems to us that her pomp is more natural than her familiarity, and we trace quite as much affectation in her records of the 'packing of her trunks,' or the 'mending her gown,' as in her elaborate criticism on Hamlet, or her gorgeous descriptions of natural scenery.

With this clue in our hands we think we may venture to begin unravelling the [*Journal of F. A. Butler*].

Though she is strangely ignorant of the author of the celebrated expression—'*du sublime au ridicule il n'y a qu'un pas*'—which she attributes to 'a French *critic*,' there is hardly a page of her work in which she does not exhibit an example of it—here is one of the most moderate:—

> The *steadfast* shining of the moon held *high supremacy* in heaven. The bay lay like *molten silver* under her light, and every now and then a tiny skiff, emerging from the shade, crossed the bright waters, its dark hull and white sails relieved between the shining sea and radiant sky. Came home at nine, *tea'd*, and sat embroidering till twelve o'clock—*industrious little me*.

The *play* and the *after-piece!*

Mrs. Butler's natural good sense (and she has a great deal of it) sees the actor-style in others, but does not perceive it,—as every body else must do most strongly,—in herself.

> —— dined with us: what a handsome man he is! but oh, what a *within and without* actor. I wonder whether I carry such a brand in every limb and look of me? *if I thought so, I'd strangle myself.* An actor shall be self-convicted in five hundred. There is a *ceaseless striving at effect*, a *straining after points* in talking, and a *lamp and orange-peel twist* in every action. How odious it is to me! Absolute and unmitigated vulgarity I can put up with, and welcome; but good Heaven defend me from the genteel version of vulgarity—to see which in perfection, a country actor, particularly if he is also manager and sees occasionally people who bespeak plays, is your best occasion.

This is but too true; but we hope the offence of smelling of the stage-lamps is not quite so serious as Mrs. Butler represents it; for assuredly she is as clearly, though not so offensively, guilty of it as any stroller of her acquaintance; and if she really thinks the crime *capital*, she must, like the self-devoted ecclesiastic of the middle ages, pronounce her own sentence—*adjudico me cremari*—or, to adopt her own expression, *I condemn myself to be strangled*. And it is singular enough that the two paragraphs which immediately precede and follow this anathema against vulgarity appear to us to be not only vulgar, but something still less excusable.

Stitching the whole blessed day. Mr. —— and his daughter called; I like him: his daughter was dressed up in French clothes, and looked very stiff; but, however, a first visit is an awkward thing, and *nothing that isn't thoroughbred* ever does it quite well . . . . . . Worked till dinner-time. My dear father, *who was a little elated, made me* sing to him [the actor abovementioned], which I greatly gulped at. When he was gone, went on playing and singing. Wrote journal, and now to bed.

We hope that Mr. ——'s daughter, though 'she *isn't* thoroughbred,' would not have been guilty of the worse than vulgarity of hinting at her 'dear father's *elevation*,' nor of letting the aforesaid actor know, *through the public press*, that she thought him '*what a* handsome man!' but so *vulgar* as to deserve hanging. To console the poor fellow, we subjoin a few instances of that dramatic '*twist*' by which his harsh critic is herself unconsciously 'self-convicted:'—

> Played till I was tired; dozed, and finally came to bed. Bed! *quotha!* 'tis a frightful misapplication of terms.

> We passed a pretty house, which Colonel—— called an old mansion: mercy on me, him, and it! Old, *quotha!* the woods and waters, and hills and skies, alone are old here.

> My father told me he had been seeing Miss Clifton, the girl they want him to teach to act (to *teach* to act, *quotha!!!*); he says she is very pretty indeed, with fine eyes, a fair delicate skin, and a handsome mouth, moreover, a tall woman—and yet from the front of the house her effect is NOUGHT.

Here we must observe by the way, that one who affects the quaintness of Shakspeare's language should understand it. Mrs. Butler more than once expresses censure by saying 'the thing is *nought*'—nought, *quotha!* she means *naught*: and in a very remarkable passage in *Richard III.* (which we refrain from quoting more particularly), Shakspeare himself marks the very *broad* distinction between the two words.

Mrs. Butler seems to have a laudable reverence for religion, and frequently tells us of the assiduity with which she worked at her 'bible-cover;' but even on the most serious occasions she lays aside her 'bible-cover,' and the better thoughts it might inspire, to intersperse dramatic slang of the least decorous sound. . . . (pp. 39-43)

In the . . . style of vulgar irreverence is her reflection on the ship which had conveyed her to America:—

> Poor good ship, I wish to Heaven my feet were on her deck, and her prow turned to the east. I would not care *if the devil himself drove a hurricane* at our backs.

Does Mrs. Butler mean any harm by this? Certainly not—there is much better evidence than the 'bible-cover' that she has a strong, though we cannot say an *adequant*, religious feeling; but as the Stage has reconciled her to the publishing her . . . [*Journal of F. A. Butler*], the Stage has reconciled *her* ears to expressions which startle, and we must add offend, *ours*.

In the midst of a great affectation of simplicity of taste and manner, she contrives to display all possible vanities; and though she laughs at the Americans for their absurd admiration of titles, she takes special care to introduce, by hook or by crook, every lord or lady she was ever acquainted with. . . . [It] *accidentally* escapes her that she is not only a *universal genius,* reading Dante—writing novels—and darning shirts, with equal facility, but is, moreover, an *habituée* of the highest circles of English aristocracy—

> Finished Journal, wrote to my mother, *read a canto in Dante, and began to write a novel.* Dined at five. After dinner, put out things for this evening, played on the piano, *mended habit-shirt,* dressed myself, and at a quarter to ten went to the theatre for my father. I had on the same dress I wore *at Devonshire House,* the night of *the last ball I was at in England,* and looked at myself with amazement, to think of all the strangenesses that have befallen since then. Lord! Lord! what fools men and women do make themselves.—

They do indeed, but never so completely as when a lecturer on folly exhibits such *transparent* affectation.

This indeed is the predominant feature of Mrs. Butler's book; and, we presume (for the reasons already given), of her character. Perhaps it may not be quite exact to call *that* 'affectation,' of which probably she is often—nay, generally—unconscious, and which has become so *habitual* that she fancies it *natural.* We indeed allege it not as censure, but as defence of what, in a case not susceptible of the like apology, would be a gross indelicacy,' and, when she speaks of other persons, a breach of all the confidences of friendship and private life.

But it is not in manner and modes of thinking only that we trace this disposition to *étalage* and factitious decoration. Her description of natural objects, though in itself very clever, becomes indistinct and perplexing from an excess of colour. Within seven lines we have '*golden* skies—*green, brown, yellow,* and *dark maroon* thickets—*grey* granite, circled with *green—purple* waters—a *red* road—and all under a *rosy* light—till the eye is drunk with beauty.' Now all this '*gorgeous* and *glorious*' brilliancy which intoxicates the eye, is excellent now and then, and on special occasions; but in *every* third or fourth page—at *every* new prospect she sees—at *every* sun-rise or sun-set she witnesses, it grows intolerable. We wonder that she did not recollect, from the childish experiment of spinning a court-card, that the gaudiest hues will become, by rapid repetition, a dingy confusion; she keeps *spinning the Queen of Diamonds* so unremittingly all day long that one cannot make out what card it is. This flowery profusion of tints is very wearisome, but her metallic metaphors are still worse. No herald painter deals more largely in *or* and *argent.* It is really incredible what a quantity of gold and silver she uses up—'silver clouds'—'silver vapours'—'silver light'—'silver waves'—'silver lamp'—'silver belt'—'silver springs'—'floating silver,' and 'molten silver;' and then, on the other side of the account, we have 'golden skies'—'golden waves'—'golden shores'—'golden spray'—'golden snake'—'golden disk'—'golden fruit'—'golden wings'—'golden leaves'—'golden willows'—'golden glories,' and 'golden froth'—in short, every visible object is so *plated* and *gilt,* that the face of nature, in Mrs. Butler's sketch-book, looks like a silversmith's shop-window. And all this surprises us the more from the deep disgust she expresses at the *false finery* which she herself is forced to put on 'in the way of her vocation—*foil stone—glass beads,* and *brass tape.*'— Is it not wonderful that she does not

see that her own mode of overloading Nature is of the same tawdry fashion?—and that calling a brook 'a *silver snake,*' and a fog 'a *golden mist,*'—a cloud an '*inky curtain,*' and a shower of rain '*fringe*' to the said curtain, is very much in the style of *glass beads* and *brass tape*—indeed, some of them are rather worse; for these flimsy counterfeits pay their homage to reality, while Mrs. Butler's degrades the glories of nature into specimens of handicraft. (pp. 43-5)

Though her finished pictures are too elaborate, she is very often very successful in a sketch, and creates by a word or two a very lively image—though even in the best of these there is, generally, some mark of the craft—something more striking than natural—some '*glass beads* and *brass tape!*' (pp. 46-7)

[Where does Mrs. Butler] intend to live?—into what society does she expect to be received? She may disguise to *us* the persons she alludes to as Col. ——, and Mr. H——, and Mr. ——, and Mrs. ——, and Dr. ——, and 'his Honour the Recorder,' but they must be all as well known in America by the circumstances, as if she had written their names at full length; and though she says nothing, perhaps, positively discreditable of any of them, we cannot comprehend that her exhibition of their foibles and ridicules, and—even where there is nothing either weak or ridiculous—of the little details of their private life, should not be exceedingly disagreeable—unpardonable we should fear. Who will let a woman into his or her house, who, after spending an evening in the *abandon* and familiarity of private life, sits up half the night to record all the little frivolities she may have witnessed, with the intention of publishing them—as she herself would say—'*ere the shoes were old* in which' she trod their *bespitted* carpets—to the ridicule of Europe, and, what is worse, of the society in which the poor victims live? It is clear she must believe that 'All the world's a stage, and all the men and women *merely* players;' and that the Col. ——, and the Dr. ——, and Mr. ——, will think no more of her ridicule of their manners, than the actor who plays the Duke of Austria does of the revilings of the Lady Constance, when the play is over. This, we are satisfied, must be the explanation of her conduct. She has evidently no particle either of malignity, or even malice, in her composition. She is not satirical, nor even giddy—she writes with premeditation, and piques herself on telling what she believes to be the fearless truth; and she will, we have no doubt, be exceedingly surprised that any one should be so silly and so unreasonable as to resent her freedom of speech. But she will find, we think, that she is mistaken, and that New York or Philadelphia will no more tolerate such a domestic spy and informer, than Edinburgh or even London would do, if she had treated them with the same unpalatable sincerity.

We here end all reference to personal topics, which to our great regret have been forced on us, by the style, the subjects, and, indeed, the very nature of the work—for its essence, and that of any similar journal, must be personality; and if some of our remarks should sound harsh in Mrs. Butler's ears, we must beg her to recollect that she has only herself to blame for observations produced by her *unprecedented* publication, and the bold and challenging style in which she has, as it were, defied all man and woman kind to the field. The remainder of our task is more agreeable—her book (with the drawbacks we have been obliged to notice) is exceedingly clever and full of entertainment. She has a great deal of *naïveté*—a great deal of good humour, and some fun—her observations on national manners are acute and candid—her narrative (when she does not bedizen it with *brass tape*) rapid and lively—and there are many passages, in which she deals with and contrasts the social and political institutions of her own country and those of America, which evince a depth of observation and a soundness of judgment, rare in any one, but wonderful in a person of her age and sex. (pp. 51-2)

In the midst of a discussion of the various styles of writing, in which she expresses her superior admiration of the dignity of what she calls the 'sculptural' to the gaudy oil and canvass style, she suddenly recollects herself, and adds, *'Yet Milton was a sculptor—Shakspeare a painter;'* an illustration, to our tastes, as profound, as striking, as just, as any that we ever remember to have met with. The idea may perhaps not be absolutely new; but it is clear from the context that it is her own, and we at least never before met it *thus* forcibly and justly applied.

We shall abstain from quoting her opinions on the topic of manners, on which our American brethren show so much morbid sensibility, and we very much fear that the occasional, but sly and pungent remarks of Mrs. Butler will not be much more satisfactory at the other side of the Atlantic, than the more direct censure and broader ridicule of Mrs. Trollope, Captain Hall, and Mr. Hamilton. The Americans may and do charge these writers with prejudice and partiality, but Mrs. Butler can have had no predisposition to find fault—no adverse theory to maintain—no political object to advance. It is a subject which she never professedly treats, and unpleasant facts drop from her only incidentally when the course of her [*Journal of F. A. Butler*] forces them from her. Besides, it will be recollected, that, if she has any partiality, it must be supposed to be to the country of her adoption, to which she has united her name and her destiny. We shall not add to the annoyance which we fear her book must occasion her among her new friends, by quoting any of the many piquant passages on this subject which the volumes afford. . . . (p. 52)

There are scattered through the volumes a great many very sensible remarks on the state of society in America, as regards aristocracy and democracy. (p. 54)

Her graver matter Mrs. Butler has in general sequestered from the too colloquial text into separate notes, which are, for the most part, written with great *à plomb* and good sense; and contain remarks . . . on the political state of America—the character and pursuits of the men, and the education and habits of the women—which we can almost, without an exception, recommend even to the gravest reader. . . . (p. 55)

We should be very much mortified, if the views we have taken . . . , should prevent any one from reading this work. We have, we believe, suggested all that can be objected to it, but we have not, and within our limits could not, indicate a hundredth part of the amusement it will afford; above all, we feel that we have given a very inadequate idea of that solid good sense, and those sound principles of social and moral life, which lie at the bottom of the whole work, though they are too often concealed or obscured by the exuberant vegetation of the rank soil and hot sky of the profession with which Mrs. Butler has become so entirely assimilated and so absolutely identified. (p. 58)

[*J. W. Croker*], "Mrs. Butler's 'Journal'," in The Quarterly Review, *Vol. LIV, No. CVII, July, 1835, pp. 39-58.*

QUEEN VICTORIA (diary date 1835)

[*Queen of Great Britain from 1837 to 1901, Victoria kept a diary in her youth in which she recorded her daily activities as well as her opinions of contemporary literature. In the following excerpt from a diary entry dated August 23, 1835, Queen Victoria objects to* Journal of a Residence in America, *which she finds "very pertly and oddly written." The queen apparently later modified her criticism, however, for on September 5, 1835 she noted in her diary that Kemble's journal "amuses me" and added that "there are some very fine feelings in it."*]

After dinner I took up Mrs. Butler's [*Journal of a Residence in America*] and read a little in it. It certainly is very pertly and oddly written. One would imagine by the style that the authoress must be very pert, and not well bred; for there are so many vulgar expressions in it. It is a great pity that a person endowed with so much talent as Mrs. Butler really is, should turn it to so little account and publish a book which is so full of trash and nonsense which can only do her harm. (pp. 128-29)

Queen Victoria, in a diary entry of August 23, 1835, in The Girlhood of Queen Victoria: A Selection from Her Majesty's Diaries Between the Years 1832 and 1840, *Vol. I, edited by Viscount Esher, John Murray, 1912, pp. 128-29.*

FRASER'S MAGAZINE FOR TOWN & COUNTRY (essay date 1835)

[*In this defense of* Journal of a Residence in America, *the critic contends that many journalists who once praised Kemble highly now attack her because her* Journal *contains unkind remarks concerning their profession.*]

There was a time, and it counts not very remote from the present, when Mrs. Butler, then Miss Fanny Kemble, either was or seemed to be an especial favourite with the gentlemen of the press. From day to day, and from week to week, the public was made acquainted with her excellences. Not on the stage alone, but in private society,—not only as an actress, but as a woman, the world had seen nothing at all worthy to be brought into comparison with her since the days when Mrs. Siddons shone forth in the zenith of her glory. If falling short of perfection as a beauty, she had about her a thousand charms infinitely more attractive than beauty. Hers was the form which set all criticism at defiance, hers the features that spoke even when the voice continued mute. And as to her genius, apart from the walk of life to which she had addicted herself, that was abundantly manifested in a drama, than which nothing resembling it for richness of imagery and chastity of expression had, at least in modern times, proceeded from a female pen. Thus was the reading portion of the community entertained with the praises of Miss Fanny Kemble; for her admirers were as numerous as there were dramatic critics connected with the newspaper press, each of whom appeared desirous of surpassing his brother scribes in the extravagance of the eulogies which he heaped upon her.

Under such circumstances, we were a good deal surprised to find that when, about three months ago, her [*Journal of a Residence in America*] made its appearance, Mrs. Butler herself had fallen into utter disfavour with these discriminating judges of other people's deserts. Not satisfied to condemn the book, our friends of the daily and weekly press opened a heavy fire upon the authoress, who was pronounced vulgar, coarse-minded, destitute of all right feeling,—a thorough pretender in the department of letters,—a mere quack as an actress. "This is mighty odd," said we to ourselves; "either Miss Fanny Kemble is not such as she is now represented, or she is. If she be, what are we to think of the men who laboured so assiduously to puff into false importance a person whom they themselves now declare never to have possessed a particle of merit? If she be not, how are we to account for so remarkable a change in their bearing?'' We opened the journal eagerly, and at page 114 of volume the first the followng sentences arrested our attention:—

> We dined at three: after dinner, J—— came; he sat some time. When he was gone, I came into the drawing-room, and found a man sitting with my father, who presented him to me by some inaudible name. I sat down, and the gentleman pursued his conversation as follows:— 'When Clara Fisher came over, Barry wrote to me about her, and I wrote him back word: My dear fellow, if your bella donna is such as you describe, why, we'll see what we can do; we will take her by the hand.' *This was enough for me. I jumped up, and ran out of the room;* BECAUSE A NEWSPAPER-WRITER IS MY AVERSION.

We cannot deny that this bold announcement startled us. We thought it rash, inconsiderate—perhaps ill-judged,—so we went on till we came to page 193, when we were again struck with the lady's audacity.

> A gentleman of the press says she by name——, paid us a visit. [By the way, we don't exactly see the utility of this blank——.] He seems an intelligent young man enough; and when he spoke of the autumnal woods, by the Oneida lake, his expressions were poetical and enthusiastic; and he pleased me. *He seems to think much of having had the honour of corresponding with sundry of the small literati of London. Je lui en fais mon compliment.*

Now this is terrible; but mark, good reader, what follows in a note.

> Except where they have been made political tools, newspaper-writers and editors have never, I believe, been admitted into good society in England.

We read these passages, with several more to the same purport,—and we felt at once that the mystery which had puzzled us when we took up the journal was solved. Mrs. Butler has not only the—what shall we call it—bad taste to dislike the whole tribe of ephemeral critics, but the excessive folly to avow her aversion. No wonder that the thin-skinned gentlemen should be sore. You might as well thrust your naked hand into a hornet's nest, and expect to draw it forth again unstung, as pass sentence of condemnation, no matter how richly deserved, upon ''writers for newspapers,'' under the idea that you shall escape unscathed. (pp. 327-28)

[In] seeking to run this lady down, her assailants only convict themselves of the grossest and most impolitic prejudice. So long as they imagined that she was willing to lean upon them they were willing to do her justice. But no sooner does she fall into the error of avowing that *a newspaper-writer is her aversion,* than the newspaper-writers combine to stultify themselves, by unblushingly retracting commendations with which they had on former occasions overwhelmed her.

The mode which has been adopted for the purpose of accomplishing this end is every way worthy of the end itself, and of those who aim at it. Mrs. Butler's journal has been carefully sifted for passages offensive to good taste; and Mrs. Butler herself has been held up, on the evidence of these, as a woman essentially vulgar in her cast in mind, and depraved in her habits. Now we . . . [admit] that Mrs. Butler's [*Journal of a Residence in America*] is not faultless; there are, on the contrary, expressions here and there which we are surprised that the lady should have ever penned, still more surprised that she should have printed. But, bearing in mind that the work is strictly what it professes to be, a journal—that is to say, the record of private feelings and private impressions, as from day to day they were stirred up and created,—we cannot sufficiently wonder at the malignity of disposition which, omitting all allusion to the general tone of the performance, can drag only its blemishes into the light, and hold them up as fair samples of a book which it was resolved, by fair means or by foul, to stifle. For in point even of quantity, to what do the blemishes amount, as compared with the mass of matter which has at least escaped censure. Out of some six or seven hundred pages, to which the [*Journal of a Residence in America*] extends, there may be ten which a judicious friend, had he been consulted while the work was in manuscript, would have erased. Of the remainder, some may be more, some less, deserving of commendation. It is the nature of a journal to be egotistical; and certainly the general reader is apt to yawn over the details of trimming caps, working at Bible-covers, translating Goethe, and so forth, however deeply the journalist may have been interested in the employment while engaged in it. Still the tendency of the work is so decidedly good, the spirit that breathes through it is so lofty, there is in it so much of pure religion, of sound morality, of unaffected love of country and of veneration for native institutions, that we defy any unprejudiced person to read it without admitting, when he lays it aside, that if he has not added much to his stock of information respecting American men and manners, he has at least held communion with a mind essentially noble. Nor is this all. Mrs. Butler's remarks and criticisms, if sometimes rough, are always just. (pp. 329-30)

Far be it from us to deny that in the [*Journal of a Residence in America*] there is a good deal to grow weary upon, something to censure, and here and there a passage to condemn. But we end as we began, by declaring that the spirit of the book is excellent; and that the galled ''newspaper-writers,'' in their efforts to run it down, only convict themselves of the grossest want of candour—the most magnanimous disregard to truth and consistency. (p. 337)

> *''Miss Fanny Kemble and Her Critics,'' in* Fraser's Magazine for Town & Country, *Vol. XII, No. LXIX, September, 1835, pp. 327-37.*

FANNY KEMBLE IN AMERICA (essay date 1835)

[*Among the irate American responses to* Journal of a Residence in America *was a pamphlet purportedly written by ''an English lady, four years resident in the United States.'' In the following excerpt from this work, the critic satirically assaults both the* Journal *and Kemble personally.*]

The art of book-making, or of weaving materials for a new title page, is so well known in the old country, and so extensively practised by the would-be witlings crowding round the public press, that I might spare myself the pains of recurring to its notoriety, if it was equally well known on the continent of America.

While it remained, however, a harmless occupation, and employed itself in manufacturing voyages performed in the dark circle of a Grub street attic; or in the fabrication of travels and adventures, spun in the miserable area of the three cornered closet; it might be allowed to pass its ordeal, in public opinion, without exciting the severity of criticism. And if the book became tolerated, it might, in the harmlessness of its intentions, be permitted to continue its uninterrupted course, and reward the needy adventurer, in such species of literature, with the scanty dinner which it was written to procure. But when it leaves its old and time worn track, as no longer profitable, and, in the boldness of its daring, assumes a new mode of raising the 'necessary supplies,' by dipping the pen in gall, retailing the thrice told slander, and in fabricating more; it becomes our duty to expose the fraud, and stigmatize the offender.

Basil Hall, the travelling captain, not very celebrated for his veraciousness on any subject; Feron, the gin seller on Holburn Hill, whose shop is the daily resort of all the dissolute of the British metropolis; Mrs. Trollope, the chaste and delicate friend of Fanny Wright; the Rev. Mr. Fidler, the refugee, who, failing in his pursuits at home—as one disqualified—sought shelter in the States, to educate, to improve, and to adorn—and who, failing there, looked to indemnify himself by the malignancy of his pen, and the vulgar flippancy of his clerical wit;—each have written a book on that never failing theme, the manners and customs of the Americans, and each has received the reward of his labors in the thriving trade of slander, and malevolent misrepresentation.

Several of the smaller tribe have followed the harvestings of these veracious and disinterested personages, who have contented themselves with the mere gleanings of the abundant field: and among the last, though not the least, is to be classed Mrs. FRANCES ANNE BUTLER, according to the title page of her [*Journal of a Residence in America*]; but I see no reason why we should forget her identity with FANNY KEMBLE, the actress; and in speaking of her work I shall deal with her in her maiden name—thus endeavoring to show my respect to the several members of that honorable family into which she has been introduced, and with which she has become allied.

I feel that I have no right to enter the sanctuary of private life; and Mrs. Butler, as Mrs. Butler, is unknown to the world but by the journal now before us. As Fanny Kemble, however, from the moment she put her foot on the boards of a theatre, she became public property, as far as public opinion went; and we claim the right of stricture on her journal, her manners, and her morals, in the same degree as she has thought proper, although without the same pretensions, to exercise in the case of the manners and the morals of the Americans.

The love of slander is unhappily like the love of idleness—the polluted source from whence it springs—too prevalent; and hence such works as the journal of Fanny Kemble. These books are seized with avidity in the old world, and with not much less of relish in the new. Praise may beget pleasure, but censure insures the deepest interest, and hence the most extensive demand. So the restaurateur, by the peculiar piquancy of his stores, obtains the larger share of customers to his refectory; and he or she is indeed but a shallow book-maker, who will not profit by the same experience. But when we consider the end—that is, money making—we should also consider the means employed; and I see no reason why the public slanderer should be any more sheltered from public obloquy and scorn, than the public robber. (pp. 3-5)

In taking up my pen, in examination of the journal of the actress; and in my feeble attempt at delineating American character, as it has appeared to my judgment; I am not influenced by any considerations of a private nature. I have lived too long in America, I have mixed too much with society, to fear the expression of my mind, or the utterance of my opinions. I have never found myself restrained in the liberty of speech; and if I have never found my name adorning a title page, it is because I have had as little confidence in my own powers, as inclination for the idle trade, and perhaps less of time to abstract from the inalienable claims of my husband and my children. But as an English woman, and a resident in America, in default of an abler pen, I have felt it an imperative duty, to deny that the journal of Fanny Kemble, so far as relates to manners in America, is conceived in common candor, or with common honesty, even with the bias of prejudice on its side. I also feel it not less my duty to defend my fair countrywomen, in their purity, from the opinion which may be formed of their worth, taking Fanny Kemble as a woman in their resemblance. (p. 5)

I know not in what society Fanny Kemble may have moved; but if I am to judge by popular report, more than by her own journal, I should imagine that good society had been opened to her; but if it was not to her taste, that ought not to operate in its discommendation. There is an essential difference in taste; and the delicate manners of private life, I can easily imagine, are in as little accordance with the taste of a public performer, as the forward demeanor and presuming airs of an exhibitionist, are to the retiring deportment of a lady in private life.

The Americans, in their eagerness of patronage, in their ambition to promote the arts in their own country, are, unhappily, too much in the habit of forgetting what is due to themselves, and to their own dignity. This is a fault, and a great one. . . . (p. 6)

This fault has unhappily existed to a great extent, and has, most unhappily, been assiduously encouraged by those who have found it their interest to misrepresent the state of society at home. The Americans, in the natural warmth of their ardent disposition; unwilling that their hospitality should be questioned; believing that the talented of the stage are fostered and caressed in private circles at home; dazzled by the glare of a great name wafted across the Atlantic by newspaper writers and play-goers; and not at all familiar with that exquisite art of puffing, by which the pretender is inflated into popular notice, (but which art, by the way, has long lost its influence on the other side of the water); too frequently lead themselves away in their eagerness to commend, and yield themselves voluntarily to an association with persons not at all qualified for their private circles, and who, under other circumstances, could never have obtained an *entre* beyond the green room of the theatre—the only congenial atmosphere they may be said to breathe. (pp. 6-7)

It may be advanced that we are too sweeping in our censure; that there are many estimable characters on the stage; and that Fanny Kemble herself, in private life, is one of its brightest ornaments. In this we mean not to impugn her; but virtue, mere female virtue, undignified by that peculiar delicacy which is the sovereign charm of woman, while it is to be prized, is not of that chastened nature to win us to its love; and the profession of an actor, in its very range, is one, only to be sustained by the sacrifice of all those charms that lend to virtue brightness.

I have said, I know not in what society Fanny Kemble may have moved; but of this I am sure—the circle from which she has gleaned her knowledge of manners in America, is so limited in its extent, that its existence is almost unknown to the country in which it draws its vital air. She may have drawn her picture faithfully—she may have limned it in all its proportions; for we know of no country where vice is not to be found, where immorality does not vegetate, and where coarseness and vulgarity of manners are not to be met with. But it remains with those who basked in the sunshine of Fanny's rays—it remains with those who were attracted to her orbit, to vindicate themselves. I cannot fight with shadows; I cannot aim an effective blow at the mere monster of imagination; I know nothing of his existence, and cannot detect him in the 'Mr. D—'s,' 'Mr. H—'s,' and the 'Mr. B—'s,' and the 'Mr. J—'s,' crowding the pages of the journal.

But if there is one, who has unfortunately been led, by the love of novelty, into this degenerate circle, and should there happily be anything left of self-esteem, the blush of shame must mantle on the cheek, with a poignant sense of past humiliation and present retribution: for it cannot be denied that Fanny has taken ample vengeance of those who have been allured by her smiles, who have been fascinated by her acting, both on and off the stage, and have wantoned in the meridian of her studied playfulness.

If there is one who has been involuntarily led into this circle, guided by the popular expression of applause, that applause which was merely extended to the actress, in the discharge of her professional duties, and for the exercise of which she was brought to America, and for which she has been amply, abundantly, remunerated in American money; if there is one who has been attracted to her by the panegyrics of hired scribblers, the laudatory strains of dependent parasites, the paid menials of the diurnal press;—I say, if there is one—and I believe there are many—who have waived prudent consideration in inconsiderate zeal—he, or rather the many, will deplore the want of caution they have displayed in their forwardness of patronage; and, furnished with the lesson which this person has taught them, be very little prone to relapse into the same error on any future occasion. They will feel the force and truth of the fable of the frozen serpent—that they have fostered into life the reptile, which, coiling its fascinating folds around the bosom that had sheltered it, fixes its envenomed teeth in the hand that had fed it. They will feel this in all the fulness of its practical illustration.

The journal of Fanny Kemble is perhaps the most extraordinary publication that ever was permitted to proceed from the press. It is difficult to conceive that it has been produced in mere prejudice, for it riots in the imaginative of all sorts. It has carefully gleaned the often repeated slanders of a Hall, a Feron, a Trollope, a Hamilton, and a Fidler; and in their union, aided by a fertile fancy, it outsteps them all. It is difficult to imagine the state of that mind which has given it birth, and committed, from day to day, so gross a tissue of false impressions and wilful misrepresentation. But it is more difficult to comprehend the mind itself, in its structure, which could so powerfully mask itself in communion with the inartificial society into which she had been introduced; and could, with so many blandishments, and so much of grace and pleased demeanor, reveal itself in the treasured pages of her journal, to be published, forsooth, when a fitting time occurred. This indeed was acting, and with something more than machievalian skill. Whatever doubts may have been entertained, or opinions formed, of Fanny Kemble ON the stage, OFF the boards of a theatre, in the great theatre of life, she has indeed proved herself inimitable.

In the delivery of my opinions, in a language perhaps more forcible than it may be by some considered the case can justify, I must beg to acquit myself of any personal ill feeling towards the actress herself. I have none. I am free to admit that the profession of the stage is not one at all to my taste, and that its professors are not sufficiently in my regard to admit them as the associates of my children. I am a mother; and I claim and exercise a mother's right over their mind and morals. I never could be brought to believe that an actress, however estimable in herself, could, in the discharge of those duties on which her success depends—duties demanding the total sacrifice of feminine delicacy, the life, the grace, the charm of woman—I repeat, I never could believe them endowed with *one* of those traits of character, rendering them the fit associates of the private circle. I may be singular in this opinion, but it has and will continue to influence my conduct. If I have ever wavered, the journal of Fanny Kemble has dismissed the doubts, and confirmed me in the resolution of that reserve which I have hitherto maintained, and which I may be said to have inherited from the country of my birth.

Of the journal itself, I know it may be truly said, it is wholly unworthy of especial notice; and that such is the opinion of the most intelligent of its readers, will scarcely admit of a question. I know that 'to break a fly upon the wheel,' is not more unmerciful than unnecessary; but I am an English woman, and if *only one* American could believe a Trollope or a Kemble, as belonging to that estimable class, the ladies of my country, that fact alone would justify me in the course I am pursuing. Let Fanny Kemble stand alone; let her be judged alone, and out of her own lips.

I pass over the mawkish sensibility with which she apostrophizes 'her English flowers, her dear English flowers,' and have no objection to her journalizing the progress she makes in her Bible cover, but perhaps a little more to her expressed admiration of *Childe Harold*—a work which in my happy country is not over-prudishly considered as unfit for a lady's reading.

We glean a little more, however, of the censor on American manners, as we proceed: we are not much *ecstacised,* to use her own expression, in her remark on *flimsy morality,* and begin to doubt the propriety of her deportment in mixing with a party, 'dancing, singing, and romping like mad things, on the quarter deck.' She says,

> It was Saturday holyday on board ship; the men were all dismissed to their grog. We of the petticoats adjourned to the gentlemen's cabin, to drink "Sweethearts and Wives," according to the approved sailor's practice.

From this we should be naturally led to infer that the journalist was not a member of a temperance society, to say the least. She continues—

> It made me sad to hear them, as they lifted their glasses to their lips, pass round the toast "Sweethearts and Wives." I drank, in my heart, home and dear H.—

She concludes this bacchanalian scene—one, to which we believe a lady, English or American, is very little accustomed—with the following remark, which I extract without comment:

> They sang a song or two, and at *twelve* we left them to their meditations, which presently reached our ears in the sound, not shape, of "Health to Bacchus," in full chorus, *to which tune I said my prayers.*

The following day was the Sabbath. She says,—'I breakfasted, and then amused myself with finding the lessons, collects, and psalms for the whole ship's company.' She expatiates prettily on the sublime effect of prayers offered up at sea.

> The bright, cloudless sky and glorious sea seemed to respond, in their silent magnificence, to our Te Deum. I felt more of the excitement of prayer than I have known for many a day, and 't was good, oh very good! **** After prayers, wrote journal.

And then she concludes her Sabbath, after expressing herself in a vein which would do honor to her feelings, if they were so excited, according to the following chilling sentence, by an act of the highest indelicacy:

> Came back to our gipsy encampment, where, by the light of a lantern, we supped, and *sang sundry scraps of old songs.* At ten came to bed.

We have another Saturday night's exhibition.

> Lord bless us! What foul nonsense people do talk, and what much fouler nonsense it is to answer them! Got very sick, and *lay on the ground* till dinner time; went to table, but withdrew again, while it was yet in my power to do so gracefully. *Lay on the floor* all the evening, singing for very sea sickness. Suddenly it occurred to me that it was our last Saturday night on board; whereupon I indited a song, to the tune of "To Ladies' eyes around Boys," and having duly instructed Mr.— "how to speak the speech," we went to supper. Mr.— sung my song, and kept my secret: the song was encored, and my father *innocently* demanded the author. I gave him a tremendous pinch, and looked very silly.—(Poor, innocent, retiring creature!)—Merit, like murder, will out; so I fancy that when they drank the health of the author, the whole table was aware of the genius that sat among them. Came to bed at about half past twelve.

(pp. 8-12)

There is something singularly novel in a modern female bard of song, presiding at a bacchanalian board, joining in the shout and hurra of excited tipplers, and handing glasses round. But Fanny is speaking for herself—I will not interrupt her. I make no comment, but my readers may. Still I must enter my protest against the opinion, that anything in the shape of an English lady would or could have been so seen.

These are the night orgies of a coming Sabbath! consequently we find Fanny, having shaken her tresses in the morning, again engaged in 'tidying the cabin for prayers,' and 'looking out the lessons.' She also 'wrote journal,' and 'spent some time in seeing a couple of geese take a swim with strings tied to their legs. After dinner, sat in my cabin some time; walked on deck; when the gentlemen joined us, *we danced the sun down and the moon up*.' But this is not all. This was to be the last Sunday on ship-board; and after the dance, on the evening of the day of prayer,—but take it from Fanny's journal:

> The sky was like the jewel shop of angels; I never saw such brilliant stars, nor so deep an azure to hang them in. The moon was grown powerful, and flooded the deck where we sat

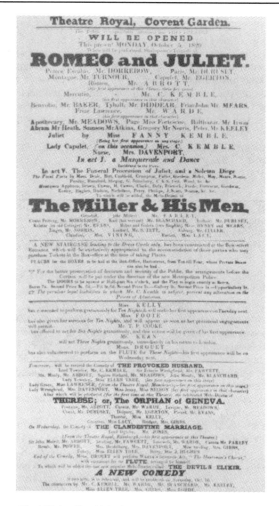

Playbill for Kemble's first performance as an actress.

> *playing at blinds man's buff, magic music, and singing and talking of shore,* till midnight— when we came to bed.

These extracts, selected from pages of rhapsody, wild without much beauty; rambling through politics and religion; wandering through the shallow mazes of poetry and philosophy, shallow only in the channel in which they flowed; will exhibit the singular mind of the intellectual Fanny, and that peculiar delicacy and refinement of sentiment, qualifying her to become the censor of the morals and the manners of the people among whom she was going for a time to sojourn.

I have no opportunity of getting at the context of this journal; but what I have extracted, has been written by herself, and of herself. And surely, it will not be denied, we could not possibly obtain a better evidence of her manners and deportment. A lady!—why, a lady's maid, or a washer-woman, proverbial for vulgarity, or the chamber maid at a public inn, even in her shamelessness, would have been ashamed of the public confession of her night broils, and would never have dared to join in the dance or blind man's buff, on the Sabbath eve. And this is the person to write a book, and scare the immoral in America! this is the woman who, by the impurity of her own example, is to check the current of immorality in others! Check—it can scarcely be called checking, to reduce to her own standard!

I might have extracted much more from this part of her exquisite journal—breathing at times the most tender sensibility, professing but without practising, and always at variance with itself. But I trust I have done enough to show from her own pen, that—to speak of her in the mildest terms we can command—she was more masculine than feminine in her nature, and wholly deficient in that chastened delicacy of conduct, which can alone give a charm to woman, even in her beauty.

The scene changes. She arrives in New-York, a candidate for public favor—the lion of the day—her den, the stage of the Park theatre. The press, in the old and the new world, had paved the way for her reception; and in the excitement, it was natural to suppose she would have many introductions to fashionable amateurs and lovers of the drama. (pp. 13-14)

A great deal of slip-slop follows; a great deal of the affectation of refinement, of abuse and ill feeling. She views New-York with a prejudice which could have been produced only by communion with a Trollope herself. But the impertinence of the following passage—the impertinence, to say the least of it—can scarcely be exceeded, and is not paralleled in the libels of any one of the junta of writers on American manners:

> I do not know how it is to be accounted for, but in spite of much lighter duties, every article of dress, particularly silks, embroideries, and all French manufactures, are more expensive here than in England. The extravagance of the American women, in this part of their expenditure, is, considering the average fortunes of this country, quite extraordinary. They never walk in the streets but in the most showy and extreme toilette; and I have known twenty, forty, and sixty dollars paid for a bonnet to wear in a morning saunter up Broadway.

But, by the bye, this extract, properly read, will show at one glance, how very little Fanny Kemble is familiar with the *haut ton* in London. The Broadway is the fashionable promenade of the *belles* of New-York, in the same degree as Bond street or Regent street is of the fashionables of the metropolis. Nothing can exceed the profusion or costliness of dress, as exhibited in the fashionable season, in these streets; but impertinence has never yet inquired into the means by which that profusion has been sustained. (pp. 15-16)

Now listen to Fanny:

> These people are happy—their wants are satisfied, their desires fulfilled—their capacities of enjoyment meet with full employment—they are well fed, well clothed, well housed. Moderate labor ensures them all this, and leaves them leisure for such recreations as they are capable of enjoying. But HOW IS IT WITH ME? and I mean not *me myself* alone, but all who, LIKE MYSELF, have received a HIGHER DEGREE OF INTELLECTUAL CULTIVATION, whose estimate of happiness is therefore so much higher, whose capacity for enjoyment is so much more expanded and cultivated. CAN I be satisfied with a race in a circular rail-road car, or a swing between the line trees?

This is truly great. I could laugh, as Fanny says, into very fits; for I cannot forget, for the life of me, the *intellectual* game of blind man's buff, on the deck of the Pacific, &c. &c. But

Fanny is now in one of her musing moods, and we must even let her proceed.

> Where are my peculiar objects of pleasure and recreation? Where are the picture galleries—(Has Fanny ever seen Peter Parley's Picture magazine?)—the sculptures—the works of art and science—the countless wonders of human ingenuity and skill—the cultivated and refined society—the intercourse with men—(Oh fie, Fanny!)—of genius, literature, scientific knowledge—where are all the sources from which I am to draw my recreations? They are not.

Oh dire calamity—unutterable woe! Fanny says, they are not! Sad, sad truth! How tenderly do I feel for her! No pictures—no sculpture—nothing, nothing but that boorish thing, content, which *a high degree of mental cultivation* would naturally feel ashamed of; nothing—nothing, but the good humor and smiling faces, indicative of a half civilized state of society; a state which the poetry of the mind sentimental cordially abhors. Poor Fanny!—but she pursues the delicate strain of intellectual refinement in a higher tone of philosophy, as follows:

> The heart of a philanthropist may indeed be satisfied, but the intellectual man feels a dearth that is inexpressibly painful; and in spite of the real and great pleasure which I derived from the sight of so much enjoyment, I could not help desiring that enjoyment of another order were combined with it. Perhaps the two are incompatible; if so, I would not alter the present state of things if I could.

Amiable, sympathizing journalist! we cannot but condole with thee, in thy etherial nature, and thy sad condition, toiling thy weary way with such unphilosophical things as these unintellectual Americans; who cannot comprehend the sweets of melancholy—who know nothing of the imaginative properties of the sublimated mind; but who, in the grossness of their appetite for vulgar enjoyments, court the shades of Hoboken for recreation and ruder health—or float in steamers on the Hudson—or in some rail-road car, darting with the rapidity of the wind, fly from the summer sun's meridian ray, to some retreat long favored, some love whispering shade or woodland height—or where the glassy stream, springing from the bosom of a lake, sweeps its wild course along the rocky ledge, and falls with impetuous roar into some deep abyss below;—this, this is freedom:—wild as nature's self, the poor American pants for its enjoyment. And I really think, my dear Fanny, we had better leave them to their irrational enjoyments. These are *their* pictures. Nature has sculptured their wild rocks entirely to *their* taste; and I believe it would be quite impossible to amalgamate your etherialized nature with their more earthly substance! Poor Fanny! (pp. 17-19)

The stage is Fanny's home. From the stage she draws all her sentimentality—all her fine and chastened feelings—all her exquisite sensitiveness of decency and decorum. She expatiates fluently on American manners; and as an example of the school in which she has been taught, I will favor my reader with the following extract from the journal of the admirer of 'blind man's buff,' and 'magic music,' on the ship's deck.

> In the parting scene—oh what a scene it was!—instead of going away from me when he said "Farewell forever," he stuck to my skirts,

though in the same breath that I adjured him, in the words of my part, *not* to leave me, I added, aside, "Get away from me, oh *do*." When I exclaimed, "Not one kiss at parting," he kept embracing and kissing me like mad; and when I ought to have been pursuing him, and calling after him, "Leave thy dagger with me," he hung himself up against the wing, and remained dangling there for five minutes. I was half crazy! and the good people sat and swallowed it all. They deserved it—by my troth they did. I prompted him constantly; and once, after struggling in vain to free myself from him, was obliged, in the middle of my part, to exclaim—"You hurt me dreadfully, Mr. Kepple." He clung to me—cramped me—crumpled me dreadfully, &c. &c. to the end of the chapter.

Now I ask, is it possible to contemplate such a scene as this, without our expressing the strongest feelings of disgust for a profession, which is to be publicly sustained by the exhibition of so much of licentiousness? Can we entertain a respectful opinion of a female, so devoid of good taste, as to blazon forth in the pages of her journal, a passage so devoid of all interest, and only to be noticed in its grossness? (p. 21)

Fanny sips the sweets of every flower, and stores her prodigious mind with gleanings of every sort. She astonishes us with the extent of her erudition.

On CHEMISTRY, she is a Sir Humphrey Davy in petticoats.

In PHILOSOPHY, she could read a lecture that would astound a Newton, a Bacon, or a Boyle.

In BELLES LETTRES, she would demonstrate the incapacity of a Blair.

In RELIGION, she is prepared to affirm the truths of Pagan theology, and to prove that Mahomet was no impostor.

In MORALS, she refutes Gisborne, Paley, and Porteus; and establishes the creed of a Byron, a Farquhar, a Shelley, and a Moore; and proves to demonstration that all the rest is 'humbug!'

In OPTICS, she would dazzle a Brewster; and satisfactorily proves that it is only a visular defect, by which we fancy we see the difference between a mountain and a mole-hill; and by a peculiarly felicitous figure of speech, she demonstrates it—by sinking the mountain to the mole-hill, and elevating the mole-hill to the mountain.

In GEOLOGY, she establishes a new doctrine—one entirely her own—by which she can discern the antiquity of America, from the *venerable* wrinkles on its face.

In NAVIGATION, she is nothing deficient.

On ATTRACTION, she is profound; and in her own surprising success, she fully establishes the perfectability of her system. She draws an essential distinction betweeen attraction and gravitation, and deduces the latter by numerous prostrations on the floor!

In POETRY, she excells—HERSELF!

In DRAMA, she proves that Shakspeare is only secondary to the author of *Francis the First*, and infinitely superior to all other writers.

In ACTING, she never mentions an O'Niel; and admits that her paternal aunt Siddons may have approached to her own excellence.

The MECHANIC, is a vulgar art, to which neither herself or her family have any pretensions; and altogether *sinks* her maternal grandfather, who was so well known as a theatrical barber.

In BOTANY, she is learned as Linnæus; and, we are told, has actually lectured on vegetable medicine to the profound founder of the Thomsonian school of physic, and Drs. Morrison and Moat, who have obtained their diplomas from the college of her foundation; and no other.

In LINGUISTRY, she is a travelling lexicon; and is about to publish a commentary on Dr. Johnson and Webster's dictionaries, with numerous corrections and additions, and an essay on 'hum-bugging!'

In RIDING, HUNTING, and in FARRIERY, Fanny is perfectly unrivalled—either by Gambado on horsemanship, Beckford, in his treatise on hunting, or Taplin, in his compendium of farriery. (pp. 27-8)

[I find Fanny] getting into tolerable good humor with the Philadelphian press. A gentleman connected with one of the journals, calls, and she says, 'He pleased me.' This mood leads her to the following passage, in a note, penned in compliment to the 'intelligent young man:'

> Except where they have been made political tools, newspaper writers and editors have never, I believe, been admitted into good society in England. It is otherwise here; newspapers are the main literature of America; and I have frequently heard it quoted, as a proof of a man's abilities, that he writes in such and such a newspaper.

Fanny, I am ashamed of you! I am ashamed of you, I say again. What!—could you not pay a compliment to this 'intelligent young man,' without disparaging the rank and condition of his brethren in the old country? 'By my troth,' Fanny—and I feel my wrath rising again—I feel ashamed of you.

When I took up your journal, I was very angry. As I proceeded, I waxed a little cooler and better tempered; and so I progressed, until at length I sat myself down quite tranquil and easy, and—but now I feel my choler rising at your ingratitude, which I call base.

Let me ask you, Fanny, where would you have been now, if it had not been for these 'penny a liners,' as they are facetiously called at home? (pp. 31-2)

The same diurnalists who had trumpeted forth your praises in England, who had elevated you to a station to which you was not only unequal, but of which, I greatly fear, you was wholly undeserving, served your cause also in America. Their elaborate praise had passed the broad waters of the Atlantic, and you followed, ere the sounds began to fade away.

You arrived. You was generously, warmly, enthusiastically received; not more for your histrionic art, than for the numerous virtues you were said to possess. Play-goers were delighted in the prospect of seeing what is termed, the legitimate drama performed with legitimate effect; while the great and good, in the benevolence of their nature, were warmed to believe that even the stage could show virtue, moral excellence, and the refinement of intellect and delicacy, combined.

I know of many persons, tempted to the boxes of the theatre to witness your performances, whom no other circumstances could attract to its threshold. They united in their patronage of you; all, all united; and I think you must admit, you made more money among them, than you did at home. To be sure, you will say, you earned it. Well, perhaps you did; but for my part, I must disagree with you. Upon my word, Fanny—and I say it with the greatest respect for your feelings—I cannot believe that a piece of base metal made to resemble a dollar, although it may pass current for a dollar, is a dollar, after all; and indeed, I am so stupidly blind to conviction, that I shall continue to be of the same opinion, in spite of all argument.

Now you know, my dear Fanny, if *your* dollars were not of a sterling quality, (you understand my meaning,) theirs were; and it seems to be straining the point rather severely, when you pocket their money abundantly, in the first instance, and then charge them two dollars extra, to laugh at their credulity in your journal, in the second. Some persons might be illiberal enough to think this not exactly fair; for myself, I abstain from offering my opinion. It is but a question of dollars, after all; and you, my dear Fanny, have them fast enough in your good keeping, and I doubt not, know well how to take care of them. (pp. 34-5)

After the preceding pages were written, and while I was yet pursuing the thread of my inquiry, a report reached my ears—of the authority of which I could entertain no doubt, from the very respectable quarter whence it was derived, and as it has since been fully confirmed, I shall give it to the reader substantially as I received it. I need not add, it immediately put an end to my labors.

On Saturday, the 2d day of May, in the 24th year of her age, at the printing office of Cary, Lea and Blanchard, Booksellers, Chesnut Street, Philadelphia, died the incomparable Fanny, surviving the death of her favorite child, her journal, only a few days.

This highly gifted lady, no less distinguished as a poet, a painter, a musician, a philosopher, a phrenologist,—no less in metaphysics, theology, and in practical and experimental chemistry, than in the useful arts,—in farriery, pharmacy and gymnastics; will be lamented so long as the record of her extraordinary powers shall remain, and gratitude for the tender interest she took in reforming the manners of society in America shall be felt. Liberal in her opinions, sound and unbiassed in her judgment, she viewed the world as formed for herself alone, and would have moulded it to her own likeness; knowing in the purity of her own heart, and in that inherent modesty which characterized her own public and private deportment, that it was good; that it was the point to which excellence may attain, and no higher.

She had been for some time drooping, and it was feared while correcting the proof sheets of her journal she would produce an abortion, and that her own most valuable life would prove the sacrifice. The event has justified the apprehension.

The following Elegy, *said* to be from the pen of an ardent admirer, has not yet we believe appeared in print: we give it as an elegant compliment to the memory of the deceased.

ELEGY ON FANNY.

Closed is the scene—the eventful Drama o'er,—
The curtain falls, and she is heard no more;
The bowl is drained, the dagger flown,
The zest of all the *Ton* in town,

And that sweet form by Keppel *rumpled*,
In Death's stern grasp is rudely *crumpled*.
Ah me! the tearful muse in vain
Woos back her tragic child again;
The Drama on her crutch appears,
Nor hopes to lengthen out her years:
And Trollope weeps, and Basil Hall,
The journalists—decline and fall.
Sad—oh most sad! the monster's got
The child of art—and she 'is not.'
Sad, that the tyrant could not spare
A wit so shrewd, a lass so fair,
Pattern of modest worth and grace,
Last of the regal Kemble race!
　　Who now th' unbroken grey shall ride,
Or musing, on the Schuylkill glide?
Or who shall ever taste again
The sparkling, creaming, bright champaigne—
Nor fail to shed one sorrowing tear
For one who loved it?—ah! how dear!
Fanny, farewell; your race is run—
Your journal's finished with your own:
But, ruthless monster, was it kind,
To leave *no* trace of her behind?
Armed by the cynic critic's wroth,
At one fell blow to level both?
Fanny, 'tis pity, pity 't is, 't is true;
Death has dealt harshly with your book and you.

EPITAPH.

BY AN UNKNOWN HAND.

Here lies one who—*never lied!*
　Save *'prostrate on the floor;'*
So *lying* lived—she *lying* died;
　And lies—to rise no more.

(pp. 46-8)

From Fanny Kemble in America; or, The Journal of an Actress Reviewed, *Light & Horton, 1835, 48 p.*

FRASER'S MAGAZINE FOR TOWN & COUNTRY **(essay date 1837)**

[*While admitting Kemble's "considerable talents," the critic censures* The Star of Seville *for vulgarity and inanity.*]

The ***Star of Seville*** is a contribution to modern dramatic literature from the pen of Mrs. Butler, some years ago Miss Fanny Kemble. . . . She here, after a considerable interval, appears before us in the fulness of womanly developement; and we shall frankly say how far she appears to us to have realised her maiden promise. . . . [The *Star of Seville*] is a most silly "play-thing,"—very dull, vapid, and insufferably vulgar. By the word "vulgar" we here convey no imputation against the kid gloves, or studied courtesies, or the personal habits or tastes of Mrs. Butler,—for of all these high matters we know nothing whatsoever: what we mean to say is, that most of her thoughts are commonplace, and many of her expressions coarse and unfeminine. This we should, perhaps, attribute to her residence in the uncivilised region from which she has just returned. But, surely, the authoress does not suppose that such Americanism of spirit can be neutralised by the mere obsolete English phrases which she scatters at hap-hazard throughout her works. In the [***Journal of a Residence in America***], we met with "quotha!" "by my two troths!" "bones of me!" &c. &c., at almost every page. And in this *Star of Seville,* there is no end of such exclamations as "marry!" "a murrain!" "by my fay!" "oons!" "lo you, now!" &c., which, as employed by this writer, have the appearance of being made to do duty in the absence of power, or thought of any kind. But it is not in *expressions* only that we trace the vulgarity of this lady's writing. She has no true elevation of soul—no moral greatness, in her views of men and things. In descriptions of American scenery she is often eloquent; and she quizzes the social peculiarities of the people with considerable humour, though this is of a masculine order. But she gives no evidence of that genial humanity which almost always accompanies true genius. The *parvenu* is eternally visible through the flimsy veil of theatrical affectation, as to the philosophy of life, and so forth. (p. 186)

[Poverty] of spirit and vulgarity of moral estimate we take to be fatal to attempts in the higher walk of dramatic writing. An all-sympathising soul is essential to the success of any such endeavour. Egotism, speaking almost the self-same language through some half-score of different characters, may be very smart reading; but it is not dramatic writing, and is, of course, not presentable on the stage. For this reason, writers of such dramas, from Byron downwards, take care to assure us either that they do not wish their plays to be acted at all, or that, if acted, their success or failure is a matter of indifference. Whether the *Star of Seville* was intended to glorify the stage, or to glimmer in the closet, we know not. It is in every respect a miserable affair. (p. 187)

It is wonderful how besetting a fancy some fair writers have for describing drinking-bouts, in the very last stage of the debauch. That they should write nonsense upon such a subject is as creditable to the inexperience of their sex as the attempt to write at all about it is a departure from feminine delicacy. (p. 188)

[The] next time [Mrs. Butler] wishes for a few lines of defiance against the morning to justify one bottle more, we shall have much pleasure in presenting her with something better than her "Hey down, my bully boys bold!" This jaw-breaking alliteration is not the most singular of the queer phrases which in Mrs. Butler's drama pass for bachelor-phraseology. . . . [We] find the following:—

> *Hyacinth.* I do protest unto you there be now
> three honourable virgins, two honest wives, and
> five chaste widows, all at this very hour sick
> in love with me.
>
> *Valentine.* O, this flogs Europe.

The usual phrase is in England, "that beats cock-fighting!" in Ireland, "that bangs Bannagher!" and so forth. "Flogs Europe!" is an expression to be used only by the late commander of the British Legion. . . . [A] coxcomb lover is requested by the lady to be seated. He answers, that "truly it is a more manly exercise to stand than to sit,—*sitting being essentially the posture of hens.*" . . . Hyacinth instructs his man Sancho to speak of him thus. "Ay, marry! he's a gallant that owns this mantle; the ladies mightily affect him:" to which Sancho answers, "Infect him." (pp. 188-89)

Sometimes we stumble on an odd simile. For instance, Don Pedro's solitariness, after his sister's marriage, is thus anticipated by the latter:—

> *Estrella.* I think he'll be as lonely as a bird
> Without its mate, sad as a silent feast,
> *Single as a stray glove, and all as purposeless.*

And after Pedro's murder Estrella exclaims,—

> His eyes dim, lightless jellies! his *kind voice*
> A tongueless bell.

This last is well intended; but it is nonsense. . . .

[We] make our bow to the *Star of Seville.* It contains abundant proof that Mrs. Butler cannot write a drama; it furnishes evidence equally conclusive that she possesses very considerable talents. What she is destined to do best we do not feel entitled, or called on, to anticipate. But the best thing she has yet done is undoubtedly her [*Journal of a Residence in America*]. She has an eye for scenery, and sketches it with a bold, fearless, yet discriminating hand. Her disquisitions, political and social, are, it is true, womanish and superficial; but throughout her work she evinces an observing and self-relying mind, which, with her opportunities and talents, might be employed to much better purpose than in concocting such playthings as that which we have been just considering. (p. 190)

> *"Three Play-Things,"* in Fraser's Magazine for Town & Country, *Vol. XVI, No. XCII, August, 1837, pp. 179-94.*

PHILIP HONE   (diary date 1838)

[*A nineteenth-century American businessman, Hone is remembered today for his diary, a portrait of life in the New York of his day. Hone became acquainted with Kemble and her father in New York, where the two were dinner guests at his home. Kemble described this evening—in terms rather unflattering to her host—in her* Journal of a Residence in America. *In 1838, Hone and Kemble met again socially for the first time since the* Journal's *publication three years earlier; in an excerpt from his diary, Hone describes their encounter.*]

We had a very pleasant ball this evening. I had an interesting conversation with Mrs. Butler, the late Fanny Kemble, who is here with her husband and two little daughters.

This lady, whom I greatly admired when she arrived in this country with her distinguished father, Charles Kemble, has seldom visited New York since the publication of her [*Journal of a Residence in America*], in which she took some foolish liberties with me and my family and others of whose hospitality she had partaken. I was never seriously offended at what she said in this book, but viewed it "more in sorrow than in anger," for I thought it a pity that a woman so brilliant and talented, who was capable of better things, should have compromised her literary reputation by giving to the world the result of her inconsiderate, girlish remarks upon the daily events which amused her excitable and lively imagination, when I knew her talents were worthy of better employment. This, then, was the first time we had met, and she felt doubtful about what I might consider our relative positions. As soon as she entered the room I seated myself at her side, told her I was happy to renew our acquaintance, the recollection of which had always given me great pleasure, and danced with her. In the course of our conservation she said to me with great earnestness and solemnity, and much agitated: "Mr. Hone, I cannot express to you how happy you have made me by the notice you have taken of me on this occasion. Believe me, I am extremely grateful." I of course turned it off as well as I could, observing that she had no reason to be grateful; my motive was selfish as I sought my own gratification in renewing an acquaintance so congenial to my feelings, etc. During this conversation the tear which stood in her flashing, expressive eye convinced me that this highly-gifted woman, with all the waywardness of thought and independence of action which the circumstances of her early introduction into life have ingrafted upon her natural disposition, possesses that warmth of heart which I thought I had formerly the sagacity to discover, and for which I have never failed to give her credit. (pp. 339-41)

> *Philip Hone, in a diary entry of August 10, 1838, in his* The Diary of Philip Hone: 1828-1851, *edited by Allan Nevins, revised edition, Dodd, Mead & Company, 1936, pp. 339-41.*

THE UNITED STATES MAGAZINE AND DEMOCRATIC REVIEW (essay date 1844)

[In this excerpt from a review of Poems, *the critic regrets that, in her lack of craftsmanship and polish, Kemble has not yet fulfilled her poetic promise.]*

The announcement which appeared in the *Democratic Review* some months since, of a forthcoming volume of poems from the pen of Mrs. Butler, must have been received with unusual pleasure, if our own individual satisfaction may be in any degree the criterion of the general feeling.... The few short poems that appeared in the newspapers and magazines while she was yet Miss Kemble, evinced the possession of great undeveloped power, of a depth of sentiment and force of expression that gave promise of a fuller and more perfect utterance. The volume has at length appeared, and to judge again from our individual experience, it has disappointed in a measure the high anticipations that were formed of it. That the interval of nine or ten years since the last appearance of Mrs. Butler before the public has not been passed in sacrificing to Apollo at the foot of Parnassus, is evident from the small number of the poems contained in the volume.... Indeed, if we are rightly informed, Pegasus has been put in harness, or what amounts to the same thing, into the hands of the publishers, to secure the welfare of a certain favorite *wingless* steed, and not with any premeditated intention of obtaining immortality. But whatever comes before the public in the questionable shape of a book, critics will speak to, without regard to the causes of its appearance. The poems themselves would confirm the suggestion that they were published without any strict reference to literary reputation, and show evidently that the fair author had not the fear of criticism before her eyes. Many of them are the mere ebullitions of her lively fancy, thrown off apparently without the slightest effort, and never re-touched afterwards. The perfection of a work of art is, doubtless, in concealing the labor that produces it; but there is a carelessness, or too evident absence of effort, that is perhaps more objectionable than the appearance of labor itself.

Many of these poems, and some among the best of them, are disfigured by lines either a syllable too long or too short, or by an unmusical arrangement of words; all of which could have been remedied by a stroke of the pen, and it is the certainty of the author's ability that renders the sin the less pardonable in the eyes of criticism. For instance, in the otherwise exquisite sonnet, **"I Would I Knew the Lady of Thy Heart,"** one line by being eleven syllables long instead of ten, and most inharmoniously arranged, mars the beauty of the whole fourteen: and in the next poem two lines are introduced of an entirely different measure, which destroy the harmony of the whole piece. The frequent recurrence of such small faults constitutes one great fault of the volume.

Another defect in many of these poems is their want of completeness, and an absence of the constructive faculty or artistic power. Too many of them are mere fragments; brilliant, to be sure, and promising well for the wealth of the mine from whence they came,—but still fragments. In the midst of a train of pleasant fancies we turn over the leaf, and lo! she has changed her theme to begin a new strain, and to end it in the same way, leaving us with taste excited but unsatisfied. But to conclude our ungracious task of fault-finding in as few words as possible, our impression is that Mrs. Butler has not done herself justice in the volume before us; but it is valuable inasmuch as it intimates what she could do, an' if she would. It is but the fluttering of wings that should soar to the empyrean.

Many of these poems indicate the intensest love of nature, a spirit exquisitely susceptible to her beautiful scenes and voices, and that finds repose as on a mother's bosom, in her leafy solitudes, by the rushing streams and the sounding ocean. (pp. 507-08)

The Poems entitled **"Absence,"** and **"The Prayer of a Lonely Heart,"** are two of the most perfect in the volume. The latter, a litany ..., will wake a response in every lonely heart.... (p. 508)

The poems of passion scattered through the volume are energetic and eloquent, as the expression of all true passion must be, and glowing as the songs of Sappho. They are the utterances of womanhood in her strength of heart, that can suffer and break, but that can never sentimentalize. (p. 509)

The prevailing tone of Mrs. Butler's poems is profoundly melancholy. In reading them, we feel too deeply the truth of her impromptu lines:

> Castalia! famed of yore, the spring divine,
>   Apollo's smile upon its current wears;
> Moore and Anacreon found its waves were wine;
>   To me it flows a sullen stream of tears.

They seem to be the wailings of a spirit that has looked appalled on the realities of life, on its friendships that change, on its love that becomes indifference, on the hollowness of fame and on death, the certain and awful consummation of this life-tragedy. This is one view of life, but it is not the highest nor the truest; nevertheless it is a view that we must take in our ascent to a higher and better. (p. 510)

That America is destined to produce a literature worthy of herself, is a question that cannot be doubted....

This country presents the widest sphere for individual influence, for here mind is most plastic. Mrs. Butler has made this country her home; with her strong original tendencies and force of character, she could not find a more ample field for their exercise, and such as she should not pass away without leaving "Footsteps on the Sands of Time." Among the voices of the *New Generation* that are now faintly heard above the uproar of business and care, and the din of party strife, we shall listen earnestly to distinguish hers in a higher and more hopeful strain. (p. 512)

> *"Mrs. Butler's Poems," in* The United States Magazine and Democratic Review, *Vol. XV, No. LXXVII, November, 1844, pp. 507-12.*

[ABRAHAM HAYWARD] (essay date 1847)

[The following excerpt is taken from a review of Kemble's A Year of Consolation *and Dora Quillinan's* Journal of a Few Months'

Residence in Portugal and Glimpses of the South of Spain. *Here, Hayward finds* A Year of Consolation, *like the earlier* Journal of a Residence in America, *alternately praiseworthy and objectionable for its subjective candor. For additional criticism by Hayward, see excerpt dated 1882.*]

[*Journal of a few months' Residence in Portugal* and *A Year of Consolation*] are of an intermediate quality. We do not believe that much pains have been taken in either case. The materials lay in the way of the writers, and they found them; and we have considerable doubts whether the fair authoress of *A few months' Residence in Portugal* had bestowed more than a few days attention on Portuguese history or literature before starting; or whether the author of *A Year of Consolation* (to be derived principally from classical associations on classic ground) knew much more of the ancient Romans than the ordinary run of her countrywomen, whom she takes or makes so many opportunities of sneering at. But it is impossible to confound either of them with the cloud of lady travellers who recently darkened the horizon. Neither of these books is a common book; and one of them (Mrs Butler's) with all its occasional faults of petulance and recklessness, is such as no one but a woman of genius, trained in the hard school of suffering, could have produced. It is from this conviction that we notice them; and we take them together for the sake rather of contrast than of similarity. (pp. 177-78)

No two female travellers, capable of writing books, could differ more widely from one another than Mrs Butler and Mrs Quillinan. The one is essentially *objective*, the other essentially *subjective;* the one draws her materials almost exclusively from without, the other almost exclusively from within; the one observes and comments, the other thinks and feels; the one, with her quiet good sense, submits patiently to privations and conventionalities—the other, with her strong fierce volition, demeans herself, when they cross her, like an eaglet in a cage. It is the Lake school against the Romantic school: the *Excursion* against *Childe Harold*—we had almost said, against *Don Juan*: Rydal Mount against Covent Garden: but Covent Garden in its zenith, with the Kembles acting Shakspeare, and (flash after flash) electrifying an audience composed of all that was most brilliant and distinguished in the land.

Our great southern contemporary was pleased to call Mrs Norton the Byron of modern poetesses. The term was a misnomer as applied to her; for in her last poems and those by which she would most wish to be known (*The Child of the Islands,* for example), self is forgotten altogether, and her entire unbroken sympathies are with the poor. But Mrs Butler's style is to all intents and purposes Byronic; and there is hardly a striking page in her *Journal of a Residence in America* or the work before us, which is not strongly coloured by her own individuality and intense self-consciousness. Occasionally she gets beyond even Byron, and startles us with a fearless, too-confiding frankness, like Rousseau's. We pointed out this peculiarity ten years ago. We pointed out at the same time sundry offences against good taste, which we suggested it might be as well to avoid in future; but as Turner goes on making his skies and water yellower and redder in exact proportion as the enlightened public exclaims against them, just so is Mrs Butler determined never to be reasoned by the pressgang (her own word) into the proprieties. Or, to take a family illustration: Once, in the height of the famous controversy about *aches,* which John Philip Kemble persevered, night after night, in pronouncing *aitches,* in defiance alike of the yells of the pit and the remonstrances of friends, who thought he was giving undue importance to a trifle,—he was overheard exclaiming to himself,

'No, I never will give up my *aitches.*' If Mrs Butler ever soliloquises—and we never yet knew a man or woman of genius who did not—we are quite sure she might be overheard exclaiming, 'No, I never will give up my indiscretions and personalities. Come what come may, I will not only utter at the time, but print for the public, any predilections or antipathies that may cross my mind, and give that same public the benefit of my passing opinion on every thing and every body, not excepting those nearest or dearest to me.'

The *Year of Consolation* commences thus:—

> *Saturday, Dec. 20th.*—Left Southampton per steamboat for Havre, at ten o'clock at night. The weather clear overhead, but blowing very hard. Horrible little boat; where, *objecting to lie close to two old women,* the only empty berths were one into which the water forced itself, or one in close proximity to the boiler. In the latter I slept.

Is Mrs Butler aware that one of the principal grounds on which Lord Eldon relied, in the Wellesley case, for depriving the father of the guardianship of his sons, was a letter recommending the persecution of old women and cats? (pp. 182-83)

We must do Mrs Butler the justice to say, that there is nothing like *malice prepense* about her, and that she does not spare her own self-love more than that of other people; or rather, (Rousseau-like again) she indulges a more refined self-love, or still higher pride, by baring all her feelings (the weak and wayward ones inclusive) to the world. As Curran said of Byron, she weeps for the press, and wipes her eyes with the public. But ought we to quarrel with the tendency, the irresistible impulse, which drives her to it? Is there not genius of a high (not perhaps the very highest) order which necessarily takes wing from egotism? Are not some of the finest efforts of the imagination owing to the faculty which enables the mind to blend itself with the sublime or beautiful in art or nature, till its own vivid conceptions take the place of the object and the very notion of reality seems lost? Is not this frequently found indissolubly connected with the intense self-consciousness we have been speaking of? And ought we to complain, or be overcritical, when we get a little dross with the gold,—when the habitual indulgence of the faculty leads now and then to the morbid, capricious, or even hurtful exercise of it?

Neither, again, should it be forgotten how character is formed by circumstances. Is there any intoxication in the world equal, while it lasts, to that produced by the applause of a crowded theatre?—is there any career in life so spirit-stirring for a period, and eventually so spirit-crushing, as that of a successful actor or actress?—did a prolonged succession of high excitements ever yet fail to create a fearful degree of morbid irritability?—or is it in human nature, to have one's vanity or self-esteem alternately depressed and elevated, from hour to hour, night after night, for years, without thinking one's feelings of more than ordinary importance to mankind? Moreover, it is far from clear that the disorders or peculiarities of genius, or those superinduced by particular modes of thinking and living, may not be inherited like gout, which occasionally skips a generation or an individual; and Mrs Butler belongs to a family whose entire existence has been one of representation; which has lived and moved, and had its being before the foot-lights; which, through the hard necessity of its position (proud, and proudly sustained, as that position was), found itself obliged for nearly half a century to weigh everything—name, fame, fortune, hopes, and prospects—in the unsteady and ill-balanced scales of popular favour.

If we read this book—as books of travels are commonly read—carelessly, superficially, and with the view of picking up a few facts or whiling away an unoccupied hour—the chances are that we shall pronounce it an unsatisfactory or uninteresting book; but if we make an effort (which Goethe used to say every fair critic ought to make) to place ourselves in the writer's point of view and situation, and then go deliberately along with her—the sense of her power, of her originality, of the depth and variety of her reflections, of the warmth and richness of her imagination, very soon comes upon us and remains with us to the end, rendering the self-imposed task a fascinating one. Yet it is not the things themselves, or the information we get regarding them, but her mode of looking at them, her *subjective* treatment (to speak aesthetically again), that constitutes the charm. (pp. 183-85)

[Thought] and feeling are blended with observation in this book. In short, it is eminently suggestive, and constantly sets us thinking, but not always in the right direction; and the pettiest provocation on the road, is often enough to unhinge the mind and disturb the judgment of the writer. Get her to Italy, and she rises with the subject; yet, even here, we often wish that her genius was of a softer character, and that she would less frequently remind us of Pope's couplet on another lady—

> Yet ne'er so sure our passion to create,
> As when she touch'd the brink of all we hate.
>
> (p. 186)

After all, the gems of this book are the poetry; and it is a curious fact that Mrs Butler, so careless, so occasionally unrefined, in her prose writings, is always uniformly correct, chastened, and refined in verse.

Rome ought never to be visited for the first time as a consolation; the mind should be entirely free from all impressions unconnected with the genius of the place. . . . But, considered merely as an eloquent, almost involuntary outpouring of melancholy thoughts, nothing can well be finer than Mrs Butler's lines beginning—

> Early in life, when hope seems prophecy,
> And strong desire can sometimes mould a fate,
> My dream was of thy shores, O Italy!

But *l'homme propose, Dieu dispose;* and when she does come, it is

> Not in that season of my life, when life
> Itself was rich enough for all its need,
> And I yet held its whole inheritance;
> But in the bankrupt days when all is spent,
> Bestow'd, or stolen, wasted, given away,
> To buy a store or bitter memories.—

It is sad to dwell upon such a picture, and know that it is a copy from the life. Yet these pages abound with indications of improvement, moral and mental; and we think we may venture to say that the wanderer has been at least partially consoled. Mixed up with the burst of indignation, the sigh of despondency, and the hardly suppressed cry of despair, are better, far better things. (p. 187)

[Abraham Hayward], "Mrs. Quillinan and Mrs. Butler—Books of Travels," in The Edinburgh Review, Vol. LXXXVI, No. CLXXIII, July, 1847, pp. 176-87.

[RICHARD FORD]   (essay date 1847)

[An English writer, Ford was the author of A Handbook for Travellers in Spain, *commonly considered the most informative guidebook of its day. In the following excerpt from a review of* A Year of Consolation, *Ford generally commends the work's poetry and descriptive prose, though he disapproves of Kemble's occasionally harsh criticism of people and places.*]

An under-tone of woe and mystery pervades the poetic portions of [Fanny Kemble's *A Year of Consolation*], exciting a compassionate curiosity, and vividly contrasting, it must be owned, with the animal spirits and comic joyousness which flash forth in the prose narrative, like sun-beams in a wintry sky. But this is all in nature;—she is a poetess—and moreover the theatre has been her nursery and her playground. No wonder then that, whenever shadows of the past, looming across the Atlantic, darkened her present dream of peace, she poured her sadness into the serious vehicle of *Il Penseroso,* and sought relief from sorrow in sympathy. In the psychology of suffering the endurance of the Spartan is often coupled with the exhibition of the martyr; many there be who, even without the excuse of her professional training, can dissect with stoic pride the morbid anatomy of their hearts, and reveal to every eye festering wounds, which the tenderest hand of friend is never permitted to probe or bind up; who, masking inner depression by outward hilarity, cherish by concealment the worm in the bud, and yet bare their stuffed bosoms to the world, for daws to peck at. (p. 441)

Perilous to all well-cut pens, and fatal to not a few of them, is the facility of blank verse. The cleverest people in the world, if they happen to be great public speakers, like Lord Robertson and Mrs. Butler, are exceedingly apt to be carried too fast and too far when they trust themselves on this broad-gauge railroad—and we conceive the jeopardy must be worst in the case of one suckled in the habits of theatrical intonation. Mrs. Siddons, we have read, used to ask for beef or porter at table in blank verse—we can vouch for it that glorious John Kemble occasionally grumbled about the Magnum being out, in lines as magniloquent as ever rolled from Lee's Alexander. In whatever fashion their niece exhibits herself, she will be sure to show the blood she is come of—but we very much prefer her rhyme to her blank, and the tighter the restraints she is pleased to adopt, the more she pleases us—best of all in the sonnet. Her Pegasus never needs the spur—the curb often. Prodigality of 'words, words, words, Horatio,' is only thus to be avoided, where, from a good ear and inveterate practice, recitative is so apt to glide into a certain cadence, that ten pages of tragic hendecasyllabics cost no more trouble than a king's speech did to William Pitt. (p. 442)

[Without] expecting her to be logical, we could desire fewer general conclusions drawn from particulars. It is too bad, because she travelled in out-of-the-way places in an out-of-the-way manner, not as other household Kates, and met with certain company and consequences, to set down la belle France as one wilderness of monkeys; but there, as everywhere, like equality-loathing Coriolanus, her heart is her mouth, and what her breast forges that her tongue must utter. Always in extremes, whether for love or hate—and a good hater she is at all events—not, perhaps, the worse lover for that—the spirit of the moment moves her, be it for good or evil. She changes character as if performing the same night both in the tragedy and farce, and enters into the genius of each with equal ardour, eagerness, and, we believe, sincerity. When despair is the order of the day, hers is terrific: now she sits among Rome's ruins wailing like the dethroned, childless queens in *Richard III.*; anon she is pelting sugar-plums at the Carnival. To hear her hoyden laughter, holding both its sides, neither black cares, men, babies, nor Butlers exist either in the old or new world, nor private feelings nor public reviewers, with such rashness and recklessness does she lay about her when her 'dander is up.'

Let us, however, repeat, even as to her prose web, what we have already said of her sombre lyrical embroideries. We do not apprehend that there is any theatrical trick or affectation in these Hamlet transitions from intense light to gloom, nor anything inconsequent and contrary to human nature, even in sufferers of less tinderlike temperament. Wrongs too deep to be forgiven, regrets too bitter to be forgotten, have been so grafted on an originally gladsome disposition as to become part and parcel of herself. Once let a mind thus jangled and out of tune surrender itself, seeking relief, to strong impressions, either of joy or sadness, and the even tenor of its course is exchanged for a condition bordering on the hysterical; the floodgates once open and the waters out, slight need be the check, the disturbing influence, which suffices to turn them from one channel to another; and as we are never nearer hate than when loving most, so melancholy dogs the heels of high excitement, like an inevitable shadow. At first, no doubt, the practice throughout these volumes of stopping short in a disquisition about some general subject, or even in a description of some gay festival scene—drawing a line with the pen—and so bounding off at once into a strain, now in verse, now in almost as musical prose, of deep personal passion and affliction—at first sight this may, no question, strike one as savouring of *hey presto!*—change the scene—let the drawing room disappear and give us the dungeon again! But, on the whole, we are satisfied that Mrs. Fanny's method is about the best she could have taken to make her pages reflect the real agitations backward and forward of her own sensitive and sorely-tried nature.

On a former occasion we too have 'said our say' on some of this young lady's own 'unpleasing peculiarities,' administering counsel with reproof, more in kindness than anger, and gently as a parent flagellates the child he loves. Gladly do we mark amendment in our interesting pupil, albeit the smack of orange-peel, Covent Garden, and Drury Lane is still perceptible. In some respects she is incorrigible. We discover outbursts of the same flippancy and bad taste, of the same habit of calling things by their right, or rather wrong, names; the same dawdling over nastinesses which she practically abhors, but has a Swift-like delight in describing. In dealing with ungentlemanlike men and their ill manners, a phraseology which takes tone and tincture from them may, perhaps, be permissible on other sides of the ocean; but in England, we are happy to say, it still grates on ears polite, and is incompatible with olfactory euphuism and lady-like water-worship. Beautiful Italy needs no such foil, and we grudge digressions on toad-stools and tittle-backs. We have constant cause to complain of tourists of both sexes, who, starting with the foregone conclusion of a book, will flesh the edge of their young curiosity at Calais, will note down what we want not to know—will waste time in seeing things not worth seeing, and then ink in the record. The whole of the French progress, in short, might as well have been cut down to half a dozen pages.

Even when she has got over both Alp and Apennine, her charges are sweeping, whether directed against classes and corporations, or tongues and peoples—not to mention principalities and powers. (pp. 445-47)

More illogical, and what is worse in the gentler sex, more ill-natured, are Mrs. Fanny's comments on her own fair compatriots and fellow Consolation-seekers. Always prone to ridicule and exaggeration, in their unlucky case her portraits are extravagant caricatures, whenever they are not actual libels. She goes out of her way to spy the motes in soft eyes, and never forgives a sister's shame. Every one she meets with is either sour-tempered, ill-bred, ill-dressed, or an awkward amazon. It is probable in these days of steam that every one of our womankind who, like herself, over-leaps the Simplon, may not be exactly suited to sit (either with or without drapery) to Mr. Gibson for one of the Graces travelling *incognita*. These, however (we must hope and believe), are the exceptions, not the rule; assuredly, so far as we have observed, nine times out of ten, whenever our Continental path has been crossed by one of those bright visions which seem lent from heaven to earth for one day, the houri has proved to be a sample of that race, the best in blood, the most beautiful in face and complexion, the most symmetrical in form, the purest in mind and body—in short, a specimen of that precious porcelain whereof are made the mothers, wives, sisters, and daughters of English gentlemen—a pretty good breed, too, and not particularly abundant across the salt seas, as we need not tell Mrs. Fanny. If she has not renounced her glorious birthright, she commits the no less egregious folly of offering up her own kith and kin, in the vain hopes of conciliating the vanity of foreign inferiority, which her former gibes have irremediably offended. (pp. 448-49)

Enough of this. Ready as we are on every occasion to stand up against any assailant, foul or fair, of the best of the only good sex, we have no wish to prolong any censure of Fanny Kemble. Far more pleasing is the task to pay sincere homage to her powers of description, her keen relish and perception of nature, her original and often masculine judgment. Occasional escapades of wilfulness may be forgiven: whenever she puts on the buskins she rises at once—like Henry V. when escaping from Eastcheap—into the rational and poetical; tone and temper are changed, and the vulgar and violent exeunt into the green-room. (p. 449)

The day before Mrs. Fanny departed, December 7th, was dark and gloomy—the rain incessant;—yet she knelt at the fountain of Trevi, and drank of its sweet waters—for those who so drink return, she had been told, to Rome—and she would carry that hope with her. May it be gratified—when the mind is more at ease, and the fascinating lady's temper less mutinous. (p. 468)

[*Richard Ford*], *"Fanny Kemble and Lear in Italy,"* in The Quarterly Review, *Vol. LXXXI, No. CLXII, September, 1847, pp. 440-68.*

HENRY WADSWORTH LONGFELLOW   (poem date 1849)

[*A poet, novelist, essayist, and translator, Longfellow was one of the most popular American writers of the nineteenth century. An admiring acquaintance of Kemble, Longfellow frequently attended her Shakespearean readings in Boston in 1849. After one such evening, he wrote the following sonnet in Kemble's honor.*]

O precious evenings! all too swiftly sped!
  Leaving us heirs to amplest heritages
  Of all the best thoughts of the greatest sages,
  And giving tongues unto the silent dead!
How our hearts glowed and trembled as she read,
  Interpreting by tones the wondrous pages
  Of the great poet who foreruns the ages,
  Anticipating all that shall be said!

O happy Reader! having for thy text
　　The magic book, whose Sibylline leaves have caught
　　The rarest essence of all human thought!
O happy Poet! by no critic vext!
　　How must thy listening spirit now rejoice
　　To be interpreted by such a voice!

> *Henry Wadsworth Longfellow, "Sonnet," in his* The
> Complete Poetical Works of Henry Wadsworth
> Longfellow, *Houghton Mifflin and Company, 1893,
> p. 112.*

THE LONDON REVIEW (essay date 1863)

[*This critic praises Kemble's unveiling of the wrongs of slavery
in* Journal of a Residence on a Georgian Plantation.]

Whenever the civil war in America comes to an end—and with
present appearances he would be a bold man who would undertake to prophesy when that will be—the sympathy which
the South has undoubtedly enjoyed in this country will end
with it. It has made an unexpected stand against superior forces,
and has supplied the want of arms and equipments by that
pluck which always commands the respect of Englishmen; and
it has followed up an obstinate resistance by a series of victories
splendid, though incomplete. Much of our good will it has also
owed to the pertinacity the North has displayed in its endeavours to lose it. But behind all this there is the vast crime of
slavery which England will not and dares not forgive, and for
which the South will have to atone either by putting an end to
it, or by enduring the shame and disgrace of its existence.
There is no plea that can be invented which will even soften
our detestation of an institution so repugnant to our feelings
as citizens, as Christians, as men. We cannot be satisfied by
being told that the negro's condition is more tolerable in the
South than in the Free States, though the argument has its force
as a satire upon the hypocritical professions of the republicans,
and the claim made by the North upon the sympathies of Europe
in right of a war waged against slaveholders. But this is an
advantage which will end when the war ends, and which even
now carries no satisfaction to the breasts of men who neither
enslave negroes nor proscribe them. Nor is it to the purpose,
even if it were true, to object that the condition of the slave
well fed, well housed and clothed, by a master whose kindness
is guaranteed by his interest, is preferable in a material point
of view to the condition of many of our own paupers. Such
an argument would go as well to prove that it is better to be
a gentleman's horse or a lady's lapdog than to be a human
being. But even this plea for slavery represents a state of things
which, though it may be found on some slave estates, is certainly not found on all, and we have reason to believe is rare
upon very many. Nor is the interest of the owner a guarantee
for the kind treatment of the slave, though it may be for his
life. A very brutal flogging, for example, will not permanently
incapacitate a slave from work, nor need a tolerably severe
one interrupt his labour for more time than it takes to inflict
it. But were there no flogging at all, and were the creature
comforts of the negro all that negro or white man could desire,
there remains the loss of freedom, and of all that depends upon
it. Not a merely sentimental loss. It includes the right to everything that can minister to the wants of mind, body, and
soul; a man's right to the profit of his labour, to his wife and
child, to the education of his mind, to the consolations of
religion. When we read in Mrs. Kemble's [*Journal of a Residence on a Georgian Plantation*] of a slave being whipped for
having asked permission to be baptized, we are not to be per-

suaded that it is any mitigation of a system so horrible, that
he is sure of being fed, because it is his master's interest to
keep him alive. We are rather moved to inquire after the fate
of those slaves who, from age or hopeless disease, are unable
any longer to work in the cotton-fields or the rice swamps; and
the question is pertinent how far the owner's interest is a protection to the slave during those long periods when he is absent
from his estate, and when his place is supplied by the overseer
who has no such interest.

But with all our horror of slavery, and our willingness to believe
the worst of it, it must be a very lively imagination indeed
which can conjure such a picture of its social working as Mrs.
Kemble presents in her journal. When we read these pages,
and are told that they represent slave life on an estate the
administration of which had the credit of being a humane one,
we are utterly at our wits' end to imagine what the condition
of the slaves can be on a badly administered estate. There is
only one thing more wonderful than their brutal degradation,
and that is the meekness and docility with which they bear it.
The estate Mrs. Kemble writes about was the property of her
husband, and it is not to be believed that the descriptions she
gives of it can be anything but true. (pp. 608-09)

There are many terrible stories in Mrs. Kemble's journal which
show how far . . . miseries can prevail even on a humanely
managed estate; but the subject is too revolting to dwell upon. . . .

Mrs. Kemble's residence on her husband's Georgian estate was
as little pleasing to that gentleman and his overseer as it was
to herself. The overseer indeed plainly hinted, that when once
she was gone, it would be long before another European lady
was permitted to come there. Better, perhaps, that it should
be so. There is a certain amount of logic in the argument,
abominable as it is, that any attempt to elevate men and women
who must bear the savage yoke of slavery, will only add to
their miseries. To qualify them for the destiny of brutes, they
must be brought as close as possible to their condition, and
for this purpose nothing can be a nearer approach to perfection
than the American system. What that system is, our readers
will have some idea, when they have read Mrs. Kemble's
journal. But apart from this view, the book is well worth
reading. Mrs. Kemble writes with grace and power. What she
describes is at once present to us; and we frequently meet with
glimpses of Georgian scenery which are very charming. (p. 609)

> *"A Residence in Georgia," in* The London Review,
> *Vol. VI, No. 153, June 6, 1863, pp. 608-09.*

THE INDEPENDENT (essay date 1863)

[*In this announcement of the publication of* Journal of a Residence
on a Georgian Plantation, *the commentator extols the realism of
the work.*]

[Mrs. Kemble's ***Journal of a Residence on a Georgian Plantation***] is the most thrilling and remarkable picture of the interior social life of the slaveholding section in this country that
has ever been published. Our previous accounts of that life
have been derived from outside observers. But the [***Journal of
a Residence on a Georgian Plantation***] of Mrs. Kemble was
jotted down from day to day as she lived upon the plantation
of which she was mistress. There is no excuse, no palliation
of facts, but the whole system is laid bare and quivering before
the eye. So faithful and final a witness we have not had. Even
Uncle Tom's Cabin is only founded upon fact. The [***Journal***

of a Residence on a Georgian Plantation] of Mrs. Kemble is fact itself.

"Mrs. Kemble's Life on a Georgian Plantation," in The Independent, *Vol. XV, No. 763, July 16, 1863, p. 6.*

THE ATLANTIC MONTHLY   (essay date 1863)

[*This critic has nothing but praise for* Journal of a Residence on a Georgian Plantation *as a penetrating exposé of the evils of slavery.*]

Those who remember the *Journal of a Residence in America* of Frances Anne Kemble, or, as she was universally and kindly called, Fanny Kemble,—a book long since out of print, and entirely out of the knowledge of our younger readers,—will not cease to wonder, as they close [the] thoughtful, tranquil, and tragical pages [of *Journal of a Residence on a Georgian Plantation in 1838-39*]. The earlier journal was the dashing, fragmentary diary of a brilliant girl, half impatient of her own success in an art for which she was peculiarly gifted, yet the details of which were sincerely repugnant to her. It crackled and sparkled with *naïve* arrogance. It criticized a new world and fresh forms of civilization with the amusing petulance of a spoiled daughter of John Bull. It was flimsy, flippant, laughable, rollicking, vivid. It described scenes and persons, often with airy grace, often with profound and pensive feeling. It was the slightest of diaries, written in public for the public; but it was universally read, as its author had been universally sought and admired in the sphere of her art; and no one who knew anything of her truly, but knew what an incisive eye, what a large heart, what a candid and vigorous mind, what real humanity, generosity, and sympathy, characterized Miss Kemble.

The dazzling phantasmagoria which life had been to the young actress was suddenly exchanged for the most practical acquaintance with its realities. She was married, left the stage, and as a wife and mother resided for a winter on the plantations of her husband upon the coast of Georgia. And now, after twenty-five years, the journal of her residence there is published. It has been wisely kept. For never could such a book speak with such power as at this moment. The tumult of the war will be forgotten, as you read, in the profound and appalled attention enforced by this remarkable revelation of the interior life of Slavery. The spirit, the character, and the purpose of the Rebellion are here laid bare. Its inevitability is equally apparent. The book is a permanent and most valuable chapter in our history; for it is the first ample, lucid, faithful, detailed account, from the actual head-quarters of a slave-plantation in this country, of the workings of the system,—its persistent, hopeless, helpless crushing of humanity in the slave, and the more fearful moral and mental dry-rot it generates in the master.

We have had plenty of literature upon the subject. (p. 260)

Yet in all this tremendous debate which resounds through the last thirty years of our history, rising and swelling until every other sound was lost in its imperious roar, one decisive voice was silent. It was precisely that which is heard in this book. General statements, harrowing details from those who had been slaveholders, and who had renounced Slavery, were sometimes made public. Indeed, the most cruel and necessary incidents, the hunting with blood-hounds, the branding, the maiming, the roasting, the whipping of pregnant women, could not be kept from knowledge. They blazed into print. But the public, hundreds

of miles away, while it sighed and shuddered a little, resolved that such atrocities were exceptional. 'T was a shocking pity, to be sure! Poor things! Women, too! Tut, tut!

Now, at last, we have no general statement, no single, sickening incident, but the diary of the mistress of plantations of seven hundred slaves, living under the most favorable circumstances, upon the islands at the mouth of the Altamaha River, in Georgia. It is a journal, kept from day to day, of the actual ordinary life of the plantation, where the slaves belonged to educated, intelligent, and what are called the most respectable people,—not persons imbruted by exile among slaves upon solitary islands, but who had lived in large Northern cities and the most accomplished society, subject to all the influences of the highest civilization. It is the journal of a hearty, generous, clear-sighted woman, who went to the plantation, loving the master, and believing, that, though Slavery might be sad, it might also be mitigated, and the slave might be content. It is the record of ghastly undeceiving,—of the details of a system so wantonly, brutally, damnably unjust, inhuman, and degrading, that it blights the country, paralyzes civilization, and vitiates human nature itself. The brilliant girl of the earlier journal is the sobered and solemnized matron of this. The very magnitude of the misery that surrounds her, the traces of which everywhere sadden her eye and wring her heart, compel her to the simplest narration. There is no writing for effect. There is not a single "sensational" passage. The story is monotonous; for the wrong it describes is perpetual and unrelieved. "There is not a single natural right," she says, after some weeks' residence, "that is not taken away from these unfortunate people; and the worst of all is, that their condition does not appear to me, upon further observation of its, to be susceptible of even partial alleviation, as long as the fundamental evil, the Slavery itself, remains."

As the mistress of the plantation, she was brought into constant intercourse with the slave-women; and no other account of this class is so thorough and plainly stated. So pitiful a tale was seldom told. It was a "model plantation"; but every day was darkened to the mistress by the appeals of these women and her observation of their condition. The heart of the reader sickens as hers despaired. (p. 261)

The life that she describes upon the model plantation is the necessary life of Slavery everywhere,—injustice, ignorance, superstition, terror, degradation, brutality; and this is the system to which a great political party—counting upon the enervation of prosperity, the timidity of trade, the distance of the suffering, the legal quibbles, the moral sophisms, the hatred of ignorance, the jealousy of race, and the possession of power—has conspired to keep the nation blind and deaf, trusting that its mind was utterly obscured and its conscience wholly destroyed.

But the nation is young, and of course the effort has ended in civil war. Slavery, industrially and politically, inevitably resists Christian civilization. The natural progress and development of men into a constantly higher manhood must cease, or this system, which strives to convert men into things, must give way. Its haughty instinct knows it, and therefore Slavery rebels. This Rebellion is simply the insurrection of Barbarism against Civilization. It would overthrow the Government, not for any wrong the Government has done, for that is not alleged. It knows that the people are the Government,—that the spirit of the people is progressive and intelligent,—and that there is no hope for permanent and expansive injustice, so long as the people freely discuss and decide. It would therefore establish a new Government, of which this meanest and most beastly despotism shall be the chief corner-stone. In a letter to C. G., in the appendix of her book, Mrs. Kemble sets this truth in the clearest light. But whoever would comprehend the real social scope of the Rebellion should ponder every page of the journal itself. It will show him that Slavery and rebellion to this Government are identical, not only in fact, but of necessity. It will teach him that the fierce battle between Slavery and the Government, once engaged, can end only in the destruction of one or the other.

This is not a book which a woman like Mrs. Kemble publishes without a solemn sense of responsibility. A sadder book the human hand never wrote, nor one more likely to arrest the thoughts of all those in the world who watch our war and are yet not steeled to persuasion and conviction. An English-woman, she publishes it in England, which hates us, that a testimony which will not be doubted may be useful to the country in which she has lived so long, and with which her sweetest and saddest memories are forever associated. It is a noble service nobly done. The enthusiasm, the admiration, the affection, which in our day of seemingly cloudless prosperity greeted the brilliant girl, have been bountifully repaid by the true and timely words now spoken in our seeming adversity by the grave and thoughtful woman. (pp. 262-63)

> *A review of "Journal of a Residence on a Georgian Plantation in 1838-39," in* The Atlantic Monthly, *Vol. XII, No. LXX, August, 1863, pp. 260-63.*

EDWARD FITZGERALD   (letter date 1875)

[*An English writer, FitzGerald is best known as the translator of the* Rubáiyát *of Omar Khayyám. In the excerpt below from a letter to Kemble, he enthuses about the installments of Kemble's "Old Woman's Gossip" appearing in the* Atlantic Monthly.]

My last Letter asked you how and where I could get at your Papers; this is to say, I have got them. . . . Now believe me; I am delighted with ["**Old Woman's Gossip**"]; and only wish it might run on as long as I live: which perhaps it may. Of course somewhat of my Interest results from the Times, Persons, and Places you write of; almost all more or less familiar to me; but I am quite sure that very few could have brought all before me as you have done—with what the Painters call, so free, full, and flowing a touch. I suppose this "**Gossip**" is the Memoir you told me you were about; three or four years ago, I think: or perhaps Selections from it; though I hardly see how your Recollections could be fuller. No doubt your Papers will all be collected into a Book; perhaps it would have been financially better for you to have so published it now. But, on the other hand, you will have the advantage of writing with more freedom and ease in the Magazine, knowing that you can alter, contract, or amplify, in any future Re-publication. It gives me such pleasure to like, and honestly say I like, this work—and—I know I'm right in such matters, though I can't always give the reason why I like, or don't like, Dr. Fell: as much wiser People can—who reason themselves quite wrong. (pp. 80-1)

> *Edward FitzGerald, in a letter to Fanny Kemble in October, 1875, in his* Letters of Edward FitzGerald to Fanny Kemble: 1871-1883, *edited by William Aldis Wright, Macmillan and Co., 1895, pp. 80-2.*

THE NATION, NEW YORK   (essay date 1878)

[*The critic praises* Record of a Girlhood *as "excellent reading" and its author as "a very interesting character."*]

Of this work [*Record of a Girlhood*], Americans have had the foretaste, under another title ["**Old Woman's Gossip**"] in the *Atlantic Monthly*. To the series which there appeared, a good deal has now been added; by no means enough, however, to console the reader for his regret that the author should not have prolonged her chronicle and carried it into her riper years. The book is so charming, so entertaining, so stamped with the impress of a strong, remarkable, various nature, that we feel almost tormented in being treated to a view only of the youthful phases of the character. Like most of the novels that we read, or don't read, these volumes are the history of a young lady's entrance into life. Mrs. Kemble's young lady is a very brilliant and charming one, and our only complaint is that we part company with her too soon. It is a pity that her easy, natural, forcible descriptive powers, her vivid memory of detail, her spontaneous pathos and humor, should not have exercised themselves upon a larger experience. What we have here, however, is excellent reading, and as the author is always tolerably definite in her characterizations of people she has met, discretion perhaps justified her in confining herself to subjects not strictly contemporaneous. Mrs. Kemble's part in these volumes is admirably done; she is naturally a writer, she has a style of her own which is full of those felicities of expression that indicate the literary sense. . . . [The work's] substance, of course, is very theatrical, but by no means exclusively so. On the contrary, nothing is more striking than the fact that Fanny Kemble, in the midst of her youthful triumph, led a life entirely independent of the stage, and had personal and intellectual interests that were quite distinct from her art. Has any young actress, before or since, ever written such letters as those addressed to Miss H. S., of which a large part of these volumes is composed? As an actress, Miss Fanny Kemble had many a confidant upon the stage; but she had the good fortune also to have one off it, to whom she poured out a thousand daily impressions and opinions, emotions and reflections of character. Taken together, these things make a very remarkable portrait—a portrait doubly remarkable when we remember that this original, positive, interrogative, reflective, generous, cultivated young girl, interested in books, in questions, in public matters, in art and nature and philosophy, was at the same time a young lady of the footlights and pursuing in this situation an extraordinarily brilliant career. (pp. 368-69)

We may add that this record is particularly interesting from what one may call a psychological point of view, on account of the singular anomaly it points out. Mrs. Kemble, during the years of her early histrionic triumphs, took no pleasure in the exercise of her genius. She went upon the stage from extrinsic considerations, and she never overcame a strong aversion to it. The talent, and the sort of activity that the talent involved, remained mutually unsympathetic. Given, in Mrs. Kemble's case, the remarkable proportions of the talent, the fact appears to be without precedent, though, if we are not mistaken, something akin to it is pointed out in the *Memoirs* of Macready. There have been people who could not act by many degrees so well as Mrs. Kemble who have had an incorrigible passion for the footlights; but we doubt whether there has been any one who, possessing so strongly the dramatic instinct, has had so little taste for the stage. The contradiction is interesting, and leads one to ask whether it takes a distinctly inferior mind to content itself with the dramatic profession. The thing is possible, though one hesitates to affirm it. We venture to say no more than that it is probable Miss Fanny Kemble would have been a more contented and ambitious actress, a more complete and business-like artist, if she had not been so generally intelligent and accomplished a young lady. She would have been happier if she could have been more "professional." But this contradiction is only a detail in the portrait of a very interesting character. (p. 369)

A review of "Record of a Girlhood," in The Nation, *New York, Vol. XXVII, No. 702, December 12, 1878, pp. 368-69.*

[ABRAHAM HAYWARD]   (essay date 1882)

[*Hayward offers unqualified praise for* Record of a Girlhood *and* Records of Later Life, *asserting that readers will find these works both amusing and interesting. For additional commentary by Hayward, see excerpt dated 1847.*]

In conversation with Washington Irving in April 1834, Mrs. Kemble was giving strong expression to her dislike of the stage as a profession, and complaining of the little leisure left by it for more congenial and improving pursuits. 'Well,' he said, 'you are living, you are seeing men and things, you are seeing the world, you are acquiring materials and heaping together observations and experience and wisdom, and by-and-by, when with fame you have acquired independence and retired from these labours, you will begin another and a brighter course with matured powers. I know of no one whose life has such a promise in it as yours.' 'Alas!' is her comment, 'my kind friend was no prophet.' Looking merely to [*Record of a Girlhood* and *Records of Later Life*], we are inclined to think that he was: that at all events he was right in supposing that she would turn her many and varied opportunities to good account: that she would hive up the results of observation and experience, and apply them in such a manner as to be pleasing and instructive to others, as well as honourable, elevating, and refining, to herself. We find much more in these volumes than ample materials for the study of a remarkable character and career. They abound in valuable reminiscences, in criticisms of a high order, in eloquent bursts of feeling and sentiment, in comments and reflections on life, manners, books and events, the boldness and originality of which are no longer marred, as in some earlier productions of her pen, by an admixture of extravagance and eccentricity not easily distinguished from affectation. We are no longer prevented by the petulance and irritability of genius from the frank and full recognition of its quality. She has emerged, soothed and softened, from the trying ordeal of domestic affliction: a memorable example of the truth embodied in the couplet which (she says) Rogers repeated to her:—

The path of sorrow, and that path alone,
Leads to the land where sorrow is unknown.

She has stood, like Byron, with all her household gods shattered round her, but, unlike Byron, she has laid aside the despairing defying tone, bravely resolving to live in charity with all men and (what is harder still) with all women: so that in the whole of the six volumes there is scarcely one unkind notice of a contemporary. It would seem, indeed, occasionally as if, startled by the strong condemnation passed on Mr. Charles Greville and Carlyle, she had rushed to the opposite extremes of unqualified admiration and overflowing amiability. (pp. 83-4)

The vividness and freshness of these Records is in no slight degree owing to the circumstance that a large portion of them consists of extracts from confidential letters to a friend, covering more than forty years and amounting to thousands, which were fortunately preserved. (p. 90)

It is a common practice with writers of Memoirs to swell their pages with the stock stories of contemporary celebrities. Mrs. Kemble restricts herself, as a rule, to her own personal reminiscences, and most of her anecdotes of the best known persons have an air of freshness and novelty. (pp. 109-10)

Where Mrs. Kemble excels is in her dramatic criticisms, and in her delineations of theatrical characters,—actors, singers, dancers, and composers. She is not wedded to a school: she can enjoy the most opposite styles and hit off their distinctive merits with combined boldness and delicacy of touch. (p. 114)

A highly-refined and cultivated Frenchwoman, who has made [*Record of a Girlhood*] the basis of a volume [*La jeunesse de Fanny Kemble* (1880) by Madame Augustus Craven], has endeavoured to deduce from it a moral which we cannot allow to pass unquestioned: 'In the first place, this book brought back to my mind's eye one of the most remarkable women I have ever met. Then, it is filled to profusion with literary beauties of all kinds. Thirdly, it must be owned, it has seemed to demonstrate clearly enough that the thought of elevating the theatrical profession to the ideal height of which I have been speaking must be ranged in the category of chimeras; since this profession, practised with the greatest success and in conditions the most favourable to the realization of this dream, has always inspired in the author of these memoirs an estrangement for which she can eloquently account. I shall be told perhaps that this, in Fanny Kemble, arose from the elevation of her soul and the rare distinction of her intellect. It may be so.' May it not have arisen from undue fastidiousness, or from having been too much behind the scenes from childhood, from having had the coarse seamy side of the calling eternally before her eyes, from having been driven to associate it with the humiliating embarrassments of the most distinguished members of her family? Mrs. Siddons, the impersonation of female dignity, who might have looked down upon it from the same moral elevation, took pride in it, left it with regret, and declared to her dying day that there was nothing worth living for like the sea of upturned faces in the pit. The argument drawn from Mrs. Kemble's dislike of the stage, is neutralized by the fact that neither she nor her illustrious aunt was sullied by it.

But whilst differing with Madame Craven as to the moral, we fully agree with her as to the distinctive merits of the book, and what she says of the *Record of a Girlhood* is true of the *Records of Later Life*, which equally abound in literary beauty and in thoughtful eminently suggestive passages, although these may not be uniformly of a kind to be discerned at a glance or grasped without an intellectual effort. 'Intelligibilia, non intellectum, fero.' The reader must be endowed with knowledge and sensibility. He should be something of a critic, something of an amateur, something of a moralist, something of a thinker, to appreciate them. Let him only come duly qualified to the perusal, and he can hardly fail to rise from it amused, interested, instructed, and improved. (pp. 122-23)

[Abraham Hayward], "Mrs. Fanny Kemble's Records of Her Life," in The Quarterly Review, *Vol. 154, No. 307, July, 1882, pp. 83-123.*

THE ATLANTIC MONTHLY   (essay date 1891)

[*In the excerpt below from an approving critique of* Further Records, *the critic salutes Kemble's "feeling, humorous perception, accurate judgment, clear-headed observation, and sympathy with life."*]

In spite of the great mass of private correspondence offered to the public within the last quarter of a century, we can think of but three women, Mrs. Carlyle, Madame Craven, and Madame Mohl, whose letters in any respect offer a parallel to those of Mrs. Kemble [in *Further Records*]. This resemblance lies not so much in the style, the keen observation, the bold diagnosis, and the pretty variegated arrows shot almost at random, which amuse the reader, but may somewhere leave a sting, in which these letters remind us of Mrs. Carlyle's; nor in the exquisite feeling for family life, for friendship, for all beauty of the intellectual and moral order, in which Mrs. Kemble is nearly akin to Madame Craven; nor yet in the capacity which belongs to the woman of the salon for a wide diversity of intimate friendships, and for keen appreciation of the exotic refinements of the most highly civilized life which characterize alike the writer and Madame Mohl; but rather in the fact that each one of these women possesses, like Mrs. Kemble, the art of embodying the facts of her environment, giving definite shape and color to her surroundings, and presenting the men and women encountered day by day as in a magic mirror, where few of the shifting lights which constitute personality and make up life are lost. There is a wide difference in the way these four women write, and in the effect their letters produce upon the reader; but in each of them we discern the artist behind the detailed and balanced impression produced,—an artist under the spur of an imperative necessity to find some clear medium of expression, that takes the form of confidential letters, which are half a self-confession and half a work of art, presenting as they do, although unconsciously, by a cunning arrangement of details and stroke upon stroke of line and color, what the artist has seen, heard, and felt, thus making up in the total more than a narrative,—an idyl or a drama. (p. 688)

If these *Further Records* lack the charm of Mrs. Kemble's wonderful *Records of a Girlhood*, which first found favor with the public in the pages of *The Atlantic* under the title of "**Old Woman's Gossip**," or if they fail to touch contemporary life and thought with the same breadth and vigor which characterized her *Later Records*, they possess their own unique advantages, and could not easily be excelled in their clear presentation of a striking individuality and its *milieu*, or in their shrewd and accurate criticism of life. The present book is made up, not like the others from a general correspondence, but of two independent series of letters, each printed continuously: the first, addressed to Miss Harriet St. Leger, beginning in January, 1874, and ending with Miss St. Leger's death, in 1877, taking up more than three quarters of the whole space, and making indeed a *journal intime;* and the second to Mr. Arthur Malkin, infrequent, desultory, but still complete enough to give a general sketch of the writer's experience from 1848 to 1883. There is a deplorable lack of good editing in the whole work, which might have been considerably shortened had the endless repetition of the same matter been omitted. Undated letters have been introduced in a way to make, at times, a bewildering jumble. Then, too, the want of chronological arrangement in the two distinct series of letters shows a singular indifference to the artistic make-up of the book on the part of author and publishers. Why those addressed to Mr. Malkin, most of which so far antedate those to Miss St. Leger, should not have been presented at the start, and finally have been

merged in the fuller correspondence, is nowhere explained. However, the sudden transition offers the charm of the unexpected. In the twinkling of an eye the writer casts off the trappings of age, and reappears as the traditional Fanny Kemble midway in her brilliant career; crossing the ocean twice a year, and delighting both England and America with her readings; climbing mountains in Switzerland; wintering in Rome and summering in Lenox. In truth, the letters to "Arthur," both in their tone and scope, afford a piquant contrast to those addressed to "H.," whose views of life, always serious, had plainly not lightened with the advance of age and loss of sight. Mrs. Kemble is evidently at not a little pains to put herself into sympathy with the deprivations of her elderly friend by herself coquetting with old age, as sexagenarians are apt to do. (p. 689)

Miss St. Leger's friendship had counted for much in Mrs. Kemble's experience, and she was generous in acknowledgments. "I have lost," remarked the younger Pliny, when Corellius Rufus died,—"yes, I have lost a witness of my own life;" and this all readers of Mrs. Kemble's various memoirs and letters know her beloved "H." to have been to her. And certainly letters like Mrs. Kemble's must have counted for much in the life of a blind invalid, past eighty years of age, written as they were with a complete absence of reserve, with marvelous facility of expression and trenchant powers of description, and out of an intellect swept clear of cobwebs. To see clearly and describe fearlessly belonged to Mrs. Kemble's temper and habit, and in this full correspondence minuteness of detail amply atones in the way of interest for possible lack of variety. (pp. 689-90)

[We regret] that Mrs. Kemble has permitted us chiefly to gather the facts of her biography from her letters, since her complete reminiscences might have been so valuable, besides being so delightful. Letters are apt to voice complaints. It is in general our disquietude, our disappointment, our *ennui*, which give the spur to self-confession; and literary work undertaken at a time of life when what is original, vital, fruitful, has largely been expended might gracefully take the form of recollections. She records an ingenious and graceful compliment from Frederika Bremer, upon whom she called one day, and found indisposed. Mrs. Kemble expressed a fear lest the exertion of receiving a visitor should be too much for her. "Oh, no!" Miss Bremer exclaimed; then added, laughing, "And yet I do not know that I ought *to see so many people at once.*" This pretty speech may be taken with two meanings; for Mrs. Kemble, one of the most brilliant and versatile women of this century, has in her time played many parts, not only on the stage, but in real life. She has been an actress, a dramatic reader, a poet, a playwriter, a voluminous writer in other literary forms, and she has throughout her career enjoyed high social distinction. Strange to say, in all her revelations of herself we nowhere see the whole woman dominated by an all-pervading idea, nor her powers fused into a single ambition. We suspect her of being most a poet, and, like other poets, *chercheur de l'infini*, whose secret goal of life dips far below the horizon, and is caught sight of only from the mountain top. (pp. 692-93)

The letters are interspersed with anecdotes of well-known people, often piquant and characteristic, and invariably interesting. But there is no running after brilliant effects, and no effort to say fine or witty things. Still, they abound in the book, and help to make up the admirably balanced impression left by the letters, in which feeling, humorous perception, accurate judgment, clear-headed observation, and sympathy with life all have free play. It may be said of Mrs. Kemble, "She brought an eye for all she saw," and brought besides the wit to understand and power to describe. (p. 694)

> "Mrs. Kemble's Letters," in The Atlantic Monthly, Vol. LXVII, No. 403, May, 1891, pp. 688-94.

THE CRITIC, NEW YORK (essay date 1891)

[*This anonymous reviewer describes and praises the "charming" reminiscences of* Further Records.]

The memoirs of an octogenarian are not often as charming as *Further Records;* but the charm of the later volume was already predicted by that of its predecessors, as an autumn rose is the exquisite fulfilled prediction of the spring. There is a pathos, too, in autumn roses which the superabounding color and scent of spring have not, just on account of their superabundance.

Mrs. Kemble-Butler's new record extends, from 1848 to 1883, over nearly forty years of sprightly correspondence with her Irish friend. A quick and agile spirit breathes through these letters, rather a French than an English spirit in its airy sarcasm and spontaneous wit. Perhaps they are not so fresh and so entertaining as the **"Old Woman's Gossip"** of *The Atlantic Monthly,* for that letter-budget was quite inimitable in style and interest, yet the winnowing of the garnered sheaves has shaken out many a jewel, and delightful reminscences abound.

Mrs. Kemble is not a Trollope, and yet she approaches perilously near her countrywoman in her frequent and passionate denunciations of American institutions. All this need not have been printed to have made a true and captivating book, and yet its sincerity and obvious foundation of truthfulness may serve an excellent purpose if it ever reach the ears of Congressmen and their constituents. The politicians and the elections draw down her overwhelming scorn, particularly during the Grant administration. Then the frightful American climate is discussed with an *Iliad* of variations, and the even more frightful servant question,—'Biddy' in all her protean manifestations,—emerges like a perpetual undercurrent running postscripturally and meteorically through all the letters. Mrs. Kemble would add a new prayer to the litany and supplicate to be delivered from her and all her Biddiness. 'Cook fever,' as she calls it, is rampant in Philadelphia whence many of these letters are written: worse than the Colorado beetles that swarmed over her potatoes, as she tells us. Every now and then she flees to a hotel from both—Biddy and beetle; to Lenox or Boston or those terrible caravansaries of the Jersey sea. She denudes herself of her hair in one of the hot spells, and declares that a climate in which the mercury sinks 40° in 24 hours is unendurable—'boiled,' 'broiled,' 'skinned,' 'scorched,' 'frozen,' are the perennial adjectives she applies to it. And yet she lives on and writes on, spiteful, fascinating, fitful, playful, climate to the contrary and Biddy militant and supreme notwithstanding. And the net result is these shining sheets brimming over with epistolary talent, interspersed with bracketed *morceaux* of reminiscences drawn from an overflowing experience, three or four hundred pages of letters for which 'Dearest Harriet' is entitled to everlasting thanks and remembrance. (p. 283)

> "Fanny Kemble's 'Further Records'," in The Critic, New York, Vol. 18, No. 387, May 30, 1891, pp. 283-84.

HENRY JAMES (essay date 1893)

[*James was an American-born English novelist, short story writer, critic, and essayist of the late nineteenth and early twentieth centuries. He is regarded as one of the greatest novelists of the English language and is also admired as a lucid and insightful critic. A friend and admirer of Kemble, James wrote a long essay after her death extolling her character, conversation, and accomplishments. In the following excerpt from this essay, he praises Kemble as a woman of letters.*]

[Mrs. Kemble's writing] had the same free sincerity as her conversation, and an equal absence of that quality which may be called in social intercourse diplomacy and in literature preoccupation or even ambition or even vanity.... [She] never dreamed of being a woman of letters—her wit and her wisdom relieved her too comfortably of such pretensions. Her various books, springing in every case but two or three straight from the real, from experience; personal and natural, humorous and eloquent, interesting as her character and her life were interesting, have all her irrepressible spirit or, if the word be admissible, her spiritedness. The term is not a critical one, but the geniality (in the Germanic sense) of her temperament makes everything she wrote what is called good reading. She wrote exactly as she talked, observing, asserting, complaining, confiding, contradicting, crying out and bounding off, always effectually communicating. Last, not least, she uttered with her pen as well as with her lips the most agreeable, uncontemporary, self-respecting English, as idiomatic as possible and just as little common. There were friends to whom she was absolutely precious, with a preciousness historic, inexpressible, to be kept under glass, as one of the rare persons (how many of her peers are left in the world?) over whom the trail of the newspaper was not. I never saw a newspaper in her house, nor in the course of many years heard her so much as allude to one; and as she had the habit, so she had the sense (a real touchstone for others) of English undefiled. French as she was, she hated Gallicisms in the one language as much as she winced at Anglicisms in the other, and she was a constant proof that the richest colloquial humor is not dependent for its success upon slang, least of all (as this is a matter in which distance gilds) upon that of the hour. I won't say that her lips were not occasionally crossed gracefully enough by that of 1840. Her attitude towards Americanisms may be briefly disposed of—she confounded them (when she didn't think, as she mostly did, that Americans made too many phrases—then she was impelled to be scandalous) with the general modern madness for which the newspaper was responsible.

Her prose and her poetical writings are alike unequal; easily the best of the former, I think, are the strong, insistent, one-sided *Journal of a Residence on a Georgia Plantation* (the most valuable account—and as a report of strong emotion scarcely less valuable from its element of *parti-pris*—of impressions begotten by that old Southern life which we are too apt to see to-day as through a haze of Indian summer), and the copious and ever-delightful *Record of a Girlhood* and *Records of Later Life,* which form together one of the most animated autobiographies in the language. Her poetry, all passionate and melancholy and less prized, I think, than it deserves, is perfectly individual and really lyrical. Much of it is so off-hand as to be rough, but much of it has beauty as well as reality, such beauty as to make one ask one's self (and the question recurs in turning the leaves of almost any of her books) whether her aptitude for literary expression had not been well worth her treating it with more regard. That she might have cared for it more is very certain—only as certain, however, as it is doubtful if any circumstances could have made her care. You can neither take vanity from those who have it nor give it to those who have it not. She really cared only for things higher and finer and fuller and happier than the shabby compromises of life, and the polishing of a few verses the more or the less would never have given her the illusion of the grand style. The matter comes back, moreover, to the terrible question of "art"; it is difficult after all to see where art can be squeezed in when you have such a quantity of nature. Mrs. Kemble would have said that she had all of hers on her hands. A certain rude justice presides over our affairs, we have to select and to pay, and artists in general are rather spare and thrifty folk. They give up for their security a great deal that Mrs. Kemble never could give up; security was her dream, but it remained her dream: practically she passed her days in peril. What she had in verse was not only the lyric impulse but the genuine lyric need. . . . She made a very honest use of it, inasmuch as it expressed for her what nothing else could express—the inexpugnable, the fundamental, the boundless and generous sadness which lay beneath her vitality, beneath her humor, her imagination, her talents, her violence of will and integrity of health. This note of suffering, audible to the last and pathetic, as the prostrations of strength are always pathetic, had an intensity all its own, though doubtless, being so direct and unrelieved, the interest and even the surprise of it were greatest for those to whom she was personally known. There was something even strangely simple in that perpetuity of pain which the finest of her sonnets commemorate and which was like the distress of a nature conscious of its irremediable exposure and consciously paying for it. The great tempest of her life, her wholly unprosperous marriage, had created waves of feeling which, even after long years, refused to be stilled, continued to gather and break.

Twice only, after her early youth, she tried the sort of experiment that is supposed most effectually to liberate the mind from the sense of its own troubles—the literary imagination of the troubles of others. She published, in 1863, the fine, sombre, poetical, but unmanageable play called *An English Tragedy* (written many years previous); and at the age of eighty she, for the first time, wrote and put forth a short novel. The latter of these productions, *Far Away and Long Ago,* shows none of the feebleness of age; and besides the charm, in form, of its old decorous affiliation (one of her friends, on reading it, assured her in perfect good faith that she wrote for all the world like Walter Scott), it is a twofold example of an uncommon felicity. This is, on the one hand, to break ground in a new manner and so gracefully at so advanced an age (did *any* one else ever produce a first fiction at eighty?), and, on the other, to revert successfully, in fancy, to associations long outlived. Interesting, touching must the book inevitably be, from this point of view, to American readers. There was nothing finer in Mrs. Kemble's fine mind than the generous justice of which she was capable (as her knowledge grew, and after the innocent impertinences of her girlish [*Journal of a Residence in America*]) to the country in which she had, from the first, found troops of friends and intervals of peace as well as depths of disaster. She had a mingled feeling and a sort of conscientious strife about it, together with a tendency to handle it as gently with one side of her nature as she was prompted to belabor it with the other. The United States commended themselves to her liberal opinions as much as they disconcerted her intensely conservative taste; she relished every obligation to them but that of living in them; and never heard them eulogized without uttering her reserves or abused without speaking her admiration. They had been the scene of some of her strongest friendships, and, eventually, among the mountains of Massachusetts,

she had for many years, though using it only in desultory ways, enjoyed the least occasional of her homes. Late in life she looked upon this region as an Arcadia, a happy valley, a land of woods and waters and upright souls; and in the light of this tender retrospect, a memory of summer days and loved pastimes, of plentiful riding and fishing, recounted her romantic anecdote, a retarded stroke of the literary clock of 1840. *An English Tragedy* seems to sound from a still earlier timepiece, has in it an echo of the great Elizabethans she cherished.

Compromised by looseness of construction, it has nevertheless such beauty and pathos as to make us wonder why, with her love of poetry (which she widely and perpetually quoted) and her hereditary habit of the theatre, she should not oftener have tried her strong hand at a play. (pp. 104-10)

Henry James, "Frances Anne Kemble," in his Essays in London and Elsewhere, *Harper & Brothers Publishers, 1893, pp. 81-120.*

ULRICH BONNELL PHILLIPS   (essay date 1929)

[*In the following excerpt from his history of the South, Phillips comments on Kemble's representation of slave life in* Journal of a Residence on a Georgian Plantation.]

In her English girlhood Fanny Kemble had acquired an abiding horror of Negro slavery which her marriage did not diminish; and resolving to keep a journal of her observations and experiences in the régime, she registered her drastic repugnance in advance: "Assuredly I *am* going prejudiced against slavery, for I am an Englishwoman, in whom the absence of such a prejudice would be disgraceful. Nevertheless I go prepared to find many mitigations in the practice to the general injustice and cruelty of the system." The resulting book [*Journal of a Residence on a Georgian Plantation*] is a monotonous view of the seamy side, and an exhibit of the critic's own mental processes. On Butler's Island the overseer's house in which the sojourners dwelt was crude and cramped, the servants unkempt and ill-smelling, the slave cabins and hospitals unclean, and all things unpleasing. The filth and stench in British and European peasant hovels, she granted, was as great; but in the case of the Negroes she said "slavery is answerable for all the evils . . . from lying, thieving and adultery to dirty houses, ragged clothes and foul smells." Again, their food and bedding were deficient and their work excessive, though in other connections it was noted that many of the workers were in perfect physique; many of them ended their tasks by the middle of the afternoon; they sold on their own account large quantities of Spanish moss, the best of materials for mattresses; and their ducks and chickens swarmed under the orange trees in the quarters and added to the filth in the cabins.

The head foreman, like several other slaves, was judged upright, intelligent, neat and self-respecting, "with a courteousness of demeanor far removed from servility." Was his a case of alleviation? No, it "exhibits a strong instance of the intolerable and wicked injustice of the system under which he lives. Having advanced thus far toward improvement in spite of all bars it puts to progress," he is forbidden further improvement.

This visiting lady, who when addressed as "Missis" begged the Negroes "For God's sake do not call me that," on occasion "addressed the girls most solemnly, showing them that they were wasting in idle riot the time in which they might be rendering their abode decent." She also addressed to her husband, who "seemed positively degraded in my eyes as he stood

Slave quarters on the Butler plantation. Margaret Davis Cate.

enforcing upon these women the necessity of their fulfilling their appointed tasks,'' so many protests that he finally forbade the further conveyance of complaints by her. Such recitals as these crowd out of the journal most of what might be expected in description of the plantation and its working. (pp. 261-62)

Ulrich Bonnell Phillips, ''Southeastern Planta- tions,'' in his Life and Labor in the Old South, Little, Brown, and Company, 1929, pp. 252-73.

LEOTA S. DRIVER   (essay date 1933)

[In the following excerpt from her study of Kemble's life and works, Driver favorably assesses her critical essays, Notes upon Some of Shakespeare's Plays.*]*

[In 1882, Mrs. Kemble published] *Notes upon Some of Shakespeare's Plays,* a volume containing interpretations of *Macbeth, Henry VIII, The Tempest,* and *Romeo and Juliet.* In addition, the author included her essay **"On the Stage"** which first appeared in 1863 in the *Cornhill Magazine.* Considering its brevity, this study contained perhaps the most careful analysis in dramatic criticism of the actor in juxtaposition with his art. English people, said the author, frequently confused the terms ''dramatic'' and ''theatrical'' and spoke of them as synonymous. She tried to correct this misconception.

The passionate, emotional, humorous element in human nature, she said, is the dramatic. Beyond its momentary excitement and gratification it claims no relation with its imitative theatrical reproduction. The dramatic is the *real* of which the theatrical is the *false.* The combination of the power to represent passion and emotion with that of imagining or conceiving it, the union of theatrical talent with dramatic temperament, is essential to the good actor. Their combination in the highest possible degree makes a great actor.

The theatrical, according to this critic's interpretation, differs from all other arts. It has neither fixed rules, specific principles, indispensable rudiments, nor fundamental laws. It has no basis in positive science such as music, painting, sculpture, or architecture has. The appearance of spontaneity is its chief merit. Although it creates nothing and perpetates nothing, it requires of its practitioners the imagination of the poet, the ear of the musician, and the eye of the painter and sculptor. In addition, it demands a faculty peculiar to itself, for the actor personally fulfills and embodies his conception. With all its demands, it requires no study worthy of the name. Actors delight only the play-going public of their own day. They cannot justly claim the rapture of creation, the glory of patient and protracted toil, or the love and honor of grateful posterity. Money and applause fitly compensate these performers.

Her notes on the various Shakespearean plays were for the most part interpretative. She designated *Macbeth* as a drama of conscience in which Lady Macbeth embodied evil strength, and Macbeth, evil weakness. *Henry VIII* presented the conflict between two types of pride—pride of power, and pride of birth. Instead of an analysis, the notes on *Romeo and Juliet* included only a few hints for the acting. Romeo seemed to represent the sentiment, and Juliet, the passion of love. The pathos was his, the power, hers. The comprehension of these distinctions furnished the key for the impersonation of these characters.

In her study of *The Tempest,* her favorite Shakespearean drama, she attempted to explain the reasons for this preference. The remoteness of setting allowed to the imagination a range permitted in no other play. The action presented the supremacy of the human soul over all things which surrounded it. The characters portrayed every plane of human life. Prospero represented wise and virtuous manhood in its relation to the combined elements of existence, the middle link in a chain of beings of which Caliban stood at the lowest and densest, and Ariel, at the most ethereal extreme. Caliban personified the more ponderous and unwieldy natural elements which, through knowledge, the wise magician compelled to serve him. Ariel embodied the keen perceiving intellect apart from all moral consciousness and sense of responsibility. Because he was a spirit only of knowledge, he became subject to the spirit of love. This wild, subtle, keen, powerful creature served the human soul with mutinous waywardness and unwilling subjection.

In these criticisms Mrs. Kemble proved herself a ready writer and the master of an easy and idiomatic English which used words exactly. Although devotees of the theatrical art severely flayed the author for her strictures upon the actor's labor and reward, her notes on the plays received favorable comment. They revealed clearness of insight and thoroughness of comprehension. (pp. 201-03)

> *Leota S. Driver, in her* Fanny Kemble, *The University of North Carolina Press, 1933, 271 p.*

ALLAN NEVINS   (essay date 1948)

[*Nevins notes both the human sympathy and the reportorial accuracy apparent in* Journal of a Residence on a Georgian Plantation.]

Fanny Kemble's *Journal of a Residence on a Georgian Plantation in 1838-39* first appeared in 1863—'a sadder book the human hand never wrote,' according to the *Atlantic Monthly* [see excerpt dated 1863]. Fanny Kemble, a niece of Mrs. Siddons and a daughter of the famous actor Charles Kemble, was born in 1809 and made her debut as Juliet at Covent Garden at the age of nineteen, at once becoming a great favorite of the public. Sheridan Knowles wrote *The Hunchback* especially for her. In 1832 she accompanied her father to America, and the two achieved an even more striking success there, being equally applauded. As she says, in these years she 'literally coined money.' Meeting Pierce Butler, a Southern planter, she married him in 1834 and went to reside on his two large estates near Darien, Georgia, in total ignorance, she assures us, of the fact that he was an extensive slave owner, or of what the condition of the slaves was.

In her solitary situation on the Darien estates, living in a comfortless frame house, without any of the amusements to which she had been accustomed, she conceived the idea of writing a journal of her daily experiences on the model of the Journal kept by Monk Lewis during his visit to his West India plantations. The Negroes on Pierce Butler's estates esteemed themselves comparatively well off, as well they might when they looked at the lot of those on neighboring tracts; while in this part of the South they were very much better off indeed than on some of the remote interior plantations. She was a clear-sighted, noble-minded, warm-hearted woman, who at the outset believed that the blacks about her were contented, and then for a time that they might be made so. Her book relates in vivid and sincere style the story of her tragic undeceiving. Its literary merits are considerable—she was later the author of various poetical and dramatic works—but it is wholly devoid of coloring for effect or of sensationalism. Her daily observations are stated in a matter-of-fact way, and such unconscious exaggeration as the book possesses arises from her excessive sensibility.

It was the slave woman, tasked with constant childbearing and field work, with whom she sympathized most deeply, and of the terrible physical ailments that resulted from the merciless combination of these two burdens she writes with proper frankness. She tells us that on Pierce Butler's well-managed plantations, as on others, the mothers were driven afield to work under the lash within three weeks after childbirth, and their infants, among whom the mortality was of course excessive, were left to the care of youngsters still not quite old enough for the field. She tells what she observed of the compulsion placed upon some of these women to cohabit with their overseers or even white masters. She tells of the floggings they received. One of her most striking passages relates at length the agony of a woman slave, Psyche, the mother of two small children, when, supposing herself the property of an overseer who had just purchased an Alabama plantation, she was in daily fear of being separated from her husband and removed thither; and the struggle that the writer, Fanny Kemble, had to wage with the overseer and with Pierce Butler to keep the family united. She describes the wretched infirmaries on the estates, and the ghastly lack of care given to the slaves on their deathbeds, in childbirth, and at other seasons of illness—no fire, no medicines, no bandages, no bedclothing, no lights. 'I groped my way out,' she states in describing one visit to an infirmary, where sick slave women were lying on the bare earth in nothing but filthy tattered clothing, 'and emerging on the piazza, all the choking tears and sobs I had controlled broke forth, and I leaned there crying over the lot of these unfortunates.'

Her description of the dirtiness and squalor of the slave huts is undoubtedly veracious. They had almost no furniture, their beds being mere wooden frames with a bark covering; they abounded with fleas and other vermin. The meals of the slaves were eaten without the aid of the most ordinary utensils, and consisted of nothing but meal or hominy. Work began at daybreak, the first food was eaten at noon—cooked over a fire kindled in the field—and the second meal was taken at night. She pictures a Negro dance and other merrymakings, but the tone of her book is one of almost unrelieved sadness. It can no more be neglected by the student of Southern society before the war than can Olmsted's volumes of Southern travels. (pp. 166-68)

> *Allan Nevins, "The Dark Side of Slavery, 1838-39,"* *in* America through British Eyes, *edited by Allan Nevins, revised edition, Oxford University Press, 1948, pp. 166-68.*

MARGARET DAVIS CATE   (essay date 1960)

[*Cate questions the truthfulness of* Journal of a Residence on a Georgian Plantation. *Concentrating on the incident (related in the* Journal) *of a territorial feud between two Georgia landowners that resulted in a fatal duel, Cate asserts that Kemble's work is factually inaccurate and unreliable. For a defense of Kemble's veracity, see excerpt by Scott dated 1961.*]

[In her *Journal of a Residence on a Georgian Plantation, 1838-1839*], Mrs. Butler stated that she would avoid the errors, which she called "misstatements, or rather mistakes," made by her countryman, Harriet Martineau, in reporting what she had been told by others. Mrs. Butler promised not to use "accounts received from others," but to furnish only "details . . . which come under my immediate observation." Had she followed this rule, she could have left a valuable record instead of this overdrawn picture of life on the Butler plantations, filled, as it is, with errors of fact and a fictitious account of events. These surely were not written while she was here, but must have been added many years after she had left Georgia. (p. 3)

[The *Journal of a Residence on a Georgian Plantation*] was advertised [in the *Independent* (see excerpt dated 1863)] as "the most thrilling and horrible picture of the interior social life of the slave holding section of this country that has ever been published . . . previous accounts . . . have been from outside observers. But the [*Journal of a Residence on a Georgian Plantation*] of Mrs. Kemble was jotted down from day to day as she lived on the plantation . . . there is no excuse, no palliation of facts. . . . So faithful and final a witness we have not had. Even *Uncle Tom's Cabin* is only founded upon the fact. The [*Journal of a Residence on a Georgian Plantation*] of Mrs. Kemble is fact itself."

And as "fact itself" this [*Journal of a Residence on a Georgian Plantation*] has been held by many during the century since it was published. But to a student of the area, of the time, and of the people covered by the [*Journal of a Residence on a Georgian Plantation*], Mrs. Kemble does not present a true picture. Furthermore, it would require one who *did* know the area, the time, and the people to find the glaring misstatements made by her in this [*Journal of a Residence on a Georgian Plantation*].

No one would deny that Mrs. Kemble did keep some kind of a journal of her stay in Georgia. (pp. 3-4)

Mrs. Kemble, herself, acknowledged that her [*Journal of a Residence on a Georgian Plantation*] was not an accurate account kept day by day while she was in Georgia. Writing in 1840 she stated, "The time that I passed in the South was so crowded with hourly and daily occupations that, though I kept a regular journal, it was hastily written, and received constant additional notes of things that occurred, and that I wished to remember, inserted in a very irregular fashion in it. . . ."

She hoped to make another trip to Georgia during the winter of 1840-41 but objections raised by her brother-in-law, John Butler, were such that she did not go. She wrote that had she made this trip she hoped to carry her journal "down to Georgia . . . ; to revise, correct, and add whatever my second experience might furnish to the chronicle."

Even then she had thoughts of publishing the journal but acknowledged that "such a publication would be a breach of confidence, an advantage taken on my part of the situation of trust, which I held on the estate . . ." and should be published only with the consent of the owners of the estate. But, she continued, "I am occupying myself, from time to time, as my leisure allows, in making a fair copy of my Georgia Journal."

If it were possible to do so, it would be interesting to secure all the manuscript copies of this [*Journal of a Residence on a Georgian Plantation*] and compare them. It could then be ascertained what Mrs. Kemble did write during the four months she spent on these Georgia plantations and what she added later to give dramatic quality to the story.

That many passages in the [*Journal of a Residence on a Georgian Plantation*] were added later is evident. It is believed that these additions were made by Mrs. Kemble when she was preparing the [*Journal of a Residence on a Georgian Plantation*] for publication. As she read the original manuscript she must have realized that it was dull reading and would excite little comment. If her purpose of arousing public indignation against the slaveholding people of the South was to be accomplished,

she must add drama to the story—and no one could know better the value of drama than this actress-author.

There are many statements in Mrs. Kemble's [*Journal of a Residence on a Georgian Plantation*] which can be proven wrong, but only one or two need be cited. Her reference to the Butler cup is one such instance. She stated that this cup was given by Major Pierce Butler to one of the Negroes "as a testimonial of approbation, with an inscription on it recording his fidelity and trustworthiness at the time of the invasion of the coast of Georgia by the English troops." She wrote that the son of the Negro who received the cup brought it to show it to her, so she *could* have seen the inscription and read it correctly. But, failing to have the correct story, she simply wrote a pretty tale.

This cup was given to Morris for a very different reason. Fanny Kemble's daughter wrote that it was given for services rendered in 1804 during a storm that came up while the Butler Negroes were working on Little St. Simons Island, where the only building was "a hurricane house." Seeing the storm break, the Negroes wanted to get in the boats and return to their homes on St. Simons Island, but Morris forced them to wait out the storm in the "hurricane house," with the result that "not a life was lost, though upwards of a hundred were drowned from a neighboring island, who had rushed into their boats and tried to reach the mainland. . . ."

The inscription on the cup reads:

TO MORRIS
from
P. BUTLER,
For his faithful, judicious, and spirited conduct in
the hurricane of September 8, 1804, whereby
the lives of more than 100 persons were,
by Divine permission, saved.

Though this instance of her inaccuracy in telling the story of the cup which Major Butler gave to the Negro shows that Fanny Kemble did not correctly report events, there is another incident which shows even better that she was far from accurate. It concerns her reference to the feud between Dr. Thomas Fuller Hazzard and Mr. John Armstrong Wylly, both of St. Simons Island.

It is in writing about this incident that Mrs. Kemble gave free rein to her imagination and her dramatic instincts. She wrote as though she were on the scene when this occurred and she described the tragic affair with gruesome details in a day by day build up.

> Saturday [March] 31st. I rode . . . to Mrs. W[ylly]'s field, . . . [on] a charming wood ride which runs between Mrs. W[ylly]'s and Colonel H[azzard]'s grounds. While going along this delightful boundary of these two neighboring estates, my mind not unnaturally dwelt upon the terms of deadly feud in which the two families owning them are living with each other. A horrible quarrel has occurred quite lately upon the subject of the ownership of this very ground I was skirting, between Dr. H[azzard] and young Mr. W[ylly]; they have challenged each other, and what I am going to tell you is a good sample of the sort of spirit which grows up among slave holders. So read it, for it is curious to people who have not lived habitually among slaves. The terms of the challenge that has passed be-

tween them have appeared like a sort of advertisement in the local paper, and are to the effect that they are to fight at a certain distance with certain weapons—fire arms, of course; that there is to be on the person of each a white paper, or mark, immediately over the region of the heart, as a point for direct aim; and whoever kills the other is to have the privilege of *cutting off his head, and sticking it up on a pole on the piece of land which was the origin of the debate;* so that, some fine day, I might have come hither as I did to-day, and found myself riding under the shadow of the gory locks of Dr. H[azzard] or Mr. W[ylly], my peaceful and pleasant neighbors.

(pp. 4-7)

A few pages farther on in the [*Journal of a Residence on a Georgian Plantation*] she told of a visit to Dr. Hazzard's plantation:

> We have been paying more friendly and neighborly visits, or rather returning them; and the recipient of these civilized courtesies on our last calling expedition were the family one member of which was a party concerned in that barbarous challenge I wrote you word about. Hitherto that brutal and bloodthirsty cartel appears to have had no result. You must not, on that account, imagine that it will have none. . . . and though this agreeable party of pleasure has not come off yet, there seems to be no reason why it should not at the first convenient season. Reflecting upon all which, I rode, not without trepidation, through Colonel H[azzard]'s grounds, and up to his house. Mr. W[ylly]'s head was not stuck up on a pole any where within sight, however, and as soon as I became sure of this, I began to look about me, and saw instead a trellis tapestried with the most beautiful roses I ever beheld, another of those exquisite Southern flowers—the Cherokee rose.

Finally, after all this fictitious build-up of incidents in connection with the Hazzard-Wylly feud, which she evidently believed would add interest to the [*Journal of a Residence on a Georgian Plantation*] and show the world the terrible people these slaveholding plantation owners were, now, she thought the time had arrived to let Mr. Wylly get killed.

On Sunday, April 14th, she recorded this as having happened. In her April 13th entry she made no mention of it. In a previous entry (without date, but during the week beginning April 7th), she wrote that "this agreeable party of pleasure has not come off yet."

She seemed to feel that she had set the stage and prepared the audience for the climax. So, it could be announced: "That horrid tragedy . . . has been accomplished . . . and [Mr. Wylly] has been brought home and buried by the little church."

The date of this entry was April 14th, 1839, and here it was that Mrs. Kemble made her BIG mistake; Mr. Wylly was killed December 3, 1838! (pp. 8-9)

Proof of the date of Mr. Wylly's death is to be found on his tombstone in Christ Church Burying Ground. . . .

Further proof of the correct date is contained in the newspaper account of the tragedy. . . . (p. 10)

Though Mrs. Kemble reported the death of Mr. Wylly in her April 14th entry, just three days later, on "Wednesday, April 17th," during her visit with Mrs. Demere and her sons, she wrote:

> The conversation turned upon Dr. H[azzard]'s trial; for there has been a trial as a matter of form, and an acquittal as a matter of course; and the gentlemen said, upon my expressing some surprise at the latter event [the acquittal], that there could not be found in 'all Georgia' a jury who would convict him, which says but little for the moral sense of all Georgia.

Had Mrs. Kemble read her [*Journal of a Residence on a Georgian Plantation*] carefully, she should have seen that she was presenting an impossible situation in reporting the death of Mr. Wylly, and, just three days later, the trial of his assailant.

Superior Court was in session at the time of the fatal encounter. The judge presiding over these sessions, the Hon. Charles S. Henry, witnessed the initial attack when Mr. Wylly struck Dr. Hazzard with a cane. The Grand Jury indicted Dr. Hazzard and the same newspaper that reported the encounter, in a paragraph on Superior Court items, stated: "The case of the State vs. Dr. Thomas F. Hazzard, indicted for manslaughter, will probably be continued till the next term of court."

The case was called at the next (April) term of Court; since it was not possible to get a jury, the case was continued. At the time that Mrs. Kemble reported he had been acquitted, Dr. Hazzard had not been tried. When the case did come to trial there was a mistrial; finally, Dr. Hazzard was acquitted.

Mrs. Kemble seemed to be striving to show that the local people were a callous, hardened group. "At the North, were it possible for a duel to be conducted on such savage terms to be a matter of notoriety, the very horror of the thing would create a feeling of grotesqueness, and the antagonists in such a proposed encounter would simply incur an immense amount of ridicule and obloquy. But here nobody is astonished and nobody ashamed of such preliminaries to a mortal combat between two gentlemen, who propose firing at marks over each other's hearts, and cutting off each other's heads; . . . ." Enjoying this theme, she repeated it a few days later: "That horrid tragedy . . . has been accomplished, and apparently without exciting anything but the most superficial sensation in this community."

However, the columns of the local newspaper told a different story. The plantation owners of St. Simons, aroused by the tragedy, met and adopted resolutions, placing themselves on the side of law and order. (pp. 11-13)

The St. Simons citizens were not the only ones who "deplored" the Hazzard-Wylly affair. The Grand Jury of Glynn County, who were in session when the killing took place and who indicted Dr. Hazzard, after the usual preamble and presentments, added:

> We deeply regret that we cannot congratulate the citizens of this County with being blessed with harmony and quietude; but, on the contrary, we have been burdened with an examination into many serious offences against the peace and good order of the community.

We deplore the unfortunate occurrence which resulted in the untimely death of our esteemed fellow-citizen, Mr. John A. Wylly; and join in condolence with the mother and relations, and surviving friends of the deceased. . . .

These statements from contemporary sources prove Fanny Kemble was mistaken when she stated that Wylly's death had excited only "the most superficial sensation in this community," that "no one seems to think anything of it," and that there was a "total absence of expression or feeling among the whole population of St. Simons." Furthermore, she was here at that time and should have recorded the true situation. (p. 14)

Fanny Kemble strayed far from her promise to write in her [*Journal of a Residence on a Georgian Plantation*] only that which she saw with her own eyes. She wrote of going along the road through the property which was the cause of the trouble, told of the challenge for the duel, and stated it had not yet taken place; yet, at that time, as given in her [*Journal of a Residence on a Georgian Plantation*], Mr. Wylly had been dead four months! In fact, he was dead and buried before Fanny Kemble left Philadelphia to come to Georgia!

The [*Journal of a Residence on a Georgian Plantation*] is not a day by day account of life on the plantations. When it is proven, as has been done here, that Mrs. Kemble must have added to it after she left Georgia, then every statement in the [*Journal of a Residence on a Georgian Plantation*] is open to suspicion.

Can anyone know *fact* from *fiction* in Mrs. Kemble's [*Journal of a Residence on a Georgian Plantation*]? (p. 17)

Margaret Davis Cate, "Mistakes in Fanny Kemble's Georgia Journal," in The Georgia Historical Quarterly, *Vol. XLIV, No. 1, March, 1960, pp. 1-17.*

JOHN ANTHONY SCOTT   (essay date 1961)

[*The excerpt below is from the introduction to Scott's edition of Kemble's* Journal of a Residence on a Georgian Plantation. *Scott discusses the literary and historical importance of the* Journal *and challenges Margaret Davis Cate's charges of untruthfulness (see the excerpt dated 1960).*]

Frances Anne Kemble recorded her stay in the Georgia Sea Islands twenty-two years before the outbreak of the Civil War; her book was the product of the fierce debate over slavery that exercised the minds of men and women on both sides of the Atlantic in the years following the end of the American Revolution. Published in the same year that the slaves were emancipated, her work was designed to contribute to the understanding of the historic struggle then being waged within the United States, to discourage British intervention in that struggle, and to spur the North to victory. Passionate in its denunciation of oppression, the *Journal of a Residence on a Georgian Plantation* painted a picture of slavery so brutal in its realism that it was unacceptable to Victorian society. Although the [*Journal of a Residence on a Georgian Plantation*] enjoyed an intensive wartime fame, it was soon forgotten by the general public and soon out of print. For nearly a hundred years it has led a twilight existence in the secondhand book stores and in the footnotes of professional historians. In this respect it stands in sharp contrast to the contemporary work of Harriet Beecher Stowe. *Uncle Tom's Cabin* has never, since its first publication in 1852, been out of print nor lost its hold upon the public's attention.

Neither as literary work nor as social study has the [*Journal of a Residence on a Georgian Plantation*] merited the oblivion that has fallen upon it. It is written by one of the most gifted women that the nineteenth century produced, and it affords insight into the life and mind of a great artist. As intense study of the ante-bellum South, it provides a fitting complement to Olmsted's classic account, *The Cotton Kingdom.* Olmsted's observations of the South were the product of a fourteen-month sojourn in which the author made three extended trips and covered many thousand miles. Kemble's picture, on the other hand, was based upon a stay of three and one half months on two small islands at the mouth of the Altamaha River. Her observations were made within an area no more than sixteen miles square, at the heart of one of the South's most important and productive cotton-, rice-, and sugar-producing zones, the home of a number of its most influential ruling families. (pp. ix-x)

A careful reading of the [*Journal of a Residence on a Georgian Plantation*] reveals a number of minor factual inaccuracies. . . . There is no reason to believe that Fanny would not have corrected the most important of these herself had she had the opportunity of a second visit to Georgia. But into one incident in the [*Journal of a Residence on a Georgian Plantation*], the Wylly-Hazzard duel, Mrs. Kemble deliberately introduced an element of fiction. In Chapters XXVII to XXXII she told the story of a quarrel between two neighboring planters on St. Simons Island which resulted in the death of one of the participants; and she gave the date of this encounter as the first week of April 1839, when in fact the quarrel occurred in 1838 and the fatal shooting on December 3 of that year. Mrs. Kemble was here recounting something that had not come under her immediate observation as if it had. How then, asks a recent writer [Margaret Davis Cate (see excerpt dated 1960)], can one distingush fact from fiction in the [*Journal of a Residence on a Georgian Plantation*]?

Fanny Kemble was a woman, evidently, who found it difficult to conceal her true thoughts and feelings. She felt obliged to take her stand on slavery before her husband even though this led to the collapse of her home, the disintegration of her marriage, and the vanishing of her hopes for happiness. We must look for some unusual reason for her decision to postdate the Wylly-Hazzard duel and to introduce it into the [*Journal of a Residence on a Georgian Plantation*] as personal experience rather than as recent St. Simons history. The fact is that shortly after returning from Georgia, Fanny had an intimate and harrowing experience. On Monday, April 15, 1844, Pierce Butler fought a duel at Bladensburg, Maryland, with a Philadelphia neighbor and friend, James Schott. Pistols were used, two rounds were fired by each man, and both escaped unharmed. It is noteworthy that the duel took place at the insistence of Pierce Butler, even after his opponent had tried to cancel it on the grounds that his heel was so painfully swollen he could not stand straight to deliver his shot accurately. The encounter came about as a result of a charge by Schott that on a visit to New York he had found Butler at midnight of March 9, 1844, in a compromising relationship with his wife, Ellen Schott. Fanny was living in Philadelphia at that time, apart from her husband and children. The charge of Butler's infidelity was a matter of public gossip, and the duel was the sensation of the hour. Fanny read the whole affair in the public press.

While she was in Georgia, Fanny had had ample opportunity to realize the role played by the duel in Southern life. The shadow of a famous murder hung over the Butler estate itself; it was there, at Hampton Point, that Aaron Burr took refuge from New Jersey justice after slaying Alexander Hamilton in 1804. The mistress of Hampton, we know, read the local newspaper, the Brunswick *Advocate,* while she was in Georgia. The March 30, 1839 issue had a lead article, evidently designed for the improvement of its readers, entitled ''The Horrors of Duelling.'' The same issue reported an encounter which resulted in the murder of George Cumberland, a commission merchant from Mobile, Alabama, by E. B. Church, also a merchant, at the latter's home; in addition it told of a duel near Moscow, Tennessee, between Alex Donelson, adopted son of the Seventh President of the United States, and Henry Robeson, in which both men were slightly wounded. Other issues of the *Advocate* reported duels in which the opponents placed their pistols in each other's mouths; and one in which a judge fought an army captain with rifles and finished his antagonist off with a bowie knife. While Fanny was on St. Simons Island the conversation must have turned constantly to the recent duel between Wylly and Hazzard. Whatever local indignation had been aroused, it was not sufficient to prevent Hazzard's acquittal upon a charge of manslaughter, and this occurred shortly after Mrs. Kemble left Georgia.

We must conclude that dueling was a fact of Fanny's Georgia experience. It was in her husband's family tradition, in his own personal conduct, and in the mental agony which she suffered as a consequence. Postdating the Wylly-Hazzard affair was a device which enabled Fanny to introduce into the [*Journal of a Residence on a Georgian Plantation*] the agonies of her own encounter with the duello without revealing the secrets of her personal life.

The picture that Mrs. Kemble paints of slavery on her husband's plantation is a dark one lightened by exquisite word pictures of the landscape, of birds, waterways, trees, skies, and flowers. Incidents, too, of a deep tenderness lighten the gloom, but also accentuate the sadness of the world of toil and misery into which the reader is plunged. If the slaves are the heroes of the scene, they are not romanticized, but presented in their dirt-incrusted, animal existence. If the planter society seems vapid and ignorant, idle and cruel, some of its members are likeable people. John Couper is shown as a kindly, thrifty old soul with a passion for flowers, and his son James Hamilton Couper, the hero of the *Pulaski,* is described in complimentary terms. Dr. James Holmes appears as courteous and friendly; Captain John Fraser and his wife, Ann, are depicted as thoughtful hosts and neighbors.

Mrs. Kemble's picture of slavery has a many-sided complexity. Its almost inexhaustible detail points up the powers of observation of a woman who reflected the varied life about her with a brilliant intensity. (pp. lv-lviii)

The [*Journal of a Residence on a Georgian Plantation*] brings to life for us both a slave community and a segment of Southern society, and because it does this, its literary and historical value is evident. Mrs. Kemble was a white woman who cast aside the apologetics which rationalized and defended the oppression of the Negro people, and who won a true perception of their strength, dignity, and beauty. This achievement was nonetheless impressive for being—as the pages of the [*Journal of a Residence on a Georgian Plantation*] bear eloquent witness— the result of a constant struggle to penetrate to the heart of things through the repulsive outer circumstance of dirt, ugliness, and disease. Fanny Kemble fought, in a difficult time, her own battle on behalf of the brotherhood of man. The [*Journal of a Residence on a Georgian Plantation*] is a contribution to the antislavery literature which constitutes an important part

of the cultural and moral heritage of the American people. (p. lix)

> *John Anthony Scott, in an introduction to* Journal of a Residence on a Georgian Plantation in 1838-1839 *by Frances Anne Kemble, edited by John A. Scott, 1961. Reprint by New American Library, 1975, pp. ix-lxi.*

ROBERT B. DOWNS (essay date 1977)

[*Downs focuses on key aspects of* Journal of a Residence on a Georgian Plantation, *which he claims is "unique in the annals of slavery."*]

Two of the most powerful documents attacking and condemning the institution of slavery in America were written by women— one in fictional and the other in factual form. Of the two, Harriet Beecher Stowe's *Uncle Tom's Cabin* unquestionably had the greater impact, because its moral lesson is wrapped up in an exciting story. Fanny Kemble's *Journal of a Residence on a Georgian Plantation* refused to mix truth and romance; except for an occasional almost poetic description of the Southern landscape, the account is a realistic picture, filled with burning indignation and pity, of slavery in operation. The book's appeal was perforce more limited than Mrs. Stowe's melodramatic tale of cruel aristocrats, stately mansions, and such memorable characters as Simon Legree, blue-eyed Eva, and black-faced Topsy. Nevertheless, the [*Journal of a Residence on a Georgian Plantation*'s] role in the Civil War and the slavery controversy is of considerable significance. (p. 82)

Fanny had resolved before undertaking the stay in Georgia that she would attempt to maintain an objective view. ''I am going to Georgia,'' she wrote, ''prejudiced against slavery, for I am an Englishwoman, in whom the absence of such a prejudice would be disgraceful.'' Nevertheless, she hoped to find mitigating factors in ''the general injustice and cruelty of the system, perhaps much contentment on the part of the slaves and kindness on that of the masters.'' Accordingly, her report was to be based on careful observation and accurate facts, avoiding malice and noting any extenuating circumstances. Here could be put to an acid test Pierce Butler's claim that ''those people are happy—happier than they would be if they were free. They love us and we are fond of them.''

As soon as she arrived in Georgia, Fanny began writing her [*Journal of a Residence on a Georgian Plantation*], pouring into it her daily experiences and impressions, character sketches, descriptions of the surrounding area, and opinions on slavery. (pp. 84-5)

Contrary to the romantic notion that the owners of Southern plantations resided in palatial mansions, nowhere on the Butler properties was there a civilized dwelling for Fanny and her family. On Butler Island, they moved into the overseer's shabby five-room cottage and while there lived under the most primitive conditions. The island itself is described by Fanny as ''a kind of mud sponge.'' She adds, ''The chief produce of this delectable spot is rice—oranges, negroes, fleas, mosquitoes, various beautiful evergreens, sundry sort of snakes, alligators, and bull rushes enough to have made cradles not for Moses alone but the whole Israelitish host besides.'' The entire island lay below high-water mark, walled in by dikes; the river water was allowed in through ditches and canals when the rice fields needed flooding. Cabbages were the only vegetable grown on the island. There were three mills for threshing rice, run by steam and tide-water, and four slave villages, where several hundred Negroes were housed in wooden shacks.

The realities of the slave system exceeded Fanny's worst fears. Her [*Journal of a Residence on a Georgian Plantation*], which her great-granddaughter, Fanny Kemble Wister, claimed "is the only firsthand account by the wife of a slave holder of the negroes' lives on a plantation," is a day-by-day record of what she saw and did. She immediately gained the confidence of the black women, and they, hoping for her intercession on their behalf, told her harrowing stories of the stripping and flogging of slave women, of hard manual labor being forced on mothers of infants within three weeks after birth of their children, of families being divided by the sale of slaves, and of women being forced to submit to the lusts of owners and overseers.

Most repulsive to Fanny was the lack of sanitation and general uncleanliness which pervaded everything. Her house servants, for example, she noted were "perfectly filthy in their persons and clothes—their faces, hands, and naked feet being literally incrusted with dirt." But, she pointed out, "this very disagreeable peculiarity does not prevent Southern women from hanging their infants at the breasts of Negresses, nor almost every planter's wife and daughter from having one or more little black pets sleeping like puppy dogs in their very bedchamber, nor almost every planter from admitting one or several of his female slaves to the still closer intimacy of his bed." Slavery, Fanny was convinced, was responsible for all such evils, "from lying, thieving, and adultery, to dirty houses, ragged clothes, and foul smells," since the system led inevitably to a total absence of self-respect.

Fanny's attempts to plead the causes of slaves that she believed to have been seriously mistreated or to reform some of the worst aspects of slavery were heard with impatience and resentment on the part of Pierce Butler, who made a few minor concessions in the beginning, and then ordered her to bring no further complaints to him. His attitude was that nothing told to Fanny by the slave women could be believed. "Why do you listen to such stuff?" he exclaimed angrily, "don't you know the niggers are all damned liars?" Her sympathy for the slaves, in Butler's view, only tended to make them discontented and idle, neglectful of their work, and therefore more liable to punishment.

Thus began the estrangement between Pierce Butler and his wife, her loss of respect for him, and later their separation and divorce.

Frustrated in her desire to alleviate the hardships of the slaves on the Butler plantation in other ways, Fanny devoted the remainder of her stay in Georgia to doing what was possible for their welfare. Ignoring Southern tradition, she went into the slave cabin used as a hospital, where there was no doctor or nurse and the Negroes lay on the earthen floor dying in their filth. There she bathed the infants and ministered to the best of her ability to the sick. She started a campaign to persuade the mothers to bathe their babies, providing soaps, and offering penny bribes. Though forbidden by law, she taught an exceptionally bright young black to read.

Fanny was impressed by the ability of the slaves to learn when given an opportunity. The blacks on the plantation were divided between field hands and mechanics or artisans. A majority, "the more stupid and brutish," were placed in the first category. The others, who were taught trades, performed as coopers, blacksmiths, bricklayers, and carpenters, becoming highly expert and assigned to construct every item of equipment used on the place.

Fanny noted that among the slaves on the Butler plantation there were men who had made considerable sums by boatbuilding in their leisure hours. She observed further that there were "instances of almost lifelong, persevering, stringent labor, by which slaves have at length purchased their own freedom and that of their wives and children." This, she asserts, is "sufficient to prove that they are capable of severe sustained effort of the most patient and heroic kind for that great object, liberty."

At the head of each group or "gang," as they were called, of Negroes was a black driver, who stood over the workers, whip in hand. A driver was allowed to inflict a dozen lashes upon any refractory slave in the field. Even more severe punishment could be meted out by the overseer to individuals considered incorrigible. Slave foremen were notoriously brutal taskmasters and, given the power, might whip more severely than white masters. Fanny Kemble observed the brutalizing effects of slavery in the "unbounded insolence and tyranny" with which the slaves treated each other. An escaped slave, Frederick Douglass, Fanny's contemporary, wrote that "everybody, in the South, wants the privilege of whipping somebody else."

The degrading effects of slavery on the whites also deeply distressed Fanny. At the lowest level were the poor who possessed no land or slaves. These "pinelanders" preferred a life of barbaric sloth and semistarvation to "working like niggers." To Fanny, "these wretched creatures" seemed hardly human, living in rude shelters, squatting on other men's land, and subsisting on wild fowl and venison and stealing from plantation gardens. In the eyes of the poor whites, physical labor was the portion of blacks and slaves alone.

More subtle was the bearing of slavery on the characters of the white masters. From a superficial point of view, Fanny pointed out, "the habit of command gives them a certain self-possession and the enjoyment of leisure a certain ease." On closer acquaintance, however, the social system to which they belonged had infected them with less pleasing traits: "haughty, overbearing irritability, effeminate indolence, reckless extravagance, and a union of profligacy and cruelty, which are the immediate result of their irresponsible power over their dependents."

In considering the condition of the people on the Butler plantations as a whole, Fanny concluded that the principal physical hardships fell on the women. Because slave women could gain favor in the eyes of their master by presenting him with a number of future slaves, some became mothers at the age of thirteen or fourteen. Because of the endless bending and lifting involved in their work, Fanny learned that many slave mothers lost more than half of their babies through miscarriages or stillbirths. After twelve or fifteen births the bodies of slave women were likely to be completely broken. The slaves had to give birth to many more children than white women; the infant mortality rate was such that no more than one out of two or three black babies could expect to grow into an ablebodied adult worker. (pp. 85-8)

What exactly was the impact of the [*Journal of a Residence on a Georgian Plantation*] on contemporary sentiment and events? Some readers thought the diary the most powerful antislavery book yet written, comparable to *Uncle Tom's Cabin* in its influence. Fanny's story of plantation life under slavery was a best seller in England. It shocked the prudish of the Victorian era by its frankness, and mothers were warned not to permit their daughters to read the book. Supporters of the South were angered, claiming erroneously that the [*Journal of a Residence on a Georgian Plantation*] had been hastily written for the occasion. . . . Generally, critics praised or condemned the [*Journal of a Residence on a Georgian Plantation*] according to the policy of their newspaper or magazine. In the North, abolitionists hailed Fanny as a bringer of light and truth, the copperheads called her a liar, and the fastidious were shocked. Some historians then and since argued that the book had little effect, that it came too late, after the tide had already turned in favor of the North.

The *Journal of a Residence on a Georgian Plantation* lacks the romantic atmosphere of *Uncle Tom's Cabin*. It is missing the aristocratic characters, opulent mansions, and beautiful country estates that fascinated the readers of Harriet Beecher Stowe's best-selling novel. Fanny herself explained that her experience had been limited and that life on a remote sea island should not be taken as typical of slave plantations everywhere in the South. Her observations were based on a stay of less than four months on two small islands at the mouth of the Altamaha River, an area about sixteen miles square, but in the center of one of the South's most productive cotton, rice, and sugar areas. (p. 90)

It is probably an exaggeration to state, as did one writer [Herbert Ravenel Sass, in a 1944 article in the *Saturday Evening Post*], that the [*Journal of a Residence on a Georgian Plantation*] "more than any other book except *Uncle Tom's Cabin* helped to smash the old South, and wipe the plantation civilization out of existence." Other powerful forces were operating to keep England from intervening in the American Civil War. Readers in general recognized the [*Journal of a Residence on a Georgian Plantation*] as a dreadful indictment of slavery as an institution. The *London Review* conceded that it would have required the imagination of a Dante to have conjured such a vision out of thin air. As the wife of a slavemaster, Fanny had reason to look for the best side of the system, and had hoped before going to Georgia to find ameliorating factors. Her "inside story," from the point of view of a cultured Englishwoman, is unique in the annals of slavery. It fills a place in the history of the "peculiar institution" occupied by no other writer. The historical and literary value of the [*Journal of a Residence on a Georgian Plantation*] is therefore incontrovertible. (p. 91)

> *Robert B. Downs, "Slave Plantation: Frances Anne Kemble's 'Journal of a Residence on a Georgian Plantation in 1838-1839'," in his* Books That Changed the South, *The University of North Carolina Press, 1977, pp. 82-91.*

J. C. FURNAS (essay date 1982)

[*In the following excerpt from his biography of Kemble, Furnas describes the early critical reception of* Journal of a Residence in America. *He explains that unfavorable accounts of American life written by other foreign visitors had often offended American readers. Furnas asserts that Kemble's descriptions of the American scene, while more complimentary and just than these earlier works, nevertheless also precipitated American outrage.*]

Foreign visitors' accounts of what-I-saw-in-America had long exasperated Americans. Much of that was, of course, hypersensitivity, an unbecoming side effect of a surviving Colonial inferiority feeling. Other versions of this eventually appeared

also in Australia and New Zealand. Britain was still patently and tactlessly elder, wealthier, more cultivated, less crude. (pp. 151-52)

In 1835, the year Fanny's [*Journal of a Residence in America*] was published, Charles Dickens's Tony Weller proposed to ship Mr. Pickwick off to America eventually to "come back and write a book about the 'Merrikins as'll pay all his expenses and more, if he blows 'em up enough." Eight years later Dickens followed this advice himself not once but twice, bearing down harshly in both *American Notes* and *Martin Chuzzlewit*. Some of the eminent players of this game openly confessed such a purpose. Mrs. Frances Trollope's preface to her *Domestic Manners of the Americans* (1832) piously renounced commenting on "the democratic form of the American government," only to acknowledge a page later that she wished "to show how greatly the advantage is on the side of those who are governed by the few, instead of the many"; and to describe the alternative as "the jarring tumult and universal degradation which invariably follow the wild scheme of placing all the power of the State in the hands of the populace." A few years later Captain Frederick Marryat admitted that in writing his conspicuous book on America "my object was to injure democracy"; and he hoped it would be read "by every [British] tradesman and mechanic; pored over by milliners' girls . . . thumbed to pieces in every circulating library," to discourage emigration among the lower classes.

Yet this was no conspiracy of propagandists. It was merely that Britain's ruling groups disliked favorable reference to American politicosocial experiments, whence publishers assumed that well-established people would like to read about how bad things actually were in the States. Unsympathetic observers had no trouble selecting large and small shortcomings for unfavorable contrast with British ways. When books thus begotten were at all conspicuous, they were also published in America. For further impact, the great British reviews, which were widely read in America, usually covered them exhaustively with extensive quotations from the nastiest passages, and American newspapers eagerly reprinted them. And reading them made for bad blood among a people already trained to be anti-British by recent memories of the War of 1812 and school textbooks presenting anglophobia as patriotism.

Both the newspaper borrowing from British reviews and the American publisher bringing out the travel commentaries of Basil Hall, Mrs. Trollope, et al. were symptoms of . . . chronic cultural colonialism . . .—a thing still lively among us. Because the book- or newspaper-reading American was culturally insecure, he was itchily inquisitive about outsiders' sneering comments, and also gratified in an I-told-you-so way as well as outraged to learn once more that listeners seldom hear good of themselves. It insulted America, his papers told him, to print that Americans spent too much time slouching in and out of barrooms and were too fond of blowing the national horn. Both observations were true, but thenceforward "Basil Hall" was a hissing and a byword. In the same year as Fanny's landing in New York, Mrs. Trollope supplied special fuel for such feeling: "I would infinitely prefer sharing the apartment of a party of well-conditioned pigs to [the cabin of a Mississippi steamboat]"; "Mr. Jefferson is said to have been the father of children by almost all of his numerous female slaves"; one "never heard Americans conversing without the word DOLLAR being pronounced," wild swings that made the lady title-holder until 1839, when Captain Marryat weighed in.

Fanny was aware of these monitory precedents. She marveled at the persistent execration of Mrs. Trollope and was glad not to have read her book, which excused her from discussing it. Long before she began to prepare her journal for print, she wrote soberly to George Combe about the inadvisability of speaking "before one has had time to reflect" and assured herself that, though she could never approve of spitting on the carpet and voting by [secret] ballat, "most of my other prejudices are melting away . . . Americans are decidedly not Hottentots . . . I have found many things to like and a few people to love." Yet her original reluctance to go to "that dreadful America" at all very probably reflected her familiarity with the reviews' steady abuse of the place and with some of its most intemperate detractors—Tom Moore, for instance, whose verses about the young nation still blister the page; and Sydney Smith, whose personal adjuration to her on one of her earlier returns to America from England was: "Be brave, my dear Lady, hoist the American flag, barbarize your manners—dissyntax your language, fling a mantle over your lively spirits & become the first of American women." It was peevishly assumed that her book on America leaned heavily on previous unfriendly accounts. A caricature of the episode of the overturned coach showed spilling out of her baggage books marked "Hall," "Trollope" and a trunk labeled "Fidler's Tour"— plus a slang dictionary. So even though what she published did not include certain things that the newspapers said it would, she was destined to the same pillory as Mrs. Trollope; and she should have known that would happen.

Fanny wrote better, true; had no ax to grind; was more intelligent; and even when American crudities outraged her, fairer. But plenty remained for the hounds to give tongue about. . . . [She] was severe about tobacco-chewing and -spitting; was scornful of not only American horses, but also American riders; was annoyed, as Britons often were, by the nasality of some and the un-English quality of most kinds of American speech; described American women as sluggish and vapid; found most American hotels slovenly managed. . . . In those and many other points her strictures coincided with those of previous observers about Washington's being only a rough sketch of where a city may be some day, and the other inevitability about American men's drinking habits.

Little of that was unjustified, certainly not the last. Fanny was on firm ground as to American men's taking brandy "in a way that would astound people of any respectability in England." She ascribed their being the very worst judges of wine in the world, always excepting Madeira, which they have in great perfection, to

> the total loss of all niceness of taste consequent upon their continual swallowing of mint julaps [sic], gin slings, brandy cocktails, and a thousand strong messes which they take *even before breakfast* . . . a practice as gross in taste, as injurious to the health. . . . Bar-rooms . . . in the theatres, in the hotels, in the bath-houses, on board the steam-boats. . . . [Yet] though the gentlemen drink more than any other *gentlemen,* the lower orders here are more temperate than with us. . . . a drunken man on the streets is comparatively rare.

Mrs. Trollope would never have written that last sentence. But in those and many other observations Fanny's indiscretion was culpable. Had she been writing a letter home, there would have been no harm; but in public print, she was sure to get American

backs up. Broadway's store personnel lacked the stylish deference that one expects of London shopmen; American wild violets lacked the scent of their English cousins; American fruits were large and beautiful but lacked the flavor of English pears and peaches ripened against walls. American oysters were grotesquely larger than British. And Fanny should have been sent to bed supperless for letting memories of the Household Troops put too much English on her description of a militia parade on the anniversary of the British evacuation of New York fifty years earlier:

> We have had firing of pop-guns, waving of star-spangled banners (some . . . the worse for wear) infantry marching through the streets, cavalry (oh Lord! what delicious objects they were,) and artillery prancing among them, to the infinite ecstacy and peril of a dense mob. . . . O, pomp and circumstance of glorious war! . . . some had gloves, and some had none; some carried their guns one way, some another; some . . . "shocking bad hats" with feathers in them. . . . Discipline, order, a peculiar carriage . . . may all be the attributes of such miserable creatures as . . . receive wages for their blood. But for free Americans! why should they not walk crooked . . . if they don't like to walk straight!

And to compound her poor judgment, the latter part of that was written a year or so after the event, when presumably she was better adjusted to American ways and things.

One part of her knew better. After a few days in New York she thought the rampant Britishness of some of her transplanted countrymen a "matter of amusement. How we English folks do cling to our own habits, our own views, our own things, our own people; how, in spite of all our wanderings . . . like so many Jews, we never . . . fail to . . . laugh at and depreciate all that differs from that country, which we delight in forsaking for any and all others." In her case one can say—as one cannot of the Marryats, Trollopes, and dozens of others—that there was no ill will involved, only brashness at worst; but a sort of destiny may have been at work. The day before landing, as the *Pacific* lay becalmed off Long Island, she half anticipated discord:

> The day was heavenly, though intensely hot, the sky utterly cloudless . . . I do not love a cloudless sky. They tell me that this is their American weather till Christmas; that's nice, for those who like frying. Commend me to dear England's soft, rich, sad, harmonious skies . . . the misty curtain of silver vapour that hangs over her September woods at morning, and shrouds them at night:—in short, I am homesick before touching land.

She was, after all, only twenty-two and had never before been anywhere but France under insulated conditions. But that is no excuse for her poor taste in printing her diary's ungracious account of the dinner party with which the Philip Hones quasiformally welcomed the Kembles to New York [for Hone's remarks, see excerpt dated 1838]. . . . In print the identities of host and guests were masked by blanks. But that, as a scholarly commentator has said, merely set New York readers playing a game of fill-in-the-blanks. (pp. 153-57)

The excerpt-greedy press never bothered, of course, to balance Fanny's indiscretions and sporadic injustices with the high ratio—far higher than Trollope's or Hall's—of American ways and things that she liked, often saying so at generous length. She was delighted with the tasteful development of Hoboken; the majestic, fast, and well-managed Hudson River steamboats; the scenery of the Hudson Highlands; shad in season, and the venerable Madeiras that emerged from good private cellars. Further, she admired William Cullen Bryant's poems (one wishes she had not also liked Nathaniel P. Willis's!), the dashing efficiency of American volunteer fire companies; New York's public bathhouses, more numerous and convenient than London's; the gentleness with which Americans handled draft horses, another strong contrast with Britain. American carriage-makers could not match the elegantly light, strong barouches and broughams at home, but New York's hackney coaches for hire were cleaner and better handled than London's.

Particularly welcome was the almost extravagant deference with which men treated women in the streets, public conveyances, churches, and hotel parlors. Within reason a woman could go practically anywhere alone with no risk of unpleasantness—except for that filthy spitting. (p. 159)

This streak-of-lean, streak-of-fat quality may be one of the things making her book so entertaining. Add the flashes of wit and frequent passages of downright good writing. Charles Francis Adams, who had met Fanny in Boston, represented responsible opinion of its merits: "A singular compound of good sense, high feeling and strong expression with coarseness, trifling and eccentricity . . . much of the truth she tells will touch the sensitive . . . far more than the severest censure." But that was in a private diary, not public print. (p. 160)

It took time for the magazines to get [their reviews] . . . into circulation. Meanwhile the newspapers . . . made Fanny's book a pre-publication *succès de scandale*. "The newspapers, whose editors she dislikes, abuse her and hers without mercy," Fitz-Greene Halleck, popular poet and convivial wit, wrote to his sister. Charles Francis Adams also understood it that way. Across the Atlantic the *Edinburgh Review* justifiably likened Fanny's "declarations against the Press-gang" to the sort of impulse "under which foolish and fearless schoolboys provoke a nest of hornets" [see excerpt by E.G.E. Bulwer-Lytton dated 1835]. . . . For Fanny had brought along from overseas a lively form of the aversion to the press strong in the British middle and upper classes. . . . Even in those simpler times such an attitude was inadvisable for actors. But the farthest she ever went toward cooperating with the press was occasionally to contribute some of her verses.

Her book made sure of war to the knife by disdainfully contrasting the social standing of American newspapermen with that of their English counterparts: "Except where they have been made political tools, newspaper writers and editors have never, I believe, been admitted into good society in England. . . . young men here . . . too often . . . accept this very mediocre mode of displaying their abilities." Then: "I do solemnly swear, never again with my own good will, to become acquainted with any man in any way connected with the public press . . . utterly unreliable people . . . their vocation requires that they should be so."

Whether adequately expurgated or not, the published [*Journal of a Residence in America*] sold handsomely—eight hundred copies the first day at Wiley and Long's New York bookstore,

for instance. And thousands on thousands who never saw the book discussed and denounced it. (pp. 161-62)

Lewis Clark, a friend of Fanny's and editor of the *Knickerbocker Magazine,* summed up for Henry Wadsworth Longfellow in Paris: "She tells a great many rough truths. . . . Some critics have treated her book with contempt . . . some have . . . sided with her, but all have lamented that, for her own sake, the author should ever have published it." (p. 162)

The consensus among those who mattered—and bought books—is clear in the successive verdicts rendered by Princess Victoria (not yet queen) reflecting first, one assumes, what her preceptors said about the book, then later her individual response: "very pertly and oddly written . . . not well bred . . . many vulgar expressions . . . full of trash and nonsense which could only do harm" [see excerpt dated 1835]; but a few days later she is reading on and on: "It amuses me . . . some very fine feelings in it." In spite of ourselves we *were* amused.

In private close friends defended it ably. . . . Lady Dacre told John Murray that "the depth of thought, the vigour of the writing, the high tone of poetry in her descriptions . . . make her work piquant and enchanting. . . . One sees her *own self,* with . . . her great qualities and her faults in every page." But the most robust rebuttal came from Francis Head, Waterloo veteran, pioneer mining explorer in South America, and in his latter years able man of letters, who, so far as I am aware, did not know Fanny personally: "She has been most unkindly and unjustly treated by the reviewers. . . . People say she is vulgar! So was Eve, for she scratched whatever part of her itched! . . . everything is vulgar nowadays . . . It is vulgar to say you are hungry or thirsty, that you perspire. . . . Poor Fanny Kemble has fallen a victim to this tyranny. Her book is full of cleverness, talent, simple-heartedness, nature, and nakedness."

That complaint that "Victorian prudery" was out of hand well before Victoria reigned over it puts the finger on a quality of Fanny's, usually but not always becoming, that reminds one she was born in the days of sedan chairs and port wine. Throughout her life she retained a strong savor of that eighteenth century in which both her parents were reared. (pp. 164-65)

The pluck—or foolhardiness—or impudence—with which she nailed her colors to the mast well before the book appeared was all her own, however. In one of the essay footnotes tucked into her [*Journal of a Residence in America*] after the explosion in the newspapers she told Americans:

> Such an unhappily sensitive public surely never existed in the world. . . . I live myself in the daily expectation of martyrdom. . . . if you express an unfavourable opinion of anything [in America], the people are absolutely astonished at your temerity. I remember . . . a lady saying to me once, "I hear you are going to abuse us dreadfully; of course, you'll wait till you go back to England . . ." I assured her I was not the least afraid of staying where I was, and saying what I thought at the same time.

One wishes that this beleaguered young woman could already have read what the *Atlantic Monthly* [see excerpt dated 1863] said of her [*Journal of a Residence in America*] twenty-eight years later in reviewing her remarkable book about black slavery: "the dashing, fragmentary diary of a brilliant girl . . . crackled and sparkled with *naïve* arrogance. It criticized a new world with the amusing petulance of a spoiled daughter of John

JOURNAL

OF

A RESIDENCE ON A

GEORGIAN PLANTATION

IN 1838–1839.

BY FRANCES ANNE KEMBLE.

SLAVERY THE CHIEF CORNER STONE.

'This stone (Slavery), which was rejected by the first builders, is become the chief stone of the corner in our new edifice.'—*Speech of* ALEXANDER H. STEPHENS, *Vice-President of the Confederate States: delivered March* 21, 1861.

NEW YORK:

HARPER & BROTHERS, PUBLISHERS,

FRANKLIN SQUARE.

1863.

Title page of the first American edition of Journal of a Residence on a Georgian Plantation.

Bull. It was flimsy, flippant, laughable, rollicking, vivid . . . often with airy grace, often with profound and pensive feeling.''

That is why the [*Journal of a Residence in America*] bobs up so buoyantly from among its companion books about America. (p. 165)

> *J. C. Furnas, in his* Fanny Kemble: Leading Lady
> of the Nineteenth-Century Stage, *The Dial Press,
> 1982, 494 p.*

CATHERINE CLINTON   (essay date 1987)

[*Clinton examines the feminist viewpoint of* Journal of a Residence on a Georgian Plantation.]

Fanny Kemble's *Journal of Residence on a Georgian Plantation*—a record of her months on her husband's Sea Island estates during the winter of 1838-39—has become one of the most frequently cited nineteenth-century descriptions of American slavery. Like those of Frederick Law Olmsted and Harriet Martineau, Kemble's account, published in 1863, is valued for the author's eye for detail and her eyewitness authenticity. Kemble's powerful prose and her stature as a literary personage lend added consequence to this record of life on a plantation.

One facet of this valuable document seems to have been neglected in many of the scholarly discussions of it: the feminist component of Kemble's attack upon slavery. Kemble was not only a writer concerned with the inhumanity of slaveowners toward slaves, but also a woman struggling against the patriarchal prerogatives within her society. (p. 74)

Kemble's political opposition to slavery was not launched directly against slaveowners, but focused on the ''system'' that allowed one human to hold another in bondage. It is fascinating to watch the way in which her views shifted radically after her brief experiment in living on her husband's rice plantations. That winter in Georgia marked the disintegration of the Butler marriage and the flowering of Kemble's commitment to the anti-slavery movement. . . .

Despite her anti-slavery bent, Fanny Kemble's cultural baggage included the common nineteenth-century racial prejudices. Unlike many of her New England and most certainly all of her southern acquaintances, however, Kemble believed that the ''racial characteristics'' ascribed to slaves were environmentally induced rather than genetically transmitted. For example, she vehemently attacked the myth that blacks were by nature filthy and smelly: ''A total absence of self-respect begets these hateful physical results, and in proportion as moral influences are remote, physical evils will abound.'' She used sarcasm as well as argument to undermine white mythology. (p. 76)

The opening sections of her journal are merciless, as Kemble pointedly scorns the hypocrisy to which she is daily witness:

> There is no law in the white man's nature which
> prevents him from making a colored woman
> the mother of his children, but there *is* a law
> on his statute books forbidding him to make
> her his wife . . . it seems almost as curious that
> laws should be enacted to prevent men mar-
> rying women toward whom they have an in-
> vincible natural repugnance.

She is utterly disgusted by the greed that underlies philosophical justifications of slavery:

> The only obstacle to immediate abolition
> throughout the South is the immense value of
> human property, and, to use the words of a
> very distinguished Carolinian, who thus ended
> a long discussion we had on the subject, ''I'll
> tell you why abolition is impossible: because
> every healthy negro can fetch a thousand dollars
> on the Charleston market at this moment.''

Fascinating in themselves, these insights are especially remarkable as observations by the wife of a slaveowner. As a woman Kemble has a special perspective on the plantation system, one that is revealed most often in a subconscious fashion. After exchanging views with her female counterparts in residence on the Georgia Sea Islands, she reports:

> We had a long discussion on the subject of
> slavery, and they took, as usual, the old ground
> of justifying the system *where* it was admin-
> istered with kindness and indulgence. It is not
> surprising that women should regard the ques-
> tion from this point of view; they are very sel-
> dom just, and are generally treated with more
> indulgence than justice by men.

Her commentary is finely tuned to sexual differences:

> I know that the Southern men are apt to deny the fact that they do live under an habitual sense of danger; but a slave population, coerced into obedience, though unarmed and half fed, *is* a threatening source of constant insecurity, and every southern *woman* to whom I have spoken on the subject has admitted to me that they live in terror of their slaves.

And her writing catalogs her increasing frustrations with those "evils of slavery" that she, as a woman, finds especially repugnant.

In her first description of life on the plantation, she explains that

> tasks of course profess to be graduated according to the sex, age, and strength of the laborer; but in many instances this is not the case, as I think you will agree when I tell you that on Mr. [Butler]'s first visit to his estates he found that the men and the women who labored in the fields had the same task to perform. This was a noble admission of female equality, was it not—and thus it had been on the estate for many years past. Mr. [Butler], of course, altered the distribution of the work, diminishing the quantity done by the women.

This passage is layered with ironies. First, Kemble plainly states that what is "professed" is not always the case on the plantation, a passing thought that multiplies into a nightmarish perspective by the journal's end, when Kemble bewails the horrors of this charade "Christianity." Kemble makes clear that plantation life and southern culture are built on deceiving appearances, fanciful exaggerations calculated to enhance the picture of slavery, which was being increasingly besmirched by the abolitionist campaign.

Second, Kemble's harsh, sarcastic comment on "female equality" when she talks about women's parallel exploitation is typical of this journal, which is one of the first methodical indictments of slavery's effects upon women. Kemble is also one of the primary critics who systematically indicts the system for its pernicious effects upon white men's morality—effects that have negative repercussions among white planter families. This charge is made with equal vehemence in the diary of Mary Chesnut, the wife of a southern slaveowner and member of the Confederate cabinet, but Kemble is almost entirely alone among prominent critics in her condemnation of slavery's effects upon black women. She provides a sustained, sympathetic treatment of the plight of slave women missing in most other accounts. (pp. 76-7)

One consistently neglected aspect of Kemble's book is the feminist rage that filters through this document. It may seem foolish to label as "feminist" yet another "strongminded" nineteenth-century woman who lived before the term was coined; who did not participate in any of the many organizations that beckoned women to feminist activism; who in fact throughout her life dissociated herself from organized feminism. Nevertheless, Kemble's analysis of slavery is informed, if not awash, with feminist ideology. She assuredly considers gender a primary category for consideration of her experiences, and factors gender into most if not all of her observations on social relations. Further, she is committed to changing the status of women within society as a key to improving society generally. Both

of these facts justify "deconstructing" Kemble's text as a feminist document.

Indeed, Kemble takes a classical "first wave" position in identifying the evils of society as bound up in patriarchal oppression of women. She is outraged by her huband's indifference to injustice. She details the punishing routine to which slave women are subjected on the plantation; she is vehement about the inhumanity that allows pregnant women and mothers to be treated so callously. She bitterly assaults a system that so casually fosters the separation of husbands from wives, and even of children from mothers. Both complaints are common in antislavery literature, but in Kemble's book, they are central, far outweighing any concerns about the effects of slavery on free labor.

Especially in documenting the sexual exploitation of women slaves, Kemble clearly articulates the sins of slavery within a feminist framework. Although, as many scholars have argued, this theme was an unconscious ploy by many abolitionists to sensationalize the attack upon slavery, Kemble had more obvious and immediate motives: she was shocked and horrified by her discoveries and committed them to paper as soon as she witnessed them. . . .

Confronted with the sexual double standard slavery fostered, with the sexual violence within their society and, in some cases, within their own homes, most white southern women, especially plantation mistresses, chose to blame the victims. Kemble made no such compromise; she laid the blame squarely on the shoulders of white southern men. Her book is laced with references to this peculiarly male "southern dishonor":

> I felt rather uncomfortable and said no more about who was like who, but came to certain conclusions in my own mind as to a young lad who had been among our morning visitors; and whose extremely light color and straight, handsome features and striking resemblance to Mr. K[ing] had suggested suspicions of a rather unpleasant nature to me, and whose sole acknowledged parent was a very black negress of the name of Minda. I have no doubt at all, now, that he is another son of Mr. K[ing], Mr. [Butler]'s paragon overseer.

Her distaste for Mr. King mounts with increasing evidence of his base character:

> [Mr. K] . . . forced her, flogged her severely for having resisted him, and then sent her off, as a farther punishment to Five Pound—a horrible swamp in a remote corner of the estate, to which the slaves are sometimes banished for such offenses as are not sufficiently atoned for by the lash.

But in Kemble's construction, King is neither an exceptional case nor the Christian gone astray on an isolated plantation. She comments on the fate of a mulatto girl condemned to a harsh life in the rice fields: "In any of the southern cities the girl would be pretty sure to be reserved for a worse fate. . . ." The debauchery of women is not accidental, she argues, but a calculated byproduct of slavery. This evil, Kemble charges, permeates all of southern society. (p. 78)

The overlapping of the personal and political was an extremely painful ordeal for Kemble, revealed in meticulous detail within the *Journal of Residence on a Georgian Plantation,* and expanded on in her other writings. Seen in historical context, her anti-slavery arguments and her attacks on slavery as a form of patriarchal oppression give us a window into an even more painful intersection of the personal and political: the plight of women slaves.

If we choose to look, we can see Kemble's text as more than descriptive, an analysis of a most powerful, political variety. And we can employ her evidence to extend our own analysis of the interdependence of systems of exploitation, the ways in which gender, race, and class interacted within nineteenth-century southern society. Used in this way, feminism is not merely a product to be manufactured by scholars, but a process, a perspective, an interpretive tool that affords us a deeper appreciation of the many-tentacled grasp slavery maintained on social interactions within the Old South, and of its legacy for us today. (p. 79)

> Catherine Clinton, *"Fanny Kemble's Journal: A Woman Confronts Slavery on a Georgia Plantation,"* in Frontiers: A Journal of Women Studies, *Vol. IX, No. 3, 1987, pp. 74-9.*

ADDITIONAL BIBLIOGRAPHY

Armstrong, Margaret. *Fanny Kemble: A Passionate Victorian.* New York: Macmillan Co., 1938, 387 p.
> A sympathetic record of Kemble's life.

Ashby, Clifford. "Fanny Kemble's 'Vulgar' Journal." *Pennsylvania Magazine of History and Biography* XCVIII, No. 1 (January 1974): 58-66.
> Describes the outrage aroused by the first publication of *Journal of a Residence in America.*

"Our Library Table." *The Athenaeum,* No. 3305 (28 February 1891): 279-80.
> Includes a brief, mixed review of *Further Records.*

Bobbé, Dorothie. *Fanny Kemble.* New York: Minton, Balch & Co., 1931, 351 p.
> An affectionate biography.

Buckmaster, Henrietta. *Fire in the Heart.* New York: Harcourt, Brace and Co., 1948, 351 p.
> A fictional retelling of Kemble's life, focused on her troubled marriage to Pierce Butler.

Gibbs, Henry. *Affectionately Yours, Fanny: Fanny Kemble and the Theatre.* London: Jarrolds Publishers, 1947, 192 p.
> A biography centered on Kemble's acting career.

Greeley, Horace. "Mrs. F. A. Kemble's Experience." *The Independent* XV, No. 765 (30 July 1863): 1.
> Uses *Journal of a Residence on a Georgian Plantation* as the basis for an exhortation against slavery.

Kahan, Gerald. "Fanny Kemble Reads Shakespeare: Her First American Tour, 1849-50." *Theatre Survey* XXIV, Nos. 1-2 (May-November 1983): 77-98.
> An assessment, reinforced by quotations from contemporary notices, of Kemble's Shakespearean readings.

Lee, Henry. "Frances Anne Kemble." *The Atlantic Monthly* LXXI, No. CCCCXXVII (May 1893): 662-75.
> An obituary tribute to Kemble.

Lombard, Mildred E. "Contemporary Opinions of Mrs. Kemble's *Journal of a Residence on a Georgia Plantation.*" *The Georgia Historical Quarterly* XIV, No. 4 (December 1930): 335-43.

Assesses the impact that *Journal of a Residence on a Georgian Plantation* had on contemporary British and American public opinion regarding slavery and the Confederacy.

MacLeod, Duncan J. "Fanny Kemble, 1809-1893." In *Abroad in America: Visitors to the New Nation, 1776-1914,* edited by Marc Pachter and Frances Wein, pp. 73-81. Reading, Mass.: Addison-Wesley Publishing Co. in association with the National Portrait Gallery, Smithsonian Institution, 1976.
> Examines Kemble's attitudes toward America and American issues, particularly slavery.

MacMahon, Ella. "Fanny Kemble." *The Living Age* CXCVII, No. 2554 (10 June 1893): 692-97.
> An anecdotal account of Kemble's girlhood and early acting career.

Marshall, Dorothy. *Fanny Kemble.* New York: St. Martin's Press, 1978, 280 p.
> A biography. Unlike earlier biographers, Marshall claims to view Kemble "from the English angle and against her English background."

My Conscience! Fanny Thimble Cutler's Journal of a Residence in America whilst Performing a Profitable Theatrical Engagement: Beating the Nonsensical Fanny Kemble Journal All Hollow!!! Philadelphia: n.p., 1835, 36 p.
> A parody of *Journal of a Residence in America.* The anonymous satirist portrays the *Journal* as crude and its author as boisterous, mercenary, and inordinately fond of mint juleps.

Myers, Andrew B. "Miss Kemble's Keys." *Columbia Library Columns* XI, No. 1 (November 1961): 3-12.
> Sheds light on Kemble's private, annotated copy of *Journal of a Residence in America.*

Oliver, Egbert S. "Melville's Goneril and Fanny Kemble." *The New England Quarterly* XVIII, No. 4 (December 1945): 489-500.
> Posits that the heartless character Goneril in Herman Melville's novel *The Confidence-Man* is a caricature of Kemble.

Parton, James. "Mrs. Frances Anne Kemble." In *Eminent Women of the Age: Being Narratives of the Lives and Deeds of the Most Prominent Women of the Present Generation,* pp. 102-27. Hartford, Conn.: S. M. Betts & Co., 1868.
> A highly complimentary account of Kemble's life and accomplishments—theatrical and literary—up to 1868.

Ritchie, Anne. "Chapters from Some Unwritten Memoirs: Mrs. Kemble." *The Living Age* CXCVIII, No. 2565 (2 September 1893): 549-55.
> Ritchie's fond reminiscences of her acquaintance with Kemble.

Robins, Edward. "Frances Ann Kemble." In his *Twelve Great Actresses,* pp. 269-302. New York: G. P. Putnam's Sons, Knickerbocker Press, 1900.
> A biographical essay focused on Kemble's stage career. Robins describes several of Kemble's individual performances and the audiences' responses to them.

Rowton, Frederic. "Frances Anne Butler." In his *The Female Poets of Great Britain, Containing the Choicest Poems of Our Female Poets, from the Time of Lady Juliana Berners to the Present Day,* pp. 477-81. London: Longman, Brown, Green, and Longmans, n.d.
> Assesses Kemble's poetic talent, praising her vivid impressions and bold sincerity.

Stevenson, Janet. *The Ardent Years.* New York: Viking Press, 1960, 374 p.
> A novel based on Kemble's marriage to Pierce Butler.

Thompson, David W. "Early Actress-Readers: Mowatt, Kemble, and Cushman." In *Performance of Literature in Historical Perspectives,* edited by David W. Thompson, pp. 629-50. Lanham, Md.: University Press of America, 1983.
> Includes a discussion of Kemble's twenty-year career as a public reader of Shakespeare, calling it "the most organized, dedicated, consistent, and profitable achievement of her whole life."

[Wilson, John]. "Miss Fanny Kemble's Tragedy." *Blackwood's Edinburgh Magazine* XXXI, No. CXCIII (April 1832): 673-92.

    Lavishly praises the poetic style and emotional power of *Francis the First,* objecting only to the unsympathetic qualities of the play's characters.

Wister, Fanny Kemble. *Fanny, the American Kemble: Her Journals and Unpublished Letters.* Tallahassee, Fla.: South Pass Press, 1972, 227 p.

    A biography of Kemble (written by her great-granddaughter) buttressed by copious quotations from previously unpublished correspondence to and from Kemble and by extracts from *Record of a Girlhood* and *Journal of a Residence in America.*

Wright, Constance. *Fanny Kemble and the Lovely Land.* New York: Dodd, Mead & Co., 1972, 242 p.

    A biographical study centered on Kemble's "relations to the times in which she lived . . . and to the land of her adoption, America."

Abraham Lincoln

1809-1865

American statesman and orator.

The sixteenth president of the United States, Lincoln is one of the best loved and most eloquent statesmen in American history. As the nation's leader during the Civil War, he was faced with the challenge of interpreting and resolving a sectional conflict precipitated by bitter disagreement over the issues of states' rights and the extension of slavery. Lincoln regarded the crisis as a test of American democracy, articulating his vision of what the war and democratic government meant in speeches and writings that are considered outstanding contributions to American political thought and literature. Critics generally agree that in such masterpieces as the "Gettysburg Address" and the *Second Inaugural Address,* he used simple but moving prose to convey both penetrating insights into profound political issues and a genuine spirit of magnanimity. Lincoln was assassinated shortly after the Civil War ended, leaving behind a reputation for honesty, compassion, and patriotism that became the foundation of his renown as a great American hero. Generations of Americans have memorized his speeches and sayings, and today scholars regard his writings as invaluable sources of insight into the Civil War crisis, the nature of American democracy, and the mind and soul of a national legend.

The son of Nancy Hanks Lincoln and Thomas Lincoln, a Kentucky backwoodsman, Lincoln was born in a log cabin in Hardin County, Kentucky, and later moved with his family to the Indiana frontier. From 1816 to 1830, he lived in Indiana, helping support his family by working as a farmhand, ferryman, and store clerk. Lincoln received a typical frontier education—less than one year of formal training in reading, writing, and arithmetic—but there is evidence that he augmented his studies by reading such works as Parson Weems's *Life of George Washington,* Daniel Defoe's *Robinson Crusoe,* Aesop's *Fables,* and John Bunyan's *The Pilgrim's Progress.* In 1830, the Lincolns moved to Macon County, Illinois, where he worked splitting wood rails and helping transport goods down the Mississippi River to New Orleans. He settled in New Salem, Illinois, in 1831, and took a job as a storekeeper. In the following year, Lincoln volunteered for service in the Black Hawk War and made an unsuccessful bid for a seat in the Illinois state legislature, afterward studying law in New Salem and working as a postmaster and surveyor. In 1834 he was elected to the state legislature on the Whig ticket, retaining that seat in four successive elections. Lincoln was admitted to the Illinois bar in 1836. The next year, he moved to the new state capitol, Springfield, where he established himself as a lawyer and courted Mary Todd, whom he married in 1842.

Lincoln advanced professionally in the 1840s, earning a reputation for lucid analysis, shrewd argumentation, and broad humor as he tried cases on the Illinois circuit court. He was elected to the United States House of Representatives in 1846, but his opposition to the Mexican War was unpopular, limiting him to one term in Congress. He withdrew from politics for several years until a national controversy arose over the implications of the Kansas-Nebraska Act of 1854 and the 1857 Supreme Court ruling in the Dred Scott case. These devel-

opments, which paved the way for the extension of slavery to the United States's western territories (previously prohibited under the Missouri Compromise) and appeared to threaten the authority of federal and state government to restrict slavery, stirred Lincoln into action. Although he was not an abolitionist, believing that the Constitution protected slavery where it currently existed, Lincoln objected to slavery on moral grounds and sought to prohibit its spread. Accordingly, he joined the newly formed antislavery Republican party in 1856 and in 1858 ran for the United States Senate seat held by Stephen A. Douglas, the author of the Kansas-Nebraska bill. Lincoln launched his senatorial campaign on 16 June 1858 with a speech delivered before the Republican state convention in which he not only attacked the Kansas-Nebraska Act and the Dred Scott decision but also spoke directly of the future of American slavery, declaring, "'A house divided against itself cannot stand.' I believe this government cannot endure, permanently half *slave* and half *free.* I do not expect the Union to be *dissolved*—I do not expect the house to *fall*—but I do expect it will cease to be divided. It will become *all* one thing, or *all* the other." The *"House Divided" Speech* presaged the depth and quality of the political discussion in the ensuing campaign, which featured a series of seven meetings now known as the Lincoln-Douglas Debates. Although Lincoln did not win the election, he challenged the morality and consistency of Douglas's position on slavery and received national recognition as a forceful and persuasive antislavery advocate. He gradually became known as a spokesperson for his party and in 1860 outlined the Republican position on slavery and other issues in an address at Cooper Institute in New York (the so-called *Cooper Union Speech*) that made him a national political figure. Later that year, Lincoln was nominated as the Republican candidate for president. Following his victory, seven slaveholding states seceded from the Union. As he left Illinois to assume the presidency, he expressed his deep sense of attachment to Springfield and his acute awareness of the difficulties facing him as president in what is considered one of the most affecting speeches of his career, the "Farewell Address at Springfield."

Lincoln's presidency—and to a large extent his presidential writings and speeches—were dominated by the Civil War. Facing a shaken and divided nation on taking office, he reassured the southern states in his *First Inaugural Address* that their constitutional right to hold slaves would continue to be protected, at the same time underscoring his commitment to maintaining the basic functions of the federal government in the seceded states. His message, containing an appeal to Americans' reason and sense of national unity, failed to avert war. Lincoln was tried severely throughout his presidency: in addition to the horde of patronage seekers who descended upon him in the White House, he encountered continual crises in military leadership and constant pressure to abolish slavery and end the war. Criticism of his stance on slavery was deeply troubling to Lincoln. In an 1862 open letter to Horace Greeley, he referred his entire policy to his concern for saving the Union, stating, "My paramount object in this struggle *is* to save the Union, and is *not* either to save or to destroy slavery. If I could save the Union without freeing *any* slave I would do it, and if I could save it by freeing *all* the slaves I would do it; and if I could save it by freeing some and leaving others alone I would also do that. What I do about slavery, and the colored race, I do because I believe it helps to save the Union; and what I forbear, I forbear because I do *not* believe it would help to save the Union." Added Lincoln, "I have here stated my purpose according to my view of *official* duty; and I intend no modification of my oft-expressed *personal* wish that all men every where could be free." Lincoln's statement loomed large in 1863 when, under increasing pressure to make advances in the war, he issued the *Emancipation Proclamation,* which declared that all slaves in the rebellious states were henceforward free. With this one act, which technically freed thousands of slaves in the deep South but made no provision for those in the border states, Lincoln established his place in American history as the "Great Emancipator." Later that year, following important victories for the North at Vicksburg, Mississippi, and Gettysburg, Pennsylvania, Lincoln was asked to speak at the dedication of the National Cemetery at Gettysburg. In what has become known as the greatest speech of his career, the "Gettysburg Address," Lincoln expressed his hope that Americans would rededicate themselves to the cause of freedom as a result of the war and experience a "new birth of freedom" that would ensure that "government of the people, by the people, for the people, shall not perish from the earth." With the war drawing to a close, Lincoln was returned for a second term in office in 1864. Idolized by many blacks as the savior of their race, revered by many Northerners as the gentle "Father Abraham," and respected by some Southerners for his restraint in victory, he took the occasion of his *Second Inaugural Address* to express a somber, spiritual vision of the war and to appeal to the nation to approach the coming period of

reconstruction "with malice toward none; with charity for all." Shortly afterward, on 14 April 1865, he was shot by John Wilkes Booth while attending a play at Ford's Theatre in Washington, D. C. He died the following day, eulogized by his secretary of war, Edwin M. Stanton, who declared at his deathbed, "Now he belongs to the ages."

Most commentators acknowledge that Lincoln's reputation for greatness is based in large part on his speeches and writings. One factor that contributed significantly to the effectiveness of Lincoln's writings was his distinctive style. The stylistic hallmarks of his works are precision, clarity, and simplicity of thought and expression, attributes that are, as Roy P. Basler notes, "the qualities of prose excellence wherever it is met with." Critics ascribe some of these elements of Lincoln's style to his humble background and legal training, yet they also detect evidence of Lincoln's familiarity with the King James Bible, the works of William Shakespeare and Robert Burns, and other literary texts. In particular, scholars observe his mastery of such technical devices as antithesis, grammatical parallelism, and repetition, which figure most prominently in the "Farewell Address at Springfield" and the "Gettysburg Address." Commentators note that Lincoln himself appears to have most valued logic and clarity of thought in his writing. He studied the works of the Greek geometer Euclid early in his career to assimilate the art of demonstration and once asserted that he was "determined to be so clear that no honest man can misunderstand me, and no dishonest one can successfully misrepresent me." Lincoln's statement underscores what critics judge to be an important dimension of his literary life: his self-consciousness as a writer. Although he was once regarded as a backwoods genius impelled by extreme circumstances to rise to unwonted literary heights, Lincoln is now considered a self-aware writer whose work displays deliberate artistry and creative development. Specifically, commentators have identified birth, death, and time as central images and themes in his writings, and they have also discerned an increasing emotional and spiritual openness in the speeches of his later years. Indeed, appreciation of Lincoln's artistry has led some scholars to characterize him as a literary genius, while it has also inspired comparisons between Lincoln's literary craftsmanship and that of Thomas Jefferson.

Critics generally agree that the ideas contained in Lincoln's speeches and writings are an important part of the American political testament. Although he is not known for framing new political doctrines in his writings, Lincoln is hailed for his ability to elucidate and exemplify established principles of American democracy. The basic instruments of that democracy—the Declaration of Independence and the United States Constitution—were the foundation for his interpretation of the complex political issues of his day. Consequently, he was able to leave to posterity a greater appreciation of democratic values both by virtue of the clearness with which he saw tests and symbols of democracy in current events and by the consistency and sincerity with which he championed them. That the Declaration of Independence was one of Lincoln's chief guides is evident, according to some scholars, in an 1858 speech in which he addressed the crucial issue of racial equality. "Certainly," he said, "the negro is not our equal in color—perhaps not in many other respects; still, in the right to put into his mouth the bread that his own hands have earned, he is the equal of every other man, white or black." As commentators have noted, the call to consider blacks and indeed all workers in light of the basic liberties affirmed in the Declaration of Independence is quite clear. In fact, one contemporary periodical averred that the proposition "All men are created equal, and are entitled to life, liberty, and the pursuit of happiness" also formed the "pith and marrow" of Lincoln's contest with Douglas, maintaining that Lincoln had "steadily upheld, defended, illustrated and applied" that proposition in every speech he made. Most critics agree that Lincoln never expressed his vision of the principles and significance of American democracy more clearly nor with more lasting effect than in the "Gettysburg Address." In this speech, described by H. L. Mencken as the "shortest and the most famous oration in American history," he illuminated the country's past, present, and future in terms of democracy. The nation was born, Lincoln said, "dedicated to the proposition that all men are created equal," thereby identifying America with the principle of human equality. The present war, he continued, was a test of whether such a nation "can long endure," thereby characterizing the Civil War as a noble battle to preserve egalitarian government. In concluding, he declared that the "great task" of the future for Americans would be to justify the sacrifices made in the war by rededicating themselves to freedom, thus ensuring that "government of the people, by the people, for the people, shall not perish from the earth." Here, scholars remark, Lincoln not only uttered a world-famous definition of democratic government, but he also advanced the influential concept that the United States was a symbol of democracy for the entire world. While the "Gettysburg Address" is considered Lincoln's greatest writing on democracy, his fame as a champion of freedom rests on a non-literary document, the *Emancipation Proclamation.* Despite its controversial character—its debatable legality and its limited scope and enforceability—Lincoln's edict ensured the demise of slavery in the United States. As the historian John Hope Franklin asserted, this liberation represented "another step toward the extension of the ideal of equality about which Jefferson had written" in the Declaration of Independence, thus making the *Emancipation Proclamation* one of the "great documents of human freedom."

While Lincoln was frequently the focus of controversy and criticism during his lifetime, he is now almost universally regarded as a national hero. Many of his contemporaries questioned his ability to rise to the dignity and intellectual challenges of the presidency, and fierce disagreements broke out concerning his military and domestic policies as chief executive. As commentators observe, however, his acute intelligence, unshakable resolve, and impeccable integrity enabled him ultimately to prevail over his staunchest critics. When Lincoln was assassinated, his death touched off mass demonstrations of grief throughout the United States, and he was immediately cast into the heroic mold of a martyr for democracy. Many Americans took his life and principles as reflections of their national character and ideals, revering him as the archetypal American. Today, scholars concede that his reputation has been inflated by hagiography; however, reinforced by modern studies of both his life and his works, they to a large extent defend his renown as a great democrat and a great American. As Henry Cabot Lodge once noted, Lincoln's fame has withstood incessant examinations into his life and character, and the solid basis on which his reputation rests promises to sustain his heroic stature for generations to come. As Lodge expressed it, "If ever a man lived who understood and loved the people to whom he gave his life, Lincoln was that man. In him no one has a monopoly; he is not now the property of any sect or party. His fame is the heritage of the people of the United States, and, as Stanton said, standing by his deathbed, 'He belongs to the ages'."

PRINCIPAL WORKS

Speech of Hon. Abram Lincoln, before the Republican Convention, June 16, 1858 (speech) 1858
Political Debates between Hon. Abraham Lincoln and Hon. Stephen A. Douglas, in the Celebrated Campaign of 1858, in Illinois (debates) 1860
Speech of Abraham Lincoln, of Illinois, Delivered at the Cooper Institute, Monday, Feb. 27, 1860 (speech) 1860
Address of Abraham Lincoln, on Taking the Oath of Office as President of the United States, March 4, 1861 (inaugural address) 1861
"Farewell Address at Springfield, Illinois" (speech) 1861; published in periodical *Harper's Weekly*
"Gettysburg Address" (speech) 1863; published in *The Gettysburg Solemnities: Dedication of the National Cemetery at Gettysburg, Pennsylvania, November 19, 1863, with the Oration of Hon. Edward Everett, Speech of President Lincoln, &c., &c., &c.*
Proclamation of Emancipation by the President of the United States, January 1st, 1863 (proclamation) 1863
Inaugural Address, March 4, 1865 (inaugural address) 1865
Complete Works of Abraham Lincoln. 12 vols. (speeches, letters, and state papers) 1905
Abraham Lincoln: His Speeches and Writings (speeches, letters, inaugural addresses, proclamations, state papers, debate, autobiography, and poetry) 1946
Abraham Lincoln: His Autobiographical Writings (autobiography) 1947
The Collected Works of Abraham Lincoln. 9 vols. (speeches, letters, inaugural addresses, proclamations, debates, and state papers) 1953-55

CHICAGO DAILY TIMES (essay date 1858)

[*The* Chicago Daily Times *responds to the* "House Divided" Speech, *focusing on Lincoln's characterization of Douglas as a "dead lion" and himself as a "living dog." In attempting to discredit him, the* Times *erroneously alleges that, as a congressman, Lincoln refused to vote supplies for volunteers in the Mexican War. These comments were originally published in the* Times *on 23 June 1858.*]

A Republican editor writing from the Springfield Republican Convention to his own paper, described the [*"House Divided" Speech*] of the Hon. A. Lincoln as abounding in strong arguments, great research, and "happy comparisons." We know Mr. Lincoln personally, and have no disposition to say one word having the slightest approach to disrespect, but as he has set himself before the people of Illinois as the competitor of Senator Douglas, and has not only invited, but actually made comparisons between himself and his opponent, we feel warranted in taking notice of what he has said in this particular.

There are a number of Republicans (as well as several Republican newspapers) who think that in a struggle for the defence of the State, and of the Constitution, and of the North, good sense would dictate that a Senator who can command support and power with the entire people of the Union, would be of more service than a mere individual whose influence would be confined to his own person, and whose power would be exhausted by the casting of his own vote. Mr. Lincoln, in his speech, after pointing out to the Republicans of Illinois the reasons why he, Lincoln, should be elected, turns to the question of whether he or Mr. Douglas would prove the most serviceable representative in the councils of the nation, and he says: (we give the extract, *italics and all,* just as we find it published in the Springfield *Journal:*)

> There are those who denounce us *openly* to their *own* friends, and yet whisper us *softly,* that *Senator Douglas* is the *aptest* instrument there is, with which to effect that object. They do *not* tell us, nor has *he* told us, that he *wishes* any such object to be effected. They wish us to *infer* all, from the facts, that he now has a little quarrel with the present head of the dynasty; and that he has regularly voted with us, on a single point, upon which, he and we, have never differed.

> They remind us that *he* is a very *great man,* and that the largest of *us* are very small ones. Let this be granted. But *"a living dog is better than a dead lion."* Judge Douglas, if not a *dead* lion *for this work,* is at least a *caged* and *toothless* one. How can he oppose the advances of slavery? He don't *care* anything about it. His avowed *mission is impressing* the "public heart" to care nothing about it.

Mr. Lincoln thinks proper to speak of his competitor as a *"dead lion,"* and to hold himself up to the people of Illinois as a *"living dog."* We have no right to question Mr. Lincoln's estimation of himself; he has applied it to himself, and has, to give it stronger significance, italicised the expression in his printed speech.

We think that for a "dead lion," or even a *"caged* and *toothless"* one, Senator Douglas possesses and displays considerable vitality. To kill a *dead* lion, all the "living dogs" of Illinois have been let loose with sharpened fangs. To fight a "toothless" lion all the living dogs from Cairo to Chicago have been lashed and whipped into the hunt. And yet there is not a "living dog" in the entire pack that does not tremble and quake, lest that dead and toothless animal, even in death, may rise and put him in jeopardy. Was the lion who stood in the pathway of Lecomptonism dead when he bid the entire power and patronage of the Government defiance, and forbid the consumation of that iniquity? Was that the voice of a dead lion, which has been heard in the mountains and valleys of Pennsylvania, upon the streams of Ohio, all over the prairies of the Northwest, and even now finds a responsive echo throughout the State of Virginia? Was that the struggle of a dead lion which forced a proud and overbearing majority in both houses of Congress, backed by all the power and appliances of the Federal Government, to abandon after a four months' struggle, their infamous measure, and send the Lecompton Constitution back to Kansas to be buried beyond all hope of resurrection by the people of that Territory? (pp. 93-4)

Who else than Douglas could have arrested that measure when he did, and as he did? A new and popular Administration just entering into office, a large Administration majority in both branches of Congress, the entire patronage of the Government undisposed of, and yet a man arose up there and bid that majority and that Administration to stop in the prosecution of

an unjust measure. Call you, Mr. Lincoln, the man who did that successfully a dead lion—a toothless animal? And pray, when do you ever expect to be able, in the Senate or out of it, anywhere, at home or abroad, to approach in power and influence that achievement of a dead lion? In that hour, of what avail would have been the barking of a "living dog?"

We remember that on one occasion, some years ago, a bill was pending in the House of Representatives at Washington for the purchase of medicines and the employment of nurses to attend the sick and dying American soldiers in the hospitals and camps of hot and burning Mexico, when our suffering soldiers—the volunteers of Illinois and of Indiana—the men who at Buena Vista had followed Hardin and Bissell, and who through the desert had accompanied Shields and Foreman—were crying out in their fever for cooling drinks and kind hands to minister to their dying wants; we know that when the bill to purchase these medicines, and furnish necessaries for the American soldiers who were sick and dying was pending, a "living dog" reared his ungainly person in the national councils, and in a yelping, barking tone, refused them succor! Let them die—let them die, the men of Illinois, who fought over and rescued the dead body of Hardin, who echoed back the cheering call of Bissell, of Richardson, of Moore, of Harris, let them die. I, a "living dog" from the State of Illinois, refuse to send these men food, clothing, or medicine. I, Abram Lincoln, of Sangamon county, refuse to vote one dollar to feed, cloth, or minister to the wants of the sick and dying volunteers from my own State, who are suffering in Mexico. Let them die like dogs! Let them die for want of medicine! Let the fever-parched lips of my Illinois neighbors crack in painful agony—not one drop of cooling liquid shall soothe them if I can help it. What if they have served their country; what if they have encountered and beaten back an enemy thrice their own number; what if they do lie on damp grounds by night, and march in blistering sunlight by day; what if they have proved, every man of them, to be a LION in his country's cause, I, Abram Lincoln, am a living dog and "a living dog is better than a dead lion."

Oh, Mr. Lincoln, the living dog at that day tried his powers with the man who is now styled a "dead lion;" you then refused succours to your countrymen in Mexico, but the "living dog" was powerless even for evil. The money was voted, and the living dog skulked back into obscurity. Was not that a deed worthy of "a living dog;" would not even a dead lion be ashamed that his memory should be stained by the record of such an act?

Democrats of Illinois, Republicans of Illinois! the man who styles himself a "living dog" asks you to support him for the United States Senate. The man who aspires to be your representative in the Senate, who offers himself to fill the place heretofore filled with such world-wide distinction by Douglas, tells you that he will go there as a living dog. He has been in Congress before, but who is there outside of the old settlers of Illinois has any recollection of his service there? What did he do? What did he say? What act is there which has rendered his service or his presence there memorable? Who is there in Illinois or in the Union that can remember any act or speech (other than the one we have mentioned) by Lincoln in the Congress of the United States. He asks you to send him there because he is better than a dead lion. But is the lion dead? Why the hostile array then that has been prepared to kill the lion who is already dead?

People of Illinois Mr. Lincoln has stated the issue—''a living dog'' or a ''lion'' not dead, nor wounded, nor toothless, nor caged, but free, bold, firm, strong, and more powerful than ever. Choose you, as your representative, the man who claims no higher rank than that of a ''living dog,'' or the man who has exercised, and forever will exercise a controlling power over the legislation of his country. (pp. 94-6)

> *''Happy Comparisons,''* in Abraham Lincoln: A Press Portrait, *edited by Herbert Mitgang, Quadrangle Books, 1971, pp. 92-6.*

NEW YORK DAILY TRIBUNE   (essay date 1858)

[*The* New York Daily Tribune *notes the great importance and interest of the Lincoln-Douglas Debates. These comments were originally published in the* Tribune *on 26 August 1858.*]

Perhaps no local contest in this country ever excited so general or so profound an interest as that now waging in Illinois, with Senator Douglas, the Federal Administration, and the Republican party headed by Messrs. Lincoln and Trumbull as the combatants. . . .

As our readers are already aware, one of the features of this remarkable contest is a series of public meetings in different parts of the State, where Mr. Douglas and Mr. Lincoln successively address the people—a mode of discussing political questions which might well be more generally adopted. The first of these [**Lincoln-Douglas Debates**] was held at Ottawa on Saturday, the 21st inst., and we publish on another page a full report of the speeches on both sides. Of the two, all partiality being left out of the question, we think Mr. Lincoln has decidedly the advantage. Not only are his doctrines better and truer than those of his antagonist, but he states them with more propriety and cogency, and with an infinitely better temper. (p. 111)

But it is not merely as a passage at arms between two eminent masters of the art of intellectual attack and defense that this discussion is worthy of study. It touches some of the most vital principles of our political system, and no man can carefully peruse it without some benefit, whatever his convictions as to the questions at issue between the disputants. (p. 112)

> *An editorial in* Abraham Lincoln: A Press Portrait, *edited by Herbert Mitgang, Quadrangle Books, 1971, pp. 110-12.*

ILLINOIS STATE JOURNAL   (essay date 1858)

[*The* Illinois State Journal *here records a victory for Lincoln in his debate with Douglas at Freeport. These comments were originally published in the* Journal *on 30 August 1858.*]

This has been a grand day for Lincoln and a glorious one for the Republican cause. The great discussion between Lincoln and Douglas [in the **Lincoln-Douglas Debate** at Freeport] has resulted in the overwhelming discomfiture of the ''little giant.'' He was completely wiped out and annihilated. To use his own choice vernacular, he was thoroughly ''trotted through.'' Lincoln ''brought him to his milk'' in a most triumphant manner. (p. 114)

What shall I say of the speaking? Lincoln made a most powerful speech, and charged home upon Douglas with a vengeance which was perfectly overwhelming. There was no escape from the coils which Lincoln wound around him, and his speech in

reply was without spirit, without power and labored throughout. His platitudes about amalgamation and nigger equality—his only political stock in trade—were too old, too stupid to be listened to with patience. Lincoln's half hour rejoinder was admirable, and clinched the argument of the first speech so that Douglas fairly squirmed under the infliction. At the close, cheer after cheer for Lincoln rent the air in prolonged shouts. The whole crowd seemed, with one voice, to join in the enthusiasm for ''Old Abe,'' while Douglas crawled off to his quarters like a whipped spaniel. (pp. 114-15)

> *''The Great Debate at Freeport between Lincoln and Douglas,''* in Abraham Lincoln: A Press Portrait, *edited by Herbert Mitgang, Quadrangle Books, 1971, pp. 113-15.*

CHICAGO TRIBUNE   (essay date 1858)

[*The* Chicago Tribune *lauds Lincoln for steadfastly upholding Republican principles in his losing effort against Douglas, claiming that Lincoln's speeches in the senatorial campaign ''will become landmarks in our political history.'' These comments were originally published in the* Tribune *on 10 November 1858.*]

Mr. Lincoln is beaten. Though Presidential management and the treachery of pretended friends may prevent Mr. Douglas' return, Mr. Lincoln cannot succeed. We know of no better time than the present to congratulate him on the memorable and brilliant canvass that he has made. He has fully vindicated the partialities of his friends, and has richly earned, though he has not achieved, success.

He has created for himself a national reputation that is both envied and deserved; and though he should hereafter fill no official station, he has done in the cause of Truth and Justice, what will always entitle him to the gratitude of his party and to the admiration of all who respect the high moral qualities and the keen, comprehensive, and sound intellectual gifts that he has displayed. No man could have done more. His speeches will become landmarks in our political history; and we are sure that when the public mind is more fully aroused to the importance of the themes which he has so admirably discussed, the popular verdict will place him a long way in advance of the more fortunate champion by whom he has been overthrown.

The Republicans owe him much for his truthfulness, his courage, his self-command, and his consistency; but the weight of their debt is chiefly in this: that, under no temptation, no apprehension of defeat, in compliance with no solicitation, has he let down our standard in the least. That God-given and glorious principle which is the head and front of Republicanism, ''All men are created equal, and are entitled to life, liberty and the pursuit of happiness,'' he has steadily upheld, defended, illustrated and applied in every speech which he has made. Men of his own faith may have differed with him when measures only were discussed; but the foundation of all—the principle which comprehends all—he has fought for with a zeal and courage that never flagged or quailed. In that was the pith and marrow of the contest.

Mr. Lincoln, at Springfield at peace with himself because he has been true to his convictions, enjoying the confidence and unfeigned respect of his peers, is more to be envied than Mr. Douglas in the Senate! Long live Honest Old Abe! (pp. 127-28)

> *''Abraham Lincoln,''* in Abraham Lincoln: A Press Portrait, *edited by Herbert Mitgang, Quadrangle Books, 1971, pp. 127-28.*

LOUISVILLE JOURNAL (essay date 1858)

[*The* Louisville Journal *responds to Douglas's and Lincoln's views concerning the legal establishment of slavery in the territories, an issue that Lincoln broached in his debate with Douglas at Freeport. These comments were originally published in the* Journal *in 1858.*]

According to Senator Douglas, the Territorial Legislatures, though prohibited by the Constitution from abolishing slavery within their respective jurisdictions, may lawfully abstain from enforcing the rights of slaveholders, and so extinguish the institution by voluntary neglect. In other words, Senator Douglas contends that the Territorial Legislatures may lawfully evade the Constitution by deliberately omitting to protect the rights which it establishes. He holds that the people of the Territories may lawfully abolish slavery indirectly, though the Constitution forbids them to abolish or prohibit it directly. It is impossible to conceive of squatter sovereignty in a more contemptible shape than this. It is the scurviest possible form of the scurviest of all possible heresies. (pp. 115-16)

Mr. Lincoln's position on this point has the merit of openness if not justness. Indeed, as compared with that of his adroit but short-sighted and unscrupulous antagonist, it possesses merits considerably more substantial than simple frankness. While taking sound national ground on every other important point of the "vexed question," Mr. Lincoln avows his belief "in the right and duty of Congress to prohibit slavery in all the United States Territories." We consider this an error, involving, theoretically at least, very grievous injustice to the citizens of the slaveholding States. It is undoubtedly a serious error, regarded in itself. Yet every impartial mind must perceive and admit that it is the pink of truth and justice compared with the wretched doctrine announced by Senator Douglas. In the name of common sense and common fairness, if slavery is to be prohibited or abolished in the Territories by any legislative tribunal, let it be done by one in which the whole nation is represented, and not by one composed of the representatives of the first stragglers from some over-burdened city or restless border State who happen to squat on the public domain. If slavery is to be prohibited in the Territories by legislation at all, let it be done by the people of the United States, and not by the first handful of nomadic settlers in the Territories themselves. If we must have any sovereignty in the case, apart from the Constitution, give us the sovereignty of the American people, not squatter sovereignty in its most detestable and unwarrantable shape. Senator Douglas, as we have seen [in the **Lincoln-Douglas Debate** at Freeport], gives us the latter—Mr. Lincoln the former. Between the two, no intelligent, discerning patriot can hesitate a moment. Mr. Lincoln's position, aside from its virtually speculative cast, is infinitely less unfriendly to the constitutional rights and just interests of the South. When, furthermore, we reflect that the Supreme Court has pronounced this identical position unconstitutional, and would infallibly nullify any Congressional legislation in pursuance of it, the practical consequence of Mr. Lincoln's error vanishes into all but nothing. It becomes a harmless crotchet—a political dream. But if it were as vital as it is lifeless, it would be immeasurably less pernicious than the reckless and shameless heresy of Douglas. (pp. 116-17)

"The 'Louisville Journal' on Douglas and Lincoln—Opinion of the Home Organ of Henry Clay," in Abraham Lincoln: A Press Portrait, *edited by Herbert Mitgang, Quadrangle Books, 1971, pp. 115-17.*

THE CINCINNATI ENQUIRER (essay date 1859)

[*In 1859, Lincoln was invited by his party to speak in Ohio before the fall elections. The* Cincinnati Enquirer *here reviews one of his speeches, describing him as a boorish, partisan "mountebank." These comments were originally published in the* Enquirer *between September 16 and September 20, 1859.*]

A "verbatim report" of the speech of Mr. Lincoln was given by our enterprising neighbor of the *Gazette*, in their yesterday's impression. Mr. Lincoln—so we are informed by the editor of that journal—*"is deficient in clap-trap, but excels in logic and honesty;* and herein"—our contemporary continues—"he differs from Judge Douglas." We thank him for his indorsement.

We have glanced over the speech of Mr. Lincoln in the *Gazette*. We do not say that we have read it: it is not worth reading. It contains nothing that is calculated to make any man wiser, or more learned; to make him a better citizen or a better man; to give him any insight into the character of the Government, or into his duty as a part of the governing power. It is, in a single expressive word, *trash*—trash from beginning to end; trash without one solitary oasis to relieve the dreary waste that begins with its nearest and ends with its furthest boundary.

Among public addresses from the stump, the speech of Mr. Lincoln belongs to the lowest order. It is not the speech of a statesman; it is not the speech of a politician; it is not even the speech of a fair partisan. It is the speech of a pettifogging demagogue, devoted to an uncandid and one-sided discussion of the real or presumed party and doctrinal status of a third person. It is not a business for the display of either logic or honesty, and, therefore—we beg pardon of our contemporary for disagreeing with him—there is no appearance of those qualities.

We do not propose to review the speech of Mr. Lincoln. Indeed, there is nothing to review. Its material is the ordinary slip-slop of the Republican party press, interlarded with profane ejaculations, hyperbolical expressions and staring comparisons, to fit it for delivery to a *mixed* audience. Mr. Lincoln was a candidate against Mr. Douglas for a seat in the Senate of the United States; and, after a severe contest, was defeated. Upon this fact stands his reputation—all that he ever had; and out of this fact grows his political character. He is the symbol of private and party enmity to the Senator of Illinois, accidentally endowed with voice and personality—owing his entire significance to that antagonism. Without Douglas Lincoln would be nothing; and this he virtually admits by being nothing but anti-Douglas. At once a parasite and enemy, he labors insanely to destroy that upon which depends his own existence.

The speech of Mr. Lincoln was well received. His audience was in excellent humor with itself and with its orator. His remarks were interrupted—as appears by the report—by frequent laughter and applause. One of Mr. Lincoln's strongest points is his propensity to misstate the positions and exaggerate the remarks of his antagonist, in the indulgence of which we observe he was so happy as to bring down the crowd on several occasions. When he told his hearers that "Douglas' popular sovereignty, as a principle, is simply this: 'If one man chooses to make a slave of another man, neither that other man nor any body else has a right to object,'" he was answered with "cheers and laughter." It was undoubtedly received as an excellent joke. As a truth it would not have been at all laughable; we must, therefore, take the applause as a tribute paid to the author's wit at the expense of his credit for veracity. His speech was full of jokes of a similar character—well calculated to reduce to less than nothing the reputation of their utterer as a man of truth and candor. Indeed, it appears that the crowd was not long in finding out its man; for the rambling dialogue between the orator and his hearers into which the speech degenerated indicated well enough the respect in which he had come to be holden, who was not too proud to stand up and utter palpable lies for their amusement.

We do not know but, in what we have said above, we have committed a radical error. We may have brought the address of Mr. Lincoln to a standard for which it was not intended. We have spoken of the gentleman from Illinois as the Hon. Abraham Lincoln: we remember now that by his admirers he is known as Abe and Old Abe Lincoln. Nay, so was he advertised and puffed and placarded around this city during last week: Old Abe was coming—rough old customer—great blackguard—tremendous on the stump—says just what he pleases—be after little Dug with a sharp stick. The idea was that to a good deal of native rudeness and vulgarity of character the aforesaid Abe had added something by assiduous practice—that in choosing among the various known modes to attain unsound popularity, he had chosen the habits of the boor and the vocabulary of the ruffian as best adapted at once to his taste and his capacity; and that he had, to a more than ordinary extent, succeeded in making himself the thing he desired.

Now, we will confess that if this is Mr. Lincoln, the speech was perfectly in character. Every thing is as it should have been; the audience applauded in the right places, and every feature of the transaction was in proper keeping with every other. The orator did as he was expected to do. The crowd was pleased because it got what it expected. It was not the statesman but the mountebank that was wanted. The mountebank came; and the honors were easy. (pp. 141-43)

"Mr. Lincoln and His Speech," in Abraham Lincoln: A Press Portrait, *edited by Herbert Mitgang, Quadrangle Books, 1971, pp. 137-43.*

WILLIAM CULLEN BRYANT   (essay date 1860)

[Bryant, who is considered one of the most accomplished American poets of the nineteenth century, served from 1829 to 1878 as editor-in-chief of the New York Evening Post. *In the following excerpt from the 28 February 1860 issue, Bryant discusses Lincoln's ideas on slavery and the slaveholding states as presented in his* Cooper Union Speech.]

When we have such a speech as that of Abraham Lincoln, of Illinois, delivered at the Cooper Institute last evening to a crowded, deeply interested and enthusiastic audience, we are tempted to wish that our columns were indefinitely elastic.

We have made room for Mr. Lincoln's [*Cooper Union Speech*] notwithstanding the pressure of other matters, and our readers will see that it was well worthy of the deep attention with which it was heard. That part of it in which the speaker places the Republican party on the very ground occupied by the framers of our constitution and fathers of our republic, strikes us as particularly forcible.

In this great controversy the Republicans are the real conservative party. They simply adhere to a policy which had its origin with George Washington of Virginia, Benjamin Franklin of Pennsylvania, Abraham Baldwin of Georgia, Alexander Hamilton of New York, and other men from other states worthy to be named with them.

It is remarkable how perfectly all the eminent statesmen of that age were agreed upon the great question of slavery in the territories. They never thought of erecting the slaveholding class into an oligarchy which was to control the political administration of the country, dictate to the judiciary, and invade and occupy the new regions possessed by the confederation. They regarded it—and this fully appears from authentic and undisputed records—by a consent next to unanimous, as a class which was never to exist beyond the limits of the old thirteen states.

At that time the slave holders were content to await, within the limits they occupied, the hour, which Washington, himself one of their number, benevolent and liberal-minded as he was, hoped was not far distant, when our republic should present to the world the spectacle of "a confederacy of free states."

All the clamor about northern aggression, all the menaces of a dissolution of the Union, have only this grievance as their cause, that we think as Washington thought, hope as he hoped, and act as he acted; and they have only this object in view—to force us from the course he approved and which our conscience approves still, and to compel us to adopt a new policy, new measures, new views of the meaning of the constitution, opening the gates of the territories of the barbarian institution which our fathers intended should wither into decrepitude, and pass to its dissolution within its original limits.

All this may not be new, but it is most logically and convincingly stated in the speech—and it is wonderful how much a truth gains by a certain mastery of clear and impressive statement. But the consequences to which Mr. Lincoln follows out the demands of these arrogant innovators give an air of novelty to the closing part of his argument.

What they require of us is not only a surrender of our long-cherished notions of constitutional rights, inherited from our ancestors and theirs; not only a renunciation of the freedom of speech, but a hypocritical confession of doctrines which revolt both our understanding and our conscience, a confession extorted by the argument of the highwayman, the threat of violence and murder. There is to be no peace with the South till the slaveholders shall have forced us to say that slavery is right—not merely to admit it by silence, but to shout the accursed doctrine with all the strength of our lungs.

With the renunciation of the creed of liberty must come the reconsideration and rejection of our free constitutions. Every one of the constitutions of the free states puts the stigma of public abhorrence upon slavery, and is an offense and an insult to the slaveholder. They who cannot submit to allow the natural lawfulness of slavery to be questioned in public debate, or in the discussions of the press, certainly will not tolerate the more solemn declaration of the right of all men to freedom embodied and proclaimed in the state constitutions of the North and West. One by one these state constitutions must be given up, torn in pieces, and trampled under foot at the bidding of the preachers of the new political gospel. (pp. 156-58)

William Cullen Bryant, in a report, in Abraham Lincoln: A Press Portrait, *edited by Herbert Mitgang, Quadrangle Books, 1971, pp. 156-58.*

ILLINOIS STATE JOURNAL   (essay date 1861)

[The Illinois State Journal *here reports on Lincoln's "Farewell Address at Springfield." These comments were originally published in the* Journal *on 12 February 1861.]*

At precisely five minutes before eight o'clock, Mr. Lincoln, preceded by Mr. Wood, of New York, slowly made his way from his room in the station, through the expectant masses which respectfully parted right and left at his approach to the car provided for his use. At each step of his progress towards the car, friendly hands were extended for a last greeting. On reaching the platform of the car, Mr. Lincoln turned toward the people, removed his hat, paused for several seconds, till he could control his emotions, and then slowly, impressively, and with profound emotion, uttered the ["**Farewell Address at Springfield**"]:

> Friends, no one who has never been placed in a like position, can understand my feelings at this hour, nor the oppressive sadness I feel at this parting. For more than a quarter of a century I have lived among you, and during all that time I have received nothing but kindness at your hands. Here I have lived from my youth until now I am an old man. Here the most sacred ties of earth were assumed; here all my children were born; and here one of them lies buried. To you, dear friends, I owe all that I have, all that I am. All the strange, chequered past seems to crowd now upon my mind. To-day I leave you; I go to assume a task more difficult than that which devolved upon General Washington. Unless the great God who assisted him, shall be with and aid me, I must fail. But if the same omniscient mind, and the same Almighty arm that directed and protected him, shall guide and support me, I shall not fail, I shall succeed. Let us all pray that the God of our fathers may not forsake us now. To him I commend you all—permit me to ask that with equal sincerity and faith, you all will invoke His wisdom and guidance for me. With these few words I must leave you—for how long I know not. Friends, one and all, I must now bid you an affectionate farewell.

It was a most impressive scene. We have known Mr. Lincoln for many years; we have heard him speak upon a hundred different occasions; but we never saw him so profoundly affected, nor did he ever utter an address, which seemed to us as full of simple and touching eloquence, so exactly adopted to the occasion, so worthy of the man and the hour. Although it was raining fast when he began to speak, every hat was lifted, and every head bent forward to catch the last words of the departing chief. When he said, with the earnestness of a sudden inspiration of feeling, that *with God's help he should not fail*, there was an uncontrollable burst of applause.

At precisely eight o'clock, city time, the train moved off, bearing our honored townsman, our noble chief, Abraham Lincoln to the scenes of his future labors, and, as we firmly believe, of his glorious triumph. God bless honest Abraham Lincoln. (pp. 224-25)

> *"Departure of Mr. Lincoln—Parting Address,"* in Abraham Lincoln: A Press Portrait, *edited by Herbert Mitgang, Quadrangle Books, 1971, pp. 224-25.*

NEW ORLEANS DAILY CRESCENT   (essay date 1861)

[*In this response to a speech that Lincoln gave at a stop in Indianapolis on his journey to Washington, D.C., to assume the presidency, the* New Orleans Daily Crescent *expresses disgust at Lincoln's alleged evasiveness and lack of decorum. These comments were originally published in the* Daily Crescent *on 21 February 1861.*]

If any one can read the speeches which Mr. Lincoln has made on his recent trip to Washington City without a feeling of intense disgust, we envy him not his disposition. Instead of displaying some of the qualities of a statesman and a patriot, he has, in point of fact, shown a "plentiful lack" of both. Instead of rising to the dignity of a President, he has fallen to the level of a stump orator, addressing, for temporary effect, a miscellaneous assemblage of the populace.

His speech at Indianapolis, which we believe was the first he delivered after leaving home, more especially challenges attention for its evasion of the real issue, its unnatural levity in the presence of great and serious events, and its illustrations drawn, not from anything grand or sublime in nature, but from the "passional attraction" of "free-love," and the "little pills" of the homeopathic practice of medicine! Who would have supposed that a man elevated to the Presidency of a nation would indulge in comparisons of this sort? Imagine George Washington or James Madison, on their way to the capital, making public speeches, destined to be read by the whole world, in which illustrations were drawn from such sources as these!

Mr. Lincoln betrays an utter inability to rise to the dignity of his subject. He resorts to the indirect and unsatisfactory and undignified expedient of *asking questions* of the populace before him, instead of coming out like a man, and saying flatly what he means. Too timid to express boldly his sentiments, he resorts to the roundabout way of putting interrogatories, thereby suggesting what he would not declare openly—and then, for fear of its being considered too great a committal, reminding the people that they must recollect he was only asking questions, not expressing opinions! Was there ever before such an instance of lack of directness and dignity in any one called to so high an office?

Then we discover also that the Northern President has totally misconceived the nature of the Government, and the Federative system by which the old Union was formed. He asks what the difference is between a county and a State, supposing the county to be equal to the State in population and territorial extent—deducing from this that a State has no more right of secession than a county! This absurd pretension shows how little Mr. Lincoln, like most other Northern politicians of all parties, knows of the character of the old Federal Union. He thinks that there is no sovereignty whatever in the respective States—that they are the dependencies of the Federal Government, instead of being the constituents of it, and that there is no such thing as a Federal Government without an unlimited surrender of their sovereignty on the part of the respective members. He thinks that the Union is the creature of the States, the latter losing their identity in the operation, for all purposes except that of tribute to the central authority. The doctrine of State Rights and State Sovereignty, it is plain to see, is something to which the President of the North is altogether a stranger.

It is but fair to say that Mr. Lincoln, as he traveled farther North, became more dignified in his harangues, and more cautious in his utterances. Under the manipulation of politicians more discreet than himself, he began to see that he must change his style. His later speeches are just as free from "passional attraction" comparisons as they are from the mistakes of the ill-informed politician.

Compare the Indianapolis speech of Lincoln with the inaugural address of President Davis, and how great the contrast! The reader of the latter cannot fail to be impressed with its dignified, manly, serious tone—its freedom from every kind of clap-trap—its abstinence from all insinuations or suggestions—its open, bold, honorable and fair statement of the opinions held by the distinguished orator. In nothing is the difference between Northern and Southern sentiment and morality better illustrated than in these two addresses. No wonder Seward, who, with all his anti-slavery bigotry and fanaticism, has some regard for outward appearances, should hesitate to accept a position in the Cabinet of one who has so poor an opinion of the popular intelligence, and so small an appreciation of the dignity of his office, as Mr. Lincoln displayed in his speech at Indianapolis. (pp. 465-67)

"The Northern President," in Southern Editorials on Secession, *edited by Dwight Lowell Dumond, 1931. Reprint by Peter Smith, 1964, pp. 465-67.*

NEW YORK DAILY TRIBUNE   (essay date 1861)

[*The* New York Daily Tribune *commends Lincoln's* First Inaugural Address *as a clear, firm, sagacious, and reassuring discourse addressing the leading national issues of the day: slavery and secession. These comments were originally published in the* Tribune *on 6 March 1861.*]

The almost universal satisfaction with which the [*First Inaugural Address*] of President Lincoln is received is the strongest evidence of the anxiety with which it was waited for, as well as of the high character of the document itself. For nearly four months the people of this country, strong in the power of self-government to which our institutions have bred them, have sustained themselves, as no other nation could have done, virtually without a central government, and while all the evil elements in the discontented and vicious of the community were appealed to by an apparently successful rebellion. Undoubtedly we have been drifting fast into anarchy; the reign of scoundrelism was impending, and might have already overwhelmed us but for the patient forbearance of the people with an effete and expiring government, and the patient waiting for the government to come, on which all hopes and all fears were centered. But had it been evident that the incoming Administration was to be a mere continuation of the imbecile policy of the last three months, the country sustained no longer by the hope of something better to come, would have fallen presently into general wreck and ruin, at least for a season, incapable of holding together even by that powerful cohesion of popular government, which is at once the result and the test of the excellence of our Republican system. The feeling then would necessarily be one of great relief were the Address merely an assurance of some positive firmness on the part of the new Administration.

But how much more must it gratify the public expectation when the address is found to be marked by a sagacity as striking as its courage, and by an absence of all passion as remarkable as its keen division of the line of duty, its unequivocal statement of the issues at stake, and uncompromising admissions of their precise value. Upon the question of Slavery the President frankly acknowledges all that the Constitution requires, as the Republican party has done before him, and proclaims the duty of fulfilling those requirements. But there is no hypocritical profession of a hasty alacrity at performing what is the exceptional duty under a free government, and he is careful to char-

acterize it as held by the majority of the people as strictly a "dry legal obligation." The question of Slavery in the Territories, inasmuch as the Constitution is silent in relation to it, he holds must be settled by the majority and their decision acquiesced in by the minority. Nor does he submit on this point to the *dictum* of the Supreme Court. In a few pregnant sentences, worthy the charge of a Chief Justice to a jury, and containing more sound law than is often found in charges twenty times its length, he clears away all the assumed settlement of the question by the Dred Scott decision. To the binding character of such decisions in private suits he assents, but he considers that the people would practically cease to be their own masters and resign the right of self-government into the hands of that tribunal, if they acknowledge that the policy of the Government is to be irrevocably fixed by the decisions of the Supreme Court, to which the Constitution gives no political power. And this is as sound common sense as it is good law, and sweeps away at a dash all the cobwebs of sophistry that have been woven over the public mind by the judgment in the case of Dred Scott.

But it is in the admirable treatment of the Secession question that Mr. Lincoln is most entitled to the gratitude of the country, and must certainly, it seems to us, command the support of all good citizens. The duty of the head of the Government to assert the rights of the Government itself is so self-evident a truth that the truth of the corollary is no less so—that those will be guilty of commencing civil war, if any shall arise, who shall attempt to hinder the Federal Government from occupying its own property. The avowal of his purpose, in this regard, is unequivocal, unhesitating, firm, and earnest. One thing only can be understood from it—he means to execute the laws. But as there is no hesitation, so there is no haste; and the firmness of his purpose is tempered by mercy. He means evidently to provoke no unnecessary hostilities, and only where his duty is perfectly clear to protect the rights of the whole will he assert the authority of the Federal Government. If in the interior of the Southern States foolish people will not permit the presence of Federal officers, they will be permitted to do without them, as they only are the losers; but where revenue is to be collected which belongs to the whole people, or where forts are to be reoccupied which no more belong to the section where they happen to be than they do to the people of the most distant corner of the Union, then the laws must be executed, and the power of the Federal Government asserted. But time, no doubt, will be given to the unhappy people, betrayed by an imbecile Government into excesses which four months ago they never contemplated, to return to their allegiance, and restore the property of which they have possessed themselves under a lamentable delusion.

The clearness with which the President states his position on this point is as remarkable as its firmness, and so persuaded will the country be that it is a wise plan, and that it is a plan which must confine all further disturbances to a few localities in settling the difference with the South, and that no disastrous consequences will follow it to any of the interests of the country, that we predict that the people will now turn to their several affairs, the mechanic to his craft, the farmer to his plow, the merchant to his merchandise, all men to their usual callings, satisfied that they may safely leave the question in the hands of one perfectly able to manage it, who will bring order out of seeming chaos, reason out of folly, safety out of danger, and that in so doing he will not sacrifice the national honor or jeopard any of the national interests. (pp. 640-42)

"Mr. Lincoln's Address," in Northern Editorials on Secession, *Vol. II, edited by Howard Cecil Perkins, Peter Smith, 1964, pp. 640-42.*

CHARLESTON MERCURY   (essay date 1861)

[*The* Charleston Mercury *depicts the* First Inaugural Address *as a "declaration of war" and mocks the president as "King Lincoln." These comments originally appeared in the* Mercury *on 9 March 1861.*]

President Abraham Lincoln reigns over all but six of the late United States. In the [*First Inaugural Address*] which his Excellency (?) vouchsafed to deliver on yesterday, he manifested no disposition to relinquish the pleasure of reigning over all the States. He said plainly as a man could say anything, that the Union was intended to be, and should be, perpetual, and that his purpose was to "hold, occupy and possess," or in other words to hold, take and retain all the forts and arsenals that ever belonged to the late government, and to do this by force of arms, unless "the people, his masters," refuse to sustain him with men, money and munitions of war. When he uttered this fiat of war in an emphatic tone, a great and prolonged shout rose up from all the people, one half of whom could not hear him. Evidently he had a *claque* around him.

He will also "collect the duties and imposts." Beyond the power which may be necessary for these objects, there will be no invasion, no using of force. So there *will* be *invasion,* there *will* be *force.* But not in "interior localities." In plain terms, then, the navy will be used on the seacoasts and against the rebellious ports; but the army will be reserved as yet. People of Charleston *prenez garde!* Sumter will be reinforced, if possible. Men of Pensacola, keep a sleepless eye on Pickens. I confess that this honest declaration of war is what I had not expected of Lincoln. Under Seward's adroit handling, I thought coercion would have been buttered over much more thickly. And it cannot be denied that sweet and suasive phrases are not wanting in the address; but the naked truth is none the less apparent and unmistakable for all that. King Lincoln—Rail Splitter Abraham—Imperator! We thank thee for this. It is the tocsin of battle, but it is the signal of our freedom. Quickly, oh quickly begin the fray. Haste to levy tribute. "Enforce the laws" with all possible speed! We have no money to pay, but we have treasure enough—liquid wealth, redder than any gold and infinitely more precious. Be sure, be very sure, O! lowborn, despicable tyrant, that the price of liberty will be paid—good measure, heaped up, shaken down, running over, in hot streams fresh from hearts that will not, cannot beat in the breasts of slaves. Then shall we hear the thunder from Sumter, and the fierce reply from Moultrie and from Cumming's Point. (pp. 242-43)

"The Abolition Regime," in Abraham Lincoln: A Press Portrait, *edited by Herbert Mitgang, Quadrangle Books, 1971, pp. 242-43.*

LA PATRIE   (essay date 1861)

[*The French periodical* La patrie *focuses on what it describes as the "irresolution" reflected in Lincoln's* First Inaugural Address. *These comments were originally published in* La patrie *on 29 March 1861.*]

What are we to think of Mr. Lincoln's [*First Inaugural Address*]? In view of the divergent opinions expressed in the United States, we in Europe have the right to put this question.

Whereas on the one hand *The (New York) Times, The Courier and Enquirer,* and *The (New York) Tribune* approve unreservedly of the new president, and speak of his "calm, inflexible courage in the face of any eventuality," of his "ability," of his "prudent wisdom," of his "conciliating tone"; on the other hand, *The (New York) Herald, The Express, The Journal of Commerce,* and *The United States Courier* declare that "Mr. Lincoln's language is neither candid nor worthy of a statesman"; that "he betrays at once both indecision and a strong tendency toward coercive measures." And whereas in the Senate Mssrs. Dixon and Douglas are asking that this speech be broadcast throughout the country in order to calm the people's spirits, Mr. Clingman answers that the tenor of this document could bring on civil war.

Anyone who has read the presidential document will easily understand these contradictory judgments. Irresolution fairly shines forth in every one of Mr. Lincoln's acts—in Chicago as in Cincinnati, as in the White House. Just when people are looking to him for a frank, clear statement, he finds nothing more explicit to say to the waiting nation than that he will do his duty, but, he adds prudently, "in so far as that will be possible." "The power which has been vested in me," he says, "will be used to hold, to occupy, and to possess the properties and the territories which belong to the government, and to collect taxes." Then he declares that there is no invasion, no use of force. And he indicates a means of solving this difficult problem. "To make the mystic chords of memory vibrate to the touch of the good angels of the country—chords which resound from our battlefields upon every heart which beats, in every home of this vast country."

Will this means, more poetic than practical, suffice to bring the Confederate States back into the Union? Will it restore the forts and the arsenals, the ships of the nation which the Confederates have seized or which have been handed over to them? Mr. Lincoln speaks of "holding, occupying, possessing the properties of the government." But these properties are in the hands of a power which up to the present has given proof of only skill and energy, which in six weeks has raised 50,000 militiamen and organized a small regular army. This army, just as we had foreseen, has been trained by those Southern officers who have abandoned the old Federal government: among others, General Twiggs, with nearly all the troops of Texas and New Mexico, Adjutant General Cooper, Assistant General Withers, and Major T. Beauregard of the Engineers Corps, who is to lead the attacks against Fort Sumter.

To oppose such adversaries, General Scott has gathered together in Washington 633 men from all the troops, but according to a report made to the Congress we now know that it will take *two months* to bring this corps up to 4,000 men. Assuming that this "army" is assembled, it will have to be transported to the South. Now, it takes eight days just to go from New York to New Orleans by rail, then there are forests and gigantic rivers to be crossed. These alone will offer almost insurmountable obstacles to military operations, and if and when these obstacles have been overcome, the Northern troops will arrive in the South just when the yellow fever is raging.

The Federal government, it is true, has ordered ships at distant stations to join forces at New York immediately, because Mr. Lincoln is depending on the fleet to blockade the Southern ports. But as we have already said, the loyalty of the Navy is in doubt, and it seems odd to see the Northern States attempting to blockade the Confederate States whose coastline is three or four times more extensive than their own. (pp. 249-50)

Confronted with such a situation, Mr. Lincoln's irresolution becomes more excusable, but in view of this, what is the purpose of the boasts which he has sown throughout this speech? Does he hope to deceive the Confederates of the South? We do not think so; especially after having read the vigorous reply of one of his opponents in a letter dated March 5 (1861) which has just been published. "We will never pay tribute to the United States. The only hope for a peaceful solution is the immediate abandonment of any idea of the collection of revenue by the United States, and the evacuation of all forts in the Confederacy.

"The only practical course for the Northern conservatives is to insist on a peaceful separation, or energetically to combat the Northern radicals in order to win the spring elections, then to dissolve the Union and to join our fresh, vigorous, liberal, and expanding republic. A rebuilding of the old edifice under Lincoln is a material absurdity."

There is a great gulf between this clear-cut program and that of the White House. To close it would require nothing less than reconciling the claims of the Democrats and the Republicans, the abolitionists and the advocates of slavery, the champions of free trade and the protectionists. (p. 251)

> *"Le discours de M. Lincoln,"* in Lincoln as They Saw Him, *edited by Herbert Mitgang, Rinehart & Company Inc., 1956, pp. 249-51.*

CHICAGO DAILY TIMES   (essay date 1862)

[*The* Chicago Daily Times *protests vigorously against the* Preliminary Emancipation Proclamation, *claiming that it is unconstitutional and "an act of national suicide." These comments were originally published in the* Times *on 24 September 1862.*]

Two days ago the President was wonderfully strong in the confidence of the country, not because of his military conduct of the war, for, in the opinion of all men, that had been disastrous, but because he had steadily manifested an apparently inflexible determination to adhere faithfully to the constitution in the political management of the war and in the general administration of the government. It was the merit of this adherence that, in the minds of all good and right-thinking men, covered his multitude of sins in the military conduct of the war. So long as he seemed to be fast-anchored to the constitution, good and right-thinking men never ceased to hope and believe that experience would teach him to correct and overcome his military mistakes, and that finally the government of the constitution would prevail over rebellion, and that the Union would be re-established.

Now that he has cut loose from the constitution [in the ***Preliminary Emancipation Proclamation***]—now that he has resorted to the same higher law than the constitution for the professed purpose of suppressing the rebellion by which the rebellion justifies itself—good and right-thinking men know not what to think or believe, or whither to turn for anchorage. They are smitten with a sense of alarm and dismay. They feel that the foundations of the government are unsettled, if not broken up— that the ship is adrift without master, compass or rudder, and that the chances of wreck are vastly greater than of safety.

If the policy of the proclamation were any more defensible than the President's constitutional power to issue it, the shadows which it has cast over the land would not be so impenetrable. It is an act of as bad faith to every conservative man in the North as it is a terrible blow to the Union men of the border slave States. The President has himself apprehended that it might drive fifty thousand Union soldiers, belonging to the border slave States, from the Union armies! We trust and pray that it will not, but that it will not work a most injurious revolution in the sentiment of those States we dare not hope; and as to Kentucky and Tennessee, what a time is this to hazard such a revolution! We await intelligence of its effect in those States with the most painful anxiety.

If we desired more conclusive arguments against the mere policy of the proclamation than any we have elsewhere seen, we should seek them in the answer of the President to the memorial of the religious fanatics of this city, contained in our yesterday's issue.

> What good would a proclamation of emancipation from me do, especially as we are now situated? I do not want to issue a document that the whole world will see must necessarily be inoperative, like the Pope's bull against the comet. Would *my word* free the slaves, when I cannot even enforce the constitution in the rebel States? Is there a single court or magistrate or individual that would be influenced by it there? And what reason is there to think it would have any greater effect upon the slaves than the late law of Congress, which I approved, and which offers protection and freedom to the slaves of rebel masters who come within our lines. Yet I cannot learn that that law has caused a single slave to come over to us. And suppose they could be induced, by a proclamation of freedom from me, to throw themselves upon us, *what should we do with them?* How can we feed and care for such a multitude? General Butler wrote me, a few days since, that he was issuing more rations to the slaves who have rushed to him than to all the white troops under his command. They *eat* and that is all.

Before the President issued the proclamation he would have done well to publicly answer these objections to the policy of it.

If utter desperation had not before seized the people of the rebel States, as a consequence of the abolition and confiscation measures of the Congress at Washington, it will seize them now. The war hereafter, on their part, will be a contest for existence as communities and individuals.

We protest against the proclamation, in the name of the constitution, in behalf of good faith to the conservative millions of the northern and border States, and for the sake of the only means by which it has at any time been possible to restore the Union. We protest against it as a monstrous usurpation, a criminal wrong, and an act of national suicide. (pp. 303-04)

> *"The Emancipation Proclamation,"* in Abraham Lincoln: A Press Portrait, *edited by Herbert Mitgang, Quadrangle Books, 1971, pp. 303-05.*

THE TIMES, LONDON   (essay date 1862)

[*The London* Times *denounces the* Preliminary Emancipation Proclamation *as a hypocritical and coercive war measure aimed at inciting insurrection among the slaves in the Confederacy.*

These comments were originally published in the Times *on 7 October 1862.*]

It is rarely that a man can be found to balance accurately mischief to another against advantage to himself. President Lincoln is, as the world says, a good-tempered man, neither better nor worse than the mass of his kind—neither a fool nor a sage, neither a villain nor a saint, but a piece of that common useful clay out of which it delights the American democracy to make great Republican personages. Yet President Lincoln has declared [in the ***Preliminary Emancipation Proclamation***] that from the 1st of January next to come every State that is in rebellion shall be in the eye of Mr. Lincoln a Free State. After that date Mr. Lincoln proposes to enact that every slave in a rebel State shall be for ever after free, and he promises that neither he, nor his army, nor his navy will do anything to repress any efforts which the negroes in such rebel States may make for the recovery of their freedom. This means, of course, that Mr. Lincoln will, on the 1st of next January, do his best to excite a servile war in the States which he cannot occupy with his arms. He will run up the rivers in his gunboats; he will seek out the places which are left but slightly guarded, and where the women and children have been trusted to the fidelity of coloured domestics. He will appeal to the black blood of the African; he will whisper of the pleasures of spoil and of the gratification of yet fiercer instincts; and when blood begins to flow and shrieks come piercing through the darkness, Mr. Lincoln will wait till the rising flames tell that all is consummated, and then he will rub his hands and think that revenge is sweet. This is what Mr. Lincoln avows before the world that he is about to do. Now, we are in Europe thoroughly convinced that the death of slavery must follow as necessarily upon the success of the Confederates in this war as the dispersion of darkness occurs upon the rising of the sun; but sudden and forcible emancipation resulting from ''the efforts the negroes may make for their actual freedom'' can only be effected by massacre and utter destruction. Mr. Lincoln avows, therefore, that he proposes to excite the negroes of the Southern plantations to murder the families of their masters while these are engaged in the war. The conception of such a crime is horrible. The employment of Indians sinks to a level with civilized warfare in comparison with it; the most detestable doctrines of Mazzini are almost less atrocious; even Mr. Lincoln's own recent achievements of burning by gunboats the defenceless villages on the Mississippi are dwarfed by this gigantic wickedness. The single thing to be said for it is that it is a wickedness that holds his head high and scorns hypocrisy. It does not pretend to attack slavery as slavery. It launches this threat of a servile rebellion as a means of war against certain States, and accompanies it with a declaration of general protection to all other slavery.

Where he has no power Mr. Lincoln will set the negroes free; where he regains power he will consider them as slaves. ''Come to me,'' he cries to the insurgent planters, ''and I will preserve your rights as slaveholders; but set me still at defiance, and I will wrap myself in virtue and take the sword of freedom in my hand, and, instead of aiding you to oppress, I will champion the rights of humanity. Here are whips for you who are loyal; go forth and flog or sell your black chattels as you please. Here are torches and knives for employment against you who are disloyal; I will press them into every black hand, and teach their use.'' Little Delaware, with her 2,000 slaves, shall still be protected in her loyal tyranny. Maryland, with her 90,000 slaves, shall ''freely accept or freely reject'' any project for either gradual or immediate abolition; but if Mississippi and

South Carolina, where the slaves rather outnumber the masters, do not repent, and receive from Mr. Lincoln a licence to trade in human flesh, that human flesh shall be adopted by Mr. Lincoln as the agent of his vengeance. The position is peculiar for a mere layman. Mr. Lincoln, by this proclamation, constitutes himself a sort of moral American Pope. He claims to sell indulgences to own votaries, and he offers them with full hands to all who will fall down and worship him. It is his to bind, and it is his to loose. His decree of emancipation is to go into remote States, where his temporal power cannot be made manifest, and where no stars and stripes are to be seen; and in those distant swamps he is, by a sort of Yankee excommunication, to lay the land under a slavery interdict.

What will the South think of this? The South will answer with a hiss of scorn. But what will the North think of it? What will Pennsylvania say—Pennsylvania, which is already unquiet under the loss of her best customers, and not easy under the absolute despotism of the present Government at Washington? What Boston may say or think is not, perhaps, of much consequence. But what will New York say? It would not answer the purpose of any of these cities to have the South made a howling wilderness. They want the handling of the millions which are produced by the labour of the black man. Pennsylvania desires to sell her manufactures in the South; New York wishes to be again broker, banker, and merchant to the South. This is what the Union means to these cities. They would rather have a live independent State to deal with than a dead dependency where nothing could be earnt. To these practical persons President Lincoln would be, after his black revolution had succeeded, like a dogstealer who should present the anxious owner with the head of his favourite pointer. They want the useful creature alive. The South without its cotton and its sugar and its tobacco would be of small use to New York, or even to Philadelphia; and the South without the produce of its rice and cotton, and its sugar and tobacco, would be but a sorry gain, even if it could be obtained. If President Lincoln wants such a conquest as this, the North is, perhaps, yet strong enough to conquer Hayti. A few fanatics, of course, will shout, but we cannot think that, except in utter desperation and vindictiveness, any real party in the North will applaud this nefarious resolution to light up a servile war in the distant homesteads of the South.

As a proof of what the leaders of the North, in their passion and their despair, would do if they could, this is a very sad document. As a proof of the hopelessness and recklessness which prompt their actions, it is a very instructive document. But it is not a formidable document. We gather from it that Mr. Lincoln has lost all hope of preserving the Union, and is now willing to let any quack try his nostrum. As an act of policy it is, if possible, more contemptible than it is wicked. It may possibly produce some partial risings, for let any armed power publish an exhortation to the labouring class of any community to plunder and murder, and there will be some response. It might happen in London, or Paris, or New York. That Mr. Lincoln's emancipation decrees will have any general effect bearing upon the issue of the war we do not, however, believe. The negroes have already abundantly discovered that the tender mercies of the Northerners are cruelties. The freedom which is associated with labour in the trenches, military discipline, and frank avowals of personal abhorrence momentarily repeated does not commend itself to the negro nature. General Butler could, if he pleased, tell strange stories of the ill success of his tamperings with the negroes about New Orleans. We do not think that even now, when Mr. Lincoln plays his last card, it will prove to be a trump. Powerful malignity is a dreadful reality, but impotent malignity is apt to be a very contemptible spectacle. Here is a would-be conqueror and a would-be extirpator who is not quite safe in his seat of government, who is reduced to such straits that he accepts a defeat as a glorious escape, a capitulation of 8,000 men as an unimportant event, a drawn battle as a glorious victory, and the retreat of an invading army which retires laden with plunder and rich in stores as a deliverance. Here is a President who has just, against his will, supplied his antagonists with a hundred and twenty guns and millions of stores, and who is trembling for the very ground on which he stands. Yet, if we judged only by his pompous proclamations, we should believe that he had a garrison in every city of the South. This is more like a Chinaman beating his two swords together to frighten his enemy than like an earnest man pressing on his cause in steadfastness and truth. (pp. 319-22)

A report on "Lincoln's Proclamation," in Abraham Lincoln: A Press Portrait, *edited by Herbert Mitgang, Quadrangle Books, 1971, pp. 319-22.*

[RALPH WALDO EMERSON]   (essay date 1862)

[Emerson was one of the most influential figures of the nineteenth century. An American essayist and poet, he founded the Transcendentalist movement and shaped a distinctly American philosophy that embraces optimism, individuality, and mysticism. Emerson here greets the Preliminary Emancipation Proclamation *as a momentous event in the history of political liberty, averring as well that the proclamation both relieves the United States of a tremendous moral burden and justifies the great sacrifices made in the Civil War. For additional commentary by Emerson, see excerpt dated 1865.]*

In so many arid forms which States incrust themselves with, once in a century, if so often, a poetic act and record occur. These are the jets of thought into affairs, when, roused by danger or inspired by genius, the political leaders of the day break the else insurmountable routine of class and local legislation, and take a step forward in the direction of catholic and universal interests. Every step in the history of political liberty is a sally of the human mind into the untried future, and has the interest of genius, and is fruitful in heroic anecdotes. Liberty is a slow fruit. It comes, like religion, for short periods, and in rare conditions, as if awaiting a culture of the race which shall make it organic and permanent. Such moments of expansion in modern history were the Confession of Augsburg, the plantation of America, the English Commonwealth of 1648, the Declaration of American Independence in 1776, the British emancipation of slaves in the West Indies, the passage of the Reform Bill, the repeal of the Corn-Laws, the Magnetic Ocean-Telegraph, though yet imperfect, the passage of the Homestead Bill in the last Congress, and now, eminently, President Lincoln's [*Preliminary Emancipation Proclamation*] on the twenty-second of September. These are acts of great scope, working on a long future, and on permanent interests, and honoring alike those who initiate and those who receive them. These measures provoke no noisy joy, but are received into a sympathy so deep as to apprise us that mankind are greater and better than we know. At such times it appears as if a new public were created to greet the new event. It is as when an orator, having ended the compliments and pleasantries with which he conciliated attention, and having run over the superficial fitness and commodities of the measure he urges, suddenly, lending himself to some happy inspiration, an-

nounces with vibrating voice the grand human principles involved,—the bravoes and wits who greeted him loudly thus far are surprised and overawed: a new audience is found in the heart of the assembly,—an audience hitherto passive and unconcerned, now at last so searched and kindled that they come forward, every one a representative of mankind, standing for all nationalities.

The extreme moderation with which the President advanced to his design,—his long-avowed expectant policy, as if he chose to be strictly the executive of the best public sentiment of the country, waiting only till it should be unmistakably pronounced,—so fair a mind that none ever listened so patiently to such extreme varieties of opinion,—so reticent that his decision has taken all parties by surprise, whilst yet it is the just sequel of his prior acts,—the firm tone in which he announces it, without inflation or surplusage,—all these have bespoken such favor to the act, that, great as the popularity of the President has been, we are beginning to think that we have underestimated the capacity and virtue which the Divine Providence has made an instrument of benefit so vast. He has been permitted to do more for America than any other American man. He is well entitled to the most indulgent construction. Forget all that we thought shortcomings, every mistake, every delay. In the extreme embarrassments of his part, call these endurance, wisdom, magnanimity, illuminated, as they now are, by this dazzling success.

When we consider the immense opposition that has been neutralized or converted by the progress of the war, (for it is not long since the President anticipated the resignation of a large number of officers in the army, and the secession of three States, on the promulgation of this policy,)—when we see how the great stake which foreign nations hold in our affairs has recently brought every European power as a client into this court, and it became every day more apparent what gigantic and what remote interests were to be affected by the decision of the President,—one can hardly say the deliberation was too long. Against all timorous counsels he had the courage to seize the moment; and such was his position, and such the felicity attending the action, that he has replaced Government in the good graces of mankind. "Better is virtue in the sovereign than plenty in the season," say the Chinese. 'T is wonderful what power is, and how ill it is used, and how its ill use makes life mean, and the sunshine dark. Life in America had lost much of its attraction in the later years. The virtues of a good magistrate undo a world of mischief, and, because Nature works with rectitude, seem vastly more potent than the acts of bad governors, which are ever tempered by the good-nature in the people, and the incessant resistance which fraud and violence encounter. The acts of good governors work at a geometrical ratio, as one midsummer day seems to repair the damage of a year of war.

A day which most of us dared not hope to see, an event worth the dreadful war, worth its costs and uncertainties, seems now to be close before us. October, November, December will have passed over beating hearts and plotting brains: then the hour will strike, and all men of African descent who have faculty enough to find their way to our lines are assured of the protection of American law.

It is by no means necessary that this measure should be suddenly marked by any signal results on the negroes or on the Rebel masters. The force of the act is that it commits the country to this justice,—that it compels the innumerable officers, civil, military, naval, of the Republic to range themselves on the line of this equity. It draws the fashion to this side. It is not a measure that admits of being taken back. Done, it cannot be undone by a new Administration. For slavery overpowers the disgust of the moral sentiment only through immemorial usage. It cannot be introduced as an improvement of the nineteenth century. This act makes that the lives of our heroes have not been sacrificed in vain. It makes a victory of our defeats. Our hurts are healed; the health of the nation is repaired. With a victory like this, we can stand many disasters. It does not promise the redemption of the black race: that lies not with us: but it relieves it of our opposition. The President by this act has paroled all the slaves in America; they will no more fight against us; and it relieves our race once for all of its crime and false position. The first condition of success is secured in putting ourselves right. We have recovered ourselves from our false position, and planted ourselves on a law of Nature.

If that fail,
The pillared firmament is rottenness,
And earth's base built on stubble.

The Government has assured itself of the best constituency in the world: every spark of intellect, every virtuous feeling, every religious heart, every man of honor, every poet, every philosopher, the generosity of the cities, the health of the country, the strong arms of the mechanics, the endurance of farmers, the passionate conscience of women, the sympathy of distant nations,—all rally to its support.

Of course, we are assuming the firmness of the policy thus declared. It must not be a paper proclamation. We confide that Mr. Lincoln is in earnest, and, as he has been slow in making up his mind, has resisted the importunacy of parties and of events to the latest moment, he will be as absolute in his adhesion. Not only will he repeat and follow up his stroke, but the nation will add its irresistible strength. If the ruler has duties, so has the citizen. In times like these, when the nation is imperilled, what man can, without shame, receive good news from day to day, without giving good news of himself? What right has any one to read in the journals tidings of victories, if he has not bought them by his own valor, treasure, personal sacrifice, or by service as good in his own department? With this blot removed from our national honor, this heavy load lifted off the national heart, we shall not fear henceforward to show our faces among mankind. We shall cease to be hypocrites and pretenders, but what we have styled our free institutions will be such.

In the light of this event the public distress begins to be removed. What if the brokers' quotations show our stocks discredited, and the gold dollar costs one hundred and twenty-seven cents? These tables are fallacious. Every acre in the Free States gained substantial value on the twenty-second of September. The cause of disunion and war has been reached, and begun to be removed. Every man's house-lot and garden are relieved of the malaria which the purest winds and the strongest sunshine could not penetrate and purge. The territory of the Union shines to-day with a lustre which every European emigrant can discern from far: a sign of inmost security and permanence. Is it feared that taxes will check immigration? That depends on what the taxes are spent for. If they go to fill up this yawning Dismal Swamp, which engulfed armies and populations, and created plague, and neutralized hitherto all the vast capabilities of this continent,—then this taxation, which makes the land wholesome and habitable, and will draw all

men unto it, is the best investment in which property-holder ever lodged his earnings. (pp. 638-41)

We think we cannot overstate the wisdom and benefit of this act of the Government. The malignant cry of the Secession press within the Free States, and the recent action of the Confederate Congress, are decisive as to its efficiency and correctness of aim. Not less so is the silent joy which has greeted it in all generous hearts, and the new hope it has breathed into the world.

It was well to delay the steamers at the wharves, until this edict could be put on board. It will be an insurance to the ship as it goes plunging through the sea with glad tidings to all people. Happy are the young who find the pestilence cleansed out of the earth, leaving open to them an honest career. Happy the old, who see Nature purified before they depart. Do not let the dying die: hold them back to this world, until you have charged their ear and heart with this message to other spiritual societies, announcing the melioration of our planet.

Incertainties now crown themselves assured,
And Peace proclaims olives of endless age.

Meantime that ill-fated, much-injured race which the [***Preliminary Emancipation Proclamation***] respects will lose somewhat of the dejection sculptured for ages in their bronzed countenance, uttered in the wailing of their plaintive music,—a race naturally benevolent, joyous, docile, industrious, and whose very miseries sprang from their great talent for usefulness, which, in a more moral age, will not only defend their independence, but will give them a rank among nations. (p. 642)

[*Ralph Waldo Emerson*], *''The President's Proclamation,'' in* The Atlantic Monthly, *Vol. X, No. LXI, November, 1862, pp. 638-42.*

THE TIMES, London (essay date 1863)

> [*The London* Times *expresses serious misgivings concerning the motivation behind the* Emancipation Proclamation, *its constitutionality, and its ultimate benefit to freed blacks. These comments were originally published in the* Times *on 15 January 1863.*]

Mr. Lincoln has finally adhered to the policy from which he showed at one moment some inclination to draw back. He has kept his promise to the very letter; he has declared the negroes in the States now at open war with the North free, except within certain districts occupied by the Federal forces, and has pledged the Government of the United States to recognize and support the freedom so granted by their naval and military force. . . . Missouri, Tennessee, Kentucky, and Maryland are exempt [from the ***Emancipation Proclamation***]; so that it would seem to be the policy of the President to interpose an isthmus of slavery between the two masses of free States which are to extend to the North and South of it. Pronounced under other circumstances, by another person, and at another time, such a Proclamation might well excite once more the enthusiasm which penetrated the whole mind of England in the days of Wilberforce and Clarkson. We should most unfeignedly rejoice were the words to which the President has given utterance capable of carrying with them their own fulfilment. To slavery we have ever entertained the most rooted aversion. Not all the valour, not all the success of the South, has ever blinded us to this black spot on their fair escocheon. But even tainted as they are with this foul stain they have commanded our admiration and our sympathy from the gallantry with which they have maintained their cause, and from the obvious truth that the struggle was for separation on the one part and compulsory retention on the other, the emancipation or continued slavery of the negro being only used as means to forward the ends of the North. While it was supposed that the South could be brought back by giving every security for the continuance of slavery, the North never dreamt of emancipation. When it was found that no such conciliation was possible, the North, as a weapon of war, and not as a concession to principle, has finally decided on emancipation. That this measure is no homage to principle or conviction, but merely a means of raising up a domestic enemy against the Southerners in the midst of the Southern States, is abundantly proved from the fact that slavery, so odious in Alabama, is tolerated in Kentucky. Its abolition is a punishment to rebels; its retention is a reward to patriots; it is not the accursed thing to be rooted out at all hazards. Its abolition is the punishment of rebellion; its retention is the reward of adherence to the Union.

Still, though there is little homage to principle in the President's Proclamation, any attempt on the part of the American Government, however tardily, reluctantly, and partially made, to emancipate any portion of the negro race, must have an effect on the opinion of mankind, and tend to what we have never doubted would in some way or other be the final result of this war, the abolition of slavery. But our exultation is by no means without misgivings. The President has proclaimed freedom, but he is without power to enforce his Proclamation. Except in the neighbourhood of New Orleans, where General Butler has already done all that is possible to create a servile war, the President of the United States has no power whatever to enforce his Proclamation. If the blacks are to obtain the freedom he promises them, it must be by their own hands. They must rise upon a more numerous, more intelligent, better armed, and braver community of whites, and exterminate them, their wives, and children, by fire and sword. The President of the United States may summon them to this act, but he is powerless to assist them in its execution. Nay, this is the very reason why they are summoned. The armies of the South have gained a clear superiority over the armies of the North, and it is to redress this balance that the negro, burning, ravishing, massacring, and destroying, is summoned to the conflict. If these things are not done at all, there will be, for the present at least, no emancipation; if they are done, they will provoke retaliatory action, which is but too likely to end in the extermination of their perpetrators. In neither case has the friend of humanity any cause to rejoice. It must also be remembered that this act of the President, if it purposed to strike off the fetters of one race, is a flagrant attack on the liberties of another. The attempt to free the blacks is a flagrant attack on the liberties of the whites. Nothing can be more unconstitutional, more illegal, more entirely subversive of the compact on which the American Confederacy rests, than the claim set up by the President to interfere with the laws of individual States by his Proclamation, unless, indeed, it be the attempt of Congress to dismember the ancient State of Virginia, and create a new State upon its ruins. It is preposterous to say that war gives these powers; they are the purest usurpation, and, though now used against the enemies of the Union, are full of evil presage for the liberties of the States that still adhere to it. It is true that the President advises the negroes to abstain from all violence except in self-defence, and to labour for reasonable wages. But the President well knows that not a slaveholder in the South will obey his Proclamation, that it can only be enforced by violence, and that if the negroes obtain freedom it will be by the utter destruction of their masters. In such a state of society to speak of wages—that is, of a contract between master and servant—

is a cruel mockery. In the South the negro can only exist apart from his master by a return to the savage state—a state in which, amid blood and anarchy and desolation, he may frequently regret the fetters he has broken, and even the master whom he has destroyed. He cannot hope for a better situation than that of his race in the North—a situation of degradation, humiliation, and destitution which leaves the slave very little to envy. Mr. Lincoln bases his act on military necessity, and invokes the considerate judgment of mankind and the judgment of Almighty God. He has characterized his own act; mankind will be slow to believe that an act avowedly the result of military considerations has been dictated by a sincere desire for the benefit of those who, under the semblance of emancipation, are thus marked out for destruction, and He who made man in His own image can scarcely, we may presume to think, look with approbation on a measure which, under the pretence of emancipation, intends to reduce the South to the frightful condition of St. Domingo. (pp. 330-33)

A report on "Lincoln's Emancipation Proclamation," in Abraham Lincoln: A Press Portrait, *edited by Herbert Mitgang, Quadrangle Books, 1971, pp. 330-33.*

[JAMES BURRILL ANGELL]   (essay date 1863)

[*The Providence, Rhode Island,* Daily Journal *published these comments on the "Gettysburg Address" on 20 November 1863. Louis A. Warren identifies the author as James Burrill Angell, a nineteenth-century American editor, college administrator, and diplomat.*]

We know not where to look for a more admirable speech than the brief one [the **"Gettysburg Address"**] which the President made at the close of Mr. Everett's oration. It is often said that the hardest thing in the world is to make a five minute speech. But could the most elaborate and splendid oration be more beautiful, more touching, more inspiring than those few words of the President? They had in my humble judgement the charm and power of the very highest eloquence.

[*James Burrill Angell*], *in an extract from "Press Reaction," in* Lincoln's Gettysburg Declaration: "A New Birth of Freedom" *by Louis A. Warren, Lincoln National Life Foundation, 1964, p. 144.*

[JOSIAH G. HOLLAND]   (essay date 1863)

[*The following praise of the "Gettysburg Address" was originally published in the 20 November 1863 issue of the Springfield, Massachusetts,* Republican. *Louis A. Warren attributes these remarks to Josiah G. Holland, one of the newspaper's editors.*]

Surprisingly fine as Mr. Everett's oration was in the Gettysburg consecration, the rhetorical honors of the occasion were won by President Lincoln. His little speech [the **"Gettysburg Address"**] is a perfect gem, deep in feeling, compact in thought and expression, and tasteful and elegant in every word and comma. . . . Strong feelings and a large brain were its parents—a little painstaking its accoucheur. (pp. 143-44)

[*Josiah G. Holland*], *in an extract from "Press Reaction," in* Lincoln's Gettysburg Declaration: "A New Birth of Freedom" *by Louis A. Warren, Lincoln National Life Foundation, 1964, pp. 143-44.*

CHICAGO DAILY TIMES (essay date 1863)

[*The* Chicago Daily Times *responds negatively to the "Gettysburg Address," castigating Lincoln for expressing political partisanship in an elegy and for misrepresenting the cause for which Union soldiers had died at Gettysburg. These comments were originally published in the* Times *on 23 November 1863.*]

It is not supposed by any one, we believe, that Mr. Lincoln is possessed of much polish in manners or conversation. His adherents, however, claim for him an average amount of common sense, and more than an ordinarily kind and generous heart. We have failed to distinguish his pre-eminence in the latter, and apprehend the former to be somewhat mythical, but imagine that his deficiencies herein being less palpable than in other qualities constituting a statesman have led his admirers greatly to overestimate him in these regards. These qualities are unfailing guides to appropriateness of speech and action in mixing with the world, however slight may have been the opportunities afforded their possessor for becoming acquainted with the usages of society.

The introduction of Dawdleism in a funeral sermon [such as the **"Gettysburg Address"**] is an innovation upon established conventionalities, which, a year or two ago, would have been regarded with scorn by all who thought custom should, to a greater or less extent, be consulted in determining social and public proprieties. And the custom which forbids its introduction is founded on the propriety which grows out of the fitness of things, and is not therefore merely arbitrary, or confined to special localities, but has suggested to all nations the exclusion of political partianship in funeral discourses. Common sense, then, should have taught Mr. Lincoln that its intrusion upon such an occasion was an offensive exhibition of boorishness and vulgarity. An Indian in eulogizing the memories of warriors who had fallen in battle would avoid allusion to differences in the tribe which had no connection with the prevailing circumstances, and which he knew would excite unnecessarily the bitter prejudices of his hearers. Is Mr. Lincoln less refined than a savage?

But aside from the ignorant rudeness manifest in the President's exhibition of Dawdleism at Gettysburg,—and which was an insult at least to the memories of a part of the dead, whom he was there professedly to honor,—in its misstatement of the cause for which they died, it was a perversion of history so flagrant that the most extended charity cannot regard it as otherwise than willful. That, if we do him injustice, our readers may make the needed correction, we append a portion of his eulogy on the dead at Gettysburg:

> Four score and ten [sic] years ago our fathers brought forth upon this continent a nation consecrated [sic] to liberty and dedicated to the proposition that all men are created equal. [Cheers.] Now we are engaged in a great civil war, testing whether that nation or any other [sic] nation so consecrated [sic] and so dedicated can long endure.

As a refutation of this statement, we copy certain clauses in the Federal constitution:

> Representatives and direct taxes shall be apportioned among the several States which may be included in this Union, according to their respective numbers, which shall be determined by adding to the whole number of *free* persons, including those bound to service for a term of

years, and excluding Indians not taxed, three-fifths of *all other persons*.

> The migration or importation of such persons as any of the States now existing shall think proper to admit shall not be prohibited by the Congress prior to the year 1808, but a tax or duty may be imposed on such importation, not exceeding ten dollars for each person.

> No amendment to the constitution, made prior to 1808, shall affect the preceding clause.

> No person held to service or labor in one State under the laws thereof, escaping into another, shall, in consequence of any law or regulation therein, be discharged from such service or labor, but shall be delivered up on claim of the party to whom such service or labor may be due.

Do these provisions in the constitution dedicate the nation to "the proposition that all men are created equal"? Mr. Lincoln occupies his present position by virtue of this constitution, and is sworn to the maintenance and enforcement of these provisions. It was to uphold this constitution, and the Union created by it, that our officers and soldiers gave their lives at Gettysburg. How dared he, then, standing on their graves, misstate the cause for which they died, and libel the statesmen who founded the government? They were men possessing too much self-respect to declare that negroes were their equals, or were entitled to equal privileges. (pp. 359-61)

> *"The President at Gettysburg," in* Abraham Lincoln: A Press Portrait, *edited by Herbert Mitgang, Quadrangle Books, 1971, pp. 359-61.*

HARRIET BEECHER STOWE (essay date 1864)

[*Stowe was an important nineteenth-century abolitionist and writer. Her famous novel,* Uncle Tom's Cabin; or, Life among the Lowly, *which is noted for its humanitarian tone and antislavery focus, became one of the most popular and profoundly influential novels of the nineteenth century. Here, she underscores the popular appeal of Lincoln's writing style in his state papers.*]

[Our] own politicians were somewhat shocked with [Lincoln's] state-papers at first. Why not let *us* make them a little more conventional, and file them to a classical pattern? "No," was his reply, "I shall write them myself. *The people will understand them.*" "But this or that form of expression is not elegant, not classical." "*The people will understand it*," has been his invariable reply. And whatever may be said of his state-papers, as compared with the classic standards, it has been a fact that they have always been wonderfully well understood by the people, and that since the time of Washington, the state-papers of no President have more controlled the popular mind. And one reason for this is, that they have been informal and undiplomatic. They have more resembled a father's talks to his children than a state-paper. And they have had that relish and smack of the soil, that appeal to the simple human heart and head, which is a greater power in writing than the most artful devices of rhetoric. Lincoln might well say with the apostle, "But though I be rude in speech yet not in knowledge, but we have been thoroughly *made manifest among you* in all things." His rejection of what is called fine writing was as deliberate as St. Paul's, and for the same reason—because he felt that he was speaking on a subject which must be made clear to the lowest intellect, though it should fail to captivate the highest. But we say of Lincoln's writing, that for all true, manly purposes of writing, there are passages in his state-papers that could not be better put; they are absolutely perfect. They are brief, condensed, intense, and with a power of insight and expression which make them worthy to be inscribed in letters of gold. Such are some passages of the celebrated Springfield letter, especially that masterly one where he compares the conduct of the patriotic and loyal blacks with that of the treacherous and disloyal whites. No one can read this letter without feeling the influence of a mind both strong and generous. (pp. 283-84)

In times of our trouble Abraham Lincoln has had his turn of being the best abused man of our nation. Like Moses leading his Israel through the wilderness, he has seen the day when every man seemed ready to stone him, and yet, with simple, wiry, steady perseverance, he has held on, conscious of honest intentions, and looking to God for help. All the nation have felt, in the increasing solemnity of his proclamations and papers, how deep an education was being wrought in his mind by this simple faith in God, the ruler of nations, and this humble willingness to learn the awful lessons of his providence. (p. 284)

> *Harriet Beecher Stowe, "Abraham Lincoln," in* The Littell's Living Age, *Vol. LXXX, No. 1027, February 6, 1864, pp. 282-84.*

PUNCH, OR THE LONDON CHARIVARI   (essay date 1864)

[*The following send-up of Lincoln's forthcoming* Second Inaugural Address *was originally published in the British comic periodical* Punch.]

Now I am sovereign of the sovereign people of this great and united republic for four years next ensuing the date hereof, as I used to say when I was a lawyer. *(You are! Bully for you!)* Yes, gentlemen, but you must do something more than bully for me, you must fight for me, if you please, and whether you please or not. As the old joke says, there's no compulsion, only you must. Must is for the King, they say in the rotten Old world. Well, I'm King, and you shall be Viceroys over me. But I tell you again, and in fact I repeat it, that there's man's work to do to beat these rebels. They *may* run away, no doubt. As the Irishman says, pigs may fly, but they're darned onlikely birds to do it. They must be well whipped, gentlemen, and I must trouble you for the whipcord. *(You shall have it!)* Rebellion is a wicked thing, gentlemen, an awful wicked thing, and the mere nomenclating thereof would make my hair stand on end, if it could be more standonender than it is. *(Laughter.)* Truly awful, that is when it is performed against mild, free, constitutional sway like that of the White House, but of course right and glorious when perpetrated against ferocious, cruel, bloodthirsty old tyrants like George the Third. We must punish these rebels for their own good, and to teach them the blessings of this mighty and transcendental Union. *(We will, we will!)* All very tall talking, gentlemen, but talking won't take Richmond. If it would, and there had been six Richmonds in the field, we should long since have took them all. If Richmond would fall like Jericho, by every man blowing of his own trumpet, we've brass enough in our band for that little feat in acoustics. But when a cow sticks, as Grant does, in the mud, how then? *(Great laughter.)* Incontestably, gentlemen, this great and mighty nation must give her a shove on. Shove for Richmond, gentlemen. *(That's the talk!)* Now about these eternal blacks, you expect me to say something touching

them, though I suppose we're none of us too fond of touching them, for reasons in that case made and provided, as I used to say. Well, listen. We've got them on our hands, that's a fact, and it reminds me of a nigger story. Two of these blacks met, and one had a fine new hat. "Where you got dat hat, Sambo?" says t'other. "Out ob a shop, nigger," says Sambo. "'Spex so," says t'other, "and what might be the price ob dat hat?" "Can't say, zactly, nigger, the shopkeeper didn't happen to be on the premises." *(Laughter.)* Well, we've got the niggers, and I can't exactly say—or at least I don't think you'd like to hear—what might be the price of those articles. But we must utilise our hats, gentlemen. We must make them dig and fight, that's a fact. There's no shame in digging, I suppose. Adam digged, and he is a gentleman of older line than any of the bloated and slavish aristocracies of Europe. And as for fighting, they must feel honoured at doing that for the glorious old flag that has braved for eighty-nine years and a-half, be the same little more or less, the battle and the breeze. *(Cheers.)* Yes, and when the rebellion's put down, we'll see what's to be done with them. Perhaps if the naughty boys down South get uncommon contrite hearts, we may make them a little present of the blacks, not as slaves, of course, but as legal apprentices with undefined salaries determinable on misconduct. *(Cheers.)* Meantime, gentlemen, I won't deny that the niggers are useful in the way of moral support. They give this here war a holy character, and we can call it a crusade for freedom.

> *"President Lincoln's Inaugural Speech," in* Punch, or the London Charivari, *December 10, 1864, p. 237.*

THE DAILY EXPRESS   (essay date 1865)

[*The Petersburg, Virginia,* Daily Express *here responds to Lincoln's* Second Inaugural Address, *taking issue with his account of the outbreak of the Civil War and mocking the religious aspects of his speech. These comments were originally published in the* Daily Express *on 9 March 1865.*]

[Lincoln's *Second Inaugural Address*] is a queer sort of document, being a compound of philanthropy, fanaticism and scriptural morality.—On the subject of the war, he would have the world to believe that his bosom is overflowing with the most distressing emotions in contemplating its horrors, and that he used all his efforts and influence to prevent its breaking out. But "somehow" or other the "slave interest" forced it upon him, and he had to choose between the alternatives of letting the nation survive or seeing it perish.—It is sufficient to say there were no such alternatives presented to him. The only alternatives were for him to leave eleven sovereign States to the peaceful enjoyment of their rights, or to draw the sword and compel them to live the slaves of a Union which abolitionism and the lusts of commerce had converted into an engine of oppression and impoverishment to them. He chose to draw the sword, but by a dirty trick succeeded in throwing upon the South the *seeming* blame of firing "the first gun." He was afraid to fire it himself, and resorted to craft and perfidy to get, what he considered, the advantage of a provocation that, in the eyes of his people, would justify his resort to open and active hostilities. . . . [Lincoln] has made a good deal of history, but none that will disgrace him more in the eyes of future generations than the part he acted in the Fort Sumter affair, by which he managed to precipitate hostilities without *technically* incurring the odium of having struck "the first blow." But let this pass.

A photograph of Lincoln in the prepresidential years.

The most curious portion of his Inaugural is the latter half of it, where he enacts the character of a saintly devotee. His allusions to Almighty Power and his citations from the scriptures might well become a Preacher of Righteousness. He seems to be thoroughly imbued with reverence for the Gospel of peace and with faith in Divine revelations. One would suppose that his knees were almost lacerated by his prayers and that his heart was the abode of all the Christian graces—that his whole time, except when his public duties forced him into carnal performances, were spent in prayer, and supplication, and that it was the supreme delight of his life to meditate upon Heavenly things. It is not for us to know any human heart, and still less such a heart as Lincoln's. God is the great searcher of this deceitful and most desperately wicked organ, and He alone knows whether it is always what the lips of its owner would represent it to be. So just here we will refrain from expressing our opinion, saying with Lincoln, who borrowed the idea and most of the words from our Saviour's sermon on the Mount: "Let us judge not, that we be not judged"—and so we take our leave of his Inaugural. (pp. 442-43)

> "*Lincoln's Inaugural No. 2,*" *in* Abraham Lincoln: A Press Portrait, *edited by Herbert Mitgang, Quadrangle Books, 1971, pp. 442-43.*

THE SPECTATOR   (essay date 1865)

[*The* Spectator *cites the* Second Inaugural Address *as evidence of Lincoln's growing maturity as a statesperson, addressing at the same time the issue of the president's alleged "bloodthirstiness" and despotism.*]

Mr. Lincoln was called from a humble station at the opening of a mighty civil war to form a Government out of a party in which the habits and traditions of official life did not exist. Finding himself the object of Southern abuse so fierce and so foul that in any man less passionless it would long ago have stirred up an implacable animosity, mocked at for his official awkwardness and denounced for his steadfast policy by all the Democratic section of the loyal States, tried by years of failure before that policy achieved a single great success, further tried by a series of successes so rapid and brilliant that they would have puffed up a smaller mind and overset its balance, embarrassed by the boastfulness of his people and of his subordinates no less than by his own inexperience in his relations with foreign States, beset by fanatics of principle on one side who would pay no attention to his obligations as a constitutional ruler, and by fanatics of caste on the other who were not only deaf to the claims of justice but would hear of no policy large enough for a revolutionary emergency, Mr. Lincoln has persevered through all without ever giving way to anger, or despondency, or exultation, or popular arrogance, or sectarian fanaticism, or caste prejudice, visibly growing in force of character, in self-possession, and in magnanimity, till in his [*Second Inaugural Address*] we can detect no longer the rude and illiterate mould of a village lawyer's thought, but find it replaced by a grasp of principle, a dignity of manner, and a solemnity of purpose which would have been unworthy neither of Hampden nor of Cromwell, while his gentleness and generosity of feeling towards his foes are almost greater than we should expect from either of them. It seems to us, we confess, a discreditable and hardly intelligible thing that the pro-Southern English journals which are exulting with such vehement delight over the squalid vulgarity of the new Vice-President's drunken inaugural . . . should not recognize the calm and grand impartiality displayed, even though it be by a foe, in the President's recent weighty address,—by far the noblest which any American President has yet uttered to an American Congress. Yet the fact is that its finest sentences have been deliberately distorted from their true and obvious meaning into the expression of a bloodthirsty spirit, the farthest possible from their real tenor. After confessing candidly the complicity of the North in the guilt of slavery, and the righteousness of the judgment by which North and South alike suffer its retribution, Mr. Lincoln went on to say, "Fondly do we hope, fervently do we pray, that this mighty scourge of war may speedily pass away. Yet, if God wills that it continue till all the wealth piled by the bondsman's two hundred and fifty years of unrequited toil shall be sunk, and until every drop of blood drawn with the lash shall be paid by another drawn with the sword, as was said three thousand years ago so still it must be said, that the judgments of the Lord are true and righteous altogether." Will it be believed that English journals have garbled this sentence by citing out of it the hypothetical clause, "Yet if it [the war] continues until the wealth piled by bondmen by 250 years' unrequited toil be sunk, and until every *drop of blood* drawn by the *lash* shall be paid with *another* drawn by the *sword*," without either the introductory or the final words,—decapitated and mutilated of its conclusion,—simply in order to prove Mr. Lincoln's bloodthirstiness? They might almost as fairly cite from the psalms the words, "If I forget thee, Oh! Jerusalem!" minus the clause, "let my right hand forget her cunning," to prove that the Psalmist was deliberately contemplating the renunciation of his patriotic duties and ties. But these are the critics who do not wish to understand Mr. Lincoln, who wish indeed to misunderstand him. (pp. 318-19)

The war once declared by his opponents, our readers know how he treated the slavery question,—not from any doubt that slavery was the root of the whole struggle, but from a profound doubt whether he was justified in anticipating the divine moment for its extinction. He was not placed there as God's instrument to put down slavery, but as His instrument for administering the Government of the United States "on the basis of the constitution," and the question might settle itself far better than he could settle it. Slowly he was forced, bit by bit, to see that the one duty was involved in the other, and as he saw he accepted it; but even then his only fear was lest he should interfere too much in the great forces which were working out their own end. He was chosen, as men usually are, to do that which he was most fearful of doing,—not because he did not see that it was a great work,—but because he only very gradually opened his eyes to its being a work in which he, with his defined duties, had any right to meddle. And now he speaks of it in just the same spirit as a great natural process, not entrusted to him or dependent on him, of which no one can foresee the course and the exact issue. Both North and South, he says, were equally confident in the justice of their cause, and appealed to God to justify that confidence. He has not justified either of them wholly. "The prayers of both could not be answered; that of neither has been answered fully. The Almighty has His own purposes."

Mr. Lincoln presents more powerfully than any man that quality in the American mind which, though in weak men it becomes boastfulness, is not really this in root, but a strange, an almost humiliated trust in the structural power of that political Nature which without any statesman's co-operation is slowly building up a free nation or free nations on that great continent, with an advance as steady as that of the rivers or the tides. It is the phase of political thought most opposite to, though it is sometimes compared with, the Caesarism that is growing up on the European side of the Atlantic. The Emperor of the French thinks the Imperial organ of the nation almost greater than the nation,—certainly an essential part of it. It is men like Mr. Lincoln who really believe devoutly, indeed too passively, in the "logic of events," but then they think the logic of events the Word of God. The Caesar thinks also of the logic of events, but he regards himself not as its servant but its prophet. He *makes* events when the logic would not appear complete without his aid, points the slow logic of the Almighty with epigram, fits the unrolling history with showy, rhetorical *dénouements*, cuts the knot of ravelled providences, and stills the birth-throes of revolution with the chloroform of despotism. Mr. Lincoln is a much stupider and slower sort of politician, but we doubt if any politician has ever shown less personal ambition and a larger power of trust. (p. 319)

"Mr. Lincoln," in The Spectator, *No. 1917, March 25, 1865, pp. 318-19.*

NATIONAL INTELLIGENCER (essay date 1865)

[*The Washington, D.C.,* National Intelligencer *praises the generosity and wisdom informing Lincoln's "Last Public Address." These comments were first published on 13 April 1865.*]

The country has indeed cause for congratulation in the speech of the President, reported in yesterday's *Intelligencer*. This remarkable speech is *wise* in *sentiment;* it is pervaded by the logic of the heart; while the keenness and clearness of percep-

tion and grasp of thought which distinguish it, considering the magnitude and complications of the intricate problem which he handles, are certainly remarkable. The simple and fit and familiar words in which he clothes his propositions and suggestions, and what of argument he advances, confirm the best opinions which have been entertained of the elevated character of the mind of the Chief Magistrate.

The first and great thought of the President is, *to welcome the States to their* PLACES *in the Union.* He wishes to consider the States "at Home" within the Union; and he does not desire to hear any discussion as to whether or not they have been *out* of the sisterhood. He does not even recognize that they have seceded; he speaks of them as the "so-called" seceded States. This is entirely in accord with the position which the *Intelligencer* has always ascribed to the President, and is as broad and liberal a platform, as soulful and generous an intimation, as the mind and heart of man could extend, in the matter of greeting and assurance to the *disordered* South. (pp. 457-58)

The practical statesmanship of the speech lies in what the President says about the establishment and protection of civil governments in the South, and which he enforces by the illustration of Louisiana. . . . [The] plan is the best which the President can see; and he will adhere to it until more wisely advised. In our judgment, the wit of man can do nothing better than adopt the simple process of the working of the old State machinery. It will soon grow if favorably fostered, and adjust itself to its former proportions. Assuming the theory of the Union to be unchanged, and its substance to be the same as before the war, then the Union, in contemplation of law, is intact. Shall we destroy the vine because it needs pruning? Or, to adopt the apt figure of the President, can we have the fowl if we smash the egg?

On all doubtful and involved questions, pertinent to a future day, and which are essentially secondary, the President expresses no opinion and deals in no intimations. He disposes of such obscurities as only a practical statesman can. To use his own admirable language, "An *exclusive* and *inflexible* plan would surely become a new *entanglement*. Important *principles* may and must be inflexible."

An eminent sense of justice characterizes this speech; it is from a lofty stand-point; it soars away above party; it is paternal as well as fraternal; it is Christian, and its spirit will be hailed with delight and responded to by almost the unanimous voice of the masses of the people, South as well as North. If any man says that he should have said more; that he should have obtruded opinions on the relations between Federal and State authority, as hereafter to be defined: that he should have talked dogmatically about the political future of the blacks; that he should have asserted something in behalf of Federal power and prerogative; in other words, that he should have ventured a *coup d'état* or practical dictatorship, then we respond, that the nation has just reason to thank God that Abraham Lincoln, as disclosed thus far to us, is no such man! His aim appears to be to find and to do the right, within the limits of the Constitution and the laws. And high evidence of this is found in the fact that he is not disposed to accept the questionable argument which asserts that no more than three-fourths of the States are necessary to ratify the constitutional amendment which abolishes slavery. "I do not commit myself against this (the President remarks) further than to say that such a ratification would be questionable, and sure to be persistently questioned; while a ratification of three-fourths of all the States would be unquestioned and unquestionable." This is as far above the partisan, the "radical," the "fanatic," as the highest statesmanship is above the lowest demagogism.

We breathe freely since reading this great and good speech, which seems also to reflect the present spirit of the more influential among the Republican newspapers; of those of that class of the press which have been esteemed as "radical." We cordially thank the President for the stand he has so nobly taken, notwithstanding the embarrassments that surround him, growing out of the weight of the questions which press upon him, and encountering, as he is compelled to do, great discordance of opinion among those who claim to be his especial friends. He has opened wide the gate to restoration; and thus far, he has grandly performed his part. (pp. 458-59)

> *A report on a speech by Abraham Lincoln in* Abraham
> Lincoln: A Press Portrait, *edited by Herbert Mitgang,*
> *Quadrangle Books, 1971, pp. 456-59.*

NEW YORK WORLD   (essay date 1865)

[*The* New York World *describes Lincoln's "Last Public Address"*
as vague, indecisive, and empty. These comments were originally
published in the New York World *on 13 April 1865.*]

The vagueness, indecision, and, we will venture to add, *emptiness* of the speech which we published yesterday [Lincoln's **"Last Public Address"**], cannot be attributed to the haste of a sudden extemporaneous effort, for there is evidence that it was prepared with unusual care and deliberation. On the evening previous to its delivery, Mr. Lincoln declined to hazard any expressions on the reconstruction question on the ground that he was to speak on that subject the next night, and wished to weigh his language. It is stated in a Washington dispatch that the speech was written out beforehand and read from a manuscript. Considering how little it contains, this precaution is evidence not only of care, but of timidity. The President was so afraid of misconstruction or criticism that he said nothing, or what comes so near to nothing that he might as well have not broken silence at all. As if conscious of the vacuity of his speech, he closed it by intimating that he might make proclamation to the South, and was meditating its substance.

And yet this speech, vague and vacillating as it is, stirred up the ire of the radicals; and this, too, not for its halting negation of purpose, but its assumed hostility to their policy. The Washington telegrams to the [*New York*] Tribune foam over with rage. The speech is, in the main, a mere apologetic defense of Mr. Lincoln's policy in Louisiana; but as the radicals have made that policy a special ground of attack, his faltering adherence to it is regarded as a declaration of hostility to them.

Mr. Lincoln ought to learn, from the fruits of this experiment, how little he has to gain by shirking the questions which it is his duty to meet with a statesmanlike boldness. By a speech obviously composed to deprecate the wrath of the radicals, he has incurred as strong expressions of their censure, as he could have done by the distinct avowal of a decided policy. He has let the radicals see that he fears them; and has thereby given them fresh encouragement to bully him. It is true that they have a great advantage over him in their predominance in Congress; but Congress cannot meet until December, unless he calls them together, and, meanwhile, the military *eclat* of our generals will cause the popular current to flow in the President's favor, and float any sound and reasonable policy which he espouses with courage, and supports by weight of his great position. Before December, he may carry forward the work of

reconstruction to so advanced a stage that Congress will not dare to face public odium and undo his work. But if he allows himself to be cowed by the radicals, he will drift like a hull without a helm till Congress meets, and then be driven at the mercy of the storm.

Mr. Lincoln gropes, in his speech, like a traveler in an unknown country without a map. And in the excess of that timidity which fears to make any committals as to the route he will take, he declares that the lines drawn on maps are "mere pernicious abstractions—good for nothing at all." Chief among these "pernicious abstractions," which, according to Mr. Lincoln, can have "no effect other than the mischievous one of dividing our friends," is the question whether the states which passed ordinances of secession are in, or out of, the Union. He dares not pronounce on this question for fear of dividing his party, and so calls it a "pernicious abstraction." But, in truth, it lies at the roots of the great problem of reconstruction; the restoration of the Union, *in any manner*, being impossible without taking a position on it on one side or the other. . . . (pp. 456-57)

> *A report on "President Lincoln's Speech of Recon-*
> *struction," in* Abraham Lincoln: A Press Portrait,
> *edited by Herbert Mitgang, Quadrangle Books, 1971,*
> *pp. 456-57.*

NEW YORK DAILY TRIBUNE   (essay date 1865)

[*The* New York Daily Tribune *weighs Lincoln's posthumous rep-*
utation, citing hesitancy and leniency among his shortcomings
and the ability to "elucidate profound truths" in his speeches and
debates as one of his greatest attributes. These comments were
originally published in the Tribune *on 19 April 1865.*]

Without the least desire to join in the race of heaping extravagant and preposterous laudations on our dead President as the wisest and greatest man who ever lived, we feel sure that the discerning and considerate of all parties will concur in our judgment that Mr. Lincoln's reputation will stand higher with posterity than with the mass of his contemporaries—that distance, whether in time or space, while dwarfing and obscuring so many, must place him in a fairer light—that future generations will deem him undervalued by those for and with whom he labored, and be puzzled by the bitter fierceness of the personal assaults by which his temper was tested.

One reason for this is doubtless to be found in the external, superficial, non-essential tests by which we are accustomed to gauge contemporary merit. A king without his crown and purple robes is, to the vulgar apprehension, a solecism, an impossibility. A coarsely clad, travel-stained, barefoot Jesus, could get no hearing in our fashionable synagogues, though his every discourse were a Sermon on the Mount. And Mr. Lincoln was so essentially, unchangeably a commoner—among embassadors and grandees in the White House the identical "Old Abe" that many of us had shaken by both hands at Western barbecues—his homely, pungent anecdotes so like those we had heard him relate from political stumps and by log-cabin firesides—that the masses thought of him but as one with whom they had been splitting rails on a pleasant Spring day or making a prosperous voyage down the Mississippi on an Illinois flatboat, and had found him a downright good fellow. We have had Presidents before him sprung from the loins of poverty and obscurity, but never one who remained to the last so simply, absolutely, alike in heart and manner, one of the People. No one who approached him, whether as minister or messenger, felt impelled either to stoop or to strut in his presence.

He was neither awed by assumption nor disgusted by vulgarity. He was never constrained nor uneasy in whatever presence, and he imposed no constraint nor ceremony on others. Every one found him easy of access, yet no one felt encouraged to take undue liberties. . . . (pp. 468-69)

Mr. Lincoln has suffered in the judgment of his immediate contemporaries from the fact that, of all things that he might have been required to do, the conduct of a great war was that for which he was least fitted. For War requires the utmost celerity of comprehension, decision, action; and Mr. Lincoln's mind was essentially of the "slow and sure" order. It was pretty certain to be right in the end; but in War to be right a little too late is equivalent to being wrong altogether. Besides, War sometimes requires sternness; and he was at heart tender and merciful as a woman. He might have saved many lives by prompt severity toward a few of the active traitors who thronged Baltimore and Washington directly after the fall of Sumter, and openly, ostentatiously exulted over our disaster at Bull Run. That extreme lenity which befits the close of a civil war was most unluckily evinced by him at the beginning of ours, giving every coward to understand that, while there was peril in steadfast loyalty, it was perfectly safe to be a Rebel. To human apprehension, Andrew Johnson should have been the man to grapple with and crush the Rebellion, with Abraham Lincoln to pacify the country at its close and heal the gaping wounds opened by four years of desperate, bloody conflict: but it was otherwise decreed. (pp. 469-70)

As Premier of a Government like the British, where the position requires skill and tact in debate while the duties of administration are divided, Mr. Lincoln would have been far more happily placed and would have done better service than in our Presidential chair, whereof the incumbent must mainly speak and act through others. His *forte* lay mainly in debate, or rather in the elucidation of profound truths, so that they can hardly evade the dullest apprehension. No other man ever so successfully confronted, before a prejudiced, negro-despising audience, the plausible fallacies of Senator Douglas's vaunted "Popular Sovereignty." His familiar exposition of that doctrine in his Springfield speech opening the Senatorial canvass of 1858—"If A. wants to make B. a slave, *C. shall not interfere*"—was only paralleled in that passage of one of his replies to his great antagonist, which reads:

> My distinguished friend says it is an insult to the emigrants of Kansas and Nebraska to suppose that they cannot govern themselves. We must not slur over an argument of this kind because it happens to tickle the ear. I admit that the emigrant to Kansas or Nebraska is competent to govern himself; *but I deny his right to govern any other person without that person's consent.*

Men of greater talent have made Republican speeches in this City; but Mr. Lincoln's [*Cooper Union Speech*] of March, 1860, remains to this day the most lucid, cogent, convincing argument of them all. So at the consecration of the Gettysburg National Cemetery (Nov. 19th, 1863) where Edward Everett made an elaborate and graceful oration, and others spoke fitly and well, the only address which the world will remember was that of the President. . . . (pp. 470-71)

—"I have not assumed to control events—events have controlled me," said Mr. Lincoln, in answer to a Kentucky complaint that he was more radical in 1864-5 than he had been in

1861-2. That was the simple truth, naively and tersely expressed; and in that truth is exhibited both the weakness and the strength of the utterer. He was not the man of transcendent genius, of rare insight, of resistless force of character, who bends everything to his will: On the contrary, he was one of those who have awaited opportunity, and thought long and patiently, before venturing on an important step, hearkening intently for that "voice of the people" which was to him, in most cases, "the voice of God." He hesitated to put down his foot, feeling the ground carefully, deliberately; but, once down, it was hard to make him take it up again. A striking and honored exemplar of some of the best points in our National character, he sleeps the sleep of the honored and just, and there are few graves which will be more extensively, persistently visited, or bedewed with the tears of a people's prouder, fonder affection, than that of Abraham Lincoln. (p. 472)

> *"Mr. Lincoln's Fame,"* in Abraham Lincoln: A Press Portrait, *edited by Herbert Mitgang, Quadrangle Books, 1971, pp. 468-72.*

RALPH WALDO EMERSON   (essay date 1865)

[*In this eulogy written shortly after the president's assassination in 1865, Emerson portrays Lincoln as a providential figure in American history. For additional commentary by Emerson, see excerpt dated 1862.*]

The President stood before us as a man of the people. He was thoroughly American, had never crossed the sea, had never been spoiled by English insularity or French dissipation; a quite native, aboriginal man, as an acorn from the oak; no aping of foreigners, no frivolous accomplishments, Kentuckian born, working on a farm, a flatboatman, a captain in the Black Hawk War, a country lawyer, a representative in the rural legislature of Illinois—on such modest foundations the broad structure of his fame was laid. (p. 917)

A plain man of the people, an extraordinary fortune attended him. He offered no shining qualities at the first encounter; he did not offend by superiority. He had a face and manner which disarmed suspicion, which inspired confidence, which confirmed good will. He was a man without vices. He had a strong sense of duty, which it was very easy for him to obey. Then, he had what farmers call a long head; was excellent in working out the sum for himself; in arguing his case and convincing you fairly and firmly. Then, it turned out that he was a great worker; had prodigious faculty of performance; worked easily. A good worker is so rare; everybody has some disabling quality. In a host of young men that start together and promise so many brilliant leaders for the next age, each fails on trial; one by bad health, one by conceit, or by love of pleasure, or lethargy, or an ugly temper—each has some disqualifying fault that throws him out of the career. But this man was sound to the core, cheerful, persistent, all right for labor, and liked nothing so well.

Then, he had a vast good nature, which made him tolerant and accessible to all; fair-minded, leaning to the claim of the petitioner; affable, and not sensible to the affliction which the innumerable visits paid to him when President would have brought to any one else. (pp. 918-19)

Then his broad good humor, running easily into jocular talk, in which he delighted and in which he excelled, was a rich gift to this wise man. It enabled him to keep his secret; to meet every kind of man and every rank in society; to take off the edge of the severest decisions; to mask his own purpose and sound his companion; and to catch with true instinct the temper of every company he addressed. (p. 919)

He is the author of a multitude of good sayings, so disguised as pleasantries that it is certain they had no reputation at first but as jests; and only later, by the very acceptance and adoption they find in the mouths of millions, turn out to be the wisdom of the hour. I am sure if this man had ruled in a period of less facility of printing, he would have become mythological in a very few years, like Aesop or Pilpay, or one of the Seven Wise Masters, by his fables and proverbs. But the weight and penetration of many passages in his letters, messages and speeches, hidden now by the very closeness of their application to the moment, are destined hereafter to wide fame. What pregnant definitions; what unerring common sense; what foresight; and, on great occasion, what lofty, and more than national, what humane tone! His ["**Gettysburg Address**"] will not easily be surpassed by words on any recorded occasion. This, and one other American speech, that of John Brown to the court that tried him, and a part of Kossuth's speech at Birmingham, can only be compared with each other, and with no fourth.

His occupying the chair of state was a triumph of the good sense of mankind, and of the public conscience. This middle-class country had got a middle-class president, at last. Yes, in manners and sympathies, but not in powers, for his powers were superior. This man grew according to the need. His mind mastered the problem of the day; and as the problem grew, so did his comprehension of it. Rarely was man so fitted to the event. In the midst of fears and jealousies, in the Babel of counsels and parties, this man wrought incessantly with all his might and all his honesty, laboring to find what the people wanted, and how to obtain that. It cannot be said there is any exaggeration of his worth. If ever a man was fairly tested, he was. There was no lack of resistance, nor of slander, nor of ridicule. The times have allowed no state secrets; the nation has been in such ferment, such multitudes had to be trusted, that no secret could be kept. Every door was ajar, and we know all that befell.

Then, what an occasion was the whirlwind of the war. Here was place for no holiday magistrate, no fair-weather sailor; the new pilot was hurried to the helm in a tornado. In four years—four years of battle-days—his endurance, his fertility of resources, his magnanimity, were sorely tried and never found wanting. There, by his courage, his justice, his even temper, his fertile counsel, his humanity, he stood a heroic figure in the centre of a heroic epoch. He is the true history of the American people in his time. Step by step he walked before them; slow with their slowness, quickening his march by theirs, the true representative of this continent; an entirely public man; father of his country, the pulse of twenty millions throbbing in his heart, the thought of their minds articulated by his tongue.

Adam Smith remarks that the axe, which in Houbraken's portraits of British kings and worthies is engraved under those who have suffered at the block, adds a certain lofty charm to the picture. And who does not see, even in this tragedy so recent, how fast the terror and ruin of the massacre are already burning into glory around the victim? Far happier this fate than to have lived to be wished away; to have watched the decay of his own faculties; to have seen—perhaps even he—the proverbial ingratitude of statesmen; to have seen mean men preferred. Had he not lived long enough to keep the greatest promise that ever man made to his fellow men—the practical abolition of slavery? He had seen Tennessee, Missouri and

Maryland emancipate their slaves. He had seen Savannah, Charleston and Richmond surrendered; had seen the main army of the rebellion lay down its arms. He had conquered the public opinion of Canada, England and France. Only Washington can compare with him in fortune.

And what if it should turn out, in the unfolding of the web, that he had reached the term; that this heroic deliverer could no longer serve us; that the rebellion had touched its natural conclusion, and what remained to be done required new and uncommitted hands—a new spirit born out of the ashes of the war; and that Heaven, wishing to show the world a completed benefactor, shall make him serve his country even more by his death than by his life? Nations, like things, are not good by facility and complaisance. "The kindness of kings consists in justice and strength." Easy good nature has been the dangerous foible of the Republic, and it was necessary that its enemies should outrage it, and drive us to unwonted firmness, to secure the salvation of this country in the next ages.

The ancients believed in a serene and beautiful Genius which ruled in the affairs of nations; which, with a slow but stern justice, carried forward the fortunes of certain chosen houses, weeding out single offenders or offending families, and securing at last the firm prosperity of the favorites of Heaven. It was too narrow a view of the Eternal Nemesis. There is a serene Providence which rules the fate of nations, which makes little account of time, little of one generation or race, makes no account of disasters, conquers alike by what is called defeat or by what is called victory, thrusts aside enemy and obstruction, crushes everything immoral as inhuman, and obtains the ultimate triumph of the best race by the sacrifice of everything which resists the moral laws of the world. It makes its own instruments, creates the man for the time, trains him in poverty, inspires his genius, and arms him for his task. It has given every race its own talent, and ordains that only that race which combines perfectly with the virtues of all shall endure. (pp. 919-21)

> *Ralph Waldo Emerson, "Abraham Lincoln," in* The Complete Essays and Other Writings of Ralph Waldo Emerson, *edited by Brooks Atkinson, The Modern Library, 1940, pp. 917-21.*

WALT WHITMAN   (poem date 1865-66)

[Whitman is regarded as one of America's finest nineteenth-century poets and a great literary innovator. His Leaves of Grass, *in which he celebrated the common person, democracy, and sexuality, had a major influence on modern free verse. One of Whitman's most highly acclaimed poems is "When Lilacs Last in the Dooryard Bloom'd," an elegy for Lincoln in which the poet symbolizes the slain president as a "powerful western fallen star." Reprinted below, the poem was originally published in* Sequel to Drum-Taps *in 1865-66 and later included in* Leaves of Grass.]

1

When lilacs last in the dooryard bloom'd,
And the great star early droop'd in the western sky in
    the night,
I mourn'd, and yet shall mourn with ever-returning
    spring.

Ever-returning spring, trinity sure to me you bring,
Lilac blooming perennial and drooping star in the west,
And thought of him I love.

2

O powerful western fallen star!
O shades of night—O moody, tearful night!
O great star disappear'd—O the black murk that hides
    the star!
O cruel hands that hold me powerless—O helpless soul
    of me!
O harsh surrounding cloud that will not free my soul.

3

In the dooryard fronting an old farm-house near the
    white-wash'd palings,
Stands the lilac-bush tall-growing with heart-shaped
    leaves of rich green,
With many a pointed blossom rising delicate, with the
    perfume strong I love,
With every leaf a miracle—and from this bush in the
    dooryard,
With delicate-color'd blossoms and heart-shaped leaves
    of rich green,
A sprig with its flower I break.

4

In the swamp in secluded recesses,
A shy and hidden bird is warbling a song.

Solitary the thrush,
The hermit withdrawn to himself, avoiding the
    settlements,
Sings by himself a song.

Song of the bleeding throat,
Death's outlet song of life, (for well dear brother I
    know,
If thou wast not granted to sing thou would'st surely
    die.)

5

Over the breast of the spring, the land, amid cities,
Amid lanes and through old woods, where lately the
    violets peep'd from the ground, spotting the gray
    debris,
Amid the grass in the fields each side of the lanes,
    passing the endless grass,
Passing the yellow-spear'd wheat, every grain from its
    shroud in the dark-brown fields uprisen,
Passing the apple-tree blows of white and pink in the
    orchards,
Carrying a corpse to where it shall rest in the grave,
Night and day journeys a coffin.

6

Coffin that passes through lanes and streets,
Through day and night with the great cloud darkening
    the land,
With the pomp of the inloop'd flags with the cities
    draped in black,
With the show of the States themselves as of crape-
    veil'd women standing,
With processions long and winding and the flambeaus
    of the night,
With the countless torches lit, with the silent sea of
    faces and the unbared heads,
With the waiting depot, the arriving coffin, and the
    sombre faces,

With dirges through the night, with the thousand voices
    rising strong and solemn,
With all the mournful voices of the dirges pour'd
    around the coffin,
The dim-lit churches and the shuddering organs—where
    amid these you journey,
With the tolling tolling bells' perpetual clang,
Here, coffin that slowly passes,
I give you my sprig of lilac.

7

(Nor for you, for one alone,
Blossoms and branches green to coffins all I bring,
For fresh as the morning, thus would I chant a song for
    you O sane and sacred death.

All over bouquets of roses,
O death, I cover you over with roses and early lilies,
But mostly and now the lilac that blooms the first,
Copious I break, I break the sprigs from the bushes,
With loaded arms I come, pouring for you,
For you and the coffins all of you O death.)

8

O western orb sailing the heaven,
Now I know what you must have meant as a month
    since I walk'd,
As I walk'd in silence the transparent shadowy night,
As I saw you had something to tell as you bent to me
    night after night,
As you droop'd from the sky low down as if to my
    side, (while the other stars all look'd on,)
As we wander'd together the solemn night, (for
    something I know not what kept me from sleep,)
As the night advanced, and I saw on the rim of the
    west how full you were of woe,
As I stood on the rising ground in the breeze in the cool
    transparent night,
As I watch'd where you pass'd and was lost in the
    netherward black of the night,
As my soul in its trouble dissatisfied sank, as where
    you sad orb,
Concluded, dropt in the night, and was gone.

9

Sing on there in the swamp,
O singer bashful and tender, I hear your notes, I hear
    your call,
I hear, I come presently, I understand you,
But a moment I linger, for the lustrous star has detain'd
    me,
The star my departing comrade holds and detains me.

10

O how shall I warble myself for the dead one there I
    loved?
And how shall I deck my song for the large sweet soul
    that has gone?
And what shall my perfume be for the grave of him I
    love?

Sea-winds blown from east and west,
Blown from the Eastern sea and blown from the
    Western sea, till there on the prairies meeting,
These and with these and the breath of my chant,
I'll perfume the grave of him I love.

11

O what shall I hang on the chamber walls?
And what shall the pictures be that I hang on the walls,
To adorn the burial-house of him I love?

Pictures of growing spring and farms and homes,
With the Fourth-month eve at sundown, and the gray
    smoke lucid and bright,
With floods of the yellow gold of the gorgeous,
    indolent, sinking sun, burning, expanding the air,
With the fresh sweet herbage under foot, and the pale
    green leaves of the trees prolific,
In the distance the flowing glaze, the breast of the
    river, with a wind-dapple here and there,
With ranging hills on the banks, with many a line
    against the sky, and shadows,
And the city at hand with dwellings so dense, and
    stacks of chimneys,
And all the scenes of life and the workshops, and the
    workmen homeward returning.

12

Lo, body and soul—this land,
My own Manhattan with spires, and the sparkling and
    hurrying tides, and the ships,
The varied and ample land, the South and the North in
    the light, Ohio's shores and flashing Missouri,
And ever the far-spreading prairies cover'd with grass
    and corn.

Lo, the most excellent sun so calm and haughty,
The violet and purple morn with just-felt breezes,
The gentle soft-born measureless light,
The miracle spreading bathing all, the fulfill'd noon,
The coming eve delicious, the welcome night and the
    stars,
Over my cities shining all, enveloping man and land.

13

Sing on, sing on you gray-brown bird,
Sing from the swamps, the recesses, pour your chant
    from the bushes,
Limitless out of the dusk, out of the cedars and pines.

Sing on dearest brother, warble your reedy song,
Loud human song, with voice of uttermost woe.

O liquid and free and tender!
O wild and loose to my soul—O wondrous singer,
You only I hear—yet the star holds me, (but will soon
    depart,)
Yet the lilac with mastering odor holds me.

14

Now while I sat in the day and look'd forth,
In the close of the day with its light and the fields of
    spring, and the farmers preparing their crops,
In the large unconscious scenery of my land with its
    lakes and forests,
In the heavenly aerial beauty, (after the perturb'd winds
    and the storms,)
Under the arching heavens of the afternoon swift
    passing, and the voices of children and women,
The many-moving sea-tides, and I saw the ships how
    they sail'd,
And the summer approaching with richness, and the
    fields all busy with labor,
And the infinite separate houses, how they all went on,
    each with its meals and minutia of daily usages,

And the streets how their throbbings throbb'd, and the
    cities pent—lo, then and there,
Falling upon them all and among them all, enveloping
    me with the rest,
Appear'd the cloud, appear'd the long black trail,
And I knew death, its thought, and the sacred
    knowledge of death.

Then with the knowledge of death as walking one side
    of me,
And the thought of death close-walking the other side
    of me,
And I in the middle as with companions, and as holding
    the hands of companions,
I fled forth to the hiding receiving night that talks not,
Down to the shores of the water, the path by the swamp
    in the dimness,
To the solemn shadowy cedars and ghostly pines so
    still.

And the singer so shy to the rest receiv'd me,
The gray-brown bird I know receiv'd us comrades
    three,
And he sang the carol of death, and a verse for him I
    love.

From deep secluded recesses,
From the fragrant cedars and the ghostly pines so still,
Came the carol of the bird.

And the charm of the carol rapt me,
As I held as if by their hands my comrades in the night,
And the voice of my spirit tallied the song of the bird.

Come lovely and soothing death,
Undulate round the world, serenely arriving, arriving,
In the day, in the night, to all, to each,
Sooner or later delicate death.

Prais'd be the fathomless universe,
For life and joy, and for objects and knowledge
    curious,
And for love, sweet love—but praise! praise! praise!
For the sure-enwinding arms of cool-enfolding death.

Dark mother always gliding near with soft feet,
Have none chanted for thee a chant of fullest welcome?
Then I chant it for thee, I glorify thee above all,
I bring thee a song that when thou must indeed come,
    come unfalteringly.

Approach strong deliveress,
When it is so, when thou hast taken them I joyously
    sing the dead,
Lost in the loving floating ocean of thee,
Laved in the flood of thy bliss O death.

From me to thee glad serenades,
Dances for thee I propose saluting thee, adornments
    and feastings for thee,
And the sights of the open landscape and the high-
    spread sky are fitting,
And life and the fields, and the huge and thoughtful
    night.

The night in silence under many a star,
The ocean shore and the husky whispering wave whose
    voice I know,
And the soul turning to thee O vast and well-veil'd
    death,
And the body gratefully nestling close to thee.

Over the tree-tops I float thee a song,
Over the rising and sinking waves, over the myriad
  fields and the prairies wide,
Over the dense-pack'd cities all and the teeming
  wharves and ways,
I float this carol with joy, with joy to thee O death.

15

To the tally of my soul,
Loud and strong kept up the gray-brown bird,
With pure deliberate notes spreading filling the night.

Loud in the pines and cedars dim,
Clear in the freshness moist and the swamp-perfume,
And I with my comrades there in the night.

While my sight that was bound in my eyes unclosed,
As to long panoramas of visions.

And I saw askant the armies,
I saw as in noiseless dreams hundreds of battle-flags,
Borne through the smoke of the battles and pierc'd with
  missiles I saw them,
And carried hither and yon through the smoke, and torn
  and bloody,
And at last but a few shreds left on the staffs, (and all
  in silence,)
And the staffs all splinter'd and broken.

I saw battle-corpses, myriads of them,
And the white skeletons of young men, I saw them,
I saw the debris and debris of all the slain soldiers of
  the war,
But I saw they were not as was thought,
They themselves were fully at rest, they suffer'd not,
The living remain'd and suffer'd, the mother suffer'd,
And the wife and the child and the musing comrade
  suffer'd,
And the armies that remain'd suffer'd.

16

Passing the visions, passing the night,
Passing, unloosing the hold of my comrade's hands,
Passing the song of the hermit bird and the tallying
  song of my soul,
Victorious song, death's outlet song, yet varying ever-
  altering song,
As low and wailing, yet clear the notes, rising and
  falling, flooding the night,
Sadly sinking and fainting, as warning and warning,
  and yet again bursting with joy,
Covering the earth and filling the spread of the heaven,
As that powerful psalm in the night I heard from
  recesses,
Passing, I leave thee lilac with heart-shaped leaves,
I leave thee there in the door-yard, blooming, returning
  with spring.

I cease from my song for thee,
From my gaze on thee in the west, fronting the west,
  communing with thee,
O comrade lustrous with silver face in the night.

Yet each to keep and all, retrievements out of the night,
The song, the wondrous chant of the gray-brown bird,
And the tallying chant, the echo arous'd in my soul,

With the lustrous and drooping star with the
  countenance full of woe,
With the holders holding my hand nearing the call of
  the bird,
Comrades mine and I in the midst, and their memory
  ever to keep, for the dead I loved so well,
For the sweetest, wisest soul of all my days and
  lands—and this for his dear sake,
Lilac and star and bird twined with the chant of my
  soul,
There in the fragrant pines and the cedars dusk and
  dim.

(pp. 233-39)

*Walt Whitman, "When Lilacs Last in the Dooryard
Bloom'd," in his* Complete Poetry and Selected Prose,
*edited by James E. Miller, Jr., Houghton Mifflin
Company, 1959, pp. 233-39.*

FREDERICK DOUGLASS   (speech date 1876)

[*Douglass is considered one of the most distinguished black writers in nineteenth-century American literature. An escaped slave,
he expounded on the theme of racial equality in stirring orations
and newspaper editorials in the 1840s, 1850s, and 1860s, winning
recognition by his peers as an outstanding speaker and the foremost black abolitionist of his era. Speaking on behalf of American
blacks, Douglass delivered the following tribute to Lincoln at the
unveiling of the* Freedmen's Monument *in Washington, D.C., on
14 April 1876.*]

Truth is proper and beautiful at all times and in all places, and
it is never more proper and beautiful in any case than when
speaking of a great public man whose example is likely to be
commended for honor and imitation long after his departure to
the solemn shades, the silent continents of eternity. It must be
admitted, truth compels me to admit, even here in the presence
of the monument we have erected to his memory, Abraham
Lincoln was not, in the fullest sense of the word, either our
man or our model. In his interests, in his associations, in his
habits of thought, and in his prejudices, he was a white man.

He was pre-eminently the white man's President, entirely devoted to the welfare of white men. He was ready and willing
at any time during the first years of his administration to deny,
postpone, and sacrifice the rights of humanity in the colored
people to promote the welfare of the white people of this country. In all his education and feeling he was an American of
the Americans. He came into the Presidential chair upon one
principle alone, namely, opposition to the extension of slavery.
His arguments in furtherance of this policy had their motive
and mainspring in his patriotic devotion to the interests of his
own race. To protect, defend, and perpetuate slavery in the
states where it existed Abraham Lincoln was not less ready
than any other President to draw the sword of the nation. He
was ready to execute all the supposed guarantees of the United
States Constitution in favor of the slave system anywhere inside
the slave States. He was willing to pursue, recapture, and send
back the fugitive slave to his master, and to suppress a slave
rising for liberty, though his guilty master were already in arms
against the Government. The race to which we belong were
not the special objects of his consideration. Knowing this, I
concede to you, my white fellow-citizens, a pre-eminence in
this worship at once full and supreme. First, midst, and last,
you and yours were the objects of his deepest affection and
his most earnest solicitude. You are the children of Abraham
Lincoln. We are at best only his step-children; children by

adoption, children by force of circumstances and necessity. To you it especially belongs to sound his praises, to preserve and perpetuate his memory, to multiply his statues, to hang his pictures high upon your walls, and commend his example, for to you he was a great and glorious friend and benefactor. Instead of supplanting you at his altar, we would exhort you to build high his monuments; let them be of the most costly material, of the most cunning workmanship; let their forms be symmetrical, beautiful, and perfect; let their bases be upon solid rocks, and their summits lean against the unchanging blue, overhanging sky, and let them endure forever! But while in the abundance of your wealth, and in the fullness of your just and patriotic devotion, you do all this, we entreat you to despise not the humble offering we this day unveil to view; for while Abraham Lincoln saved for you a country, he delivered us from a bondage, according to Jefferson, one hour of which was worse than ages of the oppression your fathers rose in rebellion to oppose.

Fellow-citizens, ours is no new-born zeal and devotion—merely a thing of this moment. The name of Abraham Lincoln was near and dear to our hearts in the darkest and most perilous hours of the Republic. We were no more ashamed of him when shrouded in clouds of darkness, of doubt, and defeat than when we saw him crowned with victory, honor, and glory. Our faith in him was often taxed and strained to the uttermost, but it never failed. When he tarried long in the mountain; when he strangely told us that we were the cause of the war; when he still more strangely told us to leave the land in which we were born; when he refused to employ our arms in defence of the Union; when, after accepting our services as colored soldiers, he refused to retaliate our murder and torture as colored prisoners; when he told us he would save the Union if he could with slavery; when he revoked the Proclamation of Emancipation of General Fremont; when he refused to remove the popular commander of the Army of the Potomac, in the days of its inaction and defeat, who was more zealous in his efforts to protect slavery than to suppress rebellion; when we saw all this, and more, we were at times grieved, stunned, and greatly bewildered; but our hearts believed while they ached and bled. Nor was this, even at that time, a blind and unreasoning superstition. Despite the mist and haze that surrounded him; despite the tumult, the hurry, and confusion of the hour, we were able to take a comprehensive view of Abraham Lincoln, and to make reasonable allowance for the circumstances of his position. We saw him, measured him, and estimated him; not by stray utterances to injudicious and tedious delegations, who often tried his patience; not by isolated facts torn from their connection; not by any partial and imperfect glimpses, caught at inopportune moments; but by a broad survey, in the light of the stern logic of great events, and in view of that divinity which shapes our ends, rough hew them how we will, we came to the conclusion that the hour and the man of our redemption had somehow met in the person of Abraham Lincoln. It mattered little to us what language he might employ on special occasions; it mattered little to us, when we fully knew him, whether he was swift or slow in his movements; it was enough for us that Abraham Lincoln was at the head of a great movement, and was in living and earnest sympathy with that movement, which, in the nature of things, must go on until slavery should be utterly and forever abolished in the United States.

When, therefore, it shall be asked what we have to do with the memory of Abraham Lincoln, or what Abraham Lincoln had to do with us, the answer is ready, full, and complete. Though he loved Caesar less than Rome, though the Union

was more to him than our freedom or our future, under his wise and beneficent rule we saw ourselves gradually lifted from the depths of slavery to the heights of liberty and manhood; under his wise and beneficent rule, and by measures approved and vigorously pressed by him, we saw that the handwriting of ages, in the form of prejudice and proscription, was rapidly fading away from the face of our whole country; under his rule, and in due time, about as soon after all as the country could tolerate the strange spectacle, we saw our brave sons and brothers laying off the rags of bondage, and being clothed all over in the blue uniforms of the soldiers of the United States; under his rule we saw two hundred thousand of our dark and dusky people responding to the call of Abraham Lincoln, and with muskets on their shoulders, and eagles on their buttons, timing their high footsteps to liberty and union under the national flag; under his rule we saw the independence of the black republic of Hayti, the special object of slaveholding aversion and horror, fully recognized, and her minister, a colored gentleman, duly received here in the city of Washington; under his rule we saw the internal slave-trade, which so long disgraced the nation, abolished, and slavery abolished in the District of Columbia; under his rule we saw for the first time the law enforced against the foreign slave-trade, and the first slave-trader hanged like any other pirate or murderer; under his rule, assisted by the greatest captain of our age, and his inspiration, we saw the Confederate States, based upon the idea that our race must be slaves, and slaves forever, battered to pieces and scattered to the four winds; under his rule, and in the fullness of time, we saw Abraham Lincoln, after giving the slaveholders three months' grace in which to save their hateful slave system, penning the immortal paper, which, though special in its language, was general in its principles and effect, making slavery forever impossible in the United States. Though we waited long, we saw all this and more.

Can any colored man, or any white man friendly to the freedom of all men, ever forget the night which followed the first day of January, 1863, when the world was to see if Abraham Lincoln would prove to be as good as his word? I shall never forget that memorable night, when in a distant city I waited and watched at a public meeting, with three thousand others not less anxious than myself, for the word of deliverance which we have heard read today. Nor shall I ever forget the outburst of joy and thanksgiving that rent the air when the lightning brought to us the [*Emancipation Proclamation*]. In that happy hour we forgot all delay, and forgot all tardiness, forgot that the President had bribed the rebels to lay down their arms by a promise to withhold the bolt which would smite the slave-system with destruction; and we were thenceforward willing to allow the President all the latitude of time, phraseology, and every honorable device that statesmanship might require for the achievement of a great and beneficent measure of liberty and progress. (pp. 49-52)

I have said that President Lincoln was a white man, and shared the prejudices common to his countrymen towards the colored race. Looking back to his times and to the condition of his country, we are compelled to admit that this unfriendly feeling on his part may be safely set down as one element of his wonderful success in organizing the loyal American people for the tremendous conflict before them, and bringing them safely through that conflict. His great mission was to accomplish two things: first, to save his country from dismemberment and ruin; and, second, to free his country from the great crime of slavery. To do one or the other, or both, he must have the earnest sympathy and the powerful co-operation of his loyal fellow-countrymen. Without this primary and essential condition to success his efforts must have been vain and utterly fruitless. Had he put the abolition of slavery before the salvation of the Union, he would have inevitably driven from him a powerful class of the American people and rendered resistance to rebellion impossible. Viewed from the genuine abolition ground, Mr. Lincoln seemed tardy, cold, dull, and indifferent; but measuring him by the sentiment of his country, a sentiment he was bound as a statesman to consult, he was swift, zealous, radical, and determined.

Though Mr. Lincoln shared the prejudices of his white fellow-countrymen against the negro, it is hardly necessary to say that in his heart of hearts he loathed and hated slavery. The man who could say, ''Fondly do we hope, fervently do we pray, that this mighty scourge of war shall soon pass away, yet if God wills it continue till the wealth piled by two hundred years of bondage shall have been wasted, and each drop of blood drawn by the lash shall have been paid for by one drawn by the sword, the judgments of the Lord are true and righteous altogether,'' gives all needed proof of his feeling on the subject of slavery. He was willing, while the South was loyal, that it should have its pound of flesh, because he thought that it was so nominated in the bond; but farther than this no earthly power could make him go. (pp. 52-3)

Few great public men have ever been the victims of fiercer denunciation than Abraham Lincoln was during his administration. He was often wounded in the house of his friends. Reproaches came thick and fast upon him from within and from without, and from opposite quarters. He was assailed by Abolitionists; he was assailed by slaveholders; he was assailed by the men who were for peace at any price; he was assailed by those who were for a more vigorous prosecution of the war; he was assailed for not making the war an abolition war; and he was bitterly assailed for making the war an abolition war.

But now behold the change: the judgement of the present hour is, that taking him for all in all, measuring the tremendous magnitude of the work before him, considering the necessary means to ends, and surveying the end from the beginning, infinite wisdom has seldom sent any man into the world better fitted for his mission than Abraham Lincoln. (p. 53)

Timid men said before Mr. Lincoln's inauguration, that we had seen the last President of the United States. A voice in influential quarters said, ''Let the Union slide.'' Some said that a Union maintained by the sword was worthless. Others said a rebellion of 8,000,000 cannot be suppressed; but in the midst of all this tumult and timidity, and against all this, Abraham Lincoln was clear in his duty, and had an oath in heaven. He calmly and bravely heard the voice of doubt and fear all around him; but he had an oath in heaven, and there was not power enough on the earth to make this honest boatman, backwoodsman, and broad-handed splitter of rails evade or violate that sacred oath. He had not been schooled in the ethics of slavery; his plain life had favored his love of truth. He had not been taught that treason and perjury were the proof of honor and honesty. His moral training was against his saying one thing when he meant another. The trust which Abraham Lincoln had in himself and in the people was surprising and grand, but it was also enlightened and well founded. He knew the American people better than they knew themselves, and his truth was based upon this knowledge.

Fellow-citizens, the fourteenth day of April, 1865, of which this is the eleventh anniversary, is now and will ever remain a memorable day in the annals of this Republic. It was on the evening of this day, while a fierce and sanguinary rebellion was in the last stages of its desolating power; while its armies were broken and scattered before the invincible armies of Grant and Sherman; while a great nation, torn and rent by war, was already beginning to raise to the skies loud anthems of joy at the dawn of peace, it was startled, amazed, and overwhelmed by the crowning crime of slavery—the assassination of Abraham Lincoln. It was a new crime, a pure act of malice. No purpose of the rebellion was to be served by it. It was the simple gratification of a hell-black spirit of revenge. But it has done good after all. It has filled the country with a deeper abhorrence of slavery and a deeper love for the great liberator.

Had Abraham Lincoln died from any of the numerous ills to which flesh is heir; had he reached that good old age of which his vigorous constitution and his temperate habits gave promise; had he been permitted to see the end of his great work; had the solemn curtain of death come down but gradually—we should still have been smitten with a heavy grief, and treasured his name lovingly. But dying as he did die, by the red hand of violence, killed, assassinated, taken off without warning, not because of personal hate—for no man who knew Abraham Lincoln could hate him—but because of his fidelity to union and liberty, he is doubly dear to us, and his memory will be precious forever. (pp. 55-6)

> *Frederick Douglass, ''Oration in Memory of Abraham Lincoln,'' in* What Country Have I? Political Writings by Black Americans, *edited by Herbert J. Storing, St. Martin's Press, 1970, pp. 46-56.*

JAMES C. WELLING (essay date 1880)

[*Welling was a prominent nineteenth-century editor and academician; a onetime law student, he worked on the editorial staff of the* National Intelligencer *in the 1850s and 1860s and later served as president of Columbian College, Washington, D.C. In the following excerpt from a detailed discussion of the* Emancipation Proclamation, *Welling argues that Lincoln's edict had no legal validity.*]

[I would like] to consider the force and effect of the [**Emancipation Proclamation**] viewed in the light of constitutional and of public law. . . . The questions presented by the . . . [**Emancipation Proclamation**], in the shape actually given to it by Mr. Lincoln, are these:

Firstly. Had the President of the United States, in the exercise of his war powers, a right, under the Constitution and by public law, to decree, on grounds of military necessity, the emancipation and perpetual enfranchisement of slaves in the insurgent States and parts of States?

Secondly. Did such proclamation work, by its own vigor, the immediate, the unconditional, and the perpetual emancipation of all slaves in the districts affected by it?

Thirdly. Did such proclamation, working *proprio vigore*, not only effect the emancipation of all existing slaves in the insurgent territory, but, with regard to slaves so liberated, did it extinguish the status of slavery created by municipal law, insomuch that they would have remained for ever free, in fact and law, provided the Constitution and the legal rights and relations of the States under it had remained, on the return of peace, what they were before the war?

Unless each and all of these questions can be answered in the affirmative, the **Emancipation Proclamation** was not authorized by the Constitution or by international law, and so far as they must be answered in the negative it was *brutum fulmen*. It remains, then, to make inquiry under each of these heads:

1. As everybody admits that the President, in time of peace and in the normal exercise of his constitutional prerogatives, had no power to emancipate slaves, it follows that the right accrued to him, if at all, from the war powers lodged in his hands by public law when, as Commander-in-Chief of the army and navy, he was engaged in a life-and-death struggle with insurgents, whose number, power, and legal description, gave them the character of public enemies. It is, therefore, to public law, as enfolded in time of war and for war purposes in the bosom of the Constitution, that we are primarily to look for the authority under which the President assumed to act. (pp. 176-77)

[International] law, with all its belligerent rights, was everywhere present as a potent force in the civil war between the United States and the Confederate States, so soon as that war had assumed such character and magnitude as to give the United States the same rights and powers which they might exercise in the case of a national or foreign war, and everybody admits that it assumed that character after the act of Congress of July 13, 1861. But international law, in time of war, is present with its belligerent *obligations* as well as with its belligerent *rights*, and what those obligations are is matter of definite knowledge so far as they are recognized and observed in the conduct and jurisprudence of civilized nations.

The law of postliminy, according to which persons or things taken by the enemy are restored to their former state when they come again under the power of the nation to which they formerly belonged, was anciently held to restore the rights of the owner in the case of a slave temporarily affranchised by military capture. And, if it be admitted that, as regards slaves, this fiction of the Roman law has fallen into desuetude under the present practice of nations, it is none the less true that the Government of the United States has earnestly contended, in its intercourse with other nations, for the substantial principle on which the rule is based. We insisted on restoration or restitution in the case of all slaves emancipated by British commanders in the War of 1812-'15, and the justice of our claim under the law of nations was conceded by Great Britain when she signed the Treaty of Ghent, and when, on the arbitration of Russia, she paid a round sum, by way of indemnity, to be distributed among the owners of slaves who had been despoiled of their slave property. In the face of a precedent so set and so adjudicated by these great powers acting under the law of nations (and one of them subsequently known as the leading antislavery power of the civilized world), it would seem that, as a question of law, the first interrogatory must be answered in the negative. Slaves temporarily captured to weaken the enemy and to conquer a peace are not lawful prize of war by military proceedings alone—proclamation, capture, and deportation. The more fully it be conceded that international law, in time and fact of war, knows the slave only as a person, the more fully must it be conceded that this law, by purely military measures, can take no cognizance of him as a chattel, either to preserve or to destroy the master's property right under municipal law. It leaves questions about the chattel to be settled in another forum, and by another judicature than the wager of battle. (pp. 177-78)

2. No principle of public law is clearer than that which rules the war rights of a belligerent to be correlative and commensurate only with his war powers. "To extend the rights of

military occupation or the limits of conquest by mere intention, implication, or proclamation, would be," says Halleck, "establishing a *paper conquest* infinitely more objectionable in its character and effects than a *paper blockade*." It is only so far as and so fast as the conquering belligerent reclaims "enemy territory" and gets possession of "enemy property" that his belligerent rights attach to either. And hence, when Mr. Lincoln, on the 1st of January, 1863, assumed authority, in the name of "military necessity," but without the indispensable *occupatio bellica*, to emancipate slaves in the territory held by the enemy, he contravened a fundamental principle of the public law—a principle equally applicable to the relations of a territorial civil war and of a foreign war. It is important to observe that where this principle was guarded by the rights and interests of foreign nations, as in the case of the Southern ports of entry while they were under the power of the Confederate authority, it was sacredly respected by our Government. And in the light of this doctrine it follows that the second of the questions formulated above must also be answered in the negative; for as to large parts of the South Mr. Lincoln had no *de facto* power when he assumed to liberate slaves both *de facto* and *de jure* within all the "enemy territory" at that date.

3. Since the decision of Lord Stowell in the case of the slave Grace, it has been an accepted doctrine of jurisprudence that the slave character of a liberated slave—liberated by residing on free soil—is redintegrated by the voluntary return of such slave to the country of the master. Unless, therefore, the [*Emancipation Proclamation*] is held to have extinguished the status of slavery in the States and parts of States affected by it, it would have conferred a very equivocal boon on its beneficiaries. For, unless the municipal law of slavery were wiped out by the [*Emancipation Proclamation*], and by conquest under it, what prevented a reënslavement of such emancipated blacks as should return to their homes after the war? And this fact was made apparent to Mr. Lincoln and to the whole country as soon as an occasion arose for bringing the matter to a practical test.

On the 18th of July, 1864, when the famous "peace negotiations" were pending at Niagara Falls between Mr. Greeley and certain assumed representatives of the Confederate States, Mr. Lincoln wrote that he would receive and consider "any proposition which embraced the restoration of peace, the integrity of the whole country, *and the abandonment of slavery*, and which came by and with an authority *that can control the armies now at war against the United States*." It was seen that the emancipation of individual slaves, even of *all* individual slaves in the insurgent States, was worth nothing without an abandonment of slavery itself—of the municipal status in which the slave character was radicated, and in which it might be planted anew by a voluntary return to the slave soil. It was seen, too, that the [*Emancipation Proclamation*], considered as a military edict addressed to "rebels in arms," had created a misjoinder of parties as well as a misjoinder of issues, for the authority which controlled the Confederate armies was not competent to "abandon slavery" in the insurgent States, though it *was* competent to restory "peace and union" by simply desisting from further hostilities. A misjoinder of issues was also created, for each State, under the Constitution as it stood, had a right, in the matter of slavery, to order and control its own domestic institutions according to its own judgment exclusively; and the nation, by the conquest of its own territory, "could acquire no new sovereignty, but merely maintain its previous rights." The [*Emancipation Proclamation*] proposed to leave the institution of slavery undisturbed in certain States and parts of States, while destroying it in certain other States and parts of States. Hence, on the supposition that the paper was to have full force and effect after the war, while our civil polity remained the same, a new distribution of powers as between certain States and parts of States on the one hand, and the Federal Government on the other, would have been created by edict of the Executive. Without any express change in the constitution of the United States, and without any express change in the constitutions of the insurgent States, the status of persons on one side of a State line, or even on one side of a county line, would have depended on municipal law; on the other side of such State or county line it would have depended on a military decree of the President. In this strange mixture of what Tacitus calls *"res dissociabiles—principatum ac libertatem,"* it would have been hard to tell where the former ended and the latter began; and to suppose that the civil courts, in the ordinary course of judicial decision, could have recognized such anomalies, while the rights of the States under the Constitution were still defined by that instrument, is to suppose that judges decree justice without law, without rule, and without reason. It is safe, therefore, to say that the third question above indicated must equally be answered in the negative. (pp. 179-81)

[It is also] clear that, without a change in the Constitution of the United States prohibiting slavery in the South, the Proclamation must have failed, with the rights of plenary conquest limited by the Constitution, to insure the perpetual freedom of the slaves liberated under it; for what, under the rights still reserved to the States, would have prevented the future reëstablishment of slavery at the South after the return of peace?

Nobody was more quick to perceive or more frank to admit the legal weakness and insufficiency of the *Emancipation Proclamation* than Mr. Lincoln. Determined though he was never to retract the paper, or by his own act to return to slavery any person who was declared free by its terms, he saw that, in itself considered, it was a frail muniment of title to any slave who should claim to be free by virtue of its vigor alone. And therefore it was that, with a candor which did him honor, he made no pretense of concealing its manifold infirmities either from his own eyes or from the eyes of the people, so soon as Congress proposed, in a way of undoubted constitutionality and of undoubted efficacy, to put an end to slavery everywhere in the Union by an amendment to the Constitution. Remarking on that amendment at the time of its proposal, he said: "A question might be raised whether the [*Emancipation Proclamation*] was legally valid. It might be added that it aided only those who came into our lines, and that it was inoperative as to those who did not give themselves up; or that it would have no effect upon the children of the slaves born hereafter; in fact, it could be urged that it did not meet the evil. But this amendment is a king's cure for all evils. It winds the whole thing up."

In the light of these facts, of these principles, and of Mr. Lincoln's own admissions, it would seem that the *Emancipation Proclamation* was extra-constitutional—so truly outside of the Constitution that it required an amendment to the Constitution to bring the President's engagements and promises inside of the Constitution. (pp. 181-82)

> James C. Welling, "The Emancipation Proclamation," in The North American Review, Vol. CXXX, No. CCLXXIX, February, 1880, pp. 163-85.

GEORGE S. BOUTWELL (essay date 1886)

[*Boutwell was a distinguished public servant, holding such offices during the nineteenth century as governor of Massachusetts, com-*

missioner of internal revenue, and secretary of the treasury. Here, he extols Lincoln's abilities as a debater and orator.]

In debate [Mr. Lincoln] often so combined wit, satire and statement that his opponent at once appeared ridiculous and illogical. Mr. Douglas was often the victim of these sallies in the [*Lincoln-Douglas Debates*] before the people of Illinois, and before the people of the country, in the year 1858. Douglas constantly asserted that abolition would be followed by amalgamation, and that the Republican party designed to repeal the laws of Illinois which prohibited the marriage of blacks and whites. This was a formidable appeal, to the prejudices of the people of Southern Illinois especially. "I protest now and forever," said Lincoln, "against that counterfeit logic which presumes that because I did not want a negro woman for a slave, I do, necessarily want her for a wife. I have never had the least apprehension that I or my friends would marry negroes if there were no law to keep them from it, but as Judge Douglas and his friends seem to be in great apprehension that they might, if there were no law to keep them from it, I give him the most solemn pledge that I will to the very last stand by the law of this State, which forbids the marrying of white people with negroes."

Thus in two sentences did Mr. Lincoln overthrow Douglas in his logic and render him ridiculous in his position. Douglas claimed special credit for the defeat of the Lecompton bill, although five-sixths of the votes were given by the Republican Party. Said Lincoln: "Why is he entitled to more credit than others for the performance of that good act, unless there was something in the antecedents of the Republicans that might induce every one to expect them to join in that good work, and, at the same time, leading them to doubt that he would. Does he place his superior claim to credit on the ground that he performed a good act which was never expected of him?" He then gave Mr. Douglas the benefit of a specific application of the parable of the lost sheep.

In the last debate at Alton, October 15, 1858, Mr. Douglas proceeded to show that Buchanan was guilty of gross inconsistencies of position. Lincoln did not defend Buchanan, but after he had stated the fact that Douglas had been on both sides of the Missouri Compromise, he added: "I want to know if Buchanan has not as much right to be inconsistent as Douglas has? Has Douglas the exclusive right in this country of being *on all sides of all questions?* Is nobody allowed that high privilege but himself? Is he to have an entire monopoly on that subject?"

There are three methods in debate of sustaining and enforcing opinions, and the faculty and facility of using these several methods are the tests of intellectual quality in writers and speakers. First, and lowest intellectually, are those who rely upon authority. They gather and marshal the sayings of their predecessors, and ask their hearers and readers to indorse the positions taken, not because they are reasonable and right under the process of demonstration, but because many persons in other times have thought them to be right and reasonable. As this is the work of the mere student, and does not imply either philosophy or the faculty of reasoning, those who rely exclusively upon authority are in the third class of intellectual men. Next, and of a much higher order, are the writers and speakers who state the facts of a case, apply settled principles to them, and by sound processes of reasoning maintain the position taken. But high above all are the men who by statement pure and simple, or by statement argumentative, carry conviction to thoughtful minds. Unquestionably Mr. Lincoln belongs to this class. Those who remember Douglas's theory in regard to "squatter sovereignty," which he sometimes dignified by calling it the "sacred right of self-government," will appreciate the force of Lincoln's statement of the scheme in these words: "The phrase, 'sacred right of self-government,' though expressive of the only rightful basis of any government, was so perverted in the attempted use of it as to amount to just this: *That if any one man choose to enslave another, no third man shall be allowed to object.*"

In the field of argumentative statement, Mr. Webster, at the time of his death, had had no rival in America; but he has left nothing more exact, explicit, and convincing than this extract from Lincoln's first speech of the great debate. Here is a statement in less than twenty words, *If any one man choose to enslave another, no third man shall be allowed to object,* which embodies the substance of the opinion of the Supreme Court of the United States in the case of Dred Scott, the theory of the Kansas-Nebraska bill, and exposes the sophistry which Douglas had woven into his arguments on "squatter sovereignty."

Douglas constantly appealed to the prejudices of the people, and arrayed them against the doctrine of negro equality. Lincoln, in reply, after asserting their equality under the Declaration of Independence, added: "In the right to eat the bread, without the leave of anybody else, which his own hand earns, he is my equal, and the equal of Judge Douglas, and the equal of every living man." Douglas often said—and he commanded the cheers of his supporters when he said it—"I do not care whether slavery is voted up or voted down." In his final speech at Alton, Lincoln reviewed the history of the churches and of the government in connection with slavery, and he then asked: "Is it not a false statesmanship that undertakes to build up a system of policy upon the basis of caring nothing about the very thing that everybody does care the most about?" He then, in the same speech, assailed Douglas's position in an argument, which is but a series of statements, and, as a whole, it is, in its logic and moral sentiment, the equal of anything in the language:

> He may say he doesn't care whether an indifferent thing is voted up or down, but he must logically have a choice between a right thing and a wrong thing. He contends that whatever community wants slaves has a right to have them. So they have, if it is not a wrong. But if it is a wrong, he cannot say people have a right to do wrong. He says that, upon the score of equality, slaves should be allowed to go into a new territory like other property. This is strictly logical, if there is no difference between it and other property. If it and other property are equal, his argument is entirely logical. But if you insist that one is wrong and the other right, there is no use to institute a comparison between right and wrong. You may turn over everything in the Democratic policy from beginning to end—whether in the shape it takes on the statute-book, in the shape it takes in the Dred Scott decision, in the shape it takes in conversation, or in the shape it takes in short maxim-like arguments—it everywhere carefully excludes the idea that there is anything wrong in it. That is the real issue. That is the issue that will continue in this country when these poor tongues

of Judges Douglas and myself shall be silent. It is the eternal struggle between these two principles, right and wrong, throughout the world. They are the two principles that have stood face to face from the beginning of time, and will ever continue to struggle. The one is the common right of humanity; and the other, the divine right of kings. It is the same principle in whatever shape it develops itself. It is the same spirit that says, 'You work and toil and earn bread, and I'll eat it.' No matter in what shape it comes, whether from the mouth of a king who seeks to bestride the people of his own nation and live by the fruit of their labor, or from one race of men as an apology for enslaving another race, it is the same tyrannical principle.

(pp. 113-18)

His mastery over Douglas in the debate of 1858 was complete. . . .

[However] I ask a judgment upon Mr. Lincoln, not as a competitor with Mr. Douglas for a seat in the Senate of the United States, but as a competitor for fame with the first orators of this and other countries, of this and other ages. (p. 130)

We all remember his simple, earnest, persuasive appeals to the South, in his [*First Inaugural Address*]. At the end he says: "I am loath to close. We are not enemies, but friends. We must not be enemies. Though passion may have strained, it must not break our bonds of affection. The mystic cords of memory, stretching from every battle-field and patriot grave to every living heart and hearthstone all over this broad land, will yet swell the chorus of the Union when again touched, as surely they will be, by the better angels of our nature." There is nothing elsewhere in our literature of plaintive entreaty to be compared with this. It combines the eloquence of the orator with the imagery and inspiration of the poet. But the three great papers on which Lincoln's fame will be carried along the ages are [the ***Emancipation Proclamation,*** the **"Gettysburg Address,"** and the ***Second Inaugural Address***]. The oration [at Gettysburg] ranks with the noblest productions of antiquity, with the works of Pericles, of Demosthenes, of Cicero, and rivals the finest passages of Grattan, Burke or Webster. This is not the opinion of Americans only, but of the cultivated in other countries, whose judgment anticipates the judgment of posterity.

When we consider the place, the occasion, the man, and, more than all, when we consider the oration itself, can we doubt that it ranks with the first of American classics? That literature is immortal which commands a permanent place in the schools of a country, and is there any composition more certain of that destiny than Lincoln's oration at Gettysburg? . . . But if all that Lincoln said and was should fail to carry his name and character to future ages, the emancipation of four million human beings by his single official act is a passport to all of immortality that earth can give. There is no other individual act performed by any person on this continent that can be compared with it. The Declaration of Independence, the Constitution, were each the work of bodies of men. The [***Emancipation Proclamation***] in this respect stands alone. The responsibility was wholly upon Lincoln; the glory is chiefly his. No one can now say whether the Declaration of Independence, or the Constitution of the United States, or the [***Emancipation Proclamation***] was the highest, best gift to the country and to mankind. With the curse of slavery in America there was no hope for republican institutions in other countries. In the presence of slavery the Declaration of Independence had lost its power; practically, it had become a lie. In the presence of slavery we were to the rest of mankind and to ourselves a nation of hypocrites. The gift of freedom to four million negroes was not more valuable to them than to us; and not more valuable to us than to the friends of liberty in other parts of the world. (pp. 131-34)

George S. Boutwell, "Chapter VI," in Reminiscences of Abraham Lincoln, *edited by Allen Thorndike Rice, North American Publishing Company, 1886, pp. 101-38.*

WILLIAM H. HERNDON AND JESSE W. WEIK (essay date 1892)

[*Herndon was Lincoln's law partner from 1844 to 1861. With the assistance of Weik, he published a biography of Lincoln that many commentators regard as an important source of information concerning the "private Lincoln." In the following excerpt, Herndon shares his impressions of Lincoln's mind and character.*]

[Mr. Lincoln perceived] all things through a perfect mental lens. There was no diffraction or refraction there. He was not impulsive, fanciful, or imaginative; but cold, calm, and precise. He threw his whole mental light around the object, and, after a time, substance and quality stood apart, form and color took their appropriate places, and all was clear and exact in his mind. His fault, if any, was that he saw things less than they really were; less beautiful and more frigid. He crushed the unreal, the inexact, the hollow, and the sham. He saw things in rigidity rather than in vital action. He saw what no man could dispute, but he failed to see what might have been seen. (p. 300)

His mind was his standard. His mental action was deliberate, and he was pitiless and persistent in pursuit of the truth. No error went undetected, no falsehood unexposed, if he once was aroused in search of the truth. The true peculiarity of Mr. Lincoln has not been seen by his various biographers; or, if seen, they have failed woefully to give it that importance which it deserves. Newton beheld the law of the universe in the fall of an apple from a tree to the ground; Owen saw the animal in its claw; Spencer saw evolution in the growth of a seed; and Shakespeare saw human nature in the laugh of a man. Nature was suggestive to all these men. Mr. Lincoln no less saw philosophy in a story and an object lesson in a joke. His was a new and original position, one which was always suggesting something to him. The world and man, principles and facts, all were full of suggestions to his susceptible soul. They continually put him in mind of something. His ideas were odd and original for the reason that he was a peculiar and original creation himself. (pp. 300-01)

His language indicated oddity and originality of vision as well as expression. Words and language are but the counterparts of the idea—the other half of the idea; they are but the stinging, hot, leaden bullets that drop from the mould; in a rifle, with powder stuffed behind them and fire applied, they are an embodied force resistlessly pursuing their object. In the search for words Mr. Lincoln was often at a loss. He was often perplexed to give proper expression to his ideas; first, because he was not master of the English language; and secondly, because there were, in the vast store of words, so few that contained the exact coloring, power, and shape of his ideas. This will account for the frequent resort by him to the use of stories, maxims, and jokes in which to clothe his ideas, that they might be comprehended. So true was this peculiar mental vision of

his that, though mankind has been gathering, arranging, and classifying facts for thousands of years, Lincoln's peculiar standpoint could give him no advantage over other men's labor. Hence he tore down to their deepest foundations all arrangements of facts, and constructed new ones to govern himself. He was compelled from his peculiar mental organization to do this. His labor was great and continuous.

The truth about Mr. Lincoln is that he read less and thought more than any man in his sphere in America. No man can put his finger on any great book written in the last or present century that he read thoroughly. When young he read the Bible, and when of age he read Shakespeare; but, though he often quoted from both, he never read either one through. He is acknowledged now to have been a great man, but the question is what made him great. I repeat, that he read less and thought more than any man of his standing in America, if not in the world. He possessed originality and power of thought in an eminent degree. Besides his well established reputation for caution, he was concentrated in his thoughts and had great continuity of reflection. In everything he was patient and enduring. These are some of the grounds of his wonderful success.

Not only were nature, man, and principle suggestive to Mr. Lincoln, not only had he accurate and exact perceptions, but he was causative; his mind, apparently with an automatic movement, ran back behind facts, principles, and all things to their origin and first cause—to that point where forces act at once as effect and cause. . . . Before he could form an idea of anything, before he would express his opinion on a subject, he must know its origin and history in substance and quality, in magnitude and gravity. He must know it inside and outside, upside and downside. . . . When all these exhaustive processes had been gone through with he could form an idea and express it; but no sooner. He had no faith, and no respect for "say so's," come though they might from tradition or authority. Thus everything had to run through the crucible, and be tested by the fires of his analytic mind; and when at last he did speak, his utterances rang out with the clear and keen ring of gold upon the counters of the understanding. He reasoned logically through analogy and comparison. All opponents dreaded his originality of idea, his condensation, definition, and force of expression; and woe be to the man who hugged to his bosom a secret error if Lincoln got on the chase of it. (pp. 301-04)

The great predominating elements of Mr. Lincoln's peculiar character were: first, his great capacity and power of reason; second, his conscience and his excellent understanding; third, an exalted idea of the sense of right and equity; fourth, his intense veneration of the true and the good. His conscience, his heart and all the faculties and qualities of his mind bowed submissively to the despotism of his reason. He lived and acted from the standard of reason—that throne of logic, home of principle—the realm of Deity in man. It is from this point Mr. Lincoln must be viewed. Not only was he cautious, patient, and enduring; not only had he concentration and great continuity of thought; but he had profound analytical power. His vision was clear, and he was emphatically the master of statement. His pursuit of the truth, as before mentioned, was indefatigable. He reasoned from well-chosen principles with such clearness, force, and directness that the tallest intellects in the land bowed to him. He was the strongest man I ever saw, looking at him from the elevated standpoint of reason and logic. He came down from that height with irresistible and crashing force. His Cooper Institute and other printed speeches will prove this; but his speeches before the courts—especially the

Supreme Court of Illinois—if they had been preserved, would demonstrate it still more plainly. Here he demanded time to think and prepare. The office of reason is to determine the truth. Truth is the power of reason, and Lincoln loved truth for its own sake. It was to him reason's food.

Conscience, the second great quality of Mr. Lincoln's character, is that faculty which induces in us love of the just. Its real office is justice; right and equity are its correlatives. As a court, it is in session continuously; it decides all acts at all times. Mr. Lincoln had a deep, broad, living conscience. His reason, however, was the real judge; it told him what was true or false, and therefore good or bad, right or wrong, just or unjust, and his conscience echoed back the decision. His conscience ruled his heart; he was always just before he was generous. It cannot be said of any mortal that he was always absolutely just. Neither was Lincoln always just; but his general life was. It follows that if Mr. Lincoln had great reason and great conscience he must have been an honest man; and so he was. He was rightfully entitled to the appellation "Honest Abe." Honesty was his polar star.

Mr. Lincoln also had a good understanding; that is, the faculty that comprehends the exact state of things and determines their relations, near or remote. The understanding does not necessarily enquire for the reason of things. While Lincoln was odd and original, while he lived out of himself and by himself, and while he could absorb but little from others, yet a reading of his speeches, messages, and letters satisfies us that he had good understanding. But the strongest point in his make-up was the knowledge he had of himself; he comprehended and understood his own capacity—what he did and why he did it—better perhaps than any man of his day. He had a wider and deeper comprehension of his environments, of the political conditions especially, than men who were more learned or had had the benefits of a more thorough training. (pp. 307-09)

[Many] contradictory opinions prevail in reference to Mr. Lincoln's heart and humanity. . . . As many people perhaps contend that he was cold and obdurate as that he was warm and affectionate. The first thing the world met in contact with him was his head and conscience; after that he exposed the tender side of his nature—his heart, subject at all times to his exalted sense of right and equity, namely his conscience. In proportion as he held his conscience subject to his head, he held his heart subject to his head and conscience. His humanity had to defer to his sense of justice and the eternal right. . . . [If, therefore,] a man, woman, or child approached him, and the prayer of such an one was granted, that itself was not evidence of his love. The African was enslaved and deprived of his rights; a principle was violated in doing so. Rights imply obligations as well as duties. Mr. Lincoln was President; he was in a position that made it his duty, through his sense of right, his love of principle, the constitutional obligations imposed upon him by the oath of office, to strike the blow against slavery. But did he do it for love? He has himself answered the question; "I would not free the slaves if I could preserve the Union without it." When he freed the slaves there was no heart in the act. (pp. 309-10)

"But was not Mr. Lincoln a man of great humanity?" asks a friend at my elbow; to which I reply, "Has not that question been answered already?" Let us suppose it has not. We must understand each other. What is meant by his humanity? Is it meant that he had much of human nature in him? If so, I grant that he was a man of humanity. If, in the event of the above definition being unsatisfactory or untrue, it is meant that he

Lincoln in 1860.

was tender and kind, then I again agree. But if the inference is that he would sacrifice truth or right in the slightest degree for the love of a friend, then he was neither tender nor kind; nor did he have any humanity. The law of human nature is such that it cannot be all head, all conscience, and all heart in one person at the same time. Our Maker so constituted things that, where God through reason blazed the way, we might boldly walk therein. The glory of Mr. Lincoln's power lay in the just and magnificent equipoise of head, conscience, and heart; and here his fame must rest or not at all. (p. 311)

Of Mr. Lincoln's will-power there are two opinions also: one that he lacked any will; the other that he was all will. (p. 312)

Remembering that Mr. Lincoln's mind moved logically, slowly, and cautiously, the question of his will and its power is easily solved. Although he cared but little for simple facts, rules, and methods, he did care for the truth and right of principle. In debate he courteously granted all the forms and non-essential things to his opponent. Sometimes he yielded nine points out of ten. The nine he brushed aside as husks or rubbish; but the tenth, being a question of substance, he clung to with all his might. On the underlying principles of truth and justice his will was as firm as steel and as tenacious as iron. It was as solid, real, and vital as an idea on which the world turns. He scorned to support or adopt an untrue position, in proportion as his conscience prevented him from doing an unjust thing. Ask him to sacrifice in the slightest degree his convictions of truth—as he was asked to do when he made his [*"House Divided" Speech*]—and his soul would have exclaimed with indignant scorn, "The World perish first!"

Such was Lincoln's will. Because on one line of questions— the non-essential—he was pliable, and on the other he was as immovable as the rocks, have arisen the contradictory notions prevalent regarding him. It only remains to say that he was inflexible and unbending in human transactions when it was necessary to be so, and not otherwise. At one moment he was pliable and expansive as gentle air; at the next as tenacious and unyielding as gravity itself.

Thus I have traced Mr. Lincoln through his perceptions, his suggestiveness, his judgement, and his four predominant qualities: powers of reason, understanding, conscience, and heart. In the grand review of his peculiar characteristics, nothing creates such an impressive effect as his love of the truth. It looms up over everything else. His life is proof of the assertion that he never yielded in his fundamental conception of truth to any man for any end. (pp. 314-16)

As illustrative of a combination in Mr. Lincoln's organization, it may be said that his eloquence lay in the strength of his logical faculty, his supreme power of reasoning, his great understanding, and his love of principle; in his clear and accurate vision; in his cool and masterly statement of principles around which the issues gather; and in the statement of those issues and the grouping of the facts that are to carry conviction to the minds of men of every grade of intelligence. He was so clear that he could not be misunderstood or long misrepresented. He stood square and bolt upright to his convictions, and anyone who listened to him would be convinced that he formed his thoughts and utterances by them. His mind was not exactly a wide, broad, generalizing, and comprehensive mind, nor yet a versatile, quick, and subtle one, bounding here and there as emergencies demanded; but it was deep, enduring, strong, like a majestic machine running in deep iron grooves with heavy flanges on its wheels. (p. 317)

The universal testimony, "He is an honest man," gave [Mr. Lincoln] a firm hold on the masses, and they trusted him with a blind religious faith. His sad, melancholy face excited their sympathy, and when the dark days came it was their heart-strings that entwined and sustained him. Sympathy, we are

told, is one of the strongest and noblest incentives to human action. With the sympathy and love of the people to sustain him, Lincoln had unlimited power over them; he threw an invisible and weightless harness over them, and drove them through disaster and desperation to final victory. The trust and worship by the people of Lincoln were the result of his simple character. He held himself not aloof from the masses. He became one of them. They feared together, they struggled together, they hoped together; thus melted and moulded into one, they became one in thought, one in will, one in action. If Lincoln cautiously awaited the full development of the last fact in the great drama before he acted, when longer waiting would be a crime, he knew that the people were determinedly at his back. Thus, when a blow was struck, it came with the unerring aim and power of a bolt from heaven. A natural king—not ruling men, but leading them along the drifts and trends of their own tendencies, always keeping in mind the consent of the governed, he developed what the future historian will call the sublimest order of conservative statesmanship.

Whatever of life, vigor, force, and power of eloquence his peculiar qualities gave him; whatever there was in a fair, manly, honest, and impartial adminstration of justice under law to all men at all times; whatever there was in a strong will in the right governed by tenderness and mercy; whatever there was in toil and sublime patience; whatever there was in these things or a wise combination of them, Lincoln is justly entitled to in making up the impartial verdict of history. These limit and define him as a statesman, as an orator, as an executive of the nation, and as a man. They developed in all the walks of his life; they were his law; they were his nature, they were Abraham Lincoln. (pp. 318-19)

William H. Herndon and Jesse W. Weik, "Chapter XI," in Abraham Lincoln: The True Story of a Great Life, *Vol. II, D. Appleton and Company, 1892, pp. 292-320.*

JOHN G. NICOLAY   (essay date 1894)

[*Nicolay, who served as private secretary to Lincoln during his presidency, here comments on the "influences from without and influences from within" that affected Lincoln's early literary development.*]

Perhaps no point in the career of Abraham Lincoln has excited more surprise or comment than his remarkable power of literary expression. It is a constant puzzle to many men of letters how a person growing up without the advantage of schools and books could have acquired the art which enabled him to write the [*"Gettysburg Address"* and the *Second Inaugural Address*]. . . . The prime factor in such phenomena always consists of natural gifts—of the element we call genius. It is not because of their condition and surroundings, but in spite of them, that individuals occasionally manifest and develop these exceptional qualities. We find no such manifestations or results in the lives of the relatives, neighbors, or companions of Abraham Lincoln, who grew up with and about him in the woods and the cabins of Kentucky and Indiana, and who shared alike his experiences, his privations, and his opportunities, but were without his natural ability. This view, however, does not lessen our curiosity and interest in his educational processes. . . .

[Lincoln has given] us certainly not the full picture, but at least a vivid suggestion of the early influences acting upon his intellectual development—his isolation in childhood and boyhood; the personal privations under which he grew up; the ignorance and mental poverty of his parents, companions, and neighbors; the rudeness of the manners amid which he lived; the absence of example and emulation to prompt him to study and improvement; the lamentable insufficiency of tuition which came to him from the two or three school-masters competent to give only the most primary instruction; the scarcity of books, and their elementary contents,—always excepting the Bible,— which could fall into his hands.

These conditions, which followed him from his birth until he attained his majority, impressed upon him certain characteristics that never afterward left him,—a certain plainness of manner, of thought, and of speech, differentiating him in a marked and unmistakable degree from the boy and youth who, during the same period, had grown up in comfort and plenty, in schools and colleges, in intelligent society and social refinement. . . . (p. 823)

Yet these disadvantages, which were destructive clogs to sluggish or ordinary intellects, brought some compensations to a quick and energetic mind. Though the range of ideas and experiences was narrow, and confined to the routine of farm work, hunting, and neighborhood merrymaking, though thought and speech were simple, they were at least clear and direct. Though the vocabulary was scanty, the words were short and forcible. If one inquired after the health of an ailing neighbor, and received for answer that he felt "mighty weak," the faulty construction was somewhat mitigated by the intended vigor of the statement. Most valuable of all was the aid these experiences afforded in the judgment of human nature. If Lincoln, when a barefoot country boy, or after he had grown to the stature and strength of a backwoods rail-splitter, was ever prompted to imagine the feelings and actions of a practising lawyer, or a member of Congress, or a President of the United States, when he in turn became a practising lawyer, a member of Congress, and a President of the United States, he never had need to imagine the feelings and actions of barefoot boys, or of stalwart rail-splitters, or of the plain people of the nation: he knew them by heart. (pp. 823-24)

His first political address or circular is dated March 9, 1832, and was printed in the *Sangamon Journal* of March 15. As there had been neither time nor opportunity for schooling in any form since his arrival in Illinois, this written address gives us the measure of the intellectual development he must have brought with him from Indiana. It is an earnest, well-arranged, and clearly expressed statement of his political views, discussing not merely the improvement of the Sangamon River, which was the local political hobby, but also railroads, usury, education, and the amendment of several specific statutes. As a literary production, no ordinary college graduate would need to be ashamed of it; as the program of an embryo legislator, it was probably fully up to the average of the best-educated of his competitors. The evidence is unmistakable that when he came of age he already possessed acquirements far beyond the mere ability to "read, write, and cipher to the rule of three."

The educational experiences of what may be called his second period, beginning with this first political venture in March, 1832, and extending to the end of his term in Congress in 1849, a period of seventeen years, partake of . . . [a] twofold character, the concurrent result of influences from without and influences from within. The influences from without consisted in his active participation in practical politics—party consultation or caucusing, personal electioneering, and political discussion on the stump; such elementary statesmanship as he could learn during eight years of membership in the State leg-

islature, and two years of membership in Congress; such a study of the principles of law as was necessary to obtain an attorney's license; and such an examination and criticism of statutes as occurred in his consequent law-practice before local courts. Perhaps the most powerful outside influence was the change in his social status: he had moved from New Salem to Springfield, and had been thrown into the companionship and rivalry of a group of young men as talented, brilliant, and ambitious as ever graced the history of a State capital.

But even these outside influences now produced a twofold effect: all this while the conditions surrounding him kept him in close contact and association with the "plain people," with primitive pioneer life. Social intercourse, argument before a court, debate on the stump or legislative discussion with Douglas, Stuart, Logan, Browning, Baker, Hardin, Trumbull, Calhoun, McDougal, and others extended his knowledge, sharpened his wit, and improved his oratory; but when he went to the cabins of the settlers to solicit their votes, or when as surveyor he located their roads and ran out their farm lines, the simple modes of thought and strong rural phraseology he had learned as boy and youth were renewed and deepened, and the tendency to express extravagant ideas in high-sounding words was repressed and chastened. And this was not alone the exercise of good judgment, but a measure of immediate utility. . . . The aspiring local candidate of those days was lucky if he found a gathering of twenty or thirty settlers at a shooting-match, a raising, or other neighborhood occasion, to whom he could propose his reforms in State legislation, or his national views on tariff and internal improvement. Sometimes it was an evening meeting assembled in a district log school-house, lighted by two or three tallow candles, with an audience of ten or fifteen persons. Only those who have been through experiences of this kind can appreciate the chilling effect of such surroundings upon oratorical enthusiasm. Here the speaker needed all his epigrams and anecdotes to dissipate the expectant gravity, the staring solemnity, of his auditors in the ghostly half-light inside and the dismal darkness and loneliness outside the little cabin. These talks were uncongenial soil for rhetoric and literary style. They needed to be seasoned with pithy argument and witty illustration, and rendered in a vocabulary that had the flavor of the cabin and the energy of the frontier. It was this kind of training in Lincoln's art which not only helped him to four successive elections to the legislature, but became to a certain degree ingrained in his literary development; for its better and higher effects are distinctly traceable in the most successful writings and utterances of his later life. (pp. 824-25)

With the exception of arguments addressed to juries, the law furnished him one of the strongest safeguards against rambling thought and redundant speech. The text-books of that science afford no encouragement to the misuse of words or logic. Their formulas of legal principles are nearly as cold and rigid as the multiplication table. To these we may confidently trace Lincoln's strong tendency to definitions and axioms in his political discussions; while from the briefs and declarations he was compelled to write he gained invaluable habits of brevity and conciseness.

It is a popular and suggestive, if not entirely correct, saying that only three books are needed to make up a sufficient library—that in the Bible, Blackstone, and Shakspere, a man may find all that is best in philosophy, law, and literature. It is certain that Lincoln worked with industry in these great intellectual quarries, and the solidity and grace that they gave to his temple of fame are plainly discernible.

If he had been a man possessing merely an average intellect, his literary and political growth would have been limited as well as fashioned by the outside influences which have been mentioned. He would have become a shrewd and successful jury lawyer, and a valuable "rabble-rousing" party lieutenant with a local fame. But all this time the influences within himself were as active and fruitful as the exterior ones. His ambition, however much hampered by the want of school training or by primitive surroundings, always prompted him to seek a better mode of expression, as well as finer thought. (p. 825)

The remarkable thing was that while nature and opportunity gave him talent and great success at story-telling and extemporaneous talking, he learned to write—learned to appreciate the value of the pen as an instrument to formulate and record his thought, and the more clearly, forcibly, and elegantly to express it.

Doubtless he made slow progress. Without books, without teachers, without a "literary" atmosphere to excite emulation, his efforts were probably only secondary—only incidental to the more engrossing occupations of law and politics. The list of his writings of this class is not large, and yet it is enough to create the inference that much similar labor must have gone to waste. In 1837 he wrote, delivered, and printed a lecture on ["**The Perpetuation of Our Political Institutions**"]. In 1839 he wrote out and printed a speech that he made in one of the political debates with which the young men of Springfield enlivened their winters. In 1842 he wrote and printed a "Washingtonian" temperance address. All his longer speeches in Congress were prepared with great care, both as to argument and handwriting; and when his political idol, Henry Clay, died in 1852, he delivered and printed a long and able eulogy on his life and character.

It will thus be seen that in the course of his self-education Lincoln from time to time engaged in composition as an art. . . . [While these "literary experiments"] call for no special admiration on account of intrinsic merit, they are of exceeding interest as stepping-stones to the attainment of that literary style and power which, in his later speeches and writings, have elicited the enthusiasm of the best scholars and critics. (pp. 825-26)

[Nicolay here quotes from Lincoln's poem "**My Childhood's Home I See Again**"; "**Fragment: Notes for a Lecture**"; "**Fragments: Notes for Law Lecture, July 1, 1850**"; and "**Lecture on 'Discoveries, Inventions, and Improvements'.**"]

It would obviously be unjust to devote any serious criticism to the foregoing quotations from Mr. Lincoln's miscellaneous writings. They must be regarded in the light of mere recreation to satisfy the craving for a change from the monotony of law and politics. In the United States, where the extended circulation of newspapers stimulates not alone the habit of reading, but also the taste for writing, and affords abundant opportunity to gratify it, even versification becomes contagious. . . .

[Lincoln tells us that he wrote his verses] in the fall of 1844, when, as a candidate for presidential elector, he was making stump speeches in Indiana for Henry Clay. Weary with the monotony of political harangues, a visit to the graves of his mother and only sister touched and gave utterance to emotions which the hard, practical duties of his life, perhaps even more than the consciousness of literary imperfection, held in patient subjection. (p. 831)

The strong probability is that ["**Lecture on 'Discoveries, Inventions, and Improvements'**"] was at least partly composed within that period of comparative leisure when, in March, 1849, his service of one term in Congress ended, and before the Nebraska Bill in January, 1854, unchained the new political controversy in which Lincoln became so conspicuous an actor and so dominant a leader. It was during that five years' lull following his congressional service that, he tells us, he took up and worked through the first six books of Euclid, by way of practice in the art of reasoning and demonstration; and the supposition is not a violent one that he may have added occasional literary composition as attractive by-play. . . .

[On February 27, 1860, five days after he delivered his "**Lecture on 'Discoveries, Inventions, and Improvements'**" in Springfield, Lincoln] was in New York, and delivered there his famous [*Cooper Union Speech*], which showed that he had trained himself for better uses than writing newspaper verses, describing Niagara, or extolling the material achievements of Young America. A gigantic moral and patriotic crusade was about to open, to which his thoughts, his words, his patience, his will, were destined to give voice, courage, perseverance, victory. (p. 832)

John G. Nicolay, "Lincoln's Literary Experiments," in The Century, Vol. XLVII, No. 6, April, 1894, pp. 823-32.

THE LIVING AGE   (essay date 1909)

[*The anonymous critic depicts Lincoln as the product, proof, and justification of American democracy.*]

The really representative American was Abraham Lincoln. The greatness of Lincoln was that of a common man raised to a high dimension. The possibility, still more the existence, of such a man is itself a justification of democracy. We do not say that so independent, so natural, so complete a man cannot in older societies come to wield so large a power over the affairs and the minds of men; we can only say he has not done so, amid all the stirring movements of the nineteenth century. (p. 678)

[Lincoln] was no "sport"; his career is a triumphant refutation of the traditional views of genius. He had no special gift or quality to distinguish him; he was simply the best type of American at a historic juncture when the national safety wanted such a man. The confidence which all Americans express that their country will be equal to any emergency which threatens it is not so entirely superstitious as it seems at first sight. For the career of Lincoln shows how it has been done in a country where the "necessary man" can be drawn not from a few leading families, or an educated class, but from the millions. Born in a log-cabin of a frontier camp, rail-splitter and farm lad in his early teens, roaming with his nomad father over the newly opening West, inured to labor, sport and fight of wits and fists from boyhood, trader and boatman down the Mississippi, storekeeper, road-surveyor, soldier, when he began to settle down to law and politics in Illinois at twenty-one he had already gathered into his personality a wider knowledge of the real life of a people than it is possible for the product of Eton and Oxford in this country, or of the most efficient pedagogy of Germany, to furnish for the service of the State. . . . Abraham Lincoln, though fond at times of reading, owed little to books, and would have gained little, if he had not lost, from the best literary education of his time and country. For an inquisitive mind, with a Shakespearean power of assimilation, this early wandering life, with its direct knowledge of all kinds of people and of work, filled with incessant talk and streaks of love-making and physical adventure among unsophisticated, hard-living men and women, was an incomparably good nourishment. This method he kept up through all his early political career, as he "rode the circuit" or "took the stump" for some election. In a democracy what is pre-eminently wanted for a man who is to "save the people" is well-grounded confidence, in himself, in the people, and in his power to do what is wanted. So it was that when the great issue of slavery was moving swiftly towards open rebellion, a certain miraculous stroke of popular perspicacity saw and demanded Lincoln. For the conditions of a society whch made it possible for an obscure small country lawyer-politician to enter the lists with so renowned an antagonist as Douglas, to arouse a swiftly expanding recognition of his powers, and to force himself untried to the helm of the State, were not fortuitous, but of the very substance of American democracy. Lincoln was truly the choice of the wisdom of the mass, recognizing the hazard of the situation and the need, not for an Eastern wirepuller or a statesman from the Harvard law school, but for a man of the people. (pp. 678-79)

His supreme greatness as statesman and as man is, of course, tested by the iron rod of single purpose with which he set himself to the policy of saving the Union, and for which he relentlessly kept under all other objects, even the suppression of the slavery he loathed. . . . To pursue an inevitable war with just the maximum of humanity circumstances would permit, to stifle the passion of abolition until the time was fully ripe and the Union was safe, to steer a devious path of necessary opportunism through years of unceasing and unforeseen crises, when the cauldron of human passions kept boiling up towards anarchy, such an achievement of the indomitable will of man has not before been witnessed.

A fiercer light beats upon such a man than upon any throne, and exhibits many flaws and deficiencies. His was no tight-spun efficiency or immaculate morality. His long, awkward, loose figure was characteristic of the man. "He always loafed a little," one of his most intelligent biographers informs us. Probably he would have endorsed Lamb's saying, "It is good sometimes to take an airing outside the strict diocese of the conscience," as a maxim of practical utility. But no man capable of such a burden as he bore could be a lighthearted or light-living man, and no little part of the fascination of his influence is due to what those who write of him, for lack of a better term, call his mysticism, or some dark, impenetrable undercurrent of his life, perhaps deriving from the puritanic inheritance reformed under the early solitude and struggles with the untamed powers of nature in his childhood. Whatever its source, this tragic background of melancholy always remained a softening and a healing influence in his dealing with his fellow-men; it neither weakened the exuberance of his sympathy nor marred his steadiness of judgment.

Though the representative American even of this generation has shifted from the type of Lincoln, he stands, and long will stand, as the most effective personality which democracy has yet produced, testifying in his own manhood, as in his own words [in the **"Gettysburg Address"**], to the meaning of the American Commonwealth, the resolve "that government of the people, by the people, for the people shall not perish from the earth." The restoration of such government is surely the great duty which the American people of to-day owes to itself, to the world, and to Abraham Lincoln, as his rightful monument. (p. 680)

"The Genius of Lincoln," in The Living Age, *Vol. CCLX, No. 3375, March 13, 1909, pp. 677-80.*

HENRY CABOT LODGE   (lecture date 1913)

[*Lodge was an American politician, historian, and author who coedited the* North American Review *with Henry Adams from 1873 to 1876 and who later served as associate editor of the* International Review. *His remarks below are drawn from "The Democracy of Abraham Lincoln," an address that he delivered in 1913 to the students of Boston University School of Law. Lodge cites Lincoln as an elucidator and guardian of constitutional democracy, focusing on his opinions concerning the role of the Supreme Court in the American system of representative government.*]

The greatness of Abraham Lincoln is admitted by the world and his place in history is assured. Yet to us he has a significance and an importance which he cannot have to other people. It is impossible to translate a beautiful poem without losing in some degree the ineffable quality, the final perfection which it possesses in the language in which it was written. In its native speech the verse is wedded to the form and to the words and has tones in its voice which only those who are "to the manner born" can hear. So Lincoln, whose life, rightly considered, was a poem, speaks to his own people as he does to no other. What he was, and what he did and said, is all part of our national life and of our thoughts as well. We see in him the man who led in the battle which resulted in a united country and we have watched his crescent fame as it has mounted ever higher with the incessant examination of his life and character. No record has ever leaped to light by which he could be shamed. Apart from all comparisons it is at least certain that he is the greatest figure yet produced by modern democracy which began its onward march at the little bridge in Concord. If ever a man lived who understood and loved the people to whom he gave his life, Lincoln was that man. In him no one has a monopoly; he is not now the property of any sect or any party. His fame is the heritage of the people of the United States and, as Stanton said, standing by his deathbed, "He belongs to the ages."

For all these reasons, it seems to me, in these days of agitation and disquiet, when the fundamental principles upon which our government rests and has always rested are assailed, that nothing could be more profitable and more enlightening than to know just what Lincoln's opinions were as to democracy and the true principles of free government. (pp. 123-24)

Lincoln's convictions and opinions are to be found in only one place, in his own speeches and writings which, like his fame, belong to his countrymen and to mankind. Fortunately we need not grope about to discover his meaning. Few men who have ever lived and played a commanding part in the world have had the power of expressing their thoughts with greater clearness or in a style more pellucid and direct than Lincoln. Of him it may truly be said that his statements are demonstrations. You will search far before you will find a man who could state a proposition more irresistibly, leaving no avenue of escape, or who could use a more relentless logic than the President of the Civil War. We feel as we read his life that he had in him the nature of a poet, the imagination which pertains to the poetic nature and which was manifested not only in what he said and did but in his intuitive sympathy with all sorts and conditions of men. Combined with these attributes of the poetic genius, which is as rare as it is impalpable, were qualities seldom found in that connection. He was an able lawyer and had the intellectual methods of the trained legal mind. He was also the practical man of affairs, as well as the great statesman, looking at facts with undazzled eyes and moulding men and events to suit his purpose. There is no occasion for guesswork, assertion, or speculation in regard to him when he turned away from the visions of the imagination to confront and deal with the hard problems of life and government, never to any man harder than they were to him.

Let us then examine his writings and speeches and see what light they throw upon the questions now subject to public discussion, which relate to the Constitution of the United States and to the principles upon which that great instrument was based. (pp. 125-27)

[Let] me define the questions upon which it seems to me well that we should seek his guidance at this time. They are two in number—representative government as involved in the agitation in favor of the compulsory initiative and referendum, and the independence of the courts which is at stake in the demand for the recall of judges and the review of judicial decisions by popular vote. (p. 128)

[In his **"Gettysburg Address"**] Lincoln told the world what the government was for which the people whom he led were pouring out their treasure and offering up their lives. (p. 133)

He defined this government to which he gave his life as a "government of the people, by the people and for the people." This famous definition, familiar in our mouths as household words, was applied to the government of the United States as created, established, and conducted by and under the Constitution adopted in 1789. With the exception of the three war amendments, and that just adopted establishing the income tax, it is the same Constitution and the same government to-day that it was in November, 1863. Lincoln thought it a popular government. He did not regard it as a government by a president, or by a congress, or by judges, but as a government of, by and for the people, and in his usual fashion he stated his proposition so clearly and with such finality that there is no escape from his meaning. (p. 135)

[Representative] government rests upon certain broad principles in regard to which Lincoln spoke clearly and decisively. The basic theory of representative government is that the representative body represents all the people, and that a majority of that body represents a majority of all the people. To the majority in Congress the power of action is committed, and it is so guarded as to exclude so far as human ingenuity can do it any opportunity for the control of the government by an organized minority either among the voters or their representatives. (pp. 137-38)

Having thus established majority rule through the representative system, the framers of the Constitution with their deep-rooted distrust of uncontrolled power anywhere, then proceeded to put limitations upon the power of the majority. They were well aware that a majority of the voters at any given moment did not necessarily represent the enduring will of the people. They knew equally well that in the end the real will of the people must be absolute, but they desired that there should be room for deliberation and for second thought and that the rights of minorities and of individuals should be so far as possible protected and secured. Hence the famous limitations of the Constitution. I need not rehearse them all; the most vital are those embodied in the first ten amendments which constitute a bill of rights, the rights of men, or human rights, and any violation of those rights is forbidden to Congress and to the majority. As further restraints upon the majority they gave the

executive a veto, which raised the necessary majority for action to two-thirds, while upon the courts they conferred, by implication, opportunity to declare, in specific cases, any law to be in violation of the general principles laid down by the Constitution.

Upon this first point of the limitation upon the majority, whether of voters or representatives, which is the essence of our constitutional system of representation, Lincoln spoke in a manner which cannot be misunderstood. He said in the [*First Inaugural Address*]:

> If by the mere force of numbers a majority should deprive a minority of any clearly written constitutional right, it might, in a moral point of view, justify revolution—certainly would if such a right were a vital one. But such is not the case. All the vital rights of minorities and of individuals are so plainly assured to them by affirmations and negations, guarantees and prohibitions, in the Constitution, that controversies never arise concerning them. . . .
>
> A majority held in restraint by constitutional checks and limitations, and always changing easily with deliberate changes of popular opinions and sentiments, is the only true sovereign of a free people.

Nothing could be clearer than these sentences. In Lincoln's opinion the violation of a vital constitutional right was moral justification for revolution, and the last sentence gives a definition of free and real popular government upon which it would be difficult indeed to improve.

I have just said that one of the checks placed upon the power of the majority was the opportunity which of necessity devolved upon the courts to declare, when a specific case was brought before them, their opinion that the law involved in the suit was in violation of the Constitution. It is this judicial power, asserted by Marshall, which has led to the present movement to destroy the independence of the courts by subjecting the judges to the recall and their decisions to review at the ballot-box. On this point Lincoln spoke often and with great elaboration. He did so because the famous Dred Scott case was a very burning issue in the years immediately preceding the Civil War. If an opinion was ever delivered by a court which justified resistance to or an attack upon the judicial authority it was that one known by the name of a poor negro—Dred Scott. The opinion against which the conscience of men revolted did not decide the case. It was an obiter dictum. It was delivered solely for the purpose of settling a great political question by pronouncement from the Supreme Court. There was no disguise as to what was intended. Mr. Buchanan, informed as to what was coming after his arrival in Washington, announced in his inaugural that the question of slavery in the territories would soon be disposed of by the Supreme Court. The wise practice of the Supreme Court is to decline jurisdiction of political questions, holding that such questions belong solely in Congress and the executive. In this case the court deliberately travelled outside the record in order to speak upon a purely political question which then divided the whole country. For such action there is no defence. Born of the passions of the slavery contest, the Dred Scott case stands in our history as a flagrant attempt by the Supreme Court to usurp power. . . . The attack upon the dictum of the court began with the masterly dissenting opinion of Mr. Justice Curtis, which wrecked Taney's argument both in the law and the facts. From the courtroom the attack spread over the country and the utterances of the chief justice were assailed with all the bitterness characteristic of that period and defended with equal fervor by those who supported slavery and who declared that a refusal to accept the decision was tantamount to treason. Lincoln, as one of the leaders of the new Republican party, was obliged to deal with it. He did so fully and thoroughly. All that he said deserves careful study, for there is no more admirable analysis of the powers of the courts and of the attitude which should be taken in regard to them. (pp. 138-41)

[This] is how he dealt with [the Dred Scott opinion], a little more than three months after it was delivered, in a speech at Springfield, Illinois, on June 26, 1857:

> He (Senator Douglas) denounces all who question the correctness of that decision, as offering violent resistance to it. But who resists it? Who has, in spite of the decision, declared Dred Scott free and resisted the authority of his master over him?
>
> Judicial decisions have two uses—first, to absolutely determine the case decided, and secondly, to indicate to the public how other similar cases will be decided when they arise. For the latter use, they are called ''precedents'' and ''authorities.''
>
> We believe as much as Judge Douglas (perhaps more) in obedience to, and respect for, the Judicial department of the government. *We think its decisions on constitutional questions, when fully settled, should control not only the particular cases decided, but the general policy of the country, subject to be disturbed only by amendments of the Constitution as provided in that instrument itself. More than this would be revolution.* But we think the Dred Scott decision is erroneous. We know the court that made it has often overruled its own decisions, and we shall do what we can to have it overrule this. We offer no resistance to it.
>
> Judicial decisions are of greater or less authority as precedents according to circumstances. That this should be so accords both with common sense and the customary understanding of the legal profession.
>
> If this important decision had been made by the unanimous concurrence of the judges, and without any apparent partisan bias, and in accordance with legal public expectation and with the steady practice of the departments throughout our history and had been in no part based on assumed historical facts, which are not really true; or, if wanting in some of these, it had been before the court more than once, and had there been affirmed or reaffirmed through a course of years, it then might be, perhaps would be, factious, nay, even revolutionary, not to acquiesce in it as a precedent.
>
> But when, as is true, we find it wanting in all these claims to the public confidence, it is not resistance, it is not factious, it is not even dis-

respectful, to treat it as not having yet quite established a settled doctrine for the country.

Contrast these calm words, uttered under the greatest provocation, with the violent attacks now made on the courts for two or three decisions which are in no respect political and which are as nothing compared to the momentous issue involved in the Dred Scott case, where the freedom of human beings and the right of the people to decide upon slavery in the territories were at stake. There is not a proposition which is not stated with all Lincoln's unrivalled lucidity, and there is not the faintest suggestion of breaking down the power of the courts or of taking from them their independence.

A year later, just before the great . . . [**Lincoln-Douglas Debates**], Lincoln at Chicago on July 10, 1858, again took up the Dred Scott case and spoke as follows:

> I have expressed heretofore, and I now repeat, my opposition to the Dred Scott decision; but I should be allowed to state the nature of that opposition, and I ask your indulgence while I do so. What is fairly implied by the term Judge Douglas has used: ''Resistance to the decision''? I do not resist it. If I wanted to take Dred Scott from his master, I would be interfering with property, and that terrible difficulty that Judge Douglas speaks of, of interfering with property, would arise. But I am doing no such thing as that; all that I am doing is refusing to obey it as a political rule. If I were in Congress, and a vote should come up on a question of whether slavery should be prohibited in a new territory, in spite of the Dred Scott decision, I would vote that it should.
>
> That is what I would do. Judge Douglas said last night that before the decision he might advance his opinion, and it might be contrary to the decision when it was made; but after it was made he would abide by it until it was reversed. Just so! We let this property abide by the decision, but we will try to reverse that decision. We will try to put it where Judge Douglas would not object, for he says he will obey it until it is reversed. Somebody has to reverse that decision since it is made; and we mean to reverse it, and we mean to do it peaceably.
>
> What are the uses of decisions of courts? They have two uses. As rules of property they have two uses. First, they decide upon the question before the court. They decide in this case that Dred Scott is a slave. Nobody resists that. Not only that, but they say to everybody else that persons standing just as Dred Scott stands are as he is. That is, they say that when a question comes up upon another person, it will be so decided again, unless the court decides in another way, unless the court overrules its decision. Well, we mean to do what we can to have the court decide the other way. That is one thing we mean to try to do.

(pp. 143-45)

He discussed the great question many times, but I will make only one more quotation, the passage in the first inaugural, where on the eve of secession and civil war he gave expression, every word weighed and meditated, to his opinions and intentions. On that solemn occasion he spoke thus of the courts:

> I do not forget the position, assumed by some, that constitutional questions are to be decided by the Supreme Court; nor do I deny that such decisions must be binding, in any case, upon the parties to a suit, as to the object of that suit, while they are also entitled to very high respect and consideration in all parallel cases by all other departments of the government. And while it is obviously possible that such decisions may be erroneous in any given case, still the evil effect following it, being limited to that particular case, with the chance that it may be overruled and never become a precedent for other cases, can better be borne than could the evils of a different practice. At the same time, the candid citizen must confess that if the policy of the government, upon vital questions affecting the whole people, is to be irrevocably fixed by the decisions of the Supreme Court, the instant they are made, in ordinary litigation between the parties in personal actions, the people will have ceased to be their own rulers, having to that extent practically resigned their government into the hands of the eminent tribunal. Nor is there in this view any assault upon the courts or the judges. It is a duty from which they may not shrink to decide cases properly brought before them, and it is no fault of theirs if others seek to turn their decisions to political purposes.

From these extracts we may see that Lincoln held that the courts had no right to lay down a rule of political action and that if they did so no one was bound by it. That now is, indeed, the position of the court itself. He said that no one should resist the decision in the Dred Scott case, but that it was the duty of all who believed that doctrine contrary to freedom and to American principles to seek to have it overruled—not reviewed by the voters at the ballot-box, or changed by the recall of its authors, but simply overruled by the court itself. Again, no one will dissent. But beyond this he did not go. On the contrary, he upheld the judicial authority within its proper domain, and there is no suggestion to be found, even under that bitter provocation, of any attempt to make the courts subservient to any outside power by any such device as a recall. Still less is there any thought of reversing the decision by a popular vote. (pp. 148-49)

There is no need to comment further upon the passages which have just been quoted. It is enough for me to say that Lincoln's discussion of the Dred Scott case seems to me to contain the strongest arguments for an independent judiciary that can be found anywhere. We may also be sure, I think, that Lincoln did not forget in his righteous indignation at the Dred Scott opinion that every slave who set foot on English soil became a free man by Lord Mansfield's decision in Somersett's case (1772), or that slavery had been ended in Massachusetts by a decision of the Supreme Court of the State in 1783 under the sentence, that "all men are born free and equal," inserted in the constitution of that State for that precise purpose by John Lowell.

Passing now from the particular to the general, let me by a few brief quotations show you what Lincoln thought of our government under the Constitution as a whole. In a speech at Columbus, Ohio, on September 16, 1859, he said:

> I believe there is a genuine popular sovereignty. I think a definition of genuine popular sovereignty, in the abstract, would be about this: That each man shall do precisely as he pleases with himself, and with all those things which exclusively concern him. Applied to government, this principle would be, that a general government shall do all those things which pertain to it, and all the local governments shall do precisely as they please in respect to those matters which exclusively concern them. I understand that this Government of the United States under which we live is based upon this principle; and I am misunderstood if it is supposed that I have any war to make upon that principle.

(pp. 149-50)

In his reply to the Mayor of Philadelphia, on February 21, 1861, he spoke as follows:

> Your worthy mayor has expressed the wish, in which I join with him, that it were convenient for me to remain in your city long enough to consult your merchants and manufacturers; or, as it were, to listen to those breathings rising within the consecrated walls wherein the Constitution of the United States, and, I will add, the Declaration of Independence, were originally framed and adopted. I assure you and your mayor that I had hoped on this occasion, and upon all occasions during my life, that I shall do nothing inconsistent with the teachings of these holy and most sacred walls. All my political warfare has been in favor of the teachings that came forth from these sacred walls. May my right hand forget its cunning and my tongue cleave to the roof of my mouth if ever I prove false to those teachings.

So he spoke at the threshold of the great conflict. Listen to him now as he spoke three years later, with the war nearing its close and when the hand of fate could almost be heard knocking at his door. (p. 151)

He said, on August 22, 1864, in his address to the 166th Ohio Regiment:

> It is not merely for to-day, but for all time to come, that we should perpetuate for our children's children that great and free government which we have enjoyed all our lives. I beg you to remember this, not merely for my sake, but for yours. I happen, temporarily, to occupy this White House. I am a living witness that any one of your children may look to come here as my father's child has. It is in order that each one of you may have, through this free government which we have enjoyed, an open field and a fair chance for your industry, enterprise and intelligence: that you may all have equal privileges in the race of life, with all its desirable human aspirations. It is for this the struggle should be maintained, that we may not lose our birthright—not only for one, but for two or

three years. The nation is worth fighting for,
to secure such an inestimable jewel.

And on August 31, 1864, in an address to the 148th Ohio
Regiment, he said:

> But this government must be preserved in spite
> of the acts of any man or set of men. It is worthy
> of your every effort. Nowhere in the world is
> presented a government of so much liberty and
> equality. To the humblest and poorest amongst
> us are held out the highest privileges and po-
> sitions. The present moment finds me at the
> White House, yet there is as good a chance for
> your children there as there was for my father's.

With these noble words, uttered as the dark shadows of the
past were fleeing away and the light of the coming victory was
beginning to shine upon him, let us leave him. As at Gettysburg, over the graves of the dead soldiers, he declared that the
great battle had been fought in order that "government of the
people, by the people, for the people" should not perish from
the earth, so now to the living soldiers he said that nowhere
in the world was presented a "government of so much liberty
and equality." . . . Thus he described his conception of democracy, and that conception he found fulfilled in the Constitution of the United States and in the great principles of
ordered freedom and guarded rights which are there embodied.
(pp. 152-54)

> *Henry Cabot Lodge, "The Democracy of Abraham
> Lincoln," in his* The Democracy of the Constitution
> and Other Addresses and Essays, *Charles Scribner's
> Sons, 1915, pp. 122-59.*

LUTHER EMERSON ROBINSON (essay date 1918)

[*In the following excerpt from his full-length study* Abraham Lincoln as a Man of Letters, *Robinson sheds light on the distinguishing features of three of Lincoln's speeches: the* Cooper Union
Speech, *"Gettysburg Address," and* Second Inaugural Address.]

In conception and content the [*Cooper Union Address*] is remarkable. It was perhaps the best fortified as well as the most
convincing and effective political address of an argumentative
nature before an American audience up to that time. It aimed
to promote the popular endorsement of the Republican party
at the next national election. It sought to confirm in the faith
of that party any who were doubtful which of the parties or
principles it would be wiser to support. It purposed to show a
distinct and unanswerable difference in goal between the Douglas policy and that maintained by the Republicans. Moreover,
it intended to disarm the leaders of the South of disunion arguments, to present with exactness the attitude of Lincoln's
party toward slavery, and to inspire the nation with confidence
in the high moral purpose and sense of justice which he believed
to be the soul of that attitude.

Lincoln's unusual capacity for research and exposition is fully
shown in his answer to a statement made by Douglas at Columbus, Ohio:

> Our fathers, when they framed the government
> under which we live, understood this question
> just as well, and even better, than we do now.

This statement Lincoln endorsed. Then he proceeded to show
from historical facts that "our fathers" had actually favored
the opinion that Congress possessed the power to prohibit slavery in the Territories. He showed that certain of the "thirty-
nine" men who framed and signed the Constitution participated, as members of Congress under the Articles of Confederation, in framing the Ordinance of 1784 and the Ordinance
of 1787, and voted for the provision against slavery in the
Northwest Territory. Only one of these six men had voted
against the anti-slavery proviso. He pointed out that, in the
first Congress under the Constitution, the sixteen members who
had been among the "thirty-nine" voted unanimously "to enforce the ordinance of '87, including the prohibition of slavery
in the Northwestern Territory"; that President Washington,
another of the "thirty-nine," signed the bill. Subsequent history disclosed the probability or the fact that members of the
"thirty-nine" surviving in Congress had voted for laws to
control the relation of slavery to the Territory of Mississippi
and the Louisiana purchase. The last act of Congress on Federal
control of slavery in which signers of the Constitution voted
was the Missouri Compromise. Here the two survivors divided
for and against on that mesure. The question which Douglas
had raised was the attitude of the Fathers on the constitutional
division of local and Federal control of slavery in the Territories. Douglas maintained that the Fathers favored local control; Lincoln showed conclusively that twenty-one out of the
twenty-three Fathers who acted on the question, had voted
favorably for Federal control, while none of the sixteen others,
including Franklin, Hamilton, and Gouverneur Morris, was
known to be unfavorable to Federal control. None of these was
known to be favorable to slavery, "unless it may be John
Rutledge, of South Carolina."

In similar manner he punctured the reasoning of the Supreme
Court, which based the Dred Scott decision upon the Fifth
amendment, and Douglas's intrenchment behind the Tenth
amendment, by showing that these amendments were "in progress toward maturity" under the same Congress which voted
to enforce the Ordinance of 1787. He demonstrated the inconsistency of the South in calling for congressional authority to
revive the slave-trade, or in supporting "popular sovereignty,"
and at the same time opposing the right of Congress under the
Constitution to prohibit slavery in the Territories. He quoted
Jefferson's hope of the ultimate emancipation of the slaves,
maintained the impossibility of the South's charge of connection between the Republicans and the John Brown raid, and
explained what must, it seems, become the historic feeling
upon that episode. "John Brown's effort," he said, "was peculiar. It was not a slave insurrection. It was an attempt by
white men to get up a revolt among slaves, in which the slaves
refused to participate. . . . An enthusiast broods over the
oppression of the people till he fancies himself commissioned
by Heaven to liberate them. . . . Orsini's attempt on Louis
Napoleon, and John Brown's attempt at Harpers Ferry were,
in their philosophy, precisely the same. The eagerness to cast
blame on Old England in the one case, and on New England
in the other, does not disprove the sameness of the two things."
(pp. 98-102)

[In the **Lincoln-Douglas Debates,** Lincoln] had insisted on fidelity to the constitutional provision for a fugitive slave law.
He deprecated, now, on the same principle of observance of
the law, the attempt of John Brown and his associates to fly
into its face in an effort to subvert a system they regarded as
iniquitous. His opposition to the South's desire to extend slavery would require him at the same time to oppose the acts of
northern States to obstruct the return of slaves escaped from
their owners. But his position in favor of law observance would
not justify the South in maintaining against him that the Su-

preme Court decision had supported the desire of the South to extend slavery to Federal Territories in spite of Congress, for the "bare majority of the judges" in that decision "disagree with one another in the reasons for making it." The decision was "mainly based upon a mistaken statement of fact—the statement . . . that the right of property in a slave is distinctly and expressly affirmed in the Constitution." Since the Constitution contains no such affirmation as the Court asserts, Lincoln held it would doubtless reconsider the decision based upon it.

Lincoln closed his *Cooper Union Address* by arguing that the South, now threatening disunion, would not be satisfied with the unconditional surrender of the Territories; it would eventually demand the overthrow of free-State constitutions which forbid slavery. This his party could not grant, because it believed slavery to be wrong. But in the face of the wrong, the party could afford to "let it alone where it is, because that much is due to the necessity arising from its actual presence in the nation"; but a sense of duty called for opposition to its spread to the Territories. "Let us not be slandered from our duty by false accusations. . . . Let us have faith that right makes might, and in that faith let us to the end dare to do our duty as we understand it." (pp. 102-03)

To his New York audience, Lincoln's address was a revelation of fresh strength and hope for America. No one before him had assembled the facts and ideals of the republic into a declaration so compact of knowledge and persuasion, so profoundly relevant to the supreme issue of the time. His words were simple, sincere, and cheering. Here was a new and unexpected pilot, with chart and compass in his hand, with direction in his mind, speaking the decisive word in a moment of cloud and confusion. Strong men heard him, and went away to deliberate upon his message. The people read his words, and saw in them a higher meaning the more they reflected. They felt there was character in what he said, and a fair promise of success in what he proposed. There was something dawning in his lofty earnestness; and his conclusions were clear, far-seeing, and fraught with insight. He seemed to many to be the only man in the nation whose courage, integrity, and comprehension gave ample assurance against rashness in action, a sufficient and steady wisdom for the present task. The [*Cooper Union Address*] is not Lincoln's masterpiece, but it is a substantial contribution to our literature of knowledge and power. (pp. 105-06)

There are those who regard [the **"Gettysburg Address"**] as the most important literary performance growing out of the Civil War—that of all that was written during that period, it will longest endure. Certain it is that this Address is our most perfect hymn in prose. It has the quiet yet stately roll of cathedral harmony. In thought and emotion it is deeply impressive and spiritual. Miltonic in conception and rhythm, it is a rich and satisfying intellectual possession to those who have stored up its sacred lines in memory. (p. 169)

There is much unconscious poetry in the . . . deeply-felt utterances of Abraham Lincoln. No other writer of American prose has quite matched him in this respect. His masterpieces have often the cadence of epic lines, and easily fall into the movement of musical measures. Any one with an elementary knowledge of metrics may test for himself this quality of certain passages in Lincoln's writings. It will be found that his best prose has as much of the modulation of rhythm as the best of Ruskin's, without the over-fluent character of the latter. (pp. 172-73)

[Yet] the final argument for [the musical character of Lincoln's prose compositions] is revealed in their thought-content. They fit De Quincey's description of the "literature of power." They move, but not so much by their beautiful words, like Poe's poems, as by the thought which commands the words. Lincoln is to be interpreted first of all as a man who brought powerful thought to bear upon the theme in which he was deeply interested. He wrote slowly, because he found that words were but feeble media for the expression of great consciousness and its atmosphere of feeling. Therefore he seems partial to simple, idiomatic language when it will more swiftly meet and carry his thought. It has been customary to mention the large proportion of Anglo-Saxon derived words in the **"Gettysburg Address."** . . . As a matter of fact, Lincoln, when he was in the writing mood, brooded over his words, tried his verbal resources to their utmost, and then chose the best he had in hand. His letter to Colonel Allen, in his young manhood, more than twenty-five years before the **"Gettysburg Address,"** shows a decided leaning toward words of foreign derivation, while his letters to his step-brother, Johnson, fifteen years later than the Allen letter, prefer words of English ancestry. Lincoln had little interest in the philology of language. His main concern was with the meaning and extent of his vocabulary, and his leading principle of composition seems to have been to use the expression, from whatever origin, that would satisfy the reader's or listener's understanding. His devotion to this principle, or method, sometimes led him into the use of words or phrases of less dignity than the context would call for.

There may be some question whether the actual words of the **"Gettysburg Address"** are chosen in every instance with as excellent discrimination as the thought indicated was conceived. It is, however, the special consciousness they embody that is the soul of the poetry they suggest. Lincoln's unique personality, the moral character of the great problem round which his political experience turned, his whole-souled sympathy for the welfare of the mass of mankind, together with his righteous hatred of special privilege and oppression of any kind, gave him the power, after the victories over Lee and Pemberton, to pen this ripened conception of democracy in America. In the Gettysburg speech, he seems to have taken the body of his conviction, derived from many elements of observation and study, and fashioned it, like a master artist, into a single life-like conception. His thought is sculptured more nearly after the lines of the classical than the Gothic. Like Angelo, he arrived at beauty by striking out the superfluous. (pp. 175-78)

The spiritual triumph of Abraham Lincoln is clothed in the unfading words which, in the *Second Inaugural*, tell the story of the Civil War with the same fidelity which the address at Gettysburg gave to the philosophy of American democracy. Both addresses unite, in Lincoln's characteristic manner, the intellectual and emotional elements of style. The first of these elements predominates in the dedication address; the second element is the more impressive in the inaugural. The theme of the earlier speech is directed to a single end. That of the inaugural has a double purpose: to comment upon the more striking events of the pending tragedy and to divine their meaning in the light of religion. The thought of the first is more elevated; that of the second is familiar and touching. The language of the one is a prophecy of freedom; that of the other is radiant with the Christian spirit of peace. One addresses the historic sense and discernment; the other appeals directly and powerfully to the heart. Both incite to high ideals of conduct, one in the accents of epic, the other in the voice of lyric, song.

In the first part of the *Second Inaugural,* one reads a truthful survey of the war. A parallel study is made of the motives and expectations of both sides. There is a certain staccato effect in the emotions that succeed each other as the sentences approach the relation of the terrible contest to the purposes of the Almighty. It was an unaccustomed step for a statesman to speak with such frankness and intimacy of a great war as God's means of purging a nation of its inveterate vices. He bears in his words the burden of shame long felt by those—by generations, even—whose spirit had bowed under the humiliation of human slavery in their midst. He speaks the prayer of a repentant nation "that this mighty scourge of war may speedily pass away." Was so fierce a slaughter, among men of the same race equally devoted to liberty, in accord with "those divine attributes which the believers in a living God always ascribe to him"? And was the blood poured out on the battlefields due to the judgment of the Lord, which is "true and righteous altogether"? Such was Lincoln's faith. He found no contradiction between that faith and that perfection of the human spirit which could battle with equal firmness and regret. With the picture of the death-grapple before him, he could still say:

> With malice toward none; with charity for all; with firmness in the right, as God gives us to see the right, let us strive on to finish the work we are in; to bind up the nation's wounds; to care for him who shall have borne the battle, and for his widow, and his orphan—to do all which may achieve a just and lasting peace among ourselves, and with all nations.

Lincoln's own modest commentary on the *Second Inaugural* was drawn out by a letter of appreciation from the distinguished journalist, Thurlow Weed. Lincoln's acknowledgment [March 15, 1865] is a precious bit of interpretation of his own feeling and purpose as he composed this remarkable state-paper:

> Dear Mr. Weed: Every one likes a compliment. Thank you for yours on my little notification speech and on the recent inaugural address. I expect the latter to wear as well as—perhaps better than—anything I have produced; but I believe it is not immediately popular. Men are not flattered by being shown that there has been a difference of purpose between the Almighty and them. To deny it, however, in this case is to deny that there is a God governing the world. It is a truth which I thought needed to be told, and, as whatever of humiliation there is in it falls most directly on myself, I thought others might afford for me to tell it.
>
> Truly yours,
>
> A. Lincoln.
>
> (pp. 188-91)

Luther Emerson Robinson, in his Abraham Lincoln as a Man of Letters, *1918. Reprint by G. P. Putnam's Sons, 1923, 344 p.*

H. L. MENCKEN (essay date 1922)

[*Mencken was one of the most influential social and literary critics in the United States during the early twentieth century. His strongly individualistic, irreverent outlook on life and his vigorous, invective-charged writing style helped establish the iconoclastic spirit of the Jazz Age and significantly shaped the direction of American literature. In his literary criticism, Mencken encouraged Amer-ican writers to shun the anglophilic, moralistic bent of the nineteenth century and to practice realism. In the following commentary on Lincoln's speeches, Mencken devotes special attention to the "Gettysburg Address." His remarks were originally published in 1922 in* Five Men at Random, Prejudices: Third Series.]

Like William Jennings Bryan, [Lincoln] was a dark horse made suddenly formidable by fortunate rhetoric. The [**Lincoln-Douglas Debates**] launched him, and the [*Cooper Union Speech*] got him the Presidency. His talent for emotional utterance was an acomplishment of late growth. His early speeches were mere empty fireworks—the hollow rhodomontades of the era. But in middle life he purged his style of ornament and it became almost baldly simple—and it is for that simplicity that he is remembered today. The [**"Gettysburg Address"**] is at once the shortest and the most famous oration in American history. Put beside it, all the whoopings of the Websters, Sumners and Everetts seem gaudy and silly. It is eloquence brought to a pellucid and almost gem-like perfection—the highest emotion reduced to a few poetical phrases. Nothing else precisely like it is to be found in the whole range of oratory. Lincoln himself never even remotely approached it. It is genuinely stupendous.

But let us not forget that it is poetry, not logic; beauty, not sense. Think of the argument in it. Put it into the cold words of everyday. The doctrine is simply this: that the Union soldiers who died at Gettysburg sacrificed their lives to the cause of self-determination—"that government of the people, by the people, for the people," should not perish from the earth. It is difficult to imagine anything more untrue. The Union soldiers in that battle actually fought *against* self-determination; it was the Confederates who fought for the right of their people to govern themselves. What was the practical effect of the battle of Gettysburg? What else than the destruction of the old sovereignty of the States, *i.e.,* of the people of the States? The Confederates went into battle free; they came out with their freedom subject to the supervision and veto of the rest of the country—and for nearly twenty years that veto was so effective that they enjoyed scarcely more liberty, in the political sense, than so many convicts in the penitentiary. (pp. 221-22)

H. L. Mencken, "Statesmen: Abraham Lincoln," in his A Mencken Chrestomathy, *Alfred A. Knopf, 1949, pp. 221-23.*

DANIEL KILHAM DODGE (essay date 1924)

[*Dodge examines Lincoln's public statements prior to his emergence as a national figure, comparing select elements of his early and later styles of public address.*]

In choosing his vocation Lincoln unconsciously paved the way for his career as orator and statesman. Having in mind the experience of Scott and Stevenson, of Bryant and Lowell, to mention only two examples each from English and American authors, we are apt to think of the profession of law as inimical to success in literature. We must remember, however, that in the early days of Illinois the practice of the law, with its regular semi-annual following of the circuit court from county seat to county seat, was something in the nature of an adventure, offering all the opportunity for the study of human nature that Dan Chaucer found in the motley company assembled at the Tabard Inn five hundred years ago. And Lincoln had much of the kindly, humorous, social nature that we attribute to the author of *The Canterbury Tales.* If he could not songs indite he could tell stories with rare skill and enjoyment and he never seemed to tire of communing with his fellow men of every degree. As a lawyer he made a careful study of human nature and his eminent success as a jury pleader—and he had no superior in this difficult art—was due far more to his knowledge of practical psychology than to his mastery of the principles of the law, profound as this latter was. In addressing Illinois juries, too, Lincoln developed a simplicity of expression that is reflected in the **"Gettysburg Address"** and the *Second Inaugural Address*. Another Illinoisian, who is still living and who is known for the clearness and simplicity of his spoken and written word, was once asked how he had developed his wonderful style. He replied that for many years he had been addressing farmers' institutes on scientific subjects related to agriculture and that he had tried to use terms that combined accuracy of scientific statement with simplicity of vocabulary. Something of the same combination may be found in the style of Lincoln. The daily practice of his profession in the county seats of the eighth Illinois district was the best possible preparation for the [**Lincoln-Douglas Debates**] of 1858 and the state papers of the early 'sixties. The simplicity of statement that was necessary in order to convince the juries of the early Illinois days is no less convincing to the most critical readers of Lincoln's speeches two generations after his voice has ceased to be heard.

Although the earliest specimen of Lincoln's political writings that has been preserved is not a speech at all, it may properly be considered in connection with his early political speeches, as it is a natural preparation for them. This is the "Communication" to voters, in which Lincoln presented his platform as a candidate for the first time for the Illinois state legislature, published in the Sangamon *Journal*, known later as the Springfield *Journal*, in 1832. (pp. 4-7)

[We] may find in [the style of the "Communication"] some of the elements that were developed and refined twenty years later. We note, in the first place, the clear thinking that is the basis of all clear writing. The paragraph construction is admirable, the theme of each paragraph being stated in the opening sentence and its development following in severe logical order. Some of the sentences are rather awkward and there is an occasional infelicitous phrase and commonplace thought, but it would be strange if this were not the case in so inexperienced and untrained a writer. The claim has been made, apparently on good authority, that some of the grammatical errors were corrected by a friend before publication. This, too, seems perfectly natural. Even in later speeches, though never in the state papers, we occasionally find solecisms and to the end of his life Lincoln showed a tendency to use the split infinitive and myself instead of I. The Illinois bar in those days was not as critical, in the minutiae of spoken English, at least, as it is to-day and grammatical slips would have made no special impression on the general public. (pp. 7-9)

The "Communication" sounds a personal note, which Lincoln in his later writings usually avoids: "But, if the good people in their wisdom shall see fit to keep me in the background, I have been too familiar with disappointment to be much chagrined." In addressing his friends and neighbors Lincoln allowed himself a freedom and intimacy of speech that would have been improper in his later and broader appeals. In spite of his indifference to what he regarded as unimportant conventions, Lincoln had a keen sense of propriety. He was always more concerned about principles than personalities and he appealed to reason rather than to prejudice. (pp. 11-12)

During the early period of his public speaking Lincoln showed a tendency that is in marked contrast to the simplicity and restraint of his later writings, a rhetorical tendency, which may fairly be regarded as a sort of infantile writer's disease, verbal mumps or measles. It will be recalled that Shakespeare shows a similar fondness for fine writing of a different sort in his earliest comedy, *Love's Labour's Lost*. This outbreak occurs, not in connection with the political speeches proper, but in a form which the later Lincoln seldom used—the occasional address. Lincoln might properly have paraphrased the words of Marc Antony and said, "I am no orator, as Webster or Everett is." Like Clay, he never seems to have sought occasions to speak in public and when he did speak he usually had some immediate end in view. He once said, during the presidential period, "I believe I shall never be old enough to speak without embarrassment when I have nothing to talk about." He spoke, not to entertain or to impress, but to persuade and convince his hearers. In his speaking he suggests the lawyer addressing the jury rather than an orator appearing before an audience. (pp. 18-19)

The earliest specimen of rhetorical speech that has been preserved is the address before the Young Men's Lyceum of Springfield, of January 23, 1837, and its subject is **"The Perpetuation of Our Political Institutions."** The opening sentence is what Lincoln himself might later have called "highfalutin'": "In the great journal of things happening under the sun, we, the American people, find our account running date of the nineteenth century." This eulogy of our country is more suggestive of Mr. Jefferson Brick than of Lincoln, as we know him now: "All the armies of Europe, Asia, and Africa, combined with all the treasure of the earth (our own excepted) in their military chest, with a Bonaparte for a commander, could not by force take a drink from the Ohio or make a track on the Blue Ridge in a trial of a thousand years."

But the speech is not all mere rhetoric, "full of sound and fury, signifying nothing." In the description of the fathers of the American Revolution there is a passage not unworthy of the later Lincoln at his best:

> They were a forest of great oaks; but the all-restless hurricane has swept over them and left only here and there a lonely trunk, despoiled of its verdure, shorn of its foliage, unshading and unshaded, to murmur in a few more gentle breezes, and to combat with its mutilated limbs a few more ruder storms, then to sink and be no more.

Here is a fine prose-rhythm together with a nice selection of words and an appeal to the historical imagination that is possible only to one gifted with a feeling for style of the first order. The concluding sentence, both in form and content, is wholly in the spirit of the later Lincoln: "Upon these let the proud fabric of freedom rest, as the rock for its basis; and as truly as has been said of the only greater institution, 'the gates of hell shall not prevail against it'."

But not only does the speech contain many purple patches like these, it is fully justified by its clearness and unity of thought. The main argument presented is the sanctity of law and order, a failure to honor which the speaker regards as a fatal blow to freedom. Lincoln never departed from this principle. No plea of expediency could ever urge him, as President, to support any measure however important, that, in his opinion, was not in agreement with the Constitution, though at times his understanding of constitutional limitations was severely criticized. (pp. 19-22)

In December, 1839, Lincoln made his first purely political speech that has been preserved and at the same time crossed swords with Stephen A. Douglas, nineteen years before the great Debates. . . . Although the speech resembles the Debates in its general style, being throughout serious and argumentative, it differs from them in subject matter, which was the national bank, of which Lincoln was a warm supporter, in opposition to the Democratic plan of the subtreasury. In one respect the speech is in marked contrast to the Debates in that it contains a highly rhetorical peroration. This difference is undoubtedly due to the fact that it was a carefully prepared speech, perhaps written out in full before its delivery, whereas the Debates were extempore, so far as the exact language was concerned. The rather hyperbolical style of the peroration reflects Lincoln's less severe taste from this early period. This brief extract will suffice to show its character:

> Many free countries have lost their liberty, and ours may lose hers: but if she shall, be it my proudest plume, not that I was the last to desert, but that I never deserted her. I know that the great volcano at Washington, aroused and directed by the evil spirt that reigns there, is belching forth the lava of political corruption in a current broad and deep, which is sweeping with frightful velocity over the whole length and breadth of the land, bidding fair to leave unscathed no green spot or living thing; while on its bosom are riding, like demons on the waves of hell, the imps of that evil spirit, and fiendishly taunting all those who dare resist its destroying course with the hopelessness of their effort; and, knowing this, I cannot deny that all may be swept away. Broken by it I, too, may be; bow to it I never will. The probability that we may fail in the struggle ought not to deter us from the support of a cause we believe to be just; it shall not deter me. If ever I feel the soul within me elevate and expand to those dimensions not wholly unworthy of its almighty Architect, it is when I contemplate the cause of my country, deserted by all the world beside, and I standing up boldly and alone, and hurling defiance at her victorious oppressors. . . . But if, after all, we shall fail, be it so. We still shall have the proud consolation of saying to our consciences, and to the departed shade of our country's freedom, that the cause approved of our judgment, and adored of our hearts, in disaster, in chains, in torture, in death, we never faltered in defending.
>
> (pp. 23-5)

Although Lincoln served only a single term in Congress, he made a number of speeches, one of which, really a stump speech, is distinguished by its markedly humorous character. This positive quality of his principal congressional speech affords an opportunity to note a negative quality of most of Lincoln's other speeches, including all his formal addresses. Famous as he was as a teller of funny stories and fond as he was at all times of illustrating a point in conversation by an appropriate anecdote, in his public speaking Lincoln is usually serious. He himself once explained his reason for abstaining from using this obvious help in the Debates, when urged to do so by a friend, by saying: "The occasion is too serious, the issues are too grave. I do not seek applause, or to amuse the people, but to convince them." As we have already noted, the persuasion of people, not their amusement, was always Lincoln's first purpose. As a political speaker he dealt with serious subjects at a critical period and he dealt with them in an appropriately serious and substantial manner. It is possible that in the Campaign Speeches, from 1840 to 1856, which have been reported in very small part and in fragmentary form, Lincoln resorted to funny stories to clinch his political arguments, but if he did so there is no record of the fact. (pp. 27-9)

[Lincoln's first speech before Congress] was delivered January 12, 1848, and it deals with the burning party question of that day—the Mexican War. Like most whigs, Lincoln was strongly opposed to the war, for which he could find no justification, and although he never failed to vote in favor of granting supplies to the army, he took advantage of every opportunity to voice his disapproval of the democratic policy. Although the speech is in the main a very clear and close argument against the President's war policy, it is occasionally relieved by passages of real beauty and imagination, as in the following:

> Let him remember he sits where Washington sat, and so remembering, let him answer as Washington would answer. As a nation should not, and the Almighty will not, be evaded, so let him attempt no evasion—no equivocation. . . . But if he cannot or will not do this— if on any pretense or no pretense he shall refuse or omit it—then I shall be fully convinced of what I more than suspect already—that he is deeply conscious of being in the wrong; that he feels the blood of this war, like the blood of Abel, is crying to heaven against him; that originally having some strong motive—what, I will not stop now to give my opinion concerning—to involve the two countries in a war, and trusting to escape scrutiny by fixing the public gaze upon the exceeding brightness of military glory—that attractive rainbow that rises in showers of blood, that serpent's eye that charms to destroy—he plunged into it, and was swept on and on till, disappointed in his calculation of the ease with which Mexico might be subdued, he now finds himself he knows not where. How like the half-insane mumbling of a fever dream is the whole part of his late message.

The conclusion is no less effective and severe than the passage just quoted:

> After all this, this same President gives a long message, without showing us that as to the end he himself has even an imaginary conception. As I have before said, he knows not where he is. He is a bewildered, confounded, and miserably perplexed man. God grant he may be able to show there is not something about his conscience more painful than his mental perplexity.

The note of strong, personal invective heard here is one seldom sounded by Lincoln, who, both in his law practice and in his public speaking, relied in the main upon sober argument. Even in the Debates, where the temptation to indulge in personalities must have been especially great, he seldom attacks Douglas.

In even more striking contrast to his usual form of oratory is the speech of July 27, 1848, entitled, **"General Taylor and the Veto."** It is really a stump speech and distinctly humorous and at times ironical. The personal note of the earlier speech is again sounded, not in the form of invective but of ridicule. The person thus assailed is the democratic candidate for the presidency, General Cass. A single extract will suffice to show the character of the criticism:

> But I have introduced General Cass' accounts here chiefly to show the wonderful physical capacities of the man. They show that he not only did the labor of several men at the same time, but that he often did it at several places, many hundreds of miles apart, at the same time. And at eating, too, his capacities are shown to be quite as wonderful. From October, 1821, to May, 1822, he ate ten rations a day in Michigan, ten rations a day here in Washington, and near five dollars' worth a day on the road between the two places! And then there is an important discovery in his example—the art of being paid for what one eats, instead of having to pay for it. Hereafter, if any nice, young man should owe a bill which he cannot pay in any other way, he can just board it out. Mr. Speaker, we have all heard of the animal standing in doubt between two stacks of hay and starving to death. The like of that would never happen to General Cass. Place the stacks a thousand miles apart, he would stand stock-still midway between them, and eat them both at once, and the green grass along the line would be apt to suffer, too, at the same time. By all means make him President, gentlemen. He will feed you bounteously—if—if there is any left after he shall have helped himself.
>
> (pp. 30-5)

During his second year in Congress Lincoln presented two resolutions of immense interest, the first favoring compensated emancipation of slaves in the District of Columbia and freedom for all children of slave mothers born in the District on or after January 1, 1850. Although the House refused to act favorably on this suggestion, this resolution may be regarded as the first step in the direction that culminated in the passing of the thirteenth amendment to the Constitution, abolishing slavery throughout the United States. The second resolution, presented in September, expressed sympathy with the cause of Hungarian freedom. . . . Like Clay, Lincoln had a keen sense of justice and a passionate love of liberty and the resolutions, which were almost certainly written as well as presented by him, expressed the sincere feelings of the speaker. They read in part as follows:

> *Resolved,* That in their present glorious struggle for liberty, the Hungarians command our highest admiration and have our warmest sympathy.
>
> *Resolved,* That they have our most ardent prayers for their speedy triumph and final success.

Owing to political conditions Lincoln was not renominated for Congress, but during his single term he achieved a reputation, both on the floor and in committee, equaling that of many of the oldest members. Apparently he could always command a hearing and, although he was in the minority and most of the measures supported by him failed of passage, there is ample evidence that he was one of the most popular members of the Lower House. (pp. 35-7)

The main significance of the congressional period, so far as this study is concerned, lies in the fact that it brought Lincoln in close personal touch with many of the whig leaders of the day and introduced him as a speaker to a larger and more varied audience than he had hitherto been able to command. During the early years of his political career Lincoln had developed into one of the leading politicians of Illinois. From now on he must be regarded as an important national figure. (p. 39)

> *Daniel Kilham Dodge, in his* Abraham Lincoln: Master of Words, *D. Appleton and Company, 1924, 178 p.*

VERNON LOUIS PARRINGTON (essay date 1927)

[*An American historian, biographer, and critic, Parrington is best known for his unfinished literary history of the United States,* Main Currents in American Thought. *Though modern scholars disagree with many of his conclusions, they view Parrington's work as a significant first attempt at fashioning an intellectual history of America based on a broad interpretive basis. In the following excerpt from* Main Currents, *Parrington focuses on the relationship between style and emotion in Lincoln's speeches.*]

[Lincoln] was rarely eloquent—never after the ornate fashion of the time; and the bits of Hebraic poetry that have come to be associated with his name are singularly few and belong to the last years of his life. His usual style was plain homespun, clear and convincing, but bare of imagery and lacking distinction of phrase. The thought seems to break into speech hesitatingly, in the way of a man visibly seeking to adapt his words to his meaning. Matter he judged to be of greater significance than manner. Few men who have risen to enduring eloquence have been so little indebted to rhetoric. Very likely his plainness of style was the result of deliberate restraint, in keeping with the simplicity of his nature. When he let himself go he discovered a well of poetry in his heart. When he chose he could even play the rhetorician. In those rare moments when he put caution behind him, his words fell into a stately rhythm that suggests the orator. (p. 151)

But he did not often let himself go. As one reads his speeches one feels that an English diffidence held him back—this and the strong prose of his environment. Like a true Anglo-Saxon he was reluctant to speak out, afraid to let his emotions seize upon his speech. Only at the last did that diffidence yield to complete unconsciousness. The [**"Gettysburg Address"**] and the *Second Inaugural* are marked by the sincerity and self-effacement that ennobled the words of John Brown in the Virginia court-room—it is the eloquence which rises from the heart when life has been felt in its tragic reality, an eloquence that Webster could not rise to. Such words come only to those who have been purified by fire; they are the distillation of bitter experience. But the mass of his speeches are in quite another manner—that of the simple, everyday world that bred him. He had none of the itch of publicity that afflicts the second-rate mind. Webster was a magnificent poseur; Edward Everett repeated the same academic oration a hundred times; but Lincoln was too modest to pose and too honest to turn parrot and speak by rote. He was a man who loved to talk with his neighbors in homely metaphor, and it was then that his thought clothed itself in whimsical humor. He did not wear his heart on his sleeve, but like Mark Twain he let it slip out in a witticism. (p. 152)

Vernon Louis Parrington, "Two Spokesmen of the West," in his Main Currents in American Thought, An Interpretation of American Literature from the Beginnings to 1920: The Romantic Revolution in America, 1800-1860, *Vol. 2, Harcourt Brace Jovanovich, 1927, pp. 138-53.*

WILLIAM E. BARTON   (essay date 1930)

[*In the following excerpt from his* Lincoln at Gettysburg, *Barton briefly reflects on the fame of Lincoln's dedication address.*]

Abraham Lincoln delivered addresses which, even as read at this distance, display the power of the true orator; but the speeches that made him famous, those that displayed his power to inform the mind, convince the reason, sway the passions and determine the action of his audiences, are little read now. The world did not fail to note but it does not now remember his real orations. That part of the world that listened to his "lost speech" at Bloomington, his State Fair speech at Springfield, his Peoria address and his Cooper Union masterpiece was deeply moved by his utterance; but these orations now, in thick volumes diligently perused by the special student, are, for the general reader, "folioed and forgot." Abraham Lincoln never suspected that almost the only scrap of oratory by which the world would remember him would be his **"Gettysburg Address."**

Abraham Lincoln said at Gettysburg, "The world will little note nor long remember what we say here, but it can never forget what they did here." He was never more mistaken in all his life. The men who fought on that red field did more than they knew while they were fighting; more than they understood after they had won the victory. They did more even than Lincoln realized four months later as he stood on the spot and paid tribute to their sacrifice. But memorable as were the deeds they wrought there, the world will longer remember the words he spoke there. The **"Gettysburg Address"** will be printed and recited and translated and cast in durable bronze long after it shall have become necessary to append foot-notes to explain that Gettysburg was neither a battle in the Revolutionary War, nor a field somewhere amid the poppies of Flanders. Deeds are memorable, but words rightly chosen and well spoken are immortal.

> We and the gods depart,
> And all things else except the Word.

And yet at the time it seemed wholly possible that Lincoln's statement might be literally true. The world appeared not to note the words he uttered, and it is not certain that a majority of those who heard him expected that what he said would be long remembered. The auditors saw the President, whom most of them had never seen before; they heard him in his brief and subordinate part in an important celebration; so much they were not likely to forget; but not all of them thought his words to be significant. No one doubts their significance now.

Many of the battle-fields of the Civil War are almost forgotten. Bull Run is a place of farms and forests. Shiloh is as desolate as the site of the ancient sanctuary whose name it bears. Appomattox has been reconquered by the wilderness. But Gettysburg lives. Vicksburg, fought on the same days, can be and is declared by competent military authorities to have been more notable as a battle and more significant as a victory than Gettysburg; it certainly is not of negligible importance in comparison with the latter; but Vicksburg is not a place of pilgrimage as Gettysburg is. Innumerable paths lead the tourist and the imagination to Gettysburg. What makes Gettysburg immortal is less the military victory than the speech of Lincoln. His words already serve to give immortality to memorable deeds. The world has nearly forgotten what brave men did on many another battle-field of the war that saved the Union and overthrew slavery, but not Gettysburg. The world remembers longer and more vividly what they did there because it so definitely remembers what he said there. (pp. 124-26)

William E. Barton, in his Lincoln at Gettysburg: What He Intended to Say; What He Said; What He Was Reported to Have Said; What He Wished He Had Said, *The Bobbs-Merrill Company, 1930, 263 p.*

EDGAR LEE MASTERS   (essay date 1931)

[*Masters was one of the first major twentieth-century American authors to use the theories of modern psychology to examine human thought and motivation. A prolific writer, he is best known for the monumental poetic cycle* Spoon River Anthology, *a collection of free-verse epitaphs on the men and women buried in a small-town churchyard. Masters also was one of the first biographers to consider Lincoln in an unfavorable light; in the excerpt below from his study* Lincoln: The Man, *he condemns the* Second Inaugural Address *as an amalgam of hypocrisy, sophistry, and "Hebraic Puritan" superstition.*]

With the background of Sherman's march to the sea, with all its horrors, and with the pathetic futility of the [peace] conference in Hampton Roads still fresh in Lincoln's memory, he stood up on March 4, 1865, and delivered his **Second Inaugural.** When he said, "With malice toward none, with charity for all, with firmness in the right as God gives us to see the right," he was too saturated with the hypocrisy of Hebraic-Puritanism to realize the enormity of such blasphemy against human nature and human reason. The gigantic inconsistency of such words was totally unperceived by his mind, now fed by war, and by imperial power, by intellectual arrogance completely reared out of old humilities often professed, until his dual nature no longer knew its divided self, if indeed what was insensitive and egocentric, and triple-hardened resolution, in it was not incomplete possession of a manner of thinking that had been double-faced all along, many colored, but which hid its change of hue by a genius for mimesis. Was it not fixed now in the black of sternest Puritanism?

Long years before Herndon had read to Lincoln one of Theodore Parker's sermons, and after doing so made this shallow revivalistic observation: "I have always noticed that ill-gotten wealth does no man any good. This is as true of nations as of individuals. I believe that all the ill-gotten gain wrenched by us from the negro through his enslavement will eventually be taken from us, and we will be set back where we began." Lincoln thought my prophecy rather direful." This Hebraic-Puritan idea took root in Lincoln's mind; and so in his **Second Inaugural** he developed it into these demonical words: "The Almighty has his own purposes. 'Woe unto the world because of offenses! for it must needs be that offenses come; but woe to that man by whom the offense cometh.' If we shall suppose that American slavery is one of those offenses which, in the providence of God, must needs come, but which having continued through his appointed time, he now wills to remove, and that he gives to both North and South this terrible war, as the woe due to those by whom the offense came, shall we discern therein any departure from those divine attributes which the believers in a living God always ascribe to him?" Not Jonathan Edwards in

Part of the handwritten text from which Lincoln delivered the ''Gettysburg Address.''

his maddest Calvinism ever uttered words to equal these of Lincoln. They mean that slavery, which the New World did not want, had to pay for it in agony and blood, but that the debt had to be paid by those who did not contract the debt. They mean that a just God willed this, and effected his will by a war which cost the country from 750,000 to 1,000,000 lives and $22,000,000,000 of money. If God was now willing the removal of slavery it was through men like Lincoln, who had given the North and the South this war, without any need for it at all, and who within a few weeks of the day of this Inaugural willed that the war should go on, and that the peace proposals of Stephens should come to nothing save upon terms of ignominious capitulation, without promises or assurances of any sort as to the fate of the South. There are only two ways of interpreting these words of Lincoln: either one interprets them as a Christian and accepts what he said as true and just, because it is taken from the Bible; or else one has retained his reasoning faculties, and abhors them as the incredible out-pouring of a mind at last completely fanaticized.

Just preceding these words Lincoln said in his [**Second Inaugural**]: ''It may seem strange that any men should dare to ask a just God's assistance in wringing their bread from the sweat of other men's faces; but let us judge not, that we be not judged.'' Let us not judge, but let us put our judgment into the obscene mouth of the Jewish Jehovah. Let us utter the

monstrous curse, but have no responsibility in it. Let us not judge; but let us prosecute with utter remorselessness the war, just as if we had passed a judgment upon the South. Killing, and burning, and conquering can be as effectually done without words of condemnation as with them. In truth, to look daggers, and to use them, but not to speak them may be a way of keeping the victim ignorant of what the strife is about. By not judging in express words, however, we shall not be judged. Let us be careful therefore what we say, lest we take the wrong stand for God's work. Do God's work and keep a shut mouth. Who at the time of war exhaustion had time to disentangle so many irrelevant ideas double criss-crossed with so many irrelevant conclusions, and sealed together with Hebraic-Puritan poetry? Today a whole volume could be written to separate and lay out for view the complexed strands of this sophistry and su-perstition. Consider by way of one wholly revealing glance how such moral hypocrisy as this would have fallen upon an audience of Pericles' Athens. If it be strength to utter words that only great analysis can blow to nothing, and since great analysis cannot exist in vacuo, but must have an audience, then Lincoln had strength of mind. Here he was to the very last, when thousands were dropping with fatigue, and many who could have put him to flight were either dead or silenced by war madness, still uttering the puerilities of his young manhood and of his first message to Congress. He was thus a strong man; and indeed a stubborn man. To a correspondent who wrote Lincoln in compliment upon his inaugural address he replied that he expected it to wear as well as anything that he had produced. But ''men are not flattered by being shown that there has been a difference of purpose between the Almighty and them.'' That is, there has been no judgment, but just a showing that God condemned the South! (pp. 471-73)

Edgar Lee Masters, in his Lincoln: The Man, *Dodd, Mead & Company, Inc., 1931, 520 p.*

ROY P. BASLER   (essay date 1939)

[Basler, a noted Lincoln scholar, explores Lincoln's use of tech-nical rhetorical devices.]

Repetition, grammatical parallelism, and antithesis may be considered the most obvious technical devices of Lincoln's general style. He uses these devices with such frequency and variety of effect that it seems to have been a consistent habit of his mind to seek repetitive sequences in both diction and sentence structure for the alignment of his thought. That these devices were the result of Lincoln's deliberate seeking for an emphasis and simplicity which would prove effective with the common man we may infer from the often repeated testimony given by William H. Herndon: ''he used to bore me terribly by his methods, processes, manners, etc., etc. Mr. Lincoln would doubly explain things to me that needed no explana-tion. . . . Lincoln's ambition in this line was this: he wanted to be distinctly understood by the common people. . . .'' This inference seems to be strengthened by the fact that Lincoln's favorite ideas—those which appear again and again in his works and which he turned over and over in his mind through months and even years—and his most memorable phrases almost in-variably betray this repetitive pattern.

The most rigid example of Lincoln's use of parallelism is the letter written in reply to Horace Greeley's ''Prayer of Twenty Millions.'' Here the parallelism is not merely a sentence pat-tern, but a pattern for the whole letter. It arranges with such geometric precision the measured parts of a complex idea that an almost deceptive simplicity is the result. In no other piece can one find quite the heavy, reduplicating blows which Lincoln employs as, over Greeley's shoulder, he speaks to the average citizen:

> As to the policy I "seem to be pursuing," as you say, I have not meant to leave any one in doubt.
>
> I would save the Union. I would save it the shortest way under the Constitution. The sooner the national authority can be restored, the nearer the Union will be "the Union as it was." If there be those who would not save the Union unless they could at the same time save slavery, I do not agree with them. My paramount object in this struggle is to save the Union, and is not either to save or to destroy slavery. If I could save the Union without freeing any slave, I would do it; and if I could save it by freeing all the slaves, I would do it; and if I could save it by freeing some and leaving others alone, I would also do that. What I do about slavery and the colored race, I do because I believe it helps to save the Union; and what I forbear, I forbear because I do not believe it would help to save the Union. I shall do less whenever I shall believe what I am doing hurts the cause, and I shall do more whenever I shall believe doing more will help the cause. I shall try to correct errors when shown to be errors, and I shall adopt new views so fast as they shall appear to be true views.
>
> I have here stated my purpose according to my view of official duty; and I intend no modification of my oft-expressed personal wish that all men everywhere could be free.

For a more subtle use of parallel pattern in conjunction with antithesis we may consider a paragraph from the [*Cooper Union Speech*]. As in the above, Lincoln here employs a characteristic amount of repetition, chiefly of the text which he has taken from a speech delivered by Stephen A. Douglas. Throughout the address Lincoln quotes this sentence in part and in whole, until it becomes at this climax the fulcrum of his antithesis.

> If any man at this day sincerely believes that a proper division of local from Federal authority, or any part of the Constitution, forbids the Federal Government to control as to slavery in the Federal territories, he is right to say so, and to enforce his position by all truthful evidence and fair argument which he can. But he has no right to mislead others, who have less access to history, and less leisure to study it, into the false belief that "our fathers who framed the government under which we live" were of the same opinion—thus substituting falsehood and deception for truthful evidence and fair argument. If any man at this day sincerely believes "our fathers who framed the government under which we live" used and applied principles, in other cases, which ought to have led them to understand that a proper division of local from Federal authority, or some part of the Constitution, forbids the Federal Government to control as

to slavery in the Federal territories, he is right to say so. But he should, at the same time, brave the responsibility of declaring that, in his opinion, he understands their principles better than they did themselves; and especially should he not shirk that responsibility by asserting that they "understood the question just as well, and even better, than we do now."

Further, Lincoln's writings abound in single sentence antithesis such as the following: "I have endured a great deal of ridicule without much malice; and have received a great deal of kindness, not quite free from ridicule."

This conjunction of grammatical parallelism with antithesis is natural enough, and where one is found to be characteristic of an author's style we may expect the other. But with Lincoln such antithesis seems not merely a technique, but like parallelism, a habit of mind. His faculties seized upon differences in opinion and contrasts in fact. In the [**Lincoln-Douglas Debates**] he rarely missed a chance to turn to advantage the contrast between himself and his opponent in appearance, and in personality, and in thought. It is perhaps to this faculty for perceiving and stressing antithesis as much as to any other quality of Lincoln's mind that we may trace whatever victory he won over Douglas. Even Douglas's so-called "Freeport Heresy" was the result of Lincoln's seizing upon an antithetical idea and literally placing it in his opponent's mouth: that a territorial legislature had not the power to exclude slavery, but that slavery could not exist in a territory unless the people desired it and gave it protection by legislation. (pp. 167-70)

On this basic pattern of parallelism in thought, Lincoln often elaborated a distinctly poetical cadence which suggests comparison with the cadenced prose of the seventeenth century. Although balanced rhythms with caesurae are indigenous to English poetry and perhaps to English prose, Hebrew literature through the King James Bible probably provided the literary examples which Lincoln knew best; and to his fondness for biblical phraseology we may trace at least a part of his mastery of the technique.

In his emotive, lyrical passages balance becomes most striking, as it enriches his melancholy reflections or his fervent appeals to the hearts of his audience. Within single sentences it occurs in two forms: in a balanced sentence of two parts with a caesura approximately midway; and in a series of phrases or clauses separated by caesurae and grouped in balanced staves of two or more phrase units. Within an individual phrase or clause internal balance and parallelism often occur. As an example of the first type, we may consider the following sentence typical:

> The grateful task commonly vouchsafed to the mournful living, of casting the mantle of charitable forgetfulness over the faults of the lamented dead, is denied us; for although it is much to say, for any of the erring family of man, we believe we may say, that he whom we deplore was faultless.

As an example of the second type, we may take the concluding sentence of the *Second Inaugural Address*:

> With malice toward none; with charity for all; with firmness in the right, as God gives us to see the right, let us strive on to finish the work we are in; to bind up the nations wounds; to care for him who shall have borne the battle,

and for his widow, and his orphan—to do all which may achieve and cherish a just and lasting peace among ourselves, and with all nations.

Sometimes this rhythm pattern extends over an entire group of sentences, or even the whole of a short address. The **"Farewell Address"** is an example:

I. *My Friends:* No one, not in my situation, can appreciate my feeling of sadness at this parting.
II. To this place,
   and the kindness of these people,
   I owe everything.
III. A. Here I have lived a quarter of a century,
      and have passed from a young to an old man.
   B. Here my children have been born,
      and one lies buried.
IV. I now leave,
   not knowing when or whether ever I may return,
   with a task before me greater than that which rested upon Washington.
V. A. Without the assistance of that Divine Being who ever attended him, I cannot succeed.
   B. With that assistance, I cannot fail.
VI. A. Trusting in Him who can go with me,
      and remain with you, and be everywhere for good,
      let us confidently hope that all will yet be well.
   B. To His care commending you,
      as I hope in your prayers you will commend me,
      I bid you an affectionate farewell.

In this address there are two parallel patterns, of thought and of rhythm. Within and between some sentences (III, for example) they become identical. In others they merely coincide (V or VI). Between others there is a compensating balance of phrases and pauses, although the thought pattern is reversed from periodic to loose structure, and the rhythm pattern is varied (as II is to IV). The only sentence which is without a compensating rhythm is the first, which stands alone as a topic statement. Within this general pattern of close parallels there is enough variety in individual sentences to avoid monotony but sufficient regularity of rhythm patterns to produce distinct cadence, in some phrases approximating loose metrical effect.

As these balanced rhythms sometimes approach meter in their regularity, Lincoln tends to heighten their effect with an occasional metrical phrase or sentence. Such phrases occur most frequently in perorations or passages of high emotional effect. As examples we may take a phrase from the *Second Inaugural Address* as quoted above— "... to do all which may achieve and cherish a just and lasting peace among ourselves ..."; or from the **"Gettysburg Address"**—"The world will little note nor long remember what we say here"; or from the *First Inaugural Address*—"The mystic chords of memory, stretching from every battlefield and patriot grave to every living heart and hearthstone...."

Repetition of sounds, as well as words, is another marked characteristic of his style. For the obvious purpose of emphasis, the reiteration of words in the letter to Greeley is typical of his habit of repeating key words. Along with this Lincoln often employs in poetic flashes alliteration, assonance, and even rime sounds. If we refer to the **"Farewell Address,"** quoted above, we find a typical sequence of alliterated key words in the first sentence: "friends ... situation ... appreciate ... feeling ... sadness ... parting," and in the following sentences, "place ... people; born ... buried," etc.

In the **"Gettysburg Address"** these several varieties of repetition provide an effect unique in Lincoln's prose. Computation shows that of the two hundred and seventy-two words in the address nearly half (one hundred and thirty-two, to be exact) are repetitions. For example, the pronoun *we* occurs ten times; *here,* eight times. Recurring in a variety of positions and with changing emphasis, they furnish Lincoln's theme of the preservation of democracy with a pointed meaning—*we, here.* His abundance of *that's* has been lamented even by those who praise him most. W. E. Barton, in a generally good analysis of the address, makes the natural comment that "possibly if he had thought of it he could have substituted other words in a few instances." But Lincoln did, apparently, think of it. He changed the only *that* which he could find a substitute for without jeopardizing his pattern and shifting his point of view. "The unfinished work *that* they have thus far so nobly advanced," which occurs in his first draft, he changed to "work *which*...." Instead of avoiding the word, Lincoln deliberately added it as he made his revisions, three times changing his original phrasing: "a portion of it" to "a portion of that field"; "that the nation" to "that that nation"; "This we may in all propriety do" to "It is altogether fitting and proper that we should do this." Whether we like it or not, we are confronted with the fact that Lincoln deliberately, and I think with full consciousness of the effect, chose this close parallelism and obvious reiteration which others surely would have avoided even at the expense of emphasis and point of view.

In addition to this reiterative pattern Lincoln uses more abundantly in this address than anywhere else alliteration, assonance, and rime-sound repetition. With these devices indicated by italics, and repetitions of key words by parentheses, the oral peculiarities of the address become apparent:

> *Four score* and *seven* years ago our *fathers* brought *forth* on this *continent* a *new nation, conceived* in liberty and dedicated to the *proposition* that all men are *created* equal.
>
> Now we are *engaged* in a *great civil war,* testing whether that (nation), or any (nation) so (*conceived*) and so (dedicated), can long *endure.* We are met on a (great) battle*field* of that (war). We have come to (dedicate) a *portion* of that (*field*) as a *final* resting-*place* for those who here gave their *lives* that that (nation) might *live.* It is altogether *fitting* and *proper* that we should to this.

(pp. 170-75)

In the *Second Inaugural Address* the sentence which some of Lincoln's critics have lamented as a pardonable lapse seems, in the light of this investigation, more likely to have been a deliberate choice: "Fondly do we hope—fervently do we pray—that this mighty scourge of war may speedily pass away."

Although it seems undeniable that Lincoln was conscious of sound effects, his choice of words seems to have been guided primarily by other values: meaning more than sound or connotation, concrete words more than abstract words, current idiom more than authoritarian nicety. So much has been written on the qualities of exactness, clarity, and simplicity in his style that it seems unnecessary to stress them here. They are, however, the qualities of prose excellence wherever it is met with, and as such hardly set Lincoln's style apart from that of Edmund Burke, though they do, in their degree, set his style apart from that of Stephen A. Douglas or that of William H. Seward.

Important and obvious as these qualities are, the very meat and bread of his thought, one may wonder whether Lincoln's memorable passages are remembered today because of them, or because of the unique effects of arrangement, rhythm, and sound which accompany them. (p. 175)

Roy P. Basler, "Abraham Lincoln's Rhetoric," in American Literature, Vol. 11, No. 2, May, 1939, pp. 167-82.

BERNARD DeVOTO (essay date 1940)

[*DeVoto, an editor of the* Saturday Review of Literature *and longtime contributor to* Harper's Magazine, *was a highly controversial literary critic and historian. A man whose thought enraged much of America's literary establishment during the 1930s and 1940s, he was frequently motivated by anger at authors he considered ignorant of American life and history. In the excerpt below, DeVoto discusses the source and significance of the Lincoln legend in the United States.*]

Through the greater part of 1939 Mr. Sherwood's *Abe Lincoln in Illinois* played to packed houses. Hollywood issued its version of Mr. Sherwood's play and made *Young Lincoln* a venture of its own. When the year ended another Lincoln play was in preparation, two scholars were co-operating on an important biography, and Mr. Carl Sandburg's *The War Years* . . . had begun a career certain to be momentous. The publishing business has a superstition that all Lincoln books make money, but such a heightening as this can no more be explained by economic determinism than the Civil War can be. There is only one explanation for this intensified interest in a President who has been dead for three-quarters of a century: that it is an invocation. At a time when American democracy has reached a crisis which many think it cannot survive, the American people have invoked the man who, by general consent, represents the highest reach of the American character and who, in that earlier crisis, best embodied the strength of our democracy. (p. 333)

Grave men have told us that . . . [the Lincoln legend] is in danger of becoming a christology. That anxiety may be dismissed. In the clear light Lincoln is a man whom anyone may look at, and though there is so much of him that no one has yet succeeded in seeing all there is, though the mystery that accompanies all high endeavor and great events will make him forever mysterious, the basis of our national reverence is simple and easily expressed. What America finds in Lincoln is confirmation of the best it has dared to believe of itself. There he is, the American, the man who was adequate for the task appointed, who grew when there was need for growth, who found the strength required, who seized the hour and subdued it. In him the democratic experience vindicates the democratic belief. His life, his understanding, and his triumph compose a symbol which stands for the justification of American democracy.

Herndon tells us that he was one of the limestone men, a common enough type; in the great central valley that is our true melting pot there were many who looked like him, and in truth there are portraits of his antagonist, Jefferson Davis, which could be, except for the goatee, mistaken for his portrait. Herndon, who spent twenty-five years in association with Lincoln and the rest of his life studying him, thought that Lincoln did not exceed or surpass the type but only brought it to full development. "Lincoln is unknown and possibly always will be," Herndon said, but he meant that Lincoln revealed himself to no one, that he kept his secrets. Herndon associated that secrecy with the loneliness of the forest lands where Lincoln was born, which may also be charged with at least some part of the melancholy that is as basic in him as the laughter, the melancholy that was close to insanity but had its part in armoring him against a strain such as no other President has been called upon to endure. Strong and weak, Herndon's antitheses run on, sad and cheerful, good-natured but capable of a terrible anger. All that went into the crucible, together with his ruthlessness in using men for his own ends, his willingness to think of men as tools which could be discarded when he had finished with them.

You can find in Lincoln nearly any quality that is human, nearly any trait that is called American, and there is so much of him that he continues to be "unknown." The sum made him superior to his associates and opponents, and the larger part of his superiority was sheer intelligence. From the beginning to the end, he is the better man, the better mind. From the backwoods circuits there slowly emerges a lawyer superior to his colleagues in clarifying issues and manipulating personalities. From the debris of the Whig party and the chaos of developing Republicanism there emerges an artisan who works more skillfully than those round him with the raw stuff of politics, and who sees farther ahead to where things unregarded by others now will be working out when their time comes. From the . . . [**Lincoln-Douglas Debates**] there emerges a mind much less deluded, much more realistic, and infinitely more capable of understanding how democratic desires become democratic causes. And once he is in Washington and freed to his destiny, his superiority is manifest, incontestable, and enormous. He is superior to anything in the Confederacy, superior to his Cabinet, to his Congress, to his supporters equally with his opponents, even to his generals.

Warmed by prairie earth, rooted in human tragedy, his intelligence was at once deeply intuitive and rigorously rational, and both qualities were anchored fast to the thing that *is*. He occupied himself with the possible, and he did not ask men to be more than he had learned they were. He had logic, but he was impatient with abstractions. The theoretical and the ideal might be very fine, but what, practically, could be done; what, practically, would the human material prove to be capable of? Jefferson Davis, implored by his generals to find food and munitions for their armies, replied with brilliant dissertations in logistics; Lincoln reorganized the service of supply and saw to it that the Treasury raised funds. Davis governed and made war like a geometer, Lincoln like an artisan in human lives. Charles Sumner and the associated intellectuals of the North wanted to abide by the ideal no matter if the war were lost and the nation destroyed; Lincoln would save the Union slave or free or half slave and half free. Seward came into office with a set of scale-drawn blueprints for the conduct of war and peace and a plan for foreign relations that satisfied the furthermost requirements of extrapolation. Either would have destroyed the United States in six months. Lincoln took hold of them and war, peace, and foreign relations became a controlled pragmatism, the next thing was done next, there was no commitment to the ideal plan; there were only the immediate dictates of the end in view.

That end was the preservation of the United States. He would save the Union. Some have told us that his reverence for the idea of union was a mystical thing, but there was no mysticism in it, there was only recognition of geography and of what two centuries and a half of American civilization had established.

Almost unanimously the intelligence of the eleven Confederate States was committed to a paradox in logic, an idea flatly falsified by the facts of experience, a miscalculation in judgment, and a misunderstanding so blatant that history sees it afterward as Lincoln saw it beforehand, as a delusion. Make war on us, he told them before they made war, fight it through to victory, establish your monstrosity—and it will all have to be done over again. The land will remain, the river valleys and the mountains and the prairies, the frontiers, the trade routes, and the membrane of interdependent lives they control. You cannot have a Europe in the continental area of the United States, you cannot have a South America, a Central America, or even a Confederacy. It is determined before you begin, it was determined when the glaciers retreated. And alternatively, as for the forms of government that rationalize the geography of God, they mean, if they mean anything, just what they say. If government is by the people, then it is by the people. If it is necessary for the people to assert their institutions through that lesser paradox—war in defense of majority rule—then so be it. How long can a nation endure which was conceived as the constitutional expression of popular will? If you say the word, we shall see.

That was the simplicity he fixed his eyes on, the consideration to which he made all others yield. It was enough. The ordeal began, the forces of disintegration were loosed, and with them were loosed all that goes into war and civil anarchy. There was the Confederacy to defeat; there were also, in the North, the violence of a thousand conflicting interests loosed in an interior war, the rise of despotisms, factions, fanaticisms, graft, treachery, treason, the full baseness and evil of human nature molten in a chaos which could be constrained within the established forms only—as it proved—by the character and intelligence of Lincoln. He met Washington in wartime as he had met Springfield in peace. He had, Swett says, "the most exalted tact and the wisest discrimination." He had also the fortitude to endure, the patience to let things happen and meet them as they came, the tenacity to let events show their shape, the realism to accept the means at hand, use them, abandon them when they would serve no further, find new ones, and keep on. A personal fatality spared him animosity and he had no need for retaliation. (pp. 334-36)

He did the next thing. The Border States must be kept in the Union; he kept them there. The North must be united in support of the war and kept united; never mistaking mob emotion for the public will, as his finest advisers sometimes did, he achieved and maintained that unity. The South must be subjugated by diplomatic, military, and economic means; he found the means. Then, because you could not have two nations in the United States, it followed that you could not have a half-conquering and half-conquered nation, and he was taking steps to repair the Union he had preserved when death caught up with him. Throughout this time there were plenty of occasions when he erred, but few in which his judgment was not proved better than the best offered as advice, and none in which he did not learn wisdom for the future.

That is his fascination. He is the stuff of American life shaping to the need. His ignorance becomes understanding, his fumbling becomes mastery, his weakness becomes strength. His uncouthness refines into spiritual greatness. As the necessity is laid on him he rises to it. The country lawyer becomes the greatest popular leader whom history knows. When American democracy reaches its crisis and needs a "saviour and a great one," out of its native earth, its native shrewdness and reality

and common sense, it produces Abraham Lincoln, a backwoods politician and one of the greatest statesmen in all history. . . .

He is the highest expression of American democracy. Of the democracy that survived its test. Government by the people did not perish from the earth. In the most terrible time that America has known democracy found formed within itself the instrument that was needed to save it. That is why, these days, we are invoking Father Abraham. (p. 336)

> *Bernard DeVoto, "Father Abraham," in* Harper's *Magazine, Vol. 180, February, 1940, pp. 333-36.*

JACQUES BARZUN (essay date 1959)

[*Barzun is a French-born American educator and writer who has produced distinguished works in several fields, including history, culture, musicology, literary criticism, and biography. His contributions to these various disciplines are contained in such classics of modern scholarship as* Darwin, Marx, Wagner: Critique of a Heritage, Berlioz and the Romantic Century, The House of the Intellect, *and the biography* A Stroll with William James. *In the following excerpt, Barzun portrays Lincoln as a "supremely conscious genius" who, through his superior artistic craftsmanship, helped establish "the American [literary] style par excellence."*]

Everybody knows who [Lincoln] was and what he did. But what was he like? For most people, Lincoln remains the rail splitter, the shrewd country lawyer, the cracker-barrel philosopher and humorist, the statesman who saved the Union, and the compassionate leader who saved many a soldier from death by court-martial, only to meet his own end as a martyr.

Not being a Lincoln scholar, I have no wish to deal with any of these images of Lincoln. I want only to help celebrate his sesquicentennial year by bringing out a Lincoln who I am sure is real though unseen. The Lincoln I know and revere is a historical figure who should stand—I will not say, instead of, but by the side of, all the others. . . .

I refer to Lincoln the artist, the maker of a style that is unique in English prose and doubly astonishing in the history of American literature, for nothing led up to it. The Lincoln who speaks to me through the written word is a figure no longer to be described wholly or mainly by the old adjectives, shrewd, humorous or saintly, but rather as one combining the traits that biography reports in certain artists among the greatest—passionate, gloomy, seeming-cold, and conscious of superiority.

These elements in Lincoln's make-up have been noticed before, but they take on a new meaning in the light of the new motive I detect in his prose. For his style, the plain, undecorated language in which he addresses posterity, is no mere knack with words. It is the manifestation of a mode of thought, of an outlook which colors every act of the writer's and tells us how he rated life. Only let his choice of words, the rhythm and shape of his utterances, linger in the ear, and you begin to feel as he did and, hence, to discern unplumbed depths in the quiet intent of a conscious artist. (p. 30)

Lincoln has indeed had praise as a writer, but nearly all of it has been conventional and absent-minded. The few authors of serious studies have fallen into sentimentality and incoherence. Thus, in the Hay and Nicolay edition of Lincoln's works, a famous editor of the '90's writes: "Of style, in the ordinary use of the word, Lincoln may be said to have had little. There was nothing ambitiously elaborate or self-consciously simple in Lincoln's way of writing. He had not the scholar's range of words. He was not always grammatically accurate. He would doubtless have been very much surprised if anyone had told him that he 'had' a style at all.''

Here one feels like asking: Then why discuss ''Lincoln as a writer''? The answer is unconvincing: ''And yet, because he was determined to be understood, because he was honest, because he had a warm and true heart, because he had read good books eagerly and not coldly, and because there was in him a native good taste, as well as a strain of imagination, he achieved a singularly clear and forcible style, which took color from his own noble character and became a thing individual and distinguished. . . .''

So the man who had no style had a style—clear, forcible, individual and distinguished. This is as odd a piece of reasoning as that offered by the late Senator Beveridge: ''The cold fact is that not one faint glimmer appears in his whole life, at least before his [*Cooper Union Speech*], which so much as suggests the radiance of the last two years.'' Perhaps a senator is never a good judge of what a President writes; this one asks us to believe in a miracle. One would think the ''serious'' critics had simply failed to read their author.

Yet they must have read him, to be so obviously bothered. ''How did he do it?'' they wonder. They think of the momentous issues of the Civil War, of the grueling four years in Washington, of the man beset by politicians who were too aggressive and by generals who were not enough so, and the solution flashes upon them: ''It was the strain that turned homespun into great literature.'' This is . . . to confuse a literary occasion with the literary power which rises to it. The famous documents—[the *First Inaugural Address*, the *Second Inaugural Address*, the **''Gettysburg Address,''** and the **''Letter to Mrs. Bixby''**]—marvelous as they are, do not solve the riddle. On the contrary, their subjects have such a grip on our emotions that we begin to think almost anybody could have moved us. For all these reasons—inadequate criticism, overfamiliarity with a few masterpieces, ignorance of Lincoln's early work and the consequent suppression of one whole side of his character—we must go back to the source and begin at the beginning.

Pick up any early volume of Lincoln's and start reading as if you were approaching a new author. Pretend you know none of the anecdotes, nothing of the way the story embedded in these pages comes out. Your aim is to see a life unfold and to descry the character of the man from his own words, written, most of them, not to be published, but to be felt.

Here is Lincoln at twenty-three telling the people of his district by means of a handbill that they should send him to the state legislature: ''Upon the subjects of which I have treated, I have spoken as I thought. I may be wrong in regard to any or all of them; but holding it a sound maxim that it is better to be only sometimes right than at all times wrong, so soon as I discover my opinions to be erroneous, I shall be ready to renounce them.'' And he closes his appeal for votes on an unpolitical note suggestive of melancholy thoughts: ''But if the good people in their wisdom shall see fit to keep me in the background, I have been too familiar with disappointments to be very much chagrined.''

One does not need to be a literary man to see that Lincoln was a born writer, nor a psychologist to guess that here is a youth of uncommon mold—strangely self-assertive, yet detached, and also laboring under a sense of misfortune. . . .

Everybody remembers the story of [Lincoln] reading the Bible in the light of the fire and scribbling with charcoal on the back of the shovel. But millions have read the Bible and not become even passable writers. The neglected truth is that not one but several persons who remembered his childhood remarked on the boy's singular determination to express his thoughts in the best way.

His stepmother gave an account of the boy which prefigures the literary artist much more than the rail splitter: ''He didn't like physical labor. He read all the books he could lay his hands on. . . . When he came across a passage that struck him, he would write it down on boards if he had no paper and keep it there till he did get paper, then he would rewrite it, look at it, repeat it.'' Later, Lincoln's law partner, William H. Herndon, recorded the persistence of this obsessive habit with words: ''He used to bore me terribly by his methods. . . . Mr. Lincoln would doubly explain things to me that needed no explanation. . . . Mr. Lincoln was a very patient man generally, but . . . just go at Lincoln with abstractions, glittering generalities, indefiniteness, mistiness of idea or expression. Here he flew up and became vexed, and sometimes foolishly so.'' (p. 62)

One does not read far in his works before discovering that as a writer he toiled above all to find the true order for his thoughts—order first, and then a lightninglike brevity. Here is how he writes in 1846, a young politician far from the limelight, and of whom no one expected a lapidary style: ''If I falsify in this you can convict me. The witnesses live, and can tell.'' There is a fire in this, and a control of it, which shows the master.

That control of words implied a corresponding control of the emotions. Herndon described several times in his lectures and papers the eccentric temperament of his lifelong partner. This portrait the kindly sentimental people have not been willing to accept. But Herndon's sense of greatness was finer than that of the admirers from afar, who worship rather storybook heroes than the mysterious, difficult, unsatisfactory sort of great man— the only sort that history provides.

What did Herndon say? He said that Lincoln was a man of sudden and violent moods, often plunged in deathly melancholy for hours, then suddenly lively and ready to joke; that Lincoln was self-centered and cold, not given to revealing his plans or opinions, and ruthless in using others' help and influence; that Lincoln was idle for long stretches of time, during which he read newspapers or simply brooded; that Lincoln had a disconcerting power to see into questions, events and persons, never deceived by their incidental features or conventional garb, but extracting the central matter as one cores an apple; that Lincoln was a man of strong passions and mystical longings, which he repressed because his mind showed him their futility, and that this made him cold-blooded and a fatalist.

In addition, as we know from other sources, Lincoln was subject to vague fears and dark superstitions. Strange episodes, though few, marked his relations with women, including his wife-to-be, Mary Todd. He was subject, as some of his verses show, to obsessional gloom about separation, insanity and death. We should bear in mind that Lincoln was orphaned, reared by a stepmother, and early cast adrift to make his own way. His strangely detached attitude toward himself, his premonitions and depressions, his morbid regard for truth and abnormal supression of aggressive impulses, suggest that he hugged a secret wound which ultimately made out of an apparent common man the unique figure of an artist-saint.

Lincoln moreover believed that his mother was the illegitimate daughter of a Virginia planter and, like others who have known or fancied themselves of irregular descent, he had a powerful, unreasoned faith in his own destiny—a destiny he felt would combine greatness and disaster.

Whatever psychiatry might say to this, criticism recognizes the traits of a type of artist one might call "the dark outcast." Michelangelo and Byron come to mind as examples. In such men the sense of isolation from others is in the emotions alone. The mind remains a clear and fine instrument of common sense—Michelangelo built buildings, and Byron brilliantly organized the Greeks in their revolt against Turkey. In Lincoln there is no incompatibility between the lawyer-statesman, whom we all know, and the artist, whose physiognomy I have been trying to sketch.

Lincoln's detachment was what produced his mastery over men. Had he not, as President, towered in mind and will over his cabinet, they would have crushed or used him without remorse. Chase, Seward, Stanton, the Blairs, McClellan had among them enough egotism and ability to wreck several administrations. Each thought Lincoln would be an easy victim. It was not until he was removed from their midst that any of them conceived of him as an apparition greater than themselves. During his life their dominant feeling was exasperation with him for making them feel baffled. They could not bring him down to their reach. John Hay, who saw the long struggle, confirms Herndon's judgments: "It is absurd to call him a modest man. No great man was ever modest. It was his intellectual arrogance and unconscious assumption of superiority that men like Chase and Sumner could never forgive."

This is a different Lincoln from the clumsy country lawyer who makes no great pretensions, but has a trick or two up his sleeve and wins the day for righteousness because his heart is pure. Lincoln's purity was that of a supremely conscious genius, not of an innocent. And if we ask what kind of genius enables a man to master a new and sophisticated scene as Lincoln did, without the aid of what are called personal advantages, with little experience in affairs of state and no established following, the answer is: military genius or its close kin, artistic genius.

The artist contrives means and marshals forces that the beholder takes for granted and that the bungler never discovers for himself. The artist is always scheming to conquer his material and his audience. When we speak of his craft, we mean quite literally that he is crafty.

Lincoln acquired his power over words in the only two ways known to man—by reading and by writing. His reading was small in range and much of a kind: the Bible, Bunyan, Byron, Burns, Defoe, Shakespeare and a then-current edition of *Aesop's Fables*. These are books from which a genius would extract the lesson of terseness and strength. The Bible and Shakespeare's poetry would be less influential than Shakespeare's prose, whose rapid twists and turns Lincoln often rivals, though without imagery. The four other British writers are all devotees of the telling phrase, rather than the suggestive. As for Aesop, the similarity of his stories with the anecdotes Lincoln liked to tell—always in the same words—is obvious. But another parallel occurs, that between the shortness of a fable and the mania Lincoln had for condensing any matter into the fewest words. . . . (p. 63)

In his own day, Lincoln's prose was found flat, dull, lacking in taste. It differed radically in form and tone from the accepted models—Webster's or Channing's for speeches, Bryant's or Greeley's for journalism. Once or twice, Lincoln did imitate their genteel circumlocutions or resonant abstractions. But these were exercises he never repeated. His style, well in hand by his thirtieth year and richly developed by his fiftieth, has the eloquence which comes of the contrast between transparency of medium and density of thought. Consider this episode from a lyceum lecture written when Lincoln was twenty-nine:

> Turn, then, to that horror-striking scene at St. Louis. A single victim was only sacrificed there. His story is very short; and is, perhaps, the most highly tragic of anything of its length that has ever been witnessed in real life. A mulatto man by the name of McIntosh was seized in the street, dragged to the suburbs of the city, chained to a tree, and actually burned to death; and all within a single hour from the time he had been a freeman, attending to his own business, and at peace with the world.

Notice the contrasting rhythm of the two sentences: "A single victim was only sacrificed there. His story is very short." The sentences are very short, too, but let anyone try imitating their continuous flow or subdued emotion on the characteristic Lincolnian theme of the swift passage from the business of life to death.

Lincoln's prose works fall into three categories: speeches, letters and proclamations. The speeches range from legal briefs and arguments to political debates. The proclamations begin with his first offer of his services as a public servant and end with his presidential statements of policy or calls to Thanksgiving between 1861 and 1865. The letters naturally cover his life span and a great diversity of subjects. They are, I surmise, the crucible in which Lincoln cast his style. By the time he was in the White House, he could frame, impromptu, hundreds of messages such as this telegram to General McClellan: "I have just read your despatch about sore-tongued and fatigued horses. Will you pardon me for asking what the horses of your army have done since the battle of Antietam that fatigues anything?"

Something of Lincoln's tone obviously comes from the practice of legal thought. . . . Legal thought encourages precision through the imagining and the denial of alternatives. The language of the law foresees doubt, ambiguity, confusion, stupid or fraudulent error, and one by one it excludes them. Most lawyers succeed at least in avoiding misunderstanding, and this obviously is the foundation of any prose that aims at clear expression.

As a lawyer Lincoln knew that the courtroom vocabulary would achieve this purpose if handled with a little care. But it would remain jargon, obscure to the common understanding. As an artist, therefore, he undertook to frame his ideas invariably in one idiom, but that of daily life. He had to use, of course, the technical names of the actions and documents he dealt with. But all the rest was in the vernacular. His first achievement was to translate the minute accuracy of the advocate and the judge into the words of common men.

To say this is to suggest a measure of Lincoln's struggle as an artist. He started with very little confidence in his stock of knowledge, and having to face audiences far more demanding than ours, he toiled to improve his vocabulary, grammar and logic. In the first year of his term in Congress he labored through six books of Euclid in hopes of developing the coherence of thought he felt he needed in order to demonstrate his views. Demonstration was to him the one proper goal of argument; he never seems to have considered it within his power to convince by disturbing the judgment through the emotions. In the few passages where he resorts to platform tricks, he uses only irony or satire, never the rain-barrel booming of the Fourth-of-July orator.

One superior gift he possessed from the start and developed to a supreme degree, the gift of rhythm. Take this fragment, not from a finished speech, but from a jotting for a lecture on the law:

> There is a vague popular belief that lawyers are necessarily dishonest. I say vague, because, when we consider to what extent confidence and honors are reposed in and conferred upon lawyers by the people, it appears improbable that their impression of dishonesty is very distinct and vivid. Yet the impression is common, almost universal. Let no young man choosing the law for a calling for a moment yield to the popular belief—resolve to be honest at all events; and if in your own judgment you cannot be an honest lawyer, resolve to be honest without being a lawyer.

Observe the ease with which the theme is announced: "There is a vague popular belief that lawyers are necessarily dishonest." It is short without crackling like an epigram, the word "necessarily" retarding the rhythm just enough. The thought is picked up with hardly a pause: "I say vague, because, when we consider . . ." and so on through the unfolding of reasons, which winds up in a kind of calm: "it appears improbable that their impression of dishonesty is very distinct and vivid." Now a change of pace to refresh interest: "Yet the impression is common, almost universal." And a second change, almost immediately, to usher in the second long sentence, which carries the conclusion: "Let no young man choosing the law . . ."

The paragraph moves without a false step, neither hurried nor drowsy: and by its movement, like one who leads another in the dance, it catches up our thought and swings it into willing compliance. The ear notes at the same time that none of the sounds grate or clash: The piece is sayable like a speech in a great play; the music is manly, the alliterations are few and natural. Indeed, the paragraph seems to have come into being spontaneously as the readiest incarnation of Lincoln's thoughts. (pp. 63-4)

Obviously [his written] style would make use of skips and connections unsuited to speechmaking. The member of the cabinet who received a terse memorandum had it before him to make out at leisure. But an audience requires a looser texture, just as it requires a more measured delivery. This difference between the written and the spoken word lends color to the cliché that if Lincoln had a style, he developed it in his presidential years. Actually, Lincoln, like an artist, adapted his means to the occasion. There was no pathos in him before pathos was due. When he supposed his audience intellectually alert—as was the famous gathering at Cooper Union in 1860—he gave them his concentrated prose. We may take as a sample a part of the passage where he addresses the South:

> Again, you say we have made the slavery question more prominent than it formerly was. We deny it. We admit that it is more prominent, but we deny that we made it so. It was not we,

but you, who discarded the old policy of the fathers. We resisted, and still resist, your innovation; and thence comes the greater prominence of the question. Would you have that question reduced to its former proportions? Go back to that old policy. What has been, will be again, under the same conditions. If you would have the peace of the old times, readopt the precepts and policy of the old times.

This is wonderfully clear and precise and demonstrative, but two hours of equally succinct argument would tax any but the most athletic audience. Lincoln gambled on the New Yorkers' agility of mind, and won. But we should not be surprised that in the [**Lincoln-Douglas Debates**], a year and a half before, we find the manner different. Those wrangles lasted three hours, and the necessity for each speaker to interweave prepared statements of policy with improvised rebuttals of charges and "points" gives these productions a coarser grain. Yet on Lincoln's side, the same artist mind is plainly at work:

> Senator Douglas is of world-wide renown. All the anxious politicians of his party, or who have been of his party for years past, have been looking upon him as certainly, at no distant day, to be the President of the United States. They have seen in his round, jolly, fruitful face, post offices, land offices, marshalships, and cabinet appointments, chargeships and foreign missions, bursting and sprouting out in wonderful exuberance ready to be laid hold of by their greedy hands.

The man who could lay the ground for a splendid yet catchy metaphor about political plums by describing Douglas's face as round, jolly and *fruitful* is not a man to be thought merely lucky in the handling of words. The debates abound in happy turns, but read less well than Lincoln's more compact productions. Often, Douglas's words are more polished:

> We have existed and prospered from that day to this thus divided and have increased with a rapidity never before equaled in wealth, the extension of territory, and all the elements of power and greatness, until we have become the first nation on the face of the globe. Why can we not thus continue to prosper?

It is a mistake to underrate Douglas's skill, which was that of a professional. Lincoln's genius needs no heightening through lowering others. Douglas was smooth and adroit, and his arguments were effective, since Lincoln was defeated. But Douglas, unlike Lincoln, sounds like anybody else.

Lincoln's extraordinary power was to make his spirit felt, a power I attribute to his peculiar relation to himself. He regarded his face and physique with amusement and dismay, his mind and destiny with wonder. Seeming clumsy and diffident, he also showed a calm superiority which he expressed as if one half of a double man were talking about the other.

In conduct this detachment was the source of his saintlike forbearance; in his art it yielded the rare quality of elegance. Nowhere is this link between style and emotional distance clearer than in the ["**Farewell Address**"] Lincoln spoke to his friends in Springfield before leaving for Washington. A single magical word, easy to pass over carelessly, holds the clue:

"My friends: No one, not in my situation, can appreciate my feeling of sadness at this parting. To this place, and the kindness of these people, I owe everything. . . ." If we stop to think, we ask: "This place"?—yes. But why "*these* people"? Why not "*you* people," whom he was addressing from the train platform, or "this place and the kindness of *its* people"? It is not, certainly, the mere parallel of *this* and *these* that commanded the choice. "These" is a stroke of genius, which betrays Lincoln's isolation from the action itself—Lincoln talking to himself about the place and the people whom he was leaving, foreboding the possibility of his never returning, and closing the fifteen lines with one of the greatest cadences in English speech: "To His care commending you, as I hope in your prayers you will commend me, I bid you an affectionate farewell."

The four main qualities of Lincoln's literary art—precision, vernacular ease, rhythmical virtuosity and elegance—may at a century's remove seem alien to our tastes. Yet it seems no less odd to question their use and interest to the present when one considers one continuing strain in our literature. Lincoln's example, plainly, helped to break the monopoly of the dealers in literary plush. After Lincoln comes Mark Twain, and out of Mark Twain come contemporaries of ours as diverse as Sherwood Anderson, H. L. Mencken and Ernest Hemingway. Lincoln's use of his style for the intimate genre and for the sublime was his alone; but his workaday style is the American style par excellence. (p. 64)

> *Jacques Barzun, "Lincoln the Literary Genius," in*
> The Saturday Evening Post, *Vol. 231, No. 33, February 14, 1959, pp. 30, 62-4.*

HARRY V. JAFFA (essay date 1959)

[*Jaffa is a scholar known for his writings on American political philosophy. In the excerpt below, he assesses Lincoln's "creative interpretation" of the Declaration of Independence, comparing his understanding of the proposition "all men are created equal" with that of Thomas Jefferson and the other Founders.*]

[In the course of the **Lincoln-Douglas Debate** at Alton, Lincoln stated:]

> At Galesburg, the other day . . . , I said, in answer to Judge Douglas, that three years ago there never had been a man, so far as I knew or believed, in the whole world, who had said that the Declaration of Independence did not include negroes in the term "all men". I reassert it today. I assert that Judge Douglas and all his friends may search the whole records of the country, and it will be a great matter of astonishment to me if they shall be able to find that one human being three years ago had ever uttered the astounding sentiment that the term "all men" in the Declaration did not include the negro. Do not let me be misunderstood. I know that more than three years ago there were men who, finding this assertion constantly in the way of their schemes to bring about the ascendancy and perpetuation of slavery, *denied the truth of it.* I know that Mr. Calhoun and all the politicians of his school denied the truth of the Declaration. I know that it ran along in the mouth of some Southern men for a period of years, ending at last in that shameful, though

rather forcible, declaration of Petit of Indiana, upon the floor of the United States Senate, that the Declaration of Independence was in that respect a "self-evident lie," rather than a self-evident truth. But I say . . . that three years ago there never had lived a man who had ventured to assail it in the sneaking way of pretending to believe it, and then asserting it did not include the negro. I believe the first man who ever said it was Chief Justice Taney in the Dred Scott case, and the next to him was our friend Stephen A. Douglas. And now it has become the catchword of the entire party.

While we would not attest, as a matter of historical record, that no man had ever said what Douglas and Taney were saying, prior to 1857, Lincoln's statement cannot be much of an exaggeration, if it is an exaggeration at all. That Washington, Jefferson, Adams, Madison, Hamilton, Franklin, Patrick Henry, and all others of their general philosophic persuasion understood the Declaration in its universalistic sense, and as including the Negro, is beyond doubt or cavil. All of them read the Declaration as an expression of the sentiments of Locke's *Second Treatise of Civil Government,* wherein many of them had read, almost from childhood, that all men are naturally in "a state of perfect freedom to order their actions . . . without asking leave, or depending upon the will of any other man. A state also of equality, wherein all power and jurisdiction is reciprocal, no one having more than another; there being nothing more evident than that creatures of the same species and rank . . . should also be equal one amongst another without subordination or subjection. . . ." The Declaration of Independence had said that governments are instituted "to secure these rights," which plainly implied that the security, or enjoyment, of the rights which are all men's by nature does not follow from the fact of their unalienability. The Revolution was a great stroke to better secure the unalienable rights of *some* men, but, still more, it was a promise that all men everywhere might *some* day not merely possess but enjoy their natural rights. . . . [The] inability of the Founders then and there to secure the rights of all the men whom they believed possessed unalienable rights did not in the least mean that they believed that the only people possessed of such rights were those whose rights were to be immediately secured.

"Chief Justice Taney," said Lincoln in his Springfield speech on the Dred Scott decision (June 26, 1857), "admits that the language of the Declaration is broad enough to include the whole human family,

> but he and Judge Douglas argue that the authors of that instrument did not intend to include negroes, by the fact that they did not at once, actually place them on the equality with the whites. Now this grave argument comes to just nothing at all, by the other fact, that they did not at once, *or ever afterwards,* actually place all white people on an equality with one another. And this is the staple argument of both the Chief Justice and the Senator, for doing this obvious violence to the plain, unmistakable language of the Declaration. I think the authors of that notable instrument intended to include *all* men, but they did not intend to declare all men equal *in all respects.* They did not mean to say all were equal in color, size, intellect, moral

developments, or social capacity. They defined with tolerable distinctness, in what respects they did consider all men created equal—equal in "certain inalienable rights, among which are life, liberty, and the pursuit of happiness." This they said, and this they meant. They did not mean to assert the obvious untruth, that all men were enjoying that equality, nor yet, that they were about to confer it immediately upon them. In fact, they had no power to confer such a boon. They meant simply to declare the *right*, so that the *enforcement* of it might follow as fast as circumstances should permit. They meant to set up a standard maxim for a free society, which should be familiar to all, and revered by all; constantly looked to, constantly labored for, and even though never perfectly attained, constantly approximated, and therefore constantly spreading and deepening its influence, and augmenting the happiness and value of life to all people of all colors everywhere.

(pp. 313-16)

[Lincoln's rendering of the Founders' meaning] cannot be endorsed on historical grounds without some qualification. For in the passages just quoted Lincoln treats the proposition that "all men are created equal" as a transcendental goal and not as the immanent and effective basis of actual political right. And, in so doing, he transforms and transcends the original meaning of that proposition, although he does not destroy it. His, we might say, is a creative interpretation, a subtle preparation for the "new birth of freedom." Let us try to understand it more precisely.

The idea of the equality of all men, within the eighteenth-century horizon, was connected with the idea of the state of nature, a pre-political state in which there was no government, no lawful subordination of one man to another man. It was a state which was tolerable but only barely so. Because it was but barely tolerable, "mankind are more disposed to suffer, while evils are sufferable, than to right themselves by abolishing the forms to which they are accustomed." But because it *was* tolerable, it was preferable to "absolute Despotism," which was intolerable. The concept of the state of nature, as a pre-political state, highly undesirable, yet tolerable, is among the axiomatic premises of the doctrine of the Declaration of Independence. To indicate the departure that Lincoln's interpretation represents we observe that the idea of such a pre-political state plays no significant role in his thinking. The only use Lincoln ever made of the expression "state of nature" is when he quoted or paraphrased a passage from Clay's famous Mendenhall speech. . . . This usage, however, is widely different from the idea of the state of nature presupposed in the Declaration. Lincoln and Clay presuppose a more or less virgin country and conditions which are more or less optimum. They envisage the kind of act of foundation portrayed in the dramatic dialogue of Plato's *Republic*, in which reason chooses the "elements" it would incorporate in a "good" society. The Lockean state of nature, on the other hand, although a normative concept, is normative primarily in a negative way: it specifies the conditions under which the right of revolution ought to be exercised, and it specifies the purposes for which it ought to be exercised. But because the conditions under which the right ought to be exercised are very bad conditions (although not the worst possible), the purposes for which the right of revolution ought to be exercised are minimal rather

than maximal conditions of human welfare. . . . [Within] the range of [the Founders'] experience, and from the point of view of their concept of the state of nature, they were asserting minimal rights, and they claimed they were absolved of their allegiance in the eyes of civilized mankind because of the insecurity which they had come to feel at the hands of the government of Great Britain. On the other hand, Lincoln's interpretation of "all men are created equal" is *not* that it specifies the condition of man in a pre-political state, a highly undesirable state which marks the point at which men ought to revolt, but that it specifies the optimum condition which the human mind can envisage. It is a condition *toward* which men have a *duty* ever to strive, not a condition *from* which they have a *right* to escape. It is conceived as a political, not a pre-political, condition, a condition in which—to the extent that it is realized—equality of right is secured to every man not by the natural law (which governs Locke's state of nature, in which all men are equal) but by positive human law. Lincoln's interpretation of human equality, as we have already indicated, is that every man had an equal right to be treated justly, that just treatment is a matter of intrinsic worth, that a man's rewards from society ought to be proportioned to the value of his work and not to any subjective liking or disliking.

In his Springfield speech of July 17, 1858, Lincoln said:

> Certainly the negro is not our equal in color—perhaps not in many other respects; still, in the right to put into his mouth the bread that his own hands have earned, he is the equal of every other man, white or black. In pointing out that more has been given you, you can not be justified in taking away the little which has been given him. All I ask for the negro is that if you do not like him, let him alone. If God gave him but little, that little let him enjoy. . . .

Lincoln did not, of course, involve himself in any foolish controversy as to whether the Negro did or did not have the same capacity as the white man; he confined himself to asserting that his claims, *whatever they were*, ought to be determined on the same principle as the white man's. This followed from the proposition that all men have an equal claim to just treatment—and that the Negro was a man.

To sum up: in the old, predominantly Lockean interpretation of the Declaration civil society is constituted by a movement away from the state of nature, away from the condition in which the equality of all men is actual. But in Lincoln's subtle reinterpretation civil society (i.e., just civil society) is constituted by the movement *toward* a condition in which the equality of men is actual. In the older view, which Lincoln shared as far as it went, the actual recognition of the quality of all men is really a necessary condition of the legitimacy of the claims of the government upon the governed. But it is also a sufficient condition. For the language of the Declaration at least permits the view that, if the government of King George III had not been as thoroughly despotic as it is pretended it actually was, the Revolution might not have been justified. In short, the Declaration conceives of just government mainly in terms of the relief from oppression. Lincoln conceives of just government far more in terms of the requirement to achieve justice in the positive sense; indeed, according to Lincoln, the proposition "all men are created equal" is so lofty a demand that the striving for justice must be an ever-present requirement of the human and political condition. While Lincoln most assuredly accepted the Declaration in its minimal, revolutionary meaning, he gave it a new dimension when he insisted that it provided a test not merely of legitimate government—i.e., of government that *may* command our allegiance because it is not despotic—but of *good and just* government—i.e., of a government which may be loved and revered because it augments "the happiness and value of life to all people of all colors everywhere."

Lincoln's interpretation of "all men are created equal" transforms that proposition from a pre-political, negative, minimal, and merely revolutionary norm, a norm which prescribes what civil society ought *not* to be, into a transcendental affirmation of what it *ought* to be. Lincoln does not, of course, abandon the lower-level Lockean-Jeffersonian demands, yet there is visible a tension between them and the higher ones upon which he insists.

> The assertion that "all men are created equal" [he says in the Dred Scott speech] was of no practical use in effecting our separation from Great Britain; and it was placed in the Declaration, not for that, but for future use. Its authors meant it to be, thank God, it is now proving itself, a stumbling block to those who in after times might seek to turn a free people back into the hateful paths of despotism. They knew the proneness of prosperity to breed tyrants, and they meant when such should re-appear in this fair land and commence their vocation they should find left for them at least one hard nut to crack.

Lincoln was trying to perpetuate a government, Jefferson in 1776 to overthrow one, and Lincoln clearly has exaggerated Jefferson's non-revolutionary purpose. In fact, the equality proposition was indispensable to Jefferson in building his case for the right of revolution upon Lockean ground, but the state-of-nature idea with which it was bound up was alien to Lincoln's whole way of thinking. However, Lincoln was probably right when he said that Jefferson did intend to make a statement which would have future as well as present usefulness, although he may have overstated the degree to which such a thought predominated in Jefferson's consciousness. Yet there is a difference between the use which Jefferson might have intended and the one Lincoln ascribes to him. Jefferson was always more concerned to remind the people of their rights than of their duties. He emphasized what they should demand of their government rather than what they must demand of themselves. Jefferson feared above all the usurpations which governments might commit if the people became drowsy and did not exercise that eternal vigilance which is the price of freedom. . . . While Lincoln never denied the danger of usurpations by the government, he placed far more emphasis on the danger of usurpations of a lawless people, which might become the usurpations of the government in response to popular pressure. Once the government was established upon a popular basis, the great danger, as Lincoln saw it, was the corruption of the people. Jefferson tended to see the people as sometimes careless of their own rights but as primarily motivated only by the desire not to be oppressed. Lincoln saw in the people, too, the desire to oppress. The Caesarian danger arose because of the coincidence of Caesar's ambitions with the people's desire to oppress; one without the other was powerless. (pp. 318-23)

Jefferson's attempt to conceive of a remedy for the people's corruption was vitiated by his Lockean horizon. All obligation within this horizon is conceived in terms of deductions from the state of nature, the state in which all men are actually equal. In this state, however, in which men have equal and unalienable rights, they have no real duties. The embryonic duties which exist in Locke's state of nature are not genuine duties but only rules which tell us to avoid doing those things which might impel others to injure us. Duties in any meaningful sense arise only in civil society and are conceived as logically required if civil society is to perform well its function of securing our rights. But whether in the state of nature or the state of civil society, men are not instructed, on Lockean grounds, to abstain from injuring others because it is objectively wrong, but because it is foolish: it undermines the security for their own rights. In short, there is little beyond an appeal to enlightened self-interest in the doctrine of universal equality when conceived in its pristine, Lockean form. Whereas for Lincoln, egotism and altruism ultimately coincide, inasmuch the greatest self-satisfaction is conceived as service to others; in the ethics just sketched such altruism as there is is ultimately reduced to egotism. That the patriotism engendered by the struggle for independence gave such an ethics a greater dignity than this suggests cannot be gainsaid, any more than the dignity of the character of Washington or the idealism of Jefferson can be vindicated on such low grounds. Yet it is also true that the widespread lack of concern over the moral challenge of Negro slavery to the doctrine of universal rights in the Declaration in the Revolutionary generation can be traced to the egotistic quality of these rights in their Lockean formulation. For this reason we must concede that Lincoln exaggerated the degree in which the men of the Revolution were concerned with the freedom of all men. And thus there is some color, although it is only the faintest, for Douglas's assertion that the signers would have been inconsistent if they had meant to include the Negroes in "all men" and then had continued to hold slaves themselves. In truth, their principle included the Negroes in "all men," but the Negroes' rights did *not* impose corresponding duties upon the white masters. Lincoln, we believe, gave a greater consistency and dignity to the position of the signers than was theirs originally. Let us try to understand precisely how he did so.

All men admittedly have a *right* to liberty by the doctrine of the Declaration. But so does every man have a right to life. Now, if we conceive these rights as operative within the Lockean state of nature, we will immediately see that no man is under any necessary obligation to respect any other man's rights. For example: because I have a right to life, I have a right to kill any man whom I have reason to believe might kill me. That is, I have no obligation to respect the other man's right to life until he has given me adequate pledges that he will not try to kill me. After I have received such a pledge I have an obligation to him. But I have this obligation then because, and only because, I have a prior concern to preserve myself. By respecting his pledge I increase my own safety. The same holds true of liberty: I have a right to liberty, which right *permits* me to enslave anyone who, I fear, might otherwise enslave me. (pp. 323-25)

[No] man, from the strictly Lockean standpoint, is under an obligation to respect any other man's unalienable rights until that other man is necessary to the security of his own rights. Only men bound to each other by the social contract are, in a strict sense, bound to respect each other's unalienable rights. And so far are they from being under the obligation to respect other men's rights that they may kill or enslave other men whenever in their judgment this *adds* to their own security. It would also be true, however, that the enslaved Negroes always had the right to revolt and to kill their masters. But the masters would have had no *obligation* to free them until and unless the Negroes had the physical power to make good their freedom. No one has ever expressed more clearly or candidly this view of the right of revolution than Lincoln, in his speech on the Mexican War, when he said that "any people anywhere, being inclined and having the power, have the *right* to rise up and shake off the existing government, and form a new one that suits them better." A people who are so servile as to lack the desire for freedom, *or* who lack the power, do not in any practical sense have the right. (pp. 325-26)

But if the foregoing is true, what interest did Jefferson and those minded like him have in ultimate Negro emancipation or, for that matter, in the emancipation of any one whom they could profitably enslave? The answer, we believe, may be found (apart from the matter of mere moral taste) in the concept of long-run as opposed to short-run egotism. The freedom of a free, popular republic depends upon the indoctrination of people *everywhere* in their natural, unalienable rights. Security is a matter of freedom from oppression at home *and* freedom from foreign domination. The great Enlightenment of the eighteenth century, of which Jefferson was such an ornament, was famous for nothing more than for its cosmopolitanism. And the essence of this cosmopolitanism lay in the conviction that only when the rights of man are secured everywhere will they attain their maximum security anywhere. It was expressed typically in the belief that republican governments are unwarlike, because when the government is of the people, when those whose blood and treasure pay for wars must decide between war and peace, there will be no more aggressive wars, no more wars for conquest or dynastic glory. In this vein Jefferson . . . feared that some day the Negro would rise up to enslave the white man. In short, Jefferson really did believe, as did Lincoln, that he who would not be a slave ought not to be a master. But the Lockean root of Jefferson's conviction—the deepest root for Jefferson's generation—regarded this precept as preeminently a requirement of enlightened self-interest, as a long-run requirement of the security of the rights of the self-regarding, egotistical individual. But in the short run, in the foreseeable future, there could, from this viewpoint, be no pressing conscientious objection to the continued enslavement of those whose slavery was not, but whose emancipation would be, a threat to the masters. (pp. 326-27)

Lincoln's morality then extends the full length of Jefferson's, but it also goes further. Jefferson's horizon, with its grounding in Locke, saw all commands to respect the rights of others as fundamentally hypothetical imperatives: *if* you do not wish to be a slave, then refrain from being a master. Lincoln agreed, but he also said in substance: he who wills freedom for himself must simultaneously will freedom for others. Lincoln's imperative was not only hypothetical; it was categorical as well. Because all men by nature have an equal right to justice, all men have an equal duty to do justice, wholly irrespective of calculations as to self-interest. Or, to put it a little differently, our own happiness, our own welfare, cannot be conceived apart from our well-doing, or just action, and this well-doing is not merely the adding to our own security but the benefiting of others. Civil society, for Lincoln as for Aristotle and Burke, is a partnership "in every virtue and in all perfection." And, while our duties to friends and fellow citizens take precedence over duties to those who are not friends or fellow citizens, the possibility of justice, and of injustice, exists in every relationship with every other human being. Indeed, if it was not possible to do justice to non-fellow citizens, the possibility of

justice and friendship with fellow citizens would not exist. For civil society is the realization of a potentiality which must exist whenever man encounters his fellow, or it is not a potentiality anywhere. And that potentiality, for Lincoln, found its supreme expression in the proposition that "all men are created equal." (p. 327)

> *Harry V. Jaffa, "The Universal Meaning of the Declaration of Independence," in his* Crisis of the House Divided: An Interpretation of the Issues in the Lincoln-Douglas Debates, *1959. Reprint by The University of Chicago Press, 1982, pp. 308-29.*

MARIANNE MOORE (essay date 1961)

[Moore was an American poet, translator, essayist, and editor. Known for the technical and linguistic precision with which she revealed her acute observations of human character, her writing is marked by an independence of style and vision that have established her as a unique poet. In the following excerpt, Moore considers Lincoln's approach to language, reflecting on both the technical and personal elements of his style.]

"I dislike an oath which requires a man to swear he *has* not done wrong. It rejects the Christian principle of forgiveness on terms of repentance. I think it is enough if the man does no wrong hereafter." It was Abraham Lincoln who said this— his controlled impetuosity exemplifying excellences both of the technician and of the poet. (p. 197)

"As a general rule," Lincoln said, "I abstain from reading attacks upon myself, wishing not to be provoked by that to which I cannot properly offer an answer." Expert in rebuttal, however, as in strategy, he often won juries and disinterested observers alike, by anecdote or humorous implication that made argument unnecessary. His use of words became a perfected instrument, acquired by an education largely self-attained— "'picked up,'" he said, "under pressure of necessity." That the books read became part of him is apparent in phrases influenced by the Bible, Shakespeare, *The Pilgrim's Progress, Robinson Crusoe,* Burns, Blackstone's *Commentaries;* and not least, by some books of Euclid—read and "nearly mastered," as he says, after he had become a member of Congress. The largeness of the life entered into the writing, as with a passion he strove to persuade his hearers of what he believed, his adroit, ingenious mentality framing an art which, if it is not to be designated poetry, we may call a "grasp of eternal grace"— in both senses, figurative and literal. (pp. 197-98)

Of persuasive expedients, those most constant with Lincoln are antithesis, reiteration, satire, metaphor; above all *the meaning,* clear and unadorned. A determination "to express his ideas in simple terms became his ruling passion," his every word natural, impelled by ardor. In his address at the Wisconsin Agricultural Fair, he said—regarding competitive awards about to be made—"exultations and mortifications . . . are but temporary; the victor shall soon be vanquished, if he relax in his exertion; and . . . the vanquished this year may be the victor next, in spite of all competition." At the Baltimore Sanitary Fair of 1864, in an address conspicuously combining antithesis with reiteration, he said, "The world has never had a good definition of liberty. . . . We all declare for liberty; but in using the same *word* we do not all mean the same *thing.* With some the word may mean for each man to do as he pleases with himself, and the product of his labor; while with others the same word may mean for some men to do as they please with other men, and the product of other men's labor. Here are two, not only different, but incompatible things, called by the same name—liberty. . . . The shepherd drives the wolf from the sheep's throat, for which the sheep thanks the shepherd as a *liberator*, while the wolf denounces him for the same act as the destroyer of liberty, especially as the sheep was a black one.'' (p. 198)

Crystalline logic . . . was to be his pasison. He wrote to James Conkling, ''You desire peace; and you blame me that we do not have it. But how can we attain it? There are but three conceivable ways. First, force of arms. . . . Are you for it? . . . A second way is to give up the Union. Are you for it? If you are, you should say so plainly. If not for force, not yet for dissolution, Compromise. I am against that. I do not believe any compromise is now possible.'' And to General Schurz he said, ''You think I could do better; therefore you blame me. I think I could not do better, therefore I blame you for blaming me.''

Unsurpassed in satire, Lincoln said that Judge Douglas, in his interpretation of the Declaration of Independence, offered ''the arguments that kings have made for enslaving the people in all ages of the world. They always bestrode the necks of the people, not that they wanted to do it, but that the people were better off for being ridden.'' Of slavery as an institution he said, ''Slavery is strikingly peculiar in this, that it is the only good thing which no man seeks the good of for *himself*.''

Metaphor is a force, indeed magnet, among Lincoln's arts of the word. Urgent that the new government of Louisiana be affirmed, he said, ''If we reject it, we in effect say, 'You are worthless. We will neither help nor be helped by you.' To the blacks we say, 'This cup of liberty which these, your old masters, hold to your lips, we will dash from you, . . . discouraging and paralysing both white and black. . . . If on the contrary, we recognize and sustain the new government, we are supporting its efforts to this end, to make it, to us, in your language, a Union of hearts and hands as well as of states.''' Passionate that the Union be saved, he uses a metaphor yet stronger than the cup of liberty. He says, ''By general law, life *and* limb must be protected; yet often a limb must be amputated to save a life; but a life is never wisely given to save a limb. . . . I could not feel that, . . . to save slavery, . . . I should permit the wreck of government, country, and constitution altogether.''

Diligence underlay these verbal expedients—one can scarcely call them devices—so rapt Lincoln was in what he cared about. He had a genius for words but it was through diligence that he became a master of them—affording hope to the most awkward of us. To Isham Reavis he wrote, ''If you are resolutely determined to make a lawyer of yourself, the thing is half done already. It is a small matter whether you read *with* anybody or not. . . . It is of no consequence to be in a large town. . . . I read at New Salem, which never had three hundred people living in it. The *books* and your *capacity* for understanding them, are just the same in all places.'' (pp. 199-200)

There is much to learn from Lincoln's respect for words taken separately, as when he said, ''It seems to me very important that the statute laws should be made as plain and intelligible as possible, and be reduced to as small compass as may consist with the fullness and precision of the will of the legislature and the perspicuity of its language.'' He was ''determined to be so clear,'' he said, ''that no honest man can misunderstand me, and no dishonest one can successfully misrepresent me.'' Exasperated to have been misquoted, he protested ''a specious and fantastic arrangement of words, by which a man can prove

a horse-chestnut to be a chestnut horse.'' Consulted regarding a more perfect edition of his [*Cooper Union Speech*], he said, ''Of course I would not object, but would be pleased rather . . . but I do not wish the sense changed or modified, to a hair's breadth. Striking out 'upon' leaves the sense too general and incomplete. . . . The words 'quite,' 'as,' and 'or,' on the same page, I wish retained.'' Of Stephen Douglas he said, ''Cannot the Judge perceive the difference between a purpose and an expectation? I have often expressed an expectation to die but I have never expressed a *wish* to die.'' The Declaration of Independence he made stronger by saying, ''I think the authors of that notable instrument intended to include *all* men but they did not intend to declare all men were equal *in all respects*.'' And to quibblers, after the surrender of the South, he replied, ''whether the seceded states, so-called, are in the Union or out of it, the question is bad . . . a pernicious abstraction!'' Indelible even upon a feeble memory—we recall the phrase, ''With malice toward none and charity for all,'' and in the second inaugural address, ''Let us strive on to finish the work we are in.'' We are *in*. Lincoln understood in the use of emphasis that one must be *natural*. Instead of using the word ''confidential'' in a letter to A. H. Stephens, he wrote in italics at the head of the page, *''For your eye only.''* The result of this intensified particularity was such that in his so-called Lost Speech of 1856, which unified the Republican party, ''newspaper men forgot paper and pad . . . to sit enraptured,'' and instead of taking down his eulogy of Henry Clay, ''dropped their pens and sat as under enchantment from near the beginning, to quite the end.''

Lincoln attained not force only, but cadence, the melodic propriety of poetry in fact, as in the **''Farewell Address from Springfield''** he refers to ''the weight of responsibility on George Washington''; then says of ''that Divine being without which I cannot succeed, with that assistance, I cannot fail.'' Consider also the stateliness of the three cannots in the **''Gettysburg Address''**: ''We cannot dedicate—we cannot consecrate—we cannot hallow—this ground. The brave men, living and dead, who struggled here, have consecrated it far above our poor power to add or detract. The world will little note nor long remember what we may say here, but it can never forget what they did here.'' Editors attempting to improve Lincoln's punctuation by replacing dashes with commas, should refrain—the dash, as well known, signifying prudence.

With consummate reverence for God, with insight that illumined his every procedure as a lawyer, that was alive in his every decision as a President with civilian command of an army at bay, Lincoln was notable in his manner of proffering consolation; studiously avoiding insult when relieving an officer of his command; instantaneous with praise. To General Grant—made commander of the Union army after his brilliant flanking maneuver at Vicksburg—he said, ''As the country trusts you, so, under God, it will sustain you.'' To Grant ''alone'' he ascribed credit for terminating the war. Constrained almost to ferocity by the sense of fairness, he begs recognition for ''black men who can remember that with silent tongues, and clenched teeth, and steady eye and well-poised bayonet, they have helped mankind to this consummation'' (preserving the Union). . . . In constant disfavor with officers in charge of penalties, he said, ''Must I shoot a simple soldier boy who deserts while I must not touch a hair of the wily agitator who induces him to desert? To silence the agitator and save the boy is not only constitutional but withal a great mercy.'' Of Captain McKnabb, dismissed on the charge of being a disunionist, Lincoln wrote, ''He wishes to show that the charge is false. Fair play is a jewel. Give him a chance if you can.'' (pp. 201-03)

With regard to presidental appointments, it was in 1849, during Zachary Taylor's administration, that Lincoln said, ''I take the responsibility. In that phrase were the 'Samson's locks' of General Jackson, and we dare not disregard the lessons of experience''—lessons underlying the principle which he put into practice when appointing Governor Chase Secretary of the Treasury. Pressed, in fact persecuted, to appoint Geneal Cameron, he said, ''It seems to me not only highly proper but a *necessity* that Governor Chase shall take that place. His ability, firmness, and purity of character produce the propriety.'' Purity of character—the phrase is an epitome of Lincoln. To a young man considering law as a career, he said, ''There is a vague popular belief that lawyers are necessarily dishonest. If you cannot be an honest lawyer, resolve to be honest without being a lawyer.'' Deploring bombast, yet tactful, he opposed investigating the Bank of Illinois: ''No, Sir, it is the *politician* who is first to sound the alarm (which, by the way, is a false one). It is he, who, by these unholy means, is endeavoring to blow up a storm that he may ride upon and direct it. . . . I say this with the greater freedom, because, being a politician, none can regard it as personal.'' Firm in resisting pressure, he was equally strong in exerting it, as when he wrote to ''Secretary Seward & Secretary Chase'' jointly, ''You have respectively tendered me your resignations . . . but, after most anxious consideration, my deliberate judgment is, that the public interest does not admit of it. I therefore have to request that you will resume the duties of your departments respectively. Your Obt. Servt.''

In faithfulness to a trust, in saving our constituted freedom and opportunity for all, declaring that ''no grievance is a fit object of redress by mob violence,'' made disconsolate by what he termed ''a conspiracy'' to ''nationalize slavery,'' Lincoln— dogged by chronic fatigue—was a monumental contradiction of that conspiracy. An architect of justice, determined and destined to win his ''case,'' he did not cease until he had demonstrated the mightiness of his ''proposition.'' It is a Euclid of the heart. (pp. 203-04)

> Marianne Moore, ''Abraham Lincoln and the Art of the Word,'' in her *A Marianne Moore Reader, The Viking Press,* 1961, pp. 197-204.

ROBERT LOWELL   (speech date 1963)

[*Winner of two Pulitzer Prizes and a National Book Award, Lowell is generally considered the premier American poet of his generation. One of the original proponents of the confessional school of poetry, he frequently gave voice to his personal as well as his social concerns, leading many to regard him as the prototypical liberal intellectual writer of his time. Lowell made the following observations concerning the ''symbolic and sacramental'' character of the ''Gettysburg Address'' in a ceremony commemorating the centenary of Lincoln's speech.*]

Abraham Lincoln was the last President of the United States who could genuinely use words. He and Thomas Jefferson are perhaps the only presidents with this gift. Without his best speeches, Lincoln would have been less great as a man of action; had he not been a great statesman, he could not have written his speeches. He knew his occasion and sensed that whatever he said must have the gravity and brevity of an act of state.

Last spring I was talking about the **''Gettysburg Address''** to a friend who is also a man of letters. He pointed out to me its curious, insistent use of birth images: ''brought forth,'' ''conceived,'' ''created,'' and finally, a ''new birth of freedom.''

Birth and Death!

The **''Gettysburg Address''** is a symbolic and sacramental act. Its verbal quality is resonance combined with a logical, matter of fact, prosaic brevity. It is part of the battle, a last military push that alters and adds significance to the previous military maneuvers. In his words, Lincoln symbolically died, just as the Union soldiers really died—and as he himself was soon really to die. By his words, he gave the field of battle a symbolic significance that it had lacked. For us and our country, he left Jefferson's ideals of freedom and equality joined to the Christian sacrificial act of death and rebirth. I believe this is a meaning that goes beyond sect or religion and beyond peace and war, and is now part of our lives as a challenge, obstacle, and hope. Lincoln's occasional speech of a hundred years ago still rings today when our country struggles with four almost insoluble spiritual problems: how to join equality to excellence, how to join liberty to justice, how to avoid destroying or being destroyed by nuclear power, and how to complete the emancipation of the slaves. (pp. 88-9)

> Robert Lowell, ''On the Gettysburg Address,'' in *Lincoln and the Gettysburg Address: Commemorative Papers, edited by Allan Nevins, University of Illinois Press,* 1964, pp. 88-9.

REINHOLD NIEBUHR   (speech date 1963)

[*Niebuhr was an important and influential Protestant theologian. The author of such works as* The Children of Light and the Children of Darkness *and* Christian Realism and Political Problems, *he persistently stressed the reality of original sin and emphasized the tragic condition of fallen humanity, opposing the tendency toward explaining human misery in economic and political rather than moral terms. The excerpt below is taken from ''The Religion of Abraham Lincoln,'' a speech Niebuhr delivered at a 1963 ceremony commemorating the centenary of the ''Gettysburg Address.'' Niebuhr here extols Lincoln as a man of superior religious convictions, focusing on the purity and depth of his sense of providence and the morality of his position on slavery.*]

An analysis of the religion of Abraham Lincoln in the context of the traditional religion of his time and place and of its polemical use on the slavery issue, which corrupted religious life in the days before and during the Civil War, must lead to the conclusion that Lincoln's religious convictions were superior in depth and purity to those, not only of the political leaders of his day, but of the religious leaders of the era.

This judgment may seem extravagant, and the casual reader may suspect that the hagiography which envelopes the heroes of a nation, substituting symbolic myths for sober reality, may have influenced the judgment. It is true, of course, that Lincoln, the savior, and therefore the second father of his nation, is enveloped in historical myth, because nothing but poetic symbol is adequate to express the status of Lincoln as a symbol representing American democracy more accurately than the eighteenth century aristocrat, George Washington, who has first place in the national pantheon as the ''father'' of his country.

It is nevertheless easy to validate the judgment as sober history, uninfluenced by the usual hagiography of the nations and their heroes. Lincoln's superior religious convictions are partly attested by the fact that, though of deeply religious temperament, he never explicitly joined the religious sects of the frontier.

This fact has given occasion for some historians to number Lincoln among the religious sceptics. Lincoln was not a sophisticated modern, but he was a thoughtful and well-read man, and one must suppose that he, therefore, did not share the orthodox beliefs of the frontier, or make common cause with the frontier evangelist, Peter Cartright, incidentally a political opponent of his. Lincoln's religious faith was primarily informed by a sense of providence, an inclination which he shared with most of the world's statesmen.

In his eloquent *Second Inaugural* Lincoln expressed this sense of providence in these words, "The Almighty has His own purposes. 'Woe unto the world because of offences! for it must needs be that offences come; but woe to that man by whom the offence cometh!' If we shall suppose that American Slavery is one of those offences, which, in the providence of God, must needs come, but which, having continued through His appointed time, He now wills to remove, and that He gives to both North and South, this terrible war, as the woe due to those by whom offence came, shall we discern therein any departure from those divine attributes, which the believers in a Living God always ascribe to Him?'' (pp. 72-4)

Lincoln spells out the dilemma of faith, as he expounds the idea of providence on the issue of slavery; for in the words of Scripture, his conception involves that the "sins of the fathers" are visited on the children of another generation. Lincoln continues "Fondly do we hope—fervently do we pray—that this mighty scourge of war will speedily pass away. Yet, if God wills that it continue, until all the wealth piled by the bondman's two hundred and fifty years of unrequited toil shall be sunk, and until every drop of blood drawn with the lash shall be paid by another drawn with the sword, as was said three thousand years ago, so still it must be said 'the judgments of the Lord are true and righteous altogether.'" Lincoln's faith is identical with that of the Hebraic prophets, who first conceived the idea of a meaningful history. If there was an element of scepticism in this grand conception, one can only observe that the Scripture itself, particularly in the book of Job, expressed some doubts about the exact definition in neat moral terms of the providential meanings of history. Incidentally, this eloquent passage surely expresses Lincoln's moral abhorrence of slavery. The point is important because the abolitionists expressed some doubt on this issue, since Lincoln was, as a responsible statesman, not primarily an abolitionist; but confessed "my primary purpose is to save the Union."

But the chief evidence of the purity and profundity of Lincoln's sense of providence lies in his ability, though the responsible leader of a great nation, embattled with secessionist States and naturally tempted to do what all political leaders, indeed all men, have done through the ages, to avoid the error of identifying providence with the cause to which the agent is committed. He resisted this temptation. Among all the statesmen of ancient and modern periods, Lincoln alone had a sense of historical meaning so high as to cast doubt on the intentions of both sides and to place the enemy into the same category of ambiguity as the nation to which his life was committed. Lincoln thus put the whole tragic drama of the Civil War in a religio-dramatic setting: "Neither party expected for the war, the magnitude, or the duration, which it has already attained. Neither anticipated that the *cause* of the conflict might cease with, or even before, the conflict itself should cease. Each looked for an easier triumph, and a result less fundamental and astounding. Both read the same Bible, and pray to the same God; and each invokes His aid against the other."

There follows an eloquent passage which puts the relation of our moral commitments in history to our religious reservations about the partiality of our moral judgments, more precisely than, I think, any statesman or theologian has put them. First the moral judgment, "It may seem strange that any men should dare to ask a just God's assistance in wringing their bread from the sweat of other men's faces." Then the religious reservation: "but let us judge not that we be not judged. The prayers of both could not be answered; that of neither has been answered just as they intended."

Surely this nice balance of moral commitment and religious reservation about the partiality of all historic commitments of biased men is a unique achievement and is particularly remarkable for a responsible political leader. For it is the very nature of political commitments that they make more ultimate claims for their cause, whether for the nation or their party, than either a transcendent providence or a neutral posterity would validate. Religious mystics and modern radical eschatologists have been neutral in specific disputes of history. But in that case they were morally uncommitted in a cause which was historically important. The ultimate consequence of this form of religious neutrality was to empty all historical striving of meaning and to invest the final end of history or an indifferentiated eternity with the fulfillment of human meaning at the price of reducing all historical striving to triviality.

It was Lincoln's achievement to embrace a paradox which lies at the center of the spirituality of all western culture; namely, the affirmation of a meaningful history and the religious reservation about the partiality and bias which the human actors and agents betray in the definition of meaning.

It was an important achievement to embrace this paradox. For the evil by-product of the historical dynamism of western cul-

Picture taken during Lincoln's last photographic sitting.

ture was the fanaticism which confused partial meanings and contingent purposes with the ultimate meaning of life itself. The lack of fanaticism and the spirit of magnanimity in Lincoln were revealed in many of his policies, but most of all in his spirit toward the defeated secessionists, a spirit eloquently expressed in his *Second Inaugural:* ''With malice toward none; with charity for all . . . let us strive on to finish the work we are in.'' (pp. 74-7)

[We] must turn to Lincoln's scheme of moral principles, his hierarchy of values to ascertain the complexity of his compound of political and personal moral preferences. His abhorrence of slavery was variously expressed, but most eloquently in the previously quoted *Second Inaugural.* Yet he was not an abolitionist. He was quite frank in his letter to Horace Greeley in stating: ''My primary purpose is to save the Union.'' This was the preference of a responsible statesman who felt himself sworn to ''defend the Constitution.'' The secessionist, he said, ''had no oath, registered in heaven,'' to destroy the Union. He himself had an oath to defend the Union. One might regard this preference as that of a patriot who expressed a nation's primal impulse of collective survival. But Lincoln's preference expressed not merely a national patriotism.

Lincoln had a Jeffersonian belief in the mission of the new nation to initiate, extend, and preserve democratic self-government. Thus not only national survival but the survival of democracy was involved in the fortunes of the Civil War.

In his brief and eloquent **"Gettysburg Address"** he defined the mission of the new nation in Jeffersonian terms: ''Four score and seven years ago our fathers brought forth upon this continent, a new nation, conceived in Liberty, and dedicated to the proposition that all men are created equal. Now we are engaged in a great civil war, testing whether that nation, or any nation so conceived, and so dedicated, can long endure.'' Lincoln evidently believed that the whole democratic cause was being tested in the destiny of our own nation, a belief which was natural in the middle of the nineteenth century, when many European critics prophesied the failure of our system of government and when the trends of history which would make democracy a universal pattern of government in western Europe were not yet apparent. The peroration of the **"Gettysburg Address"** returned to the same theme: ''That we were highly resolve that these dead shall not have died in vain— that this nation, under God, shall have a new birth of freedom— and that the government of the people, by the people, for the people shall not perish from the earth.''

Lincoln's passion for saving the Union was held by some critics to express a personal, and not necessarily a historical, concept of the irrevocable character of the covenant of the Constitution. A very high-minded leader of the secessionist states, Robert E. Lee, had a different conception. Though he abhorred slavery, he felt himself bound in loyalty to his State of Virginia, rather than to the nation. Since the Civil War itself, not to speak of the many unifying forces which made the nation one, subsequently altered the loyalties of our citizens, making state loyalty very subordinate to national loyalty, it is safe to say that, if Lincoln's conception of the irrevocable character of the national covenant was a personal conviction, it was also a conviction which his own contribution to the national destiny, and many forces even more far reaching than the Civil War, transmuted into a national conviction. (pp. 78-80)

Of course, there was a residue of moral ambiguity in his devotion to the national union. Sometimes his devotion included his abhorrence of slavery, for the [**Lincoln-Douglas Debates**] were primarily on the question of allowing new states to decide the issue of slavery in each state. Lincoln, in opposing the policy, was a pure Jeffersonian. Thus he argued: ''When he [Douglas] invites any people willing to have slavery, to establish it, he is blowing out the moral lights around us. When he says 'he cares not whether slavery is voted down or voted up,' that it is the sacred right of self government, he is in my judgment penetrating the human soul and eradicating the light of reason and the love of liberty in this American people.''

This absolute rejection of slavery seems at variance with the sentiment expressed in a letter to Horace Greeley, assuring him that his primary purpose is to save the Union and that, if he could save it half slave and half free, he would do it. The contradiction in the two attitudes may be explained by the fact that the point at issue in the Douglas debates was the extension of slavery into the free territories, as provided in the Kansas-Nebraska Act. Lincoln was violently opposed to this policy, the more so since he believed that if the institution were restricted to the original slave states, it would gradually die.

In this position he felt himself in firm accord with the founding fathers of the nation. He argued: ''The framers of the Constitution found the institution of slavery among their other institutions at the time. They found that by an effort to eradicate it, they might lose much of what they had already gained. They were obliged to bow to the necessity. They gave power to Congress to abolish the slave trade at the end of twenty years. They also prohibited slavery in the territories where it did not yet exist. They did what they could and yielded to necessity for the rest. I also yield to all which follows from that necessity.''

In short, Lincoln's opposition to slavery cannot be questioned. If there is moral ambiguity in his position, it is an ambiguity which he shared with the founding fathers, indeed with the author of the Declaration of Independence, and, for that matter, with all responsible statesmen, who pursue their ideals within the frame of the harmony and survival of their community. In short, he exhibited not his own ambiguity, but the moral ambiguity of the political order itself.

Lincoln's attitude to the principle of the Declaration of Independence ''that all men are created equal'' was of course informed by the ethos of his day. It was not the same as the ethos of our own time, which is charged with eliminating the last vestiges of slavery from our national life. Lincoln's attitude on race equality exhibited the same fusion between the ideal of equality and the customary inequality which the institution of slavery had introduced into the ethos of the nation, which presumably characterized the attitude of Thomas Jefferson, the author of the Declaration.

In one of his debates with Senator Douglas, Lincoln said: ''Last night Judge Douglas tormented himself with horrors about my disposition to make negroes perfectly equal with white men in social and political relations. I have said that I do not understand the Declaration to mean that all men are equal in all respects. They are not equal in color. But they are equal in their right to 'life, liberty and the pursuit of happiness'. Certainly the negro is not our equal in color, but still in the right to put into his mouth the bread his own hand earned, he is equal to every man, white or black.'' The affirmation of basic human equality is unexceptional. One might quarrel with the assumption that difference in color implies inequality. Lincoln either shared the color prejudices of his and our day, or he was political enough not to challenge popular prejudices too radically.

The chief source of tension between Lincoln and the abolitionists was Lincoln's hesitancy in freeing the slaves. That hesitancy was not personal, but motivated by a political calculation of a responsible statesman, namely, the loyalty of the border states. Lincoln reprimanded the commanders who freed the slaves in the border states, and when he issued the *Preliminary Emancipation Proclamation,* postponed for a time until victory would insure that it was not regarded as a final desperate effort of a defeated nation, it was made applicable only to the Negroes in territories under Union arms. In the words of a distinguished historian, "It had the eloquence of a bill of lading."

Not only our own abolitionists, but the critical British liberals were not moved by the [*Emancipation Proclamation*]. But both its timing and its immediate scope were the fruits of statesmanlike calculations. They merely revealed that Lincoln was not a moral prophet in the first place, but a responsible statesman. All of his actions and attitudes can be explained and justified by his hierarchy of values, succinctly expressed in his statement to Horace Greeley, "My primary purpose is to save the Union."

A responsible statesman is compelled to relate all the moral aspirations and all the moral hesitancies of the social forces of a free society to the primary purpose of the survival of the community. In the political order justice takes an uneasy second place behind the first place of the value of internal order. In reviewing Lincoln's hierarchy of values, one must come to the conclusion that his sense of justice was strong enough to give that value an immediate position under the first purpose of national survival; and that the purpose of national survival included not only the physical life of the nation, but the system of democratic self-government, which he identified, perhaps too simply, as all our fathers did, with the survival of democracy throughout the world.

It may be significant that the moral ambiguities in the idealism of a responsible statesman proved themselves religiously superior to the pure moral idealism of the abolitionists, the Horace Greeleys, William Lloyd Garrisons, and Wendell Phillipses. This fact does not prove that responsible statesmen are morally superior to the pure idealists. In any case their idealist opposition to slavery was an indispensable contribution to the dramatic struggle which saved the nation and purged it of the hated institution of human bondage. In his message to Congress in 1862 Lincoln admirably revealed both the moral imperatives which prompted the emancipation and the political considerations which made him more cautious than the abolitionists approved.

The caution was prompted by diverse sentiments on the issue within the Union. Lincoln wrote: "Among the friends of the Union, there is great diversity, of sentiment, and of policy, in regard to slavery, and the African race amongst us. Some would perpetuate slavery; some would abolish it suddenly, and without compensation; some would abolish it gradually, and with compensation; some would remove the freed people from us, and some would retain them with us, and there are yet other minor diversities. Because of these diversities, we waste much strength in struggles among ourselves. By mutual concession we should harmonize, and act together."

But Lincoln, as President, acted for the nation, and the moral imperative of the emancipation was eloquently expressed in the words: "In *giving* freedom to the *slave,* we *assure* freedom to the free—honorable alike in what we give, and what we preserve. We shall nobly save, or meanly lose, the last hope

of earth. Other means may succeed; this could not fail. The way is plain, peaceful, generous, just—a way which, if followed, the world will forever applaud, and God must forever bless." (pp. 80-5)

But Lincoln's moral superiority over the idealists was not primarily due to his conscientiousness and power as a statesman. It was due to the depth and weight of his religious sense of the meaning of the drama of history, and his consequent sensitivity to the problem of the taint of self-interest in the definitions of meaning, by which human agents corrupt the meaning in which they are involved. It was due, finally, to the magnanimity which was the natural fruit of this sensitivity.

The idealists were, like most if not all idealists, self-righteous and consequently vindictive. Garrison may have made the southern response to the abolitionist movement more stubborn because he interpreted social attitudes and evils as if they were the fruits of criminal tendencies. He did not understand that good men may inherit social attitudes and become the bearers of social evil, although their own consciences are not perverse, but merely conventional.

This failure to understand the complex causes of historical and socially embedded evil helped generate the vindictiveness of the victors of the Civil War and the consequent horrors of Reconstruction days. As we try now, a century after the Civil War, to eliminate the last vestiges of slavery from our national life, we frequently encounter resentments in the South which are not so much the fruits of the terrible conflict as of the vindictiveness of Reconstruction; that is, of the harsh years when the North proved that, without humility, idealism can be easily transmuted into a cruel vindictiveness.

If we analyze the whole import of the relation of moral idealism to fanaticism, and of religious humility and contrition to magnanimity, and if we set the tension between Lincoln and the abolitionist in the context of this problem, the conclusion is inevitable that Abraham Lincoln is not only a statesman who saved the nation in the hour of its peril; he was also that rare and unique human being who could be responsible in executing historic tasks without equating his interpretation of the task with the divine wisdom.

It is, in short, not too much to claim that Lincoln embraced the paradox of all human spirituality, and of western historical dynamism in particular, more adequately than any statesman of modern history. (pp. 86-7)

> *Reinhold Niebuhr, "The Religion of Abraham Lincoln," in* Lincoln and the Gettysburg Address: Commemorative Papers, *edited by Allan Nevins, University of Illinois Press, 1964, pp. 72-87.*

JOHN HOPE FRANKLIN   (essay date 1963)

[*A modern historian, Franklin is the author of numerous studies of American history, including* From Slavery to Freedom: A History of American Negroes, The Militant South: 1800-1861, Reconstruction: After the Civil War, *and* The Emancipation Proclamation—*the work excerpted below. Taking the impact of the* Emancipation Proclamation *as his subject, Franklin here portrays the edict as a powerful document that far surpassed its immediate purpose as a war measure and ultimately served to validate and extend the principles of democracy and equality expressed in the* Declaration of Independence.]

The character of the Civil War could not possibly have been the same after the President issued the *Emancipation Procla-*

mation as it had been before January 1, 1863. During the first twenty months of the war, no one had been more careful than Lincoln himself to define the war merely as one to save the Union. He did this not only because such a definition greatly simplified the struggle and kept the border states fairly loyal, but also because he deeply felt that this was the only legitimate basis for prosecuting the war. When, therefore, he told Horace Greeley that if he could save the Union without freeing a single slave he made the clearest possible statement of his fundamental position. And he was holding to this position despite the fact that he had written the first draft of the *Emancipation Proclamation* at least six weeks before he wrote his reply to Greeley's famous "Prayer of Twenty Millions."

Lincoln saw no contradiction between the contents of his reply to Greeley and the contents of the *Emancipation Proclamation.* For he had come to the conclusion that in order to save the Union he must emancipate *some* of the slaves. His critics were correct in suggesting that the Proclamation was a rather frantic measure, an act of last resort. By Lincoln's own admission it was, indeed, a desperate act; for the prospects of Union success were not bright. He grabbed at the straw of a questionable victory at Antietam as the occasion for issuing the *Preliminary Proclamation.* If anything convinced him in late December that he should go through with issuing the final Proclamation, it was the ignominious defeat of the Union forces at Fredericksburg. *Something* needed to be done. Perhaps the *Emancipation Proclamation* would turn the trick!

The language of the Proclamation revealed no significant modification of the aims of the war. Nothing was clearer than the fact that Lincoln was taking the action under his authority "as Commander-in-Chief of the Army and Navy." The situation that caused him to take the action was that there was an "actual armed rebellion against the authority and government of the United States." He regarded the *Emancipation Proclamation,* therefore, as "a fit and necessary war measure for suppressing said rebellion." In another place in the Proclamation he called on the military and naval authorities to recognize and maintain the freedom of the slaves. Finally the President declared, in the final paragraph of the Proclamation, that the measure was "warranted by the Constitution upon military necessity." This was, indeed, a war measure, conceived and promulgated to put down the rebellion and save the Union.

Nevertheless, both by what it said and what it did not say, the Proclamation greatly contributed to the significant shift in 1863 in the way the war was regarded. It recognized the right of emancipated slaves to defend their freedom. The precise language was that they should "abstain from all violence, unless in necessary self-defence." It also provided that former slaves could now be received into the armed services. While it was clear that they were to fight to save the Union, the fact remained that since their own fate was tied to that of the Union, they would also be fighting for their own freedom. The Negro who, in December 1862, could salute his own colonel instead of blacking the boots of a Confederate colonel, as he had been doing a year earlier, had a stake in the war that was not difficult to define. However loyal to the Union the Negro troops were—and they numbered some 190,000 by April 1865—one is inclined to believe that they were fighting primarily for freedom for themselves and their brothers in the months that followed the issuance of the *Emancipation Proclamation.*

Despite the fact that the President laid great stress on the issuance of the Proclamation as a military necessity, he did not entirely overlook the moral and humanitarian significance of the measure. And even in the document itself he gave some indication of his appreciation of this particular dimension that was, in time, to eclipse many other considerations. He said that the emancipation of the slaves was "sincerely believed to be an act of justice." This conception of emancipation could hardly be confined to the slaves in states or parts of states that were in rebellion against the United States on January 1, 1863. It must be recalled, moreover, that in the same sentence that he referred to emancipation as an "act of justice" he invoked "the considerate judgment of mankind and the gracious favor of Almighty God." This raised the Proclamation above the level of just another measure for the effective prosecution of the war. And, in turn, the war became more than a war to save the integrity and independence of the Union. It became also a war to promote the freedom of mankind.

Throughout the previous year the President had held to the view that Negroes should be colonized in some other part of the world. And he advanced this view with great vigor wherever and whenever possible. He pressed the Cabinet and Congress to accept and implement his colonization views, and he urged Negroes to realize that it was best for all concerned that they should leave the United States. It is not without significance that Lincoln omitted from the *Emancipation Proclamation* any reference to colonization. It seems clear that the President had abandoned hope of gaining support for his scheme or of persuading Negroes to leave the only home they knew. Surely, moreover, it would have been a most incongruous policy as well as an ungracious act to have asked Negroes to perform one of the highest acts of citizenship—fighting for their country—and then invite them to leave. Thus, by inviting Negroes into the armed services and omitting all mention of colonization, the President indicated in the Proclamation that Negroes would enjoy a status that went beyond mere freedom. They were to be free persons, fighting for their *own* country, a country in which they were to be permitted to remain.

The impact of the Proclamation on slavery and Negroes was profound. Negroes looked upon it as a document of freedom, and they made no clear distinction between the areas affected by the Proclamation and those not affected by it. . . . The celebration of the issuance of the Proclamation by thousands of Negroes in Norfolk illustrates the pervasive influence of the document. President Lincoln had said that Norfolk slaves were not emancipated by his Proclamation. Norfolk Negroes, however, ignored the exception and welcomed the Proclamation as the instrument of their own deliverance.

Slavery, in or out of the Confederacy, could not possibly have survived the *Emancipation Proclamation.* Slaves themselves, already restive under their yoke and walking off the plantation in many places, were greatly encouraged upon learning that Lincoln wanted them to be free. They proceeded to oblige him. There followed what one authority has called a general strike and another has described as widespread slave disloyalty throughout the Confederacy. Lincoln understood the full implications of the Proclamation. That is one of the reasons why he delayed issuing it as long as he did. Once the power of the government was enlisted on the side of freedom in one place, it could not successfully be restrained from supporting freedom in some other place. It was too fine a distinction to make. Not even the slaveholders in the excepted areas could make it. They knew, therefore, that the *Emancipation Proclamation* was the beginning of the end of slavery for them. (pp. 136-40)

The critics of the Lincoln Administration stepped up their attack after January 1, 1863, because they fully appreciated the fact that the Proclamation changed the character of the war. Orestes A. Brownson, Clement L. Vallandigham, William C. Fowler, Samuel S. Cox, and others insisted that the Proclamation represented a new policy that made impossible any hasty conclusion of the struggle based on a compromise. The President had become the captive of the abolitionists who had persuaded him to change the war aims from preservation of the Union to abolition of slavery. (pp. 140-41)

In the light of the demands they had been making, the language of the *Emancipation Proclamation* could hardly have been the source of unrestrained joy on the part of the abolitionists. The Proclamation did not represent the spirit of "no compromise" that had characterized their stand for a generation. There was no emancipation in the border states, with which the abolitionists had so little patience. Parts of states that were under Union control were excepted, much to the dismay of the abolitionists, whose view was ably set forth by Chase. Obviously, the President was not completely under their sway, despite the claims of numerous critics of the Administration. For the most part, the Proclamation represented Lincoln's views. It was in no sense the result of abolitionist dictation.

And yet, when the Proclamation finally came, the abolitionists displayed a remarkable capacity for accommodating themselves to what was, from their point of view, an obvious compromise. (pp. 141-42)

For thirty years William Lloyd Garrison had never been known to make concessions as far as slavery was concerned. Yet, he declared the *Emancipation Proclamation* to be a measure that should take its place along with the Declaration of Independence as one of the nation's truly important historic documents. Frederick Douglass, the leading Negro abolitionist, said that the Proclamation changed everything. "It gave a new direction to the councils of the Cabinet, and to the conduct of the national arms." Douglass realized that the Proclamation did not extend liberty throughout the land, as the abolitionists hoped, but he took it "for a little more than it purported, and saw in its spirit a life and power far beyond its letter. Its meaning to me was the entire abolition of slavery," he concluded, "and I saw that its moral power would extend much further." (pp. 142-43)

The enthusiasm of the abolitionists was greater than that of a group that had reached the conclusion that half a loaf was better than none. Their initial reaction of dissatisfaction with the [*Preliminary Emancipation Proclamation*] had been transformed into considerable pleasure over the edict of January 1. Most of them seemed to agree with Douglass that the Proclamation had, indeed, changed everything. Even if the Proclamation did not free a single slave, as Henry Ward Beecher admitted, it gave liberty a moral recognition. It was a good beginning, the most significant step that had been taken in a generation of crusading. (p. 144)

[Britons] made known their enthusiastic support of the Lincoln policy in a dozen different ways. As Henry Adams, writing from London, put it, the Proclamation was creating "an almost convulsive reaction in our favor all over this country." He chided the London *Times* [see excerpt dated 1863] for behaving like a "drunken drab," but he was certain that its hostility represented no substantial segment of the middle and lower classes. "Public opinion is deeply stirred here and finds expression in meetings, addresses to President Lincoln, deputations to us, standing committees to agitate the subject and to affect opinion, and all the other symptoms of a great popular movement peculiarly unpleasant to the upper classes here because it rests on the spontaneous action of the laboring classes and has a pestilous squint at sympathy with republicanism."

Within a few weeks after the issuance of the Proclamation, some important public figures in Britain began to speak out in public—at first timidly, then more boldly—in support of the Northern policy. In late March, the Prime Minister, speaking in Edinburgh on the Civil War, expressed a feeling of horror of any war that brought in its wake so much suffering and bloodshed. This was the Palmerston style, to which the people had become accustomed. But this time there was a reply. On the following evening the Duke of Argyll said that when civil wars involved a high moral purpose, he for one was not ashamed of the ancient combination of the Bible and the sword. . . . Soon the British government became more respectful of what Argyll had called the combination of the Bible and the sword.

The broadening of the Union's war aims to include a crusade against slavery coincided with another important development. Serious grain shortages at home were forcing the British to look elsewhere for foodstuffs. . . . [The] British had come to rely heavily on Northern wheat. Indeed, many thought it was indispensable. Perhaps, under the circumstances, the British government should not risk a rupture with the North, some leaders began to reason. As Her Majesty's Government began to look seriously at this problem, it also began to take cognizance of the pressures of the rank and file of the British people and the pressures of the Washington government. Hope for recognition of the Confederacy by Britain and the Continental powers faded away. The *Emancipation Proclamation* had played an important role in achieving this signal diplomatic victory. (pp. 146-48)

The President hoped that the Proclamation would be the instrument for the further prosecution of the war and the emancipation of slaves in states and parts of states excepted by the Proclamation. He followed with great interest the recruitment and activity of Negro troops that followed in the wake of emancipation. He noticed that the Confederates attacked Negro troops fiercely, and that was to be expected. "It is important to the enemy that such a force shall *not* take shape, and grow, and thrive, in the South; and in precisely the same proportion, it is important to us that it shall." In May the President said he would gladly receive "ten times ten thousand" colored troops and would protect all who enlisted. (p. 149)

[Lincoln] praised the conduct of Negroes under fire and said that some of the generals who had been most successful in the field "believe the emancipation policy, and the use of colored troops, constitute the heaviest blow yet dealt to the rebellion; and that, at least one of those important successes, could not have been achieved when it was, but for the aid of black soldiers." The President had no doubt of the loyalty of Negroes to the Union, but he felt that their interest in their own freedom was an additional motive. This grew out of the government's emancipation policy, the wisdom of which Lincoln was even more certain before the end of the year.

Although the Proclamation did not apply to the border slave states—Missouri, Kentucky, Maryland, and Delaware—Lincoln hoped that it would be a stimulus for the development of emancipation policies in those areas. He was pleased to learn in the spring of 1863 that the state of Missouri was considering a plan for gradual emancipation. (pp. 150-51)

Despite the fact that the immediate results of the *Emancipation Proclamation* were not always measurable, Lincoln was pleased with what he had done. Over and over again he expressed the view that he had done the right thing. It had not had an adverse effect on the course of the war. The war, he told a correspondent in the summer of 1863, had "certainly progressed as favorably for us, since the issue of the proclamation as before." The Proclamation was valid, and he would never retract it. Moreover, it reflected his own repugnance to slavery. As an antislavery man, he wrote Major General Nathaniel P. Banks, he had a motive for issuing the Proclamation that went beyond military considerations. At last he had been able to strike the blow for freedom that he had long wanted to do.

Finally, Lincoln hoped that the Proclamation would provide the basis for a new attitude and policy for Negroes. That all slaves would soon be free was a reality that all white men should face. "Those who shall have tasted actual freedom I believe can never be slaves, or quasi slaves again." He hoped, therefore, that the several states would adopt some practical system "by which the two races could gradually live themselves out of their old relation to each other, and both come out better prepared for the new." He hoped that states would provide for the education of Negroes, and he went so far as to suggest to Governor Michael Hahn of Louisiana that his state might consider extending the franchise to free Negroes of education and property.

Thus, in many ways the Proclamation affected the course of the war as well as Lincoln's way of thinking about the problem of Negroes in the United States. Abroad, it rallied large numbers of people to the North's side and became a valuable instrument of American foreign policy. At home it sharpened the issues of the war and provided a moral and humanitarian ingredient that had been lacking. It fired the leaders with a new purpose and gave to the President a new weapon. Small wonder that he no longer promoted the idea of colonization. Small wonder that he began to advocate education and the franchise for Negroes. They were a new source of strength that deserved to be treated as the loyal citizens that they were.

For the last hundred years the *Emancipation Proclamation* has maintained its place as one of America's truly important documents. Even when the principles it espoused were not universally endorsed and even when its beneficiaries were the special target of mistreatment of one kind or another, the Proclamation somehow retained its hold on the very people who saw its promises unfulfilled. It did not do this because of the perfection of the goal to which it aspired. At best it sought to save the Union by freeing *some* of the slaves. Nor did it do it by the sublimity of its language. It had neither the felicity of the Declaration of Independence nor the simple grandeur of the **"Gettysburg Address."** But in a very real sense it was another step toward the extension of the ideal of equality about which Jefferson had written.

Lincoln wrote the *Emancipation Proclamation* amid severe psychological and legal handicaps. Unlike Jefferson, whose Declaration of Independence was a clean break with a legal and constitutional system that had hitherto restricted thought and action, Lincoln was compelled to forge a document of freedom for the slaves within the existing constitutional system and in a manner that would give even greater support to that constitutional system. This required not only courage and daring but considerable ingenuity as well. As in so many of Lincoln's acts, the total significance and validity of the measure were not immediately apparent, even among those who were sympathetic with its aims. Gradually, the greatness of the document dawned upon the nation and the world. Gradually, it took its place with the great documents of human freedom.

When English America was settled in the seventeenth century it soon became the haven for people who were religiously and socially discontent, economically disadvantaged, and politically disoriented. It was not until they broke away from the mother country that they began effectively to realize the existence of which they had dreamed. The break was so complete and the ideology of the break so far-reaching that the only valid base on which to build the New World republic was one characterized by democracy and equality. The tragedy of this republic was that as long as human slavery existed its base had a fallacy that made it both incongruous and specious. The great value of the *Emancipation Proclamation* was that in its first century it provided the base with a reinforcement that made it at long last valid and worthy. Perhaps in its second century it would give real meaning and purpose to the Declaration of Independence. (pp. 151-54)

> *John Hope Franklin, "Victory More Certain," in his* The Emancipation Proclamation, *Doubleday & Company, Inc., 1963, pp. 136-54.*

DAVID D. ANDERSON   (essay date 1970)

[*In this excerpt from his literary study* Abraham Lincoln, *Anderson critiques three verse fragments composed by Lincoln.*]

All three of [Lincoln's] 1846 poems are sentimental ballads, each of them a nostalgic evocation of the past in the Romantic tradition of the safe Victorian poets whose works were found in every American home aspiring to gentility. This verse tradition was imitated in country newspapers throughout America west of the Appalachians and east of the Mississippi during the nineteenth century. Although Lincoln's verse was in the vein satirized by Mark Twain in *Huckleberry Finn*, Lincoln was neither an Emmaline Grangerford; nor, thanks to his memories of the grim nature of his childhood environment and occasional flashes of wry humor, did he become, like Julia A. Moore, a sweet singer of Indiana.

But to see in the weak, unskilled, and theatrical verse that he produced at this time a foreshadowing of the prose poems at Gettysburg, as some critics have unfortunately done, is to stretch a coincidental authorship to an unacceptable extent; they are conventional bad poems. Lincoln had worked at revising the verses and had allowed Andrew Johnston to publish them anonymously, but he knew that he was no poet in the conventional sense. Of William Knox's "Mortality" he wrote, "I would give all I am worth, and go in debt, to be able to write so fine a piece as I think that is"; and in respect to his own verse he was under no illusions. But he was not ashamed of his venture into verse, as he recounted its inception to Johnston:

> In the fall of 1844, thinking I might aid some to carry the State of Indiana for Mr. Clay, I went into the neighborhood in that State in which I was raised, where my mother and only sister were buried, and from which I had been absent about fifteen years. That part of the country is, within itself, as unpoetical as any spot of the earth; but still, seeing it and its objects and inhabitants aroused feelings in me which were certainly poetry; though whether my expression of those feelings is poetry is quite another question.

In seeking to express the depth of those feelings in the conventional jingle-like ballad form that he chose, Lincoln did not write the poetry that he might have on that occasion and that he was to do on equally or more stirring occasions in the future. The regularity of rhyme and rhythm inevitably distorted and cheapened the emotions that he felt. But his effort at creative expression at this time is important, not for its accomplishment but for its intent. Emotion, Lincoln was beginning to learn, is neither shameful nor to be feared, nor is it to be rejected by reason. Instead, it can elevate man to a new awareness, a new insight into himself and the human experience.

The verses as they survive in fragments fall naturally into three parts, two of them cantos of what was a projected or actual four-canto work, and the third a rousing narrative that may have been the third of the projected four cantos. Cantos one and two, revised by Lincoln in the spring and summer of 1846, describe the nostalgic impact of the return to boyhood scenes and the sense of loss, of death, of emptiness that those scenes engendered. The first ["**My Childhood's Home I See Again**"] is a general recollection of emotion, and the second ["**Poor Mathew**"] explores in detail the microcosmic tragedy of a mad boy before pondering again on the unknowable logic of death. He began by examining the memory of his childhood emotions as he looked about the scene:

> My childhood's home I see again,
>   And sadden with the view;
> And still, as memory crowds my brain,
>   There's pleasure in it too.
>
> O Memory! thou midway world
>   'Twixt earth and paradise,
> Where things decayed and loved ones lost
>   In dreamy shadows rise,
>
> And, freed from all that's earthly vile,
>   Seem hallowed, pure and bright,
> Like scenes in some enchanted isle
>   All bathed in liquid light.
>
> As dusky mountains please the eye
>   When twilight chases day;
> As bugle-notes that, passing by,
>   In distance die away;
>
> As, leaving some grand waterfall,
>   We, lingering, list its roar—
> So memory will hallow all
>   We've known, but know no more.
>
> Near twenty years have passed away
>   Since here I bid farewell
> To woods and fields, and scenes of play,
>   And playmates loved so well.
>
> Where many were, but few remain
>   Of old familiar things;
> But seeing them, to mind again
>   The lost and absent brings.
>
> The friends I left that parting day,
>   How changed, as time has sped!
> Young childhood grown, strong manhood gray,
>   And half of all are dead.
>
> I hear the loved survivors tell
>   How naught from death could save,
> Till every sound appears a knell
>   And every spot a grave.

> I range the fields with pensive tread,
>   And pace the hollow rooms,
> And, feel (companion of the dead)
>   I'm living in the tombs.

Like much of the graveyard poetry of the eighteenth century, the period that provided the model and inspiration for Lincoln's adherence to reason, this introductory canto is bathed in Romantic pathos, platitudes, and a morbid awareness of the omnipresence of death, a commonplace on the frontier as in the lives of the folk in Thomas Gray's famous churchyard. The sentiments are genuine, as Lincoln commented in his accompanying letter to Johnston; but the result is not. Instead, he was forced into stereotyped diction by the narrow regularity of the form. The clichés are only occasionally redeemed by an original image. But the unbroken tone of mournful regret, the regularity of rhythm and rhyme, make the poem expressive neither of Lincoln nor of the harsh impact of a past softened by time. Instead, its nostalgia is conventionally sentimental.

In the second canto, in spite of close adherence to the conventions of the first, Lincoln moved toward mythmaking in the frontier tradition as he dealt with a story that had its counterpart in almost every area of the mid-American frontier, many of which have become part of the Midwestern literary heritage. This is the story of Mathew Gentry, a former schoolmate of Lincoln's who had gone violently mad and then became harmlessly insane. In moving from the pensive to the descriptive, Lincoln's verse takes on an active movement and vitality at odds with the first canto; and the subject permits a blunt diction taken from life. Finally, however, the verse bogs down in the same pensive wonder that marked the first. Like the other canto, this verse retains its grimness from first to last; but the violence has the force of reality:

> But here's an object more of dread
>   Than ought the grave contains—
> A human form with reason fled,
>   While wretched life remains.
>
> Poor Mathew! Once of genius bright,
>   A fortune-favored child—
> Now locked for aye, in mental night,
>   A haggard mad-man wild.
>
> Poor Mathew! I have n'er forgot,
>   When first, with maddened will,
> Yourself you maimed, your father fought,
>   And mother strove to kill;
>
> When terror spread, and neighbors ran,
>   Your dange'rous strength to bind;
> And soon, a howling crazy man
>   Your limbs were fast confined.
>
> How then you strove and shrieked aloud,
>   Your bones and sinews bared;
> And fiendish on the gazing crowd,
>   With burning eyeballs glared—
>
> And begged, and swore, and wept, and prayed
>   With maniac laughter joined—
> How fearful were those signs displayed
>   By pangs that killed thy mind!
>
> And when at length, tho' drear and long,
>   Time soothed thy fiercer woes,
> How plaintively thy mournful song
>   Upon the still night rose.

I've heard it oft, as if I dreamed,
  Far distant, sweet and lone—
The funeral dirge, it ever seemed
  Of reason dead and gone.

To drink its strains, I've stole away,
  All stealthily and still,
Ere yet the rising God of day
  Had streaked the Eastern hill.

Air held his breath; trees, with the spell,
  Seemed sorrowing angels round,
Whose swelling tears in dew-drops fell
  Upon the listening ground.

But this is past; and naught remains,
  That raised thee o'er the brute.
Thy piercing shrieks, and soothing strains,
  Are like, forever mute.

Now fare thee well—more thou the *cause,*
  Than *subject* now of woe,
All mental pangs, by time's kind laws,
  Has lost the power to know.

O death! Thou awe-inspiring prince,
  That keepest the world in fear;
Why doest thou tear more blest ones hence,
  And leave him ling'gring here?

Certainly more original and vivid than the first canto, this one is at the same time less unified in statement as Lincoln found himself restricted by a form demanding a more conventional subject than the violence of insanity. Consequently, in contrast to the first, distortions abound, the verse is less polished, and irregularities recur. But much of the diction is startlingly fresh, with the vivid Anglo-Saxon force of the frontier; and mournful monotony is allayed by primitive vitality.

The third verse, perhaps intended as the third canto, carries on the original strain of **"Poor Mathew,"** but the mournful nostalgia is gone; and the subject is a lively recounting of a bear hunt, its intensity relieved by wry humor. Less strained in its structure, it is less pretentious and less polished; and at its core is an unfeeling, unfelt violence at home in its setting. Even the infrequent nostalgic notes take on the atmosphere of violence in which there is neither strain nor falsity. As Lincoln describes it, the bear hunt *is:*

A wild-bear chace, didst never see?
  Then hast thou lived in vain.
Thy richest bump of glorious glee,
  Lies desert in thy brain.

When first my father settled here,
  'Twas then the frontier line:
The panther's scream, filled night with fear
  And bears preyed on the swine.

But wo for Bruin's short lived fun,
  When rose the squealing cry;
Now man and horse, with dog and gun,
  For vengeance, at him fly.

A sound of danger strikes his ear;
  He gives the breeze a snuff;
Away he bounds, with little fear,
  And seeks the tangled *rough.*

From this point it is a merry, confused chase as the hue and cry bring on the dogs and the "merry *corps*"; then, cornered at bay, worn from the chase, the bear stands to fight and die:

And furious now, the dogs he tears,
  And crushes in his ire.
Wheels right and left, and upward rears,
  With eyes of burning fire.

But leaden death is at his heart,
  Vain all the strength he plies.
And, spouting blood from every part,
  He reels, and sinks, and dies.

But at this moment there is no questioning or pondering; death, sudden and bloody, is a necessary fact for the bear; and Lincoln wastes no time on false sentiment. Instead, in keeping with the lusty tradition of which the hunt is a part, he portrays the comedy of the confusion and the universality of its human aftermath:

And now a dinsome clamor rose,
  'Bout who should have his skin;
Who first draws blood, each hunter knows,
  This prize must always win.

But who did this, and how to trace
  What's true from what's a lie,
Like lawyers, in a murder case
  They stoutly *argufy.*

Sentiment is gone, replaced by a gentle contempt devoid of the emotion in the early poems. The human comedy, in contrast to the dumb courage of the bear, is ludicrous. And that ultimate irony is emphasized in the last lines, when a dog who had hung back comes forward to attack the corpse. Emulating his human companions, he parodies their nonsense, giving Lincoln additional opportunity for wry, pointed comment as the dog moves to the attack,

And swells as if his skin would tear,
  And growls and shakes again;
And swears, as plain as dog can swear,
  That he has won the skin.

Conceited whelp! we laugh at thee—
  Nor mind, that not a few
Of pompous, two-legged dogs there be,
  Conceited quite as you.

No poet in the conventional sense, Lincoln's eye and ear at this time were for the real, as was his innate sense of language, forceful, clear, simple, and active. In letting form control idea in the earlier verse, sentiment was distorted to unreality; and in this verse, it impedes action. But the mock-heroic satire of this verse, together with the keen sense of ironic comedy and the shrewd insight into pompous nonsense, give **"The Bear Hunt"** a verisimilitude that transcends its form by using its story as well as its form as a comic device. The rude, forceful combination produces a rough humor in which the hunt is like the ridiculous paradox of life, and violence is only a passing shadow to be ignored in the spirit of fun. Lincoln focuses not on tragedy but on foolishness, the sympathy for animals so much a part of the Lincoln myth is strangely absent, and the stark comedy of frontier life and humor prevails.

In spite of the obvious weaknesses in this brief collection of verse, it is evident that Lincoln—who largely continued to regard words pragmatically although he read widely in imaginative verse—was beginning to see language as more than a

precision instrument. During this respite from preparing legislative documents, bills, and speeches, he attempted to explore
the esthetic and emotional use of language, and the result suggests that, had he pursued it, he might have become one of
the many minor poets who achieved local and regional fame
as the stabilizing Midwest sought to compensate for the crude-
ness of its recent past. Fortunately, Lincoln did not join this
movement; equally fortunate was his increasing awareness of
the emotional and aesthetic potential of words. That awareness,
purged of its naïve adherence to the conventional demands of
popular verse, was to lead to a personal restraint in the poetically provocative prose of the future. But the emotional maturity and simplicity of those later statements were not yet
apparent. (pp. 71-8)

> *David D. Anderson, in his* Abraham Lincoln, *Twayne
> Publishers, Inc., 1970, 205 p.*

MORTIMER J. ADLER AND WILLIAM GORMAN (essay date 1975)

[*Adler is an American philosopher and educator best known as
the originator—with Robert Maynard Hutchins—of the "Great
Books" program of studies, in connection with which he prepared
the index of ideas for and helped edit the program's monumental
set of texts,* Great Books of the Western World. *In 1974, Adler
and Gorman moderated a conference at which the participants
discussed the significance of three historic political statements:
the Declaration of Independence, the Preamble to the Constitution, and the "Gettysburg Address." Adler and Gorman then
issued commentaries on the political doctrines reflected in each
statement, which they regard collectively as the "American Testament." Below, the authors explicate the concept of democracy
implied in Lincoln's reference to "government of the people, by
the people, for the people" in the "Gettysburg Address."*]

[In the **"Gettysburg Address"** Lincoln asserts:]

> Now we are engaged in a *great* civil war, test-
> ing whether that nation or *any nation* so con-
> ceived and so dedicated can long endure. We
> are met on a *great* battlefield of that war.

Was it unseemly to speak of the terrible civil war as a *great*
war, of Gettysburg as a *great* battlefield? Lincoln was surely
not speaking of the intensity or of the unexpected duration of
the war. He was thinking of the magnitude of the issue that
was being tested. It was not just whether *this* nation but whether
any nation so conceived and so dedicated could long endure.

With the words "or any nation," Lincoln raised the question
of the worldwide significance of the American model. In his
First Inaugural Address Washington had said: "The sacred fire
of liberty and the destiny of the republican model of government are justly considered, perhaps, as *deeply,* as *finally,* staked
on the experiment entrusted to the hands of the American
people." Washington was echoing what every major revolutionary leader had said about the world meaning of the American Revolution—John Adams, James Madison, Alexander
Hamilton, Thomas Jefferson.

Lincoln had many times spoken in the same vein. On the way
to his first inauguration, Lincoln addressed the New Jersey
Senate. After recalling his boyhood reading, in Parson Weems's
Life of Washington, of the military struggles around Trenton,
he said:

> I recollect thinking then, boy even though I
> was, that there must have been something more

than common that those men struggled for. I
am exceedingly anxious that that thing which
they struggled for—that something even more
than National Independence; that something that
held out a great promise to all the people of the
world for all time to come—I am exceedingly
anxious that this Union, the Constitution, and
the liberties of the people shall be perpetuated
in accordance with the original idea for which
that struggle was made, and I shall be most
happy indeed if I shall be an humble instrument
in the hands of the Almighty, and of this, his
almost chosen people, for perpetuating the object of that great struggle.

For Lincoln, what came into being with the war that gave the
nation its birth, and held out a great promise to the people of
the world for all time to come, was *the* issue in the Civil War.
(pp. 127-28)

["Saving the Union"], taken by itself, did not yield the moral
justification for the Civil War. Saving the Union was of such
awesome importance only because the preservation of the Union
was indispensable to this nation's promotion of "that something," struggled for in the War of Independence, which "held
out a great promise to all the people of the world for all time
to come." This point becomes firmly clear at the end of the
["**Gettysburg Address**"].

After words of deep respect for the dead, Lincoln turns to what
the living must take from the dead:

> It is rather for us to be here dedicated to the
> great task remaining before us—that from these
> honored dead we take increased devotion to that
> cause for which they gave the last full measure
> of devotion, that we here highly resolve that
> these dead shall not have died in vain, *that this
> nation, under God, shall have a new birth of
> freedom; and that government of the people,
> by the people, for the people shall not perish
> from the earth.*

The "unfinished work," "the great task remaining before us,"
"that cause for which they gave the last full measure of devotion"—these are articulated in the last two clauses of the
["**Gettysburg Address**"], which are statements of purpose.
The first purpose concerns "*this* nation"—that *it* "shall have
a new birth of freedom." The second concerns the historical
future of an idea—the idea of democracy—that it "shall not
perish from the earth."

Some, if not all, of the revolutionary leaders believed that
somehow, by the very circumstances of the nation's birth, the
idea of democracy was held in trust by America. For Lincoln
it was precisely that trust which was being tested in a great
Civil War.

Lincoln formulated the idea of democracy in what has become
a world-famous trinity of prepositional phrases:

> . . . government of the people, by the people,
> for the people . . .

This tripartite formula has acquired widespread talismanic power.
It has always been invoked by the American people as an
inspired formula. However, if we take this triad of prepositional
phrases as a compressed formulation of the idea of democracy,

it is necessary to ask a number of questions which aim at explicating its meaning. (pp. 129-30)

In a paper entitled *What is Democracy?*, written in 1958 for a conference on "Representative Government and Public Liberties in the New States," [Bertrand] De Jouvenel found Lincoln's "formula" a ludicrous failure, even something of a hoax. De Jouvenel's findings are useful as yielding the questions that we must ask about Lincoln's formula.

In regard to "*government of the people*," De Jouvenel writes: "Let me first note that any *de facto* authority, habitually obeyed and acknowledged by a people, is its government; the first term, therefore, merely tells us that a government must be obeyed and acknowledged by the people; if not, it is not the government of the people, but then it is no government at all."

In regard to "*government by the people*," De Jouvenel interprets it to mean that "all decisions are jointly taken by all members of the community assembled for that purpose"; this, he says, describes "no government as we know it"; it is applicable only to ancient Athens and a few anomalous, small, short-lived communities in Western history.

In regard to "*government for the people*," De Jouvenel writes: "The last term reminds us that a government has a moral obligation of seeking the good of the people; this is valid for a government of whatever origin or form." Accordingly, in his view, Lincoln's third term in no way catches something distinctive about democracy.

Our reponse to De Jouvenel must begin by conceding that the only way to counter his attack is by treating Lincoln's triad of phrases as an *oracle*—compressed, cryptic, expressing deep truths.

... government *of* the people ...

Grammarians have long since noted an ambiguity in the use of the genitive case. On the one hand, the phrase, "the love of God" (by man) can be used to designate the love that is directed to God as an object of love. The genitive is then an *objective genitive*. On the other hand, "the love of God" can be used to designate the love that God has for man. The genitive is then a *possessive genitive*.

Lincoln's oracular "of" is what might be called a "deliberate double-genitive." He did not need to be told by De Jouvenel that "government" is a relative term, so that where there is "government," there has to be a "governed." Democracy is not anarchy. It involves government and therefore those who are governed—the subjects or objects of government. (pp. 130-31)

However, in a democracy that is genuine, the people are governed by a government that is *theirs,* by a government that belongs to them, as an instrument belongs to its user. It is, therefore, necessary to distinguish between a people conceived as submitting to a government that claims to derive its authority and power from sources which are wholly extraneous to them (as is the case in an absolute monarchy or despotism), and a people conceived as under a government that derives its authority and power from their consent.

Given the privileges of the oracular style, Lincoln's first prepositional phrase contains a possessive genitive at the same time that it contains an objective genitive. That possessive genitive calls attention to the fundamental distinction between constitutional and despotic government—a government of laws as contrasted with a government by men. Constitutional govern-

ment is government that derives its authority and power from the consent of the people, and is therefore *their* government. Constitutional government takes different forms: It is oligarchical or democratic depending on the meaning of the words "the people" in the phrase "government of the people," as well as in the other two phrases associated with it. If "the people" stands for the whole human population of the political community—all except the few who can be justly excepted, such as infants or hospitalized mental incompetents—then we have the specific form of government known as constitutional democracy. Lincoln's adherence to the proposition about human equality in the Declaration, together with its consequential avowal of the possession by all of the same inherent and unalienable human rights, must persuade us that when he spoke of "government of the people, by the people, and for the people," he had constitutional democracy in mind, not merely as one specific form of government among others, but as the only just form of government—more just than a constitutional oligarchy in which the consenting people are a privileged few, and much more just than a despotic or absolute government in which the people are the subjects of a government that is in no sense theirs because it in no way involves their consent or participation.

The significance of the possessive genitive in the initial phrase—"government of the people"—can be summarized in the following propositions that any defender of the rightness of constitutional government should affirm as true. They provide us with the definitive solution of a problem that has persisted throughout the whole tradition of Western political thought—the problem about the source of the authority and the grounds for the legitimacy of governments.

1. Authority is not possessed by a government merely as a result of the *de facto* submission of the governed to the power it is able to exert over them.

2. A government has genuine authority—the right to govern—only when such authority is conferred on it, or transmitted to it, by acts of the people as its consenting constituents, originating, constitutive acts, interim acts of consent, and periodically recurring electoral acts.

3. While such authority is possessed and exercised by the office-holders or officials in a constitutional government, it is held and exercised by them in dependence on the people to whom it principally and inalienably belongs.

4. Just as in the physical world, an instrumental cause, such as the painter's brush, has its causal power imparted to it by the principal cause, the painter's art, so in the political realm, the governing bodies in a constitutional government function as an instrument empowered by the people.

... government ... *by* the people ...

At the time that Lincoln spoke, he was the head of a government in a not-all-that-small society. It is way off the mark for De Jouvenel or anybody else to suggest that Lincoln, in a spasm of rhetorical excitement, was trying to suggest that the government of the United States was a government-of-everybody-by-everybody—government by the assembly of all the citizens, as in Athens or in a New England town.

The leaders of the revolutionary and constitutional period had spoken of "self-government," even though, because of the size of the society, such government would involve representation in a legislative body rather than the direct participation of the citizens in a public assembly. In *Federalist #39*, Madison wrote: "It is evident that no other form of government would be reconcilable with the genius of the people of America; with the fundamental principles of the Revolution; or with that honorable determination which animates every votary of freedom, to rest all our political experiments on the capacity of mankind for self-government." The fathers of the republic were not intimidated by the paradoxes often supposed to lie in the term "self-government." Those paradoxes, largely verbal, can be discounted by considering the relation between rulers and ruled under a constitutional government.

Aristotle had pointed out, many centuries before, that under constitutional government the citizens rule and are ruled in turn. They are both rulers and ruled. The office of citizenship is the primary and permanent office in a constitutional regime; all other offices, including that of the chief magistrate, are secondary offices, to which citizens are eligible and which some of them fill for a period of time, to resume their status as private citizens when they leave public office.

The people—the body of the citizens constituting the ruling class—must, therefore, be regarded as the permanent principal rulers in a constitutional democracy. The officeholders, the public officials or magistrates to whom the administration of the government is entrusted while they hold office, are by contrast with the citizens the transient instrumental rulers, directly or indirectly elected by the people and responsible to them. . . . [The] citizens remain the principal rulers and the temporary occupants of public offices function as their instruments of self-government.

Under the Constitution of the United States, officeholders wield whatever authority and power are vested in their office by the Constitution. Neither the authority nor the power belongs to them personally, but rather to the office they hold. They exercise it only as officeholders. Their exercise of it is subject, even concurrently with that exercise, to such critical inspection and control by the people as will not render them impotent for the performance of their designated instrumental functions. In addition, they are liable to impeachment and removal from office when they exceed the constitutional authority vested in their office or usurp powers not allotted to them, as well as when they commit other high crimes and misdemeanors. A constitutional government is thus a government of laws in the sense that no man is above the law and no man has political authority or legitimate power except that which is conferred upon him by the people who govern themselves through the services of their political instruments—public officials or officeholders.

To say that constitutional democracy is both government *of* the people and government *by* the people is to say that the people are both the constituents of government through acts of consent to the constitution which they have adopted as the framework of government, and also that they are enfranchised citizens participating through the exercise of their suffrage in self-government—not directly, but indirectly through their representatives upon whom they have conferred the authority to administer the functions of government. In the last analysis, government in a democracy, even if it is through representatives rather than through the direct action of the citizens, is government by the people.

. . . government . . . *for* the people . . .

As De Jouvenel pointed out, the phrase, taken by itself, refers to something that is common to all forms of government which are good or just; namely, that they consist in government for the public good, the good of the governed or the community as a whole, not government in the service of the private interests of those who administer the functions of government.

However, democratic governments are charged with doing more *for* the people than are benevolent monarchies and wise aristocracies, precisely because constitutional democracy is fundamentally an experiment in self-government. Just as government *by* the people takes on a special significance from the fact that it is, first of all, the people's government, so too government *for* the people draws its full force from the antecedent fact that it is both government *of* and also *by* the people.

The idea of democracy presupposes that all men are not only equal under the law but equal as well in their claim to the rights of life, liberty, and the pursuit of happiness that a just government must try to make secure for them. Accordingly, democratic governments have an obligation that is inherent in the idea of democracy but alien to the idea of monarchy and the idea of aristocracy—the obligation to secure for all the rights to which all have an equal claim.

The Preamble's statement of the purposes of our government enunciates an articulation of the common good. Of the six purposes or objectives of government there stated, the last calls for something that is specific to a constitutional democracy and that enlarges—and immeasurably deepens—the conception of the common good. No other form of government is called upon by its constituents "to secure the blessings of liberty for ourselves and our posterity."

Being a limited government, a constitutional democracy is restrained from invading certain precincts of purely personal liberty. Being accountable to the people, it must not only respect, but it must also strive to enhance, those freedoms which the people need for the mature, critical control of government—freedom of thought, freedom of expression, freedom of association and of public assembly, freedom to dissent and to petition for the redress of grievances.

Because the idea of democracy entails such additional things that a democratic government is obliged to do *for* the people, democracy is pre-eminently "government *for* the people," and, therefore, once again in Jefferson's words, "the only truly just form of government."

If the idea of democracy became at this nation's birth something it regarded itself as holding in trust for the world and for the future, and if Lincoln's oracular triad of prepositional phrases indeed epitomizes that idea, then we have not been wrong in regarding Lincoln's last ten words as the focal point of the American Testament. (pp. 131-36)

> *Mortimer J. Adler and William Gorman, "The Gettysburg Address," in their* The American Testament, *Praeger Publishers, 1975, pp. 121-36.*

JAMES HURT (essay date 1980)

[*Hurt examines several "characteristic images" in Lincoln's speeches, explaining their significance as expressions of both Lincoln's self-perception and the self-perception of the nation.*]

Lincoln's greatest speeches have the kind of resonance that we associate with poetry, a reverberation through multiple levels of experience, both public and private. And the mediating force that links these levels of experience is his imagery. During the period of intensive self-examination and self-development which Lincoln underwent between the ages of about twenty-two and twenty-eight, he seems to have come to define himself and his lifework in terms of images already well established in his culture, images of family rivalry, of distant perspectives, and of the earth and the span of human life. These images, commonplace as they were, seem to have become deeply and personally meaningful to Lincoln and to have provided a way of resolving conflicts in his own personality that threatened to become paralyzing. But the fact that they had a public dimension as well meant that, in the speeches of his maturity, the more personal and deeply felt his expression was, the more, paradoxically, he seemed to speak for his followers and for the age itself. The bullets of his words were driven by the powder not only of his own complicated personality but of the deepest self-perceptions of the nation itself. The few simple words of the **"Gettysburg Address"** seem to capture a wholeness because they are at once a luminously clear and moving response to the immediate situation, a profoundly personal expression of Lincoln's own identity, and an equally profound expression of the self-perception of the nation. And the links among these layers—the "mystic chords" that resonate through these levels of experience, to use a Lincolnesque phrase—are the speech's simple but rich images. (p. 353)

The crucial period for the study of Lincoln's personality is the New Salem years, between 1831 and 1837, when Lincoln was twenty-two to twenty-eight years old. (pp. 353-54)

Lincoln was confronting during these years the classic challenges of young manhood: the challenge to achieve intimacy, in friendship as well as sexuality; the challenge of occupational choice, of finding a life task that would allow the full exercise of his abilities; the challenge of competition, of measuring himself against his fellows; and the challenge of self-definition, of determining who he was, both personally and socially. (p. 356)

How did Lincoln meet the multiple life challenges of the years of his young manhood in New Salem? Judging from indirect, external evidence, the only kind we have, his struggle was against everything his father stood for, and he resolved the struggle by wiping his personal slate clean of his father's values. Lincoln came to New Salem a country man, heir to a paternal tradition of manual labor, Jacksonian democratic principles, and fundamentalist religion. He left a city man, a lawyer, a Whig, and a religious skeptic. There have been a number of attempts to document Lincoln's undoubted alienation from his father, on very scanty evidence. But the personal alienation is ultimately less important than the extent to which Lincoln rejected his father's entire world. His father had led the unsettled, individualistic life of subsistence farming on a series of farms, each farther west. Lincoln cast his lot with the city, life as a professional man in a fixed place among his fellows. The choice of the law itself was a repudiation of frontier values. To men of Thomas Lincoln's background, the law was the instrument of the rich and powerful, who could use its complexities to outwit the common man and do him out of his property; he himself had left Kentucky to avoid a tangle of litigation over titles to all three of the farms he had owned in Kentucky. Lincoln came to see the law not as trickery or showmanship, though he could employ showmanship when it suited his purposes, but as the instrument of reason and justice, a way of bringing order to the entanglements of human affairs.

Along with his father's nomadic, frontier way of life, Lincoln rejected, during his New Salem years, his father's Jacksonian political faith. There was much in Jacksonian democracy which Lincoln never repudiated, including its reverence for the people and its goal of allowing maximum opportunity to the common

man. But during his New Salem years, he came to distrust Jacksonian egalitarianism and emotionalism and, under the influence of reading Henry Clay's speeches, took the politically dangerous step of casting his lot with the Whigs and their ideal of an open and democratic society led by a natural aristocracy of ability and reason. (pp. 357-58)

Lincoln's mature religious views, formed during the New Salem years, similarly involved a rejection of frontier emotionalism in favor of reason. Both Thomas Lincoln and Sarah Bush Lincoln were active members of the Pigeon Baptist Church during Lincoln's childhood, and Thomas Lincoln served both on the discipline committee and as a trustee. It may be possible to trace some reminiscences of his father's faith in Lincoln's mature beliefs, but consciously and intellectually Lincoln rejected it, along with his father's economics and his politics. . . . John T. Stuart, Lincoln's first law partner, wrote Herndon, "He was an avowed and open infidel, and sometimes bordered on atheism . . . went further against Christian beliefs and doctrines and principles than any man I ever heard; he shocked me. I don't remember the exact line of his argument; suppose it was against the inherent defects, so-called, of the Bible, and on grounds of reason. Lincoln always denied that Jesus was the Christ of God—denied that Jesus was the son of God as understood and maintained by the Christian Church." The evolution of Lincoln's religious views, any more than his political views, did not stop in New Salem, but for the time at least, he seems to have defined himself in opposition, rather than in conformity, to paternal values. (pp. 358-59)

In attempting to understand Lincoln's development after 1837, we can draw upon more direct evidence than for the earlier years, since we have not only Herndon's detailed and persuasive account but a substantial body of Lincoln's own writings, comparatively sparse and unrevealing before 1837. In the brilliant final chapter of his biography, Herndon chose to emphasize five qualities of Lincoln as more important than any other: his melancholy, his ambition, his emotional coldness, his reverence for reason, and his inclination to view experience from a distant, philosophical perspective. (p. 359)

Lincoln's depressions were a recurring element in his personality. . . . "He was a sad-looking man," Herndon wrote; "his melancholy dripped from him as he walked. His apparent gloom impressed his friends, and created sympathy for him—one means of his great success. He was gloomy, abstracted, and joyous—rather humorous—by turns; but I do not think he knew what real joy was for many years."

No satisfactory answer has ever been given as to the causes of Lincoln's depressions. But their nature and their timing suggest that they may have been related to his ambition and guilt over the radical revolt against his father's world to which it had led him. . . . Herndon's controversial emphasis upon Lincoln's marital unhappiness as a source of his melancholy has obscured the fact that he also connected Lincoln's depressions with his ambition, which Herndon called "a little engine that knew no rest." He regarded Lincoln's depressions as hereditary and therefore finally inexplicable, but he thought the contributory causes were not only Lincoln's domestic trials but also, "unquestionably," "the knowledge of his own obscure and lowly origin" and the contrast with his own lofty hopes. (pp. 359-60)

The lifting of Lincoln's most crippling depression coincided with the beginning of his rise to professional success as a lawyer and legislator, with its implications of consolidation of values and beliefs, success in adult competition, and self-confirmation in rewarding work. The challenge of establishing and maintaining intimate personal relationships was still largely unresolved and would remain so to some extent for the rest of his life. Herndon concluded that ''In general terms his life was cold—at least characterized by what many persons would deem great indifference. He had, however, a strong latent capacity to love: but the object must first come in the guise of a principle, next it must be right and true—then it was lovely in his sight. He loved humanity when it was oppressed—an abstract love as against the concrete love centred in an individual.'' (pp. 360-61)

A view of Lincoln's personality during the 1840s as recurringly absorbed in the problem of defining himself and ''making a place for himself'' against paternal values, undergoing severe depressions over the conflicts inherent in that problem, and finding personal intimacy difficult and threatening helps to illuminate two other characteristics of Lincoln which Herndon found striking and which appear prominently in the writings of the forties: an idealization of reason and an inclination to minimize immediate circumstances by taking a distant temporal and spatial perspective. Both, whatever their virtues as ways of thinking, are also modes of transcendence, of ''rising above'' a painful subjectivity into a comparatively safe objectivity. Lincoln wrote, in his 1842 [''**Temperance Address Delivered before the Springfield Washington Temperance Society**'']: ''Happy day, when, all appetites controlled, all passions subdued, all matters subjected, *mind,* all conquering *mind,* shall live and move the monarch of the world. Glorious consummation! Hail, fall of Fury! Reign of Reason, all hail!'' This is conventional fustian which nevertheless expresses an emotional truth, as Herndon makes clear: ''His conscience, his heart and all the faculties and qualities of his mind bowed submissively to the despotism of his reason. He lived and acted from the standard of reason—that throne of logic, home of principle— the realm of Deity in man.'' . . . Lincoln was always strongly attracted to abstract logical systems, and his course of self-improvement at New Salem included the study of mathematics, logic, and grammar. Later, he studied and ''nearly mastered'' the six books of Euclid and practiced writing out propositions in three different forms. The connection between such clear, hard-edged studies and personal autonomy is suggested by the association of ideas in his statement in his 1860 third-person autobiography: ''After he was twenty-three and had separated from his father, he studied English grammar—imperfectly, of course, but so as to speak and write as well as he does now.''

Lincoln's attraction toward the generalized and the abstract also appears in a tendency which Herndon noted to take ''the long view,'' to habitually view experience in a long and even cosmic perspective. . . . [This tendency] appears in his works as a habitual concern with history, both national and personal. He is preoccupied with beginnings and endings, with the origins of present political conditions in the national past and on the individual level with birth and death, the entire span of man's life.

Lincoln's capacity for clear reasoning and his ability to see the immediate and the particular in the context of historical process were major factors in his success; as were also his ambition, his cool control over personal relationships, and perhaps, as Herndon suggests, even his melancholy. Lincoln's personality was a magnificently integrated one; whatever the emotional source of the elements of his personality, by 1858, when he came upon the national political scene, he had so mastered and balanced these elements as to ''make a place'' for himself in history.

The speech on ''**The Perpetuation of Our Political Institutions**'' which Lincoln delivered before the Young Men's Lyceum of Springfield in 1838 is full of the imagery of filial revolt, distanced by being placed in a broad, impersonal, philosophical perspective. Very much a product of its age, the speech expresses the dominant political mythology of pre-Civil War America. But it is at the same time a personal statement; Lincoln found in the public imagery of his time a language for expressing the complex tension and conflicts in his own personality. (pp. 361-64)

Lincoln's subject is what he regards as ''the increasing disregard for law which pervades the country; the growing disposition to substitute the wild and furious passions, in lieu of the sober judgment of Courts; and the worse than savage mobs, for the executive ministers of justice''; he cites several examples of mob violence and places them against the background of a broad interpretation of the course of American history. In the first half of the speech, Lincoln vividly describes the incidents which concern him and calls upon his listeners to adhere strictly to the laws of the country. He turns, in the second half, to a much broader consideration of the problem. Why, he asks, are our political institutions in particular jeopardy at this time? His answer is that the present generation stands in a new and particularly dangerous relation to the Fathers of the Revolution. The Revolution provided a glorious field of achievement for the Fathers; their own glory was inseparably linked with the success of the democratic experiment. But ''this field of glory is harvested, and the crop is already appropriated.'' Equally ambitious men of the present generation will find that the work of building up has been accomplished and that the only challenge which remains is the lesser one of preserving what the Fathers have created. Bold, ambitious men may appear who are not content with this comparatively humble mission and who will seek to win glory, not by building up but by pulling down what has been created. How can we deal with this threat to our institutions? Only, Lincoln concludes, by renouncing the lofty passion which spurred the Fathers and placing our faith in reason, ''cold, calculating, unimpassioned reason . . . moulded into *general intelligence, sound morality,* and, in particular, *a reverence for the constitution and laws.*''

The domestic metaphor and the father-son rivalry implicit in this view of American history were very much a part of the conventional attitudes of Lincoln's age, as George B. Forgie has recently persuasively argued and massively documented. A powerful and widespread domestic metaphor was established and disseminated not only by patriotic oratory but by childhood patriotic training. The Union was a home, the founders were fathers, the land itself was a nurturing mother, and the sons were brothers in a family, charged with the duty of honoring the Fathers and preserving their legacy. The effect of this metaphor, which was so deeply embedded in the national consciousness as partially to lose its status as metaphor, was to color political conflicts with the emotions and fantasies of private, family life. The generation which, in the 1820s, succeeded the generation of the founding fathers almost universally adopted the view which Lincoln expressed, that theirs was a diminished age, that the days of heroic achievement were over, and that they could only win the lesser glory of preserving what their fathers had created.

Lincoln not only states this view of American history in its fullest form in the Lyceum speech, he also goes on to examine its implications in a way that leads Forgie to call the speech ''the most profound contemporary study . . . of the problem of ambition in the post-heroic age.'' Lincoln's view of the Fathers is deeply ambivalent. Although he begins by paying conventional homage to the Fathers, that ''*once* hardy, brave, and patriotic, but *now* lamented and departed race of ancestors,'' he goes on to reject the view that the Fathers were more virtuous than their Sons. They acted, after all, out of self-interest; they sought ''celebrity and fame, and distinction'' in the success of their experiment. And they were just as subject to the baser passions of ''jealousy, envy, and avarice'' as their Sons; they were merely more fortunate to live in a time which either subdued such passions or directed them against the British. Therefore, that they succeeded was ''not much to be wondered at.''

The combination of homage and hostility in Lincoln's treatment of the Fathers reflects the paradoxes inherent in the domestic metaphor. The Sons were challenged from the cradle to ''be like Washington,'' but grew up in a world that presented no greater opportunities for heroic action than a seat in Congress. It was common to accept this paradox and resign oneself to diminished opportunities. Thus Charles Francis Adams wrote, in 1834, ''It is for us to *preserve,* and not to create,'' and Daniel Webster, in 1843, ''Heaven has not allotted to this generation an opportunity of rendering high services, and manifesting strong personal devotion, such as [the fathers] rendered and manifested. . . . But we may praise what we cannot equal, and celebrate actions which we were not born to perform.'' Lincoln initially agrees that his generation should accept the comparatively humble task of preserving the Father's legacy, but he thinks it likely that eventually ambitious men will arise who will be dissatisfied with such contracted horizons. Such a man will seek distinction above all else, and although he may be as inclined to win it by creation as by destruction, ''that opportunity being past, and nothing left to be done in the way of building up, he would set boldly to the task of pulling down.'' The only defense against such a rebellious spirit is ''cold, calculating, unimpassioned reason.''

In addressing the immediate problem of the rising violence and lawlessness in the United States, Lincoln thus called upon a prevailing mythology and cast the problem in its terms. He reaffirms the heroism of the Fathers and the duty of the Sons to preserve their legacy. Violence, passion, and lawlessness are acts of bad sons: ''Let every man remember that to violate the law, is to trample on the blood of his father.'' Good sons must accept the unheroic task of ''supporting and maintaining an edifice that has been erected by others'' and must be prepared to erect a bulwark of reason and law against the threat of rebellious bad sons.

But **''The Perpetuation of Our Political Institutions''** is a personal statement as well as a restatement and critique of a national myth. On the personal level, its subject is still the one which preoccupied Lincoln through his early manhood: ''making a place for oneself.'' Lincoln describes the potential rebel in romantic, Byronic terms which reveal the figure's deep attraction for Lincoln himself. Some ''great and good men'' may be found who will be satisfied with a seat in Congress, a governorship, or even the presidency,

> but such belong not to the family of the lion, or the tribe of the eagle. What! think you these places would satisfy an Alexander, a Caesar, or a Napoleon?—Never! Towering genius disdains a beaten path. It seeks regions hitherto unexplored.—It sees *no distinction* in adding story to story, upon the monuments of fame,

A view of the presidential box in Ford's Theatre, where Lincoln was assassinated.

> erected to the memory of others. It *denies* that it is glory enough to serve under any chief. It *scorns* to tread in the footsteps of any predecessor, however illustrious. It thirsts and burns for distinction; and, if possible, it will have it, whether at the expense of emancipating slaves, or enslaving freemen.

This rebel is a strictly hypothetical figure, of course, the product of Lincoln's own imagination, and he is described in such heroic terms that he would seem, even if it were not for the rather startling reference to emancipation, to be a projection of the speaker's own potentialities. (pp. 364-67)

The ambivalent figure of the heroic rebel reflects the central problem of self-realization for Lincoln and for his age: how to achieve full selfhood without incurring the guilt of overthrowing the father. The solution in the speech, as in Lincoln's life, is reason. The forces of murderous filial rebellion can be held in check only by ''cold, calculating, unimpassioned reason,'' a political theory which corresponds precisely to a personal policy which idealizes reason as a bulwark against the urgent but threatening demands of self-realization.

But Lincoln's argument does not end by counseling the renunciation of heroic ambition in favor of repressive reason, either politically or personally. Ultimately he rejects both romantic rebellion and resignation to perpetual inferiority to the heroic fathers in favor of a third alternative: winning immortal glory through overthrowing and expelling the rebel. Preserving the Fathers' legacy can be in itself a heroic task if it involves, not mere petty administration, but challenging and defeating the lawless rebel who threatens that legacy. Law and reason can thus become not the enemy of ambition but its instrument, and the good son, by expelling the bad son, can win not only glory but the gratitude of the fathers, when "the last trump shall awaken our Washington."

The role of the lonely hero defending the Union was a particularly congenial one for Lincoln, perhaps because it reconciled so powerfully the competing claims of ambition and filiopiety. Less than two years after the Lyceum speech, Lincoln ended an otherwise fairly routine speech on the Sub-Treasury thus: "If ever I feel the soul within me elevate and expand to those dimensions not wholly unworthy of its Almighty Architect, it is when I contemplate the cause of my country, deserted by all the world beside, and I standing up boldly alone, and hurling defiance at her victorious oppressors." . . . By 1858, he was saying to his listeners, in defending the principles of the Declaration of Independence, "You may do anything with me you choose, if you will but heed these sacred principles. You may not only defeat me for the Senate, but you may take me and put me to death." And in 1861, on his way to Washington for his inauguration, he told a crowd in Philadelphia that if the country could not be saved on the basis of the principles in the Declaration of Independence, he "would rather be assassinated on this spot" than surrender them.

To Forgie, Lincoln's fantasy of "the besieged house," with himself cast in the role of the hero defending the Fathers' legacy against a rebellious tyrant, decisively shaped his political career and contributed to the outbreak of the Civil War. Lincoln found his anticipated tyrant in the person of Stephen A. Douglas, overthrew him, and devoted the remainder of his life to restoring the Fathers' "house divided." . . . Lincoln's attitudes and behavior were undoubtedly colored by his private fantasies, but there is no reason to believe that he ever lost the distinction between fantasy and reality. Black slavery and the loss of civil rights under the slavocracy that ruled the South were real threats to American democracy, as was Douglas, to the extent that his politics contributed to the perpetuation and extension of slavery. One might argue, perhaps more validly, that the myth of the besieged house which Lincoln shared with his followers did not warp their view of reality but gave them an instrument to confront wrongs that had been covered up and protected by the conventional rationalizations of majority opinion.

The besieged house myth which Lincoln presented so fully and with such romantic rhetoric in the Lyceum speech was to reappear in chaster form in the ["*House Divided" Speech*] of 1858 and its elements were to form the major images of the great speeches of the War years. At once deeply rooted in Lincoln's own self-perceptions and expressive of the self-perception of the nation, it was a major factor in the complex interweaving of personality and history that made Lincoln's voice so powerful a force in the last eight years of his life. (pp. 368-70)

[It] is generally agreed that Lincoln's personality and manner of expression changed noticeably during the last years. He was elected as the frontier scrapper of the [**Lincoln-Douglas Debates**] and the formidable logician of the [*Cooper Union Speech*]; by the time of his assassination, he had become "Father Abraham," a gentle, compassionate, melancholy figure already being compared to Christ. The shift in emphasis from logic to emotion in his thought has been attributed, probably correctly, to the crucible of responsibility and suffering he passed through in his final years. . . . But the emergence of a new emotional quality may also be related, at a deeper level, to the resolution of long-standing conflicts in his personality. Emotion had been linked for him with the dangerous claims of self-realization and filial rebellion; logic had been the instrument for holding these impulses in check. But now, the mission of saving the

Union reconciled the claims of self-realization and filiopiety, and the urgent need for logic as a defense against his own impulses receded. The terms in which Lincoln perceived reality and himself remained the same, however, throughout the last years of his life, even as he shifted his emphasis from logic to emotion, from defense to mission. He continued his preoccupation with father-son relationships, the maternal earth, and the distancing, objectifying power of large temporal and spatial perspectives. The "**Farewell to Springfield**" and the "**Gettysburg Address**" may be taken as representative of the great speeches Basler singles out as containing the new note of emotion in Lincoln's last years. (pp. 370-71)

An important element in the tone of [the "**Farewell to Springfield**"] is the long temporal perspective Lincoln adopts. He places the present moment in the large context of his own life and of the nation's life, structuring the speech around past, present, and future, underscored by the parallel verb phrases "Here I have lived . . . ," "I now leave . . . ," and "let us confidently hope. . . ." Temporal change, in this large perspective, is represented as decline, and the speech is thus heavily nostalgic. In Springfield, Lincoln has "passed from a young to an old man," and this biological pattern is transferred to the present situation. The past is idealized ("To this place, and the kindness of these people, I owe everything"), while the present is ominous ("I now leave, not knowing when or whether ever I may return"), and the future imponderable ("Let us confidently hope that all will yet be well"). Furthermore, the pattern of aging and decline is applied to the nation's life as well as his own. The task before him is "greater than that which rested upon Washington"; in the three quarters of a century since the nation was founded, the threats to its existence have become greater rather than lesser. In a phrase, Lincoln implies the same view of American history he had developed more melodramatically in the Lyceum speech: the Fathers were a "forest of giant oaks" of which there remained only "here and there, a lonely trunk" and "pillars of the temple of liberty," now "crumbled away."

The strong orientation to the past in Lincoln's references to both his personal life and the life of the nation serve an obvious emotional function for Lincoln at this moment. On the train, about to be carried away from long-time friends to an uncertain and threatening future, he naturally turns with nostalgia to the past. But it also touches a responsive chord in the spirit of the nation, the tendency in the 1850s toward what Forgie calls "sentimental regression," Ann Douglas designates "the feminization of American culture," and Elizabeth Akers expressed in the most popular song of 1861: "Backward, turn backward, O Time, in your flight,/Make me a child again just for to-night!" The vigorous, forward-looking spirit of the "Young America" movement of the 1830s and forties gave way in the fifties to a widespread domesticization of American life, which amounted to an attempt to escape the rising conflicts of political life by returning Americans, in Forgie's words, to "their childhood, the security of their early homes, and even to the bosom of their mothers." (pp. 372-73)

The note of domestic regression is struck in the "**Farewell to Springfield**" not only in the treatment of time, with its strong pull toward the past, but in the treatment of space, with a suggestion of the idealization of the maternal earth. The speech is literally a farewell to Springfield, the physical place as well as the people, as Lincoln emphasizes in the second sentence: "To this place, and the kindness of these people, I owe everything." In the rest of the speech, he deals with the place and then with the people, a second structure overlaying the past-present-future pattern. ''Here I have lived a quarter of a century,'' he says, clearly referring to the physical place, and ''here my children have been born, and one is buried,'' associating the earth with both the maternal womb and the grave. It is only with the final sentence that he turns decisively away from the place to the people: ''To His care commending you, as I hope in your prayers you will commend me, I bid you an affectionate farewell.''

The regressive qualities of the imagery of the past and the earth in the speech are, however, balanced by a third set of images in the speech which deal with fatherhood. Lincoln begins by representing himself as a father: here I have ''passed from a young to an old man,'' and ''here my children have been born.'' He turns next to another kind of father; the task before him is ''greater than that which rested upon Washington.'' And he turns finally to a third kind of father: the ''Divine Being'' who can ''go with me, and remain with you, and be everywhere for good.'' To the patterns of past-present-future and place-people, we can thus add a third structure; personal father-national father-divine Father. This sequence embodies the domestic metaphor; the three kinds of father are equated, and political and religious matters are seen to some degree in terms of family relationships.

The sense of mission is very strong in the [''**Farewell to Springfield**''], and it is significant that Lincoln has come to see himself as a father rather than a son.... But in being a good father, he is also being a good son. He has found a way to rival the Fathers in glory, while remaining loyal to them. His task is ''greater than that which rested upon Washington,'' but he will be found true to the Fathers ''when the last trump shall awaken our Washington.'' (pp. 373-74)

Lincoln's characteristic imagery nowhere appears more explicitly and fully than in the **''Gettysburg Address.''** At the same time, nowhere is it expressed in a tighter, more highly controlled form. It seems that Lincoln, in baring such primitive emotional material as that in the [''**Gettysburg Address**''], felt intuitively the need to impose correspondingly powerful formal controls. Hence the highly wrought rhetoric of the [''**Gettysburg Address**''], the complex patterns of repetition of sounds, words, and phrases, the subtle allusiveness, and the cadence-like rhythms.

Like the **''Farewell to Springfield''**, the **''Gettysburg Address''** is built upon a simple pattern of past-present-future. It is shaped like an hour-glass, beginning with the point most general and most distant in time, narrowing rapidly to the specific, immediate occasion, and then broadening again to the distant perspective of the future. In the opening sentence, Lincoln's characteristic homage to the age of the Revolution becomes thoroughly mythologized, distanced not only by time but by a network of echoes of the King James Bible. ''Four score and seven years ago'' recalls ''the days of our years are three score and ten,'' ''our fathers,'' echoes the opening of the Lord's Prayer, and ''brought forth'' reminds us, however faintly, of ''and she brought forth a babe and wrapped him in swaddling clothes and laid him in a manger.''

After the sinuous rhythms of the opening sentences, Lincoln brings us in three comparatively abrupt, parallel sentences from the mythic past to the present occasion: ''Now we are engaged....,'' ''We are met...,'' and ''We have come to dedicate....'' In the three central sentences that form the heart of the [''**Gettysburg Address**''], Lincoln considers the present,

and in these sentences he implies quietly and unpolemically the conception of ''mission'' he had made explicit in the Lyceum speech. The ''brave men, living and dead, who struggled here'' are implicitly balanced against ''our fathers'' and are found at least equally worthy of glory. The fathers ''brought forth'' the new nation, but the sons have given their lives ''that that nation might live.'' On the one hand, the sons have remained true to the fathers; they have given ''the last full measure of devotion'' to preserve the fathers' heritage. But they have succeeded at the same time in rivaling and perhaps surpassing the fathers; preservation, in the midst of ''a great civil war,'' is at least as glorious a task as the act of creation. But we are sons, too, and in the last three sentences of the speech, Lincoln turns to the future and the living. The dead have won immortal glory: the world ''can never forget what they did here.'' We cannot win comparable glory by ''what we say here''—the world will ''little note, nor long remember'' that—but we can adopt their sacrifice as a model for our own actions and seek our fame in preservation of the father's legacy.

This fundamental past-present-future structure of the speech is undergirded by a tight symmetry of sentence groups, which consist of an arrangement of threes. After the introductory sentence, the speech consists of three groups of three sentences each devoted respectively to the past, the present, and the future. By far the longest and most complex sentences are the first and last: their stately rhythms, contrasted with the comparative speed and simplicity of the central sentences, reenforce our sense of broad perspectives framing the immediate occasion.

The meaning of history, in the **''Gettysburg Address,''** lies in the relationship of fathers and sons, and this imagery is the dominant imagery of the speech. But closely related to this imagery and constituting another broad structural pattern in the [''**Gettysburg Address''**] is imagery of birth-death-rebirth. The Biblical association of ''brought forth'' is with birth, an association reenforced by the ambiguity of ''conceived in Liberty.'' On the one hand, ''conceived'' anticipates ''proposition'' and suggests the roots of the national experiment in reason. On the other hand, it rhymes conceptually with ''brought forth'' and suggests an identification of the national life with the individual life. Life and death are treated paradoxically in the central section of the speech. Individual men are dead, but the nation lives; they gave their lives ''that the nation might live.'' And yet, metaphorically, the nation itself has died, so closely intertwined are the national and the individual life. The nation itself, after these deaths, must have a ''new birth of freedom,'' this time into immortality, so that it shall never ''perish from the earth.''

The imagery of birth, death, and rebirth in the **''Gettysburg Address''** is not only emotionally evocative in itself, it also serves, characteristically, to provide an emotional distance from the barely concealed material of filial rivalry. This imagery, like the distant historical perspective of the temporal imagery, suggests an almost cosmic perspective upon human conflict, with beginnings and endings held simultaneously in the mind. In this respect, it recalls the **''Farewell to Springfield,''** with its similar emphasis upon birth and death: ''Here I... have passed from a young to an old man. Here my children have been born, and one is buried.''

The connection of this imagery to a third chain of images in the [''**Gettysburg Address**''] is suggested by the rhyme of birth/earth in the last sentence. And here again we may recall the **''Farewell to Springfield,''** with its strong sense of a physical place and its maternal associations. The word ''earth'' does not appear in the ["**Gettysburg Address**"] until the end; it is the last word of the speech. But it is anticipated by a number of conceptual rhymes which appear throughout: "continent," "battlefield" and "ground." The phrase "our fathers brought forth on this continent" establishes a strong maternal association for the physical land. But by the middle of the speech, the womb has become a tomb: the "field" is a "final resting place." At the same time, by their sacrifice, the dead have "hallowed" this ground, and "hallowed" takes on overtones of fertilization in the context of the act as performed so "that nation might live." This suggestion is reenforced by the final reference to the physical earth, which associates it with "a new birth of freedom."

The major images of the "**Gettysburg Address**"—fathers and sons, time, birth and death, and the earth—are all domestic in the general sense. Lincoln's subject is public and collective and he casts his remarks in a tone of public ceremoniousness. But underlying the explicit meaning of his words is a rich imagery of individual and family life. These images are rooted deep in Lincoln's own emotional experiences and in his view of himself. But Lincoln's imagery was drawn from the imagery of a nation in a "post-heroic" age, simultaneously worshipful and resentful of "the fathers," and continually drawn both toward lofty, glorious achievement and toward withdrawal into a safe domesticity. Perhaps we perceive the "**Gettysburg Address**," along with Lincoln's other central works, as capturing a "wholeness" in "a few simple words" because their imagery touches so many of these chords in the national experience. (pp. 377-80)

> *James Hurt, "All the Living and the Dead: Lincoln's Imagery," in* American Literature, *Vol. 52, No. 3, November, 1980, pp. 351-80.*

ADDITIONAL BIBLIOGRAPHY

Abraham Lincoln Association Papers. Springfield, Ill.: Abraham Lincoln Association, 1929-39.
> An annual publication featuring commentary by noted scholars on various aspects of Lincoln's life, work, and times. From 1924 to 1928, this periodical was published under the title *Lincoln Centennial Association Papers.*

Anderson, David. "Abraham Lincoln, Man of Letters." *University College Quarterly* 12, No. 2 (January 1967): 3-8.
> Attributes Lincoln's literary greatness to his ability to capture the "essence of the American experience" in words.

Angle, Paul M. *A Shelf of Lincoln Books: A Critical, Selective Bibliography of Lincolniana.* New Brunswick, N.J.: Rutgers University Press in association with The Abraham Lincoln Association of Springfield, Illinois, 1946, 142 p.
> A highly regarded annotated bibliography of writings basic to the study of Lincoln. Angle covers both nineteenth-century Lincolniana and twentieth-century Lincoln books published through 1946.

———. "The Changing Lincoln." In *The John H. Hauberg Historical Essays,* edited by O. Fritiof Ander, pp. 1-17. Augustana Library Publications, edited by Lucien White, no. 26. Rock Island, Ill.: Denkmann Memorial Library, Augustana College, 1954.
> Summarizes developments in modern Lincoln scholarship, noting changes in historians' views concerning such issues as Lincoln's relationship with Ann Rutledge and his policy regarding the secession crisis.

———. Introduction to *Created Equal? The Complete Lincoln-Douglas Debates of 1858,* by Abraham Lincoln and Stephen A. Douglas, pp. v-xxx. Chicago: University of Chicago Press, 1958.
> A historical introduction to the Lincoln-Douglas Debates, focusing on the political background of the candidates' discussion of the slavery issue.

Barondess, Benjamin. *Three Lincoln Masterpieces: "Cooper Institute Speech," "Gettysburg Address," "Second Inaugural."* Charleston: Education Foundation of West Virginia, 1954, 156 p.
> Discusses the background, content, and reception of the *Cooper Union Speech,* "Gettysburg Address," and *Second Inaugural Address.*

Barton, William E. *A Beautiful Blunder: The True Story of Lincoln's Letter to Mrs. Lydia A. Bixby.* Indianapolis, Ind.: Bobbs-Merrill Co., 1926, 135 p.
> Presents information concerning the origin of Lincoln's "Letter to Mrs. Bixby" and the history of the Bixby family.

Basler, Roy P. *The Lincoln Legend: A Study in Changing Conceptions.* Boston: Houghton Mifflin Co., Riverside Press, 1935, 336 p.
> A critical examination by a noted Lincoln scholar of the mythology surrounding Lincoln.

———. "Abraham Lincoln—Artist." *The North American Review* 245, No. 1 (Spring 1938): 144-53.
> Hails Lincoln as a "literary genius," predicting that "his prose may yet be recognized as his most permanent legacy to humanity."

———. "Lincoln's Development as a Writer." In *Abraham Lincoln: His Speeches and Writings,* by Abraham Lincoln, edited by Roy P. Basler, pp. 1-49. Cleveland: World Publishing Co., 1946.
> An extensive discussion of Lincoln's literary evolution. Basler's essay is generally considered one of the best treatments of Lincoln as a writer.

Bauer, Marvin G. "Persuasive Methods in the Lincoln-Douglas Debates." *The Quarterly Journal of Speech Education* XIII, No. 1 (February 1927): 29-39.
> Explores the candidates' attempts to use personal character as a factor in the Lincoln-Douglas Debates.

Berkelman, Robert. "Lincoln's Interest in Shakespeare." *Shakespeare Quarterly* II (October 1951): 303-12.
> A general discussion of Lincoln's knowledge of and enthusiasm for Shakespeare's works.

Betts, William W., Jr., ed. *Lincoln and the Poets.* Pittsburgh: University of Pittsburgh Press, 1965, 140 p.
> An anthology of poems on Lincoln composed by James Russell Lowell, Paul Laurence Dunbar, Carl Sandburg, Vachel Lindsay, and other distinguished writers.

Blegen, Theodore C. *Lincoln's Imagery: A Study in Word Power.* La Crosse, Wis.: Sumac Press, 1954, 32 p.
> Highlights Lincoln's use of figures of speech in writing and conversation.

Charnwood, Lord. *Abraham Lincoln.* New York: Henry Holt and Co., 1917, 482 p.
> Widely admired as one of the best early biographies of Lincoln.

Current, Richard N. *The Lincoln Nobody Knows.* New York: McGraw-Hill Book Co., 1958, 314 p.
> Explores several controversial aspects of Lincoln's life, including his marriage, military strategy, and assassination.

Dana, Richard H. "Nullity of the Emancipation Edict." *The North American Review* CXXXI, No. 285 (August 1880): 128-34.
> Contends that the *Emancipation Proclamation* was invalid.

De Alvarez, Leo Paul S., ed. *Abraham Lincoln, "The Gettysburg Address," and American Constitutionalism.* Irving, Tex.: University of Dallas Press, 1976, 203 p.
> A collection of essays focused on Lincoln's "political religion" as revealed in the "Gettysburg Address." Contributors to the

volume include DeAlvarez, Laurence Berns, Eva Brann, Glen E. Thurow, and George Anastaplo.

Dodd, William E. *Lincoln or Lee: Comparison and Contrast of the Two Greatest Leaders in the War between the States; The Narrow and Accidental Margins of Success*. New York: Century Co., 1928, 177 p.
    A study of the two Civil War leaders, whom Dodd describes as "representative of everlasting differences among men."

Dodge, Daniel Kilham. "Abraham Lincoln: The Evolution of His Literary Style." *The University Studies* (University of Illinois) I, No. 1 (May 1900): 3-58.
    An early consideration of Lincoln's development as a writer.

Donald, David. *Lincoln Reconsidered: Essays on the Civil War Era*. New York: Alfred A. Knopf, 1956, 200 p.
    Indicates fresh means of approaching the study of Lincoln and the Civil War.

Douglas, William O. *Mr. Lincoln and the Negroes: The Long Road to Equality*. New York: Atheneum, 1963, 237 p.
    Credits Lincoln with playing a key role in the struggle for racial equality in the United States.

Dumond, Dwight Lowell, ed. *Southern Editorials on Secession*. 1931. Reprint. Gloucester, Mass.: Peter Smith, 1964, 529 p.
    Reprints Southern newspaper editorials concerning the issue of secession. The volume includes several editorials on the *First Inaugural Address* and other Lincoln speeches.

Fehrenbacher, D. E. *The Changing Image of Lincoln in American Historiography: An Inaugural Lecture Delivered before the University of Oxford on 21 May 1968*. Oxford: Clarendon Press, 1968, 24 p.
    Reviews the evolution of Lincoln's image among historians.

Greeley, Horace. "Greeley's Estimate of Lincoln." *The Century* XLII, No. XX (July 1891): 371-82.
    An assessment of Lincoln's life and career written in about 1868.

Hochmuth, Marie. "Lincoln's *First Inaugural*." In *American Speeches*, edited by Wayland Maxfield Parrish and Marie Hochmuth, pp. 21-71. New York: Longmans, Green and Co., 1954.
    Discusses the background and reception of the *First Inaugural Address* and evaluates the speech from a rhetorical perspective.

Hofstadter, Richard. "Abraham Lincoln and the Self-Made Myth." In his *The American Political Tradition and the Men Who Made It*, pp. 92-134. New York: Alfred A. Knopf, 1948.
    Depicts Lincoln as an ambitious man who, in taking a pragmatic approach to political issues, purchased worldly success at the expense of spiritual tranquility.

Jaffa, Harry V., and Johannsen, Robert W. Introduction to *In the Name of the People: Speeches and Writings of Lincoln and Douglas in the Ohio Campaign of 1859*, by Abraham Lincoln and Stephen A. Douglas, edited by Harry V. Jaffa and Robert W. Johannsen, pp. 1-57. Columbus: Ohio State University Press for The Ohio Historical Society, 1959.
    Details Lincoln's and Douglas's involvement in the 1859 Ohio state elections and examines the issues that they addressed in their speeches and writings.

Kranz, Henry B., ed. *Abraham Lincoln: A New Portrait*. New York: G. P. Putnam's Sons, 1959, 252 p.
    A collection of essays designed to underscore Lincoln's multifaceted personality. The volume includes discussions of such topics as Lincoln and music, Lincoln as a man of letters, and Lincoln and the sciences.

Lowell, James Russell. "Abraham Lincoln." In his *Essays, Poems, and Letters*, edited by William Smith Clark II, pp. 69-93. New York: Odyssey Press, 1948.
    Includes Lincoln's style of public address among the factors that enhanced his national leadership during the Civil War. Lowell first published this essay, a revised version of his 1864 article "The President's Policy," in 1888.

Luthin, Reinhard H. *The Real Abraham Lincoln: A Complete One Volume History of His Life and Times*. Englewood Cliffs, N.J.: Prentice-Hall, 1960, 778 p.
    A modern biography written by an esteemed Lincoln scholar.

Masters, Edgar Lee. "How to Debunk Abraham Lincoln." *The American Mercury* XXXVII, No. 146 (February 1936): 241-44.
    Reviews Basler's *The Lincoln Legend* (see entry above), urging the complete deflation of the Lincoln "myth."

Mitgang, Herbert, ed. *Abraham Lincoln: A Press Portrait; His Life and Times from the Original Documents of the Union, the Confederacy, and Europe*. Chicago: Quadrangle Books, 1971, 519 p.
    Reprints responses to Lincoln in the contemporary press, both foreign and domestic.

Monaghan, Jay. *Lincoln Bibliography, 1839-1939*. 2 vols. Collections of the Illinois State Historical Library, edited by Paul M. Angle, vols. XXXI-XXXII; Bibliographical Series, vols. IV-V. Springfield: Illinois State Historical Library, 1943-45.
    An authoritative annotated bibliography of books and pamphlets by and about Lincoln that covers the years 1839-1939.

Nevins, Allan. *The Emergence of Lincoln*. 2 vols. New York: Charles Scribner's Sons, 1950.
    A detailed study of Lincoln's emergence as a national leader during the years 1857-61.

————, ed. *Lincoln and the "Gettysburg Address": Commemorative Papers*. Urbana: University of Illinois Press, 1964, 133 p.
    A collection of reprinted speeches honoring the centenary of the "Gettysburg Address." The volume includes addresses by John Dos Passos, Arthur Lehman Goodhart, and others.

"President Lincoln's Proclamation of Freedom to the Slaves." *The New Englander* XXIV, No. XC (January 1865): 178-86.
    Defends the validity and effectiveness of the *Emancipation Proclamation*.

Nicolay, John G., and Hay, John. *Abraham Lincoln: A History*. 10 vols. New York: Century Co., 1914.
    An important early chronicle of Lincoln's life and times, written by his secretaries.

Perkins, Howard Cecil, ed. *Northern Editorials on Secession*. 2 vols. 1942. Reprint. Gloucester, Mass.: Peter Smith, 1964.
    Reprints Northern newspaper editorials concerning the secession crisis of 1860-61. The volumes include numerous essays on Lincoln's policies and speeches.

Quarles, Benjamin. *Lincoln and the Negro*. New York: Oxford University Press, 1962, 275 p.
    A detailed study of the relationship between Lincoln and blacks. In addition to examining his political stand on race-related issues, Quarles investigates Lincoln's personal and professional interactions with blacks.

Randall, J. G. *Lincoln the President*. 4 vols. New York: Dodd, Mead & Co., 1946-55.
    An influential re-examination of Lincoln's presidency by a distinguished Lincoln scholar. Randall's study is divided into three parts: *Lincoln the President: Springfield to Gettysburg; Lincoln the President: Midstream;* and *Lincoln the President: Last Full Measure* (completed by Richard N. Current).

Recollections of Lincoln and Douglas Forty Years Ago. New York: Privately printed, 1899, 49 p.
    A contemporary observer recalls the Lincoln-Douglas senatorial contest and Lincoln's nomination for president.

Rice, Allen Thorndike, ed. *Reminiscences of Abraham Lincoln by Distinguished Men of His Time*. New York: North American Publishing Co., 1886, 656 p.
    Memories of Lincoln recounted by such notable contemporaries as Ulysses S. Grant, Frederick Douglass, Benjamin Franklin Butler, and Walt Whitman.

Rourke, Constance. "The Comic Poet." In her *American Humor: A Study of the National Character,* pp. 138-62. New York: Harcourt Brace Jovanovich, A Harvest Book, 1931.
    Includes a discussion of Lincoln's comic storytelling, in which Rourke finds traces of both Western and Yankee humor.

Sandburg, Carl. *Abraham Lincoln: The Prairie Years.* 2 vols. New York: Harcourt, Brace & Co., 1926.

———. *Abraham Lincoln: The War Years.* 4 vols. New York: Harcourt Brace & Co., 1939.
    A two-part, panoramic chronicle of Lincoln's life and times. Sandburg's work is one of the most famous Lincoln biographies.

Sparks, Edwin Erle, ed. *The Lincoln-Douglas Debates of 1858,* by Abraham Lincoln and Stephen A. Douglas. Collections of the Illinois State Historical Library, vol. III; Lincoln Series, vol. I. Springfield: Illinois State Historical Library, 1908, 627 p.
    An edition of the Lincoln-Douglas Debates featuring a discussion of the background of the meetings, numerous excerpts from contemporary newspaper articles on the debates, and an extensive bibliography.

Stevenson, Adlai E. "A Call to a New Battle: Unfinished Emancipation." In his *Looking Outward: Years of Crisis at the United Nations,* pp. 244-48. New York: Harper & Row, 1963.
    Reprints a speech commemorating the centennial of the *Emancipation Proclamation.* Stevenson invokes Lincoln's example as he urges Americans to complete the "unfinished work of emancipation."

Thomas, Benjamin P. *Abraham Lincoln.* New York: Alfred A. Knopf, 1952, 548 p.
    Regarded by many scholars as the best single-volume Lincoln biography.

Thompson, Seymour D. "Lincoln and Douglas: The Great Freeport Debate." *The American Law Review* Vol. XXXIX, No. 2 (March-April 1905): 161-77.
    A contemporary observer recalls the debate between Lincoln and Douglas at Freeport, Illinois.

Vidal, Gore. "A Note on Abraham Lincoln." In his *The Second American Revolution and Other Essays (1976-1982),* pp. 273-78. New York: Random House, 1982.
    Debunks the idealistic "Sandburg-Mount Rushmore" image of Lincoln, portraying the "real Lincoln" as a great man who yet had common weaknesses.

Warren, Louis A. *Lincoln's Gettysburg Declaration: "A New Birth of Freedom."* Fort Wayne, Ind.: Lincoln National Life Foundation, 1964, 236 p.
    Sheds light on numerous aspects of the "Gettysburg Address," including the historical and rhetorical background of the speech, the circumstances under which it was written and delivered, and contemporary and posthumous response to the address.

Wecter, Dixon. "Lincoln: The Democrat as Hero." In his *The Hero in America: A Chronicle of Hero-Worship,* pp. 222-72. Ann Arbor: University of Michigan Press, Ann Arbor Paperbacks, 1963.
    Explores the factual and fictive bases of Lincoln's identity as a national hero.

Whitman, Walt. "Memories of President Lincoln." In his *Complete Poetry and Selected Prose,* edited by James E. Miller, Jr., pp. 233-40. Riverside Editions, edited by Gordon N. Ray. Boston: Houghton Mifflin Co., 1959.
    Contains four Lincoln elegies: "When Lilacs Last in the Dooryard Bloom'd" (see poem dated 1865-66), "O Captain! My Captain!," "Hush'd Be the Camps To-day," and "This Dust Was Once the Man."

———. "Memories of President Lincoln." In his *Walt Whitman's Civil War,* edited by Walter Lowenfels and Nan Braymer, pp. 257-80. New York: Alfred A. Knopf, 1960.
    A collection of writings concerning Lincoln drawn from Whitman's letters, unpublished manuscripts, and set pieces. The text of Whitman's lecture "Death of Abraham Lincoln" is included among these materials.

Wilson, Edmund. "Abraham Lincoln: The Union as Religious Mysticism." *The New Yorker* XXIX, No. 4 (14 March 1953): 116, 119-26, 129-36.
    A frequently cited review of *The Collected Works of Abraham Lincoln.* Seeking to discover the "authentic" Lincoln through his writings and the memoirs of his close associates, Wilson focuses his remarks on Lincoln's conception of the Civil War.

Wilson, Henry. "The Lincoln and Douglas Debate." In his *History of the Rise and Fall of the Slave Power in America,* Vol. II, 7th ed., pp. 566-77. Boston: Houghton, Mifflin and Co., Riverside Press, n.d.
    Provides a critical overview of the Lincoln-Douglas Debates, which Wilson interprets as a contest between the forces of freedom, represented by Lincoln, and the forces of slavery, represented by Douglas.

Wilson, Rufus Rockwell, ed. *Lincoln among His Friends: A Sheaf of Intimate Memories.* Caldwell, Idaho: Caxton Printers, 1942, 506 p.
    A collection of firsthand accounts of Lincoln.

Zarefsky, David. "The Lincoln-Douglas Debates Revisited: The Evolution of Public Argument." *The Quarterly Journal of Speech* 72, No. 2 (May 1986): 162-84.
    Analyzes prominent argument patterns in the Lincoln-Douglas Debates.

Abraham (ben Jekutiel) Mapu

1808-1867

Lithuanian novelist.

Mapu is recognized as the first novelist to write in the Hebrew language. His novels *Ahavat Zion (The Shepherd Prince)*, *'Ayit zahvu'a*, and *Ashmat Shomeron* attracted a large audience among Eastern European Jews in the nineteenth century and had an important influence on later Hebrew writers. In *The Shepherd Prince* and *Ashmat Shomeron,* Mapu blended elements of European Romanticism with biblical language, settings, and themes to fashion a new type of historical romance, the biblical novel. Thus, although his works are now almost unknown, Mapu remains of interest to scholars as a pioneer in the use of Hebrew in secular literature and as the creator of the biblical romance.

The son of an impoverished Hebrew schoolmaster and his wife, Mapu was born in Slobodka-Kovno, Lithuania. He began the traditional course of instruction in talmudic texts at an early age, proving an adept scholar. At fifteen, under the guidance of his father and other scholars of the community, he delved with enthusiasm into the mystic philosophies of the medieval Jewish cabala, even attempting to make himself invisible through ritual incantations. In 1825, his family arranged for his marriage to the daughter of a wealthy resident of a nearby town. In the following years, supported by his father-in-law, Mapu devoted himself to his studies and pursued his interest in mysticism through his association with members of the Hasidic revivalist movement, who espoused the teachings of the cabala. Eventually, however, Mapu became disenchanted with mysticism and came to support Haskalah, a movement among Eastern European Jews that promoted intellectual enlightenment. Inspired by the proponents of Haskalah, Mapu taught himself Latin by studying a Latin translation of the Psalms and learned French, German, and Russian by reading contemporary romantic novels. When his father-in-law suffered financial ruin, Mapu was obliged to find work as an itinerant tutor to support his wife and children. Overcoming harsh living conditions, meager pay, and poor health, he began to write *The Shepherd Prince*, a romance set in the ancient nation of Israel. His financial difficulties increased in the mid-1840s, and in 1846, his wife died. By 1848, however, he had found more satisfactory work, which, coupled with his domestic happiness in a second marriage, resulted in a period of literary productivity. In 1853, his career as a published author began with the appearance of *The Shepherd Prince*, widely regarded as the first novel in the Hebrew language.

The Shepherd Prince portrays a world vastly different from Mapu's own impoverished surroundings. In this historical novel Mapu chronicles the love stories of two couples—Amnon and Tamar, and Teman and Peninnah—in the idyllic Judean countryside during the times of the prophet Isaiah. The work proved a popular success with its Eastern European Jewish audience, for whom Mapu's romanticized recreation of biblical life, language, and settings engendered pride in their cultural heritage. In his second novel, *'Ayit zahvu'a*, which he published in five parts from 1858 to 1864, Mapu dealt with contemporary Jewish life from the viewpoint of the Haskalah, savagely denouncing hypocrisy and ignorance. Like its predecessor, *'Ayit zahvu'a* was well received. While writing *'Ayit zahvu'a*, Mapu was

also at work on his most ambitious undertaking, a lengthy novel entitled *Hoze hezyonot* set in the seventeenth century in the time of the false messiah, Shabbethai Zebi. However, government censors, influenced by conservative factions who objected to Mapu's pleas for reform in *'Ayit zahvu'a* and his advocacy of Haskalah, suppressed the work; the manuscript was lost and only a fragment of seven chapters remains. Mapu returned to ancient Israel for the subject of his final novel, *Ashmat Shomeron,* which appeared in 1865-66. Set in the times of Ahaz, king of Judah, *Ashmat Shomeron* contrasts the righteous, enlightened Jerusalemites with the evil idolaters of Samaria, making an obvious parallel between the two ancient kingdoms and contemporary proponents of Haskalah and Hassidism. In addition to his four novels, Mapu wrote three innovative and influential textbooks designed to promote a more liberal and enlightened Hebrew education. Despite the success of both his novels and his textbooks, Mapu profited little from sales. Poverty and illness continued to plague him until his death in 1867 on Yom Kippur, the Jewish Day of Atonement.

Criticism of Mapu's works in English is limited and does not reflect the depth of study afforded them by Hebrew-language critics, who consider him the father of the Hebrew novel and an important influence on the subsequent development of Hebrew literature. Mapu's achievement, scholars suggest, lies primarily in his pioneering use of biblical language and settings in his historical novels, but *'Ayit zahvu'a* is also valued for the insights it offers into the culture and concerns of nineteenth-century Jewry. Mapu's works have received minimal praise on literary grounds: critics agree that the novels are flawed by overly complicated and melodramatic plots, poorly developed characters, and repetitiveness. Nevertheless, Mapu remains a seminal figure in modern Hebrew literature and is remembered as the author of innovative novels that enjoyed unparalleled popularity among Jewish readers in the nineteenth century.

PRINCIPAL WORKS

Ahavat Zion (novel) 1853
  [*Amnon, Prince and Peasant,* 1887; also published as *In the Days of Isaiah,* 1902; *The Sorrows of Noma,* 1919; and *The Shepherd Prince,* 1922]
'Ayit zahvu'a (novel) 1858-64
Ashmat Shomeron (novel) 1865-66
*Hoze hezyonot (novel fragment) 1939; published in *Kol kitebei Abraham Mapu*
Kol kitebei Abraham Mapu (novels) 1939
Mikhteve Avraham Mapu (letters) 1970

*This work was written in 1858.

Portions of *Ahavat Zion,* '*Ayit zahvu'a,* and *Ashmat Shomeron* are available in English translation as "The Love of Zion," "The Hypocrite," and "The Guilt of Samaria" in *Abraham Mapu: The Creator of the Modern Hebrew Novel,* by David Patterson.

NAHUM SLOUSCHZ (essay date 1903)

[*In this excerpt from his 1903 survey of modern Hebrew literature, Slouschz examines the importance of Mapu's historical novels to the development of Eastern European Jewish culture.*]

Romantic fiction in Hebrew, which the strait-laced life and the austerity of the educated had rendered impossible up to [the mid-nineteenth century], . . . made its first appearance in the form of translations of modern romances. They were received with acclaim by a well-disposed public greedy for novelties. The creators of original romances were not long in coming. The first master in the department, the father of Hebrew romance, was Abraham Mapu. (p. 134)

Infatuated with the works of the romanticists, especially the novels of Eugène Sue, his favorite author, he began to think out the first part of his historical romance [*Ahavat Zion* (The Love of Zion)] as early as 1830. Twenty-three years were to pass before it saw the light of day. During that interval he led a life of never-ceasing privation and toil, laboring by day, dreaming by night. The Haskalah had created humanist centres in the little towns of Lithuania. In some of these, in Zhagor and in Rossieny, "the city of the educated, of the friends of their people and of the sacred tongue", Mapu finally found the opportunity to display his talents. But his material condition, bad enough to begin with, grew worse and worse. . . . [The] success obtained by the Hebrew translation of [Sue's] *The Mysteries of Paris* emboldened him to publish his [*Ahavat Zion*], and the timid author was overwhelmed, stupefied almost, when he realized the enthusiasm with which the public had greeted his first literary product.

Into the ascetic and puritanic environment in which the world of sentiment and the life of the spirit were unknown, Mapu's romance descended like a flash of lightning, rending the cloud that enveloped all hearts. A century after Rousseau, there was still a corner in Europe in which pleasure, the joy of living, the good things of this life, and nature, were considered futilities, in which love was condemned as a crime, and the passions as the ruin of the soul. Such were the surroundings amid which [*Ahavat Zion*], a Jewish *Nouvelle Héloïse,* appeared as the first plea for nature and love.

[*Ahavat Zion*] is an historical romance. It re-tells a chapter in the life of the Jewish people at the time of the prophet Isaiah. The poet could not exercise any choice as to his subject—it was forced upon him inevitably. In order to be sure of touching a responsive chord in his people, it was necessary to carry the action twenty-five centuries back. A Jewish novel based on contemporaneous life would have been incongruous both with truth and with the spirit of the ghetto.

The time of his novel was the golden age of ancient Judea. It was the epoch of a great literary and prophetic outburst. Also it was an agitated time, presenting striking contrasts. At Jerusalem, an enlightened king was making a firm stand against the limitation of his power from within and against an almost invincible enemy from without. On the one side, society was decadent, on the other side arose the greatest moralists the world has ever seen, the prophets, the intrepid assailants of corruption. It was, finally, the period in which the noblest dreams of a better, an ideal humanity were dreamed. That is the time in which the author lets his story take place. (pp. 139-42)

[*Ahavat Zion*] recalls the wonder-tales of the eighteenth century. From the point of view of romantic intrigue, study of character, and development of plot, it is a puerile work. The interest does not reside in the romantic story. Borrowed from modern works, the fiction rather injures Mapu's novel, which is primarily a poem and an historical reconstruction. [*Ahavat Zion*] is more than an historical romance, more than a narrative invented by an imaginative romancer—it is ancient Judea herself, the Judea of the prophets and the kings, brought to life again in the dreams of the poet. The reconstruction of Jewish society of long ago, the appreciation of the prophetic life, the local color, the majesty of the descriptions of nature, the vivid and striking figures of speech, the elevated and vigorous style, everything is so instinct with the spirit of the Bible that, without the romantic story, one would believe himself to be perusing a long-lost and now recovered book of poetry of ancient Judea.

Dreamy, guileless, ignorant of the actual and complicated phenomena of modern life, Mapu was able to identify himself with the times of the prophets so well that he confounded them with modern times. He committed the anachronism of transporting the humanist ideas of the Lithuanian Maskil to the period of Isaiah. But by reason of wishing to show himself modern, he became ancient. He was not even aware of the fact that he was restoring the past with its peculiar civilization, its manners, and ideas.

None the less his aim as a reformer was attained. Guided by prophetic intuition, Mapu accomplished a task making for morality and culture. To men given over to a degenerate asceticism, or to a mystic attitude hostile to the present, he revealed a glorious past as it really had been, not as their brains, weighed down by misery and befogged by ignorance, pictured it to have been. He showed them, not the Judea of the Rabbis, of the pious, and the ascetics, but the land blessed by nature, the land where men took joy in living, the land of life, flowing with gaiety and love, the land of the Song of Songs and of Ruth. He drew Isaiah for them, not as a saintly Rabbi or a teller of mystical dreams, but a poetic Isaiah, patriot, sublime moralist, the prophet of a free Judea, the preacher of earthly prosperity, of goodness, and justice, opposing the narrow doctrines and minute and senseless ceremonialism inculcated by the priests, who were the predecessors of the Rabbis.

The lesson of the novel is an exhortation to return to a natural life. It presents a world of pleasure, of feeling, of joyous living, justified and idealized in the name of the past. It sets forth the charms of rural life in a succession of poetic pictures. Judea, the pastoral land, passes under the eyes of the reader. The blithe humor of the vine-dressers, the light-heartedness of the shepherds, the popular festivals with their outbursts of joy and high spirits, are reproduced with masterly skill. The moral grandeur of Judea appears in the magnificent description of a whole people assembled to celebrate the Feast in the Holy City, and in the impassioned discourses of the prophets, who openly criticise the great and the priests in the name of justice and truth. But especially it is love that pervades the work, love, chaste and ingenuous, apotheosized in the relation of Amnon and Tamar.

The impression that was made by the book is inconceivable. It can be compared with nothing less than the effect produced by the publication of the *Nouvelle Héloïse*.

At last the Hebrew language had found the master who could make the appeal to popular taste, who understood the art of speaking to the multitude and touching them deeply. The success of the book was impressive. In spite of the fanatical intriguers, who looked with horror upon this profanation of the holy language, the novel made its way everywhere, into the academies for Rabbinical students, into the very synagogues. The young were amazed and entranced by the poetic flights and by the sentimentalism of the book. A whole people seemed to be reborn unto life, to emerge from its millennial lethargy. Upon all minds the comparison between ancient grandeur and actually existing misery obtruded itself.

The Lithuanian woods witnessed a startling spectacle. Rabbinical students, playing truant, resorted thither to read Mapu's novel in secret. Luxuriously they lived the ancient days over again. The elevated love celebrated in the book touched all hearts, and many an artless romance was sketched in outline.

But the greatest beneficiary of the new movement ushered into being by the appearance of [*Ahavat Zion*] was the Hebrew language, revived in all its splendor.

> I have searched out the ancient Latin in its majestic vigor, the German with its depth of meaning, the French full of charm and ravishing expressions, the Russian in the flower of its youth. Each has qualities of its own, each is crowned with beauty. But in the face of all of them, whose voice appeals unto me? Is it not thy voice, my dove? How pellucid is thy word, though its music issues from the land of destruction! . . . The melody of thy words sings in my ear like a heavenly harp.

This idealization of a language of the past, and of that past itself, produced an enormous effect upon all minds, and it prepared the soil for an abundant harvest. The success won by [*Ahavat Zion*] encouraged Mapu to publish his other historical

romance, the action of which is placed in the same period as the first work. *Ashmat Shomeron* (The Transgression of Samaria) . . . is an epic in the true sense. It reproduces the conflicts set afoot by the rivalry betwen Jerusalem and Samaria. The underlying idea in this novel is not unlike that of [*Ahavat Zion*]. But the author allows himself to run riot in the use of antitheses and contrasts. He arraigns the poor inhabitants of Samaria with pitiless severity. Whatever is good, just, beautiful, lofty, and chaste in love, proceeds from Jerusalem; whatever savors of hypocrisy, crookedness, dogmatism, absurdity, sensuality, proceeds from Samaria. The author is particularly implacable toward the hypocrites, and toward the blind fanatics with their narrow-mindedness. The personification of certain types of ghetto fanatics is a transparent ruse. The book excited the anger of the obscurantists, and, in their wrath, they persecuted all who read the works of Mapu.

[*Ashmat Shomeron*] shares a number of faults of technique with the first novel, but also it is equally with the other a product of rich imaginativeness and epic vigor. In reproducing local color and the Biblical life, the author's touch is even surer than in [*Ahavat Zion*].

If one were inclined to apply to Mapu's novels the standards of art criticism, a radical fault would reveal itself. Mapu is not a psychologist. He does not know how to create heroes of flesh and blood. His men and women are blurred, artificial. The moral aim dominates. The plot is puerile, and the succession of events tiresome. But these shortcomings were not noticed by his simple, uncultivated readers, for the reason that they shared the artless *naïveté* of the author. (pp. 146-52)

> *Nahum Slouschz, "The Romantic Movement—Abraham Mapu," in his* The Renascence of Hebrew Literature (1743-1885), *The Jewish Publication Society of America, 1909, pp. 124-58.*

ABRAHAM SOLOMON WALDSTEIN (essay date 1916)

> [*Waldstein evaluates the characteristic strengths and weaknesses of Mapu's novels, concluding that while all his works are flawed by poorly developed characters, they are redeemed by his engaging style and the simple appeal of his plots.*]

[The influence of Russian, German, and French romantic literature upon Mapu] was in accord with his temperament. For, with a nature such as his, mild, timid, dreamy, and impressible, he could not but fall under the influence of the fantastic novels of a Eugene Sue rather than of the matter-of-fact stories of a Balzac. Add to this, moreover, the circumstances under which he lived: his being confined to the stifling atmosphere of the Talmudic academy, and to the narrow limits of a small town, with its monotonous, stagnant life,—and it will readily be understood why his creative powers sought an outlet in the romantic, distant past rather than in the petty, uninteresting present of his surroundings.

The literary heritage of Mapu is not large: four novels in all, only three of which are extant. Of the fourth we have but a fragment, the rest having been destroyed in manuscript, through the machinations of his conservative adversaries. Three of these novels deal with historic subjects and one with modern life. [*Ahavat Zion*] (The Love of Zion) was the first work produced by him. It deals with the times of the prophet Isaiah and of the kings Ahaz and Hezekiah. (pp. 18-19)

[*Ahavat Zion*] created a sensation with the Hebrew reading public,—a sensation due, to be sure, not so much to the literary value of the book as to the novelty of the enterprise. For, regarded from the artistic point of view, this novel—and for that matter, all Mapu's novels—has very great defects. There is, for example, no attempt at character drawing. His heroes are not individualities; nor do they even represent types. They are simply idealizations, the offspring of the author's fancy: gentle, kind, of dove-like sweetness and angelic beauty; in short, embodiments of virtue and loveliness. Their activities are wholly determined by external circumstances. They themselves are endowed with all the weakness and timidity of the author, are at times rather cowardly, afraid to run in the face of Providence or of society, and prone to seek their ends through intrigue rather than through an open display of courage. In one respect, however, Mapu's heroes are Homeric, in that they are ever ready to weep, whether the occasion call for tears or not.

All this is generally true of Mapu's virtuous heroes. His villains—ordinarily as misshapen in body as in soul—do show some individuality and strength of character. This fact manifests more than anything else the influence of the French romantic novelists of the Eugene Sue type, in whose novels, as in those of Mapu, we admire the rogues more than the namby-pamby, washed-out heroes. Take, for example, Reumah, one of the characters in Mapu's second historical novel, *Ashmath Shomeron* (The Guilt of Samaria), a sort of depraved Joan of Arc, of the kingdom of Ephraim, who is the daughter of a profligate mother and of Zichri, "the hero of Ephraim," the prototype of the cruel, corrupt mediaeval robber-knight. The author designed to embody in this heroine the cruelty of her father as well as the depravity of her mother. Yet, Reumah is not entirely unsympathetic. It is true that she is the rallying point of the wild orgies in Ephraim; but she is, at the same time, the object of inspiration for the Ephraimitish young men in honest warfare, and though violent in love, she is constant. Similarly Mapu's other rogues, though more villainous than the one described above, are imposing at least with their strenuous wickedness.

The native powers of Mapu, then, lie not in character drawing, but rather in his plot and in the charm of his story telling. This charm arises from a naivity, from an innocent, firm belief in the final victory of good over evil,—and in it, as well as in a successful imitation of the picturesqueness, though not of the strength, of the Isaianic style, lies his success. All this is particularly true of the first novel of Mapu, [*Ahavat Zion*]. Here, the plot is simple and smooth, and it runs swiftly along, carrying the interest of the reader with it. Yet, even in this story there are some unfilled gaps and a number of questionable knots in the weaving of the plot. This defect is still more apparent in his longer novels: *Ashmath Shomeron* (two parts) and [*'Ayit zahvu'a*] (five parts). Here, especially in the latter, the thread of the story is much more of a tangle than in [*Ahavat Zion*]. The intricacies of the plot, though skillfully formed, are rather hard to follow; and the same is true of their unravelling in the denouement,—where the discrepancies are more apparent in these two novels than in his first book. Some unnecessary incidents are conjured up for no other reason apparently than to lend more complication to the incidents, and interstices are often left open, because the heroes do not possess the strength to carry their decisions into action. Mapu, in his romantic zeal, moreover, sometimes overdraws the situation. Placing the scenes of activity of his first two novels in Palestine, during the decadence of the northern kingdom, Ephraim, he contrasts the life of the Judeans with that of the Ephraimites, painting the former in the most ideal and the latter in the darkest colors. Zion, or, more specifically, Jerusalem, is for Mapu an enchanted Cam-

elot, where the people, at least, the aristocracy, are knights *sans peur et sans reproche;* and if there chance to be a plotter or rogue among them, he generally hails from Samaria. Ephraim, on the other hand, is represented in all that drunkenness and vile corruption, against which the prophet Isaiah launches his most effective denunciations.

The tendencies and ideas represented in Mapu's novels are rather conservative. The heroes are usually born into the aristocracy—the nobility or the money-aristocracy,—with whom he sympathizes more than with the masses. In general, his romanticism is not of the revolutionary, Byronic, type. Neither is it pessimistic of the type of Leopardi, or mystical of the German type. He was too gentle for the first kind and too much of a modern Jew for the other two,—his indulgence in the Kabbalah being merely a youthful vagary. His was rather a romanticism of the type of the "Lake School" poets: dreamy, idyllic, quietistic,—indulging in the vague rather than in the mystic. To these characteristics is due the fact that Mapu's heroes always yearn for the quiet to be found in the bosom of nature. This longing stands in sharp contrast to the stirring incidents and vicissitudes which they undergo,—incidents in which, it is true, they play rather a passive part. It is natural, therefore, that we find in his novels some fine romantic descriptions of nature, coupled with praise and admiration for idyllic life.

These characteristics are, to a greater or lesser degree, true of all Mapu's novels. In [*'Ayit zahvu'a*] (The Painted Hawk), however, a story of modern life, we find ourselves in a different atmosphere from that of his other two novels, aside from the fact that the latter represent a different mode of life. The publication of [*'Ayit zahvu'a*] falls in a new period in the life of eastern Jewry and Hebrew literature. . . . Here, it may be said in brief, that the tendencies of the new period were those of the Haskalah movement in its second stage. At that time the demand for religious reforms became loud and the struggle acute between old beliefs and a modern interpretation of religion. And these tendencies are reflected in Mapu's novel of modern times, [*'Ayit zahvu'a*]. Traces of this conflict may be found, to be sure, even in his historic novels. Zimri, in [*Ahavat Zion*], for example, is a type of hypocrite later developed by Mapu in Rabbi Zadok, the villain of [*'Ayit zahvu'a*], and the false Ephraimite prophet in *Ashmath Shomeron* is an earlier version of the wonder-worker of the nineteenth century. But it is in [*'Ayit zahvu'a*] that we find ourselves right in the midst of the struggle. Upon religious reforms as such, Mapu, indeed, touches only off-handedly; but the atmosphere of the novel is militant. The hypocrites, that is to say, the extreme orthodox, are arrayed in battle against the enlightened, the Maskilim, the religious reformers,—with the natural result—natural from the point of view of Mapu—that the latter ultimately carry off the victory.

Such is Mapu the romantic and the father of the Hebrew novel. He is no creator of character; nor is his plot flawless. His success lies in the charm of his story telling rather than in the logical sequence of events. By dint of this and by his successful application of Biblical phraseology to his subject, he exerted considerable influence upon the further development of Hebrew literature; and by reason of this charm his [*Ahavat Zion*] became a classic read with delight by old and young even in our own time. (pp. 19-23)

Abraham Solomon Waldstein, "Romanticism: The Creation of the Hebrew Novel," in his The Evolution of Modern Hebrew Literature: 1850-1912, *Columbia University Press*, 1916, pp. 14-23.

ROBERT DICK WILSON   (essay date 1922)

[*Wilson was an important archaeologist and scholar of biblical Hebrew. In the following excerpt from his introduction to* The Shepherd Prince, *Wilson praises Mapu's depiction of life in ancient Israel and recommends the novel to modern Christian readers for its uplifting tone and captivating setting.*]

The perusal of ***The Shepherd-Prince*** . . . will show how possible it is for the spirit and "atmosphere" of a people, as well as the environment and setting of ages long past, to be brought out so vividly as to make them real to the consciousness of readers of today. To achieve this is a distinction, the height of literary art.

This work is to be warmly commended to Christian readers because it presents in graphic form the ideas of a modern Israelite with regard to the life and ideals, the emotions and aspirations, of the Ancient Chosen People.

The period of this intensely interesting love story is that of the time of Isaiah, the greatest in the long list of prophets from Moses to Christ. And the incidents of the love-idyl and love-tragedy throughout its course, which, as in all human experience, did not run smooth, but was ultimately triumphant, are admirably developed and in language so felicitous that one feels almost as if it were from the Bible-fount itself.

Love—the greatest thing in the world—found expression in ancient times just as it does today; although the setting differed, the essentials are the same, and the reader of modern fictional literature will find something refreshing in the pure and ardent affection of the hero and heroine, in their tribulations and joys. We believe that this book will be uplifting and that it will have a healthful influence on readers of the present time; for, as has been well said, "There is no time in life when books do not influence a man," and the potency and sway of a good book are incalculable.

The love story—the leading motive of the book—illustrates the theme of the Song of Songs: that love is stronger than death. It is interesting to observe that love at first sight was, in the estimation of Mapu, as common a thing as it is in our own times, and that the course of love ran no more smoothly then than now. The manner in which the passion was manifested, especially of the heroine, may shock the sensibilities of some of the readers, because of the departure from certain conventionalities to which they are accustomed; but it is well to learn how other people express their affection and how a great Hebrew scholar imagines the passion and the practice of love among the Israelites 2,700 years ago.

Mr. Schapiro has [by translating this work] put the reading public unfamiliar with Hebrew language and literature under a deep debt of gratitude for the excellent manner in which he has rendered into English this masterpiece of Abraham Mapu, whose fame is known to the uttermost ends of the earth as the "Father of Jewish Fiction." (pp. xi-xii)

Robert Dick Wilson, in an introduction to The Shepherd-Prince: A Historical Romance of the Days of Isaiah *by Abraham Mapu, translated by Benjamin A. M. Schapiro, 1922. Reprint by Brookside Publishing Company, 1937, pp. xi-xiv.*

JOSEPH KLAUSNER   (essay date 1932)

[*Klausner provides an appreciative appraisal of Mapu's two biblical novels and describes the impact they had on Jewish readers in Eastern Europe.*]

Mapu had an unusually rich imagination and a lively and emotional temperament. Few knew the Scriptures, or, rather, felt them, as he did—their spirit, their stately oriental beauty, and the secret of the living history that wells up from them so vigorously. As he meditated on the books of the Prophets, Mapu's spirit was transported to ancient times. He breathed the atmosphere of ancient Judaea in the days of Hezekiah, king of Judah, and Isaiah, the son of Amoz; and he can transport us also to the same distant past. His novel, [***Ahavat Zion*** (The Love of Zion)] . . . marks a new epoch in Hebrew literature. Mapu did not merely describe that ancient epoch in the usual manner of the historical novelist: he lived within himself the life of the Zion of Bible times, and described that life like a contemporary and an eye-witness. In reading the novel, it is almost impossible to escape the feeling that we have here a work written 2,500 years ago by one of the Prophets, or by the poet of the Song of Songs, or by the author of the Book of Ruth.

The plot of the novel is complicated and artificial, and at the same time naive almost to the point of puerility. Its leading figures are of the type that is found in the eighteenth-century French pastoral romances, with a certain admixture of Eugène Sue and the elder Dumas. Yet this does not detract from the value of the novel as a whole. The reader marvels at the inner illumination, the veritable "holy spirit" by which Mapu's insight has succeeded in penetrating the innermost life of the time, a life so distant and different from the life of his day. No historian or archaeologist specialising in the period could show us so realistically as Mapu the life of Judaea and Samaria, with their true prophets and their false prophets, their kings and priests, masters and servants, their customs and their manners, their conversation and affairs, and their winding processions and moving crowds. Yet with Mapu it is all as simple and natural as in the Bible itself. And with it all he is so lucid and interesting that the reader feels the big, uncomplicated life rustling by him as on some day in the time of Isaiah and Hezekiah—that unique manner of life, so rich in great men, the teachers of the human race, veritable pillars of the world, yet at the same time utterly simple and primitive: a life at once so small and so large.

The impression which [***Ahavat Zion***] made on its Hebrew readers was immense. For the Russian Jew of the 'fifties, this work, besides the qualities that we have enumerated, had a quite special appeal. The Ghetto Jew, with his spiritual horizon bounded by arid religious routine, was suddenly confronted with a picture of a new life, untrammelled, youthful, exuberant, with no trace of Ghetto or subjection or servitude, no merely mechanical religious ceremonial; and this life was the life of his own people, that genuine Hebrew life which had given to the Jewish people and to humanity the most precious gifts of the spirit, had given the prophets themselves, the very Isaiah who appeared in Mapu's pages as a living and active hero. The young Jew, who had hitherto thought of the kings and Prophets of Israel as occupied only with religious matters, found in this glorious past, re-created for him by Mapu, the ideal of national freedom which his people had lost in the Dark Ages. Thus this novel became a sort of stepping-stone to the Zionist idea.

The Jewish heart was stirred to new life. The luxuriant scenery of the East; Jerusalem's intoxicating beauty; the joy of harvest and vintage; the pure, artless love of Tamar, daughter of Jedidiah the Judaean nobleman, for the shepherd Amnon, who had saved her from the lion's jaws; her brother Teman's burning love for Peninah the reaper; and, finally, the great motley crowds which, at the "Three Feasts," came thronging up to Jerusalem from all parts of the land of Israel—what a pageant of joy and magic for the young Jew, who had never known anything before except the tractates of the Talmud and the hairsplitting casuistries of the rabbinical commentators! Thus it came about that Mapu's novel did more to spread *Haskalah* among the frequenters of the rabbinical seminaries than hundreds of volumes that directly preached the doctrines of "enlightenment."

[*Ahavat Zion*] had yet another quality of inestimable value. The Prophets had risen in revolt against the pretensions of charlatans and hypocrites. "To what purpose is the multitude of your sacrifices unto me? saith the Lord . . . your hands are full of blood." Such is the substance of many chapters in the book of Isaiah. Thus Chapter 58 denounces the fastings in which the ungodly "bow down their heads like a rush" at the very time when they call "for strife and contention" and "smite with the fist of wickedness." To them the Prophet says, "Is not this the fast that I have chosen? to loose the bonds of wickedness . . . to let the oppressed go free," "to deal thy bread to the hungry and that thou bring the poor that are cast out to thy house; when thou seest the naked, that thou cover him, and that thou hide not thyself from thine own flesh?"

These ideas are the background both of [*Ahavat Zion*] and of Mapu's second and longer novel, *Ashmath Shomeron*, "The Sin of Samaria." The latter deals with the same period, and contains descriptions drawn with even greater art than those in [*Ahavat Zion*]; but its plot is hopelessly confused, and it characters are so numerous that they pass before the reader like shadows and fail to leave the necessary impression. In these two novels Mapu depicts the hostility of the true prophets to the priests and the false prophets (more particularly to the priests, whom the true prophets condemned because they urged the multiplication of sacrifices even though they were offered without true religious intention, and thus laid all the stress on routine observance). Priests and false prophets alike appear as deceivers and hypocrites, who make outward observance of religious forms a cloak for their evil practices and offences against the moral law, which is the sovereign principle in the eyes of God and His prophets. Thus these ancient hypocrites were made to represent the religious humbugs of Mapu's own day. Zimri, who appears as the villain in both novels, is shown as the archetype of all charlatans and hypocrites, and not only of those who were contemporary with Isaiah and Hezekiah. Through the thin, transparent, historical wrapping it is easy to see that Mapu was not castigating the ancient Zimris so much as the charlatans and hypocrites of his own time, who also rated the externals of religion and the conventional lies of stereotyped tradition more highly than loving-kindness and sincere piety. This explains why Mapu and all his readers were the target for persecution by the more bigoted among the orthodox, although at first sight there would seem to be no harm in the historical subject-matter of the books, and although the orthodox themselves profess to hold the Prophets in great veneration. The forces of obscurantism realised that the Prophets as painted by Mapu were a source of light—and darkness dreads the light. The orthodox saw that the false prophets and hypocrites, the Mattans, Zimris and Pashhurs and their like, could

serve as a mirror from which their own degraded image was reflected; and they felt also that soon Mapu would not rest content with historical types only, but would pass on to the life of his own time, and the bigots of Kovno would replace the bigots of Jerusalem. Hence to read [*Ahavat Zion*] was, in the eyes of the Jewish orthodoxy of the time, as bad as to read heretical writings—a fact which rather increased than diminished the number of Mapu's readers. (pp. 45-51)

> *Joseph Klausner, "The Romantic Period," in his* A History of Modern Hebrew Literature (1785-1930), *edited by Leon Simon, translated by Herbert Danby, 1932. Reprint by Greenwood Press, Publishers, 1972, pp. 21-51.*

MEYER WAXMAN (essay date 1936)

[*Waxman surveys Mapu's novels and suggests that his importance to the development of Hebrew literature lies in his descriptive power and original form. Waxman's remarks were first published in 1936.*]

Judging the first and probably the best novel of Mapu [*Ahavat Zion*] by the canons of modern literary criticism, we must conclude that its great value lies not in its content, but in its form. The most important elements of the plot were . . . borrowed from Moses Hayyim Luzzatto's dramas, *la-Yeshorim Tehillah* and *Migdal Oz*. The exchange of Nabal for Azrikam which is the backbone of the story is taken from the first where the whole story is built around the fact that *Rahab* is exchanged for *Yosher* in time of siege, while the dream of Ḥannanel which plays such an important part in the tale is modelled after the dream of King Rom in the second. Likewise, can we trace other features in this plot to these dramas. Nor are the development and construction of the story very original, but an imitation of the methods employed by contemporary French writers of romantic novels. There is little sequence in the progress of events, changes are sudden and arise in a miraculous manner. The delineation of the characters is also deficient. There is no attempt at a psychological analysis and the heroes possess little individuality, but are more or less types.

Yet with all these deficiencies, the [*Ahavat Zion*] is a real work of art, even if the art consists entirely in its form. Its greatest value lies in the vividness of description of the life of the period. In this Mapu displayed great power. He actually resuscitated the life of a long-forgotten time. There is so much naturalness in the recital of the story that the reader is carried away from contemporary life to a distant time and place and becomes an onlooker of the events transpiring around him. It is marvelous how a man like Mapu who spent his life in the ghetto of Kovno with its crooked and muddy streets could visualize a life of beauty and pastoral tranquillity as is described in some of the chapters of the novel. He completely immersed himself in the atmosphere which he created by his own imagination. In [*Ahavat Zion*], the long pent-up yearning of the Jew of the ghetto for the beauty of nature, which was frequently though sporadically expressed by various writers and poets throughout the Haskalah period, found its culmination. Hence, the exceptional skill displayed by our author in the portrayal of pastoral and vintage scenes. Mapu does not only depict rural scenes masterfully but also the life of the city. He penetrates with deep insight into the life of the past and revives before us the events and actions which had transpired in Jerusalem in the time of Hezekiah. One by one these pass before our eyes, the joyous scenes of the celebration of the festivals of Passover and Succoth by the pilgrims who crowded the Holy City, the siege which divided the populace into factions, and finally the scene of redemption when the army of the mighty conqueror was smitten by the hand of God. In all these kaleidescopic descriptions, there is not a trace of artificiality, all fit so well into their natural setting and are expressed in such pure Biblical language that we imagine that these pages are in reality leaves taken out from some lost Scriptural book.

Another valuable characteristic of the book is the brevity of expression. Our author succeeded in drawing vivid pictures in a few words. With simple but select colors and several chosen strokes, the artist delineates a scene which impresses itself upon the mind of the reader. Finally, there is the quality of the language. True, Mapu did not invent a new style, for his is primarily an imitation of that of the Bible, but there is originality in his use of it. It is completely adapted to the narrative and the events of the story and is distinguished by its simplicity and economy. Even the euphuisms with which the book abounds do not seem out of place and sound quite natural in the mouths of ordinary people who were among the auditors of Isaiah. Mapu proved that the language of the Bible can be used to great advantage not only for the expression of lofty thoughts but also for the narrating of a well-connected story.

All these qualities are of a permanent and lasting nature, which make the book valuable even today. We must not forget though that its value was much greater for its generation. For the readers of the day, it was a real revelation. It took them out of the miserable life of the ghetto with its squalor and sordidness and brought them into a new world of broad fields and blossoming vines, a world where love was not forbidden, where young people moved freely and enjoyed life moderately, without external restraint. It aroused in them a desire for a life of nature and evoked in their hearts a sense of beauty. In addition, it also expressed the philosophy of life of the Haskalah for though it was an historical novel, it reflected the ideas of the age. The heroes are all enlightened people who strive for knowledge, and on the other hand, the ''villain,'' Zimri, is represented as a hypocrite who parades as a pious man and uses his apparent piety for his own purpose, a characteristic frequently attributed by the Maskilim to their opponents. Mapu's beautiful descriptions of rural life and the happiness enjoyed by those who labor with their hands, spread the ideals of the movement of enlightenment which propagated the cultivation of the soil and the engaging in manual labor as the proper ways of life. Mapu also performed a national service, for indirectly his [Ahavat Zion] was a forerunner of the national sentiment which found expression a generation later. His vivid description brought his readers the scent of the lilies of Sharon and the fragrance of Lebanon. There passed before their eyes the waving green of the Carmel, the pastures of Bethlehem, and the vineyards of Judea, all of which aroused in their hearts the dormant love for Zion.

His second great historical novel, *Ashmat Shomron* (The Guilt of Samaria) shares both the faults and the good qualities of the first. There is not much advancement in the construction of the plot nor in the psychological analysis of the characters of the story. In fact, as far as the plot is concerned, it resembles greatly that of the [Ahavat Zion], as both possess common elements. One of the principal characters in the second novel, Elifelet, grows up, like Amnon, under an assumed name, and his noble descent is only revealed at the end of the story. Moreover, several characters of the former novel are reintroduced in the later production. These devices prove that Mapu was more of the poet and the seer than the story writer

and did not possess much ability for inventing new plots and many new episodes. Yet the *Ashmat Shomron* displays some improvement in plot construction and in the concatenation of events. The story is more complicated, the number of characters larger, and the scenes of life portrayed more varied and considerably more colorful. In the [Ahavat Zion], the idyllic predominates, while in the second work we feel the pulse of the rushing life of the capital of Israel, Samaria; we hear the din of battle, and are introduced to the variegated machinations of the priests of Beth El who exploit both religion and politics for their own purposes.

In the *Ashmat Shomron,* Mapu drew his portraits on a large canvas which embraced both Judah and Israel. The time is that of the last days of the kingdom of Israel, when the kings were merely shadows and puppets in the hands of the generals on the one hand, and the crafty priests on the other hand. The moral situation in Judah was not much better, for it was the reign of Ahaz who strove to imitate the northern kingdom in its cult and in its glittering social life. It is this tumultuous rushing life, filled with strife, cunning, and riotous orgies in the name of religion, which the author undertook to delineate and succeeded in a large measure. It is true that the multiplicity of events and the numerous episodes which he tried to combine in the story proved too difficult for him to master. Consequently, there are many lacunae in the sequence, while on the other hand, many acts on the part of the characters are unnecessary and only unduly accentuate the frightful picture the author wished to draw of them. But here, as in the first work, the real value of the production lies in the form.

The power of description and the presentation of the life of the past is revealed in Mapu's second novel to a greater extent than in the first. With the help of a few prophetic books of the Bible, the author pieced together the isolated stray incidents recorded there and constructed them into a narrative breathing with vividness. His thirteenth chapter in Part I is a masterful portrayal of a religious orgy on the mountains around Beth El. We see before us groups of young men and young women heated by wine and inflamed both by lust and ecstasy of a false religion, madly dancing to the strains of the pipe and the harp. We hear the flowing oratory of the false prophets who encourage the people in the deceptive trust of their strength and hide from them the approaching doom. We also see the crafty priests of Baal gliding furtively through the crowds rejoicing at the sight. There is, of course, no lack of the idyllic and the pastoral in the book, for the exaltation of that life was one of the principal aims of our author. In fact, the first chapter consists entirely of an excellent description of the Lebanon mountains, of their cliffs, valleys, and precipices, and the reader feels the moisture of the dew of Hermon and the rustling of the tall cedars. The tendency to exalt the ideal and the good life is felt in the entire progress of both stories. In both works, there is an underlying conflict between men who champion the cause of goodness, knowledge, and justice, and men to whom falsehood, hypocrisy, and evil are second nature; and the author, of course, makes the good triumph. In this we hear an echo of the war of the enlightened with their opponents. Due to this tendency, Mapu made his characters paragons of virtue, almost perfect in their conduct. It is especially manifest in the characters of the women in the novels. With few exceptions he endowed them with good qualities, such as beauty, sweetness, and nobility of soul, veritable ideal daughters of Israel.

The influence of the two historical novels of Mapu was, at the time of their appearance, exceedingly great, and they formed the most frequented path to Haskalah for numerous students of the Yeshibah and the Ḥeder. Even the opponents of the enlightenment felt instinctively that these books were its powerful weapons and they prohibited their reading with great zeal and vigor.

In his third novel, ['Ayit zahvu'a], Mapu turned from the distant past to depict the life of his own generation. It was a bold attempt, for the story is a lengthy one consisting of five parts and the plot is complicated; it was on the whole unsuccessful. All the defects and shortcomings of the writer in plot construction and his inability to present the concatenation of events in systematic sequence are displayed in the novel in a most atrocious manner. It is a typical Haskalah story, for its theme pictures the struggle between the champions of the old order of life in Jewry and those of the enlightened, and its purpose was to depict the former in the darkest colors, and the latter in the brightest. It thus appears that the opponents of the Haskalah were mostly hypocrites who committed many crimes in secret, but appeared outwardly pious, using their piety as a cloak to cover their evil deeds. The animosity which they displayed towards the enlightened served them only as a means of increasing their influence upon the people who, as a whole, were superstitious and followers of the old order. The enlightened, on the other hand, were people who were models of truth and honesty and who strove to improve Jewish life. We have, therefore, in the story two sets of characters, villains and noble men. The first oppress and persecute the second, but only for a stated time. The author, anxious to have truth and justice triumph, turns the tables upon the villains and reveals them in their true character and the noble men and women receive their reward. (pp. 272-76)

[In 'Ayit zahvu'a] the development of the plot is most amateurish. It proceeds in a haphazard manner without cause or reason. Events take sudden turns in a most mysterious way. The characters in the story, which takes place in a small Lithuanian town, hail from all countries, from Italy, from the East, and from the Balkans. Thus, his chief villain, Rabbi Ẓadok, is an Italian Jew, son of a non-Jewish father and Jewish mother, who lived in Turkey, Macedonia, and the Balkans for years. Later he came to Lithuania, posed as a wonder-performing rabbi, and finally married the daughter of Gaal. How such a man could adapt himself to the conditions of a small Lithuanian town and be considerd a holy man and a scholar is difficult to understand. Similarly several of his other characters hail from distant places and suddenly appear on the scene, almost simultaneously in London and in Lithuania.

The characters are not persons but types. In fact, Mapu himself admitted that Rabbi Ẓadok is a purely imaginary character not taken from life. Still, we might have expected some semblance of orderly delineation of the personality of his types, but there is almost none. All the multifarious deeds of Ẓadok are not shown to us but merely told by the author and that in fragmentary manner. Likewise, Nehemiah, who plays such an important part in the story, is almost a shadow, as we are not even told his occupation. At times he appears as a preacher (Maggid), at other times as a teacher, and suddenly he is revealed as a wine-seller. How great was the naïveté of the author can be seen from the following: The last chapter in the book represents a masquerade presided over by the Prince, the lord of the town. To that masquerade, all the leading Jews are invited, including Rabbi Ẓadok, who appears there without arousing any protest on the part of the pious Jews who consider him a holy man. Of course, his scandalous deeds are revealed

there. Yet what a strange setting for a concluding scene, a masquerade ball attended by a holy man.

However, in spite of all these defects, the book reveals the life of the period. Several characters are truly depicted and the work is permeated with the breath of life of the Lithuanian town in the fifties of the last century. We have there also all the ideals of the Maskilim, their idealization of pure love, the glorification of manual labor and chiefly of agriculture, and the denunciation of the rights of parents to force their daughters into marriages against their will. All these tendencies are strongly reflected in that book, so that after all it is a novel close to life. Mapu also did not forget to weave into his story some Palestinian scenes, as he makes one of his characters settle in the Holy Land and describe in his letters to his friends the beauties of the land, even in its desolation. To all these qualities, we must add the author's power of description which sheds a special lustre upon the book.

It is no wonder then that notwithstanding its shortcomings which were already noted even by contemporary critics, the ['Ayit zahvu'a] exerted considerable influence upon the readers of the generation. It was the first long novel which depicted contemporary life and they saw in its kaleidoscopic panorama reflections of their own life and struggles. The influence of Mapu, though, was not limited to the readers but extended also to the writers. He was the father of the modern Hebrew novel. He was the first to express the aspirations and ideals of a whole period in a new form, that of story and fiction, and he showed his followers a new way to reach the heart of their fellow Jews and mould their opinions, that of description and living examples. (pp. 277-78)

> *Meyer Waxman, "The Novel of the Haskalah," in his* A History of Jewish Literature: From the Middle of the Eighteenth Century to 1880, *Vol. III, Thomas Yoseloff, 1960, pp. 265-312.*

D. PATTERSON (essay date 1956)

[Patterson has written extensively on the history of Hebrew literature. In the following excerpt, he explores Mapu's use of poetry and songs in his novels. For additional criticism by Patterson, see excerpts dated 1964.]

[Within] the framework of his stories Mapu has interspersed a considerable number of poems in the form of songs, of which eight appear in [Ahavat Zion], five in *Ashmat Shomron*, two in ['Ayit zahvu'a] and one—in the form of a *Piyyut*—in the fragment *Ḥoze Ḥezyonot*. In addition there is a passage in rhymed prose in ['Ayit zahvu'a], and several passages in rhymed prose in *Ḥoze Ḥezyonot*. Only in [Ahavat Zion], however, may they be regarded as an integral and important element, by virtue both of their comparative frequency in proportion to the length of the novel and of the specific atmosphere which they are intended to create. Little of this intention can be discerned in the songs which appear in *Ashmat Shomron*. Both here, and more particularly in the case of the other examples cited, their very infrequency makes them incidental. Their interest, therefore, is mainly intrinsic.

The songs in general, and those found in the historical novels in particular, are distinguished primarily by the lack of poetic inspiration and the unsuitablity of the form. With regard to the latter, their entire structure, within the framework of a biblical setting, is a complete anachronism. It is true that the prose of the Hebrew Bible is not infrequently interspersed with fragments of poetry, and Mapu may have been motivated by a desire to emphasize this tendency. But the poetry of the Old Testament is characterized by parallelism and by a rhythmic system of stress accents, while the conception of a regular, syllabic metre does not exist. Moreover, with the exception of a few, isolated instances, there is no trace of rhyme. But Mapu regularly uses a thoroughgoing system of rhyme together with types of syllabic metres, which are wanting not merely in the poetry of the Old Testament, but also in Paitanic and Medieval Hebrew literature, and which, indeed, first make their appearance in the literature of the *Haskalah* movement, modelled entirely on the European pattern. The very fidelity which Mapu demonstrated in the handling of his biblical material, in the setting, in the style and particularly in the language, and the real measure of success he attained in recreating a genuine, historical atmosphere only serve to emphasize the anachronistic nature of his songs—a glaring discrepancy made even more obvious by the paucity of poetic inspiration.

In the sense that Milton felt himself to be writing prose with his left hand, Mapu displays a similar awkwardness in poetic composition. It is strange that the rich admixture of imagery, rhythm and dexterity of language, which infuses his prose with a poetic quality of very high order, is sadly lacking in the poetry itself. One searches in vain for the calm balance, the illuminating phrase and the economy of expression, which everywhere abound in his prose. But particularly conspicuous is the want of rich inspiration, the essential element of poetry, which conjures up the vivid picture and arouses daring associations in the mind. Mapu's poetry is clumsy and wooden, obviously laboured and forced. Its emotional content is flat and the general impression one of artificiality. Frequently too, it would appear that his musical ear is faulty—in spite of his well known love of music—for the rhythm is halting and the scansion often imperfect. It is as though the very quality of rhythmic lyricism, which distinguished his prose, refused to be encompassed within the confines of poetic form.

Mapu's purpose in introducing the songs into [*Ahavat Zion*] is clear. The lyric song is closely allied to the pastoral idyll, of which a strong element pervades the novel, and the connexion between shepherd-hero and singer is exemplified traditionally by King David. Mapu believed—and rightly so—that the spirit of [*Ahavat Zion*] might well be enhanced by the interspersion of a number of songs. But he was faced with the problem either of couching these songs in the form of psalms, more in keeping with the biblical setting of the novel, or of resorting to a poetic mould in normal use among his contemporaries, but in this case constituting an anachronism. It is suggested that his choice of the latter may have been influenced by Bulwer Lytton's *The Last Days of Pompeii,* in which many songs in European form are introduced anachronistically into an historical framework, and with which Mapu may have been familiar in its German or French translation. But it is more likely that Mapu, essentially a Romantic, was influenced by the lyric poetry of the French, German and English romantic movements in literature, some of whose spirit had penetrated the second period of *Haskalah* and profoundly influenced the lyric poetry of that movement, as best exemplifed by Mapu's contemporary, Micah Joseph Lebensohn. In either case an experiment of this nature can prove successful only in the hands of a genuine poet, and Mapu's inadequate self-criticism with regard to his poetic creations sadly undermines the effect.

Of the eight songs in [*Ahavat Zion*] five are sung by the hero, Amnon, and revolve upon three principal themes—the supe-

riority of pastoral to city life, the pain of a hopeless love that cannot be requited, and the praise of Zion. They provide a foil to the hero's character, bearing witness to the sweet voice that accompanies his many natural virtues, and are quite compatible with the idyllic background of his shepherd upbringing. His last song takes the form of a letter written to the heroine, Tamar. Of the remaining three, the first is a drinking song, the second a song of the city watchmen and the third a temple song. The latter is woven into the soliloquy which heralds Amnon's reappearance after a long absence and exercises a certain dramatic effect. The drinking song retains a flavour of the boisterousness which the villains contribute to the story, its last line being reminiscent of the famous student-song ''Gaudeamus Igitur.'' But the song of the watchmen—consisting of a single stanza—is particularly unconvincing, and gives the impression of being more in the tradition of comic opera than the romantic novel.

Mapu's favourite stanza consists of six lines with a rhyme scheme a.a.b.c.c.b. in each verse. This form is found in the second, fifth, sixth, seventh and eighth songs. Elsewhere he uses a four-line stanza with a rhyme scheme a.b.a.b., with the exception of the first song, which contains sixteen lines in a single stanza with a rhyme scheme a.b.a.b.c.d.c.d., etc. By and large the rhymes are accurate, although from time to time the metre fluctuates unsteadily. (pp. 382-86)

Whereas the purpose of the songs in [*Ahavat Zion*] is clear, no ready explanation is forthcoming for those introduced into **Ashmat Shomron**, where they are not connected with such idyllic elements as the story contains. Of the five songs the first three are very short, the third, indeed, consisting of only two lines—the second with a medial rhyme—in which the kingdoms of Judah and Israel are compared, to the great detriment of the latter. The song is reminiscent of the Old Testament in its conciseness of expression and use of contrast, more in keeping with the biblical setting. The first two songs each consist of a single stanza of four lines, with a rhyme scheme a.b.a.b. The former appears during the drunken orgy of the priests of Beth-El, and is a cursing song aimed against the kingdom of Judah, while the latter is a song of rejoicing on the death of King Ahaz. Both songs are of inferior quality, remarkable only for the contrast they make with the magnificent prose description, in which they are embedded. The fourth song is a coronation ode, the choir singing in two parts. The five stanzas are of unequal length and have a complicated rhyme scheme a.a.a.a.b.b.c.c.d.b.d.b.—b.b.—e.b.e.b.b.b.—f.f.g.g.b.—h.h.h., the last three lines being in praise of the queen mother. The entire form of the song is an anachronism, although the rhythm is at times quite effective. In the fifth song the hero, Uzziel, succumbs to the prophetic spirit . . . and sings a song of Zion, but once more the form is quite unbiblical. There are six stanzas, each of six lines and again Mapu uses the rhyme scheme a.a.b.c.c.b. But the very short lines and swift metre give the impression not of prophetic inspiration, but rather of doggerel verse.

Of the two songs which appear in [*'Ayit zahvu'a*] the first has a double interest. It is contained in a letter from Naaman to Elisheba, consisting of four stanzas of six lines each—the rhyme scheme being a.a.b.c.b.c.—together with an introduction, the first two lines of which are reminiscent of the Psalms. In the first place the young lovers are represented by the names Amnon and Tamar, thus forming a conscious reference to [*Ahavat Zion*] and helping to set the fashion of the day. Secondly the last two lines of each verse constitute a recurring refrain, which contains an acrostic on the names Amnon and Tamar in the manner of Paitanic and Medieval Hebrew poetry. The lyric feeling of this poem is far more genuine, and it remains one of Mapu's happier creations, possibly because the form, in the framework of a novel of contemporary life, is no longer an anachronism. The second song is a youthful composition of the boy Raphael and consists of two verses in rhymed couplets, the first containing eighteen lines and the second sixteen; but the lines are short, the metre uneven and the quality poor. (pp. 386-87)

> *D. Patterson, "The Use of Songs in the Novels of Abraham Mapu," in* Journal of Semitic Studies, *Vol. I, No. 4, October, 1956, pp. 382-88.*

D. PATTERSON (essay date 1964)

[*Here, Patterson examines Mapu's use of epistolary devices in his novels as a means of developing plot, providing place descriptions, creating dramatic irony, and delineating character. For additional criticism by Patterson, see excerpts dated 1956 and 1964.*]

The text of Abraham Mapu's lengthy novel [*'Ayit zahvu'a*] makes reference to more than sixty letters, of which the great majority are quoted in full. Many of the letters are substantial, more than half exceeding 500 words with a few even approaching 5000 words. Indeed, the sum total of the various sections of the novel written in letter-form amounts to more than 42,000 words, a figure equalling the length of an entire novel of small compass. Admittedly, [*'Ayit zahvu'a*] is a very long story, whose five parts embrace almost a quarter of a million words. Nevertheless the epistolary elements comprise no less than one sixth of the whole so that their place in the overall scheme of the novel deserves serious consideration. [*'Ayit zahvu'a*], indeed, shares a number of features in common with the class of epistolary novels exemplified by Richardson's *Pamela*. Mapu's adoption of a hybrid form, with the epistolary element comprising only about one sixth of the whole, while nevertheless employing a far greater number of letters than one might expect to find in a non-epistolary novel published in the second half of the nineteenth century, provides an interesting example of the time lag separating much of the Hebrew literature of the period from the European models which influenced its development.

In European literature epistolary fiction progressed along two fairly distinct paths, although the dividing line is sometimes blurred. In the first place there was the approach of the "outsider", whereby society was subjected to the observation of a visitor from abroad, who was thus enabled to assume the role of onlooker and comment on the rough and tumble of society while safely standing on the touchlines. (p. 132)

The second major division of epistolary fiction adopts the approach of the "insider", with the correspondent or correspondents forming an integral element in the events they describe or the pattern of society they portray. Far from remaining a detached observer, the correspondent is generally characterized by a deep and often passionate commitment to the narrative, which thus provides an admirable backcloth for the detailed expression and analysis of emotion. (p. 133)

In proceeding to a closer survey of the methods favoured by the Hebrew authors in the nineteenth century in adapting the letter form for their own purposes, two further aspects of epistolary technique require brief consideration. One of the devices employed in epistolary fiction of the satirical type consisted of

the introduction of a cumbersome footnote apparatus as an accompaniment to the text, partly to generate an aura of authenticity and trustworthiness and partly as a grotesque parody of the object of attack. (p. 134)

The second aspect of epistolary technique which deserves consideration has a far wider application and concerns the role of the letter itself. The epistolary element of a novel is by no means confined to the form. The framework of a letter-novel is, indeed, important in itself and possesses many advantages and disadvantages over and against the plain, narrative novel. But that is by no means all. [As A. D. McKillop wrote of epistolary techniques in Richardson's novels:] "The writing of the letters is only the beginning; they are copied, sent, received, shown about, discussed, answered, even perhaps hidden, intercepted, stolen, altered or forged. The relation of the earlier letters in an epistolary novel to the later may thus be quite different from the relation of the earlier chapters of a novel to the later."

The letter, therefore, may equally readily be used as a factor in the plot or serve as a framework for the plot. But the more that letters are introduced as factors in the plot—particularly where the plot is in any case tortuous or complex—the more likely are they to take a melodramatic form and serve as little more than crude fictional devices. Whenever the reader is able to accept the epistolary method unquestioningly without feeling

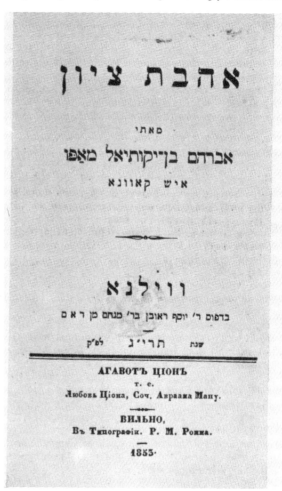

The title page of the first edition of Ahavat Zion.

any improbability in its use and without any awareness of artificial stratagems on the author's part, the more likely is that method to be successfully employed. On the whole, it would appear that the letter lends itself to the novel more naturally as a means of presentation than as an agent forcibly dragged into the narrative. But where the author has in any case deliberately adopted a grotesque framework for satirical purposes, the extravagant use of letters for melodramatic effect may be regarded with a certain indulgence. (pp. 135-36)

An examination of the influences of the European epistolary tradition upon Hebrew literature in the nineteenth century leads inevitably to the conclusion that while the satirical *genre* in the tradition of Montesquieu's *Persian Letters* eventually finds its way into Hebrew literature in the fully-fledged guise of Perl's *Megalleh Ṭemirin* and *Boḥan Ṣaddiq,* which take advantage of the principal techniques of a long literary chain, the epistolary novel of manners, in the tradition of Richardson's *Pamela,* has no real counterpart in Hebrew. Due to the long time lag separating European and Hebrew literature previously mentioned, the Hebrew novel makes its appearance not merely long after the classical form of the epistolary novel had disappeared but at a time when even the hybrid novel has spent its force. As a result the full epistolary form, with all the subtleties of construction and shifting points of view that it can offer, was restricted in Hebrew literature to satirical writing; and although Mapu and his successors throughout the period of Enlightenment endow their novels with a copious supply of letters, their function largely consists of introducing improbable or melodramatic turns into the plot, sometimes of a baffling nature. In addition, as will be seen, they serve as a medium for sketching character, as well as for conveying information either relevant to the plot or of a generally didactic nature.

Although the epistolary element assumes quantitative importance only in Mapu's novel of contemporary life ['*Ayit zahvu'a*], letters occur or are mentioned in both his historical romances, [*Ahavat Zion*] (The Love of Zion) and [*Ashmat Shomeron*] (The Guilt of Samaria). In the former they are used for the advancement of the plot and as vehicles for description or reflection. Their comparative infrequency in the historical romances reflects a similar phenomenon in European literature. It would appear that an atmosphere of intimacy which the familiar letter can create so well in a contemporary setting is more difficult to effect within the framework of a remote period. Certainly the historical and Gothic fiction which became so popular in English literature in the first half of the nineteenth century had little resort to the letter.

In spite of their infrequency, however, the letters in [*Ahavat Zion*] play an important role in the somewhat tortuous plot. Early in the story the wicked Zimri escapes from captivity after the fall of Samaria and brings a letter from a fellow captive Hananeel, describing a dream according to which a young man, who claims to be the lover of his granddaughter, Tamar, appears to Hananeel and promises to rescue him. But Hananeel has also entrusted his personal seal to Zimri, who later uses it to send a false message from Hananeel, stating that the latter is dying and thereby destroying confidence in the dream with its description of a youth resembling the hero Amnon. In a further attempt to alienate Tamar's affections from Amnon after first arousing her suspicions that he loves another, Zimri advises the hero to send Tamar a letter seeking reconciliation together with a bottle of wine which Zimri promptly poisons, and then informs the heroine of Amnon's "treachery."

The letter serves as a two-fold source of dramatic irony. In the first instance Amnon writes it at the suggestion of Zimri whose advice he has sought in order to win back Tamar's affection, unaware of Zimri's villainous resolve to achieve exactly the opposite result. Secondly Amnon includes the following ironic statement in his letter: ''I am sending a bottle of wine as usual. If you accept it from me as wine of love, then all is well and I shall again hold up my head. But if it rebounds on me like treacherous wine, then it will be a sign that God has decreed that I must become a wanderer in a foreign land.'' It is hardly surprising that the heroine returns the bottle of wine together with a letter written in biting if somewhat euphuistic terms telling him literally to go to hell. ''Fly for your life,'' the letter concludes, ''why let me witness your blood being spilled over the ground like water? For my kinsmen burn with anger, and should they catch you they will rend your soul in their rage and show no mercy in the day of wrath. Perhaps you will ask: Whither can I flee from them? Surely you know the path that leads to hell. No pure-minded man would traverse it, but it is yours. You have taken your stand astride it and you shall walk upon it until you find yourself in mourning for your soul, and then you will regret your end.'' The dramatic effect is heightened further by the fact that the letter does not specifically mention the reason for Amnon's rejection. The hero is utterly baffled, although he begins to suspect that he may have been slandered!

The remaining correspondence in [*Ahavat Zion*] comprises a number of love-letters. A daring innovation at the time, these love-letters are important not so much because of their role in the plot, which is in any case slight, but because they reflect one of the principal aims of the exponents of Enlightenment in the Hebrew literature of the period, namely the free expression of romantic love in the attempt to awaken the emotional aspect of personality in the pursuit of a wider and more meaningful life. As poetry was considered a most helpful means towards the attainment of that end, it is perhaps only to be expected that one of these love-letters should be written in the form of a poem, in which the hero pours out his heart to his beloved in very stilted verse. The heroine is suitably impressed. Similar in tone, if not in form, is a letter from the second heroine, Shoshanah, in which she too pours out her hopeless love for her darling Teman. Her final plea to him may serve to illustrate the nature of the missive: ''Take pity on a wretched soul, and forget her as though she had never been, and give your love to one more fortunate than she.'' One further love-letter, however belongs to a somewhat different category. The lengthy epistle encompassing almost an entire chapter which Amnon despatches to Tamar from Nineveh ranks partly as a love-letter, but also contains an historico-political survey of the Near East in Isaiah's time as well as a wealth of natural description. Highly romantic in tone and written in characteristic, high-flown style the letter serves as a refreshing interlude after the tortuous machinations of the previous chapter. This particular epistolary stratagem occurs again in ['*Ayit zahvu'a*] in more developed form.

Mapu's second historical novel, [*Ashmat Shomeron*], although twice the length of the [*Ahavat Zion*], makes less resort to the letter form. In four cases the letters are not even quoted, although the contents of all but one is revealed. Nor, for the most part, do they seem to play any significant role in the story. Only one of them has some importance for the plot. Unaware that Uzziel is his father, Eliphelet discovers him making love to Miriam his mother, and departs in high dudgeon, leaving behind a letter for Miriam full of reproaches, but fortunately not quoted. One substantial letter, however, is worthy of comment, for it represents Mapu's writing at its best. Jehosheba's letter to Miriam contains a self-revelation by one mature matron to another, unfolded with sensitive insight and poignant irony. In the course of her narrative the widowed Jehosheba outlines in stately language the affection she has conceived for Eliada, whom she commends to Miriam's care, advising her to employ him as her agent, while confessing that she herself may marry him. But the name Eliada is, in fact, a symbolic pseudonym for Uzziel, Miriam's husband, who has been forced into hiding for many years because of the anger of the wicked King Ahaz. The letter concluded as follows,

> Why should I conceal from you, my dear, what I have in mind? Elkanah for all the glory that surrounded him will never return, and my grief and sorrow will pass eventually, and then I shall want to resume the threads of life. How nice it would be to settle down under the protection of this splendid man. I know you will understand me, my dear. If it is bad for a man to live alone, how much worse is the fate of a woman who has to live alone. You know that only too well. So tell Manoah of your decision so that dear Eliada may know where he stands, and may God bring your husband back from exile, and may you have the joy of seeing him return at a propitious hour. You may be sure that your friend Jehosheba will share your joy.

In the event it is comforting to learn that with Miriam's consent Uzziel finally takes the unhappy Jehosheba as a second wife.

While the role performed by letters in the historical novels is clearly limited, the sheer volume of correspondence scattered throughout [*'Ayit zahvu'a*] inevitably gives the novel a certain epistolary flavour. For all their weight of numbers and widespread distribution, however, the letters do not constitute an integral and well-planned element in the overall structure. With the important exception of one series, which will be examined later, the arrangement of the letters makes an haphazard impression, and for all the variety of device which they are made to serve, they fail to exert the cohesive force which their number might have warranted. So much so, that apart from the one series mentioned above, the critics seem to have overlooked them altogether. This seemingly haphazard introduction of letters into the novel, however, is the more readily understandable in view of Mapu's inability to weave a convincing plot. The structure of his novels is remniscent rather of a clumsy amateur than of a polished craftsman.

Nevertheless, as individual units the letters are important in the novel, and the sum total of units embraces or determines in great measure the numerous twists and turns of a long and complex narrative. The letters may be divided broadly into three main categories, although a number of letters contain elements pertaining to all three. To the first category belong all those which have some bearing on the plot, whether in the form of a dramatic device or as a vehicle for supplying the reader with information not previously known; they are also used to effect an interruption of the narrative or for purposes of dramatic irony. The second category embraces such letters as are included primarily for characterization, and which serve to throw additional light upon the *dramatis personae,* apart from the information which the reader may glean by direct observation. In the third category may be included all the letters used by the author for reflection on or criticism of the various

aspects of society, or for the propagation of certain ideas or the advocacy of particular policies.

A closer examination of these three main categories may serve to illustrate Mapu's success in exploiting a wide range of the techniques associated with the epistolary novel and at the same time his failure to take advantage of the more subtle aspects of the *genre.* As far as the plot is concerned, the letter is most frequently encountered in the guise of melodramatic device or as a vehicle for the portrayal of melodramatic action. As a device the letter furnished Mapu with a wide range of application in the classical manner. Letters are regularly forged by the arch-villain Zadok, a master of the art, in order to direct events to his own advantage. They are cunningly planted on virtuous but unsuspecting heroes, who are dragged off to gaol in consequence. The heroes also suffer misfortune and distress by having their letters either stolen or intercepted, a device which affords the villains access to the private plans and activities of their enemies, and facilitates their machinations to harm their innocent victims by means of scandal, slander or persecution.

Many of the letters contain warnings about the nefarious activities of villains masquerading in the guise of righteousness, although the warnings usually go unheeded! One letter, in particular, is worthy of note. After betrothing his sister to a rich old money-lender Achbor, Eliab receives a letter from a friend warning him against the old man's meanness, wickedness and hypocrisy in the strongest possible terms. The writer approaches his theme without any preliminary niceties: "I have heard a rumour which makes my blood boil, that you are selling your poor sister to the devil, and I feel constrained to outline for you without delay the sort of man he is and the kind of life he leads." After a prolonged and vehement exposure of the old man's thorough nastiness the writer concludes: "You see, my dear Eliab, that I have let you know something of Achbor's wiles, and I warn you not to give your gentle sister to him. Be sure to take my words of warning seriously, and you will have cause to be grateful for my advice." Fortunately, on this occasion the warning achieves its desired effect.

Apart from such admonitory letters addressed to individuals, the novel contains two interesting examples of what may be termed warning circulars. Both letters describe the villainous past of the arch-hypocrite, Zadok *alias* Alkum *alias* Hophni—and incidently, a pirate's son—and unfold a melodramatic sequence of murder, forgery and theft. In the earlier letter Heman recounts how he had previously placed implicit trust in Alkum, unaware that the villain was responsible for the death by poisoning of Heman's wife. While together on a business trip, however, Heman is startled by a murderous attack launched upon him in the night, which shakes his confidence in the trustworthiness of his associate:

> One day I was making my way to a market town, well supplied with money, and with Alkum accompanying me as usual. We reached an inn where Alkum and I shared a room. The candle was still alight, and I was sleeping restlessly, troubled by all sorts of nightmares. Suddenly I half awoke only to feel blood trickling down my neck. I tried to pull myself together and tell myself that it was only a bad dream. Then I woke up properly and found—O horrible sight!—Alkum the pirate's son standing over me brandishing a razor to slit my throat from ear to ear, his face aflame, his eyes bulging

terrifyingly in their sockets. Bracing myself I sprang out of bed to defend my life, with only my bare fists to ward off the forces of evil. I wanted to scream: Help, murder! But I realized that if I shouted with such a wound in my throat, the veins would burst and all would be lost. Seeing my end in sight, I summoned all my reserves of strength. . . .

The narrative is continued for some time in similar strain, both letters concluding with the information that they are being circulated through the Jewish communities far and wide as a warning, and in an attempt to trace the culprit. The suitability of the device as a medium for the introduction of crude melodrama scarcely requires further demonstration.

The examples furnished above, however, by no means exhaust the dramatic possibilities of the letter utilized by Mapu in [*'Ayit zahvu'a*]. Letters are conveniently found in books, whether deliberately planted there, or by sheer accident as when Hamul discovers a letter in Othniel's book just as he is about to burn it! They may be deliberately anonymous, in which form they serve excellently for spreading slander or conveying bad news. The arrival of a letter may produce consternation or result in the recipients fainting away. Again, when the young Zerah's clothes are discovered on a river bank, they contain a letter explaining that the cause of his suicide is unrequited love. The cloying self-pity and euphuistic expression of the letter may be seen from the following extract: "The joy of living has been taken from me, so why should I face a life of bitterness when death is preferable. That is why I have composed this document, which contains my last words. Perhaps Elisheba, too, will read them and realize that my death is due to her, so that my memory will remain embedded in her heart, to embitter all her happiness and joy. . . ."

Apart from melodramatic devices, letters are employed extensively as a means of conveying information, and as such constitute an important element in the plot. To effect an introduction of these letters, Mapu frequently utilizes the technique of allowing one character to hand over a letter written by a second for the perusal of a third. The events prior to the opening of this story, for example, are described in a series of letters which Jeroham has received from his grandson Naaman, and which he allows Saul his grandson's benefactor to read. These three letters which together comprise an entire chapter, supply both Saul and the reader with much important information. Saul returns the compliment by reading to Jeroham a further series of letters from or via Naaman of even greater length and of no less importance for the understanding of the plot. A similar purpose is achieved when the wicked Zaphnath shows Levi her paramour a letter which she has abstracted from her husband's bag, and which contains an account of Alkum's villainous exploits. The technique is taken one step further when Zibiah asks Hogeh—one of the good characters—to read her a letter written by Elisheba to Othniel which she, Zibiah, has intercepted but cannot read. She blandly pretends that the letter must have been lost!

Elsewhere, however, letters are used to convey information directly to the intended recipient. This somewhat obvious procedure is the more acceptable in so far as it obviates the second-hand flavour inherent in the technique of using two third parties. This is particularly the case, for example, in the letter describing Eden's dramatic nocturnal encounter with a band of robbers and his timely deliverance, or when Naaman receives a letter sent to him in London by his grandfather to acquaint him with news of all the latest intrigues since his departure. Nevertheless, the substantial proportion of the plot presented in letter-form inevitably tends to deaden its impact, so that at times it appears as if the action were being unfolded in reported speech. This unfortunate impression is further strengthened where the letter depicts a minimum of action while consisting largely of inconsequential gossip—an unhappy combination to which [*'Ayit zahvu'a*] is in any case only too prone.

More successful, structurally, is the insertion of letters which interrupt the narrative at moments of tension, and allow the reader's emotions to subside in readiness for the next crisis. Azriel's letters from Palestine, which comprise perhaps the most refreshing element in the story and form a natural connecting link with the historical novels, virtually constitute a self-contained frame-story. Interspersed in segments throughout the novel, they represent a valuable cohesive force in a sprawling and somewhat shapeless work. The technique of interruption is sometimes applied even to the letters themselves. While reading an exciting episode in Azriel's letters, for example, Elisheba is handed an impassioned love letter from Zerah which she reds before returning to Azriel's narrative. The same lengthy missive—almost 5000 words in all—iself quotes another letter, which attempts to account for the real Zadok's renunciation of Shiphrah. It is, of course, a forgery from the pen of pseudo-Zadok! Again, a letter may be interrupted while the reader comments on it, or in another case by the sounds of the Passover *Haggadah* being recited in the next room and skilfully illustrating the situation described in the letter.

Among the more attractive of the dramatic devices is Mapu's employment of the letter-form for dramatic irony. On two occasions the wicked Zadok (alias Hophni alias Alkum) receives letters enlisting his aid in bringing Hophni or Alkum to justice for their many crimes! On another occasion a marriage-broker who is anxious to prevent the hero from marrying the heroine, so as to further his own ends, shows Obadiah the heroine's grandfather a letter written by the hero to a friend, in which he confesses his passionate love for Elisheba in spite of her grandfather's opposition, and bluntly declares: "After all Obadiah will not live for ever." Not unnaturally, the old man finds the sentiment less than endearing!

Quite apart from their role in the plot, letters are frequently employed for the delineation of character. The direct method is normally followed, with the characterization confined to a narrow canvas and a single plane. In the early part of the story, for example, Jeroham's enemies are outlined in letters written by Naaman and his friend Ahitub, which constitute a kind of dossier, and seem at times more suitable for a record office than a novel. Although the descriptions may, on occasion, be quite powerful, the characterization is almost entirely of the black and white variety, which leaves little scope for development. The subtlety to be derived from varying viewpoints, which constitutes one of the great advantages of the epistolary *genre*, is conspicuously absent.

This failure to make use of so successful a technique is all the more surprising in view of Perl's skilful employment of multiple perspective. But it is not the only aspect of characterization in which Mapu falls short of his predecessor. Perl resorts to a skilful use of language to denote the affiliation of characters to the movement of Enlightenment, *Haskalah*, or to Hasidism, and even marks the gradual transition of his main character from support for the latter movement to the former by a marked change in his literary style. Mapu's characterizations, on the other hand, suffer from a uniformity of style, which tends to make their rigid stratification into black and white still less convincing. Indeed, when Mapu does attempt to differentiate, the result scarcely reflects the author's intention. Whereas the virtuous characters are apt to write their epistles in the high-flown, euphuistic and over-florid style which was regarded as "good taste" by most of the Hebrew writers of the period, the wicked characters—except when they are deliberately forging letters in the manner of their opponents—adopt a rather more straightforward and hence more pleasing style. It may well be that Mapu was temperamentally incapable of writing the barbarous jargon which Perl foists upon the opponents of Enlightenment in his stories. Certainly, the obscurantism of many of Mapu's villains is not noticeably reflected in their choice of language.

Letters, however, do provide Mapu with one additional means of characterization. On occasion, the author chooses the letter-form to furnish a character with a medium for self-portraiture. Unlike the more frequent use of letters, already noticed, in which one character describes a second for the benefit of a third, the reader in this case is able to form an estimate of personality as it unfolds in the writer's letter. Such, for example, is the case when Elisheba writes a letter to Naaman, in which the generosity of her nature becomes immediately apparent. Indeed, it is this very generosity which the villains, who have intercepted the letter, plan to exploit for their own nefarious purposes. It is a pity that Mapu did not make greater use of this effective method for his characterization.

In spite of the serious shortcomings in Mapu's copious use of letters for the construction of the plot of [*'Ayit zahvu'a*] and the depiction of its characters, a third epistolary category plays a more successful role. Those letters which are employed for reflections on contemporary life and social criticism or for the propagation of the author's pet ideas constitute a far more satisfactory element in the novel. The suitability of the letter-form for such purposes has been pointed out above, but in the context of [*'Ayit zahvu'a*] it possesses the additional advantage of directness of approach, in contrast to many of the letters which seem to relegate the action and characterization of the novel to the third person. Indeed, for Mapu the exponent of Enlightenment and advocate of social reform, the letter served as an excellent medium for expounding his views, without appearing to emphasize the author's didactic aims too blatantly.

A life-long pedagogue, Mapu lost no opportunity of pointing out what he considered to be the shortcomings of the old traditional type of education with its narrow horizons and inefficient methods. Time and again the letters sing the praises of a secular education, and a training which will enable the student to earn a dignified livelihood, and at the same time develop his aesthetic appreciation of the beauties of the world. They might almost be regarded as tracts for the propagation of the movement of *Haskalah*. Of particular interest is his support for equal educational opportunities for women, and Elisheba's letter to her grandfather, in which she defends her right to study, represents an important advance in the struggle for emancipation. Again, his enthusiasm for the learning of foreign languages appears in Elisheba's ability to cope with a letter of invitation written in French—an unusual accomplishment in her environment. The frequent insertion of arguments advocating the development of a refined literary taste belongs to the same category.

Finally, the letters afforded Mapu ample scope for the free expression of romantic love, which the exponents of Enlight-

enment considered so important a step towards Jewish regeneration. Many of the letters written by the hero and the heroine of the novel display a tenderness and sensitivity of considerable charm. In the mental climate of Mapu's environment the portrayal of such outright declarations of love was an act of considerable daring, and it is a little difficult to realize quite how revolutionary Zerah's impassioned letter to Elisheba must have appeared to Mapu's contemporaries. After praising her beauty and charm in somewhat elegant style Zerah continues: "From that time (when I first saw you) I became conscious of a new world, a world which God had planted in my heart to plague and delight me by turns, as successive waves of hope and fear swept over me. From the day when I beheld the symbol of love in your beautiful face and felt the pangs of jealousy—from that day I have been mad for love of you, and I am terrified lest you might not feel well disposed towards me." Mild as such sentiments may appear to a modern reader of sophisticated tastes, their impact upon a society in which it was customary for young couples to see each other for the first time on their wedding day was startling, and it is scarcely surprizing that Mapu's stories were read with such avidity.

It is, indeed, in the realm of sentiment that Mapu's use of letters proved most effective. His employment of the epistolary device for the mechanics of plot and characterization reflects the less satisfactory aspects of the European tradition, and relies too often on crude melodrama or third-party account, while neglecting the subtle advantages which may accrue from a more skilful use of epistolary techniques. In utilizing the letter-form for the exposition of his own ideas, however, and for reflections on the social conditions of his time, and in particular for the introduction of sentiment into his novels, Mapu performed a genuine service for Hebrew literature comparable with Perl's exploitation of the letter-form for satirical purposes. The importance of that service may be perceived in the copious supply of letters included in most of the Hebrew novels composed during the twenty years following Abraham Mapu's death. . . . (pp. 136-46)

> *D. Patterson, "Epistolary Elements in the Novels of Abraham Mapu," in* The Annual of Leeds University Oriental Society, *Vol. IV, 1964, pp. 132-49.*

DAVID PATTERSON   (essay date 1964)

[*In his* Abraham Mapu: The Creator of the Modern Hebrew Novel, *Patterson discusses Mapu's life and works and provides synopses and translations of selected portions of his three completed novels. In the following excerpt from that study, Patterson considers Mapu's pioneering use of a neo-biblical style, his attempts to write spoken dialogue in a biblical idiom, his didactic purpose, and finally, his influence on later Hebrew writers. For additional criticism by Patterson, see excerpts dated 1956 and 1964.*]

[In **Ahavat Zion, Ashmat Shomeron,** and **'Ayit zahvu'a,** the source of Mapu's style] lies in the self-imposed limitation of modelling his work primarily upon the style and language of the Bible. In the absence of any prior Hebrew novel to influence his choice of style, the predilection of the exponents of *Haskalah* for the purity of Biblical Hebrew inevitably determined his medium. Moreover, it is reasonable to concede that many of the elements essential for his creations were to be found in the Bible. The Prophets, Psalms and Job provided the materials for natural description; the Song of Songs furnished him with the raw materials of romantic love; the books of Samuel and Kings afforded a simple but powerful model for narrative, while the point of view of the Bible with its clear-cut distinction between right and wrong, good and evil, provided the mould from which the 'black and white' characters might be cast. Upon these basic elements Mapu directed the powerful beam of his imagination, harnessed to a highly developed faculty for creating historical atmosphere, and a most sensitive feeling for language. These are the raw ingredients of Mapu's novels to which he adhered with remarkable fidelity.

For his reading public, too, the adoption of such a method possessed an immediate advantage. Familiarity with the content, language and style of the Bible provided a natural bridge to this new, literary domain. The transition was so natural, the framework so well remembered, that to many [*Ahavat Zion*] appeared almost as an extension of the Bible itself, and young lovers began to call each other 'Amnon' and 'Tamar'. It is unquestionable that his delightful use of Biblical language must have been one of the chief reasons for the popularity of his novels—his readers would have felt so much at home! Moreover, the consistent employment of Biblical language provides a large measure of artistic unity, which prevails in spite of the weakness and intricacies of the plots. (pp. 63-5)

But the premise that the linguistic foundations of [*Ahavat Zion, Ashmat Shomeron*] and in great measure [*'Ayit zahvu'a*] are Biblical is in itself a striking reflection of Mapu's creative powers. The initial problems facing the author in this choice of medium were as difficult as they were obvious. How could Biblical language adequately satisfy the very different demands of the novel? How could words and phrases, sanctified by religion and made authoritative by thousands of years of tradition, be adapted to a secular and fictitious context? Finally— and perhaps most seriously of all—how could such usage fail to suffer by comparison with the unassailable grandeur of the original? Each formidable in itself, the three problems together formed a seemingly insuperable obstacle.

The strength of Biblical narrative lies, moreover, in the brevity of the stories. Its adaptation for the purposes of a full-length novel confronted the author with the very serious problem of maintaining the interest over long periods in a medium especially suited to conciseness of expression. Mapu was compelled to paint atmosphere and create detail, while using a Biblical style which concentrates only on essentials. The sublimity of Biblical narrative arises from the restraint displayed at moments of great dramatic tension. At such moments, when an explanation might destroy the entire effect, a terse phrase can arouse the deepest emotion. Such is the force of Abraham's answer when Isaac seeks the victim for sacrifice. Herein lies the poignancy of the description of the dead concubine with her hands upon the threshold. The imagination is inflamed to the point of outrage, yet in the first example the Hebrew uses six words and in the second example three.

The Bible story is characterized by a hardness of outline, by a rigid economy of expression, by a relentless exposition of consecutive facts, with almost no attempt at psychological analysis or philosophic speculation which may serve as motivation. . . . The significant facts are singled out and hammered home. All extraneous detail is ignored, or left to the reader to supply. The Bible story is a narrative of events arranged in their time sequence. It is a skeleton narrative that bites into the imagination to supply the flesh and blood, and therein lies its strength. (pp. 66-7)

As a novelist Mapu had to supply those very elements . . . which Biblical narrative is so careful to omit, while at the same time using a medium of expression which derives its force from such omission. It is hardly surprising that he sometimes fails badly; it is all the more surprising that he has achieved so large a measure of success.

Mapu's answer to these problems consisted of a direct attack upon his material, without reservation and without apology. The Bible in its entirety became grist for the mill of his invention. Complete appropriation was followed by analysis and refashioning. The ingredients remained, but the treatment was varied at need. The emergent pattern retained much of its original colouring, entire phrases and suitable images being introduced unaltered, or slightly modified for the new situations. But more often the reshuffling amounted to a new creation, without losing the spirit of the original. If the final result had not the sublimity of the Bible, it was nevertheless inspired. Although the peaks could not be reached, a very high general level was achieved. With the dangers of plagiarism and parody confronting him at every step, Mapu succeeded in threading his way to the height of originality. That he has had no successors, in spite of the popularity of his novels, is ample testimony of the difficulties that beset the way.

The authenticity of the Biblical scene, which forms the background of both Mapu's historical novels, is engendered by this constant and thoroughgoing employment of the characteristics of Biblical language. There is, indeed, an interpenetration of Biblical idiom which forges between these novels and the Bible a link so genuine and so organic that it is not without reason that they have been described as a new commentary on the Bible. From the Biblical language stems the Biblical quality of setting, atmosphere, dialogue—and hence characters—and even to some extent action.

Mapu appears to have been so steeped in the language of the Bible that he thought in it and lived it—as though he had inherited the mould of thought of its ancient authors. His art resides in his ability to introduce Biblical phrases or adapt Biblical passages while preserving an impression of natural and organic expression. The appeal lies in the familiarity yet aptness of the transmutation. The well-known passage is adapted to serve a new purpose, without destroying the original spirit. Innumerable short snatches of phrase are drawn from the Bible either in their entirety or with a subtle modification, which leaves no doubt of their origin. Yet the Biblical association of such phrases inevitably reinforces their effect upon the reader.

The merit of such application must be sought in the delicate restraint which the author exercised. His prose does not glitter with Biblical gems, painstakingly quarried from the mine of the Bible, as is the case with so many of the writers of *Haskalah*. Only on rare occasions does a Biblical phrase project abruptly from his writing. Close examination reveals his novels to be alive with the phrases of the Bible, but almost always so skilfully placed that the picture is clear, while the countless jigsaw pieces that comprise it remain invisible.

The danger that the method might produce a jumbled patchwork of Biblical phrases was always present. Every turn of phrase threatened distortion of context or interruption of the smooth course of narrative. His success consists in the fact that the attention is excited but not distracted. The reader is able to appreciate the Biblical allusion without being diverted from the story. Recognition is simple but not obvious. The phrases are clear, but they do not leap out of the text. Whether drawn directly from the Bible or original creation the language is subtly fused into a single harmony. (pp. 67-9)

· · · · ·

For the author writing in a living language the acquisition of the materials for dialogue presents no great problem; he has only to use his ears. . . . For Mapu the problem was very different and far more difficult. He set out to write novels in a language which had not been used in common speech for tens of centuries. . . . In the virtual absence of a spoken idiom from which he might draw inspiration, this task must be regarded almost as a *creatio ex nihilo,* and represents one of Mapu's major contributions to the development both of Hebrew literature and of the very conception that Hebrew might be revived as a spoken language. Even to the present generation, long familiar with the phenomenon of Hebrew as a natural and accepted instrument of daily speech, Mapu's success is impressive if somewhat quaint. To Mapu's contemporaries and near contemporaries the effect must have been startling, and the significance of the achievement clear. It would be unfair to expect that at one fell swoop Mapu should forge an instrument sufficiently flexible to portray the infinite variety of expression required by the novelist to suit every conceivable time and situation. Mapu, clearly, could do no more than pave the way. The criterion for criticism in this instance must be that he succeeded at all—that the dialogue was actually written.

But Mapu was faced with an added difficulty. As his specific aim was to create a novel in the language of the Bible, he was compelled to renounce the characteristic language of subsequent strata of Hebrew literature, which would have rendered him invaluable assistance in the formation of dialogue. As if the difficulty of creating a living idiom from a literary language were not enough, he had in addition to confine himself to one section of that literature, a section, moreover, whose vocabulary is limited in the extreme. Within the framework of this literature—the primary source upon which Mapu could draw— the passages couched in the form of conversation comprise a comparatively small proportion of the whole. Yet from these flimsy materials Mapu succeeded in constructing the dialogue of two entire novels, together with by far the greater part of a third.

Interspersed in the Bible there are, of course, elements of dialogue full of the freshness and spontaneity of living speech, such as the conversations in the book of Ruth or those between God and Satan in Job or the scene in which Solomon is confronted by two women, each claiming to be the mother of a child. It has, indeed, been pointed out that Mapu was the first to make full use of these elements, which were invaluable by virtue of their scarcity, and which had to be exploited to the maximum. But apart from these primary sources the Bible contains numerous secondary sources of dialogue, that is material which, although not in the actual form of conversation, can be adapted to dialogue quite naturally and with little alteration. Elements of dialogue lurk beneath the surface of the numerous stories of the narrative books. They may be sought in God's injunctions to the Israelites and in the passionate outbursts of the later prophets. One feels them in the soliloquies of the Psalms and, in didactic form, in the conside epigrams of the book of Proverbs. The emotions of sadness may be expressed in the words of the book of Lamentations, and the intimate love conversations arise naturally from the language of the Song of Songs. Again a tertiary—or even less direct— source of material for dialogue may be discerned in the natural description embodied in the Bible, which is found in sufficient quantity in the latter Prophets, in the Psalms and in Job to form the basis for the more imaginative and descriptive elements of dialogue.

But in the final analysis the sum total of all the possible materials for dialogue which can be derived from the various strata of the Bible, even by a master of that medium, remains sadly meagre compared to the resources which the novelist, writing in a living idiom, has constantly at his disposal. In [*Ahavat Zion*] the problem is not so acute. The comparative brevity of the story, the greater part of which is narrative and descriptive, with the dialogue playing a minor role, alleviates the difficulty; moreover the historical background is, if anything, enhanced by the old-fashioned flavour of the conversation. In some measure, even if to a lesser extent, the same factors mitigate the problem in [*Ashmat Shomeron*]; although here the greater length and complexity of the novel, with the accompanying greater emphasis on dialogue, tend to make the deficiencies of the medium more obvious. Only the prophetic soliloquies sound a convincing note of truth. . . . (pp. 78-81)

But with [*'Ayit zahvu'a*] the limits of Biblical dialogue are finally reached. In this novel, which is approximately five times the length of [*Ahavat Zion*] and which depicts the life of his own period, Mapu was compelled to face the inadequacy of his chosen medium. The Biblical flavour of the dialogue is manifestly unsuitable for a novel of contemporary life. (pp. 81-2)

It must, then, be conceded *a priori* that the greater part of the dialogue is stilted and artificial, and that despite Mapu's heroic efforts to hammer out his material into pliable form, the direct speech only too frequently lacks vitality. This defect is enhanced by a tendency—found commonly in Biblical Hebrew, and not unknown even in Modern Hebrew—to couch polite conversation in the oblique form. The stilted nature of much of the incidental dialogue may be illustrated from the first meeting of Amnon and Jedidiah, the father of Tamar, whose life has been saved by Amnon's bravery:

> And Jedidiah raised his eyes and said: 'Is your name Amnon?'
>
> And the youth said to him: 'Amnon is the name of your servant.'
>
> 'Are you the one that saved Tamar, my daughter, from the savage lion?'—Jedidiah asked him further.
>
> 'The Lord was pleased to strengthen the hand of your servant'—Amnon answered with modest grace.
>
> 'May the Lord bless you, my son!'—Jedidiah said—'And you will be an honourable man in Zion. Behold! I am in your debt for this deed, and I shall reward you accordingly.'

Not infrequently, however, a more genuine spirit is infused, and the dialogue comes to life. This is especially the case with the villains, who tend to be more convincing than the righteous characters, and whose conversations are often spiced, and on occasion leavened with humour—a quality which the heroes lack entirely! This quality tends to assert itself during bouts of heavy drinking, as when Bukkiah remarks to Carmi, the rascally inn-keeper:

> . . . Now both of us are empty fellows, while our vessels are full of wine. But if the vessels are emptied inside us, we shall become full and the vessels empty. . . .

Of a similar order is Omri's comment when he meets Zimri, his companion in villainy, after a long absence, and attempts to rouse him from sleep with the cutting observation:

> . . . But what are you doing asleep on your feet?
> Don't you know you've slept right through the
> end of Ahaz's reign to the beginning of
> Hezekiah's? . . .

Even more spirited is the lively altercation which takes place between Pethahiah and Jerahmeel, and which, quite apart from the dramatic irony involved, has elements of slapstick humour and colourful phraseology. A similar raciness is found, too, in the preceding passage, in which Pethahiah assures Zadok of his ability to ensure that his rest will not be disturbed, while a brave attempt to portray the language of the street occurs in the lively scene in which Nehemiah's house is picketed. Again a more genuine note is found in the love scenes, where the imaginative language is in keeping with romantic emotions involved, and which nevertheless—as in the reunion of Uzziel and Miriam after many long years of separation—are handled with delicate restraint. In general a gradual maturing of dialogue is observable in the later novels as Mapu acquired more experience in this form of expression; while the longer speeches, which are here much more frequent than in [*Ahavat Zion*], tend to be more successful than the short, casual snatches of conversation, which, as is well known to students of language, present the greatest idiomatic difficulties. (pp. 82-4)

[The limitations of Mapu's vernacular are] pathetically obvious and must be admitted even while recognizing the greatness of Mapu's feat in creating dialogue and the large measure of success which he achieved in the attempt. Nevertheless, there can be little doubt that Mapu's novels, both by virtue of their own merit, and through the great influence which they exerted on subsequent Hebrew novelists, helped in no small measure to prepare the ground for the extraordinary revival of Hebrew as a spoken language, which Mapu had, himself, so dramatically prophesied. (p. 85)

· · · · ·

Although in so many respects a revolutionary in the realm of Hebrew literature from the point of view of the form, setting and conception of his novels, Mapu was too much a child of his generation to remain aloof from its missionary spirit. On the contrary he felt himself a conscious champion of the cause of *Haskalah,* and the ideals of that movement, as reflected in the cultural, religious, social and economic struggles of the time, are inextricably embedded in the body of his writings.

The principal ideas, which comprise the element of didacticism in Mapu's novels, and which roughly correspond with the main aims of the movement of *Haskalah,* may be divided into five categories:
1 The glorification of the Jewish past.
2 The encouragement of a discriminating use of the Hebrew language with an attendant refinement of taste.
3 The dissemination of knowledge and enlightenment.
4 The inculcation of a lofty, ethical attitude to life.
5 The improvement of the social and economic position of the Jewish people.

These several aspects, however, are not treated as separate themes, but rather interwoven one with the other to such an extent that the aims appear synonymous and mutually dependent.

The glorification of the Jewish past is, of course, inherent in the very conception of the two historical novels, and embodied in the name [*Ahavat Zion*]. . . . [Apart] from their historical interest, these stories contained a living message for Mapu's own generation. The full, free life of the individual and the national independence, so clearly portrayed in these novels, as well as the healthy and organic connection with the soil, presented such a striking contrast to the harsh reality and meagre existence of contemporary life, that his readers could not but have been awakened to a longing for better things and to the need to break the fetters of gradual decay which enveloped the Jewish community.

It is clearly an exaggeration to portray Mapu as a creator of the Zionist movement. . . . But there can be no doubt that the influence exerted by these novels and the deep longings they aroused helped to prepare a mental climate suitable for the growth of the Zionist idea. It may be doubted whether Mapu's personal conception of a physical return to Palestine went beyond the traditional idea expressed by the ageing Obadiah:

> But be sure of this, that Zion's paths are in my
> heart, and that as soon as my money is returned,
> I shall take my staff in my hand and journey
> to the holy city; for who is there, or what is
> there, to keep me here?

What is more certain, however, is that his stories represent a symbolic, indeed prophetic, call for national revival, and as such have exercised a profound influence on subsequent generations of young readers. (pp. 86-7)

Mapu's love of the Hebrew language was equalled only by his earnest desire to foster its widespread use among his own contemporaries and to raise the aesthetic level of publications in that medium. His motives for writing in Hebrew and his choice of the imaginative story—which he refers to as *Hazon* (a vision)—are described in the introduction to the third part of [*'Ayit zahvu'a*] and the introduction to [*Hoze hezyonot*]. With the publication of his novels in Hebrew, Mapu hoped to attract the young generation to a deeper attachment to that language, and thereby counteract the tendency towards assimilation so conspicuous among the Jewish communities of France and Germany. In addition he believed that by stirring their imagination and widening their mental horizons he would encourage the youth to seek learning and wisdom. Mapu felt deeply the pressing need to raise the general level of taste, and the emphasis on *Ṭub Ta'am* (good taste) is maintained constantly throughout his writings. . . . (p. 88)

Closely connected with the call for refinement of language is Mapu's constant plea for the dissemination of knowledge and enlightenment. Indeed, apart from its intrinsic value, the former concept is regarded as the instrument of the latter. No less than the 'Age of Reason' in France and the 'Enlightenment' in Germany of the previous century, the movement of *Haskalah* believed that the spread of the ideas of reason and understanding would eradicate the evils of society and advance the cause of civilization. In consequence the need for popular enlightenment was regarded as a matter of paramount importance, towards which every effort should be expended. Hence, too, the constant stress on the importance of learning foreign languages—an occupation regarded by the orthodox as anathema. All the virtues required for the new type of being, whose every action would be guided by reason, were embodied in the ideal figure of the *Maskil*. As the spearhead of the attack on the forces of darkness and ignorance, and in spite of all the harm

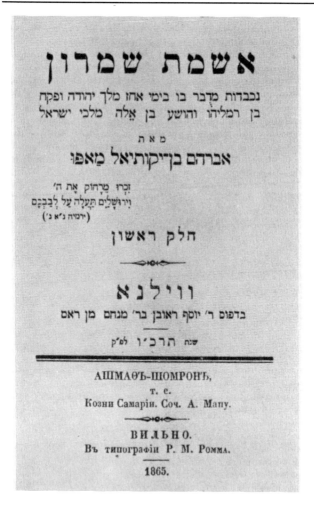

The 1865 title page of Ashmat Shomeron.

perpetrated by foolishness and superstitious prejudice, the *Maskil* would eventually conquer with the weapons of wisdom, moral superiority and good taste. The concept is stressed continually in Mapu's writings. . . . (p. 90)

Moral and religious sentiments—modelled on the prophetic books and Wisdom Literature of the Bible, and in the historical novels actually uttered by Biblical prophets—occupy a prominent place in all three stories. They all end happily with a generous reward for the good characters and the shameful exposure and punishment of the villains, who, moreover, regularly repent. In spite of the numerous occasions on which the evil schemes seem certain of victory, in the end truth will out, and no grounds are left for uncertainty that the issue was ever really in doubt. Only too willing to admit his mistake in placing a too naïve trust in men, now unmasked as hypocrites, Jedidiah discerns the hand of God in the final turn of events. His wife Tirzah readily echoes his sentiments:

> But God is good to them that hope for him,
> and in him we place our trust. . . .

No less expressive of deep faith is Shulamit's cry:

> The Lord sees the tears of every afflicted soul,
> and my tears too, and he will heal the broken-
> hearted, and redeem the captives of war.

Again the two villains Hepher and Bukkiah are described as having lost God's grace on the day of their crimes, and never prospering subsequently. Even if, at times, a suggestion of the problem of the book of Job emerges as in the outburst:

> O righteous God! Why do the violent flourish?

in the end poetic justice prevails. (pp. 92-3)

Wretchedly poor all his life and himself a victim of the crushing poverty in which the Jews of eastern Europe lived, Mapu could hardly refrain from suggesting improvements in the social and economic conditions of his people. In the historical novels he portrays the varied pursuits of the individuals of an independent nation, with due emphasis on the agricultural backbone of the economy, and the satisfaction to be derived from such a livelihood. (p. 94)

Frequently, too, the story serves as a forum for his ideas on education, wherein he forcefully portays the bad effects of harsh and exclusive book-learning, so widely practised by the Pietists, and advocates his own use of more gentle methods. The barbaric practice of burning secular books is censured severely, while the underhand methods of the traditional 'matchmaker', quite indifferent to the happiness of the young couples whose marriages he is so anxious to arrange, receive a due share of satire! A further reform, strongly advocated, is the emancipation of woman. Elisheba is the representative of the new type of woman, independent, cultured, demanding equality of education with her male counterpart. It is significant, too, that Mapu stresses her interest in handicrafts as a field of creative and aesthetic expression. His advocacy of economic and social reform, however, is generally moderate and restrained in comparison to the bitter polemics which abound in the novels of his successors, who frequently resort to cutting satire and biting irony for the propagation of their views.

But the solutions put forward for the social and economic evils of Jewish life are sketchy and inadequate. It is, indeed, doubtful whether the problems involved were deeply understood. There are, at least, indications that Mapu did not always feel sure of his ground. . . . But for the most part Mapu points his lesson in good faith, on the one hand fighting to preserve the finer elements of Jewish tradition, and on the other indicating the new values to be adopted in a changing world. (pp. 94-5)

[Proof of] Mapu's creative power must not be sought in the form of his novels. The structure, the dramatic technique and the characterizations all lean heavily on previous writers, and all display grave weaknesses and limitations. From a technical standpoint Mapu resembles a clumsy apprentice rather than a finished craftsman. He never mastered the art of weaving a convincing plot, and his inability to sustain interest over long periods is particularly evident in his more lengthy novels. Nevertheless, Mapu's writings are stamped with a freshness and originality which more than atone for all his borrowings and limitations, and display an element of genius.

Mapu's main contribution to Hebrew literature appears in the overall conception of his works. He possessed an imagination and descriptive power that could bring dry bones to life. In his historical novels he made the Bible live and endowed a remote period in history with a vividness and freshness of appeal such as no commentary or explanation can offer. His greatness consisted not so much in the intrinsic vlaue of his writings as in the possibilities that he revealed, which placed him at the head of a new literary epoch. His strength lay in the portrayal of setting, in the smoothness of his style, in his mastery of Biblical language. He clearly indicated that the Hebrew language might eventually be forged into an adequate medium of expression and adapted to serve the manifold needs of modern life. And above all he gave vent to the free expression of emotion, transfusing a somewhat dry and intellectual literature with the feelings of heroism and love. His novels provided an emotional stimulus to generations of young readers, fostering a pride in the national past and focusing attention upon the Holy Land. Hence, their influence on the Jewish national movement from which Zionism later emerged constitutes an important factor in modern Jewish history.

His importance is almost equally in evidence in another direction. The ideas on social and educational reform, expounded in ['*Ayit zahvu'a*], helped to set a fashion among the Hebrew writers who followed him. The influence of the elements of realism in his novel of contemporary life may be traced in the writings of P. Smolenskin . . . , J. L. Gordon, R. A. Braudes . . . , M. D. Brandstätter . . . and Mendele Mocher Sefarim, who developed the positivist and social aspects of their work still further. Indeed, the realist novel depicting the problems of contemporary society has continued to occupy the dominant position in Hebrew literature to the present day. It is of interest, however, that none of the major novelists who succeeded Mapu attempted to imitate his strict Biblical style. Little by little they began to follow Mapu's own advice in utilizing the linguistic resources of later strata of Hebrew literature. Either they lacked Mapu's facility and mastery of the language of the Bible, or they felt that his three novels had exhausted the possibilities of that medium, and sought a richer and more flexible instrument of language. But in any case, the clumsiness of Biblical Hebrew as a means of depicting the complex phenomena of the modern world became increasingly apparent as the range of subject-matter depicted in the Hebrew novel widened.

Of the three novels [*Ahavat Zion*] remains the most significant. It was this first novel that really broke fresh ground, that opened up the prospect of a free and independent life to a people hopelessly cramped and fettered by political, social and economic restrictions. For Mapu's contemporary public [*Ahavat Zion*] depicted a new world. This achievement, as a pointer to Mapu's contribution as a novelist, deserves serious attention. As F. R. Leavis has remarked [in *The Great Tradition*]:

> . . . it is well to start by distinguishing the few really great—the major novelists who count in the same way as the major poets, in the sense that they not only change the possibilities of the art for practitioners and readers, but that they are significant in terms of the human awareness they promote; awareness of the possibilities of life.

If this criterion has real validity, then [*Ahavat Zion*] must bear the stamp of greatness. For not only did it create—not merely change—the possibilities for a Hebrew novel, but in addition it gave open expression to the mute longings and half-sensed gropings of a whole people towards a fuller and richer life. (pp. 104-07)

> *David Patterson, in his* Abraham Mapu: The Creator of the Modern Hebrew Novel, *East and West Library, 1964, 178 p.*

ADDITIONAL BIBLIOGRAPHY

Brainin, R. *Abraham Mapu.* Piotrkow, Poland, 1900.
      A respected biographical and critical study written in Hebrew.

Cohen, Israel. "Religious and Literary Activities, c. 1700-1900." In his *Vilna*, pp. 304-32. Jewish Communities Series. Philadelphia: Jewish Publication Society of America, 1943.
      A history of the Jewish settlement in Vilna, Lithuania, that includes scattered references to Mapu.

Halkin, Simon. *Modern Hebrew Literature: Trends and Values.* New York: Schocken Books, 1950, 238 p.
      Contains several passages concerning Mapu's works and their place in the development of modern Hebrew literature.

Kravitz, Nathaniel. "Enlightenment and Emancipation." In his *Three Thousand Years of Hebrew Literature: From the Earliest Time through the Twentieth Century*, pp. 425-80. Chicago: Swallow Press, 1972.
      A survey of Hebrew proponents of Haskalah, including Mapu.

Patterson, David. "Mendele Mokher Sepharimo." In his *The Foundations of Modern Hebrew Literature*, pp. 5-30. London: Liberal Jewish Synagogue, 1961.
      Briefly remarks upon Mapu's importance in the development of modern Hebrew literature.

———. "Some Linguistic Aspects of the Nineteenth-Century Hebrew Novel." *Journal of Semitic Studies* VII, No. 2 (Autumn 1962): 309-24.
      A study of linguistic development in Hebrew literature. Patterson notes Mapu's contribution of the neo-biblical style.

———. "A Growing Awareness of Self: Some Reflections on the Role of Nineteenth Century Hebrew Fiction." *Modern Judaism* 3, No. 1 (February 1983): 23-37.
      Includes a discussion of Mapu as a proponent of enlightenment.

Raisin, Jacob S. "Russification, Reformation, and Assimilation." In his *The Haskalah Movement in Russia*, pp. 222-67. Philadelphia: Jewish Publication Society of America, 1913.
      A history of the enlightenment movement in Eastern Europe incorporating commentary on '*Ayit zahvu'a*.

Spiegel, Shalom. *Hebrew Reborn.* New York: Macmillan Co., 1930, 479 p.
      A general history of modern Hebrew literature that includes scattered references to Mapu's works.

Percy Bysshe Shelley

1792-1822

(Also wrote under pseudonyms of Victor and The Hermit of Marlow) English poet, essayist, dramatist, translator, and novelist.

Shelley is known as a major English Romantic poet. His foremost works, including *Prometheus Unbound, Adonais, The Revolt of Islam,* and *The Triumph of Life,* are recognized as leading expressions of radical thought written during the Romantic age, while his odes and shorter lyrics are often considered among the greatest in the English language. In addition, his essay *A Defence of Poetry* is highly valued as a statement of the role of the poet in society. Thus, although Shelley was one of the early nineteenth century's most controversial literary figures, his importance to English literature is today widely acknowledged.

Shelley's brief life was colorful. The eldest son of Sir Timothy and Elizabeth Shelley, landed aristocrats living in Horsham, Sussex, he was educated first at Syon House Academy, then Eton, and finally University College, Oxford. His idiosyncratic, sensitive nature and refusal to conform to tradition earned him the name "Mad Shelley," but during his years as a student he enjoyed several close friendships and pursued a wide range of interests in addition to his prescribed studies; he experimented in physical science, studied medicine and philosophy, and wrote novels and poetry. Before the age of twenty he had published two wildly improbable Gothic novels, *Zastrozzi* and *St. Irvyne,* and two collections of verse. *Original Poetry by Victor and Cazire,* written with his sister, continued in the Gothic mode, while *Posthumous Fragments of Margaret Nicholson,* coauthored with his Oxford friend Thomas Jefferson Hogg, was a collection of treasonous and erotic poetry disguised as the ravings of a mad washerwoman who had attempted to stab King George III. In 1811, during his second term at Oxford, Shelley turned to philosophical concerns with his *The Necessity of Atheism,* a pamphlet challenging theological proofs for the existence of God. Assisted by Hogg, he published the tract, distributed it to the clergymen and deans of Oxford, and invited a debate. Instead, he and Hogg were expelled, an event that estranged him from his family and left him without financial means. Nonetheless, later that year he eloped to Scotland with Harriet Westbrook, a sixteen-year-old schoolmate of his sisters. The three years they spent together were marked by financial difficulties and frequent moves to avoid creditors. Despite these pressures, Shelley was actively involved in political and social reform in Ireland and Wales, writing radical pamphlets in which he set forth his views on liberty, equality, and justice. He and Harriet enthusiastically distributed these tracts among the working classes, but with little effect.

The year 1814 was a pivotal one in Shelley's personal life. Although their marriage was faltering, he remarried Harriet in England to ensure the legality of their union and the legitimacy of their children. Weeks later, however, he fell in love with Mary Godwin, the sixteen-year-old daughter of the radical English philosopher William Godwin and his first wife, the feminist author Mary Wollstonecraft. Shelley and Mary eloped and, accompanied by Mary's stepsister, Jane (Claire) Clair-

mont, spent six weeks in Europe. On their return, Shelley entered into a financial agreement with his family that ensured him a regular income. When Harriet declined to join his household as a "sister," he provided for her and their two children, but continued to live with Mary.

In the summer of 1816, Shelley, Mary, and Claire traveled to Lake Geneva to meet with Lord Byron, with whom Claire had begun an affair. Though Byron's interest in Claire was fleeting, he developed an enduring friendship with Shelley that proved an important influence on the works of both men. Shortly after Shelley's return to England in the fall, Harriet drowned herself in Hyde Park. Shelley thereupon legalized his relationship with Mary and sought custody of his children, but the Westbrook family successfully blocked him in a lengthy lawsuit. Citing his poem *Queen Mab,* in which he denounced established society and religion in favor of free love and atheism, the Westbrooks convinced the court that Shelley was morally unfit for guardianship. Although Shelley was distressed by his separation from his daughter and infant son, he enjoyed the stimulating society of Leigh Hunt, Thomas Love Peacock, John Keats, and other literary figures during his residence at Marlow in 1817. The following year, however, motivated by ill health, financial worries, and the fear of losing custody of his and Mary's two children, Shelley relocated his family in Italy.

There, they moved frequently, spending time in Leghorn, Venice, Naples, Rome, Florence, Pisa, and Lerici. Shelley hastened to renew his relationship with Byron, who was also living in Italy, and the two poets became the nucleus of a circle of expatriots that became known as the "Satanic School" because of their defiance of English social and religious conventions and promotion of radical ideas in their works. The years in Italy were predominantly happy and productive for Shelley despite the deaths of his and Mary's children Clara and William and the increasing disharmony of their marriage. Shortly before his thirtieth birthday, Shelley and his companion, Edward Williams, drowned when their boat capsized in a squall off the coast of Lerici. Shelley's body, identified by the works of Keats and Sophocles in his pockets, was cremated on the beach in a ceremony conducted by his friends Byron, Hunt, and Edward John Trelawny. His ashes, except for his heart, which Byron plucked from the fire, were buried in the Protestant cemetery in Rome.

Much of Shelley's writing reflects the events and concerns of his life. His passionate beliefs in reform, the equality of the sexes, and the powers of love and imagination are frequently expressed in his poetry. Shelley's first mature work, *Queen Mab*, was printed in 1813, but not distributed due to its inflammatory subject matter. It was not until 1816, with the appearance of *Alastor; or, The Spirit of Solitude, and Other Poems*, that he earned recognition as a serious poet. In *Alastor*, a visionary and sometimes autobiographical poem, Shelley describes the experiences of the Poet who, rejecting human sympathy and domestic life, is pursued by the demon Solitude. Shelley also used a visionary approach in his next lengthy work, *Laon and Cythna; or, The Revolution of the Golden City*, written in friendly competition with Keats. An imaginative account of a bloodless revolution led by a brother and sister, the poem deals with the positive power of love, the complexities of good and evil, and ultimately, spiritual victory through martyrdom. *Laon and Cythna* was immediately suppressed by the printer because of its controversial content, and Shelley subsequently revised the work as *The Revolt of Islam*, minimizing its elements of incest and political revolution.

In 1819 Shelley wrote two of his most ambitious works, the verse dramas *Prometheus Unbound* and *The Cenci*. Usually regarded as his masterpiece, *Prometheus Unbound* combines myth, political allegory, psychology, and theology. Shelley transformed the Aeschylean myth of Prometheus, the fire-giver, into an allegory on the origins of evil and the possibility of regenerating nature and humanity through love. The variety of verse forms Shelley employed exhibits his poetic virtuosity and makes it one of his most challenging works. *The Cenci* differs markedly from *Prometheus Unbound* in tone and setting. Shelley based this tragedy on the history of a sixteenth-century Italian noble family. The evil Count Cenci rapes his daughter, Beatrice; she determines to murder him, seeing no other means of escape from continued violation, and is executed for parricide. Although Shelley hoped for a popular success on the English stage, his controversial treatment of the subject of incest outraged critics, preventing the play from being produced.

One of Shelley's best-known works, *Adonais: An Elegy on the Death of John Keats,* was written in 1821. Drawing on the formal tradition of elegiac verse, Shelley laments Keats's early death and, while rejecting the Christian view of resurrection, describes his return to the eternal beauty of the universe. In the same year, Shelley wrote *Epipsychidion,* in which he chronicles his search for ideal beauty through his relationships with

women—Harriet, Mary, Claire, and finally Emilia Viviani, an Italian girl he and Mary befriended and to whom the poem is addressed. Although Shelley's interest in Emilia soon diminished, the work she inspired is considered one of his most revealing and technically accomplished poems. Shelley's last work, *The Triumph of Life,* left unfinished at his death, describes the relentless march of life that has destroyed the aspirations of all but the sacred few who refused to compromise to worldly pressures. Despite its fragmentary state, many critics consider *The Triumph of Life* a potential masterpiece and evidence of a pessimistic shift in Shelley's thought.

Throughout his career Shelley wrote numerous short lyrics that have proved to be among his most popular works. Characterized by a simple, personal tone, his minor poems frequently touch on themes central to his more ambitious works: the "Hymn to Intellectual Beauty" and "Mont Blanc" focus on his belief in an animating spirit, while "Ode to the West Wind" examines opposing forces in nature. In other lyrics, including "Lines Written among the Euganean Hills," "Stanzas Written in Dejection, Near Naples," and "Lines Written in the Bay of Lerici," Shelley explores his own experiences and emotions. Political themes also inspired several of his most famous short poems, among them "Ode to Liberty," "Sonnet: England in 1819," and *The Masque of Anarchy.* Shelley's shorter lyrics, praised for their urbane wit and polished style, have established him as a preeminent poet of nature, ideal love, and beauty.

Mary Shelley took on the challenge of editing and annotating Shelley's unpublished manuscripts after his death. Her 1840 collection included Shelley's greatest prose work, *A Defence of Poetry.* Writing in response to *The Four Ages of Poetry,* an essay by his friend Peacock, Shelley detailed his belief in the moral importance of poetry, calling poets "the unacknowledged legislators of the world." In addition to several other philosophical essays and translations from the Greek, Shelley's posthumous works include the highly personal odes addressed to Edward Williams's wife, Jane. "To Jane: The Invitation," "To Jane: The Recollection," and "With a Guitar: To Jane" are considered some of his best love poems. At once a celebration of his friends' happy union and an intimate record of his own attraction to Jane, these lyrics are admired for their delicacy and refined style.

The history of Shelley's critical reputation has been characterized by radical shifts. During his lifetime he was generally regarded as a misguided or even depraved genius; critics frequently praised portions of his poetry in passing and deplored at length his atheism and unorthodox philosophy. Serious study of his works was hindered by widespread rumors about his personal life, particularly those concerning his desertion of Harriet and his supposed involvement in an incestuous love triangle with Mary and Claire. In addition, because of their limited publication and the scant critical attention given his works, he found only a small audience. Those few critics who voiced their admiration of his talents, particularly Hunt, who defended him vigorously in the *Examiner,* were ironically responsible for further inhibiting his success by causing him to be associated in the public mind with the despised "Cockney School" of poets belittled by John Gibson Lockhart and others in *Blackwood's Magazine.* Nevertheless, Shelley was known and admired by his great contemporaries: Byron, Keats, William Wordsworth, Samuel Taylor Coleridge, and Robert Southey regarded his works with varying degrees of sympathy and approval.

After his death, Shelley's reputation was greatly influenced by the efforts of his widow and friends to portray him as an angelic visionary. Biographies by Trelawny, Peacock, and Hogg, though frequently self-serving, inaccurate, and sensationalized, succeeded in directing interest toward Shelley's life and character and away from the controversial beliefs expressed in his works. Critics in the second half of the nineteenth century for the most part ignored Shelley's radical politics, celebrating instead the spiritual and aesthetic qualities of his poetry. In the Victorian age he was highly regarded as the poet of ideal love, and the Victorian notion of the poet as a sensitive, misunderstood genius was largely modeled after Shelley.

Shelley's works, however, fell into disfavor around the turn of the century. Many critics, influenced by Matthew Arnold's assessment of Shelley as an "ineffectual angel," objected to his seemingly vague imagery, nebulous philosophy, careless technique, and, most of all, his apparent intellectual and emotional immaturity. In the late 1930s Shelley's reputation began to revive: as scholars came to recognize the complexity of his philosophical idealism, serious study was devoted to the doctrines that informed his thought. Since that time, Shelley scholarship has covered a wide array of topics, including his style, philosophy, and major themes. In examining his style commentators have generally focused on his imagery, use of language, and technical achievements. The importance of neoplatonism, the occult, the Bible, the French Revolution, and Gothicism, as well as the works of individual philosophers—Wollstonecraft, Jean-Jacques Rousseau, and Godwin—to Shelley's thought and writings has been explored by other critics. Attention has also been devoted to recurring themes in Shelley's work. His doctrines of free love and sexual equality have particularly attracted commentary on the poet as an early proponent of feminism. Recent criticism of Shelley's works is generally marked by increasing respect for his abilities as a poet and his surprisingly modern philosophy. In addition, the details of his personal life continue to fascinate students of English literature, inspiring numerous biographies and peripheral studies about his life and friends.

Shelley remains a central figure in English Romanticism. His major works are respected as challenging credos of revolutionary philosophy, and his odes and shorter lyrics are widely known for their stylistic mastery. Furthermore, his *Defence of Poetry* stands as a powerful statement of the Romantic ideal of art and the artist. These accomplishments, combined with Shelley's remarkable life and friendships, assure his continuing prominence in English literary history.

PRINCIPAL WORKS

Original Poetry by Victor and Cazire [as Victor, with Elizabeth Shelley] (poetry) 1810
Posthumous Fragments of Margaret Nicholson [with Thomas Jefferson Hogg] (poetry) 1810
Zastrozzi (novel) 1810
The Necessity of Atheism (essay) 1811
St. Irvyne; or, The Rosicrucian (novel) 1811
An Address to the Irish People (essay) 1812
A Declaration of Rights (essay) 1812
Queen Mab (poetry) 1813
A Refutation of Deism (dialogue) 1814
Alastor; or, The Spirit of Solitude, and Other Poems (poetry) 1816
An Address to the People on the Death of Princess Charlotte [as The Hermit of Marlow] (essay) 1817

"Hymn to Intellectual Beauty" (poetry) 1817; published in periodical *The Examiner*
A Proposal for Putting Reform to the Vote [as The Hermit of Marlow] (essay) 1817
Laon and Cythna; or, The Revolution of the Golden City: A Vision of the Nineteenth Century (poetry) 1818; also published in revised form as *The Revolt of Islam*, 1818
The Cenci [first publication] (verse drama) 1819
Rosalind and Helen: A Modern Eclogue, with Other Poems (poetry) 1819
Prometheus Unbound, with Other Poems (verse drama and poetry) 1820
Adonais: An Elegy on the Death of John Keats (poetry) 1821
Epipsychidion (poetry) 1821
Hellas [first publication] (verse drama) 1822
"Julian and Maddalo" (poetry) 1824; published in *Posthumous Poems of Percy Bysshe Shelley*
Posthumous Poems of Percy Bysshe Shelley (poetry and verse drama) 1824
The Triumph of Life (unfinished poetry) 1824; published in *Posthumous Poems of Percy Bysshe Shelley*
"The Witch of Atlas" (poetry) 1824; published in *Posthumous Poems of Percy Bysshe Shelley*
*The Masque of Anarchy (poetry) 1832
**A Defence of Poetry (essay) 1840; published in *Essays, Letters from Abroad, Translations, and Fragments by Percy Bysshe Shelley*
Essays, Letters from Abroad, Translations, and Fragments by Percy Bysshe Shelley. 2 vols. (essays, letters, translations, and prose) 1840
The Works of Percy Bysshe Shelley (poetry, verse dramas, and essays) 1847
The Complete Works of Percy Bysshe Shelley. 10 vols. (poetry, verse dramas, essays, and translations) 1924-30
The Letters. 2 vols. (letters) 1964
The Complete Poetical Works of Percy Bysshe Shelley. 2 vols. to date. (poetry) 1972-

*This work was written in 1819.

**This work was written in 1821.

THE CRITICAL REVIEW AND ANNALS OF LITERATURE (essay date 1810)

[*In this excerpt from an 1810 review of* Zastrozzi *published in the* Critical Review and Annals of Literature, *the critic condemns the novel on moral grounds.*]

Zastrozzi is one of the most savage and improbable demons that ever issued from a diseased brain. (p. 33)

The story [of *Zastrozzi*] itself, and the style in which it is told, are so truly contemptible, that we should have passed it unnoticed, had not our indignation been excited by the open and barefaced immorality and grossness displayed throughout. Mathilda's character is that of a lascivious fiend, who dignifies vicious, unrestrained passion by the appellation of love.

Does the author, whoever he may be, think his gross and wanton pages fit to meet the eye of a modest young woman? Is this the instruction to be instilled under the title of a romance?

Such trash, indeed, as this work contains, is fit only for the inmates of a brothel. It is by such means of corruption as this that the tastes of our youth of both sexes become vitiated, their imaginations heated, and a foundation laid for their future misery and dishonour. When a taste for this kind of writing is imbibed, we may bid farewell to innocence, farewell to purity of thought, and all that makes youth and virtue lovely.

We know not when we have felt so much indignation as in the perusal of this execrable production. The author of it cannot be too severely reprobated. Not all his "scintillated eyes," his "battling emotions," his "frigorific torpidity of despair," nor his "Lethean torpor," with the rest of his nonsensical and stupid jargon, ought to save him from infamy, and his volume from the flames. (pp. 34-5)

> *"The Juvenile Period: The 'Critical Review' Exposes Corruption," in* The Unextinguished Hearth: Shelley and His Contemporary Critics, *edited by Newman Ivey White, 1938. Reprint by Octagon Books, 1966, pp. 33-5.*

THE BRITISH CRITIC   (essay date 1811)

[*This anonymous critic dismisses* Original Poetry by Victor and Cazire *as a work of little merit, citing its absurdities and stylistic faults.*]

When we ventured to say that poetical taste and genius abound in the present day, we by no means intended to assert, that we always meet with either the one or the other. Miserable, indeed, are the attempts which we are often doomed to encounter; so miserable sometimes, that it seems quite wonderful how any individuals, fancying themselves able to write, should be so far behind their contemporaries. One of the unknown authors of [*Original Poetry by Victor and Cazire*] begins by complaining, most sincerely, we are convinced, of the difficulty of writing grammatically; but there is another difficulty, which seems never to have entered the lady's head, (if a lady!)—that is, the difficulty of writing *metrically*. In this she is still less successful than in the other; and does not seem at all to suspect it. The verse intended to be used, is that of the Bath Guide: and so it is, *sometimes*: but sometimes also not. For example:

> This they friendly will tell, and ne'er make you blush,
> With a jeering look, taunt, or an O fie! tush!
> Then straight all your thoughts in black and white put,
> Not minding the *if's*, the *be's*, and the but.

Again,

> My excuse shall be humble, and faithful, and true,
> *Such as I fear can be made but by few.*

This *humble* and *faithful* lady lays claim *only* to "sense, wit, and grammar!"—Yet she tells her friend;

> Be not a coward, *shrink* not a tense,
> But read it all over, and *make it out sense.*
> *What a tiresome girl!*—pray soon make an end.

The last line, if not measure, contains at least truth in the first part, and a very reasonable wish in the second.

Two epistles, in this exquisite style, begin this volume, which is filled up by songs of sentimental nonsense, and very absurd tales of horror. It is perfectly clear, therefore, that whatever we may say in favour of the poetry of this time, such volumes as this have no share in the commendation. (pp. 408-09)

> *A review of "Original Poetry; by Victor and Cazire," in* The British Critic, *Vol. XXXVII, April, 1811, pp. 408-10.*

THE ANTIJACOBIN REVIEW   (essay date 1812)

[*Reviewing* St. Irvyne, *this anonymous critic deplores its Gothic excesses and deviations from moral and religious standards.*]

Had not the title-page informed us that this curious "Romance" [*St. Irvyne; or, The Rosicrucian*] was the production of "a gentleman," a *freshman* of course, we should certainly have ascribed it to some "Miss" in her teens; who, having read the beautiful and truly poetical descriptions, in the unrivalled romances of Mrs. Radcliffe, imagined that to admire the writings of that lady, and to imitate her style, were one and the same thing. Here we have *description run mad;* every uncouth epithet, every wild expression, which either the lexicographer could supply, or the disordered imagination of the romance writer suggest, has been pressed into the service of "the Rosicrucian." Woe and terror are heightened by the expressions used to describe them. Heroes and heroines are not merely distressed and terrified, they are "*enanguish'd*" and "*enhorrored.*"

Nor are the ordinary sensations of *joy,* or even *delight,* sufficient to gratify such exalted beings. No, when the hero was pleased, not only did he experience "a transport of delight;—*burning ecstacy revelled through his veins; pleasurable coruscations were emitted from his eyes.* Even hideous sights acquire additional deformity under the magic influence of this "gentleman's" pen. We read, of "a form more hideous than the imagination of man is capable of pourtraying, whose proportions, gigantic and deformed, were seemingly blackened by the *inerasible traces of the thunderbolts of God.*"

From one who, disdaining the common forms and modes of language, aims at sublimity both of thought and expression, a slavish subjection to the vulgar restrictions of grammar, a tame submission to the *Jus et Norma loquendi,* cannot reasonably be extracted. Exalted genius ever spurns restraint; and the mind, accustomed to indulge in "*a train of labyrinthic meditations,*" cannot very well bear with the trammels of common sense.

Were he, however, only enthusiastical and nonsensical, we should dismiss his book with contempt. Unfortunately he has subjected himself to censure of a severer cast. In the fervor of his illustrations he is, not unfrequently, impious and blasphemous. And his notions of *innocence* and *virtue* are such as, were they to pass current in the world, would very soon leave society without one innocent or virtuous being. His two heroines are represented as women of rank, family, and education; yet one of them, Megaline, is made to fall in love, at first-sight, with a member of a company of banditti, residing in a cavern in the Alps, who had just robbed and murdered her father. And to this man, who is the hero of the piece, she surrenders herself, without a struggle, and becomes his mistress. The other heroine, Eloise, who has had a religious education, and who has just buried her mother, also falls in love at first sight with a man wholly unknown to her, and whom she had seen under very suspicious circumstances. To him she, also, surrenders her virgin charms; lives with him, as his mistress, becomes pregnant by him; then leaves, and becomes the mistress of another stranger.

Yet, under these circumstances, the reader is insulted with the assertion that "her soul was susceptible of *the most exalted virtue* and expansion.'' Fitzeustace, the man with whom she lives, at length proposes to take her with him to England, when the following dialogue ensues between them.

> ''But before we go to England, before my father will see us, it is necessary that we should be married—nay, do not start, Eloise; I view it in the light that you do; I consider it an human institution, and incapable of furnishing that bond of union by which, alone can intellect be conjoined; I regard it as but a chain, which, although it keeps the body bound, still leaves the soul unfettered: it is not so with love. But still, Eloise, to those who think like us, it is at all events harmless; 'tis but yielding to the prejudices of the world wherein we live, and procuring moral expediency, at a slight sacrifice of what we conceive to be right.''
>
> ''Well, well, it shall be done, Fitzeustace,'' resumed Eloise; ''but take the assurance of *my* promise, that I cannot love you more.''
>
> They soon agreed on a point of, in their eyes, so trifling importance, and arriving in England, tasted that happiness which love and *innocence* alone can give. Prejudice may triumph for a while, but *virtue* will be eventually the conqueror.

His penetration must be much deeper than any to which we can form pretensions, who can discover, in this denouement, any thing bearing the most distant resemblance to the triumph of virtue. It exhibits, however, a tolerable fair criterion by which the standard of the writer's intellectual powers, and his peculiar system of ethics, may be estimated.

A third female character, Olympia, a young lady of the first rank in Genoa, is introduced, for no other imaginable purpose, than to increase the reader's contempt and abhorrence of the sex. She, setting aside all dignity and decorum, as well as every feature of virtue, seeks, at night, the residence of a man, whom she believes to be married, and courts prostitution. He, however, who has never restrained his passions in any one instance, during his whole life, and who, for their gratification, has committed the most enormous crimes, suddenly displays a virtue, wholly foreign from his disposition and character, and resolutely resists the most powerful temptation, presenting itself under the most alluring form. Olympia, thus unable to become a prostitute, commits suicide.

But 'tis not surprising, that the writer who can outrage nature and common sense, in almost every page of his book, should libel a sex, of whom, we should suppose, he has no knowledge, but such as may be collected in the streets, or in a brothel.

Of his hero Wolfstein, and *his* mistress, Megalina, he disposes in a very summary way. The latter is found dead in the vaults of the Castle of St. Irvyne; though how she came there, we are not informed. To these vaults Wolfstein repairs, for the purpose of being taught the secret of obtaining eternal life. Here the Devil himself, ''borne on the pinions of hell's sulphurous whirlwind,'' appears to him and calls on him to deny his Creator. This Wolfstein refuses; then, ''blackened in terrible convulsions, Wolfstein expired; over him, had the power of hell no influence.''—*Why* he was made to expire, and *why* hell had no power over him, we are left to conjecture. Wolf-

stein, be it observed, had lived in the habitual commission of atrocious crimes, and died an impenitent sinner.

Of such a rhapsody we have, perhaps, said too much. But it is a duty due from critics to the public to mark every deviation from religious and moral principle, with strong reprobation; as well to deter readers from wasting their time in the perusal of unprofitable and vicious productions, as to check silly and licentious writers, at an early period of their literary career. If this duty were performed with greater punctuality, the press would be more purified than it is.—As to this Oxford gentleman, we recommend him to the care of his tutor, who, after a proper *jobution* for past folly, would do well, by *imposition,* to forbid him the use of the pen, until he shall have taken his *bachelor's degree.* (pp. 69-71)

> *''Romance,'' in* The Antijacobin Review, *Vol. XLI, January, 1812, pp. 69-71.*

PERCY BYSSHE SHELLEY (essay date 1818)

[*In the following excerpt from his preface to* The Revolt of Islam, *published in 1818, Shelley outlines his intentions in writing the poem and discusses his conception of his role as poet. For additional commentary by Shelley, see excerpts dated 1819, 1820, and 1821.*]

The Poem which I now present to the world [**The Revolt of Islam**], is an attempt from which I scarcely dare to expect success, and in which a writer of established fame might fail without disgrace. It is an experiment on the temper of the public mind, as to how far a thirst for a happier condition of moral and political society survives, among the enlightened and refined, the tempests which have shaken the age in which we live. I have sought to enlist the harmony of metrical language, the etherial combinations of the fancy, the rapid and subtle transitions of human passion, all those elements which essentially compose a Poem, in the cause of a liberal and comprehensive morality: and in the view of kindling within the bosoms of my readers, a virtuous enthusiasm for those doctrines of liberty and justice, that faith and hope in something good, which neither violence, nor misrepresentation, nor prejudice, can ever totally extinguish among mankind.

For this purpose I have chosen a story of human passion in its most universal character, diversified with moving and romantic adventures, and appealing, in contempt of all artificial opinions or institutions, to the common sympathies of every human breast. I have made no attempt to recommend the motives which I would substitute for those at present governing mankind by methodical and systematic argument. I would only awaken the feelings, so that the reader should see the beauty of true virtue, and be incited to those inquiries which have led to my moral and political creed, and that of some of the sublimest intellects in the world. The Poem, therefore (with the exception of the first Canto, which is purely introductory), is narrative, not didactic. It is a succession of pictures illustrating the growth and progress of individual mind aspiring after excellence, and devoted to the love of mankind; its influence in refining and making pure the most daring and uncommon impulses of the imagination, the understanding, and the senses; its impatience at ''all the oppressions which are done under the sun;'' its tendency to awaken public hope and to enlighten and improve mankind; the rapid effects of the application of that tendency; the awakening of an immense nation from their slavery and degradation to a true sense of moral dignity and freedom; the bloodless dethronement of their oppressors, and the unveiling of the religious frauds by which they had been deluded into submission; the tranquility of successful patriotism, and the universal toleration and benevolence of true philanthropy; the treachery and barbarity of hired soldiers; vice not the object of punishment and hatred, but kindness and pity; the faithlessness of tyrants; the confederacy of the Rulers of the World, and the restoration of the expelled Dynasty by foreign arms; the massacre and extermination of the Patriots, and the victory of established power; the consequences of legitimate despotism, civil war, famine, plague, superstition, and an utter extinction of the domestic affections; the judicial murder of the advocates of Liberty; the temporary triumph of oppression, that secure earnest of its final and inevitable fall; the transient nature of ignorance and error, and the eternity of genius and virtue. Such is the series of delineations of which the Poem consists. And if the lofty passions with which it has been my scope to distinguish this story, shall not excite in the reader a generous impulse, an ardent thirst for excellence, an interest profound and strong, such as belongs to no meaner desires—let not the failure be imputed to a natural unfitness for human sympathy in these sublime and animating themes. It is the business of the Poet to communicate to others the pleasure and the enthusiasm arising out of those images and feelings, in the vivid presence of which within his own mind, consists at once his inspiration and his reward.

The panic which, like an epidemic transport, seized upon all classes of men during the excesses consequent upon the French Revolution, is gradually giving place to sanity. It has ceased to be believed, that whole generations of mankind ought to consign themselves to a hopeless inheritance of ignorance and misery, because a nation of men who had been dupes and slaves for centuries, were incapable of conducting themselves with the wisdom and tranquillity of freemen so soon as some of their fetters were partially loosened. That their conduct could not have been marked by any other characters than ferocity and thoughtlessness, is the historical fact from which liberty derives all its recommendations, and falsehood the worst features of its deformity. There is a reflux in the tide of human things which bears the shipwrecked hopes of men into a secure haven, after the storms are past. Methinks, those who now live have survived an age of despair.

The French Revolution may be considered as one of those manifestations of a general state of feeling among civilized mankind, produced by a defect of correspondence between the knowledge existing in society and the improvement or gradual abolition of political institutions. The year 1788 may be assumed as the epoch of one of the most important crises produced by this feeling. The sympathies connected with that event extended to every bosom. The most generous and amiable natures were those which participated the most extensively in these sympathies. But such a degree of unmingled good was expected, as it was impossible to realize. If the Revolution had been in every respect prosperous, then misrule and superstition would lose half their claims to our abhorrence, as fetters which the captive can unlock with the slightest motion of his fingers, and which do not eat with poisonous rust into the soul. The revulsion occasioned by the atrocities of the demagogues and the re-establishment of successive tyrannies in France was terrible, and felt in the remotest corner of the civilized world. Could they listen to the plea of reason who had groaned under the calamities of a social state, according to the provisions of which, one man riots in luxury whilst another famishes for want of bread. Can he who the day before was a trampled slave, suddenly become liberal-minded, forbearing, and in-

dependent? This is the consequence of the habits of a state of society to be produced by resolute perseverance and indefatigable hope, and long-suffering and long believing courage, and the systematic efforts of generations of men of intellect and virtue. Such is the lesson which experience teaches now. But on the first reverses of hope in the progress of French liberty, the sanguine eagerness for good overleapt the solution of these questions, and for a time extinguished itself in the unexpectedness of their result. Thus many of the most ardent and tender-hearted of the worshippers of public good have been morally ruined by what a partial glimpse of the events they deplored, appeared to shew as the melancholy desolation of all their cherished hopes. Hence gloom and misanthropy have become the characteristics of the age in which we live, the solace of a disappointment that unconsciously finds relief only in the wilful exaggeration of its own despair. This influence has tainted the literature of the age with the hopelessness of the minds from which it flows. Metaphysics, and enquiries into moral and political science, have become little else than vain attempts to revive exploded superstitions, or sophisms like those of Mr. Malthus, calculated to lull the oppressors of mankind into a security of everlasting triumph. Our works of fiction and poetry have been overshadowed by the same infectious gloom. But mankind appear to me to be emerging from their trance. I am aware, methinks, of a slow, gradual, silent change. In that belief I have composed the following Poem.

I do not presume to enter into competition with our greatest contemporary Poets. Yet I am unwilling to tread in the footsteps of any who have preceded me. I have sought to avoid the imitation of any style of language or versification peculiar to the original minds of which it is the character, designing that even if what I have produced be worthless, it should still be properly my own. Nor have I permitted any system relating to mere words, to divert the attention of the reader from whatever interest I may have succeeded in creating, to my own ingenuity in contriving to disgust them according to the rules of criticism. I have simply clothed my thoughts in what appeared to me the most obvious and appropriate language. A person familiar with nature, and with the most celebrated productions of the human mind, can scarcely err in following the instinct, with respect to selection of language, produced by that familiarity.

There is an education peculiarly fitted for a Poet, without which, genius and sensibility can hardly fill the circle of their capacities. No education indeed can entitle to this appellation a dull and unobservant mind, or one, though neither dull nor unobservant, in which the channels of communication between thought and expression have been obstructed or closed. How far it is my fortune to belong to either of the latter classes, I cannot know. I aspire to be something better. The circumstances of my accidental education have been favourable to this ambition. I have been familiar from boyhood with mountains and lakes, and the sea, and the solitude of forests: Danger, which sports upon the brink of precipices, has been my playmate. I have trodden the glaciers of the Alps, and lived under the eye of Mont Blanc. I have been a wanderer among distant fields. I have sailed down mighty rivers, and seen the sun rise and set, and the stars come forth, whilst I have sailed night and day down a rapid stream among mountains. I have seen populous cities, and have watched the passions which rise and spread, and sink and change, amongst assembled multitudes of men. I have seen the theatre of the more visible ravages of tyranny and war, cities and villages reduced to scattered groups of black and roofless houses, and the naked inhabitants sitting famished upon their desolated thresholds. I have conversed with living men of genius. The poetry of antient Greece and Rome, and modern Italy, and our own country, has been to me like external nature, a passion and an enjoyment. Such are the sources from which the materials for the imagery of my Poem have been drawn. I have considered Poetry in its most comprehensive sense, and have read the Poets and the Historians, and the Metaphysicians whose writings have been accessible to me, and have looked upon the beautiful and majestic scenery of the earth as common sources of those elements which it is the province of the Poet to embody and combine. Yet the experience and the feelings to which I refer, do not in themselves constitute men Poets, but only prepare them to be the auditors of those who are. How far I shall be found to possess that more essential attribute of Poetry, the power of awakening in others sensations like those which animate my own bosom, is that which, to speak sincerely, I know not; and which with an acquiescent and contented spirit, I expect to be taught by the effect which I shall produce upon those whom I now address.

I have avoided, as I have said before, the imitation of any contemporary style. But there must be a resemblance which does not depend upon their own will, between all the writers of any particular age. They cannot escape from subjection to a common influence which arises out of an infinite combination of circumstances belonging to the times in which they live, though each is in a degree the author of the very influence by which his being is thus pervaded. Thus, the tragic Poets of the age of Pericles; the Italian revivers of ancient learning; those mighty intellects of our own country that succeeded the Reformation, the translators of the Bible, Shakspeare, Spenser, the Dramatists of the reign of Elizabeth, and Lord Bacon; the colder spirits of the interval that succeeded;—all resemble each other, and differ from every other in their several classes. In this view of things, Ford can no more be called the imitator of Shakspeare, than Shakspeare the imitator of Ford. There were perhaps few other points of resemblance between these two men, than that which the universal and inevitable influence of their age produced. And this is an influence which neither the meanest scribbler, nor the sublimest genius of any æra, can escape; and which I have not attempted to escape.

I have adopted the stanza of Spenser (a measure inexpressibly beautiful) not because I consider it a finer model of poetical harmony than the blank verse of Shakspeare and Milton, but because in the latter there is no shelter for mediocrity; you must either succeed or fail. This perhaps an aspiring spirit should desire. But I was enticed also, by the brilliancy and magnificence of sound which a mind that has been nourished upon musical thoughts, can produce by a just and harmonious arrangement of the pauses of this measure. Yet there will be found some instances where I have completely failed in this attempt, and one, which I here request the reader to consider as an erratum, where there is left most inadvertently an alexandrine in the middle of a stanza.

But in this, as in every other respect, I have written fearlessly. It is the misfortune of this age, that its Writers, too thoughtless of immortality, are exquisitely sensible to temporary praise or blame. They write with the fear of Reviews before their eyes. This system of criticism sprang up in that torpid interval when Poetry was not. Poetry, and the art which professes to regulate and limit its powers, cannot subsist together. Longinus could not have been the contemporary of Homer, nor Boileau of Horace. Yet this species of criticism never presumed to assert an understanding of its own: it has always, unlike true science, followed, not preceded the opinion of mankind, and would

even now bribe with worthless adulation some of our greatest Poets to impose gratuitous fetters on their own imaginations, and become unconscious accomplices in the daily murder of all genius either not so aspiring or not so fortunate as their own. I have sought therefore to write, as I believe that Homer, Shakspeare, and Milton wrote, with an utter disregard of anonymous censure. I am certain that calumny and misrepresentation, though it may move me to compassion, cannot disturb my peace. I shall understand the expressive silence of those sagacious enemies who dare not trust themselves to speak. I shall endeavour to extract from the midst of insult, and contempt, and maledictions, those admonitions which may tend to correct whatever imperfections such censurers may discover in this my first serious appeal to the Public. If certain Critics were as clear-sighted as they are malignant, how great would be the benefit to be derived from their virulent writings! As it is, I fear I shall be malicious enough to be amused with their paltry tricks and lame invectives. Should the Public judge that my composition is worthless, I shall indeed bow before the tribunal from which Milton received his crown of immortality, and shall seek to gather, if I live, strength from that defeat, which may nerve me to some new enterprise of thought which may *not* be worthless. I cannot conceive that Lucretius, when he meditated that poem whose doctrines are yet the basis of our metaphysical knowledge, and whose eloquence has been the wonder of mankind, wrote in awe of such censure as the hired sophists of the impure and superstitious noblemen of Rome might affix to what he should produce. It was at the period when Greece was led captive, and Asia made tributary to the Republic, fast verging itself to slavery and ruin, that a multitude of Syrian captives, bigotted to the worship of their obscene Ashtaroth, and the unworthy successors of Socrates and Zeno, found there a precarious subsistence by administering, under the name of freedmen, to the vices and vanities of the great. These wretched men were skilled to plead, with a superficial but plausible set of sophisms, in favour of that contempt for virtue which is the portion of slaves, and that faith in portents, the most fatal substitute for benevolence in the imaginations of men, which, arising from the enslaved communities of the East, then first began to overwhelm the western nations in its stream. Were these the kind of men whose disapprobation the wise and lofty-minded Lucretius should have regarded with a salutary awe? The latest and perhaps the meanest of those who follow in his footsteps, would disdain to hold life on such conditions.

The Poem now presented to the Public occupied little more than six months in the composition. That period has been devoted to the task with unremitting ardour and enthusiasm. I have exercised a watchful and earnest criticism on my work as it grew under my hands. I would willingly have sent it forth to the world with that perfection which long labour and revision is said to bestow. But I found that if I should gain something in exactness by this method, I might lose much of the newness and energy of imagery and language as it flowed afresh from my mind. And although the mere composition occupied no more than six months, the thoughts thus arranged were slowly gathered in as many years.

I trust that the reader will carefully distinguish between those opinions which have a dramatic propriety in reference to the characters which they are designed to elucidate and such as are properly my own. The erroneous and degrading idea which men have conceived of a Supreme Being, for instance, is spoken against, but not the Supreme Being itself. The belief which some superstitious persons whom I have brought upon the stage entertain of the Deity, as injurious to the character of his benevolence, is widely different from my own. In recommending also a great and important change in the spirit which animates the social institutions of mankind, I have avoided all flattery to those violent and malignant passions of our nature, which are ever on the watch to mingle with and to alloy the most beneficial innovations. There is no quarter given to Revenge, or Envy, or Prejudice. Love is celebrated every where as the sole law which should govern the moral world.

In the personal conduct of my Hero and Heroine, there is one circumstance which was intended to startle the reader from the trance of ordinary life. It was my object to break through the crust of those outworn opinions on which established institutions depend. I have appealed therefore to the most universal of all feelings, and have endeavoured to strengthen the moral sense, by forbidding it to waste its energies in seeking to avoid actions which are only crimes of convention. It is because there is so great a multitude of artificial vices, that there are so few real virtues. Those feelings alone which are benevolent or malevolent, are essentially good or bad. The circumstance of which I speak, was introduced, however, merely to accustom men to that charity and toleration which the exhibition of a practice widely differing from their own, has a tendency to promote. Nothing indeed can be more mischievous, than many actions innocent in themselves, which might bring down upon individuals the bigotted contempt and rage of the multitude. (pp. 239-47)

> *Percy Bysshe Shelley, in a preface to "Laon and Cythna (The Revolt of Islam)" in his* The Complete Works of Percy Bysshe Shelley: Poems, Vol. I, *edited by Roger Ingpen and Walter E. Peck, 1926. Reprint by Gordian Press, 1965, pp. 239-47.*

J. T. COLERIDGE (essay date 1819)

[*In this excerpt from a review of* The Revolt of Islam, *Coleridge—nephew of the poet Samuel Taylor Coleridge—censures Shelley's philosophy of religious and social reform. The critic's remarks are challenged by Lockhart (see excerpt dated 1819).*]

Of all his brethren Mr. Shelley carries to the greatest length the doctrines of the sect. He is, for this and other reasons, by far the least pernicious of them; indeed there is a naiveté and openness in his manner of laying down the most extravagant positions, which in some measure deprives them of their venom; and when he enlarges on what certainly are but necessary results of opinions more guardedly delivered by others, he might almost be mistaken for some artful advocate of civil order and religious institutions. This benefit indeed may be drawn from his book [*Laon and Cythna; or, The Revolution of the Golden City*], for there is scarcely any more persuasive argument for truth than to carry out to all their legitimate consequences the doctrines of error. But this is not Mr. Shelley's intention; he is, we are sorry to say, in sober earnest:—with perfect deliberation, and the steadiest perseverance he perverts all the gifts of his nature, and does all the injury, both public and private, which his faculties enable him to perpetrate.

Laon and Cythna is the same poem with the *Revolt of Islam*—under the first name it exhibited some features which made 'the experiment on the temper of the public mind,' as the author calls it, somewhat too bold and hazardous. This knight-errant in the cause of 'a liberal and comprehensive morality' had already sustained some 'perilous handling' in his encounters with Prejudice and Error, and acquired in consequence of it a

small portion of *the better part of valour*. Accordingly *Laon and Cythna* withdrew from circulation; and happy had it been for Mr. Shelley if he had been contented with his failure, and closed his experiments. But with minds of a certain class, notoriety, infamy, any thing is better than obscurity; baffled in a thousand attempts after fame, they will still make one more at whatever risk,—and they end commonly like an awkward chemist who perseveres in tampering with his ingredients, till, in an unlucky moment, they take fire, and he is blown up by the explosion.

Laon and Cythna has accordingly re-appeared with a new name, and a few slight alterations. If we could trace in these any signs of an altered spirit, we should have hailed with the sincerest pleasure the return of one whom nature intended for better things, to the ranks of virtue and religion. But Mr. Shelley is no penitent; he has reproduced the same poison, a little, and but a little, more cautiously disguised, and as it is thus intended only to do the more mischief at less personal risk to the author, our duty requires us to use his own evidence against himself, to interpret him where he is obscure now, by himself where he was plain before, and to exhibit the 'fearful consequences' to which he would bring us, as he drew them in the boldness of his first conception.

Before, however, we do this, we will discharge our duty to Mr. Shelley as poetical critics—in a case like the present, indeed, where the freight is so pernicious, it is but a secondary duty to consider the 'build' of the vessel which bears it; but it is a duty too peculiarly our own to be wholly neglected. Though we should be sorry to see the *Revolt of Islam* in our readers' hands, we are bound to say that it is not without beautiful passages, that the language is in general free from errors of taste, and the versification smooth and harmonious. In these respects it resembles the latter productions of Mr. Southey, though the tone is less subdued, and the copy altogether more luxuriant and ornate than the original. Mr. Shelley indeed is an unsparing imitator; and he draws largely on the rich stores of another mountain poet, to whose religious mind it must be matter, we think, of perpetual sorrow to see the philosophy which comes pure and holy from his pen, degraded and perverted, as it continually is, by this miserable crew of atheists or pantheists, who have just sense enough to abuse its terms, but neither heart nor principle to comprehend its import, or follow its application. We shall cite one of the passages to which we alluded above, in support of our opinion: perhaps it is that which has pleased us more than any other in the whole poem.

> An orphan with my parents lived, whose eyes
> Were loadstars of delight, which drew me home
> When I might wander forth, nor did I prize
> *Aught* (any) human thing beneath Heaven's mighty
>   dome
> Beyond this child; so when sad hours were come,
> And baffled hope like ice still clung to me;
> Since kin were cold, and friends had now become
> Heartless and false, I turned from all, to be,
> Cythna, the only source of tears and smiles to thee.
>
> What wert thou then? a child most infantine,
> Yet wandering far beyond that innocent age
> In all but its sweet looks, and mien divine;
> Even then, methought, with the world's tyrant rage
> A patient warfare thy young heart did wage,
> When those soft eyes of scarcely conscious thought

Some tale or thine own fancies would engage
To overflow with tears, or converse fraught
With passion o'er their depths its fleeting light had
    wrought.

She moved upon this earth, a shape of brightness,
A power, that from its object scarcely drew
One impulse of her being—in her lightness
Most like some radiant cloud of morning dew
Which wanders through the waste air's pathless blue
To nourish some far desert; she did seem
Beside me, gathering beauty as she grew
Like the bright shade of some immortal dream
Which walks, when tempest sleeps, the waves of life's
    dark stream.

As mine own shadow was this child to me,
A second self—far dearer and more fair,
Which clothed in undissolving radiancy
All those steep paths, which languor and despair
Of human things had made so dark and bare,
But which I trod alone—nor, till bereft
Of friends and overcome by lonely care,
Knew I what solace for what loss was left,
Though by a bitter wound my trusting heart was cleft.

These, with all their imperfections, are beautiful stanzas; they are, however, of rare occurrence:—had the poem many more such, it could never, we are persuaded, become popular. Its merits and its faults equally conspire against it; it has not much ribaldry or voluptuousness for prurient imaginations, and no personal scandal for the malicious; and even those on whom it might be expected to act most dangerously by its semblance of enthusiasm, will have stout hearts to proceed beyond the first canto. As a whole, it is insupportably dull, and laboriously obscure; its absurdities are not of the kind which provoke laughter, the story is almost wholly devoid of interest, and very meagre; nor can we admire Mr. Shelley's mode of making up for this defect—as he has but one incident where he should have ten, he tells that one so intricately, that it takes the time of ten to comprehend it.

Mr. Shelley is a philosopher by the courtesy of the age, and has a theory of course respecting the government of the world; we will state in as few words as we can the general outlines of that theory, the manner in which he demonstrates it, and the practical consequences, which he proposes to deduce from it. It is to the second of these divisions that we would beg his attention; we despair of convincing him directly that he has taken up false and pernicious notions; but if he pays any deference to the common laws of reasoning, we hope to shew him that, let the goodness of his cause be what it may, his manner of advocating it is false and unsound. This may be mortifying to a teacher of mankind; but a philosopher seeks the truth, and has no vanity to be mortified.

The existence of evil, physical and moral, is the grand problem of all philosophy; the humble find it a trial, the proud make it a stumbling-block; Mr. Shelley refers it to the faults of those civil institutions and religious creeds which are designed to regulate the conduct of man here, and his hopes in a hereafter. In these he seems to make no distinction, but considers them all as bottomed upon principles pernicious to man and unworthy of God, carried into details the most cruel, and upheld only by the stupidity of the many on the one hand, and the selfish conspiracy of the few on the other. According to him the earth is a boon garden needing little care or cultivation, but pouring forth spontaneously and inexhaustibly all innocent delights and luxuries to her innumerable children; the seasons have no inclemencies, the air no pestilences for man in his proper state of wisdom and liberty; his business here is to enjoy himself, to abstain from no gratification, to repent of no sin, hate no crime, but be wise, happy and free, with plenty of 'lawless love.' This is man's natural state, the state to which Mr. Shelley will bring us, if we will but break up the 'crust of our outworn opinions,' as he calls them, and put them into his magic cauldron. But kings have introduced war, legislators crime, priests sin; the dreadful consequences have been that the earth has lost her fertility, the seasons their mildness, the air its salubrity, man his freedom and happiness. We have become a foul-feeding carnivorous race, are foolish enough to feel uncomfortable after the commission of sin; some of us even go so far as to consider vice odious; and we all groan under a multiplied burthen of crimes *merely conventional;* among which Mr. Shelley specifies with great *sang froid* the commission of *incest!*

We said that our philosopher makes no distinction in his condemnation of creeds; we should rather have said, that he makes no exception; distinction he does make, and it is to the prejudice of that which we hold. In one place indeed he assembles a number of names of the founders of religions, to treat them all with equal disrespect.

And through the host contention wild befell,
As each of his own God the wondrous works did tell;
And Oromaze and Christ and Mahomet,
Moses and Buddh, Zerdusht, and Brahm and Foh,
A tumult of strange names.

But in many other places he manifests a dislike to Christianity which is frantic, and would be, if in such a case any thing could be, ridiculous. When the votaries of all religions are assembled with one accord (this unanimity by the bye is in a vision of the *nineteenth* century) to stifle the first breathings of liberty, and execute the revenge of a ruthless tyrant, he selects a Christian priest to be the organ of sentiments outrageously and pre-eminently cruel. The two characteristic principles upon which Christianity may be said to be built are repentance and faith. Of repentance he speaks thus:—

Reproach not thine own soul, but know thyself;
Nor hate another's crime, nor loathe thine own.
It is the dark idolatry of self
Which, when our thoughts and actions once are gone,
Demands that we should weep and bleed and groan;
O vacant expiation! be at rest—
The past is death's—the future is thine own;
And love and joy can make the *foulest* breast
A paradise of flowers where peace might build her nest.

Repentance then is selfishness in an extreme which amounts to idolatry! but what is Faith? our readers can hardly be prepared for the odious accumulation of sin and sorrow which Mr. Shelley conceives under this word. 'Faith is the Python, the Ogress, the Evil Genius, the Wicked Fairy, the Giantess of our children's tales;' whenever any thing bad is to be accounted for, any hard name to be used, this convenient monosyllable fills up the blank. (pp. 460-64)

Mr. Shelley is neither a dull, nor, considering all his disadvantages, a very ignorant man; we will frankly confess, that with every disposition to judge him charitably, we find it hard to convince ourselves of his belief in his own conclusions. . . .

Mr. Shelley argues for the necessity of a change; we must bestow a word or two upon the manner in which he brings that change about, before we come to the consequences which he derives from it. Laon and Cythna, his hero and heroine, are the principal, indeed, almost the sole agents. The latter by her eloquence rouses all of her own sex to assert their liberty and independence; this perhaps was no difficult task; a female tongue in such a cause may be supposed to have spoken fluently at least, and to have found a willing audience; by the same instrument, however, she disarms the soldiers who are sent to seize and destroy her,—

> even the torturer who had bound
> Her meek calm frame, ere yet it was impaled
> Loosened her weeping then, nor could be found
> One human hand to harm her.
>
> (p. 466)

These peaceable and tender advocates for 'Universal Suffrage and *no* representation' assemble in battle-array under the walls of the Golden City, keeping night and day strict blockade (which Mr. Shelley calls 'a watch of love,') around the desperate bands who still adhere to the maintenance of the iron-hearted monarch on the throne. Why the eloquence of Cythna had no power over *them*, or how the monarch himself, who had been a slave to her beauty, and to whom this model of purity and virtue *had borne a child*, was able to resist the spell of her voice, Mr. Shelley leaves his readers to find out for themselves. In this pause of affairs Laon makes his appearance to complete the revolution. . . . A good deal of mummery follows, of national fetes, reasonable rites, altars of federation, &c. borrowed from that store-house of cast-off mummeries and abominations, the French revolution. In the mean time all the kings of the earth, pagan and christian, send more sanguine slaves, who slaughter the sons of freedom in the midst of their merry-making; Plague and Famine come to slaughter them in return; and Laon and Cythna, who had chosen this auspicious moment in a ruined tower for the commencement of their 'reign of love,' surrender themselves to the monarch and are burnt alive.

Such is Mr. Shelley's victory, such its security, and such the means of obtaining it! (p. 467)

Mr. Shelley is a very vain man; and like most very vain men, he is but half instructed in knowledge, and less than half-disciplined in his reasoning powers; his vanity, wanting the controul of the faith which he derides, has been his ruin; it has made him too impatient of applause and distinction to earn them in the fair course of labour; like a speculator in trade, he would be rich without capital and without delay, and, as might have been anticipated, his speculations have ended only in disappointments. They both began, his speculations and his disappointments, in early childhood, and even from that period he has carried about with him a soured and discontented spirit—unteachable in boyhood, unamiable in youth, querulous and unmanly in manhood,—singularly unhappy in all three. (pp. 469-70)

[Mr. Shelley] is still a young man, and though his account be assuredly black and heavy, he may yet hope to redeem his time, and wipe it out. He may and he should retain all the love for his fellow-creatures, all the zeal for their improvement in virtue and happiness which he now professes, but let that zeal be armed with knowledge and regulated by judgment. Let him not be offended at our freedom, but he is really too young, too ignorant, too inexperienced, and too vicious to undertake the task of reforming any world, but the little world within his own breast; that task will be a good preparation for the difficulties which he is more anxious at once to encounter. There is a book which will help him to this preparation, which has more poetry in it than Lucretius, more interest than Godwin, and far more philosophy than both. But it is a sealed book to a proud spirit; if he would read it with effect, he must be humble where he is now vain, he must examine and doubt himself where now he boldly condemns others, and instead of relying on his own powers, he must feel and acknowledge his weakness, and pray for strength from above. (p. 470)

> *J. T. Coleridge, "Shelley's 'Revolt of Islam'," in* The Quarterly Review, *Vol. XXI, No. XLII, April, 1819, pp. 460-71.*

[JOHN GIBSON LOCKHART] (essay date 1819)

[*Although Lockhart wrote several novels, his fame rests on his biography of Sir Walter Scott and his critical contributions to* Blackwood's Edinburgh Magazine *and the* Quarterly Review. *He is notorious for his series of scathing articles in* Blackwood's *on the "Cockney School" of poetry, in which he assailed John Keats and Leigh Hunt on the basis of political differences and, indirectly, for their inferior education and upbringing. In contrast, Lockhart recognized the talents of William Wordsworth, Samuel Taylor Coleridge, and Shelley, despite his aversion to their political principles. Reviewing* Alastor *with praise for Shelley's developing talents, Lockhart defends the poet against John Taylor Coleridge's attack on* The Revolt of Islam *in the* Quarterly Review *(see excerpt dated 1819). For further criticism by Lockhart, see excerpt dated 1820.*]

We believe [*Alastor; or, The Spirit of Solitude and Other Poems*] to be Mr Shelley's first publication; and such of our readers as have been struck by the power and splendour of genius displayed in the *Revolt of Islam,* and by the frequent tenderness and pathos of *Rosalind and Helen,* will be glad to observe some of the earliest efforts of a mind destined, in our opinion, under due discipline and self-management, to achieve great things in poetry. It must be encouraging to those who, like us, cherish high hopes of this gifted but wayward young man, to see what advances his intellect has made within these few years, and to compare its powerful, though still imperfect display, in his principal poem with its first gleamings and irradiations throughout this production almost of his boyhood. (p. 148)

We beg leave . . . to say a few words about the treatment which Mr Shelley has, in his poetical character, received from the public. By our periodical critics he has either been entirely overlooked, or slightingly noticed, or grossly abused. There is not so much to find fault with in the mere silence of critics; but we do not hesitate to say, with all due respect for the general character of that journal, that Mr Shelley has been infamously and stupidly treated in the *Quarterly Review.* His Reviewer there, whoever he is, does not shew himself a man of such lofty principles as to entitle him to ride the high horse in company with the author of the *Revolt of Islam.* And when one compares the vis inertiae of his motionless prose with the "eagle-winged raptures" of Mr Shelley's poetry, one does not think indeed of Satan reproving Sin, but one does think, we will say it in plain words and without a figure, of a dunce rating a man of genius. If that critic does not know that Mr Shelley is a poet, almost in the very highest sense of that mysterious word, then, we appeal to all those whom we have enabled to judge for themselves, if he be not unfit to speak of poetry before the people of England. If he does know that Mr

Shelley is a great poet, what manner of man is he who, with such conviction, brings himself, with the utmost difficulty, to admit that there is any beauty at all in Mr Shelley's writings, and is happy to pass that admission off with an accidental and niggardly phrase of vague and valueless commendation. This is manifest and mean—glaring and gross injustice on the part of a man who comes forward as the champion of morality, truth, faith, and religion. This is being guilty of one of the very worst charges of which he accuses another; nor will any man who loves and honours genius, even though that genius may have occasionally suffered itself to be both stained and led astray, think but with contempt and indignation and scorn of a critic who, while he pretends to wield the weapons of honour, virtue, and truth, yet clothes himself in the armour of deceit, hypocrisy, and falsehood. He *exults* to calumniate Mr Shelley's moral character, but he *fears* to acknowledge his genius. And therefore do we, as the sincere though sometimes sorrowing friends of Mr Shelley, scruple not to say, even though it may expose us to the charge of personality from those from whom alone such a charge could at all affect our minds, that the critic shews himself by such conduct as far inferior to Mr Shelley as a man of worth, as the language in which he utters his falsehood and uncharitableness shews him to be inferior as a man of intellect.

In the present state of public feelings, with regard to poets and poetry, a critic cannot attempt to defraud a poet of his fame, without paying the penalty either of his ignorance or his injustice. So long as he confines the expression of his envy or stupidity to works of moderate or doubtful merit, he may escape punishment; but if he dare to insult the spirit of England by contumelious and scornful treatment of any one of her gifted sons, that contumely and that scorn will most certainly be flung back upon himself, till he be made to shrink and to shiver beneath the load. It is not in the power of all the critics alive to blind one true lover of poetry to the splendour of Mr Shelley's genius—and the reader who, from mere curiosity, should turn to the **Revolt of Islam** to see what sort of trash it was that so moved the wrath and the spleen and the scorn of the Reviewer, would soon feel, that to understand the greatness of the poet, and the littleness of his traducer, nothing more was necessary than to recite to his delighted sense any six successive stanzas of that poem, so full of music, imagination, intellect, and passion. We care comparatively little for injustice offered to one moving majestical in the broad day of fame—it is the injustice done to the great, while their greatness is unknown or misunderstood that a generous nature most abhors, in as much as it seems more basely wicked to wish that genius might never lift its head, than to envy the glory with which it is encircled.

There is, we firmly believe, a strong love of genius in the people of this country, and they are willing to pardon to its possessor much extravagance and error—nay, even more serious trangressions. Let both Mr Shelley and his critic think of that—let it encourage the one to walk onwards to his bright destiny, without turning into dark or doubtful or wicked ways— let it teach the other to feel a proper sense of his own insignificance, and to be ashamed, in the midst of his own weaknesses and deficiencies and meannesses, to aggravate the faults of the highly-gifted, and to gloat with a sinful satisfaction on the real or imaginary debasement of genius and intellect.

And here we ought, perhaps, to stop. But the Reviewer has dealt out a number of dark and oracular denunciations against the Poet, which the public can know nothing about, except that

they imply a charge of immorality and wickedness. Let him speak out plainly, or let him hold his tongue. There are many wicked and foolish things in Mr Shelley's creed, and we have not hitherto scrupled, nor shall we henceforth scruple to expose that wickedness and that folly. But we do not think that he believes his own creed—at least, that he believes it fully and to utter conviction—and we doubt not but the scales will yet all fall from his eyes. The Reviewer, however, with a face of most laughable horror, accuses Mr Shelley in the same breath of some nameless act of atrocity, and of having been rusticated, or expelled, or warned to go away from the University of Oxford! He seems to shudder with the same holy fear at the violation of the laws of morality and the breaking of college rules. He forgets that in the world men do not wear caps and gowns as at Oriel or Exeter. He preaches not like Paul—but like a Proctor.

Once more, then we bid Mr Shelley farewell. Let him come forth from the eternal city, where, we understand, he has been sojourning,—in his strength, conquering and to conquer. Let his soul watch his soul, and listen to the voice of its own noble nature—and there is no doubt that the future will make amends for the past, whatever its error may have been—and that the Poet may yet be good, great, and happy. (pp. 153-54)

[*John Gibson Lockhart*], *in a review of ''Alastor; or, The Spirit of Solitude and Other Poems,''* in Blackwood's Edinburgh Magazine, *Vol. 6, November, 1819, pp. 148-55.*

PERCY BYSSHE SHELLEY   (essay date 1819)

[*In the following excerpts from Shelley's dedication and preface to* The Cenci, *published in 1819, he describes the story that inspired his drama and explains his artistic decisions concerning its composition. For additional commentary by Shelley, see excerpts dated 1818, 1820, and 1821.*]

Those writings which I have hitherto published, have been little else than visions which impersonate my own apprehensions of the beautiful and the just. I can also perceive in them the literary defects incidental to youth and impatience; they are dreams of what ought to be, or may be. The drama which I now present to you [*The Cenci*] is a sad reality. I lay aside the presumptuous attitude of an instructor, and am content to paint, with such colours as my own heart furnishes, that which has been. (p. 67)

• • • • •

A manuscript was communicated to me during my travels in Italy, which was copied from the archives of the Cenci Palace at Rome, and contains a detailed account of the horrors which ended in the extinction of one of the noblest and richest families of that city, during the pontificate of Clement VIII., in the year 1599. The story is, that an old man, having spent his life in debauchery and wickedness, conceived at length an implacable hatred towards his children; which showed itself towards one daughter under the form of an incestuous passion, aggravated by every circumstance of cruelty and violence. This daughter, after long and vain attempts to escape from what she considered a perpetual contamination both of body and mind, at length plotted with her mother-in-law and brother to murder their common tyrant. The young maiden, who was urged to this tremendous deed by an impulse which overpowered its horror, was evidently a most gentle and amiable being, a creature formed to adorn and be admired, and thus violently thwarted from her nature by the necessity of circumstance and opinion. The deed was quickly discovered, and in spite of the most earnest prayers made to the Pope by the highest persons in Rome, the criminals were put to death. The old man had, during his life, repeatedly bought his pardon from the Pope for capital crimes of the most enormous and unspeakable kind, at the price of a hundred thousand crowns; the death therefore of his victims can scarcely be accounted for by the love of justice. The Pope, among other motives for severity, probably felt that whoever killed the Count Cenci deprived his treasury of a certain and copious source of revenue. Such a story, if told so as to present to the reader all the feelings of those who once acted it, their hopes and fears, their confidences and misgivings, their various interests, passions, and opinions, acting upon and with each other, yet all conspiring to one tremendous end, would be as a light to make apparent some of the most dark and secret caverns of the human heart.

On my arrival at Rome, I found that the story of the Cenci was a subject not to be mentioned in Italian society without awakening a deep and breathless interest; and that the feelings of the company never failed to incline to a romantic pity for the wrongs, and a passionate exculpation of the horrible deed to which they urged her, who has been mingled two centuries with the common dust. All ranks of people knew the outlines of this history, and participated in the overwhelming interest which it seems to have the magic of exciting in the human heart. (pp. 69-70)

This national and universal interest which the story produces and has produced for two centuries, and among all ranks of people in a great City, where the imagination is kept for ever active and awake, first suggested to me the conception of its fitness for a dramatic purpose. In fact it is a tragedy which has already received, from its capacity of awakening and sustaining the sympathy of men, approbation and success. Nothing remained, as I imagined, but to clothe it to the apprehensions of my countrymen in such language and action as would bring it home to their hearts. The deepest and the sublimest tragic compositions, *King Lear,* and the two plays in which the tale of Aedipus is told, were stories which already existed in tradition, as matters of popular belief and interest, before Shakspeare and Sophocles made them familiar to the sympathy of all succeeding generations of mankind.

This story of the Cenci is indeed eminently fearful and monstrous: anything like a dry exhibition of it on the stage would be insupportable. The person who would treat such a subject must increase the ideal, and diminish the actual horror of the events, so that the pleasure which arises from the poetry which exists in these tempestuous sufferings and crimes, may mitigate the pain of the contemplation of the moral deformity from which they spring. There must also be nothing attempted to make the exhibition subservient to what is vulgarly termed a moral purpose. The highest moral purpose aimed at in the highest species of the drama, is the teaching the human heart, through its sympathies and antipathies, the knowledge of itself; in proportion to the possession of which knowledge, every human being is wise, just, sincere, tolerant, and kind. If dogmas can do more, it is well: but a drama is no fit place for the enforcement of them. Undoubtedly no person can be truly dishonoured by the act of another; and the fit return to make to the most enormous injuries is kindness and forbearance, and a resolution to convert the injurer from his dark passions by peace and love. Revenge, retaliation, atonement, are pernicious mistakes. If Beatrice had thought in this manner she would have been wiser and better; but she would never have been a tragic character: the few whom such an exhibition would have

interested, could never have been sufficiently interested for a dramatic purpose, from the want of finding sympathy in their interest among the mass who surround them. It is in the restless and anatomising casuistry with which men seek the justification of Beatrice, yet feel that she has done what needs justification; it is in the superstitious horror with which they contemplate alike her wrongs and their revenge, that the dramatic character of what she did and suffered, consists.

I have endeavoured as nearly as possible to represent the characters as they probably were, and have sought to avoid the error of making them actuated by my own conceptions of right or wrong, false or true: thus under a thin veil converting names and actions of the sixteenth century into cold impersonations of my own mind. They are represented as Catholics, and as Catholics deeply tinged with religion. To a Protestant apprehension there will appear something unnatural in the earnest and perpetual sentiment of the relations between God and man which pervade the tragedy of the Cenci. It will especially be startled at the combination of an undoubting persuasion of the truth of the popular religion with a cool and determined perseverance in enormous guilt. But religion in Italy is not, as in Protestant countries, a cloak to be worn on particular days; or a passport which those who do not wish to be railed at carry with them to exhibit; or a gloomy passion for penetrating the impenetrable mysteries of our being, which terrifies its possessor at the darkness of the abyss to the brink of which it has conducted him. Religion coexists, as it were, in the mind of an Italian Catholic, with a faith in that of which all men have the most certain knowledge. It is interwoven with the whole fabric of life. It is adoration, faith, submission, penitence, blind admiration; not a rule for moral conduct. It has no necessary connexion with any one virtue. The most atrocious villain may be rigidly devout, and, without any shock to established faith, confess himself to be so. Religion pervades intensely the whole frame of society, and is, according to the temper of the mind which it inhabits, a passion, a persuasion, an excuse, a refuge; never a check. Cenci himself built a chapel in the court of his palace, and dedicated it to St. Thomas the Apostle, and established masses for the peace of his soul. Thus in the first scene of the fourth act at Lucretia's design in exposing herself to the consequences of an expostulation with Cenci after having administered the opiate, was to induce him by a feigned tale to confess himself before death; this being esteemed by Catholics as essential to salvation; and she only relinquishes her purpose when she perceives that her perseverance would expose Beatrice to new outrages.

I have avoided with great care in writing this play the introduction of what is commonly called mere poetry, and I imagine there will scarcely be found a detached simile or a single isolated description, unless Beatrice's description of the chasm appointed for her father's murder should be judged to be of that nature.

In a dramatic composition the imagery and the passion should interpenetrate one another, the former being reserved simply for the full development and illustration of the latter. Imagination is as the immortal God which should assume flesh for the redemption of mortal passion. It is thus that the most remote and the most familiar imagery may alike be fit for dramatic purposes when employed in the illustration of strong feeling, which raises what is low, and levels to the apprehension that which is lofty, casting over all the shadow of its own greatness. In other respects I have written more carelessly; that is, without an over-fastidious and learned choice of words. In this respect,

I entirely agree with those modern critics who assert that in order to move men to true sympathy we must use the familiar language of men. And that our great ancestors the ancient English poets are the writers, a study of whom might incite us to do that for our own age which they have done for theirs. But it must be the real language of men in general, and not that of any particular class to whose society the writer happens to belong. So much for what I have attempted; I need not be assured that success is a very different matter; particularly for one whose attention has but newly been awakened to the study of dramatic literature.

I endeavoured whilst at Rome to observe such monuments of this story as might be accessible to a stranger. The portrait of Beatrice at the Colonna Palace is admirable as a work of art: it was taken by Guido during her confinement in prison. But it is most interesting as a just representation of one of the loveliest specimens of the workmanship of Nature. There is a fixed and pale composure upon the features: she seems sad and stricken down in spirit, yet the despair thus expressed is lightened by the patience of gentleness. Her head is bound with folds of white drapery, from which the yellow strings of her golden hair escape, and fall about her neck. The moulding of her face is exquisitely delicate; the eye-brows are distinct and arched; the lips have that permanent meaning of imagination and sensibility which suffering has not repressed and which it seems as if death scarcely could extinguish. Her forehead is large and clear; her eyes, which we are told were remarkable for their vivacity, are swollen with weeping and lustreless, but beautifully tender and serene. In the whole mien there is a simplicity and dignity which united with her exquisite loveliness and deep sorrow are inexpressibly pathetic. Beatrice Cenci appears to have been one of those rare persons in whom energy and gentleness dwell together without destroying one another: her nature was simple and profound. The crimes and miseries in which she was an actor and a sufferer are as the mask and the mantle in which circumstances clothed her for her impersonation on the scene of the world. (pp. 70-3)

> *Percy Bysshe Shelley, in a dedication and a preface to "The Cenci" in his* The Complete Works of Percy Bysshe Shelley: Poems, Vol. II, *edited by Roger Ingpen and Walter E. Peck, 1926. Reprint by Gordian Press, 1965, pp. 67-8, 69-74.*

THE LONDON MAGAZINE   (essay date 1820)

[*In this excerpt from a mixed review of* The Cenci, *the critic praises Shelley's poetic genius while deploring his apparent depravity.*]

[It] is no more than fair towards Mr. Shelley to state, that the *style* of his writings betrays but little affectation, and that their matter evinces much real power of intellect, great vivacity of fancy, and a quick, deep, serious feeling, responding readily, and harmoniously, to every call made on the sensibility by the imagery and incidents of this variegated world. So far Mr. Shelley has considerable advantages over some of those with whom he shares many grave faults. In the extraordinary work now under notice [*The Cenci*], he, in particular, preserves throughout a vigorous, clear, manly turn of expression, of which he makes excellent use to give force, and even sublimity, to the flashes of passion and of phrenzy,—and wildness and horror to the darkness of cruelty and guilt. His language, as he travels through the most exaggerated incidents, retains its correctness and simplicity;—and the most beautiful images,

the most delicate and finished ornaments of sentiment and description, the most touching tenderness, graceful sorrow, and solemn appalling misery, constitute the very genius of poesy, present and powerful in these pages, but, strange and lamentable to say, closely connected with the signs of a depraved, nay mawkish, or rather emasculated moral taste, craving after trash, filth, and poison, and sickening at wholesome nutriment. There can be but little doubt that *vanity* is at the bottom of this, and that weakness of *character* (which is a different thing from what is called weakness of *talent*) is also concerned. Mr. Shelley likes to carry about with him the consciousness of his own peculiarities; and a tinge of disease, probably existing in a certain part of his constitution, gives to these peculiarities a very offensive cast. This unlucky tendency of his, is at once his pride and his shame: he is tormented by more than suspicions that the general sentiment of society is against him— and, at the same time, he is induced by irritation to keep harping on sore subjects. Hence his stories, which he selects or contrives under a systematic predisposition as it were,—are usually marked by some anti-social, unnatural, and offensive feature:—whatever "is not to be named amongst men," Mr. Shelley seems to think has a peculiar claim to celebration in poetry;—and he turns from war, rapine, murder, seduction, and infidelity,—the vices and calamities with the description of which our common nature and common experience permit the generality of persons to sympathise,—to cull some morbid or maniac sin of rare and doubtful occurrence, and sometimes to found *a system* of practical purity and peace on violations which it is disgraceful even to contemplate. (pp. 547-48)

[In Mr. Shelley's preface to **The Cenci**] we have considerable incoherency, and more improbability, to begin with. What are we to understand by an old man conceiving "an implacable *hatred* against his children, which showed itself towards one daughter under the form of an incestuous *passion*" [see excerpt dated 1819]? A passion resulting from hatred, as well as a hatred showing itself in a passion, must be considered quite new at least. Luckily the language of common-sense is not applicable to these monstrous infamies: they are not reduceable even to the forms of rational communication: they are so essentially absurd that their very description slides necessarily into nonsense; and a person of talent who has taken to this sort of *fancy*, is sure to stultify himself in committing the atrocious act of insulting the soul of man which is the image of his maker. If it be really true that an individual once existed who hated his children, and under the impulse of hatred, committed an outrage on his daughter, that individual was *mad*; and will any who are not the same, or worse, pretend that the horrors of madness, the revolting acts of a creature stripped of its being's best part, can properly furnish the principal interest of a dramatic composition, claiming the sympathy of mankind as a representation of human nature? The author informs us, with reference to his present work, that "the person who would treat such a subject must INCREASE *the ideal, and* DIMINISH *the actual horror* of the events, so that the *pleasure which arises from the poetry that exists in these tempestuous sufferings and crimes,* may mitigate the pain of the contemplation of the moral deformity from which they spring." Now the necessity which Mr. Shelley here admits, finally condemns his attempt; for it is a hopeless one. It is quite impossible to increase the ideal, or to diminish the actual horror of *such* events: they are therefore altogether out of the Muse's province. (p. 549)

[Mr. Shelley's] object, he says, is "*the teaching* the *human heart the knowledge of itself,* in proportion to the possession of which knowledge every human being is wise, just, sincere, *tolerant, and kind.''* He therefore considers that his work, *The Cenci,* is ''subservient to a moral purpose.'' We think he is mistaken in every respect. His work does not teach the human heart, but insults it:—a father who invites guests to a splendid feast, and then informs them of the events they are called together to celebrate, in such lines as the following, has neither heart nor brains, neither human reason nor human affections, nor human passions of any kind;—nothing, in short, of human about him but the external form, which, however, in such a state of demoniac frenzy, must flash the wild beast from its eyes rather than the man.

> Oh, thou bright wine whose purple splendour leaps
> And bubbles gaily in this golden bowl
> Under the lamp light, as my spirits do,
> To hear the death of my accursed sons!
> Could I believe thou wert their mingled blood,
> Then would I taste thee like a sacrament,
> *And pledge with thee the mighty Devil in Hell,*
> Who, if a father's curses, as men say,
> Climb with swift wings after their children's souls,
> And drag them from the very throne of Heaven,
> Now triumphs in my triumph!—But thou art
> Superfluous; I have drunken deep of joy
> And I will taste no other wine to night.
> Here, Andrea! Bear the bowl around.

In this way Mr. Shelley proposes to *teach* the human heart, and thus to effect *''the highest moral purpose!''* His precepts are conveyed in the cries of Bedlam; and the outrage of a wretched old maniac, long passed the years of appetite, perpetrated on the person of his miserable child, under motives that are inconsistent with reason, and circumstances impossible in fact, is presented to us as a mirror in which we may contemplate a portion at least, of our common nature! (p. 550)

The radical foulness of moral complexion, characterizing such compositions as this one now before us, we shall never let escape unnoticed or unexposed, when examples of it offer themselves. It is at once disgusting and dangerous; our duty, therefore, is here in unison with our taste. In *The Cenci* however, the fault in question is almost redeemed, so far as literary merit is concerned, by uncommon force of poetical sentiment, and very considerable purity of poetical style. There are gross exceptions to the latter quality . . . , but the praise we have given will apply generally to the work. (p. 551)

This tragedy is the production of a man of great genius, and of a most unhappy moral constitution. (p. 555)

> *A review of ''The Cenci,'' in* The London Magazine, *Vol. V, No. 1, May, 1820, pp. 546-55.*

JOHN KEATS   (letter date 1820)

[*Keats is considered a key figure in the English Romantic movement and a major poet in the English language. Critics note that though his creative career spanned only four years, he achieved remarkable intellectual and artistic development. In this excerpt from a letter to Shelley, Keats offers advice after reading* The Cenci.]

There is only one part of [*The Cenci*] I am judge of; the Poetry, and dramatic effect, which by many spirits now a days is considered the mammon. A modern work it is said must have a purpose, which may be the God—*an artist* must serve Mammon—he must have ''self concentration'' selfishness perhaps. You I am sure will forgive me for sincerely remarking that

you might curb your magnanimity and be more of an artist, and 'load every rift' of your subject with ore. The thought of such discipline must fall like cold chains upon you, who perhaps never sat with your wings furl'd for six Months together. And is not this extraordina[r]y talk for the writer of *Endymion?* whose mind was like a pack of scattered cards—I am pick'd up and sorted to a pip. My Imagination is a Monastry and I am its Monk—you must explain my [metaphysics] to yourself. I am in expectation of *Prometheus* every day. Could I have my own wish for its interest effected you would have it still in manuscript—or be but now putting an end to the second act. I remember you advising me not to publish my first-blights, on Hampstead heath—I am returning advice upon your hands. (pp. 322-23)

> *John Keats, in a letter to Percy Bysshe Shelley on August 16, 1820, in his* The Letters of John Keats: 1814-1821, *Vol. 2, edited by Hyder Edward Rollins, Harvard University Press, 1958, pp. 322-23.*

PERCY BYSSHE SHELLEY   (essay date 1820)

[*In his 1820 preface to* Prometheus Unbound, *reprinted below, Shelley discusses such topics as his sources, imagery, and philosophy of poetry. For further commentary by Shelley, see excerpts dated 1818, 1819, and 1821.*]

The Greek tragic writers, in selecting as their subject any portion of their national history or mythology, employed in their treatment of it a certain arbitrary discretion. They by no means conceived themselves bound to adhere to the common interpretation or to imitate in story as in title their rivals and predecessors. Such a system would have amounted to a resignation of those claims to preference over their competitors which incited the composition. The Agamemnonian story was exhibited on the Athenian theatre with as many variations as dramas.

I have presumed to employ a similar licence [in *Prometheus Unbound*]. The *Prometheus Unbound* of Aeschylus supposed the reconciliation of Jupiter with his victim as the price of the disclosure of the danger threatened to his empire by the consummation of his marriage with Thetis. Thetis, according to this view of the subject, was given in marriage to Peleus, and Prometheus, by the permission of Jupiter, delivered from his captivity by Hercules. Had I framed my story on this model, I should have done no more than have attempted to restore the lost drama of Aeschylus; an ambition, which, if my preference to this mode of treating the subject had incited me to cherish, the recollection of the high comparison such an attempt would challenge might well abate. But, in truth, I was averse from a catastrophe so feeble as that of reconciling the Champion with the Oppressor of mankind. The moral interest of the fable, which is so powerfully sustained by the sufferings and endurance of Prometheus, would be annihilated if we could conceive of him as unsaying his high language and quailing before his successful and perfidious adversary. The only imaginary being resembling in any degree Prometheus, is Satan; and Prometheus is, in my judgment, a more poetical character than Satan, because, in addition to courage, and majesty, and firm and patient opposition to omnipotent force, he is susceptible of being described as exempt from the taints of ambition, envy, revenge, and a desire for personal aggrandisement, which, in the Hero of *Paradise Lost*, interfere with the interest. The character of Satan engenders in the mind a pernicious casuistry which leads us to weigh his faults with his wrongs, and to excuse the former because the latter exceed all measure. In the minds of those who consider that magnificent fiction with a religious feeling it engenders something worse. But Prometheus is, as it were, the type of the highest perfection of moral and intellectual nature, impelled by the purest and the truest motives to the best and noblest ends.

This Poem was chiefly written upon the mountainous ruins of the Baths of Caracalla, among the flowery glades, and thickets of odoriferous blossoming trees, which are extended in ever winding labyrinths upon its immense platforms and dizzy arches suspended in the air. The bright blue sky of Rome, and the effect of the vigorous awakening spring in that divinest climate, and the new life with which it drenches the spirits even to intoxication, were the inspiration of this drama.

The imagery which I have employed will be found, in many instances, to have been drawn from the operations of the human mind, or from those external actions by which they are expressed. This is unusual in modern poetry, although Dante and Shakspeare are full of instances of the same kind: Dante indeed more than any other poet, and with greater success. But the Greek poets, as writers to whom no resource of awakening the sympathy of their contemporaries was unknown, were in the habitual use of this power; and it is the study of their works, (since a higher merit would probably be denied me,) to which I am willing that my readers should impute this singularity.

One word is due in candour to the degree in which the study of contemporary writings may have tinged my composition, for such has been a topic of censure with regard to poems far more popular, and indeed more deservedly popular, than mine. It is impossible that any one who inhabits the same age with such writers as those who stand in the foremost ranks of our own, can conscientiously assure himself that his language and tone of thought may not have been modified by the study of the productions of those extraordinary intellects. It is true, that, not the spirit of their genius, but the forms in which it has manifested itself, are due less to the peculiarities of their own minds than to the peculiarity of the moral and intellectual condition of the minds among which they have been produced. Thus a number of writers possess the form, whilst they want the spirit of those whom, it is alleged, they imitate; because the former is the endowment of the age in which they live, and the latter must be the uncommunicated lightning of their own mind.

The peculiar style of intense and comprehensive imagery which distinguishes the modern literature of England, has not been, as a general power, the product of the imitation of any particular writer. The mass of capabilities remains at every period materially the same; the circumstances which awaken it to action perpetually change. If England were divided into forty republics, each equal in population and extent to Athens, there is no reason to suppose but that, under institutions not more perfect than those of Athens, each would produce philosophers and poets equal to those who (if we except Shakspeare) have never been surpassed. We owe the great writers of the golden age of our literature to that fervid awakening of the public mind which shook to dust the oldest and most oppressive form of the Christian religion. We owe Milton to the progress and development of the same spirit: the sacred Milton was, let it ever be remembered, a republican, and a bold inquirer into morals and religion. The great writers of our own age are, we have reason to suppose, the companions and forerunners of some unimagined change in our social condition, or the opinions which cement it. The cloud of mind is discharging its collected lightning, and the equilibrium between institutions and opinions is now restoring, or is about to be restored.

As to imitation, poetry is a mimetic art. It creates, but it creates by combination and representation. Poetical abstractions are beautiful and new, not because the portions of which they are composed had no previous existence in the mind of man or in nature, but because the whole produced by their combination has some intelligible and beautiful analogy with those sources of emotion and thought, and with the contemporary condition of them: one great poet is a masterpiece of nature which another not only ought to study but must study. He might as wisely and as easily determine that his mind should no longer be the mirror of all that is lovely in the visible universe, as exclude from his contemplation the beautiful which exists in the writings of a great contemporary. The pretence of doing it would be a presumption in any but the greatest; the effect, even in him, would be strained, unnatural, and ineffectual. A poet is the combined product of such internal powers as modify the nature of others; and of such external influences as excite and sustain these powers; he is not one, but both. Every man's mind is, in this respect, modified by all the objects of nature and art; by every word and every suggestion which he ever admitted to act upon his consciousness; it is the mirror upon which all forms are reflected, and in which they compose one form. Poets, not otherwise than philosophers, painters, sculptors, and musicians, are, in one sense, the creators, and, in another, the creations, of their age. From this subjection the loftiest do not escape. There is a similarity between Homer and Hesiod, between Aeschylus and Euripides, between Virgil and Horace, between Dante and Petrarch, between Shakspeare and Fletcher, between Dryden and Pope; each has a generic resemblance under which their specific distinctions are arranged. If this similarity be the result of imitation, I am willing to confess that I have imitated.

Let this opportunity be conceded to me of acknowledging that I have, what a Scotch philosopher characteristically terms, "a passion for reforming the world:" what passion incited him to write and publish his book, he omits to explain. For my part, I had rather be damned with Plato and Lord Bacon, than go to Heaven with Paley and Malthus. But it is a mistake to suppose that I dedicate my poetical compositions solely to the direct enforcement of reform, or that I consider them in any degree as containing a reasoned system on the theory of human life. Didactic poetry is my abhorrence; nothing can be equally well expressed in prose that is not tedious and supererogatory in verse. My purpose has hitherto been simply to familiarize the highly refined imagination of the more select classes of poetical readers with beautiful idealisms of moral excellence; aware that until the mind can love, and admire, and trust, and hope, and endure, reasoned principles of moral conduct are seeds cast upon the highway of life which the unconscious passenger tramples into dust, although they would bear the harvest of his happiness. Should I live to accomplish what I purpose, that is, produce a systematical history of what appear to me to be the genuine elements of human society, let not the advocates of injustice and superstition flatter themselves that I should take Aeschylus rather than Plato as my model.

The having spoken of myself with unaffected freedom will need little apology with the candid; and let the uncandid consider that they injure me less than their own hearts and minds by misrepresentation. Whatever talents a person may possess to amuse and instruct others, be they ever so inconsiderable, he is yet bound to exert them: if his attempt be ineffectual, let

the punishment of an unaccomplished purpose have been sufficient; let none trouble themselves to heap the dust of oblivion
upon his efforts; the pile they raise will betray his grave which
might otherwise have been unknown. (pp. 171-75)

> *Percy Bysshe Shelley, in a preface to "Prometheus
> Unbound," in his* The Complete Works of Percy
> Bysshe Shelley: Poems, Vol. II, *edited by Roger
> Ingpen and Walter E. Peck, 1926. Reprint by Gor-
> dian Press, 1965, pp. 171-75.*

[JOHN GIBSON LOCKHART] (essay date 1820)

> [*While admitting Shelley's artistic mastery, particularly in the
> odes and in* The Sensitive Plant, *Lockhart denounces the poet's
> antireligious themes and liberal philosophy in* Prometheus Un-
> bound, with Other Poems. *For additional commentary by Lock-
> hart, see excerpt dated 1819.*]

Whatever may be the difference of men's opinions concerning
the measure of Mr Shelley's poetical power, there is one point
in regard to which all must be agreed, and that is his Audacity.
In the old days of the exulting genius of Greece, Aeschylus
dared two things which astonished all men, and which still
astonish them—to exalt contemporary men into the personages
of majestic tragedies—and to call down and embody into tragedy, without degradation, the elemental spirits of nature and
the deeper essences of Divinity. . . . But what shall we say of
the young English poet who has now attempted, not only a
flight as high as the highest of Aeschylus, but the very flight
of that father of tragedy—who has dared once more to dramatise Prometheus—and, most wonderful of all, to dramatise
the *deliverance* of Prometheus?. . . (p. 679)

It would be highly absurd to deny, that [Mr Shelley] has manifested very extraordinary powers of language and imagination
in his treatment of the allegory, however grossly and miserably
he may have tried to pervert its purpose and meaning. . . .
[What] can be more deserving of reprobation than the course
which he is allowing his intellect to take, and that too at the
very time when he ought to be laying the foundations of a
lasting and honourable name. There is no occasion for going
round about the bush to hint what the poet himself has so
unblushingly and sinfully blazoned forth in every part of his
production. With him, it is quite evident that the Jupiter whose
downfall has been predicted by Prometheus, means nothing
more than Religion in general, that is, every human system of
religious belief; and that, with the fall of this, he considers it
perfectly necessary (as indeed we also believe, though with far
different feelings) that every system of human government also
should give way and perish. The patience of the contemplative
spirit in Prometheus is to be followed by the daring of the
active Demagorgon, at whose touch all "old thrones" are at
once and for ever to be cast down into the dust. It appears too
plainly, from the luscious pictures with which his play ter-
minates, that Mr Shelley looks forward to an unusual relaxation
of all moral *rules*—or rather, indeed, to the extinction of all
moral feelings, except that of a certain mysterious indefinable
kindliness, as the natural and necessary result of the overthrow
of all civil government and religious belief. It appears, still
more wonderfully, that he contemplates this state of things as
the ideal SUMMUM BONUM. In short, it is quite impossible
that there should exist a more pestiferous mixture of blasphemy, sedition, and sensuality, than is visible in the whole
structure and strain of this poem—which, nevertheless, and
notwithstanding all the detestation its principles excite, must
and will be considered by all that read it attentively, as abound-

ing in poetical beauties of the highest order—as presenting
many specimens not easily to be surpassed, of the moral sublime of eloquence—as overflowing with pathos, and most magnificent in description. Where can be found a spectacle more
worthy of sorrow than such a man performing and glorying in
the performance of such things? His evil ambition,—from all
he has yet written, but most of all, from what he has last and
best written, his **Prometheus,**—appears to be no other, than
that of attaining the highest place among those poets,—enemies, not friends, of their species,—who, as a great and virtuous poet has well said (putting evil consequence close after
evil cause).

Profane the God-given strength, and *mar the lofty line.*

(p. 680)

[Among the miscellaneous pieces in this volume, there] is an
"Ode to the Westwind," another **"To a Sky-lark,"** and several
smaller pieces, all of them abounding in richest melody of
versification, and great tenderness of feeling. But the most
affecting of all is *The Sensitive Plant,* which is the history of
a beautiful garden, that after brightening and blossoming under
the eye of its lovely young mistress, shares in the calamity of
her fate, and dies because she is no more there to tend its
beauties. . . . [This piece contains] passages which we do not
scruple to place upon a level with the very happiest productions
of the greatest contemporaries of Mr Shelley. (pp. 685-86)

Mr Shelley, as a man of genius, is not merely superior, either
to Mr Hunt, or to Mr Keats, but altogether out of their sphere,
and totally incapable of ever being brought into the most distant
comparison with either of them. It is very possible, that Mr
Shelley himself might not be inclined to place himself so high
above these men as we do, but that is his affair, not ours. We
are afraid that he shares, (at least with one of them) in an
abominable system of belief, concerning Man and the World,
the sympathy arising out of which common belief, may probably sway more than it ought to do on both sides. But the truth
of the matter is this, and it is impossible to conceal it were we
willing to do so, that Mr Shelley is destined to leave a great
name behind him, and that we, as lovers of true genius, are
most anxious that this name should ultimately be pure as well
as great.

As for the principles and purposes of Mr Shelley's poetry,
since we must again recur to that dark part of the subject, we
think they are on the whole, more undisguisedly pernicious in
this volume, than even in his *Revolt of Islam.* There is an **"Ode
to Liberty"** at the end of the volume, which contains passages
of the most splendid beauty, but which, in point of meaning,
is just as wicked as any thing that ever reached the world under
the name of Mr Hunt himself. . . .

Let us hope that Percy Bysshe Shelley is not destined to leave
behind him, like that great genius [Voltaire], a name for ever
detestable to the truly FREE and the truly WISE. He talks in
his preface about MILTON, as a "Republican," and a "bold
inquirer into Morals and religion." Could any thing make us
despise Mr Shelley's understanding, it would be such an instance of voluntary blindness as this! Let us hope, that ere long
a lamp of genuine truth may be kindled within his "bright
mind;" and that he may walk in its light the path of the true
demigods of English genius, having, like them, learned to
"fear God and honour the king." (p. 687)

> [*John Gibson Lockhart*], *in a review of "Prometheus
> Unbound," in* Blackwood's Edinburgh Magazine,
> *Vol. 7, September, 1820, pp. 677-87.*

EDWARD E. WILLIAMS   (letter date 1821)

[*Williams and his wife were close friends of the Shelleys, sharing a house with them in Pisa. In the following excerpt from a letter to Trelawny, Williams describes Shelley and mentions his influence on Byron.*]

Shelley is certainly a man of most astonishing genius in appearance, extraordinarily young, of manners mild and amiable, but withal full of life and fun. His wonderful command of language, and the ease with which he speaks on what are generally considered abstruse subjects, are striking; in short, his ordinary conversation is akin to poetry, for he sees things in the most singular and pleasing lights: if he wrote as he talked, he would be popular enough. Lord Byron and others think him by far the most imaginative poet of the day. The style of his lordship's letters to him is quite that of a pupil, such as asking his opinion, and demanding his advice on certain points, &c. I must tell you, that the idea of the tragedy of Manfred, and many of the philosophical, or rather metaphysical, notions interwoven in the composition of the fourth Canto of *Childe Harold,* are of his suggestion; but this, of course, is between ourselves. (pp. 8-9)

> *Edward E. Williams, in a letter to E. J. Trelawny in April, 1821, in* Trelawny's Recollections of the Last Days of Shelley and Byron *by E. J. Trelawny, 1906. Reprint by Humphrey Milford, 1923, pp. 8-9.*

BLACKWOOD'S EDINBURGH MAGAZINE   (essay date 1821)

[*The following excerpt was drawn from a negative review of* Adonais. *In addition to ridiculing Shelley's elegiac style and obscurity, the critic condemns his treatment of religion as blasphemous.*]

Mr. P. B. Shelley having been the person appointed by the *Pisan* triumvirate to canonize the name of this apprentice [John Keats], "nipt in the bud," as he fondly tells us, has accordingly produced an Elegy, in which he weeps "after the manner of Moschus for Bion." The canonizer is worthy of the saint.— "*Et tu, Vitula!*"—Locke says, that the most resolute liar cannot lie more than once in every three sentences. Folly is more engrossing; for we could prove, from the present Elegy, that it is possible to write two sentences of pure nonsense out of every three. A more faithful calculation would bring us to ninety-nine out of every hundred, or,—as the present consists of only fifty-five stanzas,—leaving about five readable lines in the entire. It thus commences:—

> O weep for Adonais—he is dead!
> O, weep for Adonais! though our tears
> *Thaw not the frost* which binds so dear a head!
> And thou, sad hour! selected from all years
> *To mourn our loss,* rouse thy obscure compeers,
> *And teach them thine own sorrow, say with me*
> *Died* Adonais! till the *future does*
> *Forget the past.* His fate and fame shall be
> An echo and a light!! unto eternity.

Now, of this unintelligible stuff the whole fifty-five stanzas are composed. Here an hour—a *dead* hour too—is to say that Mr J. Keats died *along with it!* yet this hour has the heavy business on its hands of mourning the loss of its *fellow-defunct,* and of rousing all its *obscure compeers* to be taught its *own sorrow,* &c. Mr Shelley and his tribe have been panegyrized in their turn for power of language; and the man of "Table-talk" [Samuel Taylor Coleridge] swears by all the gods he

owns, that he has a great command of words, to which the most eloquent effusions of the Fives Court are *occasionally* inferior. But any man may have the command of every word in the vocabulary, if he will fling them like pebbles from a sack; and even in the most fortuitous flinging, they will sometimes fall in pleasing though useless forms. The art of the modern *Della Cruscan* is thus to eject every epithet that he can conglomerate in his piracy through the Lexicon, and throw them out to settle as they will. He follows his own rhymes, and shapes his subject to the close of his measure. He is a glutton of all names of colours, and flowers, and smells, and tastes, and crowds his verse with scarlet, and blue, and yellow, and green; extracts tears from every thing, and makes moss and naud hold regular conversations with him. "A goose-pye talks,"—it does more, it thinks, and has its peculiar sensibilities,—it smiles and weeps, raves to the stars, and is a listener to the western wind, as fond as the author himself.

On these principles, a hundred or a hundred thousand verses might be made, equal to the best in **Adonais,** without taking the pen off the paper. The subject is indifferent to us, let it be the "Golden age," or "Mother Goose,"—"Waterloo," or the "Wit of the Watchhouse,"—"Tom Thumb," or "Thistlewood." We will undertake to furnish the requisite supply of blue daisies and dandelions, not with the toilsome and tardy lutulence of the puling master of verbiage in question, but with a burst and torrent that will sweep away all his weedy trophies. (pp. 697-98)

Percy Bysshe has figured as a sentimentalist before, and we can quote largely without putting him to the blush by praise. What follows illustrates his power over the language of passion. In the **Cenci,** Beatrice is condemned to die for parricide, a situation that, in a true poet, might awaken a noble succession of distressful thought. The mingling of remorse, natural affection, woman's horror at murder, and alternate melancholy and fear at the prospect of the grave, in Percy Bysshe works up only this frigid rant:—

> ——How comes this hair undone?
> Its wandering strings must be what bind me so,
> And yet I *tied it fast!!*——

> (p. 698)

So much for the history of "Glue"—and so much easier is it to rake together the vulgar vocabulary of rottenness and reptilism, than to paint the workings of the mind. This raving is such as perhaps no excess of madness ever raved, except in the imagination of a Cockney, determined to be as mad as possible, and opulent in his recollections of the shambles.

In the same play, we have a specimen of his "art of description." He tells of a ravine—

> And in its depths there is a mighty Rock,
> Which has, from unimaginable years,
> Sustain'd itself with *terror and with toil!*
> Over a gulph, and with *the agony*
> *With which it clings,* seems slowy coursing down;
> Even as a wretched soul, hour after hour,
> Clings to the mass of life, yet clinging *leans,*
> And leaning, makes *more dark* the dread abyss
> In which it fears to fall. Beneath this crag,
> *Huge as despair,* as if *in weariness,*
> The *melancholy* mountain *yawns* below, &c. &c.

And all this is done by a rock—What is to be thought of the *terror* of this novel sufferer—its *toil*—the *agony* with which so sensitive a personage clings to its paternal support, from *unimaginable* years? The magnitude of this *melancholy* and injured monster happily is measured by its being the *exact size of despair!* Soul becomes substantial, and *darkens a dread abyss.* Such are Cockney darings before "the Gods, and columns" that abhor mediocrity. And is it to this dreary nonsense that is to be attached the name of poetry? Yet on these two passages the whole lauding of his fellow-Cockneys has been lavished. But *Percy Bysshe* feels his hopelessness of poetic reputation, and therefore lifts himself on the stilts of blasphemy. He is the only verseman of the day, who has dared, in a Christian country, to work out for himself the character of direct ATHEISM! In his present poem, he talks with impious folly of "the *envious* wrath of man or GOD!" Of a

> Branded and ensanguined brow,
> Which was like *Cains's* or CHRIST'S.

Offences like these naturally come before a more effective tribunal than that of criticism. We have heard it mentioned as the only apology for the predominant irreligion and nonsense of this person's works, that his understanding is unsettled. But in his Preface, there is none of the exuberance of insanity; there is a great deal of folly, and a great deal of bitterness, but nothing of the wildness of his poetic fustian. The Bombastes Furioso of these stanzas cools into sneering in the preface; and his language against the *death-dealing "Quarterly Review,"* which has made such havoc in the Empire of Cockaigne, is merely malignant, mean, and peevishly personal. (pp. 698-99)

The seasons and a whole host of personages, ideal and otherwise, come to lament over Adonais. They act in the following manner:

> Grief made the young Spring *wild,* and she threw down
> Her kindling buds, as if the Autumn were,
> Or they dead leaves, since her delight is flown,
> For whom should she have wak'd the sullen year?
> To Phoebus was not Hyacinth so dear,
> Nor to himself Narcissus, as to both,
> Thou, Adonais; wan they stand, and sere,
> Amid the drooping comrades of their youth,
> With dew all turn'd to tears, odour to sighing ruth.

Here is left, to those whom it may concern, the pleasant perplexity, whether the lament for Mr J. Keats is shared between Phoebus and Narcissus, or Summer and Autumn. It is useless to quote those absurdities any farther *en masse*, but there are flowers of poesy thickly spread through the work. . . . (p. 699)

> *"Remarks on Shelley's 'Adonais',"* in Blackwood's Edinburgh Magazine, *Vol. 10, December, 1821, pp. 696-700.*

PERCY BYSSHE SHELLEY (essay date 1821)

[*In this excerpt from his* A Defence of Poetry, *which he wrote in 1821, Shelley addresses such issues as the meaning of imagination; the nature, function, and effect of poetry; and the role of the poet. For additional commentary by Shelley, see excerpts dated 1818, 1819, and 1820.*]

Poetry, in a general sense, may be defined to be "the expression of the imagination": and poetry is connate with the origin of man. Man is an instrument over which a series of external and internal impressions are driven, like the alternations of an ever-changing wind over an Aeolian lyre, which move it by their motion to ever-changing melody. But there is a principle within

the human being, and perhaps within all sentient beings, which acts otherwise than in the lyre, and produces not melody, alone, but harmony, by an internal adjustment of the sounds or motions thus excited to the impressions which excite them. It is as if the lyre could accommodate its chords to the motions of that which strikes them, in a determined proportion of sound; even as the musician can accommodate his voice to the sound of the lyre. A child at play by itself will express its delight by its voice and motions; and every inflexion of tone and every gesture will bear exact relation to a corresponding antitype in the pleasurable impressions which awakened it; it will be the reflected image of that impression; and as the lyre trembles and sounds after the wind has died away, so the child seeks, by prolonging in its voice and motions the duration of the effect, to prolong also a consciousness of the cause. In relation to the objects which delight a child, these expressions are, what poetry is to higher objects. (pp. 109-10)

In the youth of the world, men dance and sing and imitate natural objects, observing in these actions, as in all others, a certain rhythm or order. And, although all men observe a similar, they observe not the same order, in the motions of the dance, in the melody of the song, in the combinations of language, in the series of their imitations of natural objects. For there is a certain order or rhythm belonging to each of these classes of mimetic representation, from which the hearer and the spectator receive an intenser and purer pleasure than from any other: the sense of an approximation to this order has been called taste by modern writers. Every man in the infancy of art, observes an order which approximates more or less closely to that from which this highest delight results: but the diversity is not sufficiently marked, as that its gradations should be sensible, except in those instances where the predominance of this faculty of approximation to the beautiful (for so we may be permitted to name the relation between this highest pleasure and its cause) is very great. Those in whom it exists in excess are poets, in the most universal sense of the word; and the pleasure resulting from the manner in which they express the influence of society or nature upon their own minds, communicates itself to others, and gathers a sort of reduplication from that community. Their language is vitally metaphorical; that is, it marks the before unapprehended relations of things and perpetuates their apprehension, until the words which represent them, become, through time, signs for portions or classes of thoughts instead of pictures of integral thoughts; and then if no new poets should arise to create afresh the associations which have been thus disorganised, language will be dead to all the nobler purposes of human intercourse. . . . In the infancy of society every author is necessarily a poet, because language itself is poetry; and to be a poet is to apprehend the true and the beautiful, in a word, the good which exists in the relation, subsisting, first between existence and perception, and secondly between perception and expression. Every original language near to its source is in itself the chaos of a cyclic poem: the copiousness of lexicography and the distinctions of grammar are the works of a later age, and are merely the catalogue and the form of the creations of poetry.

But poets, or those who imagine and express this indestructible order, are not only the authors of language and of music, of the dance, and architecture, and statuary, and painting; they are the institutors of laws, and the founders of civil society, and the inventors of the arts of life, and the teachers, who draw into a certain propinquity with the beautiful and the true, that partial apprehension of the agencies of the invisible world which is called religion. Hence all original religions are allegorical, or susceptible of allegory, and, like Janus, have a double face of false and true. Poets, according to the circumstances of the age and nation in which they appeared, were called, in the earlier epochs of the world, legislators, or prophets: a poet essentially comprises and unites both these characters. For he not only beholds intensely the present as it is, and discovers those laws according to which present things ought to be ordered, but he beholds the future in the present, and his thoughts are the germs of the flower and the fruit of latest time. Not that I assert poets to be prophets in the gross sense of the word, or that they can foretell the form as surely as they foreknow the spirit of events: such is the pretence of superstition, which would make poetry an attribute of prophecy, rather than prophecy an attribute of poetry. A poet participates in the eternal, the infinite, and the one; as far as relates to his conceptions, time and place and number are not. The grammatical forms which express the moods of time, and the difference of persons, and the distinction of place, are convertible with respect to the highest poetry without injuring it as poetry; and the choruses of Aeschylus, and the book of Job, and Dante's *Paradise,* would afford, more than any other writings, examples of this fact, if the limits of this essay did not forbid citation. The creations of sculpture, painting, and music, are illustrations still more decisive.

Language, colour, form, and religious and civil habits of action, are all the instruments and materials of poetry; they may be called poetry by that figure of speech which considers the effect as a synonyme of the cause. But poetry in a more restricted sense expresses those arrangements of language, and especially metrical language, which are created by that imperial faculty, whose throne is curtained within the invisible nature of man. And this springs from the nature itself of language, which is a more direct representation of the actions and passions of our internal being, and is susceptible of more various and delicate combinations, than colour, form, or motion, and is more plastic and obedient to the control of that faculty of which it is the creation. For language is arbitrarily produced by the imagination, and has relation to thoughts alone; but all other materials, instruments, and conditions of art, have relations among each other, which limit and interpose between conception and expression. The former is as a mirror which reflects, the latter as a cloud which enfeebles, the light of which both are mediums of communication. Hence the fame of sculptors, painters, and musicians, although the intrinsic powers of the great masters of these arts may yield in no degree to that of those who have employed language as the hieroglyphic of their thoughts, has never equalled that of poets in the restricted sense of the term; as two performers of equal skill will produce unequal effects from a guitar and a harp. The fame of legislators and founders of religions, so long as their institutions last, alone seems to exceed that of poets in the restricted sense; but it can scarcely be a question, whether, if we deduct the celebrity which their flattery of the gross opinions of the vulgar usually conciliates, together with that which belonged to them in their higher character of poets, any excess will remain.

We have thus circumscribed the meaning of the word Poetry within the limits of that art which is the most familiar and the most perfect expression of the faculty itself. It is necessary, however, to make the circle still narrower, and to determine the distinction between measured and unmeasured language; for the popular division into prose and verse is inadmissible in accurate philosophy.

Sounds as well as thoughts have relation both between each other and towards that which they represent, and a perception of the order of those relations has always been found connected with a perception of the order of those relations of thoughts. Hence the language of poets has ever affected a certain uniform and harmonious recurrence of sound, without which it were not poetry, and which is scarcely less indispensable to the communication of its action, than the words themselves, without reference to that peculiar order. (pp. 111-14)

An observation of the regular mode of the recurrence of this harmony in the language of poetical minds, together with its relation to music, produced metre, or a certain system of traditional forms of harmony of language. Yet it is by no means essential that a poet should accommodate his language to this traditional form, so that the harmony, which is its spirit, be observed. The practice is indeed convenient and popular, and to be preferred, especially in such composition as includes much form and action: but every great poet must inevitably innovate upon the example of his predecessors in the exact structure of his peculiar versification. The distinction between poets and prose writers is a vulgar error. (p. 114)

A poem is the image of life expressed in its eternal truth. There is this difference between a story and a poem, that a story is a catalogue of detached facts, which have no other bond of connexion than time, place, circumstance, cause and effect; the other is the creation of actions according to the unchangeable forms of human nature, as existing in the mind of the creator, which is itself the image of all other minds. The one is partial, and applies only to a definite period of time, and a certain combination of events which can never again recur; the other is universal, and contains within itself the germ of a relation to whatever motives or actions have place in the possible varieties of human nature. Time, which destroys the beauty and the use of the story of particular facts, stript of the poetry which should invest them, augments that of Poetry, and for ever develops new and wonderful applications of the eternal truth which it contains. Hence epitomes have been called the moths of just history; they eat out the poetry of it. The story of particular facts is as a mirror which obscures and distorts that which should be beautiful: Poetry is a mirror which makes beautiful that which is distorted.

The parts of a composition may be poetical, without the composition as a whole being a poem. A single sentence may be considered as a whole, though it be found in a series of unassimilated portions; a single word even may be a spark of inextinguishable thought. And thus all the great historians, Herodotus, Plutarch, Livy, were poets; and although the plan of these writers, especially that of Livy, restrained them from developing this faculty in its highest degree, they make copious and ample amends for their subjection, by filling all the interstices of their subjects with living images.

Having determined what is poetry, and who are poets, let us proceed to estimate its effects upon society.

Poetry is ever accompanied with pleasure: all spirits on which it falls open themselves to receive the wisdom which is mingled with its delight. In the infancy of the world, neither poets themselves nor their auditors are fully aware of the excellence of poetry: for it acts in a divine and unapprehended manner, beyond and above consciousness; and it is reserved for future generations to contemplate and measure the mighty cause and effect in all the strength and splendour of their union. Even in modern times, no living poet ever arrived at the fulness of his fame; the jury which sits in judgment upon a poet, belonging as he does to all time, must be composed of his peers: it must be impanneled by Time from the selectest of the wise of many generations. A Poet is a nightingale, who sits in darkness and sings to cheer its own solitude with sweet sounds; his auditors are as men entranced by the melody of an unseen musician, who feel that they are moved and softened, yet know not whence or why. (pp. 115-16)

The whole objection . . . of the immorality of poetry rests upon a misconception of the manner in which poetry acts to produce the moral improvement of man. Ethical science arranges the elements which poetry has created, and propounds schemes and proposes examples of civil and domestic life: nor is it for want of admirable doctrines that men hate, and despise, and censure, and deceive, and subjugate one another. But Poetry acts in another and diviner manner. It awakens and enlarges the mind itself by rendering it the receptacle of a thousand unapprehended combinations of thought. Poetry lifts the veil from the hidden beauty of the world, and makes familiar objects be as if they were not familiar; it reproduces all that it represents, and the impersonations clothed in its Elysian light stand thenceforward in the minds of those who have once contemplated them, as memorials of that gentle and exalted content which extends itself over all thoughts and actions with which it coexists. The great secret of morals is love; or a going out of our own nature, and an identification of ourselves with the beautiful which exists in thought, action, or person, not our own. A man, to be greatly good, must imagine intensely and comprehensively; he must put himself in the place of another and of many others; the pains and pleasures of his species must become his own. The great instrument of moral good is the imagination; and poetry administers to the effect by acting upon the cause. Poetry enlarges the circumference of the imagination by replenishing it with thoughts of ever new delight, which have the power of attracting and assimilating to their own nature all other thoughts, and which form new intervals and interstices whose void for ever craves fresh food. Poetry strengthens that faculty which is the organ of the moral nature of man, in the same manner as exercise strengthens a limb. A Poet therefore would do ill to embody his own conceptions of right and wrong, which are usually those of his place and time, in his poetical creations, which participate in neither. By this assumption of the inferior office of interpreting the effect, in which perhaps after all he might acquit himself but imperfectly, he would resign the glory in a participation in the cause. There was little danger that Homer, or any of the eternal Poets, should have so far misunderstood themselves as to have abdicated this throne of their widest dominion. Those in whom the poetical faculty, though great, is less intense, as Euripides, Lucan, Tasso, Spenser, have frequently affected a moral aim, and the effect of their poetry is diminished in exact proportion to the degree in which they compel us to advert to this purpose. (pp. 117-18)

We have more moral, political and historical wisdom, than we know how to reduce into practice; we have more scientific and economical knowledge than can be accommodated to the just distribution of the produce which it multiplies. The poetry in these systems of thought, is concealed by the accumulation of facts and calculating processes. There is no want of knowledge respecting what is wisest and best in morals, government, and political economy, or at least, what is wiser and better than what men now practise and endure. But we let *"I dare not wait upon I would,* like the poor cat i' the adage.'' We want the creative faculty to imagine that which we know; we want the generous impulse to act that which we imagine; we want the poetry of life: our calculations have outrun conception; we have eaten more than we can digest. The cultivation of those

sciences which have enlarged the limits of the empire of man over the external world, has, for want of the poetical faculty, proportionally circumscribed those of the internal world; and man, having enslaved the elements, remains himself a slave. To what but a cultivation of the mechanical arts in a degree disproportioned to the presence of the creative faculty, which is the basis of all knowledge, is to be attributed the abuse of all invention for abridging and combining labour, to the exasperation of the inequality of mankind? From what other cause has it arisen that these inventions which should have lightened, have added a weight to the curse imposed on Adam? Thus Poetry, and the principle of Self, of which Money is the visible incarnation, are the God and Mammon of the world.

The functions of the poetical faculty are twofold; by one it creates new materials for knowledge, and power and pleasure; by the other it engenders in the mind a desire to reproduce and arrange them according to a certain rhythm and order which may be called the beautiful and the good. The cultivation of poetry is never more to be desired than at periods when, from an excess of the selfish and calculating principle, the accumulation of the materials of external life exceed the quantity of the power of assimilating them to the internal laws of human nature. The body has then become too unwieldy for that which animates it.

Poetry is indeed something divine. It is at once the centre and circumference of knowledge; it is that which comprehends all science, and that to which all science must be referred. It is at the same time the root and blossom of all other systems of thought; it is that from which all spring, and that which adorns all; and that which, if blighted, denies the fruit and the seed, and withholds from the barren world the nourishment and the succession of the scions of the tree of life. It is the perfect and consummate surface and bloom of things; it is as the odour and the colour of the rose to the texture of the elements which compose it, as the form and the splendour of unfaded beauty to the secrets of anatomy and corruption. What were Virtue, Love, Patriotism, Friendship—what were the scenery of this beautiful Universe which we inhabit; what were our consolations on this side of the grave, and what were our aspirations beyond it, if Poetry did not ascend to bring light and fire from those eternal regions where the owl-winged faculty of calculation dare not ever soar? Poetry is not like reasoning, a power to be exerted according to the determination of the will. A man cannot say, ''I will compose poetry.'' The greatest poet even cannot say it: for the mind in creation is as a fading coal, which some invisible influence, like an inconstant wind, awakens to transitory brightness: this power arises from within, like the colour of a flower which fades and changes as it is developed, and the conscious portions of our natures are unprophetic either of its approach or its departure. Could this influence be durable in its original purity and force, it is impossible to predict the greatness of the results; but when composition begins, inspiration is already on the decline, and the most glorious poetry that has ever been communicated to the world is probably a feeble shadow of the original conception of the Poet. I appeal to the great poets of the present day, whether it be not an error to assert that the finest passages of poetry are produced by labour and study. The toil and the delay recommended by critics, can be justly interpreted to mean no more than a careful observation of the inspired moments, and an artificial connexion of the spaces between their suggestions by the intertexture of conventional expressions; a necessity only imposed by the limitedness of the poetical faculty itself. For Milton conceived the *Paradise Lost* as a whole before he executed it in portions.

We have his own authority also for the Muse having "dictated" to him the "unpremeditated song," and let this be an answer to those who would allege the fifty-six various readings of the first line of the *Orlando Furioso*. Compositions so produced are to poetry what mosaic is to painting. This instinct and intuition of the poetical faculty is still more observable in the plastic and pictorial arts; a great statue or picture grows under the power of the artist as a child in the mother's womb; and the very mind which directs the hands in formation is incapable of accounting to itself for the origin, the gradations, or the media of the process.

Poetry is the record of the best and happiest moments of the happiest and best minds. We are aware of evanescent visitations of thought and feeling sometimes associated with place or person, sometimes regarding our own mind alone, and always arising unforeseen and departing unbidden, but elevating and delightful beyond all expression: so that even in the desire and the regret they leave, there cannot but be pleasure, participating as it does in the nature of its object. It is as it were the interpenetration of a diviner nature through our own; but its footsteps are like those of a wind over a sea, which the coming calm erases, and whose traces remain only, as on the wrinkled sand which paves it. These and corresponding conditions of being are experienced principally by those of the most delicate sensibility and the most enlarged imagination; and the state of mind produced by them is at war with every base desire. The

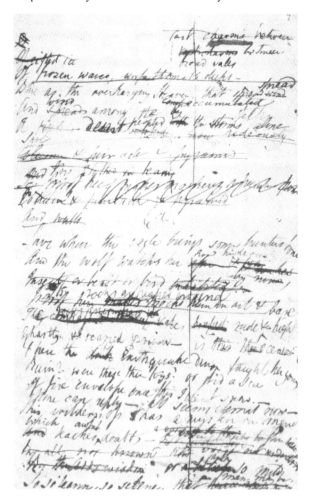

A draft copy of "Mont Blanc."

enthusiasm of virtue, love, patriotism, and friendship, is essentially linked with these emotions; and whilst they last, self appears as what it is, an atom to a Universe. Poets are not only subject to these experiences as spirits of the most refined organisation, but they can colour all that they combine with the evanescent hues of this ethereal world; a word, or a trait in the representation of a scene or a passion, will touch the enchanted chord, and reanimate, in those who have ever experienced these emotions, the sleeping, the cold, the buried image of the past. Poetry thus makes immortal all that is best and most beautiful in the world; it arrests the vanishing apparitions which haunt the interlunations of life, and veiling them, or in language or in form, sends them forth among mankind, bearing sweet news of kindred joy to those with whom their sisters abide—abide, because there is no portal of expression from the caverns of the spirit which they inhabit into the universe of things. Poetry redeems from decay the visitations of the divinity in Man.

Poetry turns all things to loveliness; it exalts the beauty of that which is most beautiful, and it adds beauty to that which is most deformed; it marries exultation and horror, grief and pleasure, eternity and change; it subdues to union under its light yoke, all irreconcilable things. It transmutes all that it touches, and every form moving within the radiance of its presence is changed by wondrous sympathy to an incarnation of the spirit which it breathes; its secret alchemy turns to potable gold the poisonous waters which flow from death through life; it strips the veil of familiarity from the world, and lays bare the naked and sleeping beauty, which is the spirit of its forms.

All things exist as they are perceived; at least in relation to the percipient. "The mind is its own place, and of itself can make a Heaven of Hell, a Hell of Heaven." But poetry defeats the curse which binds us to be subjected to the accident of surrounding impressions. And whether it spreads its own figured curtain, or withdraws life's dark veil from before the scene of things, it equally creates for us a being within our being. It makes us the inhabitants of a world to which the familiar world is a chaos. It reproduces the common Universe of which we are portions and percipients, and it purges from our inward sight the film of familiarity which obscures from us the wonder of our being. It compels us to feel that which we perceive, and to imagine that which we know. It creates anew the universe, after it has been annihilated in our minds by the recurrence of impressions blunted by reiteration. It justifies that bold and true word of Tasso: *Non merita nome di creatore, se non Iddio ed il Poeta.*

A poet, as he is the author to others of the highest wisdom, pleasure, virtue and glory, so he ought personally to be the happiest, the best, the wisest, and the most illustrious of men. As to his glory, let Time be challenged to declare whether the fame of any other institutor of human life be comparable to that of a poet. That he is the wisest, the happiest, and the best, inasmuch as he is a poet, is equally incontrovertible: the greatest Poets have been men of the most spotless virtue, of the most consummate prudence, and, if we could look into the interior of their lives, the most fortunate of men. . . . (pp. 134-38)

For the literature of England, an energetic development of which has ever preceded or accompanied a great and free development of the national will, has arisen as it were from a new birth. In spite of the low-thoughted envy which would undervalue contemporary merit, our own will be a memorable age in intellectual achievements, and we live among such philosophers and poets as surpass beyond comparison any who have appeared since the last national struggle for civil and religious liberty. The most unfailing herald, companion, and follower of the awakening of a great people to work a beneficial change in opinion or institution, is Poetry. At such periods there is an accumulation of the power of communicating and receiving intense and impassioned conceptions respecting man and nature. The persons in whom this power resides, may often as far as regards many portions of their nature, have little apparent correspondence with that spirit of good of which they are the ministers. But even whilst they deny and abjure, they are yet compelled to serve, the Power which is seated upon the throne of their own soul. It is impossible to read the compositions of the most celebrated writers of the present day without being startled with the electric life which burns within their words. They measure the circumference and sound the depths of human nature with a comprehensive and all-penetrating spirit, and they are themselves perhaps the most sincerely astonished at its manifestations; for it is less their spirit than the spirit of the age. Poets are the hierophants of an unapprehended inspiration; the mirrors of the gigantic shadows which futurity casts upon the present; the words which express what they understand not; the trumpets which sing to battle, and feel not what they inspire; the influence which is moved not, but moves. Poets are the unacknowledged legislators of the world. (p. 140)

> *Percy Bysshe Shelley, "A Defence of Poetry," in his* The Complete Works of Percy Bysshe Shelley: Prose, Vol. VII, *edited by Roger Ingpen and Walter E. Peck, revised edition, Gordian Press, 1965, pp. 109-40.*

LORD BYRON   (conversation date 1821?)

[*Byron was an English poet and dramatist who is now considered one of the most important poets of the nineteenth century. In this brief excerpt from a conversation recorded by Trelawny and thought to have been held in 1821, Byron speaks highly of Shelley's character.*]

To-day I had another letter warning me against the Snake (Shelley). He, alone, in this age of humbug, dares stem the current, as he did to-day the flooded Arno in his skiff, although I could not observe he made any progress. The attempt is better than being swept along as all the rest are, with the filthy garbage scoured from its banks.

> *Lord Byron, in a conversation with Edward John Trelawny in 1821?, in* Trelawny's Recollections of the Last Days of Shelley and Byron *by E. J. Trelawny, 1906. Reprint by Humphrey Milford, 1923, p. 26.*

[WILLIAM HAZLITT]   (essay date 1824)

[*One of the most important commentators of the Romantic age, Hazlitt was an English critic and journalist. He is best known for his descriptive criticism in which he stressed that no motives beyond judgment and analysis are necessary on the part of the critic. In this excerpt from a review of Shelley's* Posthumous Poems, *Hazlitt characterizes the poet as a flawed genius, deploring his obscurity and abstract approach in such works as "Julian and Maddalo" and* The Triumph of Life, *but praising the shorter odes and lyrics.*]

Mr Shelley's style is to poetry what astrology is to natural science—a passionate dream, a straining after impossibilities, a record of fond conjectures, a confused embodying of vague abstractions,—a fever of the soul, thirsting and craving after what it cannot have, indulging its love of power and novelty at the expense of truth and nature, associating ideas by contraries, and wasting great powers by their application to unattainable objects.

Poetry, we grant, creates a world of its own; but it creates it out of existing materials. Mr Shelley is the maker of his own poetry—out of nothing. Not that he is deficient in the true sources of strength and beauty, if he had given himself fair play ([his ***Posthumous Poems***], as well as his other productions, contains many proofs to the contrary): But, in him, fancy, will, caprice, predominated over and absorbed the natural influences of things; and he had no respect for any poetry that did not strain the intellect as well as fire the imagination—and was not sublimed into a high spirit of metaphysical philosophy. Instead of giving a language to thought, or lending the heart a tongue, he utters dark sayings, and deals in allegories and riddles. His Muse offers her services to clothe shadowy doubts and inscrutable difficulties in a robe of glittering words, and to turn nature into a brilliant paradox. We thank him—but we must be excused. Where we see the dazzling beacon-lights streaming over the darkness of the abyss, we dread the quicksands and the rocks below. Mr Shelley's mind was of 'too fiery a quality' to repose (for any continuance) on the probable or the true—it soared 'beyond the visible diurnal sphere,' to the strange, the improbable, and the impossible. He mistook the nature of the poet's calling, which should be guided by involuntary, not by voluntary impulses. He shook off, as an heroic and praiseworthy act, the trammels of sense, custom, and sympathy, and became the creature of his own will. He was 'all air,' disdaining the bars and ties of mortal mould. He ransacked his brain for incongruities, and believed in whatever was incredible. Almost all is effort, almost all is extravagant, almost all is quaint, incomprehensible, and abortive, from aiming to be more than it is. Epithets are applied, because they do not fit: subjects are chosen, because they are repulsive: the colours of his style, for their gaudy, changeful, startling effect, resemble the display of fire-works in the dark, and, like them, have neither durability, nor keeping, nor discriminate form. Yet Mr Shelley, with all his faults, was a man of genius; and we lament that uncontrollable violence of temperament which gave it a forced and false direction. He has single thoughts of great depth and force, single images of rare beauty, detached passages of extreme tenderness; and, in his smaller pieces, where he has attempted little, he has done most. If some casual and interesting idea touched his feelings or struck his fancy, he expressed it in pleasing and unaffected verse: but give him a larger subject, and time to reflect, and he was sure to get entangled in a system. The fumes of vanity rolled volumes of smoke, mixed with sparkles of fire, from the cloudy tabernacle of his thought. The success of his writings is therefore in general in the inverse ratio of the extent of his undertakings; inasmuch as his desire to teach, his ambition to excel, as soon as it was brought into play, encroached upon, and outstripped his powers of execution.

Mr Shelley was a remarkable man. His person was a type and shadow of his genius. His complexion, fair, golden, freckled, seemed transparent with an inward light, and his spirit within him

> ——so divinely wrought,
> That you might almost say his body thought.

He reminded those who saw him of some of Ovid's fables. His form, graceful and slender, drooped like a flower in the breeze. But he was crushed beneath the weight of thought which he aspired to bear, and was withered in the lightning-glare of a ruthless philosophy! He mistook the nature of his own faculties and feelings—the lowly children of the valley, by which the skylark makes its bed, and the bee murmurs, for the proud cedar or the mountain-pine, in which the eagle builds its eyry, 'and dallies with the wind, and scorns the sun.'—He wished to make of idle verse and ilder prose the frame-work of the universe, and to bind all possible existence in the visionary chain of intellectual beauty—

> More subtle web Arachne cannot spin,
> Nor the fine nets, which oft we woven see
> Of scorched dew, do not in th' air more lightly flee.

Perhaps some lurking sense of his own deficiencies in the lofty walk which he attempted, irritated his impatience and his desires; and urged him on, with winged hopes, to atone for past failures, by more arduous efforts, and more unavailing struggles.

With all his faults, Mr Shelley was an honest man. His unbelief and his presumption were parts of a disease, which was not combined in him either with indifference to human happiness, or contempt for human infirmities. There was neither selfishness nor malice at the bottom of his illusions. He was sincere in all his professions; and he practised what he preached—to his own sufficient cost. He followed up the letter and the spirit of his theoretical principles in his own person, and was ready to share both the benefit and the penalty with others. He thought and acted logically, and was what he professed to be, a sincere lover of truth, of nature, and of human kind. To all the rage of paradox, he united an unaccountable candour and severity of reasoning: in spite of an aristocratic education, he retained in his manners the simplicity of a primitive apostle. An Epicurean in his sentiments, he lived with the frugality and abstemiousness of an ascetick. His fault was, that he had no deference for the opinions of others, too little sympathy with their feelings (which he thought he had a right to sacrifice, as well as his own, to a grand ethical experiment)—and trusted too implicitly to the light of his own mind, and to the warmth of his own impulses. . . . We wish to speak of the errors of a man of genius with tenderness. His nature was kind, and his sentiments noble; but in him the rage of free inquiry and private judgment amounted to a species of madness. Whatever was new, untried, unheard of, unauthorized, exerted a kind of fascination over his mind. The examples of the world, the opinion of others, instead of acting as a check upon him, served but to impel him forward with double velocity in his wild and hazardous career. Spurning the world of realities, he rushed into the world of nonentities and contingencies, like air into a *vacuum.* If a thing was old and established, this was with him a certain proof of its having no solid foundation to rest upon: if it was new, it was good and right. Every paradox was to him a self-evident truth; every prejudice an undoubted absurdity. The weight of authority, the sanction of ages, the common consent of mankind, were vouchers only for ignorance, error, and imposture. Whatever shocked the feelings of others, conciliated his regard; whatever was light, extravagant, and vain, was to him a proportionable relief from the dulness and stupidity of established opinions. The worst of it however was, that he thus gave great encouragement to those who believe in all received absurdities, and are wedded to all existing abuses: his extravagance seeming to sanction their grossness and selfishness, as theirs were a full justification of his folly and eccentricity. (pp. 494-97)

The volume before us is introduced by an imperfect but touching Preface by Mrs Shelley, and consists almost wholly of original pieces, with the exception of **"Alastor, or the Spirit of Solitude"** . . . and the admirable Translation of the "Mayday Night," from Goethe's *Faustus.*

"Julian and Maddalo" (the first Poem in the collection) is a Conversation or Tale, full of that thoughtful and romantic humanity, but rendered perplexing and unattractive by that veil of shadowy or of glittering obscurity, which distinguished Mr Shelley's writings. The depth and tenderness of his feelings seems often to have interfered with the expression of them, as the sight becomes blind with tears. A dull, waterish vapour, clouds the aspect of his philosophical poetry, like that mysterious gloom which he has himself described as hanging over the *Medusa's Head* of Leonardo da Vinci. The metre of this poem, too, will not be pleasing to every body. It is in the antique taste of the rhyming parts of Beaumont and Fletcher and Ben Jonson—blank verse in its freedom and unbroken flow, falling into rhymes that appear altogether accidental—very colloquial in the diction—and sometimes sufficiently prosaic. (pp. 499-500)

The march of [the lines in **"Julian and Maddalo"**] is, it must be confessed, slow, solemn, sad: there is a sluggishness of feeling, a dearth of imagery, an unpleasant glare of lurid light. It appears to us, that in some poets, as well as in some painters, the organ of colour (to speak in the language of the adepts) predominates over that of form; and Mr Shelley is of the number. We have every where a profusion of dazzling hues, of glancing splendours, of floating shadows, but the objects on which they fall are bare, indistinct, and wild. There is something . . . that reminds us of the arid style and matter of Crabbe's versification, or that apes the labour and throes of parturition of Wordsworth's blank-verse. It is the preface to a story of Love and Madness—of mental anguish and philosophic remedies—not very intelligibly told, and left with most of its mysteries unexplained, in the true spirit of the modern metaphysical style—in which we suspect there is a due mixture of affectation and meagreness of invention.

This poem is, however, in Mr Shelley's best and *least mannered* manner. If it has less brilliancy, it has less extravagance and confusion. It is in his stanza-poetry, that his Muse chiefly runs riot, and baffles all pursuit of common comprehension or critical acumen. The **"Witch of Atlas,"** the *Triumph of Life,* and **"Marianne's Dream,"** are rhapsodies or allegories of this description; full of fancy and of fire, with glowing allusions and wild machinery, but which it is difficult to read through, from the disjointedness of the materials, the incongruous metaphors and violent transitions, and of which, after reading them through, it is impossible, in most instances, to guess the drift or the moral. They abound in horrible imaginings, like records of a ghastly dream;—life, death, genius, beauty, victory, earth, air, ocean, the trophies of the past, the shadows of the world to come, are huddled together in a strange and hurried dance of words, and all that appears clear, is the passion and paroxysm of thought of the poet's spirit. The poem entitled the *Triumph of Life,* is in fact a new and terrific *Dance of Death;* but it is thus Mr Shelley transposes the appellations of the commonest things, and subsists only in the violence of contrast. How little this poem is deserving of its title, how worthy it is of its author, what an example of the waste of power, and of genius 'made as flax,' and devoured by its own elementary ardours, let the reader judge. . . . Any thing more filmy, enigmatical, discontinuous, unsubstantial than this, we have not seen; nor yet more full of morbid genius and vivifying soul. We cannot help preferring **"The Witch of Atlas"** to **"Alastor, or the Spirit of Solitude"**; for, though the purport of each is equally perplexing and undefined, (both being a sort of mental voyage through the unexplored regions of space and time), the execution of the one is much less dreary and lamentable than that of the other. In the **"Witch,"** he has indulged his fancy more than his melancholy, and wantoned in the felicity of embryo and crude conceits even to excess. (pp. 502-04)

[It] is curious to remark every where the proneness to the marvellous and supernatural, in one who so resolutely set his face against every received mystery, and all traditional faith. Mr Shelley must have possessed, in spite of all his obnoxious and indiscreet scepticism, a large share of credulity and wondering curiosity in his composition, which he reserved from common use, and bestowed upon his own inventions and picturesque caricatures. To every other species of imposture or disguise he was inexorable; and indeed it is his only antipathy to established creeds and legitimate crowns that ever tears the veil from his *ideal* idolatries, and renders him clear and explicit. Indignation makes him pointed and intelligible enough, and breathes into his verse a spirit very different from his own boasted spirit of Love.

The **"Letter to a Friend in London"** shows the author in a pleasing and familiar, but somewhat prosaic light; and his **"Prince Athanase, a Fragment,"** is, we suspect, intended as a portrait of the writer. It is amiable, thoughtful, and not much overcharged. (p. 505)

[The] **"Ode for Liberty,"** though somewhat turbid and overloaded in the diction, we regard as a fair specimen of Mr Shelley's highest powers—whose eager animation wanted only a greater sternness and solidity to be sublime. The poem is dated *September* 1820. Such were then the author's aspirations. He lived to see the result,—and yet Earth does not roll its billows over the heads of its oppressors! (pp. 507-08)

We pass on to some of Mr Shelley's smaller pieces . . . , which we think are in general excellent and highly interesting. His **"Hymn of Pan"** we do not consider equal to Mr Keats's sounding lines in the *Endymion*. His **"Mont Blanc"** is full of beauties and of defects; but it is akin to its subject, and presents a wild and gloomy desolation. **"Ginevra,"** a fragment founded on a story in the first volume of the *Florentine Observer*, is like a troublous dream, disjointed, painful, oppressive, or like a leaden cloud, from which the big tears fall, and the spirit of the poet mutters deep-toned thunder. We are too much subject to these voluntary inflictions, these 'moods of mind,' these effusions of 'weakness and melancholy,' in the perusal of modern poetry. It has shuffled off, no doubt, its old pedantry and formality; but has at the same time lost all shape or purpose, except that of giving vent to some morbid feeling of the moment. The writer thus discharges a fit of the spleen or a paradox, and expects the world to admire and be satisfied. We are no longer annoyed at seeing the luxuriant growth of nature and fancy clipped into arm-chairs and peacocks' tails; but there is danger of having its stately products choked with unchecked underwood, or weighed down with gloomy nightshade, or eaten up with personality, like ivy clinging round and eating into the sturdy oak! The *Dirge*, at the conclusion of this fragment, is an example of the manner in which this craving after novelty, this desire 'to elevate and surprise,' leads us to 'overstep the modesty of nature,' and the bounds of decorum.

> Ere the sun through heaven once more has roll'd,
> *The rats in her heart*
> *Will have made their nest,*

And the worms be alive in her golden hair,
While the spirit that guides the sun,
Sits throned in his flaming chair,
    She shall sleep.

The 'worms' in this stanza are the old and traditional appendages of the grave;—the 'rats' are new and unwelcome intruders; but a modern artist would rather shock, and be disgusting and extravagant, than produce no effect at all, or be charged with a want of genius and originality. In the unfinished scenes of *Charles I.*, (a drama on which Mr Shelley was employed at his death) the *radical* humour of the author breaks forth, but 'in good set terms' and specious oratory. We regret that his premature fate has intercepted this addition to our historical drama. (pp. 508-09)

> *[William Hazlitt], "Shelley's 'Posthumous Poems'," in* The Edinburgh Review, *Vol. XL, No. LXXX, July, 1824, pp. 494-514.*

CHARLES LAMB   (letter date 1824)

[*An English essayist, critic, and poet, Lamb is chiefly remembered for his "Elia" essays, a series renowned for its witty, idiosyncratic treatment of everyday subjects. In this excerpt from a letter to Bernard Barton, Lamb offers a predominately negative appraisal of Shelley's poetry.*]

I can no more understand Shelley than you can. His poetry is 'thin sewn with profit or delight.' Yet I must point to your notice a sonnet [**"Lines to a Reviewer"**] conceivd and expressed with a witty delicacy. It is that addressed to one who hated him, but who could not persuade him to hate *him* again. His coyness to the other's passion (for hate demands a return as much as Love, and starves without it) is most arch and pleasant. Pray, like it very much.

For his theories and nostrums they are oracular enough, but I either comprehend 'em not, or there is miching malice and mischief in 'em. But for the most part ringing with their own emptiness. Hazlitt said well of 'em—Many are wiser and better for reading Shakspeare, but nobody was ever wiser or better for reading Sh—y. (pp. 436-37)

> *Charles Lamb, in a letter to Bernard Barton on August 17, 1824, in his* The Letters of Charles Lamb, *Vol. 2, edited by E. V. Lucas, J. M. Dent & Sons Ltd., and Methuen & Co. Ltd., 1935, pp. 436-38.*

SAMUEL TAYLOR COLERIDGE   (letter date 1830)

[*A poet and critic, Coleridge was central to the English Romantic movement and is considered one of the greatest literary critics in the English language. His most important contributions include his formulation of Romantic theory, his introduction of the ideas of the German Romantics to England, and his Shakespeare criticism. In the following excerpt from a letter to John E. Reade, Coleridge comments on Shelley's atheism and the effect his meeting with the poet Robert Southey had upon his beliefs. For Southey's response to Coleridge's remarks, see excerpt dated 1838.*]

I think as highly of Shelley's Genius—yea, and of his *Heart*—as you can do. Soon after he left Oxford, he went to the Lakes, poor fellow! and with some wish, I have understood, to see me; but I was absent, and Southey received him instead. Now, the very reverse of what would have been the case in ninety-nine instances of a hundred, I *might* have been of use to him, and Southey could not; for I should have sympathised with his poetico-metaphysical Reveries, (and the very word metaphysics is an abomination to Southey,) and Shelley would have felt that I understood him. His Atheism would not have scared *me*—for *me*, it would have been a semi-transparent Larva, soon to be *sloughed*, and, through which, I should have seen the true *Image; the final metamorphosis. Besides, I have ever thought *that* sort of Atheism the next best religion to Christianity—nor does the better faith, I have learnt from Paul and John, interfere with the cordial reverence I feel for Benedict Spinoza. As far as Robert Southey was concerned with him, I am quite certain that his harshness arose entirely from the frightful reports that had been made to him respecting Shelley's moral character and conduct—reports essentially false, but, for a man of Southey's strict regularity and habitual self-government, rendered plausible by Shelley's own wild words and horror of hypocrisy. (pp. 849-50)

> *Samuel Taylor Coleridge, in a letter to John E. Reade in December, 1830, in his* Collected Letters of Samuel Taylor Coleridge: 1826-1834, Vol. VI, *edited by Earl Leslie Griggs, Oxford at the Clarendon Press, Oxford, 1971, pp. 849-50.*

LEIGH HUNT   (essay date 1832)

[An English poet and essayist, Hunt is remembered as a literary critic who encouraged and influenced several Romantic poets, especially Shelley and Keats. In this excerpt from his 1832 introduction to The Masque of Anarchy, *Hunt describes the circumstances of the poem's composition, noting Shelley's devotion to liberty and political equality.]*

[*The Masque of Anarchy*] was written by Mr. Shelley on occasion of the bloodshed at Manchester, in the year 1819. I was editor of the *Examiner* at that time, and it was sent to me to be inserted or not in that journal as I thought fit. I did not insert it, because I thought that the public at large had not become sufficiently discerning to do justice to the sincerity and kind-heartedness of the spirit that walked in this flaming robe of verse. His charity was avowedly more than proportionate to his indignation; yet I thought that even the suffering part of the people, judging, not unnaturally, from their own feelings, and from the exasperation which suffering produces before it produces knowledge, would believe a hundred-fold in his anger, to what they would in his good intention; and this made me fear that the common enemy would take advantage of the mistake to do them both a disservice. Mr. Shelley's writings have since aided the general progress of knowledge in bringing about a wiser period; and an effusion, which would have got him cruelly misrepresented a few years back, will now do unequivocal honour to his memory, and shew everybody what a most considerate and kind, as well as fervent heart, the cause of the world has lost.

The poem, though written purposely in a lax and familiar measure, is highly characteristic of the author. It has the usual ardour of his tone, the unbounded sensibility by which he combines the most domestic with the most remote and fanciful images, and the patience, so beautifully checking, and, in fact, produced by, the extreme impatience of his moral feeling. His patience is the deposit of many impatiences, acting upon an equal measure of understanding and moral taste. His wisdom is the wisdom of a heart overcharged with sensibility, acquiring the profoundest notions of justice from the completest sympathy, and at once taking refuge from its pain, and working out its extremest purposes, in the adoption of a stubborn and loving fortitude which neutralizes resistance. His very strokes

of humour, while they startle with their extravagance and even ghastliness, cut to the heart with pathos. The fourth and fifth stanzas, for instance, of this Poem, involve an allusion, which becomes affecting from our knowing what he must have felt when he wrote it. It is to his children, who were taken from him by the late Lord Chancellor, under that preposterous law, by which every succeeding age might be made to blush for the tortures inflicted on the opinions of its predecessor.

"Anarchy, the Skeleton," riding through the streets, and grinning and bowing on each side of him,

> As well as if his education
> Had cost ten millions to the nation,

is another instance of the union of ludicrousness with terror. Hope, looking "more like Despair," and laying herself down before his horses' feet to die, is a touching image. The description of the rise and growth of the Public Enlightenment,

> —upborne on wings whose grain
> Was as the light of sunny rain,

and producing "thoughts" as he went,

> As stars from night's loose hair are shaken,

till on a sudden the prostrate multitude look up,

> and ankle-deep in blood,
> Hope, that maiden most serene,
> Was walking with a quiet mien,

is rich with the author's usual treasure of imagery and splendid words. The sixty-third is a delicious stanza, producing a most happy and comforting picture in the midst of visions of blood and tumult. We see the light from its cottage window. The substantial blessings of Freedom are nobly described; and lastly, the advice given by the poet, the great national measure recommended by him, is singularly striking as a *political anticipation*. It advises what has since taken place, and what was felt by the grown wisdom of the age to be the only thing which *could* take place, with effect, as a final rebuke and nullification of the Tories; to wit, a calm, lawful, and inflexible preparation for resistance in the shape of a protesting multitude,—the few against the many,—the laborious and suffering against the spoilt children of monopoly—Man-kind against Tory-kind. It is true the Poet recommends that there should be no active resistance, come what might; which is a piece of fortitude, however effective, which we believe was not contemplated by the Political Unions: yet, in point of the spirit of the thing, the success he anticipates has actually occurred, and after his very fashion; for there really has been no resistance, except by multitudinous protest. The Tories, however desirous they showed themselves to draw their swords, did not draw them. The battle was won without a blow. (pp. 225-27)

> *Leigh Hunt, in a preface to "The Masque of Anarchy," in* The Complete Works of Percy Bysshe Shelley: Poems, Vol. III *by Percy Bysshe Shelley, edited by Roger Ingpen and Walter E. Peck, 1926. Reprint by Gordian Press, 1965, pp. 225-33.*

ROBERT SOUTHEY   (letter date 1838)

[A late eighteenth- and early nineteenth-century English man of letters, Southey was a key member of the so-called Lake School of poetry, a group that included William Wordsworth and Samuel Taylor Coleridge. Responding to comments made by Coleridge

in a letter to Reade (see excerpt dated 1830), Southey describes to Reade his acquaintance with Shelley.]

Coleridge was entirely mistaken in what he says of my manner towards Shelley. So far from there having been any thing harsh or intolerant in it, I took a great liking to him, believed (most erroneously as it proved) that he would outgrow all his extravagances, that his heart would bring him right, and that the difference between us was that at that time he was just nineteen and I was eight and thirty. The observation appeared not to please him, for he would not allow that that could make any difference.

Coleridge was equally mistaken in saying that the reports of Shelley's moral character and conduct were essentially false. *I know them to be true,* and the story is the most frightful tragedy that I have ever known in real life. His metaphysics would never have shocked me. I told him that he was wrong in calling himself an Atheist which he delighted in doing, for that as far as he might be called any thing, he was a Pantheist. He had never heard the word before, and seemed much pleased at discovering what he really was. When he left this place where he resided some months we parted in mutual good will. He had not then entered upon his career of guilt.

The late Duke of Norfolk who knew Shelley's father, requested a neighbour of mine to notice him, and be of any use to him that he could. That neighbour introduced him to me, and as long as he remained here he was upon the most familiar terms in this house, coming to it whenever he pleased and always finding a cordial reception. His only complaint of me was that I would not talk Metaphysicks with him. (pp. 474-75)

Robert Southey, in a letter to John Edmund Reade on June 12, 1838, in New Letters of Robert Southey: 1811-1838, Vol. II, *edited by Kenneth Curry, Columbia University Press, 1965, pp. 474-75.*

MARY W. SHELLEY (essay date 1839)

[*Mary Shelley, best known for her novel* Frankenstein; or, The Modern Prometheus, *also wrote criticism, short stories, and travel essays. In this excerpt from her preface to a collection of Shelley's poems, Mary Shelley describes her husband's character and summarizes the central themes of his poetry.*]

The qualities that struck any one newly introduced to Shelley, were, first, a gentle and cordial goodness that animated his intercourse with warm affection, and helpful sympathy. The other, the eagerness and ardour with which he was attached to the cause of human happiness and improvement; and the fervent eloquence with which he discussed such subjects. His conversation was marked by its happy abundance, and the beautiful language in which he clothed his poetic ideas and philosophical notions. To defecate life of its misery and its evil, was the ruling passion of his soul: he dedicated to it every power of his mind, every pulsation of his heart. He looked on political freedom as the direct agent to effect the happiness of mankind; and thus any new-sprung hope of liberty inspired a joy and an exultation more intense and wild than he could have felt for any personal advantage. Those who have never experienced the workings of passion on general and unselfish subjects cannot understand this; and it must be difficult of comprehension to the younger generation rising around, since they cannot remember the scorn and hatred with which the partisans of reform were regarded some few years ago, nor the persecutions to which they were exposed. He had been from youth the victim of the state of feeling inspired by the reaction of the French

Revolution; and believing firmly in the justice and excellence of his view, it cannot be wondered that a nature as sensitive, as impetuous, and as generous as his, should put its whole force into the attempt to alleviate for others the evils of those systems from which he had himself suffered. Many advantages attended his birth; he spurned them all when balanced with what he considered his duties. He was generous to imprudence, devoted to heroism.

These characteristics breathe throughout his poetry. The struggle for human weal; the resolution firm to martyrdom; the impetuous pursuit; the glad triumph in good; the determination not to despair. Such were the features that marked those of his works which he regarded with most complacency, as sustained by a lofty subject and useful aim.

In addition to these, his poems may be divided into two classes,—the purely imaginative, and those which sprung from the emotions of his heart. Among the former may be classed **"The Witch of Atlas,"** *Adonais,* and his latest composition, left imperfect, *The Triumph of Life.* In the first of these particularly, he gave the reins to his fancy, and luxuriated in every idea as it rose; in all, there is that sense of mystery which formed an essential portion of his perception of life—a clinging to the subtler inner spirit, rather than to the outward form—a curious and metaphysical anatomy of human passion and perception.

The second class is, of course, the more popular, as appealing at once to emotions common to us all; some of these rest on the passion of love; others on grief and despondency; others on the sentiments inspired by natural objects. Shelley's conception of love was exalted, absorbing, allied to all that is purest and noblest in our nature, and warmed by earnest passion; such it appears when he gave it a voice in verse. Yet he was usually averse to expressing these feelings, except when highly idealised; and many of his more beautiful effusions he had cast aside, unfinished, and they were never seen by me till after I had lost him. Others, as for instance, **"Rosalind and Helen,"** and **"Lines written among the Euganean Hills,"** I found among his papers by chance; and with some difficulty urged him to complete them. There are others, such as the **"Ode to the Sky Lark,"** and **"The Cloud,"** which, in the opinion of many critics, bear a purer poetical stamp than any other of his productions. They were written as his mind prompted, listening to the carolling of the bird, aloft in the azure sky of Italy; or marking the cloud as it sped across the heavens, while he floated in his boat on the Thames.

No poet was ever warmed by a more genuine and unforced inspiration. His extreme sensibility gave the intensity of passion to his intellectual pursuits; and rendered his mind keenly alive to every perception of outward objects, as well as to his internal sensations. Such a gift is, among the sad vicissitudes of human life, the disappointments we meet, and the galling sense of our own mistakes and errors, fraught with pain; to escape from such, he delivered up his soul to poetry, and felt happy when he sheltered himself from the influence of human sympathies, in the wildest regions of fancy. His imagination has been termed too brilliant, his thoughts too subtle. He loved to idealise reality; and this is a taste shared by few. We are willing to have our passing whims exalted into passions, for this gratifies our vanity; but few of us understand or sympathise with the endeavour to ally the love of abstract beauty, and adoration of abstract good, . . . with our sympathies with our kind. In this Shelley resembled Plato; both taking more delight in the abstract and the ideal, than in the special and tangible. This did not result from imitation; for it was not till Shelley resided in Italy that he made Plato his study; he then translated his *Symposium* and his *Ion;* and the English language boasts of no more brilliant composition, than Plato's "Praise of Love," translated by Shelley. To return to his own poetry. The luxury of imagination, which sought nothing beyond itself, as a child burthens itself with spring flowers, thinking of no use beyond the enjoyment of gathering them, often showed itself in his verses: they will be only appreciated by minds which have resemblance to his own; and the mystic subtlety of many of his thoughts will share the same fate. The metaphysical strain that characterises much of what he has written, was, indeed, the portion of his works to which, apart from those whose scope was to awaken mankind to aspirations for what he considered the true and good, he was himself particularly attached. There is much, however, that speaks to the many. When he would consent to dismiss these huntings after the obscure, which, entwined with his nature as they were, he did with difficulty, no poet ever expressed in sweeter, more heart-reaching or more passionate verse, the gentler or more forcible emotions of the soul.

A wise friend once wrote to Shelley "You are still very young, and in certain essential respects you do not yet sufficiently perceive that you are so." It is seldom that the young know what youth is, till they have got beyond its period; and time was not given him to attain this knowledge. It must be remembered that there is the stamp of such inexperience on all he wrote; he had not completed his nine-and-twentieth year when he died. The calm of middle life did not add the seal of the virtues which adorn maturity to those generated by the vehement spirit of youth. Through life also he was a martyr to ill health, and constant pain wound up his nerves to a pitch of susceptibility that rendered his views of life different from those of a man in the enjoyment of healthy sensations. Perfectly gentle and forbearing in manner, he suffered a good deal of internal irritability, or rather excitement, and his fortitude to bear was almost always on the stretch; and thus, during a short life, had gone through more experience of sensation, than many whose existence is protracted. "If I die to-morrow," he said, on the eve of his unanticipated death, "I have lived to be older than my father." The weight of thought and feeling burdened him heavily; you read his sufferings in his attentuated frame, while you perceived the mastery he held over them in his animated countenance and brilliant eyes.

He died, and the world showed no outward sign; but his influence over mankind, though slow in growth, is fast augmenting, and in the ameliorations that have taken place in the political state of his country, we may trace in part the operation of his arduous struggles. His spirit gathers peace in its new state from the sense that, though late, his exertions were not made in vain, and in the progress of the liberty he so fondly loved. (pp. xi-xiv)

Mary W. Shelley, "Mrs. Shelley's Preface to the Collected Poems, 1839," in *The Complete Works of Percy Bysshe Shelley: Poems,* Vol. I, by Percy Bysshe Shelley, edited by Roger Ingpen and Walter E. Peck, 1926. Reprint by Gordian Press, 1965, pp. xi-xv.

EDGAR ALLAN POE (essay date 1849)

[*Considered one of America's most outstanding men of letters, Poe was a distinguished poet, novelist, essayist, journalist, short story writer, editor, and critic. Although Poe and his literary criticism were subject to controversy in his own lifetime, he is*

now valued for his literary theories. In this excerpt from an essay first published in 1849, Poe offers his response to Shelley, noting particularly his sincerity and originality.]

If ever mortal "wreaked his thoughts upon expression," it was *Shelley.* If ever poet sang—as a bird sings—earnestly—impulsively—with utter abandonment—to himself solely—and for the mere joy of his own song—that poet was, the author of *The Sensitive Plant.* Of Art—beyond that which is instinctive with Genius—he either had little or disdained all. He *really* disdained that rule which is an emanation from Law, because his own soul was Law in itself. His rhapsodies are but the rough notes—the stenographic memoranda of poems—memoranda which, because they were all sufficient for his own intelligence, he cared not to be at the trouble of writing out in full for mankind. In all his works we find no conception thoroughly wrought. For this reason he is the most fatiguing of poets. Yet he wearies in saying too little rather than too much. What, in him, seems the diffuseness of one idea, is the conglomerate concision of many: and this species of concision it is, which renders him obscure. With such a man, to imitate was out of the question. It would have served no purpose; for he spoke to his own spirit alone, which would have comprehended no alien tongue. Thus he was profoundly original. His quaintness arose from intuitive perception of that truth to which Bacon alone has given distinct utterance:—"There is no exquisite Beauty which has not some strangeness in its proportions." But whether obscure, original, or quaint, Shelley had no *affectations.* He was at all times sincere. (p. 1445)

Edgar Allan Poe, "Marginalia," in his Essays and Reviews, *Viking Press, 1984, pp. 1445-72.*

MARGARET FULLER OSSOLI (essay date 1850?)

[*A distinguished critic and early feminist, Fuller (later Ossoli) played an important role in the developing cultural life of the United States during the first half of the nineteenth century. She wrote social, art, and music criticism, but she is most acclaimed as a literary critic; many rank her with Poe as the finest of her era. Here, Fuller expresses her great admiration for Shelley's poetry. As the date of Fuller's remarks is unknown, the year of her death has been used to date this entry.*]

In Europe the fame of Shelley has risen superior to the clouds that darkened its earlier days, hiding his true image from his fellow-men, and from his own sad eyes oftentimes the common light of day. As a thinker, men have learned to pardon what they consider errors in opinion for the sake of singular nobleness, purity, and love in his main tendency or spirit. As a poet, the many faults of his works having been acknowledged, there are room and place to admire his far more numerous and exquisite beauties.

The heart of the man, few, who have hearts of their own, refuse to reverence, and many, even of devoutest Christians, would not refuse the book which contains *Queen Mab* as a Christmas gift. For it has been recognized that the founder of the Christian church would have suffered one to come unto him, who was in faith and love so truly what he sought in a disciple, without regard to the form his doctrine assumed.

The qualities of his poetry have often been analyzed, and the severer critics, impatient of his exuberance, or unable to use their accustomed spectacles in the golden mist that broods over all he has done, deny him high honors; but the soul of aspiring youth, untrammelled by the canons of taste, and untamed by scholarly discipline, swells into rapture at his lyric sweetness, finds ambrosial refreshment from his plenteous fancies, catches fire at his daring thought, and melts into boundless weeping at his tender sadness—the sadness of a soul betrothed to an ideal unattainable in this present sphere.

For ourselves, we dispute not with the *doctrinaires* or the critics. We cannot speak dispassionately of an influence that has been so dear to us. Nearer than the nearest companions of life actual has Shelley been to us. Many other great ones have shone upon us, and all who ever did so shine are still resplendent in our firmament, for our mental life has not been broken and contradictory, but thus far we "see what we foresaw." But Shelley seemed to us an incarnation of what was sought in the sympathies and desires of instinctive life, a light of dawn, and a foreshowing of the weather of this day.

When still in childish years, the **"Hymn to Intellectual Beauty"** fell in our way. In a green meadow, skirted by a rich wood, watered by a lovely rivulet, made picturesque by a mill a little farther down, sat a party of young persons gayer than, and almost as inventive, as those that told the tales recorded by Boccaccio. . . . [One day] we sought relief in personating birds or insects; and now it was the Libellula who, tired of wild flitting and darting, rested on the grassy bank and read aloud the **"Hymn to Intellectual Beauty,"** torn by chance from the leaf of a foreign magazine.

It was one of those chances which we ever remember as the interposition of some good angel in our fate. Solemn tears marked the change of mood in our little party, and with the words

Have I not kept my vow?

began a chain of thoughts whose golden links still bind the years together.

Two or three years passed. The frosty Christmas season came; the trees cracked with their splendid burden of ice, the old wooden country house was banked up with high drifts of the beautiful snow, and the Libellula became the owner of Shelley's *Poems*. It was her Christmas gift, and for three days and three nights she ceased not to extract its sweets; and how familiar still in memory every object seen from the chair in which she sat enchanted during those three days, memorable to her as those of July to the French nation! The fire, the position of the lamp, the variegated shadows of that alcoved room, the bright stars up to which she looked with such a feeling of congeniality from the contemplation of this starry soul,—O, could but a De Quincey describe those days in which the bridge between the real and ideal rose unbroken! He would not do it, though, as *Suspiria de Profundis,* but as sighs of joy upon the mountain height.

The poems we read then are what every one still reads, the **"Julian and Maddalo,"** with its profound revelations of the inward life; **"Alastor,"** the soul sweeping like a breeze through nature; and some of the minor poems. *Queen Mab,* the *Prometheus,* and other more formal works we have not been able to read much. It was not when he tried to express opinions which the wrongs of the world had put into his head, but when he abandoned himself to the feelings which nature had implanted in his own breast, that Shelley seemed to us so full of inspiration, and it is so still.

In reply to all that can be urged against him by people of whom we do not wish to speak ill,—for surely "they know not what they do,"—we are wont simply to refer to the fact that he was the only man who redeemed the human race from suspicion to

the embittered soul of Byron. "Why," said Byron, "he is a man who would willingly die for others. *I am sure of it.*"

Yes! balance that against all the ill you can think of him, that he was a man able to live wretched for the sake of speaking sincerely what he supposed to be truth, willing to die for the good of his fellows! (pp. 149-52)

Margaret Fuller Ossoli, "Shelley's Poems," in her Life Without and Life Within; or, Reviews, Narratives, Essays, and Poems, *edited by Arthur B. Fuller, 1859. Reprint by The Tribune Association, 1869, pp. 149-52.*

JAMES THOMSON (essay date 1860)

[A poet, essayist, and translator, Thomson published what is considered one of the most powerful poems of the Victorian era, yet he is largely overshadowed by the major writers of his time. His reputation rests primarily on "The City of Dreadful Night," which is praised as a compelling expression of religious despair in Victorian society. In this excerpt from an essay first published in 1860, Thomson decries the lack of respect given Shelley in the Victorian age, praising the poet's "musicalness" and evaluating his subject matter, intelligence, emotional point of view, and depth of inspiration.]

Probably no man of this century has suffered more and more severely, both in person and reputation, from . . . rash convictive bigotry than Percy Bysshe Shelley. Florence to the living Dante was not more cruelly unjust than England to the living Shelley. Only now, nearly forty years after his death, do we begin to discern his true glory. It is well that this glory is such as can afford to wait for recognition; that it is one of the permanent stars of heaven, not a rocket to be ruined by a night of storm and rain. I confess that I have long been filled with astonishment and indignation at the manner in which he is treated by the majority of our best living writers. Emerson is serenely throned above hearing him at all; Carlyle only hears him "shriek hysterically;" Mrs. Browning discovers him "blind with his white ideal;" Messrs. Ruskin and Kingsley treat him much as senior schoolboys treat the youngster who easily "walks over their heads" in class,—with reluctant tribute of admiration copiously qualified with sneers, pinches, and kicks. Even Bulwer (who, intellectually worthless as he is, now and then serves well as a straw to show how the wind blows among the higher and more educated classes), even Bulwer can venture to look down upon him with pity, to pat him patronisingly on the back, to sneer at him—in *Ernest Maltravers*—with a sneer founded upon a maimed quotation. . . . Now, I do not expect that Shelley—any more than piety and lofty thought and heroic action—will ever be extensively popular; I admit that to himself more than to most poets are his own grand words applicable,—"the jury that sits in judgment upon a poet, belonging as he does to all time, must be composed of his peers: it must be impanneled by time from the selectest of the wise of many generations." (pp. 14-15)

A poet, in our restricted sense of the term, may be defined, an inspired singer; the singing, the spontaneous musical utterance being essential to the poetical character. Great learning, profound thought, and keen moral insight may all enrich a volume, which shall yet, lacking this instinctive harmony, be no poem—Verse equally with prose may be unpoetic through this fatal want. (p. 16)

In musicalness, in free and, as it were, living melody, the poems of Shelley are unsurpassed, and on the whole, I think, unequalled by any others in our literature. Compared with that of most others his language is as river to a canal,—a river ever flowing "at its own sweet will," and whose music is the unpurposed result of its flowing. So subtly sweet and rich are the tones, so wonderfully are developed the perfect cadences, that the meaning of the words of the singing is lost and dissolved in the overwhelming rapture of the impression. I have often fancied, while reading them, that his words were really transparent, or that they throbbed with living lustres. Meaning is therein, firm and distinct, but "scarce visible through extreme loveliness;" so that the mind is often dazzled from perception of the surpassing grandeur and power of his creations. I doubt not that Apollo was mightier than Hercules, though his divine strength was veiled in the splendour of his symmetry and beauty more divine.

But when we have allowed that a man is pre-eminently a singer, the question naturally follows, what is the matter of his song? Does his royal robe of verse envelop a real king of men, or one who is intrinsically a slave? And here may fitly be adduced Wordsworth's remark, that the style is less the *dress* than the *incarnation* of the thought. Noble features have been informed by ignoble natures, and beautiful language has expressed thoughts impure and passions hateful; great hearts have pulsed in unsightly bodies, and grand ideas have found but crabbed utterance: yet still it is true that generally the countenance is a legible index to the spirit, and the style to the thought.

With this presumption in his favour, we enter upon four inquiries. (I.) What are the favourite subjects of Shelley's song—great or small? (II.) Is his treatment of these great-minded? (III.) Is it great-hearted? And, rising to the climax. (IV.) Is it such as to entitle him to the epithet *inspired?*

(I.)The favourite subjects of Shelley's song, the speculations to which his intellect continually gravitates from the petty interests of the hour, are certainly great and important above all others. (I omit one theme, whose treatment is common to all poets, so that we conceive it as inseparable from the poetic character,—the beauty and harmony of the visible universe: in the celebration of which, however, Shelley displays an intense fervour of admiration and love which almost isolates him above his compeers.) The questions concerning the existence of God, the moral law of the universe, the immortality of the soul, the independent being of what is called the material world, the perfectibility of man; these and their kindred perpetually fascinate his mind to their investigation. It may be considered by many—and not without some show of reason—that mere addictedness to discourse on great subjects is no proof of a great mind: crude painters always daub "high art," adolescent journalists stoop to nothing below Epics; nay, Macaulay long since told us that the very speculations of which we speak are distinctive of immaturity both in nations and in men. Nevertheless, believing that the essence of poetry and philosophy is communication with the Infinite and the Eternal, I venture to conclude that to be strongly inclined to such communication is to be gifted with the first requisite for a poet and a philosopher. The valiant heart may prove victorious without the strong arm, but the strong arm without the valiant heart must be beaten ignominiously for ever.

(II.) But have his thoughts and his conceptions a magnanimity befitting these subjects? He upholds strenuously the Manichean doctrine, that the world is the battle-field of a good and an evil spirit, each aboriginal; of whom the evil has been and still is the more powerful, but the good shall ultimately triumph. Let those who scoff so liberally at this, account for the existence of evil and a devil created by an omnipotent all-holy God. How magnificent is his conception of these hostile powers, symbolised in the eagle and serpent, in the opening of *The Revolt of Islam;* how sublime is it in the *Prometheus Unbound,* where they are represented by Jupiter and Prometheus!

He proclaims enthusiastically the Idealism of Plato, of Spinoza, of Berkeley, of Kant. Let those who so stolidly sneer at this, expound by what possibility spirit and matter can influence each other without one attribute in common; or let them demonstrate the existence of matter apart from our perception; or let them show, if there be but one existing substance, that it is such as we should call matter rather than spirit. How glorious are his expositions of this philosophy in the **"Ode to Heaven"** and the speeches of Ahasuerus in *Hellas!*

He devoted himself heart and mind to the doctrine of the perfectibility of human nature; an intrinsic perfectibility to eventuate in a heaven on earth realised by the noble endeavours of man himself; not that which is complacently patronised by many so-called Christians, who are agreed to die and accept a perfect nature as a free gift, when they can no longer live imperfect. As if the severe laws of the universe permitted partial gifts, any more than they permit gainful robberies! Though I must consider Shelley mistaken in this belief, I yet honour and not blame him for it. For his nature must have been most pure and noble, since it could persuade his peculiarly introspective mind of its truth. Right or wrong, it is the very mainspring of his philosophic system. In *Queen Mab,* in *The Revolt of Islam,* in the *Prometheus Unbound,* its expression glows with the solemn inspiration of prophecy. As Scott was the poet of the past, and Goethe of the present, so was Shelley of the future; the thought of whose developed triumphs always kindles him into rapture. However dissident, we cannot but reverence so sublime and unselfish an enthusiasm: perchance, were we more like him in goodness, we would be more like him in faith. Expand the stage from our earth to the universe; the time from one life to an infinite succession of lives, let the *dramatis personae* be not men only but all living souls; and this catastrophe, if catastrophe there must be, is the most righteous and lofty conclusion ever suggested for the great drama.

Of his opinions concerning the right relations of the sexes, I can only say that they appear to me radically correct. And of his infidelity, that he attacked not so much Christianity as Priestianity—that blind unspiritual orthodoxy which freezes the soul and fetters the mind, vilifying the holiest essence of all religion. . . . [In] all his thoughts one is struck by a certain loftiness and breadth characteristic of the best minds. It is as if they looked around from the crest of a mountain, with vision unbaffled by the crowd and the chimney-tops. Now, exactly as the height at which a person stands may be calculated from any one object on his horizon as well as from a hundred, so one of these superior thoughts is in itself proof sufficient of an elevated mind. For quantity is the measure of low things, but quality of high. Ten small apples may be worth more than one large; but not any number of small thoughts can equal one great: ten weak arms may be stronger than one stalwart; but what number of weak minds can equal one that is powerful?

(III.) What moral emotion, pure or impure, noble or mean, generous or selfish, does Shelley effuse through his works? The question has been partly answered already; for in a poet, whose theme is concrete with man and abstract with destiny, the spirit refuses to be analysed into thought and passion, being the identity of the two. Morally, he is indeed sainted. Never yet did man thrill and glow with more love of his fellows, more self-sacrificing sympathy with all life, more hatred of fraud and cruelty—yet hatred interfused with the tenderest pity, more noble independence, candour, and intrepidity, more devoted reverence for goodness and truth. In what is understood by the present age as a truly Christian spirit, he bears comparison with the holiest of Christians. The creeds, the rituals, the ceremonies,—those media which common men require to temper the else intolerable splendour of divine truth,—he did not need: his eagle eye could gaze unblenching upon the cloudless sun. And his life incarnated his poetry. He was his own Prometheus. . . . He perceived—who better?—the symbolism of the visible world; he appreciated—who more rapturously?— its divine beauty; but he did not rest here: he lived higher to the beauty of that which is symbolised, to the beauty of that which is called "of holiness," to the laws of that realm which is eternal. He was not "master of the revels to mankind," but prophet and preacher. His music was as the harping of David to charm away the evil spirit from Saul.

And thus we have crossed the threshold of our last inquiry,— is he entitled, in a high sense, to be called *inspired?* That he was a singer who sang songs beautiful, wise, and pure, may be affirmed of many a poet, though of no two with the same emphasis. What is it then which differentiates him from the second-class poets, and exalts him to sit with Isiah and Dante as one of that small choir of chief singers who are called transcendent? It is that of which I but now spoke; it is that of which he is so often accused under the name of mysticism. I dare affirm that no great writer is less obscure in manner, in expression, than he: obscure in matter he is, and ever must be, to those in whom is not developed the faculty correlative to those ideas in whose expression he supremely delights. Were the most of us born deaf, we should reprobate as obscure and mystical those gifted men who dilated upon the ravishment of music. And to the ideal or spiritual harmonies, perfect and eternal, to whose rhythm and melody the universe is attuned, so that it is fitly named Cosmos,—to these we *are* most of us deaf; and whoever with reverence and love and rapture is devoted to their celebration—be it Plato or Swedenborg, Emerson or Shelley—shall for ever to the great mass be as one who is speaking in an unknown tongue, or who is raving of phantasies which have no foundation in reality.

Therefore the accusations of mysticism but ignorantly affirm that he was most intensely and purely a poet. Plato in the "Ion" (Shelley's translation), says:—"For the authors of those great poems which we admire, do not attain to excellence through the rules of any art; but they utter their beautiful melodies of verse in a state of inspiration, and, as it were, *possessed* by a spirit not their own." And again, "For a poet is indeed a thing ethereally light, winged and sacred; nor can he compose anything worth calling poetry until he becomes inspired, and, as it were, mad . . . For whilst a man retains any portion of the thing called reason, he is utterly incompetent to produce poetry or to vaticinate." This great truth has been enounced or implied by all true philosophers; though sadly abused by uninspired poetasters, and as obviously obnoxious as the Berkeleyan Idealism to stupid and unavailing sneers. Shelley himself, in that *Defence of Poetry* which is one of the most beautiful prose-pieces in the language, and which in serene elevation of tone, and expanse and subtlety of thought is worthy of Plato or Emerson, repeatedly and throughout insists upon it as the essential law of poetic creation.

The only true, or inspired poetry, is always from within, not from without. The experience contained in it has been spiritu-

ally transmuted from lead into gold. It is severely logical, the most trivial of its adornments being subservient to, and suggested by, the dominant idea; any departure from whose dictates would be the "falsifying of a revelation." It is unadulterated with worldly wisdom, deference to prevailing opinions, mere talent or cleverness. Its anguish is untainted by the gall of bitterness, its joy is never selfish, its grossness is never obscene. It perceives always the profound identity underlying all surface differences. It is a living organism, not a dead aggregate, and its music is the expression of the law of its growth; so that it could no more be set to a different melody than could a rose-tree be consummated with lilies or violets. It is most philosophic when most enthusiastic; the clearest light of its wisdom being shed from the keenest fire of its love. It is a synthesis not arithmetical, but algebraical; that is to say, its particular subjects are universal symbols, its predicates universal laws: hence it is infinitely suggestive. It is ever-fresh wonder at the infinite mystery, ever-young faith in the eternal Soul. Whatever be its mood, we feel that it is not self-possessed but God-possessed; whether the God come down serene and stately as Jove, when a swan he wooed Leda; or with overwhelming might insupportably burning, as when he consumed Semele.

These distinctive marks of the highest poetry I find displayed in the works of Shelley more gloriously than in those of any other poet in our language. As we must study Shakespeare for knowledge of idealised human nature, and Fielding for knowledge of human nature unidealised, and Carlyle's *French Revolution* as the unapproached model of history, and Currer Bell's *Villette* to learn the highest capabilities of the novel, and Ruskin for the true philosophy of art, and Emerson for quintessential philosophy; so must we study, and so will future men more and more study, Shelley for quintessential poetry. It was a good nomenclator who first called him the poet of poets. (pp. 16-24)

> *James Thomson, "Shelley," in his* Shelley, a Poem: With Other Writings Relating to Shelley, *n.p., 1884, pp. 14-25.*

H. A. TAINE   (essay date 1863-64)

[*Taine was a French philosopher, critic, and historian who studied the influence of environment and heredity on the development of human character. In his well-known work,* Histoire de la littérature anglaise, *from which the following excerpt is drawn, Taine describes the otherworldly qualities of Shelley's life and poetry, noting particularly the importance of nature to the poet. Taine's comments were first published in 1863-64.*]

[Shelley], one of the greatest poets of the age, son of a rich baronet, beautiful as an angel, of extraordinary precocity, gentle, generous, tender, overflowing with all the gifts of heart, mind, birth, and fortune, marred his life, as it were, wantonly, by allowing his conduct to be guided by an enthusiastic imagination which he should have kept for his verses. From his birth he had "the vision" of sublime beauty and happiness; and the contemplation of an ideal world set him in arms against the real. Having refused at Eton to be a fag of the big boys, he was treated by boys and masters with a revolting cruelty; suffered himself to be made a martyr, refused to obey, and, falling back into forbidden studies, began to form the most immoderate and most poetical dreams. He judged society by the oppression which he underwent, and man by the generosity which he felt in himself; thought that man was good, and society bad, and that it was only necessary to suppress established institutions to make earth "a paradise." He became a republican, a communist, preached fraternity, love, even abstinence from flesh, and as a means the abolition of kings, priests, and God. We can fancy the indignation which such ideas roused in a society so obstinately attached to established order—so intolerant, in which, above the conservative and religious instincts, Cant spoke like a master. Shelley was expelled from the university; his father refused to see him; the Lord Chancellor, by a decree, took from him, as being unworthy, the custody of his two children; finally, he was obliged to quit England. I forgot to say that at eighteen he married a young girl of inferior rank, that they separated, that she committed suicide, that he undermined his health by his excitement and suffering, and that to the end of his life he was nervous or ill. Is not this the life of a genuine poet? Eyes fixed on the splendid apparitions with which he peopled space, he went through the world not seeing the high road, stumbling over the stones of the roadside. He possessed not that knowledge of life which most poets share in common with novelists. Seldom has a mind been seen in which thought soared in loftier regions, and more removed from actual things. When he tried to create characters and events—in *Queen Mab,* in "Alastor," in *The Revolt of Islam,* in *Prometheus*—he only produced unsubstantial phantoms. Once only, in the *Cenci,* did he inspire a living figure (Beatrice) worthy of Webster or old Ford; but in some sort this was in spite of himself, and because in it the sentiments were so unheard of and so strained that they suited superhuman conceptions. Elsewhere his world is throughout beyond our own. The laws of life are suspended or transformed. We move in Shelley's world between heaven and earth, in abstractions, dreamland, symbolism: the beings float in it like those fantastic figures which we see in the clouds, and which alternately undulate and change form capriciously, in their robes of snow and gold.

For souls thus constituted, the great consolation is nature. They are too finely sensitive to find amusement in the spectacle and picture of human passions. Shelley instinctively avoided that spectacle; the sight re-opened his own wounds. He was happier in the woods, at the sea-side, in contemplation of grand landscapes. The rocks, clouds, and meadows, which to ordinary eyes seem dull and insensible, are, to a wide sympathy, living and divine existences, which are an agreeable change from men. No virgin smile is so charming as that of the dawn, nor any joy more triumphant than that of the ocean when its waves swell and shimmer, as far as the eye can reach, under the lavish splendor of heaven. At this sight the heart rises unwittingly to the sentiment of ancient legends, and the poet perceives in the inexhaustible bloom of things the peaceful soul of the great mother by whom every thing grows and is supported. Shelley spent most of his life in the open air, especially in his boat; first on the Thames, then on the Lake of Geneva, then on the Arno, and in the Italian waters. He loved desert and solitary places, where man enjoys the pleasure of believing infinite what he sees, infinite as his soul. And such was this wide ocean, and this shore more barren than its waves. This love was a deep Teutonic instinct, which, allied to pagan emotions, produced his poetry, pantheistic and yet full of thought, almost Greek and yet English, in which fancy plays like a foolish, dreamy child, with the splendid skein of forms and colors. A cloud, a plant, a sunrise,—these are his characters: they were those of the primitive poets, when they took the lightning for a bird of fire, and the clouds for the flocks of heaven. But what a secret ardor beyond these splendid images, and how we feel the heat of the furnace beyond the colored phantoms, which it sets afloat over the horizon! Has any one since Shak-

speare and Spenser lighted on such tender and such grand ecstasies? Has any one painted so magnificently the cloud which watches by night in the sky, enveloping in its net the swarm of golden bees, the stars:

> The sanguine sunrise, with his meteor eyes,
> And his burning plumes outspread,
> Leaps on the back of my sailing rack,
> When the morning star shines dead . . .
> That orbed maiden with white fire laden,
> Whom mortals call the moon,
> Glides glimmering o'er my fleece-like floor,
> By the midnight breezes strewn.

Read again those verses on the garden, in which the sensitive plant dreams. Alas! they are the dreams of the poet, and the happy visions which floated in his virgin heart up to the moment when it opened out and withered. (pp. 535-37)

Every thing lives [in *The Sensitive Plant*], every thing breathes and yearns for something. This poem, the story of a plant, is also the story of a soul—Shelley's soul, the sensitive. Is it not natural to confound them? Is there not a community of nature amongst all the dwellers in this world? Verily there is a soul in every thing; in the universe is a soul; be the existence what it will, uncultured or rational, defined or vague, ever beyond its sensible form shines a secret essence and something divine, which we catch sight of by sublime illuminations, never reaching or penetrating it. It is this presentiment and yearning which sustains all modern poetry,—now in Christian meditations, as with Campbell and Wordsworth, now in pagan visions, as with Keats and Shelley. They hear the great heart of nature beat; they wish to reach it; they try all spiritual and sensible approaches, through Judea and through Greece, by consecrated doctrines and by proscribed dogmas. In this splendid and fruitless effort the greatest become exhausted and die. Their poetry, which they drag with them over these sublime tracks, is torn to pieces. (p. 537)

> *H. A. Taine, "Modern Life: Ideas and Productions,"*
> *in his* History of English Literature, *translated by H.*
> *Van Laun, 1873. Reprint by John B. Alden, Pub-*
> *lisher, 1887, pp. 507-38.*

RALPH WALDO EMERSON   (letter date 1868)

[Emerson was one of the most influential figures of the nineteenth century. An American essayist and poet, he founded the Transcendental movement and shaped a distinctly American philosophy which embraces optimism, individuality, and mysticism. In the following excerpt from a letter to James Hutchinson Stirling, Emerson comments briefly on Shelley.]

But Shelley,—was he the poet? He was a man in whom the spirit of the Age was poured,—man of aspiration, heroic character; but poet? Excepting a few well known lines about a cloud & a skylark, I could never read one of his hundreds of pages. . . . (p. 19)

> *Ralph Waldo Emerson, in a letter to James Hutch-*
> *inson Stirling on June 1, 1868, in his* The Letters of
> Ralph Waldo Emerson, *Vol. 6, edited by Ralph L.*
> *Rusk, Columbia University Press, 1939, pp. 18-19.*

WILLIAM M. ROSSETTI   (lecture date 1886)

[An English art critic and man of letters and one of the original members of the Pre-Raphaelite Brotherhood, Rossetti was an ap-

preciative critic of Shelley's poetry. In this excerpt from a lecture delivered to the Shelley Society in 1886, Rossetti summarizes his interpretation of Prometheus Unbound.]

[In my view of **Prometheus Unbound**] Prometheus is the Mind of Man, Asia is Nature, Jupiter is the Vicissitude of the World transmuted into anthropomorphic deity, and Demogorgon is Eternity. . . . I will with utmost succinctness say a few words to sum up the intellectual and moral bearing of a poem than which, as *Blackwood's Magazine* averred in 1820 [see excerpt above by Lockhart], ''it is quite impossible that there should exist a more pestiferous mixture of blasphemy, sedition, and sensuality.'' I read it thus.

The Universe (spoken of as Heaven, Earth, and Light) is eternal and self-existing: it had no creator. The primary powers of the Universe, or (as we may say) its spiritual functions, are Love, Fate, Occasion, Chance, and Change. Of these no beginning and no origin can be predicated, nor yet any end. Of Man, the earliest age is called the Saturnian Age, when Time became a factor in the world. Men in that age, being intellectually undeveloped, lived a natural and therefore so far a happy life, like animals, as indeed like plants. Ultimately Human Mind was evolved, or, mythically speaking, Prometheus came into being, and was united to Nature, as in the espousals of man and wife. One of the first acts of Human Mind was to create a God in his own image: he assigned wisdom to Jupiter—that is, to the Vicissitude of the World—and ascribed to him the dominion of Heaven, stipulating only that man should be free—free in will and in act. The mere animal happiness, or natural conformity, of man had lapsed with the birth of Mind: under the theocracy which the mind of man had established, everything went amiss. The natural operations of the Vicissitude of the World, such as want, toil, and disease, became grievously oppressive when they were regarded as the decree of Omniscient Omnipotence; and the spirit of mankind was a theatre of dismal cravings and chafings. To this catastrophe of all human well-being the Mind of Man supplied numerous and noble palliatives; but it sank beneath the stern theocratic sway—Prometheus was bound and tortured. Still the potential remedy for the multiform and monstrous evil remained in the human mind itself—it remains in the human mind at this moment. When the mind shall finally have rejected the delusions (such Shelley considered them) of theocracy, and shall have purged itself on the dark passions of hatred and revenge, then will the moment of emancipation be sounding. Eternity itself will conspire with the human mind to launch the world of man upon a new career—a career of boundless progression, in which even the planet which man inhabits will participate. The theocracy, with all its attendant evils, will vanish into nothingness; the Human Mind will be re-united to Nature in indissoluble and boundless concord; and only chance and death and mutability will dispute with man the future of his globe. (pp. 71-2)

> *William M. Rossetti, ''Shelley's 'Prometheus Unbound': A Study of Its Meaning and Personages,'' in* The Shelley Society's Papers, *1888. Reprint by AMS Press, 1975, pp. 50-72.*

MATTHEW ARNOLD   (essay date 1888)

[*Arnold is considered one of the most influential authors of the later Victorian period in England. While he is well known today as a poet, in his own time he asserted his greatest influence through his prose writings. Arnold's forceful literary commentary, which is based on his humanistic belief in the value of balance and clarity in literature, significantly shaped modern critical the-*

ory. Arnold's description of Shelley as an ''ineffectual angel'' in the essay excerpted below had a substantial influence on later criticism.]

It is [Shelley's] poetry, above everything else, which for many people establishes that he is an angel. . . . Let no one suppose that a want of humour and a self-delusion such as Shelley's have no effect upon a man's poetry. The man Shelley, in very truth, is not entirely sane, and Shelley's poetry is not entirely sane either. The Shelley of actual life is a vision of beauty and radiance, indeed, but availing nothing, effecting nothing. And in poetry, no less than in life, he is 'a beautiful *and ineffectual* angel, beating in the void his luminous wings in vain.' (pp. 251-52)

> *Matthew Arnold, ''Shelley,'' in his* Essays in Criticism, *second series,* Macmillan and Co., Limited, *1888, pp. 205-52.*

ALGERNON CHARLES SWINBURNE   (poem date 1892)

[*Swinburne, an English poet renowned during his lifetime for the technical mastery of his lyric poetry, is remembered today as a preeminent symbol of rebellion against the Victorian age. In a time when poets were expected to reflect and uphold contemporary morality, Swinburne believed that his only vocation was to express beauty. The following poem is Swinburne's tribute to Shelley on the centenary of his birth.*]

Now a hundred years agone among us came
Down from some diviner sphere of purer flame,
Clothed in flesh to suffer, maimed of wings to soar,
One whom hate once hailed as now love hails by name,
Chosen of love as chosen of hatred. Now no more
Ear of man may hear or heart of man deplore
Aught of dissonance or doubt that mars the strain
Raised at last of love where love sat mute of yore.

Fame is less than love, and loss is more than gain,
When the sweetest souls and strongest, fallen in fight,
Slain and stricken as it seemed in base men's sight,
Rise and lighten on the graves of foemen slain,
Clothed about with love of all men as with light,
Suns that set not, stars that know not day from night.

> *Algernon Charles Swinburne, ''The Centenary of Shelley,'' in* The Athenaeum, *No. 3379, July 30, 1892, p. 159.*

BERNARD SHAW   (essay date 1892)

[*Shaw is generally considered to be the greatest and best-known dramatist to write in the English language since Shakespeare. During the late nineteenth century, he was prominent as a literary, art, music, and drama critic, and his reviews were known for their biting wit and brilliance. In this excerpt from an 1892 essay, Shaw urges that Shelley be remembered as the radical atheist that he was.*]

In politics Shelley was a Republican, a Leveller, a Radical of the most extreme type. He was even an Anarchist of the old-fashioned Godwinian school, up to the point at which he perceived Anarchism to be impracticable. He publicly ranged himself with demagogues and gaol-birds like Cobbett and Henry Hunt (the original ''Man in the White Hat''), and not only advocated the Plan of Radical Reform which was afterwards embodied in the prosposals of the Chartists, but denounced the rent-roll of the landed aristocracy as the true pension list, thereby classing himself as what we now call a Land Nationalizer. He echoed Cobbett's attacks on the National Debt and the Funding System in such a manner as to leave no reasonable doubt that if he had been born half a century later he would have been advocating Social-Democracy with a view to its development into the most democratic form of Communism practically attainable and maintainable. (pp. 236-37)

In religion, Shelley was an Atheist. There is nothing uncommon in that; but he actually called himself one, and urged others to follow his example. He never trifled with the word God: he knew that it meant a personal First Cause, Almighty Creator, and Supreme Judge and Ruler of the Universe, and that it did not mean anything else, never had meant anything else, and never whilst the English language lasted would mean anything else. Knowing perfectly well that there was no such person, he did not pretend that the question was an open one, or imply, by calling himself an Agnostic, that there might be such a person for all he knew to the contrary. He did know to the contrary; and he said so. Further, though there never was a man with so abiding and full a consciousness of the omnipresence of a living force, manifesting itself here in the germination and growth of a tree, there in the organization of a poet's brain, and elsewhere in the putrefaction of a dead dog, he never condescended to beg off being an Atheist by calling this omnipresent energy God, or even Pan. He lived and died professedly, almost boastfully, godless. In his time, however, as at present, God was little more than a word to the English people. What they really worshipped was the Bible; and our modern Church movement to get away from Bible fetishism and back to some presentable sort of Christianity . . . had not then come to the surface. The preliminary pick-axing work of Bible smashing had yet to be done; and Shelley, who found the moral atmosphere of the Old Testament murderous and abominable, and the asceticism of the New suicidal and pessimistic, smashed away at the Bible with all his might and main.

But all this . . . was mere eccentricity compared to Shelley's teaching on the subject of the family. He would not draw any distinction between the privilege of the king or priest and that of the father. He pushed to its extremest consequences his denial that blood relationship altered by one jot or tittle the relations which should exist between human beings. One of his most popular performances at Eton and Oxford was an elaborate curse on his own father, who had thwarted and oppressed him: and the entirely serious intention of Shelley's curses may be seen in his solemn imprecation against Lord Eldon, ending with the words:

I curse thee, though I hate thee not.

His determination to impress on us that our fathers should be no more and no less to us than other men, is evident in every allusion of his to the subject, from the school curse to *The Cenci*, which to this day is refused a licence for performance on the stage.

But Shelley was not the man to claim freedom of enmity, and say nothing about freedom of love. If father and son are to be as free in their relation to one another as hundredth cousins are, so must sister and brother. The freedom to curse a tyrannical father is not more sacred than the freedom to love an amiable sister. In a word, if filial duty is no duty, than incest is no crime. This sounds startling even now, disillusioned as we are by Herbert Spencer, Elie Reclus, and other writers as to there being anything "natural" in our code of prohibited

degrees; but in Shelley's time it seemed the summit of impious vice. . . . Nevertheless, he did not shrink from it in the least: the hero and heroine of *Laon and Cythna* are brother and sister; and the notion that the bowdlerization of this great poem as *The Revolt of Islam* represents any repentance or withdrawal on Shelley's part, cannot be sustained for a moment in the face of the facts. . . . And no one who has ever reasoned out the consequences of such views can doubt for a moment that Shelley regarded the family, in its legal aspect, as a doomed institution.

So much for the opinions which Shelley held and sedulously propagated. Could Sussex be reconciled to them on the ground that they were mere "views" which did not affect his conduct? Not a bit of it. (pp. 237-39)

Shelley was not a hot-headed nor an unpractical person. All his writings, whether in prose or verse, have a peculiarly deliberate quality. His political pamphlets are unique in their freedom from all appeal to the destructive passions; there is neither anger, sarcasm, nor frivolity in them; and in this respect his poems exactly resemble his political pamphlets. Other poets, from Shakespear to Tennyson, have let the tiger in them loose under pretext of patriotism, righteous indignation, or what not: he never did. His horror of violence, cruelty, injustice, and bravery was proof against their infection. Hence it cannot for a moment be argued that his opinions and his conduct were merely his wild oats. His seriousness, his anxious carefulness, are just as obvious in the writings which still expose their publishers to the possibility of a prosecution for sedition or blasphemy as in his writings on Catholic Emancipation, the propriety and practical sagacity of which are not now disputed. And he did not go back upon his opinions in the least as he grew older. By the time he had begun *The Triumph of Life,* he had naturally come to think *Queen Mab* a boyish piece of work, not that what it affirmed seemed false to him or what it denied true, but because it did not affirm and deny enough. Thus there is no excuse for Shelley on the ground of his youth or rashness. If he was a sinner, he was a hardened sinner and a deliberate one. (p. 240)

[The cry has gone up], "We want our great Shelley, our darling Shelley, our best, noblest, highest of poets. We will not have it said that he was a Leveller, an Atheist, a foe to marriage, an advocate of incest. He was a little unfortunate in his first marriage; and we pity him for it. He was a little eccentric in his vegetarianism; but we are not ashamed of that; we glory in the humanity of it [with morsels of beefsteak, fresh from the slaughter house, sticking between our teeth]. We ask the public to be generous—to read his really great works, such as the **"Ode to a Skylark,"** and not to gloat over those boyish indiscretions known as *Laon and Cythna, Prometheus,* **"Rosalind and Helen,"** *The Cenci, The Masque of Anarchy,* etc., etc. Take no notice of the Church papers; for our Shelley was a true Christian at heart. Away with Jeaffreson; for our Shelley was a gentleman if ever there was one. (p. 241)

Why not be content to say, "I abhor Shelley's opinions; but my abhorrence is overwhelmed by my admiration of the exquisite artistic quality of his work," or "I am neither an Atheist nor a believer in Equality nor a Free Lover; and yet I am willing to celebrate Shelley because I feel that he was somehow a good sort," or even "I think Shelley's poetry slovenly and unsubstantial, and his ideas simply rot; but I will celebrate him because he said what he thought, and not what he was expected to say he thought." Instead of this, each of us gets up and says, "I am forced for the sake of my wife and family and social position to be a piffler and a trimmer; and as all you fellows are in the same predicament, I ask you to back me up in trying to make out that Shelley was a piffler and a trimmer too.'' As one of the literary brotherhood myself, I hope I am clubbable enough to stand in with any reasonable movement in my trade; but this is altogether too hollow. It will not do: the meanest Shelley reader knows better. If it were only to keep ourselves from premature putrefaction, we must tell the truth about somebody; and I submit that Shelley has pre-eminent claims to be that somebody. (p. 246)

> Bernard Shaw, ''Shaming the Devil About Shelley,'' in his Pen Portraits and Reviews, revised edition, Constable and Company Limited, 1932, pp. 236-46.

W. B. YEATS (essay date 1900)

[Yeats was an Irish poet, playwright, and essayist of the late nineteenth and early twentieth centuries. The leading figure of the Irish Renaissance, Yeats was also an active critic. In the following excerpt from an essay dated 1900, he stresses the importance of understanding Shelley's system of belief, concluding that he approached a mystical, revolutionary faith.]

When I was a boy in Dublin I was one of a group who rented a room in a mean street to discuss philosophy. My fellow-students got more and more interested in certain modern schools of mystical belief, and I never found anybody to share my one unshakable belief. I thought that whatever of philosophy has been made poetry is alone permanent, and that one should begin to arrange it in some regular order, rejecting nothing as the make-believe of the poets. I thought, so far as I can recollect my thoughts after so many years, that if a powerful and benevolent spirit has shaped the destiny of this world, we can better discover that destiny from the words that have gathered up the heart's desire of the world, than from historical records, or from speculation, wherein the heart withers. Since then I have observed dreams and visions very carefully, and am now certain that the imagination has some way of lighting on the truth that the reason has not, and that its commandments, delivered when the body is still and the reason silent, are the most binding we can ever know. I have re-read **Prometheus Unbound**, which I had hoped my fellow-students would have studied as a sacred book, and it seems to me to have an even more certain place than I had thought among the sacred books of the world. I remember going to a learned scholar to ask about its deep meanings, which I felt more than understood, and his telling me that it was Godwin's *Political Justice* put into rhyme, and that Shelley was a crude revolutionist, and believed that the overturning of kings and priests would regenerate mankind. I quoted the lines which tell how the halcyons ceased to prey on fish, and how poisonous leaves became good for food, to show that he foresaw more than any political regeneration, but was too timid to push the argument. I still believe that one cannot help believing him, as this scholar I know believes him, a vague thinker, who mixed occasional great poetry with a fantastic rhetoric, unless one compares such passages, and above all such passages as describe the liberty he praised, till one has discovered the system of belief that lay behind them. It should seem natural to find his thought full of subtlety, for Mrs. Shelley has told how he hesitated whether he should be a metaphysician or a poet, and has spoken of his 'huntings after the obscure' with regret, and said of the **Prometheus Unbound**, which so many for three generations have thought *Political Justice* put into rhyme,

It requires a mind as subtle and penetrating as his own to understand the mystic meanings scattered throughout the poem. They elude the ordinary reader by their abstraction and delicacy of distinction, but they are far from vague. It was his design to write prose metaphysical essays on the nature of Man, which would have served to explain much of what is obscure in his poetry; a few scattered fragments of observations and remarks alone remain. He considered these philosophical views of Mind and Nature to be instinct with the intensest spirit of poetry.

From these scattered fragments and observations, and from many passages read in their light, one soon comes to understand that his liberty was so much more than the liberty of *Political Justice* that it was one with Intellectual Beauty, and that the regeneration he foresaw was so much more than the regeneration many political dreamers have foreseen, that it could not come in its perfection till the Hours bore 'Time to his tomb in eternity.' In *A Defence of Poetry* [see excerpt dated 1821], he will have it that the poet and the lawgiver hold their station by the right of the same faculty, the one uttering in words and the other in the forms of society his vision of the divine order, the Intellectual Beauty.

> Poets, according to the circumstances of the age and nation in which they appeared, were called in the earliest epoch of the world legislators or prophets, and a poet essentially comprises and unites both these characters. For he not only beholds intensely the present as it is, and discovers those laws according to which present things are to be ordained, but he beholds the future in the present, and his thoughts are the germs of the flowers and the fruit of latest time.

> Language, colour, form, and religious and civil habits of action are all the instruments and materials of poetry.

Poetry is

> the creation of actions according to the unchangeable process of human nature as existing in the mind of the creator, which is itself the image of all other minds.

> Poets have been challenged to resign the civic crown to reasoners and merchants. . . . It is admitted that the exercise of the imagination is the most delightful, but it is alleged that that of reason is the more useful. . . . Whilst the mechanist abridges and the political economist combines labour, let them be sure that their speculations, for want of correspondence with those first principles which belong to the imagination, do not tend, as they have in modern England, to exasperate at once the extremes of luxury and want. . . . The rich have become richer, the poor have become poorer, . . . such are the effects which must ever flow from an unmitigated exercise of the calculating faculty.

The speaker of these things might almost be Blake, who held that the Reason not only created Ugliness, but all other evils.

The books of all wisdom are hidden in the cave of the Witch of Atlas, who is one of his personifications of beauty, and when she moves over the enchanted river that is an image of all life, the priests cast aside their deceits, and the king crowns an ape to mock his own sovereignty, and the soldiers gather about the anvils to beat their swords to ploughshares, and lovers cast away their timidity, and friends are united; while the power which, in *Laon and Cythna,* awakens the mind of the reformer to contend, and itself contends, against the tyrannies of the world, is first seen as the star of love or beauty. And at the end of the **"Ode to Naples"**, he cries out to 'the spirit of beauty' to overturn the tyrannies of the world, or to fill them with its 'harmonising ardours.' He calls the spirit of beauty liberty, because despotism, and perhaps, as 'the man of virtuous soul commands not, nor obeys,' all authority, pluck virtue from her path towards beauty, and because it leads us by that love whose service is perfect freedom. It leads all things by love, for he cries again and again that love is the perception of beauty in thought and things, and it orders all things by love, for it is love that impels the soul to its expressions in thought and in action, by making us 'seek to awaken in all things that are, a community with what we experience within ourselves.' 'We are born into the world, and there is something within us which, from the instant that we live, more and more thirsts after its likeness.' We have 'a soul within our soul that describes a circle around its proper paradise which pain and sorrow and evil dare not overleap,' and we labour to see this soul in many mirrors, that we may possess it the more abundantly. He would hardly seek the progress of the world by any less gentle labour, and would hardly have us resist evil itself. He bids the reformers in [*A Philosophical View of Reform*] receive 'the onset of the cavalry,' if it be sent to disperse their meetings, 'with folded arms,' and 'not because active resistence is not justifiable, but because temperance and courage would produce greater advantages than the most decisive victory'; and he gives them like advice in *The Masque of Anarchy,* for liberty, the poems cries, 'is love,' and can make the rich man kiss its feet, and, like those who followed Christ, give away his goods and follow it throughout the world.

He does not believe that the reformation of society can bring this beauty, this divine order, among men without the regeneration of the hearts of men. Even in *Queen Mab,* which was written before he had found his deepest thought, or rather perhaps before he had found words to utter it, for I do not think men change much in their deepest thought, he is less anxious to change men's beliefs, as I think, than to cry out against that serpent more subtle than any beast of the field, 'the cause and effect of tyranny.' He affirms again and again that the virtuous, those who have 'pure desire and universal love,' are happy in the midst of tyranny, and he foresees a day when the 'Spirit of Nature,' the Spirit of Beauty of his later poems, who has her 'throne of power unappealable' in every human heart, shall have made men so virtuous that 'kingly glare will lose its power to dazzle,' and 'silently pass by,' and, as it seems, commerce, 'the venal interchange of all that human art or nature yield; which wealth should purchase not,' come as silently to an end.

He was always, indeed in chief, a witness for that 'power unappealable.' Maddalo, in **"Julian and Maddalo,"** says that the soul is powerless, and can only, like a 'dreary bell hung in a heaven-illumined tower, toll our thoughts and our desires to meet below round the rent heart and pray'; but Julian, who

is Shelley himself, replies, as the makers of all religions have replied:—

> Where is the love, beauty, and truth we seek
> But in our mind? And if we were not weak,
> Should we be less in deed than in desire?

while **"Mont Blanc"** is an intricate analogy to affirm that the soul has its sources in 'the secret strength of things which governs thoughts, and to the infinite dome of heaven is as a law.' He even thought that men might be immortal were they sinless, and his Cythna bids the sailors be without remorse, for all that live are stained as they are. It is thus, she says, that time marks men and their thoughts for the tomb. And the 'Red Comet,' the image of evil in *Laon and Cythna,* when it began its war with the star of beauty, brought not only 'Fear, Hatred, Fraud and Tyranny,' but 'Death, Decay, Earthquake, and Blight and Madness pale.'

When the Red Comet is conquered, when Jupiter is overthrown by Demogorgon, when the prophecy of Queen Mab is fulfilled, visible Nature will put on perfection again. Shelley declares, in one of the notes to *Queen Mab,* that 'there is no great extravagance in presuming . . . that there should be a perfect identity between the moral and physical improvement of the human species,' and thinks it 'certain that wisdom is not compatible with disease, and that, in the present state of the climates of the earth, health, in the true and comprehensive sense of the word, is out of the reach of civilised man.' In *Prometheus Unbound* he sees, as in the ecstasy of a saint, the ships moving among the seas of the world without fear of danger—

> by the light
> Of wave-reflected flowers, and floating odours,
> And music soft,

and poison dying out of the green things, and cruelty out of all living things, and even the toads and efts becoming beautiful, and at last Time being borne 'to his tomb in eternity.'

This beauty, this divine order, whereof all things shall become a part in a kind of resurrection of the body, is already visible to the dead and to souls in ecstasy, for ecstasy is a kind of death. The dying Lionel hears the song of the nightingale, and cries:—

> Heardst thou not sweet words among
> That heaven-resounding minstrelsy?
> Heardst thou not, that those who die
> Awake in a world of ecstasy?
> That love, when limbs are interwoven,
> And sleep, when the night of life is cloven,
> And thought, to the world's dim boundaries clinging,
> And music, when one beloved is singing,
> Is death? Let us drain right joyously
> The cup which the sweet bird fills for me.

And in the most famous passage in all his poetry he sings of Death as of a mistress. 'Life, like a dome of many-coloured glass, stains the white radiance of Eternity.' 'Die, if thou wouldst be with that which thou dost seek'; and he sees his own soon-coming death in a rapture of prophecy, for 'the fire for which all thirst' beams upon him, 'consuming the last clouds of cold mortality.' When he is dead he will still influence the living, for though Adonais has fled 'to the burning fountain whence he came,' and 'is a portion of the Eternal which must glow through time and change, unquenchably the same,' and has 'awakened from the dream of life,' he has not gone from the 'young Dawn,' or the caverns and the forests, or the 'faint flowers and fountains.' He has been 'made one with Nature,' and his voice is 'heard in all her music,' and his presence is felt wherever 'that Power may move which has withdrawn his being to its own,' and he bears 'his part' when it is compelling mortal things to their appointed forms, and he overshadows men's minds at their supreme moments, for—

> when lofty thought
> Lifts a young heart above its mortal lair,
> And love and life contend in it for what
> Shall be its earthly doom, the dead live there,
> And move like winds of light on dark and stormy air.

'Of his speculations as to what will befall this inestimable spirit when we appear to die,' Mrs. Shelley has written,

> a mystic ideality tinged these speculations in Shelley's mind; certain stanzas in the poem of **The Sensitive Plant** express, in some degree, the almost inexpressible idea, not that we die into another state, when this state is no longer, from some reason, unapparent as well as apparent, accordant with our being—but that those who rise above the ordinary nature of man, fade from before our imperfect organs; they remain in their ''love, beauty, and delight,'' in a world congenial to them, and we, clogged by ''error, ignorance, and strife,'' see them not till we are fitted by purification and improvement to their higher state.

Not merely happy souls, but all beautiful places and movements and gestures and events, when we think they have ceased to be, have become portions of the Eternal.

> In this life
> Of error, ignorance and strife,
> Where nothing is, but all things seem,
> And we the shadows of the dream,
>
> It is a modest creed, and yet
> Pleasant, if one considers it,
> To own that death itself must be,
> Like all the rest, a mockery.
>
> That garden sweet, that lady fair,
> And all sweet shapes and odours there,
> In truth have never past away;
> 'Tis we, 'tis ours, are changed, not they.
>
> For love, and beauty, and delight
> There is no death nor change; their might
> Exceeds our organs, which endure
> No light, being themselves obscure.

He seems in his speculations to have lit on that memory of Nature the visionaries claim for the foundation of their knowledge; but I do not know whether he thought, as they do, that all things good and evil remain for ever, 'thinking the thought and doing the deed,' though not, it may be, self-conscious; or only thought that 'love and beauty and delight' remain for ever. The passage where Queen Mab awakes 'all knowledge of the past,' and the good and evil 'events of old and wondrous times,' was no more doubtless than a part of the machinery of the poem, but all the machineries of poetry are parts of the convictions of antiquity, and readily become again convictions in minds that brood over them with visionary intensity.

Intellectual Beauty has not only the happy dead to do her will, but ministering spirits who correspond to the Devas of the East,

and the Elemental Spirits of mediaeval Europe, and the Sidhe of ancient Ireland, and whose too constant presence, and perhaps Shelley's ignorance of their more traditional forms, give some of his poetry an air of rootless fantasy. They change continually in his poetry, as they do in the visions of the mystics everywhere and of the common people in Ireland, and the forms of these changes display, in an especial sense, the flowing forms of his mind when freed from all impulse not out of itself or out of supersensual power. These are 'gleams of a remoter world which visit us in sleep,' spiritual essences whose shadows are the delights of all the senses, sounds 'folded in cells of crystal silence,' 'visions swift, and sweet, and quaint,' which lie waiting their moment 'each in its thin sheath, like a chrysalis,' 'odours' among 'ever-blooming Eden-trees,' 'liquors' that can give 'happy sleep,' or can make tears 'all wonder and delight'; 'the golden genii who spoke to the poets of Greece in dreams'; 'the phantoms' which become the forms of the arts when 'the mind, arising bright from the embrace of beauty,' 'casts on them the gathered rays which are reality'; 'the guardians' who move in 'the atmosphere of human thought,' as 'the birds within the wind, or the fish within the wave,' or man's thought itself through all things; and who join the throng of the happy Hours when Time is passing away—

> As the flying-fish leap
> From the Indian deep,
> And mix with the sea-birds half asleep.

It is these powers which lead Asia and Panthea, as they would lead all the affections of humanity, by words written upon leaves, by faint songs, by eddies of echoes that draw 'all spirits on that secret way,' by the 'dying odours' of flowers and by 'the sunlight of the sphered dew,' beyond the gates of birth and death to awake Demogorgon, eternity, that 'the painted veil called life' may be 'torn aside.'

There are also ministers of ugliness and all evil, like those that came to Prometheus:—

> As from the rose which the pale priestess kneels
> To gather for her festal crown of flowers
> The aërial crimson falls, flushing her cheek,
> So from our victim's destined agony
> The shade which is our form invests us round;
> Else we are shapeless as our mother Night.

Or like those whose shapes the poet sees in **The Triumph of Life,** coming from the procession that follows the car of life, as 'hope' changes to 'desire,' shadows 'numerous as the dead leaves blown in autumn evening from a poplar-tree'; and resembling those they come from, until, if I understand an obscure phrase aright, they are 'wrapt' round 'all the busy phantoms that were there as the sun shapes the clouds.' Some to sit 'chattering like restless apes,' and some like 'old anatomies' 'hatching their bare broods under the shade of demon wings,' laughing 'to reassume the delegated power' they had given to the tyrants of the earth, and some 'like small gnats and flies' to throng 'about the brow of lawyers, statesmen, priest and theorist,' and some 'like discoloured flakes of snow' to fall 'on fairest bosoms and the sunniest hair,' to be 'melted by the youthful glow which they extinguished,' and many to 'fling shadows of shadows, yet unlike themselves,' shadows that are shaped into new forms by that 'creative ray' in which all move like motes.

These ministers of beauty and ugliness were certainly more than metaphors or picturesque phrases to one who believed the 'thoughts which are called real or external objects' differed but in regularity of recurrence from 'hallucinations, dreams, and the ideas of madness,' and lessened this difference by telling how he had dreamed 'three several times, between intervals of two or more years, the same precise dream,' and who had seen images with the mind's eye that left his nerves shaken for days together. Shadows that were—

> as when there hovers
> A flock of vampire-bats before the glare
> Of the tropic sun, bringing, ere evening,
> Strange night upon some Indian isle,

could not but have had more than a metaphorical and picturesque being to one who had spoken in terror with an image of himself, and who had fainted at the apparition of a woman with eyes in her breasts, and who had tried to burn down a wood, if we can trust Mrs. Williams' account, because he believed a devil, who had first tried to kill him, had sought refuge there.

It seems to me, indeed, that Shelley had reawakened in himself the age of faith, though there were times when he would doubt, as even the saints have doubted, and that he was a revolutionist, because he had heard the commandment, 'If ye know these things, happy are ye if ye do them.' I have re-read his *Prometheus Unbound* for the first time for many years, in the woods of Drim-na-Rod, among the Echtge hills, and sometimes I have looked towards Slieve ná nOg where the country people say the last battle of the world shall be fought till the third day, when a priest shall lift a chalice, and the thousand years of peace begin. And I think this mysterious song utters a faith as simple and as ancient as the faith of those country people, in a form suited to a new age, that will understand with Blake that the Holy Spirit is 'an intellectual fountain,' and that the kinds and degrees of beauty are the images of its authority. (pp. 65-78)

> *W. B. Yeats, "The Philosophy of Shelley's Poetry,"*
> *in his* Essays and Introductions, *The Macmillan Company, 1961, pp. 65-95.*

ARCHIBALD T. STRONG   (essay date 1921)

[*In this excerpt, Strong discusses Shelley as a poet of decay, tracing his preoccupation with death, the demonic, and the supernatural throughout his career.*]

[Shelley] is best remembered by such passages as Asia's long and exquisite speech in the second act of *Prometheus Unbound,* or **"Life of Life"**, or the soaring close of *Epipsychidion,* or that perfect flower piece, **"The Question"**, or **"Mutability"**, or **"Rarely, rarely, comest thou"**. The unearthliness which is the distinctive note of all his higher poetry is here celestial, and this not less in the passages of despair than in those of ecstasy. The same glory is upon him when he stands 'at noon upon the peak of Heaven', as when, in **"Prince Athanase"**, he passes through the 'Night of the Soul', or, remaining with his kind, becomes the 'nerve o'er which do creep the else unfelt oppressions of this earth'. It flames forth in such an ecstasy of joy as this:

> Her voice is hovering o'er my soul—it lingers
> O'ershadowing it with soft and lulling wings,
> The blood and life within those snowy fingers
> Teach witchcraft to the instrumental strings.

> My brain is wild, my breath comes quick—
> The blood is listening in my frame,
> And thronging shadows, fast and thick,
> Fall on my overflowing eyes;
> My heart is quivering like a flame;
> As morning dew, that in the sunbeam dies,
> I am dissolved in these consuming ecstasies.

But it is hardly less strong and lovely in the despairing

> Swifter far than summer's flight—
> Swifter far than youth's delight—
> Swifter far than happy night,
> Art thou come and gone—
> As the earth when leaves are dead,
> As the night when sleep is sped,
> As the heart when joy is fled,
> I am left lone, alone.

> The swallow summer comes again—
> The owlet night resumes her reign—
> But the wild-swan youth is fain
> To fly with thee, false as thou.—
> My heart each day desires the morrow;
> Sleep itself is turned to sorrow;
> Vainly would my winter borrow
> Sunny leaves from any bough.

In both of these passages, opposite as is their mood, there is a common element of beauty and feeling, and even of rhythm. Innumerable instances of the same quality might be cited. In all of these places Shelley walks with an angel, even though it be in darkness—with the angel who was his true and most constant guardian. There were other times when he could walk in darkness, and in daylight too, in the grip of a devil of the pit. For our present purpose, the antithesis is not the easy one between joy and gloom, ecstasy and despair. In the darkest of the passages just cited there is no touch of what he himself calls the 'daemonic': conversely, there is another beauty in Shelley, and a very real one, suffused by no gleam of celestial light. So far we have not met the sinister in him: and it is the sinister we seek. (pp. 112-13)

From earliest childhood [Shelley] had taken the liveliest interest in the supernatural. 'Sometimes', Hogg tells us [see Additional Bibliography], 'he watched the livelong nights for ghosts', and his researches into electricity and galvanism, which were to be resumed so ardently in his Oxford days, were varied by the eager perusal of volumes on magic and witchcraft. With the help of the rules herein presented, he even tried to raise a ghost himself, uttering incantations and drinking thrice out of a human skull (or its substitute) as he bestrode a running stream. His sister Helen testifies to his early love of ghost stories, and of Monk Lewis's weirdly grotesque poems. Later, *The Monk* itself, with all its wonders and horrors, became one of his 'especial favourites', and Medwin tells us that he was also enraptured by 'a strange wild romance entitled *Zofloya the Moor,* a Monk Lewisy production where his Satanic Majesty, as in *Faust,* plays the chief part'. He was also entranced by Bürger's eery and gripping *Lenore,* by the witch Lorrinite in *Kehama,* and by the legend of the headless spectre of St. Leonard's forest. This course of reading was at once the cause and the effect of his fervent preoccupation with the supernatural, and it affected his life no less powerfully than it did his novels and his poetry. . . . [Of] this period he tells us himself, in the **"Hymn to Intellectual Beauty"**:

> While yet a boy I sought for ghosts, and sped
>   Through many a listening chamber, cave, and ruin,
>   And starlight wood, with fearful steps pursuing
> Hopes of high talk with the departed dead.
> I called on poisonous names with which our youth is fed.

Medwin tells us that at this period he was subject to dreams of fearful vividness, to somnambulism, and to waking visions. Hogg informs us that even at Oxford Shelley had a 'decided inclination for magic, daemonology, incantations, raising the dead, evoking spirits and devils, seeing ghosts, and chatting familiarly with apparitions.' While at Oxford, too, he read *Gebir* eagerly, and we may well believe that he had a special liking for that Book of it which tells how, at Masar,

> Yet were remaining some of ancient race,
> And ancient arts were now their sole delight.
> With Time's first sickle they had marked the hour
> When at their incantation would the Moon
> Start back, and shuddering shed blue blasted light.

Several years later, in a letter of 1816, he speaks sympathetically of the belief in ghosts, and condemns as illogical the theory of Byron and 'Monk' Lewis that none could entertain that belief without also believing in God. Like Blake at this time he believed that the atmosphere surrounding the earth was peopled with the spirits of the departed. Less frequently than Blake he was vouchsafed, or conceived himself to have been vouchsafed, a vision of such beings. Shortly before his death and after Allegra's, while walking by the moonlit ocean, he claimed to have seen a naked child (Allegra) 'rise from the sea and clap its hands as in joy, smiling at him'. A month later, while walking on the terrace of Villa Magni after a succession of frightful dreams, he declared that he had encountered his own wraith, which addressed to him the boding question, 'How long do you mean to be content?' The voice which he heard at Rome calling on him to write *The Cenci* was probably merely the casual utterance of a passing ragcrier, but the fact that he construed it as supernatural, and at once applied it to himself, illustrates at once the speed and the unruliness of his imagination. His mind constantly became the prey of his rebellious fancy: thus, after repeating aloud the passage of *Christabel* describing the gruesome mystery of Geraldine's bosom, he ran shrieking from the room, saying 'that he had suddenly thought of a woman he had heard of who had eyes instead of nipples; which taking hold of his mind horrified him'. This visionary faculty of Shelley's had its counterpart in his extraordinarily sensitive physical organization, and displayed itself vividly in his everyday demeanour. He tells us that during a period of ill-health his feelings were 'awakened to a state of such unnatural and keen excitement that, only to instance the organ of sight, I find the very blades of grass and the boughs of distant trees present themselves to me with microscopial distinctness'. To beholders, during and after his visions he had the look of one possessed, and his eyes were filled with an unearthly light of heaven or of hell. It is curious to compare Medwin's description of him during these visitations with Hogg's: 'He was given to waking dreams', says Medwin, 'a sort of lethargy and abstraction that became habitual to him, and after the *accès* was over, his eyes flashed, his lips quivered, his voice was tremulous with emotion, a sort of ecstasy came over him, and he talked more like a spirit or an angel than a human being.' Hogg lays still greater stress on the daemonic aspect which Shelley sometimes assumed. 'Bysshe looked as he al-

ways looked, wild, intellectual, unearthly; like a spirit that had just descended from the sky; like a demon risen at that moment out of the ground'; and he adds, 'his poems seem to have been breathed, not by a mere mortal, but by some God or demon. His writings are invariably demoniacal, plainly the compositions of a demoniacal man.' It is curious that Shelley, in talking to Medwin, refers to himself as being occasionally daemoniacally possessed: 'The poet is a different being from the rest of the world. Imagination steals over him—he knows not whence. Images float before him—he knows not their home. Struggling and contending powers are engendered within him, which no outward impulse, no inward passion awakened. He utters sentiments he never meditated. He creates persons whose original he had never seen. But he cannot command the power that called them out of nothing. He must wait till the God or daemon genius breathes it into him.' (pp. 121-24)

In all these cases we find Shelley's mind working in strange and sometimes sinister fashion, through abnormal, or supernormal, correlation to the phenomenal world. Out of his very yearning for the Absolute he had lost sure footing in the Particular. Striving to soar into the empyrean before the day appointed to the human soul for flight, he fell repeatedly to earth, and, dazed by that shock, at times saw the things around him dizzily and brokenly. Olympian at soul, he had not the Titan's gift of embracing mother earth and gaining strength and sanity thereby. Like the cave-dwellers of his beloved Plato, when he returned to the cavern from the daylight, he saw the shadows on its walls less clearly than they were seen by his fellows of the lower vision who had never looked upon the sun. Had he dwelt longer in the world's cave perhaps his eyes would have grown clear and steady, would have focussed to the mean distances of earth, while abating nothing of their heavenly range and brightness. Certainly this steadier tendency seems to have been growing in him when his death at twenty-nine thwarted its full realization.

As things were, his preoccupation with the ideal warped his views of men and women no less than his views of the external world, and frequently resulted in conduct not the less cruel and unjust to its victims because it was perfectly sincere on his part. (pp. 124-25)

When we leave Shelley's life for his writings, the 'daemonic' element manifests itself under different forms. Among the most common of them is his constant preoccupation with putrefaction and decay. It is easy to dismiss this as a mere youthful foible of excess derived from his reading of *The Monk* and *Zofloya*; but unless he had already had that in him which responded eagerly to these wild volumes, he would never have read them so keenly nor have followed them so closely as he did in his own romances, *Zastrozzi* and *St. Irvyne.* (pp. 129-30)

Outside gruesome dreams, neither novel deals greatly in the supernatural variety of the sinister which occurs elsewhere in Shelley. Both thus differ considerably from their prototype *The Monk.* The initiation of Ginotti and the death of Wolfstein in *St. Irvyne* do, it is true, partake of the crudely miraculous: but apart from the horrors and surprises scattered throughout the pages, the most sinister element in each novel, and especially in *Zastrozzi,* is its master-motive of revenge. These stories must, of course, be regarded for the most part as mere exercises of boyish fancy: but their pages, spattered with blood and hate, are in striking contrast to the lesson so emphatically preached a year later by Shelley in *The Address to the Irish People,* that revolutionists can under no circumstances be justified in asserting their national rights by bloodshed. As a matter of fact,

The trial scene in a 1959 production of The Cenci. *Photograph by Angus McBean.*

we know from Hogg that Shelley hated the idea of taking life in any form. Yet constantly throughout his earlier poems does one encounter the reek of the slaughter-yard and whiff of the charnel-vault. In his fragmentary poem of 1807, the night-raven sings tidings of approaching death. In **"A Dialogue"** Death appears indeed as the consoler, and love is exempted from his touch: and in **"To Death"**, the mortal triumphs over his dissolution. But when we come to the *Poems of Victor and Cazire*, and other of Shelley's juvenile poems, we find **"St. Edmund's Eve"** to be a crude study in the terrible, and **"Revenge"** and **"Ghasta"** to be mere metrical novelettes of sensation written in the vein of *Zastrozzi*. The scene, crude and unreal as some melodrama staged in a child's theatre, is lit, as it were, from the wings, with stage lightnings, blue firelight, and the 'midnight pestiferous meteor's blaze'—illuminations afterwards to be flung with quite other effect on Shelley's later work. And beneath this rococo heaven stalk daemons, nightmares, tombless ghosts, and even the skeleton of a dead man, its half-eaten eyeballs illuminated by two pale flames. Fiends laugh and howl over the corpse of a man who has sold his soul to hell. Other corpses rot and stink around, and 'the loathsome worm' gnaws below in 'the dark mansions of the dead'. Nor in *Queen Mab*, for all its promise, and occasional achievement, of beauty, are we ever far from that 'gloomy power whose reign is in the tainted sepulchres'. Putrefaction persists everywhere, even if it does not utterly prevail. Even when Nature is invoked in her own fair shrine we are forbidden to forget the worm 'that lurks in graves and fattens on the dead'. In every corner pestilence 'lowers expectant'. Human flesh poisons the atmosphere with putrid smoke, and over the whole scene there is moonlight, not soft and gracious as at the close of *The Merchant of Venice*,

but weird and lurid as in that great poem of Landor's in which Shelley had just been steeping his keenly responsive imagination. Among Shelley's later poems there is scarcely one of any length which is totally free from the atmosphere of corruption. Especially common are the references to the 'charnel' and the 'worm'. Early in *The Revolt of Islam* we meet 'Death, Decay, Earthquake and Blight and Want and Madness pale, wingèd and wan diseases'. Later, when Pestilence meets Laon, she prints on his lips 'the Plague's blue kisses'. Later still she lays a mocking feast of bread, and sets around it 'a ring of cold, stiff babes'. Again, we inhale the 'rotting vapour' that passes from the unburied dead, and are told that when the beasts' food fails, they inhale 'the breath of its decay', while a strange disease glows in their green eyes: the sea-shore stinks with dead and putrid fish: human flesh is sold for food in the market place: blue Plague falls upon the race of man, and near the great fountain in the public square, a pyramid of corpses crumbles beneath the noonday sun. The zest with which Shelley's imagination works on this subject may be gauged from such a stanza as the following:

> It was not hunger now, but thirst. Each well
>   Was choked with rotting corpses, and became
> A cauldron of green mist made visible
>   At sunrise. Thither still the myriads came,
>   Seeking to quench the agony of the flame,
> Which raged like poison through their bursting veins;
>   Naked they were from torture, without shame,
> Spotted with nameless scars and lurid blains,
> Childhood, and youth, and age, writhing in savage pains.

The union of passion with decay developed with such sinister mastery in Swinburne's *The Leper* appears in these lines:

> A woman's shape, now lank and cold and blue,
>   The dwelling of the many-coloured worm,
> Hung there; the white and hollow cheek I drew
>   To my dry lips—what radiance did inform
>   Those horny eyes? whose was that withered form?
> Alas, alas! it seemed that Cythna's ghost
>   Laughed in those looks, and that the flesh was warm
>   Within my teeth!—A whirlwind keen as frost
> Then in its sinking gulfs my sickening spirit tossed.

It is re-echoed in Fiordispina's longing to lie beside her dead love in her shroud:

>   'And if my love were dead,
>   Unless my heart deceives me, I would lie
> Beside him in my shroud as willingly
> As now in the gay night-dress Lilla wrought.' . . .

In **"Rosalind and Helen"** we again come upon the dead in their 'putrid shrouds', and upon the couplet:

>   When she was a thing that did not stir
>   And the crawling worms were cradling her:

in **Prometheus** the victims of the Fury are 'linked to corpses in unwholesome cells'. But perhaps no better instance could be given of Shelley's preoccupation with putrefaction than *The Sensitive Plant*. As soon as the lady dies, we are prepared for the horrors to follow by being told that the Plant felt

>   the smell, cold, oppressive, and dank,
>   Sent through the pores of the coffin-plank.

As the garden becomes

>   cold and foul
>   Like the corpse of her who had been its soul,

the lilies grow

>   drooping, and white, and wan,
>   Like the head and the skin of a dying man.

A still more sinister passage appeared in the edition of 1820 but was subsequently cancelled:

>   Their moss rotted off them, flake by flake,
>   Till the thick stalk stuck like a murderer's stake,
>   Where rags of loose flesh yet tremble on high,
>   Infecting the winds that wander by.
>
>   (pp. 130-34)

The above cases are mainly ones of direct description: even more significant of Shelley's preoccupation with decay and the sinister are the similes which he constantly introduces in contexts where they are not strictly necessary:

> Two days thus passed—I neither raved nor died—
>   Thirst raged within me, like a scorpion's nest
> Built in mine entrails.

>   These things dwelt in me, even as shadows keep
>   Their watch in some dim charnel's loneliness,
> A shoreless sea, a sky sunless and planetless!

>   The twilight's gloom
>   Lay like a charnel's mist within the radiant dome.

> The hope of torturing him smells like a heap
> Of corpses, to a death-bird after battle.

> And one sweet laugh, most horrible to hear,
> As of a joyous infant waked and playing
> With its dead mother's breast.

> As from an ancestral oak
> Two empty ravens sound their clarion,
> Yell by yell, and croak by croak,
> When they scent the noonday smoke
>   Of fresh human carrion.

> From the cities where from caves,
> Like the dead from putrid graves,
> Troops of starvelings gliding come,
> Living tenants of a tomb.

>   The heavy dead hulk
> On the living sea rolls an inanimate bulk,
> Like a corpse on the clay which is hungering to fold
> Its corruption around it.

>   They stand aloof,
> And are withdrawn—so that the world is bare;
> As if a spectre wrapped in shapeless terror
> Amid a company of ladies fair

> Should glide and glow, till it became a mirror
> Of all their beauty.

> As dogs bay the moonlight clouds,
> Which, like spectres wrapped in shrouds,
> Pass o'er night in multitudes.
>
>   (pp. 135-36)

In view of the foregoing considerations it is not too much to claim that Shelley ranks with Baudelaire and Poe as one of the poets of decay. His preoccupation with the charnel and the worm, as exemplified in the passages quoted above, suggest affinities with *The Conqueror Worm,* or the conclusion of *Annabel Lee,* or that strange story in which the corpse of M. Valdemar, when unmesmerized, rots suddenly away and lies on the bed 'a nearly liquid mass of loathsome, of detestable, putridity'. A similar, though not identical, quality appears in Baudelaire's poem, *Une Charogne,* in which a lover, walking with his beloved, espies a piece of decaying carrion, and moralizes thereon concerning his passion.

Apart from descriptions of decay, Shelley's imagination has a strange power both of word and idea over the sinister in nature. There is a grim strength, for instance, in this recurring image of the scorpion wreaking venomed death upon itself under torture:

> The truths of their pure lips, that never die,
> Shall bind the scorpion falsehood with a wreath
>   Of ever-living flame,
> Until the monster sting itself to death.

>   Each girt by the hot atmosphere

> Of his blind agony like a scorpion stung
>   By his own rage upon his burning bier
> Of circling coals of fire.

There is a kindred variety of the sinister in such lines as:

>   The slow soft toads out of damp corners creep,

and

>   foodless toads
>   Within voluptuous chambers panting crawled.

Such are the more striking instances of what is perhaps the most conspicuous form of the sinister in Shelley's poetry. It is quite impossible to dismiss this as either a youthful foible or a melodramatic trick of literary practice. It corresponds to something deep and lasting in Shelley's soul. It seems to be partly the result of a violent reaction against his ecstatic optimism and belief in the ultimate perfectibility of all nature, human and cosmic. Beaten at certain crises from this hope, his mind fled desperately into the extreme of horror. Seen in this aspect, the sinister in his verse has strong analogy with the sinister in his character, especially as manifested in his relations with women. . . . [We] find him speaking of himself as desiring more in this world 'than any understand'. Stripped of the ideal and its armour, his soul was laid bare to the torments of reality, and became the nerve 'o'er which do creep the else unfelt oppressions of this earth'. The ecstatic physical intensity both of his yearning and of the subsequent reaction, is well illustrated in **"To Constantia Singing"**. . . . If one reads this poem carefully and compares with it Shelley's own account of the extraordinary acuteness which his senses developed during states of sickness, one can easily understand how inevitable it became that he who had seen and felt the beautiful with such abnormal vividness, should, when flung back on the terrible and horrible, feel and portray them also with appalling vividness in their minutest particulars. Equally applicable to his poetic vision and the hallucinations of his everyday life, is his description of 'that state of mind in which ideas may be supposed to assume the force of sensations through the confusion of thought with the objects of thought, and the excess of passion animating the creatures of imagination'. (pp. 136-39)

[There is] another striking characteristic of Shelley's thought and verse. On the one hand he believed with all his heart that evil is not the primary but the secondary principle of life, that the human soul is in its nature good, and only needs awakening to understand and realize a golden perfection of charity and brotherhood; and that the basic principle of all existence, human and cosmic, is love. This belief is the central tenet of his faith; it inspires many of his most perfect lyrics, and is the soul of *The Revolt of Islam, Prometheus Unbound*, and *Hellas*. Yet side by side with this strain in Shelley, a totally different one sounds throughout his poetry, and constitutes him one of the great poets of despair. The self-portrayal which had begun in **"Alastor"** deepens in **"Prince Athanase"** into a settled gloom of heart and brain. It has never been doubted that in this poem Shelley is attempting a portrait of himself, part dream, part reality. Here we are told that he is consumed by a grief unmirrored in other minds, by 'thoughts on thoughts, unresting multitudes', which worked within him 'as the fiends which wake and feed an everliving woe'. At the end of the First Part of this poem, Shelley relinquished as morbid his description of Athanase, after having written the following lines:

like an eyeless nightmare grief did sit

Upon his being; a snake which fold by fold
Pressed out the life of life, a clinging fiend
Which clenched him if he stirred with deadlier hold;
And so his grief remained—let it remain—untold!

He touches the inmost secret of his own character, in all its inconsistency and aspiration and disillusion, when he says of the Prince

all who knew and loved him then perceived
That there was drawn an adamantine veil

Between his heart and mind,—both unrelieved
Wrought in his brain and bosom separate strife.

It would seem that with Shelley himself, heart and brain, taken separately, were true and strong: the pity was that in the fight against circumstance they so seldom joined forces, and were thus so often vanquished and led captive by disillusion and despair. Hence the mood and the music we find in **"Mutability"**, the song, **"Rarely, rarely, comest thou, Spirit of Delight"**, and **"Lines Written in Dejection near Naples"**. . . . Hence, too, the famous portrait he draws of himself in *Adonais* as 'a herd-abandoned deer struck by the hunter's dart', and as

A pardlike Spirit beautiful and swift—
A love in desolation masked;—a Power
Girt round with weakness;—it can scarce uplift
The weight of the superincumbent hour;
It is a dying lamp, a falling shower,
A breaking billow;—even whilst we speak
Is it not broken? On the withering flower
The killing sun smiles brightly: on a cheek
The life can burn in blood, even while the heart may
    break.

(pp. 140-42)

[In] *Queen Mab* and *The Sensitive Plant,* Shelley evidently scorns beauty of subject, and strives to portray the sinister for its own sake, trusting his own imagination to envelop it with daemonic glamour: a more positive and acceptable phase of the same instinct is his constant attempt to discover beauty in things generally considered sinister. This effort is evident in the original theme of the relationship between the lovers in *The Revolt of Islam,* in Shelley's development of a kindred motive in *The Cenci,* and in his famous remark that this motive is 'a very poetical circumstance'. It appears again in his portrayal of the Spirit of Good as a snake in *The Revolt of Islam,* in his making the Woman take it to her bosom and scornfully repudiate any fear of it, and in the eventual absorption of its serpentine beauty in the transfigured glory of Laon:

Then first, two glittering lights were seen to glide
    In circles on the amethystine floor,
Small serpent eyes trailing from side to side,
    Like meteors on a river's grassy shore,
    They round each other rolled, dilating more
And more—then rose, commingling into one,
    One clear and mighty planet hanging o'er
A cloud of deepest shadow, which was thrown
Athwart the glowing steps and the crystalline throne.

Again, in **"Rosalind and Helen"** the pale snake floats on the 'dark and lucid flood in the light of his own loveliness'. In *Adonais* 'the green lizard and the golden snake like unimprisoned flames out of their trance awake'. And again, in *Prometheus Unbound,* after the transfiguration occurring in the Third Act, toads, snakes and efts become at once beautiful 'with little change of shape or hue.'

The simile of the meteors in the lines just quoted from *The Revolt of Islam* is itself a good case in point. The meteor, a thing of fear or evil with most poets, is constantly in Shelley beautiful and benignant. Here it is used as a symbol of the snake, which is frequently itself the symbol of Shelley's antinomianism, and of his conviction that the highest good is often what the world holds to be most evil. He was as great a transvaluer of values as Nietzsche, and this in art not less than in life. It is noteworthy that the rare beauty of Laon's hall is compounded of

> Starry shapes between
> And hornèd moons and meteors strange and fair.

Yet another benignant meteor, speeding from its home of decay, appears later in the poem to light the reunited pair in their love, and reappears under a form of strange beauty in **"Marenghi"**:

> And the marsh-meteors, like tame beasts, at night
>   Came licking with blue tongues his veined feet;
> And he would catch them, as, like spirits bright,
>   In many entangled figures quaint and sweet
> To some enchanted music they would dance—
> Until they vanished at the first moon-glance.

'The tempestuous loveliness of terror' is hymned with a different reference in the lines on the *Medusa* of Leonardo da Vinci, 'whose horror and whose beauty are divine':

> Yet it is less the horror than the grace
>   Which turns the gazer's spirit into stone,
> Whereon the lineaments of that dead face
>   Are graven, till the characters be grown
> Into itself, and thought no more can trace;
>   'Tis the melodious hue of beauty thrown
> Athwart the darkness and the glare of pain,
> Which humanize and harmonize the strain.

Akin to this is the homage Shelley pays to the Hermaphrodite, that 'sweet marble monster of both sexes', dear also to Gautier and Swinburne.

A main characteristic of his genius, and one closely akin to the foregoing, and definitely connected with his use of the sinister, is his desire to restore their full dues to objects whose beauty has been undervalued: thus in **"The Witch of Atlas"** he says:

> Men scarcely know how beautiful fire is—
>   Each flame of it is as a precious stone
> Dissolved in ever-moving light, and this
>   Belongs to each and all who gaze upon.

And in the same way he tells how Prometheus

>   tamed fire, which, like some beast of prey,
> Most terrible, but lovely, played beneath
> The frown of man.

Here it is once more the combination of loveliness and terror which fascinates him, as it had previously fascinated Collins.

Some of Shelley's most beautiful poetry of Nature possesses a peculiar unearthliness which seems due to a desire to get as far away as possible from the normal and everyday aspects of her which were so dear to Wordsworth. A good example of this is the picture of the sea-bed and its flowers given in the **"Ode to the West Wind"**. . . . A like magic appears in *Prometheus Unbound,* in the Second Faun's description of the spirit's home:

> I have heard those more skilled in spirits say,
> The bubbles, which the enchantment of the sun
> Sucks from the pale faint water-flowers that pave
> The oozy bottom of clear lakes and pools,
> Are the pavilions where such dwell and float
> Under the green and golden atmosphere
> Which noontide kindles through the woven leaves;

> And when these burst, and the thin fiery air,
> The which they breathed within those lucent domes,
> Ascends to flow like meteors through the night,
> They ride on them, and rein their headlong speed,
> And bow their burning crests, and glide in fire
> Under the waters of the earth again.

Nor does this unearthliness depend merely on Shelley's choice of subject: it recurs constantly in the colour given by his imagination even to the normal features of Nature. Nobody but he would have conceived this image for the Moon:

> And like a dying lady, lean and pale,
> Who totters forth, wrapped in a gauzy veil,
> Out of her chamber, led by the insane
> And feeble wanderings of her fading brain,
> The moon arose up in the murky East,
> A white and shapeless mass.

This unearthly colouring is sometimes extended even to Nature's homeliest aspects: witness the strange beauty given to the simplest flowers in **"The Question"**—beauty due in large measure to the hues of night cast upon the spring daylight by the 'moonlight-coloured may', and by the water lilies

> Which lit the oak that overhung the hedge
> With moonlight beams of their own watery light.

Starting from the merely horrible and sinister, we have arrived almost insensibly at one of the most real and distinctive kinds of beauty in all Shelley's verse. It would be as easy as it is unnecessary to follow the chain on to its final link, and show how that beauty passes into the simpler, more usual and normal, and perhaps also more perfect, beauty of **"Life of Life"**, or **"The Hymn of Apollo"**, or **"Love's Philosophy"**. It would be easy, too, to enlarge further on the psychological aspect of the matter, and to continue the parallel between Shelley's poetry and his life. In each he had a vision of glory withheld from his fellows, and, when this was eclipsed, he at times moved dizzily amid a night of tombs and terrors. In the darker places of his soul's adventure amid poetry, he was haunted by spectres of his own imagining, even as in life he had been haunted by his phantom assailant of the Pisa post-office, and the visionary assassin of Tanyrallt. And even when he came forth into the daylight and caught and sang its beauty, his song had constantly something in it of the night's witchery and terror. 'The oracular vapour' he had 'drunk wandering in his youth' would at times turn to other things than 'truth, virtue, love or joy'. Of the two powers to which he had ascribed poetic inspiration, God or the daemon genius, it was often the daemon that held him, or in his own words,

> This fiend whose ghastly presence ever
> Beside thee like thy shadow hangs.

The condition described in this and similar passages was, one must repeat, a deadly reality with Shelley, and is on no account to be dismissed as a mere literary affectation or extravagance: on the other hand, we must never forget that if there was something of the sinister deep in his soul and song, this was but the obverse of that celestial effluence hardly touched on here—the effluence of Love, whom he

>   sent to bind
> The disunited tendrils of that vine
> Which bears the wine of life, the human heart,

the effluence of Beauty through which his hearers walk

> exempt from mortal care
> Godlike, o'er the clear billows of sweet sound.
>
> (pp. 142-47)

> *Archibald T. Strong, "The Sinister in Shelley," in
> his* Three Studies in Shelley and An Essay on Nature
> in Wordsworth and Meredith, *Oxford University Press,
> London, 1921, pp. 107-47.*

T. S. ELIOT (lecture date 1933)

[*Eliot was perhaps the most influential poet and critic to write in
the English language during the first half of the twentieth century.
Here, he explains why he dislikes Shelley's writing, emphasizing
the immaturity of Shelley's ideas. Eliot originally presented his
commentary in a lecture delivered at Harvard University on 17
February 1933.*]

Shelley both had views about poetry and made use of poetry
for expressing views. With Shelley we are struck from the
beginning by the number of things poetry is expected to do;
from a poet who tells us, in a note on vegetarianism, that "the
orang-outang perfectly resembles man both in the order and
the number of his teeth," we shall not know what not to expect.
The notes to **Queen Mab** express, it is true, only the views of
an intelligent and enthusiastic schoolboy, but a schoolboy who
knows how to write; and throughout his work, which is of no
small bulk for a short life, he does not, I think, let us forget
that he took his ideas seriously. The ideas of Shelley seem to
me always to be ideas of adolescence—as there is every reason
why they should be. And an enthusiasm for Shelley seems to
me also to be an affair of adolescence: for most of us, Shelley
has marked an intense period before maturity, but for how
many does Shelley remain the companion of age? I confess
that I never open the volume of his poems simply because I
want to read poetry, but only with some special reason for
reference. I find his ideas repellant; and the difficulty of separating Shelley from his ideas and beliefs is still greater than
with Wordsworth. And the biographical interest which Shelley
has always excited makes it difficult to read the poetry without
remembering the man: and the man humourless, pedantic, self-
centered, and sometimes almost a blackguard. Except for an
occasional flash of shrewd sense, when he is speaking of someone else and not concerned with his own affairs or with fine
writing, his letters are insufferably dull. He makes an astonishing contrast with the attractive Keats. On the other hand, I
admit that Wordsworth does not present a very pleasing personality either; yet I not only enjoy his poetry as I cannot enjoy
Shelley's, but I enjoy it more than when I first read it. I can
only try to fumble (abating my prejudices as best I can) for
reasons why Shelley's abuse of poetry does me more violence
than Wordsworth's.

Shelley seems to have had to a high degree the unusual faculty
of passionate apprehension of abstract ideas. Whether he was
not sometimes confused about his own feelings, as we may be
tempted to believe when confronted by the philosophy of *Epipsychidion,* is another matter. I do not mean that Shelley had
a metaphysical or philosophical mind; his mind was in some
ways a very confused one: he was able to be at once and with
the same enthusiasm an eighteenth-century rationalist and a
cloudy Platonist. But abstractions could excite in him strong
emotion. His views remained pretty fixed, though his poetic
gift matured. It is open to us to guess whether his mind would
have matured too; certainly, in his last, and to my mind greatest

though unfinished poem, *The Triumph of Life,* there is evidence
not only of better writing than in any previous long poem, but
of greater wisdom:

> Then what I thought was an old root that grew
> To strange distortion out of the hillside,
> Was indeed one of those (*sic*) deluded crew
> And that the grass, which methought hung so wide
> And white, was but his thin discoloured hair
> And that the holes he vainly sought to hide
> Were or had been eyes . . .

There is a precision of image and an economy here that is new
to Shelley. But so far as we can judge, he never quite escaped
from the tutelage of Godwin, even when he saw through the
humbug as a man; and the weight of Mrs. Shelley must have
been pretty heavy too. And taking his work as it is, and without
vain conjectures about the future, we may ask: is it possible
to ignore the "ideas" in Shelley's poems, so as to be able to
enjoy the poetry? (pp. 79-82)

I am not a Buddhist, but some of the early Buddhist scriptures
affect me as parts of the Old Testament do; I can still enjoy
Fitzgerald's *Omar,* though I do not hold that rather smart and
shallow view of life. But some of Shelley's views I positively
dislike, and that hampers my enjoyment of the poems in which
they occur; and others seem to me so puerile that I cannot enjoy
the poems in which they occur. And I do not find it possible
to skip these passages and satisfy myself with the poetry in
which no proposition pushes itself forward to claim assent.
What complicates the problem still further is that in poetry so
fluent as Shelley's there is a good deal which is just bad jin-
gling. The following, for instance:

> On a battle-trumpet's blast
> I fled hither, fast, fast, fast,
> Mid the darkness upward cast.
> From the dust of creeds outworn,
> From the tyrant's banner torn,
> Gathering round me, onward borne,
> There was mingled many a cry—
> Freedom! Hope! Death! Victory!

Walter Scott seldom fell as low as this, though Byron more
often. But in such lines, harsh and untunable, one is all the
more affronted by the ideas, the ideas which Shelley bolted
whole and never assimilated, visible in the catchwords of creeds
outworn, tyrants and priests, which Shelley employed with
such reiteration. And the bad parts of a poem can contaminate
the whole, so that when Shelley rises to the heights, at the end
of the poem:

> To suffer woes which Hope thinks infinite;
> To forgive wrongs darker than death or night;
> To defy Power, which seems omnipotent;
> To love, and bear; to hope till Hope creates
> From its own wreck the thing it contemplates . . .

lines to the content of which belief is neither given nor denied,
we are unable to enjoy them fully. One does not expect a poem
to be equally sustained throughout; and in some of the most
successful long poems there is a relation of the more tense to
the more relaxed passages which is itself part of the pattern of
beauty. But good lines amongst bad can never give more than
a regretful pleasure. In reading *Epipsychidion* I am thoroughly
gravelled by lines like:

> True love in this differs from dross or clay,
> That to divide is not to take away . . .
> I never was attached to that great sect

> Whose doctrine is, that each one should select
> Out of the crowd, a mistress or a friend
> And all the rest, though fair and wise, commend
> To cold oblivion . . .

so that when I come, a few lines later, upon a lovely image like:

> A vision like incarnate April, warning
> With smiles and tears, Frost the anatomy
> Into his summer grave,

I am as much shocked at finding it in such indifferent company as pleased by finding it at all. And we must admit that Shelley's finest long poems, as well as some of his worst, are those in which he took his ideas very seriously. It was these ideas that blew the "fading coal" to life; no more than with Wordsworth can we ignore them without getting something no more Shelley's poetry than a wax effigy would be Shelley.

Shelley said that he disliked didactic poetry; but his own poetry is chiefly didactic, though (in fairness) not exactly in the sense in which he was using that word. Shelley's professed view of poetry is not dissimilar to that of Wordsworth. The language in which he clothes it in the **Defence of Poetry** [see excerpt dated 1821] is very magniloquent, and with the exception of the magnificent image which Joyce quotes somewhere in *Ulysses* ("the mind in creation is as a fading coal, which some invisible influence, like an inconstant wind, awakens to transitory brightness") it seems to me an inferior piece of writing to Wordsworth's great preface. He says other fine things too; but the following is more significant of the way in which he relates poetry to the social activity of the age:

> The most unfailing herald, companion and follower of the awakening of a great people to work a beneficial change in opinion or institution, is poetry. At such periods there is an accumulation of the power of communicating and receiving intense and impassioned conceptions respecting man and nature. The persons in whom this power resides may often, so far as regards many portions of their nature, have little apparent correspondence with that spirit of good of which they are the ministers. But even whilst they deny and abjure, they are yet compelled to serve, the power which is seated on the throne of their own soul.

I know not whether Shelley had in mind, in his reservations about "the persons in whom this power resides," the defects of Byron or those of Wordsworth; he is hardly likely to have been contemplating his own. But this is a statement, and is either true or false. If he is suggesting that great poetry always tends to accompany a popular "change in opinion or institution," that we know to be false. Whether at such periods the power of "communicating and receiving intense and impassioned conceptions respecting man and nature" accumulates is doubtful; one would expect people to be too busy in other ways. Shelley does not appear, in this passage, to imply that poetry itself helps to operate these changes, and accumulate this power, nor does he assert that poetry is a usual by-product of change of these kinds; but he does affirm some relation between the two; and in consequence, a particular relation between his own poetry and the events of his own time; from which it would follow that the two throw light upon each other. This is perhaps the first appearance of the kinetic or revolu-

tionary theory of poetry; for Wordsworth did not generalise to this point.

We may now return to the question how far it is possible to enjoy Shelley's poetry without approving the use to which he put it; that is, without sharing his views and sympathies. Dante, of course, was about as thoroughgoing a didacticist as one could find; and I have maintained elsewhere, and still maintain, that it is not essential to share Dante's beliefs in order to enjoy his poetry. If in this instance I may appear to be extending the tolerance of a biased mind, the example of Lucretius will do as well: one may share the essential beliefs of Dante and yet enjoy Lucretius to the full. Why then should this general indemnity not extend to Wordsworth and to Shelley? Here Mr. Richards [in his *Practical Criticism*] comes very patly to our help:

> Coleridge, when he remarked that a "willing suspension of disbelief" accompanied much poetry, was noting an important fact, but not quite in the happiest terms, for we are neither aware of a disbelief nor voluntarily suspending it in these cases. It is better to say that the question of belief or disbelief, in the intellectual sense, never arises when we are reading well. If unfortunately it does arise, either through the poet's fault or our own, we have for the moment ceased to be reading and have become astronomers, or theologians, or moralists, persons engaged in quite a different type of activity.

We may be permitted to infer, in so far as the distaste of a person like myself for Shelley's poetry is not attributable to irrelevant prejudices or to a simple blind spot, but is due to a peculiarity in the poetry and not in the reader, that it is not the presentation of beliefs which I do not hold, or—to put the case as extremely as possible—of beliefs that excite my abhorrence, that makes the difficulty. Still less is it that Shelley is deliberately making use of his poetic gifts to propagate a doctrine; for Dante and Lucretius did the same thing. I suggest that the position is somewhat as follows. When the doctrine, theory, belief, or "view of life" presented in a poem is one which the mind of the reader can accept as coherent, mature, and founded on the facts of experience, it interposes no obstacle to the reader's enjoyment, whether it be one that he accept or deny, approve or deprecate. When it is one which the reader rejects as childish or feeble, it may, for a reader of well-developed mind, set up an almost complete check. I observe in passing that we may distinguish, but without precision, between poets who employ their verbal, rhythmic and imaginative gift in the service of ideas which they hold passionately, and poets who employ the ideas which they hold with more or less settled conviction as material for a poem; poets may vary indefinitely between these two hypothetical extremes, and at what point we place any particular poet must remain incapable of exact calculation. And I am inclined to think that the reason why I was intoxicated by Shelley's poetry at the age of fifteen, and now find it almost unreadable, is not so much that at that age I accepted his ideas, and have since come to reject them, as that at that age "the question of belief or disbelief," as Mr. Richards puts it, did not arise. It is not so much that thirty years ago I was able to read Shelley under an illusion which experience has dissipated, as that because the question of belief or disbelief did not arise I was in a much better position to enjoy the poetry. I can only regret that Shelley did not live to put his poetic gifts, which were certainly of the first order, at the service of more tenable beliefs—which need not have been, for my purposes, beliefs more acceptable to me. (pp. 82-8)

T. S. Eliot, "Shelley and Keats," in his The Use of Poetry and the Use of Criticism: Studies in the Relation of Criticism to Poetry in England, *Cambridge, Mass.: Harvard University Press, 1933, pp. 78-94.*

HERBERT READ   (essay date 1936)

[*Read was a prolific English poet, critic, and novelist who championed "organic" artistic expression and who was deeply concerned with the role of art in furthering human development. Comparing Shelley with his contemporaries Keats and Landor, Read defines the "particular quality" of Shelley's poetry as his expression of two principles: liberty and tolerance.*]

The particular quality of Shelley's poetry still remains to be defined. It is a quality directly related to the nature of his personality.... Understanding the personality, we may more easily, more openly, appreciate the poetry.

Byron, who was a very honest critic, even of his friends, was the first to be aware of Shelley's *particular* quality. "You know my high opinion of your own poetry," he wrote to Shelley, and added the reason: "—because it is of *no* school." To Byron all the rest of his contemporaries seemed "secondhand" imitators of antique models or doctrinaire exponents of a mannerism. Shelley alone could not be so simply classified; his verse was too honestly original, too independently thought and wrought, to be accepted as "fashionable literature." For there are always these two types of originality: originality that responds like the Aeolian harp to every gust of contemporary feeling, pleasing by its anticipation of what is but half-formed in the public consciousness; and originality that is not influenced by anything outside the poet's own consciousness, but is the direct product of his individual mind and independent feeling. The latter type is always long in winning recognition, and since Shelley's originality was essentially of this type, we need not be surprised that only a few of his contemporaries appreciated his poetry for its proper qualities.

The reaction of Keats is the most interesting, for he had perhaps a profounder understanding of the nature of poetry than any man of that age—profounder, I would say, than Bryon and even profounder than Coleridge. We only discern this from the occasional statements made in his letters—there is unfortunately no formal essay to compare with Shelley's. Nor did Keats live to write poetry with which he was personally satisfied; we must not, that is to say, treat the poetry of Keats as an exemplification of his poetic ideals. A detailed comparison of the poetry of Keats and Shelley would not therefore be of great value. But Keats's reaction to Shelley's poetry, expressed in a letter to Shelley [see excerpt dated 1820], is most definitely critical:

> ... You might curb your magnanimity and be more of an artist, and load every rift of your subject with ore. The thought of such discipline must fall like cold chains upon you, who perhaps never sat with your wings furled for six months together.

We cannot doubt the force of the impact which Shelley's poetry had made on Keats. The poetry had been felt, but felt as something strange or inadequate. And actually we can see that what is involved is a clash of personalities. There is no need to describe Keats's personality at length; but it was in no way

parallel to Shelley's. Keats was not, of course, a normal type—no genius is; but compared with Shelley he was far more fully adjusted to his environment; physically more masculine and heterosexual; and though a sick man ("when I shook him by the hand there was death"), not a morbid one.... Now though much of Keats's poetry is anything but definite and objective, he was very conscious of an intolerable hiatus between his personality and the poetic diction he had derived from traditional models and current fashions; and his whole effort, as expressed in his short but intense poetic development, is towards objective virtues.

The whole tendency of Shelley, on the contrary, is towards a clarification and abstraction of thought—away from the personal and the particular towards the general and the universal. Between the transcendental intellectualism of Shelley and the concrete sensualism of Keats there could be, and was no contact.

The highest beauties of Keats's poetry are enumerative: a positive evocation of the tone and texture of physical objects. Even when describing an abstract conception like Melancholy, the imagery of physical sensation is dominant:

Ay, in the very temple of Delight
  Veil'd Melancholy has her sovran shrine,
    Though seen of none save him whose strenuous tongue
  Can burst Joy's grape against his palate fine ...

But the highest beauties of Shelley's poetry are evanescent and imponderable—thought so tenuous and intuitive, that it has no visual equivalent; no positive impact:

> Life of Life! thy lips enkindle
>   With their love the breath between them;
> And thy smiles before they dwindle
>   Make the cold air fire; then screen them
> In those looks, where whoso gazes
> Faints, entangled in their mazes.
>
> Child of Light! thy limbs are burning
>   Through the vest which seems to hide them;
> As the radiant lines of morning
>   Through the clouds ere they divide them;
> And this atmosphere divinest
> Shrouds thee whereso'er thou shinest.
>
> Fair are others; none beholds thee,
>   But thy voice sounds low and tender
> Like the fairest, for it folds thee
>   From the sight, that liquid splendour,
> And all feel, yet see thee never,
> As I feel now, lost for ever!
>
> Lamp of Earth! where'er thou movest
>   Its dim shapes are clad with brightness,
> And the souls of whom thou lovest
>   Walk upon the winds with lightness,
> Till they fail, as I am failing,
> Dizzy, lost, yet unbewailing!

In such a poem—and it is the supreme type of Shelley's poetic utterance—every image fades into air, every outline is dissolved in fire. The idea conveyed—the notional content—is almost negligible; the poetry exists in the suspension of meaning, in the avoidance of actuality.

In other words, such poetry has no precision, and the process of its unfolding is not logical. It does not answer to a general definition of any kind. It is vain to apply to it that method of criticism which assumes that the ardour of a verse can be analysed into separate vocables, and that poetry is a function of sound. Poetry is mainly a function of language—the exploitation of a medium, a vocal and mental material, in the interests of a personal mood or emotion, or of the thoughts evoked by such moods and emotions. I do not think we can say much more about it; according to our sensitivity we recognise its success. The rest of our reasoning about it is either mere prejudice, ethical anxiety, or academic pride.

Among his contemporaries, Shelley was perhaps nearest in poetic quality to Landor, whose *Gebir* was a lasting joy to him. A critical justification for this attraction would not be far to seek. The next nearest analogies are with Schiller and Goethe, both of whom Shelley read with enthusiasm; the influence of *Faust* has been traced in *The Triumph of Life*, but between Goethe and Shelley there is a general sympathy of poetic outlook which is not explained by direct contacts. Other analogies . . . are remoter: "the gentle seriousness, the delicate sensibility, the calm and sustained eneregy" of Ariosto; and above all "the first awakener of entranced Europe . . . the congregator of those great spirits who presided over the resurrection of learning; the Lucifer of that starry flock which in the thirteenth century shone forth from republican Italy as from a heaven, into the darkness of the benighted world"—Dante. All great poetry, said Shelley in the same reference to Dante, is *infinite;* and that is the final quality of his own poetry, the quality which lifts it into regions beyond the detractions of moralists and sciolists.

Shelley is of no school; that is to say, Shelley is above all schools, universal in the mode of his expression and the passion of his mind. That passion, the force that urged him to abundant voice, was simple, almost single, in its aim. "I knew Shelley more intimately than any man," wrote Hogg, "but I never could discern in him any more than two fixed principles. The first was a strong, irrepressible love of liberty; of liberty in the abstract, and somewhat after the pattern of the ancient republics, without reference to the English constitution, respecting which he knew little and cared nothing, heeding it not at all. The second was an equally ardent love of toleration of all opinions, but more especially of religious opinions; of toleration, complete, entire, universal, unlimited; and, as a deduction and corollary from which latter principle, he felt an intense abhorrence of persecution of every kind, public or private." Liberty and toleration—these words have a tortured history, and are often perverted for a moral purpose. But that was not Shelley's intention. "The highest moral purpose aimed at in the highest species of the drama, is the teaching the human heart, through its sympathies and antipathies, the knowledge of itself; in proportion to the possession of which knowledge, every human being is wise, just, sincere, tolerant and kind." Inasmuch as the final quality of Shelley's poetry is infinitude, so the final quality of his mind is sympathy. Sympathy and infinitude—these are expansive virtues, not avowed in the dry air of disillusion, awaiting a world of peace and justice for their due recognition. (pp. 80-86)

Herbert Read, "In Defence of Shelley," in his In Defence of Shelley and Other Essays, *William Heinemann Ltd., 1936, pp. 1-86.*

CARLOS BAKER (essay date 1948)

[*In this excerpt from his widely respected study of Shelley's most important works, Baker provides a detailed explication of* The Triumph of Life, *concluding with possible answers to Shelley's final question, "What is life?"*]

The long poem on which Shelley was at work when he was drowned was called *The Triumph of Life,* and the likelihood is that, if he had been able to finish what he had begun, the result would have been a fourth great poem to add to the *Prometheus,* the *Epipsychidion,* and the *Adonais. The Triumph* is filled with solemn music, charged with deep melancholy, more nearly mature in its inward control and majestically dignified in its quiet outward demeanor than anything Shelley had done before. The movement is *andante;* the language is intentionally subdued. There is no avid searching after the proper epithet as there was in the *Epipsychidion;* the word that Shelley wants, or something near it, is the word most frequently chosen. Once chosen, it is placed with a precision about which he had never cared quite so much until at least the time of *Adonais.*

Because it is melancholy, solemn, quiet, muted, controlled and majestic—because it is, so to speak, a return from paradise to purgatory, a fashion has arisen which looks upon *The Triumph of Life* as the first work of Shelley's second, and greater, maturity, or as the commencement of something to which he had gradually grown up through years of experimentation with "ideal" poems—something in itself fundamentally new. This stress on the newness has led in turn to the frequent implication that *The Triumph of Life* is in some sort a palinode to many of Shelley's previous philosophic affirmations.

But *The Triumph of Life* is rather a reaffirmation that a palinode. In it Shelley reexamines, from a slightly different point of view than was usual in his "ideal" poems, two connected problems which had engaged his attention in *The Sensitive Plant, Epipsychidion, A Defence of Poetry,* and *Adonais*: the poet's relation to the worldly life around him, and his relation to the divine light which, in Shelley's view, informs the highest efforts of the best poets. Though the fragment breaks off before the reexamination has been completed, it provides, as it stands, a quiet corroboration of the position endorsed in Shelley's most recent work.

Putting aside for the moment the difference in tone already mentioned, there appear to be three major differences between this last poem and those which precede it. The first is that *The Triumph* focuses on worldly life almost to the exclusion of the eternal life, though the values implicit in the latter are everywhere assumed, and in a strange way are visible *through* the unlovely but awesome and pitiable vision which Shelley is at pains to keep in immediate focus. Both *Epipsychidion* and *Adonais* had pointed a similar contrast between the temporal and the eternal, though not by means of this oddly effective device of the double vision.

The second major differences is that Shelley (if we may identify him with the Dantean narrator) is spectator rather than protagonist. In *Epipsychidion,* Shelley (or his creative soul) was a direct participant; in *Adonais* he had moved a little to one side in order to give Keats the center of the stage, but his idealized self-portrait had a prominent place in the poem, and it was his own aspiration of which he spoke in its closing stanzas. There is a new objectivity in *The Triumph of Life,* and Shelley is the curious questioning bystander trying to understand the complexity of the vision. Aside from the central allegorical procession, the center of interest is Rousseau and his psychomachia, rather than Shelley and his own struggle with the world.

The third major change from antecedent poems is a shift of the image by which the scene of worldly life is presented. The "dreary cone of our life's shade" (*Epipsychidion*) and the lowering mist, charnel-house gloom, and night-shadow (*Adonais*) have now become an ice-cold brassy glare "intenser than the noon"—light so harsh that it "obscures" the supernal sun. This new figure is preferable to the Cimmerian desert figure of *Adonais* or the "cone of shade" figure of *Epipsychidion* because it is in closer conformity with natural fact. But it had been anticipated at the close of *Adonais* in the dome of many-colored glass, which refracted, diffused, distorted, and stained the white radiance of eternity without excluding all supernal light. It will be seen that none of these differences from preceding poems is complete—most of Shelley's poems feed into one another—but the over-all difference is marked enough to give *The Triumph of Life* a complexion and a tone which are different from those of any earlier production.

Those who have previously examined this poem have thrown valuable light on its literary analogues and on some aspects of its allegorical significance. But *The Triumph* has never been viewed as a whole in the full perspective of Shelley's theory of the relation of the poet to society and to the cosmos. To accomplish this task, one must first answer the question: What happens in the poem?

The theme of *The Triumph of Life* is partly summarized in Wordsworth's lines about the light of heaven in the *Ode on Intimations of Immortality*.

> At length the Man perceives it die away,
> And fade into the light of common day.

For the ice-cold glare which emanates from the Chariot of Life in Shelley's poem is a more intensely felt version of Wordsworth's "light of common day" which intercedes against and eventually supersedes the "vision splendid" which the youth has known. Another aspect of the same theme is expressed in Byron's *The Prophecy of Dante*, which Shelley read with great admiration in the fall of 1821. Especially in the third and fourth cantos of this poem, Byron put into Dante's mouth an impassioned statement of a problem which troubled Shelley increasingly in his last years: the corrupting forces in human society which destroy the artist's integrity.

> They shall ring
> Many of love, and some of liberty,
> But few shall soar upon that eagle's wing,
> And look in the sun's face with eagle's gaze
> All free and fearless as the feather'd king,
> But fly more near the earth; how many a phrase
> Sublime shall lavish'd be on some small prince
> In all the prodigality of praise!
> And language, eloquently false, evince
> The harlotry of genius, which, like beauty,
> Too oft forgets its own self-reverence
> And looks on prostitution as a duty.

The dramatic method employed in *The Triumph of Life* is analogous to that of the *Inferno*, with Shelley and Rousseau in the place of Dante and Vergil, although instead of moving from place to place like the observer and the commentator of the *Inferno* and the *Purgatorio*, Shelley and Rousseau stand in one place to watch the approach, the passage, and the departure of the swiftly moving car of worldly life. The idea of the pageant is derived from Petrarch's *Trionfi*, with clear reminiscences of the procession of Lucifera in Spenser's *Faerie Queene*.

The fragment consists of a prologue, three unnumbered sections, and a final question. The prologue is an extraordinarily beautiful description of the physical setting (the seer lies under a chestnut tree on a slope of the Apennines, facing westward to the sea, with sunrise behind him) in which transpires the waking trance which overspreads his mind as the advancing light overspreads matutinal earth. Part the first is a detailed and graphic description of the visionary pageant, the advancing *triumphus* of the car of Worldly Life and its victims. Part the second discovers the commentator Rousseau, who, like Vergil in the *Inferno*, first identifies himself and then helps the spectator to identify certain historical characters among Worldly Life's countless victims. Part the third is Rousseau's "idealized history" of his "life and feelings" and occupies all the rest of the fragment except the final question of line 544 (which is probably Shelley's): "Then, what is life?"

The vision opens with the picture of a dusty and sterile public highway on which millions of aimless people hurry to and fro, pursuing "their serious folly as of old" and unaware of the contiguous forests, fountains, caverns, and banks of violets which lie beyond their beaten track. Heralded by an ice-cold glare which widely activates the madding crowd now comes swiftly the triumphal chariot with the deformed, caped and hooded figure of Worldly Life as its passenger, "wonder-wingèd" hours as its steeds, and a "Janus-visaged Shadow" with four faces and four pairs of eyes (all blindfolded) as the highly inefficient charioteer. The nearer approach of the car stirs the crowd to frenzy. The vanguard of the procession is made up of youths and maidens wild as bacchanals and maenads, convulsed in "agonizing pleasure" of insane mutual attraction, commingling and falling senseless to be rolled over by the chariot of "her who dims the sun" with her icy glare. The rear is brought up by obscene "old men and women foully disarrayed" who vainly strive to keep up with the car and the cold light which emanates from it, and who wheel about "with impotence of will" until "ghastly shadows" close round them and they sink in hopeless corruption. The allegorical significance of this pageant will be obvious to anyone who has read the Lucifera passage in *The Faerie Queene* on which this section of the poem is chiefly founded. The car of Worldly Life with its deformed occupant attracts the millions who blindly follow its cold light or run ahead in breathless haste, torn by wild passions. The vanguard and the rearguard represent respectively passionate love and spiritual impotence, and the fierce Spirit whose "unholy leisure" the youths and maidens serve is evidently the lower Venus.

Somewhat more difficult, however, is the identification of the "Janus-visaged Shadow" with blindfolded eyes who serves as charioteer. One who has read through Rousseau's account of his own life (where he makes it plain that his failure was a failure of vision as poet, so that he plunged too soon into the cold light of common day) will return to the Janus-figure with a stronger sense of what it stands for: it is the type of the poet who has been hoodwinked by the worldly life, and does not therefore own the skill—which for Shelley was the true use of great poetry—to guide aright the chariot of worldly life. Shelley's conception of ideal [see excerpt dated 1821] poets, as outlined in the *Defence*, included not only the progenitors of all the arts but also "institutors of laws . . . founders of civil society . . . inventors of the arts of life, and the teachers, who draw into a certain propinquity with the beautiful and the true, that partial apprehension of the agencies of the invisible world which is called religion." Hence, Shelley added, "all original religions are allegorical . . . and, like Janus, have a double face of false and true." The ideal poets, "those who imagine and express" the "indestructible order" are both legislators and prophets, and can "behold intensely the present as it is" as well as see "the future in the present." Suppose that these ideal poets are corrupted by the false shows of worldly life into losing contact with the "indestructible order" of things. They are, in effect, putting blindfolds on their great visionary powers; they can neither "behold intensely the present as it is," nor see "the future in the present." It is the generic type of the blindfolds on their great visionary powers; they can neither "behold intensely the present as it is," nor see "the future in the present." It is the generic type of the blindfolded poet who has "assumed the guidance" of the wonder-wingèd team of hours which draws the chariot of Worldly Life.

Besides the bacchic rout of youth and age who are crushed beneath or fall behind the chariot are another "captive multitude" who include all those grown old in power or misery, all the men of action and martyrs who subdued their respective worlds, and all those known to worldly fame or infamy. The reminiscence of Petrarch's *Triumph of Fame* is clear enough in this group. But the captives of the worldly life do not include the "sacred few" of Athens and Jerusalem

> who could not tame
> Their spirits to the conqueror—but, as soon
> As they had touched the world with living flame,
> Fled back like eagles to their native noon.

The "sacred few" were those who established contact with the "living flame" of heavenly light and did not lose it by taming their spirits to the cold glare of the worldly life. Evidently Christ and Socrates are foremost among the sacred few.

When the first part of the vision has been enacted, and the spectator wonders, half aloud, about the meaning of the pageant, and the identity of the shape within the car, a voice answers, "Life!" Out of the near hillside rises then the owner of the voice, who identifies himself as the corrupt and half-destroyed shade of Rousseau. "Who are those chained to the car?" asks the spectator. Rousseau answers that they are the great and famous who established "thought's empire over thought" but never learned to know themselves. Among them is the giant Napoleon

> Whose grasp had left the giant world so weak
> That every pigmy kicked it as it lay.

And as the phantasm of Napoleon passes, the spectator falls to grieving that the opposition of power and will is the badge of mortal experience, and to wondering why God made "good and the means of good" irreconcilable. Others of Life's victims pass in heterogeneous array—Plato, whose heart Life conquered by earthly love, Aristotle and Alexander the Great; Catherine the Great and Frederick the Great; Gregory the Great and other institutionalizers of Christianity who, in Shelley's view, "rose like shadows between man and God," corrupted the purity of Christian doctrine, and thus produced a false idol which still prevails and is worshiped in place of "the true sun" it superseded. But the spectator soon sickens of the historic pageantry and turns to the commentator to learn how it came about that Rousseau should be here beside the highway of the worldly life.

The idealized history of Rousseau's life and feelings which ensues closely parallels the idealized history of Shelley's life and feelings in *Epipsychidion* up to the point at which the "Being" he had dreamed of in his youth passed "into the dreary cone of our life's shade." The difference between the two careers is that when Rousseau's supernal vision faded, he

did not, like the creative soul of *Epipsychidion,* continue to search, but plunged instead into the worldly life and

> bared [his] bosom to the clime
> Of that cold light, whose airs too soon deform.

This is the central doctrine in which the whole fragment of *The Triumph of Life* is directed: that the poet must not abandon his search for the "living flame" he has known in his youth, though, as he grows up, the Worldly Life does all she can with her icy glare "intenser than the noon" to amaze his eyes, like Spenser's Lucifera, and to draw him into the killing airs which "too soon deform" the creative spirit. It is noteworthy that Shelley does not, like Wordsworth in the "Ode on Intimations of Immortality" embrace, though with sadness, the "homely nurse" of common life who seeks to make her foster-child ("her inmate man") forget the glories he has known. He will not take stoical consolation in the thought that advancing years will bring the philosophic mind because he has observed too often in literary history the Worldly Life's corrupting force. Indeed, as he showed in **"Peter Bell the Third,"** he regarded Wordsworth as a conspicuous victim of that force. He knows what Wordsworth means by "the light that never was on sea or land" and by "the consecration and the poet's dream." He knows, out of his own experience, how that nascent glory passes away from the earth into the dreary cone. But he will seek it still. "I go on until I am stopped," said Shelley, "and I am never stopped." *The Triumph of Life* is not a palinode against his previous affirmations about the poet's aspirations towards divine fire, but rather a palinode against Wordsworth's reluctant acceptance of what Shelley (and even Wordsworth) would regard as a lesser substitute. With Keats, of course, it was otherwise. In *Adonais* he is represented as one who never surrendered, and as one who, for all his alleged frailty, dared "the unpastured dragon in his den." Shelley admired the *Hyperion,* fragmentary though it was, as a great poem in that idealistic mode to which he was devoting his own efforts in the year of Keats' death. "Poetry," he asserted in the *Defence,* "lifts the veil from the hidden beauty of the world, and makes familiar objects be as if they were not familiar; it re-produces all that it re-presents, and the impersonations clothed in its Elysian light stand thenceforward in the minds of those who have once contemplated them, as memorials of that gentle and exalted content which extends itself over all thoughts and actions with which it coexists." The cold glare of the light around the triumphal car of worldly life was a anathema to one whose eyes were trained upon the Elysian light. "Poetry," said he again, "defeats the curse which binds us to be subjected to the accident of surrounding impressions" and "creates for us a being within our being. It makes us the inhabitants of a world to which the familiar world is a chaos. It reproduces the common [i.e. shared] universe of which we are portions and percipients, and it purges from our inward sight the film of familiarity which obscures from us the wonder of our being." The film of familiarity was a phrase of Coleridge's, and was another way of describing the cold light to which Rousseau and Wordsworth, and dozens of other great poets, had surrendered.

[As he had before], though objectively now in Rousseau's life-story, Shelley reincarnated in woman's shape his conception of the source of true poetic power—this time as Iris, many-colored goddess of the rainbow, prismatic reflector of the rays of the supernal sun. On an April morning long past, says Rousseau, he was laid asleep under a mountain. Running through the base of the mountain was a high-roofed cavern out of which flowed a limpid stream of water which filled the grove with pleasant sounds and "kept for ever wet" the stems of the flowers that grew nearby. Back beyond this sweet oblivious sleep Rousseau cannot remember:

> And whether life had been before that sleep
> The Heaven which I imagine, or a Hell
> Like this harsh world in which I wake to weep,
> I know not.

The sleep-figure is a symbolic representation of Rousseau's birth. "I arose," says he, and for a little while, though it was now broad day, the scene of woods and water seemed to retain a gentle trace

> Of light diviner than the common sun
> Sheds on the common earth, and all the place
> Was filled with magic sounds woven into one
> Oblivious melody, confusing sense.

To put the matter in Wordsworthian terms, Rousseau after his birth retained intimations ("a gentle trace") of a previous immortal state.

Now comes Rousseau's vision of the supernal influence. Shelley has worked out the phenomenal aspects of this vision in such careful detail that one must place himself in full possession of the picture which was evidently in Shelley's mind. The hulking mountain (the great divide between the antenatal and postnatal condition) runs as it were, on a north-south axis, blocking out the direct rays of the rising sun to the eastward. But the mountain is pierced straight through, on an east-west axis, by a cavern high and deep, through which the soul, in the unconscious act of being born, has just come from the sun-filled regions of the east. Within the cavern is a well or fountain. From it flows, the west-running stream beside which the soul has awakened after birth. But the rays of the eastern sun strike through the cavern, and the sun's image, "radiantly intense," burns on the waters of the well. It must be understood that the youthful soul is now on the western side of the mountain facing eastward toward the cavern where the sun's rays strike in upon the waters of the fountain. In the midst of this blaze is seen "on the vibrating floor of the fountain"

> A shape all light, which with one hand did fling
> Dew on the earth, as if she were the dawn,
> And the invisible rain did ever sing
> A silver music on the mossy lawn;
> And still before me on the dusky grass
> Iris her many-colored scarf had drawn.

The emanation from the "shape all light" is Iris, the rainbow, caused by the action of the sun's rays on the waters of the well. The same care which Shelley lavished on the setting for this phenomenon is applied in the development of the rainbow image. This vision is eventually to fade from Rousseau's sight and to lose itself in the light of common day just as a rainbow fades and vanishes. But for a while, as the youth Rousseau moves westward along the stream which flows from the cavern and the well, she remains visible to him, and all her actions and manifestations are such as would suggest, still, the rainbow.

It has sometimes been quite wrongly supposed that the Iris-figure is intended to be a creature with evil connotations. Thus she is said to blot out "the thoughts of him" who watches her swift movement, and one by one to trample them out, like sparks or embers, into "the dust of death." But from what follows it is plain that these are dark and evil thoughts, not thoughts in general, for her action is compared to that of day

"upon the threshold of the east" treading out the lamps of night. Similarly, when Rousseau asks for some explanation of the mysteries of his origin and his present condition, the goddess offers him her cup of Nepenthe, the bright cordial of her own Elysium, with the invitation: "Quench thy thirst [for knowledge]." But even as he touches "with faint lips" the cup which she raises, his brain becomes as sand and a new vision (that of Worldly Life and the "cold bright car") bursts on his sight. The usual explanation is that as a result of drinking from Iris' cup, Rousseau's spiritual senses were overcome by the cold new vision. Actually, however, he is not said to drink, but only to touch his lips to the cup. Had he drunk the bright Nepenthe, he could have quenched his youthful thirst for knowledge of the mysteries. But at the crucial moment his courage failed, his brain became "as sand," his thirst remained unquenched, and the bright cold vision of worldly life burst in.

Even in the severe excess of the cold light of the worldly life, Rousseau was sadly aware of the waning rainbow-vision, which still moved downstream by his side as he continued his journey through the wilderness. But it was dim now as

> A light of heaven, whose half-extinguished beam
> Through the sick day in which we wake to weep,
> Glimmers, for ever sought, for ever lost.

And turning his eyes to the triumphal procession of worldly life, Rousseau was swept up and borne along by the "loud million," baring his breast to the cold light "whose airs too soon deform."

As he closes the account of his great failure of nerve, Rousseau recalls one more phenomenon which he witnessed just after he had joined the "loud million." It was, he says, a wonder worthy to have been recorded by Dante. As the chariot of Worldly Life left the valley of the stream he had been following, he saw a convocation of fury-like phantoms filling the air along the chariot's tracks. And as he watched, all beauty, strength, and freshness slowly waned and fell from each of the human forms who followed the chariot, so that

> long before the day
> Was old, the joy which waked like heaven's glance
> The sleepers in the oblivious valley, died.

The situation here, as some commentators observe, is precisely the opposite of that which takes place at the end of *Prometheus Unbound*, after Prometheus has achieved his act of self-reform. At that time, the masks of ugliness fall from all created things. Now, in the procession of the Worldly Life, the masks are gradually assumed, and grow on. One who has observed the doffing of the masks in *Prometheus* and the assumption of them in *The Triumph*, might wish to use the observation as an argument that *The Triumph* is a palinode. But the argument would rest on a fundamental misconception of Shelley's intention in the two poems. The end of *Prometheus* is not intended as a picture of the actual, but only of what "ought to be." The beginning of the play, with Prometheus in chains, is Shelley's picture of the world as it is at present. The pageant of worldly life in *The Triumph* is, in effect, another vision of the conditions which obtain in the Prometheus up to the time of the hero's recantation. The voluntary or involuntary assumption of the loathsome masks is the equivalent of what happened to mankind when Prometheus granted sovereignty to Jupiter, god of hate and despair within the mind.

The fragmentary state of **The Triumph** leaves uncertain the identity of the asker of the final question, ''What is life?'' But whether the asker is Shelley or Rousseau, it is the answer which is important. If, as one strongly suspects, the ''life'' of the question is that which has been talked about through the greater part of the fragment, the answer to the question is clear, for worldly life is a corrupting force, a slow strain, a cold light whose effect is to deform. Shelley had discussed this question at some length in a passage of the **Defence** where he contrasted the Greek erotic poets (presumably those of the Hellenistic decadence) with Homer and Sophocles. The imperfection of the erotic poets, said he, consisted not in what they had but in what they had not. ''It is not inasmuch as they were poets, but inasmuch as they were not poets, that they can be considered with any plausibility as connected with the corruption of their age.'' That corruption did not extinguish in them all sensibility to pleasure, passion, and natural scenery; had it done so ''the last triumph of evil would have been achieved.'' For, as Shelley went on to say, ''the end of social corruption is to destroy all sensibility to pleasure'' and it spreads like a ''paralysing venom'' through imagination, intellect, affections, and even ''into the very appetites,'' until the whole mind becomes ''a torpid mass in which hardly sense survives.'' But the true poetic principle is at perpetual war with social corruption, and a given age can corrupt a given poet only to the extent that the poet has cut himself off from his greatest source of power. The shade of Rousseau in **The Triumph,** a mere root or misshapen stump of a being, serves as the *exemplum:* one who turned his back on the visionary splendor and followed the millions who accompanied the chariot of life.

To the poet who would avoid what Shelley called in **Adonais** ''the contagion of the world's slow strain,'' death is one of three alternatives. Shelley outlined the other two in a letter to his wife, written while he was visiting Byron at Ravenna in August, 1821. One device ''would be utterly to desert all human society,'' retiring with Mary and his son to a ''solitary island in the sea'' and shutting up ''the floodgates of the world.'' On this plan, said Shelley, he would be alone, and ''would devote either to oblivion or to future generations the overflowings of a mind which, *timely withdrawn from the contagion,* should be kept fit for no baser object.'' A more feasible alternative, said Shelley would be ''to form for ourselves a society of our own class, as much as possible in intellect, or in feelings; and to connect ourselves with the interests of that society.''

As it turned out, death by drowning in the Gulf of Spezzia was the alternative which preserved Shelley's spirit from the fate of those chained to the chariot of the Worldly Life. In the isolation of Lerici, on the shores of that gulf, he had been trying, surrounded by a little coterie, to put into practice the second plan. Without the solution chance forced upon him, Shelley might have succeeded in the great double task of preserving his integrity and maintaining, clear and unsullied before his mind's eye, the vision by which his best poetry was exalted. On the other hand, he sometimes felt, in the last year of his life, that his powers were beginning to wane. ''I try to be what I might have been,'' he said of **Hellas,** the last major poem he was able to complete, ''but am not successful.'' He summarized his feeling by quoting the first two lines of the following passage from Goethe's *Faust:*

> Over the noblest gift, the spirit's splendour.
> There floods an alien, ever alien stream;
> When this world's wealth is won, our souls surrender,
> The larger hope we call a lying dream.

> Our life of life, the visions grave and glorious,
> Fade, and the earthly welter is victorious.
> Imagination once, fire-winged with hope,
> Filled all eternity, and flamed to heaven;
> But now it dwindles to a petty scope,
> While joy on joy falls round us, wrecked and riven.

This is the great problem to which Shelley addressed himself in **The Triumph of Life**: the impingement of the mundane and the meretricious upon the higher life of the mind. From the perhaps inevitable stain upon the spirit's splendor Shelley was saved, if he needed saving, in the late afternoon of July 8, 1822. (pp. 255-70)

> *Carlos Baker, in his* Shelley's Major Poetry: The Fabric of a Vision, *Princeton University Press, 1948, pp. 255-75.*

JAMES A. NOTOPOULOS (essay date 1949)

[*In this excerpt from his book on Shelley's platonism, Notopoulos discusses the relationship between Plato's philosophy of art and the beliefs Shelley expresses in* A Defence of Poetry.]

The Platonism in [*A Defence of Poetry*] goes deeper than incidental borrowing. Plato no less than Peacock had attacked poetry, and the defense of poetry in Shelley's essay must be interpreted as an answer to both. But Shelley rejects Plato's attack on art in the tenth book of the *Republic*, only to accept Plato's view of poetry in the *Ion* and the *Phaedrus*. Plato offered Shelley two contradictory views of poetry: in the *Republic* Plato attacks not only bad poets but poetry itself, yet in the *Ion* and *Phaedrus* he states that poetry is an emanation of divinity. Shelley's defense makes use of the latter thesis to attack the former. In order to understand Shelley's defense of poetry we must understand Plato's attack on art in the tenth book of the *Republic*. This may be regarded from two points of view: (1) the standard of perfection in art being such and such, all the works which fall short of it are bad, or (2) all art is bad because it has no standards. One might maintain the first view because the art of Plato's day failed to come up to the standard of perfection. It is wrong, however, to think that Plato attacked only bad art. Plato's fundamental view about art is as follows: In sense perception the objects that we perceive are ambiguous and contradictory, and the emotions we experience in their perception are equally various and conflicting. Nothing can be valuable which is not organized by a standard of its own. This standard is supplied both for perceptions and emotions by philosophy and ultimately in both cases by the Idea of the Good. A work of art claims to be something other than a mere recording of sense perceptions and a mere feeling of perceptions. The artist selects, but qua artist he has no standard of selection except pleasure. . . . His services may be valuable in so far as the pleasure he provides may for the undeveloped man sugar the pill of logical or moral instruction. But if we turn to art for an independent standard of artistic excellence, then we are in a state of logical and moral delusion. Plato's real position in art is stated in the *Republic:* ''This, then, was what I wished to have agreed upon when I said that poetry, and in general the mimetic art, produces a product that is far removed from truth in the accomplishment of its task, and associates with the part in us that is remote from intelligence, and is its companion and friend for no sound and true purpose.'' The essence then of Plato's attack is that the artist has no standard. Shelley's defense rests essentially on Plato's view of poetry as something divine. . . . ''Poetry,'' he says, "is indeed something divine. It is at once the centre and circumference of knowledge; it is that which comprehends all science, and that to which all science must be referred." This is Shelley's reply to Plato's attack in the *Republic*.

Woven into the texture of Shelley's essay are all the fundamental doctrines of Plato about Intellectual Beauty, immortality, the relative and absolute world. Poetry for Shelley is philosophy itself: "a poet," he says, "participates in the eternal, the infinite, and the one." Poetry has for Shelley the same function as Eros in the *Symposium:* it is an intermediary daemon between man and the divine; like Love it leads us from the earthly to the divine; it strips the world of the veil of unreality and enables us to see the Ideal Beauty. In his essay Shelley has refracted all the rays of the Platonism that had previously appeared in his poetry through the prism of poetry; the doctrines of the *Symposium*, the *Phaedrus*, and the *Ion*, and the metaphysics of the *Republic* all emerge in the essay with Shelleyan coloration. Poetry, says Shelley, "strips the veil of familiarity from the world, and lays bare the naked and sleeping beauty, which is the spirit of its forms"; it "purges from our inward sight the film of familiarity which obscures from us the wonder of our being." Thus poetry, like philosophy, reveals reality and Intellectual Beauty. It "makes immortal all that is best and most beautiful in the world"; it "redeems from decay the visitations of the divinity in Man"; it "defeats the curse which binds us to be subjected to the accident of surrounding impressions". . .; "what were the scenery of this beautiful Universe which we inhabit; what were our consolations on this side of the grave, and what were our aspirations beyond it, if Poetry did not ascend to bring light and fire from those eternal regions?" In all these statements we see the Platonic immortality of the *Phaedo*, which, as seen in *Adonais* and *Epipsychidion*, is always an attribute of Ideal Beauty. Furthermore, poetry "creates for us a being within our being." What is this but the Platonic soul as described in *Epipsychidion* and the fragment **"On Love"**? Poetry for Shelley is the Platonic quest for beauty in all the planes of life, the physical, moral, and intellectual. In this essay the cloud of Shelley's own mind is "discharging its collected lightning" from Plato into a vast, comprehensive, and all-inclusive conception of the nature of poetry. Although Shelley does not unify all these Platonic strands, nevertheless we see in all of them a restatement of the Platonic philosophy that Shelley expressed in his poetry. Poetry, like Shelley's Platonic women, is but the means by which Intellectual Beauty finds expression in the world of time and space. As Professor White puts it, ". . . poetry is to Shelley simply the voice of Intellectual Beauty,. . . Intellectual Beauty is itself the sum of all true Imagination conceivable and inconceivable,. . . the individual human imagination flows from this fountain and back into it and is the nearest human contact with the Divine."

Even though Plato and Shelley do not agree as to the nature of poetry, they do agree about the use of poetry in the regeneration of man. Poetry, Shelley maintains, improves man morally and awakens the human spirit. "The great secret of morals," says Shelley, "is love; or a going out of our own nature, and an identification of ourselves with the beautiful which exists in thought, action, or person, not our own. A man, to be greatly good, must imagine intensely and comprehensively; he must put himself in the place of another and of many others. . . . The great instrument of moral good is the imagination; and poetry administers to the effect by acting upon the cause." Like Shelley, Plato recognizes the propaedeutic power of poetry in the habituation of moral feeling. "Let our artists," says Plato, "rather be those who are gifted to discern the true nature of beauty and grace; then will our youth dwell in a land of health, amid fair sights and sounds, and receive the good in everything; and beauty, the effluence of fair works, shall flow into the eye and ear, like a health-giving breeze from a purer region, and insensibly draw the soul from earliest years into likeness and sympathy with the beauty of reason." By supplanting reason with imagination Shelley makes poetry not a mere stage at a certain level of education, but education itself. Thus Plato and Shelley agree as to the function of poetry in education, but differ as to the primacy of reason or imagination in the educational process.

In Shelley's conception of poetry we also see a similarity to Plotinus. Like Keat's soul in *Adonais,* poetry is to Shelley a portion of the Eternal which flows from and returns to this fountain, bringing with it "the light and fire from those eternal regions." Shelley has woven into his conception of poetry the Plotinean theory of emanation which he expresses in *Adonais* and in particular in the *Essay on Christianity*. Furthermore, Shelley's view of art is Plotinian rather than Platonic. . . . [In] **"A Discourse on the Manners of the Antient Greeks,"** he restates Plato's theory of Ideas and their relation to particulars in terms of imagination rather than reason. He bases poetry on imagination rather than on reason; imagination is an active creative agent which synthesizes rather than analyzes.

This conception reappears in *A Defence of Poetry* as "Poetry enlarges the circumference of the imagination by replenishing it with thoughts of ever new delight, which have the power of attracting and assimilating to their own nature all other thoughts, and which form new intervals and interstices whose void for ever craves food."

The affinities of this view of poetry with Plotinus rather than Plato are marked, though in the absence of proof we must be cautious about deducing any derivative relation, for if Shelley's essay shows anything clearly, it shows his own creative powers of thought. . . . Plotinus, unlike Plato, does not view the artist as one who imitates imitations. The question which Plotinus asked and answered was,. . . "Why . . . did not Plato, taught by his own technique, understand that the great artist has his eye fastened not on nature or manufactured objects as on an opaque veil, but is really looking through these to the Ideas behind the curtain? Why did he not see that the artist is no slave of nature, but at once her lover and, as it were, her corrector and finisher, and more truly a maker than he who fashions works of utility with his hands?" The answer which Shelley gave to Plato is the same as that Plotinus gave to Plato, and in so doing we may . . . apply to Shelley More's appraisal of Plotinus's theory of art: ". . . he justified Platonism as the artist's philosophy *par excellence*."

Yet the influence of direct Platonism on the essay is great. Shelley had translated the *Symposium* and had read in the preceeding year Plato's *Phaedo, Phaedrus,* and *Republic*. In acknowledging the receipt of Peacock's essay which provoked the composition of his own essay, Shelley wrote, "I was at the moment reading Plato's *Ion,* which I recommend you to reconsider." This statement gives us an insight into Shelley's Platonic frame of mind in writing the essay. Coupled with such indirect Platonism as is found in Sir Philip Sidney's *Defence of Poesie*. . ., the dialogues of Plato which Shelley read form an important contribution to the color of phraseology and the texture of Shelley's thoughts. Shelley found in Plato a kindred spirit, despite their differences of outlook on poetry. He used the treasure of Plato's dialogues in the spirit of the statement in the *Essay on Christianity:* "Among true and real friends all is common.'' As this introduction and . . . detailed analysis of Platonic passages show, the Platonism in [*A Defence of Poetry*] represents the high-water mark of Shelley's Platonism. (pp. 346-50)

> *James A. Notopoulos, in his* The Platonism of Shelley: A Study of Platonism and the Poetic Mind, *1949. Reprint by Octagon Books, 1969, 671 p.*

DONALD DAVIE (essay date 1952)

[*An English poet, critic, educator, and translator, Davie is well respected for both his creative and critical contributions to literature. The following commentary first appeared in Davie's 1952 work* The Purity of Diction in English Verse, *in which he argued for a return to the prose-like syntax, formal structures, and conservative metaphors of the eighteenth-century Augustan poets. Davie discusses Shelley's sublime and familiar styles, focusing on the success of his diction in each.*]

However we look at it, Shelley affects the sublime. We may not know what the sublime is, and yet know that, to be acceptable, it must include *The Triumph of Life* and *Prometheus Unbound*. Whatever we think of these poems (and the latter at any rate makes dull reading in my experience), there can be no doubt how high the poet aims in them, what large pretensions he makes. In short, whatever his performace, Shelley promises in these poems to move on a level where (for instance) 'urbanity' cannot count.

But this is what makes criticism of Shelley so difficult; he evades so many standards. In this he is peculiar even among the poets of the sublime. His sublimity is peculiarly indefinite and impalpable. From one point of view his poetry is certainly sensuous; but the sensuousness is not of a sort to bring into poetry the reek and grit of common experience. For Shelley goes as far as poetry can go, while it uses intelligible language, in cutting the hawsers which tie his fancies to the ground. His metaphors are tied so tenuously to any common ground in experience that it is peculiarly hard to arrive at their mooring in common logic or association. It was this, for instance, which gave Mr. Eliot so much trouble with an image in **"To a Skylark"**:

> Keen as are the arrows
>   Of that silver sphere,
> Whose intense lamp narrows
>   In the white dawn clear
> Until we hardly see—we feel that it is there.

It is typical of Shelley's obscurity that as it happens I find no difficulty here, but only the accurate register of a sense-perception—the fading of the morning-star. For Shelley evades as many standards as he can, and when he cannot evade them, makes their application as difficult as he can; or so it must seem to the harassed critic. And as a result we can expect to find the critics even further than usual from agreement about the nature of his achievement. All one can say is that the period of uncritical adulation is past, and that we have learnt, since Dr. Leavis' damaging scrutiny, to be on our guard when Shelley is most sublime.

At any rate, if Shelley is great, in *Prometheus Unbound*, in *The Triumph of Life*, even in such shorter poems as **"The Cloud,"** he is so by virtue of *invention*, the characteristic virtue of the sublime. And the eighteenth-century critics would agree that in poems of this sort the poet has considerable licence. We can expect (and it is only right) that the diction of an epic or a hymn will be less chaste than the diction of a familiar

epistle. And we can go so far as to say that in the case of such poems the question of diction should not be introduced at all. But this is not quite true. There are always limits. As Keats remarked, 'English must be kept up'—even in the epic. And Shelley as usual goes to the limit, or over it.

"The Cloud" is a good example:

> Sublime on the towers of my skiey bowers,
>   Lightning my pilot sits;
> In a cavern under is fettered the thunder,
>   It struggles and howls at fits;
> Over earth and ocean, with gentle motion,
>   This pilot is guiding me,
> Lured by the love of the genii that move
>   In the depths of the purple sea;
> Over the rills, and the crags, and the hills,
>   Over the lakes and the plains,
> Wherever he dream, under mountain or stream,
>   The Spirit he loves remains;
> And I all the while bask in Heaven's blue smile,
>   Whilst he is dissolving in rains.

The image is audacious to begin with. There is no reason in natural philosophy to give a basis in logic to the notion that a cloud is directed by electric charges. The image depends entirely on association, and the leap of association is something of a strain. However, it is made easier by the elaboration which makes the thunder a prisoner in the dungeons of the cloud. Natural philosophy lends its aid to the logical association of a cloud with the genii of the sea; and the lightning is supposed amorous of the sea—a link sanctioned by neither logic nor association (however 'free'), but carried as it were on the cloud's back. The real difficulty comes with the 'he,' appearing three times in the last six lines. Is this 'he' the lightning, the actual cloud, or the idea of the cloud which is always present even in a cloudless sky? We are given no indication that this 'he' is any other than 'the pilot,' i.e., the lightning. And yet this is surely impossible in the last two lines:

> And I all the while bask in Heaven's blue smile,
>   Whilst he is dissolving in rains.

Shelley means to say, I think, that the ideal cloud continues to bask while the actual cloud dissolves in rains; but in fact he says that the cloud, ideal or actual, rides high, while the lightning dissolves. And this is lunacy.

The fault here lies in the conduct and development of a metaphor, not, in the first place, in choice of language. And yet the two cannot be distinguished since the metaphor only comes to grief on the loose use of a personal pronoun. This looseness occurs time and again:

> The stars peep behind her and peer;
> And I laugh to see them whirl and flee,
>   Like a swarm of golden bees,
> When I widen the rent in my wind-built tent,
>   Till the calm rivers, lakes, and seas,
> Like strips of the sky fallen through me on high,
>   Are each paved with the moon and these.

The grotesque 'and these' is an affront to all prosaic discipline. So again:

> I am the daughter of Earth and Water,
>   And the nursling of the Sky;
> I pass through the pores of the ocean and shores;
>   I change but I cannot die. . . .

—where 'ocean and shores' is unthinkable in speech or prose. And finally:

> From cape to cape, with a bridge-like shape,
>   Over a torrent sea,
> Sunbeam-proof, I hang like a roof,—
>   The mountains its columns be.

Here the language is quite indiscriminate; the adjectival 'torrent' is a Latinate urbanity, 'sunbeam-proof' is an audacious coining, and 'The mountains . . . be' is a *naïveté*.

Obviously the conduct of the metaphor in the second stanza is a more serious flaw than any of these later examples. And obviously too, Shelley pitches his poem in a high key, to advise us not to expect nicety of discrimination and prosaic sense. The poem offers compensations. But all the same when the barbarities are so brutal and the carelessness so consistent, it may be doubted whether we can let them pass on any understanding. In poems of this sort, the weight to be given to diction and invention respectively is something that must be left to the taste of the reader. But this may serve as an example of how, even in sublime poems, the poet may take such liberties with his diction as to estrange his reader's sympathies. For one reader, at any rate, **"The Cloud"** remains a poem splendid in conception but ruined by licentious phrasing.

This does not dispose of Shelley's pretensions to sublimity. They confuse at almost every point the issue of his diction. In reading Wordsworth it is comparatively easy to distinguish the 'sublime' poems from the others, and to say that this poem begs the question of diction, this other does not. In the case of Shelley this is not so easily done. And yet there are poems by Shelley which plainly make no sublime pretensions. It was Ernest de Selincourt, I think, who proposed Shelley as one of the masters of the familiar style. The term, like all those which we find we need, is out of fashion; but plainly it refers to a quality of tone, of unflurried ease between poet and reader, in short to urbanity, the distinctive virtue of a pure diction.

It is worth remarking how unlikely this was, in the period when Shelley wrote. Plainly urbanity will come most easily to a poet who is sure of his audience, sure that he and his reader share a broad basis of conviction and assumption. The whole pressure of Shelley's age was against anything of the kind. Urbanity, except in the raffish version of Byron and Praed, was out of fashion among critics and readers; but that was the least of the difficulties. In the Elizabethan, the Caroline and the Augustan ages, the poet moved in a society more or less stable and more or less in agreement about social propriety. Most poets moved in circles where manners were ceremonious. The courteous usages were mostly hypocritical, but at least they were consistent; and they furnished the poet with a model urbanity which he could preserve in the tone of his writing. This was as true of the ponderous decorum of Mrs. Thrale's drawing-room as of the elaborate frivolity of the court of Charles II. Presumably, the violent dislocation of English society at the end of the eighteenth century (the Industrial Revolution) had destroyed the established codes of social behaviour. At any rate, in the Godwin household, in the family of Leigh Hunt, in the extraordinary domestic arrangements of Lord Byron, personal suffering and passion broke through into conversation and social demeanour. These were people who lived on their nerves, whom an established code of behaviour no longer protected. Therefore we cannot expect to find in the poetry of 1820 the exquisite assurance, the confident communication between poet and reader, which dignifies the slightest pieces of Thomas Carew or Thomas Parnell. We cannot expect it; but we find it. It is only natural that Spenser and Dryden, Carew and Parnell, enjoy this assurance. It is anything but natural, it seems almost impossible, that Shelley should do so.

The familiar style in this sense derives from the mean style of the Elizabethans, distinguished by them from the high style, proper to the heroic poem and the hymn, and from the base style of satire and pastoral. It is related too, to what Coleridge, in *Biographia Literaria*, called the 'neutral' style. It is distinguished from the other styles, in the nineteenth century as in the sixteenth, by being comparatively prosaic. Now, according to Johnson, a diction was pure when it was sanctioned by speech-usage on the one hand, and by literary precedent (classic and neo-classic) on the other. The poet's needs tugged him now one way, now the other; to tread a middle course, in touch with both sorts of usage, was to write a pure diction. But as the literary models varied (Juvenal for satire, Virgil for epic), so did the spoken models. The speech of a cobbler was not the model for epic, nor the speech of bishops for satire. There survived, in fact, though mostly unacknowledged, Puttenham's rule that the model for the high style was the speech of courtiers and governors; for the mean style, the speech of merchants and yeomen; for the base style, the speech of peasants and menial trades. In theory Wordsworth ignored the other criterion, literary precedent, and, as Coleridge confusedly saw, came near to asserting that the only permissible style was the mean. In any of the styles, to maintain a pure diction was to preserve 'the tone of the centre' which Arnold was to esteem in Attic prose. It is one way of explaining 'the sublime,' to say that, as England in the eighteenth century became a bourgeois state, the spoken model for the high style disappeared, and in poetry which 'affected the sublime' (the Augustan version of the high style) the question, whether the diction was pure, became meaningless. We are usually asked to acknowledge that Shelley's greatest poetry was of this sort. But there are other poems which are in the base and the mean styles; and it is among these that we have to look for Shelley the master of the familiar style.

The clearest example of Shelley's base style is the **"Letter to Maria Gisborne."** If we . . . talk in terms of Elizabethan decorum, this corresponds to "The Shepheard's Calender," as **"Julian and Maddalo,"** in the mean style, to "Colin Clout's Come Home Again," as **"The Cloud,"** in the high style, to "Fowre Hymnes." Shelley himself invites the Spenserian parallel:

> Near those a most inexplicable thing,
> With lead in the middle—I'm conjecturing
> How to make Henry understand; but no—
> I'll leave, as Spenser says, with many mo,
> This secret in the pregnant womb of time,
> Too vast a matter for so weak a rhyme.

The archaism, like others ('I wist' . . . 'they swink') is used partly as Spenser used it in "The Shepheard's Calender" or "Mother Hubberd's Tale," partly as Byron used it in *Don Juan*, to draw attention to its ungainly self. But the **"Letter to Maria Gisborne"** is neither Spenserian nor Byronic. It belongs to the tradition of Donne and Browning, who use the base style to unusual ends. There is no gainsaying that Shelley's verse resembles Browning's more than Donne's; it is an exercise in agility, not energy. Still, it is heartening, not hearty; and affectionate without being mawkish. It is too exuberant to be called urbane in the usual sense. But it is so, in the sense that the poet is sure of his relationship with the person he addresses, that he knows what is due to her and to himself, that he maintains a consistent tone towards her. She is not a peg to hang a poem on, nor a bosom for him to weep on, but a person who shares with him certain interests and certain friends and a certain sense of humour.

This poem is prosaic only in the relatively unimportant sense that it introduces things like hackney-coaches, Baron de Tott's Memoirs, 'self-impelling steam-wheels,' and 'a queer broken glass With ink in it.' But like Donne's verse or Browning's, Shelley's is far more figurative than normal prose. For truly lean and bare prosaic language, we turn to **"Julian and Maddalo"**:

> I rode one evening with Count Maddalo
> Upon the bank of land which breaks the flow
> Of Adria towards Venice; a bare strand
> Of hillocks, heaped from ever-shifting sand,
> Matted with thistles and amphibious weeds,
> Such as from earth's embrace the salt ooze breeds
> Is this; an uninhabited sea-side,
> Which the lone fisher, when his nets are dried,
> Abandons; and no other object breaks
> The waste, but one dwarf tree and some few stakes
> Broken and unrepaired, and the tide makes
> A narrow space of level sand thereon,
> Where 'twas our wont to ride while day went down.

This of course represents a specifically Romantic purity—the adoption, from prose or careful conversation, of a vocabulary of natural description. At their best, the eighteenth-century poets had good reason for believing that features of natural appearance had to be dignified by figures, if they were to be pleasing and instructive; but more often their fussing with metaphors and personifications represented an impurity even by their own standards, for there can be little doubt that their practice in this particular was very far from any spoken usage. Shelley's assumption, that accuracy confers its own dignity, produced a much purer diction; and there are satisfying examples of this elsewhere in **"Julian and Maddalo,"** as elsewhere in his work. But what the Romantics gained with one hand they lost from the other. For if Johnson, for example, was 'intolerably poetical' when he essayed natural description, he had an enviable prosaic assurance in his dealings with the abstractions of moral philosophy. And it is in this province that Shelley's diction is woefully impure. He expressed, in *The Defence of Poetry* [see excerpt dated 1821], his concern for these large abstractions, and his Platonic intention to make them apprehensible and 'living' in themselves. In **"The Witch of Atlas"** he came near to effecting this; but more often, this programme only means that an abstraction such as Reason or Justice must always be tugged about in figurative language. The moment they appear in Shelley's verse (and they always come in droves) the tone becomes hectic, the syntax and punctuation disintegrate. In **"Julian and Maddalo,"** by inventing the figure and the predicament of the maniac, Shelley excuses this incoherency and presents it (plausibly enough) as a verbatim report of the lunatic's ravings: and in this way he preserves the decorum of the conversation piece (the poem is subtitled 'A Conversation'). As a result, the whole of this passage, tiresome and unpoetic as it is, impairs but does not ruin the whole. The urbanity is resumed in the close:

> If I had been an unconnected man
> I, from this moment, should have formed some plan
> Never to leave sweet Venice,—for to me
> It was delight to ride by the lone sea;

> And then, the town is silent—one may write
> Or read in gondolas by day or night,
> Having the little brazen lamp alight,
> Unseen, uninterrupted; books are there,
> Pictures, and casts from all those statues fair
> Which were twin-born with poetry, and all
> We seek in towns, with little to recall
> Regrets for the green country. I might sit
> In Maddalo's great palace, and his wit
> And subtle talk would cheer the winter night
> And make me know myself, and the firelight
> Would flash upon our faces, till the day
> Might dawn and make me wonder at my stay.

The conversation we have attended to in the poem is just as civilized as the intercourse of Maddalo and Julian here described. It is in keeping that Julian should know little of Maddalo and not approve of all that he knows, but should be prepared to take him, with personal reservations, on his own terms. It is the habit of gentlemen; and the poet inculcates it in the reader, simply by taking it for granted in his manner of address. The poem civilizes the reader; that is its virtue and its value.

"To Jane; the Invitation" and **"To Jane: the Recollection"** were originally two halves of one poem, called "The Pine Forest of the Cascine near Pisa." In the second working over, **"The Invitation"** gained enormously, **"The Recollection"** hardly at all. The evolution of the latter poem illustrates very forcibly the process . . . by which the characteristically Shelleyan attitude emerges from a Wordsworthian base. The original version is strikingly Wordsworthian in metre and diction:

> A spirit interfused around,
>   A thinking, silent life;
> To momentary peace it bound
>   Our mortal nature's strife;—
>
> And still, it seemed, the centre of
>   The magic circle there,
> Was one whose being filled with love
>   The breathless atmosphere.

This becomes:

> A spirit interfused around,
>   A thrilling, silent life,—
> To momentary peace it bound
>   Our mortal nature's strife;
> And still I felt the centre of
>   The magic circle there
> Was one fair form that filled with love
>   The lifeless atmosphere.

[The] changes ('thrilling' for 'thinking,' 'being' to 'fair form,' and 'lifeless' for 'breathless') are all in the direction of eroticism. It is more pertinent to the present enquiry to notice that they all remove the discourse further from prosaic sense. One could write, in sober prose, of a *breathless* atmosphere; one could never describe it as *lifeless.* And by the same token a prose-writer can make us conceive how a person can seem to imbue a locality or a moment with a peculiar spiritual flavour; but that the emanation should be physical, an attribute of 'form' rather than 'being,' is something far more difficult. It is, of course, part of the poetic function to persuade us of realities outside the range of prosaic sense. But this can hardly be done by the familiar tone; and certainly Shelley does not do it here. He does not persuade us of the novelty, he only tricks us into it. His verse neither appeals to an old experience, nor creates a new one. These passages are a serious flaw in such a short poem.

The other piece, "**The Invitation,**" is a nonpareil, and one of Shelley's greatest achievements. It maintains the familiar tone, though in highly figured language, and contrives to be urbane about feelings which are novel and remote. This poem presents the experience which "**The Recollection**" tries to define and rationalize; and the definition is there, already, in the expression. Jane's influence upon the scene where she moved is here entirely credible; what Shelley afterwards tried to express, first in Wordsworthian and then in erotic terms, here persuades us from the start with no fuss or embarrassment. It is the lack of fuss, the ease and assurance, which persuades us throughout. In other words, the poem is first and foremost a triumph of tone. We can accept Jane as 'Radiant Sister of the Day,' largely because the lyrical feeling has already accommodated such seemingly unmanageable things as unpaid bills and unaccustomed visitors. It is an achievement of urbanity to move with such ease from financial and social entanglements to elated sympathy with a natural process; just as it is a mark of civilization to be able to hold these things together in one unflurried attitude.

It is important that we should understand the reservations we have to make about "**The Recollection.**" We dislike Shelley's eroticism, in the end, because it seems a vicious attitude, morally reprehensible; but we dislike it in the first place only because it produces a vicious diction, a jargon. In the end every true literary judgment is a moral judgment. But many critics go wrong, and many readers misunderstand them, because they pass too rapidly into the role of moralist. Even so, those critics are doing their duty better than others who think that moral judgment is no part of their business. I think we should value the significant ambiguity in such phrases as '*chaste* diction,' '*pure* diction,' '*vicious* style,' 'the *conduct* of a fable.' But I am willing to let the ambiguity tell its own tale and to stop short, in this argument, before the point at which literary criticism moves over and becomes philosophical. It is best to think, therefore, that we condemn Shelley's eroticism (as we do) because it produces a jargon, and not because we dislike it 'in itself.' (pp. 307-16)

[The] best of Shelley's love-songs (not those like "**Love's Philosophy,**" which figure in the anthologies) are distinguished, like the best Caroline lyrics, by urbanity. As early as 1814, the 'Stanza, written at Bracknell' can control self-pity by controlled and judicious phrasing:

> Thy dewy looks sink in my breast;
>   Thy gentle words stir poison there;
> Thou has disturbed the only rest
>   That was the portion of despair!
> Subdued to Duty's hard control,
>   I could have borne my wayward lot:
> The chains that bind this ruined soul
>   Had cankered then—but crushed it not.

It is not serious, of course, only album-verse; as is some of Carew. It all depends on how good the album is; in other words, on the degree of civilization in the society which calls for such trifles. And of course there is no question of comparison with Carew. But the Caroline neatness in the third and fourth lines, and the Augustan echo in the fifth, represent an urbane control which Shelley later threw away. More urbane still are the stanzas, "**To Harriet,**" written in the same year. . . . Of course

we cheapen the idea of urbanity by applying it to such polished nothings. . . . But in their brittle elegance they represent a tradition which could have made Shelley's later love-verse a source of delight instead of embarrassment. (pp. 316-17)

[It] appears from parts of "**Peter Bell the Third**" that Shelley quite deliberately worked erotic elements into the Wordsworthian base of many of his poems. He seems to have mistaken for prudery the master's natural frigidity. No doubt, too, the erotic jargon was bound up with his dedicated flouting of all the sexual morality of his society. For whatever reason Shelley in his love-lyrics adopted a hectic and strident tone, and the urbanity of his early pieces never bore fruit. At the same time he threw into lyrical form more and more of his poetry. The lyric became confused with the hymn and so moved into the orbit of the sublime.

But the jargon came to be habitual with him, whatever sort of poem he wrote, until it taints them nearly all, sublime or not. One of the least tainted is *The Sensitive Plant*, which I find one of his greatest achievements, and of great interest from the point of view of diction. In this poem and "**The Witch of Atlas**" Shelley is as daring as ever in invention, making his fable as wayward and arbitrary as possible. In both poems the sensuousness is of his peculiar sort which makes the familiar remote. (He takes a common object such as a rose or a boat, and the more he describes it, the less we remember what it is.) In short, the vision in both these poems has all the difficulties of the Shelleyan sublime, impalpable and aetherial. What distinguishes these poems, however, from such a similar (and maddening) piece as "**Alastor,**" is the presence, at the end of each of them, of a tough hawser of sober sense which at once pulls the preceding poem into shape and (what amounts to the same thing) gives it as much prose meaning as it will bear.

The Sensitive Plant is in three parts, with a conclusion. The first part presents in ecstatic detail the garden in summer, and dwells with particular weight upon one plant in the garden, which appears endowed with almost human intelligence in so far as it seeks to express the love it feels and the beauty it aspires to. Devoid of bloom and scent, it is unable to do so. But this predicament is subordinate to the poet's more general purpose, which is, in Part I, to make the garden seem like a dream. He does so with persuasive ease, partly by metrical resourcefulness (the metres induce a dream, not a pre-Raphaelite swoon), partly by deliberate confusion between the five senses, and partly by exploiting the vaporous, atmospheric and luminous features in the scene which he describes. Part II is short and concerned with the presiding human deity of the garden, a woman who is a sort of human counterpart of the Sensitive Plant. Part III begins with the death of the lady and describes how the garden, through autumn and winter into the next spring, falls into unweeded ruin.

In the scheme of this fable there is plainly room for an erotic element. The garden, for all its dream-like quality, pulses with germinating energy; and this 'love' is what the sensitive plant seeks to express:

> But none ever trembled and panted with bliss
> In the garden, the field, or the wilderness,
> Like a doe in the noontide with love's sweet want,
> As the companionless Sensitive Plant.

We know Shelley's eroticism is vicious only by the vicious diction it produces. Therefore we can have no complaints about the third line of this stanza, at the same time as we condemn the first. There the trembling and the panting and the bliss, coming thus together, are Shelleyan jargon, reach-me-down words which obviate the need for thinking and feeling precisely. The vice in question is not lasciviousness but more generally self-indulgence which betrays itself in lax phrasing as in lax conduct. Once we have read a certain amount of Shelley's verse, we recognize and dislike words from the private jargon, even when they are used with propriety:

> And the hyacinth purple, and white, and blue,
> Which flung from its bells a sweet peal anew
> Of music so delicate, soft, and intense,
> It was felt like an odour within the sense.

This is deliberate confusion between the senses, not used as later poets used it for definition of a compound sense-experience, nor only for intensification, but to throw over waking experience the illusion of a dream. Unfortunately 'intense' is a word we learn to suspect in Shelley, and it irritates. So again:

> The plumed insects swift and free,
> Like golden boats on a sunny sea,
> Laden with light and odour, which pass
> Over the gleam of the living grass;
>
> The unseen clouds of the dew, which lie
> Like fire in the flowers till the sun rides high,
> Then wander like spirits among the spheres,
> Each cloud faint with the fragrance it bears;
>
> The quivering vapours of dim noontide,
> Which like a sea o'er the warm earth glide,
> In which every sound, and odour, and beam,
> Move as reeds in a single stream.

Here the confusion between the senses is particularly persuasive, for it appeals to known facts about atmospheric conditions, or else to the evidence of the senses in such conditions. Unfortunately 'faint' and 'dim' are words from the jargon; and this perturbs the reader, even though both are plausible in this context.

Occasionally, too, there are flagrant violations of prosaic discipline:

> But the Sensitive Plant which could give small fruit
> Of the love which it felt from the leaf to the root,
> Received more than all, it loved more than ever,
> Where none wanted but it, could belong to the giver . . .

and:

> The snowdrop, and then the violet,
> Arose from the ground with warm rain wet,
> And their breath was mixed with fresh odour, sent
> From the turf like the voice and the instrument

—which is culpably ambiguous like Byron's lines which appalled Wordsworth:

> I stood in Venice on the Bridge of Sighs
> A palace and a prison on each hand.

And yet at the very crux of the argument lies the beautiful stanza:

> And the beasts, and the birds, and the insects were drowned
> In an ocean of dreams without a sound;
> Whose waves never mark, though they ever impress
> The light sand which paves it, consciousness.

This is memorably poetic, and yet, in the distinction between 'mark' and 'impress,' and in the logical tautness of the whole image, it is 'strong' with . . . prosaic strength. . . . (pp. 318-21)

The object of these many examples is not to pick holes in a masterpiece, still less to reduce judgment to some ridiculous balancing of good stanzas against bad. They are meant to illustrate what is after all the capital difficulty in reading Shelley—his unevenness. He has hardly left one perfect poem, however short. In reading him one takes the good with the bad, or one does without it altogether. The business of private judgment on his poems is not a weighing of pros and cons but a decision whether the laxity, which is always there, lies at the centre of the poem (as it often does) or in the margin. I have no doubt that the faults of *The Sensitive Plant* are marginal, and that at the centre it is sound and strong.

In any case, the second and third parts of the poem are an improvement on Part I. Part III, in particular, presents a rank and desolate scene as in **"Julian and Maddalo"** but in greater detail. It is done more poetically than by Crabbe, but no less honestly.

The six stanzas of the 'Conclusion' are of a quite different kind. They ask to be judged on the score of diction, and they triumphantly pass the test they ask for:

> Whether the Sensitive Plant, or that
> Which within its boughs like a Spirit sat,
> Ere its outward form had known decay,
> Now felt this change, I cannot say.
>
> Whether that Lady's gentle mind,
> No longer with the form combined
> Which scattered love, as stars do light,
> Found sadness, where it left delight,
>
> I dare not guess; but in this life
> Of error, ignorance, and strife,
> Where nothing is, but all things seem,
> And we the shadows of the dream,
>
> It is a modest creed, and yet
> Pleasant if one considers it,
> To own the death itself must be,
> Like all the rest, a mockery.
>
> That garden sweet, that lady fair,
> And all sweet shapes and odours there,
> In truth have never passed away:
> 'Tis we, 'tis ours are changed; not they.
>
> For love, and beauty, and delight,
> There is no death nor change: their might
> Exceeds our organs, which endure
> No light, being themselves obscure.

There is not a phrase here which would be out of place in unaffected prose. If that is strange praise for a piece of poetry, it is what one can rarely say of the poetry of Shelley's period. If these stanzas stood by themselves, they might seem tame and flat. In their place in the longer poem they are just what is needed to vouch for the more florid language of what has gone before. (pp. 321-22)

The poet I have considered here is a poet of poise and good breeding. Shelley was the only English Romantic poet with the birth and breeding of a gentleman, and that cannot be irrelevant. What is more surprising is the evidence that in other poems Shelley failed chiefly for want of the very tact which

A drawing, reputedly of Shelley, by Edward Williams.

is here conspicuous. I am at a loss to explain how a poet so well aware of what he was doing should also have written *The Cenci*. But if urbanity depends on the relation between poet and public, then it may be that Shelley's failures in tact were connected with his being unread and neglected. In her notes on the poems of 1821, Mrs. Shelley hinted as much:

> Several of his slighter and unfinished poems were inspired by these scenes, and by the companions around us. It is the nature of that poetry, however, which overflows from the soul, oftener to express sorrow and regret than joy; for it is when oppressed by the weight of life, and away from those he loves, that the poet has recourse to the solace of expression in verse.

It is, alas, too true that many of Shelley's poems are the products of self-pity looking for 'solace' or compensation; and it is not strange that the 'slighter and unfinished poems,' inspired by 'the companions around us,' should be some of Shelley's best work. This is not the poetry 'which overflows from the soul,' but the considered expression of an intelligent man. (pp. 324-25)

> *Donald Davie, "Shelley's Urbanity," in* English Romantic Poets: Modern Essays in Criticism, *edited by M. H. Abrams, Oxford University Press, 1960, pp. 307-25.*

HAROLD BLOOM   (essay date 1965)

[*Bloom, an American critic and editor, is best known as the formulator of "revisionism," a controversial theory of literary creation based on the concept that all poets are subject to the influence of earlier poets and that, to develop individual voices,* they attempt to overcome this influence through a deliberate process of "creative correction," which Bloom calls "misreading." In this excerpt from an essay first published in 1965, Bloom provides a general introduction to Shelley's poetry.]

Percy Bysshe Shelley, one of the greatest lyrical poets in Western tradition, has been dead for more than a hundred and forty years, and critics have abounded, from his own day to ours, to insist that his poetry died with him. Until recently, it was fashionable to apologize for Shelley's poetry, if one liked it at all. Each reader of poetry, however vain, can speak only for himself, and there will be only description and praise in this introduction, for after many years of reading Shelley's poems, I find nothing in them that needs apology. Shelley is a unique poet, one of the most original in the language, and he is in many ways *the* poet proper, as much so as any in the language. His poetry is autonomous, finely wrought, in the highest degree imaginative, and has the spiritual form of vision stripped of all veils and ideological coverings, the vision many readers justly seek in poetry, despite the admonitions of a multitude of churchwardenly critics. (p. 87)

The urbane lyricism of the **"Hymn of Apollo,"** and the harshly self-conscious, internalized dramatic quality of *The Triumph of Life* are both central to Shelley. Most central is the prophetic intensity, as much a result of displaced Protestantism as it is in Blake or in Wordsworth, but seeming more an Orphic than Hebraic phenomenon when it appears in Shelley. Religious poet as he primarily was, what Shelley prophesied was one restored Man who transcended men, gods, the natural world, and even the poetic faculty. Shelley chants the apotheosis, not of the poet, but of desire itself:

> Man, oh, not men! a chain of linkèd thought,
>   Of love and might to be divided not,
> Compelling the elements with adamantine stress;
>   As the sun rules, even with a tyrant's gaze,
>   The unquiet republic of the maze
> Of planets, struggling fierce towards heaven's free wilderness.
>   Man, one harmonious soul of many a soul,
>   Whose nature is its own divine control,
> Where all things flow to all, as rivers to the sea. . . .

The rhapsodic intensity, the cumulative drive and yet firm control of those last three lines in particular, as the high song of humanistic celebration approaches its goal—that seems to me what is crucial in Shelley, and its presence throughout much of his work constitutes his special excellence as a poet.

Lyrical poetry at its most intense frequently moves toward direct address between one human consciousness and another, in which the "I" of the poet directly invokes the personal "Thou" of the reader. Shelley is an intense lyricist as Alexander Pope is an intense satirist; even as Pope assimilates every literary form he touches to satire, so Shelley converts forms as diverse as drama, prose essay, romance, satire, epyllion, into lyric. To an extent he himself scarcely realized, Shelley's genius desired a transformation of all experience, natural and literary, into the condition of lyric. More than all other poets, Shelley's compulsion is to present life as a direct confrontation of equal realities. This compulsion seeks absolute intensity, and courts straining and breaking in consequence. When expressed as love, it must manifest itself as mutual destruction:

> In one another's substance finding food,
> Like flames too pure and light and unimbued
> To nourish their bright lives with baser prey,

Which point to Heaven and cannot pass away:
One Heaven, one Hell, one immortality,
And one annihilation.

Shelley is the poet of these flames, and he is equally the poet of a particular shadow, which falls perpetually between all such flames, a shadow of ruin that tracks every imaginative flight of fire:

O, Thou, who plumed with strong desire
    Wouldst float above the earth, beware!
A Shadow tracks thy flight of fire—
    Night is coming!

By the time Shelley had reached his final phase, of which the great monuments are *Adonais* and *The Triumph of Life,* he had become altogether the poet of this shadow of ruin, and had ceased to celebrate the possibilities of imaginative relationship. In giving himself, at last, over to the dark side of his own vision, he resolved (or perhaps merely evaded, judgment being so difficult here) a conflict within his self and poetry that had been present from the start. Though it has become a commonplace of recent criticism and scholarship to affirm otherwise, I do not think that Shelley changed very much, as a poet, during the last (and most important) six years of his life, from the summer of 1816 until the summer of 1822. The two poems of self-discovery, of mature poetic incarnation, written in 1816, **"Mont Blanc"** and the **"Hymn to Intellectual Beauty,"** reveal the two contrary aspects of Shelley's vision that his entire sequence of major poems reveals. The head and the hearts, each totally honest in encountering reality, yield rival reports as to the name and nature of reality. The head, in **"Mont Blanc,"** learns, like Blake, that there is no natural religion. There is a Power, a secret strength of things, but it hides its true shape or its shapelessness behind or beneath a dread mountain, and it shows itself only as an indifference, or even pragmatically a malevolence, toward the well-being of men. But the Power speaks forth, through a poet's act of confrontation with it that is the very act of writing his poem, and the Power, rightly interpreted, can be used to repeal the large code of fraud, institutional and historical Christianity, and the equally massive code of woe, the laws of the nation-states of Europe in the age of Castlereagh and Metternich. In the **"Hymn to Intellectual Beauty"** a very different Power is invoked, but with a deliberate and more austere tenuousness. A shadow, itself invisible, of an unseen Power, sweeps through our dull dense world, momentarily awakening both nature and man to a sense of love and beauty, a sense just beyond the normal range of apprehension. But the shadow departs, for all its benevolence and despite the poet's prayers for its more habitual sway. The heart's responses have not failed, but the shadow that is antithetically a radiance will not come to stay. The mind, searching for what would suffice, encountered an icy remoteness, but dared to affirm the triumph of its imaginings over the solitude and vacancy of an inadvertent nature. The emotions, visited by delight, felt the desolation of powerlessness, but dared to hope for a fuller visitation. Both odes suffer from the evident straining of their creator to reach a finality, but both survive in their creator's tough honesty and gathering sense of form. (pp. 88-90)

Shelley was anything but a born poet, as even a brief glance at his apprentice work will demonstrate. Blake at fourteen was a great lyric poet; Shelley at twenty-two was still a bad one. He found himself, as a stylist, in the autumn of 1815, when he composed the astonishing **"Alastor,"** a blank verse rhapsodic narrative of a destructive and subjective quest. **"Alas-**tor,"** though it has been out of fashion for a long time, is nevertheless a great and appalling work, at once a dead end, and a prophecy that Shelley finally could not evade. (p. 91)

The poem is an extremely subtle internalization of the quest-theme of romance, and the price demanded for the internalization is first, the death-in-life of what Yeats called "enforced self-realization," and at last, death itself. The Alastor or avenging demon of the title is the dark double of the poet-hero, the spirit of solitude that shadows him even as he quests after his emanative portion, the soul out of his soul that Shelley later called the epipsyche. Shelley's poet longs to realize a vision, and this intense and overconstant yearning destroys natural existence, for nature cannot contain the infinite energy demanded by the vision. Wordsworthian nature, and not the poet-hero, is the equivocal element in **"Alastor,"** the problem the reader needs to, but cannot, resolve. (p. 92)

Prometheus Unbound is a remarkably subtle and difficult poem. That a work of such length needs to be read with all the care and concentration a trained reader brings to a difficult and condensed lyric is perhaps unfortunate, yet Shelley himself affirmed that his major poem had been written only for highly adept readers, and that he hoped for only a few of these. *Prometheus Unbound* is not as obviously difficult as Blake's *The Four Zoas,* but it presents problems comparable to that work. Blake has the advantage of having made a commonplace understanding of his major poems impossible, while Shelley retains familiar (and largely misleading) mythological names like Prometheus and Jupiter. The problems of interpretation in Shelley's lyrical drama are as formidable as English poetry affords, and are perhaps finally quite unresolvable. (p. 96)

Published with *Prometheus Unbound* in 1820 were a group of Shelley's major odes, including **"Ode to the West Wind,"** **"To a Skylark,"** and **"Ode to Liberty."** These poems show Shelley as a lyricist deliberately seeking to extend the sublime mode, and are among his finest achievements.

Wallace Stevens, in one of the marvelous lyrics of his old age, hears the cry of the leaves and knows, "it is the cry of leaves that do not transcend themselves," knows that the cry means no more than can be found "in the final finding of the ear, in the thing / Itself." From this it follows, with massive but terrible dignity, that "at last, the cry concerns no one at all." This is Stevens' modern reality of *decreation,* and this is the fate that Shelley's magnificent **"Ode to the West Wind"** seeks to avert. Shelley hears a cry of leaves that do transcend themselves, and he deliberately seeks a further transcendence that will metamorphosize "the thing itself" into human form, so that at last the cry will concern all men. But in Shelley's **"Ode,"** as in Stevens's "there is a conflict, there is a resistance involved; / And being part is an exertion that declines." Shelley too feels the frightening strength of the *given,* "the life of that which gives life as it is," but here as elsewhere Shelley does not accept the merely "as it is." The function of his **"Ode"** is apocalyptic, and the controlled fury of his spirit is felt throughout this perfectly modulated "trumpet of a prophecy."

What is most crucial to an understanding of the **"Ode"** is the realization that its fourth and fifth stanzas bear a wholly antithetical relation to one another. The triple invocation to the elements of earth, air, and water occupies the first three stanzas of the poem, and the poet himself does not enter those stanzas; in them he is only a voice imploring the elements to hear. In the fourth stanza, the poet's ego enters the poem, but in the guise only of a battered Job, seeking to lose his own humanity.

From this nadir, the extraordinary and poignantly ''broken'' music of the last stanza rises up, into the poet's own element of fire, to affirm again the human dignity of the prophet's vocation, and to suggest a mode of imaginative renovation that goes beyond the cyclic limitations of nature. Rarely in the history of poetry have seventy lines done so much so well.

Shelley's other major odes are out of critical favor in our time, but this is due as much to actual misinterpretations as to any qualities inherent in these poems. **"To a Skylark"** strikes readers as silly when they visualize the poet staring at the bird and hailing it as nonexistent, but these readers have begun with such gross inaccuracy that their experience of what they take to be the poem may simply be dismissed. The ode's whole point turns on the lark's being out of sight from the start; the poet *hears* an evanescent song, but can see nothing, even as Keats in the ''Ode to a Nightingale'' never actually sees the bird. Flying too high almost to be heard, the lark is crucially compared by Shelley to his central symbol, the morning star fading into the dawn of an unwelcome day. What can barely be heard, and not seen at all, is still discovered to be a basis upon which to rejoice, and indeed becomes an inescapable motive for metaphor, a dark justification for celebrating the light of uncommon day. In the great revolutionary **"Ode to Liberty,"** Shelley successfully adapts the English Pindaric to an abstract political theme, mostly by means of making the poem radically its own subject, as he does on a larger scale in **"The Witch of Atlas"** and *Epipsychidion.*

In the last two years of his life, Shelley subtly modified his lyrical art, making the best of his shorter poems the means by which his experimental intellectual temper and his more traditional social urbanity could be reconciled. The best of these lyrics would include **"Hymn of Apollo," "The Two Spirits: An Allegory," "To Night," "Lines . . . on . . . the Death of Napoleon,"** and the final group addressed to Jane Williams, or resulting from the poet's love for her, including **"When the lamp is shattered," "To Jane: The Invitation," "The Recollection," "With a Guitar, to Jane,"** and the last completed lyric, the immensely moving **"Lines Written in the Bay of Lerici."** Here are nine lyrics as varied and masterful as the language affords. Take these together with Shelley's achievements in the sublime ode, with the best of his earlier lyrics, and with the double handful of magnificent interspersed lyrics contained in *Prometheus Unbound* and *Hellas,* and it will not seem as if Swinburne was excessive in claiming for Shelley a rank as one of the two or three major lyrical poets in English tradition down to Swinburne's own time.

The best admonition to address to a reader of Shelley's lyrics, as of his longer poems, is to slow down and read very closely, so as to learn what Wordsworth could have meant when he reluctantly conceded that ''Shelley is one of the best *artists* of us all: I mean in workmanship of style.''

The Cenci occupies a curious place in Shelley's canon, one that is overtly apart from the sequence of his major works that goes from *Prometheus Unbound* to *The Triumph of Life.* Unlike the pseudo-Elizabethan tragedies of Shelley's disciple Beddoes, *The Cenci* is in no obvious way a visionary poem. Yet it is a tragedy only in a very peculiar sense, and has little in common with the stageplays it ostensibly seeks to emulate. Its true companions, and descendants, are Browning's giant progression of dramatic monologues, *The Ring and the Book,* and certain works of Hardy that share its oddly effective quality of what might be termed dramatic solipsism, to have recourse to a desperate oxymoron. Giant incongruities clash in *Prometheus*

Unbound as they do in Blake's major poems, but the clashes are resolved by both poets in the realms of a self-generated mythology. When parallel incongruities meet violently in *The Cenci,* in a context that excludes myth, the reader is asked to accept as human characters beings whose states of mind are too radically and intensely pure to be altogether human. Blake courts a similar problem whenever he is only at the borderline of his own mythical world, as in *Visions of the Daughters of Albion* and *The French Revolution.* Shelley's Beatrice and Blake's Oothoon are either too human or not human enough; the reader is uncomfortable in not knowing whether he encounters a Titaness or one of his own kind.

Yet this discomfort need not wreck the experience of reading *The Cenci,* which is clearly a work that excels in character rather than in plot, and more in the potential of character than in its realization. At the heart of *The Cenci* is Shelley's very original conception of tragedy. Tragedy is not a congenial form for apocalyptic writers, who tend to have a severe grudge against it, as Blake and D. H. Lawrence did. Shelley's morality was an apocalyptic one, and the implicit standard for *The Cenci* is set in *The Mask of Anarchy,* which advocates a nonviolent resistance to evil. Beatrice is tragic because she does *not* meet this high standard, though she is clearly superior to every other person in her world. Life triumphs over Beatrice because she does take violent revenge upon an intolerable oppressor. The tragedy Shelley develops is one of a heroic character ''violently thwarted from her nature'' by circumstances she ought to have defied. This allies Beatrice with a large group of Romantic heroes, ranging from the Cain of Byron's drama to the pathetic daemon of Mary Shelley's *Frankenstein* and, on the cosmic level, embracing Shelley's own Prometheus and the erring Zoas or demigods of Blake's myth. (pp. 103-04)

The aesthetic power of *The Cenci* lies in the perfection with which it both sets forth Beatrice's intolerable dilemma, and presents the reader with a parallel dilemma. The natural man in the reader exults at Beatrice's metamorphosis into a relentless avenger, and approves even her untruthful denial of responsibility for her father's murder. The imaginative man in the reader is appalled at the degeneration of an all-but-angelic intelligence into a skilled intriguer and murderess. This fundamental dichotomy *in the reader* is the theater where the true anguish of *The Cenci* is enacted. The overt theme becomes the universal triumph of life over integrity, which is to say of death-in-life over life. (p. 105)

In the spring of 1820, at Pisa, Shelley wrote *The Sensitive Plant,* a remarkably original poem, and a permanently valuable one, though it is little admired in recent years. As a parable of imaginative failure, the poem is another of the many Romantic versions of the Miltonic Eden's transformation into a wasteland, but the limitations it explores are not the Miltonic ones of human irresolution and disobedience. Like all of Shelley's major poems, *The Sensitive Plant* is a skeptical work, the skepticism here manifesting itself as a precariously posed suspension of judgment on the human capacity to perceive whether or not natural *or* imaginative values survive the cyclic necessities of change and decay. (pp. 105-06)

The tone of *The Sensitive Plant* is a deliberate exquisitiveness, of a more-than-Spenserian kind. . . .

The dark melancholy of *The Sensitive Plant* is not Spenserian, but everything else in the poem to some extent is. Like many poems in this tradition, the lament is for mutability itself, for change seen as loss. What is lost is innocence, natural harmony, the mutual interpenetrations of a merely given condition that is nevertheless whole and beyond the need of justification. The new state, experiential life as seen in Part III of the poem, is the world without imagination, a tract of weeds. When Shelley, in the noblest quatrains he ever wrote, broods on this conclusion he offers no consolation beyond the most urbane of his skepticisms. The light that puts out our eyes is a darkness to us, yet remains light, and death may be a mockery of our inadequate imaginations. The myth of the poem—its garden, lady, and plant—may have prevailed, while we, the poem's readers, may be too decayed in our perceptions to know this. Implicit in Shelley's poem is a passionate refutation of time, but the passion is a desperation unless the mind's imaginings can cleanse perception of its obscurities. Nothing in the poem proper testifies to the mind's mastery of outward sense. The "Conclusion" hints at what Shelley beautifully calls "a modest creed," but the poet is too urbane and skeptical to urge it upon either us or himself. The creed appears again in "The Witch of Atlas," but with a playful and amiable disinterestedness that removes it almost entirely from the anguish of human desire.

"The Witch of Atlas" is Shelley's most inventive poem, and is by any just standards a triumph. In kind, it goes back to the English Renaissance epyllion, the Ovidian erotic-mythological brief epic, but in tone and procedure it is a new departure, except that for Shelley it had been prophesied by his own rendition of the Homeric **"Hymn to Mercury."** Both poems are in *ottava rima*, both have a Byronic touch, and both have been characterized accurately as possessing a tone of visionary cynicism. Hermes and the Witch of Atlas qualify the divine grandeurs among which they move, and remind us that imagination unconfined respects no orders of being, however traditional or natural. (pp. 106-07)

"The Witch of Atlas," as Shelley says in the poem's highly ironic dedicatory stanzas to his wife, tells no story, false or true, but is "a visionary rhyme." If the Witch is to be translated at all into terms not her own, then she can only be the mythopoeic impulse or inventive faculty itself, one of whose manifestations is the Hermaphrodite, which we can translate as a poem, or any work of art. The Witch's boat is the emblem of her creative desire, and like the Hermaphrodite it works against nature. The Hermaphrodite is both a convenience for the Witch, helping her to go beyond natural limitations, and a companion of sorts, but a highly inadequate one, being little more than a robot. The limitations of art are involved here, for the Witch has rejected the love of every mortal being, and has chosen instead an automation of her own creation. In the poignant stanzas in which she rejects the suit of the nymphs, Shelley attains one of the immense triumphs of his art, but the implications of the triumph, and of the entire poem, are as deliberately chilling as the Byzantine vision of the aging Yeats.

Though the Witch turns her playful and antinomian spirit to the labor of upsetting church and state, in the poem's final stanzas, and subverts even the tired conventions of mortality as well as of morality, the ultimate impression she makes upon us is one of remoteness. The fierce aspirations of *Prometheus Unbound* were highly qualified by a consciously manipulated prophetic irony, yet they retained their force, and aesthetic immediacy, as the substance of what Shelley passionately desired. The ruin that shadows love in *Prometheus Unbound,* the *amphisbaena* or two-headed serpent that could move downward and outward to destruction again, the warning made explicit in the closing stanzas spoken by Demogorgon; it is these antithetical hints that survived in Shelley longer than the vehe-

ment hope of his lyrical drama. *The Sensitive Plant* and "**The Witch of Atlas**" manifest a subtle movement away from that hope. *Epipsychidion,* the most exalted of Shelley's poems, seeks desperately to renovate that hope by placing it in the context of heterosexual love, and with the deliberate and thematic self-combustion of the close of *Epipsychidion* Shelley appears to have put all hope aside, and to have prepared himself for his magnificent but despairing last phase, of which the enduring monuments are *Adonais* and *The Triumph of Life.* (pp. 107-08)

Except for Blake's *Visions of the Daughters of Albion,* which it in some respects resembles, *Epipsychidion* is the most outspoken and eloquent appeal for free love in the language. Though this appeal is at the heart of the poem, and dominates its most famous passage (lines 147-54), it is only one aspect of a bewilderingly problematical work. *Epipsychidion* was intended by Shelley to be his *Vita Nuova,* celebrating the discovery of his Beatrice in Emilia Viviani. It proved however to be a climactic and not an initiatory poem, for in it Shelley culminates the quest begun in "**Alastor,**" only to find after culmination that the quest remains unfulfilled and unfulfillable. The desire of Shelley remains infinite, and the only emblem adequate to that desire is the morning and evening star, Venus, at whose sphere the shadow cast by earth into the heavens reaches its limits. After *Epipsychidion,* in *Adonais* and *The Triumph of Life,* only the star of Venus abides as an image of the good. It is not Emilia Viviani but her image that proves inadequate in *Epipsychidion,* a poem whose most turbulent and valuable element is its struggle to record the process of image-making. Of all Shelley's major poems, *Epipsychidion* most directly concerns itself with the mind in creation. **"Mont Blanc"** has the same position among Shelley's shorter poems, and has the advantage of its relative discursiveness, as the poet meditates upon the awesome spectacle before him. *Epipsychidion* is continuous rhapsody, and sustains its lyrical intensity of a lovers' confrontation for six hundred lines. The mind in creation, here and in *A Defense of Poetry,* is as a fading coal, and much of Shelley's art in the poem is devoted to the fading phenomenon, as image after image recedes and the poet-lover feels more fearfully the double burden of his love's inexpressibility and its necessary refusal to accept even natural, let alone societal limitations.

There is, in Shelley's development as a poet, a continuous effort to subvert the poetic image, so as to arrive at a more radical kind of verbal figure, which Shelley never altogether achieved. Tenor and vehicle are imported into one another, and the choice of natural images increasingly favors those already on the point of vanishing, just within the ken of eye and ear. The world is skeptically taken up into the mind, and there are suggestions and overtones that all of reality is a phantasmagoria. Shelley becomes an idealist totally skeptical of the metaphysical foundations of idealism, while he continues to entertain a skeptical materialism, or rather he becomes a fantasist pragmatically given to some materialist hypotheses that his imagination regards as absurd. This is not necessarily a self-contradiction, but it is a kind of psychic split, and it is exposed very powerfully in *Epipsychidion.* Who wins a triumph in the poem, the gambler with the limits of poetry and of human relationship, or the inexorable limits? Space, time, loneliness, mortality, wrong—all these are put aside by vision, yet vision darkens perpetually in the poem. "The world, unfortunately, is real; I, unfortunately, am Borges," is the ironic reflection of a great contemporary seer of phantasmagorias, as he brings his refutation of time to an unrefuting close. Shelley too is swept along by what destroys him and is inescapable, the reality that will not yield to the most relentless of imaginings. In that knowledge, he turns to elegy and away from celebration.

Adonais, Shelley's formal elegy for Keats, is a great monument in the history of the English elegy, and yet hardly an elegy at all. Nearly five hundred lines long, it exceeds in scope and imaginative ambition its major English ancestors. . . .

Like [Yeats's] *Byzantium* poems (which bear a close relation to it) *Adonais* is a high song of poetic self-recognition in the presence of foreshadowing death, and also a description of poetic existence, even of a poem's state of being.

Whether Shelley holds together the elegiac and visionary aspects of his poem is disputable; it is difficult to see the full continuity that takes the poet from his hopeless opening to his more than triumphant close, from:

> I weep for Adonais—he is dead!
> O, weep for Adonais! though our tears
> Thaw not the frost which binds so dear a head!

to:

> I am borne darkly, fearfully, afar;
> Whilst, burning through the inmost veil of Heaven,
> The soul of Adonais, like a star,
> Beacons from the abode where the Eternal are.

From frost to fire as a mode of renewal for the self: that is an archetypal Romantic pattern, familiar to us from *The Ancient Mariner* and the *Intimations* Ode. . . . But *Adonais* breaks this pattern, for the soul of Shelley's Keats burns through the final barrier to revelation only by means of an energy that is set against nature, and the frost that no poetic tears can thaw yields only to "the fire for which all thirst," but which no natural man can drink, for no living man can drink of the whole wine of the burning fountain. As much as Yeats's "All Souls' Night," *Adonais* reaches out to a reality of ghostly intensities, yet Shelley as well as Yeats is reluctant to leave behind the living man who blindly drinks his drop, and *Adonais* is finally a *Dialogue of Self and Soul,* in which the Soul wins a costly victory, as costly as the Self's triumph in Yeats's "Dialogue." The Shelley who cries out, in rapture and dismay, "The massy earth and spherèd skies are riven!" is a poet who has given himself freely to the tempest of creative destruction, to a reality beyond the natural, yet who movingly looks back upon the shore and upon the throng he has forsaken. The close of *Adonais* is a triumph of character over personality, to use a Yeatsian dialectic, but the personality of the lyric poet is nevertheless the dominant aesthetic element in the poem's dark and fearful apotheosis. (pp. 108-11)

Though *Adonais* has been extensively Platonized and Neoplatonized by a troop of interpreters, it is in a clear sense a materialist's poem, written out of a materialist's despair at his own deepest convictions, and finally a poem soaring above those convictions into a mystery that leaves a pragmatic materialism quite undisturbed. Whatever supernal apprehension it is that Shelley attains in the final third of *Adonais,* it is not in any ordinary sense a religious faith, for the only attitude toward natural existence it fosters in the poet is one of unqualified rejection, and indeed its pragmatic postulate is simply suicide. Nothing could be more different in spirit from Demogorgon's closing lines in *Prometheus Unbound* than the final stanzas of *Adonais,* and the ruthlessly skeptical Shelley must have known this.

He knew also though that we do not judge poems by pragmatic tests, and the splendor of the resolution to *Adonais* is not impaired by its implications of human defeat. Whether Keats lives again is unknown to Shelley; poets are among "the enduring dead," and Keats "wakes *or* sleeps" with them. The endurance is not then necessarily a mode of survival, and what flows back to the burning fountain is not necessarily the *human* soul, though it is "pure spirit." Or if it is the soul of Keats as well as "the soul of Adonais," then the accidents of individual personality have abandoned it, making this cold comfort indeed. Still, Shelley is not offering us (or himself) comfort; his elegy has no parallel to Milton's consolation in *Lycidas:*

> There entertain him all the Saints above,
> In solemn troops, and sweet Societies
> That sing, and singing in their glory move,
> And wipe the tears forever from his eyes.

To Milton, as a Christian poet, death is somehow unnatural. To Shelley, for all his religious temperament, death is wholly natural, and if death is dead, then nature must be dead also. The final third of *Adonais* is desperately apocalyptic in a way that *Prometheus Unbound,* Act IV, was not. For *Prometheus Unbound* ends in a Saturnalia, though there are darker implications also, but *Adonais* soars beyond the shadow that the earth casts into the heavens. Shelley was ready for a purgatorial vision of earth, and no longer could sustain even an ironic hope. (pp. 111-12)

There are elements in *The Triumph of Life*, Shelley's last poem, that mark it as an advance over all the poetry he had written previously. The bitter eloquence and dramatic condensation of the style are new; so is a ruthless pruning of invention. The mythic figures are few, being confined to the "Shape all light," the charioteer, and Life itself, while the two principal figures, Shelley and Rousseau, appear in their proper persons, though in the perspective of eternity, as befits a vision of judgment. The tone of Shelley's last poem is derived from Dante's *Purgatorio,* even as much in *Epipsychidion* comes from Dante's *Vita Nuova,* but the events and atmosphere of *The Triumph of Life* have more in common with the *Inferno.* Still, the poem is a purgatorial work, for all the unrelieved horror of its vision, and perhaps Shelley might have found some gradations in his last vision, so as to climb out of the poems' impasse, if he had lived to finish it, though I incline to doubt this. As it stands, the poem is in hell, and Shelley is there, one of the apparently condemned, as all men are, he says, save for "the sacred few" of Athens and Jerusalem, martyrs to vison like Socrates, Jesus, and a chosen handful, with whom on the basis of *Adonais* we can place Keats, as he too had touched the world with his living flame, and then fled back up to his native noon.

The highest act of Shelley's imagination in the poem, perhaps in all of his poetry, is in the magnificent appropriateness of Rousseau's presence, from his first entrance to his last speech before the fragment breaks off. Rousseau is Virgil to Shelley's Dante, in the sense of being his imaginative ancestor, his guide in creation, and also in prophesying the dilemma the disciple would face at the point of crisis in his life. Shelley, sadly enough, was hardly in the middle of the journey, but at twenty-nine he had only days to live, and the imagination in him felt compelled to face the last things. Without Rousseau, Shelley would not have written the **"Hymn to Intellectual Beauty"** and perhaps not **"Mont Blanc"** either. . . . Shelley knew that the spirit of Rousseau was what had moved him most in the spirit of the age, and temperamentally (which counts for most in a poet) it makes more sense to name Shelley the disciple and heir of Rousseau than of Godwin, or Wordsworth, or any of the later French theorists of Revolution. Rousseau and Hume make an odd formula of heart and head in Shelley, but they are the closest parallels to be found to him on the emotional and intellectual sides respectively.

Chastened and knowing, almost beyond knowledge, Rousseau enters the poem, speaking not to save his disciple, but to show him that he cannot be saved, and to teach him a style fit for his despair. The imaginative lesson of *The Triumph of Life* is wholly present in the poem's title: life always triumphs, for life our life is after all what the Preface to "Alastor" called it, a "lasting misery and loneliness." One Power only, the Imagination, is capable of redeeming life, "but that Power which strikes the luminaries of the world with sudden darkness and extinction, by awakening them to too exquisite a perception of its influences, dooms to a slow and poisonous decay those meaner spirits that dare to abjure its dominion." In *The Triumph of Life,* the world's luminaries are still the poets, stars of evening and morning, "heaven's living eyes," but they fade into a double light, the light of nature or the sun, and the harsher and more blinding light of Life, the destructive chariot of the poem's vision. The chariot of Life, like the apocalyptic chariots of Act IV, *Prometheus Unbound,* goes back to the visions of Ezekiel and Revelation for its sources, as the chariots of Dante and Milton did, but now Shelley gives a demonic parody of his sources, possibly following the example of Spenser's chariot of Lucifera. Rousseau is betrayed to the light of Life because he began by yielding his imagination's light to the lesser but seductive light of nature, represented in the poem by the "Shape all light" who offers him the waters of natural experience to drink. He drinks, he begins to forget everything in the mind's desire that had transcended nature, and so he falls victim to Life's destruction, and fails to become one of "the sacred few." There is small reason to doubt that Shelley, at the end, saw himself as having shared in Rousseau's fate. The poem, fragment as it is, survives its own despair, and stands with Keats's *The Fall of Hyperion* as a marvelously eloquent imaginative testament, fit relic of an achievement broken off too soon to rival Blake's or Wordsworth's, but superior to everything else in its own age. (pp. 112-14)

> Harold Bloom, "The Unpastured Sea: An Introduction to Shelley," in his The Ringers in the Tower: Studies in Romantic Tradition, *The University of Chicago Press, 1971, pp. 87-116.*

STUART CURRAN (essay date 1970)

[*In this excerpt from his book on* The Cenci, *Curran discusses Shelley's presentation of Beatrice's moral dilemma in terms of his attitudes toward evil.*]

With the exception of Beatrice the characters of *The Cenci* are fixed, changing only in intensity. Whether this indicates Shelley's immaturity as a playwright is, like other such questions, debatable, and the dramatic effect is at any rate far more important than its possible causes. The villainy and the weakness that circumscribe the experience of Beatrice Cenci do not alter during the course of the tragedy, but they do intensify, making her own insecure position more and more acute. She is driven to suffer between fixed poles, which reverse the ordinary values of her world to the extent that the only positive force is evil; the good of Lucretia or Camillo is negative. Beatrice's slow recognition, first, of these reversed values and, second, of her inability to withstand the magnetic power of the evil confront-

ing her, determines the underlying structure of Shelley's tragedy. His play is a psychological study whose focus is Beatrice, the Romantic Everyman with whom we identify and in whose defeat we are forced to see our own. The development of her awareness can be precipitated by the action, but can only partially be explained by it. Thus, the very structure of the play necessitates Shelley's heavy reliance on patterns of imagery: in their combination he can set for any given moment the precarious balance between Beatrice and the evil forces threatening her, as well as illuminate the basic characteristics of the world in which she is forced to act. That world is remarkably similar to the pessimistic conceptions of our own time.

In the commonplaces of twentieth-century philosophy Beatrice Cenci would be considered an existential heroine. She endures both a crisis of faith and a crisis of identity. If we examine in the abstract her progress through the play, we find a familiar path at least to a point: that of Kierkegaard, who, confronting a Nothingness where values were without meaning, posited with ruthless persistence a God who would give them meaning. But *The Cenci* is the tragic history of a human being, not the record of a victorious logician. Though the play often moves in the realms of philosophical argument, the final questions that it asks are subordinate to a dramatic purpose resolved only in the concluding lines. Beatrice is another Shelleyan "Spirit that strove / For truth, and like the Preacher found it not." Beginning as a sensitive and basically good human being whose values are civilized, she finds herself inhabiting a bestial world whose denizens satisfy only a selfish appetite for power and personal gain. Always these men are alone, alienated from the world on which they prey, isolating their victims in turn. Both Cenci and Orsino bar her exit from the prison of their separate designs. And then that external savage chaos is perpetrated upon her person—not simply upon, but within as well. To keep from being swirled into that vortex of evil, Beatrice must use evil means to support good, to destroy the bestiality that would destroy her. But the external forms of the world unite to prevent her return to normal human society. God has allowed evil to disfigure her; man has acquiesced; and now neither God nor man will act to save her. Beatrice is forced into her own alienation from the world, in which she questions the very roots of human society, the values that she has been taught to accept. To her condition they have nothing to say; they contradict the history of her life. The elemental paradoxes she confronts on every hand resolve only in meaninglessness, whose acceptance leads to despair. Through the development of the play Beatrice has increasingly been forced to uphold her universal values simply through the force of her belief. Her final act—and a singular triumph in the face of despair—is to accept the meaninglessness of the external world without relinquishing the meaningfulness of her internal values, to posit order in the face of chaos even as she must succumb to it. Having passed through the dark night of the soul and having resolved the deepest crises of her existence, Beatrice can die in peace with herself, "fear and pain / Being subdued."

The values preserved through her mere act of faith allow Beatrice to face death with measured equanimity, but such an internal commitment would appear inadequate to sustain her life in a world where these values can have no reality beyond the confines of the mind. Beatrice's experience has proved the world insidious and treacherous. Here, nothing is as it seems: beneath the deceptive appearance lies a vicious and implacable reality, whose effect on pure ideals and hopes is corrosive. It is both symbol and symptom of the conditions under which man must live that Beatrice comes forward during her trial, not to admit complicity in her father's murder and to explain its necessity, but to deny the parricide in the elaborate and impassioned paradox that restoration of divine order can be no crime. The greater paradox, however, is that societal institutions, themselves organized to impose what is construed to be God's order upon this fallen world, destroy Beatrice through their inflexible machinery. For Beatrice, for Everyman, there is no refuge from the savagery of the world: the logical order descending from the supreme Good does not exist, and all experience thus resolves in paradox.

But a firm distinction separates Beatrice's experience from that of her audience. If she is an existential heroine, confronted with a total ambiguity of values, our vision is larger, less immediate than hers. Shelley allows his audience the perspective Beatrice lacks, and, comprehending design where she sees chaos, we are enabled to resolve the ambiguity. The regulatory principle of human affairs, casually but prophetically enunciated by Beatrice in the third scene, is "ill must come of ill." An evil act sows the seeds of future evil. Beatrice, who is Cenci's offspring, precipitates her own destruction as he does his, for any human who resorts to evil means unleashes a devastation he cannot control. "Ill must come of ill" is the premise, but beyond that there is no logic to evil either. That Cenci courts his own destruction makes him no more and no less susceptible to it than is Beatrice, who in murdering her father to preserve herself unwittingly brings on the destruction she sought to forestall. What is ultimately terrifying about this world, however, is that Beatrice has no choice. Within the perverse framework of this tragedy, to act is to commit evil. The tragic premise admits of a second and less obvious reading: an evil act can only be met by another evil act. Good is by its nature fundamentally passive. The good people of this world are, like Christ, sufferers until made aware that martyrdom is upon them, at which point, if they would live, they must deny their Christian precepts and counter with evil. The single representative of the good who does not follow this pattern is Camillo, who purchases salvation with ignorance. He shuffles through the play, kindly, soothing, a true Christian priest—blissfully unaware that he is the lackey of evil. Because he is a good Christian, he is impotent.

To participate in an evil world is to become, like Cenci, suspicious of the motives of all others, to distrust any impulses but one's own—and, indeed, not even to be certain of these—in effect, to become isolated from human society. Shelley's imagery . . . emphasizes this at every turn. The world is a nest of Chinese boxes, prison within prison: the evil world, the evil castle, the evil self. But one cannot retreat into that last fortress, because even it is not secure. At every turn there is a treacherous threat to one's integrity. The result is the curiously static milieu distinguishing Shelley's tragedy and often criticized without being understood. The ultimate justification for a drama where there is almost no action is a world where action is necessary, but feared. To impose one's will upon the formless savagery of an irrational world is an absolute imperative, but any such act can precipitate a cataclysm. Thus, the drama poises between the necessity of these isolated figures to establish their will in fact and their fear lest it cannot be accomplished safely, between an agony of decision and an agony of indecision. "What hast thy father done?" asks Lucretia of her ravished daughter. Beatrice, clinging still to the logic of a Christian universe, answers with a question, "What have I done?" But a few lines later she accepts the demands of the world—"Ay, something must be done"—which she affirms again during the scene: "Ay, / all must be suddenly resolved

and done." The ensuing scene between Orsino and Giacomo ends with the priest's exclamation, "When next we meet may all be done—" to which Giacomo adds a hope impossible of fulfillment in this world—"And all / Forgotten."

The conspirators are naturally anxious that the murder be accomplished quickly and fearful that Cenci may escape and destroy them all; but this linguistic pattern is not simply confined to that part of the tragedy lying between their resolve and its accomplishment. Orsino ends the second scene of Act II with the assertion that success in his world can only proceed from clever flattery of the dark spirit ruling it—"as I will do." This remark, uttered at the end of his soliloquy, stands not only as a reiteration of his resolve, but as the culmination of his self-indictment. The two previous scenes have concluded with a similar imprecation falling from Cenci's lips. He has whetted his appetite with plans for his most insidious crime; he has contemplated his artistry with a relish that he realizes the deed will end; but his delay is caused less by his professed delight in caressing the design than it is by a nameless fear of Beatrice. After confronting and subduing his daughter at the banquet scene, Cenci ends the act by urging himself to the ravishment: "It must be done; it shall be done, I swear." But Beatrice, the family's "protecting presence," quells Cenci's resolution, and at the end of Act II, Scene i, he betrays his fear in a second curtain line: "Would that it were done!" In the Ellis Concordance to Shelley's poems fully half of the citations for the active verb "do" and the past participle "done" come from ***The Cenci***. For a drama of so little action, that fact is significant.

In the dark wilderness of ***The Cenci*** exists a principle of natural selection as inexorable as that of Darwin's primeval rain-forest. The unscrupulous have at least a chance of survival, where the weak must succumb. Man is at once both the savage devourer of his own species and prey to savagery in a cycle of meaningless, endless destruction. Shelley has turned Christian values on end in depicting this world: they survive only in Camillo's ignorance or Beatrice's resolute act of will, both of which are only possible through a denial of the evidence so powerfully documented by experience. Beatrice refuses to accept what everything substantiates and what she herself tentatively poses in the great monologue of the final scene: that the principle upon which this univese is based is evil. The divine trinity that rules her fortunes consists of God the Father, God the Holy Father, and God the Count, whose vindictive power is supported by the scheme of things on earth. The one consolation—and it is scarcely a firm support for the denizens of this world—is that evil is incapable of logical order. Breeding chaos, it is the prey of itself. . . . Cenci will be murdered; Clement VIII will either die or be destroyed. A new figure will represent the "dark spirit" on earth, himself to fall prey to the bestial disorder. The cycle grinds remorselessly toward infinity.

And toward infinity, too, Shelley pursues the dimensions of this oxymoronic order, perversely rendered like a Miltonic universe from elemental Chaos and ancient Night and issuing in torments without qualification or exception. Isolated in his roof-top terrace in the embroiled summer of personal miseries, Shelley, like Orsino, saw "from a tower, the end of all," compressing his vision into one epitomizing metaphor:

> And we are left,—as scorpions ringed with fire,
> What should we do but strike ourselves to death?

In popular superstition encircling a scorpion with fire compelled the tail forward until the venomous sting at its tip penetrated the head, causing instantaneous death. Similarly, man carries within him the seed of his own destruction, a poison less of the body than of the mind. As Shelley develops his image in the events of the tragedy, he poses not the conquest of spirit by flesh that it first suggests, but an apocalyptic shattering of all pretensions to an ideal order erupting from the brutal, irrational forces abstracted in Count Cenci. Racked like Lear on a wheel of fire, all men and all men's ideals succumb to the insidious thrust of evil. And from the ashes of that fire no phoenix arises.

Shelley, fresh from the sublime conceptions of *Prometheus Unbound* to which he was again soon to return, could hardly have been insensitive the the iconographical significance of his symbol. His *felo-de-se* is a parody of the "snake / That girds eternity," the . . . tail-eating serpent, which, forming a circle without beginning or end, where the tail of death resolves into the head of life, was a Platonic and Cabalistic emblem for the One. . . . The scorpion is, in truth, an inverted One, the symbol for an eternity of destructive evil, of everlasting hell, as the poet had intimated when he invoked the figure in a previous poem. And if the One, that creative Eternity of pure ideals, is forever beyond the reach of mortal man, this second, Cencian eternity is immediate, admitting no escape short of death (and even that, as Beatrice comes to realize, is uncertain). The line circumscribed by the agonized scorpion's self-destruction is enclosed by a second circle, the wall of fire representing destructive experience. Together, the two interlock with an ultimate geometric precision to form the superstructure of a sphere, the perfect symbolic prison of Beatrice's tragic condition and the only aspect of eternity she has known.

Against this extreme and total vision Shelley's contemporary critics mounted their vituperative attack, castigating the Manichean heresy with which Shelley had invested his tragedy. In retrospect, however, they were too easy on the poet. His heresy was far more radical, if we understand the Manichean belief to be that good and evil are equal forces on earth. James Rieger [in his *The Mutiny Within: The Heresies of Percy Bysshe Shelley* (see Additional Bibliography)], terms Shelley's conception 'Paterin,' meaning that in this world evil is the dominating force, but even this is, perhaps, inadequate to characterize the extremity of Shelley's vision. In the world of *The Cenci* evil is the only force. Good can exist as a principle, even, like Beatrice, as a presence; but good, transferred into action, into force, as a deterrent to evil, becomes evil. Shelley's curious foray into dark humor, the essay **"On the Devil, and Devils,"** which probably was written shortly after *The Cenci*, explains the principles underlying his tragedy. He notes two main interpretations of the Christian devil, the first bearing the likeness of Cenci—"a fiend appointed to chastise / The offenses" of the world, the sadistic deputy of a sadistic God, the Cenci who serves a "dark spirit." The second interpretation mirrors the relationship of Cenci to his daughter so closely that in his essay Shelley adopts the words in which the Count explained his design. This devil is Shelley's version of Lucifer, like Beatrice a bearer of light who rebelled against an evil Omnipotence:

> . . . the benevolent and amiable disposition which
> distinguished his adversary, furnished God with
> the true method of executing an enduring and
> a terrible vengeance. He turned his good into
> evil, and, by virtue of his omnipotence, in-
> spired him with such impulses, as, in spite of
> his better nature, irresistibly determined him to
> act *what he most abhorred,* and to be a minister

of those designes and schemes of which he was
the chief and the original victim."

In such terms does Beatrice understand the nature of her father's sexual attack. She can withstand an exterior evil, an exterior assault. But the "clinging, black, contaminating mist" suffuses her, becoming an interior evil that subverts good and subdues the girl to her father's will as long as he exists to exercise it. The incestuous act is both profoundly sexual and profoundly metaphysical: if Beatrice is not to become, like Lucifer, the instrument of evil for a cruel God—and Cenci throughout the fourth act voices this purpose—then she must commit murder. The intense bombardment of the imagery in the third and fourth acts emphasizes the truth of Beatrice's assertion at the trial that she has not committed parricide: her crime is deicide.

This justification for Beatrice's revenge is not simply ingenious intellectualizing on Shelley's part. In the movement of his play Shelley imbeds a subtle distinction dropped from his "Preface," a distinction which every critic . . . refuses to acknowledge. The Lucifer-figure of *The Cenci* must confront a graver assault than the Lucifer-figure of *Prometheus Unbound*. The immortal Prometheus, in returning Jupiter's tyrannical oppressions with love, frees the world from the divine tyranny. The fundamental principle on which this universe rests is stated without equivocation by Demogorgon: "All things are enslaved which serve things evil." To rebel against evil is not enough: love must be substituted in its place if man would create a new heaven and earth. Shelley applies the same formula to Beatrice in his "Preface" to *The Cenci* [see excerpt dated 1819]: "Undoubtedly no person can be truly dishonoured by the act of another; and the fit return to make to the most enormous injuries is kindness and forbearance, and a resolution to convert the injurer from his dark passions by peace and love. Revenge, retaliation, atonement, are pernicious mistakes." Shelley here, it must be emphasized, is referring to the Beatrice of history; his premises are inadequate to encompass the character whom he created. She murders her father not out of revenge, but imperative self-defense; not because he raped her body, but because he ravaged her spirit, "poisoning / The subtle, pure, and inmost spirit of life," turning her "good into evil." In the first two acts of the tragedy Beatrice has returned her father's hatred with fear, but with firm forbearance as well. Like Prometheus, she has suffered; she has been chained in the dungeon, forced to eat putrid food, physically tortured, and, as she tells the guests at the banquet, her answer has been to pray that her father would change or that she would be saved. Prometheus, condemned to his rock in the Caucasus for thirty centuries of torture, suffers no more intensely than Beatrice. His spiritual integrity remains inviolate, however, whereas Beatrice's is destroyed. "Peace and love" have only inflamed her father to commit an outrage that negates the possibility of both. The Cenci legend posed for Shelley a physical situation—perhaps the only possible one—in which good was not merely made to suffer from evil, but was subjected to it so completely that *it literally embodied evil*. Beatrice is thus faced with an ethical dilemma admitting of no solution consonant with her conception of good. To become, like Lucifer, the instrument of evil is the greatest of all possible sins against her Catholic God; to commit suicide is an act of mortal sin for which the Church allows no exception; only by killing her father in line with the principles of divine justice can Beatrice hope for absolution from the evil into which her father has plunged her. But the universe does not respond to her conception of it. Her act creates further evil, from which the only relief is death—if even that is to be a relief. For, at best the after-life she conceives at the play's end will be a void; at its worst, it will be a Hell in which the evil God who rules the universe will at last and eternally commit Beatrice to Luciferian violation.

If this is an admittedly unorthodox view of Shelley's tragedy, the work itself, isolated from the rest of Shelley's poetry, leads to no other conclusion. The poet has denied himself "what is vulgarly termed a moral purpose"—in other words, the dogmatic parable expressed in *Prometheus Unbound*. He has lavished on Beatrice "the restless and anatomizing casuistry" that he asserts her history provokes among all classes of men, exercising it with such skill that he justifies her action by creating an ethical system necessitating it. Thus to condemn Beatrice, we must impose upon her world an ethic foreign to its exigencies, denying the repeated symbolism of the imagery and the carefully balanced structure of characterizations. By an objective ideal she may be wrong, but in the inescapable prison of human events, she is merely and thus profoundly tragic, beyond the realm of simple moral platitudes. One might as well argue the criminality of Cordelia, whose reticence causes fragmentation, war, and bloodshed, as impose the ideals of *Prometheus Unbound* upon this mortal woman, impelled by her fate into a no-man's-land where both action and non-action are evil and where objective ethical standards dissolve into the absurd.

Only one incident in the entire play seems to suggest that Beatrice had no need to take justice into her own hands: the arrival of Savella with a warrent for Cenci's death. It would appear that once again Demogorgon has risen to overthrow Jupiter and release Prometheus from bondage. But on the contrary, that Cenci should be ordered killed by the irrational command of a capricious tyrant who had refused aid to the distraught family only emphasizes again how vicious and illogical this world is. Beatrice, thinking that the Pope had refused her petition, knows that she can expect no relief from that quarter. But we who know that Orsino suppressed the petition are also aware that Camillo presented as strong a plea and saw it denied. And we cannot forget that had Lucretia not drugged her husband in order to make his death easier, Beatrice would have been violated again before Savella arrived with official sanction for Cenci's murder in a warrant whose immorality only intensifies the moral purpose by which Beatrice acts. In this illogical universe where Beatrice is reduced to establishing an existential moral order and where she has no reason to suppose that the Pope will suddenly move against her father, Savella's entrance does not at all obviate the imperative by which Beatrice murders the Count. The cruelest of ironies, the entrance of this hatchetman for *Realpolitik* merely substantiates the bestial evil of the world. Beatrice, who had reason to kill her father, is arrested for a crime which the Pope, who lacked any rationale, would wantonly have commanded. To presuppose Shelley's intentions in this matter is impossible, but that there is so marked a difference between the action of Demogorgon and the command of the Pope suggests once again the total disparity between the worlds of *Prometheus Unbound* and *The Cenci*.

Is it by accident, one wonders, that the determining act of both *Prometheus Unbound* and *The Cenci* should be sexual? Prometheus' fortitude culminates in his sexual union with Asia in which is symbolized the harmonious regeneration of the world. Beatrice's fortitude ends in a union symbolizing the world's degeneration, its moral cacophony. Sexual union is a metaphor for the most intense of physical and spiritual experiences, and, if we carefully distinguish how very different these worlds are,

the metaphors in each drama are of equal symbolic weight. That Shelley wrote the last act of *Prometheus,* the great hymn of joy resolving in union, after he had completed *The Cenci* does not indicate that his tragedy was to be subordinated to the ethical structure of his lyrical drama. We can never know, of course, why Shelley chose to return to the earlier work, but it is likely that it was an act of purgation and relief, designed to round off what was to him a vision of the ideal as he had completed what he called his "sad reality." The two works pose for their readers a problem unique in literature: two masterpieces, works of literary genius and intellectual profundity, written in sequence, which attack perhaps the most difficult of philosophical problems, that of evil, and issue impassioned and totally opposed conclusions. (pp. 129-43)

Shelley scholars have long assumed that in *Prometheus Unbound* the poet finally resolved the problem of evil. But, while philosophically more successful and complete than Shelley's earlier statements, his lyric drama is as tentative in its conclusions as those others. In this Manichean universe the power of evil can only be checked by an act of will through which the individual, attuning himself to the universal spirit of harmony, love—that Neo-Platonic "One warring against the Evil Principle,"—thus triumphs through forgiveness. But, when Shelley reduces the conflict from the realm of the immortals to a human reality, his One becomes, tragically, one. In *The Cenci* the poet represents a world of endless decay, where the appearance can never ultimately match the reality, where evil is ultimately triumphant. The earthly manifestation of the spirit of harmony can, like all things, be avoided.

It is all very well for critics to observe that *The Cenci* is written between the acts of *Prometheus Unbound*; but the fact can only be interpreted as a sign of Shelley's breadth of vision, not as proof that Beatrice was morally culpable because, being human and constrained by a world where all acts are evil, she could not preserve her integrity against the power of evil. It behooves us, indeed, to match the one fact of chronology with another. The final act of the cosmic drama, the ecstatic hymn in praise of harmonious regeneration, follows not one, but two works emphatically representing the world, as far as Shelley scans it, as incapable of regeneration. Universal progress, that local deity of the earth enshrined by the youthful Shelley some years in advance of the Victorian captains of industry, the mature poet rejects as a fiction. (p. 147)

Clearly . . . in Shelley's later years he at times embraced the view that the world was inherently evil and incapable of regeneration; but in affirming this, we would do wrong to repeat Mary Shelley's mistake [in her note to *The Cenci*] and too easily systematize her husband's thought. At the same time that Shelley wrote **"Peter Bell the Third,"** he also penned his stirring polemic, *The Masque of Anarchy,* urging the workingmen of England to resist the tyranny imposed by the ruling classes. And two years later, foreseeing in *Hellas* the defeat of the Greek independence movement, Shelley nevertheless subscribed to its idealistic vision of a renewed glory for Greece. But if in such poems we trace the hand of the political and philosophical liberal who wrote *Queen Mab,* in others we see the architect of elemental despair, denying any possibility for progress because man lacks the means to alter the evil condition of himself and his world. The dilemma was natural to such a man. On the one hand he was passionately devoted to ideals of social, economic, and religious justice; on the other, the calamities suffered by one who lived by those ideals seemed no more logical than Savella's entrance into Petrella. If Shelley had been able to resolve the dilemma, it would not have figured so prominently in his poetry. But his political liberalism, which is ultimately Christian, is in basic conflict with that perverse, unorthodox Neo-Platonism which conceived the world outside of man's mind to be degenerate, totally divorced from the good. (pp. 149-50)

Beatrice, in the persistence with which she tears the painted veils from the substance of life, embodies Shelley's own mental process by which he probes beyond the comfortable affirmations of *Prometheus Unbound.* In this mortal world love cannot remove the burden of evil; the most it can do is ease it. And even love, like all other ideals, can become the agency through which one's integrity is assaulted from within. In this respect Shelley's portrayal of Beatrice is an enlarged and more mature version of the dreaming poet of **"Alastor,"** who sought "in vain for a prototype of his conception. . . . [and] Blasted by his disappointment . . . descend[ed] to an untimely grave." In similar fashion, we could apply to Beatrice—as impassioned for perfect justice as the imaginary *persona* of *Epipsychidion* is for perfect love—the cancelled epitaph from Shelley's original preface to that poem: "He was an accomplished & amiable person but his error was . . . [being mortal, not to be content with mortal things],—his fate is an additional proof that 'The tree of Knowledge is not that of Life.'" (pp. 150-51)

The development of Shelley's thought, as recorded both in his poetry and his letters, would suggest that *The Cenci* is not at all the radical departure from the poet's customary ideas that has often been supposed, nor is it ethically subservient to the doctrines and ideals of *Prometheus Unbound.* From the airy heights of the Caucasus Shelley plunged into the dark abyss of *The Cenci,* to survey its depths and to test the surety of the bottom. And there he remained, against his will perhaps, to accept the central principle of mortal life as evil, to ponder its implications, and to strive toward a tragic awareness through which the burden could be endured. (p. 152)

> *Stuart Curran, in his* Shelley's "Cenci": Scorpions Ringed with Fire, *Princeton University Press, 1970, 298 p.*

JUDITH CHERNAIK (essay date 1972)

[*In the following excerpt from her study of Shelley's best-known lyrics, Chernaik examines the poems inspired by his relationship with Jane Williams, tracing both his increasing pessimism and his growing artistic mastery.*]

[Shelley's] poems to Jane Williams were written in the winter and spring of 1822, when the intimacy between Shelley and Jane and Williams was too close, perhaps, to sustain the easy friendship in which it had begun. . . . The poems to Jane were to be kept from Mary's eyes (they are headed: "For Jane and Williams alone to see;" "Not to be opened unless you are alone"—and to Williams: "If any of the stanzas should please you, you may read them to Jane, but to no one else"); and their implied or explicit subject is not only the delight the poet takes in Jane's singing, or her hand on his forehead, but his embittered "life and love," his "cold home." Jane appears to have had none of Mary's intellectual or Emilia Viviani's spiritual refinement; Shelley must have been drawn to her at least in part because she and Williams were devoted to each other. This meant that she could be kind to Shelley in a disinterested way (a "friend"), and that she could never be his—ideal circumstances, in a way, for Shelley, and thus celebrated and lamented in the poems. (p. 162)

The poems to Jane include **"The Magnetic Lady to her Patient"** and **"The keen stars were twinkling;"** **"With a Guitar"** (written to accompany a gift from Shelley), an epistle in tetrameter couplets, marked by the whimsy that characterized Shelley's social relations; the lovely pastoral, **"The Invitation,"** and its companion poem, **"The Recollection;"** and **"Lines written in the Bay of Lerici,"** possibly the last lyric Shelley wrote. We could include too the stanzas **"To Edward Williams,"** addressed really to Edward and Jane ("Dear friends, dear *friend*"). These are the most intimate as well as the most charming of Shelley's love poems. In them he breaks away from the brief lyric form, with its simplifications, into sustained analysis of the themes that dominate all the late lyrics: the perversity of human desire, its illogic and self-destructiveness, the illusory and fragile nature of happiness and love, the conflict between reason and desire, between desire and obligation. It is unlikely that Shelley would ever have turned away completely from political and prophetic poetry; but these poems, representing as they do his last work, suggest the deepening pessimism of his vision of life. For poetry in these lyrics has nothing to do with changing the world, nor does it impinge on the larger world in any way; it is rather a means of cherishing the moment of happiness, of celebrating and perhaps immortalizing "one moment's good" after long pain.

The social context of the poems is drawn in a letter Shelley wrote to John Gisborne:

> I like Jane more and more, and I find Williams the most amiable of companions. She has a taste for music, and an elegance of form and motions that compensate in some degree for the lack of literary refinement. Mrs. Gisborne knows my gross ideas of music, and will forgive me when I say that I listen the whole evening on our terrace to the simple melodies with excessive delight. I have a boat here . . . Williams is captain, and we drive along this delightful bay in the evening wind, under the summer moon, until earth appears another world. Jane brings her guitar, and if the past and future could be obliterated, the present would content me so well that I could say with Faust to the passing moment "Remain, thou, thou art so beautiful."

The poet's momentary happiness, his general unhappiness, the fact, more or less apparent to him, that he was falling in love with Jane—these are the materials of the poems, their ostensible occasion and subject. They analyze complicated adult relationships; above all they demonstrate the poet's insight into his own nature, his acute sense of the personal necessities that made it imperative for him to tame his ardor, not to "break his chain." Yet the privacy of actual lives is protected, the personal details disguised (especially those having to do with Mary), even as the emotions they cause in the poet are analyzed. In their subtlety, the poems reveal a quality of Shelley's mind he hints at with reference to his strained relations with Byron: "What is passing in the heart of another rarely escapes the observation of one who is a strict anatomist of his own."

"The Magnetic Lady to her Patient" is frank in its portrait of the relationship between Jane and Shelley. Jane is made to say at least three or four times that she pities Shelley but cannot love him, that her role is that of friend and physician, not of mistress. The explicitness of the poem (she reminds him at the outset of her own happy relationship with Williams) is part of its charm, the tone of affectionate raillery and wholly disinterested tenderness. The patient's ills are the same as those which plague the poet of **"Stanzas written in Dejection"**—"lost health," "the world's dull scorn"—but they are validated by the fact that it is not the poet but the Lady who names them. The cure, again, is forgetfulness, but the self-pity of the earlier poem ("I could lie down like a tired child") is modified by the poet's awareness of the several players in the drama, not only Jane and himself but Edward and Mary.

The occasion of the poem—Jane practicing hypnotism on the ailing poet—becomes a metaphor for their relationship, both for what Jane insists that it be, and for what he would like it to become. The metaphor of love as a sickness, the mistress as physician, is one of the oldest staples of love poetry, and it is a function of the poem's wit to raise possibilities even as their implications are denied. In hypnotism the subject is laid to sleep and forgetfulness induced; when he is entirely receptive, a new spirit is infused into him. In this last stage, the physician-patient relationship is easily confused with that of mistress and lover: "By mine thy being is to its deep / Possest."

The entry of the hypnotist's spirit into the subject suggests unmistakably the spiritual or physical union of love, a thought which no doubt the poet briefly, wistfully, entertains, before he descends to earth:

> "The spell is done—how feel you now?"
> "Better, quite well" replied
> The sleeper—"What would do
> You good when suffering and awake,
>   What cure your head and side?"
> "What would cure that would kill me, Jane,
> And as I must on earth abide
> Awhile yet, tempt me not to break
>   My chain."

The effect of the stanza lies in the shift from Jane's concern to the poet's oblique play on her words: "What would cure that would kill me, Jane." As her frankness comes from a free heart, his allusiveness, in the form of pun and metaphor, comes from the knowledge of burdens he cannot shake off. The "chain" he must not break is the chain of life; also, undoubtedly, it is the chain of his marriage.

"The keen stars were twinkling" is a poetic rendering of the experience Shelley describes in the letter to Gisborne: "we drive along this delightful bay in the evening wind, under the summer moon, until earth appears another world." The poem concentrates upon the presentness of the scene, even though the poet's delight has its source in something more, the yearning for "some world far from ours." The lyric is reminiscent of **"To Constantia,"** both in its occasion and in the relationship suggested between song and feeling, between the singer and the instrument. In both lyrics the erotic component is submerged; the emphasis is on the power of song to move the spirit to delight and to transport the hearer to another world. But the later lyric is more personal and circumstantial, not an extended analysis of the experience, like **"To Constantia,"** but a musical imitation of it.

The structure of the poem depends on the analogy between the moon, which gives splendor to the stars, and Jane's voice, which gives life to the guitar's soulless notes. Each stanza interweaves the same terms—keen stars, fair moon, sweet tones—until they are given final shape in the last lines:

> Though the sound overpowers
> Sing again, with your dear voice revealing
>   A tone

> Of some world far from ours,
> Where music and moonlight and feeling
>   Are one.

The present scene, the rising moon, the stars, the guitar, Jane's life-giving presence—all are turned into an emblem of the poet's desire for love and harmony and his sense that although the elements are present, a particular human magnetism is needed to bring them into relationship. The stanza, with its ingenious verbal and metrical patterning, its rhythmical pauses, is an imitation of the song Jane might have played (as Shelley's description of it, "words for an ariette," suggests); the syncopated rhythm approximates the pattern of a voice singing against strummed chords. The stress pattern compels one to read with "rests" included, so that the short lines are isolated: *Tonight; Delight; A tone; Are one.* In the final lines, the three stresses, which summarize the three elements of the scene, "music and moonlight and feeling," literally become "one."

The remaining three poems inscribed to Jane are essays in light tetrameter couplets, conversational in tone, intimate, analytic. Each poem idealizes Jane, partly as a compliment to her peculiar grace and serenity, party in response to the poet's needs, to which Jane is merely an accessory. For in these poems Jane, the "spirit of peace in our circle of tempests," is identified with the harmonizing and life-giving spirit described in **"The Zucca,"** that which the poet, or in the allegorical framework of the poem, the human soul, desires beyond all else. It is this spirit which the poet or lover adores—

> In winds, and trees, and streams, and all things common,
>   In music and the sweet unconscious tone
> Of animals, and voices which are human . . .
> In the soft motions and rare smile of woman,
>   In flowers and leaves, and in the grass fresh-shown

—and whose sudden and unpreventable fight he laments, since he cannot follow after.

"With a Guitar" represents the happiest side of this spring interlude. It has the overtones of social intercourse, the affectionate nicknaming and play-acting in which the Shelley circle always indulged (and which Shelley alludes to in the last section of *Epipsychidion*). Its theme, like that of **"The keen stars were twinkling,"** is the happy union of love, music, poetry, nature.

The opening section imagines the group of friends as immortal spirits temporarily imprisoned in their present bodies. Jane and Edward are Miranda and Ferdinand (ideal love), Shelley is Ariel (their guardian spirit, devoted servant, agent of poetry), and Mary, one is tempted to say, is "the silent Moon / In her interlunar swoon," sadness personified. True to the fiction, Miranda and Ferdinand are quite unaware of Ariel's long service, of which he must gently remind them; this is his excuse for the long introduction, with its ingenuous declaration of "more than ever can be spoken."

The second part of the poem turns to the guitar itself, which, in a kind or mirror image to the opening fiction (Ariel, we remember, was imprisoned for twelve years in a pine), is seen as the second and happier life of a tree. To those who know how to question it, the guitar will reveal the secrets of nature and the oracles it conceals:

> For it had learnt all harmonies
> Of the plains and of the skies,
> Of the forests and the mountains,

> And the many-voiced fountains,
> The clearest echoes of the hills,
> The softest notes of falling rills,
> The melodies of birds and bees,
> The murmuring of summer seas,
> And pattering rain and breathing dew
> And airs of evening;—and it knew
> That seldom heard mysterious sound,
> Which, driven on its diurnal round
> As it floats through boundless day
> Our word enkindles on its way—

The natural world is conceived in terms of its sounds—many-voiced fountains, echoes, pattering rain; these merge naturally into the sounds of the guitar, which both echoes and interprets natural sound. The pastoral survey, like that in **"Lines written among the Euganean Hills,"** climaxes in the intuition of a transcendent principle of unity or harmony, a "mysterious sound" (like the "soul of all" or the inconstant Spirit of Intellectual Beauty), which, though seldom heard, can be divined or sensed through its analogy with that which can be heard. The poem ends with what amounts to a definition of poetry or art, lighter in tone than those in *A Defence of Poetry* but in agreement with Shelley's general insistence on "the wise heart" and the "mind's imaginings" as the ultimate source of love, beauty, and truth:

> All this it knows, but will not tell
> To those who cannot question well
> The spirit that inhabits it:
> It talks according to the wit
> Of its companions; and no more
> Is heard than has been felt before
> By those who tempt it to betray
> These secrets of an elder day.—

Nature and natural mythology on the one hand, the grace and intuitive feeling of the pure spirit on the other—these remain Shelley's absolutes. The tribute Shelley pays them in this poem balances the sadness of other poems of this time, the despair of **"When the lamp is shattered,"** the recurrent lament for the loss of love and happiness.

The companion poems **"The Invitation"** and **"The Recollection"** are perceptibly the work of the author of **"Lines written among the Euganean Hills."** Again the poet's mood is described in relation to a scene lovingly and accurately set down, to which he is intensely responsive and yet which serves to establish beyond all question his isolation from nature. In the poems to Jane, unlike **"Lines written among the Euganean Hills,"** other persons figure in the poet's thoughts: the woman he is falling in love with, whom he identifies with all that is happy, free, and life-giving, and his wife, who has come to be associated only with "low-thoughted care," past tragedy, the poet's inescapable responsibilities. While the poet concentrates on the image of his own happiness or grief—the day, the scene—the human relationships in the background, barely hinted at, color all that he says. In addition to the human quality of these lyrics, their tenderness and nostalgia of tone, we notice as in all the late lyrics the quiet disappearance of apocalyptic hope, the ambition to change the world. The pine forest in the Cascine and the day spent there provide just such a "green isle" in the sea of agony as the day the poet spends in the Euganean Hills, but his modest joy in it—"To-day is for itself enough"—does not radically after his initial pessimism; he has no hopes of permanent relief, change, or transcendence. For in these poems the poet's personal distress takes the form of a stoicism most closely akin to that of Keats's great Odes. From a world of care and sorrow the poet imaginatively enters a closed and secret and delightful world, of nature, art, or love, from which he must at last return, tolled back to his "sole self." The psychological and artistic movement of the poems is similiar to Keats's characteristic procedure. The poet first holds the image of perfection in his mind—for Keats the song of the bird, the Greek urn, for Shelley the hour spent in the forest with Jane—then, through the process of imagining it, he appears to be physically absorbed into its reality, which becomes exclusive and absolute: "Already with thee! tender is the night . . ." But as the intensity of the imagined moment fades, as the song of the nightingale recedes over the hills, the vision dissolves, and the world's reality breaks in upon the poet with the return of his self-consciousness.

"The Invitation" is organized, like **"Lines written among the Euganean Hills,"** on an extended analogy between the physical rhythms of nature and the emotional rhythms of human life. The fair day, unexpectedly breaking into the winter, come to smile at the "rough Year," is sister to the fair Jane, come miraculously to ease the poet's sorrow:

> Best and brightest, come away—
> Fairer far than this fair day
> Which like thee to those in sorrow
> comes to bid a sweet good-morrow
> To the rough year just awake
> In its cradle on the brake.—

The poet offers a pseudo-mythological genealogy for the sweet morning, which draws closer and closer to the thought of the ministering Magnetic Lady, until the analogy is made explicit:

> The brightest hour of unborn spring
> Through the winter wandering
> Found, it seems, the halcyon morn
> To hoar February born;
> Bending from Heaven in azure mirth
> It kissed the forehead of the earth
> And smiled upon the silent sea,
> And bade the frozen streams be free
> And waked to music all their fountains
> And breathes upon the frozen mountains
> And like a prophetess of May
> Strewed flowers upon the barren way,
> Making the wintry world appear
> Like one on whom thou smilest, dear.

The analogy between the frozen earth, wintry and barren, and the desolate state of the poet leads to the second analogy, between the nature of the day—a rare halcyon day in February, with winter soon closing in again—and the nature of the poet's experience, a brief moment of peace and happy forgetfulness interrupting cares to which he must return. Given this simple framework, it is easy to see why the poem should be so modest in scope compared to **"Lines written among the Euganean Hills,"** where the terms are on the one hand the physical vista of all Italy, its cities islanded in the fair plains, on the other a metaphor for the human condition, green isles of happiness in a sea of agony. The tone reflects the difference in scope; Shelley turns next to a confession Cowperesque in its modesty and humor, its defiance of the "accustomed" demons. Yet the poetic sensibility is the same as that of **"Stanzas written in**

Dejection," "Invocation to Misery," and "Song: ('Rarely, rarely comest thou')":

> Hope, in pity mock not woe
> With smiles, nor follow where I go;
> Long having lived on thy sweet food,
> At length I find one moment's good
> After long pain—

"The Invitation" ends with a brief description of the "wild woods and the plains" reminiscent of the noon moment described in **"Lines written among the Euganean Hills."** But in **"The Invitation"** the description is limited to the physical scene, and the felt unity is an appearance, momentary and fragile:

> Where the earth and ocean meet,
> And all things seem only one
> In the universal Sun.—

The account of wintry woods and sea is the kind of natural description at which Shelley is unsurpassed, in which physical life, and the meaning it embodies and evokes, effortlessly pass one into the other. The whole of nature—land, sea, and sky— seems to have a life of its own, whose secrets are bare to the eye of the poet. It is as if nature, in its multiplicity and continual process, revealed to him the secret of unity and timelessness— in the "wild woods" where nature is not bound or limited, where day and night, winter and summer, earth and ocean, meet and appear to be merged into one. The natural scene represents innocent relationship, the more innocent, perhaps, because the elements that meet or reflect one another in love do not merge, barely touch, and bear no fruit, scent, or color. Nature under such an aspect offers still another inducement to Jane to join the poet, and demonstrates the innocence of his request.

"The Recollection" is, as Shelley says, "The epitaph of glory fled" and is therefore more serious, more complicated. It is an attempt to fix the exact quality of the scene and of the poet's happiness; more precisely, it seeks to find an image that can permanently stand for the day in the pine forest. Its formal introduction sustains the tone of epistolary verse; with an inversion of rhyme the passage ends on a sad, suspended cadence: "A frown is on the Heaven's brow." The "frown" recalls the "smile" with which **"The Invitation"** begins; the reader will guess that it is not only the earth that has returned to its wintry state. And the experience, as it is now recalled, takes on more and more the character of an interlude, a pause, marked by a silence and stillness, a profound calm, which is gradually elaborated and deepened until it takes on magical properties, like the trance of dream vision or revelation. Land, sea, and sky are drawn, each soothed to peace and harmony by the "smile of Heaven," the waves "half asleep," the clouds "gone to play," the twisted pines stilled by the "azure breath" of the wind, the "treetops . . . asleep / Like green waves on the sea, / As still as in the silent deep / The Ocean woods may be." The universal calm is finally made to include the human beings who perceive it; its source, imaged as the lovely day, the "smile of Heaven," is identified more precisely as the "Radiant Sister of the day" of **"The Invitation."**

> There seemed from the remotest seat
> Of the white mountain-waste,
> To the soft flower beneath our feet
> A magic circle traced,
> A spirit interfused around
> A thrilling silent life,

> To momentary peace it bound
> Our mortal nature's strife;—
> And still I felt the centre of
> The magic circle there
> Was one fair form that filled with love
> The lifeness atmosphere.

The "magic circle" recalls the windless bower envisaged by the poet at the end of **"Lines written among the Euganean Hills,"** its peace made permanent by "the love which heals all strife / Circling, like the breath of life, / All things in that sweet abode." But where the island paradise is an image of an Elysium, a universal source of hope, the "magic circle" is drawn around an hour of present life, the peace is momentary, the source of love is embodied in human form, hence transient and frail. And as if the statement alone is not sufficient, Shelley draws the "magic circle" in terms of a new circle image of sky and forest reflected in the forest pools (like the reflection of "old palaces and towers" in "the wave's intenser day," in **"Ode to the West Wind"**). The still reflection, while real, has the perfection and truth as well as the illusory character of dream or vision; it strangely approximates a Platonic absolute— "purer," "more boundless," "more perfect"—to which the "upper world" "our world above," is but a dim shadow.

> We paused beside the pools that lie
> Under the forest bough—
> Each seemed as 'twere, a little sky
> Gulfed in a world below;
> A firmament of purple light
> Which in the dark earth lay
> More boundless than the depth of night
> And purer than the day,
> In which the lovely forests grew
> As in the upper air,
> More perfect, both in shape and hue,
> Than any spreading there.

Just as . . . the notion of absolute peace yields imperceptibly to the idea of love which is its source and which emanates from Jane, so in lines 53-76, as the description of the reflected Elysium continues, its perfection and truth become identified with physical love: the water's desire to receive the surrounding woods.

> Sweet views, which in our world above
> Can never well be seen,
> Were imaged in the water's love
> Of that fair forest green;
> And all was interfused beneath
> With an Elysian glow,
> An atmosphere without a breath,
> A softer day below—

The poem ends with a return to reality, the "frown . . . on the Heaven's brow," the poet's melancholy; the shift is accomplished aphoristically by pun and metaphor:

> Like one beloved, the scene had lent
> To the dark water's breast,
> Its every leaf and lineament
> With more than truth exprest;
> Until an envious wind crept by,
> Like an unwelcome thought
> Which from the mind's too faithful eye
> Blots one dear image out.—

> Though thou art ever fair and kind
> And forests ever green,
> Less oft is peace in ———'s mind,
> Than calm in water seen.

(pp. 163-74)

As "**The Invitation**" and "**The Recollection**" suggest comparison with "**Lines written among the Euganean Hills,**" "**Lines written in the Bay of Lerici**" suggests "**Stanzas written in Dejection**" in its simplicity of statement, its directness. As in the earlier poem, the poet's agitation of spirit is measured against a scene so lovely and so intensely felt that it becomes an image of the serenity from which he is excluded. The displacement of emotion in the opening lines of the poem is characteristic of Shelley's last poems. Brooding about Jane, he addresses the Moon: "Bright wanderer, fair coquette of Heaven;" suffering the effects of her recent presence and her departure, he analyzes the nature of time and the relationship of the present to past and future. Thus before turning directly to the beloved, his thoughts linger over the moment of departure, which turns into an image of suspended time. And the image of this "silent time," when the moon hovers between its rise and its setting, "like an albatross asleep," anticipates the thought of the moment of happiness, the "time which is our own," suspended between past and future, which, the poet implies, possess or enchain us. It is a moment caught and imprisoned, like the noon moment of "**Lines written in the Euganean Hills,**" or the hour spent in the pine forest in the Cascine, when flux, process, physical reality are for a moment transcended by feeling and memory. The images that render this moment are similar to those which dominate "**Music, when soft voices die:**" they have to do with the analogy between the vibrations of feeling and those of sound and odor, the relation of physical cause to nonphysical effect. The effects of love are imperceptible, immeasurable, but felt by the "enchanted heart," which is not dependent upon physical presence. But the demon reassumes his throne, despite a momentary enchantment; the poet's "antient pilot, Pain" takes control of his "frail bark" once more, in the image which represents Shelley's persistent vision of the solitary human life. No sooner does he mention his "faint heart," though, than he turns again to the scene, displacing his need onto the landscape:

> . . . I dare not speak
> My thoughts; but thus disturbed and weak
> I sate and watched the vessels glide
> Along the ocean bright and wide,
> Like spirit-winged chariots sent
> O'er some serenest element
> For ministrations strange and far . . .

As in "**Stanzas written in Dejection,**" the very solitude of the poet sharpens his sensibility to the harmonies of the natural scene, as well as to its analogy with human life. The enumeration of the elements of the scene—the gliding vessels, the wind, the scent of the flowers, the coolness of dew, the sweet warmth left by day—seems to parallel the enumeration earlier in the poem of the beloved's ministrations, her tones, the "soft vibrations of her touch," her healing presence. Both passages imply the gulf between the suffering poet and the harmony of spirit toward which he yearns, whether represented by his "guardian angel" (who, like the moon, is bound after her brief stay for her own "nest"), or by the natural scene in its clarity and freshness.

The poet has instinctively turned to the scene for some easing of his pain, perhaps for a continuation of the peace ministered

by his beloved, who serves in all these poems as an extension of a beneficent nature. And the scene finally supplies its more than adequate image. With a sudden twist or tautening the quiet description ends with the vision of the fisherman with lamp and spear—the human figure in the landscape, the natural predator, as the fish are natural victims. And to this image the poet appends a moral, somewhat in the fashion of the wry aphorism that ends "**The Recollection:**" "Less oft is peace in [Shelley]'s mind / Than calm in water seen:"

> Too happy, they whose pleasure sought
> Extinguishes all sense and thought
> Of the regret that pleasure
> Seeking life not peace.

The final contrast is between not happiness and despair but the simplicity of nature, even in the urge of natural creatures toward death, and the complexity of human life, which, subject always to "sense and thought," must endure the departure of pleasure, and which survives all it loves. What the poet envies in the luring of the fish, which otherwise seems to mirror his own foolish pursuit of pleasure, is the singleness of animal instinct, the sureness of its consequences.

The image of the "delusive flame" is the last variation on a theme that runs through Shelley's poetry, the desire of every living creature:

> . . . ever from below
> Aspiring like one who loves too fair, too far,
> To be consumed within the purest glow
>
> Of one serene and unapproachèd star,
> As if it were a lamp of earthly light,
> Unconscious, as some human lovers are,
>
> Itself how low, how high beyond all height
> The heaven where it would perish!

   ("**The Woodman and the Nightingale**")

Yet the image of temptation, desire, and destruction in Shelley's last poem has a special quality entirely different from the soaring affirmations of *Adonais* and *Epipsychidion,* an objective, ironic detachment. The appended moral suggests that the choice for the aspiring soul is simply between the seeking of life—i.e., of its necessity, of light, love, delight—and the sensible pursuit of peace. Life and peace are incompatible; by implication, peace is possible only in the grave. The earlier images of present peace and happiness are set in a most somber perspective. And for the first time, the image of the flame is qualified by the suggestion that it is indeed a false lure, and that the heart which follows the flame does so because it is a "weak heart of little wit" ("**Love, Hope, Desire, and Fear**").

These last lyrics confirm the darkening of spirit that is suggested so strongly by *The Triumph of Life.* One senses an increasing pessimism on Shelley's part, the gradual withdrawal of the poet's bright Elysium until it appears to be no more than an image of what the soul in vain desires, counter to all reason, all evidence. Yet as Shelley's hope of permanent change in society and in private life recedes and its place is taken by the notion of endurance, the ideal for which his spirit longs seems suddenly to take shape in the present moment, the beloved Italian scene, the brief presence of a woman. Hence the poignancy of these poems, which celebrate present happiness in the certainty of loss, which do not seek beyond the "present and tangible object" but rather draw a magic circle around that which is mortal and doomed.

Even as Shelley's perspective seems to shift, his art is strengthened. In these last poems there is always a hard core of thought at the center, whether the poem appears to be a simple description of a natural scene, an expression of nameless joy or sorrow, or an ecstatic approximation of an ideal beyond sense experience or rational inference. Though Shelley's unique qualities as a poet come from his intense sensibility to just these things, though he is preeminently a poet of passionate feeling and commitment, his intelligence, which is essentially abstract and logical, is always in control. The precision of his thought should never be underestimated; as it is the source of difficulty, sometimes of ambiguity, so it is what finally gives his poetry its strength. (pp. 175-78)

> *Judith Chernaik, in her* The Lyrics of Shelley, *The Press of Case Western Reserve University, 1972, 303 p.*

TIMOTHY WEBB (essay date 1977)

[*Webb discusses Shelley's reaction against political and religious tryanny, focusing on* Prometheus Unbound *as a revolutionary protest against Old Testament teachings and traditional Christian theology.*]

Shelley read the Bible regularly and critically throughout his life. . . . The evidence of the letters, the prose works and the poetry . . . goes to show that the Bible was regularly in Shelley's thoughts and that its ideas and images haunted not only the rationalising side of his nature but also his creative imagination. In one way or another, the Bible is at the root of much of his work.

One reason for this continuing interest was that Shelley was genuinely attracted to the literary qualities of the Bible or, more precisely, to the literary qualities of certain books such as Job and the Psalms and some of the prophets. . . . Temperamentally, too, Shelley was well attuned to the patterns of elevation and despair which are so common in the prophets and in the Psalms. Whatever his beliefs, Shelley had a deeply religious sensibility, a readiness to open himself to the invisible energies, which must have attracted him to the poetry of the Bible and which gives to much of his work a visionary or prophetic quality.

However, this in itself would not be enough to explain the intensity and duration of Shelley's interest. The Bible also provided the traditional answers to many of the metaphysical problems which had obsessed him from an early age—was there a God? was there an existence after death? were our lives truly meaningful? Shelley showed a quite exceptional hunger for certainty in these matters and it was this which led, indirectly, to his being sent down from Oxford after publishing *The Necessity of Atheism.* In spite of its title, this little pamphlet did not proclaim that god was dead. It examined the reasons normally put forward for believing in his existence, found these inadequate and asked if anyone could answer the objections. It was a cry for help addressed to the heads of the Oxford colleges and the Bishops of England, each of whom received a copy in the post and not one of whom cared to reply. Shelley had had his first experience of the closed mind; but he persevered in his investigations. *A Refutation of Deism* which was privately printed in 1814 was a dialogue in the manner of Hume in which Shelley dispassionately explored the reasons for and against a belief in the existence of God. The discussion was buttressed by carefully selected quotations from the Bible, mostly from the Old Testament which Shelley regarded as a disgraceful record of crime and cruelty. In particular, through the mouth of Theosophus, he objected to the degraded notion of a God presented by the Old Testament: 'An unnatural monster, who sawed his fellow beings in sunder, harrowed them to fragments under harrows of iron, chopped them in pieces with axes, and burned them in brick-kilns, because they bowed before a different and less bloody idol than his own.'

The political conscience of Shelley is at work here translating Biblical history into terms which were all too intelligible to a man of his generation. Though he never abandoned his concern for metaphysics, Shelley's interest in Christianity gradually shifted its focus away from the metaphysical implications of theology towards the political realities which they embodied. He came to believe that religion was 'intimately connected with politics' and could not be dissociated from a variety of repressive systems which had prevented the vast majority of Europeans from reaching their full human potential. He was thinking specifically of institutionalised Christianity as interpreted by the Church, not of the genuine Christianity of those few individuals who had responded from their hearts to the true message of Christ.

The sanguinary God which Christianity has inherited from Judaism is a projection of man's own imperfections and his selfishness:

> What is that Power? Some moon-struck sophist stood
> Watching the shade from his own soul upthrown
> Fill Heaven and darken Earth, and in such mood
> The Form he saw and worshipped was his own,
> His likeness in the word's vast mirror shown;
> And 'twere an innocent dream, but that a faith
> Nursed by fear's dew of poison, grows thereon,
> And that men say, that Power has chosen Death
> On all who scorn its laws, to wreak immortal wrath.
>
> (***Revolt of Islam***)

If there was a God it was logically impossible that, being all-good, he could have devised the system of retaliation and revenge accepted by Christian orthodoxy. This repugnant system of an eye for an eye and a tooth for a tooth had outlived even the Greek love of liberty and destroyed Greek civilisation in a series of futile and retaliatory wars. Following in the footsteps of Aeschylus, but offering a final solution which did not involve compromising with power, Shelley devoted *Prometheus Unbound* to showing how man could and should escape from this seemingly endless cycle of retributive 'justice'. Man must be released from fear and guilt and the evil personifications of his heart must be demythologised and destroyed. The action of *Prometheus Unbound* deals largely with this— the dethronement of Jupiter, a false god who reigned simply because man's will 'made or suffered' him and who has chained Prometheus, the potential saviour, to his rock and thwarted humanity from achieving its true potential. Here Shelley is following not only the philosophers of the eighteenth century, Hume, Gibbon, Voltaire and others, but he is particularly indebted to the example of Lucretius, whose *De Rerum Natura* was designed to rid his contemporaries of the crippling fears induced by superstitious religion. *Queen Mab,* though it exhibits some youthful deficiencies, is a fair index of Shelley's approach to these matters: it bears an epigraph from Lucretius which concludes: *magnis doceo de rebus; et arctis / Religionum animos nodis exsolvere pergo* ('I tell of great matters, and I shall go on to free men's minds from the crippling bonds of superstitions'). For much of his career, that remained one of Shelley's main objectives.

In particular, he was much exercised by the Christian doctrine of eternal punishment. In the essay **"On the Devil and Devils"** he objects to the license given to the Devils to tempt mankind into offences for which they will be punished in eternity. Such behaviour could be understood in the case of an earthly tyrant who is afraid of losing power:

> But to tempt mankind to incur everlasting dam-
> nation must, on the part of God and even on
> the part of the Devil, arise from that very dis-
> interested love of tormenting and annoying which
> is seldom observed on earth except from the
> very old . . . The thing that comes nearest to it
> is a troop of idle dirty boys baiting a cat; cook-
> ing, skinning eels, and boiling lobsters alive,
> and bleeding calves, and whipping pigs to
> death. . . . It is pretended that God dislikes it,
> but this is mere shamefacedness and coquet-
> ting, for he has everything his own way and he
> need not damn unless he likes. The Devil has
> a better excuse. . . .

In this passage Shelley is characteristically downright; the brutal physicality of his images is the index of his disgust. Fur-
thermore, although he is examining a theological problem, it is clear that he is transferring it into terms which are recog-
nisably political. Since God is a projection of the darker powers within man himself, it is not surprising if he appears to behave himself in a fashion which we might expect from 'earthly tyrants'.

As soon as we have recognised this, we can see that the whole of God's behaviour with regard to the human race is consistent and explicable. God is not the spirit of God who rules over the universe; he is a peculiarly odious distortion of a human tyrant. Consider for example the collaboration between God and the Devil:

> These two considerable personages are sup-
> posed to have entered into a sort of partnership
> in which the weaker has consented to bear all
> the odium of their common actions and to allow
> the stronger to talk of himself as a very hon-
> ourable person, on condition of having a par-
> ticipation in what is the especial delight of both
> of them—burning men to all eternity. The dirty
> work is done by the Devil in the same manner
> as some starving wretch will hire himself out
> to a King or Minister with a stipulation that he
> shall have some portion of the public spoil as
> an instrument to betray a certain number of
> other starving wretches into circumstances of
> capital punishment, when they may think it
> convenient to edify the rest by hanging up a
> few of those whose murmurs are too loud.

Once again Shelley displays an unusual ability to project himself feelingly into the abstractions of theological dispute. Specifically, what he has in mind is the use by the British Gov-
ernment of informers and *agents provocateurs* to discredit radical movements. . . . It was this kind of tryannical repression of liberties he had in mind when he wrote in **"England in 1819"** of 'Golden and sanguine laws which tempt and slay'. This political system was based on money and on violent oppression,

and it provoked revolutions in order that they might be put down *pour encourager les autres.* (pp. 130-34)

[English political history is] relevant to Shelley's interpretation of orthodox theology since, on the one hand, the theology was a projection of those repressive instincts which were so obviously evidenced in politics and since, on the other, the po-
litical system was reinforced with deterrent sanctions by the theology. Orthodox theology directed man's attentions towards life after death, threatening punishment for those who did not believe in it or for those who did believe but were wicked enough to ignore it. This approach had the advantage that it diverted and frustrated attempts to alter the *status quo.* The essential message of Christianity implied a redistribution of property or, more precisely, not a strictly communistic system but a system of moral responsibility according to which every man 'considers himself with respect to the great community of mankind as the steward and guardian of their interests in the property which he chances to possess'. Christ had been quite unequivocal about this: 'Sell all that thou hast, give it to the poor, and follow me.' Likewise, his injunction that we should take no thought for the morrow was directed against the materialistic view of life: 'He simply exposes with the passionate rhetoric of enthusiastic love towards all human beings the miseries and mischiefs of that system which makes all things subservient to the subsistence of the material frame of man'. You cannot serve God and Mammon: 'it is impossible at once to be high-minded and just and wise, and comply with the accustomed forms of human society, seek honour, wealth, or empire either from the idolatry of habit or as the direct instruments of sensual gratification.' This part of Christ's message was inconvenient and therefore it was neglected since, after all, the kingdom of Heaven is not of this world.

Shelley gives us an illustration of how this system works in **The Cenci,** where he examines specifically the mind of Italian Catholicism. The action of the play exhibits a close connection between power, wealth and authority, a nexus of self-interest which binds together Count Cenci, the Pope, and God. Beatrice prays to God 'Whose image upon earth a father is' hoping that she will not be abandoned to her father's will. But it soon appears that the will of the father is the will of the Father. Cenci assumes this with great certainty:

> With what but with a father's curse doth God
> Panic-strike armèd victory, and make pale
> Cities in their prosperity? The world's Father
> Must grant a parent's prayer against his child,
> Be he who asks even what men call me.

This belief seems to be confirmed by the way in which his rebellious sons have been eliminated in one night, apparently by divine intervention. This league of force is strengthened and confirmed by God's representative on earth, the Holy Father, who refuses to intervene against the Count except for the purpose of lining his own purse. He knows that it is not in his interest to stand in the way of Cenci:

> He holds it of most dangerous example
> In aught to weaken the paternal power,
> Being, as 'twere, the shadow of his own.

The connection between sanctions and self-interest could hardly be made clearer. As Shelley put it in the **Essay on Christianity:**

> [The doctrines of Christ] are the very doctrines
> which, in another shape, the most violent as-
> sertors of Christianity denounce as impious and

seditious; who are such earnest champions for social and political disqualification as they? This alone would be a demonstration of the falsehood of Christianity, that the religion so called is the strongest ally and bulwark of that system of successful force and fraud and of the selfish passions from which it has derived its origin and permanence, against which Jesus Christ declared the most uncompromising war, and the extinction of which appears to have been the great motive of his life.

(pp. 135-36)

[Shelley was attracted to the story of Prometheus] not because of an irresistible predilection for Greek mythology as such but because he recognised the continuing relevance of the truths which it embodied. It was the responsibility of every age to reinterpret these myths for its own purposes: 'Of such truths / Each to itself must be the oracle'.

Given, then, this living relationship with the best that has been thought and said, the poet will reinterpret what he finds in terms of his own age. Thus, Shelley was able to see that the Zeus of *Prometheus Bound* (or Jupiter as Shelley calls him in *Prometheus Unbound*) was not simply the unfilial son of Saturn, the unfaithful husband of Hera, the capricious and vindictive Father of the Gods. He was all of those things but he was also only a symbol of the kind of divinity which man had duped himself into worshipping: as Aeschylus had put it, *pollōn onomatōn morphē mia* (the names are many, but the form is one) a line which Shelley was found of quoting. It followed that an interpretation of the Prometheus story which was valid for the revolutionary period of the early nineteenth century would recognize in Jupiter that daunting and vindictive God who ruled the hearts and minds of men by a combination of threats and promises. And, since the orthodox Christian view of God was a projection of man's own propensity to tryannise over his fellows, since God was no more than the magnified image of an earthly tyrant, an attack on the power of Jupiter represented an attack on the reigning monarchies of Europe. That three of these had banded together for political purposes under the title of the Holy Alliance was a fact which seemed to endorse this point of view. The theological premises of the argument implied the political and the political implied the theological: to release man from the bondage of his religious guilt and fears was to take another step toward abolishing the remaining vestiges of the *ancien régime,* while to unite men in free and brotherly love was to eliminate the system of hatred, self-contempt and retaliation on which the tyranny of religion was based. Therefore, it is wrong to see *Prometheus Unbound* simply as a poem which enacts a political revolution; likewise it is wrong to see it simply as a poem which readjusts the mental equilibrium. It does both of these things together and each readjustment or revolution implies and necessitates the other.

Once this has been understood, the peculiar potency of the language and the symbols can be seen in the appropriate focus. Throughout **Prometheus Unbound** Shelley employs the language of religion but he employs it to these heterodox and revolutionary ends. The old repressive religion is abandoned, the knots of superstition are unravelled (to use the image of Lucretius) and the new religion of love is established in its place. The negative world of the Decalogue is swept away and for it is substituted the positive injunction, 'Thou shalt love thy neighbour better than thyself'. This is in no sense an easy

commandment to fulfil but one which requires constant vigilance and self-control as well as a proper recognition of one's own true dignity: Shelley makes this point in the **"Hymn to Intellectual Beauty"** when he records how that beneficent spirit had taught him 'To fear himself, and love all human kind'.

Consider the opening speech of Prometheus in which, bound to his precipice, he turns his face to the torturing divinity who is his gaoler:

> Monarch of Gods and Daemons, and all Spirits
> But One, who throng those bright and rolling worlds
> Which Thou and I alone of living things
> Behold with sleepless eyes! regard this Earth
> Made multitudinous with thy slaves, whom thou
> Requitest for knee-worship, prayer and praise,
> And toil, and hecatombs of broken hearts,
> With fear and self-contempt and barren hope;
> Whilst me, who am thy foe, eyeless in hate,
> Hast thou made reign and triumph, to thy scorn,
> O'er mine own misery and thy vain revenge.

There is an obviously Miltonic ring to some of these lines ('Made multitudinous with thy slaves', 'Requitest for knee-worship') which immediately reminds us that one of Shelley's models for Prometheus was the Satan of *Paradise Lost.* Thus, the unjust gods of Aeschylus and Milton are fused in Jupiter, while the outspoken indignation of Prometheus and Satan burns behind the words of Shelley's hero. At the centre of this passage is the image of religious worship, a submission to divinity which is degrading and humiliating, not because worship is in itself damaging to humanity, but because the god in question is not worthy of our devotion. This system of religious worship has nothing to do with an acknowledgement of the spirit of good in the universe and everything to do with keeping the tyrant in power.

Jupiter here is a kind of Nobodaddy, a jealous, vindictive God, eager for sacrifice and self-abasement from his subjects. He is shaped, in part at least, by the Jehovah whom Shelley encountered in the Old Testament; yet the empire over which he rules is not a world of religious ceremonies and blood sacrifices, but a mental world. The hecatombs are not of oxen or of sheep but of 'broken hearts'. And the rewards of this service are 'fear and self-contempt and barren hope'. Shelley is thinking of the theological system of rewards and punishments, the system which promises requital in terms of eternal felicity in Heaven or eternal punishment in Hell. To hope for this kind of heaven after death is to be deceived by barren hope, that is, to withdraw oneself from the present possibilities of doing good for the illusory prospect of being rewarded with eternal happiness in another life. To subscribe to a belief in the reality of a hell of fire and flames is to submit to an illusory and degrading fear. This extortionate system of threats and promises leads man to undervalue himself, to misconceive his own potential, to trample on his own liberties: this is 'self-contempt'.

As Shelley saw it, any claim to virtue must be judged in terms of motivation. He explained the point in a letter of 1812: 'Paley's *Moral Philosophy* begins—Why am I *obliged* to keep my word? Because I desire Heaven and hate Hell. *Obligation* and duty therefore are words of no value as the criteria of excellence. So much for Obedience, Parents & Children. Do you agree to my definition of Virtue—Disinterestedness?'... Some years later he returned to the subject in his **"Treatise on Morals,"** where he attacks the conventional association of virtue and obligation:

Virtue is a law to which it is the will of the lawgiver that we should conform, which will we should in no manner be bound to obey, unless some dreadful punishment were attached to disobedience. This is the philosophy of slavery and superstition.

In fact, no person can be *bound* or *obliged* without some power preceding to bind and oblige. If I observe a man bound hand and foot, I know that some one bound him. But if I observe him returning self-satisfied from the performance of some action by which he has been the willing author of extensive benefit, I do not infer that the anticipation of hellish agonies, or the hope of heavenly reward, has constrained him to sacrifice . . .

These passages suggest that one way in which Prometheus is *unbound* is by being released from these obligations to behave virtuously, which are endorsed and supported by deterrent sanctions. The only authentic virtue is based on what can truly be described as free will.

In spite of this, Shelley did not discountenance Hell and Heaven: rather, he believed that they were potential in us here and now. To postpone them to the life after death was to submit ourselves to a belief in what was almost certainly illusory; it was also to avoid our serious responsibility to redeem ourselves and our society as far as was humanly possible. So, imagining the fall of Jupiter, Prometheus (as yet unregenerate) rejoices to think how he will suffer: 'How will thy soul, cloven to its depths with terror, / Gape like a hell within!' Conversely, if Hell is within man's reach, so too are the means of escape. Thus, in *Prometheus Unbound* the Spirit of the Hour describes regenerated man in terms of the internal Hell from which he has liberated himself, an *Inferno* of the mind which makes explicit reference to Dante:

> None fawned, none trampled; hate, disdain, or fear,
> Self-love or self-contempt, on human brows
> No more inscribed, as o'er the gate of Hell,
> 'All hope abandon, ye who enter here' . . .

The reversal is portrayed even more positively in the final act, where it is made clear that revolutionary man has not only freed himself from Hell, but has created his own Heaven:

> . . . Hate, and Fear, and Pain, light-vanquished
>   shadows, fleeing.
>
> Leave Man—who was a many-sided mirror,
>   Which could distort to many a shape of error
> This true fair world of things—a sea reflecting Love;
>   Which over all his kind, as the Sun's Heaven
>   Gliding o'er ocean, smooth, serene, and even,
> Darting from starry depths radiance and life, doth
>   move . . .
>
> Man, one harmonious soul of many a soul,
>   Whose nature is its own divine control,
> Where all things flow to all, as rivers to the sea;
>   Familiar acts are beautiful through love;
>   Labour, and Pain, and Grief, in life's green grove
> Sport like tame beasts—none knew how gentle they
>   could be!

These last lines approach closer to the mere personification than is usual with Shelley but this song as a whole preserves

a splendid image of harmony and unity between man and man, which is based on each man's discovery of the paradise which is latent within himself. . . .

In order to realise this paradise, Prometheus has to conquer the evil tendencies in himself, to direct himself away from the potential Hell within. Through his ministers, Jupiter tries hard to persuade Prometheus of his own essential worthlessness and to force him to acquiesce in Jupiter's world of punishments and rewards. Jupiter's agent Mercury taunts Prometheus with the prospect of eternal punishment; the Furies try to impress on him the futility of human endeavour, bringing before his eyes two notable examples of idealism betrayed by the relentless process of history—the spread of Christianity and the French Revolution. The aim is to induce fear and self-contempt, a superstitious reluctance to improve on the existing state of things. This is the temptation of the Devil and in the fragmentary draft of *Hellas* it is rejected by Christ, who rebukes Satan for being a historical determinist: 'Obdurate spirit! / Thou seest but the Past in the To-come. / Pride is thy error and thy punishment'. (This might be Julian talking to Maddalo, insisting, even in the face of unsavoury realities, that 'this is not destiny / But man's own wilful ill'.) What Christ implies here is that to take Satan's view of history is to put ourselves in bondage to the past; ultimately it is a denial both of free will and of moral responsibility. This, then, is the temptation to despair on the grounds that history inevitably repeats itself and that, since previous attempts to improve the human condition have notoriously failed, all future attempts are doomed to be equally unsuccessful.

Another subtle and insidious temptation to despair is to interpret the whole of history as a process of gradual degeneration from an imagined Golden Age. This doctrine is philosophically false: 'Later and more correct observations have instructed us that uncivilized man is the most pernicious and miserable of beings. . .'; it is also morally dangerous because it ministers to 'thoughts of despondency and sorrow'. It may, however, be turned to advantage: the 'imaginations of a happier state of human society' were 'the children of airy hope, the prophets and parents of mysterious futurity'. The important distinction is that we must look forward not back, seeking for the New Jerusalem rather than the lost Eden. Or. as Shelley expressed it in one of his footnotes to the *Essay on Christianity,* 'Jesus Christ foresaw what these poets retrospectively imagined'. Once again Christ as prophet shows the way to later generations.

Like Christ and like Julian, Prometheus is alert to the dangerous pressures of despair: from experience he notes that 'Evil minds / Change good to their own nature'. This fact is implicit in his opening speech where he acknowledges a close and subtle relationship between himself and Jupiter. In particular, this uncomfortable connection is mirrored in the richly ambivalent syntax of 'whilst me, who am thy foe, eyeless in hate, / Hast thou made reign'. Conventionally, *eyeless in hate* is taken to go with *thou;* even if the structure of this is rather jerky, no one can be surprised by such a description of the vigilant sadism of the Almighty. However, the syntax is awkward not because Shelley was too incompetent to iron it out but because it embodies a genuine ambiguity in the sense: *eyeless in hate* balances tantalisingly on the end of the line, poised between *me* (Prometheus) and *thou* (Jupiter). The hatred emanating from Jupiter has communicated itself to Prometheus: because he has allowed himself to respond in kind, he too is *eyeless in hate.* There may also be an allusive irony at work here, since one of the parallels for Prometheus as the enduring hero is Samson

Agonistes who was also, notoriously, *eyeless*. If this allusion is intended, the implication might be that Prometheus, like Samson, has erred through indulging his baser passions. At any rate, this ambiguity seems to suggest that, at this point in the play, Prometheus and Jupiter are identified. It is therefore entirely appropriate that, when Prometheus asks to hear the curse which he once invoked on Jupiter, the words of that curse are spoken by the Phantasm of Jupiter himself. Prometheus cannot recall them since he has now cast out hatred but the Phantasm of Jupiter is more than an ironical dramatic device; its appearance actually suggests that in cursing Jupiter, Prometheus became identified with him.

When the curse has been summoned from the recesses of consciousness and re-enacted in a therapeutic process well known to psychoanalysis, when hatred has been rejected and the vacuum filled by love (embodied in Asia), Jupiter necessarily falls. The suddenness of his disappearance should not be surprising since Jupiter is in fact a *nothing,* as the imagery of the play constantly proclaims. His disappearance follows logically from the end of **"Mont Blanc":**

> And what were thou, and earth, and stars, and sea,
> If to the human mind's imaginings
> Silence and solitude were vacancy?

If man can populate the universe with the divinities he imagines to himself, he also has the power to recall those images and demythologise them. So, in Act Three Prometheus has asserted his independence and dethroned the dark divinity of his own soul.

This psychological change is mirrored in imagery derived from religious ceremony and worship. Early in the play Mercury arrives to negotiate on behalf of Jupiter; the pressure he wishes to exert is an unsubtle one based on the threat of punishment. The best policy, he advises Prometheus, is submission:

> . . . bend thy soul in prayer,
> And like a suppliant in some gorgeous fane
> Let the will kneel within thy haughty heart:
> For benefits and meek submission tame
> The fiercest and the mightiest.

To kneel would be for Prometheus to acknowledge Jupiter as the divinity of his own heart: it would be to collaborate with the forces of evil. Prometheus resists this invitation; later he is tempted with greater subtlety by a Fury who recommends a passive acquiescence in the *status quo.* She tells him that even the most lofty spirits are inhibited by misgivings which they would not openly acknowledge: 'Hypocrisy and custom make their minds / The fanes [temples] of many a worship, now outworn.'

When Prometheus has surmounted these temptations and his hope and endurance have been fortified by the vivifying love of Asia, the old religion of fear is abolished and 'thrones, altars, judgment-seats, and prisons' which 'imaged to the pride of kings and priests / A dark yet mighty faith' are unregarded and abandoned. Even more significantly:

> . . . those foul shapes, abhorred by God and man,
> Which, under many a name and many a form,
> Strange, savage, ghastly, dark and execrable,
> Were Jupiter, the tyrant of the world;
> And which the nations, panic-stricken, served
> With blood, and hearts broken by long hope, and love
> Dragged to his altars soiled and garlandless
> And slain amid men's unreclaiming tears,
> Flattering the thing they feared, which fear was hate—
> Frown, mouldering fast, o'er their abandoned shrines.

Here the representative character of Jupiter becomes very clear: he is the deity of any false religion, Christian or otherwise; he is 'many fearful natures in one name.' This false deity has been worshipped in pain and fear: even Love, which is potentially the redeeming agent, has been sacrificed to this dark idolatry.

Shelley's powerful image of 'love / Dragged to his altars soiled and garlandless' almost certainly had its origin in a famous passage where Lucretius describes how, on the advice of his soothsayer, Agamemnon agreed to sacrifice his daughter Iphigenia so that the winds might blow again and give his ships passage to Troy. . . . For Lucretius, the moral of the story was the extent to which the demands of so-called religion could pervert the normal feelings of humanity; for Shelley, the moral also involved the dangerous influence of religion, but in his reading what has been so ruthlessly abandoned is not merely Iphigenia, a trembling and innocent girl, but love. This barbaric ritual is not merely a specific offence against the blood relationship binding the Atreidae one to another; it is also, and more important, an offence against the spirit of love. Therefore, in Shelley's view it is a contradiction of all that is implied by true religion. It is a measure of the seriousness of the threat which he recognised in the history of organised religion that, even at this moment of supreme triumph, when Jupiter has been overthrown and ordinary man are walking 'One with another even as spirits do', even at the end of this speech where he originally planned to finish the play, the image of man's inhumanity to man presents itself so forcibly.

Edward Williams's sketch of the Don Juan, *or* Ariel, *in which he and Shelley were drowned.*

Shelley, then, sees the sacrifice of Iphigenia as an offence against the spirit of love; in his version the brutal image is translated from the external world of dramatic action to the inner world of mental events. . . . Yet the inner world does retain a vivid and tangible connection with physical actions. The adjective *soiled* immediately transmits to these mental happenings an unforgettable reality; and *garlandless* (a word which Shelley introduced into English from the Greek *aste- phanos*) derives much of its force from the incident in Lucre- tius. This Iphigenia is not paid even the customary civility of being adorned for the sacrifice. Finally, *unreclaiming tears* is another phrase of particular resonance. On the literal level it means that, although the spectators at this sacrifice were grieved, they offered no objections, raised no voice in protest. In Lu- cretius it was Iphigenia herself who was struck dumb with fear (*muta metu*); in Shelley's new version this fear has transmitted itself to the acquiescing crowd. Metaphorically, *unreclaiming tears* takes us to the heart of Shelley's thought. In a very practical way Shelley had devoted his own services to the process of reclamation; specifically, he had helped in the fa- mous project for reclaiming land from the sea at Tremadoc. This in itself was an image, a living symbol of how man could reclaim the desert of his life and plant it with the flowers of progress. So the unreclaiming tears are not only the tears of cowardice and moral weakness but unpractical tears, tears which reject the possibilities of redemption which are open to the human race. Since Jupiter has only reigned by the consent of man, love can still be rescued from the altar of sacrifice and the human condition can still be redeemed. (pp. 142-50)

> *Timothy Webb, in his* Shelley: A Voice Not Under-
> stood, *Humanities Press, 1977, 269 p.*

WILLIAM KEACH   (essay date 1984)

[*In this excerpt from his critically acclaimed study of Shelley's style, Keach discusses the importance of reflexive imagery in Shelley's poetry.*]

'But even with so limited an instrument as the short-circuited comparison, he could do great things'—William Empson con- cludes his remarks on Shelley in *Seven Types of Ambiguity* [see Additional Bibliography] with this curiously qualified compliment, which he illustrates with two lines from *The Triumph of Life:*

> And others mournfully within the gloom
>
> Of their own shadow walked, and called it death . . .

Although Empson calls attention here to a prominent verbal pattern in Shelley's writing, he does not go on to elucidate the 'great things' Shelley does with it, and the gist of his remarks on these 'short-circuited comparisons'—what he earlier calls 'self-inwoven similes'—is negative. He sees them as products of hasty, unpremeditated composition: 'when not being able to think of a comparison fast enough he compares the thing to a vaguer or more abstract notion of itself, or points out that it is its own nature, or that it sustains itself by supporting itself.' My contention [is] that while Shelley's reflexive imagery (to broaden the terminology) does present special critical diffi- culties, it is not, as Empson implies, an inherently limited stylistic mannerism with no particular expressive function. It is, on the contrary, a characteristic form of Shelley's imagery 'drawn from the operations of the human mind', one which he uses to articulate some of his deepest poetic concerns.

I use the term 'reflexive' to refer to locutions in which an object or action is compared, implicitly or explicitly, to an aspect of itself, or is said to act upon or under the conditions of an aspect of itself. Such locutions call unusual attention to the act of mind they presuppose in the writer and provoke in the reader, an act of mind in which something is perceived as both one thing and more than one thing, as both itself and something other than itself. Reflexive images often include or appear in connection with references to literal physical reflec- tion (or shadow, as above in *The Triumph of Life*), and when they do they may appeal strongly and teasingly to the visual imagination. But the basis of the reflexive image *per se* is grammatical and syntactical; the signifying function of a phrase or clause turns back on itself, and its doing so marks an 'op- eration of the human mind' that couples analysis or division (as an aspect is separated from the idea to which it belongs) with synthesis or reunion (as the separated or divided aspect is re-identified with that same idea):

> One seat was vacant in the midst, a throne,
>   Reared on a pyramid like sculptured flame,
> Distinct with circling steps which rested on
>   Their own deep fire . . .
>
> **(The Revolt of Islam)**

'Deep fire' is simultaneously separate from 'circling steps' and thus capable of becoming the grammatical object of the phrase 'rested on', and inseparable from 'circling steps', since what the steps rest on is an aspect of themselves. In the case of 'the self-inwoven simile', a subcategory of reflexive imagery which is in fact less frequent in Shelley's writing than Empson im- plies, the separation of idea and aspect is even more conspic- uously a result of the mind's ability to perceive relational dif- ference within sameness and identity:

> He has invented lying words and modes,
> Empty and vain as his own coreless heart . . .
>
> **(Queen Mab)**

The punning paradox of 'coreless heart' ('heartless heart', as Hamlet might have said) brings to a sharp conclusion this line's turn of language and thought. Shelley's reflexive images may be thought of as extremely condensed (but not necessarily 'short- circuited') versions of the figurative situation analyzed by Wimsatt in 'The structure of Romantic nature imagery', where tenor and vehicle 'are wrought in a parallel process out of the same material'. (pp. 79-80)

Reflexive imagery is fundamentally ambivalent in *The Revolt of Islam;* the states of consciousness - especially political con- sciousness - it signals may be either auspicious or inauspicious, benign or malign. Consider the imagery of self-illumination. In Canto I the narrator is led into a vast temple of prophetic vision where 'long and labyrinthine aisles' appear 'more bright / With their own radiance than the Heaven of Day'. But in Canto V, when Laon approaches the tryant Othman, he finds him 'Upon the footstool of his golden throne, / Which, starred with sunny gems, in its own lustre shone'. Throughout the poem, as so often in Shelley's later poetry, political oppression is imaged reflexively, suggesting that to an important degree it is, at least passively, self-imposed. In Canto II Laon re- members how the citizens of his native Argolis had allowed 'one Power' to gain 'supreme control / Over their will by their own weakness lent'; in Canto V he appeals to his followers to show mercy towards their former oppressors, since ' to avenge misdeed / On the misdoer, doth but Misery feed / With her own broken heart'.

In Canto X the forces of counter-revolution brutally regain control and leave the populace prey to disease and famine:

> Many saw
> Their own lean image everywhere, it went
> A ghastlier self beside them, till the awe
> Of the dread sight to self-destruction sent
> Those shrieking victims . . .

Whether suicide is provoked by seeing one's own emaciated shadow or by seeing one's starving fellow citizens is left horrifyingly indeterminate. Related indeterminacies of reference and implication appear in instances where forces of political regeneration or liberation are imaged reflexively. An old hermit revives Laon's spirits in Canto IV by telling him how Cythna has inspired her people to try to conquer Othman's soldiers by sympathy rather than by force:

>   . . . the multitude
> Surrounding them, with works of human love,
> Seek from their own decay their stubborn minds to move.

'From their own decay' can appropriately refer either to the social and physical condition of the 'multitude', or to the moral condition of the soldiers who oppress them. In Canto V Laon returns to Argolis and leads the people to victory over Othman and his army. There is a night of rejoicing, and the canto comes to a close with this couplet:

> The multitudes went homeword, to their rest,
> Which that delightful day with its own shadow blessed.

'With its own shadow' at first seems merely intensive, a way of emphasizing the point that the end of a day of victory and celebration brings an additional reward of peaceful rest. But the reflexive syntax also enhances an ominous undertone in that last line, a suggestion that even this glorious day is shadowed by the suffering that has and is to come.

Reflexive images in *The Revolt of Islam* lack the intensely developed psychological context they have in **"Alastor"**, and rarely are they articulated with the finesse of Shelley's later writing at its best. But one can see Shelley working towards an expanded sense of the figure's possibilities in this poem— particularly in Cythna's narrative of her imprisonment, release and return to Argolis in Cantos VII and VIII. Extending what he took to be the epistemological and educational implications of the 'intellectual philosophy', Shelley has Cythna describe her isolated confinement in a seaside cave as an extreme symbolic enactment of the essential reflexive condition of mind. '"We live in our own world"', she says, in words that recall Satan's 'The mind is its own place':

> My mind became the book through which I grew
> Wise in all human wisdom, and its cave,
> Which like a mine I rifled through and through,
> To me the keeping of its secrets gave—
> One mind, the type of all, the moveless wave
> Whose calm reflects all moving things that are . . .

Cythna's mind becomes its own book and teacher, generates its own 'subtler language within language'. Like the wandering poet in **"Alastor"**, but with an access to consciousness other than her own that he never achieves, she sustains herself with her own visionary love-songs:

>   - and sweet melodies
> Of love, in that lorn solitude I caught
> From mine own voice in dream, when thy dear eyes
> Shone through my sleep, and did that utterance harmonize.

In learning to rely on the self-sustaining power of mind, however, Cythna also learns to mistrust the mind's tendency to project itself as a god-like 'Power' separate from and superior to the human imagination. When an earthquake shatters her cavern-prison and she is rescued by a passing ship, she upbraids the mariners for their superstitious belief in a personified deity:

> What is that Power? Ye mock yourselves, and give
> A human heart to what ye cannot know:
> As if the cause of life could think and live . . .
>
> What is that Power? some moon-struck sophist stood
> Watching the shade from his own soul upthrown
> Fill Heaven and darken Earth, and in such mood
> The Form he saw and worshipped was his own,
> His likeness in the world's vast mirror shown . . .

Cythna gives new force to the Miltonic adjective 'moon-struck' as she imagines the sophist lost in a lunacy of unselfconscious reflection, projecting his own 'likeness' as an object of worship. What makes her attack on this false form of reflexive projection so striking is the way in which it echoes her previous appeal to the mariners' self-reliance:

> What dream ye? Your own hands have built an home,
> Even for yourselves on a beloved shore.
>
> Is this your care? Ye toil for your own good —
> Ye feel and think - has some immortal power
> Such purposes?

The reflexive impulse weaves its way ambivalently in and out of Cythna's narrative, showing itself now as self-reliance and self-sufficiency, now as self-deception and mere selfishness. She concludes her speech to the mariners by urging them to 'know thyself' and yet to recognize and shun 'the dark idolatry of self'.

That 'One mind, the type of all' to which Cythna gains access by studying herself in *The Revolt of Islam* becomes the center of Shelley's metaphysical allegory in *Prometheus Unbound*. Here again, but with greater figurative daring and cogency than in the earlier work, reflexive imagery articulates the mind's capacity for self-imprisonment and self-liberation. Wasserman's reading of Act I is particularly powerful in its analysis of the fundamental thematic reflexiveness in Shelley's handling of the Prometheus myth. Commenting on the repetition of Prometheus's curse by the Phantasm of Jupiter, Wasserman [see Additional Bibliography] asks us

> to recognize this as the actual identification of
> the execrating Prometheus with Jupiter, the god
> he made in his own image. Not only does the
> audience watch the Phantasm uttering Prome-
> theus' curse against him of whom it is the phan-
> tom; it also observes Prometheus facing his own
> former self in Jupiter's ghost.

That such self-confrontation is a necessary and critical phase in Prometheus's liberation is indicated analogically and prophetically in the Earth's response to her immortal son's plea that the curse against Jupiter be 'recalled':

> PROMETHEUS
> But mine own words, I pray, deny me not.
>
> THE EARTH
> They shall be told.—Ere Babylon was dust,
> The Magus Zoroaster, my dead child,
> Met his own image walking in the garden.
> That apparition, sole of men, he saw.

When the Earth tells Prometheus later in the same speech to 'Call at will / Thine own ghost, or the ghost of Jupiter', her ambiguous syntactic alternation allows for the reflexive identification of Prometheus with his self-created tormenter ('I gave all / He has, and in return he chains me here').

Confronting his former self in the Phantasm of Jupiter completes this phase of the movement within Prometheus from hatred to pity ('I wish no living thing to suffer pain'). But pity alone is not enough. Prometheus's curse is not recalled just to be revoked; the words repeated by the Phantasm also contain the verbal pattern through which Prometheus will reclaim power for himself on behalf of mankind and mortal existence. When he cursed Jupiter, Prometheus had reminded him that 'O'er all things but thyself I gave thee power, / And my own will', words which again establish a reciprocal identification as well as a distinction between oppressor and oppressed. Prometheus reserved to himself a power which he denied Jupiter but which hatred had prevented him from fully realizing. In the course of Act I he reclaims this power by freeing himself from the constrictions of hate. Rhetorically, as he responds to the taunts of the Furies, he re-recalls those critical words and frees them from the context of his curse:

> Yet am I king over myself, and rule
> The torturing and conflicting throngs within
> As Jove rules you when Hell grows mutinous.

The process by which Prometheus's original defiant assertion of autonomy is recalled and transformed into its fullest political realization comes to completion at the end of ACT III, where the Spirit of the Hour extends that autonomy, and the stylistic motif which has become its signature, to man '—the King / Over himself; just, gentle, wise—but man'.

As Empson recognized, however, not all the 'self-inwoven' figures in *Prometheus Unbound* bear such immediate relation to the poem's central mythic and psychical action, nor are they always as internally coherent as the instances we have just been looking at. The figure pervades the lyric celebration of Act IV; it is no accident that all the examples queried by Empson come from this part of the poem. Shelley could be uneven in exploiting this stylistic resource in moments of extravagant visionary intensity. Consider Panthea's description of the regenerated earth and the attendant spirit asleep within its 'Ten thousand orbs involving and involved':

>   . . . they whirl
> Over each other with a thousand motions
> Upon a thousand sightless axles spinning
> And with the force of self-destroying swiftness,
> Intensely, slowly, solemnly roll on—
> Kindling with mingled sounds, and many tones,
> Intelligible words and music wild.—
> With mighty whirl the multitudinous Orb
> Grinds the bright brook into an azure mist
> Of elemental subtlety, like light,
> And the wild odour of the forest flowers,
> The music of the living grass and air,
> The emerald light of leaf-entangled beams
> Round its intense, yet self-conflicting speed,
> Seem kneaded into one aerial mass
> Which drowns the sense. Within the Orb itself,
> Pillowed upon its alabaster arms
> Like to a child o'erwearied with sweet toil,
> On its own folded wings and wavy hair
> The Spirit of the Earth is laid asleep,

> And you can see its little lips are moving
> Amid the changing light of their own smiles
> Like one who talks of what he loves in dream—

The images of 'self-destroying swiftness' and 'intense, yet self-conflicting speed' are both cogently precise in their evocation of whirling concentric spheres off-setting and counter-balancing each other's motions as together, in a paradoxical 'whirlwind harmony', they 'slowly, solemnly roll on'. But the infant Spirit of the Earth sleeping calmly at the center of all his spinning movement is presented in gratuitously reflexive terms. Empson comments on the redundancy of the simile in line 268 ('The last comparison is merely a statement of what he is'); he might also have complained about the triviality of the Spirit's lying 'On its own folded wings and wavy hair', and about the awkwardness of 'Amid the changing light of their own smiles'. This last image is troubling not because it lacks a discernible expressive function: Panthea sees the Spirit of the Earth here in a way that recalls Asia's response to Panthea's prophetic dream-vision of a liberated Prometheus in Act II.

> There is a change: beyond their inmost depth
> I see a shade—a shape—'tis He, arrayed
> In the soft light of his own smiles . . .

Like Prometheus in Act II, the Spirit of the Earth in Act IV appears in an illumination generated internally by love and radiated from within, not from an external source. But the problem with the Act IV image arises because of the odd plurals in 'their own smiles' (why not '*its* own smiles', or '*his* own smiles'?). 'Their' has its antecedent in the plural 'lips' of line 266, but the reader has to struggle with the distracting thought of each individual lip forming its own smile on the way to seeing that Shelley is referring to 'smiles' as separate, repeated actions. The image in Act IV is not carefully composed, and if many of Shelley's reflexive images were articulated with this kind of looseness, one would be inclined to agree with Empson that the figure had become a bad habit.

But elsewhere in Act IV Shelley shows that reflexive imagery is not habitually a resource he takes for granted. The first speech uttered by the Earth after Panthea's long rhapsodic introduction culminates in one of the poem's most compelling 'self-inwoven similes':

> The joy, the triumph, the delight, the madness,
> The boundless, overflowing bursting gladness,
> The vaporous exultation, not to be confined!
> Ha! ha! the animation of delight
> Which wraps me, like an atmosphere of light,
> And bears me as a cloud is borne by its own wind!

The commentators who have shown us the specificity and precision of Shelley's meteorological knowledge would be right to point out here that in thunderstorms clouds are actually moved about by their own internally generated turbulence. Shelley uses the simile's meteorological energy to animate an otherwise vapid 'vaporous exultation', and to invigorate the metaphorical life of 'an atmosphere of light'. But the simile is effective in other ways as well, as we may see by comparing it to an earlier version of itself from *The Revolt of Islam*. Laon remembers how he persisted in his cause despite being separated from Cythna:

> Doth the cloud perish, when the beams are fled
> Which steeped its skirts in gold? or, dark and lone,
> Doth it not through the paths of night unknown,
> On outspread wings of its own wind upborne
> Pour rain upon the earth?

The effect of this melodramatic cloud and wind image is wonderfully enhanced in *Prometheus Unbound* by its new dramatic context: the lightness and ebullience the Earth feels in realizing its recently acquired freedom give the simile of the cloud, with its implied contrast to the massive weight and solidity we normally associate with the Earth, a witty appropriateness. The main point of the reflexive simile is to convey the Earth's participation in the self-generated freedom and power realized by Prometheus—a freedom and power that come from within, like the wind in line 324, and initially depend on no external source. Reflexive images continue to display this fundamental condition of mind and experience right through to the end of the poem. In its antiphonal song with the Moon, the Earth celebrates the renovated human condition by elaborating once again the idea of man as 'King / Over himself':

> Man, one harmonious Soul of many a soul
> Whose nature is its own divine controul . . .

The there is Demogorgon's concluding exhortation about what must be done if oppressive evil should ever regain power:

> To defy Power which seems Omnipotent;
> To love, and bear; to hope, till Hope creates
> From its own wreck the thing it contemplates . . .

The rhyme here—'creates' and 'contemplates' reinforce each other conceptually as well as phonetically—complements the reflexive syntactic figure; together they give memorable shape to the ideal of a self-liberating and self-sustaining psychical potential.

While *Prometheus Unbound* contains Shelley's most positive exaltation of the reflexive imagination, the poem also recognizes that the same mental capacity can be negative and destructive. Prometheus replies to Mercury's request that he divulge the 'secret known / To thee and to none else of living things' by denouncing Jupiter's perversion of the very principle which will enable Prometheus to liberate himself and mankind:

> Evil minds
> Change good to their own nature.

These Satanic words could serve as an epigraph for *The Cenci*, which Shelley wrote between Acts I-III and Act IV of *Prometheus Unbound*. One of the many ways in which *The Cenci* inverts the vision of human potential expressed in *Prometheus Unbound* is in its articulation of the mind's power to know itself and to make the world over in its own image. Orsino's soliloquy at the end of Act II both anatomizes and enacts the reflexive imagination in its Cencian shape:

> It fortunately serves my close designs
> That 'tis a trick of this same family
> To analyse their own and other minds.
> Such self-anatomy shall teach the will
> Dangerous secrets: for it tempts our powers,
> Knowing what must be thought, and may be done,
> Into the depth of darkest purposes:
> So Cenci fell into the pit; even I,
> Since Beatrice unveiled me to myself,
> And made me shrink from what I cannot shun,
> Shew a poor figure to my own esteem,
> to which I grow half reconciled.

This 'trick' of infectious 'self-anatomy' and self-corruption is pervasive in *The Cenci*; a father's rape of his own daughter, a perversion of the positive incestuous bond between brother and sister which figures significantly in other of Shelley's poems,

is only one of its many manifestations. What makes this pattern of behavior so disturbing is that it springs from the same capacity of mind to become conscious of its own operations and impulses which Shelley elsewhere celebrates—in the Preface to *The Cenci* itself [see excerpt dated 1819], for instance:

> The highest moral purpose aimed at in the highest species of the drama, is the teaching of the human heart, through its sympathies and antipathies, the knowledge of itself. . . .

Cencian 'self-anatomy', like Promethean self-knowledge, is often represented in circular figures. Internally *The Cenci* offers no scape from the circle of negative reflexiveness; corrupt self-consciousness can finally only reconfigure itself as self-destruction:

> And we are left, as scorpions ringed with fire,
> What should we do but strike ourselves to death?

'The line circumscribed by the agonized scorpion's self-destruction is enclosed by a second circle, the wall of fire representing destructive experience'—Stuart Curran's comment [see excerpt dated 1970] shows why he sees this figure as emblematic of Shelley's vision of a world in which 'evil is the only force . . . good, transferred into action, into force, as a deterrent to evil, becomes evil.' As Prometheus says, 'Evil minds / Change good to their own nature'.

The deep-lying ambivalence of Shelley's reflexive imagery is nowhere more powerfully evident than in *The Triumph of Life*, the other major poem from which Empson draws his examples of this characteristic figure. The opening lines signal the importance of the reflexive pattern through what appears to be a propitious personification:

> Swift as a spirit hastening to his task
> Of glory and of good, the Sun sprang forth
> Rejoicing in his splendour . . .

But 'splendour' in *The Triumph* is only intermittently and briefly cause for rejoicing; within his 'waking dream' the narrator soon encounters 'a cold glare, intenser than the noon / But icy cold' which 'obscured with [ ] light / The Sun as he the stars'. The course of this strange new light appears in a reflexive figure which itself 'obscures', by recalling and transforming, the opening image of the sun's joyous 'splendour':

> So came a chariot on the silent storm
> Of its own rushing splendour . . .

The internal dynamics of this particular image are striking: the initial paradox of 'silent storm', which at first appears to be contradicted by the strong aural force of 'rushing', is eventually validated as that aural force is absorbed into the wholly visual effect of 'splendour'. 'Silent storm' and 'rushing splendour' stand in chiastic synaesthetic relation to each other. Empson juxtaposes these lines with a second passage from much later in Rousseau's inset narrative:

> I among the multitude
> Was swept; me sweetest flowers delayed not long,
> Me not the shadow nor the solitude,
>
> Me not the falling stream's Lethean song,
> Me, not the phantom of that early form
> Which moved upon its motion.

Although Empson does not make it clear that the 'early Form' of this second passage is not the chariot of Life referred to in the first, his juxtaposition is none the less suggestive: the 'shape all light' envisioned by Rousseau moves with the same kind of self-sustaining motion as the chariot of Life, in whose 'coming light' that 'fair shape waned'. This connection is anticipated, and linked with the sun's rising movement at the beginning of the poem, through a contrasting reflexive figure in Rousseau's account of 'that early form's' first appearance:

> . . . there stood
>
> > Amid the sun, as he amid the blaze
> > Of his own glory, on the vibrating
> > Floor of the fountain, paved with flashing rays,
> >
> > A shape all light . . .

Rousseau's 'shape' may be nothing more than an idealized reflection of the sun's 'flashing rays' at a moment of illusory stasis. Like the narrator's perception of the sun, Rousseau's perception of the 'shape all light' is paradoxically 'obscured' by the intense glare of a force whose movement duplicates and mocks both sun and 'shape'. The interlocking reflexive images provide one of the means by which Shelley suggests a complexly infolded and parallel relationship between Rousseau's experience and that of the narrator.

Empson comments directly on only one part of this sequence of images: about 'the phantom of that early form / Which moved upon its motion' he says, 'The *Form* is its own justification; it sustains itself, like God, by the fact that it exists'. This comment is actually more appropriate to the previous passage in which Life's chariot appears 'in the silent storm / Of its own rushing splendour', since Life is triumphant in Shelley's poem simply 'by the fact that it exists', and in many respects it does assume the role of God in its self-sustaining and relentless omnipotence. But Empson is right to question the apparently tautological redundancy of 'moved upon its motion'. Whether logically and verbally pointless, as he argues, or somehow strangely expressive, the phrase pushes the reflexive figure to an extreme. In *Epipsychidion* the speaker refers to Emily as 'a tender / Reflection of the eternal Moon of Love / Under whose motions life's dull billows move', but the absence of a reflexive relation here between 'motions' and 'moves' only accentuates by comparison the excessive involution of the later image. What this image is meant to convey, I would suggest, is Rousseau's attentuated memory of the 'shape all light's' increasingly faint and finally negative corporeal presence. Even when 'that early form' first appeared to him, its spectral movements seemed barely to register on the natural world:

> —the fierce splendour
> Fell from her as she moved under the mass
>
> Of the deep cavern, and with palms so tender
> > Their tread broke not the mirror of its billow,
> Glided along the river . . .
>
> As one enamoured is upborne in dream
> > O'er lily-paven lakes mid silver mist
> To wondrous music, so this shape might seem
>
> > Partly to tread the waves with feet which kist
> > The dancing foam, partly to glide along
> > The airs that roughened the moist amethyst . . .

When the 'new Vision' of Life's chariot 'Burst' upon his sight and made 'that early form' the 'phantom' which Rousseau

remembers in lines 464-5, this 'phantom' moves even more spectrally over and through the 'wilderness' of experience:

> So knew I in that light's severe excess
> The presence of that shape which on the stream
> > Moved, as I moved along the wilderness,
>
> More dimly than a day appearing dream,
> > The ghost of a forgotten form of sleep,
> A light from Heaven whose half extinguished beam
>
> > Through the sick day in which we wake to weep
> Glimmers, forever sought, forever lost.—
> > So did that shape its obscure tenour keep
>
> Beside my path, as silent as a ghost . . .

A moving shape whose 'tenour' has become as 'obscure' as this might plausibly be remembered as having attained a mode of 'presence' so infinitely remote from immediacy ('The ghost of a forgotten form of sleep') that there is nothing left that it can 'move[ ] upon' but 'its [own] motion'. To say so, however, is to turn language back on itself so severely and completely that its signifying function momentarily stalls or breaks down. At such a moment we may recall that shortly after he began speaking to the narrator, Rousseau wearily paused 'like one who with the weight / Of his own words is staggered'.

But language need not stagger in enacting the burden of reflexive consciousness, as Empson implies in praising the 'great things' Shelley does with reflexive imagery in the narrator's opening vision of Life's victims. In the passage Empson cites, the reader is asked to envision the experience of simultaneously casting a shadow and walking 'within' its 'gloom':

> And others mournfully within the gloom
>
> Of their own shadow walked, and called it death . . .

'Death', says the Earth in *Prometheus Unbound*, 'is the veil which those who live call Life'. What those who live call 'death', Shelley suggests, is the fear of physical nonexistence, the 'shadow' of our consciousness of physical existence. That this idea of death is a product of the defeated, earthbound imagination is conveyed in a reflexive image which gives us the metaphorical reverse or 'negative' of those positive visions of beings or objects seen in their own light in *Prometheus Unbound*: Asia's vision of Prometheus 'arrayed / In the soft light of his own smiles'; Earth's description of the cavern to which Prometheus and Asia will retire, surrounded by 'bright, golden globes / Of fruit, suspended in their own green heaven'. The image from *The Triumph of Life* involves a double psychic perspective reminiscent of "**Alastor**": the image is implicitly expressive of the narrator's perception as well as explicitly expressive of the perception of those among Life's followers who have seen their own shadow and 'called it death'. The narrator sees what the mourners do not—that what they call death is only the shadow cast by their mortal form of existence, by their bodies. Here again Shelley articulates the force of the reflexive image by taking precise advantage of internal semantic relationships. 'Gloom', positioned emphatically at the end of the line, is itself an image 'drawn from the operations of the human mind' and operates here in a double sense: its original meaning, 'sadness', links it behind to 'mournfully'; the figurative meaning given it by Milton, 'darkness', links it forward to 'shadow'. The double sense of 'shadow' ('image cast by a body intercepting light' but also 'spectral form, phantasm', as in the 'shades' of Hell) links it behind to the physical meaning of 'gloom' and forward to 'death'. The phrase 'and called it death' calls forth the latent mental or spiritual senses of 'gloom' and 'shadow' and provides an ironic stylistic analogue to the way in which the mourners mistake an image of their own corporeality for death. Death is not the eclipsing of bodily existence, we are left to infer, but rather the mind's experience of sadness and torment—'the veil which those who live call Life'. (pp. 97-111)

Throughout *A Defence of Poetry* seminal formulations are cast in reflexive shapes.

In the *Defence,* however, as in the rest of Shelley's writing, reflexive thinking and writing stand, sometimes unsteadily, beside fierce denunciations of selfishness, that 'dark idolatry of self' condemned in *The Revolt of Islam.*

> Poetry, and the principle of Self, of which money is the visible incarnation, are the God and the Mammon of the world.

Byron called Shelley 'the *best* and least selfish man I ever knew'; Mary Shelley, Trelawny and others made this judgement part of the Shelley myth. But Shelley's writing and his life continually make us aware that generous, altruistic self-projection and self-sacrifice may be only deceptively antithetical to those manifestations of 'the principle of Self' that Shelley hated. . . . Shelley came to see with increasing dismay that the mind's reflexive powers make possible, but also limit and vex, the self's relations with the world and with other people.

> The great secret of morals is Love; or a going out of our own nature, and an identification of ourselves with the beautiful which exists in thought, action, or person, not our own. A man, to be greatly good, must imagine intensely and comprehensively; he must put himself in the place of another and of many others; the pains and pleasures of his species must become his own.

For every movement 'out of our own nature' towards 'another' in this passage, there is a movement back towards the self: the phrase that concludes the first sentence, 'not our own', is eventually countered by the phrase that concludes the second, 'must become his own' (the shift from plural to singular is significant). Shelley's writing enacts this circle of subjectivity with boldness and originality by demonstrating the degree to which it is both a blessing and a curse—a blessing discoverable by poetry in the very fabric of the language, a curse that poetry can only partially and momentarily defeat by spreading 'its own figured curtain'. (pp. 116-17)

> *William Keach, in his* Shelley's Style, *Methuen, Inc., 1984, pp. 79-117.*

ADDITIONAL BIBLIOGRAPHY

Abbey, Lloyd. *Destroyer and Preserver: Shelley's Poetic Skepticism.* Lincoln: University of Nebraska Press, 1979, 171 p.
    Seeks to demonstrate the skepticism of Shelley's philosophy.

Allott, Miriam, ed. *Essays on Shelley.* Totowa, N.J.: Barnes & Noble Books, 1982, 282 p.
    Contains discussions of both individual works and such general topics as Shelley's critical reputation and his Gothicism.

Allsup, James O. *The Magic Circle: A Study of Shelley's Concept of Love.* National University Publications, Literary Criticism Series, ed-ited by John E. Becker. Port Washington, N.Y.: Kennikat Press, 1976, 115 p.
    Discovers a combination of Christian and platonic ideas in Shelley's writings on love.

Barcus, James E., ed. *Shelley: The Critical Heritage.* The Critical Heritage Series, edited by B. C. Southam. London: Routledge & Kegan Paul, 1975, 432 p.
    Reprints early critical assessments of Shelley's work.

Barnard, Ellsworth. *Shelley's Religion.* Minneapolis: University of Minnesota Press, 1937, 320 p.
    An extended exploration of Shelley's religious beliefs.

Barrell, Joseph. *Shelley and the Thought of His Time: A Study in the History of Ideas.* 1947. Reprint. Hamden, Conn.: Archon Books, 1967, 207 p.
    Examines the extent to which Shelley's life and works reflected early nineteenth-century philosophical trends.

Bloom, Harold. *Shelley's Mythmaking.* Yale Studies in English, edited by Benjamin Christie Nangle, vol. 141. New Haven: Yale University Press, 1959, 279 p.
    Considers Shelley as a primarily mythopoeic poet.

———. ''Percy Bysshe Shelley.'' In his *The Visionary Company: A Reading of English Romantic Poetry,* pp. 297-379. Garden City, N.Y.: Doubleday & Co., Anchor Books, 1961.
    A detailed examination of select poems in the context of poetic tradition.

Blunden, Edmund. *Shelley: A Life Story.* London: Collins, 1946, 320 p.
    A popular biography.

Brown, Nathaniel. *Sexuality and Feminism in Shelley.* Cambridge: Harvard University Press, 1979, 298 p.
    Presents Shelley as a proponent of sexual equality whose writings anticipate modern attitudes toward sexuality.

Butter, Peter. *Shelley's Idols of the Cave.* Edinburgh University Publications, Language and Literature, no. 7. Edinburgh: University Press, 1954, 228 p.
    Examines recurring images in Shelley's poetry.

Buxton, John. ''Percy Bysshe Shelley (1792-1822).'' In his *The Grecian Taste: Literature in the Age of Neo-Classicism, 1740-1820,* pp. 147-69. New York: Harper & Row Publishers, Barnes & Noble, 1978.
    Discusses Shelley's interest in Greek culture.

Cameron, Kenneth Neill. *The Young Shelley: Genesis of a Radical.* New York: Macmillan Co., 1950, 437 p.

———. *Shelley: The Golden Years.* Cambridge: Harvard University Press, 1974, 669 p.
    An acclaimed two-part account of Shelley's intellectual development and writings covering the period from 1809 to 1822.

———, and Reiman, Donald H., eds. *Shelley and His Circle, 1773-1822.* 8 vols. to date. Cambridge: Harvard University Press, 1961-.
    Provides bibliographical and critical material on Shelley, Mary Shelley, Byron, Hunt, and Peacock.

Campbell, Olwen Ward. *Shelley and the Unromantics.* New York: Charles Scribner's Sons, 1924, 307 p.
    One of the first studies of Shelley's personality and thought based primarily on his letters and other writings.

Carey, Gillian. *Shelley.* Literature in Perspective, edited by Kenneth Grose. London: Evans Brothers, 1975, 160 p.
    An introductory survey of Shelley's life and works.

Cronin, Richard. *Shelley's Poetic Thoughts.* London: Macmillan Press, 1981, 263 p.
    A highly regarded discussion of Shelley's use of language and poetic forms.

Crook, Nora, and Guiton, Derek. *Shelley's Venomed Melody.* Cambridge: Cambridge University Press, 1986, 273 p.

A study of Shelley's concern with disease, particularly syphilis, and his own state of health.

Curran, Stuart. *Shelley's Annus Mirabilis: The Maturing of an Epic Vision.* San Marino, Calif.: Huntington Library, 1975, 255 p.
  Focuses on the poems Shelley wrote in 1819 and 1820, emphasizing his use of myth.

———. "Percy Bysshe Shelley." In his *The English Romantic Poets: A Review of Research and Criticism,* 4th ed., edited by Frank Jordan, pp. 593-663. The Modern Language Association of America, Reviews of Research. New York: Modern Language Association of America, 1985.
  A guide to Shelley scholarship that emphasizes recent studies.

Dawson, P. M. S. *The Unacknowledged Legislator: Shelley and Politics.* Oxford: Clarendon Press, 1980, 312 p.
  Examines Shelley's political interests and attitudes in their historical context.

Deconstruction and Criticism. New York: Seabury Press, A Continuum Book, 1979, 256 p.
  Includes two important essays on Shelley, Paul de Man's "Shelley Disfigured" and J. Hillis Miller's "The Critic as Host."

Dunbar, Clement. *A Bibliography of Shelley Studies: 1823-1950.* Garland Reference Library of the Humanities, vol. 32. New York: Garland Publishing, 1976, 320 p.
  A guide to Shelley studies dating from his death to 1950.

Empson, William. Chapter V in his *Seven Types of Ambiguity,* 3d. ed., pp. 155-75. New York: New Directions, 1966.
  Includes a discussion of Shelley's language, particularly his use of synesthesia.

Fairchild, Hoxie Neale. "Shelley and Transcendentalism." In his *The Romantic Quest,* pp. 373-401. New York: Columbia University Press, 1931.
  An analysis of the development of Shelley's philosophy from Godwinism to the pessimism of *The Triumph of Life.*

Firkins, Oscar W. *Power and Elusiveness in Shelley.* Minneapolis: University of Minnesota Press, 1937, 187 p.
  Examines the pervasiveness of abstract imagery and ideas in Shelley's poetry.

Grabo, Carl. *The Meaning of "The Witch of Atlas."* Chapel Hill: University of North Carolina Press, 1935, 158 p.
  An explication of "The Witch of Atlas" emphasizing Shelley's language, his interest in science, and his philosophy, particularly his neoplatonism.

———. *"Prometheus Unbound": An Interpretation.* Chapel Hill: University of North Carolina Press, 1935, 205 p.
  An interpretive study of Shelley's imagery in *Prometheus Unbound* focusing on his revolutionary social philosophy, neoplatonism, and interest in scientific experimentation.

———. *The Magic Plant: The Growth of Shelley's Thought.* Chapel Hill: University of North Carolina Press, 1936, 450 p.
  Examines Shelley's ideology as manifested in his writings. This study helped influence the revival of interest in Shelley's works in the twentieth century.

Hogg, Thomas Jefferson. *The Life of Percy Bysshe Shelley.* London: London Library, 1906, 585 p.
  A controversial biography of Shelley originally published in 1858. Hogg has been criticized for altering his sources and for maliciously misrepresenting Shelley; nonetheless, his work had an important influence on the poet's reputation.

Hughes, A. M. D. *The Nascent Mind of Shelley.* 1947. Reprint. Folcroft, Pa.: Folcroft Press, 1969, 272 p.
  Explores the formative influences leading to Shelley's composition of his philosophical poem *Queen Mab.*

Keats-Shelley Journal. New York: Keats-Shelley Association of America, 1952-.

An annual publication devoted to studies on Keats, Shelley, Byron, and their circles. A detailed bibliography is included in the periodical.

King-Hele, Desmond. *Shelley: His Thought and Work.* 3d ed. London: Macmillan Press, 1984, 383 p.
  An appreciative general introduction to Shelley's poetry with emphasis on his interest in the sciences. King-Hele includes an annotated bibliography of books on Shelley published since 1970.

Kurtz, Benjamin P. *The Pursuit of Death: A Study of Shelley's Poetry.* New York: Oxford University Press, 1933, 339 p.
  A controversial study of Shelley's preoccupation with death.

Leavis, F. R. "Shelley." *Scrutiny* IV, No. 1 (June 1935): 158-80.
  An influential evaluation of Shelley centering on "Ode to the West Wind."

Matthews, G. M. "A Volcano's Voice in Shelley." *ELH* 24, No. 2 (June 1957): 191-228.
  An important essay stressing the interrelation of Shelley's political activism and poetry. Matthews's discussion focuses on the image of the volcano in *Prometheus Unbound.*

———. "'Julian and Maddalo': The Draft and the Meaning." *Studia Neophilologica* XXXV (1963): 57-84.
  An explication of the poem with reference to Shelley's draft copy and events in his life at the time of composition.

McNiece, Gerald. *Shelley and the Revolutionary Idea.* Cambridge: Harvard University Press, 1969, 303 p.
  A close examination of Shelley's revolutionary ideology in the context of the French Revolution and the philosophies of British radicals.

Norman, Sylva. *Flight of the Skylark: The Development of Shelley's Reputation.* Norman: University of Oklahoma Press, 1954, 304 p.
  Chronicles the development of Shelley's posthumous reputation, emphasizing the role his family and friends played in shaping it.

O'Malley, Glenn. *Shelley and Synesthesia.* Evanston, Ill.: Northwestern University Press, 1964, 204 p.
  An in-depth study of Shelley's use of synesthesia, primarily as revealed in *Alastor, Epipsychidion, Adonais,* and *Prometheus Unbound.*

Orel, Harold. "Another Look at *The Necessity of Atheism.*" *Mosaic* 2, No. 2 (Winter 1969): 27-37.
  Examines the meaning of Shelley's controversial tract with reference to his life and philosophy.

Peacock, Thomas Love. *Peacock's Memoirs of Shelley, with Shelley's Letters to Peacock.* Edited by H. F. B. Brett-Smith. London: Henry Frowde, 1909, 219 p.
  An early memoir of Shelley first published between 1858 and 1862. Peacock sought to rectify misrepresentations in accounts by Hogg (see entry above), Trelawny (see entry below), and others.

Pulos, C. E. *The Deep Truth: A Study of Shelley's Scepticism.* Lincoln: University of Nebraska Press, 1954, 124 p.
  A respected survey of Shelley's intellectual development.

Reiman, Donald H. *Shelley's "The Triumph of Life": A Critical Study Based on a Text Newly Edited from the Bodleian Manuscript.* Illinois Studies in Language and Literature, vol. 55. Urbana: University of Illinois Press, 1965, 272 p.
  A detailed examination of the text and imagery of Shelley's last work.

———. *Percy Bysshe Shelley.* Twayne's English Authors Series, edited by Sylvia E. Bowman, vol. 81. New York: Twayne Publishers, 1969, 188 p.
  A general introduction to Shelley's life and works.

Ridenour, George M., ed. *Shelley: A Collection of Critical Essays.* Twentieth Century Views, edited by Maynard Mack. Englewood Cliffs, N.J.: Prentice-Hall, A Spectrum Book, 1965, 182 p.

Reprints essays by such distinguished critics as Humphry House, Carlos Baker, Earl R. Wasserman, G. M. Matthews, G. Wilson Knight, and Harold Bloom.

Rieger, James. *The Mutiny Within: The Heresies of Percy Bysshe Shelley.* New York: George Braziller, 1967, 283 p.
Discusses Shelley's deviations from the accepted theological doctrines and sociopolitical thought of his time.

Robinson, Charles E. *Shelley and Byron: The Snake and Eagle Wreathed in Fight.* Baltimore: Johns Hopkins University Press, 1976, 286 p.
Explores Shelley's and Byron's influence on one another.

Rogers, Neville. *Shelley at Work: A Critical Inquiry.* Oxford: Clarendon Press, 1956, 356 p.
A study of Shelley's thought and work based on an examination of his rough-draft notebooks.

Schulze, Earl J. *Shelley's Theory of Poetry: A Reappraisal.* Studies in English Literature, Vol. XIII. The Hague: Mouton & Co., 1966, 237 p.
Considered an important study of Shelley's poetics. Schulze's central concern is Shelley's exalted conception of poetry.

Scrivener, Michael Henry. *Radical Shelley: The Philosophical Anarchism and Utopian Thought of Percy Bysshe Shelley.* Princeton, N.J.: Princeton University Press, 1982, 354 p.
An assessment of Shelley's philosophical and political thought.

Silverman, Edwin B. *Poetic Synthesis in Shelley's "Adonais."* De Proprietatibus Litterarum, Series Practica, edited by C. H. Van Schooneveld, vol. 36. The Hague: Mouton, 1972, 117 p.
Answers criticisms of *Adonais* raised by previous scholars with an examination of its formal and philosophic unity.

Trelawny, E. J. *Recollections of the Last Days of Shelley and Byron.* London: Edward Moxon, 1858, 304 p.
A lively narrative of Trelawny's friendship with the poets in Italy.

Wasserman, Earl. R. *Shelley: A Critical Reading.* Baltimore: Johns Hopkins Press, 1971, 507 p.
A highly respected study of Shelley's major poems.

Weaver, Bennett. *Toward the Understanding of Shelley.* 1932. Reprint. New York: Octagon Books, 1966, 258 p.
Investigates Shelley's familiarity with the Bible and analyzes his works in the context of biblical prophetic tradition.

White, Newman Ivey. *The Unextinguished Hearth: Shelley and His Contemporary Critics.* 1938. Reprint. New York: Octagon Books, 1972, 397 p.
Reprints all known criticism of Shelley's works published from 1810 to 1822.

————. *Shelley.* 2 vols. New York: Alfred A. Knopf, 1940.
Considered the definitive biography.

Woodman, Ross Greig. *The Apocalyptic Vision in the Poetry of Shelley.* University of Toronto Department of English, Studies and Texts, no. 12. Toronto: University of Toronto Press, 1964, 209 p.
Examines the development of Shelley's creative vision from *Queen Mab* to *The Triumph of Life.*

Wright, John W. *Shelley's Myth of Metaphor.* Athens: University of Georgia Press, 1970, 79 p.
Discusses the modernity of Shelley's poetics.

Young, Art. *Shelley and Nonviolence.* Studies in English Literature, vol. CIII. The Hague: Mouton, 1975, 172 p.
Attempts to define Shelley's philosophy of nonviolence through a study of his writings.

James Thomson

1834-1882

(Also wrote under pseudonym B. V.) Scottish-born English poet, essayist, and translator.

Thomson is known as the author of one of the most powerful poems of the Victorian era, yet he is largely overshadowed by the major writers of his time. His reputation rests primarily on ''The City of Dreadful Night,'' which has been repeatedly praised for its compelling expression of religious despair in Victorian society.

Thomson was born in Port Glasgow, Scotland. As a youth, he rarely saw his father, a merchant sailor; instead, he was raised by his mother, a devoutly religious woman who drilled him in the teachings of Edward Irving, an independent Christian minister. In 1840 Thomson's father suffered a stroke while at sea, and the family's finances quickly became desperate. Thomson began attending London's Royal Caledonian Asylum, a school for the children of poor Scottish sailors and soldiers, following his mother's death in 1842. After leaving the Royal Caledonian Asylum in 1850, Thomson prepared for a career as an army schoolmaster. He joined the military and, from 1851 to 1853, trained as a teacher's assistant at an outpost in Ballincollig, Ireland. At Ballincollig, Thomson became friends with Charles Bradlaugh, a soldier and free-thought advocate who was to play an important role in his career. In addition, he met and reportedly fell in love with Matilda Weller, the fourteen-year-old daughter of an army sergeant. Thomson left Ballincollig in 1853 to complete his education at the Royal Military Asylum in Chelsea, where he received word that Matilda had died. Some nineteenth-century critics suggested that this loss was the source of Thomson's pessimism and that it may have contributed to his alcoholism. However, this supposition has been largely rejected by modern biographers, who downplay the effect of Matilda's death on Thomson.

Thomson served as schoolmaster at several army posts from 1854 to 1862. During these years, he composed both poetry and prose, read prolifically, and studied several languages. His philosophical outlook in his writings gradually changed, shifting from the religious faith of his childhood, to Emersonian pantheism, then to a doubting rationalism, and finally to a complete negation of Christian faith and idealism. Beginning in 1858, Thomson began publishing his first poems and essays in several periodicals, including the *National Reformer*, a controversial secularist weekly edited by his friend Bradlaugh. He signed his pieces with a number of pseudonyms, most notably B. V., which became his recognized alias. Signifying Bysshe Vanolis, B. V. was a tribute to two poets, Percy Bysshe Shelley and Novalis, whom Thomson admired and viewed as kindred, tortured spirits.

Thomson was discharged from military service in 1862, ostensibly for a minor offense but very likely for his compulsive drinking bouts as well. He then moved to London, where he lived with the Bradlaugh family, working at a variety of jobs while contributing literary reviews, iconoclastic essays, and a small amount of poetry to the *Reformer*. By 1866, however, Thomson's alcoholism had worsened, and he left the Bradlaugh's home. Suffering from chronic financial difficulties, he

lived in dismal rooms and labored at the few low-paying jobs available to him. His writings for the *Reformer* were his only reliable source of income, but they did little to further his literary reputation. From 1867 to 1869, Thomson's major literary activity consisted of translating and analyzing the works of the nineteenth-century Italian poet Giacomo Leopardi. Thomson's personal difficulties continued, and in 1869 he decided to burn nearly all of his accumulated notes, manuscripts, and letters, later commenting in his diary, ''I felt myself like one who, having climbed halfway up a long rope . . . cuts off all beneath his feet; he must climb on, and can never touch the old earth again without a fatal fall.''

This realization, however, did not deter Thomson from pursuing his literary career. In 1870 he began drafting his masterpiece, ''The City of Dreadful Night,'' which he published in the *Reformer* four years later. In this twenty-four stanza poem describing the nocturnal wanderings and musings of the inhabitants of a surreal London, Thomson sought to shatter the idealistic, Romantic, and Christian conceptions of life ingrained in Victorian society. Thus, a speaker in the poem proclaims: ''Good tidings of great joy for you, for all; / There is no God; no Fiend with names divine / Made us and tortures us; if we must pine, / It is to satiate no Being's gall.'' Although some reviews of ''The City of Dreadful Night'' were hostile,

Thomson also received favorable notices. After he sent a copy of the poem to George Eliot, she responded in a brief, complimentary letter, encouraging him to continue writing but admonishing him for his one-sided outlook on humanity. Thomson was also encouraged by the bookseller Bertram Dobell, who befriended him and vowed to see his first volume of poetry published. Thomson had finally gained some longed-for critical attention, and the poem sparked a surge of public curiosity concerning the identity of the talented poet B. V.

Thomson's success was short-lived, however, and he experienced a number of setbacks. In 1875, following an argument with Bradlaugh, he severed all ties with his longtime benefactor. Furthermore, Dobell had considerable difficulty interesting publishers in Thomson's work. For the next several years, Thomson wrote little poetry and supported himself with regular prose contributions to a business magazine, *Cope's Tobacco Plant,* that also published some literary material. The most notable of these contributions were his essays on Heinrich Heine, Walt Whitman, and Stendhal, which critics have praised for anticipating modern critical thought. During the final years of his life, Thomson published two volumes of poetry, *The City of Dreadful Night and Other Poems* and *Vane's Story, Weddah and Om-el-Bonain,* as well as a collection of prose pieces, *Essays and Phantasies.* Although Thomson enjoyed the support of such literary figures as Philip Bourke Marston, George Meredith, and William Michael Rossetti, he had little hope for widespread recognition of his talent. In the spring of 1882, Thomson spent several weeks with close friends who tried unsuccessfully to help him overcome his alcoholism and aid him financially. Following more alcoholic binges later that year, some of which landed him in jail, Thomson died of intestinal hemorrhaging.

Interest in Thomson following his death was prompted by the publication of several biographical accounts and various collections of his writings, including *Satires and Profanities* and *Poetical Works.* Much of this commentary centered on the despairing tone of Thomson's works, and by the early 1900s he was widely recognized as the preeminent pessimistic poet of his time. Thomson's pessimism has continued to be the major topic of critical discussion throughout the twentieth century, and today scholars agree that what he portrayed in his best works, but most completely in "The City of Dreadful Night," was a world view that introduced such modern literary themes as alienation, social disintegration, and psychological torment. Numerous critics have noted Thomson's considerable influence on the subgenre of city poetry, focusing particularly on T. S. Eliot's seminal work, *The Waste Land.* However, some scholars have protested the emphasis on Thomson's pessimism, arguing that he has been pigeonholed as a minor, eccentric writer largely because of such estimates of his importance as that of Dobell, who stated that "The City of Dreadful Night" was "the one great and final poetic expression of pessimistic thought, and as such it must ever remain an unique and unsurpassable achievement." In recent times, these critics have attempted to broaden Thomson's reputation by emphasizing the diversity of his poems, the literary influences on his works, and the depth of his philosophy. Some commentators have stressed that Thomson composed successful poems treating lighter themes, including the bucolic idylls "Sunday at Hampstead" and "Sunday up the River" and the oriental love epic "Weddah and Om-el-Bonain." Many critics have also commended his progressive taste in literature, noting the influence on his poetry of such varied writers as Leopardi, Heine, Dante, Shelley, William Blake, and Robert Browning. Still

other critics have discussed how Thomson's work reflects several intellectual and aesthetic trends of the Victorian era: in both his prose and in such poems as "Insomnia," "In the Room," and "To Our Ladies of Death," Thomson addressed the emergence of Darwinism, rationalism, and industrialization; the existence of social injustice and alienation; and the death of idealism and Christianity. While twentieth-century commentary on Thomson has been generally positive, he has been censured for the derivative nature of his works and for the gloominess of his outlook.

Although few modern scholars accord Thomson greatness as a writer, some contend that his works have long been unjustifiably overlooked. He is today most admired for "The City of Dreadful Night," considered one of the most effective expressions of religious pessimism in Victorian poetry. For his highly individual poetic vision and for his introduction of many modern literary motifs, Thomson is regarded as a significant if minor Victorian poet.

(See also *Dictionary of Literary Biography,* Vol. 35: *Victorian Poets after 1850.*)

PRINCIPAL WORKS

"Mr. Save-His-Soul-Alive, O!" [as B. V.]   (poetry)
    1858; published in periodical *The London Investigator*
The Story of a Famous Old Jewish Firm   (essay) 1876
The City of Dreadful Night and Other Poems   (poetry)
    1880
Essays and Phantasies   (essays and prose poetry) 1881
Vane's Story, Weddah and Om-el-Bonain, and Other Poems
    (poetry) 1881
Satires and Profanities   (essays) 1884
A Voice from the Nile and Other Poems   (poetry) 1884
Selections from Original Contributions by James Thomson to
    "Cope's Tobacco Plant"   (essays and poetry) 1889
Poems, Essays, and Fragments   (poetry and essays) 1892
The Poetical Works of James Thomson (B. V.). 2 vols.
    (poetry) 1895
Biographical and Critical Studies   (essays) 1896
Poems of James Thomson   (poetry) 1927
Poems and Some Letters of James Thomson   (poetry and
    letters) 1963
The Speedy Extinction of Evil and Misery: Selected Prose of
    James Thomson (B. V.)   (essays and prose poetry)
    1967

[GEORGE ELIOT]   (letter date 1874)

[*Eliot was one of the greatest English novelists of the nineteenth century. Her work, including the novels* The Mill on the Floss *and* Middlemarch: A Study of Provincial Life, *is informed by penetrating psychological analysis and profound insight into human character. In the following letter to Thomson, Eliot comments favorably on his poetic potential as revealed in "The City of Dreadful Night."*]

Dear Poet

I cannot rest satisfied without telling you that my mind responds with admiration to the distinct vision and grand utterance in the poem ["**The City of Dreadful Night**"] which you have been so good as to send me.

Also, I trust that an intellect informed by so much passionate energy as yours will soon give us more heroic strains with a wider embrace of human fellowship in them—such as will be to the labourers of the world what the odes of Tyrtaeus were to the Spartans, thrilling them with the sublimity of the social order and the courage of resistance to all that would dissolve it. To accept life and write much fine poetry, is to take a very large share in the quantum of human good, and seems to draw with it necessarily some recognition, affectionate and even joyful, of the manifold willing labours which have made such a lot possible.

> *[George Eliot], in a letter to James Thomson on May 30, 1874, in* Selections from George Eliot's Letters, *edited by Gordon S. Haight, Yale University Press, 1985, p. 444.*

[EDITH SIMCOX] (essay date 1874)

[*Simcox stresses the power and originality of "The City of Dreadful Night."*]

The admirers of Leopardi, of Shelley, of Richter's "Dream," of picturesque melancholy, sonorous despair, and the sombre philosophy which finds moral consolation in atheism—may be interested to know of a really remarkable poem, lately published in four numbers of the *National Reformer.* . . . The spirit of the work is akin to that of Leopardi, but the writer (who uses the signature B. V.) has thought out his philosophy of the universe in more detail, and presents it by the help of wider range of illustration and imagery. The versification in places recalls Shelley more nearly than any other well-known author, but it is only a passing resemblance of the sweet, fluent cadence, and in the greater part of the poem (about 1,500 lines) the originality of the writer is as unquestionable as his power. The work is called **"The City of Dreadful Night,"** and is simply a series of visions representing the despair of minds doomed by their own constitution to revolve, through a dark dreamlike life, round the ruined shrines of "dead Faith, dead Love, dead Hope." But the poetical merits of the whole are quite out of proportion to the truth or morality of the general thesis. The following stanzas are near the end: a shorter quotation would hardly do the author justice:—

> I sat me weary on a pillar's base,
>   And leaned against the shaft; for broad moonlight
> O'erflowed the peacefulness of cloistered space,
>   A shore of shadow slanting from the right:
> The great cathedral's western front stood there,
> A wave-worn rock in that calm sea of air.
>
> Before it, opposite my place of rest,
>   Two figures faced each other, large, austere;
> A couchant sphinx in shadow to the breast,
>   An angel standing in the moonlight clear;
> So mighty by magnificence of form,
> They were not dwarfed beneath that mass enorm.
>
> Upon the cross-hilt of a naked sword
>   The angel's hands, as prompt to smite, were held;
> His vigilant intense regard was poured
>   Upon the creature placidly unquelled,
> Whose front was set at level gaze which took
> No heed of aught, a solemn trance-like look.
>
> And as I pondered these opposèd shapes
>   My eyelids sank in stupor, that dull swoon
> Which drugs and with a leaden mantle drapes

The outworn to worse weariness. But soon
A sharp and clashing noise the stillness broke,
And from the evil lethargy I woke.

> The angels' wings had fallen, stone on stone,
>   And lay there shattered; hence the sudden sound:
> A warrior leaning on his sword alone
>   Now watched the sphinx with that regard profound;
> The sphinx unchanged looked forthright, as aware
> Of nothing in the vast abyss of air.
>
> Again I sank in that repose unsweet,
>   Again a clashing noise my slumber rent;
> The warrior's sword lay broken at his feet;
>   An unarmed man with raised hands impotent
> Now stood before the sphinx, which ever kept
> Such mien as if with open eyes it slept.
>
> My eyelids sank in spite of wonder grown;
>   A louder crash upstartled me in dread;
> The man had fallen forward, stone on stone,
>   And lay there shattered, with his trunkless head
> Between the monster's large quiescent paws,
> Beneath its grand front changeless as life's laws.
>
> The moon had circled westward full and bright,
>   And made the temple-front a mystic dream,
> And bathed the whole enclosure with its light,
>   The sworded angel's wrecks, the sphinx supreme:
> I pondered long that calm majestic face
> Whose vision seemed of infinite void space.

(pp. 632-33)

> *[Edith Simcox], in a review of "The City of Dreadful Night," in* The Academy, *Vol. 5, June 5, 1874, pp. 632-33.*

THE SPECTATOR (essay date 1874)

[*In the following response to Simcox's review of "The City of Dreadful Night" in the* Academy *(see excerpt dated 1874), the critic highlights Thomson's lack of originality and his professed belief in determinism, or Necessity.*]

The *Academy* . . . called attention last week, by some highly appreciative words, to a poem printed in a place where one scarcely expects poems, the *National Reformer.* Struck by an extract, in which the poet seemed to express in admirable lines his grief at the victory of Doubt, at the impossibility, or rather the distantness, of any solution for the problem of life, we obtained, with some difficulty—all numbers containing the verses being out of print—a copy of the entire production, only to find that the stanzas which had attracted us were at variance with the whole remainder of its thought; or at least, if they were not, if the thought might still be traced, the poet's skill had failed him in some way so strange as to suggest that he had been over-mastered by his own inner consciousness, till he had been compelled to invest the infernal figure he was trying to shape, with a humanity which had not entered into his original design. Shelley he is none, though the critic of the *Academy* seems to hint at a resemblance, for he could no more have written the "Revolt of Islam" than the "Ode to the Skylark;" and his melody, where he is melodious—and he very often is not—is not that of Shelley's silver trumpet, but of Edgar Poe's brass horn. Nevertheless, though annoyed with many harshnesses and many excessive inequalities, the reader cannot deny to the unknown writer the true lyric cry, which marks the poet who is not merely a versifier, or only a thinker;

or to his work some praise which Dante would have sanctioned. Dante delirious might have written **"The City of Dreadful Night."** Nor do we see the marked originality of thought of which the *Academy* speaks, though there is originality of illustration of the ghastly kind; for he does but use his power to teach, in striking verse, the melancholy doctrine, old as the Nile, that man is but a self-deluded fool to think himself either divine, or immortal, or noteworthy at all; that Necessity alone exists, and that Necessity is cruel. A Hindoo Pundit would understand all his philosophy, and wonder calmly how all that had come to be discussed again. . . . The originality of the writer's thought consists not in his creed, which men thought out and rejected before Job, but in his own horror of his creed; in the ghastliness with which he invests it, the fervour with which he hates it, the energy with which he depicts all the degradation it involves, and yet goes on believing it. Necessity alone exists, and Necessity is a fiend. . . . No man escapes the City of Dreadful Night; no effort avails him, no manner of life can save him; the same pall envelopes alike the just and the unjust, the good and the evil, the priest and the prowler, those who believe and those who reject, the patriot and the actor, the statesman and the scholar. . . . (pp. 780-81)

Through fifteen hundred lines, with endless iteration, with ever-varying illustration, the singer preaches the creed he at once trusts and loathes—the latter, it may be, unconsciously—sometimes in harsh croakings, sometimes in passionate lyrics;—and the poem would be unique in its long-drawn gloom, a gloom which, however artificial, is yet impressive, but for the strange stanzas that the *Academy* has quoted, and which seem to have shaped themselves against their author's will. . . . He meant those verses to be as gloomy as the rest, and as indicative of the imbecility of human hope, of the passionless cruelty of Nature or of Law; but as if to confute his own theory, he has not found the fitting words, and angel and hero and penitent fall prostrate, not before Despair, but before the gigantic figure in which the Egyptian hierophants embodied Doubt. The Sphinx is calm and dreadless, and unmoved by the generations of men, but still she looks into the abyss of air in unending expectation. It is Doubt, not Despair, which has for the hour achieved the victory.

The body of the poem, however, is all gloom, and it is in this gloom that the answer to the poet's argument seems to us to be found. No man may prove by mere logic that Necessity does not exist, for even if he believes in God, God like man may be a necessity; but why, if Necessity be the only cause, should the effect be gloom, and not light,—why, that is, should man, of all that lives, be the only being in whom his impersonal ruler excites so deep a fear, that even the occasionally artificial and strained horror of this writer will touch in all men some hidden chord of sympathy? If the doubt be solved, and this be certainty—if the meaningless mill grinds on for ever—what, if we can get that certainty, is there to be so horrified about? If there has been no past and will be no hereafter, and life is but a dream within a dream, as the writer says, and copies Poe in saying, why moan over man in mournful numbers, as over a being who endures some exceptional lot? The true fatalist, did such a man ever exist, would not be a horror-struck semi-maniac, but a lotus-eater, or a calm sage, or even a man devoted to philanthropy. . . . Why squeal so, when at the worst you may be a lotus-eater, or at the best, work yourself out in the determination that mankind shall be happier than it has been, though there will be no reward to you? It is surely the most inartistic of work, for a convinced Necessitarian to go on talking of gloom and want of light and groping in the dark, and

dead faith and dead hope and dead love in the higher sense. What, if Necessity reigns, and he believes that sovereignty, does he want with them all? Why fight the Sphinx, or bother about her "unquelled eyes," or think about her at all, when he knows contest to be useless, the eyes immovable, the monster always at rest? The truth is, he does not believe it, and cannot believe it, and must fight, whether he wants to or not; and in that instinctive unbelief and instinctive determination to contend is the answer to the whole theory of Necessity,—the certainty, otherwise so difficult to gain whenever man has risen to the consciousness of Law, that the will is free. And if the will be free, Necessity is not Queen. (pp. 781-82)

> *"A Necessitarian Poet," in* The Spectator, *Vol. 47, No. 2399, June 20, 1874, pp. 780-82.*

GEORGE MEREDITH   (letter date 1880)

[Meredith was a respected nineteenth-century British poet, novelist, and critic. He and Thomson began corresponding in late 1879, after which time they became close friends. Thomson was among the first English critics to fully appreciate Meredith's literary powers and, conversely, Meredith was among the early champions of Thomson's talents. In the following letter to Thomson, Meredith lauds The City of Dreadful Night and Other Poems.]

I will not delay any longer to write to you on the subject of [*The City of Dreadful Night and Other Poems*], though I am not yet in a condition to do justice either to the critic or the poet, for owing to the attack I suffered under last year, I have been pensioned off all work of any worth of late; and in writing to you about this admirable and priceless book of verse I have wished to be competent to express my feeling for your merit, and as much as possible the praise of such rarely equalled good work. My friends could tell you that I am a critic hard to please. They say that irony lurks in my eulogy. I am not in truth frequently satisfied by verse. Well, I have gone through your volume, and partly a second time, and I have not found the line I would propose to recast. I have found many pages that no other English poet could have written. Nowhere is the verse feeble, nowhere is the expression insufficient; the majesty of the line has always its full colouring, and marches under a banner. And you accomplished this effect with the utmost sobriety, with absolute self-mastery. I have not time at present to speak of the City of Melancolia. There is a massive impressiveness in it that goes beyond Dürer, and takes it into upper regions where poetry is the sublimation of the mind of man, the voice of our highest. What might have been said contra poet, I am glad that you should have forestalled and answered in **"Philosophy"**—very wise writing. I am in love with the dear London lass who helped you to the [**"Sunday up the River"**]. You give a zest and new attraction to Hampstead Heath. . . . (pp. 307-08)

> *George Meredith, in a letter to James Thomson on April 27, 1880, in his* Letters of George Meredith: 1844-1881, *Vol. I, edited by W. M. Meredith, Charles Scribner's Sons, 1912, pp. 307-08.*

GEORGE SAINTSBURY   (essay date 1880)

[Saintsbury was a late nineteenth- and early twentieth-century English literary historian and critic. A prolific writer, he composed several histories of English and European literature as well as numerous critical works on individual authors, styles, and periods. In the following excerpt, Saintsbury offers an appreciative overview of The City of Dreadful Night and Other Poems.]

Readers of the *Academy* will remember the interest which was excited by the publication some six or seven years ago in a little-read periodical of "**The City of Dreadful Night**," extracts from which appeared with comment in our columns [see excerpt by Edith Simcox dated 1874]. The republication of the complete poem with others of earlier and later composition is very welcome for more reasons than one. The poems comprised in the volume range over twenty years, and do not quite fill ten times that number of pages. Now nothing can be more certain than that it is for the soul's health of English poetry that the present deplorable fashion of rapid composition should come to an end. In other days, when a poet had produced something that was liked, he did not think it necessary thenceforward to be delivered yearly of a new volume. Considering especially that the poets who make money out of poetry nowadays may be counted on one hand, this haste of production is nearly as inexplicable as it is lamentable. Evidently Mr. Thomson has escaped the contagion, and, in the case of a poet whose work was so favourably received as was "**The City of Dreadful Night**," this is something to compliment him upon. The results, as well as the mere fact of this reticence, justify the compliment. The present volume of verse [*The City of Dreadful Night and Other Poems*] is an unusually interesting one, testifying, indeed, to a certain lack of range in the author's thought, and to a concentration of his ideas upon certain riddles which the wise indifference of the wise is apt to leave unattempted, but singularly melodious in expression, dignified and full in meaning, and bearing witness to reading as well as to meditation. "The City of Dreadful Night" is, as may be readily apprehended, the abode of those who, seeing no hereafter, fret themselves at the prospect or, rather, the lack of it. . . . He writes, he says,

> Because a cold rage seizes one at whiles
>   To show the bitter, old, and wrinkled truth
> Stripped naked of all vesture that beguiles,
>   False dreams, false hopes, false masks and modes of
>   youth,
> Because it gives some sense of power and passion
> In helpless impotence to try to fashion
>   Our woes in living words, howe'er uncouth.

Mr. Thomson's words, however, are by no means uncouth, as this stanza and, still more, the following will testify:—

> For life is but a dream, whose shapes return,
>   Some frequently, some seldom, some by night,
> And some by day, some night and day: we learn
>   The while all change and many vanish quite,
> In their recurrence with recurrent changes
> A certain seeming order. Where this ranges
>   We count things real. Such is memory's might.

This is good poetry and good philosophy. We cannot follow the lugubrious visions of the seer, the most powerful of which perhaps is that of a great cathedral, whither everyone presses and enters with a pass-verse, each describing some occupation of civilised life, and all ending with the refrain "I wake from day dreams to this real night." The congregation are addressed by a preacher who announces blank atheism to them, and requests them to be comforted thereby, which as a rule they fail to be. The poem ends with two descriptively allegorical passages of extreme beauty, but unfortunately too long to quote. The one is a vision of a sphinx and an angel, who face each other, undergoing metamorphoses as the spectator gazes, so that the angel, at first armed and winged, loses his wings, then his sword, and then falls prostrate at the feet of the unchanging

sphinx. The other is a description of the *Melencolia* not unworthy to be inscribed as a legend under the print itself.

The smaller poems give not merely bulk but variety to the book, and relieve Mr. Thomson from the charge of seeing all things in black, though they display for the most part a certain inconsolableness. "**Sunday at Hampstead**" and "**Sunday up the River**" have cheerful passages in praise of love and whisky. "**Life's Hebe**" is an allegorical poem of considerable beauty, telling how the golden cup of life is received, rejected, or misused by those to whom it is offered; and "**The Naked Goddess**" has something of the same moral. Some smaller and directly philosophical and religious poems please us less, and indeed it must be confessed that the determination to preach occasionally possesses Mr. Thomson with undue strength. His "**Lord of the Castle of Indolence**" has the drawback of being conceived and written in a key and a language utterly different from those of Thomson's masterpiece; and the two Browning-esque poems, "**A Polish Insurgent**" and "**L'Ancien Régime**," are not very successful. But it is exceedingly rare to find a volume in which so large a number of the pieces contained have a distinct and individual poetic attractiveness. Mr. Thomson suffers, as we have said, from a want of range in his verse, and also from a certain lack of spontaneity, in which he by no means stands alone nowadays. Sometimes, but rarely, his language is not what it might be. For instance, "tenebriously" is a form which we cannot possibly consent to. But, as a rule, no objections on the ground of scholarship can be brought against him. The echo of the pulpit drone is occasionally obvious—a drone which is terribly frequent in modern poetry, and which is apt to sound in the critic's ears very much as that of Io's gadfly did in hers. However, we have endeavoured to preserve our own equanimity, and indeed the pleasure of reading Mr. Thomson has decidedly the better of the pain. That he has what somebody once called a fine gloomy imagination is not contestable, and, fortunately, he is not always given up to it. His book, if it were ever possible to induce Englishmen to buy poetry except as they buy wine—not because of its goodness, but because of the name of the seller—ought to be widely read. (pp. 432-33)

The volume closes with some translations from Heine, modestly called "Attempts," and really as fair endeavours at the impossible as we have seen. On the whole, the interest and the attraction of the volume are of the most considerable, though we cannot help wishing that Mr. Thomson had read Shakspere more and Leopardi less. Byronism was bad enough, but Leopardism would be something to shudder at. (p. 433)

> *George Saintsbury, in a review of "The City of Dreadful Night," in* The Academy, *n.s. Vol. 17, No. 423, June 12, 1880, pp. 432-33.*

JOEL BENTON (essay date 1881)

[Benton offers a mixed review of Thomson's first two volumes of poetry, holding that his pessimism clouds his literary talents.]

The arrival of a new poet who has something new to say, or who sets the discourse of old matters to new music, has not been a frequent thing of late—in English literature, at least—and we are ready to rub our eyes now, and look sharply at the first portent of this kind that makes its appearance. Without doubting that, out of the rich soil which has produced in recent times Wordsworth and Tennyson, there are many further fruitful poetic growths to arise, it must be confessed that the tendency of mental activity, of late, has been most noticeable in the sphere of science, and is least prominent in the field of the imagination. A few of the English critical journals, however, profess lately to have found a real poet, and more; and think they can discern him in Mr. Thomson, whose two books furnishing them their evidence have but just appeared—the first having been followed by the second within a very few weeks. But, though the books themselves are so new, the poems which distend their covers into only moderate dimensions have been dropped from time to time into the various magazines from as far back as 1857.

We do not know, of course, who Mr. Thomson is, except that he is the author of this body of verse—using when it was separately published the signature of "B. V."—and that he is, on the probable supposition that his earliest effort here was produced no earlier than in his later teens, already over forty years of age. It is our purpose to emphasize this point; because, while some difference of literary quality in the various pieces is to be observed, the reader may, by keeping the foregoing fact in mind, take notice that the one chord of despair which began with the earliest poem is struck through them all to the very last.

"**The City of Dreadful Night**," which gives the title to the first volume, furnishes the key-note to all that Mr. Thomson has to offer. It shows our author to be a determined, if not a predetermined, pessimist. The world which he depicts, which is supposed to be the world we all live in, is one without faith, hope, or love, or any good thing. (pp. 468-69)

The poem is allegorical, and much of its elaborate machinery of symbolism is distressingly vague and incoherent. (p. 469)

[It] ranges through several meters, but with one persistent monotone, and at last a sphinx and an angel come together—the former staring the latter out of existence—and we find the meaning of the poem to be—

> The sense that every struggle brings defeat,
>   Because Fate holds no prize to crown success;
> That all the oracles are dumb or cheat,
>   Because they have no secret to express;
> That none can pierce the vast black veil uncertain
> Because there is no light beyond the curtain;
>   That all is vanity and nothingness.

And yet we dare to say Mr. Thomson is tolerably well and hearty; and, whether he lives in London or in the country, manages to dispose of good dinners, discerns at times some beauties in art or nature, nourishes some tender friendships, and is not worse off, perhaps, on the average, than the rest of us. In "**Two Sonnets**," printed in the second volume, he ventures to tell us why he sings so sadly:

> A spirit lifts me where I lie alone,
>   And thrills me into song by its own laws;
> That which I feel but seldom know, indeed,
>   Tempering the melody it could not cause.
>
>   .   .   .   .   .
>
> Striving to sing glad songs, I but attain
>   Wild discords sadder than grief's saddest tune;
> As if an owl with his harsh screech should strain
>   To over-gratulate a thrush of June:
>
>   .   .   .   .   .
>
> My mirth can laugh and talk, but can not sing;
> My grief finds harmonies in everything.

The more important poems in the earlier volume are "**To our Ladies of Death**," "**The Naked Goddess**," and "**The Lord of the Castle of Indolence**." The second of these has as little somberness, perhaps, as any of the three, and is clothed in graceful diction, and sparkles with some pleasant fancies. In "**Life's Hebe**" a very pretty conceit is quite prettily caught and carried out; and, though not without the costume of shadow, shows as "**Virtue and Vice**" and many of the briefer pieces do, that Mr. Thomson has the power to do good lyrical work if he chooses. In fact his longer pieces, with their fondness for allegory, are not without positive technical merit too, and poised beauty of expression. They give assurance that this writer might do something of real worth—something which sane minds could welcome, if it were possible for him to escape from the spiritual neurasthenia—the dumps and the dolors—in which he so delights to revel.

The rollicking poems of "**Sunday at Hampstead**" and "**Sunday up the River**" almost seem as if they wished to let in the sunlight; but they appear to us a little too crude in form, and are grotesquely coarse in certain passages. This volume closes with some modestly titled "Attempts at Translation from Heine," which, as we should easily have expected, are quite admirably done. The mocking sarcasm and light raillery of Heine are in close accordance with Mr. Thomson's own natural vein, and he has taken elsewhere no pains to conceal his sympathy with this genuine but morbid genius. (pp. 469-79)

By far the most unobjectionable production, the most perfect, we may say, taking all points of view into consideration, in Mr. Thomson's two books, is "**Weddah and Om-El-Bonain**." . . .

[With] its various episodes, Mr. Thomson has succeeded in making a poem of somewhat unique quality and indisputable power. It is sad, of course, with seething passion and bitter fate, or Mr. Thomson would not have chosen the theme; but the fixed limits of the Arabic original have served to give it a coherence, a want of which is one of the marked deficiencies in our author's more exclusively original work. Delicate touches of fancy and verses of rare beauty are quite frequent in it, and the high plane of merit attained in the first stanza is well kept up to the end. (p. 470)

In "**L'Ancien Régime**," or, "**The Good Old Rule**," a piece of moderate brevity, our author hits the character of the traditional and unbeloved monarch—a hated kingly head—with no mean ability and with pungent force. It is a fairly striking production, and might cause the blood of liberty or reprobation to tingle in the most sluggish vein. The memorial verses on "**E. B. B.**" have also an appropriate significance (Elizabeth Barrett Browning is the subject); but here, as in frequent other instances, there is a certain realistic baldness in the verse that makes it just miss the requisite melody. In none of the poems, long or brief—and there are many we shall have no opportunity to even mention—do you find the luxuriant, airy wing-power of Swinburne, the rich quality of Rossetti, or the captivating magic of Morris, when Morris is at his best. There are passages in all these writers we are sometimes compelled to remember and repeat; but in Mr. Thomson it is not the phrase or the form or the meaning that stays by us, so much as the murky gloom and the dark and formless atmosphere.

Mr. Thomson dedicates [*The City of Dreadful Night and Other Poems*] "to the memory of the younger brother of Dante, Giacomo Leopardi, a spirit as lofty, a genius as intense, with a yet more tragic doom"; and the newer volume [*Vane's Story,*

Weddah and Om-el-Bonain, and Other Poems] he inscribes "to the memory of the poet of poets, and purest of men, Percy Bysshe Shelley, with the gratitude and love and reverence of the author."

It is not for us to say how far the picturesque apotheosis of melancholy is natural to this author, or how much of it is affectation and posture. The problems of evil and human existence are as old as the world itself; and, long before Leopardi and Shelley and the whole weeping choir of modern times had uttered a wail or note, the sepulchral singer of grief and despair was a frequent and periodically recurring phenomenon. Omar Khayyam voiced this philosophy hundreds of years ago, and not one of his successors has done it with more touching pensiveness, or set its perspective in finer shades of gloom and darkness. We listen to his melody, but is passes like a ripple on the ocean; there is neither nutriment nor permanence in it. One passage from Shakespeare, or one breath from Wordsworth's "Ode on the Intimations of Immortality," or one of Milton's best sonnets, is worth the whole body of this bibliography of grief. It would bring Mr. Thomson untold benefits if he should read sympathetically Shakespeare's matchless utterances upon the scheme of Nature and life which now so bewilders him, and imbibe their health and wholeness. Or he would gain immeasurably if he should take up the tone of his namesake and brother bard of an older time, and go out from his own mephitic catacombs and charnel-house into the bright sunshine with the author of "The Seasons." He has gifts and an ear for melody, and a strength of both fancy and imagination which could be made eminently serviceable, if he could be taught how to apply them. But a hundred years of this singing which he offers will never place him on any high or secure pedestal of the English Parnassus. Nothing is more inevitably true than the fact that moral as well as physical suicide ends in death, and that, as some writer has well said, the disparagement of and disbelief in immortality can not lead its advocate into the company of the immortals. (p. 471)

> Joel Benton, "A New English Poet," in *Appleton's Journal*, n.s. Vol. X, No. 59, May, 1881, pp. 468-71.

E. D. A. MORSHEAD (essay date 1881)

[*Morshead reviews* Essays and Phantasies, *praising Thomson's prose poetry and literary criticism but condemning his religious beliefs.*]

It is impossible to criticise [*Essays and Phantasies*] without a feeling of what Carlyle used to call "sorrowful dubiety;" first, because the extremely heterogeneous character of its contents makes it hard to appreciate as a whole; secondly, because, when a veiled and sardonic humour appears heavy, ill-sustained, and dull to the critic, he cannot but remember that *Sartor Resartus* also seemed so on its first appearance; lastly, because a writer so warmly commended and encouraged by "George Eliot" [see letter dated 1874] as Mr. Thomson has been must have spiritual qualities and insight of no common kind. She, we may feel assured, did not lightly ascribe such qualities as "distinct vision and grand utterance."

The book may be divided into three parts—(1) Prose-poetry; (2) Theology; (3) Literary Criticism. Of these, the first—as exhibited in the opening piece, called "A Lady of Sorrow"—seems to be a very able but, at the same time, a very laboured imitation of De Quincey. "A Lady of Sorrow" is a dream of bereaved solitude in London. And there is pathos and poetry, too, in the description of Sorrow, personified first as the Angel—

the "image in beatitude of her who died so young"—then as the Siren, the blind and sorry impulse that drives her victim, a second Faust, through a weary round of gaudy but debasing pleasures, very happily compared to the tavern of Omar Khayyam, till the world is "laughed back into chaos;" finally, as the Shadow, the veiled goddess of Despair, the "dominant metamorphosis" of Sorrow. The style is that of De Quincey, but the voice is that of Heine or Leopardi. Whether pessimism has a sound philosophy may be a question; that it has a real poetry cannot be doubted. The only criticism I should venture to make on this part of Mr. Thomson's work is that it is dream-literature without the *persuasiveness* of dreams. The unforgettable charm of works like De Quincey's "Dream-Fugue," or Coleridge's "Kubla Khan," is that they combine the fantasticality of dreams with their apparently effortless reality; surprising as they are in our waking hours, they never surprise the dreamer. This quality is not reached by Mr. Thomson. His work reminds one rather of such works as George Macdonald's *Phantastes*, or *Alton Locke*, where dream-land is reproduced rather by eloquence and literary force than by the indefinable touch of inspired personal experience.

The second, or theological, side of the volume is mainly represented by a long essay entitled **"Proposals for the Speedy Extinction of Evil and Misery."** This essay is introduced by a wearisome mystification, wherein the question of the author's sanity is raised, the verdict of the critics forestalled by parodying their manner, and counsel is darkened and comprehension obscured by a tiresome indirectness. The essay itself is a long pessimistic diatribe against Christianity and most other religions, against modern politics and social arrangements, without any tangible suggestion for their amendment—unless the absurd oracle that Nature can be coerced by a threat of universal suicide on the part of Man be considered such. The ruling influence is clearly that of Swift, for whom Mr. Thomson elsewhere expresses his profound admiration. But of that great writer's bitter sincerity, his "saeva indignatio," his intense pity for the miseries and inequalities of the human lot, there is here no trace. One power of Swift's—that of producing nausea by a single phrase—Mr. Thomson has got indeed. With apologies to the readers of the *Academy,* I present an instance of this. The eulogies of the dead, in a certain journal, are said to be so "rancidly unctuous that . . . the corpse of the victim thus lubricated has turned and vomited its heart up in the grave." If this is a specimen of the invective of the kingly pessimistic man of the future, one may be allowed a satisfaction, hitherto unfelt, that one lives in the days of the journal thus assailed.

So ugly a lapse in taste and feeling might be pardoned if it stood alone. I am constrained to say that in this essay it has parallels. The very thought of certain religious doctrines—particularly that of the Trinity—seems to goad the writer to a veritable frenzy of abuse. . . . Mr. Thomson writes like a person excoriated beyond endurance by facile and popular orthodoxy, till in sheer desperation he breaks into offensiveness. But in truth, if a new temple be required, it is better to unbuild than to shatter the old one. Mr. Thomson's sketch of Christianity is just such a distempered picture as is so often and so harmfully drawn by orthodox hands and labelled Doubt, or Comtism, or Free-thinking. The picture is a hopeless daub, but the *animus* of the artist is provoking—then follow reprisals, and all is obscured in abusive polemics. But the victory will be to that side that comes to comprehend its opponent best, not that which abuses him most loudly. Neither can the heavy humour, which here and there gives a touch of irony to the essay, succeed in redeeming it from polemical dulness. "A committee of seven

archangels.'' ''Jesus Christ hauling up an editor into heaven.''
There is taste and style! ''Humanity and even womanity.'' ''A
new Jerusalem—as if one wasn't enough!'' There is humour
and satire! Serious or ironical, this essay only proves to what
level a writer of great power may sink if he is determined to
think everything worthless which is imperfect. (pp. 367-68)

It is pleasant to turn from this kind of work to the more purely
literary part of the volume. The panegyric of Spenser's poetry
shows fine critical insight, though it is hard to realise the justice
of the last two pages, which seem to ascribe to Spenser a carnal,
antinomian, defiant mood; no examples of which are given,
nor would it, I think, be easy to find them. Very happy also
is the definition of G. Meredith as ''the Browning of our novelists.'' . . . The influence of Dante is very traceable, particularly in the final essay, **''In our Forest of the Past.''** It is only
by a play of fancy, however, that Mr. Thomson calls him
''Dante Durante, the long-enduring Giver.'' Dante never meant
''the Giver;'' the name is only an abbreviation of Durante.

In fine, the general character of Mr. Thomson's book seems
to me to be as follows:—The poetry is good, though of a
somewhat laboured sombreness. The literary criticism is keen
and striking. The theology, and especially the humour applied
to the theology, is deplorably vulgar. (p. 368)

E. D. A. Morshead, in a review of ''Essays and
Phantasies,'' in The Academy, *Vol. 19, No. 472,*
May 21, 1881, pp. 367-68.

JOHN M. ROBERTSON (essay date 1892)

[*A Scottish-born English journalist, Robertson succeeded Brad-*
laugh as editor of the National Reformer *and later served as editor*
of the Free Review. *In the following excerpt from his preface to*
Poems, Essays, and Fragments, *Robertson defends Thomson's*
talents, particularly as revealed in his prose writings.]

The works of James Thomson the Second, who still needs to
be distinguished from his little-read namesake by his pen-name
initials of ''B. V.'', have thus far had a ''success of esteem''
rather than a success of popularity. Popular, indeed, they are
not likely ever to be: neither his pessimism nor his criticism
ministers enough to the normal judgment to win him a large
audience. But some addition there must be, year by year, to
the audience for his most remarkable work; and among these
there must be some to whom it will be a matter of course that
all the literary work of a man of literary genius is interesting.
For such readers [*Poems, Essays, and Fragments*] has been
compiled. (p.v)

Taken as representing his earlier literary performance, these
[pieces] . . . seem to me of great illustrative interest, and at the
same time to possess an independent value. I incline to claim
this, on the whole, more emphatically for the prose than for
the verse; not only because few of the poems here given were
such as Thomson would have wished to put beside his most
important work, but because it is arguable that he was more
perfectly at home in prose than in verse. In his prose, to a
critical eye, he is almost always a quite secure and accomplished craftsman; in his verse, even the greatest, he was always
capable of lapsing from perfection, of eking out his gold with
putty. This happens here and there in **''The City of Dreadful**
Night''; and in such strong work as **''Insomnia''**; and it happens
repeatedly in the poem which stands first in this volume, **''The**
Dead Year''. That poem challenges attention at a glance as
testifying strongly to the artistic influence of Shelley, and in

a less degree to the influence of Keats. The rapid and copious
phrasing are quite Shelleyan, with an occasional suggestion of
Keats in a searched-out epithet. It is not the spirit but the form
that is imitative: what happened evidently was that Thomson's
receptive sense was colored by writer after writer till he found
his own style, so definite but so free from mannerism; he all
along expressing his own thought under copied manners, till
his style and his thought were alike his own. This holds good
of the prose as well as of the longest poem in the present
collection. It is remarkable how the critical essays tell, one
after another, of the writers who had been influencing the young
reader: that on Emerson echoing its subject; that on Burns partly
keeping the same note; that on Shelley speaking of Mr. Ruskin
and hinting of Mr. Swinburne and Mr. Kingsley; that on Blake,
the most remarkable, bringing much of the critical manner and
attitude of Ruskin and the critical tone and temper of Swinburne, curiously because ably combined, to the utterance of a
quite original stream of critical opinion. This last essay, written
in 1863, when Thomson was twenty-nine years old, shows him
maturing his aesthetic judgment and his powers sufficiently to
be near the end of his time of imitative style; and in the paper
on Walt Whitman we have his own voice and key-note as well
as his own cordial enthusiasm for greatness and nobleness of
spirit, and freshness and mastery of utterance. His pessimism,
which fully reveals itself so early as **''The Dead Year''**, never
ate away this native zest; and his malady, which was so much
worse a bane, never extinguished though it sometimes clouded
the ardency of his higher affections.

What in these days will most strike readers of Thomson's early
criticisms is the confident and incisive censure of Tennyson as
a thinker in poetry. I do not know that it can be otherwise
rebutted than by pointing out that Thomson considerably over-
estimated the intellectual depth of the poets he praised, and
that he did not recognise as he should have done how inevitably
perfection of art ultimately tells in poetry, if only its emotional
basis be sufficient, as against philosophical or metaphysical
range with imperfection of art. And it may be that his failure
to recognise this was correlative with his own defect in artistic
austerity and patient devotion. In this he fell below Tennyson
as every contemporary has done. One would be apt to explain
the shortcoming in terms of his constitutional flaw, were it not
that on the one hand the long-lived Tennyson himself seems
to have had a pretty bad nervous system, and that on the other
hand Thomson's prose is so perfectly competent. He writes
prose so well and with such security that, remembering how
neither Tennyson nor Browning could write praiseworthy prose,
we are led to think him primarily a prosist and only secondarily
a poet. Indeed it is as much the peculiar impressiveness of his
theme as of his song in his greatest poem [**''The City of Dread-**
ful Night''] that has struck his contemporaries. On the other
hand his dissection of the *Saturday Reviewer's* paragraph on
Bright . . . shows how peculiarly vigilant he was on the logic
of prose expression; and as regards his notably wide vocabulary
I take this opportunity of saying that the charge of unsoundness
made against some of his terms, such as ''tenebrous'', is quite
unfounded, that for instance being a perfectly lawful derivation
from the Latin *tenebrosus*, through the French *ténébreux*. As
a linguist he was always scholarlike, and the felicity of his
German translations is not more striking than their faithfulness.

Yet we are forced back to the recognition that Thomson remained fundamentally if he was not altogether a poet. A man
who at thirty reasoned as he did concerning mysticism and
idealism could hardly become predominantly scientific. He
indeed grew out of the views on these points set forth in his

essay on Blake; and he came to be a trenchant disputant enough, but never, I think, a rigorous analyst of ultimate mental processes. His very clever paper on **"Liberty and Necessity"**, reprinted from the *National Reformer* in his *Essays and Phantasies*, does not carry its point for those who know the ground, and was speedily refuted by a reader. It is in the sphere of cogitated feeling—in the "comment of the emotions on the propositions of the intellect", to apply Mr. Spencer's sufficiently poetic definition of music—that Thomson finds his literary field; and that field, though broad, is largely within the realm of poetry. His was a mind of rare impressionableness, and of rare vivacity of expression; and whether he is giving out his keen appreciation of moral and artistic beauty, or putting into cadence his undersong of "teen and threne", he is always tending towards aesthesis rather than philosophy. As from his flaying of the flabby reviewer he turned to Heine and the Lorelei for solace and repose, so does his whole performance, on retrospect, seem in spirit to set towards song. And if the best or greatest of the song be mostly sad, there is humor withal. And if the humor, whether translated or original, seems to some irreverent, it has only to be said that it belongs to the same period as that in which Thomson thought much of mystics, and anticipated the conception of Jesus as a Mahatma, and allegorised on the supremacy of King Pisteus (Faith) over Erosal (Instinct, Love, or Goodwill) and Phrenos (Brain or Reason). It is not at all a product of Atheism, so that if apologies be wanted it is not clear who could offer them. (pp. vi-xi)

> *John M. Robertson, in a preface to* Poems, Essays, and Fragments *by James Thomson ("B. V."), edited by John M. Robertson, Bertram Dobell, 1892, pp. v-xi.*

PHILIP BOURKE MARSTON (essay date 1893)

[*Marston was a popular though minor nineteenth-century English poet, novelist, and short story writer. A friend of Thomson, Marston offered him assistance when he was ill and homeless shortly before his death. Here, Marston praises Thomson's contributions to English poetry, especially his "intense sincerity, joined to a vivid imagination."*]

James Thomson, though his works were few and his death comparatively early, was still one of the remarkable poets of this century. Most of the poets of our time have flirted with pessimism, but through their beautifully expressed sorrow we cannot help seeing that on the whole they are less sad than they seem, or that, like Mr. Matthew Arnold, they have laid hold of a stern kind of philosophic consolation. It was reserved for Thomson to write the real poem of despair; it was for him to say the ultimate word about melancholia: for, of course, it is the result of that disorder which is depicted in **"The City of Dreadful Night."** It was for him to gauge its horrible shapes, to understand its revelations of darkness, as Shelley and others have understood revelations of light. As soon as we have read the opening pages of **"The City of Dreadful Night,"** we feel transported to a land of infinite tragedy. It has been contended that because life itself is so tragic, such poems as Thomson's are worse than needless; but the true reason for the existence of this particular poem is given by its author in the following lines:—

> Yes, here and there some weary wanderer
> In that same city of tremendous night,
> Will understand the speech, and feel a stir
> Of fellowship in all-disastrous fight;

> I suffer mute and lonely, yet another
> Uplifts his voice to let me know a brother
> Travels the same wild paths though out of sight.

Happily all men have not walked in Thomson's City of Despair, but too many have done so, and they must feel a bitter kind of comfort, such comfort as comes of tears, in having all its horrors so faithfully and sympathetically recorded.

In the gloomy delineation of life Thomson has had of course many predecessors, but perhaps none of them have equalled him in the intense spirit of desolation revealed in **"The City of Dreadful Night,"** not only in direct utterance, but in imagery large and terribly majestic, and in the thorough keeping of the illustrations of the poem with its general sentiment. The colossal imagination of both idea and symbol show the influence of no other writer. Equally graphic and equally earnest, though in a distinctly different vein, are two poems in the same volume called **"Sunday at Hampstead,"** and **"Sunday up the River."** They are genuine idyls of the people, yet without any trace of vulgarity. They are charged with brightness and healthy joy in living, as fully as the leading poem of the book is fraught with darkness and despair.

In these days of poetic schools, to some one of which a man must generally be relegated, if his work is to be considered at all, there is something remarkable in the solitariness of this poet, who can be classed in no poetic fraternity. It is not likely that **"The City of Dreadful Night,"** through the awful blackness of which no ray of light penetrates, will ever be a popular poem, but amid the uncertainties of modern speculation, the hesitating lights which still too often discover no sure track, the poem will stand out as a monument of solemn and uncompromising gloom. Intense sincerity, joined to a vivid imagination, constitute Thomson's claims to be remembered. Whether he speaks to us from the fastnesses of his Dreadful City, or in a happier mood breaks into snatches of song as he drifts down stream in his boat, one feels brought in contact with a strong personal individuality. This strong individuality, whether expressing itself in life or poetry, is not welcome to all persons, but those on whom it seizes find in it a fascination which it is difficult for any other quality to substitute. (pp. 621-22)

> *Philip Bourke Marston, "James Thomson (1834-1882)," in* The English Poets: Wordsworth to Rossetti, Vol. IV, *edited by Thomas Humphry Ward, revised edition, Macmillan and Co., 1893, pp. 621-22.*

[ARTHUR SYMONS] (essay date 1895)

[*Symons was a critic, poet, dramatist, short story writer, and editor who first gained notoriety in the 1890s as an English decadent. Eventually, he established himself as one of the most important critics of the modern era. In the following excerpt, Symons both acknowledges Thomson's talents and notes his limitations.*]

The author of **"The City of Dreadful Night"** had to wait long for recognition; but it cannot be said that he failed, before the end, to receive at least the recognition that was his due. Of late his name has almost dropped out of sight; the critics of the hour have been too busy discussing the immortals of the moment. Yet [in *The Poetical Works of James Thomson (B. V.)*] we have a considerable body of work, work which certainly aims at great things, work planned on a large scale, and carried out with an unquestionable force; work, too, which has been praised by those whose praise is scrupulous and weighty. How far does the work, looked at to-day, seem to justify the neglect of yesterday, or the appreciation of the day before yesterday?

It is a difficult question to answer, even to oneself. There is that about Thomson's work which is at all events interesting; it has a human appeal, almost like that of a distressed face, seen in passing, in the street. Incorrect, commonplace, slovenly, as it so frequently is, there is a certain breath of life in it; there is, too, an unusual quality of mind, unusual in a poet, at work behind all these tawdry and slipshod lines. . . . His work is the story of his own life, with its momentary jollities (as in **"Sunday up the River"**), its customary gloom (as in **"The City of Dreadful Night"**), and that strange, occasional mingling of tragedy and comedy in a fantastic transformation of reality (as in **"Vane's Story"**). It was not merely circumstances that made Thomson miserable; it is difficult to imagine a temperament such as his being anything else. His extreme sense of sin, which he tried to silence by blaspheming, would have done credit to the most devout Puritan. He was always, in his own despite, and to his own despair, a moralist; and his Hyde Park atheism is only the counterpart of the belief of the Hyde Park salvationist. He is incessantly concerned with spiritual problems, with the order of the universe and with his own individual peace of mind; and it is to escape from his own mental tortures that he cries aloud:

> Because a cold rage seizes one at whiles
>   To show the bitter, old, and wrinkled truth
> Stripped naked of all vesture that beguiles,
>   False dreams, false hopes, false masks and modes of
>   youth;
> Because it gives some sense of power and passion
> In helpless impotence to try to fashion
> Our woe in living words howe'er uncouth.

And so the burden of his main poem is one of

> Infections of unutterable sadness,
> Infections of incalculable madness,
> Infections of incurable despair.

This tragic pessimism, so obviously and rootedly sincere, is as much a matter of temperament, demanding as purely pathological an explanation, as the inherited craving for drink which ruined the man's body. It is in this "anatomy of melancholy," in which he is generally engaged, that we see what was most intimate in Thomson; it is here, really, that he is at his best, despite the brilliance and novelty of some of his lighter work in livelier veins.

Among this lighter work there is much that demands consideration in any view of Thomson as a poet. He was ahead of the fashion in aiming at what we now call modernity; his work is, in a certain sense, more modern than that of any other considerable writer in verse. But in regard to his actual success in so difficult an endeavour, it is not quite easy to define the precise measure of attainment. The great problem presented itself to him, as it does to every writer: how to be real, true to life, and yet poetic, true to art. Thomson never quite mastered the problem: how few have ever mastered it! More than most, he cared for the trivial details, the casual accidents, of "Sundays out," and shop-girls' dancing-halls; and he tried to get the full value out of these things by a certain crudity in his transference of them to the canvas. To render vulgar life, it seemed to him necessary to be vulgar. Now here, surely, was a radical misapprehension. . . . [He] did not realize that to be modern is of all achievements the most difficult, that it requires the most perfect command of oneself and one's material, consummate art; and that here, more than elsewhere, a flaw, a

lapse, is fatal alike to the illusion and to the distinction of success.

Thomson's poetic style, though it has breadth and at times dignity, and is almost always both impressive and incisive, is never, even in his most serious work, really finished. There is always thought at the back of it, but, when it seems to him that he has expressed his thought clearly and trenchantly, it does not occur to him that the process is not ended; he does not labour, as the true artist labours, to find the one, perfect, final expression of that thought. . . . At his best in such large movements as the three polysyllabic lines we quoted from **"The City of Dreadful Night,"** he is rarely without a suspicion of commonness, which slips out, like a vulgarism in speech, at just the crucial moment. He formed his style, we should say, laboriously; it appears to be the result of much study, and the study of many models, of whom the chief were Shelley, Browning, and Heine. It was probably from Shelley that he acquired his fondness for vague symbolism; from Browning that he learnt a certain trick of writing verse in almost the same key as prose; from Heine that he copied, not always successfully, a manner of executing discords with intention. Out of these varying styles he built up a style which he made individual, indeed, but with an individuality which, above all things, lacked distinction. Contrast, for instance, **"Vane's Story"** with an equally modern poem in the same metre, Rossetti's "Jenny." Here we see at once the difference between a perfectly finished work of art and an exceedingly clever and interesting impromptu. Carelessness or incapacity, it matters not: poetic work which is not perfectly finished can never really prove satisfying, and in Thomson's very best work there is always something not quite satisfying. Yet how many qualities of almost the first order went to the making of what we cannot justly call a success! And there is always that personal interest, which, associated as it is with the pathos of Thomson's career, will perhaps do more than anything else to preserve his work from oblivion. (pp. 215-16)

[*Arthur Symons*], "James Thomson," in The Saturday Review, *London, Vol. 79, No. 2051, February 16, 1895, pp. 215-16.*

RODEN NOEL (essay date 1905)

[In the following excerpt, Noel reveals his preference for Thomson's celebrative rather than pessimistic verse.]

[Thomson's] early poetry is all idealistic, mystical, exhaling impassioned affection, and breathing the "difficult iced air" of Faith's mountain top. It is the unmistakable utterance of a true poet, unduly neglected because showing a less consummate shaping power than the **"City of Dreadful Night."** In **"Bertram to the Lady Geraldine,"** and in **"Tasso to Leonora,"** . . . we have only to read between the lines to behold Mathilda [Thomson's dead love] as the ideal mistress, raised above the poet's reach for awhile by destiny, yet reserved for him in all fulness when both attain to the profound spiritual union of Eternity. For one main characteristic of Thomson was his love for allegory and symbol; this we find early and late in him. His pessimistic vein indeed is not to be regarded as that most proper and essential to the man merely because it came latest, when his spirit was over-clouded by the dark environments of his career, cooperating with and evoking those demons of gloom and intemperate disease which lurked within, only waiting their sinister opportunity. His healthy period was surely that middle time when he worked strong and hopeful, full of human sympathy, and of trust in the great, sound, universal Heart of all, in that overruling Providence which is ever preparing man's undying spirit for larger spheres of life and labour.

The "**Doom of a City**" is in parts as fine as the more celebrated poem of which it is the anticipation,—more brilliant in imagery and metaphor, and with more ethereal insight, though less concentration, and command of the artist over his resources. The poem, indeed, has an undertone of deep personal desolation, but it represents men as not quite irresponsible for their sins; the righteous Nemesis visits them with doom, while the excellent are rewarded with more excellence and fuller life. The pseudo-scientific, immoral doctrine, which teaches that unconscious force, producing conscious good and evil, swallows all alike in one senseless annihilation, has not yet been arrived at. Though there is here a personal wail, as of a lost soul, there is more hope for the world.

The purport and substance of Thomson should be gauged by his earlier, quite as much as by his later work, and the manner in that is often good also. We get an exuberant exultation in life, a glad, immense embrace of all Nature (including even Death, the renovator), as characterising the true and "happy poet." Here we have the "**Lord of the Castle of Indolence**," as lovely, I think, as anything Thomson wrote in his maturity, yet composed at the early age of twenty-five, where the Spenserian measure is used with the skill of his namesake in the masterpiece bearing the same title. (pp. 673-75)

The "**Sunday up the River**" and the "**Sunday at Hampstead**" of his middle period are gay, jubilant, and full of sympathy with external nature. They have all the vital charm of Clough's beautiful "Bothie." The former is of rare lyrical beauty, . . . while the latter poem, containing a splendid little lyric, "As we rush, as we rush in the train," though an offence to Bumble, and the "superior person," is also full of vernal joy and playful humour. Seldom, on the other hand, have appeared such terribly veracious creations as the "**Insomnia**," and "**City of Dreadful Night**," with their visions of unmitigated pain. Distinct and palpable as sculpture, carven out of Solid Night, these pervade and subdue us with an atmosphere of prevailing horror; and were such poetry the whole of Thomson, despite its stern pagan stoicism, I confess that I for one could hardly regret the neglect to which his masterly, though unhealthy, and devastating work was long consigned. (pp. 676-77)

Roden Noel, "James Thomson (1834-1882)," in The Poets and the Poetry of the Nineteenth Century: Charles Kingsley to James Thomson, *edited by Alfred H. Miles, 1905. Reprint by AMS press, 1967, pp. 671-96.*

PAUL ELMER MORE   (essay date 1908)

[*More was an American critic who, along with Irving Babbitt, formulated the doctrines of New Humanism in early twentieth-century American thought. The New Humanists were strict moralists who adhered to traditional conservative values in reaction to an age of scientific and artistic self-expression. In regard to literature, they believed that a work's implicit reflection of support for the classic ethical norms was as important as its aesthetic qualities. More is especially esteemed for the philosophical and literary erudition of his multi-volume* Shelburne Essays. *In the following excerpt from that work, he accords Thomson a unique position in English literature for the "rounded philosophy of pessimism" that emerges from his four poems "In the Room," "In-*

somnia," "The City of Dreadful Night," and "To Our Ladies of Death."]

As a critic [Thomson] is shrewd and original, somewhat over-romantic in taste, but always judicial in tone; the studies of Ben Jonson are particularly rich and variegated in interest. The miscellaneous essays show a surprising vein of humour and satire, with now and then a flaunting of gorgeous rhetoric which suggests a union of De Quincey and Poe. The probability is that his greater name as a poet of pessimism has deprived him of a good many readers who have been frightened away by that ugly word; in a very literal sense his reputation has become to him *nominis umbra*. And this is quite natural, for it is, after all, by his four pessimistic poems—"**In the Room**," "**Insomnia**," "**The City of Dreadful Night**," and "**To Our Ladies of Death**"—that he has taken a unique place in English literature and will be remembered. Some, I dare say, would reckon "**Vane's Story**," or "**Weddah and Om-El-Bonain**," or one of his two Sunday idyls ["**Sunday at Hampstead**" and "**Sunday up the River**"] as more notable pieces of writing than "**In the Room**"; but there is something so singularly characteristic in this poem that it groups itself imperatively with the three acknowledged masterpieces. And in the grave and geometric simplicity of the stanzas; in the naïve complaints of mirror and table and curtain over their master, who, like another Chatterton, lies heedless of everything; in the slow heightening of wonder and mistrust . . . : in all this tragic-comic inversion of life wherein the man alone acts the dumb part, there is a literary effect which we so commonly hear about, but so rarely feel— a veritable shudder of the nerves. How often must Thomson himself as he sat in his London lodgings, in that rigid tension, perhaps, which preluded a return of dipsomania, have prefigured to himself a day when he too might lie "unconscious of the deep disgrace":

> And while the black night nothing saw,
>   And till the cold morn came at last,
> That old bed held the room in awe
>   With tales of its experience vast.
> It thrilled the gloom; it told such tales
>   Of human sorrows and delights,
> Of fever moans and infant wails,
>   Of births and deaths and bridal nights.

I could wish that the flat twenty-fifth stanza had been blotted; and in the penultimate line of the eighth "and" is apparently a slip for *or*.

After "**In the Room**" the natural transition and contrast is "**Insomnia**" with its burden of torture that impelled the poet night after night to rove the streets of London. The stanza, more complicated in structure than Thomson generally employed, is handled with notable skill; the language is at once analytic and magnificent; here, as in the *Opium-Eater* of De Quincey, "the fierce chemistry of his dreams burns daily objects into insufferable splendour"; and yet withal the poem, owing to its overwrought artificiality, or, it may be, to its too visibly pathologic basis, leaves one colder than any of its three companion pieces. Its chief value (thematically, not chronologically) is as a preparation for "**The City of Dreadful Night**," seen particularly in the form and imagery of one of the concluding stanzas:

> Against a bridge's stony parapet
>   I leaned, and gazed into the waters black;
> And marked an angry morning red and wet

Beneath a livid and enormous rack
Glare out confronting the belated moon,
Huddled and wan and feeble as the swoon
Of featureless Despair:
When some stray workman, half-asleep but lusty,
Passed urgent through the rainpour wild and gusty,
I felt a ghost already, planted watching there.

(pp. 181-84)

In the sharpness of its outlines, in the balance of its members, there is something in **"The City of Dreadful Night"** that borders on the geometry of delirium. The body of the work is composed of a series of brief cantos in a stanza of seven lines . . . which, for its perfect fitness to the theme, must be reckoned one of the few remarkable inventions of prosody. The idea of the stanza was taken, as Thomson himself admits, from that of Browning's "Guardian Angel" in the *Dramatic Lyrics,* but the changes introduced by Thomson make it completely his own. Browning, to begin with, rhymed the seventh line with the first and third; by shifting this arrangement so as to rhyme together the second, fourth, and seventh, Thomson reduced eccentric formlessness to form, and gave to the three concluding lines the effect of a slow, melancholy refrain. A different use of the metrical pauses also, immediately felt by the reader but not easily described, adds a heavy, brooding quality to the rhythm quite foreign to Browning's impulsive temperament. Alternating with these descriptive cantos is a series of episodes, in which the narrative parts are in a common six-line stanza (ababcc), while the confessions, so to speak, of the *dramatis personæ* vary in metrical form according to their mood. The whole poem is like the phantasmagoria of a fever subdued to mathematical restraint, or the clamour of mad grief trained into remorseless logic. (pp. 184-85)

No one knew better than Thomson himself that this is not the City of all the world; indeed, the very sting of his grief is the feeling of isolation from the common lot. Few men tread those streets of denial and gloom habitually, but many have been there at one time of their lives and carry with them always, somewhere hidden from view, the badge of citizenship in that "sad Fraternity." To these, as well as to the few like-fated with the poet, his words will still have a meaning:

Yes, here and there some weary wanderer
In that same city of tremendous night,
Will understand the speech, and feel a stir
Of fellowship in all disastrous fight;
"I suffer mute and lonely, yet another
Uplifts his voice to let me know a brother
Travels the same wild paths though out of sight."

The sequel to **"The City of Dreadful Night"** is the poem **"To Our Ladies of Death,"** written in the same seven-line stanza. The only change is the substitution of a single for a double rhyme in the couplet, reducing the lyrical clangour of the rhythm to a more contemplative calm. The idea was suggested, as Thomson records, by "the sublime sisterhood of Our Ladies of Sorrow, in the "Suspiria de Profundis" of De Quincey"; but for the three Sorrows we now have the three conceptions of Death—Our Lady of Beatitudes, the gracious mother, on whom the broken and hopeless dare not call; Our Lady of Annihilation, who waits with her scourge "the selfish, fatuous, proud, and pitiless"; and, last, Our Lady of Oblivion, who gathers to her breast "the weak, the weary, and the desolate," and to whom the wanderer in the City of Night makes his plea:

Take me, and lull me into perfect sleep;
Down, down, far-hidden in thy duskiest cave;
While all the clamorous years above me sweep

Unheard, or, like the voice of seas that rave
On far-off coasts, but murmuring o'er my trance,
A dim vast monotone, that shall enhance
The restful rapture of the inviolate grave.

And so the cycle is made complete—from the sordid tragedy of the poet's room, through the terrible unforgetfulness of insomnia, to the conception of all life as a City of Night, and the despairing cry for the consummation of oblivion. Together the four poems present a rounded philosophy of pessimism, which stands quite alone in English literature, and which has, I believe, no precise equivalent in any language. (pp. 186-88)

Paul Elmer More, "James Thomson ('B. V.')," in his Shelburne Essays, *fifth series, G. P. Putnam's Sons, 1908, pp. 170-95.*

BERTRAM DOBELL   (essay date 1910)

[*An English bookseller, publisher, and poet, Dobell is remembered especially for his discovery and editorship of Thomas Traherne's lost manuscripts and for his help in financing the publication of* The City of Dreadful Night and Other Poems. *Following Thomson's death, Dobell edited and published other collections of his verse, including* A Voice from the Nile and Other Poems. *Here, he characterizes Thomson's artistic nature as "intensive rather than extensive" and establishes the ascendancy of his pessimistic thought.*]

It has been said that there can be no justification for the writing of such a poem as the **"City of Dreadful Night,"** because the poet's object should be to increase the sum of human happiness, and not to render man's existence yet more insupportable. But a view of the poet's office which reduces him to a mere purveyor of mental syrup for the benefit of the soft-headed and soft-hearted will hardly commend itself to a robust intelligence. If Shakespeare was justified in writing *King Lear* or *Hamlet,* then Thomson was no less justified in writing **"The City of Dreadful Night."** If ever any man was born to accomplish a particular task, Thomson was born for the purpose of writing his great masterpiece, and he would have lived in vain had he failed to write it. It is the one great and final poetic expression of pessimistic thought, and as such it must ever remain an unique and unsurpassable achievement. (p. 44)

If we are interested in Thomson's writings we shall find, when we come to analyse our feelings about them, that it is because we are interested in the author's personality. In other words, he was rather a subjective than an objective writer. He belonged to the school of Shelley, Coleridge and Rossetti, rather than to that of Scott, Tennyson and Morris. His genius was intensive rather than extensive. He does not often attempt the dramatic presentation of the world outside himself: he prefers rather to study the workings of his own mind than to observe the evolutions of the great drama of humanity. His own thoughts and emotions were almost exclusively the subjects of his writings. Perhaps his works, while gaining in intensity from this cause, lost something in breadth of sympathy and in sanity of outlook upon life. But every author must work according to the law of his own nature; and it is not given, even to a Shakespeare, to combine incompatible excellences. Thomson would, doubtless, have been happier if he had not been so constantly engaged in analysing and dissecting his own emotions, sensations and impulses. He did not sufficiently realise the thought that, since destiny could not in any way be moved to favour him, it would be wise on his part to submit, as far as possible, to its decrees. He did not—or could not—avail himself of the common method of assuaging or deadening his sorrows. Most men and women find a way of escape from their too-insistent griefs or too-tormenting thoughts in joining in the social life around them, and so sinking, in a great degree, their own existence in that of the community. To escape in this way from themselves is, indeed, the great object of the lives of most persons, for few can endure, for any length of time, to be alone with themselves, or care to indulge in solitary reflection. That this is the wisest, as well as the most natural course for the generality of mankind can hardly be doubted; and it is this truth that Walt Whitman most constantly dwells upon. Though Thomson had much admiration for Whitman, and was, in his later life, influenced to some extent by him, no two writers ever differed more in character and in outlook upon life than did the authors of *Leaves of Grass* and **"The City of Dreadful Night."** The one rejoiced in the thought of his kinship to the multitude around him—

> In all people I see myself, none more and not one a
>   barleycorn less,
> And the good or bad I say of myself I say of them—

the other was only too conscious that he had little in common with "the average sensual man." Conscious as he was of his intellectual superiority to those around him, he was unable to free himself—or at least not till late in life—from the delusion that he was a sinner who had sinned the unpardonable sin. "The Christian conscience," says a discerning critic, "survived in him to torment the sceptic." He had in him the blood, tinctured with fanaticism and intolerance, of long generations of Scotsmen, who had bequeathed to him something of their religious fervour, together with their not less fervent love of the national drink. His vigorous intellect enabled him to free himself from the bondage of Calvinistic theology, but its poison could not be altogether eliminated from his system. Few of us can hope to be entirely emancipated from the evil influences of our ancestry and early education. It is not possible for many of us to attain the serene and impartial, if somewhat ironic, attitude of Walt Whitman—

> I do not despise you priests: all time, the world over:
> My faith is the greatest of faiths, and the least of faiths,
> Enclosing worship ancient and modern, and all between
>   ancient and modern.

The unquestioning optimism and equal acceptance of the good and evil of human existence which characterised the American poet were impossible to Thomson. Most of Whitman's writings seem as if they had been written in sunshine and open air; some of Thomson's might have been written within the walls of a prison, with ink compounded from his own blood. There is no greater contrast in all literature than that between the spirit of *Leaves of Grass* and that of **"The City of Dreadful Night."** Yet there is a likeness between them in at least one point. Both of them express with absolute truth and sincerity the inmost nature and deepest convictions of their authors. They are not works which please the reader because of their exquisite literary form rather than by their power of thought or depth of meaning. Neither was the product of a mind at ease, sporting with its own fancies, and solicitous rather about the form than the substance of its creations. Thomson's art, indeed, though it was never, I think, his first consideration, was yet always adequate to his subject, and he seldom or never failed in wedding a fine thought to its fitting expression. I need not say that this was hardly the case with Whitman, whose artlessness too often degenerates into incoherence or mere formlessness. (pp. 58-61)

Men are made what they are chiefly by their innate dispositions, and only in a very minor degree by the force of outward circumstances. It is truer to say that our inner qualities create our surroundings than that we are ruled by the accidents of our environment. I am of course aware that this view will not be universally accepted, for I know that there are good people who hold that man is the creature of circumstances, and that he can be moulded by education and training into a pattern of perfect excellence. In other words, they think that by suppressing his most distinctively human qualities he can be converted into a sort of moral and intellectual eunuch, or into such a bloodless mockery of manliness as Tennyson's King Arthur. Well, let those who will entertain that belief: doubtless it pleases them, and it does no harm, I suppose, to anyone else. But I must be excused myself from thinking that the best way of dealing with human beings is to begin by assuming that it is possible to divest them of their human nature.

Thomson himself called his life "a long defeat"; yet was it really that? As regards himself and his personal misfortunes, it was certainly a failure; but so was that of Robert Burns, who, at the close of his brief career, might almost have used the same words. Yet what seemed failure and defeat to themselves, we can now see was but the necessary discipline which was to fit them for their allotted tasks—

> 'Tis pain and passion form the poet's soul,
> Without them he will never reach his goal:
> He must be racked by grief and tried by fire;
> See just beyond his reach his great desire;
> View mediocrity the prize attain,
> And seldom till too late the laurel gain:
> Yet what he is his high reward shall be,
> None else may know such ecstasy as he.

Yes! the poets who, through their own sufferings, learn to understand and to sympathise with the sufferings of humanity at large, and who, by their power of expression, are able to voice the else-inarticulate griefs and repinings of their fellow-mortals, have one great compensation for all the sorrows they have to endure. "The fine madness" of the poet's brain, which is in truth the faculty by which he sees and apprehends things unseen and unapprehended by the multitude, is to him the source of the most exquisite delight, the most ecstatic exaltation, even though it may be also the source of his most poignant pains, his heaviest afflictions. What king or emperor, however great his power, or however wide his dominions, is the peer of a Traherne or a Blake, who, landless and wealthless as he may be, is yet the owner of an infinite realm, the possessor of the only kind of wealth which is indeed "beyond the dreams of avarice"? (pp. 63-64)

> *Bertram Dobell, in his* The Laureate of Pessimism: A Sketch of the Life and Character of James Thomson ("B. V."), *Bertram Dobell, 1910, 64 p.*

HENRY S. SALT (essay date 1914)

[*Salt published the first full-length biography of Thomson in 1889. In the following excerpt from the revised edition of this work, he surveys Thomson's writings, commenting on the pessimism, individualism, careful workmanship, and clarity of expression evident in his poetry and prose.*]

"The City of Dreadful Night" has been generally accepted as the masterpiece of its author, and rightly; for if this poem does not take its place amidst the permanent works of English literature, it is difficult to believe that any of Thomson's writings will do so. It has not the rapturous idealism of the early poems, nor the brilliant fancy of "Vane's Story"; but it has, in far greater measure, the massive strength and reality of a great allegorical work; we feel in reading it that we are in the presence of one who has not only been profoundly moved by the mysteries of existence, but has *seen* what he has felt, as only a great poet can see it; and who, moreover, is gifted with the rare poetical faculty of translating his visions into words which impress themselves on the mind of the reader with all the vividness and intensity of a picture. (p. 79)

Thomson's pessimism is the expression of a dominant mood, amounting to a personal conviction—a mood with which all thinking men must be acquainted at times, but which is felt by some far more often and more strongly than by others. "I wish," he says, in his essay on "Sympathy,"

> to draw into clear light the facts that, in two moods of two several hours not a day asunder, a man's relations to the most serious problems of life may be, and often are, essentially opposite; that the one may burn with hope and faith, and the other lour black with doubt and despair; and that there is no possibility of conciliating (philosophically) this antagonism, since the two are mutually unintelligible.

In the same essay he asserts that there are cases, though not frequent ones, in which "a dark mood has dominated a whole life." But though the dark mood was the one with which he was specially familiar, and though in "The City of Dreadful Night" and similar writings he dilated and insisted on this mood to the exclusion of the other, yet he was himself well aware that it was a half-truth and not the whole truth to which he was then giving expression. "Is it true," he asks of his own pessimistic doctrine in the introduction to "A Lady of Sorrow"—

> Is it true in relation to the world and general life? I think true, but not the whole truth. There is truth of winter and black night, there is truth of summer and dazzling noonday. On the one side of the great medal are stamped the glory and triumph of life, on the other side are stamped the glory and triumph of death; but which is the obverse and which the reverse none of us surely knows. It is certain that both are inseparably united in every coin doled out to us from the universal mintage.

The sense of "sanctitude and piety," finding action in services of gentleness and tenderness to suffering fellow-beings, is a most important and characteristic feature of Thomson's pessimism, relieving it altogether from any suspicion of misanthropic churlishness, and allying it not only with the most valuable part of Schopenhauer's philosophy, in which compassion is made the principle of moral action, but also with the tender and benevolent sadness of Buddha. [In Thomson's "Arthur Schopenhauer, by H. Zimmern"] he expresses a strong dislike for the tinge of sullenness and vanity that disturbed the philosophic composure of the great German pessimist, while he refers to Buddhism as "the venerable, the august, the benign, so tender, so mystic, so profound, so solemnly supernal." This frank human sympathy is the one ray of light that relieves the deepening gloom of Thomson's despondency. If we regard Leopardi as the source of his most pessimistic in-

spiration, so in like manner must we attribute to Shelley's example much of the gentleness and humanity that pervade even his most sombre productions; and we note that while "The City of Dreadful Night" was appropriately dedicated to Leopardi, the "younger brother of Dante," "Vane's Story," which is conceived in a somewhat more tender spirit, was dedicated to Shelley, the "poet of poets and purest of men." Next to these two literary sponsors, Heine and Novalis must not be overlooked as having strongly affected his imagination and line of thought; Novalis perhaps in a minor degree, and more by a sense of spiritual relationship and the similarity between their lives than by direct force of teaching, whereas Heine's influence is very noticeable in all his mature thoughts and writings. (pp. 150-52)

But if Thomson owed much to Leopardi and Shelley and Heine—a debt which he himself openly and gratefully avowed—he was none the less perfectly independent and original in his methods of thought and in the conclusions at which he arrived. Both by nature and conviction he was far too jealous an upholder of the freedom of private judgment to be in danger of blindly following any intellectual lead; indeed, he was more likely, if he erred at all, to err in the opposite direction, "obstinately individual" being the description applied to him by one of his friends. Nor does he betray the least tendency to preach his pessimistic gospel in an over-positive or dogmatic spirit, exhibiting it, as I have already said, simply as that side of the great medal of life which most men would gladly overlook, but which had presented itself to him as the more important and significant one. The insolubility of the mystery of existence is the chief point in Thomson's pessimistic creed, from which he deduces the entire worthlessness of all metaphysical systems, and mercilessly satirizes those theologians and philosophers who expatiate on the origin of the universe. He compares such metaphysicians to a colony of mice in a great cathedral getting "a poor livelihood out of communion-crumbs and taper-droppings," and speculating confidently on "the meaning of the altar, the significance of the ritual, the clashing of the bells, the ringing of the chants, and the thunderous trepidations of the organ." (pp. 153-54)

Like De Quincey, he possesses the gift of distinct mental vision finding utterance in sublime imagery; those who read "The City of Dreadful Night," or "Insomnia," cannot doubt that the forms there described were actually existent to the eye of the poet. He himself tells us how, during his sojourn in London with his "Lady of Sorrow"—the life-long grief that is thus allegorically represented—he lived in a spiritual world of his own, not less real than the actual world around him. . . . (p. 155)

Yet this same visionary was also one of the shrewdest logicians, one of the keenest critics, and one of the most trenchant satirists of the age in which he lived.

At the time when Thomson first entered on his literary career the most prominent representatives of English poetry were Tennyson, Arnold, and the Brownings, Landor's star having already practically set, and the names of Swinburne, Morris, and Rossetti being as yet unknown. The influence most discernible in Thomson's early writings is that of Shelley; but as his style matured it became Dantesque rather than Shelleyan in the gravity and conciseness of its expression, and it is evident that Dante, whom Thomson had studied till he knew him almost by heart, had made a profound impression on his mind. Heine, too, became before long a very potent influence, as is proved by the affinity of thought and tone, the numerous references to his writings that are scattered through his works, and what he modestly called the "attempts at translations."

But such receptivity is perfectly compatible with independence; and original Thomson undoubtedly was, if ever poet was so. The strong, clear impression of his very marked personality is stamped on the thought, style, and diction of every poem he wrote. He has, of course, something in common with those contemporary writers who rose to fame and celebrity while he was still condemned to struggle with obscurity and neglect; but the similarity, where any similarity exists, is only such as must necessarily be found between all poets of the same social and political epoch. The dates, moreover, which are in most cases prefixed to Thomson's poems, often show that, though published later, they were in reality written earlier than those to which a resemblance may be traced. (pp. 156-57)

[There is a] striking resemblance between "**The City of Dreadful Night**" and the prose piece entitled "**A Lady of Sorrow**," which had been written ten years earlier. During all that time the writer was carrying in his mind the sombre imagery, and even actual phrases, which he afterwards converted with such effect into a poetical form. In this patient workmanship, and conscientious elaboration of the details of his art, we see the secret of much of his success in the creation of vivid word-pictures which fix themselves indelibly on the mind.

Many of Thomson's writings, whether belonging to his early or his late period of authorship, are subjective in a high degree, being full of a marked and easily discernible individuality. Through the medium of his poems, grave or gay, we see him as he was actually seen in his lifetime; now overshadowed by the profound gloom of pessimistic thought, now forgetting his sorrows for a time, in some interval of hearty and almost boisterous merriment; and now in the intermediate mood, half pensive, half playful—the mood of "**Vane's Story**"—in which he was most familiar to his friends. Yet the scope of his genius was perhaps wider than would be supposed by those who know him only by his published volumes of poems, for his prose works and scattered pieces show that he was also gifted with a very keen power as satirist, critic, and journalist—a power which would certainly have brought him to the fore if it had been enlisted in a more popular cause, and exerted under less depressing circumstances.

His masterpiece in prolonged narrative is "**Weddah and Om-el-Bonain**," which is a model throughout of severe concentration and artistic finish; but his power of strong, vivid description is made evident in many scattered passages, of which one of the most notable is the poetical reproduction, in the closing section of "**The City of Dreadful Night**," of Albert Dürer's "**Melencolia**"—a piece of writing certainly not surpassed by anything of its kind in contemporary literature.... (pp. 157-58)

In addition to this quality of picturesque vision, Thomson was gifted with a remarkable faculty of clear and lucid expression. His love of allegory may occasionally lead him in a few of his earlier writings into something approaching to mysticism, but otherwise I doubt if there is a single passage in his works which is not perfectly plain, intelligible, and perspicuous. His pure, racy, idiomatic English is free from any trace of fastidiousness; yet at the same time he possessed the cultured taste of a man who is a master of several languages. But the main power which underlay all his literary powers, and enabled him to use them with real and lasting effect, was the genuineness of feeling which lends to his word-pictures an intensity which could not have been supplied by any external culture. (p. 159)

A page from the manuscript of "The City of Dreadful Night."

Thomson's prose writings are scarcely less excellent than his poems, though they have attracted far less attention in the literary world. Here, too, the juxtaposition of the imaginative and logical faculties is seen to stand him in good stead, and we might say of his best essays what he himself has said of Shelley's, that, "with the enthusiasm and ornate beauty of an ode, they preserve throughout the logical precision and directness of an elegant mathematical demonstration." His style is strong, simple, and perspicuous, yet inspired by the same intensity of feeling that has been noted in his poetry. In the prose "**Phantasies**," which are in reality prose-poems, and closely akin to the dream-fugues of De Quincey, there is a certain amount of deliberate word-structure and carefully balanced melody; but even here his sentences are quite free from unnecessary ornament, his manner being that of a writer who knows exactly what is to be said and the most effective way of saying it. Owing to his affinity to De Quincey, some critics have been over hasty in accusing Thomson of plagiarism; but in reality there is as much distinction in his prose as in his poems, the same strong-minded thinker speaking unmistakably through both. (pp. 161-62)

As an essayist pure and simple, he is seen at his best in such pieces as those on "**Indolence**," "**Sympathy**," and "**Open Secret Societies**." It has been well remarked that a really fine essayist is one of the rarest of literary phenomena, because the mere suspicion of any didactic tendency is often sufficient to destroy the peculiar charm and indefinable aroma of the essay. Thomson, though too much of a metaphysician and revolutionist to be a model essayist, was endowed nevertheless with a considerable portion of the genuine Addisonian faculty of lambent humour and gentle raillery of human foibles, as appears to a marked extent in the essays just mentioned. In letter-writing, where somewhat similar qualities are indispensable to success, he also excelled; his letters . . . being remarkable for their ease, directness, versatility of style, and incisive vigour of expression. Serious or humorous, descriptive or critical, these letters seldom fail to wield the charm of high artistic finish united with perfect freshness and spontaneity; even in Shelley's famous "Letters from Abroad" it would be difficult, I think, to find many finer pieces of descriptive writing than the long letter to Mr. W. M. Rossetti from Central City, Colorado.

Thomson's critical writings give evidence of his wide literary sympathies, catholicity of taste, and natural insight into what is best in contemporary literature, as well as in that of past periods. For Dante he is said to have expressed unbounded reverence in private talk, accepting Mr. Ruskin's statement that Dante is "the central intellect" of the world. His love of the Elizabethan poets is shown in his delightful essay entitled **"An Evening with Spenser,"** where he declares Spenser and his fellows to be "peers of the noblest men that have existed since the human race was born"; for Milton he seems to have felt a less hearty admiration, if it is fair to judge by a few scattered references to parts of "Lycidas" and *Paradise Lost.* His most notable criticisms of the modern school are those which deal with Burns, Blake, Browning, Garth Wilkinson, Whitman, Meredith, and Shelley. He was the first writer who, recognizing in Shelley the teacher as well as the singer, ventured to drop the tone of timid apology which even the most favourable reviewers had previously considered necessary. (pp. 162-64)

The **"Note on George Meredith"** is one of his finest pieces of criticism, a splendid testimony to the high qualities of a great novelist whose name at that time was comparatively unknown. (p. 164)

When we take into consideration Thomson's whole body of work, poetry and prose together, it must in justice be said that he possesses the two prime qualities that are essential to the making of a great writer. In the first place, he has that strong sense of humanity which lies at the back of all really memorable literature; pessimist though he may be, his sympathies are entirely human; the subject, in one shape or another, of all his writings is that great struggle between Love and Death, the pessimistic view of which must present itself, in certain moods and at certain times, to the mind of every thoughtful person. Secondly, he is gifted with the not less indispensable faculty of poetic and artistic expression—the rich tone, the massive strength, the subtle melody of his language will scarcely be denied by those who have made it their study. Popular he perhaps can never be, in the ordinary sense, since his doctrines all point to a conclusion disagreeable to the popular taste; but when once his claim to immortality is impartially considered, it will be impossible to deny that his position in English literature is unique; a special niche will have to be set apart for him in the gallery of poets. (pp. 165-66)

Henry S. Salt, in his The Life of James Thomson *("B. V."), revised edition, Watts & Co., 1914, 169 p.*

J. EDWARD MEEKER (essay date 1917)

[*Meeker attempts to redeem Thomson's reputation by explaining that his philosophy and style stemmed from the contradictory nature of his genius.*]

The defense of a poet is usually poor enough criticism, for the writer must at once plunge into the dust and heat of partizanship. It is very difficult for the advocate to weigh evidence rather than shape it to his purpose. Yet in the case of Thomson, any fair and intelligent criticism must necessarily be a defense, for the poet's name and works survive chiefly as horrible hearsay phantoms. Men who have never read a word of his poetry or his prose gain somehow, year after year, the general impression that Thomson was an immoral and blasphemous man who wrote, some years since, several very pessimistic poems in a rough, harsh style that quite lacks distinction. Be it our task to inquire into the more significant phases of this wan, hearsay reputation which the poet at present possesses, that we may do even a scant justice to one of the most original, powerful and sincere poets of the last century. (p. 136)

Like Coleridge, Thomson became fatally absorbed in himself, and from brooding upon his own irresolute powers of mind, became a pessimist. Coleridge in his "Ode on Dejection" had written:

> O Lady! We receive but what we give,
> And in our life alone does Nature live:
> Ours is her wedding-garment, ours her shroud!
> And would we aught behold, of higher worth,
> Than that inanimate cold world allowed
> To the poor loveless ever-anxious crowd,
> Ah! from the soul itself must issue forth
> A light, a glory, a fair luminous cloud
>   Enveloping the Earth—
> And from the soul itself there must be sent
>   A sweet and potent voice, of its own birth,
> Of all sweet sounds the life and element!

Thomson came to know the truth of this poem only too well. Yet his brooding melancholy was largely inherent in his nature from his earliest days. Novalis has somewhere said that "Character is Fate," and in Thomson's case the epigram is tragically true. His love died early in his career, his youthful religious beliefs were so rigid that they could not survive the inevitable doubtings of maturity, a life of action was prevented by his literary tendencies, his literary labors went almost without notice or approval most of his life, and he could not identify himself with Nature because of his self-awareness and his city life. Thomson was thus unable to sink himself into any external interest, and so save himself from his terrible self-analysis. Under immediate stimulus, his talk and his letters were almost invariably cheerful, but when leisure allowed him to ponder, his poems were usually dark and sorrowful.

Yet this fatalism of his is not at all ignoble. It should be pitied, not reprehended. Thomson believed when his despairing mood was upon him, that

> I find no hint throughout the Universe
> Of good or ill, of blessing or of curse;
>   I find alone Necessity supreme.

Yet until the last two months of his life, he fought bitterly against the inevitable. Except perhaps in the **"Lord of the Castle of Indolence,"** his poetry shows no signs of the Oriental submission to Fate. Certainly the generation which reads the *Rubaiyat* of Fitzgerald with relish, can scarcely afford to censure the heroic struggle with Destiny which Thomson maintains in the conclusion to the **"City."** Like the greatest writers of his race, from the unknown author of the *Beowulf* to Thomas Hardy, he never ceased to oppose Fate with all the power that was in him, and the passionate intensity of **"Mater Tenebrarum,"** the **"Ladies of Death,"** or the **"City"** is a tribute to a mighty courage. Since he would not bend, he broke at the last.

Much also has been made of his occasional cynicism, as in **"Art"** or **"Vane's Story."** These cynical passages, however, represent merely the comparatively infrequent moments when he found himself too worn out with the sad difference between the ideal and the actual world, to blaze with his usual fiery indignation at the tragic disparity. Although he lacked any sort of formal religious faith, few poets have loved the truth as much, or sought for it as eagerly. (pp. 137-39)

As to Thomson's blasphemy, much understanding is again needed. Sincere blasphemy of the kind which he occasionally wrote, as in **"Vane's Story"** or **"Bill Jones on Prayer,"** is, paradoxically enough, the sign of a profoundly religious nature. There is no casual impudence about it. The poet has been unable to escape his early upbringing in an atmosphere of original sin, total depravity, and all the other morbid horrors of Calvinism against which Burns and Carlyle have spoken with no uncertain tone. It is not for most of us, who smile at Mid-Victorian theology, to criticise Thomson for nobler, wiser and more acute criticisms of it than our own. Actually, Thomson was never an unreligious man, nor could he for long escape spiritual problems. His blasphemies were caused by the failure of the actual church which he saw to correspond to the lofty ideal which his poetic idealism had created for it.

Many critics have objected to the rough, harsh style of his poetry, and this objection cannot be dismissed so lightly. Even William Sharp's charge of "rhetorical verbiage, and a vulgar recklessness of expression" is not without foundation. The poet's use of archaic and original words, of double words, of monotonous epithets and imperfect rhymes, is indeed too pronounced, even in his mature work. Thomson was for the most part self-educated in literature, and his sense of poetic form was sometimes more mathematical than artistic. There are occasional touches like those of "Johnny Keats," except that Thomson sins in clumsy over-seriousness rather than mawkish prettiness. Certain phases of the crudely powerful and earnest style of Thomson's poetry, remind one of Carlyle's prose. Yet this charge of harsh diction, true as it is, can be pressed too far. In a private conversation, Alfred Noyes once remarked to me that Thomson was too rough and lacked art. Afterwards, as is usually the case, I thought of the reply I should have made at the time. According to the old Greek myth, out of Chaos came order, and out of order came the Muses. In plain language, poetry organizes the world in order to extract meaning out of it. The poet's world is usually consistent because it has been well ordered. Just as his world is more regular and patterned than the real world, so his language is more regular and more patterned than the ordinary unmetrical language of prose or speech. Tennyson's line is smooth because it is expressing a world which he has smoothed out beforehand. Hence it comes that readers expect the poet to organize a meaning out of the world, and consequently write rather smooth verses about it. But Thomson differs from most poets in that very often he is attempting to express Chaos, and not an ordered universe at all. What he was trying to express was not the harmony of life, but the meaningless discords of it, and to do this successfully uncouthness is absolutely necessary. So Lu-

cretius had found it in *De Rerum Natura,* so did that master of poetic technique, Milton, find it in the *Paradise Lost* when he wrote of

> Rocks, caves, lakes, fens, bogs, dens, and
> shades of death—

Had Thomson forgotten the truth of what he was writing for the mere beauty of insincere expression, such a rough stanza as

> The world rolls round for ever like a mill;
> It grinds out death and life and good and ill;
> It has no purpose, heart or mind or will

would lack its powerful sincerity. Consequently, his rough lines are very often not only justifiable but felicitous in expressing what he was attempting to express. Despite Tennyson and the school of Tennyson, poetry cannot be measured only by its smoothness. Browning's assertion of much the same principle finds more consent now than it did when Tennyson's influence on English poetry was supreme. Thomson satirized this insincere oversmoothness in his **"Real Vision of Sin,"** and was usually far too much in earnest to disguise his real meaning with a bland beauty of utterance. In this respect, it is natural though unfortunate that he should have the defects of his qualities.

Thomson has also been severely criticised for his receptivity. Critics have pointed out in his poems the strong and successive influence of Shelley, Browning, Leopardi, Arnold, Dante, Heine, Swinburne, Rossetti, and even Tennyson, especially in the poems written before 1862, and during the period when his powers were maturing. Yet such imitation is indeed the general rule among young poets. But as he grew older, his prolix flow of rich and original metaphors was curbed, and his best poems are in a stern and inevitably powerful style. In such spirit, at least, **"In the Room,"** the **"City," "Weddah," "The fire that filled my heart of old"** and **"Insomnia"** were composed. Certainly no other poet in English literature could well have written these poems. At his best Thomson possesses an almost unique balance between his relentless logical faculties and his intense and sweeping imagination. Shelley was too imaginative and Browning too intellectual to attain such Dantean power as the best passages of the **"City"** reveal. In fact, the resemblance between Thomson and the Florentine is not as superficial as on first sight it might seem. Both poets' loves died young, to both the universe seemed stern and predetermined. The fact that one took a single City to embody human life, while the other found it necessary to employ the whole known universe, is after all a difference in degree rather than kind. Thomson once called Dante "the central intellect of the world," and consciously imitated his style. In Thomson's several experiments with *terza rima,* and in his frequent allusions to the great Italian, the younger poet shows the results of constant and intense reading of the *Divina Commedia.*

But the chief and perhaps least valid of the stock objections to Thomson's poetry is its pessimism. That all great poets have a streak of this in their natures is obvious. That Thomson's peculiar pessimism is neither ignoble nor his only attitude toward life, has been sufficiently illustrated. The question, therefore, which the critic of poetry must ask himself, is whether he has expressed this feeling fully, sincerely and powerfully, and few who read Thomson's best poems can deny that he has done this.

In the **"Proem"** to the **"City,"** as well as in many other poems, Thomson declared that he well knew that his poetry was not a true expression of the lives of everyone. He did not wish, as Swift had, to kill the whole human race, and he declined upon reflection to kill himself. He bore the habitual optimist no envy, but much of his best poetry he addressed to the "sad confraternity" who like himself wandered hopelessly in the "dolent city." He is not therefore insanely unbalanced at all, nor does he exaggerate. Dante could never have written the *Inferno* had he not also been capable of writing the *Paradiso*. Thomson's gloom is intense because he could also rejoice greatly. As a matter of fact, very few of the critics who shake their heads in disapproval over his pessimism, ever felt half the beauty or the joy which Thomson has put into **"Sunday up the River."** According to these men, Thomson must be a formula, an unswerving type of something or other. They cannot seem to see that he was a man, self-contradictory as any living man always is, constantly wavering between joy and despair, a love of beauty and a hatred of life, a passionate yearning for his dead love and a stern desire for oblivion. Thomson expressed these things because he was a poet, and his expression of them is intense because he was a genius. His pessimism, when it was upon him, was the sincere conviction of a man of industry, high ideals, strong will, sound brain and great poetical ability. It cannot be lightly set aside by men who dare no irreverence to the heath scenes in *Lear*, or the Malebolge in the *Inferno*. (pp. 139-45)

Pessimism may prevent Thomson from ever being popular, as it has Leopardi and, despite conventional sentiment to the contrary, Dante himself. Yet at least his poetry must always be respected by the "judicious reader," as it will always be understood and appreciated by such as themselves have "paced that dolent city," overcome by the "melancholia that transcends all wit." (pp. 147-48)

> *J. Edward Meeker, in his* The Life and Poetry of James Thomson (B. V.), *Yale University Press, 1917, 148 p.*

FRANK HARRIS (essay date 1919)

[*Harris was a highly controversial English editor, critic, and biographer. A man frequently referred to in colorfully insulting terms by major critics, he was by most accounts a remarkable liar and braggart, traits that deeply color the quality of his works and their critical reception. Harris's fame as a critic rests primarily upon his five-volume* Contemporary Portraits, *which contains essays marked by the author's characteristically vigorous style and patronizing tone. In the following excerpt from that work, Harris expresses his profound admiration for Thomson's poetic and critical talents.*]

There is an old story that tells how a man went about without a shadow and what a sensation the loss caused when it was discovered. For the greater part of the nineteenth century the majority of men went about without souls in drear discomfort, yet they only realized their loss when it was pointed out to them by poets and idealists. Every one had got drunk with greed and was mad to get rich; the things of the spirit were thrust aside; the soul ignored.

Karl Marx proved in *Das Kapital* that working men, women and children were never so exploited as towards the middle of the nineteenth century in the factories of England; mere wage slaves they were, worse treated than they would have been had the employers owned them body and soul; for then at least they would have been fed and housed decently.

The poets were naturally the first to revolt against the sordid life of capitalistic exploitation. Hood's "Song of the Shirt" and "One More Unfortunate" were the lyrics of that sad time when men "wore the name of freedom graven on a heavier chain."

The greatest poets were in all countries the most convinced pessimists; Leopardi in Italy, Heine in Germany and Thomson in England. Their souls had been maimed and wounded in the squalid struggle.

Thomson interested me very early by what seemed pure chance. In 1874 or thereabouts Charles Bradlaugh spoke in Lawrence, Kan., and though not so good a speaker as Ingersoll made an even deeper impression on me by dint of force of character and personality. I began reading *The National Reformer* and soon noticed "jottings" by "B. V.," which excited my curiosity and admiration. One day I came across the first verses of **"The City of Dreadful Night"**; the title appealed to me and the poem made a tremendous impression on me: I was young and had not found my work in life.

The weary weight of this unintelligible world lay heavy on me and the builded desolation and passionate despair of Thomson's poem took complete possession of my spirit. Verse after verse once read, printed itself in my brain unforgettably; ever since they come back to me in dark hours, and I find myself using them as a bitter tonic. Take such a verse as this:

> The sense that every struggle brings defeat
>   Because Fate holds no prize to crown success;
> That all the oracles are dumb or cheat
>   Because they have no secret to express;
> That none can pierce the vast black veil uncertain
> Because there is no light beyond the curtain;
>   That all is vanity and nothingness.
>   Such words sink deep into the heart as meteors
> into the earth dropped from some higher sphere.

Or this:

> *We* do not ask a longer term of strife,
>   Weakness and weariness and nameless woes;
> We do not claim renewed and endless life
>   When this which is our torment here shall close,
> An everlasting conscious inanition!
> We yearn for speedy death in full fruition,
>   Dateless oblivion and divine repose.

That "dateless oblivion and divine repose" sings itself in my memory still with an imperishable cadence. Almost every verse of this long poem has the same high finish; it would puzzle one to find a weak stanza. (pp. 158-60)

After living in that terrible **"City"** for weeks I dug up a good many of Thomson's translations and critical essays and found everywhere the same masculine grasp of truth and deep comprehension of all high gifts and qualities. A critic's value is not to be gauged by his agreement with the established estimates of great men, but by the degree in which he can enlarge and enrich these secular judgments of humanity. And if he cannot rise to this height he should be esteemed for the alacrity with which he discovers and proclaims men of genius neglected in his own time.

I still remember the surprise I felt when Thomson wrote his essay on **"The Poems of William Blake,"** and allayed my fears by beginning with praise of the "magnificent prose as well as poetry" in the book.

I don't set much store on his high and just praise of Blake, for already Dante Rossetti, at least, if not Swinburne, had been before him in appreciation, but when he wrote on the ''Improvisations from the Spirit,'' by Garth Wilkinson, Thomson had no forerunners, to my knowledge, yet his understanding is just as complete and his eulogy as finely balanced. He wrote about Wilkinson's work as ''A Strange Book''; he does not for a moment accept his mysticism and again and again points out that these ''improvisations'' might be bettered by a little painstaking and self-criticism. On the whole, his praise is more than generous, though finely qualified. (pp. 161-62)

Thomson was, perhaps, the first to tell us that the passion of the creative artist, the wish to do our work, to mould the gold in us into perfect form, is one of the chief incentives to living:

> So potent is the Word, the Lord of Life,
>   And so tenacious Art,
> Whose instinct urges to perpetual strife
>   With Death, Life's counterpart;
> The magic of their music, might and light,
> Can keep one living in his own despite.

A year or so later I was staying at Argenteuil, near Paris, when I read of Thomson's death, and the curt posthumous notices showed that he had practically drunk himself to death. (p. 168)

Frank Harris, ''James Thomson,'' in his Contemporary Portraits, second series, *Frank Harris, 1919, pp. 158-78.*

JEANNETTE MARKS (essay date 1926)

[Marks argues that Thomson's poetry is marred by imitation, but affirms the value of a few great, dark works.]

[Meredith] wrote after Thomson's death:

> He probably had, as most of us have had, his heavy suffering on the soft side. But he inherited the tendency to the things which slew him. And it is my opinion that, in consideration of his high and singularly elective mind, he might have worked clear of it to throw it off, if circumstances had been smoother and brighter about him. For thus he would have been saved from drudgery, have had time to labor at conceptions that needed time for the maturing and definition even before the evolvement of them. He would have had what was also much needed in his case, a more spacious home, a companioned life, more than merely visiting friends, good and true to him though they were. A domestic center of any gracious kind would have sheathed his overactive, sensational imaginativeness, to give it rest, and enable him to feel the delight of drawing it forth bright and keen of edge.

These are the best and wisest words that have been written about James Thomson. Yet I cannot agree with them.

Youth spends all its strength and makes most of its mistakes in trying to come into closer contact with the lives of others, trying indeed to escape into the life of another,—the age old presumption of youth with its bubble of possession and its obliviousness to that separateness, that ''deep ordained'' strangeness we bear one to another. This is the solitude which comes with the years. How would the nature of James Thomson have borne this inevitable realization? What would it have done

to the balance of Thomson's forces? Sent them forward as a blow sends a valiant nature forward? Or struck them down as a blow will do to a nature less valiant? The outlook for dipsomania is not good,—and his was a genuine case of dipsomania, an entailment from his father. If Matilda Weller had lived, would not the struggle have involved two rather than setting free one? Would his have been the commonplace heroism which knows that it is harder to live and make the best of life than to die and find escape? . . . The way in which his mind returns to Matilda as life goes on is just the psychology of the man dying in the desert of thirst, in his eyes the mirage of a remembered oasis. Matilda was fourteen when she died and Thomson was eighteen. G. W. Foote writes: ''I do not agree with Mr. Dobell in regarding this bereavement as the *cause* of his lifelong misery. She was, I hold, merely the peg on which he hung the raiment of his sorrow; without her, another object might have served the same purpose. He carried with him his proper curse, constitutional melancholia.'' The nature and the symbol of sorrow in Thomson's poetry assuredly have the quality of an *idée fixe* with its touch of the abnormal. Even his very pseudonym ''B. V.'' (Bysshe Vanolis) ''Bysshe'' commemorates Shelley and ''Vanolis'' Novalis the German lyric poet, Friedrich von Hardenberg, who lost his beloved, also named Matilda. One feels that this carefully maintained devotion after death has in it the quality of imitation and that it is shot through, not with fact and experience and a great vision of love as part of life, but with sentimentality. There is some delegated emotion here not wholly his own.

This quality of imitation is felt in James Thomson's art. His early poetry shows no approach, no traits of emotion, no thought different from any other young poet adequately gifted with sensuous perceptions. There are immaturities in Keats, Shelley, Coleridge, in their earliest poetry, but great gifts too. In James Thomson's *Juvenilia* there are immaturities but no great gifts. . . . These *Juvenilia* in essays and verse might be entitled ''Echoes from Swift, Keats, Shelley, Arnold, Rossetti, and Tennyson.'' Even the very titles of the essays are imitative—as, for example—**''Proposals for the Speedy Extinction of Evil and Misery''** with its Swiftlike sound; and of his poems, to take a single illustration, **''Ronald and Helen.''** It would seem that many who bear the name of poet exercise what must be called the executive, which in art is craftsmanship, rather than the creative faculty. William Morris has power to swing and shape lines, to assemble, to retell. He can scarcely be said to create. The creative faculty is something deeper than the executive: it is slow of growth, stamped with originality, marked often by inequalities. There is a pleasant executive faculty in Thomson's **''Weddah,'' ''Vane's Story,''** and other poems. The bulk of Thomson's work is more extensive than that of Keats. It cannot be said that there is not enough by which to judge it. Here is nothing, unless it be by imitation of those flame-shod feet of Shelley, nothing of the clairvoyant transcendentalism of Wordsworth, nothing of the phantasmagoric power of Coleridge, in their youth. And no where in this young poetry is there a love poem so perfect as Keats' ''La Belle Dame Sans Merci.'' I do not find anything worthy the name of ''great'' either in promise or in achievement in James Thomson's poetry except **''In the Room,'' ''The City of Dreadful Night,''** possibly **''Insomnia.'' ''Up the River,'' ''Weddah,'' ''Vane's Story,''** and a few other poems which have been so exaggeratedly praised are attractive here and there—charming poetry it might be called, but assuredly not considerable. Some critics of James Thomson have been too trustful of what others have said.

Even in progression and grouping, as in **"The Dead Year,"** as well as in word and sound, many of his poems bear every mark of close imitation of Shelley. But where Shelley blazes cometlike or is ethereal, Thomson is confused or high-falutin' or both. Yet Thomson was twenty-seven when he wrote his poem about **"Shelley"** and thirty when he wrote **"Ronald and Helen."** In other words at an age when not only Shelley's youthful work but *all* his work was done. Thomson wrote with the uncertain hand of the tyro. At twenty-seven he was one year older than Keats when all Keats' work was finished. His attempt at Shelley translucence, the boat, the sea, the storm, the phantoms, the sense of being driven and hunted, the hysterical despair, are all dyed in Shelley's color of word and thought. In **"The Doom of a City"** the lyrics and the long-drawn-out cadence of "Oh, wait!" are unmistakably Shelley-like. Even the quick change from one stanza form to another is imitative of Shelley in his longer work. I suppose there is a degree beyond which imitation is not a wholesome sign. In my opinion Thomson reached and passed that degree.

The vocabulary of these Shelley imitations is interesting. Thomson gives again so many of Shelley's actual words and phrases: as, for example, in the poem called **"Shelley"**:— "vultures of despair," "fierce ambition," "Promethean gloom," "vision," "universal ether," "life and light and music," "heavy with anguish," "blind with blood and tears," "pant after them," and so on. He "swoons," of course, like Shelley. It is not unpleasant to find Shelley "swooning,"—he should to be Shelley. And he was so very charming. But this compact muscular little poet with his touch of the Cockney, that is different! In Thomson's case the swoons "melt him." They never did melt Shelley: he continued to soar. But, somehow, in **"Ronald and Helen,"** one feels as if the liquefaction of James Thomson had become vast, almost final. Possibly it is only the liquefaction of youth.

He used words and phrases Shelley could not under any circumstances have used, "paths steep and drear," "happy home," "laggard feet," "healing balm," "billows rage," "tempests blow," "pure peace below," "harp strings," "palm branch," "noble fight," "enduring all," "holy visions blest," "sharp wounds," "love and life and bliss,"—undoubtedly Irvingite influence. One is not without a sense of wicked amusement in contemplating Shelley strewn over with all this wreckage of a sentimental, outworn hymnology! This collection of phrases is sufficient to prove that if on one who had capacity for powerful poetry, sentimental hymns could have so disastrous an effect, their harmfulness to those with less capacity is too widespread to measure. The time should come when anything so important to the human race as its hymns should be censored. In his poem called **"Suggested by Matthew Arnold's 'Stanzas from the Grande Chartreuse',"** Thomson gravely discusses "Conquerors of the Promised Land." Imagine Arnold's state of mind upon discovering this introduction of the "Promised Land" into his thought and his poetry! And he indulges in such Victorianisms as "feeble limbs" when he means weak legs, and such verbal properties as "fountain" are never long absent from his poems,—not even from **"The City of Dreadful Night."** In the Shelley imitations the last injury to those who love words sensitively is given in **"Ronald and Helen"** where Thomson writes: "Life's faded flowers." Wordsworth never talked about "Life's faded flowers." Shelley never did. Keats never did. One can only wish that nobody ever had!

He was a man thirty years old when he wrote some of this. It is totally without distinction. One reads on and on wearily wondering what much of it is about; nothing clear-etched; nothing firm,—just "poetry" that beats its varying rhythms with the help of trite phrases, tedious sentimentality, blurred meanings. In the lesser poems the only memorable passages are those which have the strength of experience. It is as if at once his verse becomes better where suffering cuts into him and mixes with him the only originality he possesses. As suffering creates his greatness, fustian phrases and cliché words drop away. Atrocities, too, there are, the odious pausing for a pun in the midst of some solemn thought. In art the trivial almost vulgar touch on a great subject is not lightly forgiven. And it should never be forgotten in any appraisal of James Thomson as an artist that in **"Vane's Story"** he was capable of such a line as "The music 'gan again arise." Beating on a tin can could not be worse. Or those atrocious lines from **"Ronald and Helen"**:

> But, O my steamer, how you crawl!
> I would your horse-power were a horse indeed,
> Thin-flanked and spur-able!

They were followed on the next page by:

> A letter she had read a hundred times,
> And still found always new,—like some old song,
> Some old sweet song of simple passionate rhymes,
> And more than mortal tenderness—a lay
> Fit for a wedding and a dying day.

This is good, musical, simple, genuine, very human. One remembers as one reads the music of Wordsworth's "Solitary Reaper":

> Will no one tell me what she sings?—
> Perhaps the plaintive numbers flow
> For old, unhappy, far-off things,
> And battles long ago.

And the comparison still leaves one with a liking for Thomson's lines.

One feels everywhere the loose articulation of these poems, their flabby sinews, their anemic blood. Of the thing that is hard or clear or perfectly shaped his poems have nothing. Like the poetry of William Morris, they come too easily. Thomson labels his divisions Part I, Part II, Part III, and so on in **"Ronald and Helen."** But they divide nothing. There is not enough structure to mark anything by division. He passes from one lyric form to another. But that too means nothing. He was writing this poem between the ages of 27 and 30. Had he been a great artist, having finished it at 30, he would have flung it away. In that Thomson destroyed personal papers which he thought might embarrass others he was a gentleman in the only and democratic sense in which that word is valid for an American. Confidence in him as an artist would be greater if he had destroyed such lethal stuff as some of his verses are.

So much of the speech of James Thomson is of the old and tattered garments of an outworn poetry,—or supposedly "poetical" speech. It is difficult to analyze why all this seems so feeble. It is not alone that it is unforgivably sentimental but it seems so without point. It rumbles with sound and rolls on and on as if the ear of the one who made it reveled in its empty reverberations. There is, however, a kind of wide-mouthed emptiness of meaning about many of the poems that makes one feel alcohol already at work blurring thought and outlines of form, nevertheless boisterously congratulating itself on the achievement of great work. This is the old, old trick of overstimulation.

There is about Thomson's imitations of Tennyson a certain "accepted" use of words; the tawdry domestic; the vulgar Cockney,—a sort of unprivileged Tennysonianism, these lodging house miller's daughters, these inexpensive princesses,—this well-bustled and well-corseted muse. True, in Thomson's **"A Real Vision of Sin,"** we find him throwing himself against Tennyson. But he is more often imitative than critical of him. Curiously enough the author of **"The City of Dreadful Night"** was capable of close absorption through Tennyson and other poets not only of that sentimentality with which we seek to put blinders on the truth, but also of trite optimistic moralizing,—a type of sentimental poem so dear to the heart of the English nation that it might be called a "box office" success! In **"Bertram"** he wrote:

> My mind, long world-filled, was empowered to see
> That Life has sacred mysteries unrevealed,
> And grander trusts than Earth and Time can yield.

This is indeed one of those platitudes which leave one with nothing to say! It was against the sentimental moralizing characteristics of English poetry that Thomson rebelled, yet he was capable of this! It is the misfortune of the imitative tendency that it is altogether too likely to retain the weakness rather than the strength of that which it follows, for strength is largely self-made. Of the great artist at work, as Tennyson was, Thomson seems to have perceived but little,—not even the delicacy with which Tennyson will grip some detail of the commonplace.

Other influences besides Shelley, Arnold, Tennyson, we have in Thomson's poetry: Poe, Blake, the Bible, Keats, Rossetti, Browning, and, it is said, Meredith. Of Poe's "Raven" there is Thomson's constant use of its refrain; of Blake here or there a bit of philosophy or the lisp of some little lyric or such a line as this from **"The City of Dreadful Night,"** "If tigers burn with beauty and with might;" of the Bible, its rhythm in some stately line of poetry or prose; of Keats some gleam of jeweled color; of Rossetti some suggestion of the great artist's sense of form, as in **"The Purple Flower of the Heather."** On Thomson's poetry, Browning's influence is not marked, but the amount of prose Thomson devotes to Browning is large. I do not know that I can account for the fact that there is so little evidence of Browning's influence in Thomson's poetry when in his thoughts he is so prominent. (pp. 93-104)

Thomson tells us that the only true or inspired poetry is always from within, not from without,—that is, a good poem cannot be created with the mind alone. "Ah then," we say, "so he knew that!" Yes, he knew that,—he knew several of the inmost secrets of great creative work. In his essay on **"Whitman"** he wrote: "To speak in literature with the perfect rectitude and *insouciance* of the movements of animals, and the unimpeachableness of the sentiment of trees in the woods and grass by the roadside, is the flawless triumph of art." This is wonderful and true. But it was never true of Thomson except where, as in the case of **"The City of Dreadful Night,"** he paid his very life for what was produced. He sins so often as an artist. The words he uses are sometimes as ludicrous as buttons sewed on in wrong places. The unusual word in Thomson seldom becomes part of the whole garment of the artist. Thomson shows himself rather the amateur at work. Let it be remembered that the word means "loving," for Thomson loved what he did. He is like a child making a collection of buttons that please him for their individual colors or shapes. But like poppy seed for narcotizing his meaning, he scatters such words as "treen," "brigue," "pereceant," "eyne," "colure," "ænomel" about in his poems,—delightful, no doubt, as a course in Middle

English or in "Gothick" influence, but no part of the texture of his poem as such. There is a fine verbal simplicity about good poetry. Yet Thomson seeks trophies of the erudite or the obsolete. There is nothing applied externally in great poetry to its fabric woven in one piece from heart and mind. A word is precious because of its human value. It can have no other value; in science as service; in common speech as community of interest; in art as revelation and healing. The instant a word is so used that it robs its context of *human* value, that instant there is loss of power. Indeed his "error" as artist goes deeper than the attachment of button trophies to the garment of his work. For me the great error of even his greatest work lies in a certain point of view, for in the very instance of his most impressive poem, **"The City of Dreadful Night,"** I detect the quality of one who sees life as an intellectually gifted and tragically condemned member of the Salvation Army might see it, rather than as pure poet. (pp. 105-06)

Is it accident or a sort of composite significance of all his work that so often makes a poet known chiefly by one poem? I feel that it is composite significance. In his greatest poems, **"In the Room," "The City of Dreadful Night"** and **"Insomnia,"** James Thomson works free from imitation of any one. No, even at this instant my eyes see the form and my ears hear the cadence of the stanzas of Tennyson's "The Two Voices." Thomson died on June 3, 1882. Between the writing of **"Insomnia"** and his death, he had two spring months in which to travel his *via crucis,*—April and May, months most beloved of the poets. I find nothing of James Thomson's equal to **"The City of Dreadful Night"** in power of thought; in impressive imagery, dull or flashing, but always full of doom; and in sustained firmness of form. **"Insomnia"** touches it; **"In the Room"** is kin to it; but no other poem of Thomson's equals it. This thought of the "City" may be said to be peculiarly Thomson's own, unless some suggestion for it came to him through his adoration for Shelley. It haunted Thomson in **"The Doom of a City,"** written when he was twenty-three. It is ever present in prefigurative imagery in his essay **"Our Lady of Sorrow,"** written ten years before **"The City of Dreadful Night."** (pp. 110-11)

It is a mystery to know why in art one thing is good and another bad. But in art it is not a problem of that which is shop-work and that which is not, so much as it is a question of that which remains plastic and that which has become fixed. So much of **"The City of Dreadful Night"** is the poetry of thought. In respect of its art it is a bigger poem than Tennyson's "Two Voices." Great poetry works outward from itself. The outward movement of Tennyson's "Two Voices" is imperceptible; its self-analysis holds it in bondage. Argumentation does not make verse. But the supreme power of Thomson's **"City of Dreadful Night"** lies in the fact that personal tragedy sets the poet free. And his line does indeed "march under a banner." But that "banner" is pessimism, sinister destiny, what you will. . . . (p. 112)

Tennyson's "Two Voices" tells us that life and love are worth living because they continue in another world beyond the senses. Thomson answers quite differently; and in lines that might well be satire on Tennyson:

> It leads me back
> From this accursed night without a moon,
> And through the deserts which have else no track,
> And through vast wastes of horror-haunted time,
> To Eden innocence in Eden's clime:

Or these lines strangely suggestive of Tennyson's golden art, but about the meaning of which there is no mistaking:

> The world rolls round forever like a mill;
> It grinds out death and life and good and ill;
> It has no purpose, heart or mind or will.

Indeed **"The City of Dreadful Night"** might be called Thomson's answer to the material of Tennyson's "Two Voices" and *In Memoriam*. Yet out of the conflict in each of these poems how different the "voice": in the one the soul that comes to know itself through struggle, to know how distinct it is from the body, conscious of an illimitable future rending the shards of its old self for flight in an eternity of time; the other with its terrible response, waking from "day dreams to a real night" of "dead Faith, dead Love, dead Hope!" Hear these two voices:

> Cry, faint not, climb: the summits slope
> Beyond the furthest flights of hope
> Wrapt in dense cloud from base to cope.

And Thomson:

> Nay, does it treat him harshly as he saith?
> It grinds him some slow years of bitter breath,
> Then grinds him back into eternal death.

Even in this only citadel of his greatest poem—the sole creation we could hope to call wholly and adequately his own—there is too close analogy between intellectual inquiry and outward form to leave us any choice, but still to place Thomson among the imitative. How was it that Meredith, the master, did not himself feel this closeness? The correspondence between certain portions of **"The City of Dreadful Night"** and Tennyson's "Two Voices" is not merely that of terza rima, of a similar subject, of figures much alike. The correspondence goes deeper than that: it is dependence,—the dependence of James Thomson on Alfred Tennyson. There must always be similarities, debts of poet to poet, of thinker to thinker, even "properties" as, for example, in the pastoral. Yet there is no question of undue dependence of Shelley or Arnold, let us say, on Theocritus, Bion, and Moschus. **"The City of Dreadful Night"** is a more powerful poem than "The Two Voices." Both its figures and its imaginative quality are greater. I think Thomson felt, as many have felt, the inner weakness of "The Two Voices." Yet he had neither the intellectual nor the spiritual strength to travel further than Tennyson. And setting his goal beyond that of Tennyson and failing to reach it, the whole poem becomes enfeebled by failure. (pp. 113-16)

It was tragedy reagent that kept James Thomson from sinking into the fat lethargies of English sentimental poetry. Had destiny touched him with a gentler hand he would have sought in self-expression one of two extremes, shallow and optimistic sentimentality or mordant satire,—both moods disturbed reflexes of what is the truth. The great work—and there can be no question but that **"The City of Dreadful Night"** has the quality of greatness—that Thomson did was hewn out through the agency of his own tragedy. This is a clear case of where through the reagency of tragedy disaster has *made* poetry. One has only to study the dates of Thomson's poems to see at work in them—for Thomson—the master shaping hand of his tragedy. His habits were destroying him, but they were shaping his poetry into a terrible graven image of human sorrow like unto Thomson's own. For Thomson, always, the "real night" was alcoholism, not opium taking. I feel that—if it may be said that disease can make even its pain contribute to beauty and no one has yet been able to prove that it does not—I feel

that it is the morbid experience of alcohol which does more for Thomson than opium did, in any relation, in deepening, when he is at his highest as an artist, that rough magnificence of terror in his poetry. The poems he wrote while he had a fair degree of health have no value. I am drawing no conclusions. I am merely stating facts. (pp. 121-22)

Jeannette Marks, "Disaster and Poetry," in her Genius and Disaster: Studies in Drugs and Genius, *second edition, Adelphi Company, 1926, pp. 77-126.*

MORTON DAUWEN ZABEL (essay date 1928)

[*Zabel was an American poet, critic, and scholar. From 1928 to 1937 he was associate editor, then editor, of Harriet Monroe's magazine* Poetry, *which was the only journal at that time devoted solely to contemporary poetry. Here, he focuses on two primary characteristics of Thomson's verse: its derivativeness and its powerful evocation of despair and desolation.*]

[In Thomson's] work two unmistakable traits may be discerned: on the one hand, a lame imitative servility; and on the other, a profound impassioned desolation in the face of the world's confusions. The first quality accounts for Thomson's obscurity among the secondary figures of nineteenth-century poetry. It is in his aping of the grandiose forms, the blatant symbolism, and the windy eloquence of the later romantics that his weaknesses lie. When he wrote **"Vane's Story"** or **"Weddah and Om-el-Bonain,"** he was attempting to project his feeble historical sense into themes for whose development he had little aptitude. Although his subtler sensibilities appear in various lines, particularly where he allows himself to speak in accents of quiet reflective candor, the general effect of such poems is unfortunate. They appear as inflated copies of Blake or William Morris, lacking the structural variety and imaginative vigor of the one and the descriptive range of the other.

But in showing his other quality, Thomson gives us his truer self. Desolation is commonly regarded as a stock-in-trade of poets; but when this despair prevails unduly it awakens a real suspicion. We demand justification for unmitigated sorrow in the actual experience, and we never wholly sanction Matthew Arnold's or Thomas Hardy's oppression of heart, because their physical lives deny the bitterness of which their spirits made a cry. But Thomson put up a miserable protest against his surroundings, and he failed to improve them. His life, beginning with the foundling hospital, continued through various episodes in vagrancy and disgrace to his wretched death.

Yet he saw beauty in the classics:

> O antique fables!—for a little light
> Of that which shineth in you evermore!

And in moments of clean singing health he expressed a happy response to life with its vigorous joys and ever-tantalizing mysteries, particularly in the graceful songs he put together under the title **"Sunday up the River"**:

> We will rush ever on without fear;
>   Let the goal be far, the flight be fleet!
> For we carry the heavens with us, dear,
>   While the earth slips from our feet!

And in the earlier part of his career, while he was still groping for his convictions through the underwoods of surprise and incredulity, he was able, in poems like **"A Festival of Life,"** to temper his resentment by recognizing a source of final truth:

> This is the Vision solely,
> Trancing all aspirations with content!
> Beauty all-perfect, blessedness all-holy,
> Are veiled beyond that crystal firmament.
> The breathless concave yearneth to the hymn
> Of all the hosts of stars and seraphim;
> The hallelujah's raptured monotone. . . .

But this was before the exact key of that monotone fixed itself in his mind. During the heavy hours he describes in **"Insomnia,"** or through the sorrows which in **"To Our Ladies of Death"** he addressed in terms of De Quincey's symbolism, he gradually came to hear the one supreme sound that echoed in every corner of the world. It was the song of grief rising out of man's ignorance, the hymn of a mysterious futility with which his own spirit found her essential harmony:

> My mirth can laugh and talk, but cannot sing;
> My grief finds harmonies in everything.

Realizing his plight with a pathetic sincerity . . . , he set about recasting an early work, **"The Doom of a City,"** which in its final version we know as his masterpiece, **"The City of Dreadful Night."**

Here is the Victorian's deepest confession of despair, his acknowledgment of those realities around whose laws so much confusion had been thrown. It is a rejection of all Will and Mind from the universe, the victory of that negation which hovers like a threat over the period. In the stanzas whose appeal to us now is damaged by their verbosity and heavy pomp, we see what an Inferno a sensitive weakling made of his environment. The imagery of the dreadful city is Thomson's one design of real mastery: the dark stronghold of denials, mysteries, and dispirited fancies, shot through, at times, by a saving light, but in the end brooding eternally on the banks of its River of Death. In the massive pictorial effect, built as it is out of dreams and longings, a strong insight defines itself. The distorted prospects and vistas over which Melancholia presides give a panorama of nightmare and delusion, it is true, but the poem mounts unforgettably toward the somber majesty of grief. In the city the poet sees men destined,

> The strong to drink new strength of iron endurance,
> The weak new terrors; all, renewed assurance
> And confirmation of the old despair.

But he is that city's lonely hero, realizing his isolation and knowing that his fellows never admit the idea of brotherhood or the leadership of new wisdom.

His book, in its finest pages, wins our pity, for its outline is not weak, its intention is rarely hindered by self-deception, and it escapes that fallacy of spiritual compromise—the note of the "somehow good"—which is the surest clue to human dishonor. Thomson's great contemporaries achieved their stature through unequivocal affirmation, and if we place his lament beside their stauncher testaments of victory, it is because he, failing where they succeeded, honored the same truth, the same conviction and integrity of spirit. He left a sheaf of poems which discern profoundly one aspect of experience in his age, and often anticipate, in form and attitude, a new and braver art. (pp. 230-33)

> *Morton Dauwen Zabel, "James Thomson," in Poetry, Vol. XXXII, No. 1, July, 1928, pp. 229-33.*

JOHN HEATH-STUBBS (essay date 1950)

[*An English poet and critic, Heath-Stubbs has written studies on John Dryden, Charles Williams, and—in his* The Darkling Plain— *a number of neglected Victorian writers. In the following excerpt from that work, he argues that "The City of Dreadful Night" is preeminent among Thomson's verse, considering it in light of poems by several major writers.*]

In Arnold and Clough we encounter a characteristic Victorian mentality—that of the Wistful Unbeliever, unable to square his intellectual convictions with the traditional faith he has lost, whose passing he continually mourns. From such an attitude—fundamentally inconsistent and sentimental—great poetry cannot be expected to spring. Something more strenuously intellectual, a recapturing of lost metaphysic, or a more desperate and courageous denial, were necessary. In one poem of the [Victorian] period, this absolute rejection, not only of faith, but also of hope, is made; and **"The City of Dreadful Night,"** approaches, in my opinion, near to being great poetry. (p. 111)

[Thomson's] poems, other than **"The City of Dreadful Night,"** do not call for much serious consideration. Some may be regarded as imperfect essays in the mood of his masterpiece. His lighter verses, such as **"Sunday up the River"** and **"Sunday at Hampstead"** sometimes sink to incredible depths of vulgarity:

> My shirt is of the soft red wool,
> My cap is azure braided,
> My two white hands so beautiful,
> My tie mauve purple-shaded.
>
> It is not brandy, it is not wine,
> It is Jameson's Irish whisky:
> It fills the heart with joy divine,
> And makes the fancy frisky.

But I am not sure that these "Idylls" have not also an absurd kind of charm. Their tawdry imagery and sentiment really do render the cockney jocularity and the pathos of the poor clerks and shop-girls who are the characters—liberated for a few brief hours from the monotony and ugliness of their working lives. Nevertheless, it is impossible to rate them very high as poetry.

"The City of Dreadful Night" stands in a class by itself. It has qualities which makes it unique in the poetry of the century—a link between the last point of development reached by the earlier Romantics, and that reunion of concrete image and symbol and direct intellectualization which is achieved in the best of modern poetry. The reassertion by the Romantics of the infinite scope of the human imagination—that imagination which since the death of Milton had tended to become more and more restricted by the social-rhetorical conventions of Augustan poetry—had coincided with a rediscovery of the greatness of the poetry of the Middle Ages and the Renaissance. Not only were the merits of earlier English poetry brought into prominence, but that of the Italians also. Leigh Hunt's influence was one of the factors which led the younger Romantic poets of his circle to the study of Dante. Cary's well-known translation of the whole of the *Divine Comedy* (1814)—which so unfortunately distorts Dante's style, misrepresenting it by an elaborate Miltonic manner—must also be taken into account. The influence of Dante can be seen in many places in Shelley's poetry, and in Keats's "Fall of Hyperion." But only in the latter poem, and in Shelley's "Triumph of Life" do we detect these two English poets, at the very end of their lives, finding their way to a method, allegorical and yet more than merely allegorical, whereby, as in Dante himself, the dream-images of romantic fancy are related organically to a conscious metaphysic, and a unity of sensibility is achieved. But after the death of Shelley and Keats, their Victorian successors for the most part neglected to develop this method, and contented themselves with using the romantic imagery in a merely decorative manner, bearing no relation to their intellectual aspirations. Thomson, in **"The City of Dreadful Night,"** is the one notable exception. His style, to a large extent, derives directly from that of Shelley, but he follows the direction indicated by the unfinished "Triumph of Life," and has rid himself of the sensuous vagueness and diffuseness which were the main faults of his master. Though, of course, it is on an infinitely smaller scale, and cannot for one moment be compared to it either for range or profundity, **"The City of Dreadful Night"** does really approach nearer, as regards atmosphere, to the *Inferno* of Dante than does any other English poem.

Besides Shelley and Dante two other poets are known strongly to have influenced Thomson—Novalis and Leopardi. The German poet is akin to Thomson in his worldweariness, his symbolism of Night, and that whereby he erected the figure of the girl he had loved and lost in early youth to a central position in his poem. From Leopardi (whose prose works he translated, and on whom he wrote an essay comparing him with Pascal) Thomson took his intellectual pessimism, though it is interesting to note how the latter has become cruder and more violent in the work of the Scotch poet, as compared with the classical, quasi-Lucretian point of view of Leopardi. (pp. 113-15)

Both in form and style **"The City of Dreadful Night"** is strikingly different from all other Victorian poems. It consists of a series of cantos written in an eight-line stanza, descriptive of the City itself, which alternate with episodes composed in a variety of different metres. This structure gives to the whole poem a unity akin to that of symphonic music, while at the same time opportunities are given for the introduction of passages whose forms are subjectively determined.

The style and diction have been stigmatized as flat—and so they will seem to those who look only for the thrilling evocative phrases, whose taste has been formed by a preference for the self-conscious richness of imagery provided by Tennyson. In fact, the style of Thomson's poem, though unequal and not always free from the crudities of his early work, is in general excellent. The verse has a slow, sonorous movement, produced largely by the skilful placing of Latin polysyllables. The language is largely free from affectation and inversions. The poet's visual sensibility is acute, and the imagery he employs is always precise and concrete; there is little vague rhetoric. The apparent plainness arises from the pictorial method characteristic of Thomson. He builds up, often through a number of stanzas, a single visual image, often of a striking magnitude, and it is these images which are the units of his poetry. In this he is akin to the mediæval poets who followed the method of allegory—a tradition carried on by Spenser. (p. 116)

Thomson was able to make use of the plainest words without falling into flatness, partly, no doubt, through his study of the crystalline Italian of Dante and Leopardi, but also, I think, because of the extreme consistency of his intellectual position. His utter rejection of religious belief becomes itself a sort of inverted dogma, and he is able to use words as precisely, and with as accurate and significant effect as the mediæval poets who wrote with the force of a universally accepted metaphysic underlying their use of language.

This leads us to one of the most remarkable features of the poem. Although it deliberately rejects all religious faith, and

there is none of the sentimental repining of Arnold, Clough, or Hardy, this poetry is itself the product of a religious mind. In describing the city of dreadful night into which nineteenth-century scientific scepticism had driven him, Thomson unconsciously defines a state, where, in theological terms, God is immanent, but where his power is not actively revealed—precisely the character given in orthodox doctrine to Hell itself. The continual protest of his spirit against the City implies the existence of its opposite; and everywhere a kind of inverted religious symbolism is detectable.

In the passage following immediately upon the section in which Thomson gives his first general description of the City, one marked feature of his style is immediately apparent. Though the poem is represented as a dream, the images have an extraordinary concreteness and reality of detail. The City, with its "great piers and causeways, many noble bridges", its streetlamps which always burn, is a modern, nineteenth-century industrial city—the Glasgow of Alexander Smith's terrible poem, or the London of Thomson's later sufferings—seen through the darkened curtain of nightmare; not merely a romantic, hazy place where:

> Shrines and palaces and towers—
> Time-eaten towers that tremble not—
> Resemble nothing that is ours

—as in Poe's "City of the Sea." It is this bringing together of the dream-symbol and the object of waking experience which gives to Thomson's poem a power not found in the dream-poetry of Shelley and Keats, and links him to the mediæval writers of allegory. Dante displays the same detailed preciseness, and makes continually a like direct reference to the scenery and landscape of the normal world with which his readers were familiar, in describing Hell.

In this same Canto an atmosphere not only of gloom and hopelessness but also of sterility is suggested by the "salt tides" of the river that surrounds the city, the "waste marshes" that "shine and glitter to the moon" beyond, the trackless wilderness that lies to the north and west. Pictures such as these make up the main theme of the poem, culminating in the great transcription of Dürer's *Melancholia* with which it closes—the vast, brooding mother-figure which is, significantly, the presiding goddess of the place. From these recurring visions the sharp, episodical passages detach themselves, and, miraculously, redeem the poem from monotony. (pp. 116-118)

The preciseness of the intellectual statement conveyed by the last-mentioned episode, the first of the particular incidents with which the poem is diversified is noteworthy:

> As whom his one intense thought overpowers,
> He answered coldly, "Take a watch, erase
> The signs and figures of the circling hours,
> Detach the hands, remove the dial-face,
> The works proceed until run down; although
> Bereft of purpose, void of use, still go."

There is a similar quality in a later episode: the vision of a sculptured angel, winged and holding a sword, which is confronted by a stone sphinx. From the angel fall first its wings, next its sword, leaving it an unarmed man with impotent raised hands. Then the human figure itself crashes to the ground, and lies broken beneath the feet of the implacable and immobile sphinx.

Very different, both from scenes such as the foregoing, and each other are the two passages in which the early death of

Matilda Weller is alluded to. The first is the story told by the traveller who has come through the desert. Here the images of violence and cruelty—the "bleeding eyeless socket" presented by the eclipsed sun, the "hoarse and heavy and carnivorous breath" of distorted animal forms that pursue the speaker and pluck at him from the bushes with "sharp claws, swift talons, fleshless fingers cold"—combine to produce a nightmare atmosphere. Into this enters a figure which seems to promise love—a woman who carries, instead of a lamp, her own bleeding heart. But she vanishes, and bears away the better part of the pilgrim with her, leaving what remains of him only to renewed and augmented despair.

In the second of these two episodes the poet enters a mansion whose windows, in striking contrast to all the others in the City, are ablaze with light. He finds it hung everywhere with images of the same beautiful woman, and finally comes upon a young man who, clasping a crucifix, mourns before the dead body of his beloved, the Lady of the images. The lyric put into his mouth has a simplicity which is exceedingly moving:

> The chambers of the mansion of my heart
> In every one whereof thine image dwells,
> Are black with grief eternal for thy sake.
>
> I kneel beside thee and I clasp the cross,
> With eyes for ever fixed upon that face,
> So beautiful and dreadful in its calm.
>
> I kneel here patient as thou liest there;
> As patient as a statue carved in stone,
> Of adoration and eternal grief.
>
> While thou dost not awake I cannot move;
> And something tells me that thou wilt not wake,
> And I alive feel turning into stone.
>
> Most beautiful were death to end my grief,
> Most hateful to destroy the sight of thee,
> Dear vision better than all death or life.
>
> But I renounce all choice of life or death;
> For either shall be ever at my side,
> And thus in bliss or woe be ever one.

Not only the subject of this scene, but the atmosphere of luxury—the fragrant garden lawn and high trees that surround the mansion, the heavily draped hall, balustrade and broad stairway within—recall many similar passages in Poe's prose. Both men, be it noted, lost their mothers at about the same early age, and the obsession with the death of a beautiful, beloved woman which haunts their work, can, psychologically, doubtless be related to this event, and points to the existence of a similar type of abnormal mentality in both.

Like Poe, Thomson shows us the obverse side of Puritanism (Novalis also had a Puritan upbringing). They take us behind the façade of the century's material prosperity and liberal smugness to a Waste Land whose existence was not yet suspected. The sexual repression and distortions to which the manners of the age conduced had doubtless much to do with this underworld of nightmare. The following lines in **"The City of Dreadful Night"**—

> The phantoms have no reticence at all:
> The nudity of flesh will blush though tameless,
> The extreme nudity of bone grins shameless,
> The unsexed skeleton mocks shroud and pall.

are highly significant. They illuminate not only Thomson's own work, but much else in the literature of an age which loved to dwell upon funerals and death-bed scenes, in which melodrama pervaded novel and poem, and the writing of ghost stories and tales of horror was brought to a fine art.

In the intellectual quality of his poetry Thomson is the superior of Poe—though lacking the peculiar analytical mind revealed in the latter's prose. The ally of Bradlaugh, whatever his failings, avoided the vague aestheticism of the rootless American. In some respects Thomson comes nearer to a greater poet—to Poe's disciple, Baudelaire, another explorer of the underworld. The claim that he was, unconsciously, and by temperament, at bottom a Christian and Catholic spirit, delineating an evil whose very existence implied the possibility of its opposite, has been made for Baudelaire and could be made for Thomson. It is curious to observe on how many occasions the latter makes use of religious imagery—as when, in the vast cathedral which stands in the centre of the City, the inhabitants gather to listen to the words of a prophet; one who has penetrated the ultimate secrets of existence. He has brought back from the beyond a message—not indeed of hope, but only of the certainty of despair; this figure suggests, nevertheless, a kind of inverted Messiah.

Thomson's imaginative vision, like that of his master, Shelley, transcends the crude rationalism which is his intellectual starting-point. Like his own traveller, he strides austere, having neither hope nor fear. Although he does not know it, with his courage he has all but traversed the Darkling Plain. He is within reach of gaining a new intelligible vision of the universe, for which the images of the faith he had abandoned will once more provide a relevant symbolism. (pp. 118-21)

> *John Heath-Stubbs, "The Poetry of Doubt and of Despair," in his* The Darkling Plain: A Study of the Later Fortunes of Romanticism in English Poetry from George Darley to W. B. Yeats, *Eyre & Spottiswoode, 1950, pp. 98-121.*

IMOGENE B. WALKER   (essay date 1950)

[*Walker outlines the philosophical ideas presented in the poetry Thomson wrote between 1862 and 1866, the years he lived in London with the Bradlaugh family.*]

The best known of Thomson's works [written between 1862 and 1866] are his Cockney poems, **"Sunday up the River," "Sunday at Hampstead," "Polycrates," "Shameless," "Low Life,"** and **"Aquatics."** . . . These poems, differing from both his earlier and later verse, show certain common characteristics. The first of these is the subject matter, doubtless suggested by Thomson's associates at the time. At the Secular Society parties his fellow guests were members of the working class, clerks, shopkeepers' assistants, underground guards, seamstresses, charwomen, provisioners. In **"Vane's Story"** he described such a party and the people who attended it:

> The mere tame weekly gathering
> Of humble tradesmen, lively clerks,
> And fair ones who befit such sparks:
> Few merry meetings could look duller;
> No wealth, no grandeur, no rich colour.
> Yet they enjoy it: give a girl
> Some fiddle-screech to time her whirl,
> And give a youth the limpest waist
> That wears a gown to hold embraced.

These are the figures that move through the Cockney poetry, and their activities are its subject.

In all these poems Thomson's approach was impersonal and objective; he wrote of what he saw, not of what he felt or thought. This deviation from his usual attitude he pointed out in a chance but significant remark. When told of a criticism of the colors he had used in describing the costume of a rower in **"Sunday up the River,"** he answered "with a slight sneer," "Do they think *I* ever went rowing in that style? I write what I have seen." Whether his readers liked the characters was a matter of indifference to Thomson; his purpose was to give a photographic picture.

Throughout these poems the tone is the same; to any might be attached the subtitle of **"Sunday at Hampstead,"** "An idle idyll by a very humble member of the great and noble London mob." And the tone is set by the action: the events, usually of a holiday or some part of it, in the life of a pair of young lovers of the working class. A fair sample of the group is **"Sunday up the River"**—more than fair, perhaps, since it contains a few fine lyrics and a few felicitous descriptions.

Ever since their first appearance critics have, in my opinion, consistently overvalued these poems and in their enthusiasm they have ignored two serious faults. In the first place, because the detail is usually photographic rather than significant, as in the case of the "mauve purple shaded" cravat and the red wool shirt to which objection was made, it distracts the reader. And in the second place, the poems are not raised above the commonplace by any depth of emotion or any meaning beyond the surface one. Only in **"Low Life,"** the most successful of the group, did Thomson go below the surface. In it, by means of a short episode, he suggested that man is by nature so egocentric that his sympathies are at best weak, shallow, and short-lived.

In seeking for an explanation of these faults, which are not characteristic of Thomson's other works, I come to an aspect of the poems which has never been pointed out, their reflection of Thomson's attitude towards his own life at the time they were written. This attitude is made clear by more than a half-dozen works but especially in the essay **"Per Contra: The Poet, High Art, Genius."** The essay makes two major points. First, the finest expression of life must be immediate; it is perfect in proportion to its spontaneity. No art is immediate; since it is always mediate, it can never be completely spontaneous. Therefore, art is not the best, the perfect form of expression; the perfect forms are such immediate and spontaneous reactions as laughter, dancing, tears, impulsive physical action. The second of the two points is that "artistry accuses weakness and lack of vitality in the artist." The artist is an artist because he has neither the strength nor the virility to participate actively in life; he stands aloof, not because of circumstances or personal inclination but because a lack in his own nature forces him to do so. (pp. 62-4)

Entirely different from the impersonal Cockney poems are the two frankly personal works, **"Vane's Story"** and **"A Lady of Sorrow."** These, the most significant works of this period, are closely associated with **"The Doom of a City"** and **"To Our Ladies of Death,"** both written before Thomson came to London. In the earlier poems Thomson had expressed for the first time certain of the ideas which were to become parts of his mature philosophy; in these later works he stated the same ideas with more sureness and added to them. **"The City of Dreadful Night"** is, of course, the culmination of all four; in

fact, it might be said that they are but a series of studies leading to that great poem.

Neither **"Vane's Story,"** in verse, nor **"A Lady,"** in prose, is of high literary quality; both show many faults, most serious of which is their structural weakness. This fault is especially obvious in **"Vane's Story,"** a long, episodic piece which fails almost completely to give any sense of unity; the episodes, each treated in a different style, no two of comparable weight, have little in common save the characters, and these are not so handled as to weld the parts into an organic whole.

Of these episodes, that which has engaged the most attention from Matilda-enamored critics is the one wherein Vane (Thomson) likens his life to a fountain hitherto stopped up by dead leaves and stones but now released by an unnamed vision, obviously Matilda. Much more revealing than this romantic allegory, however, is an earlier episode in which Vane and Matilda converse, Matilda questioning and accusing and Vane answering and explaining. In Vane's responses, of course, are the principle autobiographical material and the deepest emotion.

The depth of emotion is expressed by means of a contrast between form and feeling. The use of commonplace, often colloquial, diction, of a half-bantering tone established partially by the diction and partially by light touches of mocking exaggeration, and of undignified couplets and short lines of only three or four feet to convey thoughts on subjects traditionally treated with polysyllabic solemnity gives a first impression of flippant, almost cheap, cynicism. Yet underneath the apparent shallowness there runs a current of sincerity and honesty that is frequently harsh because it is somewhat defensive and somewhat belligerent. (pp. 65-7)

The major idea in this episode is that the laws of the universe are immutable and unconscious of human existence. In **"The Doom of a City"** Thomson had presented one aspect of this concept in his consideration of the indifference of nature to man, but he had shown his reluctance to accept it by insisting at the same time on the idea of a divine plan. Now, seven years later, he expresses the full concept without reservations and emphasizes its deterministic implications. Of these the most important is that in a universe so governed man is not only not perfectible but not even capable of improvement through his own efforts. (p. 67)

The second of the autobiographical works of this period, **"A Lady of Sorrow,"** offers even more material than **"Vane's Story."** This prose phantasy starts out as the story of Thomson's grief at the death of Matilda. He is visited first by the Angel, who comforts him with the hope of reunion after death; but soon she becomes the Siren, symbol of futile rebellion, born of reckless, passionately bitter despair. Shortly, the Siren is replaced by the Shadow, who promises oblivious death. The first two sections, dealing with the Angel and the Siren, are both very short, together making up but one-fifth of the whole, and are of comparatively little interest. The third part, that of the Shadow, however, is worthy of detailed consideration.

The mood of this section, one of weariness of spirit and a longing for the repose of death, is apparent throughout; but its most striking expression is in the litany of death, chanted by the Shadow. This litany, made up of twenty-eight quotations from Plato, the Bible, Chaucer, Shakespeare, Keats, Arnold, and others, all voicing the same deep desire for the peace of death, has a cumulative effect of emotional lassitude, almost exhaustion. One cannot state categorically that such was the predominant mood of Thomson during these years; in fact, an examination of all his writings would seem unquestionably to refute any such assumption. Yet that he had at hand such a collection of quotations on the subject of the peace of death and that the mood permeated a work which he took two years to write bears evidence that this weariness and desire for release was more than a thing of the moment.

It is in this section also that Thomson expressed most directly the philosophic ideas with which he was chiefly concerned during these years. These ideas fall into two groups, one reflecting the earlier stages in the development of his thought and the other looking forward to his final philosophy.

The first group includes two ideas which Thomson had considered, the one only casually, the other seriously, in his efforts to find a substitute for orthodox Christianity. The former is that of reincarnation, touched on briefly in **"To Our Ladies of Death"** and expanded only a little more fully here. That Thomson saw fit to expand it at all at this later date should not, however, be taken as significant; the idea is presented as a picture, the flat monotony and unvarying rhythm of which gives rise to idle wondering but not to considered thought. The other of these earlier ideas is that of pantheism, [which can be] pointed out in **"The Doom"** and **"A Happy Poet."** The expression of it in **"A Lady"** differs from the earlier expressions only in a slight shift of emphasis from the concept of a universal soul to the promise of immortality that lies in that concept.

The second and more important group of ideas in this section of **"A Lady"** Thomson had first expressed in a somewhat hesitant, incomplete form in **"Our Ladies of Death"**; in the phantasy he developed them more fully and expressed them with more sureness. The first of these ideas he derived from the law of the indestructibility of matter: however great may be the physical changes of a substance, every atom of it remains in existence throughout all time. Thus, that which is commonly called the mortal body is in truth immortal. Again and again in the course of his life, Thomson insisted on this concept of immortality. In **"Our Ladies of Death,"** he had written,

> One part of me shall feed a little worm,
> And it a bird on which a man may feed;

In **"A Lady of Sorrow"** he put the same thought into prose: "Let no atom in the world be proud; it is now in the heart of a hero, it may soon be in a serpent's fang. Let no atom in the world be ashamed; it is now in the refuse of a dung-hill, it may soon be in the loveliest leaf of a rose."

The second major idea is that of the omnipotence and unconsciousness of the laws of nature. This idea Thomson handled in different ways in his writings but always as it related to man. In **"The Doom"** he had expressed the thesis that nature was indifferent to man; in **"Vane's Story"** he had emphasized the impotence of man under such laws; in **"A Lady"** he stressed man's insignificance in a universe so ruled. Far from being the center of the universe for whom all things were created, man he now saw as a small and unimportant step in a great order prescribed by the laws of the universe.

> When will you freely and gladly own the truth
> that whatever is born in Time must decay and
> perish in Time? As your race studies fossil rel-
> ics of plant and shell and gigantic animal, so
> shall future existences (to you in their kind in-
> conceivable) study fossil relics of your race.

This concept of man's place in the universe clearly appealed to Thomson, for he expressed it repeatedly and frequently in his later writings.

In addition to the mood and the philosophic ideas presented in **"A Lady,"** the phantasy shows a trait of Thomson's character exhibited throughout his work, though difficult to document by line reference, a trait related equally to his analytical thinking and his imaginative sympathy. In one of the finest prose passages he ever wrote he insisted on his agnosticism: "Know this only, that you can never know; of this only be assured, that you shall never be assured; doubt not that you must doubt to the end—if ever end there be. . . ." Despite his various assertions of atheistic beliefs, this creed he held, both intellectually and emotionally, to be more nearly true than any other. And that he did hold it and permitted it to exercise a restraining influence on his mind and work at all times saved his writings from dogmatism. It is true that he codified his beliefs and wrote of them as though they were indisputable facts; but no passage in his work, however intense in feeling, however positive in form, makes the reader feel that he is being shouted at. Sympathy and tolerance pervade even the most arbitrary sections. It is this attitude of moderation that makes incorrect the use of the word *atheist;* Thomson was not an atheist, he was an agnostic. (pp. 68-72)

> *Imogene B. Walker, in her* James Thomson (B. V.):
> A Critical Study, *Cornell University Press, 1950,*
> *212 p.*

HOXIE NEALE FAIRCHILD (essay date 1957)

[*An American educator, Fairchild is the author of numerous essays and books on literary and religious subjects. His major works include the six-volume* Religious Trends in English Poetry, *in which he traces religious thought and feeling in English poetry from the eighteenth to the twentieth century, and* The Noble Savage: A Study in Romantic Naturalism, *in which he discusses the depiction of the unspoiled primitive life in literature and its relationship to romantic naturalism. In the following excerpt from the former work, Fairchild describes Thomson's intellectual progression toward atheistic negation.*]

James Thomson's unfortunate childhood became firmly linked in his memory with the least attractive manifestations of Christianity. At the Royal Caledonian Asylum, however, the orphan boy supplemented his meager schooling with books which admitted him to a world much pleasanter than his actual environment. At fifteen, Byron was for him the ideal romantic poet, but during the following year Shelley became the polestar. De Quincey, himself a wanderer in the City of Dreadful Night, was another favorite. Fielding, Smollett, and Defoe helped to shape the realistic side of his divided character. In later years romance and renunciation of romance would combine in his admiration for Heine. (p. 456)

In 1851, while serving as an assistant teacher in a village near Cork, he had become engaged to the fourteen-year-old Matilda Weller. Her death in 1853 provided a favorite theme for Thomson's poetry during the next ten years. It gave him his first conclusive evidence of the impotence of man's desires. It also, however, gave him a flattering analogy: by thinking of her as Sophie von Kühn he was able to think of himself as Novalis. He claimed spiritual kinship with both Shelley and Novalis in adopting the pen-name "Bysshe Vanolis" (almost always abbreviated as "B. V."). Whether the loss of Matilda was a major cause of his melancholy or mainly a medium for the release of hitherto unfocused neurotic feelings is a disputed question. I incline strongly to the latter view without being able to substantiate it. That a seventeen-year-old should enter into a ''some day we'll marry'' sort of engagement with a girl of fourteen is not a disquieting circumstance. But a well-adjusted boy does not find his ideal lover in Friedrich von Hardenberg or rest long content with the knowledge that he has a little heavenly soul-bride—especially if he does not believe in heaven. What Thomson writes about the dead Matilda does not sound quite healthy. There is too much talk of her purity, too much uneasiness about his own carnality. He seems to have shrunk from the physical side of love as if it were shameful. He never married and apparently had no sex-life at all. The horse-boat-pipe-girl manliness of ''**Sunday Up the River**'' is factitious. In his attitude toward Matilda, in his alcoholism, and in the general manic-depressive pattern of his nature, he reminds one of Poe. No, there was already something wrong with Thomson when he met Matilda-Sophie-Ulalume. He used her as a love-less way of being ''in love.''

In 1851 he also made friends with an army private who was destined to achieve fame in fields other than military. There is no reason to suppose that Charles Bradlaugh was wholly responsible for Thomson's conversion to secularistic rationalism. By the time they met, the disturbed young schoolmaster had doubtless reacted sharply against what he took to be Christianity. But Bradlaugh introduced him to a well-defined tradition of aggressive unbelief; gave him a cause and comrades, arguments and ammunition, and eventually a sort of trade. At least up to the time of his discharge, however, the dead Matilda claimed Thomson's heart about as strongly as Bradlaugh claimed his brains. She had been more pious than he and had sometimes voiced gentle Gretchen-like distress at her Faust's bold opinions. After her death, her purity and her piety combined to preserve early influences which would otherwise have been cast off without much hesitation. Always in need of something to feel guilty about, he felt guilty about his irreligion. It was a sin. Yet, would not acceptance of her beliefs constitute a sin against reason? Either way he could be sure of sinning. That was something, but not enough.

Hence the poems written between 1853 and 1862 point in several incongruous directions. The somber tone of ''**The Doom of a City**'' predicts that of his masterpiece, but the poem shows him still trying to reconcile the reality of evil with the reality of a benevolent God. In ''**A Recusant**'' he longs to go to church but feels a moral obligation to remain outside:

> How sweet to enter in, to kneel and pray
>   With all the others whom we love so well!
> All disbelief and doubt might pass away,
>   All peace float to us with its Sabbath bell.
>
> Conscience replies, There is but one good rest,
> Whose head is pillowed upon Truth's pure breast.

But the breast of truth, as Thomson conceives of truth, is no less flinty than pure. In 1860 he can derive no ray of hope for human betterment from ''**The Dead Year**'' which has just passed. He tries to rejoice in the ''heathen manhood'' of ''**Robert Burns**'':

> He felt scant need
> Of church or creed,
> He took small share
> In saintly prayer,

> His eyes found food for his love;
> He could pity poor souls condemned to hell,
> But sadly neglected endeavours to dwell
>   With the angels in luck above.

But healthy animalistic paganism was impossible for Thomson. He was never able to suppress his awareness that a godless life is a devaluated life. When he tries to be sheerly naturalistic he shows us nothing but the bestial horrors of ''**A Real Vision of Sin**.'' According to a note penciled by the author on his manuscript, this poem was ''Written in disgust of Tennyson's, which is very pretty and clever, and silly, and truthless.'' The characters in this Zolaesque slice of life are a vile old thieving beggar, his vile old doxy, and their vile old dog, each consumed with hatred of the other two. Urged on by his mate, who possesses a nihilistic philosophy too sophisticated for her station, the old man agrees to commit suicide with her in the nearby stream; but he craftily pulls back at the last moment and leaves her to drown alone. His glee is short-lived, for the dog, whom he has recently beaten, leaps at his throat; they fall into the stream and drown each other.

From such labored loathesomeness Thomson's imagination recoils in quest of some faith which will replace the one he has rejected. A poem of 1855 was ''**Suggested by Matthew Arnold's 'Stanzas from the Grande Chartreuse'**,'' which Thomson regards as a fitting ''dirge for a mighty Creed outworn.'' Part I assumes that Christ is dead; but Part II, in a way which reminds us more strongly of Clough than of Arnold, avers that although ''the great Form'' is dead ''the Divine'' is an undying spirit which requires some new mode of expression. In Part III, however, Thomson fears that no man of this age can be looked to for a modernized revelation. We had better maintain provisional loyalty to the dead Christ ''Till the diviner One appear.''

> Nay,—our adoring love should have
>   More faith than to believe that He,
> Before Another comes to save,
>   Can leave us in blind misery
> Without a Guide: God never can
> So utterly depart from man.
>
> We will move onward!—let us trust
>   That there is life and saving power
> In this dear Form which seems but dust.

If dead *men* can inspire us, he asks, why not a dead *God*? From such pathetic nonsense he rather often turns, during this period, to a pantheism which he vainly attempts to reconcile with both the struggle-for-existence conception of nature and with the religion of humanity. ''**Shelley**'' hails that poet as an angelic spirit sent down from heaven to teach a corrupted world that the Soul of the Universe is ''infinite love for all things that exist.'' How these poor souls gravitate toward Shelley!

Such ideas continued to exert some emotional appeal even after his intellect had rejected them. His admiration for Shelley, Novalis, and—inevitably—for Blake and Whitman was maintained to the end of his life. His tastes, as his critical essays bear witness, were always more affirmatively romantic than his official philosophy. After 1862, however, his gropings toward a romantic substitute-religion are largely though not quite completely abandoned in favor of more thoroughgoing unbelief. (pp. 456-59)

If he was to externalize his deepest self in authentic poetry he must affirm despair, not seek to suppress it. He had reached the point where he could satisfy the romantic desire for power only through a powerful expression of the impossibility of being romantic:

> Because it gives some sense of power and passion
> In helpless impotence to try to fashion
> Our woe in living words, howe'er uncouth.
>
> (pp. 465-66)

[Not] all of the poems which he continues to write in soberer moments are utterly devoid of light. To be sure **"Insomnia,"** devoted to a major theme of his masterpiece, voices the hysterical dread that he alone will be denied the boon of sleep even in the grave. In the **"Proem"** to an unwritten work which might well have been a slightly softer sequel of the **"City,"**

> We stagger under the enormous weight
> Of all the heavy ages piled on us.

And we have lost the illusions which made life endurable for our forebears: "Our world is all stript naked of their dreams." For us there can be "No God . . . / No Heaven . . . / No life beyond death." Our only remaining hope is that of a better life for future generations. If *that* prove a mirage, then there remains

> In all our world, beneath, around, above,
> One only refuge, solace, triumph,—Love,
> Sole star of light in infinite black despair.

At least there is a star. Thomson views the shattered dreams of the past not with the arid glee of a triumphant rationalist but with the sentimental regret of a thwarted romantic, for the **"Proem"** ends:

> O antique fables! beautiful and bright,
> And joyous with the joyous youth of yore;
> O antique fables! for a little light
> Of that which shineth in you evermore,
> To cleanse the dimness from our weary eyes,
> And bathe our old world with a new surprise
> Of golden dawn entrancing sea and shore.
>
> (p. 467)

It is not surprising that Thomson, largely released from doctrinaire commitments and moving further and further into the fragments of his disintegrating nature, should slightly have relaxed the utter pessimism of **"The City of Dreadful Night"** in favor of "wistful yearnings toward unsated loves." Moreover the last seven years of his life do not constitute one unbroken downward plunge. They derive peculiar pathos from gleams of hope like those which sometimes delude the hero of a Greek tragedy just before the catastrophe. Prior to 1874, Thomson lived and wrote in a specialized circle which had little connection with the literary world. Rossetti, with his flair for such discoveries, had read and admired some of his earlier poems, but otherwise Thomson was practically unknown among his peers. **"The City of Dreadful Night,"** however, possessed a power which swept beyond the bounds of the Secularist Society. Men like George Meredith, Philip Marston, Roden Noel, and Bertram Dobell praised the poem and sought his acquaintance. Here was an excellent poet, a sensitive literary critic, an interesting though difficult human being, a wreck well worth salvaging. Just as Thomson approached his nadir, he saw that he had a chance of becoming a reputable man of letters if only he could pull himself together. Through Dobell he published two volumes of verse in 1880 and a volume of prose *Essays and Phantasies* in the following year.

Hence the mixture of real midnight and false dawn in **"The Poet and His Muse."** Oppressed by deepest melancholy, he calls upon the muse to help him sing more joyously. She appears in answer to his summons, but she is no less pale and worn and sad than he. Bitterly she reproaches him:

> Lo, you have ravaged me with dolorous thought
> Until my brain was wholly overwrought,
>   Barren of flowers and fruit;
> Until my heart was bloodless for all passion,
> Until my trembling lips could no more fashion
> Sweet words to fit sweet airs of trembling lyre and lute.

Now she is dead, and ghosts can sing no songs. But the poet refuses to accept her message of despair,

> For lo, this beating heart, this burning brow,
> This spirit gasping in keen spasms of dread,
>   This agony of the sting:
> What soulless clod could have these tears and
>   sobbings,
> These terrors that are hopes, these passionate
>   throbbings?
> Dear Muse, revive! we yet may dream and love and
>   sing!

If he could still feel agony, he had not lost all capacity of feeling joy. So long as his heart leaps in passionate throbbings, Bysshe Vanolis need not admit complete frustration.

Too late. By this time the depressive troughs of the curve were much deeper than the manic peaks were high. **"The Poet and His Muse"** was written in 1882. Before the year was out he had died of intestinal hemorrhage after a six-day bout of drinking. We are told that his last words were so extravagantly blasphemous that no one has ever ventured to print them. I should be quite willing to break the silence if I knew what they were, for in my opinion all facts and ideas about important matters deserve to be in print, no matter how shocking they may be to this person or that. At all events, it is clear that he did not permit himself to be scared into affirming beliefs which he did not possess, and for this he deserves our respect. What God thought (and eternally thinks) about James Thomson is no business of ours, but we are entitled to hope that the Recording Angel may have been directed to file the case under "Invincible Ignorance": the poor soul had so little chance, on this side of the grave, to learn the real meaning of the faith which he denied.

"The City of Dreadful Night" may be lengthy, repetitive, and awkwardly constructed, but it is one of the most powerful poems produced within the nineteenth century. Both before and after 1874, . . . Thomson could write more hopefully in more hopeful moods, but it is right that he should be remembered for his greatest and blackest poem. Its importance for our subject is obvious. Its ideas and feelings are far from unique in this period, but nowhere else are they set forth with such uncompromising intensity of despair. After observing so many attempts to extract from unbelief the satisfactions of belief, we are delighted to meet a good honest atheist who has the courage to write:

> All substance lives and struggles evermore
> Through countless shapes eternally at war,
>   By countless interactions interknit;
> If one is born a certain day on earth,
> All times and forces tended to that birth,
>   Not all the world could change or hinder it.

I find no hint throughout the Universe
Of good or ill, of blessing or of curse;
    I find alone Necessity Supreme,
With infinite Mystery, abysmal, dark,
Unlighted ever by the faintest spark
    For us the flitting shadows of a dream.

Now at last we know where we are. This is rock bottom. Such negation is radical enough to raise the possibility of affirmation.

But this is a strange poem to have been published in a journal devoted to making the godless life attractive. Perhaps Bradlaugh felt that its impressiveness as a statement of thoroughgoing unbelief outweighed the misery which it depicted, or perhaps he could not resist the temptation to show that really "high class" poetry could bloom from the dry soil of the Secularist Society. For whatever reason, he printed in the *National Reformer* a crushingly pessimistic interpretation of the principles which official rationalism advocated as a source of enlightenment, freedom, and happiness:

The world rolls round forever like a mill;
It grinds out death and life and good and ill;
It has no purpose, heart or mind or will.
            .   .   .   .   .   .

Man might know one thing were his sight less dim;
That it whirls not to suit his petty whim,
That it is quite indifferent to him.

Nay, does it treat him harshly as he saith?
It grinds him some slow years of bitter breath,
Then grinds him back into eternal death.

Though probably not many readers of the *National Reformer* were orthodox Comtian Positivists, practically all of them would accept Comte's view of human history as ascending from the religious through the metaphysical to the positive or scientific stage of development. In Section XX of his poem Thomson allegorizes this theory with grimmest irony. The angel (man believing in God), the warrior (man believing in his own powers), and the unarmed man (man believing in nothing) successively collapse in impotence before the steady gaze of the sphinx. The symbolism of the sphinx herself is complex. She is "Necessity Supreme," but she is also "infinite Mystery"—Demogorgon, and the black void which enshrouds Demogorgon. She means knowing too much, and she means knowing nothing at all. In the next section she melts into the figure of Melancholia, "That City's somber Patroness and Queen." Then she reveals herself as

The sense that every struggle brings defeat
    Because Fate holds no prize to crown success;
That all the oracles are dumb or cheat
    Because they have no secret to express;
That none can pierce the vast black veil uncertain
Because there is no light beyond the curtain;
    That all is vanity and nothingness.

Not much consolation can be drawn from the discovery that "There is no God . . . / Whom we must curse for cursing us with life." The loss of any such object of vital hatred is perhaps the bitterest deprivation which an unbeliever can suffer. Equally unconvincing—to Thomson no less than to us—is the mock-stoicism of "No hope could have no fear." The City is not the abode of ataraxy: it reeks with

Infections of unutterable sadness,
Infections of incalculable madness,
    Infections of incurable despair.

This poem is not the tragedy of a convinced positivist: positivism in itself knows no tragedy. It is the tragedy of Bysshe Vanolis, a romantic who has cast off the chains of Christianity in order to enjoy "All the sublime prerogatives of Man" and who finds that the aspirations of Shelley are no less completely thwarted by "Necessity Supreme."

We cannot say, however, that **"The City of Dreadful Night"** simply shows us what "science" has done to romantic aspiration. When Thomson asserts that the universe has "no secret to express . . . no light beyond the curtain," he has no firm belief that he is stating the objective truth about the real nature of things. The poem represents the nemesis of subjectivism rather than the power of ineluctable fact to crush the heart's illusion. Thomson knows very well that the emptiness of the universe is the product of his imagination. Both *In Memoriam* and **"The City of Dreadful Night"** say "I have felt"; the difference is that Tennyson and Thomson feel differently. Thomson declares that he is not describing the world of "the hopeful young, / Or those who think their happiness of worth," or the superficially contented Philistines,

Or pious spirits with a God above them
To sanctify and glorify and love them,
    Or sages who foresee a heaven on earth.

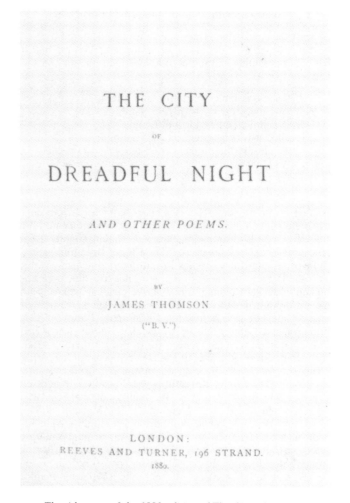

THE CITY

OF

DREADFUL NIGHT

AND OTHER POEMS.

BY

JAMES THOMSON

("B. V.")

LONDON:
REEVES AND TURNER, 196 STRAND.
1880.

The title page of the 1880 edition of The City of Dreadful Night and Other Poems.

No, he is addressing, and representing, a very special "sad Fraternity" of doomed souls,

> . . . desolate, Fate-smitten,
> Whose faith and hope are dead, and who would die—

men who have come "through the desert," who suffer from Leopardian *noia*, who have lost their Matildas, who cannot sleep, who drink too much. These are the sole inhabitants of the City of Dreadful Night, and they are not very numerous in proportion to the population of the globe. Every one of them, in fact, is James Thomson.

But of course, although he has no criterion of the reality of anything except its existence as a vivid impression in the mind, Thomson wants his misery to be *both* unique and universal. The poem certainly implies that those who have been initiated into the "sad Fraternity" are peculiarly qualified

> To show the bitter old and wrinkled truth
> Stripped naked of all vesture that beguiles,
>   False dreams, false hopes, false masks and modes of
>   youth.

On the other hand, since "life is but a dream," how is one to distinguish between "false dreams" and the real truth? The City itself is an illusion,

> For it dissolveth in the daylight fair;
> Dissolveth like a dream of night away.

The dream, however, is real for those who habitually dream it, since

> . . . when a dream night after night is brought
> Throughout a week, and such weeks few or many
> Recur each year for several years, can any
>   Discern that dream from real life in aught?
>
> For life is but a dream, whose shapes return,
>   Some frequently, some seldom, some by night,
> And some by day, some night and day; we learn,
>   The while all change and many vanish quite,
> In their recurrence with recurrent changes
> A certain seeming order; where this ranges
>   We count things real; such is memory's might.

Thus Thomson's pessimism arises not from acceptance of "the findings of science," but from a morbid subjective state of mind. Reality is the consistency of your dream. The subjectivism which enables happier romantics to assert the divinity of man has deprived Thomson of everything but "infinite void space." Perhaps the saddest feature of the poem is the absence of conviction that anything is really true or really false. The Inner Light has willed to extinguish itself. (pp. 468-73)

> Hoxie Neale Fairchild, "Thomson," in his *Religious Trends in English Poetry: 1830-1880, Christianity and Romanticism*, Vol. IV, *1957. Reprint by Columbia University Press, 1964, pp. 456-73.*

JEROME J. McGANN (essay date 1963)

[*In this discussion of Thomson as a "direct descendant of the Visionary Romantic type," McGann examines Thomson's rejection of an entirely pessimistic world view and shift toward Romanticism near the end of his life.*]

From 1870 to 1874 James Thomson (B. V.) spent his poetic efforts in the composition of what was to be his masterpiece, **"The City of Dreadful Night."** Like most of his poetry up to

1875, the poem was published in Charles Bradlaugh's radical magazine *The National Reformer,* in four installments. It embodied nearly all his accumulated convictions and attitudes: God does not exist, man's spirit is not immortal, necessity is the supreme law of Nature. These ideas, coupled with his pessimistic views about the likelihood of happiness on earth (opinions which undoubtedly resulted from the misery and wretchedness he experienced throughout his life), produced the most famous poem of pessimism written in our language. After completing **"The City"** Thomson ceased writing poetry. The "seven songless years," 1874-1881, followed. During this period he wrote a number of prose essays of various kinds—satire, criticism, fantasy—but his poetry was limited to a few short lyrics and an occasional political satire.

Critics have long been aware that the poems written during the last year of Thomson's life contrast sharply with **"The City of Dreadful Night,"** which is the culmination of the thoroughly pessimistic vision toward which Thomson had been moving throughout the latter part of the 1850's and the whole of the 1860's. Occasionally during this period an "optimistic" poem was written (e.g., **"Sunday at Hampstead,"** and **"Sunday up the River"**), but in general both the poetry and prose unmistakably foreshadow **"The City of Dreadful Night."** All the significant poetry of 1881-1882, on the other hand, bears the stamp of a new vision. **"The Sleeper," "At Belvoir," "Proem," "He Heard Her Sing,"** and even the famous **"Insomnia"**—a poem invariably categorized with **"The City"** and frequently called Thomson's most pessimistic poem—all without exception illustrate the change that Thomson's poetic attitudes had undergone since the publication of **"The City."** There is, in fact, substantial evidence from Thomson's writings between 1874 and 1881 to support the view that this new vision had been slowly developing even before his last outburst of poetic activity.

"Proem" and **"Insomnia,"** two poems written during this last period, are much alike in that they seem to evidence pessimistic moods similar to those that controlled nearly all his earlier work. The other poems, particularly **"He Heard Her Sing"** and **"At Belvoir,"** patently embody attitudes that are completely at variance with **"The City of Dreadful Night."** A close inspection reveals, however, that the case is no different for **"Proem"** and **"Insomnia."** Despite the wanness that pervades **"Proem,"** something not to be found in **"The City"** emerges from it. The poem begins with an apostrophe to the beauty of ancient legends and a wish that some of that beauty might "cleanse the dimness from our weary eyes, And bathe our old world with a new surprise." Immediately after the first stanza a doleful note is sounded: "We stagger under the enormous weight Of all the heavy ages piled on us, With all their grievous wrongs inveterate." A litany of woe then carries the poem forward. The poet cries out that "Our world is all stript naked of [the] dreams" bequeathed to us by the ages. The earth is a mere inert mass whirling in space; God can no longer be seen in what was thought to be His own universe; heaven likewise is not to be expected. There is, in fact, "No life beyond death—coming not too soon." To this point, at least, the poem scarcely seems to advance beyond the attitude of despair anatomized earlier in **"The City of Dreadful Night."** There the poet, seeing nothing but torment in this world, turned toward death as a passage to oblivion, extinction, escape from the griefs of earth. In **"Proem,"** however, a new attitude is adopted. An anodyne for grief which has rarely even been hinted at in Thomson's poetry for fifteen years is set against the "Dateless oblivion and divine repose" of **"The City of Dreadful Night"**—human love, ''Sole star of light in infinite black despair.'' That love can act as a healing agent for all forms of human grief is hardly a novel idea, but for James Thomson such a suggestion is startling indeed. Not that the poet, in the last year of his life, underwent any sort of theistic conversion. He remained a confirmed atheist to his death. Nevertheless, the lines indicate that his personal vision as expressed in **"The City"** had been seriously modified.

To see the essential difference between **"The City"** and **"Insomnia"** is not quite so easy. Critics have always considered these poems as kindred pieces, and it can hardly be denied that pessimism and depression—in the broadest senses of those terms—are integral elements in both poems. Yet there is a difference, and an important one, which is obscured by the very breadth of the terms ''pessimism'' and ''depression.'' **"Insomnia"** is not a poem written within the limits of the vision that controls **"The City of Dreadful Night"** and the other poems truly kindred to it, for example, **"In the Room,"** **"Philosophy,"** **"To Our Ladies of Death,"** **"Night,"** and **"Mater Tenebrarum."** As nearly all of Thomson's critics have already pointed out, the controlling tone of **"The City"** is a calm acceptance of a miserable existence. The mood is epitomized by the statue of ''Melancolia'' presiding over the city from its position of prominence in the poem's final canto. **"Insomnia,"** on the other hand, has a vital new element: not a hope precisely, but rather a longing, an aspiration. It is, in fact, just this sense of yearning that makes **"Insomnia"** an even more depressing poem than **"The City of Dreadful Night."** The misery of humanity's lot is insisted upon equally in both poems, but the attitude of the poet toward this misery is manifestly different in each case.

Aspiration denies the vision proposed by **"The City"** and it is, reciprocally, denied by that poem. Here we arrive at the precise difference between the poetry of 1881-1882 and the poetry associated with Thomson's masterwork. Recognizing this difference is naturally important for a whole view of Thomson's life and work, but it is far more important for the light it can shed upon the methodology of the Romantic poet, or—more exactly—of a certain type of Romantic poet that we might call Visionary. This poet is the mythmaker, and Shelley and Blake are its obvious modern prototypes. Thomson's admiration for both of these men is, then, just the attitude we should expect from one who is a direct descendant of the Visionary Romantic type. He too sees visions, dreams dreams, makes myths. (pp. 493-95)

"The City of Dreadful Night" is a visionary poem and the dreadful city is itself a vision in the strictest sense of that word. The significance of this fact can be easily overlooked if you lose sight of the principal concern of the poem: what is real, what is unreal? This problem is, in fact, central to the poetry of all the Romantic Visionaries. Shelley, for example, employed his celebrated ''veil image'' as a means of solving this very problem of appearance and reality. He saw that if the tangible world of appearances and the imaginative world of Platonic reality were kept apart, that is, if the poet (or the man) opted for either one or the other rather than both simultaneously, then the whole unity of experience would collapse. The best of both appearance and reality would be lost, leaving the searcher with only the worst of both. This is precisely the fate of the poet-youth of ''Alastor,'' who fails in his attempt to get a unified grasp of the ''real'' and the ''imaginative'' worlds. To prevent this catastrophe of diverseness—to prevent, as Eliot puts it, ''the Shadow'' from falling between ''the idea

And the reality''—Shelley hit upon this wonderful image, whereby the veil and the thing veiled are seen as one, as interpenetrating. The beauty hidden behind the veil of the material world is not separate from that veil; it shines beautifully only because it can shine *through* the veil. For example, in *Prometheus Unbound* a spirit choir sings to Asia: ''Child of Light! thy limbs are burning Through the vest which seems to hide them; As the radiant lines of morning Through the clouds ere they divide them.'' Thomson also employs the veil image in three important sections of **"The City,"** each time with the same purpose, to the same end. In Canto XXI.x, he writes of

> The sense that every struggle brings defeat
> Because Fate holds no prize to crown success;
> That all the oracles are dumb or cheat
> Because they have no secret to express;
> That none can pierce that vast black veil uncertain
> Because there is no light beyond the curtain;
> That all is vanity and nothingness.

The two views are perfectly antithetical. In Shelley, the radiance beyond the cloud-vest is magnificent because the covering is inseparable from the entire ''atmosphere divinest'': ''idea'' suffuses ''reality'' and the Shelleyan dream-myth of love is thereby made real. In Thomson, too, the ''idea'' suffuses the ''reality,'' but with manifestly different results. Reality, what Thomson called earlier the ''pleasant veil of various error,'' is here seen to be as ''black'' and ''uncertain'' as that which it is supposed to be veiling because ''there is no light beyond the curtain.'' The burning, radiant vest is for Shelley the symbol of the interpenetration of ''idea'' and ''reality'' within the framework of a basically mythic—because vital and holistic—vision of love. The idea and brightness of love seeps through the whole of reality. In Thomson, on the other hand, the idea of death and nothingness infects reality by blackening its symbol, the ''pleasant veil of various error.'' Thus, the visionary methodology of both men is essentially the same, although they employ it in different ways, for different purposes, with different results. (pp. 496-97)

Consider the poem's final two stanzas. There a symbol of despair (Melancolia) is raised up to a position where it presides over the entire poem: ''Titanic from her high throne in the north . . . In bronze sublimity she gazes forth.'' Because the vision is mythic, however, the statue is made to preside over the whole of reality as well. This is why the lines are so alarming. Thomson says, in effect, that it must be so, always; and he says it with such quiet, almost meek assurance that the horror becomes not only acceptable but necessarily acceptable. The poet allows his reader no room for revolt of any kind in the well-modulated lines that conclude the poem:

> Her subjects often gaze up to her there:
> The strong to drink new strength of iron endurance,
> The weak new terrors; all, renewed assurance,
> And confirmation of the old despair.

The world postulated by such a vision is the Shelleyan world turned on its head. Suffering and pain are purposeless in a universe without the possibility of faith, love, and hope. In Canto II the narrator asks one of the city's inhabitants how life can proceed under such conditions. His answer is significant:

> Take a watch, erase
> The signs and figures of the circling hours,
> Detach the hands, remove the dial-face;
> The works proceed until run down; although
> Bereft of purpose, void of use, still go.

"Bereft of purpose, void of use," life in the city of dreadful night continues until the mechanism runs itself out. The myth of creativity is inverted; matter is not conserved, life is not renewed, but the world slowly plunges toward "oblivion," "blackness," annihilation. This is anti-myth.

If accepted, however, such a vision of reality has one serious drawback: it mitigates against life, any form of life—for example, poetic creation. The anti-myth is self-destructive by its very nature. Thomson brought **"The City of Dreadful Night"** into being and gave unity to his own experience; but by so doing he dammed up the springs of his creative energies. The "seven songless years" were the natural consequence of the poem. When he again began to write poetry in 1881, his new efforts showed marked deviations from the pattern he had established up to the publication of **"The City."** The poems of 1881-1882 not only represent a departure from that attitude; they are, in fact, written upon premises that deny the myth of the metropolis of nightmare. In February 1882, Thomson finished **"The Poet and his Muse,"** and the conclusion to that piece is indicative of what he tried to accomplish in the short time that was left to him. Here is the last stanza:

I am half-torpid yet I spurn this lore,
I am long silent yet cannot avow
My singing voice is lost for evermore;
For lo, this beating heart, this burning brow,
This spirit gasping in keen spasms of dread
And fierce revulsion that it is not dead,
This agony of the sting:
What soulless clod could have these tears and sobbings,
These terrors that are hopes, these passionate throbbings?
Dear Muse, revive! we yet may dream and love and sing!

He was right. The fact that he speaks of a longing to dream indicates that he has not, as a poet, left the methodology of the Romantic Visionary behind (or advanced beyond it to something entirely new). The particular vision of **"The City of Dreadful Night"** was that of the anti-myth achieved through the uncreative dream of death. In his last poems Thomson groped toward what Shelley had achieved—the dream of creativity, the Romantic vision of hope.

But Thomson would not complete his attempt to establish his creative vision. He had not enough time, even if he had had the imaginative strength. His poetic and moral faculties were struggling against a dream of death at least forty years in the making, and it was no easy matter to destroy that vision, much less supplant it with another. The fact that he felt impelled to destroy it is clear from his last poems, although it is equally clear that he only managed to make partially and temporarily successful assaults upon his earlier creation. **"Insomnia,"** his last poem of any consequence, indicates clearly, despite its depressing scenes, that Thomson was seeking to redirect his poetry. Because the poem expresses through its highly personalized symbolism only a doleful longing for a renewal of visionary creativity, we are forced to conclude that Thomson had not been able to submit himself completely to his new dream of love and hope and life. Undoubtedly his physical and mental deterioration, recorded by his biographers, had progressed too far; the spiritual, moral, and physical release needed to produce such a dream—and, indeed, it had to be produced, not simply reached—could not be generated by James Thomson, the poet so long accustomed to self-bondage.

Nevertheless, Thomson's attempt to generate the dream of love resulted in one poem that merits attention, the partially suc-

cessful **"He Heard Her Sing."** Though the poem is not great, large portions of it are very fine. Probably the best single passage is the narrator's visionary description of the song of love that bursts from the spirit of the girl in the poem. She lifts her voice and the whole surrounding creation springs to life with the vitality of her emotion. Since the passage is lengthy I can give here only a general account of its content and effects. The spirit of love is made to assume a number of physical forms. Through these it is then envisioned as mixing with the universe in all its parts and as giving the universe life and meaning thereby. The resultant emotion is one of joy and exultation. Put discursively, the lines detail the interpenetration of matter and spirit: matter becoming spiritualized ("For the stars were the notes of the singing and the moon was the voice of the song"), and spirit becoming clothed in the newly radiant garb of the contingent universe ("A most unendurable burning consuming the soul with the sense").

The effect of a complex and continually ramifying cosmic unity is achieved not only through the use of such "life" metaphors as the living tree, the swelling song, and the pulsating body. Even more effective is the device of envisioning each of these metaphors as perpetually flowing into and out from each other throughout the created universe. The lines, reminiscent of the antiphonal singing in the last act of *Prometheus Unbound*, are patently the product of a Visionary Romantic working in the direction of the Shelleyan dream-myth of love and life ("a passion and a yearning of limitless scope"). This fact is strongly confirmed if we contrast the passage with Canto XVII of **"The City,"** where an almost identical situation is suffused with the aura of the death vision. The antithesis between the two passages is complete. Indeed, in comparing them one discovers that the conceptual (or visionary) disparity operates down through the smallest particulars. Take, for example, the line in Canto XVII where the poet says that men "think the heavens respond to what they feel." In **"The City"** Thomson has little difficulty disposing of this characteristic "daydream": "There is no heart or mind in all [the] splendour" of the heavens. The whole point of **"He Heard Her Sing,"** however, is embodied in the poet's joyful and visionary apprehension of a mutual "response" between man and universe: the girl sings and the vast "abyss of the night" answers with a chant "Through the vault of the firmament ringing and swelling resistlessly strong." The question of life and death, process and inertia, is also to the point. Whereas in **"He Heard Her Sing"** the cosmos is seen as vital and self-regenerating, in Canto XVII "The empyrean is a void abyss" because it is "self-consuming." The two passages, at odds on every point, illustrate quite clearly, I think, the transformation that Thomson's poetry had undergone between 1874 and 1881. (pp. 504-07)

Jerome J. McGann, "James Thomson (B. V.): The Woven Hymns of Night and Day," in Studies in English Literature, 1500-1900, *Vol. III, No. 4, Autumn, 1963, pp. 493-507.*

ANNE RIDLER (essay date 1963)

[Ridler contrasts the prosody and language of Thomson's lesser works with that of his greatest pieces: "The City of Dreadful Night" and "In the Room."]

Mr. Robert Graves has told us that the nest of the Muse is 'littered with the jawbones and entrails of poets', and certainly a glance at the lives of nineteenth-century poets discovers much evidence in his support. Yet

> I will not see myself the desolate bard,
> His natural friendships cast and his loves buried,
> Auguring doom like some black carrion bird

was Mr. Graves's own early protest against such a view, and something of this ambivalence is to be found, I think, in James Thomson, the 'laureate of pessimism' as some admirers named him; a poet who often saw himself as dedicated to despair and as a son of the devil, who yet had in him a tough, practical capacity for humdrum work, and a longing for the delightful state that is disparaged as 'ordinary bourgeois happiness'. He had too keen a sense of the ridiculous to maintain a consistently Byronic pose, though he enjoyed referring to himself as an outcast and Ishmael, and as he grew older he came to think that no one would write poetry unless he were thwarted of the more satisfactory means of self-expression to be found in action.

> Who gives the fine report of the feast?
> He who got none and enjoyed it least.
>
> ["Art"]
> (p. ix)

'As for this **"City of Dreadful Night"**, it is so alien from common thought and feeling that I knew well . . . that scarcely any readers would care for it'—so wrote Thomson to Dobell about his poem, and in writing to his sister-in-law he describes it as 'sombre and atheistical and generally incomprehensible', advising her to skip the first 77 pages of his book, as they will only distress her. Yet to us, as we look back on the poetry of the last half of the nineteenth century, it seems that Thomson is much more typical of his time than the Victorian of solid and bewhiskered optimism who has often been presented to us. Certainly, the nostalgia and despair of the poets alternated with bursts of exaggerated manliness, and even Thomson might be judged a cheerful poet of the great outdoors by anyone who looked only at the quite untypical selection of his work printed by Quiller-Couch in the *Oxford Book of English Verse*. (p. xxx)

In [**"In the Room"**] Thomson perhaps comes nearest to a pure pessimism, because the death is presented as completely without significance, importance or consolation. **"Insomnia"** impresses one as the fruit of terrible experience, certainly, but the piling up of superlatives, the overplus of adjectives—

> Death's ghastly aureole,
> Pregnant with overpowering fascinations,
> Commanding by repulsive instigation
> Despair's envenomed anodyne to tempt the Soul . . .

inevitably dull the impact. In the early poems, death is yearned for like the 'easeful death' of Keats—

> [I] yearn for Thee, divinely tranquil Death,
>   To come and soothe away my bitter pain.

As to the **"City"** itself, though Herman Melville called it 'the modern book of Job', there is in it a consolation of stoicism akin to Housman's

> O never fear man, nought's to dread,
>   Look not left or right,
> In all the endless road you tread
>   There's nothing but the night.

As Paul Elmer More says in an interesting essay on Thomson: 'So necessary for the soul is some place of stability outside of

nature's vortex that, if no other peace is allowed, it will make its account with death.'

> Her subjects often gaze up to her there:
>   The strong to drink new strength of iron endurance,
> The weak new terrors; all, renewed assurance
>   And confirmation of the old despair.

There is something in common between the pessimism of Thomson, Arnold, Clough and Hardy—indeed, two of Clough's lines were quoted by Kipling as coming from the **"City"**. But a comparison shows that the element of self-pity, present in some degree in Arnold if not in the others, is considerably more dominant in Thomson. The mood, as a literary habit, was no doubt derived to some extent from Thomson's sources: from Novalis, and perhaps from Leopardi, with his 'stanco mio cor', though an enervating, inward-gazing, self-pity is rarer in him than in Thomson. Leopardi cannot have influenced Thomson's early poetry, since he did not begin to learn Italian until 1866, but the pessimism of his later poems is undoubtedly coloured by Leopardi's expression of his own, and especially in the conviction that Nature is indifferent to man, an idea which Thomson often repeats in prose and in verse, but most strikingly in the **"City"**. . . . (pp. xxxii-xxxiii)

Despair becomes a fruitful ground for poetry in proportion as the poet has power to express the common lot through his own: a power which depends partly on sheer technical ability, partly on sincerity of artistic purpose, and partly on the breadth of his sympathies. The sense of isolation from one's fellows, known to every human being as a mood, and very pervasive in Matthew Arnold for instance, is damaging to poetry if it becomes absolute, and the experience of life as 'one dark maze of dreams' ends in sterility. Thomson maintained easy surface relationships with his fellows . . . , but his inner life became more and more divorced from these, and from any sense of reality.

> Of old I was conscious of an impenetrable veil
> between myself and nature: of late I have been
> conscious also of an impenetrable veil between
> my inner and outer self; I have to live, think
> and work with the latter, and cannot get at the
> former, cold and vague and dim aloof. This is
> a painful puzzle, to be shut out and cut off from
> one's very self, and conscious of the disabling
> separation.

So it happened that Thomson's power of apprehending reality and transmuting his experience into poetry did not develop after the **"City"**, finished when he was forty. Of his later poems, the only really valuable part expresses hallucination in one form or another: his attempts to write of the natural world or the emotion of love become more and more derivative from other literature. To write good love-poetry, one must have a vivid sense of another person's existence, but in Thomson the sense of separation is the only reality. This had always been true of his serious love poems:

> You were an Angel then; as clean
> From earthly dust-speck, as serene
> And lovely and beyond my love
> As now in your far world above . . .
>
> [**"Vane's Story"**]

but in the playful vein there had once been something more alive.

> Oh, what are you waiting for here, young man?
>   What are you looking for over the bridge?
> A little straw hat with the streaming blue ribbons
> Is soon to come dancing oover the bridge.
>
> ["**Sunday up the River**"]

In the late love-poems nothing gets through but the second-hand image, the stock response: the pure neck burns, the little white arms cling, maidens murmur like doves, and the nightingale is in attendance as inevitably as Koplik's spots attend upon measles.

As to technical ability, Thomson undoubtedly had a remarkable imitative facility from his earliest days, and one wonders what his poetry might have been if, like Hardy, he had learnt his technique from William Barnes rather than from Shelley and Swinburne. J. M. Robertson remarks [see excerpt dated 1892] on his 'defect in artistic austerity and patient devotion' in the craft of poetry, which made him fail fully to appreciate those qualities in Tennyson—a defect which Robertson thought was not present in his prose, 'which he writes with perfect ease'. And J. M. Cohen cites "**The Poet, High Art, Genius**", to support this view—an essay in which Thomson develops his theory that art is only a second-best substitute for life. Yet Thomson did toil at his poems, as the verbal alterations in his manuscripts show, and I feel that the stale diction he employed and his insensitive use of words were due more to the bad influence of Shelley (a great poet but a bad model) and the prevailing acceptance of a worn-out coinage, than to a failure of care. The lack of perception which made him adopt some of Shelley's worst faults of style—the inflated sentiment and the profusion of generalised adjectives—may also have been partly due to his inadequate training: after all, he achieved everything for himself. And however much Shelley may teach a disciple about the imagination, he does not teach him to use his eyes. Thomson's Colorado notebook shows that he *could* use his eyes, but in his poetry the colours are always 'literary' colours—azure, vermeil, crimson—the landscapes are dream scenes.

I do not think, therefore, that Thomson should be accused of a want of devotion, but rather of a want of taste, and of auditory imagination. . . . 'It was congenial to him to be thorough', as the passage quoted above said of his journalistic work: he was accustomed to mark with underscorings and a tick in the margin the lines in his poems which he wanted to improve, and there are many such marks in his manuscripts, with attempts at improvement. In the "Proem" to the ["**City of Dreadful Night**"] he changes 'To blot the sunshine of *exulting* years' to 'exultant', as the first version would have conveyed 'exulting ears'; he notes fortuitous internal rhymes and the ambiguity caused by the *s* in 'torrent swirled'; he writes to Rossetti that if the animal in Dürer's engraving is indeed a wolf-hound and not a sheep, he will have to alter his line to

> With the keen wolf-hound sleeping undistraught

'a villainous makeshift'. Yes indeed, and the worse because 'undistraught' has been brought in for makeshift duty in other places in his verse. But those shifts for the purpose of rhyme did not really seem as villainous to Thomson as they did to a purer tradition, or to poets writing after the revolution of the early twentieth century: they seemed regrettable perhaps, but not unforgivable.

Where ideas were concerned, Thomson was not in the least tied to the fashions of his day. . . . [He] admired Blake when his poetry was little known; he was among the first to admire Walt Whitman; he knew Leopardi before translations had appeared in England. It is curious that he does not seem to have read Baudelaire, since he knew French quite as well as he knew Italian—Balzac meant much to him, and he drew on Stendhal for some of his subjects. Dante also Thomson knew well—the *Inferno* at any rate, as we could deduce from the "**City**", especially section II, and the 'rooted congregation' swaying 'as black fir-groves in a large wind bow' of section XIV. Some of his contemporaries thought him 'terse', an adjective which certainly does not spring to the mind of one who peruses, say "**The Doom of a City**", or even its greater successor: he does in fact need space for his effects, which are cumulative and not epigrammatic. He has an ear for a grand-sounding line, a sonorous word—

> Most cold, imperial, unlamenting Bride.
>
> ["**The Doom of a City**"]

One is never quite sure that such a line may not come from some other poet, however, as with

> Islanded in the boundless sea of air
>
> ["**A Voice from the Nile**"]

which turns out to be a borrowing from Shelley's "A Boat on the Serchio", though an improvement on its original:

> Islanded in the immeasurable air.

The refrain, too, Thomson used with splendid effect in his major poem

> As I came through the Desert, thus it was

and

> I wake from daydreams to this real night . . .

the more so because an effect of monotony is one of the legitimate aims of the poetry here. Elsewhere the monotony cannot be so defended, and there are few of his poems which would not be the better for cutting.

Thomson has little or no auditory imagination—the power that enables a poet to recreate a word by his use of it in certain contexts, and to make coined or technical or archaic words serve his purpose. He is fatally fond of the word *riant*, which occurs in his work from first to last, and *fulgent* is another unresisted temptation. In a letter to Bertram Dobell which refers to some criticisms of "**Our Ladies of Death**", he quotes the dictionary in support of his use of sombrous, tenebriously, ruth, but adds: 'I looked into the Dictionaries, not knowing whether their authority would sustain or condemn me, as I am used to trust in careful writing to my own sense of what is right; this, naturally, having been modified and formed by reading of good authors'—a defence effective enough if the 'sense of what is right' had in fact been alert to the associations of words, their evocative power. (pp. xxxiii-xxxvi)

It is now time to consider Thomson's major poem in more detail, and with it the early poem ("**The Doom of a City**") which foreshadows it both in form and content. Passages in the prose "**A Lady of Sorrow**" are also relevant, but I want here to show how the form of the "**City of Dreadful Night**" developed from the much more diffuse shape of the "**Doom**", written some thirteen years earlier. This is a remarkable work for a young man of twenty-three, and has value in its own right: it shows the influence of Shelley's "Triumph of Life" (a favourite poem of Thomson's), but not overwhelmingly, and the main theme is derived from the *Arabian Nights,* while the "Judgements" are reminiscent of those books of Edward Irving which Thomson recalled reading as a little boy.

The narrator leaves his native city (where, as in the later poem, the lamps burning in streets deserted save for himself are a symbol of gloom and loneliness)

> To dare the desert sea . . .
> The unknown awful realm where broods Eternity.

The reiteration which follows his arrival at another City across the ocean, foreshadows the terrible reiterations of the ["**City of Dreadful Night**"].

> What saw I in the City, which could make
>   All thought a frenzy and all feeling madness?
> What found I in the City . . .

The horror is that its inhabitants are all turned to stone, and he hears a Judgement pronounced upon them, and sees destruction overtake all but the few 'spirits who had conquered Life' (compare the "Triumph of Life"), who are beckoned to join a company of the blessed on their mountain—

> And still the glory-stream flowed back to God;
>   And they with it were floated up the sky;
>   Whose gates shut blank against my straining eye,
> And left the earth a dark and soulless clod . . .

The Avenging Justice withdraws from 'Penal smitings dire' (Miltonic phrase), and the Narrator sees the statues begin to be brought back to life, whereon he returns to his boat and to his own city, with a message of warning and of hope.

The noticeable thing about the Argument of the poem, as compared with Thomson's later philosophy expressed in the "**Dreadful Night**", is that doom falls as a retribution for wrongdoing, and the Narrator himself, after first renewing his self-dedication to Misery and Death, comes to realize that it is a madness which has made him cut himself off from his fellows and from life. It is a sad commentary on the poet's own later sense of isolation.

> Dire Vanity! to think to break the union
> That interweaveth strictly soul with soul
> In constant, sane, life-nourishing communion:
> The rivers ever to the ocean roll,
> The ocean-waters feed the clouds on high
> Whose rains descending feed the flowing rivers:
> All the world's children must how quickly die
> Were they not all receivers and all givers!

The form is very diffuse: a series of long irregularly-rhymed stanzas, varied in the later parts of the poem by sections of couplets, octosyllables, and long dactylic or trochaic lines. Thomson kept something of this variety in the ["**City of Dreadful Night**"], but he must have realized that a long poem needed a backbone, so that he there employed two main stanza-forms, one of six lines for most of the narrative, and the other, of seven, for meditation and commentary. (pp. xxxix-xl)

In the later poem there is no definite journey to reach the City—

> How he arrives there none can clearly know . . .
> To reach it is as dying fever-stricken—

in fact, 'Hell is a City much like London' the reader feels— but once having visited it, Thomson says, no one can escape it for long. The Narrator passes through the City and its suburbs, and the visions which he sees, the circles of its Inferno, are all aspects of Thomson's own mental misery, the forms of his obsession—so much is clear to anyone who has studied his other writings. First, is a man tracing out an endless round, revisiting the places where died Faith, and Love, and Hope— and Thomson has a mathematical footnote:

$$\text{Life divided by that persistent three } = \frac{\text{LXX}}{333} \overset{\cdot\cdot}{.210.}$$

The poetry of this, the first part of the poem that Thomson wrote, seems to me to look back to Dante and forward to Mr. Eliot.

Next is an orator (his 'stalwart shape, the gestures full of might, The glances burning with unnatural light' perhaps reminiscent of Bradlaugh, as is the second orator in section XIV with the 'organ-like vibrations of his voice'), declaiming to no one his schizophrenic vision on a shore, where a woman carrying her own burning heart bears off his corpse, leaving behind the 'vile me', the part of him that watches, alone on the shore.

Next comes a strange episode of two spirits who could not enter Hell because they could find no hope to abandon at the portal. This is, to me, the least satisfactory of the episodes, because of the intellectual contradiction contained in such a situation, where two people wishing to enter the place of the hopeless, are forbidden because they *are* hopeless. Next follows a dialogue (already quoted) between the defiant and the fatalistic—as it might be Thomson in his earlier blasphemous mood, and the calmer voice of Leopardi: the one indicts the Maker of the Universe, and the other responds that there is no such Being—

> Man might know one thing were his sight less dim;
> That it whirls not to suit his petty whim,
> That it is quite indifferent to him.

Next appears a 'mansion' which, unlike the other houses of the City, is lighted up—but only to reveal a young man kneeling by the dead body of his love, whose picture is in all the rooms of the house, 'the mansion of (his) heart'. Then the Narrator enters a cathedral, where all who enter 'wake from daydreams to this real night', and hears the preacher (speaking the doctrines which Thomson must often have heard Bradlaugh enunciate) give comfort to the assembly by telling them that all illusions have vanished—

> There is no God, no Fiend with names divine
> Made us and tortures us . . .

such a sad comfort as Thomson perhaps himself found in abandoning a faith which held too many contradictions for him. A man in the assembly laments his lost chance—again with Thomson's own bitter backward-looking glance—the one chance of happiness 'frustrate from my birth'.

Next, the Narrator, meeting a man who is trying to retrace the thread of his life in order to begin it again, sees the folly of it, for 'His life would grow, the germ uncrushed', whereas death lies close at hand for the taking. A meditation on suicides follows, with the arguments that Thomson must often have had with himself, as to why he did not put that 'End it when you will' into practice. Then comes the episode of the angel defeated by the sphinx. And last, in the seven-line stanza, the vision of 'Melencolia' which had been in the poet's mind for so long, with its consolation of stoicism.

The poem is wonderfully comprehensive: at the close, the reader feels that he has travelled the whole range of despair, and although the light is the lurid one of nightmare, the City is so consistently and passionately seen that it becomes for ever a part of experience for those who have read the poem, even if they are not among those who 'Travel the same wild paths though out of sight'. It has been blamed for monotony, and even though hell be monotonous, it will always be a question how far its reproduction in art is permissible. Certainly, one or two of the intervening meditations could be cut without damage to the matter of the poem, but this would damage the musical structure, and we can see from the manuscript that this was carefully planned. (pp. xli-xliii)

"In the Room", written some three years earlier, is perhaps Thomson's best poem after the **"City"**. The way in which the inanimate objects surrounding a lonely man in lodgings come to appear to him to have an actual, and hostile, life of their own; the dramatic delay of the clue—that the tenant of the room is lying there dead while the furniture is talking; the ironic contrast between his deadness and the comparative liveliness of objects that can still be used; and the sudden harsh introduction of the 'hero'—

> It lay, the lowest thing there, lulled
>   Sweet-sleep-like in corruption's truce;
> The form whose purpose was annulled,
>   While all the other shapes meant use.
> It lay, the *he* become now *it*,
>   Unconscious of the deep disgrace,
> Unanxious how its parts might flit
>   Through what new forms in time and space—

all these are masterly. The flat, dull rhythm of the stanza is exactly right, and the reminiscence of *Lear* (whether conscious or unconscious) only enriches the irony:

> I know when men are good or bad,
>   When well or ill, he [the bed] slowly said;
> When sad or glad, when sane or mad,
>   And when they sleep alive or dead . . .

which is followed by the mirror's reminiscence of how a relation of hers was brought to prove whether a man was still alive to 'blur her with his breath' or not.

What has Thomson to say to a mid-twentieth-century reader? Before I read Mr. T. S. Eliot's preface to a recent selection of John Davidson's poems, it had struck me that the 'unreal City' of the *Waste Land* owed something to Thomson as well as to Baudelaire, and that Thomson might even have some part in the 'familiar compound ghost' of "Little Gidding", Part IV:

> Because he seemed to walk with an intent
>   I followed him; who, shadowlike and frail,
> Unswervingly though slowly onward went . . .
> Thus step for step with lonely sounding feet
> We travelled many a long dim silent street.

The preface confirmed me at least in that Mr. Eliot there acknowledges an early debt to the **"City"**. (p. xliii)

The uncompromising courage with which Thomson rejected all facile consolations is sympathetic to an age in which disillusion has seemed the only honest starting-place. Moreover, in his 'cold rage' to 'show the bitter old and wrinkled truth' he seems very close to our time. His own contemporaries, though recognizing the power of the **"City"**, turned with relief to his love poems and his lyrics, which seem to us . . . largely derivative and written in a worn-out mode. It is no use looking

to him for freshness of diction, for subtleties of metrical variation, or for the natural observation which illumines the flattest page of Barnes or the most ornate page of Hopkins; the colloquial rhythms which give life to the poems of Browning and Clough are rarely found in him. But the unromantic pessimism of his maturity, his midnight view of an unhomely city, his 'dingy urban images', these speak directly to us. (pp. xliv-xlv)

> *Anne Ridler, in an introduction to* Poems and Some
> Letters of James Thomson *by James Thomson, edited
> by Anne Ridler, Southern Illinois University Press,
> 1963, pp. ix-xlv.*

GEOFFREY GRIGSON   (essay date 1963)

[*Grigson is an English poet, critic, editor, and journalist whose direct style characterizes both his criticism and his poetry. As founder and editor of the short-lived periodical* New Verse, *a forum for avant-garde poetry, Grigson distinguished himself as a strongly principled and sometimes polemical critic. In the following excerpt from a review of Ridler's edition of Thomson's poems, he offers a highly negative assessment of Thomson's work. Grigson's comments first appeared in the* New Statesman *in 1963.*]

[Miss Anne Ridler] says that the poetry of the earlier part of the **"City of Dreadful Night"** seems to her 'to look back to Dante and forward to Mr Eliot' [see excerpt dated 1963].

I can't believe this is a very useful statement, though it does suggest a parlour game of making parallels (the Albert Memorial looks back to Ghiberti and forward to Robert Rauschenberg). Certainly the poet of the **"City of Dreadful Night"** read *The Inferno* (if rather in the sense of estimating it through the illustrations by Gustave Doré?), and Mr Eliot when young read the **"City of Dreadful Night,"** and we are all at some time or another affected by inferior influences. But this does not elevate the **"City of Dreadful Night"** into a poem it is at all necessary to read. Dismal—abysmal, fate—gate, frail—veil, tomb—gloom (or —doom), mighty fane—organ strain, it is a monument stickier than fudge to a confusion between life and poetry which we should regret, and be ashamed of, in as far as we ourselves encourage it.

Thomson was a Victorian pessimist; he was a cosmical unbeliever, a friend of Bradlaugh—so far so good. He was a melancholic, he drank, he was poor, he was alone, he was a failure. He walked about London in frayed bedroom slippers in the winter night by the gas flares, he collapsed, with internal bleeding, in the rooms of the blind poet Marston. The Secularist Burial Service was read over him in Highgate Cemetery. His poems paid for the coffin. But if you are a sad and saddening creature of our race (mental hospitals are full of them), and if you write poems, and if your poems are related to a mood better voiced by others, it does not follow that you yourself are a Leopardi, or anything else than a fudger and rubbisher. Outside the sloppy hell of the **"City of Dreadful Night,"** 'capital of teen and threne', there is not much fun in discovering that Thomson wrote even more weakly—most weakly of all when he leaves such haunts (the *mot juste*) as the ravine, the blackest stormiest night, the centre of the fire, the middle of Waterloo Bridge, or the desert (the eager vultures hanging overhead):

> And in the spot most thrilling-sweet
>   Of all this Love-Realm rosy
> Our truant pair had found retreat,
>   Unblushing, calm and cosy:

> Where seats too wide for one are placed,
>   And yet for two but narrow,
> It's 'Let my arm steal round your waist,
>   And be my winsome marrow!'

—which wouldn't need to be quoted if there were not some idea around that James Thomson, rightly considered, is a Waste Land poet, for ourselves, of existential courage.

In contrast or support Miss Ridler positions around him Shelley, Clough, Browning, Melville, Leopardi, Baudelaire, Novalis, Kipling, Housman, Hardy, Wilfred Owen, Edwin Muir, Robert Graves, Mario Praz, and Paul Elmer More, as well as Dante and Eliot. She does her best (but how did she forget Charles Williams?); and I am grateful—mildly—to have learned from her introduction why this sad creature she mothers, distinguished himself from that superior fellow-Scot, Thomson, the poet of *The Seasons,* as James Thomson (B. V.).

B. V. stood for Bysshe Vanolis, his pen name: Bysshe for Shelley, from whose faults—O World, O Life, O Time and Bird thou never wert (doesn't 'wert' stick in your throat like a sticky jack?)—he derived many of his own; Vanolis for the romantic Novalis of the blue flower and the *Hymnen an die Nacht,* a night of less lugubrious illumination. I could of course have discovered about B. V. from the nearest encyclopedia, but I mention that bracketed B. V. as an indication, in shorthand, of what may happen when a great surge in the arts is at last in its dotage or decay. (pp. 168-70)

> Geoffrey Grigson, "Four Ways of Making Fudge," in his The Contrary View: Glimpses of Fudge and Gold, Macmillan, 1974, pp. 166-76.

KENNETH HUGH BYRON (essay date 1965)

[*Byron examines Thomson's pessimistic philosophy in the context of nineteenth-century intellectual movements.*]

James Thomson's importance as a literary figure of the Victorian period stems from the fact that his writings reflect in miniature the many aspects of that period's strong undercurrent of pessimism. His writings also reflect the constant sense of conflict which gave the period its transitional character. Above all, Thomson was unable to come to a satisfactory resolution; and while we have innumerable examples of compromise in his time, we have few representatives of the prominent thread of pessimism who are as eloquent as Thomson. We can trace throughout his creative life the development of each facet of his pessimism. We can see that no one factor by itself is a sufficient explanation, a sufficient cause for the lack of compromise expressed in his greatest work, the ultimate of atheistic pessimism, **"The City of Dreadful Night."** Each of the factors contributing to his pessimism contains an easily detected conflict: the highly charged religious atmosphere of his early years gave way to a thorough disbelief in the precepts of Christianity; he desperately desired an end to life's sufferings, but to commit suicide attributed a value to life; his attempts to find emotional stability in life were destroyed by the loss of his sweetheart and the consequences of his dipsomania; and, finally, when he sought a resolution to his dilemma in reason and Necessity, they failed, and he was unable to realize existential freedom. (pp. 159-60)

Thomson had no sudden revelation of the fallibility of the Bible, or of Christianity, for his was a long, anguished process of doubt and soul searching self-reproach, which can be traced through his works in successive stages from fear of disbelief,

through disbelief in the divinity of Christ, in God, and finally in the soul and immortality. His personal conflict reflected the dispute between the adherents of pessimism and the adherents of religious authority. The foes of pessimism, J. Radford Thomson, Mark Wenley, John Hopps, struck hard for the authority of divine guidance and felt that Christianity alone could save for mankind a sense of the relativity of values. The proponents of divine authority themselves felt a need for a belief in Christianity and that need was echoed by a vast number of Englishmen. . . . Thomson expressed his divergence from the central tenets of Christianity in his [**"Stanzas Suggested by Matthew Arnold's 'Stanzas from the Grande Chartreuse'"**]. Although he still believed in a soul and a deity when he wrote **"The Doom of a City",** his lessening belief produced a deepening despair which culminated in utter disbelief and utter despair. **"Vane's Story"** and **"To Our Ladies of Death"**, and his prose-poem, **"A Lady of Sorrow"** lead us to this declaration of disbelief and despair in his greatest poem, **"The City of Dreadful Night"**; his last poems simply reaffirm his atheistic pessimism.

The same sort of two-fold classification holds true for Thomson's philosophy of pessimism as well, for according to Schopenhauer we are under the dominion of Will, Will which causes us to exist—the only escape is death. However, as long as we are conscious, we are involved with, always oriented to, an object, whether it be something real, perceived by the senses, or a fantasy of our imaginings. Balanced against this will to exist was Thomson's frequently expressed longing for death, for the eternal rest of something akin to a Buddhist *nirvana,* or for the complete cessation of pain and anguish in annihilation. He had at almost any time in his life the power to end it when he wished, but to commit suicide is to place too high a value on life. The most startling expression of the dichotomy is the juxtaposition of the phenomenal and noumenal worlds in **"The City of Dreadful Night"**; for Thomson depicts both worlds in the poem as his striving to escape the world of the limbo of the lost, which to him is reality, into the real city, which by a reversal, represents annihilation. This same curious reversal is repeated over and over as each of the supplicants enters the cathedral and leaves his everyday activities by telling the hooded figure that they wake from day dreams to this real life—in the city of fantasy. Thomson, however, had an intense interest in life; he did not shut himself off from the world, at least until his last year. The similarity between Schopenhauer's philosophy and Thomson's pessimism is striking, but the philosopher was speaking from the mind. Thomson turned to the Italian poet-philosopher Giacomo Leopardi as a kindred soul who felt from the heart, as did Thomson, the pessimism expressed in his writings. That Thomson was familiar with Schopenhauer's philosophy is more than a possibility, but it is a fact that he translated with great sympathy the "Operette Morali" and "Pensieri" of Leopardi.

The reality-unreality dichotomy of Thomson's religious despair is repeated in his emotional pessimism, for romantic melancholy comes under the same head. Thomson was a poet of his time, and his time was romantically influenced by Rousseau, Goethe, Heine, and the English romantics. From Byron's subjective melancholy Thomson learned the loneliness and isolation of the subjective melancholiac, and he suffered from the solitude imposed by his attacks of dipsomania. In Heine he saw a reflection of his own personal misery caused by the death of Matilda Weller, an emotional effect almost mystic in its intensity transcending the cold expression of philosophical pessimism. Shelley, whom Thomson admired above all other English poets, taught him the distinction between the feigner of melancholy and the sincere sufferer of worldsorrow. Despite his lack of belief in man's ultimate self-perfectibility, Thomson was fully aware that man was the unfortunate victim of social and political inequalities of his period and believed in a reformation of the past. Understanding, as did many in his time, the portents of evolution, he could not transfer his belief to the powers of nature; he could form no new ideal, no peg upon which to hang his life. When a man places absolute value in an ideal—be it his conception of God or of love—and if this prove unobtainable, or obtainable and prove meaningless, the result is utter, futile despair. **"The City of Dreadful Night"** is a poem of profound emotional force whose apparent monotony reveals, in a careful reading, subtle variations of form, meter, and dramatic intensity, all within the framework of a single mood.

In looking at **"The City of Dreadful Night"** from a modern viewpoint, we can see that this poem is at once the beginning and the culmination of the history of Thomson's pessimism. Thomson's existential view of life entailed the loss of absolutes (the death of God) and his encounter with Nothingness. His reaction to that view of life resulted in dread, the fear of meaninglessness, and despair, the fear of Nothingness exemplified by the death of Hope. His futile attempt at a resolution of his dilemma included reason, which did not suffice to reconcile the value of life with the misery in the world, and the freedom of the individual in which Thomson could not believe. Thomson chose, rather, an anti-existential aspect, Necessity, and failed to realize existential freedom; or in the words of F.C.S. Schiller, Thomson's great poem "cannot be pooh-poohed as a drunken raving: it must be treated on its merits, as a superb poetic statement of the case against optimism, as a poignant expression of the utter desolation of a soul that abandons itself to a belief in a godless, mindless, ruthless, and mechanical universe". It is precisely this that prevented Thomson from realizing existence in the existentialist sense of separating subject and object; because he attempted to transcend human subjectivity, he failed of the essential meaning of existence. (pp. 160-63)

The twentieth century "Wasteland school" of poetry reflects Thomson's nineteenth century pessimism. The city he describes in his early **"The Doom of a City"** is, perhaps, a "prelude to Eliot's 'Unreal City'—which symbolized for him the pain of human existence resulting from an awareness of the futile ordering of the universe" [see entry by R. A. Forsyth in Additional Bibliography]. Thomson's journey through life has also been described as a journey through the Waste Land of his times. If his poetry did not contribute to the bitterness of much of the poetry of his own times and of the post World War I era, it certainly gave an ample foretaste of the desolate, disillusioned literature of those periods. (p. 164)

Kenneth Hugh Byron, in his The Pessimism of James Thomson (B. V.) in Relation to His Times, *Mouton & Co., 1965, 174 p.*

WILLIAM DAVID SCHAEFER (essay date 1967)

[*In the following excerpt from his introduction to the most complete edition of Thomson's prose, Schaefer underscores Thomson's heretofore largely overlooked talents as an essayist and satirist.*]

During a literary career that spanned nearly a quarter of a century, Thomson naturally altered a good many of his beliefs.

He was raised as an orthodox Christian, and, although in the 1850's his Christianity was tempered by his reading of Carlyle, Emerson, and Shelley, as late as 1863 his world view, as indicated in his attitude toward Frederic Harrison's *Meaning of History*, was still Christian-oriented. But by 1864, after a few years of life in London with Bradlaugh and the National Reformers, he completely rejected Christianity and became a pantheist; as he explains in his "Introductory Note" to **"A Lady of Sorrow,"** he "believed in the soul's immortality as a Materialist believes in the immortality of matter; he believed that the universal soul subsists for ever, just as a Materialist believes that universal matter subsists for ever." Inextricably involved with this new pantheistic faith was a new philosophy of life, an optimistic sort of *carpe diem* in which he implored his fellowmen, as he states it in the "sermon" that concludes **"A Lady of Sorrow,"** to "really live, knowing, and gladly accepting, and bravely working out your little part in the sublime economy of the universe." Becoming convinced that Christianity was a major stumbling block to "really living life," he also at this time began to write the blasphemous antichristian satires that during the next decade were to earn him, in the eyes of National Reformers, the prose-laureateship of free thought. But although the attacks upon religion continued well into the 1870's, both the "live life" philosophy and the pantheism that gave rise to it had faded out by the end of the 1860's, to be replaced by a bleak atheism; thus by 1873 and the completion of **"The City of Dreadful Night,"** Thomson was able to bring "authentic word" that "there is no God," that

> The world rolls round for ever like a mill;
> It grinds out death and life and good and ill;
> It has no purpose, heart or mind or will.

In spite of his long association with the *National Reformer*, Thomson never became actively involved in reform movements, believing with Carlyle that reform must begin—and end—with the individual. Although a Republican "in principle," he never actively participated in the Republican movement, his major contribution to the cause being his attacks upon despotism and imperialism as revealed in such essays as **"A Commission of Inquiry on Royalty"** and the bitterly biased criticism of Disraeli (**"In the Valley of Humiliation"**). Thomson's social criticism centered, for the most part, simply upon a denunciation of what he called "Bumbleism"—in effect, the dullness, dishonesty, conservatism, and complacency of his century. And it was only when he came to realize that Bumble was impervious to change, that there was in fact a natural savagery in the human heart, that his atheism became combined with a pessimism as to any hope for improvement in mankind. **"The City of Dreadful Night"** is a pessimist's manifesto for a select group, those "whose faith and hope are dead, and who would die," but in his **"Proposals for the Speedy Extinction of Evil and Misery"** Thomson involves the entire human race, ridiculing the prospect of progress, laughing at man's dreams of perfectibility.

As a literary critic, Thomson discovered different values to accord with his changing views on God and man. While a Christian, and later as a pantheist, he was strongly attracted to the English Romantic poets and to the idea that the "inspired" poet was God's messenger, a divine hierophant sent to reveal the beauty and harmony of the visible universe. But as he gradually moved toward the position of atheist and pessimist, he became increasingly convinced that the great works were those that depicted life realistically, the great authors those who were not afraid to show the "bitter old and wrinkled truth / Stripped naked of all vesture that beguiles." Thus, in his many reviews and biographical essays of the 1870's, Thomson was attracted to men like Swift, Burns, Browning, and Meredith; his early interest in Novalis was replaced by admiration for Heine; and it was Leopardi, not Dante; Epictetus, not Plato; Whitman and Melville, not Emerson, whose works he attempted to learn and to propagate. For Thomson, always retaining a touch of the army schoolmaster, was at heart a moralist and humanist who, even after he had lost faith in both God and man, paradoxically attempted to enlighten and to teach, however unpleasant the lesson for the day.

It is no longer necessary to make apologies for the subject matter of the satires Thomson wrote for the secularists, and it is most unlikely that anyone today will write to the publisher of this edition, as did one Victorian gentleman after reading a Thomson "profanity," and suggest that "your paper, yourself, and all your supporters ought to be burned." Indeed, many of the ideas expressed in Thomson's "profanities" are now commonplace, and the modern reader will probably be less shocked by the content than by the freshness of expression, whether Thomson is writing about Jehovah, Son, and Company as *The Story of a Famous Old Jewish Firm,* or describing Jesus as a "poor sexless Jew with a noble feminine heart, and a magnificent though uncultivated and crazy brain," or proudly proclaiming that "the man is a fool who in his heart says there is no God, and has not the courageous wisdom to publish it abroad with tongue or pen." Such views are, of course, no more cheerful today, or any less blasphemous to Christians, than they were in the 1860's and 1870's, but, if we are to judge by the continued interest in **"The City of Dreadful Night,"** there is considerable attraction even in repulsion, and few modern readers (attracted or not) would agree with an early reviewer that a work such as **"Proposals for the Speedy Extinction of Evil and Misery"** is "deplorably vulgar" [see excerpt by E.D.A. Morshead dated 1881]. Readers of **"The City,"** first approaching Thomson's prose with expectations of gloom and melancholy, will, in fact, be pleasantly surprised by the wealth and variety of his humor. In the **"Proposals,"** for instance, Thomson wisely harnessed his talents to the genius of Jonathan Swift, and, if the satire lacks the delightful morbidity of Swift's baby eating, the moral to be drawn from Thomson's modest proposal—that universal suicide is the key to eliminating evil and misery—has all the black charm of the conclusion of *Gulliver's Travels.* (pp. 4-7)

Many of these free-thought articles from the *National Reformer* and the *Secularist,* as well as the tobacco articles written for *Cope's Tobacco Plant,* were, of course, little more than hackwork. Not even Ruskin or Huxley could have written for more than five years on the subject of tobacco without staining their reputations, and Thomson's long association with tobacco and free thought has undoubtedly hurt his position as a serious author. He once admitted, referring to the *National Reformer,* that "I am an author thoroughly unknown, and writing for a periodical of the deepest disrepute," and, as he well knew, most of the readers of these "disreputable" journals cared "nothing for literature as literature, but only as a club to hit parsons and lords on the head with." By and large, these articles were expected to do little more than feed the apparently insatiable free-thought appetites of men long since "unconverted" from religion, and it must have been somewhat discouraging to attempt to write sophisticated satire for such an audience (on at least one occasion the editor had to publish a note explaining to a confused if freethinking reader that

"B. V.'s" recent reference to "merciful providence" had been ironic). But it is a tribute to both his sincerity and his skill that Thomson succeeds as consistently as he does, even when merely "hacking out" another article to amuse and edify secularist iconoclasts who, for the most part, were too busily engaged in hurling bricks at a God no longer there to recognize Thomson's true value.

Of course not all of Thomson's prose is in this vein. His social criticism—to Thomson, at least, the more important aspect of his work—is in the great tradition of Victorian prose. This work reminds us somewhat of Matthew Arnold's, lacking Arnold's range and urbane sophistication, no doubt, but at one with Arnold in expressing the belief that Hebraism was definitely not the *unum necessarium* for the nineteenth century (as Thomson put it, the "continual cry of Work! Work! Work! is simply the Imperative mood of a doctrine which, couched in the quiet Indicative, reads, 'Mankind is a damned rascal'"). Thomson's attack upon Bumbledom was partly inspired by Arnold's comments on the Philistines, and, like Arnold, Thomson devoted much of his career to writing "biographical essays" and "introductory reviews" that were intended to propagate some of the best "known and thought in the world." Thomson, however, distrusting what he considered to be Arnold's kid-glove aloofness, offered a more down-to-earth "message" than Arnold's plea for "sweetness and light" Hellenism, calling for a sort of workingman's realism, encouraging men to live their lives fully and honestly while facing up to harsh reality. The message is neither original nor profound, but there is a clean masculinity and directness in Thomson's statement which avoid both the sentimental "robust optimism" of Browning or Henley and the limp-wristed hedonism of the later aesthetes. (pp. 7-8)

Thomson's achievement as a literary critic and reviewer is the most remarkable, and least known, aspect of his work, remarkable particularly when we remember that he lacked the advantages of intimacy with a literary circle, or even of a university background. He was at one with his age in admiring Carlyle, Ruskin, Mill, and George Eliot (and Dante and Goethe for that matter); he was outrageously wrong in his early championing of Garth Wilkinson and in his failure to recognize Dickens' genius. But Thomson was far in advance of his age in his other evaluations—in his virtual worship of Shelley as early as the 1840's; in his early disillusionment with Tennyson and recognition of Browning as the greatest poet of the age, and this at a time when most of his contemporaries were still considering the author of *Men and Women* to be Mrs. Browning's lesser half ("Tennyson is a rare 'literary luxury' for us all, and especially for our youths and maidens; but Robert Browning is indeed the poet of Men and Women"); in his appreciation of Blake, his essay on Blake's poems anticipating even Swinburne's famous early study; and in his praise of Meredith, whom, long before most Victorians were aware of his work, Thomson was proclaiming as "the Robert Browning of our novelists." Thomson was one of the first to appreciate and to translate Leopardi; he was one of few Victorians to read Swift and Burns for the right reasons; at a time when "Rabelais," "Flaubert," "Baudelaire," and "Whitman" were dirty words to most Englishmen, Thomson was extolling these men's works; and decades before twentieth-century criticism was to launch its attack upon Victorian literature, Thomson recognized that "it is astonishing what a large part of even a good modern book has been written without any exercise of the faculty of thought," had praised works by Pope and Swift because "nearly every sentence has required a distinct intellectual effort [that shames] by their powerful virility our effeminate modern books.''

The phantasies, on the other hand—although Thomson himself probably considered "**A Lady of Sorrow**" to be his finest work in prose—may not prove very exciting to the modern reader. This is unfortunate because "**A Lady of Sorrow**," in spite of its excessive length and the flimsiness of the pseudo-Darwinian pantheism preached by the Shadow woman in Part III, does have passages at least equaling the best of De Quincey. From the terse opening line (''I lived in London, and alone''), through the nightmare journey into labyrinthic caverns with the culminating carnival orgy (''the maddest and most lawless in a world all mad and lawless''), right up to the conclusion when, after the dolorous march of death, the ''gloom grows deeper still and yet more awful,'' Thomson reaches toward a terrible beauty seldom attained even in the best passages of "**The City**." And even more emphatically than "**The City**" or the "**Proposals for the Speedy Extinction of Evil and Misery**," the phantasy titled "**In Our Forest of the Past**," where the moanings of all the wasted and frustrated lives echo back from the past and blend with the swelling storm, could serve as Thomson's final and most pessimistic statement as to the futility of life.

I do not know whether Thomson's prose is better than his poetry; I suspect that it is. That his collected prose would fill ten or twelve volumes, while his poetry could be collected in one, is no indication as to quality; but it is unfortunate that in the five books, some twenty articles, and seven doctoral dissertations devoted to Thomson in the past quarter century, so little attention has been paid to his prose. It would be absurd to suggest that he deserves the same recognition afforded to men like Carlyle, Ruskin, or Arnold; his prose exerted absolutely no influence, stylistically or intellectually, upon his age or ours. But Thomson is perhaps our finest example of a ''middleclass,'' self-educated Victorian author, and his works provide a fascinating portrait of one man's struggle to come to terms with the new ideas and shifting values of a dynamic century. We can hardly say that in Thomson's prose we have found God's plenty; but we can say that his prose is of greater value and of considerably greater interest than has yet been recognized. (pp. 9-11)

> *William David Schaefer, in an introduction to* The Speedy Extinction of Evil and Misery: Selected Prose of James Thomson (B. V.) *by James Thomson (B. V.), edited by William David Schaefer, University of California Press, 1967, pp. 1-12.*

IAN CAMPBELL   (essay date 1978)

[*Campbell focuses on the techniques Thomson employed to externalize and vivify his personal vision in "The City of Dreadful Night."*]

"**The City of Dreadful Night**" has won a good deal of recognition as a powerful poem, successful in stating a point of view sometimes unbearably vivid, powerfully expressing the negative philosophy of its creator. Running counter to much that was successful in the poetry of its time (though by no means unique in its philosophy and conclusions), it gives uncomfortable shape to doubts possessed by the writer, to a lesser extent probably familiar to the reader, but doubts which the prevalent attitudes or taboos of the time might make difficult to publish. Compared to the achieved faith and certainties of *In Memoriam*, "**The City**" seems often unsteady and irregular

in the focus of its vision; yet it has the advantage of seeking to awaken feelings latent in the reader, rather than transmitting something so personal that it can be transferred sympathetically to the reader only at great length and with numerous interpretive passages. Thomson's stated intention is to set to work on readers already partly prepared to hear him:

> O sad Fraternity, do I unfold
>   Your dolorous mysteries shrouded from of yore?
> Nay, be assured; no secret can be told
>   To any who divined it not before:
> None uninitiate by many a presage
> Will comprehend the language of the message,
>   Although proclaimed aloud for evermore.
>
> (**"Proem"**)

We are closer here to the leap of dreadful welcome Jekyll experiences on meeting Hyde, or Young Goodman Brown on meeting the devil-figure in the forest, than to the fantasy world of *Phantastes,* or the anguish of *In Memoriam*. The City is there to be recognized with mixed emotions, perhaps with guilt, perhaps with shock at the public expression of private doubt. Nevertheless the city is there, recognizable; and (we will argue) it is one of Thomson's intentions to convince us that he ''burns'' too with the immediacy of a feeling so intense that it moves from the status of unfamiliar or shocking, to the status of normality, or something close to it, in the mind of a reader affected by this lonely and often corrosive poem. (pp. 123-24)

[Thomson] was a poet who aimed for control, for complete expression of a wide variety of emotion and experience in well-finished verse. His notebooks were one avenue of self-criticism, another the inner voice which he saw as controlling him when he degenerated into merely ''exhaling'' emotion:

> I often now write, as I wonder whether others ever write, conscious of a sort of dim veil separating the inner from the dictating mind. Reading over such exterior writing, I may judge It is correct, it will do; but my inner self disclaims all responsibility for it, & simply refuses to be concerned in or about it.
>
> (**"Book of Aphorisms"**)
(p. 126)

In "**The City of Dreadful Night**," success is manifested by the relatively few occurrences of weak, badly composed work springing from the dictating mind: the inner mind seems to speak consistently, burning with the intensity which convinces the reader he is reading genuinely felt emotion, not second-hand poetry put together from building-blocks. In claiming this success, we may distinguish among several techniques perfected by Thomson to achieve the immediacy desired.

In the first place, one can point to a skillful and sustained use of literary allusion and reference. It may seem redundant to point to Dante, but Thomson, like T. S. Eliot, saw that the *Divina Commedia* could be used for much more than scene-setting. Thomson employs the relatively simple verbal echo of the inscription above the portals of Hell, rephrased to ''Leave hope behind, all ye who enter here.'' More delicately, he uses a scene (curiously enough, also used by Eliot in "Little Gidding") in which Dante meets with surprise and shock Ser Brunetto, in life a respected teacher and friend, grovelling below him in the burning plains of Hell. ''What, you here, Ser Brunetto? you!'' Ser Brunetto takes time from his journey across the burning plains to make friendly talk with Dante, praising him for his work while Ser Brunetto was his living teacher and friend, and prophesying in general good fortune, though with some adversity, for Dante. Thomson's scene recalls this, yet changes it in important details. His pain-wracked muddy creature is

> something crawling in the lane below;
> It seemed a wounded creature prostrate there
> That sobbed with pangs in making progress slow.

This creature's torture is in mud, not heat; it recalls more the grovelling of Milton's fallen angels. Yet it "had been a man," and the reader may consciously or unconsciously relate Thomson's picture to Dante's. Thomson's creature (a savage commentary on Blake, it has been suggested) crawls through Hell trying to retrace the thread that will lead him to primeval innocence, the "sacred steel of the clue":

> It leads me back
> From this accursed night without a morn,
> And through the deserts which have else no track,
> And through vast wastes of horror-haunted time,
> To Eden innocence in Eden's clime.

He is in agony; he lacks Brunetto's pervasive neutral or good humor: Dante was told, "Follow but thy star; / Thou canst not fail to win the glorious haven" (*Inferno*), but Thomson, in a scene reminiscent of Browning's "The Laboratory" (of which there are distinct verbal echoes) is hissed at with scorn, threatened with a poisoned knife-blade and phials of chemicals unless he leave the monster alone to find his Eden. The overall effect of Thomson's section XVIII is of pervasive melancholy, a wasted life searching for an impossible ideal, no more than escape "Beyond the reach of man-evolving Doom" which is never achieved. The surface melancholy is reinforced by the echoes of the similar scene from Dante: the irony of the scene is reinforced by the differences between the interviews in the two pictures of Hell.

Literary allusion does not merely heighten interest, or make possible implicit ironies: it can also help condition the reader's attitude to a "difficult" and potentially unpopular message. Thomson, claiming that "no secret can be told / To any who divined it not before," fills his section XII with people who state an ideal, then awaken from these "daydreams" to the "real night" of the city, a gloomy horror which shows them the futility of their previous ideals. In richly allusive stanzas Thomson includes as futile the dreams of men like Milton, awakening

> From writing a great work with patient plan
> To justify the ways of God to man,
> And show how ill must fade and perish quite.

Not only Milton's success, but Tennyson's more recent one in *In Memoriam,* might be thought to be devalued in these lines. So might Coleridge's,

> wandering through many a solemn scene
> Of opium visions, with a heart serene
> And intellect miraculously bright.

But then we have seen how far from Coleridge was Thomson's idea of the poet. Coleridge's hermit in "The Ancient Mariner" is as devalued as the mystic vision of earlier and later poets (including "Little Gidding"):

> prayer and fasting in a lonely cell,
> Which brought an ecstasy ineffable
> Of love and adoration and delight

stands no chance against "this real night." King and comic, mimic, hero-fighter, plastic artist, "great" poet—all alike are discredited. The allusiveness is *not* to discredit through jealousy, but to affect the reader's attitude. Thomson's problem is to make the reader share a mood of pervasive gloom, and the discrediting of others who have written more optimistically is legitimate.

Other allusiveness can easily be demonstrated, particularly the consistent use of Biblical, apocalyptic language, whether openly in the superlative scene of the "preaching" in the dark cathedral in section XIV, or in more oblique ways such as the discussions of geological and evolutionary problems familiar from many more sources than just *In Memoriam*. (pp. 127-29)

Vivid pictorial effects are one avenue of attack used by Thomson on his readers; another is the use of echoes, repetitions, orchestrations. These are not always successful, particularly when Thomson falls into errors of over-elaboration and pastiche, such as the Tennysonian description of light which "from roof to basement / Doth glow or gleam athwart the mirk air cast." Here excessive elaboration slows down the poem to the point of ridicule. In IV. 30-31, the failure is an unnecessary (and again slowly-spoken) French interpolation, "A Sabbath of the Serpents, heaped pell-mell / For Devil's roll-call and some *fête* of Hell," successfully emphasizing the serpents with the sibilant sounds, but jarring the ear overall. Another such failure is in XIV. 59-60, "Infinite aeons after the last man / Has joined the mammoth in earth's tomb and womb," with a ridiculous internal rhyme. Yet these failures illustrate sharply the truth of Thomson's observation, quoted earlier, that only a very small verbal difference lies between success and failure.

Well handled, Thomson's verbal successes are extraordinary. Incantatory repetition is one of his strongest effects—witness the menacing effect in section IV of the repeated introductory "As I came through the desert thus it was, / As I came through the desert," counterpointed with the skillfully modulating closing lines of each stanza, moving deeper into despair:

> But I strode on austere
> No hope could have no fear,
>   .   .   .   .   .
> And as she came more near
> My soul grew mad with fear,
>   .   .   .   .   .
> They love; their doom is drear,
> Yet they nor hope nor fear;
> But I, what do I here?

The eye and ear are conditioned to a two-line rhyming conclusion: the third, bewildered, line interrupts the rhythm brilliantly to express the waking from a dream—to "real night," no doubt. The conditioning of eye and ear is still more subtle in section VIII, where the dialogue is expressed in unsettling blocks of alternating stanza forms, contrasting again with the homogenous verse of recent sections, particularly section VI. Individual lines, too, are used in this echoing and allusive way, the "End it when you will" of section XIV recurring in section XVI, and the mocking use of "I wake from daydreams to this real night" in section XII.

The qualities of technique noted here are important to the success of **"The City,"** which undeniably suffers from a narrowness of range and tone, in its intense concentration to catch a mood, and convey the vividness of the mood to the reader. The hellishness is disturbing (particularly the "pandora's box" of lost hopes in section VI), but the really disturbing thing is the hellish nature of "reality," the normality of the city which by the end of the poem has come to replace the normality of the reader. Just as the blasphemer must restrict himself to what he really believes to be holy and dreadful, so Thomson's reader must restrict his vision to what Thomson sees as "real night," not the "daydreams" which affect most readers and writers. To achieve this Thomson alludes to his own work and freely to the work of others, he constructs vivid patterns of imagery to assault and wound the reader, and he orchestrates individual effects to sustain the shock, and to convince. "The City" is an attempt to transfer poetry to this hitherto dubious ground; yet he regarded it as honest ground. He wrote with scorn in a translation from Heine of the classical gods whom he rejected, yet with sympathy

> when I think how mean and blatant
> The Gods are who have overcome you,
> The new, dominant, melancholy Gods,
> So malignant in their sheep's clothing of humility.

His "City" seeks rather to create its own rules, and its own mood. "It is strange how limited & uncouth is the gamut of expression of joyousness, especially among our lower classes: hoarse shouts & horseplay. Sorrow for us has so much dignity in itself, that we seldom note critically its expression" ("**Book of Aphorisms**"). This is from Thomson's notes of 1878; in a nutshell, it was his achievement in writing a successful poem like "**The City of Dreadful Night**," and in firing his burning arrows at his audience, that he succeeded in convincing them of the burning immediacy of *his* feelings; he burned too. Yet he also tried to be critical about the expression of his burning vision, and the success of this poem (which more than outweighs its failures) testifies to the intensity of his cheerless personal philosophy, which tried to convince the Victorian readers that his city too, like Weissnichtwo and Coketown, was part of the ambiguous totality of the Victorian age. (pp. 132-33)

> *Ian Campbell, " 'And I Burn Too': Thomson's 'City of Dreadful Night'," in* Victorian Poetry, *Vol. 16, Nos. 1 & 2, Spring & Summer, 1978, pp. 123-33.*

WILLIAM SHARPE   (essay date 1984)

[*In the following explication of "The City of Dreadful Night," Sharpe explores Thomson's handling of the themes of collective identity and human fellowship.*]

As the chief Victorian ancestor of *The Waste Land*, "**The City**" continues to strike readers as "the most faithful and magnificent expression of the spirit of despair in all modern poetry" [see entry by Gordon Hall Gerould in Additional Bibliography].

But few students of the work notice that the poem also attempts to overcome the very isolation and despair it so vividly conveys. The "Laureate of Pessimism," as Thomson has come to be called, in fact employs many of the traditional doctrines of Stoicism to resist the typically Victorian sense of estrangement and disorientation evoked by the city. What makes this work remarkable among Victorian poems about the city is that it offers a solution to the familiar catalogue of urban complaints and fears, a way of dealing and living with the urban despair to which it at first appears to succumb.

Like *Idylls of the King*, "**The City**" relies on a monumental use of the city metaphor for its structure, so that the "City of Night" becomes not only a trope for the disintegration of the self, the darkest hour of an individual soul, but also a figure for the human condition in the modern world—a city, a country, a civilization in decline where "all things good . . . have been . . . strangled by that City's curse." Confronting the image of the city in its largest implications, Thomson utilizes the formal qualities of the episodic long poem to modify step by step the attitude of his audience toward the city. By learning to "read" "**The City**," both as poem and place, the poet and his audience can come to terms with their shared plight of living in a world without hope or faith. The act of reading the poem reenacts the poet's process of self-education and discovery, gradually mapping and reordering the urban landscape of fractured identity and bitter disillusion. The narrator of the poem participates in the dreamlike scenes of the even-numbered episodes (II-XX), then later composes and intersperses the odd-numbered commentaries (I-XXI) which attempt to elucidate them. Finally, he writes the "**Proem**" that introduces the work. Forced to retrace his steps and relive his nightmare in order to explain it, the poet finds himself in a labyrinth paralleling the urban one he wishes to explore. (pp. 65-6)

Through its reliance on the participation of the reader, the poem paradoxically functions as a map or thread, the key to itself, as well as a skein of despair wherein the self may be lost. As the emphasis in the "**Proem**" on serving its special audience makes clear, the poet takes seriously the task of aiding the lost and weary. Therefore, although read first, the "**Proem**" calls attention to its having been written last, as an impassioned final word directly addressing its readers, an inviting open-ended coda that contrasts with the austere impersonality of the actual ending of the poem. Through this apostrophe the work comments on its own legibility; it is written specifically for urban "initiates" who share the poet's sense of alienation and loss:

> no secret can be told
> To any who divined it not before:
> None uninitiate by many a presage
> Will comprehend the language of the message,
> Although proclaimed aloud for evermore.

Yet Thomson does not plan merely to reiterate the familiar; rather, he intends that by threading the labyrinth of the poem itself the members of his "Freemasonry" will learn more about the City and each other. . . . The insulating quality of urban experience compels each individual obliquely to pick out his own way to consciousness, unaware of fellow seekers whose paths may cross his continually. Not until 1870, at the age of thirty-six, had Thomson become convinced that each man was spiritually alone in the universe, and among other reasons he wrote "**The City**" to share that discovery, wishing to draw his *semblables* closer together in the knowledge of their common condition.

But instead of proffering any consolation so crude as hope or even resignation, "**The City**" attempts to alleviate suffering through the presentation of a truth that should make each man's life more his own, and less vulnerable to the indifferent cruelties of existence. The poet writes

> Because a cold rage seizes one at whiles
>   To show the bitter old and wrinkled truth
> Stripped naked of all vesture that beguiles,
>   False dreams, false hopes, false masks and
>   modes of youth;
> Because it gives some sense of power and passion
> In helpless impotence to try to fashion
>   Our woe in living words howe'er uncouth.

The controlled anger that engenders the poem consistently opposes the sleep, suicide, and death which the work at first seems to praise. Rather, the poet's harsh honesty acts like cold water dashed over the heads of the drugged and weary automatons the City creates. Ruthlessly exposing the "false masks" of Victorian complacency, he will instead produce "power and passion" through the potency of his indictment. Insisting on the power of poetry to keep the denizens of his city wide awake, the poet argues that the only responsible attitude toward life lies in the conscious experience of it, in the process of speaking the truth and refusing to accept the mind-forged manacles which shackle the poor and rebellious in the benighted streets of Britain.

Indeed, it is possible to see Thomson's poem in the context of the "discovery of poverty" in the East End that had been begun by Henry Mayhew a decade earlier and which culminated during the eighties and nineties. For although **"The City"** is as much a psychological as a physical "construct," it bears an important kinship to that literature of "exotic" travel through English slums which titillated and shocked the genteel bourgeois of the time. The pestilent gloom that Charles and William Booth, George Gissing, and Andrew Mearns saw emanating from "darkest London" was no less noxious than that which clouds the pages of **"The City."** (pp. 67-9)

Despite its forbidding atmosphere, in **"The City of Dreadful Night"** one can discover the solace Thomson intended his poetry to furnish: he uncovers the links, however hidden or perverted by city life, between all men living there and brings them to "self-knowledge" and identity, changing dispirited phantoms into unflinching endurers of urban emptiness. In this project, Thomson has much in common with traditional Stoic teaching. The apparently conflicting ideals of trying to achieve a brotherhood of man while at the same time seeking detachment from the miseries of the external world are both Stoic, as are the goals toward which Thomson applies them: self-awareness and survival. Therefore the conventional concept of "stoic endurance," the Victorian poet's response to a godless universe, gains a more precise meaning when played against the framework of a classical system of belief. For Thomson, the path toward self-possession begins with a gradual rejection of the many misleading avenues of action. (pp. 69-70)

Though the sections which expound Thomson's philosophy are often examined in isolation, they are seldom seen as a gradual progression of alternatives into which the episodes of despair logically fit. The last two sections Thomson wrote in 1870 begin a process of recognition, culminating in the cathedral scene (1873), that through fraternity men can achieve some measure of relief. In section VI the narrator, walking by the river, overhears one phantom tell another how he was ready to go even to hell to escape the City. He

> would have passed in, gratified to gain
> That positive eternity of pain,
> Instead of this insufferable inane.

But as a resident of the City he was denied entrance: he had no hope to abandon. His companion's response, however, brings a revolutionary idea into the atomized, solitary world of **"The City"**:

> The other sighed back, Yea; but if we grope
> With care through all this Limbo's dreary scope,
> We yet may pick up some minute lost hope;

The cover of the 1895 edition of The Poetical Works of James Thomson.

> And, *sharing it between us,* entrance win,
> In spite of fiends so jealous for gross sin:
> Let us without delay our search begin. (my italics)

Such deluded quests may be fruitless, yet in this episode Thomson begins to hint at the major theme of the poem: by sharing, though not necessarily in conventional consolations like hope, men can eventually forge identity through unflinching consciousness of their situation. The idea arises naturally out of the City's desolation, since values based on human commiseration are alone possible. Thomson is groping toward an answer which his later lines will make explicit: collective action, or at the least dialogue, helps men to combat "the insufferable inane."

The four stanzas of section III, the last which Thomson wrote in 1870, indicate that although he had inklings of how to resolve the problems he had set himself, he was too uncertain and weary of this intensely personal project to proceed. Struggling for a way out of the City's wasteland of grief, helplessness, and utter disillusion, the poet at first boldly asserts, "And soon the eye a strange new vision learns." But unable to see his way clear of "the gloom intense," he gives up and prefaces what was to be a two-and-a-half year hiatus in the composition of the poem with these lines:

> Crushed impotent beneath this reign of terror,
> Dazed with such mysteries of woe and error,
> The soul is too outworn for wondering.

The breaking point is significant, because in May, 1873, when he took up the poem again, Thomson had formulated that "new vision" which makes the latter portions so forceful. With "renewed assurance" and a clearer sense of the whole, he confidently resumes at the same point where he had left off, the riverside (section VIII). Another man complains that destiny has singled him out for punishment, but his companion argues instead for "the supreme indifference of Fate":

> "The world rolls round for ever like a mill;
> It grinds out death and life and good and ill;
> It has no purpose, heart or mind or will."

In the monosyllables of these lines one hears the pounding of Blake's Satanic mills, and recalls the opening pages of *Hard Times*. By insisting on the mindless mechanical functioning of the universe, Thomson readjusts traditional Stoic fatalism to suit life in a godless industrial era. The Stoics had held that man should strive for harmony with nature because all its laws and actions inevitably stem from the directing intelligence of the first cause, God. But Thomson substitutes blind Necessity for a divine Fate, thereby describing what man in the city has been reduced to in the most effective terms possible—those of the ubiquitous industrial process. Here Thomson anticipates Eliot's lifeless parade down King William Street: Life and Death are as mechanical as that "automatic hand" of the typist in "The Fire Sermon."

Yet **"The City of Dreadful Night"** offers an insight into the minds of the "so many" that Eliot's more exterior view omits. This is the radical difference between the two poets and the chief contribution of the 1873 sections. Still, we should be aware that the germ of the later sections is present even in section XI, written in 1870. Truly concerned about the masses, Thomson relentlessly examines the crowd until he can fathom "What men are they who haunt these fatal glooms?" Penetrating the superficialities, he finds in all a common delusion and fate: "rational and yet insane," they foresee their ruin but refuse to acknowledge it. This is what the poem must change, and the narrator, grasping this universal problem, makes the most important discovery in the poem, that whatever their roles in life, all men share the same condition: "these and those are brothers, / The saddest and the weariest men on earth." Only the camaraderie of weariness and freedom from delusion can somehow make their plight bearable.

In 1873 Thomson articulated this intuition more fully in the explicit question which opens section XII. What if "Our isolated units could be brought / To act together for some common end?" he inquires. Prompted by the sight of a long line of the City's residents, "each silent with his thought," winding slowly toward the cathedral, the poet searches for a way out of the shackles of non-communication. The poem subtly shifts from thinking of the prison to "thinking of the key."

The long procession they form on the way up to the cathedral indicates the power of the City to transform any life it touches. It is actually antiprocessional, exposing how the modern city produces individual alienation while still enforcing outward forms of the old social order. . . . Yet as Thomson's inverted procession of isolation toward a cathedral of atheism demonstrates, the more men realize their separation, the more they can see in each other a common despair or, worse, the consequences of their own seemingly isolated actions. Thomson's

procession serves an authentic purpose finally, beneath its silent, dissociative demeanor and godless destination, for it requires total participation and a renunciation of individual identity for the common acceptance of "this real night." This becomes the advantage of this community over the residents of Eliot's "unreal city"—their awareness of each other.

At the door of the cathedral a porter asks each man what he did before he came to the City. Significantly, the first is a social reformer just come from pleading "for some scant justice to our countless hordes / Who toil half-starved with scarce a human right." He represents the younger, more idealistic Thomson who in **"The Doom of a City"** made the ameliorating possibilities of the brotherhood of men his theme.

However, his own urban experience later compelled Thomson to surrender hope of any material aid. Like the Stoic Epictetus, Thomson comes to believe in a human fellowship that does not depend on the futile hope of doing anything to improve men's physical well-being. Given the grim indifference of life, philosophical enlightenment and increased self-awareness are the only consolations he feels he can legitimately offer. A kind of fatalistic nobility, later to be embodied in Melancholia's "indomitable will," allows his fellow victims to confront their fate. Thus the reformer must admit that his efforts were useless: "I wake from daydreams to this real night." The recognition of this painful reality marks the turning point in the poem, and soon others join the reformer in his confession. An opium smoker, a clown, a monk, a poet with the vain Miltonic intent to "justify the ways of God to man," even a revolutionary—all concede the reality of this night, and enter the cathedral. Finally the narrator also acquiesces and follows after them.

The next episode, XIV, is the intellectual focal point of the poem, as sections XV and XVI are its emotional ones. Here in the cathedral the men of the City enter into a perverse communion, as they did in the procession. Their preacher unites the themes of desolation and fraternity in his first, Miltonic words: "O melancholy Brothers, dark, dark, dark!" Confiding that "Your woe hath been my anguish," the preacher stands in the same relation to the crowd as the poet does to his readers, and he tells them how he has searched the universe for some news to ease their suffering:

> Good tidings of great joy for you, for all:
> There is no God; no Fiend with names divine
> Made us and tortures us; if we must pine
> It is to satiate no Being's gall.

Rather than merely shocking his readers, Thomson wishes to convince them that these ideas can be liberating as well. As the preacher concludes, "you are free to end it when you will, / Without the fear of waking after death." The key word "free" suggests why everyone has not leapt into the River of Suicides. Though they take suicide very seriously, its real value, as poet and preacher realize in **"The City,"** is as an emancipating concept, not as an act of defiance or desperate escape.

The fifteenth and shortest section of the poem celebrates the congregation's new-found self-awareness and freedom to act. In a ritual expression of collective suffering it recognizes that only human activity and belief can create value and meaning in an impersonal universe. Revising Christ's words implying spiritual immanence, "Where two or three are gathered together in my name, there am I," the poet asserts that only Man is there: "Wherever men are gathered, all the air / Is charged with human feeling, human thought.'' The air is ''with our life fraught and overfraught,'' so that no man breathes alone,

> But nourishes warm life or hastens death
>   With joys and sorrows, health and foul disease,
> Wisdom and folly, good and evil labours,
> Incessant of his multitudinous neighbours;
>   He in his turn affecting all of these.

In a few lines Thomson sketches the vast entanglement of social and moral activity that is a vital part of city literature from Blake's ''London'' to *Bleak House*. Like Blake and Dickens, Thomson insists on the almost endless repercussions of each man's deeds.

The rest of the poem acts as a response to the powerful climax of the cathedral scene. In section XVI, for example, a member of the ''shadowy congregation'' seconds the preacher's revelation. He complains that he had only one opportunity in all eternity for a happy life with a wife and children, ''And this sole chance was frustrate from my birth, / A mockery, a delusion.'' Encapsulating what is apparently the poet's view, he proclaims, ''Our life's a cheat, our death a black abyss.'' Thomson's decision not to end the scene here indicates his willingness to sacrifice dramatic effect to the larger didactic purpose of the poem. The preacher concludes the section instead on a more positive note: ''I ponder these thoughts and they comfort me.'' The poet appears convinced that they will comfort his readers, too.

In fact, even the ending—usually viewed as a resounding anthem of pessimism—seems to undermine the supposed edifice of unremitting despair of ''The City.'' In the center of a park that overlooks the city from the north sits the ''stupendous superhuman'' image of Dürer's *Melancholia*. After describing her in detail (from the engraving, of which Thomson owned a copy) the narrator admits he derives solace from her stoic self-possession. Moreover, he admires her almost transcendent endurance in the face of the terrible fact that ''all is vanity and hopelessness'':

> Unvanquished in defeat and desolation,
> Undaunted in the hopeless conflagration
> Of the day setting on her baffled prime.
>
> Baffled and beaten back she works on still,
>   Weary and sick of soul she works the more,
> Sustained by her indomitable will.

Despite the characteristically gloomy philosophy, here Thomson sounds surprisingly like William Ernest Henley in ''Invictus,'' that anti-decadent paean to perseverance written about this time. Indeed, the last lines of ''The City'' suggest that the poet's final intention is to fortify his readers, not, as is usually assumed, to dismay them further:

> Her subjects often gaze up to her there:
> The strong to drink new strength of iron endurance,
> The weak new terrors; all, renewed assurance
>   And confirmation of the old despair.

(pp. 75-80)

The syntactic ambiguity that enables ''renewed assurance'' to form its own unit free of ''confirmation of the old despair'' seems especially telling. Moreover, anything proposed as a symbol of the City's unity in the face of the void must inevitably take on positive overtones for those it strengthens. By concluding his poem with Dürer's arresting emblem of emotional

stamina, Thomson freezes, glorifies, and mythologizes its final moment into a monument of ''indomitable will.''

The narrator in ''The City,'' then, is searching for a way to come to terms with the meaninglessness of a universe ruled by blind Necessity. His journey gradually uncovers the hidden connections between the isolated members of his suffering fraternity, eventually showing that freedom and comfort can be achieved through a shared stoic confrontation of the City. Seen in this light, the poem functions like the sacred texts it parodies, bringing ''cheer'' to those who participate in the bleak routine of the Necropolis. Though an antipilgrimage toward a Cathedral of Despair, the poem has much in common with the literature which guides the wanderer toward the Heavenly City. (pp. 80-1)

Thomson's metropolis is a true anti-city to the City of God— not an infernal city, which is still theological, but rather a construct with no meaning except what human action assigns. Therefore, Dante lies behind the poem only indirectly, and the references in the poem to the Inferno as a desirable place underline this. Thomson makes it explicit that, despite its torments, the City is not Hell, for his poem is a Book of Job without God in it. (p. 82)

Thomson largely banishes nature from his secular, artificial city, and one reason why ''The City'' steadfastly refuses to fall in with the typical Victorian notion of city as earthly reflection of heaven or hell is simply that these terms have no personal meaning for him. The ''trackless wilderness'' surrounding the City provides no Wordsworthian mirror of eternity, for Thomson starts from an antithetic premise: he sees the City as a permanent condition. The cities of Blake or Tennyson represent otherworldly destinations, but the horror of Thomson's City derives from there being nothing beyond it: it is a nightmare from which one cannot wake. In the ongoing misery of a life spent in darkened streets, one finds ''a certain seeming order'' whose grim logic insists that ''where this ranges / We count things real.'' (p. 83)

What the City does to its inhabitants—implacably eroding love, hope, communication, sanity—must be resisted through self-awareness, fellowship, and sober contemplation. The Victorian victim of the city must fight back with the weapons of the modern urban artist. Out of his ''great expression of the spirit of despair,'' Thomson fashions a persuasive program for collective identity and defiant self-consciousness, which each weary wanderer can achieve through learning to read ''The City.'' (p. 84)

> *William Sharpe, ''Learning to Read 'The City','' in* Victorian Poetry, *Vol. 22, No. 1, Spring, 1984, pp. 65-84.*

ADDITIONAL BIBLIOGRAPHY

Church, Richard. ''Pale Melancholy.'' *The Spectator* 141, No. 5233 (13 October 1928): 479-80.
    A highly favorable assessment of Thomson.

Crawford, Robert. ''A Little More 'B. V.'.'' *Notes and Queries* n.s. 30, No. 4 (August 1983): 307-09.
    Discusses the discovery of Thomson's annotated copies of *Cope's Tobacco Plant* at Glasgow University Library. On this evidence, Crawford attributes nine unsigned reviews from the journal to Thomson.

————. "James Thomson and T. S. Eliot." *Victorian Poetry* 23, No. 1 (Spring 1985): 23-41.

Documents Eliot's close familiarity with Thomson's works and examines the influence of "The City of Dreadful Night" on the theme and language of *The Waste Land*.

DeCamp, David. "Thomson's 'The City of Dreadful Night'." *The Explicator* VII, No. 4 (February 1949): 29.

Stresses the structural and thematic importance of the Thames River in the poem.

Evans, Ifor. "James Thomson." In his *English Poetry in the Later Nineteenth Century*, rev. ed., pp. 226-35. London: Methuen & Co., 1966.

A biographical and critical assessment of Thomson.

Foakes, R. A. "The Vanity of Rhetoric: Matthew Arnold's Poetry and James Thomson's 'The City of Dreadful Night'." In his *The Romantic Assertion: A Study in the Language of Nineteenth Century Poetry*, pp. 149-79. New Haven: Yale University Press, 1958.

Discusses "The City of Dreadful Night" as a forthright negation of the idealistic Romantic vision of earthly existence.

Forsyth, R. A. "Evolutionism and the Pessimism of James Thomson (B. V.)." *Essays in Criticism* 12, No. 2 (1962): 148-66.

Suggests that the decline of Christianity and the rise of scientific evolutionism contributed greatly to Thomson's pessimistic philosophy.

Gerould, Gordon Hall. Introduction to *Poems of James Thomson "B. V."*, by James Thomson, edited by Gordon Hall Gerould, pp. vii-xviii. New York: Henry Holt and Co., 1927.

A biographical and critical survey that lauds Thomson as "among the most important literary figures of his time."

Grierson, Herbert J. C., and Smith, J. C. "Mid-Victorian Poetry: Patmore, Thomson, and Other Minors." In their *A Critical History of English Poetry*, 2d ed., pp. 453-60. 1947. Reprint. London: Chatto & Windus, 1965.

A general, brief appreciation of Thomson's verse.

LeRoy, Gaylord C. "James Thomson." In his *Perplexed Prophets: Six Nineteenth-Century British Authors*, pp. 104-20. Philadelphia: University of Pennsylvania Press for Temple University Publications, 1953.

Traces Thomson's loss of faith and its effect on his pessimistic ideas.

Noel-Bentley, Peter C. "'Fronting the Dreadful Mysteries of Time': Dürer's *Melencolia* in Thomson's 'City of Dreadful Night'." *Victorian Poetry* 12, No. 3 (Autumn 1974): 193-203.

Examines the impact of Albrecht Dürer's engraving entitled *Melencolia I* on the setting and symbolism of Thomson's poem.

Piestrzyńska-Wdowik, Danuta. "'The City of Dreadful Night' and Some Other Victorian Poetry and Prose." *Anglica Wratislaviensia* VIII (1981): 37-44.

Discusses "The City of Dreadful Night" in relation to other Victorian poems that deal with city life.

Powys, Llewelyn. "A Tragedy of Genius." *The Freeman* V, No. 130 (6 September 1922): 609-11.

A sympathetic biographical tribute containing a brief estimation of "The City of Dreadful Night."

Schaefer, William D. "The Two Cities of Dreadful Night." *PMLA* LXXVII, No. 5 (December 1962): 609-16.

Reconstructs the order in which Thomson composed the stanzas of "The City of Dreadful Night," thereby illuminating the ambiguity and thematic unevenness of its various sections.

————. *James Thomson (B. V.): Beyond "The City."* Berkeley and Los Angeles: University of California Press, 1965, 208 p.

Traces Thomson's intellectual development through his poetry, regularly referring to pivotal events in his life.

Steele, Michael R. "James Thomson's Angel and Sphinx: A Possible Source." *Victorian Poetry* 12, No. 4 (Winter 1974): 373-76.

Investigates the possibility that Winwood Reade's atheistic world history, *The Martyrdom of Man*, significantly influenced a central portion of "The City of Dreadful Night."

Talbot, Norman. "Best of Three Falls: James Thomson (B. V.) v Alfred, Lord Tennyson." *Southern Review* XII, No. 3 (November 1979): 227-45.

Discusses part XX of "The City of Dreadful Night" as a parodic inversion of the "Holy Grail" section of Tennyson's *Idylls of the King*.

Wallis, N. Hardy. "James Thomson and His 'City of Dreadful Night'." *Essays by Divers Hands* n.s. XIV (1935): 137-65.

The text of a 1934 lecture commemorating the 100th anniversary of Thomson's birth. Following a summary of his career, Wallis offers a general, appreciative study of "The City of Dreadful Night."

Woodbridge, Benjamin M. "Poets and Pessimism: Vigny, Housman, et Alii." *The Romantic Review* XXXV, No. 1 (February 1944): 43-51.

Compares the religious pessimism of Alfred de Vigny, A. E. Housman, Leopardi, Leconte de Lisle, and Thomson.

Appendix

The following is a listing of all sources used in Volume 18 of *Nineteenth-Century Literature Criticism*. Included in this list are all copyright and reprint rights and acknowledgments for those essays for which permission was obtained. Every effort has been made to trace copyright, but if omissions have been made, please let us know.

THE EXCERPTS IN NCLC, VOLUME 18, WERE REPRINTED FROM THE FOLLOWING PERIODICALS:

The Academy, v. 5, June 5, 1874; n.s. v. 17, June 12, 1880; v. 19, May 21, 1881.

The Albemarle Review, September, 1982.

American Imago, v. 20, Spring, 1963 for ''Wilkie Collins and 'The Moonstone' '' by Lewis A. Lawson. Copyright 1963 by The Association for Applied Psychoanalysis, Inc. Reprinted by permission of the Wayne State University Press and the author.

American Literature, v. 11, May, 1939./ v. 52, November, 1980. Copyright © 1980 Duke University Press, Durham, NC. Reprinted by permission of the publisher.

The Annual of Leeds University Oriental Society, v. IV, 1964. © copyright 1964 by Leeds University Oriental Society. All rights reserved. Reprinted by permission of the publisher.

The Antijacobin Review, v. XLI, January, 1812.

Appleton's Journal, n.s. v. X, May, 1881.

The Athenaeum, n. 3379, July 30, 1892.

The Atlantic Monthly, v. X, November, 1862; v. XII, August, 1863; v. LXVII, May, 1891.

Bentley's Miscellany, v. XX, August, 1846.

Blackwood's Edinburgh Magazine, v. 6, November, 1819; v. 7, September, 1820; v. 10, December, 1821.

The Bookman, New York, v. LXX, February, 1930.

The British Critic, v. XXXVII, April, 1811; n.s. v. VII, April, 1830; v. XXX, October, 1841.

Browning Institute Studies, v. 10, 1982. Copyright © 1982 by the Browning Institute, Inc. Reprinted by permission of the publisher.

The Century, v. XLVII, April, 1894.

Charleston Mercury, March 9, 1861.

Chicago Daily Times, June 23, 1858.

Chicago Times, September 24, 1862; November 23, 1863.

Chicago Tribune, November 10, 1858.

The Christian Examiner, n.s. v. I, January, 1844.

The Christian Remembrancer, n.s. v. VIII, October-December, 1844.

The Church Quarterly Review, v. CLXII, April-June, 1961. Reprinted by permission of the Society for Promoting Christian Knowledge, London.

Cincinnati Enquirer, September 16-20, 1859.

The Critic, New York, v. 18, May 30, 1891.

The Critical Review and Annals of Literature, n. 21, November, 1810.

Criticism, v. XX, Fall, 1978 for "The Completed Story in the 'Mystery of Edwin Drood' " by Roy Roussel. Copyright, 1979, Wayne State University Press. Reprinted by permission of the publisher and the author.

The Daily Express, March 9, 1865.

Daily Journal, November 20, 1863.

Dickens Quarterly, v. II, March, 1985. Copyright 1985 by the Dickens Society. Reprinted by permission of the publisher.

Dickens Studies Annual, v. I, 1970. Copyright © 1970 by Southern Illinois University Press. All rights reserved. Reprinted by permission of AMS Press, Inc.

The Edinburgh Review, v. XL, July, 1824; v. LXI, July, 1835; v. LXXVI, January, 1843; v. LXXXI, January, 1845; v. LXXXVI, July, 1847.

The Fortnightly Review, n.s. v. CLX, August, 1946.

Fraser's Magazine for Town & Country, v. XII, September, 1835; v. XVI, August, 1837; v. XXXIII, May, 1846.

Frontiers: A Journal of Women Studies, v. IX, 1987. © copyright 1987, by the Frontiers Editorial Collective. Reprinted by permission of the publisher.

The Georgia Historical Quarterly, v. XLIV, March, 1960. Copyright © 1960 by the Georgia Historical Society, Savannah, Georgia. Reprinted by permission of the publisher.

Harper's Magazine, v. 180, February, 1940. Copyright 1940, renewed 1967, by *Harper's Magazine.* All rights reserved. Reprinted by special permission.

Illinois State Journal, August 30, 1858; February 12, 1861.

The Independent, v. XV, July 16, 1863.

Journal of Semitic Studies, v. I, October, 1956.

Judy; or, The London Serio-Comic Journal, April-June, 1870.

Lippincott's Magazine of Literature, Science and Education, v. II, December, 1868.

The Littell's Living Age, v. LXXX, February 6, 1864.

The Living Age, v. CCLX, March 13, 1909.

The London Magazine, v. V, May, 1820.

The London Review, v. VI, June 6, 1863.

London Times, January 15, 1863.

Louisville Journal, 1858.

The Monthly Review, London, n.s. v. 127, April, 1832.

The Nation, New York, v. VII, September 17, 1868; v. XXVII, December 12, 1878.

National Intelligencer, April 13, 1865.

New Orleans Daily Crescent, February 21, 1861.

New York Daily Tribune, August 26, 1858; March 6, 1861.

New York Evening Post, February 28, 1860.

New York Tribune, April 19, 1865.

New York World, April 13, 1865.

The New Yorker, v. LI, September 8, 1975. © 1975 by The New Yorker Magazine, Inc. Reprinted by permission of the publisher.

The North American Review, v. CXXX, February, 1880.

Novel: A Forum on Fiction, v. 13, Winter, 1980 for "From 'Roman Policier' to 'Roman-Police': Wilkie Collins's 'The Moonstone'" by D. A. Miller. Copyright © Novel Corp., 1980. Reprinted by permission of the author.

The Pall Mall Magazine, v. XXXVII, June, 1906.

Philological Quarterly, v. 63, Summer, 1984 for "Wilkie Collins's 'Little Jewel': The Meaning of 'The Moonstone'" by Patricia Miller Frick. Copyright 1984 by The University of Iowa. Reprinted by permission of the publisher and the author.

Poetry, v. XXXII, July, 1928.

Proceedings of the American Antiquarian Society, v. 57, 1947.

The Prospective Review, v. I, 1845.

The Psychoanalytic Quarterly, v. XXVI, April, 1957 for "Detective Story: Psychoanalytic Observations" by Charles Rycroft. Copyright © 1957, renewed 1985, by The Psychoanalytic Quarterly, Inc. Reprinted by permission of the publisher and A. D. Peters & Co. Ltd.

Punch, or the London Charivari, December 10, 1864.

The Quarterly Review, v. XXI, April, 1819; v. XLVII, March, 1832; v. LIV, July, 1835; v. LXXIV, October, 1844; v. LXXXI, September, 1847; v. 154, July, 1882.

Republican, November 20, 1863.

The Saturday Evening Post, v. 231, February 14, 1959. © 1959 The Curtis Publishing Company. Reprinted from *The Saturday Evening Post* by permission.

The Saturday Review, London, v. 30, September 17, 1870; v. 79, February 16, 1895.

The Southern Literary Messenger, v. I, May, 1835; May, 1849.

Southern Review, Australia, v. IX, 1976 for "'Awful Images and Associations': A Study of Wilkie Collins's 'The Moonstone'" by R. P. Laidlaw. Copyright 1976 by the author. Reprinted by permission of the author.

The Spectator, n. 1917, March 25, 1865; v. 43, October 1, 1870; v. 47, June 20, 1874; v. 63, September 28, 1889; v. 68, June 18, 1892; v. 186, April 6, 1951.

Studies in English Literature, 1500-1900, v. III, Autumn, 1963 for ''James Thomson (B. V.): The Woven Hymns of Night and Day'' by Jerome J. McGann. © 1963 William Marsh Rice University. Reprinted by permission of the publisher and the author.

The Times, London, October 7, 1862; October 3, 1868; April 2, 1870; July 17, 1896.

The Times Literary Supplement, November 3, 1905.

The United States Magazine and Democratic Review, v. XV, November, 1844.

Victorian Poetry, v. 16, Spring & Summer, 1978; v. 22, Spring, 1984. Both reprinted by permission of the publisher.

The Westminster Review, v. XXXIX, February, 1843.

THE EXCERPTS IN NCLC, VOLUME 18, WERE REPRINTED FROM THE FOLLOWING BOOKS:

Anderson, David D. From *Abraham Lincoln.* Twayne, 1970. Copyright 1970 by Twayne Publishers. All rights reserved. Reprinted with the permission of Twayne Publishers, Inc., a division of G. K. Hall & Co., Boston.

Anderson-Imbert, Enrique. From *Spanish American Literature: A History.* Edited by Elaine Malley, translated by John V. Falconieri and Elaine Malley. Second edition. Wayne State University Press, 1969. Copyright © 1969 Wayne State University Press, Detroit, Michigan 48202, USA. All rights reserved. Reprinted by permission of the Wayne State University Press and the author.

Arnold, Matthew. From *Essays in Criticism, second series.* Macmillan and Co., Limited, 1888.

Arnold, Matthew. From *The Works of Matthew Arnold: Poems, Vol. I.* Macmillan and Co., Limited, 1903-04.

Arnold, Thomas. From *The Life and Correspondence of Thomas Arnold, D.D., Vol. I.* By Arthur Penrhyn Stanley. B. Fellowes, 1844.

Arnold, Thomas. From *The Life and Correspondence of Thomas Arnold, D.D., Vol. II.* By Arthur Penrhyn Stanley. B. Fellowes, 1844.

Baker, Carlos. From *Shelley's Major Poetry: The Fabric of a Vision.* Princeton University Press, 1948. Copyright 1948, renewed 1976, by Princeton University Press. Reprinted with permission of the publisher.

Bamford, T. W. From an introduction to *Thomas Arnold on Education: A Selection from His Writings.* By Thomas Arnold, edited by T. W. Bamford. Cambridge at the University Press 1970. © Cambridge University Press 1970. Reprinted with permission of the publisher.

Barton, William E. From *Lincoln at Gettysburg: What He Intended to Say; What He Said; What He Was Reported to Have Said; What He Wished He Had Said.* The Bobbs-Merrill Company, 1930. Copyright, 1930 by Macmillan Publishing Company. Renewed 1957 by Bruce Barton. Reprinted with permission of Macmillan Publishing Company.

Bloom, Harold. From an introduction to *Selected Poetry and Prose of Shelley.* By Percy Bysshe Shelley, edited by Harold Bloom. New American Library, 1966. Reprinted by permission of the editor, Harold Bloom.

Boutwell, George S. From "Chapter VI," in *Reminiscences of Abraham Lincoln.* Edited by Allen Thorndike Rice. North American Publishing Company, 1886.

Bradby, G. F. From *The Brontës and Other Essays.* Oxford University Press, London, 1932.

Butler, Frances Anne. From *Journal of a Residence in America.* A. and W. Galignani and Co., 1835.

Byron, Kenneth Hugh. From *The Pessimism of James Thomson (B. V.) in Relation to His Times.* Mouton, 1965. © copyright 1965 Mouton & Co., Publishers. Reprinted by permission of Mouton de Gruyter, a Division of Walter de Gruyter & Co.

Byron, Lord. From a conversation in *Recollections of the Last Days of Shelley and Byron.* By E. J. Trelawny. Edward Moxon, 1858.

Cawelti, John G. From *Adventure, Mystery, and Romance: Formula Stories as Art and Popular Culture.* University of Chicago Press, 1976. © 1976 by The University of Chicago. All rights reserved. Reprinted by permission of The University of Chicago Press and the author.

Chernaik, Judith. From *The Lyrics of Shelley.* Press of Case Western Reserve University, 1972. Copyright © 1972 by Judith Chernaik. All rights reserved. Reprinted by permission of the author.

Clough, Arthur Hugh. From *The Poems of Arthur Hugh Clough.* Edited by F. L. Mulhauser. Second edition. Oxford at the Clarendon Press, 1974. © Oxford University Press, 1974. All rights reserved. Reprinted by permission of Oxford University Press.

Cockshut, A. O. J. From " 'Edwin Drood': Early and Late Dickens Reconciled," in *Dickens and the Twentieth Century.* Edited by John Gross and Gabriel Pearson. Routledge and Kegan Paul, 1962. © Routledge & Kegan Paul Ltd 1962. Reprinted by permission of Routledge & Kegan Paul PLC.

Cockshut, A. O. J. From "Arnold, Hook, Ward: A Wiccamical Sidelight on Nineteenth-Century Religion," in *Winchester College: Sixth-Centenary Essays.* Edited by Roger Custance. Oxford University Press, Oxford, 1982. © Warden and Fellows of Winchester College 1982. All rights reserved. Reprinted by permission of Oxford University Press.

Coester, Alfred. From *The Literary History of Spanish America.* Macmillan, 1916. Copyright 1916 by Macmillan Publishing Company. Copyright renewed 1944 by Alfred Coester.

Coleridge, Samuel Taylor. From *Collected Letters of Samuel Taylor Coleridge: 1826-1834, Vol. VI.* Edited by Earl Leslie Griggs. Oxford at the Clarendon Press, 1971. © Oxford University Press, 1971. Reprinted by permission of Oxford University Press.

Collins, Philip. From *Dickens and Crime.* St. Martin's Press, 1962. Copyright © 1962 by Philip Collins. All rights reserved. Used with permission of St. Martin's Press, Inc.

Collins, Wilkie. From prefaces to *The Moonstone.* Harper & Brothers, 1868. Smith, Elder & Co., 1871.

Curran, Stuart. From *Shelley's "Cenci": Scorpions Ringed with Fire.* Princeton University Press, 1970. Copyright © 1970 by Princeton University Press. All rights reserved. Reprinted with permission of the publisher.

Davie, Donald. From *Purity of Diction in English Verse.* Chatto & Windus, 1952.

Dickens, Charles. From *Letters of Charles Dickens to Wilkie Collins: 1851-1870.* Edited by Georgina Hogarth and Laurence Hutton. James R. Osgood, McIlvaine & Co., 1892.

Dobell, Bertram. From *The Laureate of Pessimism: A Sketch of the Life and Character of James Thomson ("B. V.").* Bertram Dobell, 1910.

Dodge, Daniel Kilham. From *Abraham Lincoln: Master of Words.* D. Appleton and Company, 1924.

Douglass, Frederick. From *Oration.* Gibson Brothers, Printers, 1876.

Downs, Robert B. From *Books That Changed the South.* University of North Carolina Press, 1977. Copyright © 1977 by The University of North Carolina Press. All rights reserved. Reprinted by permission of the publisher and the author.

Driver, Leota S. From *Fanny Kemble.* The University of North Carolina Press, 1933.

Dyson, A. E. From *The Inimitable Dickens: A Reading of the Novels.* Macmillan and Co. Ltd., 1970. © A. E. Dyson 1970. Reprinted by permission of Macmillan, London and Basingstoke.

Eliot, George. From *The George Eliot Letters: 1874-1877, Vol. VI.* Edited by Gordon S. Haight. Yale University Press, 1955. Copyright © 1955 by Yale University Press. Renewed 1983 by Gordon S. Haight. All rights reserved. Reprinted by permission of the Literary Estate of Gordon S. Haight.

Eliot, T. S. From an introduction to *The Moonstone.* By Wilkie Collins. Oxford University Press, London, 1928.

Eliot, T. S. From *The Use of Poetry and the Use of Criticism: Studies in the Relation of Criticism to Poetry in England.* Cambridge, Mass.: Harvard University Press, 1933. Copyright 1933 by the President and Fellows of Harvard College. Renewed © 1961 by T. S. Eliot. All rights reserved. Excerpted by permission of the publishers.

Emerson, Ralph Waldo. From *The Complete Essays and Other Writings of Ralph Waldo Emerson.* Edited by Brooks Atkinson. The Modern Library, 1940.

Emerson, Ralph Waldo. From *The Letters of Ralph Waldo Emerson, Vol. 6.* Edited by Ralph L. Rusk. Columbia University Press, 1939. Copyright, 1939, renewed 1967, by Ralph Waldo Emerson Association. Reprinted by permission of the publisher.

Fairchild, Hoxie Neale. From *Religious Trends in English Poetry: 1830-1880, Christianity and Romanticism, Vol. IV.* Columbia University Press, 1957.

Fanny Kemble in America; or, the Journal of an Actress Reviewed. Light & Horton, 1835.

FitzGerald, Edward. From *Letters of Edward FitzGerald to Fanny Kemble: 1871-1883.* Edited by William Aldis Wright. Macmillan and Co., 1895.

Flores, Angel. From *The Literature of Spanish America, 1825-1885: A Critical Anthology, Vol. 2.* Edited by Angel Flores. Las Américas Publishing Company, 1967. Copyright © 1967 by Angel Flores. Reprinted by permission of the publisher.

Forster, John. From *The Life of Charles Dickens: 1852-1870, Vol. III.* J. B. Lippincott & Co., 1874.

Franco, Jean. From *An Introduction to Spanish-American Literature.* Cambridge at the University Press, 1969. © Cambridge University Press 1969. Reprinted with permission of the publisher and the author.

Franco, Jean. From *Spanish American Literature Since Independence.* Barnes & Noble Books, 1973. © Jean Franco 1973. Reprinted by permission of the publisher.

Franklin, John Hope. From *The Emancipation Proclamation*. Doubleday & Company, Inc., 1963. Copyright © 1963 by John Hope Franklin. All rights reserved. Reprinted by permission of Doubleday, a division of Bantam, Doubleday, Dell Publishing Group, Inc.

Furnas, J. C. From *Fanny Kemble: Leading Lady of the Nineteenth-Century Stage*. The Dial Press, 1982. Copyright © 1982 by J. C. Furnas. All rights reserved. Reprinted by permission of Doubleday, a division of Bantam, Doubleday, Dell Publishing Group, Inc.

Gloyn, Cyril Kennard. From *The Church in the Social Order: A Study of Anglican Social Theory from Coleridge to Maurice*. Pacific University, 1942.

Gooch, G. P. From *History and Historians in the Nineteenth Century*. Second edition. Longmans, Green, and Co., 1913.

Grigson, Geoffrey. From *The Contrary View: Glimpses of Fudge and Gold*. Macmillan, London, 1974. © Geoffrey Grigson 1974. All rights reserved. Reprinted by permission of the author.

Harris, Frank. From *Contemporary Portraits, second series*. Frank Harris, 1919.

Heath-Stubbs, John. From *The Darkling Plain: A Study of the Later Fortunes of Romanticism in English Poetry from George Darley to W. B. Yeats*. Eyre & Spottiswoode, 1950.

Henríquez-Ureña, Pedro. From *Literary Currents in Hispanic America*. Cambridge, Mass.: Harvard University Press, 1945. Copyright 1945, renewed 1972, by the President and Fellows of Harvard College. Excerpted by permission of the publishers.

Herndon, William H. and Jesse W. Weik. From *Abraham Lincoln: The True Story of a Great Life, Vol. II*. D. Appleton and Company, 1892.

Hone, Philip. From *The Diary of Philip Hone: 1828-1851*. Edited by Allan Nevins. Revised edition. Dodd, Mead & Company, Inc., 1936.

Hughes, Thomas. From *Tom Brown's School Days*. Macmillan & Co., 1857.

Hunt, Leigh. From a preface to *The Masque of Anarchy*. By Percy Bysshe Shelley. Edward Moxon, 1832.

Jaffa, Harry V. From *Crisis of the House Divided: An Interpretation of the Issues in the Lincoln-Douglas Debates*. Doubleday & Company, Inc., 1959. Copyright © 1959 by Harry V. Jaffa. All rights reserved. Reprinted by permission of the author.

James, Henry. From *Essays in London and Elsewhere*. Harper & Brothers Publishers, 1893.

Johnson, Edgar. From *Charles Dickens: His Tragedy and Triumph, Vol. 2*. Simon and Schuster, 1952. Copyright, 1952, renewed 1980, by Edgar Johnson. All rights reserved. Reprinted by permission of Georges Borchardt, Inc. for the author.

Keach, William. From *Shelley's Style*. Methuen, 1984. © 1984 William Keach. All rights reserved. Reprinted by permission of Methuen & Co. Ltd.

Keats, John. From a letter in *Shelley Memorials*. By Lady Shelley. Smith, Elder & Co., 1859.

Kenney, Lucy. From *Description of a Visit to Washington*. N.p., 1835.

Klausner, Joseph. From *A History of Modern Hebrew Literature (1785-1930)*. Edited by Leon Simon, translated by Herbert Danby. M. L. Cailingold, 1932.

Knowlton, Edgar C., Jr. From *Esteban Echeverría*. Dorrance & Company, Incorporated, 1986. Copyright © 1986 by Edgar C. Knowlton, Jr. All rights reserved. Reprinted by permission of the publisher.

Lamb, Charles. From *The Letters of Charles Lamb, Vol. 2*. Edited by E. V. Lucas. J. M. Dent & Sons, Ltd. and Methuen & Co. Ltd., 1935.

Lodge, Henry Cabot. From *The Democracy of the Constitution and Other Addresses and Essays*. Charles Scribner's Sons, 1915.

Longfellow, Henry Wadsworth. From *The Complete Poetical Works of Henry Wadsworth Longfellow*. Houghton Mifflin and Company, 1893.

Lowell, Robert. From ''On the Gettysburg Address,'' in *Lincoln and the Gettysburg Address: Commemorative Papers*. Edited by Allan Nevins. University of Illinois Press, 1964. © 1964 by the Board of Trustees of the University of Illinois. Reprinted by permission of the publisher.

Mack, Edward C. From *Public Schools and British Opinion, 1780-1860: The Relationship between Contemporary Ideas and the Evolution of an English Institution.* Methuen & Co. Ltd, 1938.

Marks, Jeannette. From *Genius and Disaster: Studies in Drugs and Genius.* Second edition. Adelphi Company, 1926.

Marshall, William H. From *Wilkie Collins.* Twayne, 1970. Copyright 1970 by Twayne Publishers. All rights reserved. Reprinted with the permission of Twayne Publishers, a division of G. K. Hall & Co., Boston.

Marston, Philip Bourke. From ''James Thomson (1834-1882),'' in *The English Poets: Wordsworth to Rossetti, Vol. IV.* Edited by Thomas Humphry Ward. Revised edition. Macmillan and Co., 1893.

Masters, Edgar Lee. From *Lincoln: The Man.* Dodd, Mead & Company, Inc., 1931. Copyright 1931 by Edgar Lee Masters. Renewed 1958 by Ellen C. Masters. All rights reserved. Reprinted by permission of the Literary Estate of Edgar Lee Masters.

Meeker, J. Edward. From *The Life and Poetry of James Thomson (B. V.).* Yale University Press, 1917.

Mencken, H. L. From ''Statesmen: Abraham Lincoln,'' in *A Mencken Chrestomathy.* Knopf, 1949. Copyright 1924 by Alfred A. Knopf, Inc. Renewed 1942 by H. L. Mencken. Reprinted by permission of the publisher.

Menton, Seymour. From *The Spanish American Short Story: A Critical Anthology.* Edited by Seymour Menton. University of California Press, 1980. Copyright © 1980 by The Regents of the University of California. Reprinted by permission of the publisher.

Meredith, George. From *Letters of George Meredith: 1844-1881, Vol. I.* Edited by W. M. Meredith. Charles Scribner's Sons, 1912.

Mitgang, Herbert, ed. From ''Le discours de M. Lincoln,'' in *Lincoln as They Saw Him.* Rinehart and Company, Inc. 1956. Copyright © 1956, renewed 1984, by Herbert Mitgang. Reprinted by permission of the editor.

Moore, Marianne. From *A Marianne Moore Reader.* The Viking Press, 1961. Copyright © 1961 by Marianne Moore.

More, Paul Elmer. From *Shelburne Essays, fifth series.* G. P. Putnam's Sons, 1908.

Murch, A. E. From *The Development of the Detective Novel.* Philosophical Library, Inc., 1958.

Nevins, Allan. From *America through British Eyes.* Edited by Allan Nevins. Revised edition. Oxford University Press, 1948. Copyright 1948 by Oxford University Press, Inc. Renewed 1975 by Mrs. Allan Nevins. Reprinted by permission of the Trustees of Columbia University in the City of New York.

Niebuhr, Reinhold. From ''The Religion of Abraham Lincoln,'' in *Lincoln and the Gettysburg Address: Commemorative Papers.* Edited by Allan Nevins. University of Illinois Press, 1964. © 1964 by the Board of Trustees of the University of Illinois. Reprinted by permission of the publisher and the Literary Estate of Reinhold Niebuhr.

Noel, Roden. From ''James Thomson (1834-1882),'' in *The Poets and the Poetry of the Nineteenth Century: Charles Kingsley to James Thomson.* Edited by Alfred H. Miles. George Routledge & Sons, Ltd., 1905.

Notopoulos, James A. From *The Platonism of Shelley: A Study of Platonism and the Poetic Mind.* Duke University Press, 1949.

Ossoli, Margaret Fuller. From *Life Without and Life Within; or, Reviews, Narratives, Essays, and Poems.* Edited by Arthur B. Fuller. Brown, Taggard and Chase, 1859.

Parrington, Vernon Louis. From *Main Currents in American Thought, An Interpretation of American Literature from the Beginnings to 1920: The Romantic Revolution in America, 1800-1860, Vol. 2.* Harcourt Brace Jovanovich, 1927. Copyright 1927, 1930 by Harcourt Brace Jovanovich, Inc. Renewed 1955, 1958 by Vernon L. Parrington, Jr., Louise P. Tucker and Elizabeth P. Thomas. Reprinted by permission of the publisher.

Patterson, David. From *Abraham Mapu: The Creator of the Modern Hebrew Novel.* East and West Library, 1964. Copyright © 1964 Hebrew Publishing Company. All rights reserved. Reprinted by permission of the publishers, Hebrew Publishing Company.

Pfleiderer, Otto. From *The Development of Theology in Germany since Kant and Its Progress in Great Britain since 1825.* Translated by J. Frederick Smith. Third edition. Swan Sonnenschein & Co., Ltd. 1909.

Phillips, Ulrich Bonnell. From *Life and Labor in the Old South.* Little, Brown, and Company, 1929. Copyright 1929 by Little, Brown, and Company. Renewed 1956 by Mrs. Ulrich B. Phillips. All rights reserved. Reprinted by permission of the publisher.

Price, B. From a letter in *The Life and Correspondence of Thomas Arnold, D.D., Vol. I.* By Arthur Penrhyn Stanley. B. Fellowes, 1844.

Pritchett, V. S. From *The Living Novel & Later Appreciations*. Revised edition. Random House, 1964. Copyright © 1964, 1975 by V. S. Pritchett. All rights reserved. Reprinted by permission of Sterling Lord Literistic, Inc.

Read, Herbert. From *In Defence of Shelley and Other Essays*. William Heinemann, Ltd., 1936.

Reed, John R. From *Victorian Conventions*. Ohio University Press, 1975. © 1975 by John R. Reed. All rights reserved. Reprinted by permission of the publisher.

Ridler, Anne. From an introduction to *Poems and Some Letters of James Thomson*. By James Thomson, edited by Anne Ridler. Centaur Press, 1963. © Centaur Press Ltd., 1963. Reprinted by permission of the publisher.

Robertson, John M. From a preface to *Poems, Essays, and Fragments*. By James Thomson (''B. V.''), edited by John M. Robertson. Bertram Dobell, 1892.

Robinson, Kenneth. From *Wilkie Collins: A Biography*. The Bodley Head, Ltd., 1951.

Robinson, Luther Emerson. From *Abraham Lincoln as a Man of Letters*. The Reilly & Britton Co., 1918.

Rossetti, William M. From ''Shelley's 'Prometheus Unbound': A Study of Its Meaning and Personages,'' in *The Shelley Society's Papers*. By William M. Rossetti and others. Reeves and Turner, 1888.

Russell, Bertrand. From *Education and The Good Life*. Boni & Liveright, 1926. Published in England as *On Education Especially in Early Childhood*. G. Allen & Unwin Ltd., 1926. Copyright 1926 by Horace Liveright. Renewed 1954 by Bertrand Russell. Reprinted by permission of Liveright Publishing Corporation. In Canada by Unwin Hyman Ltd.

Salt, Henry S. From *The Life of James Thomson (''B. V.'')*. Revised edition, Watts & Co., 1914.

Sayers, Dorothy L. From an introduction to *The Moonstone*. By Wilkie Collins. J. M. Dent & Sons Ltd., 1944.

Schaefer, William David. From an introduction to *The Speedy Extinction of Evil and Misery: Selected Prose of James Thomson (B. V.)*. By James Thomson (B. V.), edited by William David Schaefer. University of California Press, 1967. Copyright © 1967 by The Regents of the University of California. Reprinted by permission of the publisher.

Scott, John Anthony. From an introduction to *Journal of a Residence on a Georgian Plantation in 1838-1839*. By Frances Anne Kemble, edited by John A. Scott. Knopf, 1961. Copyright © 1961 by Alfred A. Knopf, Inc. All rights reserved. Reprinted by permission of the publisher.

Shelley, Mary W. From *The Poetical Works of Percy Bysshe Shelley*. Edited by Mary W. Shelley. Edward Moxon, 1839.

Shelley, Percy Bysshe. From *The Cenci: A Tragedy in Five Acts*. C. & J. Ollier, 1819.

Shelley, Percy Bysshe. From *Essays, Letters from Abroad: Translations and Fragments*. Edited by Mrs. Shelley. E. Moxon, 1840.

Shelley, Percy Bysshe. From *Prometheus Unbound*. C. and J. Ollier, 1820.

Shelley, Percy Bysshe. From *The Revolt of Islam: A Poem, in Twelve Cantos*. C. and J. Ollier, 1818.

Slouschz, Nahum. From *The Renascence of Hebrew Literature (1743-1885)*. The Jewish Publication Society of America, 1909.

Southey, Robert. From *New Letters of Robert Southey: 1811-1838, Vol. II*. Edited by Kenneth Curry. Columbia University Press, 1965. Copyright © 1965 Columbia University Press, Ltd. Reprinted by permission of the publisher.

Stanley, Arthur Penrhyn. From *The Life and Correspondence of Thomas Arnold, D.D. Vol. I*. B. Fellowes, 1844.

Strachey, Lytton. From *Eminent Victorians: Cardinal Manning, Florence Nightingale, Dr. Arnold, General Gordon*. G. P. Putnam's Sons, 1918.

Strong, Archibald T. From *Three Studies in Shelley and An Essay on Nature in Wordsworth and Meredith*. Oxford University Press, London, 1921.

Taine, H. A. From *History of English Literature*. Translated by H. Van Laun. J. W. Lovell Company, 1873.

Thomson, James. From *Shelley, a Poem: With Other Writings Relating to Shelley*. N.p., 1884.

Victoria, Queen of England. From *The Girlhood of Queen Victoria: A Selection from Her Majesty's Diaries Between the Years 1832 and 1840, Vol. I.* Edited by Viscount Esher. John Murray, 1912.

Waldstein, Abraham Solomon. From *The Evolution of Modern Hebrew Literature: 1850-1912.* Columbia University Press, 1916.

Walker, Imogene B. From *James Thomson (B. V.): A Critical Study.* Cornell University Press, 1950. Copyright 1950 by Cornell University. Renewed 1977 by Imogene B. Walker. Used by permission of the publisher, Cornell University Press.

Waxman, Meyer. From *A History of Jewish Literature from the Close of the Bible to Our Own Days, Vol. III.* Bloch Publishing Co., 1936.

Webb, Timothy. From *Shelley: A Voice Not Understood.* Manchester University Press, 1977. © Timothy Webb 1977. All rights reserved. Reprinted by permission of the publisher.

Whitman, Walt. From *Sequel to Drum-Taps.* N.p., 1865-66.

Williams, Edward E. From a letter in *Recollections of the Last Days of Shelley and Byron.* By E. J. Trelawny. Edward Moxon, 1858.

Wilson, Angus. From an introduction to *The Mystery of Edwin Drood.* By Charles Dickens, edited by Arthur J. Cox. Penguin, 1974. Introduction copyright © Angus Wilson, 1974. Reprinted by permission of Curtis Brown Ltd., London, and the author.

Wilson, Edmund. From *The Wound and the Bow: Seven Studies in Literature.* Houghton Mifflin Company, 1941. Copyright 1929, 1932, 1938, 1939, 1940, 1941 by Edmund Wilson. Copyright renewed © 1966, 1968, 1970, by Edmund Wilson. All rights reserved. Reprinted by permission of Farrar, Straus and Giroux, Inc.

Wilson, Robert Dick. From an introduction to *The Shepherd-Prince: A Historical Romance of the Days of Isaiah.* By Abraham Mapu, translated by Benjamin A. M. Schapiro. Benjamin A. M. Schapiro, 1922.

Wordsworth, William. From a letter in *Letters of the Wordsworth Family from 1787 to 1855, Vol. III.* Edited by William Knight. Ginn and Company, 1907.

Yeats, W. B. From *Essays and Introductions.* The Macmillan Company, 1961. © Mrs. W. B. Yeats, 1961. All rights reserved. Reprinted with permission of Macmillan Publishing Company. In Canada by A. P. Watt Ltd. on behalf of Michael B. Yeats and Macmillan, London, Ltd.

ISBN 0-8103-5818-2

9 780810 358188   90000>